NEW WORLD COMPACT

DICTIONARY OF AMERICAN ENGLISH

Based upon

**WEBSTER'S
NEW WORLD DICTIONARY**
Of The American Language
Second College Edition

Editor in Chief
DAVID B. GURALNIK

SIMON AND SCHUSTER

CONTENTS

EDITORIAL STAFF

Supervising Editor
Clark C. Livensparger

Managing Editor
Thomas Layman

Editors
Jonathan L. Goldman, Ruth Kimball Kent,
Paul B. Murry, Andrew N. Sparks

Assistants
Yvonne Boyd, Mary Shulman, Betty Thompson

FOREWORD

This is a dictionary for those who need a simple, accurate, modern aid to a sound working knowledge of the language. It has been prepared from the vast resources of the *Second College Edition* of WEBSTER'S NEW WORLD DICTIONARY of the AMERICAN LANGUAGE, the dictionary of first reference for the major wire services and for hundreds of newspapers. The words defined have been carefully selected to include all the commonly used terms that make up the basic vocabulary of English. The word stock of more than 38,000 vocabulary entries contains hundreds of newer terms and newer senses of established terms not to be found in other dictionaries of similar scope.

It has been the intent of the editors of this dictionary to incorporate as much information as possible within the limited space available. As a result, in addition to the clear, but brief definitions, there will be found a large number of idiomatic expressions and numerous prefixes and suffixes to help the user determine the meanings of words that do not appear in this book, and levels of usage are identified where necessary. In the interest of conserving space, many words derived from main words, such as nouns ending in *-tion*, *-er*, or *-ness*, adjectives ending in *-like* or *-less*, and adverbs ending in *-ly*, have been run in at the end of the entry for the base word and the suffix.

Pronunciations are given for those words which might present some difficulty. These pronunciations are recorded in a simplified but precise phonemic key which appears on page vi.

Another feature of this dictionary is the number of useful reference supplements that it contains. These include a list of abbreviations, demographic data on nations of the world and States of the United States, a table of presidents of the United States, and others.

A careful examination of the *Guide to the Use of the Dictionary* on

Foreword

pages VIII, IX, and x will make clear the kinds of information available in this book and increase its usefulness to the reader.

The type for this dictionary was created on the Fototronic CRT Typesetter, controlled by a Univac 1108 computer at Ecotran-Chi Corporation in Beachwood, Ohio. The database for the dictionary was created and maintained by the publisher's staff in his own office using a video editing terminal connected via phone to the Univac computer.

The Editors

KEY TO PRONUNCIATION

Symbol	Key Words	Symbol	Key Words
a	ask, fat	u	up, cut
ā	ape, date	ʉr	fur, fern
ä	car, lot		
		ə	a in ago
e	elf, ten		e in agent
er	berry, care		e in father
ē	even, meet		i in unity
			o in collect
i	is, hit		u in focus
ir	mirror, here		
ī	ice, fire	ch	chin, arch
		ŋ	ring, singer
ō	open, go	sh	she, dash
ô	law, horn	th	thin, truth
oi	oil, point	*th*	then, father
o͞o	look, pull	zh	s in pleasure
o͞o	ooze, tool		
yo͞o	unite, cure	,	as in (a′ b'l)
yo͞o	cute, few		
ou	out, crowd		

ABBREVIATIONS
USED IN THIS DICTIONARY

a.	adjective	**N.**	North
adv.	adverb	**n.**	noun
alt.	alternate	**Naut.**	nautical
Am.	American	**NE**	northeastern
Ar.	archaic	**NW**	northwestern
Biol.	biology	**Obs.**	obsolete
Br.	British	**orig.**	originally
c.	circa, century	**pl.**	plural
Can.	Canadian	**Poet.**	poetic
cf.	compare	**pp.**	past participle
Col.	colloquial	**pref.**	prefix
con.	conjunction	**prep.**	preposition
cu.	cubic	**pres. t.**	present tense
Dial.	dialectal	**pron.**	pronoun
E	eastern	**prp.**	present participle
E.	East	**pt.**	past tense
Elec.	electricity	**R.C.Ch.**	Roman Catholic
esp.	especially		Church
etc.	et cetera	**S**	southern
fem.	feminine	**S.**	South
Fr.	French	**SE**	southeastern
G.	German	**sing.**	singular
Geom.	geometry	**Sl.**	slang
Gr.	Greek	**sp.**	spelled, spelling
Gram.	grammar	**Sp.,Span.**	Spanish
int.	interjection	**spec.**	specifically
It.	Italian	**suf.**	suffix
L.	Latin	**superl.**	superlative
masc.	masculine	**SW**	southwestern
Math.	mathematics	**Theol.**	theology
Mil.	military	**TV**	television
Mus.	music	**v.**	verb
Myth.	mythology	**W**	western
N	northern	**W.**	West

Other abbreviations will be found on pages 609-617.

GUIDE TO THE USE OF THE DICTIONARY

I. THE MAIN ENTRY WORD

A. *Arrangement of Entries* –
All main entries, including
single words, compounds, prefixes
and suffixes, are listed in strict
alphabetical order.

a *a.* indefinite article **1.** ...
a- *pref.* not
aard'vark (ärd'-) *n.* ...
ab- *pref.* away; from; down
a·back' *adv.* [Ar.] back ...

Idiomatic phrases are listed
alphabetically after a main entry.

get *v.* ... —**get over** recover
from—**get through 1.** finish

B. *Variant Spellings & Forms* –
When variant spellings of a word
are far apart alphabetically, the
definition appears with the most
common spelling. If two commonly used variant spellings are
alphabetically close to each other,
they are entered as a joint entry.

cook'ie, cook'y *n.* ...

Variant spellings that are
alphabetically close to the prevailing spelling are given at the
end of the entry block.

co·op'er·ate *v.* to work
together: also **co-operate,**
coöperate

C. *Cross-references* – An entry may be cross-referenced to
another term meaning the same
but more frequently used.

hoo'li·gan *n.* ruffian

D. *Foreign Terms* – Foreign
words and phrases that are not
fully naturalized in English are
shown by an abbreviation, as Fr.
or Sp., in brackets.

bon jour (bôn zhōōr') [Fr.] ...

E. *Prefixes & Suffixes* –
Prefixes are indicated by a hyphen
following the entry form. Suffixes
are indicated by a hyphen preceding the entry form.

hemo- *pref.* blood
-hood *suf.* **1.** state or quality

F. *Syllabification* – The syllab-
ifications in this dictionary are
indicated by centered dots in the
entry words or by stress marks.

ca·bal·le·ro (ka'bə le'rō) *n.*
cab'i·net-mak'er *n.* ...

II. PRONUNCIATION

A. *Key to Pronunciation* – The
key is to be found on page vi.
B. *Styling of Pronunciation* –
Pronunciations are given only
when needed and are put inside
parentheses. A primary, or
strong, stress is marked by a
heavy stroke (′) after the syllable so stressed. A secondary, or
weak, stress is marked by a lighter stroke (′) after the syllable so
stressed. Truncation is used
wherever possible.

cache·pot (kash'pät, -pō) ...
cac'tus ...
caf·e·te·ri·a (-tir'ē ə) ...

Guide To The Use Of The Dictionary

Where the pronunciation changes for a different part of speech within an entry block, it is shown after that part-of-speech label.

con·flict′ *v.* be in opposition — *n.* (kän′flikt) **1.** a fight **2.** ...

III. PART-OF-SPEECH LABELS

Part-of-speech labels are given for main entries that are solid or hyphenated, except prefixes and suffixes. A long dash introduces each different part-of-speech label within an entry block.

con·verse′ *v.* to talk *a.* opposite —*n.* (kän′vars) ...

Two or more part-of-speech labels may be given jointly for an entry when the same definition or definitions will serve for both or all.

hoo·ray′ *int., n.* hurrah
Aus′tri·an *n., a.* (native) of Austria

IV. INFLECTED FORMS

Inflected forms not regular in spelling are entered in capitals within brackets after the part-of-speech label. They are usually truncated.

au·thor′i·ty *n.* [*pl.* -TIES]
hem *v.* [HEMMED, HEMMING]

Certain inflected forms are not entered. These include past tenses

and past participles that are formed by adding -ed to the infinitive, as *waited*, or -d, as *closed*; present participles formed by adding -ing to the infinitive, as *waiting*, or -ing, after dropping the e, as *closing*; comparatives and superlatives formed by adding -er and -est to the base of an adjective or adverb, as *taller*, *tallest* or *sooner*, *soonest*; and plurals formed by adding -s or -es to the singular, as *bats*, *boxes*.

Where two inflected forms are given for a verb, the first is the past tense and the past participle, and second is the present participle.

make *v.* [MADE, MAKING]

Where three forms are given, the first is the past tense, the second the past participle, and the third the present participle.

give *v.* [GAVE, GIVEN, GIVING]

Alternative principal parts are given where needed.

bid (bid) *v.* [BADE or BID, BIDDEN or BID, BIDDING]
dive *v.* [*alt. pt.* DOVE]

V. THE DEFINITIONS

A. *Capitalization* – A main entry that is capitalized may have a sense that is not. Or a lower-case main entry may have a sense that

ix

is capitalized. Such senses are shown thus.

A·pos'tle (-päs''l) *n.* **1.** any of the disciples of Jesus **2.** [a-] leader of a new movement

maj·es·ty *n.* **1.** grandeur; dignity **2.** [M-] title for a sovereign

B. *Verbs Followed by Prepositions or Objects* – Prepositions that customarily follow certain verbs are italicized inside parentheses. The typical objects of certain verbs may appear inside parentheses.

VI. RUN-IN DERIVED ENTRIES

It is possible in English to form an almost infinite number of derived forms, simply by adding certain prefixes or suffixes to the base word. The editors have included as run-in entries, in boldface type, as many of these common derived words as space permitted, but only when the meaning of such words can be immediately understood from the meanings of the base word and the prefix or suffix. Thus, **liveliness** and **madness** are run in at the end of the entries for **lively** and **mad**, the suffix **-ness** being found as a separate entry meaning "quality; state." Many words formed with common suffixes, such as **-able**, **-er**, **-less**, **-like**, **-ly**, **-tion**, etc. are similarly treated as run-in entries with the base word from which they are derived. All such entries are syllabified and either accented to show stress in pronunciation or, where necessary, pronounced in full or in part.

When a derived word has a meaning or meanings different from those that can be deduced from the sum of its parts, it has been given separate entry, pronounced, and fully defined (for example, **folder**).

A

a *a.* *indefinite article* **1.** one **2.** each; any one

a- *pref.* not

aard·vark (ärd'-) *n.* African mammal that eats ants

ab- *pref.* away; from; down

a·back' *adv.* [Ar.] back — **taken aback** surprised

ab'a·cus *n.* frame with beads for doing arithmetic

ab·a·lo'ne *n.* sea mollusk

a·ban'don *v.* **1.** give up entirely **2.** to desert —*n.* lack of restraint

a·ban'doned *a.* **1.** deserted **2.** shamefully wicked **3.** unrestrained

a·base' *v.* to humble

a·bash' *v.* embarrass

a·bate' *v.* lessen —**a·bate'- ment** *n.*

ab·at·toir' (-ə twär') *n.* slaughterhouse

ab·bé (a'bā) *n.* priest's title in France

ab'bess *n.* woman who is head of a nunnery

ab'bey (-ē) *n.* [*pl.* -BEYS] monastery or nunnery

ab'bot *n.* man who is head of a monastery

ab·bre'vi·ate *v.* shorten, as a word

ab·bre·vi·a'tion *n.* **1.** a short-ening **2.** shortened word or phrase, as *Dr.* for *doctor*

A B C *n.* [*pl.* A B C's] **1.** *usually pl.* alphabet **2.** basics; rudiments

ab'di·cate *v.* give up, as a throne —**ab'di·ca'tion** *n.*

ab'do·men (or ab dō'-) *n.* part of the body between chest and pelvis; belly —**ab·dom'i·nal** (-däm'-) *a.*

ab·duct' *v.* kidnap **ab·duc'- tion** *n.* —**ab·duc'tor** *n.*

a·bed' *adv.* in bed

ab·er·ra'tion *n.* deviation from normal, right, etc. —**ab·er'- rant** (a ber'ənt) *a.*

a·bet' *v.* [ABETTED, ABET-TING] to help, esp. in crime — **a·bet'tor, a·bet'ter** *n.*

a·bey'ance (-bā'-) *n.* temporary suspension

ab·hor' *v.* [-HORRED, -HOR-RING] shun in disgust, hatred, etc. —**ab·hor'rence** *n.*

ab·hor'rent *a.* detestable

a·bide' *v.* [ABODE or ABIDED, ABIDING] **1.** remain **2.** [Ar.] reside **3.** await **4.** endure — **abide by** keep (a promise) or obey (rules)

a·bid'ing *a.* enduring

a·bil'i·ty *n.* [*pl.* -TIES] **1.** a being able **2.** talent

ab'ject *a.* miserable

ab·jure' v. renounce on oath — **ab'ju·ra'tion** n.

a·blaze' a. on fire

a'ble a. 1. having power (to do) 2. talented; skilled —**a'bly** adv.

-able suf. 1. that can or should be 2. tending to

a'ble-bod'ied a. healthy

able-bodied seaman skilled seaman: also **able seaman**

ab·lu'tion n. a washing of the body, esp. as a rite

ab'ne·gate v. renounce; give up —**ab'ne·ga'tion** n.

ab·nor'mal a. not normal — **ab·nor'mal·ly** adv.

ab'nor·mal'i·ty n. 1. abnormal condition 2. [pl. -TIES] abnormal thing

a·board' adv., prep. on or in (a train, ship, etc.)

a·bode' n. home

a·bol'ish v. do away with

ab'o·li'tion n. an abolishing, spec. [A-] of slavery in U.S. — **ab'o·li'tion·ist** n.

A'-bomb' n. atomic bomb

a·bom'i·na·ble a. 1. disgusting 2. very bad —**a·bom'i·na·bly** adv.

a·bom'i·nate v. loathe — **a·bom'i·na'tion** n.

ab'o·rig'i·ne (-rij'ə nē) n. native of original stock —**ab'o·rig'i·nal** a., n.

a·bort' v. 1. have or cause to have a miscarriage 2. cut short (a flight, etc.), as because of equipment failure

a·bor'tion n. miscarriage, esp. if done on purpose

a·bor'tive a. unsuccessful; fruitless

a·bound' v. be plentiful

a·bout' adv. 1. around 2. near 3. in an opposite direction 4. nearly —a. astir —prep. 1. around 2. near to 3. just starting 4. concerning

a·bout'-face' n. a reversal

a·bove' adv. 1. higher 2. earlier on a page —prep. 1. over 2. higher than —a. mentioned above

a·bove'board' a., adv. in plain view; honest (ly)

ab·rade' (ə brād') v. scrape away

ab·ra'sion n. 1. an abrading 2. abraded spot

ab·ra'sive a. causing abrasion —n. substance, as sandpaper, used for grinding, polishing, etc.

a·breast' adv., a. 1. side by side 2. informed (of)

a·bridge' v. shorten, as in wording; lessen —**a·bridg'ment, a·bridge'ment** n.

a·broad' adv. 1. far and wide 2. outdoors 3. to or in foreign lands —from abroad from a foreign land

ab'ro·gate v. abolish; repeal — **ab'ro·ga'tion** n.

a·brupt' a. 1. sudden 2. brusque 3. steep —**a·brupt'ly** adv. —**a·brupt'ness** n.

ab'scess (-ses) n. inflamed, pus-filled area in body

ab·scond' (-skänd') v. flee and hide to escape the law

ab'sent a. 1. not present; away 2. lacking —v. (ab sent') keep (oneself) away —**ab'sence** n.

ab·sen·tee' n. one who is absent, as from work —a. of, by, or from one who is absent — **ab·sen·tee·ism** n.

absentee ballot ballot marked and sent to a board of elections by a voter (**absentee voter**) who cannot be present to vote in an election

ab·sent-mind·ed a. **1.** not attentive **2.** forgetful

absent without leave Mil. absent from duty without official permission

ab·sinthe, ab·sinth (-sinth) n. green, bitter liqueur

ab·so·lute a. **1.** perfect **2.** complete **3.** not mixed; pure **4.** certain; positive **5.** real —**ab'·so·lute·ly** adv.

ab'so·lu'tion n. **1.** forgiveness **2.** remission (of sin)

ab·solve' v. to free from guilt, a duty, etc.

ab·sorb' v. **1.** suck up **2.** engulf wholly **3.** interest greatly —**ab·sorp'tion** n. —**ab·sorp'tive** a.

ab·sorb'ent a. able to absorb moisture, etc.

ab·stain' v. do without; refrain —**ab·sten'tion** n.

ab·ste'mi·ous (-stē'-) a. not eating or drinking too much

ab'sti·nence n. an abstaining from food, liquor, etc.

ab·stract' a. **1.** apart from material objects; not concrete **2.** theoretical —v. summarize —n. (ab'strakt) summary —**ab·strac'tion** n.

ab·stract'ed a. preoccupied

ab·struse' a. hard to understand —**ab·struse'ly** adv. —**ab·struse'ness** n.

ab·surd' a. ridiculous —**ab·surd'i·ty** n. [pl. -TIES] —**ab·surd'ly** adv.

a·bun'dance n. more than is needed —**a·bun'dant** a. —**a·bun'dant·ly** adv.

a·buse' (-byōōz') v. **1.** use wrongly **2.** mistreat **3.** berate —n. (-byōōs') **1.** wrong use **2.** mistreatment **3.** corrupt practice **4.** vile language —**a·bu'sive** a. —**a·bu'sive·ly** adv.

a·but' v. [ABUTTED, ABUTTING] to border (on or upon)

a·but'ment n. part supporting an arch, strut, etc.

a·bys'mal (-biz'-) a. **1.** too deep to be measured **2.** very bad —**a·bys'mal·ly** adv.

a·byss' (-bis') n. deep or bottomless gulf

a·ca'cia (-kā'shə) n. tree with yellow or white flowers

ac·a·dem'ic a. **1.** of schools or colleges **2.** of liberal arts **3.** merely theoretical —**ac·a·dem'i·cal·ly** adv.

a·cad'e·my n. [pl. -MIES] **1.** private high school **2.** school for special study **3.** society of scholars, etc.

a·can'thus n. plant with large, graceful leaves

a cap·pel·la (ä kə pel'ə) with no instruments accompanying: said of choral singing

ac·cede' (-sēd') v. **1.** agree (to) **2.** enter upon the duties of (an office)

ac·cel'er·ate (-sel'-) v. **1.** increase in speed **2.** make happen sooner —**ac·cel'er·a'tion** n. —**ac·cel'er·a'tor** n.

ac'cent n. **1.** stress on a syllable in speaking **2.** mark showing this **3.** distinctive way of pronouncing **4.** rhythmic stress —*v.* emphasize

ac·cen′tu·ate (-choo-) *v.* to accent; emphasize; stress

ac·cept′ *v.* **1.** receive willingly **2.** approve **3.** agree to **4.** believe in

ac·cept′a·ble *a.* worth accepting; satisfactory —**ac·cept′a·bil′i·ty** *n.* —**ac·cept′a·bly** *adv.*

ac·cept′ance *n.* **1.** an accepting **2.** approval **3.** belief in

ac·cept′ed *a.* generally regarded as true, proper, etc.; conventional; approved

ac′cess *n.* **1.** right to enter, use, etc. **2.** means of approach

ac·ces′si·ble *a.* **1.** easy to enter, etc. **2.** obtainable —**ac·ces′si·bil′i·ty** *n.* —**ac·ces′si·bly** *adv.*

ac·ces′sion *n.* **1.** an attaining (the throne, etc.) **2.** an addition or increase

ac·ces′so·ry *n.* [*pl.* -RIES] **1.** thing added for decoration, etc. **2.** helper in a crime

ac′ci·dent *n.* **1.** unexpected happening **2.** mishap **3.** chance

ac′ci·den′tal *a.* happening by chance; unplanned —**ac′ci·den′tal·ly** *adv.*

ac′ci·dent-prone′ *a.* prone or apt to be in or have accidents

ac·claim′ *v.* greet with applause —*n.* great approval

ac′cla·ma′tion *n.* **1.** great applause **2.** spoken vote of "yes" by many

ac·cli·mate (ak′lə māt, ə klī′mət) *v.* get used to a new climate or situation: also **ac·cli′ma·tize**

ac′co·lade *n.* high praise

ac·com′mo·date *v.* **1.** adjust **2.** do a favor for **3.** have room for; lodge

ac·com′mo·dat·ing *a.* obliging

ac·com′mo·da′tion *n.* **1.** adjustment **2.** willingness to do favors **3.** a help **4.** [*pl.*] lodgings **5.** [*pl.*] traveling space, as a seat on a plane

ac·com′pa·ny *v.* [-NIED, -NY·ING] **1.** add to **2.** go with **3.** play music supporting a soloist —**ac·com′pa·ni·ment** *n.* —**ac·com′pa·nist** *n.*

ac·com′plice (-plis) *n.* partner in crime

ac·com′plish *v.* do; complete

ac·com′plished *a.* **1.** done; completed **2.** skilled; expert

ac·com′plish·ment *n.* **1.** completion **2.** work completed **3.** a social art or skill

ac·cord′ *v.* **1.** agree **2.** grant —*n.* agreement —**according to 1.** consistent with **2.** as stated by —**of one's own accord** voluntarily —**ac·cord′ance** *n.*

ac·cord′ing·ly *adv.* **1.** in a fitting way **2.** therefore

ac·cor′di·on *n.* musical instrument with a bellows

ac·cost′ *v.* approach and speak to

ac·count′ *v.* **1.** give reasons (*for*) **2.** judge to be —*n.* **1.** *pl.* business records **2.** bank account **3.** charge account **4.** worth **5.** explanation **6.** a report —**on account** as part payment —**on account of** because of —**on no account** under no circumstances —**take into account** consider —**turn to account** get use or profit from

ac·count'a·ble a. 1. responsible 2. explainable

ac·count'ant n. one whose work is accounting

ac·count'ing n. the keeping of business records

ac·cou'ter (-kōō'-) v. equip

ac·cou'ter·ments n.pl. 1. outfit; clothes 2. soldier's equipment

ac·cred'it v. 1. authorize; certify 2. believe in —**ac·cred'it·a'tion** n.

ac·cre'tion n. 1. growth in size 2. accumulated matter 3. growing together of parts

ac·crue' (-krōō') v. be added, as interest on money

ac·cu'mu·late v. pile up; collect —**ac·cu'mu·la'tion** n.

ac'cu·rate (-rit) a. exactly correct —**ac'cu·ra·cy** n. —**ac'cu·rate·ly** adv.

ac·curs'ed a. damnable

ac·cuse' (-kyōōz') v. 1. to blame 2. charge with doing wrong —**ac·cu·sa'tion** n.

ac·cus'tom v. make familiar by habit or use

ac·cus'tomed a. 1. usual; customary 2. used (to)

ace n. 1. playing card with one spot 2. expert —a. [Col.] first-rate

ace in the hole [Sl.] any advantage held in reserve

ac'er·bate (as'-) v. 1. make sour or bitter 2. irritate

a·cer'bi·ty (-sur'-) n. sourness; sharpness —**a·cerb'**, **a·cer'bic** a.

ac·et·an·i·lide (as'ə tan'ə lid') n. drug used to lessen pain and fever

ac'e·tate (as'-) n. 1. salt or ester of acetic acid 2. fabric made of an acetate of cellulose

a·ce'tic acid sour acid found in vinegar

ac'e·tone n. liquid solvent for certain oils, etc.

a·cet'y·lene (-set''l-) n. gas used in a blowtorch

ache (āk) n. dull, steady pain —v. have such pain

a·chieve' v. 1. do; accomplish 2. get by effort —**a·chieve'ment** n.

ac'id (as'-) n. 1. sour substance 2. chemical that reacts with a base to form a salt —a. 1. sour; sharp 2. of an acid —**a·cid'i·ty** n.

acid test crucial, final test

a·cid'u·lous (-sij'ōō-) a. somewhat acid or sour

ac·knowl'edge v. 1. admit or recognize 2. respond to (a greeting, invitation, etc.) 3. express thanks for —**ac·knowl'edg·ment** n.

ac'me (-mē) n. highest point

ac'ne (-nē) n. pimply skin

ac'o·lyte n. altar boy

ac'o·nite n. poisonous plant with hoodlike flowers

a'corn n. nut of the oak

acorn squash winter squash, acorn-shaped with green skin

a·cous'tics (-kōōs'-) n. 1. science of sound 2. [with pl.v.] qualities of a room that affect sound —**a·cous'tic**, **a·cous'**-

ti·cal *a.* —a·cous'ti·cal·ly *adv.*

ac·quaint' *v.* 1. make familiar (*with*) 2. inform

ac·quaint'ance *n.* 1. personal knowledge 2. person one knows slightly

ac·qui·esce' (-kwē es') *v.* consent without protest —ac·qui·es'cence *n.* —ac·qui·es'cent *a.*

ac·quire' (-kwīr') *v.* get as one's own —ac·quire'ment *n.*

ac'qui·si'tion (-kwə zish'-) *n.* 1. an acquiring 2. something acquired

ac·quis'i·tive (ə kwiz'ə-) *a.* eager to acquire money, etc. —ac·quis'i·tive·ness *n.*

ac·quit' (ə kwit') *v.* [-QUITTED, -QUITTING] 1. declare not guilty 2. conduct (oneself) —ac·quit'tal *n.*

a·cre (ā'kər) *n.* measure of land, 43,560 sq. ft.

a'cre·age (-ij) *n.* acres collectively

ac'rid *a.* sharp or bitter

ac'ri·mo·ny *n.* bitterness, as of manner or speech —ac'ri·mo'ni·ous *a.*

ac'ro·bat *n.* performer on the trapeze, tightrope, etc. —ac'ro·bat'ic *a.*

ac'ro·bat'ics *n.pl.* acrobat's tricks

ac'ro·nym *n.* word formed from the first letters of several words, such as *radar*

ac'ro·pho'bi·a *n.* fear of being in high places

a·cross' *adv.* from one side to the other —*prep.* 1. from one side to the other of 2. on the other side of 3. into contact with

a·cryl'ic (-kril'-) *a.* 1. of certain synthetic fibers used to make fabrics 2. of certain clear, synthetic resins

act *n.* 1. thing done 2. a doing 3. a law 4. division of a play or opera —*v.* 1. perform in a play, etc. 2. behave 3. function 4. have an effect (*on*)

act'ing *a.* substitute

ac·tin'ic *a.* designating rays causing chemical change

ac'tion *n.* 1. a doing of something 2. thing done 3. *pl.* behavior 4. way of working 5. lawsuit 6. combat

ac'ti·vate *v.* make active —ac'ti·va'tion *n.*

ac'tive *a.* 1. acting; working 2. busy; lively; agile —ac'tive·ly *adv.*

ac·tiv'i·ty *n.* [*pl.* -TIES] 1. a being active 2. liveliness 3. specific action

ac'tor *n.* one who acts in plays —ac'tress *n.fem.*

ac'tu·al (-choo-) *a.* existing; real —ac'tu·al'i·ty *n.*

ac'tu·al·ize *v.* 1. make actual or real 2. make realistic —ac'tu·al·ly *adv.* really

ac'tu·ar'y *n.* [*pl.* -IES] insurance statistician —ac'tu·ar'i·al *a.*

ac'tu·ate *v.* 1. put into action 2. impel to action

a·cu'i·ty (-kyoō'-) *n.* keenness of thought or vision

a·cu'men *n.* keenness of mind

ac'u·punc'ture *n.* the practice, esp. in China, of piercing the body with needles to treat disease or pain

a·cute′ *a.* 1. sharp-pointed 2. shrewd 3. keen 4. severe 5. critical 6. less than 90°: said of angles —**a·cute′ly** *adv.* —**a·cute′ness** *n.*

ad *n.* [Col.] advertisement

A.D. of the Christian era

ad′age (ij) *n.* proverb

a·da·gio (ə dä′jō, -zhō) *adv., a. Music* slow(ly)

ad′a·mant *a.* unyielding

Ad′am's apple bulge in the front of a man's throat

a·dapt′ *v.* fit or adjust as needed —**a·dapt′a·ble** *a.* —**ad′ap·ta′tion** *n.*

add *v.* 1. join (*to*) so as to increase 2. increase 3. find the sum of 4. say further —**add up** seem reasonable —**add up to** signify; mean

ad·den′dum *n.* [*pl.* -DA] thing added, as an appendix

ad′der *n.* small snake, sometimes poisonous

ad·dict′ *v.* give (oneself) up (*to* a habit) —*n.* (ad′ikt) one addicted, as to a drug —**ad·dic′tion** *n.* —**ad·dic′tive** *a.*

ad·di′tion *n.* 1. an adding 2. part added —**in addition** (*to*) besides

ad·di′tion·al *a.* added; more; extra —**ad·di′tion·al·ly** *adv.*

ad′di·tive *n.* something added —*a.* of addition

ad′dle *v.* make or become confused —**ad′dled** *a.*

ad·dress′ *v.* 1. speak or write to 2. write the destination on (mail, etc.) 3. apply (oneself *to*) —*n.* 1. a speech 2. (or ad′-

res) place where one lives or receives mail

ad·dress·ee (ad res ē′) *n.* person to whom mail, etc. is addressed

ad·duce′ *v.* give as proof

-ade *suf.* 1. the act of 2. participants in 3. drink made from

ad′e·noids *n.pl.* growths in the throat behind the nose

a·dept′ *a.* highly skilled —*n.* (ad′ept) an expert

ad′e·quate (-kwət) *a.* enough or good enough —**ad′e·qua·cy** *n.* —**ad′e·quate·ly** *adv.*

ad·here′ *v.* 1. stick fast 2. give support (*to*) —**ad·her′ence** *n.* —**ad·her′ent** *n.*

ad·he′sion *n.* 1. a being stuck together 2. body tissues abnormally joined

ad·he′sive *a.* sticking —*n.* sticky substance, as glue

ad hoc (häk′) for a specific purpose

a·dieu (ə dyōo′) *int., n.* [Fr.] goodbye

ad in·fi·ni·tum (-nī′-) [L.] endlessly

a·di·os (ä dē ōs′, ä dyōs′) *int.* [Sp.] goodbye

ad′i·pose (-pōs) *a.* fatty

ad·ja′cent *a.* near or next

ad′jec·tive (-tiv) *n.* word that qualifies a noun —**ad′jec·ti′val** (-tī′-) *a.*

ad·join′ *v.* be next to —**ad·join′ing** *a.*

ad·journ′ (-jurn′) *v.* suspend (a meeting, etc.) for a time —**ad·journ′ment** *n.*

ad·judge′ *v.* judge, declare, or award

ad·ju'di·cate (-jōō'-) v. act as judge (in or on)

ad'junct n. a nonessential addition

ad·jure' v. 1. order solemnly 2. ask earnestly

ad·just' v. 1. alter to make fit 2. regulate 3. settle rightly —**ad·just'a·ble** a. —**ad·just'ment** n.

ad'ju·tant n. 1. assistant, esp. to a commanding officer 2. large stork of India and Africa

ad-lib' v. [-LIBBED, -LIBBING] [Col.] improvise (words, etc.) —n. [Col.] ad-libbed remark —adv. [Col.] as one pleases: also **ad lib**

ad'man n. [pl. -MEN] a man whose work is advertising

ad·min'is·ter v. 1. manage; direct 2. give; attend (to) —**ad·min'is·tra'tor** n.

ad·min'is·tra'tion n. 1. an administering 2. executive officials; management —**ad·min'is·tra'tive** a.

ad'mi·ra·ble a. worth admiring —**ad'mi·ra·bly** adv.

ad'mi·ral n. high-ranking naval officer

ad'mi·ral·ty n. department of naval affairs

ad·mire' v. have high regard for —**ad·mi·ra'tion** n.

ad·mis'si·ble a. acceptable

ad·mis'sion n. 1. an admitting 2. entrance fee 3. confession or concession

ad·mit' v. [-MITTED, -MITTING] 1. let enter 2. concede or confess —**ad·mit'tance** n.

ad·mit'ted·ly adv. by general agreement

ad·mix'ture n. mixture

ad·mon'ish v. 1. warn or advise 2. reprove mildly —**ad'mo·ni'tion** n. —**ad·mon'i·to·ry** a.

ad nau'se·am (nô'ze-, -nô'shē-) [L.] to the point of disgust

a·do' (-dōō') n. fuss; trouble

a·do'be (-dō'bē) n. unburnt, sun-dried brick

ad'o·les'cence n. the time of life between childhood and adulthood; youth

ad'o·les'cent a. of or in adolescence —n. a person during adolescence

a·dopt' v. 1. take legally as one's child 2. take as one's own 3. choose or accept —**a·dop'tion** n.

a·dop'tive a. that has become so by adoption

a·dor'a·ble a. [Col.] delightful; charming

a·dore' v. 1. worship 2. love greatly 3. [Col.] like very much —**ad'o·ra'tion** n.

a·dorn' v. decorate; ornament —**a·dorn'ment** n.

ad·re'nal glands two ductless glands on the kidneys

Ad·ren'al·in trademark for a hormone that is a heart stimulant —n. [a-] this hormone

a·drift' adv., a. floating aimlessly

a·droit' a. skillful and clever —**a·droit'ly** adv.

ad·u·late (aj'ə-) v. flatter servilely —**ad·u·la'tion** n.

a·dult' a. grown-up; mature —n. mature person, animal, or plant —**a·dult'hood** n.

a·dul'ter·ant n. substance that

adulterates —*a*. adulterating
a·dul'ter·ate *v*. make impure
by adding things —a·dul'ter·
a'tion *n*.

a·dul'ter·y *n*. [*pl*. -IES] sexual
intercourse between a married
person and another person not
the spouse —a·dul'ter·er *n*.
—a·dul'ter·ess *n.fem*. —
a·dul'ter·ous *a*.

ad·vance' *v*. 1. bring or go
forward 2. pay before due 3.
rise or raise in rank —*n*. 1. a
move forward 2. *pl*. approaches
to get favor 3. payment made
before due —*a*. 1. in front 2.
beforehand —in advance 1.
in front 2. ahead of time —ad·
vance'ment *n*.

ad·vanced' *a*. 1. in front 2.
old 3. ahead or higher in progress, price, etc.

ad·van'tage *n*. 1. superiority
2. gain; benefit —take advantage of 1. use for one's own
benefit 2. impose upon —ad'-
van·ta'geous *a*.

ad·ven·ti'tious (-ti'-) *a*. not
inherent; accidental

ad·ven'ture *n*. 1. dangerous
undertaking 2. exciting experience —ad·ven'tur·ous *a*. —
ad·ven'ture·some *a*.

ad·ven'tur·er *n*. 1. one who
has adventures 2. one who
tries to get rich by shady
schemes —ad·ven'tur·ess
n.fem.

ad'verb *n*. word that modifies
a verb, adjective, or other adverb —ad·ver'bi·al *a*.

ad'ver·sar'y *n*. [*pl*. -IES] foe;
opponent

ad·verse' (*or* ad'vərs) *a*. 1. op-

posed 2. harmful —ad·
verse'ly *adv*.

ad·ver'si·ty (-vur'-) *n*. 1. misfortune 2. *pl*. [-TIES] calamity;
disaster

ad·vert' *v*. refer (*to*)

ad'ver·tise (-tīz) *v*. tell about
publicly to promote sales, etc.
—ad'ver·tis'er *n*. —ad'ver·
tis'ing *n*.

ad'ver·tise'ment (*or* ad·vur'-
tiz-) *n*. public notice, usually
paid for

ad·vice' *n*. opinion on what to
do

ad·vis'a·ble (-vīz'-) *a*. being
good advice; wise —ad·vis'a·
bil'i·ty *n*.

ad·vise' *v*. 1. give advice (*to*)
2. offer as advice 3. inform —
ad·vis'er, ad·vi'sor *n*.

ad·vis·ed·ly *adv*. with due
consideration

ad·vise'ment *n*. careful consideration

ad·vi'so·ry *a*. advising or em-
powered to advise —*n*. [*pl*.
-RIES] a report, esp. about
weather conditions

ad'vo·cate *v*. support or urge
—*n*. (-kit) one who supports
another or a cause —ad'vo·
ca·cy (-kə sē) *n*.

adz, adze *n*. axlike tool

ae·gis (ē'jis) *n*. sponsorship

ae·on (ē'ən) *n*. very long time

aer'ate (er'-) *v*. expose to air
—aer·a'tion *n*.

aer'i·al (er'-) *a*. 1. of or like
air 2. of flying —*n*. radio or
TV antenna

aero- *pref*. 1. air; of air 2. of
aircraft

aer'o·nau'tics (-nô'-) *n*. the

science of making and operating aircraft —**aer·o·nau'ti·cal** *a.*

aer'o·sol' (-sôl', -säl') *a.* **1.** of a container in which gas under pressure is used to dispense liquid or foam **2.** so dispensed

aer'o·space *n.* earth's atmosphere and outer space —*a.* of missiles, etc. for flight in aerospace

aes·thete (es'thēt) *n.* one who is sensitive to art and beauty, or pretends to be

aes·thet'ic (-thet'-) *a.* **1.** of beauty or aesthetics **2.** sensitive to art and beauty

aes·thet'ics *n.* philosophy or study of beauty

a·far' *adv.* far away

af'fa·ble *a.* pleasant; sociable —**af'fa·bil'i·ty** *n.*

af·fair' *n.* **1.** matter; event **2.** *pl.* matters of business **3.** amorous episode

af·fect' *v.* **1.** act on; influence **2.** stir emotionally **3.** like to wear, use, etc. **4.** pretend to be or feel

af'fec·ta'tion *n.* **1.** pretense **2.** artificial behavior

af·fect'ed *a.* **1.** artificial **2.** diseased **3.** influenced **4.** emotionally moved **5.** behaving in an artificial way

af·fect'ing *a.* emotionally moving

af·fec'tion *n.* **1.** fond feeling **2.** disease

af·fec'tion·ate (-it) *a.* tender and loving; fond —**af·fec'tion·ate·ly** *adv.*

af·fi'ance *v.* betroth

af·fi·da·vit (-dā'-) *n.* sworn statement in writing

af·fil'i·ate *v.* join as a member; associate —*n.* (-it) affiliated member —**af·fil'i·a'tion** *n.*

af·fin'i·ty *n.* [*pl.* -TIES] **1.** close relationship or kinship **2.** attraction to a person or thing

af·firm' *v.* assert or confirm —**af'fir·ma'tion** *n.*

af·firm'a·tive *a.* affirming; positive —*n.* assent

af·fix' *v.* attach —*n.* (af'-) thing affixed, as a prefix

af·flict' *v.* cause pain to; distress —**af·flic'tion** *n.*

af'flu·ence *n.* **1.** plenty **2.** riches

af'flu·ent *a.* **1.** plentiful **2.** rich; wealthy

af·ford' *v.* **1.** have money enough for **2.** provide

af·for'est *v.* turn (land) into forest —**af·for'est·a'tion** *n.*

af·front' *v.*, *n.* insult

af'ghan (-gan) *n.* crocheted or knitted blanket

a·field' *adv.* away; astray

a·fire' *adv.*, *a.* on fire

a·flame' *adv.*, *a.* in flames

a·float' *a.* **1.** floating **2.** at sea **3.** current **4.** flooded, as a ship's deck

a·flut'ter *adv.*, *a.* in a flutter

a·foot' *adv.* **1.** on foot **2.** in motion; astir

a·fore'men'tioned *a.* mentioned before

a·fore'said *a.* said before

a·fore'thought *a.* thought out beforehand; premeditated

a·foul' *adv.*, *a.* in a tangle or

collision —**run** (or **fall**) **afoul of** get into trouble with

a·fraid' *a.* **1.** frightened **2.** regretful

a·fresh' *adv.* anew; again

Af'ri·can *n.*, *a.* (native) of Africa

Af'ro *n.* bouffant hair style

aft *adv.* near the stern

af'ter *adv.* **1.** behind **2.** later —*prep.* **1.** behind **2.** in search of **3.** later than **4.** because of **5.** in spite of **6.** in imitation of **7.** for —*con.* later than —*a.* later

af'ter·birth *n.* placenta, etc. expelled after childbirth

af'ter·ef·fect *n.* an effect coming later, or as a secondary result

af'ter·life *n.* life after death

af'ter·thought *n.* (bad) result

af'ter·math *n.* time from noon to evening —*a.* in the afternoon

af'ter·thought *n.* a thought coming later or too late

af'ter·ward *adv.* later; subsequently: also **af'ter·wards**

a·gain' *adv.* **1.** once more **2.** besides —**again and again** repeatedly —**as much again** twice as much

a·gainst' *prep.* **1.** opposed to **2.** so as to hit **3.** next to **4.** in preparation for

a·gape' *adv.*, *a.* with mouth wide open

ag·ate (ag'ət) *n.* **1.** hard, semiprecious stone, often striped **2.** a playing marble made of or like this

a·ga've (-gä'vē) *n.* desert plant with thick leaves

age *n.* **1.** length of time of existence **2.** stage of life **3.** old age **4.** historical period **5.** *often pl.* [Col.] long time —*v.* grow or make old —**of age** old enough to qualify for full legal rights

-age *suf.* act or state of; amount of; place of or for; cost of

a'ged *a.* **1.** old **2.** (ājd) of the age of —**the aged** old people

age'less *a.* **1.** seemingly not growing older **2.** eternal

a'gen·cy (-jən sē) *n.* [*pl.* **-CIES**] **1.** action or means **2.** firm that acts for another **3.** administrative government division

a·gen'da (-jen'-) *n.* list of things to be dealt with

a'gent *n.* **1.** force, or cause of an effect **2.** one that acts for another

age'-old' *a.* ancient

ag·gran'dize (or ag'rən-) *v.* to increase in power, riches, etc. —**ag·gran'dize·ment** *n.*

ag'gra·vate *v.* **1.** make worse **2.** [Col.] vex; annoy —**ag'gra·va'tion** *n.*

ag'gre·gate (-git; *for v.*, -gāt) *a.*, *n.*, *v.* total; mass —**ag'gre·ga'tion** *n.*

ag·gres'sion *n.* unprovoked attack —**ag·gres'sor** *n.*

ag·gres'sive (-siv) *a.* **1.** quarrelsome **2.** bold and active —**ag·gres'sive·ly** *adv.*

ag·grieve' (-grēv') *v.* offend

a·ghast' (-gast') *a.* horrified

ag·ile (aj'l) *a.* quick; nimble —**ag'ile·ly** *adv.* —**a·gil'i·ty** (-jil'-) *n.*

ag'i·tate (aj'-) *v.* **1.** stir up **2.**

disturb 3. talk to arouse support (for) —**ag'i·ta'tion** n. —**ag'i·ta·tor** n.

a·glow' adv., a. in a glow

ag·nos'tic n. one who doubts the existence of God —**ag·nos'ti·cism** n.

a·go' adv., a. (in the) past

a·gog' a. eager; excited

ag'o·nize v. 1. cause agony 2. be in agony 3. to torture

ag'o·ny n. great suffering

a·grar'i·an a. of land and farming

a·gree' v. 1. to consent 2. be in harmony or accord 3. be of the same opinion 4. be suitable, healthful, etc.

a·gree'a·ble a. 1. pleasing 2. willing to consent —**a·gree'a·bly** adv.

a·gree'ment n. 1. an agreeing 2. a contract

ag'ri·cul'ture n. farming —**ag'ri·cul'tur·al** a. —**ag'ri·cul'tur·al·ly** adv.

a·ground' adv., a. on or onto the shore, a reef, etc.

a·gue (ā'gyōō) n. fever with chills

ah int. cry of pain, delight, etc.

a·ha' int. cry of satisfaction, triumph, etc.

a·head' adv., a. in front; forward; in advance

a·hoy' int. Naut. hailing call

aid v. help; assist —n. 1. help; assistance 2. helper

aide (ād) n. 1. assistant 2. aide-de-camp

aide'-de-camp' n. [pl. AIDES-] military officer assisting a superior: also sp. **aid'-de-camp'** [pl. AIDS-]

ail v. 1. to pain 2. be ill

ai'le·ron (ā'-) n. hinged flap of an airplane wing

ail'ment n. chronic illness

aim v. 1. direct (a gun, blow, etc.) 2. intend —n. 1. an aiming 2. direction of aiming 3. intention; goal —**take aim** aim a weapon

aim'less a. having no purpose —**aim'less·ly** adv.

ain't 1. [Col.] am not 2. [Substandard] is not; are not; has not; have not

air n. 1. mixture of gases around the earth 2. appearance 3. pl. haughty manners 4. tune —v. 1. let air into 2. publicize —a. of aviation —**on the air** broadcasting on TV or radio

air base base for military aircraft

air'borne a. 1. carried by or through the air 2. aloft or flying

air conditioning controlling of humidity and temperature of air in a room, etc. —**air'-con·di'tion** v. —**air'-con·di'tion·er** n.

air'craft n.sing. & pl. machine or machines for flying

Aire'dale (er'-) n. large terrier with a wiry coat

air'field n. field where aircraft can take off and land

air force aviation branch of a country's armed forces

air lane route for air travel

air'lift n. the transporting of troops, supplies, etc. by aircraft —v. transport by airlift

air'line n. air transport system

or company —a. of or on an airline

air'lin'er n. large passenger aircraft of an airline

air'mail n. mail transported by aircraft

air'man n. [pl. -MEN] 1. aviator 2. enlisted person in the U.S. Air Force

air'plane n. motor-driven or jet-propelled aircraft with wings

air'port n. airfield with facilities for repair, etc.

air pressure pressure of the atmosphere or of compressed air

air raid attack by aircraft

air'ship n. steerable aircraft that is lighter than air

air'sick a. nauseated because of air travel

air'tight a. too tight for air to enter or escape

air'way n. air lane

air'y a. [-IER, -IEST] 1. open to the air 2. flimsy as air 3. light; graceful 4. gay —**air'i·ly** adv.

aisle (īl) n. passageway between rows of seats

a·jar' adv., a. slightly open

a·kim'bo adv., a. with hands on hips

a·kin' a. similar; alike

-al suf. 1. of; like; fit for 2. act or process of

al'a·bas'ter n. whitish, translucent gypsum

a la carte with a separate price for each dish

a·lac'ri·ty n. quick willingness; readiness

a la mode 1. in fashion 2. served with ice cream

a·larm' n. 1. signal or device

to warn or waken 2. fear —v. frighten

alarm clock clock with device to sound at set time

a·larm'ist n. one who expresses needless alarm

a·las' int. cry of sorrow, etc.

alb n. priest's white robe

al'ba·core n. kind of tuna

al'ba·tross n. large, webfooted sea bird

al·be'it (ôl-) con. although

al·bi'no (-bī'-) n. [pl. -NOS] individual lacking normal coloration

al'bum n. 1. blank book for photographs, stamps, etc. 2. booklike holder for phonograph records 3. single LP or tape recording

al·bu'men (al byōō'mən) n. white of an egg

al·bu'min n. protein in egg, milk, muscle, etc.

al'che·my (-kə-) n. chemistry of the Middle Ages —**al'che·mist** n.

al'co·hol n. colorless, intoxicating liquid got from fermented grain, fruit, etc.

al'co·hol'ic a. of alcohol —n. one addicted to alcohol

al'co·hol·ism n. addiction to alcohol; drinking too much

al'cove n. recess; nook

al'der (ôl'-) n. small tree of the birch family

al'der·man n. [pl. -MEN] member of a city council

ale n. kind of beer

a·lert' a. watchful; ready —n. an alarm —v. warn to be ready —**a·lert'ly** adv. —**a·lert'ness** n.

al·fal'fa n. plant used for fodder, pasture, etc.

al'gae (-jē) n.pl. primitive water plants

al'ge·bra n. mathematics using letters and numbers in equations —**al'ge·bra'ic** a.

a'li·as (ā'-) n. assumed name —adv. otherwise named

al'i·bi (-bī) n. [pl. -BIS] 1. plea that the accused was not at the scene of the crime 2. [Col.] any excuse —v. [Col.] give an excuse

al·ien (āl'yən) a. foreign —n. foreigner

al'ien·ate v. make unfriendly —**al'ien·a'tion** n.

al'ien·ist n. psychiatrist

a·light' v. 1. dismount 2. land after flight —a. lighted up

a·lign' (-līn') v. 1. line up 2. make agree —**a·lign'ment** n.

a·like' a. similar —adv. 1. similarly 2. equally

al'i·men'ta·ry canal the passage in the body that food goes through

al'i·mo'ny n. money paid to support one's former spouse

a·live' a. 1. living; in existence 2. lively —**alive with** teeming with

al'ka·li (-lī) n. [pl. -LIS, -LIES] substance that neutralizes acids —**al'ka·line** a. —**al'ka·lize** v.

al'ka·loid n. alkaline drug from plants, as cocaine

al'kyd (-kid) n. synthetic resin used in paints, etc.

all a. 1. the whole of 2. every one of 3. complete —pron. 1. [with pl. v.] everyone every-thing 3. every bit —n. a whole —adv. entirely —**after all** nevertheless —**all in** [Col.] very tired —**all the same** 1. nevertheless 2. unimportant —**at all** 1. in the least 2. in any way

all- pref. 1. entirely 2. for every 3. of everything

Al'lah God: Muslim name

all'-A·mer'i·can a. chosen as the best in the U.S. —n. all-American team player

all'-a·round' a. having many abilities, uses, etc.

al·lay' v. to calm; quiet

all'-clear' n. siren or signal that an air raid is over

al·lege' (-lej') v. declare, esp. without proof —**al'le·ga'tion** (-gă?-) n. —**al·leg'ed·ly** adv.

al·le'giance (-lē'jəns) n. loyalty, as to one's country

al'le·go'ry n. [pl. -RIES] story in which things, actions, etc. are symbolic

al'le·gret'to a., adv. Music moderately fast

al·le'gro a., adv. Music fast

al'ler·gen (-jən) n. allergy-causing substance

al'ler·gy n. [pl. -GIES] sensitive reaction to certain food, pollen, etc. —**al·ler'gic** a.

al·le'vi·ate (-lē'-) v. relieve; ease —**al·le'vi·a'tion** n.

al'ley n. [pl. -LEYS] 1. narrow street 2. bowling lane

al·li'ance (-lī'-) n. 1. an allying 2. association; league

al·lied' a. 1. united by treaty, etc. 2. related

al'li·ga'tor n. large lizard like a crocodile

alligator pear avocado

all'·im·por'tant *a.* necessary

all'·in·clu'sive *a.* comprehensive

al·lit'er·a'tion *n.* use of the same initial sound in words

al'lo·cate *v.* 1. set apart for a purpose 2. distribute or allot —**al'lo·ca'tion** *n.*

al·lot' *v.* [-LOTTED, -LOTTING] 1. distribute in shares 2. assign —**al·lot'ment** *n.*

all'-out' *a.* thorough

all'o'ver *a.* over the whole surface

al·low' *v.* 1. to permit 2. let have 3. grant —**allow for** leave room, time, etc. for —**al·low'a·ble** *a.*

al·low'ance *n.* 1. thing allowed 2. amount given regularly

al'loy *n.* metal mixture —*v.* (ə loi') mix (metals)

all'-pur'pose *a.* useful in many ways

all right 1. satisfactory 2. unhurt 3. correct 4. yes

all'spice *n.* pungent spice from a berry

all'-star' *a.* made up entirely of star performers

all'-time' *a.* unsurpassed until now

al·lude' *v.* refer; mention

al·lure' *v.* tempt; attract —**al·lur'ing** *a.*

al·lu'sion *n.* indirect or casual mention

al·lu'sive *a.* 1. containing an allusion 2. full of allusions

al·ly' (-lī') *v.* [-LIED, -LYING] unite; join —*n.* (al'ī) [*pl.* -LIES]

country or person joined with another

al'ma ma'ter college or school that one attended

al'ma·nac *n.* calender with miscellaneous data

al·might'y *a.* all-powerful —**the Almighty** God

al·mond (ä'mənd) *n.* edible, nutlike, oval seed of a tree of the peach family

al'most *adv.* very nearly

alms (ämz) *n.* money, food, etc. given to the poor

al'oe (-ō) *n.* African plant whose juice is a laxative

a·loft' *adv.* high up

a·lo'ha *n., int.* love: Hawaiian "hello" or "goodbye"

a·lone' *a., adv.* with no other —**let alone** not to mention

a·long' *prep.* on or beside the length of —*adv.* 1. onward 2. together (*with*) 3. with one —**all along** from the beginning —**be along** [Col.] come —**get along** 1. to advance 2. succeed 3. agree

a·long'shore' *adv.* near or beside the shore

a·long'side' *adv.* at the side —*prep.* beside

a·loof' *adv.* apart —*a.* cool and reserved

a·loud' *adv.* loudly

al·pac'a (-pak'ə) *n.* 1. kind of llama 2. cloth from its long, silky wool

al'pha *n.* first letter of the Greek alphabet

al'pha·bet *n.* letters of a language, in the regular order —**al'pha·bet'i·cal** *a.*

al'pha·bet·ize' v. arrange in alphabetical order

alpha particle a positively charged particle given off by a radioactive substance

alpha ray stream of alpha particles

al·read'y adv. by or before the given time; previously

al'so adv. in addition; too

al'so·ran' n. [Col.] defeated contestant in a race, etc.

al'tar (ôl'-) n. table, etc. for sacred rites, as in a church

altar boy boy or man who helps a priest at religious services, esp. at Mass

al'ter v. change; modify —**al'ter·a'tion** n.

al'ter·ca'tion n. a quarrel

al'ter e'go 1. one's other self 2. constant companion

al'ter·nate (-nit) a. 1. succeeding each other 2. every other —n. a substitute —v. (-nāt) do, use, act, etc. by turns —**al'ter·na'tion** n.

alternating current electric current that reverses direction periodically

al·ter'na·tive (-tiv) n. choice between two or more —a. giving such a choice

al'ter·na'tor n. generator producing alternating current

al·though' (-thō') con. in spite of the fact that

al·tim'e·ter n. instrument for measuring altitude

al'ti·tude n. height, esp. above sea level

al'to n. [pl. -TOS] lowest female voice

al'to·geth'er adv. wholly

al'tru·ism' n. unselfish concern for others —**al'tru·ist** n. —**al'tru·is'tic** a.

al'um n. astringent salt

a·lu'mi·num n. silvery, lightweight metal, a chemical element: also [Br.] **al'u·min'i·um**

a·lum'nus n. [pl. -NI (-nī)] former student of a certain school or college —**a·lum'na** [pl. -NAE (-nē)] n.fem.

al'ways adv. 1. at all times 2. continually

am pres. t. of **be**, with I

AM amplitude modulation

A.M., a.m. before noon

a·mal'gam n. alloy of mercury and another metal

a·mal'ga·mate v. unite —**a·mal'ga·ma'tion** n.

a·man'u·en'sis (-yoo wen'-) n. [pl. -SES (-sēz)] a secretary: now used jokingly

am'a·ranth n. plant with showy flowers

am'a·ryl'lis (-ril'-) n. bulb plant with lilylike flowers

a·mass' v. pile up; collect

am'a·teur (-chər) n. 1. one who does something for pleasure, not pay 2. unskillful person —**am'a·teur'ish** a.

a·maze' v. astonish; surprise —**a·maze'ment** n.

am'a·zon n. strong woman

am·bas'sa·dor n. top-ranking diplomatic official

am'ber n. 1. yellowish fossil resin 2. its color

am'ber·gris (-grēs) n. waxy secretion of certain whales, used in perfumes

am'bi·ance (-bē-) *n.* milieu; environment: also **amblence**

am'bi·dex'trous *a.* using both hands with equal ease

am·big'u·ous *a.* having two or more meanings; vague —**am'bi·gu'i·ty** [*pl.* -TIES] *n.*

am·bi'tion *n.* 1. desire to succeed 2. success desired —**am·bi'tious** *a.*

am·biv'a·lence *n.* simultaneous conflicting feelings —**am·biv'a·lent** *a.*

am'ble *v.* move in an easy gait —*n.* easy gait

am·bro'sia (-zhə) *n.* Gr. & Rom. Myth. food of the gods

am'bu·lance (-byə-) *n.* car to carry sick or wounded

am'bu·late *v.* walk

am'bu·la·to'ry *a.* 1. of walking 2. able to walk

am·bus·cade' *n., v.* ambush

am'bush *n.* 1. a hiding for a surprise attack 2. the hiding place or group —*v.* to attack from hiding

a·me'ba (-mē-) *n.* amoeba

a·mel'io·rate (-mēl'yə-) *v.* improve —**a·mel'io·ra'tion** *n.*

a·men' *int.* may it be so!

a·me'na·ble (-mē'nə-, -men'ə-) *a.* willing to obey or heed advice; responsive —**a·me'na·bly** *adv.*

a·mend' *v.* 1. to correct 2. improve 3. revise, as a law

a·mend'ment *n.* 1. correction 2. improvement 3. revision proposed or made in a law

a·mends' *n.* a making up for injury, loss, etc.

a·men'i·ty *n.* [*pl.* -TIES] 1. pleasantness 2. *pl.* courtesies 3. *pl.* conveniences

a·ment *n.* spike of small flowers, as on a willow

A·mer'i·can *a.* 1. of America 2. of the U.S. —*n.* 1. native of America 2. U.S. citizen

A·mer'i·can·ism *n.* 1. U.S. custom 2. word or idiom originating in American English 3. devotion to the U.S.

A·mer'i·can·ize' *v.* make or become American

am'e·thyst *n.* (-thist) purple quartz for jewelry

a'mi·a·ble (ā'-) *a.* friendly; good-natured

am'i·ca·ble *a.* friendly; peaceable —**am'i·ca·bly** *adv.*

a·mid', a·midst' *prep.* among

a·mid'ship *adv.* in or toward the middle of a ship: also **amidships**

a·mi'go (-mē'-) *n.* [*pl.* -GOS] [Sp.] friend

a·mi'no acids (-mē'-) basic matter of proteins

a·miss' *adv., a.* wrong

am'i·ty *n.* friendship

am'me'ter *n.* instrument for measuring amperes

am'mo *n.* [Sl.] ammunition

am·mo'ni·a *n.* 1. acrid gas 2. water solution of it

am'mu·ni'tion *n.* bullets, gunpowder, bombs, etc.

am·ne'sia (-zhə) *n.* loss of memory

am'nes·ty *n.* general pardon for political offenses

a·moe'ba (-mē'-) *n.* [*pl.* -BAS, -BAE (-bē)] one-celled animal —**a·moe'bic** *a.*

a·mok′ (-muk′) *a., adv.* in a frenzy to kill

a·mong′, a·mongst′ *prep.* **1.** surrounded by **2.** in the group of **3.** to or for each of

a·mon′til·la′do (-män′tə lä′-) *n.* pale, rather dry sherry

a·mor′al (ā-) *a.* with no moral sense or standards

am′o·rous *a.* **1.** fond of making love **2.** full of love

a·mor′phous *a.* **1.** shapeless **2.** of no definite type

am′or·tize *v.* provide for gradual payment of

a·mount′ *v.* **1.** add up (*to*) **2.** be equal (*to*) —*n.* **1.** sum **2.** quantity

a·mour′ (-moor′) *n.* love affair

am′per·age (-ij) *n.* strength of an electric current in amperes

am′pere (-pir) *n.* unit of electric current

am′per·sand *n.* sign (&) meaning *and*

am·phet′a·mine (-mēn) *n.* drug used as a stimulant and to lessen appetite

am·phib′i·an *n.* **1.** land-and-water animal, as the frog **2.** land-and-water vehicle —*a.* amphibious

am·phib′i·ous *a.* adapted to both land and water

am′phi·the·a·ter *n.* open theater with central space circled by tiers of seats

am′ple *a.* **1.** large **2.** adequate; plenty —**am′ply** *adv.*

am′pli·fy *v.* make stronger, louder, or fuller —**am′pli·fi·ca′tion** *n.* —**am′pli·fi′er** *n.*

am′pli·tude *n.* **1.** extent or breadth **2.** abundance

amplitude modulation changing of the amplitude of the radio wave according to the signal being broadcast

am′pul (-pool) *n.* small glass container for one dose of a hypodermic medicine; also **am′pule** (-pyool)

am′pu·tate (-pyə-) *v.* to cut off, esp. by surgery —**am′pu·ta′tion** *n.*

am·pu·tee′ *n.* one who has had a limb amputated

a·muck′ (-muk′) *a., adv.* amok

am′u·let (-yə-) *n.* charm worn against evil

a·muse′ *v.* **1.** entertain **2.** make laugh —**a·mus′ing** *a.* —**a·muse′ment** *n.*

amusement park outdoor place for entertainment, with a merry-go-round, roller coaster, etc.

am′yl·ase (-ə lās) *n.* enzyme that helps change starch into sugar, found in saliva

an *a., indefinite article* **1.** one **2.** each; any one

-an *suf.* **1.** of **2.** born in; living in **3.** believing in

a·nach′ro·nism (-nak′-) *n.* thing out of proper historical time —**a·nach′ro·nis′tic** *a.*

an′a·con′da *n.* large S. American boa snake

a·nae′mi·a (-nē′-) *n.* anemia

an′aer·o′bic (-er-) *a.* able to live without air or free oxygen, as some bacteria

an′a·gram *n.* word made by rearranging the letters of another word

a′nal *a.* of the anus

an·al·ge·sic (-əl jē'zik) n., a. (drug) that eases pain

an'a·log computer (-lôg) computer working by electrical analogy with a mathematical problem to be solved

an'a·logue, an'a·log (-lôg) n. something analogous

a·nal'o·gy (-jē) n. [pl. -GIES] similarity in some ways —a·nal'o·gous (-gəs) a.

a·nal'y·sis (-ə sis) n. [pl. -SES (-sēz)] 1. separation of a whole into its parts to find out their nature, etc. 2. psychoanalysis —an'a·lyst (-list) n. —an'a·lyt'i·cal a. —an'a·lyze (-līz) v.

an'arch·ism (-ər kiz'm) n. opposition to all government —an'arch·ist n.

an·arch·y n. 1. absence of government and law 2. great disorder —an·ar'chic a.

a·nath'e·ma n. 1. person or thing accursed or detested 2. ritual curse —a·nath'e·ma·tize' v.

a·nat'o·mize v. 1. dissect, as animals 2. analyze

a·nat'o·my n. 1. science of plant or animal structure 2. structure of an organism —an'a·tom'i·cal a.

-ance suf. 1. action or state of 2. a thing that (is)

an·ces·tor (-ses-) n. person from whom one is descended

an·ces·try n. 1. family descent 2. all one's ancestors —an·ces'tral a.

an'chor (-kər) n. metal weight lowered from a ship to prevent drifting —v. hold secure —at

anchor anchored —an'chor·age n.

an'cho·rite (-kə-) n. hermit

anchor man newscaster coordinating various reports

an'cho·vy (-chō-) n. [pl. -VIES] tiny herring

an·cient (ān'shənt) a. 1. of times long past 2. very old —n. pl. people of ancient times

an'cil·lar'y a. auxiliary

and con. 1. also 2. plus 3. as a result

an·dan'te a., adv. Mus. moderately slow

and'i'rons n.pl. metal stands for logs in a fireplace

an'dro·gen (-jən) n. male sex hormone

an'droid n. in science fiction, human-looking robot

an'ec·dote n. brief story

a·ne'mi·a (-nē'-) n. deficiency of red blood cells —a·ne'mic a.

an·e·mom'e·ter n. gauge measuring wind velocity

a·nem'o·ne (-nē) n. plant with cup-shaped flowers

a·nent' prep. [Now Rare] concerning

an·es·the·sia (-zhə) n. loss of the sense of pain, touch, etc.

an·es·the·si·ol'o·gist (-zē-) n. doctor specializing in giving anesthetics

an·es·thet'ic n., a. (drug, gas, etc.) that produces anesthesia —an·es'the·tize v.

an·es'the·tist n. nurse or other person trained to give anesthetics

an·eu·rysm, an'eu·rism (-yər

iz'm) *n.* sac formed by swelling in an artery wall

a·new' *adv.* **1.** once more **2.** in a new way

an'gel (ān'jəl) *n.* messenger of God, pictured with wings and halo —**an·gel'ic** (an-) *a.*

an'gel·fish *n.* spiny-finned, bright-colored tropical fish

angel cake light, spongy, white cake: in full, **angel food cake**

an'ger *n.* hostile feeling; wrath —*v.* make angry

an·gi·na pec'to·ris (an jī'nə) heart disease with chest pains

an'gle *n.* **1.** space formed by two lines or surfaces that meet **2.** point of view —*v.* **1.** bend at an angle **2.** fish with hook and line **3.** use tricks to get something —**an'gler** *n.*

angle iron piece of iron bent at a right angle, for joining two beams, etc.

an'gle·worm *n.* earthworm

An'gli·cize (-sīz) *v.* make English in form, sound, etc.

Anglo- *pref.* English (and)

An'glo-Sax'on *n.* **1.** native of England before 12th century **2.** person of English descent **3.** Old English

An·go'ra *n.* silky wool from longhaired goat or rabbit

an'gry *a.* [-GRIER, -GRIEST] **1.** feeling anger; enraged **2.** stormy —**an'gri·ly** *adv.*

ang'strom (-strəm) *n.* one hundred-millionth of a centimeter, unit for measuring length of light waves

an'guish (-gwish) *n.* great pain, worry, or grief

an'gu·lar (-gyə-) *a.* having angles —**an'gu·lar'i·ty** *n.*

an'i·line (-'l in) *n.* oily liquid made from benzene, used in dyes, etc.

an'i·mad·vert' *v.* criticize —**an'i·mad·ver'sion** *n.*

an'i·mal *n.* **1.** living organism able to move about **2.** any four-footed creature —*a.* **1.** of an animal **2.** bestial

an'i·mal·cule (-mal'kyool) *n.* very small animal

an'i·mate *v.* **1.** give life to **2.** make gay —*a.* (-mit) **1.** living **2.** lively —**an'i·mat'ed** *a.* —**an'i·ma'tion** *n.* —**an'i·ma'tor** *n.*

animated cartoon movie made by filming series of cartoons

an'i·mism *n.* belief that all things in nature have souls —**an'i·mis'tic** *a.*

an'i·mos'i·ty *n.* strong hatred; ill will

an'i·mus *n.* ill will

an'ise (-is) *n.* plant whose seed is used as flavoring

an'i·sette' *n.* a sweet, anise-flavored liqueur

ankh (aŋk) *n.* cross with a loop at the top, ancient Egyptian symbol of life

an'kle *n.* joint connecting foot and leg

an'klet *n.* short sock

an'nals *n.pl.* historical records, year by year

an·neal' (-nēl') *v.* toughen (glass or metal) by heating and then cooling slowly

an'ne·lid *n.* any worm with a body of joined segments or rings, as the earthworm

an·nex' v. attach or join to a larger unit —n. (an'eks) something annexed —**an'nex·a'tion** n.

an·ni'hi·late (-nī'ə-) v. destroy —**an·ni'hi·la'tion** n.

an'ni·ver'sa·ry n. [pl. -RIES] yearly return of the date of some event

an'no·tate v. provide explanatory notes for —**an'no·ta'tion** n.

an·nounce' v. make known; tell about —**an·nounc'er** n. —**an·nounce'ment** n.

an·noy' v. to bother or anger —**an·noy'ance** n.

an'nu·al a. yearly —n. 1. plant living one year 2. yearbook —**an'nu·al·ly** adv.

an·nu'i·ty n. [pl. -TIES] investment yielding fixed annual payments

an·nul' v. [-NULLED, -NULLING] make null and void —**an·nul'ment** n.

an·nun'ci·a'tion n. 1. an announcing 2. [A-] announcement to Mary, mother of Jesus, that she would bear Jesus

an'ode (-ōd) n. positive electrode

an'o·dize (-dīn) n. put a protective oxide film on (a metal) by an electrolytic process

an'o·dyne (-dīn) n. anything that relieves pain

a·noint' v. put oil on, as in consecrating

a·nom'a·ly n. [pl. -LIES] unusual or irregular thing —**a·nom'a·lous** a.

a·non' adv. 1. soon 2. at another time

a·non'y·mous (-ə məs) a. with name unknown or withheld; unidentified —**an'o·nym'i·ty** (-nim'ə tē) n. —**a·non'y·mous·ly** adv.

a·noph'e·les (-näf'ə lēz) n. mosquito that can transmit malaria

an·oth'er a., pron. 1. one more 2. a different (one)

an'swer (-sər) n. 1. thing said or done in return; reply 2. solution to a problem —v. 1. reply (to) 2. serve or suit 3. be responsible —**answer back** [Col.] reply insolently —**an'swer·a·ble** a.

ant n. small insect living in colonies

-ant suf. 1. that has, shows, or does 2. one that

ant·ac'id n., a. (substance) counteracting acids

an·tag'o·nism n. hostility —**an·tag'o·nis'tic** a.

an·tag'o·nist n. opponent

an·tag'o·nize v. incur the dislike of

ant·arc'tic a. of or near the South Pole —n. antarctic region

an'te (-tē) n. player's stake in poker —v. [-TEED or -TED, -TEING] put in one's stake

ante- pref. before

ant'eat'er n. long-snouted mammal that feeds on ants

an'te·ced'ent (-sēd'-) a. prior —n. 1. thing prior to another 2. word or phrase to which a pronoun refers

an'te·date v. occur before

an·te·di·lu′vi·an *a.* **1.** before the Flood **2.** outmoded

an′te·lope *n.* horned animal like the deer

an·ten′na *n.* [*pl.* **-NAE** (-nē), **-NAS**] **1.** feeler on the head of an insect, etc. **2.** [*pl.* **-NAS**] wire or wires for sending and receiving radio waves

an·te′ri·or *a.* **1.** toward the front **2.** earlier

an′te·room *n.* room leading to another room

an′them *n.* religious or patriotic choral song

an′ther *n.* pollen-bearing part of a stamen

an·thol′o·gize *v.* include in an anthology

an·thol′o·gy *n.* [*pl.* **-GIES**] collection of poems, stories, etc. — **an·thol′o·gist** *n.*

an′thra·cite *n.* hard coal

an′thrax *n.* disease of cattle

an′thro·poid *a.* manlike —*n.* an anthropoid ape

an′thro·pol′o·gy *n.* study of the races, customs, etc. of mankind —**an′thro·pol′o·gist** *n.*

an′thro·po·mor′phism *n.* a giving of human qualities to gods, things, etc. —**an′thro·po·mor′phic** *a.*

an′ti *n.* [*pl.* **-TIS**] [Col.] a person opposed to something —*a.* [Col.] opposed

anti- *pref.* **1.** against **2.** that acts against

an′ti·air′craft *a.* used against hostile aircraft

an′ti·bal·lis′tic missile ballistic missile for stopping enemy ballistic missile

an′ti·bi·ot′ic *n.* substance produced by some microorganisms, able to kill or weaken bacteria

an′ti·bod′y *n.* [*pl.* **-IES**] protein produced in body to neutralize an antigen

an′tic *n.* silly act; prank

an·tic′i·pate (-tis′-) *v.* **1.** expect **2.** act on before —**an·tic′i·pa′tion** *n.*

an′ti·cli′max (-klī′-) *n.* sudden drop from the important to the trivial —**an′ti·cli·mac′tic** *a.*

an′ti·co·ag′u·lant *n.* drug that delays or prevents the clotting of blood

an′ti·de·pres′sant *n.* drug that lessens emotional tension

an′ti·dote *n.* remedy to counteract a poison or evil

an′ti·freeze′ *n.* substance used to prevent freezing

an′ti·gen (-jan) *n.* substance to which the body reacts by producing antibodies

an′ti·his′ta·mine′ (-mēn′) *n.* drug used to treat allergies

an′ti·knock′ *n.* substance added to fuel of internal-combustion engines to do away with noise of too rapid combustion

an′ti·mat′ter *n.* matter in which the electrical charge of each particle is the reverse of that in the usual matter

an′ti·mo′ny *n.* silvery metal in alloys, a chemical element

an′ti·par′ti·cle *n.* any particle of antimatter

an′ti·pas′to (-päs′-) *n.* [It.]

appetizer of spicy meat, fish, etc.

an·tip'a·thy (-thē) n. [pl. -THIES] strong dislike

an'ti·per·son·nel' a. meant to destroy people rather than buildings or objects

an'ti·per·spir·ant n. skin lotion, cream, etc. to reduce perspiration

an'ti·phon (-fän) n. hymn, psalm, etc. sung in responsive, alternating parts —**an·tiph'o·nal a.**

an·tip'o·des (-dēz) n.pl. opposite places on the globe

an'ti·quar'i·an (-kwer'-) a. of antiques or antiquaries —n. antiquary

an'ti·quar'y n. [pl. -IES] collector or student of antiquities

an'ti·quate v. make obsolete —**an'ti·quat'ed a.**

an·tique' (-tēk') a. 1. of a former period 2. out-of-date —n. piece of furniture, etc. of earlier times

an·tiq'ui·ty (-tik'wə-) n. [pl. -TIES] 1. ancient times 2. great age 3. ancient relic, etc.

an'ti·Sem'i·tism n. prejudice or hostility against Jews —**an'ti-Se·mit'ic** (-mit'-) a.

an'ti·sep'tic a. preventing infection by killing germs —n. antiseptic substance

an'ti·slav'er·y a. against slavery

an'ti·so'cial a. 1. not sociable 2. harmful to society

an'ti·tank' a. for use against tanks in war

an·tith'e·sis n. [pl. -SES (-sēz)] exact opposite

an'ti·tox'in n. serum that counteracts a disease

an'ti·trust' a. regulating business trusts

an'ti·viv'i·sec'tion·ist n. one opposing vivisection

ant'ler n. branched horn of a deer, elk, etc.

an'to·nym n. word opposite in meaning

a'nus n. opening at rear end of the alimentary canal

an'vil n. block on which to hammer metal objects

anx·i·e·ty (aŋ zī'ə tē) n. [pl. -TIES] 1. worry about what may happen 2. eager desire

anx·ious (aŋk'shəs) a. 1. worried 2. eagerly wishing —**anx'-ious·ly adv.**

an'y a. 1. one of more than two 2. some 3. every —pron. sing., pl. any person(s) or amount —adv. at all

an'y·bod'y pron. anyone

an'y·how adv. 1. in any way 2. in any case

an'y·one pron. any person

an'y·thing pron. any thing — anything but not at all

an'y·way adv. anyhow

an'y·where adv. in, at, or to any place

A-OK a. [Col.] excellent, fine, etc.: also **A'-O·kay'**

A one [Col.] superior; first-class: also **A1, A number 1**

a·or'ta (ā-) n. main artery leading from the heart

a·pace' adv. swiftly

a·part' adv. 1. aside 2. away from (one) another 3. into pieces —a. separated

a·part'heid (-hāt, -hīt) n. strict

racial segregation as practiced in South Africa

a·part'ment *n.* room or set of rooms to live in

ap'a·thy *n.* lack of feeling or interest —**ap'a·thet'ic** *a.*

ape *n.* large, tailless monkey — *v.* imitate

a·pe·ri·tif' (-pā rə tēf') *n.* alcoholic drink before meals

ap'er·ture (-chər) *n.* opening

a'pex *n.* highest point

a·pha'sia (-fā'zha) *n.* loss of power to use or understand words

a'phid *n.* insect that sucks the juices of plants

aph'o·rism *n.* wise saying

aph'ro·dis'i·ac *n., a.* (drug, etc.) arousing sexual desire

a'pi·ar'y (-ē-) *n.* [*pl.* -IES] collection of beehives

a·piece' *adv.* to or for each

a·plen'ty *a., adv.* [Col.] in abundance

a·plomb (ə pläm') *n.* poise

a·poc'ry·phal *a.* of doubtful authenticity

ap'o·gee *n.* point farthest from heavenly body in a satellite's orbit

a'po·lit'i·cal (ā'-) *a.* not concerned with political matters — **a'po·lit'i·cal·ly** *adv.*

a·pol'o·get'ic *a.* showing apology or regret —**a·pol'o·get'i·cal·ly** *adv.*

a·pol'o·gist *n.* defender of a doctrine, action, etc.

a·pol'o·gize (-jīz) *v.* to make an apology

a·pol'o·gy (-jē) *n.* [*pl.* -GIES] expression of regret for a fault, etc. 2. defense of an idea, etc.

ap'o·plex'y *n.* paralysis caused by a broken blood vessel in brain —**ap'o·plec'tic** *a.*

a·pos'tate *n.* one who abandons his faith, principles, etc. —**a·pos'ta·sy** *n.*

A·pos'tle (-päs''l) *n.* 1. any of the disciples of Jesus 2. [a-] leader of a new movement — **ap'os·tol'ic** *a.*

a·pos'tro·phe (-fē) *n.* sign (') indicating: 1. omission of letter(s) from a word 2. possessive case

a·poth'e·car'y *n.* [*pl.* -IES] druggist

a·poth'e·o'sis *n.* 1. deifying of a person 2. glorification of a person or thing 3. glorified ideal

ap·pall', **ap·pal'** (-pôl') *v.* to dismay —**ap·pall'ing** *a.*

ap'pa·ra'tus (-ra'-, -rā'-) *n.* 1. tools, etc. for a specific use 2. complex device

ap·par'el *n.* clothes; attire —*v.* clothe; dress

ap·par'ent *a.* 1. obvious; plain 2. seeming —**ap·par'ent·ly** *adv.*

ap'pa·ri'tion *n.* ghost

ap·peal' *n.* 1. request for help 2. attraction 3. request for rehearing by a higher court —*v.* 1. make an appeal 2. be attractive

ap·pear' (-pir') *v.* 1. come into sight 2. seem 3. come before the public

ap·pear'ance *n.* 1. an appearing 2. look; aspect 3. pretense —**keep up appearances** seem to be proper, etc.

ap·pease' v. quiet by satisfying —**ap·pease'ment** n.

ap·pel'lant n. one who appeals to a higher court

ap·pel'late court (-it) court handling appeals

ap·pel·la'tion n. a name

ap·pend' v. add or attach

ap·pend'age (-ij) n. attached part, as a tail

ap'pen·dec'to·my n. [pl. -MIES] surgical removal of the appendix

ap·pen'di·ci'tis n. inflammation of the appendix

ap·pen'dix n. [pl. -DIXES, -DICES (-də sēz)] 1. extra material at the end of a book 2. small, closed tube attached to large intestine

ap·per·tain' v. pertain

ap'pe·ten·cy n. [pl. -CIES] 1. appetite 2. propensity 3. natural attraction

ap'pe·tite n. desire (esp. for food)

ap'pe·tiz'er n. tasty food that stimulates the appetite

ap'pe·tiz'ing a. stimulating the appetite; savory

ap·plaud' v. show approval, esp. by clapping the hands; praise —**ap·plause'** n.

ap'ple n. 1. round, fleshy fruit 2. tree it grows on

apple butter jam made of stewed apples

ap'ple·jack n. brandy distilled from apple cider

ap'ple·sauce' n. 1. apples boiled to a pulp and sweetened 2. [Sl.] nonsense

ap·pli'ance n. device or machine, esp. for home use

ap'pli·ca·ble a. appropriate — **ap'pli·ca·bil'i·ty** n.

ap'pli·cant n. one who applies, as for a job

ap'pli·ca'tion n. 1. an applying 2. thing applied 3. formal request

ap'pli·ca'tor n. device for applying medicine, paint, etc.

ap'pli·qué' (-kā') n. decoration of one fabric on another

ap·ply' v. [-PLIED, -PLYING] 1. to put on 2. put into use 3. devote (oneself) diligently 4. ask formally 5. be relevant

ap·point' v. 1. set (a time, etc.) 2. name to an office 3. furnish —**ap·point'ee'** n. — **ap·point'ive** a.

ap·point'ment n. 1. an appointing or being appointed 2. position filled by appointing 3. engagement to be somewhere

ap·por'tion v. portion out — **ap·por'tion·ment** n.

ap'po·site (-zit) a. fitting

ap'po·si'tion n. placing of a word or phrase beside another in explanation —**ap·pos'i·tive** a., n.

ap·praise' v. estimate the value of —**ap·prais'al** n. — **ap·prais'er** n.

ap·pre'ci·a·ble (-sha-) a. significant; enough to be noticed —**ap·pre'cia·bly** adv.

ap·pre'ci·ate (-shē-) v. 1. value; enjoy 2. recognize rightly or gratefully —**ap·pre'ci·a'tion** n.—**ap·pre'ci·a·tive** a.

ap·pre·hend' v. 1. arrest 2. understand 3. fear —**ap·pre·hen'sion** n.

ap·pre·hen'sive a. anxious

ap·pren'tice (-tis) n. helper who is being taught a trade — v. place as apprentice —**ap·pren'tice·ship** n.

ap·prise', ap·prize' (-prīz') v. inform; notify

ap·proach' v. 1. come nearer (to) 2. speak to —n. 1. a coming near 2. way of beginning 3. access

ap'pro·ba'tion n. approval

ap·pro'pri·ate v. 1. take for one's own use 2. set (money) aside for some use —a. (-it) suitable —**ap·pro'pri·ate·ly** adv. —**ap·pro'pri·a'tion** n.

ap·prov'al n. 1. an approving 2. favorable attitude 3. formal consent

ap·prove' v. 1. consent to 2. have a favorable opinion (of)

ap·prox'i·mate v. be about the same as —a. (-mit) nearly exact or correct —**ap·prox'i·ma'tion** n.

ap·pur'te·nance n. 1. adjunct 2. additional right

ap·pur'te·nant a. pertaining

a'pri·cot (ā'-, ā'-) n. small peachlike fruit

A'pril n. fourth month

a'pron n. garment to protect the front of clothes

ap·ro·pos' (-pō') a. fitting —apropos of regarding

apse (aps) n. domed or vaulted projection of a church

apt a. 1. fitting; suitable 2. likely (to) 3. quick to learn

ap'ti·tude n. 1. ability 2. quickness to learn

aq·ua (ak'wə, äk'wə) n. water —a. bluish-green

aq·ua·cul'ture n. cultivation of water plants and animals for human use

Aq'ua·lung' trademark for apparatus for breathing under water —n. [usually a-] such apparatus

aq'ua·ma·rine' n., a. bluish green

aq'ua·naut (-nôt) n. one who does undersea experiments in a watertight chamber

a·quar'i·um (-kwer'-) n. tank, etc. for keeping fish or other water animals

A·quar'i·us 11th sign of the zodiac; Water Bearer

a·quat'ic (-kwät'-) a. 1. living in water 2. taking place in water

aq'ue·duct (ak'wə-) n. large pipe or channel bringing water from a distance

a'que·ous (ā'kwē-) a. of or like water

aqueous humor watery fluid between the cornea and the lens of the eye

aq·ui·line (ak'wə lin) a. curved like an eagle's beak

Ar'ab, A·ra'bi·an n. one of a nomadic people native to Arabia, etc. —a. of the Arabs — **Ar'a·bic** a., n.

Arabic numerals figures 1, 2, 3, 4, 5, 6, 7, 8, 9, and 0

ar'a·ble a. fit for plowing

a·rach'nid (-rak'-) n. small, eight-legged animal, as the spider or mite

ar'bi·ter n. judge; umpire

ar'bi·trar'y a. using only one's own wishes or whim —**ar'bi·trar'i·ly** adv.

ar·bi·trate v. settle (a dispute) by using or being an arbiter —**ar·bi·tra'tion** n. —**ar'bi·tra'tor** n.

ar'bor n. place shaded by trees, shrubs, or vines

ar·bo're·al a. of, like, or living in trees

ar·bo·re'tum n. [pl. -TUMS, -TA] place where many kinds of trees are grown

ar·bor·vi'tae (-vī'tē) n. small kind of pine tree

ar·bu'tus n. evergreen trailing plant

arc n. **1.** curved line, as part of a circle **2.** band of light made by electricity leaping a gap

ar·cade' n. **1.** covered passage, esp. one lined with shops **2.** row of arches on columns

ar·cane' a. secret or esoteric

arch n. curved support over an opening —v. form (as) an arch —a. **1.** chief **2.** mischievous; coy

arch- pref. chief; main

ar'chae·ol'o·gy (ärˈkē-) n. study of ancient peoples, as by excavation of ruins: also sp. **ar'che·ol'o·gy**   **ar'chae·o·log'i·cal** a.

ar·cha'ic (-kāˈ-) a. **1.** out-of-date **2.** now seldom used

arch·an'gel (ärkˈ-) n. angel of the highest rank

arch'bish'op (ärchˈ-) n. bishop of the highest rank

arch'dea'con n. church official ranking just below a bishop

arch'di·o·cese n. diocese of an archbishop

arch'en'e·my n. [pl. -MIES] chief enemy

arch'er n. one who shoots with bow and arrow

arch'er·y n. a shooting with bow and arrow

ar'che·type (-kə-) n. original model

ar'chi·pel'a·go' (-kə-) n. [pl. -GOES, -GOS] chain of islands in a sea

ar'chi·tect (-kə-) n. one who designs buildings

ar'chi·tec'ture (-chər) n. art or science of designing and constructing buildings —**ar'·chi·tec'tur·al** a.

ar'chives (-kīvz) n.pl. public records or place to store them

arch'way n. passage under an arch

arc lamp (or **light**) lamp in which light is made by an arc between electrodes

arc'tic a. of or near the North Pole —n. arctic region

ar'dent a. passionate; eager —**ar'dent·ly** adv.

ar'dor n. passion; zeal

ar'du·ous (-joo-) a. laborious or strenuous

are pres. t. of **be**, used with you, we, and they

ar'e·a n. **1.** region **2.** total surface, measured in square units **3.** scope

area code telephone code number for any of the areas into which U.S. and Canada are divided

a·re'na (-rēˈ-) n. **1.** center of amphitheater, for contests, etc. **2.** area of struggle

arena theater theater with a central stage surrounded by seats

aren't are not

ar'gon n. chemical element, gas used in radio tubes, etc.

ar'go·sy n. [pl. -SIES] [Poet.] large merchant ship or fleet

ar'got (-gō, -gət) n. special vocabulary, as of thieves

ar'gue v. 1. give reasons (*for* or *against*) 2. dispute; debate —**ar'gu·ment** n. —**ar'gu·men·ta'tion** n.

ar'gu·men·ta'tive a. apt to argue

ar'gyle (-gīl) a. knitted or woven in a diamond-shaped pattern, as socks

a·ri·a (är'ē-) n. solo in an opera, etc.

-arian suf. one of specified age, belief, work, etc.

ar'id a. 1. dry 2. dull —**a·rid'i·ty** n.

Ar'i·es (-ēz) 1st sign of the zodiac; Ram

a·right' adv. correctly

a·rise' v. [AROSE, ARISEN, ARISING] 1. get up; rise 2. come into being

ar'is·toc'ra·cy n. 1. government by an upper class minority 2. upper class

a·ris'to·crat n. 1. member of the aristocracy 2. one with upper-class tastes, etc. —**a·ris'to·crat'ic** a.

a·rith'me·tic n. science of computing by numbers —**ar'ith·met'i·cal** a.

ark n. *Bible* boat in which Noah, etc. survived the Flood

arm n. 1. upper limb of the human body 2. anything like this 3. weapon 4. military branch 5. *pl.* heraldic symbols —v. provide with weapons —**up in arms** indignant —**with open arms** cordially —**armed** a.

ar·ma'da (-mä'-) n. fleet of warships

ar'ma·dil'lo n. [pl. -LOS] tropical mammal covered with bony plates

ar'ma·ment n. *often pl.* military forces and equipment

ar'ma·ture (-chər) n. revolving coil in an electric motor or dynamo

arm'chair n. chair with supports for one's arms

armed forces all the military, naval, and air forces of a country

arm'ful n. [pl. -FULS] as much as the arms can hold

arm'hole n. opening for the arm in a garment

ar'mis·tice (-tis) n. truce

arm'let n. ornamental band worn on the upper arm

ar'mor n. protective covering —**ar'mored** a.

armored car vehicle with armor plate, as a truck carrying money to or from a bank

ar·mor'i·al a. heraldic

armor plate protective covering of steel plates

ar'mor·y n. [pl. -IES] 1. arsenal 2. military drill hall

arm'pit n. the hollow under the arm at the shoulder

arm'rest n. support for the arm as on inside of car door

ar'my n. [pl. -MIES] 1. large body of soldiers 2. any very large group

a·ro'ma n. pleasant odor —**ar'·o·mat'ic** a.

a·rose' pt. of **arise**

a·round' adv., prep. 1. in a circle (about) 2. on all sides (of) 3. to the opposite direction 4. [Col.] nearby

a·rouse' v. wake; stir up

ar·peg'gio (-pej'ō) n. [pl. -GIOS] chord with notes played in quick succession

ar·raign' (-rān') v. 1. bring to court for trial 2. accuse —**arraign'ment** n.

ar·range' v. 1. put in a certain order 2. plan 3. Mus. adapt (a work) for certain instruments or voices —**ar·rang'er** n.

ar·range'ment n. 1. an arranging 2. result of arranging 3. usually pl. a plan 4. Mus. composition arranged

ar'rant a. out-and-out

ar'ras n. 1. elaborate tapestry 2. wall hanging

ar·ray' v. 1. place in order 2. dress finely —n. 1. orderly grouping 2. impressive display 3. finery

ar·rears' n.pl. overdue debts —**in arrears** behind in payment

ar·rest' v. 1. stop or check 2. seize 3. seize and hold by law —n. an arresting —**under arrest** in legal custody

ar·rest'ing a. interesting

ar·riv'al n. 1. an arriving 2. person or thing arriving

ar·rive' v. 1. reach one's destination 2. come

ar'ro·gant a. haughty; overbearing —**ar'ro·gance** n.

ar'ro·gate v. seize arrogantly —**ar'ro·ga'tion** n.

ar'row n. 1. pointed shaft shot from a bow 2. sign (←) to show direction

ar'row·head n. pointed tip of an arrow

ar'row·root n. starch from a tropical plant root

ar·roy'o n. [pl. -OS] 1. dry gully 2. stream

ar'se·nal n. place for making or storing weapons

ar'se·nic n. silvery-white, poisonous chemical element

ar'son n. crime of purposely setting fire to property —**ar'·son·ist** n.

art n. 1. skill; craft 2. aesthetic work, as painting, sculpture, music, etc. 3. pl. academic studies 4. cunning; wile —v. [Ar.] are: used with thou

art de·co (dek'ō) decorative style of the 1920's and 1930's derived from cubism

ar·te'ri·o·scle·ro'sis n. hardening of the arteries

ar'ter·y n. [pl. -IES] 1. tube carrying blood from the heart 2. a main road —**ar·te'ri·al** (-tir'ē-) a.

ar·te'sian well (-zhan) deep well with water forced up by underground water pressure

art'ful a. 1. skillful; clever 2. crafty; cunning

ar·thri'tis n. inflammation of joints —**ar·thrit'ic** a.

ar'thro·pod (-thrə-) n. invertebrate animal with jointed legs and segmented body

ar'ti·choke n. 1. thistle-like plant 2. its flower head, cooked as a vegetable

ar'ti·cle n. 1. single item 2.

separate piece of writing, as in a magazine 3. section of a document 4. any of the words *a*, *an*, or *the*

ar·tic'u·late v. 1. speak clearly 2. join —*a*. (-lit) 1. clear in speech 2. jointed —**ar·tic'u·la'tion** n.

ar'ti·fact n. any object made by human work; esp., a primitive tool

ar'ti·fice (-fis) n. 1. trick or trickery 2. clever skill

ar'ti·fi'cial a. 1. made by man; not natural 2. not genuine; affected —**ar'ti·fi'ci·al'i·ty** n. —**ar'ti·fi'cial·ly** adv.

artificial respiration artificial maintenance of breathing, as by forcing breath into the mouth

ar·til'ler·y n. 1. mounted guns, as cannon 2. military branch using these

ar'ti·san (-z'n) n. skilled craftsman

art'ist n. person with skill, esp. in any of the fine arts

ar·tis'tic a. 1. of art or artists 2. skillful —**ar·tis'ti·cal·ly** adv.

art'is·try n. artistic quality, ability, work, etc.

art'less a. 1. unskillful 2. simple; natural

art'y a. [-IER, -IEST] [Col.] affectedly artistic

ar'um (er'-) n. plant with flowers inside hooded leaf

as adv. 1. equally 2. for instance —**con.** 1. in the way that 2. while 3. because 4. though —**pron.** that —**prep.** in the role of —**as for** (or **to**)

concerning —**as if** (or **though**) as it (or one) would if —**as is** [Col.] just as it is

as·bes'tos n. fibrous mineral used in fireproofing

as·cend' (-send') v. go up; climb —**as·cen'sion** n.

as·cend'an·cy n. domination: also **as·cend'en·cy**

as·cend'ant a. 1. rising 2. dominant Also sp. **as·cend'-ent**

as·cent' n. 1. an ascending 2. upward slope

as·cer·tain' (-sər tān') v. find out with certainty

as·cet'ic (-set'-) a. austere; self-denying —n. one who denies himself pleasures —**as·cet'i·cism** n.

as·cor'bic acid vitamin C

as'cot n. scarflike necktie

as·cribe' v. assign or attribute —**as·crip'tion** n.

a·sep'tic a. free from disease germs

a·sex'u·al a. sexless

ash n. 1. often pl. grayish powder left from something burned 2. shade tree —**ash'en** a. —**ash'y** a.

a·shamed' a. feeling shame

a·shore' adv., a. to or on shore

ash'tray n. container for smokers' tobacco ashes: also **ash tray**

A'sian (-zhən), **A'si·at'ic** n., a. (native) of the continent of Asia

a·side' adv. 1. on or to one side 2. away 3. apart —n. actor's words spoken aside —**aside from** except for

as·i·nine (-nīn) *a.* stupid; silly —**as'i·nin'i·ty** (-nin'-) [*pl.* -TIES] *n.*

ask *v.* 1. call for an answer to 2. inquire of or about 3. request 4. invite

a·skance' *adv.* 1. sideways 2. with suspicion

a·skew' (-skyōō') *adv., a.* awry

asking price price asked by a seller, to begin bargaining

a·slant' *adv., a.* on a slant —*prep.* slantingly across

a·sleep' *a.* 1. sleeping 2. numb —*adv.* into sleep

a·so'cial (-ā-) *a.* not social; avoiding others

asp *n.* poisonous snake

as·par'a·gus *n.* plant with edible green shoots

as'pect *n.* 1. look or appearance 2. side or facet

as'pen *n.* poplar tree with fluttering leaves

as·per'i·ty *n.* [*pl.* -TIES] harshness; sharpness

as·per'sion (-pur'-) *n.* a slur; slander

as'phalt *n.* tarlike substance used for paving, etc.

as'pho·del *n.* plant like a lily, with white or yellow flowers

as·phyx'i·ate (-fik'sē-) *v.* overcome by cutting down oxygen in the blood —**as·phyx'i·a'tion** *n.*

as'pic *n.* jelly of meat juice, tomato juice, etc.

as'pir·ant (as'par-, ə spīr'-) *n.* one who aspires

as'pi·rate *v.* 1. begin (a syllable, etc.) with sound of English *h* 2. suck in or suck up

as'pi·ra'tion *n.* 1. ambition 2. thing desired 3. a drawing in by suction

as'pi·ra'tor *n.* apparatus using suction to remove air, fluids, etc.

as·pire' *v.* be ambitious (*to*)

as'pi·rin *n.* drug that relieves pain or fever

ass *n.* 1. donkey 2. fool

as·sail' *v.* attack

as·sail'ant *n.* attacker

as·sas'sin *n.* murderer

as·sas'si·nate *v.* murder, esp. for political reasons —**as·sas'si·na'tion** *n.*

as·sault' (-sôlt') *n., v.* attack

assault and battery *law* the carrying out of threatened physical harm

as'say (or a sā') *n.* 1. a testing 2. analysis of what is in an ore, drug, etc. —*v.* (a sā') make an assay of; test

as·sem'blage (-blij) *n.* 1. an assembling 2. group gathered together 3. sculptural collage

as·sem'ble *v.* 1. gather in a group 2. put together

as·sem'bly *n.* [*pl.* -BLIES] 1. an assembling 2. group 3. [A-] legislative body

assembly line line of workers in a factory who assemble a product as it passes along

as·sem'bly·man *n.* [*pl.* -MEN] member of a legislative assembly

as·sent' *v., n.* consent

as·sert' *v.* 1. declare 2. defend, as rights —**assert oneself** insist on one's rights

as·ser'tion *n.* 1. an asserting 2. positive statement

as·ser'tive *a.* persistently confident

as·sess' *v.* 1. set a value on for taxes 2. impose a fine, tax, etc. —**as·sess'ment** *n.* —**asses'sor** *n.*

as'set *n.* 1. valuable thing 2. *pl.* property, cash, etc.

as·sev'er·ate *v.* declare

as·sid'u·ous (-sij'-) *a.* diligent

as·sign' *v.* 1. designate 2. appoint 3. allot; give —**as·sign'ment** *n.*

as'sig·na'tion *n.* secret appointment of lovers to meet

as·sim'i·late *v.* merge; absorb —**as·sim'i·la'tion** *n.*

as·sist' *v., n.* help; aid —**as·sist'ance** *n.* —**as·sist'ant** *a., n.*

as·so'ci·ate *v.* 1. join 2. connect in the mind 3. join (*with*) as a partner, etc. —*n.* (-it) partner, colleague, etc. —*a.* (-it) associated

as·so'ci·a'tion *n.* 1. an associating 2. partnership 3. organization or society

association football soccer

as'so·nance *n.* likeness of sound

as·sort'ed *a.* 1. miscellaneous 2. sorted

as·sort'ment *n.* variety

as·suage' (ə swāj') *v.* ease (pain, hunger, etc.)

as·sume' *v.* 1. take on (a role, look, etc.) 2. undertake 3. take for granted 4. pretend to have —**as·sump'tion** *n.*

as·sure' (-shoor') *v.* 1. make sure; convince 2. give confidence to 3. promise 4. guarantee —**as·sur'ance** *n.*

as·sured' *a.* 1. certain 2. self-confident

as'ter *n.* daisylike flower

as'ter·isk *n.* sign (*) used to mark footnotes, etc.

a·stern' *a., adv.* at or toward the rear of a ship

as'ter·oid *n.* any of the small planets between Mars and Jupiter

asth'ma (az'-) *n.* chronic disorder characterized by coughing, hard breathing, etc. —**asth·mat'ic** *a., n.*

a·stig'ma·tism *n.* eye defect that keeps light rays from focusing to one point

a·stir' *adv.* 1. in motion

as·ton'ish (ə stän'-) *v.* fill with sudden surprise —**aston'ish·ing** *a.* —**as·ton'ish·ment** *n.*

as·tound' *v.* astonish greatly —**as·tound'ing** *a.*

a·strad'dle *adv.* in a straddling position

as'tra·khan (-kən) *n.* curled fur from young lamb pelts

as'tral *a.* of, from, or like the stars

a·stray' *adv., a.* off the right path

a·stride' *adv., a., prep.* with a leg on either side (of)

as·trin'gent (-jənt) *n., a.* (substance) contracting body tissue and blood vessels

as·trol'o·gy *n.* pseudo-science of effect of stars, etc. on human affairs —**as·trol'o·ger** *n.* —**as'tro·log'i·cal** *a.*

as'tro·naut (-nôt) *n.* traveler in outer space —**as'tro·naut'ics** *n.*

as'tro·nom'i·cal *a.* 1. of astronomy 2. huge, as numbers

as·tron'o·my *n.* science of the stars and other heavenly bodies —**as·tron'o·mer** *n.*

as·tute' *a.* shrewd; keen

a·sun'der *adv., a.* apart

a·sy'lum *n.* 1. place of safety 2. institution for the mentally ill, aged, etc.

a·sym'me·try (ā-) *n.* lack of symmetry —**a'sym·met'ri·cal** *a.*

at *prep.* 1. on; in; near 2. to or toward 3. busy with 4. in the state of 5. because of

at'a·vism *n.* a throwback

ate *pt. of* **eat**

-ate *suf.* 1. make, become, or form 2. to treat with 3. of or like

at'el·ier (-yā) *n.* studio

a'the·ism (-thē-) *n.* belief that there is no God —**a'the·ist** *n.* —**a'the·is'tic** *a.*

ath'er·o·scle·ro'sis *n.* formation of nodules on hardening artery walls

a·thirst' *a.* eager

ath'lete *n.* one skilled at sports requiring strength, speed, etc. —**ath·let'ic** *a.* —**ath·let'i·cal·ly** *adv.*

athlete's foot ringworm of the feet

ath·let'ics *n.* athletic sports, games, etc.

a·thwart' (ə thwôrt') *prep., adv.* 1. across 2. against

a·tilt' *a., adv.* tilted

a·tin'gle *a.* tingling

-ation *suf.* act, condition, or result of

-ative *suf.* of or relating to; serving to

at'las *n.* book of maps

at'mos·phere *n.* 1. the air surrounding the earth 2. general feeling or spirit —**at'mos·pher'ic** *a.*

at·oll' (-ôl) *n.* coral island surrounding a lagoon

at'om *n.* smallest particle of a chemical element, made up of electrons, protons, etc. —**a·tom'ic** *a.*

atomic bomb, atom bomb bomb whose immense power derives from nuclear fission

atomic energy energy released from an atom in nuclear reactions

at'om·iz'er *n.* device for spraying liquid in a mist

a·to·nal'i·ty (ā'tō-) *n. Mus.* lack of tonality due to disregard of key —**a·ton'al** *a.*

a·tone' *v.* make amends (for) —**a·tone'ment** *n.*

a·top' *a., adv., prep.* on the top (of)

a'tri·um (ā'trē-) *n.* 1. central hall 2. hall or lobby rising up through several stories

a·tro'cious (-shəs) *a.* 1. cruel or evil 2. [Col.] very bad

a·troc'i·ty (-träs'-) *n.* [*pl.* -TIES] 1. atrocious act 2. [Col.] very unpleasant thing

at'ro·phy (-PHIED, -PHYING) waste away or shrink up —*n.* an atrophying

at'ro·pine (-pēn) *n.* alkaloid used to relieve spasms

at·tach' *v.* 1. fasten; join 2. tie by devotion 3. seize by legal order —**at·tach'ment** *n.*

at·ta·ché' (-shā') n. member of a diplomatic staff

attaché case flat, rectangular case for carrying papers

at·tack' v. 1. fight or work against 2. undertake vigorously —n. 1. an attacking 2. fit of illness —at·tack'er n.

at·tain' v. 1. gain; achieve 2. arrive at —at·tain'a·ble a. —at·tain'ment n.

at·tain'der (-dər) n. loss of civil rights and property by one sentenced to death or outlawed

at'tar (-ər) n. perfume made from flower petals

at·tempt' v., n. try

at·tend' v. 1. be present at 2. pay attention 3. go with —attend to take care of —at·tend'ant n.

at·tend'ance n. 1. an attending 2. number present

at·ten'tion n. 1. a giving heed 2. heed; notice 3. pl. kind acts

at·ten'tive a. 1. paying attention 2. courteous

at·ten'u·ate' v. thin out; weaken —at·ten'u·a'tion n.

at·test' v. 1. declare to be true 2. be proof of

at'tic n. space just below the roof; garret

at·tire' v. clothe; dress up —n. clothes

at'ti·tude n. 1. bodily posture 2. way of looking at things, or manner

at'ti·tu'di·nize v. to pose for effect

at·tor'ney (-tur'-) n. [pl. -NEYS] lawyer

attorney at law lawyer

attorney general chief law officer of a government

at·tract' v. 1. draw to itself 2. make notice or like one

at·trac'tion n. 1. an attracting 2. charm; fascination 3. anything that attracts

at·trac'tive a. that attracts; charming, pretty, etc. —at·trac'tive·ly adv.

at·trib'ute v. think of as belonging or owing (to) —n. (at'rə bũt) characteristic —at·trib'u·ta·ble a. —at'tri·bu'tion n.

at·tri'tion (-tri'-) n. a wearing down bit by bit

at·tune' v. bring in tune

ATV (ā'tē'vē') n. [pl. ATVs] small motor vehicle for rough ground, snow, ice, and water

a·twit'ter (-ər) a. twittering

au'burn a., n. red-brown

auc'tion n. public sale in which items go to the highest bidder —v. sell at auction —auc'tion·eer' n., v.

au·da'cious (-shəs) a. 1. bold; reckless 2. insolent —au·dac'i·ty (-das'-) n.

au'di·ble a. loud enough to be heard —au·di·bil'i·ty n. —au'di·bly adv.

au'di·ence n. 1. group seeing or hearing a play, concert, radio or TV show, etc. 2. formal interview

au'di·o a. of the sound portion of a TV broadcast

au'di·o·phile' (-fīl') n. devotee of hi-fi sound reproduction, as on phonographs

au·di·o·vis'u·al *a.* involving both hearing and sight

au'dit *v.* examine and check (accounts) —*n.* an auditing —**au'di·tor** *n.*

au·di'tion *n.* a hearing to try out a singer, actor, etc. —*v.* try out in an audition

au·di·to'ri·um *n.* hall for speeches, concerts, etc.

au'di·to·ry *a.* of hearing

au'ger (-gər) *n.* tool for boring holes in wood

aught (ôt) *n.* 1. anything 2. naught —*adv.* in any way

aug·ment' *v.* increase —**aug'men·ta'tion** *n.*

au gra'tin (ō grä'-) [Fr.] with browned cheese crust

au'gur (-gər) *v.* foretell; prophesy —**augur ill** (or **well**) be a bad (or good) omen

au'gu·ry (-gyər ē) *n.* [pl. -RIES] 1. a foretelling 2. omen

Au'gust *n.* eighth month

au·gust' *a.* imposing

au jus (ō zhōō') [Fr.] in its natural gravy

auk *n.* diving sea bird

aunt *n.* 1. sister of one's parent 2. uncle's wife

au'ra *n.* radiance or air about a person or thing

au'ral *a.* of hearing

au're·ole *n.* halo

Au·re·o·my'cin (ôr'ē ō mī'sin) *trademark for* antibiotic drug

au re·voir (ō'rə vwär') [Fr.] goodbye

au'ri·cle *n.* 1. outer part of the ear 2. an upper chamber of the heart

au·ro'ra *n.* dawn

aurora bo·re·a·lis (bôr'ē al'is)

luminous bands in the northern night sky

aus·cul·ta'tion (-kəl-) *n.* a listening to chest sounds with a stethoscope

aus'pi·ces (-pə sēz) *n.pl.* sponsorship; patronage

aus·pi'cious (-pish'əs) *a.* favorable; of good omen —**aus·pi'cious·ly** *adv.*

aus·tere' *a.* 1. strict 2. very plain; severe —**aus·ter'i·ty** [pl. -TIES] *n.*

Aus·tral'ian (-trāl'-) *n., a.* (native) of the continent or country of Australia

Aus'tri·an *n., a.* (native) of Austria

au·then'tic *a.* true, real, genuine, reliable, etc. —**au·then'ti·cal·ly** *adv.* —**au'then·tic'i·ty** (-tis'-) *n.*

au·then'ti·cate *v.* 1. make valid 2. verify —**au·then'ti·ca'tion** *n.*

au'thor *n.* writer or originator —**au'thor·ship** *n.*

au·thor·i·tar'i·an *a.* enforcing or favoring strict obedience to authority

au·thor'i·ta'tive *a.* having or showing authority

au·thor'i·ty *n.* [pl. -TIES] 1. power to command 2. *pl.* persons with such power 3. expert; reliable source

au'thor·ize *v.* 1. give official approval to 2. empower —**au'thor·i·za'tion** *n.*

au·to (ôt'ō) *n.* [pl. -TOS] [Col.] automobile

auto- *pref.* self

au'to·bi·og'ra·phy *n.* [pl. -PHIES] one's own life story written by oneself —**au'to·bi·o·graph'i·cal** a.

au'to·crat n. ruler with unlimited power —**au·toc'ra·cy** n. —**au'to·crat'ic** a.

au'to·di'dact (-dī'-) n. person who is self-taught

au'to·graph n. signature —v. write one's signature on

au'to·hyp·no'sis n. a hypnotizing of oneself

au'to·in·tox'i·ca'tion n. poisoning by toxic substances formed within the body

au'to·mat n. restaurant dispensing food from coin-operated compartments

au'to·mate v. convert to automation

au'to·mat'ic a. **1.** done without conscious effort **2.** operating by itself —**au·to·mat'i·cal·ly** adv.

automatic pilot gyroscopic instrument for piloting an aircraft, missile, etc.: also **au'to·pi'lot** n.

au'to·ma'tion n. automatic system of manufacture, as by electronic devices

au·tom'a·tism n. automatic quality, action, etc.

au·tom'a·ton n. robot

au'to·mo·bile' (-bēl') n. car propelled by its own engine, for use on streets and roads

au'to·mo'tive a. **1.** self-moving **2.** having to do with automobiles, trucks, etc.

au'to·nom'ic (-näm'-) a. of the nervous system regulating the heart, lungs, etc.

au·ton'o·mous a. **1.** self-governing **2.** existing independently —**au·ton'o·my** n.

au'top·sy n. [pl. -SIES] examination of a corpse to find cause of death, etc.

au'tumn (-təm) n. season after summer, when leaves fall —**au·tum'nal** (-n'l) a.

aux·il·ia·ry (ôg zil'yə rē) a. **1.** helping **2.** subsidiary —n. [pl. -RIES] auxiliary group, etc.

auxiliary verb helping verb, as *has* in "he has gone"

a·vail' v. be of use or help (to) —n. use or help —**avail oneself of** make use of

a·vail'a·ble a. that can be got or had —**a·vail'a·bil'i·ty** n.

av'a·lanche n. great fall of rock, snow, etc. down a hill

a·vant-garde (ä vänt' gärd') n. [Fr.] vanguard

av'a·rice (-ris) n. greed for money —**av'a·ri'cious** a.

a·vast' int. Naut. stop!

a·venge' v. get revenge for —**a·veng'er** n.

a·ve·nue n. **1.** street **2.** way to something; approach

a·ver' (-vur') v. [AVERRED, AVERRING] declare to be true

av'er·age n. **1.** sum divided by the number of quantities added **2.** usual kind, amount, etc. —a. being the average —v. **1.** figure the average of **2.** do on the average —**on the average** as an average amount, rate, etc.

a·verse' a. unwilling

a·ver'sion n. dislike

a·vert' v. **1.** turn away **2.** prevent

a·vi·ar′y (ā-) n. [pl. -IES] large cage for many birds

a′vi·a′tion n. science or work of flying airplanes

a′vi·a′tor n. airplane pilot

av′id a. eager or greedy

a′vi·on′ics n. electronics applied in aviation and astronautics

av′o·ca′do (-kä′-) n. [pl. -DOS] thick-skinned tropical fruit with buttery flesh

av′o·ca′tion (-kä′-) n. hobby

a·void′ v. keep away from; shun —**a·void′a·ble** a. —**a·void′ance** n.

av·oir·du·pois (av′ər də poiz′) n. weight system in which 16 oz. = 1 lb.

a·vouch′ v. assert; affirm

a·vow′ v. declare openly; admit; aver —**a·vow′al** n. —**a·vowed′** a. —**a·vow′ed·ly** adv.

a·vun′cu·lar (-vuŋ′kyə-) a. of an uncle

aw int. sound of protest, etc.

a·wait′ v. wait for

a·wake′ v. [pt. & alt. pp. AWOKE] rouse from sleep —a. 1. not asleep 2. alert

a·wak′en v. rouse; awake —**a·wak′en·ing** n., a.

a·ward′ v. give after judging —n. 1. decision, as by judges 2. prize

a·ware′ a. conscious; knowing —**a·ware′ness** n.

a·wash′ adv., a. 1. with water washing over the surface 2. flooded 3. afloat

a·way′ adv. 1. to another place 2. aside n. 1. from one's keeping —a. 1. absent 2. at a distance —int. begone! —**away with** go or take away —**do away with** get rid of

awe n. reverent fear and wonder —v. inspire awe in

a·weigh′ a. being weighed (hoisted): said of an anchor

awe′some a. causing awe

awe′-struck′ a. filled with awe: also **awe′-strick′en**

aw′ful a. 1. terrifying; dreadful 2. [Col.] bad —adv. [Col.] very —**aw′ful·ly** adv.

a·while′ adv. for a short time

awk′ward a. 1. clumsy 2. uncomfortable 3. embarrassing —**awk′ward·ly** adv.

awl n. pointed tool for making holes in wood, etc.

awn n. bristly fibers on a head of barley, oats, etc.

awn′ing n. overhanging shade of canvas, metal, etc.

A.WOL, a·wol (ā′wôl) a. absent without leave

a·wry (ə rī′) adv., a. 1. with a twist to a side 2. amiss

ax, axe n. [pl. AXES] tool for chopping wood, etc. —**get the ax** [Col.] be fired from a job

ax′i·om n. an evident truth —**ax′i·o·mat′ic** a.

ax′is n. [pl. AXES (-ēz)] straight line around which a thing rotates —**ax′i·al** a.

ax′le n. rod on which a wheel revolves

ax′le·tree n. axle of a wagon, carriage, etc.

ax′o·lotl (-sə lät′'l) n. dark salamander of Mexico and western U.S.

aye (ā) adv. [Ar.] always

aye, ay (ī) adv., n. yes

a·zal'ea (-zāl'yə) *n.* shrub with brightly colored flowers

az·ure (azh'ər) *a., n.* sky blue

B

baa (bä) *v., n.* bleat

bab'ble *v.* 1. talk in a foolish or jumbled way 2. murmur —*n.* babbling talk or sound —**bab'bler** *n.*

babe *n.* baby

ba'bel (bā'-) *n.* tumult

ba·boon' *n.* large monkey with doglike snout

ba·bush'ka (-boosh'-) *n.* scarf worn on the head

ba'by *n. [pl.* -BIES] very young child; infant —*a.* 1. of, for, or like a baby 2. small or young —*v.* [-BIED, -BYING] pamper —**ba'by·hood'** *n.* —**ba'by·ish** *a.*

baby beef meat from a heifer or steer one to two years old

baby carriage light carriage for wheeling a baby about: also **baby buggy**

baby grand small grand piano

ba'by's breath plant with small white or pink flowers

ba'by·sit' *v.* [-SAT, -SITTING] take care of children when parents are away —**baby sit·ter** *n.*

bac·ca·lau·re·ate (-lô'rē it) *n.* 1. bachelor's degree 2. a talk to graduating class

bac·cha·nal (bak'ə nəl) *n.* drunken orgy —**bac'cha·na'li·an** (-nā'-) *a.*

bach'e·lor *n.* unmarried man —**bach'e·lor·hood'** *n.*

Bachelor of Arts (or **Science,** etc.) college degree

ba·cil'lus (-sil'-) *n. [pl.* -LI (-ī)] kind of bacteria

back *n.* 1. rear or hind part 2. backbone 3. the reverse 4. football player behind the line —*a.* 1. at the rear 2. of the past 3. backward —*adv.* 1. at or to the rear 2. to a former time, etc. 3. in return —*v.* 1. move backward 2. support 3. provide a back for —**back down** retract an opinion, etc. —**back up** 1. to support 2. move backward 3. accumulate because stopped —**go back on** [Col.] 1. betray 2. fail to keep, as a promise —**back'er** *n.* —**back'ing** *n.*

back'ache *n.* an ache in the back

back'bite *v.* to slander

back'board *n. Basketball* board behind the basket

back'bone *n.* 1. spinal column 2. courage; firmness

back'break'ing *a.* very tiring

back'drop *n.* curtain at the back of a stage

back'field *n. Football* players behind the line

back'fire *n.* faulty ignition, as in the exhaust pipe of an engine —*v.* 1. have a backfire 2. go awry

back'gam'mon *n.* game played on a special board

back'ground n. 1. the part behind, more distant, etc. 2. past events, causes, etc.

back'hand n. backhanded stroke, as in tennis

back'hand'ed a. 1. with the back of the hand forward 2. insincere

back'lash n. sharp reaction

back'log n. piling up, as of work to be done

back order order not yet filled

back'pack n. knapsack —v. hike wearing a backpack

back'rest n. support for the back

back'side n. back part 2. rump

back'slap'per n. [Col.] effusively friendly person

back'slide' v. to fall back in morals, religious faith, etc.

back'stage' adv. in theater dressing rooms, etc.

back'stretch n. part of a race track opposite the homestretch

back'stroke n. swimming stroke made while lying face upward

back talk [Col.] insolence

back'track v. to retreat

back'ward adv. 1. toward the back 2. with the back foremost 3. into the past Also **back'-wards** —a. 1. turned to the rear or away 2. shy 3. retarded —**back'ward·ness** n.

back'woods' n.pl. remote, wooded areas —**back'woods'-man** [pl. -MEN] n.

ba'con n. cured meat from hog's back or sides

bac·te'ri·a n.pl. [sing. -RIUM] microorganisms causing diseases, fermentation, etc. —**bac-te'ri·al** a.

bac·te'ri·cide n. agent that destroys bacteria

bac·te'ri·ol·o·gy n. study of bacteria

bad a. [WORSE, WORST] 1. not good 2. spoiled 3. incorrect 4. wicked 5. severe —adv. [Col.] badly —n. anything bad —**in bad** [Col.] in trouble —**bad'ly** adv. —**bad'ness** n.

bade (bad) alt. pt. of **bid**

badge n. pin or emblem worn to show rank, membership, etc.

badg'er n. burrowing animal — v. to nag; pester

bad'man n. [pl. -MEN] desperado of the old West

bad'min·ton n. game using rackets and a feathered cork

bad'-mouth' v. [Sl.] find fault (with)

bad'-tem'pered a. irritable

baf'fle v. puzzle; bewilder —n. deflecting screen —**baf'fling** a.

bag n. 1. container made of fabric, paper, etc. 2. suitcase 3. purse —v. [BAGGED, BAGGING] 1. hang loosely 2. kill or capture —in the bag [Col.] certain —**bag'ful** [pl. -FULS] n. —**bag'gy** a.

bag·a·telle' n. a trifle

ba·gel (bā'g'l) n. hard bread roll like a small doughnut

bag'gage n. luggage

bag'pipe n. often pl. musical instrument with a bag from which air is forced into pipes

bah (bä) int. shout of scorn

bail n. money left as security to free a prisoner until trial —

v. **1.** get freed by giving bail **2.** dip out (water) from (a boat) —**bail out** to parachute

bail'iff *n.* **1.** court officer guarding prisoners and jurors **2.** sheriff's assistant

bail'i·wick *n.* one's field of interest or authority

bait *v.* **1.** torment, as by insults **2.** put food on (a hook, etc.) as a lure —*n.* anything used as a lure

baize (bāz) *n.* coarse, feltlike cloth

bake *v.* **1.** cook by dry heat in an oven **2.** harden by heat —**bak'er** *n.*

bak'er·y *n.* [*pl.* -IES] place where bread, etc. is baked

baking powder leavening powder

baking soda sodium bicarbonate, powder used as leavening and as an antacid

bal'a·lai'ka (-lī'-) *n.* Russian instrument like a guitar

bal'ance *n.* **1.** instrument for weighing, with two pans **2.** equilibrium **3.** harmonious proportion **4.** equality of or difference between credits and debits **5.** [Col.] remainder —*v.* **1.** compare **2.** offset; counteract **3.** put, keep, or be in equilibrium **4.** be equal **5.** sum up or equalize the debits and credits of (an account) —**in the balance** not yet settled

balance sheet statement of financial status of a business

bal'co·ny *n.* [*pl.* -NIES] **1.** platform projecting from an upper story **2.** tier of theater seats above main floor

bald *a.* **1.** lacking hair on the head **2.** plain and frank — **bald'ly** *adv.* —**bald'ness** *n.*

bald eagle large eagle of N. America, with white-feathered head

bal'der·dash (bôl'-) *n.* nonsense

bald'faced *a.* shameless

bald'ing *a.* becoming bald

bal'dric (bôl'-) *n.* belt over the shoulder to support a sword

bale (bāl) *n.* large bundle, as of raw cotton —*v.* make into bales

ba·leen' *n.* whalebone

bale'ful *a.* harmful; evil

balk (bôk) *v.* **1.** stop and refuse to move **2.** obstruct —*n.* obstruction; hindrance —**balk'y** [-IER, -IEST] *a.*

ball *n.* **1.** round object; sphere **2.** round or oval object used in games **3.** formal social dance **4.** [Sl.] good time —*v.* form into a ball —**on the ball** [Sl.] alert

bal'lad *n.* **1.** popular love song **2.** folk song or poem telling a story

ball-and-socket joint joint, as the hip, like a ball in a socket

bal'last (-əst) *n.* heavy matter put in a ship, etc. to keep it steady —*v.* to furnish with ballast

ball bearing 1. bearing in which the parts turn on rolling metal balls **2.** one of these balls

bal'le·ri'na (-rē'-) *n.* woman ballet dancer

bal'let (-ā) *n.* intricate, formalized group dance

ballistic missile long-range guided missile that falls free as it nears its target

bal·lis'tics *n.* science of the motion of projectiles —**bal·lis'tic** *a.*

bal·loon' *n.* bag that rises when filled with light gas —*v.* swell; expand

bal'lot *n.* **1.** paper marked in voting **2.** voting —*v.* to vote

ball'park' *n.* baseball stadium

ball'play'er *n.* baseball player

ball point pen pen with an ink cartridge and a small ball bearing instead of a point: also **ball'-point', ball'point'** *n.*

ball'room *n.* large room for social dances

bal'ly·hoo' *n.* [Col.] exaggerated talk or noisy uproar

balm (bäm) *n.* fragrant healing ointment or oil

balm'y *a.* [-IER, -IEST] soothing, mild, etc.

ba·lo'ney *n.* **1.** bologna **2.** [Sl.] nonsense

bal'sa (bôl'-) *n.* lightweight wood of a tropical tree

bal'sam (bôl'-) *n.* **1.** aromatic resin **2.** tree yielding it

bal'us·ter *n.* railing post

bal'us·trade *n.* row of balusters supporting a rail

bam·boo' *n.* tropical grass with hollow, treelike stems

bam·boo'zle *v.* [Col.] **1.** trick **2.** confuse

ban *v.* [BANNED, BANNING] forbid —*n.* formal forbidding by authorities

ba'nal (bā'-) *a.* trite —**ba·nal'i·ty** [*pl.* -TIES] *n.*

ba·nan'a *n.* long tropical fruit with creamy flesh

band *n.* **1.** strip of cloth, etc. as for binding **2.** stripe **3.** range of radio wavelengths **4.** group of people **5.** group of performing musicians —*v.* **1.** mark or tie with a band **2.** join

band'age (-ij) *n.* cloth strip to bind an injury —*v.* bind with a bandage

Band'-Aid' *trademark for* small bandage of gauze and adhesive tape —*n.* [b- a-] such a bandage: also **band'aid**

ban·dan'na, ban·dan'a *n.* large, colored handkerchief

band'box *n.* light pasteboard box for hats, etc.

ban'dit *n.* robber; brigand —**ban'dit·ry** *n.*

ban·do·leer', ban·do·lier' (-lir') *n.* broad belt holding bullets, worn over one shoulder and across the chest

band saw power saw that is an endless, toothed steel belt

band'stand *n.* (outdoor) platform for an orchestra

band'wag'on *n.* winning or popular side

ban'dy *v.* [-DIED, -DYING] toss or pass back and forth —*a.* curved or bent outward —**ban'dy-leg'ged** *a.*

bane *n.* cause of harm or ruin —**bane'ful** *a.*

bang *v.*, *n.* (make, or hit with) a loud noise

ban'gle *n.* bracelet

bangs *n.pl.* short hair worn across the forehead

ban'ish *v.* **1.** to exile **2.** dismiss —**ban'ish·ment** *n.*

ban·is·ter n. 1. baluster 2. pl. balustrade

ban·jo n. [pl. -JOS, -JOES] stringed musical instrument with a circular body —**ban·jo·ist** n.

bank n. 1. mound; heap 2. steep slope, as beside a river 3. row; tier 4. business handling savings, loans, etc. —v. 1. form a bank 2. put (money) in a bank 3. cover (a fire) to make it last —**bank on** [Col.] rely on

bank account money deposited in a bank and credited to the depositor

bank′book n. book recording a bank depositor's deposits

bank′er n. person who owns or manages a bank

bank′ing n. business of a bank

bank note promissory note issued by a bank

bank′roll n. supply of money —v. [Col.] supply with money

bank′rupt a. 1. legally declared unable to pay one's debts 2. lacking —n. bankrupt person —v. make bankrupt —**bank′rupt·cy** n.

ban′ner n. flag —a. foremost; leading

banns, bans n.pl. church notice of coming marriage

ban′quet n. formal dinner

ban·quette (-ket′) n. 1. gunner's platform in a trench 2. upholstered bench

ban′shee n. Folklore female spirit warning of death

ban′tam n. [B-] breed of small chickens —a. small

ban′ter v. tease playfully —n. genial teasing

ban′yan n. Asian fig tree with many trunks

bap′tism n. rite of admission into a Christian church by dipping in or sprinkling with water —**bap·tis′mal** a. —**bap·tize′** v.

bap·tis·ter·y (-tis trē) n. [pl. -IES] place in a church used for baptizing: also **bap′tis·try** [pl. -TRIES]

bar n. 1. long, narrow piece of wood, metal, etc. 2. oblong piece, as of soap 3. obstruction 4. band or strip 5. law court 6. legal profession 7. counter or place for serving liquor 8. Music a measure or vertical line marking it off —v. [BARRED, BARRING] 1. obstruct; close 2. oppose 3. exclude —prep. excluding

barb n. sharp, back-curving point —**barbed** a.

bar·bar·i·an (-ber′-) n. uncivilized person; savage —a. uncivilized —**bar·bar′ic** a. —**bar·bar′i·ty** n.

bar′ba·rize v. make or become barbarous

bar′ba·rous a. 1. uncivilized 2. crude; coarse 3. brutal —**bar′ba·rism** n.

bar′be·cue n. 1. animal roasted whole over open fire 2. picnic at which such meat is served —v. 1. roast whole 2. broil in spicy sauce (**barbecue sauce**)

barbed wire twisted strands of wire with barbs at close intervals: also **barb′wire′** n.

bar'bel (-b'l) *n.* a threadlike growth from lip or jaw of a fish

bar'bell *n.* metal bar with weights at each end, used in weight lifting

bar'ber *n.* one who cuts hair, shaves beards, etc.

bar'ber·ry *n.* [*pl.* -RIES] 1. spiny shrub with red berries 2. the berry

bar·bi'tu·rate (-bich'ə rit) *n.* drug used as a sedative

bar'ca·role, bar'ca·rolle (-rōl) *n.* Venetian gondolier song, or such music

bard *n.* poet

bare *a.* 1. naked 2. exposed 3. empty 4. mere —*v.* uncover —**lay bare** uncover

bare'back *adv., a.* on a horse with no saddle

bare'faced *a.* shameless

bare'foot *a., adv.* without shoes and stockings —**bare'-foot·ed** *a.*

bare'hand·ed *a., adv.* 1. with hands uncovered 2. without weapons, etc.

bare'head·ed *a., adv.* with the head uncovered

bare'leg·ged (-leg id, -legd) *a., adv.* with the legs bare

bare'ly *adv.* only just

bar'gain (-g'n) *n.* 1. agreement or contract 2. item bought at a favorable price —*v.* haggle —**bargain for** expect —**into the bargain** besides —**bar'gain·er** *n.*

bargain counter store counter with goods on sale at reduced prices

barge *n.* flat-bottomed freight boat —*v.* [Col.] enter abruptly (*into*)

bar'i·tone (bar'-) *n.* male voice, or instrument, between tenor and bass

bar'i·um *n.* silver-white metallic chemical element

bark *n.* 1. outside covering of trees 2. sharp cry of a dog 3. sailing vessel —*v.* 1. utter a bark 2. scrape off the skin of

bar'keep·er *n.* owner of a barroom 2. bartender

bark'er *n.* announcer at a carnival side show

bar'ley (-lē) *n.* cereal grain

bar mitz·vah (mits'və) religious ceremony for a Jewish boy when he becomes 13 years old —**bat** (or **bas**) **mitzvah** (bät, bäs) *fem.*

barn *n.* farm building for livestock, storage, etc.

bar'na·cle *n.* shellfish that clings to ships, etc.

barn'storm *v.* tour small towns, acting plays, etc.

barn'yard *n.* yard near a barn —*a.* of or fit for a barn

ba·rom'e·ter *n.* instrument to measure atmospheric pressure —**bar'o·met'ric** *a.*

bar'on *n.* nobleman of lowest rank —**bar'on·ess** *n.fem.* —**bar·o'ni·al** (-rō'-) *a.*

bar'o·net *n.* British man with hereditary rank of honor

ba·roque' (-rōk') *a.* having elaborate decoration

bar'racks *n.pl.* building(s) for housing soldiers

bar'ra·cu'da (-kōō'-) *n.* [*pl.* -DA, -DAS] fierce tropical fish

bar·rage (bə räzh′) *n.* curtain of artillery fire

barred *a.* **1.** having bars or bands **2.** closed off with bars **3.** not allowed

bar′rel *n.* **1.** round, wooden container with bulging sides **2.** tube of a gun

barrel organ musical instrument played by turning crank

bar′ren *a.* **1.** sterile **2.** unproductive

bar·rette (bə ret′) *n.* clasp for a girl's hair

bar′ri·cade *n.* barrier for defense —*v.* block with a barricade

bar′ri·er (bar′-) *n.* fence, wall, or other obstruction

bar′ring *prep.* excepting

bar′ris·ter (bar′-) *n.* British courtroom lawyer

bar′room *n.* room with a bar (*n.* 7)

bar·row (bar′ō) *n.* traylike frame for carrying loads

bar′tend′er *n.* man serving drinks at a bar (*n.* 7)

bar′ter *v.* exchange (goods) —*n.* a bartering

bas·al (bā′s'l) *a.* basic

basal metabolism quantity of energy used by any organism at rest

ba·salt (bə sôlt′) *n.* dark volcanic rock

base *n.* **1.** part that a thing rests on **2.** basis **3.** goal in some games **4.** headquarters **5.** substance reacting with an acid to form a salt —*v.* put on a base —*a.* **1.** morally low **2.** inferior —**base′ly** *adv.*

base′ball *n.* **1.** team game

played with bat and ball **2.** the ball used

base′board *n.* molding at the base of a wall

base hit *Baseball* play by a batter who hits and gets on base safely

base′less *a.* unfounded

base line 1. *Baseball* lane from one base to the next **2.** back line on a tennis court

base′man *n.* [*pl.* -MEN] *Baseball* infielder at first, second, or third base

base′ment *n.* story just below the main floor

base on balls *Baseball* a walk

base pay basic rate of pay, not counting overtime pay

base runner *Baseball* batter who is on, or trying to reach, a base

bash *v.* [Col.] hit hard —*n.* [Sl.] a party

bash′ful *a.* socially timid; shy —**bash′ful·ly** *adv.*

bas′ic *a.* of or at the base; fundamental —**bas′i·cal·ly** *adv.*

bas·il (baz′'l) *n.* an herb

ba·sil′i·ca *n.* ancient kind of church building

bas′i·lisk (bas′-) *n.* mythical, lizardlike monster whose glance could kill

ba′sin *n.* **1.** wide, shallow container for liquid **2.** a sink **3.** bay, cove, etc. **4.** area drained by a river

ba′sis *n.* [*pl.* -SES (-sēz)] **1.** base or foundation **2.** main constituent

bask *v.* warm oneself

bas′ket *n.* **1.** container made

of interwoven strips 2. goal in basketball

bas'ket·ball n. 1. team game with raised open nets through which a large ball must be tossed 2. this ball

bas'-re·lief' (bä'-) n. sculpture with figures projecting a little from the background

bass (bās) n. 1. lowest male singing voice 2. singer or instrument with low range; spec., double bass

bass (bas) n. perchlike fish

bas'set n. short-legged hound

bas·si·net' n. baby's bed like a large basket

bas·so (bas'ō, bäs'ō) n. [pl. -SOS] bass voice or singer

bas·soon' n. double-reed, bass woodwind instrument

bass viol double bass

bast n. plant fiber used for ropes, mats, etc.

bas'tard n. illegitimate child — a. 1. illegitimate 2. sham, not standard, etc.

baste v. 1. sew with loose, temporary stitches 2. moisten (a roast) with drippings, etc. 3. beat soundly —bast'ing n.

bas·tion (bas'chən) n. 1. part of a fort that juts out 2. any strong defense

bat n. 1. a club to hit a ball, as in baseball 2. a turn at batting 3. [Col.] a blow 4. nocturnal, mouselike, flying mammal —v. [BATTED, BATTING] 1. hit as with a bat 2. [Col.] blink

batch n. quantity taken, made, etc. in one lot

bat'ed (bāt'-) a. held in, as the breath in fear

bath n. 1. a washing of the body 2. water, etc. for bathing or soaking something 3. bathtub 4. bathroom

bathe (bāth) v. 1. give a bath to, or take a bath 2. put into a liquid 3. cover as with liquid —bath'er n.

bathing suit garment worn for swimming

bath'mat n. mat used in or next to a bathtub

ba'thos (bā'-) n. a shift from noble to trivial

bath'robe n. loose robe worn to and from the bath

bath'room n. room with a bathtub, toilet, etc.

bath'tub n. tub to bathe in

bath'y·scaph' (-ə skaf) n. deep-sea diving apparatus not using a cable

ba·tik' (-tēk') n. cloth with design dyed only on parts not coated with wax

ba·tiste' (-tēst') n. fine, thin cotton fabric

ba·ton' (-tän') n. 1. stick used in leading an orchestra, etc. 2. staff serving as a symbol of office 3. metal rod twirled by a drum major

bat·tal'ion n. subdivision of a regiment

bat'ten n. strip of wood —v. 1. fasten with battens 2. fatten; thrive

bat'ter v. 1. strike repeatedly 2. injure by hard use —n. 1. player at bat in baseball 2. mixture of flour, milk, etc. for making cakes

battering ram heavy beam, etc. to batter down walls

bat·ter·y n. [pl. -IES] 1. cell or cells providing electric current 2. set of artillery guns 3. pitcher and catcher in baseball 4. illegal beating of a person

bat′ting n. wadded fiber

bat′tle n., v. fight, esp. between armies —**bat′tler** n.

bat′tle-ax′, bat′tle-axe′ n. 1. heavy ax formerly used as a weapon 2. [Sl.] harsh, domineering woman

bat′tle-dore n. racket for a game like badminton

bat′tle-field n. place of battle: also **bat′tle-ground**

bat′tle-ment n. low wall on a tower with open spaces for shooting

battle royal [pl. BATTLES ROYAL] 1. a brawl 2. heated dispute

bat′tle-ship n. large warship with big guns

bat′ty a. [-TIER, -TIEST] [Sl.] crazy, odd, queer, etc.

bau′ble (bô′-) n. trinket

baux·ite (bôk′sīt, bō′zīt) n. claylike aluminum ore

bawd n. a prostitute

bawd′ry n. obscene language

bawd′y a. [-IER, -IEST] obscene —**bawd′i·ness** n.

bawl v. 1. to shout 2. weep noisily —**bawl out** [Sl.] scold angrily

bay n. 1. wide inlet of a sea or lake 2. alcove 3. recess in a wall, as for a window (**bay window**) 4. laurel tree 5. reddish brown 6. reddish-brown horse —v. bark in long, deep tones —**at bay** 1. with escape

cut off 2. held off —**bring to bay** cut off escape of

bay′ber·ry n. [pl. -RIES] 1. wax myrtle 2. its berry

bay leaf laurel leaf, dried and used as spice in cooking

bay′o·net n. blade attached to a rifle barrel —v. stab with a bayonet

bay·ou (bī′ōō) n. marshy inlet or outlet, as of a lake

ba·zaar′ (-zär′) n. 1. Oriental marketplace 2. benefit sale for a club, etc.

ba·zoo′ka n. portable rocket-firing weapon

BB (shot) tiny metal shot for an air rifle (**BB gun**)

B.C. before Christ

be v. [WAS or WERE, BEEN, BEING] 1. exist; live 2. occur 3. remain; continue Be is an important helping verb

be- pref. 1. around 2. completely 3. away 4. about

beach n. stretch of sandy shore —v. ground (a boat)

beach′comb·er n. hobo living on a beach

beach′head n. shore area taken by invading troops

bea′con n. guiding light

bead n. 1. small ball of glass, etc., pierced for stringing 2. pl. string of beads 3. pl. rosary 4. drop or bubble 5. rim edge of a rubber tire —**bead′ed** a. —**bead′y** a.

bea′dle n. minor officer who keeps order in church

bea′gle n. small, shortlegged hound

beak n. 1. bird's bill 2. any beaklike mouth part

beak′er n. broad glass container

beam n. 1. long, thick piece of timber, etc. 2. ship's greatest breadth 3. shaft of light 4. radiant look or smile 5. guiding radio signal —v. radiate in a beam

bean n. 1. edible seed of some plants 2. pod of these

bear (ber) n. 1. large, heavy mammal with shaggy fur 2. rough, rude person —v. [BORE, BORNE or BORN, BEARING] 1. carry 2. have or show 3. give birth to 4. produce 5. permit of 6. endure —**bear down** exert pressure —**bear on** relate to —**bear out** confirm —**bear up** endure —**bear** with tolerate —**bear′a·ble** a. —**bear′er** n. —**bear′like** a.

beard (bird) n. 1. hair on a man's face 2. awn —v. defy face to face —**beard′ed** a. —**beard′less** a.

bear′ing (ber′-) n. 1. way one carries oneself 2. often pl. relative position or direction 3. relation 4. ball, roller, etc. on which something turns or slides

bear′ish a. 1. bearlike 2. causing a drop in stock exchange prices

bear′skin n. 1. furry hide of a bear 2. rug, coat, etc. made from this

beast n. 1. any large four-footed animal 2. brutal, gross person

beast′ly a. [-LIER, -LIEST] 1. of or like a beast; brutal 2. [Col.] disagreeable

beast of burden any animal used for carrying things

beast of prey any animal that hunts and kills other animals for food

beat v. [BEAT, BEATEN, BEATING] 1. strike repeatedly 2. punish by striking 3. mix by stirring 4. defeat 5. throb 6. flap (wings) 7. make (a path) by tramping 8. mark (time) by tapping 9. [Col.] to puzzle 10. [Col.] to cheat —n. 1. a throbbing 2. habitual route 3. unit of musical rhythm —a. [Sl.] tired —**beat back** (or off) drive back —**beat it!** [Sl.] go away! —**beat up (on)** [Sl.] give a beating to

be·a·tif′ic a. blissful

be·at′i·fy v. [-FIED, -FYING] R.C.Ch. declare one who has died to be among the blessed in heaven

be·at′i·tude n. bliss

beat′-up′ a. [Sl.] worn-out, battered, dilapidated, etc.

beau (bō) n. [pl. BEAUS, BEAUX (bōz)] woman's lover

beau·ti·cian (byōō tish′ən) n. one who works in a beauty shop

beau′ti·ful a. having beauty: also **beau′te·ous** —**beau′ti·ful·ly** adv.

beau′ti·fy v. [-FIED, -FYING] make beautiful

beau′ty n. [pl. -TIES] 1. pleasing quality as in looks, sound, etc. 2. person or thing of beauty

beauty shop (or **salon** or

parlor) place where women go for hair styling, etc.

bea·ver (bē′-) *n.* **1.** amphibious animal with webbed hind feet **2.** its brown fur

be·calm′ *v.* **1.** make calm **2.** make (a ship) motionless from lack of wind

be·cause′ *con.* for the reason that —**because of** on account of

beck *n.* beckoning gesture

beck′on *v.* call by gesture

be·cloud′ *v.* to obscure

be·come′ *v.* [-CAME, -COME, -COMING] **1.** come to be **2.** suit —**become of** happen to

be·com′ing *a.* right or suitable; attractive

bed *n.* **1.** piece of furniture to sleep on **2.** plot of soil for plants **3.** flat bottom or foundation **4.** layer —*v.* [BEDDED, BEDDING] put or go to bed

be·daz′zle *v.* dazzle thoroughly

bed′bug *n.* small, wingless, biting insect

bed′clothes *n.pl.* bed sheets, blankets, etc.

bed′cov′er *n.* bedspread

bed′ding *n.* mattresses and bedclothes

be·deck′ *v.* adorn

be·dev′il *v.* to torment or worry —**be·dev′il·ment** *n.*

bed′fast *a.* bedridden

bed′fel′low *n.* **1.** person who shares one's bed **2.** any associate

be·dim′ *v.* [-DIMMED, -DIM MING] make (the vision) dim

bed jacket woman's jacket worn in bed over a nightgown

bed′lam *n.* noisy confusion

bed of roses [Col.] situation of ease and luxury

Bed′ou·in (-ōō win) *n.* Arab nomad

bed′pan *n.* shallow pan used as a toilet by one bedridden

be·drag′gled *a.* wet and dirty; messy

bed′rid′den *a.* confined to bed, as by long illness

bed′rock *n.* **1.** solid rock under soil **2.** base or bottom

bed′roll *n.* portable roll of bedding, used by campers

bed′room *n.* sleeping room

bed′sore *n.* sore on a bedridden person

bed′spread *n.* ornamental cover for a bed

bed′spring *n.* framework of springs under a mattress

bed′stead *n.* frame of a bed

bed′time *n.* one's usual time for going to bed

bee *n.* **1.** winged insect that makes honey **2.** meeting of group, as to work together

beech *n.* **1.** tree with gray bark and edible nuts **2.** its hard wood

beech′nut *n.* small, three-cornered nut of the beech tree

beef *n.* [*pl.* BEEVES, BEEFS] **1.** cow, bull, or steer **2.** its meat **3.** [Col.] brawn **4.** [Sl.] complaint —*v.* [Sl.] complain

beef′eat′er *n.* **1.** one who eats beef **2.** guard at the Tower of London **3.** [Sl.] Englishman

beef′steak *n.* thick cut of beef for broiling or frying

beef′y *a.* [-IER, -IEST] brawny —**beef′i·ness** *n.*

bee′hive *n.* hive for bees

bee′keep′er *n.* one who keeps bees to make honey —**bee′-keep′ing** *n.*

bee′line *n.* straight course

been pp. of **be**

beep *n.* brief, shrill sound of a horn or electrical signal —*v.* make this sound

beer *n.* mildly alcoholic drink brewed from malt, hops, etc.

bees′wax *n.* wax from bees, used in their honeycomb

beet *n.* plant with edible red or white root

bee′tle *n.* insect with hard front wings —*v.* jut out

bee′tle-browed′ *a.* 1. having bushy eyebrows 2. frowning

be·fall′ *v.* [-FELL, -FALLEN, -FALLING] happen (to)

be·fit′ *v.* [-FITTED, -FITTING] be fitting for

be·fog′ *v.* [-FOGGED, -FOGGING] 1. make foggy 2. to confuse

be·fore′ *adv.* 1. in front 2. till now 3. earlier —*prep.* 1. ahead of 2. in sight of 3. earlier than 4. rather than —*con.* earlier or sooner than

be·fore′hand *adv., a.* ahead of time

be·foul′ *v.* 1. make filthy 2. cast aspersions on

be·friend′ *v.* be a friend to

be·fud′dle *v.* confuse

beg *v.* [BEGGED, BEGGING] 1. ask for (alms) 2. entreat —**go begging** be unwanted

be·gat′ *v.* [Ar.] pt. of **beget**

be·get′ *v.* [-GOT, -GOTTEN or -GOT, -GETTING] 1. to father 2. to cause

beg′gar *n.* 1. one who lives by begging 2. very poor person —

v. 1. make a beggar of 2. make seem useless

beg′gar·ly *a.* poor; mean

be·gin′ *v.* [-GAN, -GUN, -GIN-NING] 1. start 2. originate —**be·gin′ner** *n.*

be·gin′ning *n.* 1. start 2. origin 3. first part

be·gone′ *int., v.* go away

be·go′nia (-gōn′yə) *n.* plant with showy flowers

be·grudge′ *v.* 1. envy the possession of 2. give reluctantly

be·guile′ (-gīl′) *v.* 1. deceive or trick 2. charm 3. pass (time) pleasantly

be·half′ (-haf′) *n.* support, side, etc. —**in (or on) behalf of** in the interest of

be·have′ *v.* 1. to conduct (oneself), esp. properly 2. act

be·hav′ior *n.* conduct

be·head′ *v.* cut off the head of

be·he′moth (bi hē′-, bē′ə-) *n.* huge animal

be·hest′ *n.* a command

be·hind′ *adv.* 1. in the rear 2. slow; late 3. to the back —*prep.* 1. in back of 2. later or slower than 3. supporting —*a.* 1. that follows 2. in arrears —*n.* [Col.] the buttocks

be·hind′hand *adv., a.* late in payment, time, or progress

be·hold′ *v.* [-HELD, -HOLDING] see —*int.* look! see!

be·hold′en *a.* indebted

be·hoove′ (-hōōv′) *v.* be necessary or fitting (for)

beige (bāzh) *a.* grayish tan

be′ing *n.* 1. existence; life 2. one that lives

be·la′bor *v.* beat; attack

be·lat'ed (-lāt'-) *a.* too late

be·lay' *v.* [-LAYED, -LAYING] 1. secure (a rope) around a cleat 2. [Naut. Col.] to stop

bel can'to (kän'-) [It.] brilliant singing style with purity of tone

belch *v.* 1. expel stomach gas orally 2. eject with force —*n.* a belching

be·lea'guer (-lē'gər) *v.* 1. besiege 2. beset

bel'fry *n.* [*pl.* -FRIES] bell tower

Bel'gian *n., a.* (native) of Belgium

be·lie' *v.* [-LIED, -LYING] 1. misrepresent 2. prove false

be·lief' *n.* 1. conviction; faith 2. trust 3. opinion

be·lieve' *v.* 1. take as true 2. have faith (in) 3. suppose; guess —**be·liev'a·ble** *a.* —**be·liev'er** *n.*

be·lit'tle *v.* make seem little or unimportant

bell *n.* 1. hollow metal object that rings when struck 2. sound of a bell

bel'la·don'na *n.* 1. poisonous plant yielding a drug that relieves spasms 2. the drug

bell'-bot'tom *a.* flared at the bottom, as trousers

bell'boy *n.* one who does errands at a hotel: also [Sl.] **bell'hop**

belle (bel) *n.* pretty girl

belles-let·tres (bel let'rə) *n.pl.* [Fr.] fiction, poetry, drama, etc.; literature

bel'li·cose *a.* quarrelsome — **bel'li·cos'i·ty** (-käs'-) *n.*

bel·lig'er·ent (-lij'-) *a.* warlike

—*n.* nation or person at war — **bel·lig'er·ence** *n.*

bell jar (or **glass**) glass, bell-shaped container, used to hold air, moisture, etc. in or out

bel'low *v., n.* roar or shout

bel'lows *n. sing. & pl.* collapsible device for producing a stream of air

bells *n.pl.* [Col.] bell-bottom trousers

bell'weth'er *n.* male sheep that leads a flock

bel'ly *n.* [*pl.* -LIES] 1. abdomen 2. stomach —*v.* [-LIED, -LYING] to bulge

bel'ly·ache *n.* pain in the belly —*v.* [Sl.] complain

bel'ly·but'ton *n.* [Col.] the navel: also **belly button**

bel'ly·ful *n.* 1. more than enough to eat 2. [Sl.] all that one can bear

belly laugh [Col.] hearty laugh

be·long' *v.* have a proper place —**belong to** 1. be a part of 2. be owned by 3. be a member of

be·long'ings *n.pl.* possessions

be·lov'ed *a., n.* dearly loved (person)

be·low' *adv., a.* 1. in or to a lower place; beneath 2. under in rank, amount, etc. —*prep.* lower than; beneath

belt *n.* 1. encircling band, as around the waist 2. distinct area —*v.* strike as with a belt

be·mire' *v.* 1. make dirty with mire 2. bog down in mire

be·moan' *v.* lament

be·mused' *a.* preoccupied

bench *n.* 1. long seat 2. work-table 3. seat for judges 4.

status of a judge —*v.* remove (a player) from a game

bench warrant order by judge or law court for an arrest

bend *v.* [BENT, BENDING] **1.** to curve, as by pressure **2.** (make) yield **3.** stoop —*n.* **1.** a bending **2.** bent part

be·neath' *adv.*, *a.* below; underneath —*prep.* **1.** below; under **2.** unworthy of

ben'e·dic'tion *n.* blessing, esp. one given at the end of a church service

ben'e·fac'tion *n.* **1.** act of helping **2.** money or help given

ben'e·fac'tor *n.* one who has given money or aid —**ben'e·fac'tress** *n.fem.*

ben'e·fice (-fis) *n.* endowed church position providing a living for a vicar, etc.

be·nef'i·cence *n.* **1.** kindness **2.** kindly act or gift —**be·nef'i·cent** *a.*

ben'e·fi'cial (-fish'əl) *a.* producing benefits

ben'e·fi'ci·ar'y (-fish'ē er'ē) *n.* [*pl.* -IES] one receiving benefits, as from insurance

ben'e·fit *n.* **1.** help or advantage **2.** a show, etc. to raise money for a cause —*v.* **1.** to help **2.** profit

be·nev'o·lence *n.* the wish to do good; kindness; generosity —**be·nev'o·lent** *a.*

be·night'ed *a.* ignorant

be·nign' (-nīn') *a.* **1.** kindly **2.** favorable **3.** not malignant

be·nig'nant *a.* benign

ben'i·son *n.* blessing

ben'ny *n.* [*pl.* -NIES] [Sl.] amphetamine pill

bent *a.* **1.** curved **2.** determined (*on*) —*n.* inclination

bent'grass *n.* low-growing grass that puts out runners, used for lawns

bent'wood *a.* made of pieces of wood permanently bent

be·numb' *v.* make numb

Ben·ze·drine (ben'zə drēn) *trademark for* amphetamine —*n.* [b-] this drug

ben'zene *n.* coal-tar derivative used as a solvent

ben'zine (-zēn) *n.* petroleum derivative used as a motor fuel, in dry cleaning, etc.

ben'zo·ate *n.* chemical used to preserve food

be·queath' (-kwēth', -kwēth') *v.* **1.** leave (property) by a will **2.** hand down

be·quest' *n.* **1.** a bequeathing **2.** anything bequeathed

be·rate' *v.* scold severely

be·reave' *v.* [alt. pt. & pp. -REFT] **1.** deprive **2.** leave forlorn, as by death —**be·reave'ment** *n.* —**be·reft'** *a.*

be·ret' (-rā') *n.* flat, round, soft cap

berg *n.* iceberg

ber'i·ber'i *n.* disease caused by lack of vitamin B₁

berm, berme *n.* ledge along the edge of a paved road

ber'ry *n.* [*pl.* -RIES] small, fleshy fruit with seeds

ber·serk' (bər surk') *a.*, *adv.* in(to) a violent rage

berth *n.* **1.** ship's place of anchorage **2.** built-in bed **3.** position or job

ber'yl (ber'əl) *n.* hard, bright mineral, as the emerald

be·ryl'li·um (-ril'-) n. rare, metallic chemical element used in alloys

be·seech' v. [-SOUGHT or -SEECHED, -SEECHING] ask (for) earnestly; entreat; beg —**beseech'ing·ly** adv.

be·set' v. [-SET, -SETTING] 1. attack from all sides 2. surround

be·set'ting a. always harassing

be·side' prep. 1. at the side of; near 2. as compared with 3. besides 4. aside from —**beside oneself** wild, as with fear

be·sides' adv. 1. in addition 2. else 3. moreover —prep. in addition to

be·siege' v. 1. lay siege to; hem in 2. overwhelm

be·smirch' v. to soil; sully

be·som (bē'zəm) n. broom made of twigs tied to a handle

be·sot'ted a. stupefied, as with liquor

be·speak' v. 1. speak for; reserve 2. indicate

best a. 1. most excellent 2. most suitable —adv. 1. in the best way 2. most —n. 1. best person, thing, etc. 2. the utmost —v. outdo; beat —**all for the best** ultimately good —**at best** under the most favorable conditions —**get** (or **have**) **the best of** defeat or outwit —**had best** should —**make the best of** adjust to

bes'tial (-chəl) a. like a beast; brutal

be·stir' v. stir up; busy

best man main attendant of a bridegroom

be·stow' (-stō') v. present as a gift (on or upon)

be·stride' v. [-STRODE, -STRIDDEN, -STRIDING] sit, mount, or stand astride

bet n. 1. agreement that the one proved wrong will pay something 2. thing so staked —v. [BET or BETTED, BETTING] 1. make a bet 2. stake in a bet

be·ta (bā'tə) n. second letter of the Greek alphabet

be·take' v. take (oneself); go

beta particle electron or positron ejected from an atomic nucleus during radioactive disintegration

beta ray stream of beta particles

be'tel n. pepper plant of Asia: some Asians chew its leaf, along with lime and the nut of a palm (**betel palm**)

be·think' v. think of; remind (oneself)

be·tide' v. happen (to)

be·to'ken v. be a sign of

be·tray' v. 1. be disloyal to 2. deceive 3. seduce 4. reveal —**be·tray'al** n.

be·troth' (-trōth', -trôth') v. promise in marriage —**betroth'al** n.

be·trothed' (-trōthd', -trôtht') a. engaged to be married —n. betrothed person

bet'ter a. 1. more excellent 2. more suitable 3. improved —adv. 1. in a better way 2. more —n. 1. a superior 2. better thing, etc. —v. surpass or improve —**better off** in better circumstances —**get** (or **have**) the better of defeat or outwit —had better should —think better of reconsider

bet'ter·ment (-ij) *n*. improvement

be·tween' *prep*. 1. in the space or time separating 2. involving 3. joining 4. in the common possession of 5. one of —*adv*. in the middle

be·twixt' *prep.*, *adv*. [Ar.] between

bev'el *n*. 1. angled part or surface 2. tool for marking angles —*v*. cut or slope at an angle

bev'er·age (-ij) *n*. drink

bev'y *n*. [*pl*. -IES] 1. group, as of girls 2. flock of quail

be·wail' *v*. wail over

be·ware' *v*. guard against

be·wil'der *v*. confuse —be·wil'der·ment *n*.

be·witch' *v*. enchant

bey (bā) *n*. Turkish title of respect

be·yond' *prep*. 1. farther or later than; past 2. more than —*adv*. farther away —the (great) beyond whatever follows death

bez'el *n*. 1. slanting faces of a cut jewel 2. groove and flange holding a gem or watch crystal in place

bhang (baŋ) *n*. 1. hemp plant 2. its dried leaves and flowers, used as a narcotic

bi- *pref*. two or twice

bi·an'nu·al *a*. twice a year

bi·as (bī'əs) *n*. 1. diagonal or slanting line 2. prejudice —*v*. to prejudice —on the bias diagonally

bib *n*. 1. cloth tied under a child's chin at meals 2. front upper part of overalls

bibb lettuce lettuce with loose, dark-green leaves

Bi'ble *n*. sacred book of Christians or of Jews —Bib'li·cal, bib'li·cal *a*.

bib'li·og'ra·phy *n*. [*pl*. -PHIES] list of writings on one subject or by one author

bib'li·o·phile' (-fil') *n*. one who loves and collects books

bib'u·lous *a*. addicted to or fond of alcoholic liquor

bi·cam'er·al *a*. having two legislative branches

bi·car'bon·ate of soda baking soda

bi·cen·ten'ni·al (-sen-) *n*. 200th anniversary

bi'ceps (-seps) *n*. [*pl*. -CEPS, -CEPSES] large front muscle of the upper arm

bick'er *v.*, *n*. quarrel

bi·cus'pid (-kus'-) *n*. tooth with two-pointed crown

bi'cy·cle (-si k'l) *n*. two-wheeled vehicle —*v*. ride a bicycle —bi'cy·clist *n*.

bid (bid) *v*. [BADE or BID, BIDDEN or BID, BIDDING] 1. command or ask 2. tell 3. [pt. & pp. BID] offer as a price; also, estimate tricks one will take in bridge —*n*. 1. amount bid 2. attempt —bid'der *n*.

bid'dy *n*. [*pl*. -DIES] 1. hen 2. [Sl.] gossipy old woman

bide (bid) *v*. [BODE or BIDED, BIDED, BIDING] [Ar.] 1. stay 2. dwell 3. wait —bide one's time [pt. BIDED] wait patiently for a chance

bi·det′ (-dā′) n. bathroom fixture, for bathing crotch

bi·en′ni·al a. 1. every two years 2. lasting two years —n. plant living two years

bier (bir) n. frame on which a coffin is put

bi·fo′cals n.pl. eyeglasses with lenses having two parts, for close and far focus

big a. [BIGGER, BIGGEST] 1. of great size 2. loud 3. important 4. noble —adv. [Col.] 1. boastfully 2. impressively —big′ness n.

big′a·my (-mē) n. crime of marrying again while still married —big′a·mist n.

big game large wild animals hunted for sport, as lions

big′heart′ed a. generous

big′horn n. horned, wild sheep of Rocky Mountains

bight (bit) n. 1. loop in a rope 2. a bay

big′ot n. narrow-minded, intolerant person —big′ot·ed a. —big′ot·ry n.

big shot [Sl.] important person

bike n. [Col.] 1. bicycle 2. motorcycle

bi·ki′ni (-kē′nē) n. 1. very brief, women's two-piece swimsuit 2. very brief underpants or trunks

bi·lat′er·al a. on, by, or having two sides

bile (bīl) n. 1. bitter liver secretion 2. bad temper

bilge (bilj) n. 1. lower part of a ship's hold 2. stale water that gathers there 3. [Sl.] nonsense

bi·lin′gual a. of, in, or speaking two languages

bil′ious (-yəs) a. 1. having a disorder of the bile or liver 2. bad-tempered

bilk v. to swindle

bill n. 1. statement of charges, as for goods 2. list of things offered 3. poster or handbill 4. proposed law 5. piece of paper money 6. bird's beak —v. 1. present a bill of charges to 2. advertise by bills —bill and coo act in a loving way

bill′board n. signboard

bil′let n. lodging, as for soldiers —v. assign to lodging

bill′fold n. wallet

bil′liards (-yərdz) n. game played with cue and balls on a table with raised edges —bil′liard a.

bil′lion n. thousand millions —bil′lionth a., n.

bil′lion·aire′ (-er′) n. one having at least a billion dollars

bill of fare menu

Bill of Rights first ten amendments to U.S. Constitution

bill of sale paper transferring ownership by sale

bil′low n. 1. large wave 2. swelling mass, as of smoke —v. surge or swell —bil′low·y [-IER, -IEST] a.

bil′ly n. [pl. -LIES] club, esp. a policeman's stick

billy goat [Col.] male goat

bi·month′ly a., adv. 1. once every two months 2. semimonthly

bin n. box or enclosed space for storage

bi′na·ry (bī′-) a. twofold

bin·au′ral (bīn-) a. of stereophonic sound reproduction

bind v. [BOUND, BINDING] 1. tie together 2. hold; restrain 3. encircle with (a belt, etc.) 4. bandage 5. put together (a book) with a cover 6. obligate —**bind'er** n.

bind'er·y n. [pl. -IES] place where books are bound

bind'ing n. 1. anything that binds 2. covers and backing of a book

binge (binj) n. [Sl.] spree

bin'go n. game played on cards with numbered squares

bin'na·cle (-ə k'l) n. case enclosing a ship's compass

bin·oc'u·lars (bī näk'-) n.pl. field glasses

bi'o·chem'is·try n. chemistry of living organisms

bi'o·cide (-sīd) n. poisonous chemical substance

bi'o·de·grad'a·ble a. readily decomposed by bacteria

bi'o·feed'back n. technique of trying to control one's emotions with the help of electronic devices

bi·og'ra·phy n. [pl. -PHIES] one's life story written by another —**bi·og'ra·pher** n. —**bi'o·graph'i·cal** a.

biological warfare use of microorganisms, toxins, etc. to spread disease in war

bi·ol'o·gy n. science of plants and animals —**bi'o·log'i·cal** a. —**bi·ol'o·gist** n.

bi·on'ics (-än'-) n. science of modeling instruments or systems after living organisms

bi'op·sy (-äp'-) n. [pl. -SIES] removal of living body tissue for diagnosis

bi·par'ti·san (-pär'-) a. representing two parties

bi'ped n. two-footed animal

birch n. 1. tree with smooth bark 2. its hard wood

bird n. warmblooded vertebrate with feathers and wings —**for the birds** [Sl.] ridiculous, worthless, etc.

bird'ie n. Golf score of one under par for a hole

bird's'-eye' a. seen from above; general

birth n. 1. a being born 2. descent or origin 3. beginning —**give birth to** to bring into being

birth'day n. day of birth or its anniversary

birth'mark' n. skin blemish present at birth

birth'place' n. place of one's birth or of a thing's origin

birth'rate' n. number of births per year per thousand people in an area, etc.

birth'right' n. rights a person has by birth

bis'cuit (-kit) n. 1. small bread roll 2. [Br.] cracker

bi·sect' v. divide into two equal parts —**bi·sec'tor** n.

bi·sex'u·al adj. sexually attracted by both sexes —n. bisexual person

bish'op n. 1. clergyman heading a diocese 2. chessman moving diagonally

bish'op·ric n. diocese, rank, etc. of a bishop

bis'muth (biz'-) n. metallic chemical element whose salts are used in medicine

bi'son n. [pl. BISON] shaggy, oxlike animal of N. America

bisque (bisk) *n*. thick creamy soup made from shellfish, etc. or strained vegetables

bis'tro *n*. [*pl*. -TROS] [Fr.] small café

bit *n*. 1. mouthpiece on a bridle, for control 2. cutting part of a drill 3. small piece or amount 4. short time —**bit by bit** gradually —**do one's bit** do one's share

bitch *n*. female dog, fox, etc. —*v*. [Sl.] complain

bite *v*. [BIT, BITTEN or BIT, BITING] 1. seize or cut as with the teeth 2. sting, as a bee 3. cause to smart 4. swallow a bait —*n*. 1. a biting 2. biting quality; smart 3. wound from biting 4. mouthful 5. light meal —**bit'er** *n*.

bit'ing *a*. 1. cutting; sharp 2. sarcastic

bit'ter *a*. 1. sharp to the taste 2. sorrowful, painful, resentful, etc. 3. harsh —**bit'ter·ly** *adv*.

bit'tern *n*. heronlike bird

bit'ters *n.pl*. liquor having bitter herbs, etc.

bi·tu'men *n*. natural asphalt or similar substance made from coal, etc.

bi·tu'mi·nous coal soft coal, easy to burn but smoky

bi'valve *n*. mollusk with two shells, as a clam

biv'ouac (-wak) *n*. temporary camp (of soldiers) in the open —*v*. [-OUACKED, -OUACKING] make such a camp

bi·week'ly *a., adv*. 1. once every two weeks 2. semiweekly

bi·zarre (bi zär') *a*. odd; fantastic

blab *v*. [BLABBED, BLABBING] to tattle, gossip, etc.

black *a*. 1. of the color of coal; opposite to white 2. having dark skin 3. without light; dark 4. dirty 5. evil 6. sad —*n*. 1. black color or pigment 2. Negro: *black* is now generally preferred —*v*. blacken —**black out** lose consciousness —**in the black** operating at a profit —**black'ness** *n*.

black'-and-blue' *a*. discolored by a bruise

black'ball *n., v*. vote against

black belt black belt awarded to an expert of the highest skill in judo or karate

black'ber'ry *n*. [*pl*. -RIES] 1. small, edible, dark fruit 2. bramble it grows on

black'bird *n*. bird the male of which is all black

black'board *n*. chalkboard

black'en *v*. 1. make or become black 2. slander

black eye discoloration of skin around the eye, as from a blow

black'guard (blag'ard) *n*. scoundrel; villain

black'head *n*. plug of dirt in a pore of the skin

black'jack *n*. 1. a small bludgeon 2. a card game

black light ultraviolet or infrared radiation

black list list of those to be punished, refused jobs, etc.

black lung (disease) lung disease from continual inhaling of coal dust

black'mail *n*. money extorted on threat of disclosing something disgraceful —*v*. get or try to get blackmail from — **black′mail′er** n.

black market system for selling goods illegally during rationing, etc.

black′out n. 1. concealing of light, facts, etc. 2. a faint

black sheep disgraceful member of a family, etc.

black′smith n. man who forges iron and shoes horses

black′thorn n. thorny shrub with black, plumlike fruit

black′top n. asphalt mixture used to surface roads, etc.

black widow small, poisonous spider

blad′der n. sac that collects urine from the kidneys

blade n. 1. leaf of grass 2. cutting part of a knife, tool, etc. 3. flat surface, as of an oar 4. lively young man

blame v. 1. accuse of being at fault 2. put the responsibility of (on) —n. 1. a blaming 2. responsibility for a fault —**be to blame** deserve blame — **blame′less** a. —**blame′wor′thy** a.

blanch v. 1. bleach 2. make or turn pale 3. scald (vegetables, etc.)

bland a. 1. mild and soothing 2. insipid

blan′dish v. flatter; coax — **blan′dish·ment** n.

blank a. 1. not written on 2. empty 3. utter —n. 1. (printed form with) space to be filled in 2. cartridge without a bullet — v. hold (an opponent) scoreless —**draw a blank** [Col.] be unable to remember something

blan′ket n. 1. large piece of cloth used as bed cover, etc. 2. a covering, as of snow —a. all-inclusive —v. to cover

blare v. sound loudly n. loud, harsh sound

blar′ney (blär′-) n. flattery

bla·sé (blä zā′) a. bored

blas′pheme (-fēm′) v. speak profanely of God; curse

blas′phe·my (-fə mē) n. [pl. -MIES] profane abuse of God — **blas′phe·mous** a.

blast n. 1. strong rush of air 2. loud sound of horn, etc. 3. explosion 4. outburst of criticism —v. 1. explode 2. blight; wither 3. criticize sharply — **blast off** take off, as a rocket

blast furnace furnace for smelting iron ore

blast′off′, blast′-off′ n. launching of a rocket, etc.

bla′tant (blā′-) a. 1. loud; noisy 2. boldly conspicuous or obtrusive —**bla′tan·cy** n.

blaze n. 1. burst of flame 2. bright light 3. vivid display 4. outburst 5. white spot on an animal's face —v. 1. burn or shine brightly 2. mark (a trail)

blaz′er n. light sports jacket in a solid color

bla′zon (-z′n) n. coat of arms —v. proclaim

bleach v. whiten —n. chemical that bleaches

bleach′ers n.pl. roofless stand where spectators sit

bleak a. 1. unsheltered; bare 2. cheerless; gloomy

blear′y a. [-IER, -IEST] dim or blurred, as with tears: also **blear**

bleat n. cry of a sheep or goat —v. make this cry

bleed v. [BLED, BLEEDING] 1. lose blood 2. draw blood from 3. [Col.] extort from

bleep n., v. beep

blem′ish v. mar; injure —n. defect; fault

blend v. 1. mix 2. shade into each other —n. 1. a blending 2. mixture

blend′er n. electrical appliance that can chop, whip, mix, or liquefy foods

bless v. [alt. pt. & pp. BLEST] 1. make holy 2. ask divine favor for 3. endow (with) 4. make happy

bless′ed a. 1. holy; sacred 2. fortunate 3. beatified

bless′ing n. 1. invocation 2. grace said before or after eating 3. approval

blew (blōō) pt. of blow

blight (blīt) n. 1. insect, disease, etc. that destroys plants 2. anything that destroys —v. destroy; ruin

blimp n. small airship like a dirigible

blind a. 1. without sight 2. lacking insight 3. having no outlet 4. not controlled by reason —n. 1. window shade 2. a decoy —v. 1. make sightless 2. dazzle 3. deprive of insight — **blind′ly** adv. —**blind′ness** n.

blind date [Col.] date with a stranger, arranged by a third person

blind′fold v. cover the eyes of —n. cloth used for this

blink v. 1. wink rapidly 2. flash on and off —n. 1. a

blinking 2. glimmer —**blink at** ignore —**on the blink** [Sl.] out of order

blink′er n. flashing light

blip n. luminous image on an oscilloscope

bliss n. great happiness — **bliss′ful** a.

blis′ter n. fluid-filled skin swelling caused by a burn, etc. —v. form blisters

blithe (blīth) a. gay; joyful; also **blithe′some** (-sam)

blitz n. sudden, overwhelming attack —v. subject to a blitz

bliz′zard n. severe snowstorm with high wind

bloat v. swell up

blob n. small drop or mass

bloc n. group united for a common purpose

block n. 1. solid piece 2. auction platform 3. obstruction 4. city square or street section 5. pulley in a frame 6. part taken as a unit —v. 1. obstruct 2. shape —**block in** (or out) sketch roughly

block·ade′ n. shutting off of a place by warships, etc. —v. subject to a blockade

block′bust′ing n. [Col.] frightening owners into selling homes because minority group will become neighbors

block′head n. stupid person

block′house n. 1. formerly, wooden fort 2. house for observing missile launchings

blond a. 1. having light-colored hair and skin 2. light-colored —n. blond person

blonde a. blond —n. blond woman or girl

blood *n.* **1.** red fluid in the arteries and veins **2.** lineage **3.** kinship —**bad blood** hatred —**in cold blood** deliberately —**blood′less** *a.*

blood bank supply of blood stored for transfusions

blood′cur′dling *a.* very frightening; terrifying

blood′hound *n.* large, keen-scented tracking dog

blood′mo·bile′ (mō bēl′) *n.* mobile unit for collecting blood for blood banks

blood′shed *n.* killing

blood′shot *a.* tinged with blood: said of the eyes

blood′thirst′y *a.* murderous

blood vessel artery, vein, or capillary

blood′y *a.* [-IER, -IEST] **1.** of or covered with blood **2.** involving bloodshed **3.** bloodthirsty —*v.* [-IED, -YING] stain with blood

bloom *n.* **1.** a flower **2.** time of flowering **3.** healthy glow —*v.* be in bloom

bloom′ers *n.pl.* women's baggy underpants

bloop′er *n.* [Sl.] stupid mistake

blos′som *n., v.* flower

blot *n.* spot or stain —*v.* [BLOTTED, BLOTTING] **1.** spot, as with ink **2.** erase or cancel (*out*) **3.** dry with soft paper, etc. —**blot′ter** *n.*

blotch *n.* discolored spot —*v.* mark with blotches —**blotch′y** [-IER, -IEST] *a.*

blouse *n.* shirtlike garment for girls

blow *v.* [BLEW, BLOWN, BLOWING] **1.** move, as (by) wind **2.** force air out, as with the mouth **3.** sound by blowing **4.** [Col.] spend (money) freely **5.** [Sl.] to leave **6.** [Sl.] bungle —*n.* **1.** a blowing **2.** gale **3.** a hit **4.** shock —**blow out 1.** extinguish **2.** burst —**blow over** pass over or by —**blow up 1.** explode **2.** [Col.] lose one's temper —**blow′er** *n.*

blow′gun *n.* long tube through which darts, etc. are blown

blow′out *n.* **1.** bursting of a tire **2.** [Sl.] party

blow′torch *n.* small, hot-flamed torch for welding

blow′up *n.* **1.** explosion **2.** enlarged photograph **3.** [Col.] angry outburst

blowz·y (blouz′ē) *a.* [-IER, -IEST] slovenly: also **blows′y**

blub′ber *n.* whale fat —*v.* weep loudly

bludg·eon (bluj′n) *n.* short, heavy club —*v.* to club

blue *a.* **1.** of the color of the clear sky **2.** gloomy **3.** puritanical **4.** [Col.] indecent —*n.* color of the clear sky —**the blues 1.** [Col.] depressed feeling **2.** Negro folk music having, usually, slow tempo, melancholy words, etc.

blue baby baby born with bluish skin, esp. because of a heart defect

blue′bell *n.* plant with blue, bell-shaped flowers

blue′ber′ry *n.* [pl. -RIES] small, edible, bluish berry

blue′bird *n.* small bird with blue back and wings

blue blood aristocrat: also **blue'blood** n.

blue'-col'lar a. designating or of industrial workers

blue'fish n. silvery-blue Atlantic food fish

blue'grass n. type of grass with bluish-green stems

blue jay noisy, crested bird with bluish upper part: also **blue'jay** n.

blue law puritanical law, esp. one prohibiting certain activities on Sunday

blue'-pen'cil v. edit

blue'print n. 1. photographic copy, white on blue, of architectural plans, etc. 2. any detailed plan —v. make a blueprint of

bluff v. mislead by a fake, bold front —a. rough and frank — n. 1. a bluffing 2. one who bluffs 3. steep bank

blu'ing, blue'ing n. blue rinse for white fabrics

blu'ish a. somewhat blue: also **blue'ish**

blun'der n. foolish mistake — v. 1. make a blunder 2. move clumsily

blun'der·buss n. obsolete gun with a broad muzzle

blunt a. 1. dull-edged 2. plainspoken —v. make dull

blur v. [BLURRED, BLURRING] 1. smudge 2. make or become indistinct —n. indistinct thing — **blur'ry** a.

blurb n. [Col.] exaggerated advertisement

blurt v. say impulsively

blush v. redden, as from shame —n. a blushing

blus'ter v. 1. blow stormily 2. speak noisily or boastfully —n. swaggering talk —**blus'ter·y** a.

bo·a (bō'ə) n. 1. large snake that crushes its prey in its coils 2. scarf of feathers

boar n. wild hog

board n. 1. broad, flat piece of wood, etc. 2. meals provided regularly for pay 3. council — v. 1. cover (up) with boards 2. get on (a ship, train, etc.) 3. get board (n. 2) —**on board** on a ship, etc. —**board'er** n.

board'ing·house' n. house where one can pay for meals, or room and meals: also **boarding house**

board'walk n. wooden walk along a beach

boast v. 1. talk with too much pride 2. take pride in —n. thing boasted of —**boast'er** n. —**boast'ful** a.

boat n. water craft, esp. a small one —**in the same boat** in the same situation —**rock the boat** [Col.] disturb the status quo —**boat'man** [pl. -MEN] n.

boat'ing n. rowing, sailing, etc.

boat'swain (bō's'n) n. petty officer directing deck work

bob n. 1. small hanging weight 2. float on a fishing line —v. [BOBBED, BOBBING] 1. move jerkily 2. cut short, as hair — **bob up** appear unexpectedly

bob'bin n. spool for thread

bob'ble n. [Col.] Sports awkward juggling of the ball —v. [Col.] make a bobble with

bob'by pin tight hairpin

bobby socks [Col.] girls' short socks

bob′cat n. wildcat of the eastern U.S.

bob′o·link n. songbird with a call like its name

bob′sled n. racing sled

bob′white′ n. small quail

bock (bäk) n. a dark beer

bode (bōd) v. be an omen of

bode pt. of **bide**

bod·ice (bäd′is) n. snug upper part of a dress

bod′y n. [pl. -IES] 1. whole physical structure 2. trunk of a man or animal 3. main part 4. distinct mass or group 5. [Col.] person —**bod′i·ly** a., adv.

bod′y·guard n. guard to protect a person

body language unconscious bodily movements that communicate something

body stocking one-piece, tight-fitting garment

bod′y·suit′ n. one-piece, tight-fitting garment for torso: also **body shirt**

bog n. small swamp —v. [BOGGED, BOGGING] sink (down) as in a bog —**bog′gy** a.

bo′gey (bō′-) n. [pl. -GEYS] 1. bogy 2. Golf one stroke more than par on a hole: also sp. **bo′gie**

bog′gle v. 1. be startled or hesitate (at) 2. confuse

bo′gus (bō′-) a. not genuine

bo′gy (bō′-) n. [pl. -GIES] imaginary evil spirit; goblin: also sp. **bogie**

Bo·he′mi·an n. one who lives unconventionally

boil v. 1. bubble up into vapor by heating 2. be agitated 3. cook by boiling —n. 1. boiling state 2. pus-filled pimple — **boil down** condense

boil′er n. tank for making steam or storing hot water

bois′ter·ous a. rough, noisy, lively, etc.

bold a. 1. daring; fearless 2. impudent 3. sharp and clear — **bold′ly** adv.

bo·le′ro (-ler′ō) n. [pl. -ROS] 1. Spanish dance 2. short, open vest

boll (bōl) n. pod of cotton or flax

boll weevil beetle that harms cotton bolls

bo·lo′gna (-lō′nē) n. type of smoked sausage

bol′ster (bōl′-) n. long pillow —v. prop (up)

bolt n. 1. flash of lightning 2. sliding bar that locks 3. threaded metal rod used with a nut 4. roll of cloth —v. 1. gulp (food) 2. rush out 3. fasten with a bolt 4. abandon (a party, etc.) 5. sift —**bolt upright** straight upright

bomb (bäm) n. 1. explosive device or missile 2. [Sl.] complete failure —v. 1. attack with bombs 2. [Sl.] have a failure

bom·bard′ v. attack as with artillery or bombs —**bombard′ment** n.

bom′bar·dier′ (-bə dir′) n. one

who releases bombs in a bomber

bom'bast n. pompous speech —**bom·bas'tic** a.

bomb'er n. airplane designed for dropping bombs

bomb'shell n. **1.** bomb **2.** shocking surprise

bo·na fi·de (bō′nə fid or fi′dē) in good faith; sincere

bo·nan'za n. **1.** rich vein of ore **2.** any rich source

bon'bon n. piece of candy

bond n. **1.** thing that binds or unites **2.** binding agreement **3.** interest-bearing certificate **4.** surety against theft, etc. —v. **1.** bind **2.** furnish a bond (n. 4) for

bond'age (-ij) n. slavery —**bond'man** [pl. -MEN] n. —**bond'wom·an** [pl. -WOMEN] n.

bonds'man n. [pl. -MEN] one furnishing bond (n. 4)

bone n. material of the skeleton or piece of this —v. **1.** remove the bones from **2.** [Sl.] study hard (with up) —**make no bones about** admit freely —**bone'less** a.

bone'-dry' a. very dry

bone meal crushed bones used as feed or fertilizer

bon'er (bōn′-) n. [Sl.] a blunder

bon'fire n. outdoor fire

bong n. deep ringing sound —v. make this sound

bon'go n. [pl. -GOS] either of a pair of small drums

bo·ni'to (-nē′tō) n. [pl. -TOS, -TOES] kind of tuna

bon jour (bōn zhōōr′) [Fr.] good day; hello

bon'net n. hat

bon'ny, bon'nie a. [-NIER, -NIEST] handsome or pretty

bon·sai' (-sī′) n. [pl. -SAI] dwarfed tree or shrub

bo'nus n. payment over the usual or required amount

bon voy·age (voi äzh′) pleasant journey

bon·y (bōn′ē) a. [-IER, -IEST] **1.** (full) of bones **2.** lean; thin —**bon'i·ness** n.

boo (bōō) int., n. [pl. BOOS] sound made to show disapproval or to startle —v. shout "boo" at

boo'-boo, boo'boo n. [pl. -BOOS] [Sl.] stupid mistake

boo'by n. [pl. -BIES] a fool

booby trap scheme or device for tricking one unawares

book n. **1.** a bound, printed work **2.** a division of a long literary work **3.** ledger —v. **1.** to list in a book **2.** to reserve, as rooms

book'case n. set of shelves for holding books

book end fixed piece to hold a row of books upright

book'ie n. [Sl.] bookmaker

book'ing n. engagement, as for a performance

book'ish a. **1.** inclined to read or study **2.** pedantic

book'keep·ing n. work of recording business transactions —**book'keep·er** n.

book'let n. small book

book'mak·er n. one who takes bets, esp. on horses

book'mark *n.* slip, etc. for marking a place in a book

book'worm *n.* one who reads or studies much

boom *v.* **1.** make a deep, hollow sound **2.** grow rapidly **3.** promote —*n.* **1.** deep sound **2.** long beam on a derrick **3.** spar at the foot of a sail **4.** period of prosperity

boom'er·ang *n.* **1.** Australian curved stick that returns to the thrower **2.** scheme that backfires

boon (boōn) *n.* benefit

boon'docks, the *n.pl.* [Col.] any remote rural region

boon'dog'gle *v.* [Col.] do trifling, pointless work —*n.* such work —**boon'dog'gler** *n.*

boor (boor) *n.* rude person

boost *v., n.* **1.** push upward; raise **2.** support —**boost'er** *n.*

booster shot later injection of vaccine, to keep immunity

boot *n.* **1.** outer covering for the foot and leg **2.** a kick —*v.* **1.** to kick **2.** [Sl.] dismiss — **the boot** [Sl.] dismissal —**to boot** in addition

boot'ee, boot'ie *n.* baby's knitted or cloth shoe

booth *n.* small stall or enclosure

boot'leg *v.* [-LEGGED, -LEGGING] sell (liquor) illegally —*a.* sold illegally —**boot'leg·ger** *n.*

boot'less *a.* useless

boo'ty *n.* plunder; spoils

booze *n.* [Col.] liquor —*v.* [Col.] drink too much liquor

bo'rax *n.* a white salt used in glass, soaps, etc.

bor'der *n.* **1.** edge; margin **2.** boundary **3.** narrow strip along an edge —*v.* put or be a border on —*a.* near a border — **border on** (or upon) be next to —**bor'der·land** *n.*

bor'der·line *n.* boundary —*a.* **1.** on a boundary **2.** indefinite

bore *v.* **1.** drill a hole (in) **2.** weary by being dull —*n.* **1.** inside or diameter of a tube **2.** dull person or thing —**bore'dom** *n.*

bore pt. of **bear**

bo'ric acid powder used in solution as an antiseptic

born pp. of **bear** (give birth) — *a.* **1.** brought into life **2.** by nature

borne pp. of **bear** (carry)

bo'ron *n.* nonmetallic chemical element

bor·ough (bur'ō) *n.* **1.** self-governing town **2.** division of New York City

bor'row (bär'-) *v.* **1.** take on loan **2.** adopt (an idea) —**bor'row·er** *n.*

borsch (bôrsh) *n.* beet soup, often served with sour cream: also **borsht** (bôrsht)

bor'zoi *n.* large dog with narrow head and long legs

bosh *n., int.* [Col.] nonsense

bos'om (booz'-) *n.* breast —*a.* intimate, as a friend

boss *n.* **1.** employer or supervisor **2.** head politician —*v.* **1.** supervise **2.** [Col.] be domineering —**boss'y** [-IER, -IEST] *a.*

bo'sun *n.* boatswain

bot'a·ny *n.* science of plants —

bo·tan'i·cal a. —**bot'a·nist** n.

botch v. spoil; bungle —n. bungled work

both a., pron. the two —con., adv. equally

both'er (bäth'-) v. 1. annoy; worry 2. trouble (oneself) —n. trouble —**both'er·some** a.

bot'tle n. glass container for liquids —v. 1. put into a bottle 2. stop (up)

bot'tle·neck n. 1. narrow passage 2. any hindrance

bot'tom n. 1. lowest part; base; underside 2. basis or cause; origin 3. [Col.] buttocks —a. lowest; last —**at bottom** actually —**bot'tom·less** a.

bot'u·lism (bäch'ə-) n. poisoning caused by bacteria in foods improperly preserved

bou·doir (bōō'dwär, bōōd'-) n. woman's private room

bouf·fant (bōō fänt') a. [Fr.] puffed out; full

bough (bou) n. tree branch

bought (bôt) pt. & pp. of **buy**

bouil·lon (bōōl'yän) n. clear broth

boul'der (bōl'-) n. large rock

boul'e·vard (bool'-) n. broad, tree-lined street

bounce (bouns) v. 1. spring back on impact 2. make bounce 3. leap 4. [Sl.] be returned, as a bad check —n. a bouncing

bounc'ing a. healthy

bound pt. & pp. of **bind** —a. 1. tied 2. certain (to) 3. obliged 4. with a binding 5. headed (for) 6. [Col.] determined —v. 1. leap or bounce 2. be a limit or boundary to —n. 1. a leap or bounce 2. boundary —**out of bounds** prohibited —**bound'less** a.

bound'a·ry n. [pl. -RIES] anything marking a limit

bound'er n. [Col.] cad

boun'te·ous a. 1. generous 2. abundant

boun'ti·ful a. bounteous

boun'ty n. [pl. -TIES] 1. generosity 2. gift or reward

bou·quet (bō kā', bōō-) n. 1. bunch of flowers 2. aroma

bour'bon (bur'ban) n. whiskey distilled from corn mash

bour·geoi·sie (boor zhwä zē') n. social middle class —**bour·geois'** (-zhwä') a., n.

bout (bout) n. 1. struggle; contest 2. spell or term

bou·tique (bōō tēk') n. small shop selling costly articles

bou·ton·niere, bou·ton·nière (bōō't'n ir') n. flower worn in a buttonhole

bo·vine (bō'vīn) a. cowlike

bow (bou) v. 1. bend down in respect 2. submit 3. weigh (down) —n. 1. bending of the head or body 2. front part of a ship; prow —**take a bow** acknowledge applause

bow (bō) n. 1. curved stick strung with cord for shooting arrows 2. stick strung with horsehairs, for playing a violin, etc. 3. knot with broad loops —a. curved —v. play a violin with a bow

bow'els (bou'-) n.pl. 1. intestines 2. depths

bow'er (bou'-) n. arbor

bow·ie knife (bōō′ē, bō′-) long, single-edged hunting knife

bow′knot (bō′-) *n.* knot usually with two loops and two ends

bowl (bōl) *n.* **1.** hollow, rounded dish or part **2.** amphitheater **3.** ball for the game of bowls —*v.* **1.** roll (a ball) in bowling **2.** move fast —**bowl over** knock over —**bowl′er** *n.*

bow′leg′ged (bō′-) *a.* with the legs curved out

bowl′ing *n.* game in which a ball is rolled along a wooden lane (**bowling alley**) at ten pins

bowls *n.* bowling game played on a smooth lawn (**bowling green**)

bow′man (bō′-) *n.* [*pl.* -MEN] archer

bow′sprit (bou′-, bō′-) *n.* tapered spar at bow of a ship

bow tie (bō) necktie tied in a bow

box *n.* **1.** container made of wood, cardboard, etc. **2.** enclosed group of seats **3.** blow with the hand **4.** evergreen shrub: also **boxwood 5.** *Baseball* area for the batter, pitcher, etc. —*v.* **1.** put (*in*) or shut (*up*) as in a box **2.** fight with the fists —**in a box** [Col.] in difficulty —**box′like** *a.*

box′car *n.* enclosed railroad freight car

box′er *n.* **1.** one who boxes; prizefighter **2.** medium-sized dog with a smooth coat

box′ing *n.* sport of fighting with fists, esp. in padded mittens (**boxing gloves**)

box office place in a theater to buy tickets

boy *n.* male child —**boy′hood** *n.* —**boy′ish** *a.*

boy′cott *v.* refuse to deal with —*n.* a boycotting

boy′friend *n.* [Col.] **1.** sweetheart of a girl or woman **2.** boy who is one's friend

boy scout member of the **Boy Scouts,** boys′ club stressing outdoor life

boy′sen·ber′ry *n.* [*pl.* -RIES] berry that is a cross of the raspberry, loganberry, and blackberry

bra (brä) *n.* woman's undergarment for supporting the breasts

brace *v.* **1.** strengthen with supports **2.** prepare for a shock **3.** stimulate —*n.* **1.** pair **2.** clamp **3.** supporting device **4.** *pl.* device worn for straightening the teeth **5.** rotating handle of a drilling tool (**brace and bit**) **6.** either of the signs {}, for connecting lines, etc.

brace′let *n.* decorative band for the arm

brack′en *n.* large, weedy fern of woods and meadows

brack′et *n.* **1.** projecting support **2.** either of the signs [ ], for enclosing words **3.** classification —*v.* **1.** support with brackets **2.** enclose in brackets **3.** classify together

brack′ish *a.* salty or rank

bract *n.* leaf at the base of a flower or on its stalk

brad *n.* thin wire nail

brae (brā) *n.* [Scot.] hillside

brag *n., v.* [BRAGGED, BRAG-GING] boast

brag'gart *n.* boaster

braid *v.* 1. interweave strands of 2. trim with braid —*n.* braided strip

Braille, braille (brāl) *n.* system of printing for the blind, using raised dots

brain *n.* 1. mass of nerve tissue in the head 2. *pl.* intelligence —*v.* smash the brains of —**brain'y** [-IER, -IEST] *a.*

brain'less *a.* foolish or stupid

brain'storm *n.* [Col.] sudden idea

brain'wash *v.* [Col.] indoctrinate thoroughly

brain wave 1. rhythmic electric impulses in the brain 2. [Col.] brainstorm

braise (brāz) *v.* brown (meat), then simmer it

brake *n.* 1. thicket 2. device to stop or slow a machine, etc. —*v.* stop or slow as with a brake

brake'man *n.* [*pl.* -MEN] train conductor's assistant

bram'ble *n.* prickly shrub

bran *n.* husks separated from grains of wheat, etc.

branch *n.* 1. limb of a tree 2. offshoot or division 3. tributary stream 4. local unit of an organization —*v.* put forth branches —**branch off** diverge —**branch out** broaden one's interests —**branched** *a.*

brand *n.* 1. burning stick 2. owner's mark burned on cattle 3. iron used to brand 4. stigma 5. trademark 6. make or kind —*v.* mark with a brand

bran'dish *v.* wave about

brand'-new' *a.* fully new

bran'dy *n.* [*pl.* -DIES] liquor distilled from wine or fruit juice

brash *a.* rash or insolent

brass *n.* 1. alloy of copper and zinc 2. *pl.* brass winds 3. [Col.] rude boldness 4. [Sl.] military officers —**brass'y** [-IER, -IEST] *a.*

bras·siere, bras·sière (brə zir') *n.* bra

brass tacks [Col.] basic facts

brass winds coiled musical instruments made of metal, as the trumpet, tuba, etc. —**brass'-wind'** *a.*

brat *n.* unruly child

brat'wurst *n.* spicy sausage

braun'schwei'ger (broun'-shwī'-) *n.* smoked liver sausage

brave *a.* full of courage —*n.* American Indian warrior —*v.* 1. defy 2. meet with courage —**brav'er·y** *n.*

bra'vo (brä'-) *int., n.* [*pl.* -VOS] shout of approval

brawl *v.* quarrel or fight noisily —*n.* noisy fight

brawn *n.* muscular strength —**brawn'y** [-IER, -IEST] *a.*

bray *n.* sound a donkey makes —*v.* make this sound

bra'zen *a.* 1. of or like brass 2. shameless —**brazen out** act unashamed of

bra·zier (brā'zhər) *n.* 1. pan for holding burning coals 2. person who works in brass

Bra·zil′ nut edible, three-sided, tropical nut

breach n. 1. break in something; gap 2. violation of a promise, etc. —v. make a breach in

bread n. 1. baked food of flour dough 2. livelihood 3. [Sl.] money —v. cover with bread crumbs

breadth n. width or scope

bread′win′ner n. one who supports dependents by earning money

break v. [BROKE, BROKEN, BREAKING] 1. split apart; smash 2. make or become unusable 3. tame by force 4. get rid of (a habit) 5. make poor, ill, etc. 6. surpass (a record) 7. not keep or obey (a law, promise, etc.) 8. interrupt 9. stop 10. make or become known — n. 1. a breaking 2. broken place 3. interruption 4. beginning (of day) 5. sudden change 6. [Sl.] a chance —**break down** 1. have a breakdown 2. analyze —**break in** 1. enter forcibly 2. interrupt 3. train 4. make less stiff —**break off** stop abruptly —**break out** 1. develop pimples 2. to flee —**break up** 1. to separate 2. to stop 3. [Col.] make laugh —**break′a·ble** a.

break′age (-ij) n. 1. a breaking 2. loss due to breaking

break′down n. 1. mechanical failure 2. physical or mental collapse 3. analysis

break′er n. breaking wave

break·fast (brek′fast) n. first meal of the day —v. eat breakfast

break′-in′ n. forcible entering of a building, to rob it

break′neck a. very dangerous

break′through n. 1. act of forcing a way through, as in war 2. important discovery

break′up n. a going apart

break′wa′ter n. barrier to break the impact of waves

breast (brest) n. 1. milk-secreting gland on a woman's body 2. upper front of the body 3. the emotions —v. face bravely —**make a clean breast of**, confess

breast′bone n. sternum

breast stroke swimming stroke in which arms are extended sideways from the chest

breast′work n. low barrier to protect gunners

breath (breth) n. 1. air taken into and let out of the lungs 2. easy breathing 3. life 4. slight breeze —**catch one's breath** 1. to pant 2. to pause or rest —**out of breath** breathless —**under one's breath** in a whisper

breathe (brēth) v. 1. inhale and exhale 2. live 3. whisper 4. rest

breath′er (brēth′-) n. 1. one who breathes 2. [Col.] pause for rest

breath′less a. panting

breath′tak′ing a. exciting

breech n. 1. back part 2. gun part behind the barrel

breech′es (brich′-) n.pl. 1. trousers reaching to the knees 2. [Col.] trousers

breed v. [BRED, BREEDING] 1. bring forth (offspring) 2.

produce 3. raise (animals) —n.
1. race; stock 2. type —
breed'er n.

breed'ing n. 1. producing of
young 2. good upbringing 3.
producing of plants and animals

breeze n. gentle wind —v. [Sl.]
move briskly —**breez'y** [-IER,
-IEST] a.

breeze'way n. covered passageway, as from house to garage

breth'ren n.pl. [Ar.] brothers

bre'vi·ar·y (brē'-) n. [pl. -IES]
R.C.Ch. book of daily prayer

brev'i·ty n. briefness

brew v. 1. make (beer, etc.) 2.
steep (tea, etc.) 3. plot 4. form
—n. beverage brewed —
brew'er n.

brew'er·y n. [pl. -IES] place
where beer is brewed

bri'ar n. brier

bribe n. thing given or promised as an inducement, esp. to
wrongdoing —v. offer or give a
bribe to —**brib'er·y** n.

bric-a-brac (brik'ə brak') n.
figurines, curios, etc.

brick n. 1. building block of
baked clay 2. any oblong piece
—a. built of brick —v. cover
with bricks

brick'lay'ing n. work of building with bricks —**brick'lay'er**
n.

brid'al n. wedding —a. 1. of a
bride 2. of a wedding

bride n. woman just married or
about to be married

bride'groom n. man just married or about to be married

brides'maid n. any of the
bride's wedding attendants

bridge n. 1. structure for crossing a river, etc. 2. thing like a
bridge in shape, etc. 3. mounting for false teeth 4. card
game for two pairs of players
—v. build or be a bridge over

bridge'work n. dental bridge
or bridges

bri'dle (brī'-) n. 1. head harness for a horse 2. thing that
restrains —v. 1. put a bridle
on 2. curb 3. draw one's head
back to show anger, scorn, etc.

bridle path path for horseback
riding

brief a. short; concise —n. 1.
summary, as of a law case 2.
pl. legless underpants —v.
summarize the facts for —
brief'ing n. —**brief'ly** adv.

brief'case n. flat, flexible case
for carrying papers, books, etc.

bri'er (brī'-) n. 1. thorny bush
2. heath root for making
tobacco pipes

brig n. 1. two-masted ship with
square sails 2. ship's prison

bri·gade' n. 1. military unit of
several battalions 2. group organized for a task

brig·a·dier' general (-dir') officer just above a colonel

brig'and n. roving bandit

bright a. 1. shining; full of
light 2. vivid 3. cheerful 4.
mentally quick —**bright'en** v.
—**bright'ly** adv. —**bright'ness** n.

bril'liant a. 1. shining brightly
2. splendid 3. keenly intelligent —**bril'liance** n. —**bril'liant·ly** adv.

brim *n.* 1. top edge of a cup, etc. 2. projecting rim of a hat —*v.* [BRIMMED, BRIMMING] fill or be full to the brim —**brim′ful** *a.*

brim′stone *n.* sulfur

brin′dled, brin′dle *a.* having dark streaks, as a cow

brine (brīn) *n.* 1. water full of salt 2. ocean —**brin′y** [-IER, -IEST] *a.*

bring *v.* [BROUGHT, BRINGING] cause to come or happen; fetch, get, lead to, etc. —**bring about** to cause —**bring forth** give birth to; produce **bring off** accomplish —**bring out** 1. reveal 2. offer, as a book, to the public —**bring to** revive —**bring up** 1. rear (children) 2. mention

brink *n.* edge, as of a cliff

bri·quette′, bri·quet′ (-ket′) *n.* brick of compressed coal dust, sawdust, etc.

brisk *a.* 1. quick; energetic 2. invigorating

bris′ket *n.* breast meat

bris′ling *n.* sprat canned as a sardine

bris·tle (bris′'l) *n.* short, stiff hair —*v.* 1. stiffen like bristles 2. stiffen with anger —**bris′tly** *a.*

britch′es *n.pl.* [Col.] any trousers; breeches

Brit′ish *a.* of Great Britain or its people

British thermal unit unit of heat equal to about 252 calories

brit′tle *a.* hard but easily broken —**brit′tle·ness** *n.*

broach (brōch) *n.* tapered bit for reaming out holes —*v.* 1. make a hole in 2. start a discussion of

broad *a.* 1. wide 2. obvious 3. tolerant 4. extensive; general —**broad′ly** *adv.*

broad′cast *v.* [-CAST or -CASTED, -CASTING] 1. spread widely 2. send by radio or TV —*n.* radio or TV program —*adv.* far and wide —**broad′cast′er** *n.*

broad′cloth *n.* a fine cloth

broad′en *v.* widen

broad jump long jump

broad′loom *a.* woven on a wide loom, as a carpet

broad′-mind′ed *a.* liberal

broad′side *n.* 1. firing of all guns on a ship's side 2. large sheet with advertising —*adv.* with the side facing

bro·cade′ *n.* cloth of a richly patterned weave —*v.* weave a raised design in

broc·co·li (bräk′ə lē) *n.* kind of cauliflower with loose heads of tiny green buds

bro·chette′ (brō shet′) *n.* a skewer for broiling chunks of meat

bro·chure′ (-shoor′) *n.* pamphlet

bro′gan *n.* heavy work shoe, fitting high on the ankle

brogue (brōg) *n.* 1. Irish accent 2. heavy oxford shoe

broil *v.* cook by direct heat

broil′er *n.* 1. pan or stove section for broiling 2. chicken fit for broiling

broke *pt.* of **break** —*a.* [Col.] without money

bro′ken *pp.* of **break** —*a.* 1.

fractured 2. not in working order 3. violated, as a vow 4. interrupted 5. imperfectly spoken

bro'ken-down' *a.* 1. sick or worn out 2. out of order

bro'ken-heart'ed *a.* crushed by grief

bro'ker *n.* agent hired to buy and sell

bro'ker·age (-ij) *n.* 1. broker's business 2. broker's fee

bro'mide (-mīd) *n.* 1. sedative 2. trite saying

bro'mine (-mēn) *n.* fuming liquid, a chemical element

bron'chi (-kī) *n.pl.* the two main branches of the windpipe —**bron'chi·al** (-kē-) *a.*

bron·chi'tis (-kī'-) *n.* inflammation of the bronchial tubes

bron'co *n.* [*pl.* -COS] small, wild horse of the West

bronze *n.* 1. alloy of copper and tin 2. reddish brown —*v.* make bronze in color

brooch (brōch) *n.* large ornamental pin with a clasp

brood (brood) *n.* 1. birds hatched at one time 2. offspring —*v.* 1. sit on and hatch eggs 2. dwell on moodily

brook (brook) *n.* small stream —*v.* endure or tolerate

brook trout mottled stream trout of NE N. America

broom (broom) *n.* 1. long-handled brush for sweeping 2. kind of shrub

broom'stick *n.* broom handle

broth (brôth) *n.* clear soup

broth'el *n.* house of prostitution

broth'er *n.* 1. male related to one by having the same parents 2. fellow member —**broth'er·hood** *n.* —**broth'er·ly** *a.*

broth'er-in-law' *n.* [*pl.* BROTHERS-IN-LAW] 1. brother of one's spouse 2. sister's husband

brought pt. & pp. of **bring**

brow (brou) *n.* 1. eyebrow 2. forehead 3. edge of a cliff

brow'beat *v.* [-BEAT, -BEATEN, -BEATING] to bully

brown *a.* 1. chocolate-colored 2. tanned; dark-skinned —*n.* brown color —*v.* make or become brown

brown'-bag', brown'bag' *v.* [-BAGGED, -BAGGING] carry one's lunch to work or school, as in a brown paper bag

brown'ie (-ē) *n.* 1. small, helpful elf 2. small bar cut from a flat chocolate cake

brown rice unpolished rice

brown'stone *n.* reddish-brown sandstone, used for building

brown sugar sugar with crystals coated with brown syrup

browse *v.* 1. feed on grass, etc. 2. glance through books —**brows'er** *n.*

bru'in (broo'-) *n.* a bear

bruise (brooz) *v.* injure and discolor (the skin) without breaking it —*n.* discolored injury of the skin

bruis'er *n.* pugnacious man

bruit (broot) *v.* spread (*about*) by rumor

bru·net' *a.* having dark hair and complexion —*n.* brunet person

bru·nette (-net′) *a.* brunet —
n. brunette woman or girl

brunt *n.* main impact

brush *n.* 1. device with bristles,
wires, etc. for cleaning, painting, etc. 2 a brushing 3. skir-
mish 4. underbrush 5. sparsely
settled land —*v.* 1. use a
brush on 2. touch lightly 3.
remove as with a brush —
brush off dismiss —**brush up**
refresh one's memory

brush′off *n.* [Sl.] curt dismissal

brusque (brusk) *a.* abrupt in
manner —**brusque′ly** *adv.*

Brus′sels sprouts (brus′-) 1.
plant bearing small cabbagelike heads 2. its edible heads

bru′tal *a.* savage, cruel, etc. —
bru·tal′i·ty [*pl.* -TIES] *n.* —
bru′tal·ly *adv.*

bru′tal·ize *v.* 1. make brutal
2. treat brutally

brute *a.* of or like an animal;
cruel, stupid, etc. —*n.* 1. animal 2. brutal person —**brut′-
ish** *a.*

bub′ble *n.* 1. globule of air or
gas in a liquid 2. transparent
dome —*v.* 1. rise in bubbles 2.
gurgle —**bub′bly** *a.*

bubble gum chewing gum for
blowing into large bubbles

bub′bler *n.* drinking fountain
that spurts water up from a
nozzle

bub′ble-top *n.* bulletproof,
transparent dome, as over a
car

bu·bon·ic plague (byōō
bän′ik) deadly contagious disease

buc·ca·neer′ (buk-) *n.* pirate

buck *n.* 1. male deer, goat, etc.
2. a bucking 3. [Sl.] dollar —*v.*
1. rear up, as to throw off (a
rider) 2. [Col.] resist —**buck
up** [Col.] cheer up —**pass the
buck** [Col.] shift the blame

buck′et *n.* container with a
handle, for water, etc.; pail —
buck′et·ful [*pl.* -FULS] *n.*

bucket seat single contoured
seat, as in sports cars

buck′eye *n.* 1. horse chestnut
with shiny, brown seeds 2. the
seed

buck′le *n.* clasp for fastening a
belt, etc. —*v.* 1. fasten with a
buckle 2. bend or crumple —
buckle down apply oneself

buck′ler *n.* round shield

buck′-pass′er *n.* [Col.] one
who puts the blame on someone else —**buck′-pass′ing** *n.*

buck′ram *n.* stiff cloth

buck′shot *n.* large lead shot
for a gun

buck′skin *n.* leather from
skins of deer or sheep

buck′tooth *n.* [*pl.* -TEETH]
projecting front tooth —**buck′-
toothed** *a.*

buck′wheat *n.* 1. plant with
seeds ground into dark flour 2.
this flour

bu·col·ic (byōō käl′-) *a.* rustic

bud *n.* small swelling on a
plant, start of a leaf, shoot, or
flower —*v.* [BUDDED, BUDDING]
1. put forth buds 2. begin to
develop

Bud·dhism (bood′iz'm) *n.* a
religion of Asia —**Bud′dhist**
n., a.

bud′dy *n.* [*pl.* -DIES] [Col.]
comrade

budge *v.* move slightly

budg'er·i·gar' (-gär') *n.* Australian parakeet: also [Col.] **budg'ie**

budg'et *n.* 1. plan adjusting expenses to income 2. estimated cost of operating, etc. —*v.* 1. put on a budget 2. schedule —**budg'et·ar'y** *a.*

buff *n.* 1. a brownish yellow 2. [Col.] devotee; fan —*v.* polish, as with soft leather —**in the buff** naked —**buff'er** *n.*

buf'fa·lo *n.* [*pl.* -LOES, -LOS] 1. wild ox 2. American bison —*v.* [Sl.] to bluff

buff'er *n.* anything that lessens shock

buf'fet *n., v.* blow; slap

buf·fet' (-fā') *n.* 1. cabinet for dishes, silver, etc. 2. food which guests serve themselves as from a buffet

buf·foon' *n.* a clown —**buffoon'er·y** *n.*

bug *n.* 1. crawling insect, esp. when a pest 2. [Col.] germ or virus 3. [Sl.] defect 4. [Sl.] hidden microphone —*v.* [BUGGED, BUGGING] [Sl.] 1. annoy or anger 2. hide a microphone in (a room)

bug'bear *n.* imaginary terror: also **bug'a·boo** [*pl.* -BOOS]

bug'gy *n.* [*pl.* -GIES] 1. light, one-horse carriage 2. carriage for a baby

bu'gle *n.* small, valveless trumpet —**bu'gler** *n.*

build *v.* [BUILT, BUILDING] 1. make by putting together parts 2. create, develop, etc. — *n.* form or structure —**build up** make more attractive — **build'er** *n.*

build'ing *n.* a structure

build'up, build'-up *n.* [Col.] 1. praise or favorable publicity 2. gradual increase

built'-in' *a.* 1. made as part of the structure 2. inherent

built'-up' *a.* 1. made higher or stronger with added parts 2. with many buildings on it

bulb *n.* 1. underground bud, as the onion 2. tuber, as of a crocus 3. bulblike thing, as in an electric lamp —**bul'bous** *a.*

bulge *n.* outward swelling —*v.* swell out —**bulg'y** *a.*

bulk *n.* 1. size or mass, esp. if great 2. main part —*v.* have, or gain in, size or importance —*a.* not packaged —**bulk'y** [-IER, -IEST] *a.*

bulk'head *n.* vertical partition, as in a ship

bull *n.* 1. male bovine animal, or male seal, elephant, etc. 2. edict of the Pope —*a.* male

bull'dog *n.* heavily built dog with a stubborn grip

bull'doze *v.* 1. [Col.] to bully 2. move or level with a bulldozer

bull'doz'er *n.* tractor with a large shovellike blade in front for pushing earth, etc.

bul'let *n.* shaped metal piece to be shot from a gun

bul'le·tin *n.* 1. brief news item 2. regular publication of a group

bulletin board board for posting bulletins or notices

bul'let-proof' *a.* that bullets cannot pierce

bull'fight *n.* spectacle in which a bull is goaded to fury, then killed —**bull'fight'er** n. — **bull'fight'ing** n.

bull'finch n. small European songbird

bull'frog n. large frog

bull'head'ed a. stubborn

bull'horn n. portable electronic voice amplifier

bul·lion (bool'yən) n. gold or silver ingots

bull'ish a. 1. like a bull 2. causing a rise in stock exchange prices

bull'ock n. castrated bull

bull's'-eye' n. target center

bul'ly n. [pl. -LIES] one who hurts or threatens weaker people —v. [-LIED, -LYING] act the bully (toward)

bul'rush n. tall grasslike plant, in marshes, etc.

bul'wark n. rampart; defense

bum n. [Col.] vagrant —v. [BUMMED, BUMMING] [Col.] 1. beg 2. loaf —a. [Sl.] 1. poor in quality 2. false 3. lame

bum'ble-bee n. large bee

bum'mer n. [Sl.] unpleasant experience, esp. with drugs

bump v. collide (with) —n. 1. light collision 2. swelling — **bump into** [Col.] meet unexpectedly —**bump off** [Sl.] to murder —**bump'y** [-IER, -IEST] a.

bump'er n. device, as on a car, for easing collisions —a. unusually abundant

bumper sticker slogan, etc. on a sticker for a bumper

bump'kin n. awkward or simple country person

bun n. small bread roll

bunch n. 1. cluster of similar things 2. [Col.] group of people —v. gather; group

bun'dle n. 1. number of things bound together 2. package —v. 1. make into a bundle 2. hustle (off)

bun'ga·low n. small house

bun'gler n.

bun'gle v. do clumsily; spoil — **bun'gler** n.

bun'ion n. swelling at the base of the big toe

bunk n. 1. built-in bed 2. [Col.] any narrow bed 3. [Sl.] empty talk —v. sleep in a bunk

bunk'er n. 1. large bin 2. mound that is an obstacle on a golf course 3. underground fortification

bunk'house n. barracks for ranch hands, etc.

bun'ny n. [pl. -NIES] rabbit: child's word

bunt v. Baseball to bat (a pitch) so it does not go beyond the infield —n. a bunted ball

bun'ting n. 1. thin cloth for flags, etc. 2. baby's hooded blanket 3. small finch

buoy (boo'ē, boi) n. floating marker —v. 1. keep afloat 2. lift up in spirits

buoy'an·cy n. 1. ability to float 2. cheerfulness —**buoy'ant** a.

bur n. prickly seedcase

bur'den n. 1. load carried 2. thing hard to bear —v. weigh down —**bur'den·some** a.

bur'dock n. plant with prickly burs

bu·reau (byoo'rō) n. [pl. -REAUS, -REAUX (-rōz)] 1. chest of drawers **2.** government department **3.** office

bu·reauc′ra·cy (-räk′-) *n.* [*pl.* -CIES] **1.** government by officials following rigid rules **2.** such officials —**bu′reau·crat** *n.* —**bu′reau·crat′ic** *a.*

burg *n.* [Col.] city or town

bur′geon (-jən) *v.* sprout

-burger *suf.* **1.** sandwich of ground meat, etc. **2.** hamburger and

bur′glar *n.* one who breaks into a building to steal —**bur′gla·ry** [*pl.* -RIES] *n.*

bur′glar·ize *v.* [Col.] commit burglary in

bur′gle *v.* [Col.] burglarize

bur′i·al (ber′-) *n.* burying of a dead body

burl *n.* **1.** knot on some tree trunks **2.** veneer from wood with burls —**burled** *a.*

bur′lap *n.* coarse cloth of hemp, etc., used for bags

bur·lesque′ (-lesk′) *n.* **1.** broadly comic satire **2.** type of vaudeville —*v.* imitate comically

bur′ly *a.* [-LIER, -LIEST] big and strong

burn *v.* [alt. pt. & pp. BURNT] **1.** be or set on fire **2.** destroy or be destroyed by fire **3.** hurt or be hurt by acid, friction, etc. **4.** feel or make feel hot **5.** be excited —*n.* injury from fire, acid, etc.

burn′er *n.* part of a stove, etc. producing the flame

bur′nish *v., n.* polish

bur·noose′ *n.* hooded cloak worn by Arabs

burn′out *n.* point when fuel

burns up and missile enters free flight

burp *v., n.* [Sl.] belch

burr *n.* **1.** rough ridge left on metal **2.** trilling of *r* **3.** bur

bur′ro *n.* [*pl.* -ROS] donkey

bur′row *n.* hole dug by an animal —*v.* make a burrow

bur′sa *n.* [*pl.* -SAE (-sē), -SAS] body sac with fluid, as between tendon and bone

bur′sar *n.* college treasurer

bur·si′tis *n.* inflammation of a bursa

burst *v.* [BURST, BURSTING] **1.** come apart suddenly; explode **2.** appear, enter, etc. suddenly **3.** be too full —*n.* a bursting

bur·y (ber′ē) *v.* [-IED, -YING] **1.** put in a grave, tomb, etc. **2.** cover; hide

bus *n.* [*pl.* BUSES, BUSSES] large motor coach, usually on a regular route —*v.* [BUSED or BUSSED, BUSING or BUSSING] **1.** transport or go by bus **2.** work as a busboy

bus′boy *n.* waiter's assistant

bus·by (buz′bē) *n.* [*pl.* -BIES] tall fur hat, part of some full-dress uniforms

bush *n.* **1.** low, woody plant **2.** uncleared land —**bush′y** [-IER, -IEST] *a.*

bush′el *n.* a dry measure equal to 4 pecks

bush′ing *n.* removable metal lining to reduce friction

busi·ness (biz′nis) *n.* **1.** commerce **2.** commercial or industrial establishment **3.** occupation **4.** rightful concern **5.** matter; affair —**busi′ness-man** [*pl.* -MEN] *n.*

busi'ness·like a. efficient

bus'ing, bus'sing n. a taking children by bus to a school so as to achieve racial balance

bust n. 1. sculpture of head and shoulders 2. woman's bosom —v. [Sl.] 1. to break 2. to bankrupt or demote 3. to hit 4. to arrest

bus·tle (bus''l) v. hurry busily —n. 1. a bustling 2. skirt padding in back

bus'y a. [-IER, -IEST] 1. active; at work 2. full of activity 3. in use, as a telephone —v. [-IED, -YING] make busy —**bus'i·ly** adv.

bus'y·bod'y n. [pl. -IES] meddler

but prep. except —con. 1. yet 2. on the contrary 3. unless — adv. 1. only 2. merely —all but almost —**but for** if it were not for

bu'tane (byōō'-) n. hydrocarbon used as a fuel

butch a. [Sl.] 1. designating a man's closely cropped haircut 2. masculine

butch'er n. 1. one who kills and dresses animals for meat 2. one who sells meat 3. killer —v. 1. slaughter 2. botch —**butch'er·y** n.

but'ler n. head male servant

butt n. 1. thick end 2. stub or stump, as of a cigar 3. object of ridicule 4. large cask —v. 1. join end to end 2. ram with the head —**butt in(to)** [Sl.] meddle (in)

butte (byōōt) n. small mesa

but'ter n. yellow fat churned from cream —v. 1. spread with

butter 2. [Col.] flatter (with up) —**but'ter·y** a.

butter bean 1. lima bean 2. wax bean

but'ter·cup n. yellow, cup-shaped flower

but'ter·fat n. fatty part of milk

but'ter·fly n. [pl. -FLIES] insect with four broad wings

but'ter·milk n. sour milk left after churning butter

but'ter·nut n. white walnut tree or its edible nut

but'ter·scotch n. 1. hard candy made with butter 2. syrup with the flavor of this

but'tocks n.pl. fleshy, rounded parts of the hips

but'ton n. 1. small disk for fastening a garment, etc. 2. buttonlike part —v. fasten with buttons

but'ton·hole n. slit for a button —v. detain in talk

but'tress n. 1. outer structure supporting a wall 2. a prop — v. prop up

bux·om (buk'səm) a. comely, plump, etc.: said of women

buy v. [BOUGHT, BUYING] 1. get by paying money, etc. 2. to bribe 3. [Sl.] accept as true — n. [Col.] something worth its price —**buy up** buy all one can get of —**buy'er** n.

buzz v. hum like a bee —n. buzzing sound

buz'zard n. 1. kind of large hawk 2. kind of vulture

buzz'er n. electrical device signaling with a buzz

buzz saw circular saw rotated by machinery

by *prep.* 1. near; beside 2. during 3. not later than 4. through 5. past 6. for 7. according to 8. using as multiplier or divisor —*adv.* 1. near 2. past 3. away; aside —**by and by** after a while —**by and large** in most respects —**by the by** incidentally

by'-and-by' *n.* a future time

bye'-bye' *n., int.* goodbye

by'gone *a.* past —*n.* anything past

by'law *n.* local law or rule

by'line *n.* writer's name heading a newspaper article

by'pass *n.* 1. road, pipe, etc. that gets around the main way 2. surgery or passage to route blood around diseased part —*v.* 1. to detour around 2. ignore

by'path *n.* side path

by'prod'uct *n.* anything produced in the course of making another thing

by'stand'er *n.* one standing near but not taking part

by'way *n.* side road

by'word *n.* 1. proverb 2. thing proverbially bad

C

cab *n.* 1. taxicab 2. place in a truck, etc. where the operator sits

ca·bal (kə bal') *n.* 1. group of conspirators 2. plot

ca·bal·le·ro (ka'bə le'rō) *n.* [*pl.* -ROS] [Southwest] 1. horseman 2. lady's escort

ca·ba'na (-bä'-) *n.* 1. cabin 2. small bathhouse

cab·a·ret' (-rā') *n.* café with entertainment

cab'bage *n.* vegetable with round head of thick leaves

cab'by, cab'bie *n.* [*pl.* -BIES] [Col.] one who drives a taxi

cab'in *n.* 1. hut 2. a room on a ship, etc. 3. space for passengers, crew, or cargo in an aircraft

cab'i·net *n.* 1. case with drawers or shelves 2. [C-] body of official advisers

cab'i·net-mak'er *n.* maker of fine furniture —**cab'i·net·work'** *n.*

ca'ble *n.* 1. thick rope, often of wire 2. cablegram —*v.* send a cablegram (to)

cable car car drawn up an incline by a moving cable

ca'ble·gram *n.* telegram sent by undersea cable

ca·bo·chon (ka'bə shän) *n.* precious stone cut in convex shape

ca·boo'dle *n.* [Col.] lot; group

ca·boose' (-bōōs') *n.* crew's car on a freight train

ca·ca·o (**bean**) (kə kā'ō) seed of a tropical American tree: source of chocolate and cocoa

cache (kash) *n.* 1. place for hiding food, supplies, etc. 2. anything so hidden —*v.* place in a cache

cache·pot (kash'pät, -pō) *n.* jar to hold a potted plant

ca·chet' (-shā') *n.* 1. sign of

cack′le v., n. (make) the shrill sound of a hen

ca·coph′o·ny (-käf′-) n. harsh, jarring sound —**ca·coph′o·nous** a.

cac′tus n. [pl. -TUSES, -TI (-tī)] spiny desert plant

cad n. ungentlemanly man —**cad′dish** a.

ca·dav′er (kə dav′-) n. corpse —**ca·dav′er·ous** a.

cad′die, cad′dy [pl. -DIES] n. attendant to a golfer —v. [DIED, -DYING] be a caddie

cad′dy n. [pl. -DIES] small container, as for tea

ca′dence (kā′-) n. 1. fall of the voice in speaking 2. rhythm; measured movement

ca·den′za n. elaborate passage for solo instrument in a concerto

ca·det′ (kə-) n. student at a military school or armed forces academy

cadge v. [Col.] beg —**cadg′er** n.

ca·dre (kad′rē) n. nucleus for a larger organization

ca·fe, ca·fé (ka fā′) n. 1. restaurant 2. barroom, nightclub, etc.

caf′e·te′ri·a (-tir′ē ə) n. self-service restaurant

caf·feine, caf·fein (kaf′ēn) n. alkaloid in coffee, tea, etc.: a stimulant

caf′tan n. long-sleeved robe, worn in eastern Mediterranean lands

cage n. openwork structure, esp. for confining animals —v. put in a cage

cag′er n. [Sl.] basketball player

cag′y, cag′y a. [Col.] sly; cunning —**cag′i·ly** adv.

ca·hoots′ n. [Sl.] scheming partnership

cais′son (kā′-) n. 1. ammunition wagon 2. watertight box for underwater construction work

cai′tiff (kā′-) n. mean or cowardly person —a. mean or cowardly

ca·jole′ (-jōl′) v. coax or wheedle —**ca·jol′er·y** n.

Ca′jun, Ca′jan (kā′jən) n. Canadian French native of Louisiana

cake n. 1. baked dough or batter of flour, eggs, sugar, etc. 2. solid, formed, usually flat mass —v. form into a hard mass

cal′a·bash n. 1. gourdlike fruit of a tropical tree 2. smoking pipe made from the neck of a gourd

cal′a·mine n. zinc compound used in lotions, etc.

ca·lam′i·ty n. [pl. -TIES] disaster —**ca·lam′i·tous** a.

cal′ci·fy (-sə fī) v. [-FIED, -FYING] change into stony matter —**cal′ci·fi·ca′tion** n.

cal′ci·mine n. thin, watery paint for covering plaster —v. cover with calcimine

cal′ci·um n. chemical element found combined in bone, limestone, etc.

calcium carbonate white compound found in limestone, bones, etc.

cal·cu·late (-kyə-) v. 1. figure by arithmetic 2. estimate 3. intend —**cal·cu·la·ble** a.

cal·cu·lat·ed a. deliberately planned or intended

cal·cu·lat·ing a. 1. scheming 2. shrewd; cautious

cal·cu·la·tion n. 1. a calculating 2. something deduced 3. careful planning

cal·cu·la·tor n. 1. one who calculates 2. machine doing arithmetic rapidly

cal·cu·lus (-kyə-) n. branch of higher mathematics

cal'dron (kôl'-) n. large kettle or boiler

cal·en·dar n. 1. table showing the days, weeks, and months of a year 2. schedule

cal·en·der n. machine with rollers for making paper, cloth, etc. smooth or glossy

calf n. [pl. CALVES] 1. young cow or bull 2. young elephant, seal, etc. 3. fleshy part of leg below the knee

calf'skin n. 1. skin of a calf 2. leather made from this

cal'i·ber, cal'i·bre n. 1. diameter of a bullet, bore of a gun, etc. 2. quality

cal'i·brate v. mark or fix the graduations of (a measuring device) —**cal'i·bra·tion** n. —**cal'i·bra'tor** n.

cal·i·co n. [pl. -COES, -COS] cotton cloth, usually printed

cal'i·pers n.pl. instrument for measuring diameter

ca·liph, cal·if (kā'lif) n. old title of Muslim rulers

cal·is·then·ics n.pl. athletic exercises

calk (kôk) v. caulk

call v. 1. say loudly; shout 2. summon 3. name 4. telephone 5. stop (a game) —n. 1. shout or cry 2. summons 3. demand 4. need 5. short visit —**call down** [Col.] to scold —**call for** 1. demand 2. come and get —**call off** cancel —**call on** 1. visit briefly 2. ask (one) to speak —**call up** 1. recall 2. summon for duty 3. telephone —**on call** available when called —**call'er** n.

cal·la (lily) (kal'ə) plant with yellow flower spike inside a large, white leaf

cal·lig'ra·phy n. attractive handwriting —**cal·lig'ra·pher** n.

call'ing n. vocation; trade

cal·li·o·pe (-li'ə pē) n. organlike musical instrument with steam whistles

cal·lous (kal'əs) a. 1. hardened 2. unfeeling; insensitive —**cal'·lous·ly** adv.

cal'low a. inexperienced

cal'lus n. hard, thickened place on the skin

calm (käm) n. stillness —a. still; tranquil —v. make or become calm —**calm'ly** adv. —**calm'ness** n.

ca·lor'ic a. 1. of heat 2. of calories

cal·o·rie, cal'o·ry (-rē) n. [pl. -RIES] unit of heat or of the energy got from food

cal·o·rif'ic a. producing heat

cal'u·met (-yə-) n. pipe with long stem smoked by N. American Indians in peace ceremony

ca·lum'ni·ate v. to slander — **ca·lum'ni·a'tion** n.

cal'um·ny n. [pl. -NIES] slander

calve (kav) v. give birth to (a calf)

ca·lyp'so (-lip'sō) n. [pl. -SOS] improvised ballad sung orig. in Trinidad

ca·lyx (kā'liks) n. [pl. -LYXES] sepals of a flower

cam n. projection on a wheel to give irregular motion, as to a shaft

ca·ma·ra·de·rie (kä'mə rä'dər ē) n. comradeship

cam'ber n. slight convexity

cam'bi·um (-bē-) n. cell layer under bark of plants from which new wood and bark grow

cam'bric (kām'-) n. fine linen or cotton cloth

came pt. of **come**

cam'el n. beast of burden with a humped back

ca·mel'lia (-mēl'yə) n. large, roselike flower

Cam'em·bert (cheese) (-ber) soft, creamy, rich cheese

cam'e·o n. [pl. -OS] gem with figure carved on it

cam'er·a n. 1. device for taking photographs 2. TV device that first receives the images for transmission

cam'er·a·man n. [pl. -MEN] operator of a movie or TV camera

cam'ou·flage (-ə fläzh) n. a disguising of potential targets in wartime —v. conceal by disguising

camp n. 1. place with tents, huts, etc., as for vacationers or soldiers 2. supporters of a cause —a. [Sl.] so artificial or trite as to amuse: also **camp'y** —v. set up a camp

cam·paign' (·pān') n. series of planned actions, as in war, an election, etc. —v. wage a campaign

cam·pa·ni'le (-nē'lē) n. bell tower

camp'er n. 1. vacationer at a camp 2. motor vehicle or trailer for camping out

camp'fire n. 1. outdoor fire at a camp 2. social gathering around such a fire

cam'phor n. strong-smelling crystalline substance used in moth balls, medicine, etc.

camp'site n. 1. site for a camp 2. park area for camping

cam'pus n. school or college grounds —a. of students

can v. [pt. COULD] 1. know how or be able to 2. [Col.] may

can n. metal container, as for foods —v. [CANNED, CANNING] 1. preserve (food) in cans or jars 2. [Sl.] dismiss —**can'ner** n.

Ca·na'di·an n., a. (native) of Canada

ca·nal' n. 1. artificial waterway 2. body duct

can'a·pé (-pē, -pā) n. appetizer on a cracker, etc.

ca·nard' n. false rumor

ca·nar'y n. [pl. -IES] yellow songbird kept in a cage

ca·nas'ta n. double-deck card game

can'can n. lively dance with much high kicking

can'cel (-s'l) v. 1. cross out 2. make invalid 3. abolish — **can'cel·la'tion** n.

can'cer (-sər) [C-] 4th sign of the zodiac; Crab — n. 1. malignant tumor 2. a spreading evil —**can'cer·ous** a.

can·de·la'brum n. [pl. -BRA, -BRUMS] large, branched candlestick: also **can'de·la'bra** [pl. -BRAS]

can'did a. 1. frank; honest 2. informal and not posed, as a photo —**can'did·ly** adv.

can'di·date n. one seeking office, etc. —**can'di·da·cy** n.

can'died (-dēd) a. sugary

can'dle n. wax taper with a wick, burned for light

candle power unit for measuring light

can'dle·stick n. holder for a candle or candles

can'dor n. frankness

can'dy n. [pl. -DIES] confection of sugar or syrup —v. [-DIED, -DYING] cook or preserve in sugar

cane n. 1. hollow, jointed stem, as of bamboo 2. walking stick 3. split rattan —v. beat with a cane

cane'brake n. dense growth of cane plants

ca'nine (kā'-) a. of or like a dog —n. dog

canine tooth any of the four sharp-pointed teeth

can'is·ter n. box or can for coffee, tea, etc.

can'ker n. a sore, esp. in the mouth —**can'ker·ous** a.

can'na·bis n. 1. hemp 2. female flowering tops of hemp

canned a. 1. preserved, as in cans 2. [Sl.] recorded for reproduction, as on TV

can'nel (coal) tough bituminous coal

can'ner·y n. [pl. -IES] factory for canning foods

can'ni·bal n. person who eats human flesh —**can'ni·bal·ism** n. —**can'ni·bal·is'tic** a.

can'ni·bal·ize v. strip (old equipment) for usable parts

can'non n. [pl. -NONS, -NON] large mounted gun

can'non·ade' n. continuous firing of artillery —v. to fire artillery (at)

can'not can not —**cannot but** have no choice but to

can'ny a. [-NIER, -NIEST] 1. cautious and shrewd 2. wise and well-informed —**can'ni·ly** adv.

ca·noe' (-nōō') n. narrow, light boat moved with paddles —v. paddle a canoe

can'on n. 1. body of church laws 2. any law 3. official list 4. clergyman serving in a cathedral 5. musical round — **ca·non'i·cal** a.

can'on·ize v. 1. name as a saint 2. glorify —**can'on·i·za'tion** n.

can'o·py n. [pl. -PIES] 1. covering hung over a bed, throne, etc. 2. rooflike projection —v. [-PIED, -PYING] place or form a canopy over

cant n. 1. special talk of a class; jargon 2. hypocritical talk —v. use cant

cant n., v. tilt; slant

can't cannot

can·ta·loupe, can·ta·loup (-lōp) *n.* sweet, juicy melon

can·tan·ker·ous *a.* bad-tempered; quarrelsome

can·ta·ta (-ta′-) *n.* dramatic choral composition

can·teen′ *n.* 1. place for refreshments, social activities, etc. 2. water flask

can′ter *n.* easy gallop —*v.* go at this pace

can′ti·cle (-k'l) *n.* hymn with words from the Bible

can′ti·le′ver *n.* structure anchored at only one end —*v.* to support by cantilevers —**can′ti·le′vered** *a.*

can′to *n.* [*pl.* -TOS] division of a long poem

can·ton′ment (-tän′-, -tōn′-) *n.* temporary quarters for troops

can′tor *n.* liturgical singer in a synagogue

can′vas *n.* coarse cloth used for tents, sails, oil paintings, etc.

can′vas·back *n.* wild duck with a grayish back

can′vass (-vəs) *v.* seek votes, opinions, etc. from —*n.* a canvassing

can′yon *n.* narrow valley between high cliffs

cap *n.* 1. brimless hat, often with a visor 2. caplike cover —*v.* [CAPPED, CAPPING] 1. put a cap on 2. surpass

ca′pa·ble *a.* able; skilled —**capable of** able or likely to —**ca′pa·bil′i·ty** [*pl.* -TIES] *n.* —**ca′pa·bly** *adv.*

ca·pa′cious *a.* roomy; wide

ca·pac′i·tor *n.* device for storing an electrical charge

ca·pac′i·ty *n.* [*pl.* -TIES] 1. ability to contain or hold 2. volume 3. ability 4. maximum output 5. position; function

cape *n.* 1. sleeveless coat fastened about the neck 2. land jutting into water

ca′per *v.* skip about playfully —*n.* 1. gay, playful leap 2. prank 3. tiny pickled bud used as seasoning —**cut a caper** play silly tricks

cap′il·lar′y *a.* having a tiny bore, as a tube —*n.* [*pl.* -IES] tiny blood vessel connecting an artery with a vein

cap′i·tal *a.* 1. bringing or punishable by death 2. chief; main 3. excellent —*n.* 1. see **capital letter** 2. city from which a state is governed 3. money or property owned or used in business 4. capitalists collectively 5. top of a column

capital gain profit made from sale of stocks, etc.

cap′i·tal·ism *n.* economic system in which the means of production and distribution are privately owned

cap′i·tal·ist *n.* owner of wealth used in business —**cap′i·tal·is′tic** *a.*

cap′i·tal·ize′ *v.* 1. convert into capital 2. use to advantage (with *on*) 3. supply capital for 4. write with a capital letter —**cap′i·tal·i·za′tion** *n.*

capital letter large letter used to begin a sentence, name, etc.

cap′i·tal·ly *adv.* very well

capital punishment penalty of death for a crime

cap'i·tol n. building where a legislature meets

ca·pit'u·late (-pich'ə-) v. surrender —**ca·pit'u·la'tion** n.

ca'pon n. castrated rooster

ca·price' (-prēs') n. whim

ca·pri'cious (-prish'əs) a. unpredictable

Cap'ri·corn 10th sign of the zodiac; Goat

cap·size' v. upset; overturn

cap'stan n. device around which cables are wound

cap'sule n. 1. small case, as for a dose of medicine 2. detachable compartment in a rocket —a. concise; compact

cap'tain n. 1. leader 2. army officer above lieutenant 3. navy officer above commander 4. master of a ship —v. to head —**cap'tain·cy** n.

cap'tion n. title, as of a newspaper picture

cap'tious (-shəs) a. 1. made for the sake of argument 2. quick to find fault

cap'ti·vate v. fascinate

cap'tive n. prisoner —a. 1. held prisoner 2. obliged to listen —**cap·tiv'i·ty** n.

cap'tor n. one who captures

cap'ture v. 1. take by force, surprise, etc. 2. represent in a picture, etc. —n. a capturing or being captured

car n. 1. wheeled vehicle, esp. an automobile 2. elevator

ca·rafe' (kə raf') n. bottle for water, coffee, etc.

car'a·mel n. 1. burnt sugar used to flavor 2. chewy candy

car'at (kar'-) n. 1. unit of weight for jewels 2. one 24th part (of pure gold)

car'a·van n. group traveling together for safety

car'a·van'sa·ry n. [pl. -RIES] in the Orient, inn for caravans

car'a·way (kar'-) n. spicy seeds used as flavoring

car'bide n. compound of a metal with carbon

car'bine (-bīn, -bēn) n. light, short-barreled rifle

carbo- pref. carbon

car'bo·hy'drate n. compound of carbon, hydrogen, and oxygen, as sugar or starch

car·bol'ic acid an acid used as an antiseptic, etc.

car'bon n. 1. nonmetallic chemical element found in all organic compounds: diamond and graphite are pure carbon 2. carbon paper 3. carbon copy

car'bon·ate v. charge with carbon dioxide

carbon copy copy made with carbon paper

carbon dioxide odorless gas given off in breathing

car'bon·if'er·ous a. containing carbon or coal

carbon monoxide colorless, odorless, poisonous gas

carbon paper paper coated with a carbon preparation, used to make copies of letters, etc.

carbon tet'ra·chlo'ride (-rə klôr'-) cleaning fluid

Car'bo·run'dum trademark for hard abrasive, esp. of carbon and silicon —n. [c-] such a substance

car′boy n. large bottle to hold corrosive liquids

car′bun·cle n. painful inflammation below the skin

car′bu·re′tor (-bə rā′-) n. device in an engine for mixing air with gasoline

car′cass, car′case (-kəs) n. dead body of an animal

car·cin′o·gen (-sin′-) n. substance that produces cancer — **car′ci·no·gen′ic** a.

car coat short overcoat

card n. 1. flat piece of stiff paper 2. post card 3. playing card 4. pl. game played with cards 5. metal comb for wool, etc. 6. [Col.] witty or clowning person —v. comb with a card —**put (or lay) one's cards on the table** reveal something frankly

card′board n. stiff paper

car′di·ac a. of the heart

car′di·gan n. knitted jacket-like sweater

car′di·nal a. 1. chief; main 2. bright-red —n. 1. high R.C.Ch. official 2. red American songbird

cardinal number number used in counting, as 7, 42, etc.

cardio- pref. of the heart

car′di·o·gram′ n. an electrocardiogram —**car′di·o·graph′** n.

card′sharp n. [Col.] professional cheater at cards: also **card shark**

care n. 1. worry 2. watchfulness; heed 3. liking (for) 4. charge; keeping —v. 1. be concerned 2. feel liking (for) 3. provide (for) 4. to wish (for) —

care of at the address of —**take care of** 1. attend to 2. provide for

ca·reen′ v. tilt; lurch

ca·reer′ n. 1. full speed 2. progress through life 3. profession or occupation

care′free a. without care

care′ful a. 1. cautious; wary 2. thoroughly done —**care′ful·ly** adv.

care′less a. 1. carefree 2. not paying enough attention or heed —**care′less·ness** n.

ca·ress′ v. touch lovingly —n. affectionate touch

car′et (kar′-) n. mark (∧) to show where addition is to be made in a printed line

care′tak′er n. one who takes care of a building, etc.

care′worn a. weary with care

car′go n. [pl. -GOES, -GOS] load carried by a ship, etc.

car·i·bou (kar′ə bōō) n. N. American reindeer

car·i·ca·ture (kar′ə kə chər) n. distorted imitation or picture for satire —v. do a caricature of

car·ies (ker′ēz) n. decay of teeth, bones, etc.

car′il·lon (kar′-) n. set of tuned bells

car′mine (-min, -mīn) n. red or purplish red

car′nage (-nij) n. slaughter

car′nal a. bodily; sensual — **car·nal′i·ty** n. —**car′nal·ly** adv.

car·na′tion n. 1. variety of the pink 2. its flower

car′ni·val n. 1. festivity 2. kind of fair, with rides, etc.

car·ni·vore n. carnivorous animal or plant

car·niv'o·rous a. 1. flesh-eating 2. insect-eating, as certain plants

car'ol (kar'-) n. (Christmas) song of joy —v. sing —**car'ol·er, car'ol·ler** n.

car'om (kar'-) n.. v. hit and rebound

ca·rot'id n. either of two main arteries in the neck

ca·rouse' (-rouz') v., n. (join in) a drinking party

carp n. freshwater fish —v. find fault pettily

car'pel n. modified leaf forming a pistil

car'pen·ter n. construction worker who makes wooden parts —**car'pen·try** n.

carpenter ant large, black ant that gnaws at wood

car'pet n. heavy fabric for covering a floor —v. to cover as with a carpet

car'pet·bag n. old-fashioned traveling bag of carpeting

car'pet·ing n. carpets; carpet fabric

car pool group plan to rotate cars, going to and from work

car'port n. roofed shelter for an automobile

car'rel, car'rell (kar'-) n. small enclosure for study in a library

car·riage (kar'ij) n. 1. horse-drawn vehicle 2. posture 3. moving part that holds and shifts something

car'ri·er n. 1. one that carries 2. one that transmits disease germs

car'ri·on (kar'-) n. decaying flesh of a dead body

car'rot n. plant with an edible, orange-red root

car'rou·sel, car'ou·sel (-rə-) n. merry-go-round

car'ry v. [-RIED, -RYING] 1. take to another place 2. lead, transmit, etc. 3. win (an election, etc.) 4. hold; support 5. bear (oneself) 6. keep in stock 7. cover a range —**be** (or **get**) **carried away** become very emotional or enthusiastic — **carry on** 1. do or continue 2. [Col.] behave wildly —**carry out** accomplish —**carry over** postpone

car'ry·out a. of prepared food or beverages sold to be consumed elsewhere

car'sick a. nauseated from riding in a car, etc.

cart n. small wagon —v. carry in a vehicle

cart'age (-ij) n. 1. a carting 2. charge for this

carte blanche (blänsh) [Fr.] full authority

car·tel' n. business firms forming international monopoly

car'ti·lage (-lij) n. tough, elastic skeletal tissue

car·tog'ra·phy n. map-making —**car·tog'ra·pher** n.

car'ton n. cardboard box

car·toon' n. 1. drawing that is a caricature 2. comic strip 3. motion picture of drawn figures that seem to move —v. draw cartoons (of) —**car·toon'ist** n.

car'tridge (-trij) n. 1. cylinder holding the charge and bullet or shot for a firearm 2. small container for film, etc.

cart′wheel n. handspring performed sidewise

carve v. 1. make or shape by cutting 2. slice —**carv′er** n. —**carv′ing** n.

car′wash n. business at which cars are washed

ca·sa′ba (kə sä′-) n. muskmelon with a yellow rind

cas·cade′ n. 1. waterfall 2. shower —v. fall in a cascade

case n. 1. example or instance 2. situation 3. lawsuit 4. form of a noun, etc. showing its relation to neighboring words 5. container 6. protective cover —v. 1. put in a case 2. [Sl.] examine carefully —**in any case** anyhow —**in case** if —**in case of** in the event of

ca·se·in (kā′sē in) n. protein constituent of milk

case′load n. number of cases being handled by a court, caseworker, etc.

case′ment n. hinged window that opens outward

case′work n. social work dealing with cases of personal and family maladjustment —**case′-work′er** n.

cash n. money on hand —v. give or get cash for —a. of or for cash —**cash in** turn into cash

cash′ew n. kidney-shaped, edible nut

cash·ier′ (-ir′) n. one in charge of cash transactions —v. dismiss in disgrace

cash′mere n. soft, fine goat's wool, or a cloth of this

cash register device for showing the amount of a sale

cas′ing (kās′-) n. 1. outer covering 2. door frame

ca·si′no (-sē′-) n. [pl. -NOS] hall for dancing, gambling, etc.

cask n. barrel for liquids

cas′ket n. coffin

cas·sa′va (-sä′-) n. tropical plant with starchy roots

cas′se·role n. 1. covered dish for baking and serving 2. food baked in such a dish

cas·sette′ (-set′) n. case with film or tape for a camera or tape recorder

cas·cia (kash′ə) n. 1. bark of an Asian tree, from which cinnamon comes 2. tropical plant whose leaves yield senna

ca·si′no (-sē′-) n. card game

cas′sock n. long vestment worn by clergymen

cast v. [CAST, CASTING] 1. throw 2. deposit (a vote) 3. mold 4. select (an actor) —n. 1. a throw 2. plaster form for broken limb 3. the actors in a play 4. type or quality 5. tinge —**cast about** search —**cast aside** (or **away**) discard —**cast off** 1. discard 2. free a ship from a dock, etc.

cas·ta·nets′ n.pl. two hollow pieces clicked together in one hand in rhythm

cast′a·way n. a shipwrecked person

caste (kast) n. class distinction based on birth, etc.

cast′er n. small swiveled wheel as on a table leg

cas′ti·gate v. criticize severely

—cas'ti·ga'tion n. —cas'ti·ga'tor n.

cast'ing n. metal cast in a mold

cast iron hard, brittle alloy of iron made by casting —cast'-i'ron a.

cas·tle (kas'l) n. 1. large, fortified dwelling 2. rook (n. 2)

cast'off' a. discarded —n. person or thing abandoned

cas'tor-oil' plant plant with large seeds yielding a cathartic oil (castor oil)

cas'trate v. remove the testicles of —cas·tra'tion n.

cas·u·al (kazh'oo wal) a. 1. by chance 2. careless 3. nonchalant 4. informal

cas'u·al·ty n. [pl. -TIES] one hurt or killed in an accident or in war

cas'u·ist·ry (kazh'oo-) n. subtle but false reasoning

cat n. 1. small, soft-furred animal kept as a pet 2. any related mammal, as the lion 3. spiteful woman

cat'a·clysm (-kliz'm) n. sudden, violent change —cat'a·clys'mic a.

cat'a·comb (-kōm) n. tunnel-like burial place

cat'a·falque (-falk, -fôlk) n. wooden framework for holding a coffin

cat'a·lep'sy n. loss of consciousness, with body rigidity —cat'a·lep'tic a., n.

cat'a·log, cat'a·logue (-lôg) n. complete list, as of library books —v. list

ca·tal'pa (-tal'-) n. tree with heart-shaped leaves

cat'a·lyst (-list) n. substance that affects a chemical reaction but itself remains unchanged —cat'a·lyt'ic a.

cat'a·mount n. 1. cougar 2. lynx

cat'a·pult n. device for throwing or launching —v. 1. shoot as from a catapult 2. to leap

cat'a·ract n. 1. large waterfall 2. condition of opaque lens in the eye

ca·tarrh' (-tär') n. inflammation of the respiratory passages: old-fashioned term

ca·tas'tro·phe (-trə fē) n. sudden great disaster —cat'a·stroph'ic (-sträf'-) a.

cat'bird n. songbird with a call like a cat's

cat'call n. derisive call —v. make catcalls (at)

catch v. [CAUGHT, CATCHING] 1. capture 2. deceive 3. surprise 4. get 5. grab 6. understand 7. take or keep hold of 8. [Col.] see, hear, etc. —n. 1. a catching 2. thing that catches or is caught 3. [Col.] trick —catch on [Col.] 1. understand 2. become popular —catch up 1. prove wrong 2. overtake

catch'all' n. container for holding all sorts of things

catch'er n. one who catches 2. Baseball player who catches pitched balls

catch'ing a. 1. contagious 2. attractive

catch'up n. ketchup

catch'y a. [-IER, -IEST] 1. easily remembered 2. tricky

cat'e·chism (-kiz'm) n. list of

questions and answers to teach religious beliefs

cat'e·chize v. to question searchingly: also sp. **catechise**

cat'e·gor'i·cal a. 1. of or in a category 2. positive —**cat'e·gor'i·cal·ly** adv.

cat'e·go·rize' v. place in a category; classify

cat'e·go'ry n. [pl. -RIES] any of a system of classes

ca'ter v. provide food, etc. for a party —**ca'ter·er** n.

cat'er·cor'nered a. diagonal —adv. diagonally

cat'er·pil'lar n. larva of a butterfly, moth, etc.

cat'er·waul v., n. wail

cat'fish n. fish with long feelers about the mouth

cat'gut n. tough thread made from animal intestines

ca·thar'sis n. a relieving of the emotions

ca·thar'tic a. purging —n. a laxative

ca·the'dral n. large church

cath'e·ter n. tube put in the bladder to remove urine

cath'ode n. 1. negative electrode in an electrolytic cell 2. positive terminal in a battery

cathode rays streams of electrons producing X-rays when they strike solids

cath'o·lic a. 1. universal 2. liberal 3. [C-] Roman Catholic —n. [C-] member of the R.C. Church —**Ca·thol'i·cism** n. —**cath'o·lic'i·ty** n.

cat'kin n. spike of clustered small flowers

cat'nap' n. short nap —v.

[-NAPPED, -NAPPING] to doze briefly

cat'nip n. plant like mint: cats like its odor

cat'-o'-nine'-tails' n. [pl. -TAILS] whip of nine knotted cords attached to a handle

cat's cradle game played by looping string over the fingers to make designs

cat's'-paw' n. a dupe

cat·sup (kech'əp) n. ketchup

cat'tail n. marsh plant with long, brown spikes

cat'tle n. 1. [Ar.] livestock 2. cows, bulls, steers, or oxen —**cat'tle·man** [pl. -MEN] n.

cat'ty a. [-TIER, -TIEST] spiteful; mean

cat'ty-cor'nered a., adv. catercornered: also **cat'ty-cor'ner**

cat'walk n. high narrow walk

Cau·ca'sian (kô kā'zhən) n., a. Caucasoid

Cau·ca·soid (kô'kə-) n., a. (member) of one of the major groups of human beings, loosely called the *white race*

cau'cus n. political meeting to choose party candidates, etc. —v. hold a caucus

cau'dal a. of the tail

caught pt. & pp. of **catch**

caul n. membrane enclosing the head of a fetus at birth

caul'dron n. caldron

cau'li·flow'er n. hard, white head of a cabbagelike plant

caulk (kôk) v. make watertight or airtight by stopping up cracks with a filler

caus'al a. of a cause or causes —**cau·sal'i·ty** n.

cau·sa'tion *n.* 1. a causing 2. anything making an effect

cause *n.* 1. thing bringing a result 2. motive 3. group movement with an aim 4. lawsuit — *v.* bring about

cause'way *n.* raised road, as across a marsh

caus'tic *a.* 1. corrosive 2. sarcastic —*n.* caustic substance — **caus'ti·cal·ly** *adv.*

cau'ter·ize *v.* burn dead tissue off, as with a hot iron

cau'tion *n.* 1. warning 2. prudence —*v.* warn

cau'tious *a.* careful to avoid danger —**cau'tious·ly** *adv.*

cav'al·cade *n.* procession

cav·a·lier' (-lir') *n.* 1. knight 2. gallant gentleman —*a.* 1. casual 2. arrogant —**cav·a·lier'ly** *adv.*

cav'al·ry *n.* [*pl.* -RIES] army troops on horses or in motorized vehicles —**cav'al·ry·man** [*pl.* -MEN] *n.*

cave *n.* hollow place in the earth —*v.* collapse (*in*)

cave'-in' *n.* 1. a caving in 2. place where ground, etc. has caved in

cave man prehistoric human being who lived in caves

cav'ern *n.* large cave —**cav'ern·ous** *a.*

cav'i·ar, cav'i·are (-är) *n.* fish eggs eaten as a relish

cav'il *v.* quibble

cav'i·ty *n.* [*pl.* -TIES] hole or hollow place

ca·vort' *v.* prance; caper

caw *n.* crow's harsh cry —*v.* make this sound

cay·enne' (kī-, kā-) *n.* ground hot red pepper

cay·use' (kī'ōōs) *n.* [*pl.* -USES] small Western horse

CB *a.* of radio frequencies for local use by private persons — *n.* CB radio

cease *v.* to end; stop

cease'-fire' *n.* temporary stop of warfare; truce

cease'less *a.* unceasing

ce'cum (-kəm) *n.* [*pl.* -CA] pouch at the beginning of the large intestine

ce'dar *n.* evergreen tree with fragrant wood

cede *v.* give up; transfer

ceil'ing *n.* 1. inner roof of a room 2. upper limit

cel'an·dine (-dīn, -dēn) *n.* 1. poppy 2. buttercup

cel'e·brate *v.* 1. perform (a ritual) 2. commemorate with festivity 3. honor; praise 4. [Col.] have a good time —**cel'e·bra'tion** *n.*

cel'e·brat'ed *a.* famous

ce·leb'ri·ty *n.* 1. fame 2. [*pl.* -TIES] famous person

ce·ler'i·ty *n.* speed

cel'er·y *n.* plant with edible crisp stalks

ce·les'tial (-chəl) *a.* 1. of the heavens 2. divine

cel'i·ba·cy *n.* 1. unmarried state 2. complete sexual abstinence —**cel'i·bate** (-bət) *a.*, *n.*

cell *n.* 1. small room as in a prison 2. small unit of protoplasm 3. device for generating electricity chemically 4. unit of an organization —**cel'lu·lar** *a.*

cel′lar n. room(s) below ground under a building

cel·lo, ′cel·lo (chel′ō) n. [pl. -LOS] instrument like a large violin, held between the knees in playing —**cel′list, ′cel′list** n.

cel′lo·phane (sel′ə-) n. thin transparent cellulose material, used as a wrapping

cel′lu·loid n. flammable plastic substance of cellulose

cel′lu·lose (-lōs) n. substance in plant cell walls, used in making paper, etc.

Col′si·us (-sē-) a. of a thermometer on which 0° is the freezing point and 100° the boiling point of water

ce·ment′ n. 1. mixture of lime, clay, and water, used for paving, in mortar, etc. 2. any adhesive —v. join as with cement

cem′e·ter′y n. [pl. -IES] place for burying the dead

cen′ser n. container in which incense is burned

cen′sor n. one who examines books, mail, etc. to remove things considered unsuitable — v. act as a censor of — **cen′sor·ship** n.

cen·so′ri·ous a. critical

cen′sure n., v. blame

cen′sus n. official count of population

cent n. 100th part of a dollar; penny

cen′taur (-tôr) n. Gr. Myth. monster with a man's head and trunk and a horse's body

cen·ta′vo (-tä′vō) n. [pl. -vos] 1/100th peso

cen·te′nar·y (-ten′ər ē) a., n. [pl. -IES] (of a) century or centennial

cen·ten′ni·al n. 100th anniversary

cen′ter n. 1. middle point, esp. of a circle or sphere 2. any central place, thing, or person 3. [often C-] political party between left and right —v. 1. put or be at the center 2. gather

cen′ter·fold n. center facing pages of a magazine, showing a photograph

cen′ter·piece n. ornament for the center of a table

centi- pref. 1. hundred 2. 100th part of

cen′ti·grade a. Celsius

cen′ti·gram n. 1/100 gram

cen·time (sän′tēm) n. 1/100 franc

cen′ti·me′ter n. 1/100 meter

cen′ti·pede n. wormlike animal with many pairs of legs

cen′tral a. 1. in or near the center 2. main; chief —**cen′tral·ly** adv.

cen′tral·ize v. 1. bring to a center 2. organize under one control —**cen′tral·i·za′tion** n.

cen′tre n., v. center: Br. sp.

cen·trif′u·gal force force that makes rotating bodies move away from the center

cen′tri·fuge (-fyōōj) n. machine using centrifugal force to separate particles

cen·trip′e·tal force force that makes rotating bodies move toward the center

cen′trist n. member of political party of the center

cen·tu'ri·on n. military commander in ancient Rome

cen'tu·ry n. [pl. -RIES] period of 100 years

ce·phal'ic (-fal'-) a. of, in, or on the head or skull

ce·ram'ics n. (the making of) pottery, porcelain, etc. —**ce·ram'ic** a.

ce're·al n. 1. grain used for food, as wheat, oats, etc. 2. food made from grain

cer'e·bel'lum (ser'-) n. lower rear part of the brain

cer'e·bral a. of the brain

cerebral palsy spastic paralysis due to a lesion of the brain

cer'e·brum n. upper, main part of the brain

cer'e·ment n. shroud

cer'e·mo'ni·al a. ritual; formal —n. system of rites

cer'e·mo'ni·ous a. 1. full of ceremony 2. very polite or formal

cer'e·mo'ny n. [pl. -NIES] 1. set of formal acts; rite 2. rigid etiquette 3. (empty) formality —**stand on ceremony** insist on formality

ce·rise' (-rēs') a. bright red

cer'tain a. 1. fixed; settled 2. sure; positive 3. specific, but unnamed 4. some —**for certain** surely

cer'tain·ly adv. surely

cer'tain·ty n. 1. fact of being certain 2. [pl. -TIES] anything certain

cer·tif'i·cate (-kit) n. written statement testifying to a fact, qualification, etc.

cer'ti·fy v. [-FIED, -FYING] 1. formally declare to be true,
etc. 2. guarantee 3. grant a certificate to —**cer'ti·fi·ca'tion** n.

cer'ti·tude n. assurance

ce·ru'le·an a. sky-blue

cer'vix n. necklike part —**cer'vi·cal** a.

ces·sa'tion n. stop; pause

ces'sion n. a ceding

cess'pool n. deep hole in the ground for sewage, etc.

Cha·blis (sha'blē) n. dry, white wine

chafe v. 1. make warm or sore by rubbing 2. be angry

chaff n. 1. threshed husks of grain 2. worthless stuff —v. tease; banter

chaf'ing dish (chāf'-) pan for cooking food at the table

cha·grin' (sha-) n. embarrassment because of failure or disappointment —v. make feel chagrin

chain n. 1. flexible series of joined links 2. pl. fetters 3. connected series —v. restrain as with chains

chain reaction sequence of (nuclear) reactions whose products cause new reactions

chain saw portable power saw with an endless chain of cutting teeth

chain store any of a group of retail stores owned by one company

chair n. 1. seat with a back 2. office of authority

chair'lift' n. seats on a power-driven cable, used to carry skiers up a slope

chair'man n. [pl. -MEN] one who presides at a meeting:

also **chair′per′son** —**chair′-man·ship** n.

chaise longue (shāz′lôṅ′) [pl. CHAISE LONGUES] couchlike chair with a long seat

chal·ced′o·ny (kal sed′-) n. colored waxlike quartz

cha·let (sha lā′) n. cottage with overhanging eaves

chal·ice (chal′is) n. cup

chalk (chôk) n. soft limestone for writing on a blackboard — **chalk up 1.** score, get, or achieve **2.** to charge or credit —**chalk′y** [-IER, -IEST] a.

chalk′board n. smooth surface for writing with chalk

chal·lenge n. **1.** demand for identification **2.** a calling into question **3.** call to a contest, etc. **4.** anything calling for special effort —v. put a challenge to —**chal′leng·er** n.

cham·ber (chām′-) n. **1.** room **2.** pl. judge's office **3.** assembly or council **4.** part of a gun for the cartridge

cham′ber·maid n. maid who keeps bedrooms neat

chamber music music for performance by a small group

cham′bray (sham′-) n. smooth cotton fabric

cha·me′le·on (kə mē′-) n. lizard able to change its color

cham·ois (sham′ē) n. [pl. CHAMOIS] **1.** small antelope **2.** soft kind of leather

cham·o·mile (kam′ə mīl, -mēl) n. plant with dried flower heads used in a medicinal tea

champ v. chew or bite noisily —n. [Sl.] champion

cham·pagne (sham pān′) n. effervescent white wine

cham·paign (sham pān′) n. flat, open country

cham′pi·on n. **1.** one who fights for a cause **2.** winner of first place —a. best —v. defend; support —**cham′pi·on·ship′** n.

chance n. **1.** luck; fortune **2.** risk **3.** opportunity **4.** possibility —a. accidental —v. **1.** happen **2.** risk —**by chance** accidentally

chan′cel n. place around an altar for clergy and choir

chan′cel·lor n. **1.** high state or church official **2.** university head —**chan′cel·ler·y** [pl. -IES] n.

chan·cre (shaṅ′kər) n. sore or ulcer of syphilis

chanc′y a. [-IER, -IEST] risky

chan·de·lier (shan′də lir′) n. hanging lighting fixture

chan′dler n. **1.** candle maker **2.** retailer of supplies for ships —**chan′dler·y** n.

change v. **1.** substitute **2.** exchange **3.** alter; vary **4.** leave one train, bus, etc. and board another **5.** put on other clothes —n. **1.** alteration or variation **2.** variety **3.** money returned as overpayment **4.** small coins —**change′a·ble** a.

change of life menopause

change′o′ver n. a complete change, as in goods produced

chan′nel n. **1.** bed of a river, etc. **2.** wide strait joining two seas **3.** any passage **4.** official course of action **5.** assigned frequency band, esp. in TV —

v. make, or send through, a channel

chant *n.* song with several words to each tone —*v.* utter in a chant

chant·ey (shan′tē, chan′-) *n.* sailors' work song

chan·ti·cleer *n.* rooster

Cha·nu·kah (hä′noo kä) *n.* Hanuka

cha·os (kā′-) *n.* complete disorder —**cha·ot′ic** *a.*

chap *n.* 1. jaw 2. cheek 3. [Col.] fellow —*v.* [CHAPPED, CHAPPING] become rough and red as from the cold

cha·peau (sha pō′) *n.* [*pl.* -PEAUS, -PEAUX (-pōz′)] hat

chap′el *n.* small church

chap·er·on (shap′ə rōn) *n.* older person in charge of unmarried people at social affairs —*v.* be a chaperon to Also sp. **chap′er·one**

chap′lain (-lin) *n.* clergyman in the armed forces

chap′let *n.* garland

chaps *n.pl.* leather trousers worn by cowboys

chap′ter *n.* 1. main division of a book 2. branch of an organization

char *v.* [CHARRED, CHARRING] scorch

char·ac·ter (kar′-) *n.* 1. letter or symbol 2. trait 3. kind or sort 4. personality 5. moral strength 6. person in a play, novel, etc. 7. [Col.] eccentric person

char·ac·ter·is′tic *a.* typical; distinctive —*n.* distinguishing quality

char·ac·ter·ize′ *v.* 1. describe

2. be a quality of —**char′ac·ter·i·za′tion** *n.*

cha·rade′ (shə-) *n.* word game in pantomime

char′coal *n.* pieces of incompletely burned wood

chard *n.* beet with edible leaves and stalks

charge *v.* 1. fill (*with*) 2. add electricity to 3. command 4. accuse 5. ask as a price 6. ask payment (*for*) 7. record as a debt 8. attack vigorously —*n.* 1. load 2. responsibility or care (*of*) 3. chemical energy in a battery 4. someone in one's care 5. command 6. accusation 7. cost 8. debt or expense 9. onslaught 10. [Sl.] thrill —**in charge** (of) in control (of) —**charge′a·ble** *a.*

charge account arrangement to pay within some future period

charg′er *n.* war horse

char′i·ot (char′-) *n.* ancient, horse-drawn, two-wheeled cart —**char′i·ot·eer′** *n.*

cha·ris′ma (kə riz′-) *n.* [*pl.* -MATA] inspiring quality of leadership —**char′is·mat′ic** *a.*

char′i·ta·ble *a.* 1. generous 2. of charity 3. forgiving

char′i·ty *n.* [*pl.* -TIES] 1. leniency in judging others 2. a helping those in need 3. institution for so helping

char′la·tan (shär′-) *n.* quack; impostor

char′ley horse [Col.] leg or arm cramp

charm *n.* 1. words or thing supposed to have magic power 2. trinket on a bracelet, etc. 3.

fascination; allure —v. 1. use a magical charm on 2. fascinate; delight —**charm'ing** a.

char'nel (house) place where there are corpses

chart n. 1. map, esp. for navigation 2. graph, table, etc. —v. make a chart of

char'ter n. 1. government franchise 2. constitution 3. written permission to form a local chapter of a society —v. 1. grant a charter to 2. hire (a bus, etc.) privately

charter member original member of an organization

char·treuse (shar trōōz') n., a. pale, yellowish green

char'wom'an n. [pl. -WOM-EN] cleaning woman

char·y (cher'ē) a. [-IER, -IEST] 1. cautious 2. sparing —**char'i·ly** adv.

chase v. 1. follow in order to catch 2. drive away 3. [Col.] rush 4. decorate (metal) as by engraving —n. a chasing —**give chase** pursue

chas'er n. [Col.] water, etc. taken after liquor

chasm (kaz'm) n. 1. deep crack in the earth's surface 2. break or gap; rift

chas·sis (chas'ē, shas'ē) n. [pl. -SIS (-ēz)] 1. frame, wheels, etc. of a car, but not the body or engine 2. frame, as for parts of a TV

chaste a. 1. sexually virtuous 2. decent; modest 3. simple in style

chas·ten (chās'n) v. 1. punish so as to correct 2. subdue

chas·tise v. 1. punish as by

beating 2. scold sharply —**chas·tise'ment** n.

chas'ti·ty n. 1. sexual virtue 2. celibacy or virginity 3. decency; modesty 4. simplicity of style

chat v. [CHATTED, CHATTING] n. talk in a light, informal way —**chat'ty** a.

châ·teau (sha tō') n. [pl. -TEAUX (-tōz'), -TEAUS] 1. French feudal castle 2. mansion

chat'tel n. piece of movable property

chat'ter v. 1. talk much and foolishly 2. click together rapidly —n. a chattering

chauf·feur (shō'fər) n. man hired to drive one's car —v. act as chauffeur

chau'vin·ism (shō'-) n. 1. fanatical patriotism 2. unreasoning devotion to one's race, sex, etc. —**chau'vin·ist** a., n.

cheap a. 1. low in price 2. worth more than the price 3. of little value 4. [Col.] stingy —adv. at a low cost —**cheap'ly** adv.

cheap'en v. make cheaper

cheap'skate n. [Sl.] stingy person

cheat n. 1. fraud 2. swindler —v. 1. deceive or practice fraud 2. escape 3. [Sl.] be sexually unfaithful —**cheat'er** n.

check n. 1. sudden stop 2. restraint or restrainer 3. test of accuracy, etc. 4. mark (✓) used to verify 5. token to show ownership 6. bill, as at a restaurant 7. written order to a bank to pay money 8. pattern of squares 9. *Chess* threat to the king —*int.* [Col.] right! —*v.* 1. stop or restrain 2. test, verify, etc. 3. mark with a check 4. deposit temporarily 5. agree, item for item 6. investigate —**check** in register at a hotel, etc. —**check out** 1. pay and leave a hotel, etc. 2. prove to be accurate, etc. —**check'er** *n.*

check'book *n.* book of forms for writing checks (*n.* 7)

checked *a.* having a pattern of squares

check'er *n.* flat, round piece used in checkers

check'er-board *n.* board for checkers, with 64 squares

check'ered *a.* 1. having a pattern of squares 2. varied

check'ers *n.* game for two using flat disks on a checkerboard

checking account bank account for writing checks (*n.* 7)

check'list *n.* list to be referred to: also **check list**

check'mate *n.* 1. *Chess* position from which king cannot escape, ending the game 2. total defeat —*v.* 1. put in checkmate 2. defeat totally

check'point *n.* place where road traffic is inspected

check'room *n.* room for leaving hats, coats, etc.

check'up *n.* medical examination

Ched-dar (cheese) (ched'ər) hard, smooth cheese

cheek *n.* 1. side of face below eye 2. [Col.] impudence —**tongue in cheek** jestingly

cheep *n.* young bird's short, shrill sound —*v.* make this sound

cheer *n.* 1. joy; gladness 2. shout of excitement, welcome, etc. —*v.* 1. fill with cheer 2. urge on, praise, etc. with cheers —**cheer up** make or become glad

cheer'ful *a.* 1. full of cheer 2. bright and attractive 3. willing —**cheer'ful-ly** *adv.* —**cheer'ful-ness** *n.*

cheer'lead'er *n.* leader of cheers, as at a football game

cheer'less *a.* not cheerful

cheers *int.* [Chiefly Br.] good health: used as a toast

cheer'y *a.* [-IER, -IEST] cheerful; bright

cheese *n.* solid food made from milk curds

cheese'burg'er *n.* hamburger topped with melted cheese

cheese'cloth *n.* cotton cloth with a loose weave

chees'y *a.* [-IER, -IEST] 1. like cheese 2. [Sl.] inferior; poor

chee'tah *n.* animal like the leopard

chef (shef) *n.* head cook

chem'i-cal (kem'-) *a.* of, in, or by chemistry —*n.* substance used in or got by chemistry —**chem'i-cal-ly** *adv.*

che-mise (shə mēz') *n.* a woman's undergarment

chem'is-try *n.* science dealing with the composition, reactions, etc. of substances —**chem'ist** *n.*

chem'o-ther'a-py *n.* use of chemical drugs in medicine

che·nille (shə nēl′) *n.* fabric woven with tufted cord

cheque (chek) *n.* check (*n.* 7): Br. sp.

cher′ish *v.* 1. hold or treat tenderly 2. keep in mind

cher′ry *n.* [*pl.* -RIES] 1. small, red fruit 2. tree it grows on, or its wood

cher′ub *n.* [*pl.* -UBIM, -UBS] angel, pictured as a chubby, winged child —**che·ru′bic** (-rōō′-) *a.*

chess *n.* checkerboard game for two players using various pieces (**chess′men**)

chest *n.* 1. box with a lid 2. piece of furniture with drawers 3. front part of the body above the abdomen

chest′nut *n.* 1. edible nut of a kind of beech 2. this tree, or its wood 3. [Col.] trite joke —*a.* reddish-brown

chev·i·ot (shev′ē ət) *n.* twilled wool fabric

chev′ron (shev′-) *n.* V-shaped sleeve insigne of rank

chew *v.* grind with the teeth —*n.* something for chewing —**chew′y** [-IER, -IEST] *a.*

chewing gum flavored chicle, etc. for chewing

Chi·an·ti (kē än′tē) *n.* a dry, red wine

chic (shēk) *a.* [CHICQUER, CHICQUEST] smartly stylish

chi·can·er·y (shi kān′-) *n.* [*pl.* -IES] 1. trickery 2. trick

Chi·ca·no (chē kä′nō) *n.* [*pl.* -NOS] Mexican-American

chick *n.* 1. young chicken 2. [Sl.] young woman

chick′a·dee *n.* small bird of the titmouse family

chick′en *n.* hen or rooster, or its edible flesh

chicken pox contagious virus disease with skin eruptions

chic′le (-′l) *n.* gummy substance from a tropical tree

chic′o·ry *n.* plant with leaf used in salads and root used as a coffee substitute

chide *v.* scold; rebuke

chief *n.* leader —*a.* main; most important —**chief′ly** *adv.*

chief′tain (-tən) *n.* chief of a clan or tribe

chif·fon (shi fän′) *n.* sheer silk cloth

chig′ger *n.* mite larva that causes itching

chi·gnon (shēn′yän) *n.* coil of hair worn at the back of the neck by women

Chi·hua·hua (chi wä′wä) *n.* tiny dog with large, pointed ears

chil′blain *n.* inflamed sore on the hand or foot caused by exposure to cold

child *n.* [*pl.* CHILDREN] 1. infant 2. boy or girl before puberty 3. son or daughter —**with child** pregnant —**child′hood** *n.*

child′ish *a.* silly; foolish

child′like *a.* of or like a child; innocent, trusting, etc.

chil′i (-ē) *n.* [*pl.* -IES] 1. hot dried pod of red pepper 2. spicy dish of beef, chilies, beans, etc.

chili sauce spiced sauce of chopped tomatoes, sweet peppers, onions, etc.

chill n. 1. moderate coldness 2. body coldness, with shivering 3. sudden fear —a. uncomfortably cool —v. make or become cold —**chil′ly** [-LIER, -LIEST]

chill factor combined effect of low temperatures and high winds on exposed skin

chime (chīm) n. usually pl. set of tuned bells —v. sound as a chime

chim′ney n. passage for smoke from a furnace, etc.

chim·pan·zee′ n. medium-sized African ape

chin n. face below the lips —v. [CHINNED, CHINNING] pull (oneself) up until the chin is above a bar being grasped

chi′na n. 1. porcelain, or dishes, etc. made of porcelain 2. earthenware dishes, etc.

chin·chil′la n. 1. small S. American rodent 2. its costly fur

Chi·nese′ n. [pl. -NESE] native or language of China —a. of China

chink n. 1. crack 2. clinking sound —v. to clink

chi′no (chē′-, shē′-) n. [pl. -NOS] 1. strong cotton cloth 2. pl. men's pants of chino

chintz n. glazed, printed cotton cloth

chintz′y a. [-IER, -IEST] [Col.] cheap, stingy, etc.

chip v. [CHIPPED, CHIPPING] break or cut off bits from —n. 1. fragment 2. place where bit is chipped off 3. small disk used in gambling 4. thin slice of food —**chip in** [Col.] contribute

chip′munk n. small striped squirrel

chipped beef dried or smoked beef sliced into shavings

chip′per a. [Col.] lively

chi·rop′o·dy (kə räp′-) n. podiatry —**chi·rop′o·dist** n.

chi′ro·prac′tic (kī′rə-) n. method of treatment by manipulation of body joints, etc. —**chi′ro·prac′tor** n.

chirp v. make short, shrill sounds —n. such a sound

chir′rup v., n. chirp

chis′el (chiz′-) n. tool for chipping wood, stone, etc. —v. 1. chip with a chisel 2. [Col.] swindle —**chis′el·er** n.

chit n. voucher of a sum owed for drink, food, etc.

chit′chat n. small talk

chi′tin (kī′-) n. horny covering of insects, etc.

chit′ter·lings (-lənz) n.pl. pig intestines, used for food: also sp. **chit′lins, chit′lings**

chiv′al·ry (shiv′-) n. 1. medieval system of knighthood 2. courtesy, fairness, etc. —**chiv′al·rous** a.

chives n.pl. plant like the onion with slender leaves used to flavor

chlor′dane n. very poisonous oil used as insecticide: also **chlor′dan** (-dan)

chlo′ride (klôr′-) n. compound of chlorine

chlo′ri·nate v. purify (water) with chlorine

chlo′rine (-rēn) n. greenish gas, a chemical element

chlo′ro·form n. colorless liquid

anesthetic —v. anesthetize or kill with this

chlo·ro·phyll, chlo·ro·phyl (-fil) n. green coloring in plants

chock n., v. block; wedge —adv. completely

chock'-full' a. as full as possible

choc·o·late (chôk'lət, chäk'-) n. 1. ground cacao seeds 2. drink or candy made with this 3. reddish brown

choice n. 1. selection 2. right to choose 3. the one chosen —a. excellent

choir (kwīr) n. group of singers, esp. in a church

choke v. 1. stop the breathing of; suffocate 2. obstruct; clog —n. a choking —choke back hold back (sobs, etc.)

choke collar dog collar that tightens when leash is taut

chok'er n. closefitting necklace

chol'er (käl'-) n. [Now Rare] anger —chol'er·ic a.

chol'er·a (käl'-) n. infectious intestinal disease

cho·les·ter·ol (kə-) n. substance in animal fats, etc.

chomp v. champ

choose v. [CHOSE, CHOSEN, CHOOSING] 1. take; select 2. prefer; decide

choos'y, choos'ey a. [-IER, -IEST] [Col.] fussy in choosing

chop v. [CHOPPED, CHOPPING] 1. cut by blows of sharp tool 2. cut in bits —n. 1. sharp blow 2. slice from rib or loin

chop'per n. 1. one that chops 2. pl. [Sl.] teeth 3. [Col.] helicopter

chop'py a. [-PIER, -PIEST] 1. rough with short, abrupt waves 2. abruptly starting and stopping —chop'pi·ness n.

chops n.pl. 1. jaws 2. flesh about the mouth

chop'sticks n.pl. two sticks held together in one hand, used in some Asian countries in eating

chop su·ey (sōō'ē) American-Chinese stew served with rice

cho'ral (kôr'-) a. of or for a choir or chorus

cho·rale', cho·ral' n. hymn tune 2. choir or chorus

chord n. 1. straight line joining two points on an arc 2. three or more tones sounded together in harmony

chore (chôr) n. daily task

chor'e·og'ra·phy (kôr'-) n. the devising of dances or ballets —chor'e·og'ra·pher n.

chor'is·ter n. choir member

chor'tle (chôr'-) v., n. chuckle or snort

cho'rus n. 1. group of singers or of singers and dancers 2. music for group singing 3. refrain of a song —v. sing or recite in unison

chose pt. of choose

cho'sen pp. of choose —a. selected; choice

chow n. 1. medium-sized Chinese dog 2. [Sl.] food

chow'der n. fish or clam soup with vegetables

chow mein (mān) American-Chinese stew served on fried noodles

Christ Jesus as the Messiah

chris'ten v. 1. baptize 2. name —**chris'ten·ing** n.

Chris'ten·dom n. Christians collectively

Chris'ti·an'i·ty n. religion based on teachings of Jesus — **Chris'tian** a., n.

Christ'mas n. celebration of Jesus' birth; Dec. 25

chro·mat'ic a. 1. of color 2. Music in half tones

chrome n. chromium

chro'mi·um n. hard metal in alloys, a chemical element

chro'mo·some n. any of the microscopic bodies carrying the genes of heredity

chron'ic a. 1. long-lasting or recurring 2. having a chronic illness 3. habitual —**chron'i·cal·ly** adv.

chron'i·cle n. historical record —v. tell the history of — **chron'i·cler** n.

chron'o·log'i·cal a. in order of occurrence —**chron'o·log'i·cal·ly** adv. —**chro·nol'o·gy** n.

chro·nom'e·ter n. very accurate clock or watch

chrys·a·lis (kris'-) n. pupa or its cocoon

chrys·an'the·mum n. plant with ball-shaped flowers

chub n. freshwater fish related to the carp

chub'by a. [-BIER, -BIEST] round and plump —**chub'bi·ness** n.

chuck v. 1. tap playfully 2. toss 3. [Sl.] get rid of —n. 1. tap 2. toss 3. shoulder cut of beef 4. clamplike device as on a lathe

chuck'-full' a. chock-full

chuck'hole n. rough hole in pavement

chuck'le v. laugh softly —n. soft laugh

chuck wagon wagon with kitchen for feeding cowboys

chug n. explosive sound, as of an engine —v. [CHUGGED, CHUGGING] make this sound

chuk'ka boot man's ankle-high boot

chum n. [Col.] close friend —v. [CHUMMED, CHUMMING] [Col.] be chums —**chum'my** [-MIER, -MIEST] a.

chump n. [Col.] fool

chunk n. short, thick piece

chunk'y a. [-IER, -IEST] 1. short and thick 2. stocky 3. full of chunks

church n. 1. building for public worship 2. religious service 3. [usually C-] all Christians, or a Christian sect 4. ecclesiastical government

church'go'er n. one who attends church regularly

church'yard n. yard beside a church, often a cemetery

churl n. rude, surly person — **churl'ish** a.

churn n. device for making butter —v. 1. shake (cream) in a churn to make butter 2. stir about vigorously

chute (shoot) n. 1. inclined passage for sliding things 2. [Col.] parachute

chut'ney (chut'-) n. [pl. -NEYS] relish of fruits, spices, etc.

ci·ca'da (si kā'-) n. large, fly-like insect making a shrill sound

ci'der n. juice pressed from apples

ci·gar' n. roll of tobacco leaves for smoking

cig·a·rette', **cig·a·ret'** n. tobacco cut fine and rolled in paper for smoking

cig·a·ril'lo n. [pl. -LOS] small, thin cigar

cil'i·a (sil'-) n.pl. small hair-like growths

cinch n. 1. saddle girth 2. [Sl.] thing easy to do —v. 1. [Sl.] make sure of

cin·cho'na (sin kō'-) n. tree whose bark yields quinine

cinc'ture (sink'-) n. belt or girdle —v. gird

cin'der n. 1. tiny charred piece of wood, etc. 2. pl. ashes

cin'e·ma n. 1. movie 2. movie theater —**cin'e·mat'ic** a.

cin'e·ma·tog'ra·phy n. art of photography in making movies —**cin'e·ma·tog'ra·pher** n.

cin'na·mon n. brown spice from East Indian tree bark

ci'pher n. 1. zero; 0 2. code 3. key to a code

cir·ca (sur'ka) prep. about; approximately

cir·ca'di·an (sər kā'-) a. of the body rhythms associated with earth's daily rotation

cir'cle n. 1. closed, curved line always equidistant from the center 2. cycle 3. group with interests in common 4. extent; scope —v. form or go in a circle around

cir'cuit (-kit) n. 1. boundary 2. regular, routine journey 3. theater chain 4. path for electric current

cir·cu'i·tous (sər kyōō'-) a. roundabout; indirect

cir'cuit·ry n. system or elements of an electric circuit

cir'cu·lar a. 1. round 2. roundabout —n. advertisement sent to many people

cir'cu·late v. move or spread about —**cir'cu·la·to'ry** a.

cir'cu·la'tion n. 1. movement, as of blood through the body 2. distribution

cir'cum·cise v. cut off the foreskin of —**cir'cum·ci'sion** (-sizh'ən) n.

cir·cum'fer·ence n. distance around a circle, etc.

cir'cum·flex n. pronunciation mark (ˆ)

cir'cum·lo·cu'tion n. roundabout way of talking

cir'cum·nav'i·gate v. sail around (the earth, etc.)

cir'cum·scribe' v. 1. encircle 2. limit; confine

cir'cum·spect a. cautious; discreet —**cir'cum·spec'tion** n.

cir'cum·stance n. 1. connected fact or event 2. pl. conditions affecting one, esp. financial conditions 3. mere chance 4. ceremony —**under no circumstances** never —**cir'cum·stan'tial** (-shəl) a.

cir'cum·vent' v. outwit or prevent by cleverness

cir'cus n. show with acrobats, animals, clowns, etc.

ci·ré (sə rā') a. having a smooth, glossy finish

cir·rho'sis (sə rō'-) n. degenerative disease, esp. of the liver

cir'rus (sir'-) n. fleecy, white cloud formation

cis'tern *n.* large storage tank, esp. for rain water

cit'a·del *n.* fortress

cite *v.* 1. summon by law 2. quote 3. mention as an example 4. mention in praise — **ci·ta'tion** *n.*

cit'i·zen *n.* member of a nation by birth or naturalization —**cit'i·zen·ship'** *n.*

cit'i·zen·ry *n.* all citizens

cit'ric acid weak acid in citrus fruits

cit'ron *n.* lemonlike fruit

cit'ron·el'la *n.* pungent oil that repels insects

cit'rus *n.* orange, lemon, lime, etc. —*a.* of these trees or fruits

cit'y *n.* [*pl.* -IES] large town

civ'et *n.* fatty secretion of an animal (**civet cat**): used in perfume

civ'ic *a.* of a city or citizens

civ'ics *n.* study of civic affairs and duties

civ'il *a.* 1. of citizens 2. polite 3. not military or religious — **civ'il·ly** *adv.*

civil disobedience nonviolent refusal to obey a law on grounds of one's conscience

civil engineering engineering that deals with the building of bridges, roads, etc.

ci·vil'i·an *a., n.* (of a) person not in armed forces

ci·vil'i·ty *n.* 1. courtesy 2. [*pl.* -TIES] polite act

civ'i·li·za'tion *n.* 1. high social and cultural development 2. culture of a certain time or place

civ'i·lize *v.* 1. bring out of savagery or barbarism to a higher cultural level 2. refine —**civ'i·lized** *a.*

civil liberties rights of free speech, assembly, etc.

civil rights rights of all people to equal treatment

civil servant civil service employee

civil service government employees except soldiers, etc.

civil war war between factions of the same nation

civ'vies *n.pl.* [Col.] civilian clothes: also sp. **civ'ies**

clack *v.* make an abrupt, sharp sound —*n.* this sound

clad *v.* pt. & pp. of **clothe** — *a.* clothed; dressed

claim *v.* 1. demand as rightfully one's own 2. require 3. assert —*n.* 1. a claiming 2. right to something 3. something claimed —**claim'ant** *n.*

clair·voy'ance (kler voi'-) *n.* supposed ability to perceive things not in sight —**clair·voy'ant** *a., n.*

clam *n.* a hard-shelled, often edible, bivalve mollusk —*v.* [CLAMMED, CLAMMING] dig for clams —**clam up** [Col.] keep silent

clam'bake *n.* 1. picnic with steamed or baked clams served 2. [Col.] large, noisy party

clam'ber *v.* climb clumsily

clam'my *a.* [-MIER, -MIEST] moist, cold, and sticky

clam'or *n.* 1. uproar 2. noisy demand —*v.* make a clamor — **clam'or·ous** *a.*

clamp *n.* device for clasping things together —*v.* fasten with a clamp

clan *n.* 1. group of related families 2. group with interests in common

clan·des'tine (-t'n) *a.* secret

clang *v.* make a loud ringing sound —*n.* this sound

clan'gor *n.* series of clangs

clank *v.* make a sharp metallic sound —*n.* this sound

clap *v.* [CLAPPED, CLAPPING] 1. make the sound of flat surfaces struck together 2. strike together, as the hands in applauding —*n.* sound or act of clapping

clap·board (klab'ərd) *n.* thin, tapered board for siding

clap'per *n.* thing that makes a clapping sound, as the tongue of a bell

clap'trap *n.* insincere, empty talk, meant to get applause

claque (klak) *n.* group paid to applaud at a play, opera, etc.

clar'et *n.* dry red wine

clar·i·fy *v.* [-FIED, -FYING] make or become clear —**clar'i·fi·ca'tion** *n.*

clar·i·net' *n.* a single-reed, woodwind instrument —**clar'i·net'ist, clar'i·net'tist** *n.*

clar'i·on *a.* clear and shrill

clar'i·ty *n.* clearness

clash *v.* 1. collide noisily 2. disagree —*n.* a clashing

clasp *n.* 1. device to fasten things 2. embrace 3. grip of the hand —*v.* 1. fasten 2. hold tightly

class *n.* 1. group of like people or things; sort 2. social rank 3. group of students in school 4. quality 5. [Sl.] excellence —*v.* classify

clas'sic *a.* 1. most excellent 2. in the style of ancient Greece or Rome —*n.* a book, work of art, etc. of highest excellence — **the classics** writings of ancient Greece and Rome

clas'si·cal *a.* 1. classic 2. of such music as symphonies, concertos, etc.

classified advertising advertising under such listings as *help wanted*

clas'si·fy *v.* [-FIED, -FYING] 1. arrange in classes 2. designate as secret —**clas'si·fi·ca'tion** *n.*

class'mate *n.* member of the same class at a school

class'room *n.* room where a class is taught at a school

class'y *a.* [-IER, -IEST] [Sl.] first-class; elegant

clat'ter *n.* series of sharp noises —*v.* make a clatter

clause *n.* 1. part of a sentence, with a subject and verb 2. provision in a document

claus'tro·pho'bi·a *n.* fear of enclosed places

clav'i·chord (-kôrd) *n.* early kind of piano

clav'i·cle *n.* bone connecting the breastbone with the shoulder blade

cla·vier (klə vir') *n.* 1. keyboard, as of a piano 2. any stringed keyboard instrument

claw *n.* 1. sharp nail of an animal's or bird's foot 2. pincers of a lobster, etc. —*v.* scratch as with claws

clay *n.* firm, plastic earth, used for pottery, etc.

clean *a.* 1. free from dirt 2.

sinless 3. sportsmanlike 4. neat and tidy 5. free from flaws 6. thorough —adv. completely —v. make clean — **clean up** 1. make neat 2. [Col.] to finish 3. [Sl.] make much profit —**clean'ly** adv. —**clean'ness** n.

clean'-cut' a. 1. clearly outlined 2. well-formed 3. trim, neat, etc.

clean'er n. one that cleans; esp., one who dry-cleans

clean'ly (klen'-) a. [-LIER, -LIEST] 1. having clean habits 2. always kept clean —**clean'li-ness** n.

cleanse (klenz) v. make clean or pure —**cleans'er** n.

clear a. 1. free from clouds 2. transparent 3. distinct 4. obvious 5. free from charges, guilt, obstruction, blemishes, debt, etc. —adv. 1. in a clear way 2. completely —v. 1. make or become clear 2. pass or leap over 3. make as profit —**clear away** (or **off**) remove —**clear out** [Col.] depart —**clear up** make or become clear —**in the clear** 1. in the open 2. [Col.] guiltless —**clear'ly** adv. —**clear'ness** n.

clear'ance n. clear space between two objects

clear'ing n. plot of land cleared of trees

cleat n. piece used to give firmness or secure footing

cleav'age n. 1. a cleaving; dividing 2. cleft; division

cleave v. [CLEAVED or CLEFT or CLOVE, CLEAVED or CLEFT or CLOVEN] split; sever

cleave v. adhere; cling

cleav'er n. butcher's cutting tool

clef n. musical symbol to indicate pitch

cleft a., n. split

clem-a-tis (klem'ə tis) n. vine with colorful flowers

clem'ent a. 1. lenient 2. mild —**clem'en-cy** n.

clench v. close tightly

cler'gy n. [pl. -GIES] ministers, priests, rabbis, etc. collectively

cler'gy-man n. [pl. -MEN] minister, priest, rabbi, etc.

cler'ic (kler'-) n. clergyman

cler'i-cal a. 1. of the clergy 2. of clerks

clerk n. 1. office worker who keeps records, etc. 2. salesperson in a store —v. work as a clerk

clev'er a. 1. skillful 2. intelligent —**clev'er-ness** n.

clew n. 1. ball of thread, etc. 2. clue

cli-ché (klē shā') n. trite expression or idea

click n. slight, sharp sound —v. make a click

cli'ent n. 1. person or company for whom a lawyer, etc. acts 2. customer

cli-en-tele' (-tel'-) n. clients

cliff n. high, steep rock

cliff'hang'er n. a suspenseful movie, story, etc.

cli'mate n. average weather conditions —**cli-mat'ic** a.

cli'max n. highest point, as of interest or excitement; culmination —v. bring to a climax —**cli-mac'tic** a.

climb v. go up; ascend —n. a

climbing —**climb down** descend —**climb'er** n.

clinch v. **1.** fasten (a nail) by bending the end **2.** settle (an argument, etc.) **3.** Boxing grip with the arms **4.** [Sl.] to embrace —n. a clinching

cling v. [CLUNG, CLINGING] **1.** hold fast **2.** stay near

clin'ic n. **1.** place where medical specialists practice as a group **2.** outpatient department —**clin'i-cal** a.

clink n. short, tinkling sound —v. make this sound

clink'er n. fused mass left in burning coal

clip v. [CLIPPED, CLIPPING] **1.** cut short **2.** cut the hair of **3.** [Col.] hit sharply **4.** fasten together **5.** move rapidly —n. **1.** a clipping **2.** [Col.] rapid pace **3.** fastening device

clip'per n. **1.** clipping tool **2.** fast sailing ship

clip'ping n. piece cut out, as an item from a newspaper

clique (klēk) n. small, exclusive circle of people —**cliqu'ish** a.

clit'o·ris (klit'-) n. small, sensitive organ of the vulva

cloak n. **1.** loose, sleeveless outer garment **2.** thing that conceals —v. conceal; hide

clob'ber n. [Sl.] **1.** to hit repeatedly **2.** defeat decisively

clock n. device for measuring and showing time

clock'wise adv., a. in the direction in which the hands of a clock rotate

clock'work n. mechanism of a clock —**like clockwork** very regularly

clod n. **1.** lump of earth **2.** dull, stupid fellow

clod'hop'per n. **1.** clumsy, stupid fellow **2.** coarse, heavy shoe

clog n. **1.** thing that hinders **2.** heavy shoe —v. [CLOGGED, CLOGGING] **1.** hinder **2.** block up

clois'ter n. **1.** monastery or convent **2.** covered walk along a wall —v. seclude

clomp v. walk heavily or noisily

clone n. exact duplicate of an organism produced by replacing the nucleus of an ovum with the nucleus of a body cell —v. produce as a clone

clop n. sound as of a hoofbeat —v. [CLOPPED, CLOPPING] make such sounds

close (klōs) a. **1.** confined **2.** secretive **3.** stingy **4.** humid; stuffy **5.** adjacent; near together **6.** dense **7.** near to the surface **8.** intimate **9.** careful **10.** thorough **11.** nearly alike; nearly equal —adv. in a close way or position —n. enclosed place —**close'ly** adv. —**close'ness** n.

close (klōz) v. **1.** shut or stop up **2.** end **3.** come close, as to attack —n. end —**close down** (or **up**) stop entirely —**close in** surround —**close out** dispose of (goods) by sale

close call (klōs) [Col.] narrow escape from danger: also **close shave**

closed circuit TV system only for receivers connected by cable to its circuit

close'fit'ting a. fitting tightly

close'-knit' a. closely united

clos'et (kläz'-) n. small room for clothes, etc. —v. shut in a room for private talk

close'-up' (klōs'-) n. photograph, movie, etc. taken at very close range

clot n. coagulated mass, as of blood —v. [CLOTTED, CLOTTING] coagulate

cloth (klôth) n. 1. fabric of cotton, wool, synthetics, etc. 2. tablecloth, dustcloth, etc.

clothe (klōth) v. [alt. pt. & pp. CLAD] to dress

clothes (klōz, klōthz) n. clothing; wearing apparel

cloth·ier (klōth'yər) n. dealer in clothes or cloth

cloth'ing (klōth'-) n. wearing apparel; garments

clo'ture (-chər) n. end of debate by putting a bill to the vote

cloud n. 1. mass of vapor in the sky 2. mass of smoke, dust, etc. 3. thing that darkens, etc. —v. darken as with clouds, gloom, etc. —**cloud'y** [-IER, -IEST] a.

cloud'burst n. sudden heavy rain

clout n., v. [Col.] hit

clove n. 1. pungent spice 2. segment of a bulb

clo'ven a. split

clo'ver n. small forage plant with triple leaves

clo'ver·leaf n. highway intersection with curving ramps to ease traffic

clown n. 1. clumsy person 2.

comic entertainer as in a circus —v. act like a clown

cloy v. surfeit by excess

club n. 1. stick used as a weapon, or in games 2. social group 3. playing card marked with a ♣ —v. [CLUBBED, CLUBBING] strike with a club

club'foot n. [pl. -FEET] congenitally misshapen foot

cluck n. low, clicking sound made by a hen —v. make this sound

clue n. hint or fact that helps solve a mystery —v. provide with clues

clump n. 1. lump 2. cluster —v. tramp heavily

clum'sy a. [-SIER, -SIEST] awkward —**clum'si·ly** adv

clung pt. & pp. of **cling**

clunk'er n. [Sl.] old machine or car in poor repair

clus'ter n., v. group; bunch

clutch v. 1. snatch (at) 2. hold tightly —n. 1. pl. control 2. grip 3. device for engaging and disengaging an engine

clut'ter n., v. disorder

co- pref. 1. together 2. joint 3. equally

coach n. 1. big, four-wheeled carriage 2. railroad passenger car 3. bus 4. lowest-priced class of airline seats 5. trainer of athletes, singers, etc. —v. be a coach

co·ad'ju·tor (-aj'ə tər, -ə jōō'-) n. assistant, esp. to a bishop

co·ag'u·late v. thicken to a semisolid; clot —**co·ag'u·la'tion** n.

coal n. 1. black mineral used as fuel 2. ember

co·a·lesce (kō ə les') v. unite into a single body —**co·a·les'·cence** n.

co'a·li'tion n. union

coal oil kerosene

coal tar black, thick liquid made from coal, used in dyes, medicines, etc.

coarse a. 1. made up of large particles 2. rough 3. vulgar — **coarse'ly** adv. —**coarse'·ness** n.

coars'en v. make or become coarse

coast n. seashore —v. 1. slide down an incline 2. continue moving on momentum — **coast'al** a.

coast'er n. small tray put under a glass

coast guard group defending a nation's coasts, aiding ships in distress, etc.

coast'line n. outline of a coast

coat n. 1. sleeved outer garment opening down the front 2. natural covering 3. layer, as of paint —v. cover with a layer

coat'ing n. surface layer

coat of arms heraldic symbols, as on a family escutcheon

coat'tail n. either half of the lower back part of a coat

co·au'thor n. joint author

coax v. urge or get by soothing words, etc.

co·ax'i·al cable cable for sending telephone, telegraph, and television impulses

cob n. corncob

co·balt (kō'bôlt) n. gray metallic chemical element

cob'ble v. mend (shoes)

cob'bler n. 1. one who mends shoes 2. deep-dish fruit pie

cob'ble·stone n. rounded stone once used for paving

co'bra n. poisonous snake of Asia and Africa

cob'web n. spider web

co·caine', co·cain' n. drug used as a narcotic or anesthetic

coch·i·neal (käch'ə nēl') n. red dye from tropical insect

coch·le·a (käk'lē ə) n. spiral part of the inner ear

cock n. 1. rooster 2. any male bird 3. faucet 4. cone-shaped pile —v. 1. tilt 2. turn alertly 3. set hammer of (a gun) to fire

cock·ade' n. badge on a hat

cock·a·too' n. crested Australian parrot

cocked hat three-cornered hat

cock'er·el n. young rooster

cock'er (spaniel) small spaniel with drooping ears

cock'eyed a. 1. cross-eyed 2. [Sl.] awry 3. [Sl.] absurd

cock'le n. edible shellfish — **cockles of one's heart** one's deepest feelings

cock'pit n. space for pilot in a small airplane

cock'roach n. flat-bodied, dark insect, a kitchen pest

cocks'comb n. red, fleshy growth on a rooster's head

cock'sure' a. self-confident

cock'tail n. 1. mixed alcoholic drink 2. appetizer

cock'y a. [-IER, -IEST] [Col.] conceited

co·co (kō'kō) n. [pl. -cos] coconut palm or coconut

co'coa (-kō) *n.* **1.** powder made from roasted cacao seeds **2.** drink made of this

co'co·nut, co'coa·nut *n.* hard-shelled fruit of a palm tree, with edible white meat

co·coon' *n.* silky case of certain insect larvae

cod *n.* N. Atlantic food fish: also **cod'fish**

co'da *n. Mus.* end passage

cod'dle *v.* pamper

code *n.* **1.** body of laws **2.** set of principles **3.** set of signals or symbols for messages —*v.* put in a code

co'deine (-dēn) *n.* sedative drug derived from opium

codg'er *n.* [Col.] odd person

cod'i·cil (-s'l) *n.* addition to a will

cod'i·fy *v.* [-FIED, -FYING] arrange (laws) in a code —**cod'i·fi·ca'tion** *n.*

co'ed', co'-ed' *n.* [Col.] girl at a coeducational college

co'ed·u·ca'tion *n.* education of both sexes in the same classes —**co'ed·u·ca'tion·al** *a.*

co·e'qual *a., n.* equal

co·erce' (-urs') *v.* force; compel —**co·er'cion** *n.* —**co·er'cive** *a.*

co·e'val *a., n.* contemporary

co·ex·ist' *v.* **1.** exist together **2.** live together peacefully —**co·ex·ist'ence** *n.*

cof'fee *n.* **1.** drink made from roasted seeds of a tropical shrub **2.** the seeds

coffee break brief respite from work for having coffee, etc.

cof'fee·cake *n.* cake or roll to be eaten with coffee, etc.

cof'fee·pot *n.* pot with a spout, for brewing or serving coffee

coffee table small, low table for serving refreshments

cof'fer *n.* **1.** chest for money, etc. **2.** *pl.* treasury

cof'fin *n.* case in which to bury a dead person

cog *n.* tooth on a cogwheel

co'gent (-jant) *a.* convincing —**co'gen·cy** *n.*

cog'i·tate (käj'-) *v.* think (about) —**cog'i·ta'tion** *n.*

co'gnac (-nyak) *n.* brandy

cog'nate *a.* related; kindred

cog·ni'tion *n.* knowledge

cog'ni·zance *n.* awareness; notice —**cog'ni·zant** *a.*

cog·no'men *n.* surname

cog'wheel' *n.* wheel rimmed with teeth, as in a gear

co·hab'it *v.* live together as if husband and wife —**co·hab'i·ta'tion** *n.*

co·here' *v.* **1.** stick together **2.** be connected logically

co·her'ent *a.* clear and intelligible —**co·her'ence** *n.*

co·he'sion (-zhan) *n.* a sticking together —**co·he'sive** *a.*

co'ho *n.* [*pl.* -HO, -HOS] small salmon

co'hort *n.* **1.** group, esp. of soldiers **2.** an associate

coif (koif) *n.* **1.** closefitting cap **2.** (kwäf) hair style

coif·fure (kwä fyoor') *n.* **1.** headdress **2.** hair style

coil *v.* to wind in a spiral —*n.* anything coiled

coin *n.* stamped metal piece, issued as money —*v.* 1. make into coins 2. make up (new word) —**coin'age** *n.*

co·in·cide' *v.* 1. occur at the same time 2. agree; match —**co·in'ci·dent** *a.*

co·in'ci·dence *n.* 1. à coinciding 2. accidental occurrence together of events —**co·in'ci·den'tal** *a.* —**co·in·ci·den'tal·ly** *adv.*

co'i·tus *n.* sexual intercourse: also **co·i'tion**

coke *n.* fuel made by removing gases from coal

co'la *n.* carbonated soft drink with flavoring from the nut of an African tree

col'an·der (kul'-) *n.* perforated bowl used as a strainer

cold *a.* 1. low in temperature 2. chilly 3. unfriendly 4. without feeling 5. [Col.] unprepared 6. [Sl.] perfectly memorized 7. [Sl.] unconscious —*n.* 1. absence of heat 2. cold weather 3. virus infection causing sneezing, coughing, etc. —**catch cold** become ill with a cold —**have** (or **get**) **cold feet** [Col.] be (or become) timid —**in the cold** neglected —**cold'ly** *adv.*

cold cream creamy cleanser for the skin

cold cuts variety of sliced cold meats and cheeses

cold shoulder [Col.] snub

cold sore blisters about the mouth during a cold

cold turkey [Sl.] 1. abrupt withdrawal of drugs from an addict 2. without preparing

cold war conflict between nations without actual war

cole'slaw *n.* salad made of shredded raw cabbage

col'ic *n.* sharp bowel pain

col·i·se'um *n.* large stadium

co·li'tis (kō li'-) *n.* inflammation of the colon

col·lab'o·rate *v.* 1. work together 2. help the enemy —**col·lab'o·ra'tion** *n.* —**col·lab'o·ra'tor** *n.*

col·lage' (kə läzh') *n.* bits of objects pasted on a surface to make an art work

col·lapse' *v.* 1. fall in or shrink in 2. break down; fail 3. fold together —*n.* a collapsing —**col·laps'i·ble** *a.*

col'lar *n.* a band, or the part of a garment, about the neck —*v.* 1. put a collar on 2. seize by the collar

col'lar·bone *n.* clavicle

col'lard *n.* kind of kale

col·late' *v.* compare (texts)

col·lat'er·al *a.* 1. of the same descent but in a different line 2. parallel 3. secondary —*n.* thing pledged as security for a loan

col'league (-lēg) *n.* fellow worker; associate

col·lect' *v.* 1. gather together 2. get payment for 3. regain control of (oneself) —*a., adv.* with the receiver paying —**col·lect'a·ble, col·lect'i·ble** *a.* —**col·lec'tor** *n.*

col·lect'ed *a.* 1. gathered together 2. calm

col·lec'tion *n.* 1. a collecting 2. things collected

col·lec'tive *a.* 1. of or as a group 2. singular in form, but referring to a group —*n.* 1. a collective enterprise 2. collective noun

col'lege *n.* 1. school of higher learning or special instruction 2. group with certain powers —**col·le'gi·an** (-jən) *n.* —**col·le'giate** (-jət) *a.*

col·lide' *v.* crash or clash

col'lie *n.* large, long-haired sheep dog

col·li'sion (-lizh'ən) *n.* 1. a colliding 2. conflict

col·lo'di·on (-dē ən) *n.* solution that dries into tough, elastic film

col'loid *n.* substance of insoluble particles suspended in a fluid —**col·loi'dal** *a.*

col·lo'qui·al (-kwē-) *a.* used in informal talk and writing —**col·lo'qui·al·ism** *n.*

col·lo'qui·um (-kwē-) *n.* [*pl.* -QUIA, -QUIUMS] organized conference or seminar

col·lo·quy (käl'ə kwē) *n.* [*pl.* -QUIES] conversation

col·lu'sion *n.* secret agreement for a wrong purpose

co·logne' (-lōn') *n.* scented liquid like diluted perfume

co'lon *n.* 1. mark of punctuation (:) 2. lower part of the large intestine

colo·nel (kur'n'l) *n.* officer above lieutenant colonel

co·lo'ni·al·ism *n.* economic exploitation of colonies, etc. —**co·lo'ni·al·ist** *n.*, *a.*

col·on·nade' *n.* row of evenly spaced columns

col'o·ny *n.* [*pl.* -NIES] 1. group of settlers from another, distant land 2. land ruled by a distant country 3. community with common interests —**co·lo'ni·al** *a.* —**col'o·nist** *n.* —**col'o·nize** *v.*

col'or *n.* 1. effect on the eyes of light waves of different wavelengths 2. pigment 3. complexion 4. *pl.* a flag 5. outward appearance 6. picturesque quality —*v.* 1. paint or dye 2. alter or distort 3. blush —**show one's colors** show one's true self

col·or·a'tion *n.* coloring

col'o·ra·tu'ra (-tyoor'ə) soprano with high, flexible voice: in full, **coloratura soprano**

col'or·blind' *a.* 1. unable to distinguish (certain) colors 2. not influenced by race

col'or·cast *n.* color TV broadcast

col'ored *a.* Negro

col'or·fast' *a.* with color not subject to fading or running

col'or·ful *a.* picturesque

col'or·ing *n.* 1. pigment 2. way a thing is colored 3. false appearance

col'or·less *a.* dull

co·los'sal *a.* huge; immense

co·los'sus *n.* huge or important person or thing

col'our *n.*, *v.* color: Br. sp.

colt *n.* young male horse

colt'ish *a.* frisky

col'um·bine *n.* plant with showy, spurred flowers

col'umn (-əm) *n.* 1. slender

upright structure 2. vertical section of printed matter 3. line of troops, etc. 4. regular feature article in a newspaper

col'um·nist n. writer of a column (n. 4)

com- *pref.* with; together

co'ma (kō'-) n. deep unconsciousness, as from injury — **com·a·tose** (kŏm'ə tōs) a.

comb (kōm) n. 1. flat, toothed object for grooming the hair 2. cockscomb 3. honeycomb —v. 1. groom with a comb 2. search

com'bat v. (*also* kəm bat'), n. fight; struggle —**com'bat·ant** a., n.

com·bat'ive a. ready or eager to fight

com·bi·na'tion n. 1. a combining 2. combined things, groups, etc. 3. series of numbers dialed to open a lock

com·bine' v. join; unite —n. (kăm'bīn) 1. machine for harvesting and threshing grain 2. [Col.] commercial or political alliance

com'bo n. [*pl.* -BOS] [Col.] small jazz ensemble

com·bus'ti·ble a., n. inflammable (thing)

com·bus'tion n. a burning

come v. [CAME, COME, COMING] 1. move from "there" to "here" 2. arrive or appear 3. extend; reach 4. happen 5. result 6. become 7. be available 8. amount (*to*) —**come about** happen —**come around** 1. recover 2. yield —**come by** get —**come into** inherit —**come off** 1. end up 2. [Col.] prove

effective, etc. —**come through** [Sl.] do or give what is wanted —**come to** gain consciousness —**come up** arise in discussion

come'back' n. 1. [Col.] a return, as to power 2. [Sl.] witty answer

co·me'di·an n. actor who plays comic parts —**co·me'di·enne'** (-en') n.fem.

come'down' n. loss of status

come'·dy n. [*pl.* -DIES] a humorous play

come'ly (kum'lē) a. [-LIER, -LIEST] attractive —**come'li·ness** n.

come'-on' n. [Sl.] inducement

co·mes'ti·bles n.pl. food

com'et n. starlike body with a luminous tail

come'up'pance n. [Col.] deserved punishment

com'fort (kum'-) v. soothe in distress; console —n. 1. relief from distress 2. one that comforts 3. ease

com'fort·a·ble a. 1. providing comfort 2. at ease 3. [Col.] sufficient to satisfy —**com'fort·a·bly** adv.

com'fort·er n. 1. one that comforts 2. a quilt

com'fy a. [-FIER, -FIEST] [Col.] comfortable

com'ic (kăm'-) a. 1. of comedy 2. funny: also **comical** —n. 1. comedian 2. *pl.* [Col.] comic strips

comic strip cartoon series, as in a newspaper

com'ing a. 1. approaching; next 2. promising success —n. arrival; approach

com'i·ty (käm'-) *n.* [*pl.* -TIES] courtesy

com'ma *n.* mark of punctuation (,)

com·mand' *v.* 1. to order 2. to control 3. deserve and get —*n.* 1. an order 2. control 3. military force, naval force, etc. under someone's control

com·man·dant' *n.* commanding officer

com·man·deer' *v.* seize for military or government use

com·mand'er *n.* 1. leader; officer 2. naval officer below a captain

commander in chief top commander of a nation's armed forces

com·mand'ment *n.* command; law

com·man'do *n.* [*pl.* -DOS, -DOES] member of a small force for raiding enemy territory

command post field headquarters of a military unit

com·mem'o·rate' *v.* honor the memory of —**com·mem'o·ra'tion** *n.*

com·mence' *v.* begin

com·mence'ment *n.* 1. beginning 2. graduation ceremony of a school, etc.

com·mend' *v.* 1. entrust 2. recommend 3. praise —**com·mend'a·ble** *a.* —**com'men·da'tion** *n.*

com·mend'a·to'ry *a.* praising or recommending

com·men'su·ra·ble (-shə-) *a.* measurable by the same standard or measure

com·men'su·rate (-shə rit) *a.* equal or proportionate

com'ment *n.* 1. explanatory note 2. remark 3. talk —*v.* make comments

com'men·ta'ry (-ter'-) *n.* [*pl.* -IES] series of explanatory notes or remarks

com'men·tate *v.* perform as a commentator

com'men·ta'tor *n.* news analyst, as on TV

com'merce *n.* trade on a large scale

com·mer'cial (-shəl) *a.* 1. connected with commerce 2. done for profit —*n.* Radio & TV paid advertisement —**com·mer'cial·ism** *n.*

com·mer'cial·ize' *v.* put on a profit-making basis —**com·mer'cial·i·za'tion** *n.*

com·min'gle *v.* mix; blend

com·mis'er·ate' (-miz'-) *v.* sympathize (with)

com'mis·sar *n.* formerly, government department head in the Soviet Union

com'mis·sar'y (-ser'-) *n.* store in an army camp for the sale of food, etc.

com·mis'sion *n.* 1. authority to act 2. group chosen to do something 3. percentage of a sale allotted to the agent 4. military officer's certificate of rank —*v.* 1. give a commission to 2. authorize —**in** (or **out of**) **commission** (not) usable

com·mis'sion·er *n.* governmental department head

com·mit' *v.* [-MITTED, -MITTING] 1. put in custody 2. do 3. pledge; bind —**com·mit'ment** *n.*

com·mit'tee n. group chosen to do something

com·mode' n. 1. chest of drawers 2. toilet

com·mo'di·ous a. spacious

com·mod'i·ty n. [pl. -TIES] anything bought and sold

com'mo·dore n. former naval rank

com'mon a. 1. shared by all 2. general 3. usual; ordinary 4. vulgar 5. designating a noun that refers to any of a group —n. also pl. town's public land —**in common** shared by all —**com'mon·ly** adv.

com'mon·al·ty n. [pl. -TIES] common people; public

common carrier transportation company

common denominator characteristic in common

com'mon·er n. person not of the nobility

common law unwritten law based on custom, usage, etc.

common market association of countries in economic union

com'mon·place n. 1. trite remark 2. anything ordinary — a. ordinary

common pleas civil and criminal court in some States

common sense good sense or practical judgment

com'mon·weal (-wēl) n. public welfare

com'mon·wealth n. 1. people of a state 2. democracy or republic

com·mo'tion n. turmoil

com·mu'nal (or kə myōō'-) a. 1. of a commune 2. of the community; public 3. with common ownership of property —**com·mu'nal·ly** adv.

com·mune' v. talk intimately —n. (käm'-) small group living communally

com·mu'ni·cate v. 1. transmit 2. give or exchange (information) 3. have a meaningful relationship 4. be connected —**com·mu'ni·ca·ble** a. —**com·mu'ni·ca'tive** a.

com·mu'ni·ca'tion n. 1. a communicating or means of doing this 2. message, etc.

com·mun'ion n. 1. a sharing or being close 2. group of the same religious faith 3. [C-] see **Holy Communion**

com·mu'ni·qué (-kā') n. official communication

com'mu·nism n. 1. theory or system of common ownership of property 2. [C-] socialism of Marx, Lenin, etc. —**com'mu·nist** n., a.

com·mu'ni·ty n. [pl. -TIES] 1. body of people living in the same place 2. a sharing in common

community college junior college for a certain community

com·mute' v. 1. lessen (a punishment, etc.) 2. travel by train, etc. to and from work —**com·mut'er** n.

com·pact' a. 1. firmly packed 2. taking little space 3. terse —v. 1. pack or join firmly together 2. compress; condense —n. (käm'-) 1. small case for face powder, etc. 2. smaller model of car 3. agreement —**com·pact'ness** n.

com·pac'tor n. device that compresses trash

com·pan'ion n. 1. comrade; associate 2. thing that matches another —**com·pan'ion·a·ble** a. —**com·pan'ion·ship** n.

com·pan'ion·way n. stairway from a ship's deck

com'pa·ny n. [pl. -NIES] 1. group of people associated for some purpose 2. guest(s) 3. military unit —**keep company** 1. associate (with) 2. go together, as a couple intending to marry

com'pa·ra·ble a. allowing or worthy of comparison

com·par'a·tive a. 1. involving comparison 2. relative —n. the second degree of comparison of adjectives and adverbs —**com·par'a·tive·ly** adv.

com·pare' v. 1. liken (to) 2. examine for similarities or differences 3. be worth comparing (with) 4. show three degrees in form, as *long, longer, longest* —**beyond compare** without equal —**com·par'i·son** n.

com·part'ment n. section partitioned off

com'pass (kum'-) n. 1. instrument for drawing circles, etc. 2. range; extent 3. instrument for showing direction —v. go around

com·pas'sion n. pity —**com·pas'sion·ate** (-it) a.

com·pat'i·ble a. getting along or going well together

com·pa'tri·ot n. fellow countryman

com·peer' n. peer or comrade

com·pel' v. [-PELLED, -PEL-LING] to force

com·pen'di·um n. [pl. -UMS, -A] comprehensive summary

com'pen·sate v. 1. make up for; pay —**com'pen·sa'tion** n.

com·pete' v. 1. vie; rival 2. take part (in a contest)

com'pe·tent a. 1. capable; able 2. adequate —**com'pe·tence** n.

com'pe·ti'tion (-tish'ən) n. 1. a competing; rivalry, as in business 2. contest; match —**com·pet'i·tive** a.

com·pet'i·tor n. rival, as in business

com·pile' v. compose by collecting from various sources —**com·pi·la'tion** n.

com·pla'cen·cy n. 1. contentment 2. smugness Also **com·pla'cence** —**com·pla'cent** a.

com·plain' v. 1. express pain, dissatisfaction, etc. 2. make an accusation

com·plain'ant n. plaintiff

com·plaint' n. 1. a complaining 2. cause for complaining 3. ailment

com·plai·sant (-plā'z'nt, -s'nt) a. obliging

com·plect'ed a. [Col.] complexioned

com'ple·ment (-mənt) n. 1. that which completes 2. entirety —v. (-ment') make complete —**com'ple·men'ta·ry** a.

com·plete' a. 1. lacking no parts 2. finished 3. thorough; perfect —v. make complete —**com·plete'ly** adv. —**com·ple'tion** n.

com·plex' (or käm'pleks) a. 1.

having two or more parts **2.** complicated —*n.* (käm′-) **1.** complex whole **2.** unified grouping **3.** group of unconscious impulses **4.** loosely, an obsession —**com·plex′i·ty** [*pl.* -TIES] *n.*

com·plex′ion (-plek′shən) *n.* **1.** color or texture of the skin **2.** nature; aspect

com·plex′ioned *a.* having a (specified) complexion

com·pli′ance *n.* **1.** a complying **2.** tendency to give in — **com·pli′ant** *a.*

com·pli·cate *v.* make difficult or involved —**com′pli·cat′ed** *a.* —**com′pli·ca′tion** *n.*

com·plic′i·ty (-plis′-) *n.* partnership in wrongdoing

com′pli·ment *n.* **1.** something said in praise **2.** *pl.* respects — *v.* (-ment′) pay a compliment to

com·pli·men′ta·ry *a.* **1.** giving praise **2.** given free

com·ply′ *v.* [-PLIED, -PLYING] conform (*with* rules)

com·po′nent *a.* serving as part of a whole —*n.* ingredient; element

com·port′ *v.* **1.** to conduct (oneself) **2.** accord (*with*) — **com·port′ment** *n.*

com·pose′ *v.* **1.** make by combining **2.** put in proper form **3.** write (a poem, etc.) **4.** make calm **5.** set (type)

com·posed′ *a.* calm

com·pos′ite (-päz′-) *n., a.* (thing) formed of distinct parts

com·po·si′tion (-zish′ən) *n.* **1.** composing of stories or songs **2.** makeup of something **3.** story or song

com·pos′i·tor (-päz′-) *n.* one who sets type

com′post *n.* rotting vegetation used as fertilizer

com·po′sure (-zhər) *n.* calmness; self-possession

com·pote (-pōt) *n.* **1.** stewed fruit **2.** stemmed dish

com·pound′ *v.* **1.** combine **2.** compute (compound interest) **3.** intensify by adding new parts —*a.* (käm′-) with two or more parts —*n.* (käm′-) **1.** substance with combined elements **2.** enclosed space

compound interest interest paid on both the principal and the accumulated unpaid interest

com′pre·hend′ *v.* **1.** understand **2.** include —**com′pre·hen′si·ble** *a.* —**com′pre·hen′sion** *n.*

com′pre·hen′sive *a.* wide in scope; inclusive

com·press′ *v.* **1.** press tight **2.** put (air) under pressure —*n.* (käm′pres) wet pad, put on skin —**com·pres′sion** *n.*

com·pres′sor *n.* machine for compressing air, gas, etc.

com·prise′ *v.* **1.** include **2.** consist of **3.** make up; form: a loose usage

com′pro·mise *n.* **1.** settlement made with concessions **2.** something midway —*v.* **1.** settle by compromise **2.** make suspect

comp·trol′ler (kən-) *n.* one who controls (*sense* 1)

com·pul′sion *n.* a forcing or

being forced —**com·pul'sive** a.

com·pul'so·ry a. 1. required 2. compelling

com·punc'tion n. uneasy feeling prompted by guilt

com·pute' v. calculate; figure —**com'pu·ta'tion** n.

com·put'er n. electronic machine that rapidly calculates or correlates data —**com·put'er·ize** v.

com'rade (-rad) n. 1. close friend 2. associate —**com'rade·ship** n.

con adv. against —v. [CONNED, CONNING] 1. study carefully 2. [Sl.] swindle —n. 1. opposing reason, vote, etc. 2. [Sl.] convict

con·cat'e·na'tion n. connected series, as of events

con·cave' a. curved like the inside of a sphere —**con·cav'i·ty** (-kav'-) n.

con·ceal' v. 1. hide 2. keep secret —**con·ceal'ment** n.

con·cede' v. 1. admit as true 2. grant as a right

con·ceit' n. 1. vanity; pride 2. fanciful notion

con·ceit'ed a. vain

con·ceive' v. 1. become pregnant 2. think of 3. understand —**con·ceiv'a·ble** a.

con·cen'trate v. 1. fix one's attention, etc. (on) 2. increase, as in density —n. concentrated substance —**con·cen·tra'tion** n.

concentration camp prison camp for political foes, ethnic minorities, etc.

con·cen'tric a. having a common center, as circles

con'cept n. idea; notion

con·cep'tion n. 1. a conceiving 2. concept

con·cep'tu·al a. of conception or concepts

con·cep'tu·al·ize' v. form a concept of

con·cern' v. be related to; involve —n. 1. business 2. regard 3. worry

con·cerned' a. 1. involved or interested 2. anxious

con·cern'ing prep. relating to

con·cert' n. 1. agreement 2. musical performance —**in concert** in unison

con·cert'ed a. combined

con'cer·ti'na (-tē'-) n. small accordion

con'cert·ize v. perform as a soloist in concerts on a tour

con·cer'to (-cher'-) n. [pl. -TOS, -TI (-tē)] composition for solo instrument(s) and orchestra

con·ces'sion n. 1. a conceding 2. thing conceded 3. franchise, as for selling food

con·ces'sion·aire' (-er') n. holder of a concession (sense 3)

conch (käŋk, känch) n. large spiral sea shell

con'ci·erge' (-sē urzh') n. custodian, as of an apartment house

con·cil'i·ar a. of or from a council

con·cil'i·ate v. make friendly —**con·cil'i·a'tion** n. —**con·cil'i·a'tor** n. —**con·cil'i·a·to'ry** a.

con·cise' *a.* short and clear; terse —con·cise'ly *adv.*

con'clave *n.* private meeting

con·clude' *v.* 1. finish 2. decide 3. arrange

con·clu'sion *n.* 1. end 2. judgment 3. outcome —in conclusion in closing

con·clu'sive *a.* decisive

con·coct' *v.* prepare or plan — con·coc'tion *n.*

con·com'i·tant *a.* accompanying —*n.* concomitant thing

con'cord *n.* 1. agreement 2. peaceful relations

con·cord'ance *n.* 1. agreement 2. complete list of the words used in a book

con·cord'ant *a.* agreeing

con·cor'dat *n.* formal agreement

con'course *n.* 1. a crowd 2. open space for crowds

con'crete' *a.* real; actual 2. specific —*n.* hard material made of sand, gravel, and cement —con·crete'ly *adv.*

con·cre'tion *n.* solidified mass

con'cu·bine *n.* wife of lesser status

con·cu'pis·cence *n.* lust — con·cu'pis·cent *a.*

con·cur' (-kur') *v.* [-CURRED, -CURRING] 1. occur together 2. agree —con·cur'rence *n.* — con·cur'rent *a.*

con·cus'sion *n.* 1. jarring shock 2. brain injury from a blow

con·demn' *v.* 1. disapprove of 2. declare guilty 3. doom 4. take for public use 5. declare unfit —con'dem·na'tion *n.*

con·dense' *v.* 1. make or become denser 2. express concisely —con'den·sa'tion *n.*

condensed milk thickened milk with added sugar

con·dens'er *n.* capacitor

con·de·scend' (-send') *v.* 1. be gracious about doing a thing beneath one's dignity 2. deal with others haughtily — con'de·scen'sion *n.*

con·dign' (-dīn') *a.* deserved; suitable

con'di·ment *n.* seasoning

con·di'tion *n.* 1. prerequisite 2. state of being 3. healthy state 4. [Col.] illness 5. rank —*v.* 1. make healthy 2. make accustomed (*to*) —on condition that provided that — con·di'tion·er *n.*

con·di'tion·al *a.* qualified — con·di'tion·al·ly *adv.*

con·di'tioned *a.* 1. in a desired condition 2. affected by conditioning 3. accustomed (*to*)

con·dole' *v.* show sympathy — con·do'lence *n.*

con'do·min'i·um *n.* any of the separately owned units in a multiple-unit dwelling: also con'do [*pl.* -DOS, -DOES]

con·done' (-dōn') *v.* forgive or overlook

con'dor *n.* large vulture

con·duce' *v.* tend; lead (*to*) — con·du'cive *a.*

con'duct *n.* 1. management 2. behavior —*v.* (kən dukt') 1. lead 2. manage 3. direct 4. behave (oneself) 5. transmit, as electricity —con·duc'tion *n.* —con·duc'tive *a.* —con'·duc·tiv'i·ty *n.*

con·duct'ance *n.* ability to conduct electricity

con·duc'tor *n.* **1.** orchestra leader **2.** one in charge of passengers, etc. **3.** thing that conducts heat, etc.

con'duit (-dit) *n.* pipe, tube, etc. for fluids or wires

con'dyle (-dil) *n.* rounded process at end of a bone

cone *n.* **1.** pointed, tapered figure with circular base **2.** woody fruit of evergreens

co'ney *n.* [*pl.* -NEYS] rabbit or its fur

con·fec'tion *n.* candy, ice cream, etc.

con·fec'tion·er *n.* maker or seller of candy

con·fec'tion·er'y *n.* [*pl.* -IES] confectioner's shop

con·fed'er·a·cy *n.* [*pl.* -CIES] league or alliance

con·fed'er·ate (-it) *a.* united; allied —*n.* **1.** ally **2.** accomplice —*v.* (-āt) unite; ally

con·fed'er·a'tion *n.* alliance; federation

con·fer' (-fur') *v.* [-FERRED, -FERRING] **1.** give **2.** have a conference

con'fer·ence *n.* **1.** formal meeting for discussion **2.** association of schools, etc.

con·fess' *v.* **1.** admit (a crime) **2.** tell (one's sins)

con·fes'sion *n.* **1.** a confessing **2.** something confessed

con·fes'sion·al *n.* box where a priest hears confessions

con·fes'sor *n.* priest who hears confessions

con·fet'ti *n.* bits of colored paper thrown as at carnivals

con·fi·dant' *n.* trusted friend —**con·fi·dante'** *n.fem.*

con·fide' *v.* **1.** trust (*in*) **2.** share as a secret

con'fi·dence *n.* **1.** trust **2.** assurance **3.** belief in one's own abilities **4.** something told as a secret —*a.* swindling or used to swindle

confidence game swindle by one (**confidence man**) who gains victim's confidence

con'fi·dent *a.* **1.** certain **2.** sure of oneself

con'fi·den'tial (-shəl) *a.* **1.** secret **2.** entrusted with private matters

con·fig'u·ra'tion *n.* form

con·fine' *n.* limit —*v.* (kən fīn') **1.** restrict **2.** shut up, as in prison —**con·fine'ment** *n.*

con·firm' *v.* **1.** strengthen **2.** approve formally **3.** prove to be true **4.** admit to membership in a church —**con'fir·ma'tion** *n.*

con·firmed' *a.* firmly established; habitual

con'fis·cate *v.* seize legally —**con'fis·ca'tion** *n.*

con·fis'ca·to'ry *a.* of or effecting confiscation

con'fla·gra'tion *n.* big, destructive fire

con·flict' *v.* be in opposition —*n.* (kän'flikt) **1.** a fight **2.** sharp disagreement

conflict of interest conflict between public obligation and self-interest of an official

con'flu·ence *n.* **1.** flowing together of streams **2.** crowd

con·form' *v.* **1.** be in accord **2.**

act according to rules, customs, etc. —con·form'ist n.

con'for·ma'tion n. 1. symmetrical arrangement 2. shape

con·form'i·ty n. [pl. -TIES] 1. similarity; agreement 2. conventional behavior

con·found' v. confuse

con·found'ed a. 1. confused 2. damned

con·front' v. 1. face boldly 2. bring face to face —con'fron·ta'tion n.

con·fuse' v. 1. mix up 2. bewilder —con·fu'sion n.

con·fute' v. prove wrong

con·geal' (-jēl') v. 1. freeze 2. thicken; jell

con·gen·ial (kən jēn'yəl) a. friendly; agreeable —con·ge'ni·al'i·ty n.

con·gen'i·tal (-jen'-) a. existing from birth —con·gen'i·tal·ly adv.

con'ger (eel) (-gər) large, edible, saltwater eel

con'ge·ries (-jə rēz) n. [pl. -RIES] heap or pile

con·gest' (-jest') v. fill too full, as with blood —con·ges'tion n.

con·glom'er·ate (-it) a. collected into a compact mass — n. large corporation formed by merging many companies — con·glom'er·a'tion n.

con·grat'u·late v. express to (a person) pleasure at his or her good fortune —con·grat'u·la·to'ry a.

con·grat'u·la'tions n.pl. expressions of pleasure over another's good luck, etc.

con'gre·gate v. gather into a crowd

con'gre·ga'tion n. assembly of people, esp. for worship

con'gress n. 1. assembly 2. legislature, esp. [C-] of the United States —con·gres'sion·al (-gresh'ən-) a. —con'gress·man [pl. -MEN] n.

con'gru·ent a. agreeing; corresponding

con·gru·ous a. suitable —con·gru'i·ty n.

con'i·cal a. of or like a cone: also con'ic

co'ni·for (kän'ə-, kō'nə-) n. cone-bearing tree

con·jec'ture (-chər) n., v. guess —con·jec'tur·al a.

con·join' v. join together

con'ju·gal a. of marriage

con'ju·gate v. give the inflectional forms of (a verb) — con'ju·ga'tion n.

con·junc'tion n. 1. a joining together 2. an occurring together 3. word used to join words, clauses, etc. —con·junc'tive a.

con·junc·ti'va n. [pl. -VAS, -VAE (-vē)] mucous membrane covering inner eyelid and the front of the eyeball

con·junc'ti·vi'tis n. inflammation of the conjunctiva

con·junc'ture (-junk'chər) n. combination of events creating a crisis

con·jure v. 1. practice magic 2. entreat 3. cause to appear, etc. as by magic —con'jur·er, con'jur·or n.

conk (känk) n., v. [Sl.] hit on the head —conk out [Sl.] 1.

fail suddenly 2. fall asleep from fatigue

con man [Sl.] confidence man

con·nect′ v. 1. join; link 2. show or think of as related — **con·nec′tive** a.

con·nec′tion n. 1. a connecting or being connected 2. thing that connects 3. relation 4. an associate, etc. 5. usually pl. a transferring from one train, plane, etc. to another Br. sp. **connexion**

co·nip′tion (fit) [Col.] fit of anger, hysteria, etc.: also **co·nip′tions**

con·nive′ v. 1. pretend not to look (at crime, etc.) 2. cooperate secretly in wrongdoing — **con·niv′ance** n.

con·nois·seur (kän ə sur′) n. expert, esp. in the fine arts

con·note′ v. suggest in addition to the explicit meaning — **con·no·ta′tion** n.

con·nu′bi·al a. of marriage

con′quer (-kər) v. defeat; overcome — **con′quer·or** n.

con′quest (-kwest) n. 1. a conquering 2. something conquered, as in war 3. winning of someone's affection or favor

con·quis·ta·dor (kän kwis′-, -kēs′-) n. [pl. -DORS, -DORES] 16th-c. Spanish conqueror of Mexico, Peru, etc.

con′science (-shəns) n. sense of right and wrong

con·sci·en′tious (-shē en′shəs) a. 1. scrupulous; honest 2. painstaking

con′scious (-shəs) a. 1. aware (of or that) 2. able to feel and think; awake 3. intentional

con′scious·ness n. 1. awareness 2. totality of thoughts and feelings

con·script′ v. draft (into the armed forces) — **con·scrip′tion** n.

con′se·crate v. 1. set apart as holy 2. devote — **con·se·cra′tion** n.

con·sec′u·tive a. following in order without a break — **con·sec′u·tive·ly** adv.

con·sen′sus n. general opinion

con·sent′ v. agree —n. agreement or approval

con′se·quence n. 1. a result 2. importance

con′se·quent a. resulting

con′se·quen′tial a. 1. consequent 2. important

con′se·quent·ly adv. as a result; therefore

con·ser·va′tion n. 1. a conserving 2. protection of natural resources — **con·ser·va′tion·ist** n.

con·ser′va·tive a. 1. opposed to change 2. cautious —n. conservative person

con·ser′va·to·ry n. [pl. -RIES] school of music, art, etc.

con·serve′ v. keep from being damaged, lost, etc.

con·sid′er v. 1. think over 2. keep in mind 3. have regard for 4. believe to be

con·sid′er·a·ble a. large or important — **con·sid′er·a·bly** adv.

con·sid′er·ate (-it) a. having regard for others

con·sid·er·a′tion (-shən) n. 1. deliberation 2. thoughtful regard 3. something considered

4. fee —**take into considera-**
tion keep in mind

con·sid'ered *a.* arrived at
after careful thought

con·sid'er·ing *prep.* taking
into account

con·sign' *v.* 1. entrust 2. assign 3. deliver (goods)

con·sign'ment *n.* goods sent
to an agent for sale, etc. —**on**
consignment with payment
due after sale

con·sist' *v.* be made up (*of*)

con·sist'en·cy *n.* [*pl.* -CIES] 1.
thickness, as of a liquid 2.
agreement 3. uniformity of
action

con·sist'ent *a.* 1. compatible
2. keeping the same practice

con·sole' *v.* comfort; cheer up
—con·so·la'tion *n.*

con'sole *n.* floor cabinet of an
organ, radio, TV, etc.

con·sol'i·date *v.* 1. unite 2.
strengthen —con·sol'i·da'-
tion *n.*

con·som·mé' (-mā') *n.* clear
meat soup

con'so·nant *n.* letter for a
breath-blocked sound, as *p, t, l,*
etc. —*a.* in harmony —con'-
so·nance *n.*

con'sort *n.* spouse, esp. of a
monarch —*v.* (kən sôrt') to associate

con·sor'ti·um (-shē-) *n.* international alliance, as of banks

con·spec'tus *n.* 1. general
view 2. summary

con·spic'u·ous *a.* 1. easy to
see 2. outstanding —con·
spic'u·ous·ly *adv.*

con·spire' *v.* join in a plot —

con·spir'a·cy (-spir'-) *n.* —
con·spir'a·tor *n.*

con'sta·ble *n.* 1. town peace
officer 2. [Chiefly Br.] policeman

con·stab'u·lar'y *n.* [*pl.* -IES]
1. constables, collectively 2.
militarized police force

con'stant *a.* 1. not changing;
fixed 2. faithful 3. continual —
n. unchanging thing —con'-
stan·cy *n.* —con'stant·ly
adv.

con'stel·la'tion *n.* group of
fixed stars

con'ster·na'tion *n.* great
alarm or dismay

con'sti·pate *v.* make it difficult to move the bowels —
con'sti·pa'tion *n.*

con·stit'u·en·cy *n.* voters in a
district

con·stit'u·ent *n.* 1. necessary
part 2. voter —*a.* needed to
form a whole

con'sti·tute' *v.* form; set up

con'sti·tu'tion *n.* 1. structure;
makeup 2. basic laws of a government, etc., esp. [C] of the
U.S.

con'sti·tu'tion·al *a.* 1. basic
2. in accord with the constitution, as of a government —*n.* a
walk for one's health

con·strain' *v.* force or restrain
—con·straint' *n.*

con·strict' *v.* make smaller by
squeezing, etc.; contract —
con·stric'tion *n.*

con·struct' *v.* build; devise

con·struc'tion *n.* 1. a constructing 2. structure 3. explanation 4. arrangement of
words

con·struc'tive *a.* leading to improvement

con·strue' *v.* interpret

con'sul *n.* 1. chief magistrate of ancient Rome 2. government official in a foreign city looking after his country's business there —**con'su·lar** *a.*

con'su·late *n.* position, office, or residence of a consul

con·sult' *v.* 1. confer 2. ask the advice of 3. consider — **con·sul·ta'tion** *n.*

con·sult'ant *n.* one who gives professional advice

con·sume' *v.* 1. destroy 2. use up 3. eat or drink up

con·sum'er *n.* one who uses goods and services for personal needs only

con·sum'er·ism *n.* movement to protect consumers against harmful products, etc.

con'sum·mate *v.* complete — *a.* (kən sum'it) complete — **con'sum·ma'tion** *n.*

con·sump'tion *n.* 1. a consuming 2. using up of goods 3. amount used up 4. tuberculosis of the lungs

con·sump'tive *n., a.* (one) having tuberculosis of the lungs

con'tact *n.* 1. a touching 2. being in touch (*with*) 3. connection —*v.* 1. place in contact 2. get in touch with

contact lens tiny, thin lens put in fluid over the cornea

con·ta'gion *n.* a spreading of disease, an idea, etc. —**con·ta'gious** *a.*

con·tain' *v.* 1. have in it 2. be able to hold 3. restrain

con·tain'er *n.* thing for containing something; box or can

con·tain'er·ize *v.* to ship (cargo) in huge, standardized containers

con·tam'i·nant *n.* contaminating substance

con·tam'i·nate *v.* make impure; pollute —**con·tam'i·na'tion** *n.*

con'tem·plate *v.* 1. watch intently 2. meditate 3. intend — **con'tem·pla'tion** *n.* —**con'tem·pla'tive** (or kən'tem plā'tiv) *a.*

con·tem'po·ra'ry *n.* [*pl.* -RIES], *a.* (one) living in the same period —**con·tem'po·ra'ne·ous** *a.*

con·tempt' *n.* 1. scorn 2. disgrace 3. disrespect shown for a judge, etc.

con·tempt'i·ble *a.* deserving contempt

con·temp'tu·ous *a.* scornful; disdainful

con·tend' *v.* 1. to struggle 2. to compete 3. assert —**con·tend'er** *n.*

con·tent' *a.* satisfied: also **con·tent'ed** —*v.* satisfy —*n.* satisfaction —**con·tent'ment** *n.*

con'tent *n.* 1. *pl.* all that is contained 2. meaning 3. capacity

con·ten'tion *n.* argument or struggle —**con·ten'tious** *a.*

con·test' *v.* 1. to dispute; question 2. fight for —*n.* (kän'test) 1. struggle 2. race, game, etc. with competition — **con·test'ant** *n.*

con'text *n.* words surrounding

a word or phrase that fix its meaning

con·tig′u·ous a. in contact

con′ti·nence n. self-restraint, esp. sexually —**con′ti·nent** a.

con′ti·nent n. large land mass —**con′ti·nen′tal** a.

con·tin′gen·cy (-jən-) n. [pl. -CIES] uncertain event

con·tin′gent a. dependent (on); conditional —n. quota, as of troops

con·tin′u·al a. 1. repeated often 2. continuous

con·tin′u·a′tion n. 1. a continuing 2. resumption 3. sequel

con·tin′ue v. 1. keep on; go on 2. endure; last 3. resume 4. extend 5. postpone —**con·tin′u·ance** n.

con′ti·nu′i·ty n. [pl. -TIES] 1. continuous state or thing 2. script for a movie, radio program, etc.

con·tin′u·ous a. without interruption; unbroken —**con·tin′u·ous·ly** adv.

con·tin′u·um (-yoo-) n. [pl. -UA, -UUMS] continuous whole or quantity

con·tort′ v. twist out of shape —**con·tor′tion** n.

con·tor′tion·ist n. one who can twist his body strangely

con′tour n. outline of a figure, land, etc. —v. shape to contour —a. made to fit the contour of something

contra- pref. against

con′tra·band n. smuggled goods —a. prohibited

con′tra·cep′tion n. prevention of fertilization of human ovum —**con′tra·cep′tive** a., n.

con′tract n. legally valid agreement —v. (kən trakt′) 1. undertake by contract 2. get; incur 3. shrink —**con·trac′tu·al** a.

con·trac′tile (-t′l) a. able to contract

con·trac′tion n. 1. a contracting 2. shortened form, as *don't* for *do not*

con′trac·tor n. builder, etc. who contracts to provide supplies or workers

con′tra·dict′ v. say or be the opposite of —**con′tra·dic′tion** n. —**con′tra·dic′to·ry** a.

con′trail n. white trail of condensed water vapor in the wake of an aircraft

con′tra·in′di·cate v. Med. make (the indicated drug or treatment) inadvisable

con·tral′to n. [pl. -TOS] lowest female voice

con·trap′tion n. [Col.] contrivance; gadget

con′tra·pun′tal a. of or like counterpoint

con′tra·ri·wise′ adv. 1. on the contrary 2. in the opposite way, order, etc.

con′tra·ry a. 1. opposed; different 2. (kən trer′ē) perverse —n. the opposite —**on the contrary** as opposed to what has been said —**to the contrary** to the opposite effect —**con′tra·ri·ly** adv.

con·trast′ v. 1. compare 2. show differences —n. (kän′trast) 1. striking difference when compared 2. one showing such differences

con'tra·vene' v. go against

con·tre·temps (kön' trə tän') n. [pl. -TEMPS (-tän')] awkward mishap

con·trib'ute v. 1. give, esp. to a common fund 2. furnish (an idea, article, etc.) —**contribute** to help bring about —**con'tri·bu'tion** n. —**con·trib'u·tor** n.

con·trite' a. remorseful —**con·tri'tion** (-trish'-) n.

con·trive' v. 1. devise; invent 2. manage; bring about —**con·triv'ance** n.

con·trol' v. [-TROLLED, -TROLLING] 1. regulate (finances) 2. direct 3. restrain —n. 1. authority 2. means of restraint 3. pl. regulating mechanism —**con·trol'ler** n.

con'tro·ver'sial (-shəl) a. of or causing controversy

con'tro·ver'sy n. [pl.-SIES] debate or dispute

con'tro·vert' v. to dispute —**con'tro·vert'i·ble** a.

con·tu·ma·cy n. disobedience —**con'tu·ma'cious** (-shəs) a.

con'tu·me·ly (-too mə lē) n. haughty rudeness

con·tu'sion n. a bruise

co·nun'drum n. a puzzle

con'ur·ba'tion n. vast area of a large city and its environs

con'va·lesce' (-les') v. regain health and strength —**con'va·les'cence** n. —**con'va·les'cent** a., n.

con·vec'tion n. transmission of heat in currents

con·vene' v. assemble; meet

con·ven'ience n. 1. a being convenient 2. comfort 3. thing that saves work, etc.

con·ven'ient a. easy to do, use, or get to; handy —**con·ven'ient·ly** adv.

con'vent n. community of nuns or their living place

con·ven'tion n. 1. an assembly 2. custom; usage

con·ven'tion·al a. 1. customary 2. conforming —**con·ven'tion·al·ly** adv.

con·verge' v. come together —**con·ver'gence** n. —**con·ver'gent** a.

con·ver'sant (-vur'-) a. familiar (with)

con'ver·sa'tion n. informal talk —**con'ver·sa'tion·al** a. —**con'ver·sa'tion·al·ist** n.

conversation piece something unusual, as in furnishing a room, that invites comment

con·verse' v. to talk —a. opposite —n. (kän'vərs) 1. conversation 2. the opposite —**con·verse'ly** adv.

con·vert' v. change in form, use, etc. or in religion —n. (kän'vərt) person converted —**con·ver'sion** n.

con·vert'i·ble a. that can be converted —n. automobile with a folding top

con·vex' (or kän'veks) a. curved like the outside of a sphere —**con·vex'i·ty** n.

con·vey' (-vā') v. 1. carry 2. transmit —**con·vey'er, con·vey'or** n.

con·vey'ance n. 1. a conveying 2. vehicle

con·vict' v. prove or find

guilty —n. (kän'vikt) prisoner serving a sentence

con·vic'tion n. 1. a being convicted 2. strong belief

con·vince' v. make feel sure — con·vinc'ing a.

con·viv'i·al a. sociable; gay — con·viv'i·al'i·ty n.

con·voke' v. call together — con'vo·ca'tion n.

con'vo·lut'ed a. 1. coiled 2. complicated; involved

con'vo·lu'tion n. a twist or twisting

con'voy v. escort —n. ships, etc. being escorted

con·vulse' v. shake as with violent spasms

con·vul'sion n. 1. often pl. violent spasm of the muscles 2. fit of laughter 3. violent disturbance —con·vul'sive a.

co'ny n. [pl. -NIES] coney

coo v. make the soft sound of a pigeon or dove —n. this sound

cook v. boil, bake, fry, etc. (food) —n. one who cooks — cook up [Col.] invent — cook'er n.

cook'book n. book with recipes and cooking information

cook'ie, cook'y n. [pl. -IES] small, sweet, flat cake

cook'out n. meal cooked and eaten outdoors

cool a. 1. moderately cold 2. not excited 3. unfriendly 4. [Sl.] very good —n. 1. cool place, time, etc. 2. [Sl.] cool, unexcited manner —v. make or become cool —cool'ly adv. —cool'ness n.

cool'ant n. fluid for cooling engines, etc.

cool'er n. 1. refrigerator 2. [Sl.] jail

con'lie n. unskilled worker, as formerly in India, China, etc.

coon n. raccoon

coop n. pen for poultry —v. confine as in a coop

co'-op n. a cooperative

co·op'er·ate v. to work together: also co·operate, coöperate —co·op'er·a'tion n.

co·op'er·a·tive a. 1. cooperating 2. owned collectively and profit-sharing —n. cooperative store, etc. Also co-operative, coöperative

co-opt' v. 1. elect or appoint as an associate 2. get (an opponent) to join one's side

co·or'di·nate (-nit) a. equally important —v. (-nāt) harmonize; adjust Also co·ordinate, coördinate —co·or'di·na·tor n.

co·or'di·na'tion n. 1. a coordinating 2. harmonious action, as of muscles Also co·ordination, coördination

coot n. 1. water bird 2. [Col.] fool

cop n. [Sl.] policeman —v. [COPPED, COPPING] [Sl.] seize; steal —cop out [Sl.] 1. confess to police 2. renege 3. give up

cope v. deal (with) successfully —n. priest's capelike vestment

cop'i·er n. 1. one who copies 2. duplicating machine

co'pi·lot n. assistant pilot of an aircraft

cop'ing (kōp'-) *n.* top of masonry wall

co'pi·ous *a.* abundant

cop'per *n.* a reddish-brown metal, a chemical element

cop'per·head *n.* poisonous snake

cop'ra (kōp'-) *n.* dried coconut meat

copse (käps) *n.* thicket

cop'ter *n.* [Col.] helicopter

cop'u·late *v.* have sexual intercourse —**cop'u·la'tion** *n.*

cop'y *n.* [*pl.* -IES] 1. thing made just like another 2. one of many books, etc. all alike —*v.* [-IED, -YING] 1. make a copy of 2. imitate

cop'y·cat *n.* imitator

cop'y·right *n.* exclusive rights over a book, song, etc. —*v.* protect by copyright

co·quette' (-ket') *n.,* *v.* [-QUETTED, -QUETTING] flirt — **co·quet'tish** *a.*

cor'al *n.* 1. hard mass of sea animal skeletons 2. yellowish red —*a.* of coral

cord *n.* 1. thick string 2. wood pile of 128 cu. ft. 3. ribbed fabric 4. insulated electric wire

cor'dial (-jəl) *a.* friendly —*n.* syrupy alcoholic drink —**cor'·di·al'i·ty** (-jē al'-) *n.* —**cor'·dial·ly** *adv.*

cord'less *a.* operated by batteries, as an electric shaver

cor'don *n.* a guarding group in a line —*v.* shut (*off*) with a cordon

cor'do·van *n.* soft leather

cor'du·roy *n.* ribbed cotton fabric

core *n.* 1. central part, as of an apple 2. most important part —*v.* remove the core of

co're·spond'ent (kō'ri-) *n.* person in divorce suit charged with adultery with one's spouse

cork *n.* 1. light, thick bark of a certain oak 2. stopper —*v.* stop with a cork

cork'screw *n.* spiral device for uncorking bottles

corm *n.* bulblike underground stem of certain plants

cor'mo·rant *n.* 1. voracious sea bird 2. glutton

corn *n.* 1. grain 2. grain that grows on large ears; maize 3. [Sl.] trite humor 4. horny thickening of the skin —*v.* pickle (meat, etc.)

cor'ne·a (-nē ə) *n.* clear, outer layer of the eyeball

cor'ner *n.* 1. place where lines or surfaces meet 2. region 3. monopoly —*v.* 1. put into a difficult position 2. get a monopoly on

cor'ner·back *n. Football* either of two defensive backs behind the line of scrimmage

cor'ner·stone *n.* stone at a corner of a building

cor·net' *n.* brass-wind instrument like a trumpet

corn'flow'er *n.* plant with showy disk flowers

cor'nice (-nis) *n.* molding along the top of a wall, etc.

corn'meal *n.* meal made from corn (maize)

corn'starch *n.* starch made from corn (maize), used in cooking

corn syrup sweet syrup made from cornstarch

cor·nu·co·pi·a *n.* horn-shaped container overflowing with fruits, flowers, etc.

corn'y *a.* [-IER, -IEST] [Col.] hackneyed, trite, etc.

co·rol'la (-räl'-) *n.* petals of a flower

cor·ol'lar·y *n.* [*pl.* -IES] 1. proposition following from one already proved 2. normal result

co·ro'na *n.* ring of light around the sun or moon

cor·o·nar'y *a.* of the arteries supplying the heart —*n.* [-IES] thrombosis in a coronary artery: in full, **coronary thrombosis**

cor·o·na'tion *n.* crowning of a sovereign

cor'o·ner *n.* official who investigates unnatural deaths

cor'o·net *n.* small crown worn by nobility

cor'po·ral *n.* lowest ranking noncommissioned officer —*a.* of the body

corporal punishment bodily punishment, as flogging

cor'po·ra'tion *n.* group given legal status of an individual — **cor'po·rate** (-rit) *a.*

cor·po're·al (-pôr'ē-) *a.* 1. of the body 2. material

corps (kôr) *n.* [*pl.* CORPS (kôrz)] 1. organized group 2. large military unit

corpse (kôrps) *n.* dead body

cor'pu·lent (-pyoo-) *a.* fat; fleshy —**cor'pu·lence** *n.*

cor'pus *n.* body, as of laws

cor'pus·cle (-pas 'l) *n.* cell in the blood, lymph, etc.

cor·ral' *n.* pen for horses, etc. —*v.* [-RALLED, -RALLING] 1. confine in a corral 2. capture

cor·rect' *v.* 1. make right 2. mark errors of 3. punish —*a.* right, true, etc. —**cor·rec'tive** *a.*, *n.* —**cor·rect'ly** *adv.* —**cor·rect'ness** *n.*

cor·rec'tion *n.* 1. a correcting 2. change that corrects 3. punishment —**cor·rec'tion·al** *a.*

cor're·late *v.* bring into mutual relation —**cor're·la'tion** *n.*

cor·rel'a·tive *n.* conjunction showing mutual relation, as *either . . . or* —*a.* showing mutual relation

cor·re·spond' *v.* 1. be similar or equal to 2. communicate as by letters —**cor·re·spond'ence** *n.*

cor·re·spond'ent *n.* 1. one exchanging letters with another 2. journalist sending in news to a home office

cor'ri·dor *n.* long hall

cor·rob'o·rate *v.* confirm — **cor·rob'o·ra'tion** *n.* —**cor·rob'o·ra'tive** *a.*

cor·rode' *v.* wear away; rust — **cor·ro'sion** *n.* —**cor·ro'sive** *a.*

cor'ru·gate *v.* make folds or wrinkles in

cor·rupt' *a.* 1. rotten 2. evil; depraved 3. taking bribes —*v.* make or become corrupt —**cor·rupt'i·ble** *a.* —**cor·rup'tion** *n.* —**cor·rupt'ly** *adv.*

cor·sage' (-säzh') *n.* small bouquet worn by a woman

cor'set *n.* tight undergarment to support the torso

cor·tege', **cor·tège'** (-tezh') *n.* ceremonial procession

cor'tex *n.* outer layer of a body organ —**cor'ti·cal** *a.*

cor'ti·sone *n.* hormone used to treat arthritis, etc.

co·run'dum *n.* mineral used for grinding wheels, etc.

cor'us·cate *v.* to glitter; sparkle —**cor'us·ca'tion** *n.*

co·ry'za (-rī'-) *n.* a cold in the head

co'sign' *v.* sign (a promissory note) making one liable if the maker defaults —**co'sign'er** *n.*

cos·met'ic *n., a.* (preparation) for enhancing beauty

cos·me·tol'o·gy *n.* work of a beautician —**cos·me·tol'o·gist** *n.*

cos'mic *a.* **1.** of the cosmos; orderly **2.** vast; huge

cos'mo·naut (-nôt) *n.* astronaut

cos'mo·pol'i·tan *a.* at home all over the world; worldly —*n.* a worldly person: also **cos·mop'o·lite** (-līt)

cos'mos *n.* the universe seen as an orderly system

co·spon'sor *n.* joint sponsor —*v.* be a cosponsor of

cost *v.* [COST, COSTING] require the payment, etc. of —*n.* **1.** price **2.** loss; sacrifice —**at all costs** by any means whatever

co'star *n.* any of the actors or actresses who are stars in a movie or play —*v.* (kō'stär') [-STARRED, -STARRING] make or be a costar

cos'tive (käs'-) *a.* constipated or constipating

cost'ly *a.* [-LIER, -LIEST] expensive —**cost'li·ness** *n.*

cost of living average cost of necessities, as food, shelter, and clothes

cos'tume *n.* **1.** the dress of a people, period, etc. **2.** set of outer clothes

co'sy (-zē) *a.* [-SIER, -SIEST] cozy —**co'si·ly** *adv.*

cot *n.* folding bed

cote (kōt) *n.* small shelter for birds, sheep, etc.

co·te·rie (kō'tər ē) *n.* social set; clique

co·til'lion *n.* formal dance

cot'tage *n.* small house

cottage cheese soft, white cheese made from sour milk

cot'ter pin pin with two stems that can be spread apart

cot'ton *n.* **1.** plant with heads of soft, white fibers **2.** thread or cloth from this —**cot'ton·y** *a.*

cot'ton·mouth *n.* water moccasin

cot'ton·seed *n.* seed of the cotton plant: its oil is used in margarine, soap, etc.

cot'ton·wood *n.* poplar with seeds covered with cottony hairs

cot'y·le'don *n.* first leaf or a leaf of the first pair produced by a plant embryo

couch *n.* piece of furniture to lie on —*v.* put in words

cou·gar (kōō'gər) *n.* large American wildcat

cough (kôf) *v.* expel lung air in a loud burst —*n.* **1.** a coughing

2. condition of coughing frequently

couldn't could not

coun'cil (koun'-) n. advisory or legislative body —**coun'cilman** [pl. -MEN] n.

coun'ci·lor, coun'cil·lor n. member of a council

coun'sel n. 1. advice 2. lawyer(s) —v. advise

coun'se·lor, coun'sel·lor n. 1. adviser 2. lawyer

count v. 1. add up to get a total 2. name numbers in order 3. include or be included 4. consider 5. be important — n. 1. a counting 2. total number 3. each charge in an indictment 4. nobleman —**count on** (or **upon**) rely on

count'down n. counting off of time units, in reverse order, before firing a rocket, etc.

coun'te·nance n. 1. facial expression 2. face —v. to sanction

count'er n. long table for displaying goods, serving food, etc. —adv., a. contrary —v. oppose

counter- pref. 1. opposite 2. against 3. in return

coun'ter·act' n., v. act against

coun'ter·at·tack' n., v. attack in return

coun'ter·bal'ance n. weight or influence that balances another —v. offset

coun'ter·clock'wise a., adv. like the hands of a clock moving in reverse

coun'ter·feit (-fit) a. made in imitation with intent to defraud —n. fraudulent imitation —v. 1. make counterfeits 2. pretend

coun·ter·mand' v. cancel (a command)

coun'ter·pane n. bedspread

coun'ter·part n. matching or corresponding thing

coun'ter·point n. harmonic interweaving of melodies

coun'ter·poise n., v. counterbalance

coun'ter·pro·duc'tive a. producing the opposite of what is intended

coun'ter·sign n. password —v. confirm another's signature by signing

coun'ter·sink v. sink a bolt or screw into a hole large enough to receive its head

coun'ter·ten'or n. highest tenor voice

count'ess n. wife or widow of a count or earl

count'less a. too many to count

coun'try n. [pl. -TRIES] 1. region 2. nation 3. rural area — a. rural —**coun'try·man** [pl. -MEN] n.

country club social club with a golf course, etc.

country music rural folk music, esp. of the South

coun'try·side' n. rural region

coun'ty n. [pl. -TIES] subdivision of a State

coup (kō̄o) n. [pl. COUPS (kō̄oz)] bold, successful stroke

cou'ple n. 1. a pair 2. engaged, married, etc. man and woman 3. [Col.] a few —v. join together

cou′plet *n.* two successive rhyming lines of poetry

cou′pling *n.* device for joining things together

cou′pon (kōō′-, kyōō′-) *n.* certificate, ticket, etc. redeemable for cash or gifts

cour′age *n.* fearless or brave quality —**cou·ra′geous** *a.*

cou′ri·er (koor′ē-, kur′ē-) *n.* messenger

course *n.* 1. path or channel 2. direction taken 3. regular mode of action 4. series 5. separate part of a meal 6. a study or series of studies —*v.* run —**in the course of** during —**of course** 1. naturally 2. certainly

court *n.* 1. open space surrounded by buildings or walls: also **court′yard** 2. playing area 3. royal palace 4. family, advisers, etc. of a sovereign 5. courtship 6. judge or judges 7. place where trials are held: also **court′room** —*v.* woo —**pay court** to to court or woo

cour′te·ous (kur′-) *a.* polite and gracious —**cour′te·ous·ly** *adv.*

cour′te·san (kôr′-) *n.* prostitute: also sp. **cour′te·zan**

cour′te·sy (kur′-) *n.* [*pl.* -SIES] polite behavior or act

court′house *n.* building housing the offices and courtrooms of a county

cour′ti·er (kôr′-) *n.* attendant at a royal court

court′ly *a.* [-LIER, -LIEST] dignified; elegant —**court′li·ness** *n.*

court′-mar′tial *n.* [*pl.* COURTS-MARTIAL] trial by a military or naval court —*v.* try by such a court

court′ship *n.* period or act of courting a woman

cous′in (kuz′-) *n.* child of one's uncle or aunt

cove (kōv) *n.* small bay

cov′en (kuv′-) *n.* witches' meeting

cov′e·nant (kuv′-) *n.* agreement; compact

cov′er *v.* 1. place something over 2. extend over 3. conceal 4. protect 5. include; deal with 6. travel over 7. point a firearm at 8. provide an excuse (*for*) —*n.* anything that covers —**take cover** seek shelter —**under cover** in secrecy

cov′er·age (-ij) *n.* amount covered by something

cov′er·all *n. usually pl.* one-piece work garment with legs

covered wagon large wagon with an arched canvas cover

cov′er·ing *n.* anything that covers

cov′er·let *n.* bedspread

cov′ert (kuv′-) *a.* hidden

cov′er·up′ *n.* something used for hiding one's real actions

cov′et *v.* desire ardently (what belongs to another)

cov′et·ous *a.* greedy

cov′ey (kuv′ē) *n.* small flock of birds, esp. quail

cow *n.* mature female of the ox, or of the elephant, seal, etc. —*v.* make timid

cow′ard *n.* a person who lacks courage —**cow′ard·ice** (-is) *n.* —**cow′ard·ly** *a., adv.*

cow'boy n. worker who herds cattle: also **cow'hand**

cow'er v. cringe as in fear

cow'hide n. leather made from the hide of a cow

cowl n. monk's hood

cow'lick n. tuft of hair difficult to comb flat

cowl'ing n. metal covering for an airplane engine

co'-work'er n. fellow worker

cow'slip n. 1. swamp plant with yellow flowers 2. English primrose

cox'comb (-kōm) n. fop

cox-swain (käk's'n, -swān) n. one who steers a boat or racing shell

coy a. shy or pretending to be shy —**coy'ly** adv.

coy·o·te (kī ō'tē, kī'ōt) n. small prairie wolf

coz'en (kuz'-) v. cheat

co'zy a. [-ZIER, -ZIEST] warm and comfortable; snug —n. [pl. -ZIES] padded cover to keep a teapot hot —**co'zi·ly** adv. —**co'zi·ness** n.

crab n. 1. shellfish with eight legs and two pincers 2. complainer —v. [CRABBED, CRABBING] [Col.] complain

crab apple small, sour apple

crab'by a. [-BIER, -BIEST] peevish —**crab'bi·ness** n.

crab grass weedy grass that spreads rapidly

crack v. 1. make a sudden, sharp breaking noise 2. break without separation of parts 3. solve 4. [Col.] hit hard 5. [Col.] break into 6. [Sl.] make (a joke) —n. 1. sudden, sharp noise 2. incomplete break 3.

crevice 4. [Col.] sharp blow 5. [Col.] a try 6. [Sl.] gibe —a. [Col.] first-rate —**crack down (on)** become strict with — **crack up** 1. crash 2. [Col.] have a mental breakdown 3. [Col.] to laugh

crack'down n. a resorting to strict discipline or rules

crack'er n. thin, crisp wafer

crack'le v., n. (make) a series of slight, sharp sounds

crack'pot n. [Col.] an eccentric

crack'up n. 1. crash 2. [Col.] mental breakdown

cra'dle n. 1. baby's bed on rockers 2. place of beginning — v. put as in a cradle

craft n. 1. special skill or art 2. slyness 3. [pl. CRAFT] boat or aircraft

crafts'man n. [pl. -MEN] skilled worker —**crafts'man·ship** n.

craft'y a. [-IER, -IEST] sly; cunning —**craft'i·ly** adv.

crag n. steep, projecting rock — **crag'gy** a.

cram v. [CRAMMED, CRAMMING] 1. stuff 2. [Col.] study hurriedly for a test

cramp n. 1. painful contraction of a muscle 2. pl. intestinal pain —v. hamper

cramped a. 1. confined 2. irregular and crowded

cran'ber·ry n. [pl. -RIES] sour, edible, red berry

crane n. 1. long-legged wading bird 2. machine for lifting heavy weights —v. stretch (the neck)

cra'ni·um (krā'-) n. the skull —**cra'ni·al** a.

crank n. 1. handle for turning a shaft 2. [Col.] an eccentric —v. start or work by a crank

crank'y a. [-IER, -IEST] 1. irritable; cross 2. eccentric

cran'ny n. [pl. -NIES] chink

crap n. [Sl.] 1. nonsense 2. junk; trash —**crap'py** a.

crape n. crepe

craps n.pl. dice game

crash v. 1. fall, break, drop, etc. with a loud noise 2. fail 3. [Col.] get into uninvited —n. 1. loud noise 2. a crashing 3. failure, as of a business 4. coarse linen —a. [Col.] using all possible speed and effort

crash'-land' v. bring (an airplane) down without landing gear —**crash landing**

crass a. grossly stupid

crate n. wooden packing case —v. pack in a crate

cra'ter n. bowl-shaped cavity or pit, as of a volcano

cra·vat' n. necktie

crave v. ask or long for

cra'ven a. very cowardly —n. coward

crav'ing n. intense desire

craw n. 1. bird's crop 2. stomach

crawl v. 1. move slowly, as while flat on the ground 2. swarm with crawling things —n. 1. a crawling 2. swimming stroke

cray'fish or **craw'fish** n. shellfish like a small lobster

cray'on n. small stick of chalk, wax, etc. for drawing —v. draw with crayons

craze v. make or become insane —n. fad

cra'zy a. [-ZIER, -ZIEST] 1. insane 2. [Col.] foolish 3. [Col.] eager —n. [pl. -ZIES] [Sl.] crazy person —**cra'zi·ly** adv. —**cra'zi·ness** n.

crazy quilt quilt of odd patches in no regular design

creak v., n. squeak

cream n. 1. oily part of milk 2. creamy cosmetic 3. best part —v. beat till smooth as cream —**cream of** purée of —**cream'y** [-IER, -IEST] a.

cream cheese soft, white cheese of cream and milk

cream'er n. cream pitcher

cream'er·y n. [pl. -IES] place where dairy products are made or sold

crease n. line made by folding —v. make a crease in

cre·ate' v. make; bring about —**cre·a'tor** n.

cre·a'tion n. 1. a creating 2. universe 3. anything created

cre·a'tive a. 1. creating 2. inventive —**cre'a·tiv'i·ty** n.

crea·ture (krē'chər) n. living being, animal or human

cre'dence n. belief; trust

cre·den'tials (-shəlz) n.pl. papers showing one's right to a certain position, etc.

cre·den'za n. buffet or sideboard

credibility gap disparity between a statement and the truth

cred'i·ble a. believable —**cred'i·bil'i·ty** n.

cred'it n. 1. belief; trust 2. reputation 3. praise or source of praise 4. trust that one will pay later 5. completed unit of study —v. 1. believe; trust 2. give credit for —do credit to bring honor to —on credit agreeing to pay later —cred'it·a·ble a. —cred'it·a·bly adv.

credit card card entitling one to charge bills

cred'i·tor n. one to whom another owes a debt

cre'do n. [pl. -DOS] creed

cred'u·lous (krej'-) a. believing too readily —cre·du'li·ty n.

creed n. statement of belief

creek n. small stream —up the creek [Sl.] in trouble

creel n. basket for fish

creep v. [CREPT, CREEPING] 1. go on hands and knees 2. go slowly or stealthily 3. grow along the ground, etc. —n. [Sl.] disgusting person —the creeps [Col.] feeling of fear, dislike, etc.

creep'y a. [-IER, -IEST] causing fear, disgust, etc.

cre'mate v. burn (a dead body) —cre·ma'tion n.

cre'ma·to'ry n. [pl. -RIES] furnace for cremating: also cre'ma·to'ri·um [pl. -UMS, -A]

cre'o·sote n. oily preservative distilled from tar

crepe, crêpe (krāp) n. 1. thin, crinkled silk, rayon, etc. 2. thin, crinkled paper 3. (also krep) thin pancake, rolled and filled

crept pt. & pp. of creep

cre·scen'do (-shen'-) n. [pl. -DOS] Mus. a growing louder

cres'cent n. shape of a quarter moon

crest n. 1. tuft on an animal's head 2. heraldic device 3. top; summit —v. reach a crest

crest'fall'en a. dejected

cre'tin n. deformed idiot

cre·tonne' (tän') n. printed linen or cotton cloth

cre·vasse' (kri vas') n. deep crack, as in a glacier

crev'ice (-is) n. narrow crack

crew n. group of workers, as on a ship

crew alt. pt. of crow

crew'el n. yarn used in embroidery —crew'el·work' n.

crib n. 1. box for fodder 2. baby's small bed 3. wood shed for grain —v. [CRIBBED, CRIBBING] 1. confine 2. [Col.] plagiarize

crib'bage n. card game

crick n. painful cramp

crick'et n. 1. leaping insect 2. ball game played with bats and wickets

cried pt. & pp. of cry

cri'er n. shouter of news

crime n. 1. an act in violation of a law 2. sin

crim'i·nal a. of crime —n. person guilty of crime

crim'i·nol'o·gy n. study of crime and criminals

crimp v., n. pleat or curl —put a crimp in [Col.] hinder

crim'son n. deep red —v. make or become crimson

cringe (krinj) v. 1. shrink back as in fear 2. to fawn

crin'kle v. to wrinkle or rustle —crin'kly a.

crin'o·line (-lin) n. 1. stiff cloth 2. hoop skirt

crip′ple *n.* disabled person —*v.* disable

cri′sis *n.* [*pl.* -SES (-sēz)] 1. turning point 2. crucial situation

crisp *a.* 1. brittle 2. clear 3. fresh; bracing

criss′cross *n.* crossed lines —*v.* 1. mark with crisscross 2. move crosswise —*adv.* 1. crosswise 2. awry

cri·ter′i·on (krī tir′-) *n.* [*pl.* -IA, -IONS] standard; rule

crit′ic *n.* 1. judge of books, art, etc. 2. faultfinder

crit′i·cal *a.* 1. finding fault 2. of critics or their work 3. being a crisis —**crit′i·cal·ly** *adv.*

crit′i·cism *n.* 1. literary or artistic judgments 2. a finding fault

crit′i·cize *v.* 1. judge as a critic 2. find fault (*with*) Br. sp. **criticise**

cri·tique′ (-tēk′) *n.* critical analysis or review

crit′ter *n.* [Dial.] creature

croak (krōk) *v.* 1. make a deep, hoarse sound 2. [Sl.] die —*n.* croaking sound

cro·chet (krō shā′) *n.* needlework done with one hooked needle —*v.* do crochet

crock *n.* earthenware jar

crocked *a.* [Sl.] drunk

crock′er·y *n.* earthenware

croc′o·dile *n.* large reptile of tropical streams

cro′cus *n.* small plant of the iris family

crois′sant (krə sänt′) *n.* a crescent-shaped roll

crone *n.* ugly, withered old woman

cro′ny *n.* [*pl.* -NIES] close friend

crook (krook) *n.* 1. bend or curve 2. [Col.] swindler

crook′ed *a.* 1. not straight 2. dishonest

croon (krōōn) *v.* sing in a soft tone —**croon′er** *n.*

crop *n.* 1. saclike part of a bird's gullet 2. farm product, growing or harvested 3. group 4. riding whip —*v.* [CROPPED, CROPPING] 1. cut or bite off the ends of 2. cut short —**crop out** (or **up**) appear suddenly —**crop′per** *n.*

crop′-dust′ing *n.* spraying of crops with pesticides from an airplane —**crop′-dust′** *v.*

cro·quet′ (krō kā′) *n.* game with hoops in the ground through which balls are hit

cro·quette (krō ket′) *n.* small mass of meat, fish, etc. fried in deep fat

cross *n.* 1. upright post with another across it 2. [*often* C-] figure of this, symbolic of Christianity 3. any affliction 4. mark made by intersecting lines, bars, etc. 5. hybrid —*v.* 1. place, go, or lie across 2. intersect 3. draw a line across 4. thwart 5. interbreed —*a.* 1. lying or passing across 2. irritable —**cross off** (or **out**) cancel as by drawing lines across —**cross′ness** *n.*

cross′bones *n.* two crossed bones under a skull, symbolizing death

cross′bow (-bō) *n.* medieval bow on a wooden stock

cross'breed n. hybrid —v. to breed as a hybrid

cross'-coun'try a. across open country, as a race

cross'cut a., n., v. cut across

cross'-ex·am'ine v. Law question (an opposition witness) —**cross'-ex·am'i·na'tion** n.

cross'-eyed' a. having the eyes turned toward the nose

cross'hatch v. shade with crossing parallel lines

cross'ing n. 1. intersection 2. place for crossing

cross'-pur'pose n. contrary purpose —**at cross-purposes** misunderstanding each other's purposes

cross'-ref'er·ence n. reference from one part to another

cross'road n. 1. road that crosses another 2. pl. road intersection

cross section 1. part cut straight across 2. broad sample

cross'walk n. pedestrians' lane across a street

cross'wise adv. across: also **cross'ways**

crotch n. place where branches or legs fork

crotch'et n. whim —**crotch'et·y** a.

crouch v., n. stoop with legs bent low

croup (krōōp) n. disease with cough and hard breathing

crou·pi·er (krōō'pē ā') n. one controlling a gambling table

crou·ton (krōō'tän) n. bit of toast served in soup

crow n. 1. large, black bird with a harsh call 2. rooster's cry —v. 1. make a rooster's cry 2. exult —**eat crow** [Col.] recant

crow'bar' n. long, metal bar for prying, etc.

crowd v. to throng, press, cram, etc. —n. mass of people —**crowd'ed** a.

crown n. 1. head covering of a monarch 2. power of a monarch 3. top part, position, quality, etc. 4. tooth above gum line —v. 1. make a monarch of 2. honor 3. be atop 4. climax

crow's'-foot' n. [pl. -FEET] wrinkle around outer edge of eyes

crow's'-nest' n. lookout platform on a ship's mast

cru·cial (krōō'shəl) a. 1. decisive 2. trying

cru'ci·ble n. container for melting metals

cru'ci·fix n. representation of Jesus on the cross

cru'ci·fy v. [-FIED, -FYING] execute by nailing or binding to a cross —**cru·ci·fix'ion** (-fik'shən) n.

crude a. 1. raw; unprocessed 2. rough or clumsy —**cru'di·ty**, **crude'ness** n.

cru'el a. causing suffering; pitiless —**cru'el·ty** n.

cru'et n. small bottle for vinegar, oil, etc.

cruise (krōōz) v. travel about, as by ship —n. voyage

cruis'er n. 1. police car 2. large, fast warship

crul'ler n. twisted doughnut

crumb (krum) n. small piece as of bread; bit —**crumb'y** [-IER, -IEST] a.

crum'ble v. break into crumbs —**crum'bly** [-BLIER, -BLIEST] a.

crum'my a. [-MIER, -MIEST] [Sl.] shabby, mean, etc.

crum'ple v. to crush into wrinkles

crunch v. chew or crush with a crackling sound —n. 1. crunching sound 2. [Sl.] tight situation —**crunch'y** [-IER, -IEST] a.

cru·sade' v., n. (engage in) united action against an abuse —**cru·sad'er** n.

cruse n. small container for water, oil, etc.

crush v. 1. press out of shape 2. pound into bits 3. subdue —n. 1. a crushing 2. crowded mass 3. [Col.] infatuation

crust n. 1. hard outer part of bread, earth, etc. 2. dry piece of bread 3. [Sl.] insolence —v. cover with a crust —**crust'y** a.

crus·ta'cean (-tā'shan) n. hard-shelled invertebrate, as a shrimp, lobster, etc.

crutch n. support held under the arm to aid in walking

crux n. essential point

cry v. [CRIED, CRYING] 1. utter loudly 2. sob; weep 3. clamor (for) —n. [pl. CRIES] 1. a shout 2. entreaty 3. call of a bird, etc. —**a far cry** a great difference

cry'ba·by n. [pl. -BIES] childish complainer

cry'o·gen'ics n. science dealing with very low temperatures

crypt (kript) n. underground (burial) vault

cryp'tic a. secret; mysterious —**cryp'ti·cal·ly** adv.

cryp·tog'ra·phy n. secret-code writing or deciphering —**cryp·tog'ra·pher** n.

crys'tal n. 1. clear quartz 2. clear, brilliant glass 3. solidified substance with symmetrical plane faces

crys'tal·line a. like crystal in clearness, structure, etc.

crys'tal·lize v. 1. form crystals 2. take on or give definite form —**crys'tal·li·za'tion** n.

cub n. 1. young bear, lion, etc. 2. youth or novice

cub'by·hole n. small, enclosed space

cube (kyoob) n. 1. a solid with six equal, square sides 2. product obtained by multiplying a number by its square —v. 1. get the cube (n. 2) of 2. cut into cubes

cu'bic a. 1. shaped like a cube: also **cu'bi·cal** 2. of three dimensions

cu'bi·cle n. small room

cu'bit n. ancient measure of length, about 18–22 inches

cuck'old n. man whose wife is unfaithful

cuck·oo (koo'koo) n. brown, slender bird —a. [Sl.] crazy

cu'cum·ber n. long, green-skinned, fleshy vegetable

cud n. food regurgitated by cattle and chewed again

cud'dle v. 1. embrace and fondle 2. lie close and snug

cud'dly a. [-DLIER, -DLIEST] appealingly sweet; lovable

cudg'el (kuj'-) v., n. (beat with) a short club

cue (kyo͞o) *n.* **1.** signal to begin **2.** hint **3.** rod for striking a billiard ball —*v.* [Col.] to signal

cuff *n.* **1.** band or fold at the wrist of a sleeve or the bottom of a trouser leg **2.** a slap —*v.* to slap —**off the cuff** [Sl.] offhandedly —**on the cuff** [Sl.] on credit

cui·sine (kwi zēn′) *n.* **1.** style of cooking **2.** food cooked

cul-de-sac (kul′də sak′) *n.* [*pl.* -SACS] blind alley

cu′li·nar′y (kyo͞o-) *a.* of cookery

cull *v.* pick over; select

cul′mi·nate *v.* reach its highest point —**cul′mi·na′tion** *n.*

cu·lotte (ko͞o lät′) *n.* often pl. women's trousers made to resemble a skirt

cul′pa·ble *a.* deserving blame —**cul′pa·bil′i·ty** *n.*

cul′prit *n.* one accused, or found guilty, of a crime

cult *n.* system of worship or group of worshipers

cul′ti·vate *v.* **1.** prepare (land) for crops **2.** grow (plants) **3.** develop, as the mind —**cul′ti·va′tor** *n.*

cul′ti·va′tion *n.* **1.** a cultivating **2.** refinement

cul′ture (-chər) *n.* **1.** animal or plant breeding **2.** training of the mind, taste, etc. **3.** civilization of a people or period —*v.* cultivate —**cul′tur·al** *a.*

cul′vert *n.* drain or waterway under a road, etc.

cum′ber·some *a.* unwieldy

cum′in (kum′-) *n.* aromatic fruit used for flavoring

cum′mer·bund (kum′-) *n.* wide sash worn as waistband by men

cu′mu·la·tive (kyo͞om′yə-) *a.* increasing by additions

cu′mu·lus *n.* cloud having rounded masses piled up

cu·ne′i·form (kyo͞o-) *a.* wedge-shaped —*n.* cuneiform characters used in ancient inscriptions

cun′ning *a.* **1.** sly; crafty **2.** pretty —*n.* slyness

cup *n.* **1.** small bowl with handle, for beverages **2.** cupful —*v.* [CUPPED, CUPPING] shape like a cup

cup′board (kub′ərd) *n.* cabinet for dishes, food, etc.

cup′cake *n.* small cake

cup′ful *n.* [*pl.* -FULS] as much as a cup holds; specif., 8 ounces

cu·pid′i·ty (kyo͞o-) *n.* greed

cu′po·la (kyo͞o′pə-) *n.* small dome

cu′pro·nick′el (kyo͞o′-) *n.* alloy of copper and nickel

cur *n.* **1.** mongrel dog **2.** contemptible person

cu·rate (kyoor′it) *n.* clergyman helping a vicar or rector

cur′a·tive *a.* able to cure —*n.* remedy

cu·ra′tor (kyoo rā′-) *n.* one in charge, as of a museum

curb *n.* **1.** chain or strap on a horse's bit for checking the horse **2.** thing that restrains **3.** edging along a street —*v.* restrain

curb'stone *n.* stones making up a curb: also **curb'ing**

curd *n.* coagulated part of soured milk

cur'dle *v.* form curd

cure *n.* 1. a healing 2. remedy —*v.* 1. make well; heal 2. remedy 3. preserve (meat) —**cur'a·ble** *a.*

cure'-all' *n.* something supposed to cure everything

cu'ret·tage (-tāzh′) *n.* a cleaning or scraping of the walls of a body cavity

cur'few *n.* evening deadline for being off the streets

cu'ri·o (kyoo′-) *n.* [*pl.* -os] unusual or rare article

cu'ri·os'i·ty *n.* [*pl.* -TIES] 1. desire to know 2. anything curious or rare

cu'ri·ous *a.* 1. eager to know; inquisitive 2. strange

curl *v.* 1. twist (hair, etc.) into ringlets 2. curve around; coil —*n.* 1. ringlet of hair 2. any curling —**curl'er** *n.* —**curl'y** [-IER, -IEST] *a.*

cur'lew *n.* wading bird

curl'i·cue *n.* fancy curve

curl'ing *n.* game played on ice by sliding a flat stone

cur'rant *n.* 1. small, seedless raisin 2. sour berry

cur'ren·cy *n.* [*pl.* -CIES] 1. money circulated in a country 2. general use; prevalence

cur'rent *a.* 1. of this day, week, etc. 2. commonly accepted or known —*n.* flow of air, water, electricity, etc.

cur·ric'u·lum *n.* [*pl.* -LA, -LUMS] course of study

cur'ry *n.* [*pl.* -RIES] spicy powder or sauce —*v.* [-RIED, -RYING] 1. brush the coat of (a horse, etc.) 2. try to win (favor) by flattery, etc.

curse *v.* 1. call or bring evil down on 2. swear (at) —*n.* 1. a cursing 2. evil or injury

curs'ed (*also* kurst) *a.* 1. under a curse 2. evil; hateful

cur'sive *a.* of writing in which letters are joined

cur'so·ry *a.* hastily done —**cur'so·ri·ly** *adv.*

curt *a.* so brief as to be rude —**curt'ness** *n.*

cur·tail' *v.* cut short —**cur·tail'ment** *n.*

cur'tain (-t'n) *n.* 1. piece of cloth hung, as at a window, to decorate or conceal 2. anything that conceals or separates —*v.* furnish as with a curtain

curt'sy *n.* [*pl.* -SIES] graceful bow that women make by bending the knees —*v.* [-SIED, -SYING] make a curtsy

curve *n.* line, surface, etc. having no straight part —*v.* form or move in a curve —**cur'va·ture** (-chər) *n.*

cush'ion *n.* 1. pillow or pad 2. something absorbing shock —*v.* provide with a cushion

cush'y *a.* [-IER, -IEST] [Sl.] easy; comfortable

cusp *n.* point, as on the chewing surface of a tooth

cus'pi·dor *n.* spittoon

cuss *n., v.* [Col.] curse

cus'tard *n.* 1. mixture of eggs, milk, sugar, etc., boiled or baked 2. similar frozen mixture

cus·to′di·an *n.* 1. one having custody 2. janitor

cus′to·dy *n.* guarding; care — **in custody** under arrest — **cus·to′di·al** *a.*

cus′tom *n.* 1. usual or traditional practice; usage 2. *pl.* duties on imported goods —*a.* made to order: also **cus′tom-made′**

cus′tom·ar′y *a.* usual —**cus′tom·ar′i·ly** *adv.*

cus′tom-built′ *a.* built to customer's specifications

ous′tom·er *n.* one who buys

cus′tom·ize *v.* make according to individual specifications

cut *v.* [CUT, CUTTING] 1 make an opening in with a sharp instrument 2. pierce sharply 3. divide into parts 4. hew 5. reap 6. trim 7. go (*across*) 8. reduce 9. [Col.] snub —*n.* 1. a cutting 2. part cut open or off 3. reduction 4. style 5. plate engraved for printing 6. insult 7. [Col.] unauthorized absence 8. [Sl.] share, as of profits — **cut and dried** lifeless; dull — **cut out for** suited for —**cut up** [Sl.] to clown, joke, etc.

cut′back′ *n.* reduction or discontinuing, as of production

cute *a.* [Col.] 1. clever 2. pretty or pleasing

cu′ti·cle (kyōō′-) *n.* hardened skin, as at the base and sides of a fingernail

cut′lass, cut′las (-ləs) *n.* short, thick, curved sword

cut′ler·y *n.* cutting tools, as knives, scissors, etc.

cut′let *n.* small slice of meat from the ribs or leg

cut′off′ *n.* 1. shortcut road, etc. 2. device for shutting off flow of a fluid, etc.

cut′-rate′ *a.* selling or on sale at a lower price

cut′ter *n.* small, swift ship

cut′throat *n.* murderer —*a.* merciless

cut′ting *n.* shoot cut from a plant —*a.* 1. sharp 2. piercing 3. sarcastic

cut′tle·fish *n.* mollusk with ten arms

-cy *suf.* 1. quality or state of being 2. position, rank, or office of

cy·a·nide (sī′ə nīd) *n.* poisonous white compound

cy·ber·net′ics *n.* comparative study of electronic computers and the human nervous system

cy′cla·mate (-māt) *n.* artificial sweetener

cy′cle (sī′-) *n.* 1. complete round of regularly recurring events, or period for this 2. bicycle, tricycle, etc. —*v.* ride a bicycle, etc. —**cy′clic** *a.* —**cy′clist** *n.*

cy′clone *n.* storm with heavy rain and whirling winds

cy·clo·pe′di·a *n.* encyclopedia

cy′clo·tron *n.* apparatus for giving high energy to atomic particles

cyg′net (sig′-) *n.* young swan

cyl′in·der *n.* 1. round figure with two flat ends that are parallel circles 2. revolver's turning part 3. piston chamber of an engine —**cy·lin′dri·cal** *a.*

cym′bal *n.* circular brass plate

making ringing sound when hit: often used in pairs

cyn'ic *n.* person who is cynical, pessimistic, etc.

cyn'i·cal *a.* 1. denying sincerity of motives and actions 2. sarcastic, sneering, etc. —**cyn'i·cal·ly** *adv.*

cyn'i·cism *n.* cynic's attitude or beliefs

cy'no·sure *n.* center of attention

cy'press *n.* evergreen tree

cyst (sist) *n.* sac containing fluid or hard matter —**cyst'ic** *a.*

cystic fibrosis children's disease of the pancreas

czar (zär) *n.* 1. Russian emperor 2. an autocrat

D

'd *had* or *would,* as in *I'd*

dab *v.* [DABBED, DABBING] pat or put on with light, quick strokes —*n.* soft or moist bit —**dab'ber** *n.*

dab'ble *v.* 1. splash the hands in water 2. do something superficially (with *in* or *at*) —**dab'bler** *n.*

dace *n.* small freshwater fish

dachs'hund (däks'hoond) *n.* small dog with a long body

Da'cron (dā'-) *trademark for* synthetic fabric —*n.* [*also* d-] this fabric

dad *n.* [Col.] father: also **dad'dy** [*pl.* -DIES]

dad'dy-long'legs *n. sing. & pl.* long-legged arachnid

da'do (dā'-) *n.* [*pl.* -DOES] lower part of a wall decorated differently

daf'fo·dil *n.* yellow flower

daf'fy *a.* [-FIER, -FIEST] [Col.] crazy; silly

daft *a.* 1. silly 2. insane

dag'ger *n.* 1. short, sharp-pointed weapon 2. printed reference mark (†)

dahl'ia (dal'ya) *n.* plant with large, showy flowers

dai'ly *a., adv.* (done or happening) every day —*n.* [*pl.* -LIES] daily newspaper

daily double bet won by choosing winners in two races on a program

dain'ty *a.* [-TIER, -TIEST] 1. delicately pretty 2. fastidious —*n.* [*pl.* -TIES] a choice food; delicacy —**dain'ti·ly** *adv.* —**dain'ti·ness** *n.*

dair'y (der'-) *n.* [*pl.* -IES] place where milk, butter, etc. are made or sold —**dair'y·man** [*pl.* -MEN] *n.*

da·is (dā'is) *n.* platform

dai'sy (-zē) *n.* [*pl.* -SIES] flower with white rays around a yellow disk

dale *n.* small valley

dal'ly *v.* [-LIED, -LYING] 1. to toy or flirt 2. loiter

Dal·ma'tian (-shan) *n.* large, black-and-white dog

dam *n.* 1. barrier to hold back flowing water 2. female parent of a horse, cow, etc. —*v.* [DAMMED, DAMMING] keep back; confine

dam'age *n.* 1. injury; harm 2.

pl. money paid for harm done —*v.* do damage to

dam′ask *n.* fabric with figured weave —*a.* deep-pink

dame *n.* **1.** [D-] woman's title of honor in Britain **2.** [Sl.] any woman

damn (dam) *v.* [DAMNED, DAMNING] condemn; declare bad, doomed, etc. —*a., adv.* [Col.] damned —**dam′na·ble** *a.* —**dam·na′tion** *n.*

damned *a.* **1.** condemned **2.** [Col.] outrageous —*adv.* [Col.] very

damp *n.* **1.** moisture **2.** mine gas or vapor, wet —*v.* **1.** bank (a fire) **2.** check or reduce —**damp′ness** *n.*

damp′-dry′ *v.* [-DRIED, -DRY- ING] dry with some moisture retained

damp′en *v.* **1.** moisten **2.** deaden, depress, or reduce

damp′er *n.* **1.** one that de- presses **2.** valve in a flue to control the draft

dam′sel *n.* [Ar.] girl

dam′son (-z′n) *n.* small, purple plum

dance *v.* **1.** move in rhythm to music **2.** move lightly, rapidly, etc. —*n.* **1.** rhythmic move- ment to music **2.** party or piece of music for dancing **3.** rapid movement —**danc′er** *n.*

dan′de·li′on *n.* common weed with yellow flowers

dan′der *n.* [Col.] anger

dan′dle *v.* dance (a child) up and down on the knee

dan′druff *n.* little scales of dead skin on the scalp

dan′dy *n.* [*pl.* -DIES] vain man —*a.* [Sl.] very good

dan′ger *n.* **1.** liability to in- jury, loss, etc.; peril **2.** thing that may cause injury, etc. — **dan′ger·ous** *a.*

dan′gle *v.* hang loosely

Dan′ish (dān′-) *a.* of the peo- ple or language of Denmark — *n.* **1.** language of Denmark **2.** [*also* d-] rich pastry with a fill- ing

dank *a.* disagreeably damp — **dank′ness** *n.*

dap′per *a.* trim; spruce

dap′ple *a.* spotted; mottled: also **dap′pled** —*v.* mottle

dare *v.* **1.** have the courage (to) **2.** challenge —*n.* a challenge — **dare say** think probable

dare′dev′il *n., a.* (one who is) bold and reckless

dar′ing *a.* fearless; bold —*n.* bold courage

dark *a.* **1.** with little or no light **2.** not light in color **3.** gloomy **4.** ignorant —*n.* **1.** a being dark **2.** night —**dark′ness** *n.*

dark′en *v.* make or become dark or darker

dark horse [Col.] one who wins or may win unexpectedly

dark′room *n.* darkened room for developing photographs

dar′ling *n., a.* beloved

darn *v.* **1.** mend by sewing **2.** [Col.] to damn —*a., adv.* [Col.] damned

dart *n.* **1.** small pointed weapon for throwing **2.** sudden movement **3.** short, tapered seam —*v.* throw or move quickly

dash *v.* **1.** smash **2.** strike violently against **3**. do hastily (with *off*) **4**. rush —*n*. **1**. bit of something **2**. short race **3**. vigor **4**. mark of punctuation (-)

dash'board *n.* instrument panel in an automobile

dash'ing *a.* lively or showy

das'tard *n.* mean coward — **das'tard-ly** *a.*

da'ta *n.pl.* [*often with sing. v.*] facts or figures; information

data processing handling of data by mechanical means or computer

date *n.* **1**. time of an event **2**. day of the month **3**. social engagement **4**. fruit of a tall palm —*v.* **1**. mark with a date **2**. belong to a particular time **3**. have social engagements with —**out of date** old-fashioned —**up to date** modern

daub (dôb) *v.* **1**. smear with sticky stuff **2**. paint badly

daugh'ter (dô'-) *n.* female in relation to her parents

daugh'ter-in-law' *n.* [*pl.* DAUGHTERS-IN-LAW] wife of one's son

daunt *v.* frighten or dishearten

daunt'less *a.* that cannot be daunted

dau-phin (dô'fin) *n.* eldest son of the French king

dav'en-port *n.* large sofa

daw'dle *v.* waste time; loiter — **daw'dler** *n.*

dawn *v.* **1**. begin to be day **2**. begin to be understood —*n.* **1**. daybreak **2**. beginning

day *n.* **1**. period from sunrise to sunset **2**. period of 24 hours,

esp. from midnight to midnight **3**. *also pl.* era —**day after day** every day: also **day in, day out**

day'break *n.* time of the first light in the morning

day'dream *n.* a pleasant, dreamy thinking or wishing — *v.* have daydreams

day'light *n.* **1**. sunlight **2**. daytime **3**. understanding

day'light-sav'ing time one hour later than standard

day nursery place for daytime care of preschool children: also **day-care center**

Day of Atonement Yom Kippur

day'time *n.* time between dawn and sunset

day'-to-day' *a.* daily; routine

daze *v.* **1**. stun **2**. dazzle —*n.* dazed condition

daz'zle *v.* overpower with light or brilliance

DDT powerful insecticide

de- *pref.* **1**. away from; off **2**. reverse the action of

dea'con (dē'-) *n.* **1**. cleric lower than a priest **2**. church officer who assists a minister

dead (ded) *a.* **1**. not living **2**. dull; inactive **3**. extinguished; extinct **4**. obsolete **5**. complete —*n.* time of most cold, darkness, etc. —*adv.* completely — **the dead** those who have died

dead'beat' *n.* [Sl.] one who avoids paying for things

dead'en *v.* to dull

dead end street closed at one end —**dead'-end'** *a.*

dead heat a tie in a race

dead'line *n.* time limit

dead'lock n. standstill with equal forces opposed —v. be or put in a deadlock

dead'ly a. [-LIER, -LIEST] 1. fatal 2. until death 3. like death 4. very boring 5. very accurate —adv. extremely — **dead'li·ness** n.

dead'-pan' n. [Sl.] expressionless face —a., adv. [Sl.] without expression

dead'wood n. useless thing

deaf (def) a. 1. unable to hear 2. unwilling to respond — **deaf'ness** n.

deaf'en v. 1. make deaf 2. overwhelm with noise

deaf'-mute' n. deaf person who has not learned to speak

deal (dēl) v. [DEALT (delt), DEALING] 1. distribute 2. give (a blow, etc.) 3. have to do (with) 4. do business —n. 1. distributing of playing cards 2. transaction or agreement —a good (or great) deal 1. large amount 2. very much — **deal'er** n.

deal'ing n. 1. way of acting 2. usually pl. transactions

dean (dēn) n. 1. church or college official 2. senior member of a group

dear (dir) a. 1. much loved 2. esteemed 3. costly 4. earnest —n. darling —**dear'ly** adv.

dearth (durth) n. scarcity

death (deth) n. 1. a dying or being dead 2. cause of death 3. destruction —**death'like** a.

death'less a. immortal

death'ly a. characteristic of death —adv. extremely

deb n. [Col.] debutante

de·ba·cle (di bä′k'l) n. sudden disaster

de·bar' v. [-BARRED, -BARRING] exclude (from)

de·bark' v. leave a ship or aircraft —**de'bar·ka'tion** n.

de·base' v. to lower in quality, etc. —**de·base'ment** n.

de·bate' v. argue in a formal way —n. formal argument — **de·bat'a·ble** a. —**de·bat'er** n.

de·bauch' (-bôch′) v. to corrupt —n. orgy —**de·bauch'er·y** (pl. -IES) n.

de·ben'ture n. voucher for a debt 2. interest-bearing bond

de·bil'i·tate v. make weak — **de·bil'i·ta'tion** n.

de·bil'i·ty n. weakness

deb'it n. entry in an account of money owed —v. enter as a debt

deb·o·nair' (-ner′) a. affable and jaunty: also sp. **deb·o·naire'**

de·bris', dé·bris (də brē′) n. broken, scattered remains; rubbish

debt n. 1. something owed 2. state of owing

debt'or n. one owing a debt

de·bunk' v. [Col.] expose the false claims, etc. of

de·but, dé·but (di byōō′, dā′-byōō) n. 1. first public appearance, as of an actor 2. formal introduction into society

deb'u·tante (-tänt) n. girl making a social debut

dec'ade n. ten-year period

dec·a·dence n. a declining, as in morals, art, etc. —**dec'a·dent** a., n.

de·cal'co·ma'ni·a *n.* picture for transfer from prepared paper: also **de·cal'**

Dec'a·logue, Dec'a·log (-lôg) *n.* [*sometimes* d-] Ten Commandments

de·camp' *v.* leave secretly

de·cant' *v.* pour off gently

de·cant'er *n.* decorative bottle for serving wine

de·cap'i·tate *v.* behead —**de·cap'i·ta'tion** *n.*

de·cath'lon *n.* contest of ten track and field events

de·cay' *v.* 1. fall into ruin 2. rot 3. disintegrate —*n.* a decaying; rot

de·cease' *n.* death

de·ceased' *a.* dead —**the deceased** dead person or persons

de·ceit' (-sēt') *n.* 1. act of deceiving 2. deceitful quality

de·ceit'ful *a.* 1. apt to lie or cheat 2. deceptive

de·ceive' *v.* make believe what is not true; mislead

de·cel'er·ate (-sel'-) *v.* slow down —**de·cel'er·a'tion** *n.*

De·cem'ber *n.* twelfth month

de'cent *a.* proper 2. respectable 3. not obscene 4. adequate —**de'cen·cy** [*pl.* -CIES] *n.* —**de'cent·ly** *adv.*

de·cen'tral·ize *v.* shift power from one main unit to local units —**de·cen'tral·i·za'tion** *n.*

de·cep'tion *n.* 1. a deceiving 2. illusion or fraud —**de·cep'tive** *a.*

dec'i·bel (des'-) *n.* unit for measuring loudness of sound

de·cide' *v.* settle by passing judgment 2. make up one's mind

de·cid'ed *a.* definite —**de·cid'ed·ly** *adv.*

de·cid'u·ous (-sij'ōō-) *a.* shedding leaves annually

dec'i·mal (des'-) *a.* based on the number ten —*n.* fraction with a denominator of ten or a power of ten, shown by a point (**decimal point**) before the numerator

dec'i·mate *v.* destroy or kill a large part of

de·ci'pher *v.* translate from code or illegibility

de·ci'sion *n.* 1. a deciding 2. judgment 3. determination

de·ci'sive (-sī'-) *a.* 1. conclusive 2. showing decision —**de·ci'sive·ly** *adv.*

deck *n.* 1. floor of a ship 2. pack of playing cards —*v.* adorn; trim

de·claim' *v.* speak in a loud, rhetorical way —**dec'la·ma'tion** *n.* —**de·clam'a·to'ry** *a.*

de·clare' *v.* 1. announce formally 2. say emphatically —**dec'la·ra'tion** *n.* —**de·clar'a·tive** *a.*

de·clas'si·fy *v.* make (secret documents) public and available

de·clen'sion *n.* grammatical inflection of nouns, etc.

de·cline' *v.* 1. slope downward 2. lessen, as in force 3. refuse politely 4. *Gram.* give inflected forms of —*n.* 1. a failing, decay, etc. 2. downward slope

de·cliv'i·ty *n.* downward slope

de·code' *v.* translate (a coded message) into plain language

dé·col·le·té (dā käl′ə tā′) *a.* [Fr.] cut low so as to bare the neck and shoulders

de·com·pose′ *v.* **1.** break up into basic parts **2.** rot —**de′com·po·si′tion** *n.*

de·com·press′ *v.* to free from air pressure —**de′com·pres′sion** *n.*

de′con·gest′ant *n.* medicinal relief for congestion, as of nasal passages

de·con·tam′i·nate *v.* to rid of a harmful substance

dé·cor, de·cor (dā kôr′) *n.* [Fr.] decorative scheme

dec′o·rate *v.* **1.** adorn; ornament **2.** to paint or wallpaper **3.** give a medal to —**dec′o·ra′tive** *a.* —**dec′o·ra′tor** *n.* —**dec′o·ra′tion** *n.*

de·co′rum *n.* proper behavior, speech, etc. —**de·co′rous** *a.* —**dec′o·rous·ly** *adv.*

de·cou·page, dé·cou·page (dā kōō pàzh′) *n.* the cutting out of designs from paper, etc. and mounting them on wood, etc.

de·coy′ (*also* dē′koi) *n.* thing or person used as a lure, esp. an artificial bird —*v.* lure

de·crease′ *v.* grow or make less or smaller —*n.* (dē′krēs) a decreasing

de·cree′ *n.* official order; edict —*v.* [-CREED, -CREEING] order by decree

de·crep′it *a.* old and worn out —**de·crep′i·tude** *n.*

de·crim′i·nal·ize′ *v.* eliminate the penalties for (a crime) or make less serious

de·cry′ *v.* [-CRIED, -CRYING] denounce; censure

ded′i·cate *v.* **1.** set apart formally **2.** devote **3.** inscribe —**ded′i·ca′tion** *n.*

de·duce′ *v.* conclude by reasoning; infer

de·duct′ *v.* subtract or take away —**de·duct′i·ble** *a.*

de·duc′tion *n.* **1.** a deducing or deducting **2.** amount deducted **3.** reasoned conclusion —**de·duc′tive** *a.*

deed *n.* **1.** act **2.** feat of courage, etc. **3.** legal document transferring property —*v.* transfer by deed —**in deed in fact**

deem *v.* think; believe

de·em′pha·size *v.* make less important

deep *a.* **1.** extending far down, in, or back **2.** hard to understand **3.** involved (*in*) **4.** of low pitch **5.** intense —*n.* deep place or part —*adv.* far down, etc. —**deep′ly** *adv.*

deep′-dish′ pie baked in a deep dish with top crust only

deep′en *v.* make or become deep or deeper

deep′freeze′ *v.* quick-freeze

deep′-fry′ *v.* [-FRIED, -FRYING] fry in a deep pan of boiling fat

deep′-seat′ed *a.* firmly fixed: also **deep′-root′ed**

deep space outer space

deer *n.* [*pl.* DEER] hoofed, cud-chewing animal, the male of which bears antlers

de·es′ca·late *v.* reduce in scope, etc. —**de·es′ca·la′tion** *n.*

de·face′ *v.* mar

de·fame' v. to slander or libel —**def'a·ma'tion** n.

de·fault' v. fail to do or pay as required —n. a defaulting

de·feat' v. 1. win victory over 2. frustrate —n. a defeating or being defeated

de·feat'ist n., a. (one) too readily accepting defeat —**de·feat'ism** n.

def'e·cate v. excrete waste matter from bowels —**def'e·ca'tion** n.

de·fect' (or di fekt') n. imperfection; fault —v. (di fekt') to desert one party, country, etc. for another —**de·fec'tion** n. —**de·fec'tor** n.

de·fec'tive a. imperfect; faulty

de·fend' v. 1. protect 2. support by speech or act 3. Law act for (an accused) —**de·fend'er** n.

de·fend'ant n. Law person sued or accused

de·fense' n. 1. a defending against attack 2. something that defends 3. defendant and his counsel —**de·fense'less** a.

de·fen'sive a. 1. defending 2. of or for defense —n. position of defense

de·fer' (-fur') v. [-FERRED, -FERRING] 1. postpone, as one's induction into the army 2. yield with courtesy (to)

def'er·ence n. 1. a yielding in opinion, respect 2. respect —**def'er·en'tial** a.

de·fer'ment n. a deferring or postponing

de·fi'ance (-fī'-) n. open resistance to authority —**de·fi'ant** a.

de·fi'cien·cy (-fish'ən-) n. [pl. -CIES] shortage; lack —**de·fi'cient** a.

deficiency disease disease due to lack of vitamins, minerals, etc. in the diet

def'i·cit (-sit) n. amount by which a sum of money is less than expected, etc.

de·file' v. dirty; sully —n. narrow pass

de·fine' v. 1. mark the limits of 2. state the meaning of —**def'i·ni'tion** n.

def'i·nite (-nit) a. 1. having exact limits 2. explicit 3. certain —**def'i·nite·ly** adv.

de·fin'i·tive a. 1. conclusive 2. most nearly complete

de·flate' v. 1. collapse by letting out air 2. lessen in amount, importance, etc.

de·fla'tion n. 1. a deflating 2. decrease in the currency in circulation, making it rise in value

de·flect' v. turn to one side

de·fo'li·ant n. chemical that strips plants of leaves —**de·fo'li·ate** v.

de·form' v. mar the form of —**de·formed'** a. misshapen

de·form'i·ty n. [pl. -TIES] 1. deformed part 2. ugliness

de·fraud' v. take property, etc. from by fraud; cheat

de·fray' v. pay (the cost)

de·frost' v. rid or become rid of frost or ice —**de·frost'er** n.

deft a. quick and skillful

de·funct' a. no longer existing

de·fy' v. [-FIED, -FYING] 1. resist openly 2. dare

de·gen'er·ate v. lose normal

or good qualities —*a.* (-it) **1.** deteriorated **2.** depraved —*n.* (-it) a degenerate person —**de·gen'er·a·cy** *n.* —**de·gen'er·a'tion** *n.*

de·grade' *v.* to lower in rank, moral character, etc. —**deg'ra·da'tion** *n.*

de·gree' *n.* **1.** successive step in a series **2.** intensity, extent, etc. **3.** rank given to a college graduate **4.** unit of measure, as for angles, temperature, etc. —**to a degree** somewhat

de·hu'man·ize *v.* deprive of human qualities

de'hu·mid'i·fy *v.* remove moisture from (air, etc.)

de·hy'drate (-hī'-) *v.* remove water from; dry (up)

de·ice' *v.* melt the ice from —**de·ic'er** *n.*

de·i·fy (dē'ə fī) *v.* [-**FIED**, -**FYING**] make a god of —**de'i·fi·ca'tion** *n.*

deign (dān) *v.* condescend

de'ism *n.* belief in God on purely rational grounds —**de'ist** *n.*

de'i·ty *n.* [*pl.* -**TIES**] god or goddess —**the Deity** God

de·ject'ed *a.* sad; depressed

de·jec'tion *n.* depression; sadness

de·lay' *v.* **1.** put off; postpone **2.** make late; detain —*n.* a delaying

de·lec'ta·ble *a.* delightful

de'lec·ta'tion *n.* delight

del'e·gate (or -git) *n.* representative —*v.* (-gāt) **1.** appoint as delegate **2.** entrust to another

del'e·ga'tion *n.* group of delegates

de·lete' (-lēt') *v.* take out (a word, etc.) —**de·le'tion** *n.*

del'e·te'ri·ous (-tir'ē-) *a.* harmful to health, etc.

del'i *n.* [Col.] delicatessen

de·lib'er·ate *v.* consider carefully —*a.* (-it) **1.** done on purpose **2.** not rash or hasty **3.** unhurried —**de·lib'er·ate·ly** *adv.* —**de·lib'er·a'tion** *n.*

del'i·ca·cy *n.* **1.** delicate quality **2.** [*pl.* -**CIES**] a choice food; dainty

del'i·cate *a.* **1.** fine and lovely **2.** fragile or frail **3.** needing care **4.** sensitive **5.** considerate and tactful —**del'i·cate·ly** *adv.*

del'i·ca·tes'sen *n.* **1.** prepared meats, fish, cheeses, etc. **2.** shop selling these

de·li'cious *a.* very pleasing, esp. to taste or smell

de·light' *v.* please greatly —*n.* great pleasure —**de·light'ed** *a.* —**de·light'ful** *a.*

de·lim'it *v.* fix the limits of

de·lin'e·ate *v.* **1.** draw; sketch **2.** describe

de·lin'quent *a.* **1.** not obeying duty or law **2.** overdue —*n.* one guilty of minor crimes —**de·lin'quen·cy** *n.*

del'i·quesce' (-kwes') *v.* absorb moisture from the air

de·lir'i·um *n.* **1.** temporary mental illness **2.** wild excitement —**de·lir'i·ous** *a.*

de·liv'er *v.* **1.** set free; rescue **2.** assist in birth **3.** utter **4.** hand over **5.** distribute **6.**

strike or throw —**de·liv'er·ance** n.

de·liv'er·y n. [pl. -IES] 1. a delivering or way of delivering 2. something delivered

dell n. small valley

del·phin'i·um n. tall plant with flower spikes, usually blue

del'ta n. 1. fourth letter of Greek alphabet 2. soil deposit at a river mouth

de·lude' v. mislead; deceive

del'uge (-yōōj) n. 1. great flood 2. heavy rainfall —v. 1. flood 2. overwhelm

de·lu'sion n. false, esp. psychotic, belief —**de·lu'sive** a.

de·luxe' a. extra fine; elegant —adv. in a deluxe manner

delve v. investigate

dem'a·gogue, dem'a·gog (-gäg) n. one who appeals to prejudices, etc. to win power —**dem'a·gog'y** (-gōj'ē), **dem'a·gog'uer·y** (-gäg'ər ē) n.

de·mand' v. 1. ask for boldly or as a right 2. require —n. 1. strong request 2. requirement 3. amount people are ready to buy —**on demand** when presented for payment

de'mar·ca'tion n. boundary line

de·mean' v. 1. degrade; behave (oneself)

de·mean'or n. behavior

de·ment'ed a. mentally ill

de·men'tia (-shə) n. loss of mental powers

de·mer'it n. 1. fault 2. mark for poor work, etc.

demi- pref. half

dem'i·god n. minor deity

dem'i·john n. large, wicker-covered bottle

de·mil'i·ta·rize' v. to free from military control

de·mise' (-mīz') n. death

dem'i·tasse (-tas) n. small cup of coffee

de·mo'bi·lize v. to disband (troops)

de·moc'ra·cy n. [pl. -CIES] 1. government in which the power is vested in all the people 2. equality of rights, etc. —**dem'o·crat** n. —**dem'o·crat'ic** a. —**dem'o·crat'i·cal·ly** adv.

de·mog'ra·phy (-mäg'-) n. statistical study of populations —**de'mo·graph'ic** a.

de·mol'ish v. destroy; ruin —**dem'o·li'tion** n.

de'mon n. devil; evil spirit —**de·mon'ic** a.

de·mo'ni·ac (-nē-) a. fiendish; frenzied: also **de'mo·ni'a·cal** (-nī'-)

dem'on·strate' v. 1. prove 2. explain with examples 3. show the working of 4. show feelings publicly —**de·mon'stra·ble** a. —**dem'on·stra'tion** n. —**dem'on·stra'tor** n.

de·mon'stra·tive a. 1. showing clearly 2. giving proof (of) 3. showing feelings openly

de·mor'al·ize' v. 1. to lower in morale 2. throw into confusion —**de·mor'al·i·za'tion** n.

de·mote' v. reduce in rank —**de·mo'tion** n.

de·mul'cent a., n. soothing (ointment)

de·mur' (-mur') v. [-MURRED,

-MURRING] to scruple (*at*) —*n.* objection

de·mure' (-myoor') *a.* modest or coy —**de·mure'ly** *adv.*

de·mur'rage (-mur'ij) *n.* 1. delay in shipping 2. compensation paid for this

den *n.* 1. animal's lair 2. haunt of thieves, etc. 3. small, cozy room

de·na'ture (-chər) *v.* make (alcohol) unfit to drink

de·ni'al *n.* 1. a denying 2. contradiction

de·ni·er (den'yər) *n.* unit to measure fineness of threads, as of nylon

den'i·grate *v.* defame; belittle —**den'i·gra'tion** *n.*

den'im *n.* coarse, twilled cotton cloth

den'i·zen *n.* inhabitant

de·nom'i·nate *v.* to name

de·nom'i·na'tion *n.* 1. a name 2. specific class or kind 3. religious sect

de·nom'i·na'tion·al *a.* of, or controlled by, a religious sect

de·nom'i·na'tor *n.* term below the line in a fraction

de·note' *v.* 1. indicate 2. mean explicitly —**de·no·ta'tion** *n.*

de·noue·ment (dā nōō'mäN) *n.* [Fr.] unraveling of a plot: also sp. **dé·noue'ment**

de·nounce' *v.* 1. accuse publicly 2. condemn strongly

dense *a.* 1. packed tightly 2. thick 3. stupid —**dense'ly** *adv.*

den'si·ty *n.* 1. a being dense 2. number per unit 3. ratio of

the mass of an object to its volume

dent *n.* slight hollow made in a surface by a blow —*v.* make a dent in

den'tal *a.* of the teeth

dental floss thread for removing food particles from between the teeth

den'ti·frice (-fris) *n.* substance for cleaning teeth

den'tin (-tin) *n.* hard tissue under the enamel of teeth: also **den'tine** (-tēn)

den'tist *n.* one who cares for and repairs teeth —**den'tist·ry** *n.*

den'ture (-chər) *n.* set of artificial teeth

de·nude' *v.* make bare; strip

de·nun'ci·a'tion *n.* the act of denouncing

de·ny' *v.* [-NIED, -NYING] 1. declare untrue 2. refuse to give, accept, etc. —**deny oneself** do without

de·o'dor·ant *n., a.* (substance) that masks odors

de·o'dor·ize *v.* counteract the odor of —**de·o'dor·iz'er** *n.*

de·part' *v.* 1. leave 2. deviate (*from*) —**de·par'ture** (-chər) *n.*

de·part'ment *n.* 1. division 2. field of activity, etc. —**de'·part·men'tal** *a.*

department store large retail store with different goods in each of many departments

de·pend' *v.* 1. be determined by something else 2. rely, as for support —**de·pend'ence** *n.* —**de·pend'ent** *a., n.*

de·pend'a·ble *a.* reliable —**de·pend'a·bil'i·ty** *n.*

de·pict' *v.* 1. represent by drawing, etc. 2. describe

de·pil'a·to·ry *n.* [*pl.* -RIES] substance or device for removing unwanted hair

de·plane' (dē-) *v.* leave an airplane after it lands

de·plete' *v.* 1. empty wholly or partly 2. exhaust —**de·ple'tion** *n.*

de·plore' *v.* be sorry about —**de·plor'a·ble** *a.*

de·ploy' *v. Mil.* spread out

de·po'nent (-pōn'-) *n. Law* one who testifies in writing under oath

de·pop'u·late *v.* reduce the population of

de·port' *v.* 1. behave (oneself) 2. banish

de'por·ta'tion *n.* banishment

de·port'ment *n.* behavior

de·pose' *v.* 1. remove from office 2. testify —**dep'o·si'tion** *n.*

de·pos'it *v.* 1. place for safekeeping 2. give as partial payment 3. set down —*n.* something deposited —**de·pos'i·tor** *n.*

de·pos'i·to·ry *n.* [*pl.* -RIES] place to put things for safekeeping

de·pot (dē'pō, dep'ō) *n.* 1. train or bus station 2. warehouse or storage place

de·prave' *v.* make morally bad —**de·praved'** *a.* —**de·prav'i·ty** [*pl.* -TIES] *n.*

dep're·cate *v.* express disapproval of —**dep're·ca'tion** *n.* —**dep're·ca·to'ry** *a.*

de·pre'ci·ate (-prē'shē-) *v.* 1. lessen in value 2. belittle —**de·pre'ci·a'tion** *n.*

dep're·da'tion *n.* a looting

de·press' *v.* 1. press down 2. sadden 3. make less active 4. lower in value, etc. —**de·press'ant** *n.* —**de·pressed'** *a.*

de·pres'sion *n.* 1. a depressing 2. hollow place 3. dejection 4. decrease in force, activity, etc. 5. period of reduced business and prosperity

de·prive' *v.* 1. take away from 2. withhold from —**dep'ri·va'tion** *n.*

depth *n.* 1. distance from the top or back 2. deepness 3. profundity 4. *usually pl.* deepest part —**in depth** comprehensively

dep'u·ta'tion *n.* delegation

de·pute' *v.* 1. authorize as a deputy 2. appoint in one's place

dep'u·tize *v.* make a deputy

dep'u·ty *n.* [*pl.* -TIES] substitute or agent

de·rail' *v.* run off the rails

de·rail'leur (-lər) *n.* device to shift gears on a bicycle

de·range' *v.* 1. upset or disturb 2. make insane

der·by (dur'bē) *n.* [*pl.* -BIES] stiff felt hat with a round crown

de·reg'u·late *v.* remove regulations governing

der'e·lict *a.* 1. abandoned 2. negligent —*n.* thing or person abandoned as worthless —**der'e·lic'tion** *n.*

de·ride' *v.* to ridicule —**de·ri'-**

sion (-rizh'ən) n. —de·ri'sive (-rī'-) a.

de·rive' v. 1. take or get (from) 2. deduce 3. originate 4. trace to a source —der'i·va'tion n. —de·riv'a·tive (-riv'-) n.

der·ma·ti'tis n. inflammation of the skin

der·ma·tol'o·gy n. study of the skin and its diseases — der·ma·tol'o·gist n.

der'o·gate v. detract; disparage —der'o·ga'tion n.

de·rog'a·to'ry a. detracting; disparaging

der'rick n. 1. machine for moving heavy objects 2. framework for drilling, as an oil well

der·ri·ère (der'ē er') n. [Fr.] the buttocks

der'vish (dur'-) n. Muslim ascetic

de·sal'i·na'tion (-sal'-) n. removal of salt from sea water to make it drinkable

de·scend' (-send') v. 1. move down 2. come from earlier times 3. derive 4. make a sudden attack (on) —de·scent' n.

de·scend'ant n. offspring of a certain ancestor

de·scribe' v. 1. picture in words; tell about 2. trace the outline of —de·scrip'tion n. —de·scrip'tive a.

de·scry' (-skrī') v. [-SCRIED, -SCRYING] catch sight of

des'e·crate v. violate the sacredness of; profane —des'e·cra'tion n.

de·seg're·gate v. end racial segregation (in) —de·seg're·ga'tion n.

de·sen'si·tize v. make less sensitive

de·sert' (-zurt') v. abandon — n. often pl. reward or punishment —de·ser'tion n.

des'ert (dez'-) n. arid, sandy region

de·serve' v. be worthy (of) — de·serv'ing a.

des'ic·cate v. dry up —des'ic·ca'tion n.

de·sid·er·a'tum (-sid'ər ä'-) n. [pl. -TA] something needed and wanted

de·sign' v. 1. to plan 2. contrive —n. 1. plan; scheme 2. purpose 3. pattern 4. artistic invention —by design purposely —de·sign'er n. —de·sign'ing a., n.

des'ig·nate v. 1. point out; specify 2. appoint —des'ig·na'tion n.

de·sir'a·ble a. worth having —de·sir'a·bil'i·ty n.

de·sire' v. wish or long for; want —n. 1. a wish 2. thing wished for 3. sexual appetite — de·sir'ous a.

de·sist' v. stop; cease

desk n. writing table

des'o·late (-lit) a. 1. lonely; forlorn 2. uninhabited 3. laid waste —v. (-lāt) make desolate —des'o·la'tion n.

de·spair' v. lose hope —n. loss of hope

des·per·a'do (-ä'dō) n. [pl. -DOES, -DOS] reckless outlaw

des'per·ate (-it) a. 1. reckless from despair 2. serious —des'per·a'tion n.

des·pi·ca·ble (or di spik′-) a. deserving scorn; contemptible

de·spise′ v. 1. to scorn 2. loathe

de·spite′ prep. in spite of

de·spoil′ v. rob; plunder

de·spond′en·cy n. loss of hope; dejection: also **de·spond′ence** —**de·spond′ent** a.

des′pot n. tyrant —**des·pot′ic** a. —**des′pot·ism** n.

des·sert′ (di zurt′) n. sweet dish ending a meal

des′ti·na′tion n. place to which one is going

des′tine v. head for, as by fate —**destined for** bound or intended for

des′tin·y n. [pl. -IES] (one's) fate

des′ti·tute a. needy; poor —**destitute of** lacking —**des′ti·tu′tion** n.

de·stroy′ v. 1. tear down; demolish 2. ruin 3. kill

de·stroy′er n. fast warship

de·struct′ n. deliberate destruction of a rocket, etc. —v. be automatically destroyed

de·struc′tion n. ruin —**de·struc′tive** a.

des′ul·to·ry a. 1. not methodical 2. random

de·tach′ v. unfasten and remove —**de·tach′a·ble** a.

de·tached′ a. 1. not connected 2. aloof; impartial

de·tach′ment n. 1. separation 2. troops on a special mission 3. aloofness

de·tail′ v. 1. tell minutely 2. Mil. choose for a special task —n. (also dē′tāl) 1. minute account 2. small part 3. Mil. special task —**in detail** item by item

de·tain′ v. 1. keep in custody 2. delay

de·tect′ v. discover (thing hidden, etc.) —**de·tec′tion** n. —**de·tec′tor** n.

de·tec′tive n. one who investigates crimes, etc.

de·tente (dā tänt′) n. lessening of tension between nations

de·ten′tion n. a detaining

de·ter′ v. [-TERRED, -TERRING] keep someone from an action —**de·ter′ment** n.

de·ter′gent a., n. cleansing (substance)

de·te′ri·o·rate′ (di tir′ē-) v. make or become worse —**de·te′ri·o·ra′tion** n.

de·ter′mi·nant n. thing that determines

de·ter′mine v. 1. set limits to 2. decide; resolve 3. find out exactly —**de·ter′mi·na′tion** n.

de·ter′mined a. 1. decided 2. resolute

de·ter′rent a. deterring —n. thing that deters

de·test′ v. hate —**de·test′a·ble** a. —**de·tes·ta′tion** n.

de·throne′ v. to depose (a monarch)

det′o·nate v. explode —**det′o·na′tor** n.

de′tour v., n. (use) an indirect or alternate road

de·tract′ v. take something desirable (from)

det′ri·ment n. damage; harm —**det′ri·men′tal** a.

de·tri'tus n. debris; spec., rock fragments

deuce (dōōs, dyōōs) n. 1. playing card with two spots 2. *Tennis* tic score after which one side must score twice in a row to win

de·val'ue v. lower the exchange value of (a currency) —de·val'u·a'tion n.

dev'as·tate v. destroy; ravage —dev'as·ta'tion n.

de·vel'op v. 1. grow, improve, expand, etc. 2. work out by degrees 3. treat (a film) to make the picture visible —de·vel'op·er n. —de·vel'op·ment n.

de'vi·ant a. deviating from social norms

de'vi·ate v. turn aside; diverge —de'vi·a'tion n.

de·vice' n. 1. a plan or scheme 2. mechanical contrivance 3. a design

dev'il n. 1. [*also* D-] evil spirit, esp. Satan 2. wicked or reckless person —v. 1. season (food) highly 2. tease —dev'il·ish a.

dev'il-may-care' a. reckless; careless

dev'il·ment n. mischief

dev'il's-food' cake rich chocolate cake

dev'il·try n. [*pl.* -TRIES] reckless mischief

de'vi·ous a. roundabout

de·vise' (-vīz') v. 1. to plan 2. bequeath by will

de·vi'tal·ize v. weaken

de·void' a. empty (*of*)

de·volve' v. pass (*on*) to another, as a duty

de·vote' v. 1. dedicate 2. apply to a purpose

de·vot'ed a. 1. dedicated 2. loyal —de·vot'ed·ly adv.

dev·o·tee' n. one strongly devoted to something

de·vo'tion n. 1. a devoting 2. *pl.* prayers 3. loyalty

de·vour' v. 1. eat up hungrily 2. take in eagerly

de·vout' a. pious or sincere

dew n. atmospheric moisture condensing on cool surfaces at night —dew'y [-IER, -IEST] a.

dew'lap n. loose skin under the throat of cattle, etc.

dex'ter·ous a. skillful in using one's hands, mind, etc. —dex·ter'i·ty n.

dex'trose n. sugar found in plants and animals

di- *pref.* twice; double

di·a·be·tes (dī'ə bē'tis) n. disease marked by excess sugar in the blood and urine —di·a·bet'ic a., n.

di'a·bol'ic a. fiendish: also di'a·bol'i·cal

di'a·crit'ic n. a mark to show pronunciation —di'a·crit'i·cal a.

di'a·dem n. a crown

di'ag·nose' v. make a diagnosis (of)

di'ag·no'sis n. identifying of a disease, etc. —di'ag·nos'tic a.

di·ag'o·nal a. slanting between opposite corners —n. diagonal line

di'a·gram n., v. sketch, plan, etc. to help explain —di'a·gram·mat'ic a.

di'al n. 1. face of a clock, meter, etc. for indicating some

di·a·lect *n.* form of speech peculiar to a region, group, etc. —**di·a·lec'tal** *a.*

di·a·lec'tic *n.* logical examination of ideas

di·a·logue, di·a·log (-lôg) *n.* conversation

di·am'e·ter *n.* **1.** straight line through the center of a circle, etc. **2.** its length

di·a·met'ri·cal *a.* exactly opposite

di·a·mond *n.* **1.** precious gem of great brilliance **2.** figure shaped like ◊ **3.** playing card so marked **4.** baseball field

di·a·mond·back' *n.* large, poisonous rattlesnake

di·a·per *n.* cloth worn about a baby's crotch —*v.* to put a diaper on

di·aph'a·nous *a.* gauzy

di·a·phragm (-fram) *n.* **1.** wall of muscle between chest and abdomen **2.** vibrating disk, as in an earphone **3.** vaginal contraceptive

di·ar·rhe·a (dī'ə rē'ə) *n.* very loose bowel movements

di·a·ry *n.* [*pl.* -RIES] daily record of one's experiences

di·as·to·le (dī as'tə lē) *n.* usual rhythmic expansion of the heart —**di·a·stol'ic** *a.*

di·a·ther'my *n.* use of electric current to heat tissues below the skin

di·a·ton·ic (-tän'-) *a.* of any standard musical scale of eight tones

di·a·tribe *n.* denunciation

dice *n.pl.* [*sing.* DIE] small, spotted cubes, used in gambling —*v.* cut into cubes

di·chot·o·my (dī kät'ə mē) *n.* [*pl.* -MIES] division into two parts

dick *n.* [Sl.] detective

dick'er *v.* barter; haggle

dick'ey *n.* detachable collar or shirt front

dic'tate *v.* **1.** speak (something) for another to write down **2.** command —*n.* an order —**dic·ta'tion** *n.*

dic'ta·tor *n.* absolute ruler; tyrant —**dic'ta·to'ri·al** *a.* —**dic·ta'tor·ship** *n.*

dic'tion *n.* **1.** choice of words **2.** enunciation

dic'tion·ar'y *n.* [*pl.* -IES] book of words alphabetically listed and defined

dic'tum *n.* formal opinion

did pt. of **do**

di·dac'tic (dī-) *a.* meant to teach; instructive

did'dle *v.* [Col.] **1.** to cheat **2.** waste time

did'n't did not

die *v.* [DIED, DYING] **1.** stop living **2.** to end **3.** [Col.] wish very much —*n.* **1.** sing. of **dice 2.** device for molding, stamping, etc. —**die away** (or **down**) cease gradually —**die off** die one by one until all are gone —**die out** go out of existence

die'-hard', die'hard' *n.* stubborn, resistant person

die·sel (dē'z'l) *n.* [*often* D-] internal-combustion engine that burns fuel oil

di'et n. 1. one's usual food 2. special food taken as for health —v. follow a diet, as to lose weight —**di'e·tar'y** a. —**di'et·er** n.

di'e·tet'ics n. study of food as needed for health

di'e·ti'tian, **di'e·ti'cian** (-tish'ən) n. planner of diets

dif'fer v. 1. to be different or unlike 2. disagree

dif'fer·ence n. 1. a being unlike 2. distinguishing characteristic 3. disagreement 4. amount by which two quantities differ

dif'fer·ent a. 1. not alike 2. distinct 3. unusual

dif'fer·en'tial (-shəl) a. being or showing a difference —n. 1. differentiating amount 2. differential gear

differential gear gear arrangement allowing one axle to turn faster than the other

dif'fer·en'ti·ate' (-en'shē-) v. 1. be or make different 2. distinguish between

dif'fi·cult' a. hard to do, learn, deal with, etc.

dif'fi·cul'ty n. [pl. -TIES] 1. a being difficult 2. something difficult 3. trouble

dif'fi·dent a. shy —**dif'fi·dence** n.

dif·frac'tion n. a breaking up of light as into the colors of the spectrum

dif·fuse' (-fyōōs') a. 1. spread out 2. wordy —v. (-fyōōz') spread widely —**dif·fu'sion** n.

dig v. [DUG, DIGGING] 1. turn up (soil), as with a spade 2. make or get by digging —n. 1.

[Col.] sarcastic remark 2. archaeological excavation

di'gest (-jest) n. summary —v. (di jest', dī'-) 1. change (food) in the stomach, etc. so that it can be absorbed 2. absorb mentally —**di·gest'i·ble** a. —**di·ges'tion** n.

dig'it (dij'-) n. 1. any number from 0 to 9 2. a finger or toe —**dig'it·al** a.

digital clock (or **watch**) timepiece that shows the time in a row of digits

dig'i·tal'is (dij'-) n. 1. plant with long spikes of flowers 2. heart medicine made from its leaves

dig'ni·fied a. having or showing dignity

dig'ni·fy (-fi) v. [-FIED, -FYING] give dignity to

dig'ni·tar'y n. [pl. -IES] person of high position

dig'ni·ty n. 1. worthiness 2. high repute; honor 3. calm stateliness

di·gress' v. wander from the subject, as in talking —**di·gres'sion** n. —**di·gres'sive** a.

dike n. embankment to hold back the sea, etc.

di·lap'i·dat'ed (-dāt'-) a. falling to pieces

di·late' v. 1. make or become wider 2. to speak or write at length (on or upon a subject) —**di·la'tion** n.

dil'a·tor'y a. 1. causing delay 2. slow

di·lem'ma n. perplexing situation

dil′et·tante′ (-tänt′) *n.* dabbler in the arts

dil′i·gent *a.* careful and industrious —**dil′i·gence** *n.*

dill *n.* plant with aromatic seeds

dil′ly·dal′ly *v.* [-LIED, -LYING] waste time

di·lute′ *v.* weaken as by mixing with water —*a.* diluted — **di·lu′tion** *n.*

dim *a.* [DIMMER, DIMMEST] not bright or clear —*v.* [DIMMED, DIMMING] make or grow dim — **dim′ly** *adv.*

dime *n.* coin equal to ten cents

di·men′sion *n.* 1. any measurable extent 2. *pl.* measurements in length, breadth, and, often, height

di·min′ish *v.* lessen

di·min′u·tive *a.* tiny

dim′i·ty *n.* a thin cotton cloth

dim′mer *n.* device for dimming electric lights

dim′ple *n.* small, natural hollow, as on the cheek

dim′wit *n.* [Sl.] stupid person —**dim′wit′ted** *a.*

din *n.* confused clamor —*v.* [DINNED, DINNING] 1. make a din 2. keep repeating

din′-din′ *n.* [Col.] dinner

dine *v.* 1. eat dinner 2. give dinner to

din′er (dīn′-) *n.* 1. railroad car for serving meals 2. restaurant built like this

din·ette′ (dī net′) *n.* small dining room or alcove

ding *n.* sound of a bell: also **ding′-dong′**

din·ghy (diŋ′gē) *n.* [*pl.* -GHIES] small boat

din′gy (-jē) *a.* [-GIER, -GIEST] dirty; shabby

din′ky (diŋ′-) *a.* [-KIER, -KIEST] [Col.] small

din′ner *n.* chief daily meal

din′ner·ware *n.* dishes

di′no·saur (-sôr) *n.* huge extinct reptile

dint *n.* force

di′o·cese (-sis) *n.* district headed by a bishop —**di·oc′e·san** (-äs′ə s′n) *a.*

di′ode *n.* electronic device used esp. as a rectifier

di·ox′ide *n.* oxide with two oxygen atoms per molecule

dip *v.* [DIPPED, DIPPING] 1. plunge into liquid for a moment 2. scoop up 3. sink or slope down —*n.* 1. a dipping 2. that into which something is dipped 3. downward slope

diph·the′ri·a (dif thir′ē-, dip-) *n.* acute infectious disease of throat

diph′thong *n.* sound made by gliding from one vowel to another in one syllable

di·plo′ma *n.* certificate of graduation from a school

di·plo′ma·cy *n.* 1. the conducting of relations between nations 2. tact

dip′lo·mat *n.* 1. government official who conducts relations with another government 2. tactful person

dip′lo·mat′ic *a.* 1. of diplomacy 2. tactful

dip′per *n.* long-handled cup, etc. for dipping

dip′so·ma′ni·a *n.* insatiable desire for alcoholic drink — **dip′so·ma′ni·ac** *n.*

dip·stick *n.* graduated rod for measuring depth

dire *a.* dreadful; terrible

di·rect' *a.* 1. straight 2. frank 3. immediate 4. exact —*v.* 1. manage; guide 2. order 3. aim —*adv.* directly —**di·rect'ly** *adv.* —**di·rec'tor** *n.*

direct current electric current moving in one direction

di·rec'tion *n.* 1. management; guidance 2. *pl.* instructions 3. an order 4. the point one faces or moves toward —**di·rec'tion·al** *a.*

di·rec'tive *n.* an order

di·rec'to·ry *n.* [*pl.* -RIES] book of names and addresses of a specific group

dire'ful *a.* dire

dirge *n.* song of mourning

dir'i·gi·ble *n.* airship

dirk *n.* short dagger

dirt *n.* 1. dust, filth, etc. 2. earth; soil

dirt'y *a.* [-IER, -IEST] 1. soiled 2. obscene 3. mean 4. unfair 5. stormy —*v.* [-IED, -YING] to soil —**dirt'i·ness** *n.*

dis- *pref.* 1. the opposite of 2. reverse the action of

dis·a·bil'i·ty *n.* [*pl.* -TIES] 1. disabled condition 2. that which disables

dis·a'ble *v.* make unable or unfit; cripple

dis·a·buse' *v.* rid of false ideas

dis'ad·van'tage *n.* drawback; handicap; detriment —**dis'ad'-van·ta'geous** *a.*

dis'ad·van'taged *a.* poor

dis·af·fect' *v.* make hostile —**dis'af·fec'tion** *n.*

dis·a·gree' *v.* 1. differ 2. quar-

rel 3. be harmful —**dis'a·gree'ment** *n.*

dis'a·gree'a·ble *a.* 1. unpleasant 2. quarrelsome

dis'al·low' *v.* reject

dis·ap·pear' *v.* 1. go out of sight 2. cease being —**dis'ap·pear'ance** *n.*

dis·ap·point' *v.* spoil the hopes of —**dis'ap·point'ment** *n.*

dis·ap·prove' *v.* 1. have an unfavorable opinion 2. reject —**dis'ap·prov'al** *n.*

dis·arm' *v.* 1. remove weapons from 2. make friendly 3. reduce armed forces —**dis·ar'ma·ment** *n.*

dis·ar·range' *v.* disorder

dis·ar·ray' *n., v.* disorder

dis'as·sem'ble *v.* take apart

dis'as·so'ci·ate' *v.* sever association with

dis·as'ter *n.* sudden misfortune; calamity —**dis·as'trous** *a.*

dis·a·vow' *v.* deny knowing or approving —**dis'a·vow'al** *n.*

dis·band' *v.* break up

dis·bar' *v.* [-BARRED, -BARRING] deprive of the right to practice law —**dis·bar'ment** *n.*

dis·be·lieve' *v.* refuse to believe (*in*) —**dis'be·lief'** *n.*

dis·burse' *v.* pay out

disc *n.* 1. disk 2. phonograph record

dis·card' *v.* throw away —*n.* (dis'kärd) thing discarded

disc brake brake with two pads that press on a disc

dis·cern' (di surn') *v.* perceive —**dis·cern'i·ble** *a.*

dis·cern'ing *a.* astute

dis·charge' *v.* 1. dismiss 2. unload 3. shoot 4. emit 5. do (a duty) —*n.* (dis'chärj) a discharging or thing discharged

dis·ci'ple *n.* follower; pupil

dis'ci·pli·nar'i·an *n.* enforcer of strict discipline

dis'ci·pline (-plin) *n.* 1. orderly training or conduct 2. punishment —*v.* 1. train; control 2. punish —**dis'ci·pli·nar'y** *a.*

disc jockey one who conducts a radio record program

dis·claim' *v.* 1. give up claim to 2. deny

dis·claim'er *n.* denial or rejection of responsibility

dis·close' (-klōz') *v.* reveal —**dis·clos'ure** *n.*

dis'co *n.* [*pl.* -cos] discotheque

dis·col'or *v.* to stain; tarnish —**dis·col'or·a'tion** *n.*

dis·com'fit *v.* upset; embarrass —**dis·com'fi·ture** *n.*

dis·com'fort *n.* lack of comfort or cause of this

dis·com·mode' *v.* to inconvenience

dis·com·pose' *v.* fluster —**dis'com·po'sure** *n.*

dis·con·cert' *v.* confuse

dis·con·nect' *v.* to separate

dis'con·nect'ed *a.* 1. separated 2. incoherent

dis·con'so·late (-lit) *a.* very unhappy

dis·con·tent' *a.* discontented —*n.* dissatisfaction: also **dis'con·tent'ment**

dis'con·tent'ed *a.* not contented

dis'con·tin'ue *v.* to stop

dis·con·tin'u·ous *a.* having gaps

dis'cord *n.* 1. disagreement 2. dissonance; harsh sound —**dis·cord'ant** *a.*

dis'co·thèque (-tek) *n.* place for dancing to records

dis·count *v.* 1. deduct, as from a price 2. sell at less than the regular price 3. disregard in part or entirely —*n.* reduction in price

dis·coun'te·nance *v.* embarrass

dis·cour'age *v.* 1. deprive of hope or confidence 2. dissuade 3. work against —**dis·cour'age·ment** *n.*

dis'course *n.* talk or formal lecture —*v.* (dis kôrs') to talk

dis·cour'te·ous *a.* impolite

dis·cour'te·sy *n.* 1. rudeness 2. [*pl.* -SIES] rude act

dis·cov'er *v.* 1. be the first to find, see, etc. 2. find out —**dis·cov'er·y** [*pl.* -IES] *n.*

dis·cred'it *v.* 1. disbelieve 2. cast doubt on 3. disgrace —*n.* 1. doubt 2. disgrace

dis·creet' *a.* careful; prudent —**dis·creet'ly** *adv.*

dis·crep'an·cy *n.* [*pl.* -CIES] inconsistency

dis·crete' *a.* unrelated

dis·cre'tion (-kresh'ən) *n.* 1. freedom to decide 2. prudence

dis·crim'i·nate *v.* 1. distinguish 2. show partiality or bias —**dis·crim'i·nat'ing** *a.* —**dis·crim'i·na'tion** *n.*

dis·crim'i·na·to'ry *a.* showing bias

dis·cur'sive *a.* rambling

dis·cus n. heavy disk thrown in a contest

dis·cuss' v. talk or write about —**dis·cus'sion** n.

dis·dain' v., n. scorn —**dis·dain'ful** a.

dis·ease (di zēz') n. (an) illness —**dis·eased'** a.

dis·em·bark' v. leave a ship, airplane, etc.

dis·em·bod'y v. [-IED, -YING] to free from bodily existence

dis·en·chant' v. to free from a false idea

dis·en·gage' v. disconnect

dis·en·tan'gle v. extricate

dis·fa'vor n. 1. dislike 2. a being disliked

dis·fig'ure v. spoil the looks of; mar —**dis·fig'ure·ment** n.

dis·fran'chise v. deprive of the right to vote: also **dis·en·fran'chise**

dis·gorge' v. 1. to vomit 2. pour forth

dis·grace' n. shame; dishonor —v. bring shame upon —**dis·grace'ful** a.

dis·grun'tle v. make sulky

dis·guise' (-gīz') v. make unrecognizable —n. thing used for disguising

dis·gust' n. sickening dislike; loathing —v. cause disgust in —**dis·gust'ed** a. —**dis·gust'ing** a.

dish n. 1. plate, etc. for food 2. kind of food —v. serve in a dish (up or out)

dis·ha·bille (dis a bēl') n. state of being only partly dressed

dis·heart'en v. discourage

di·shev'el v. muss up (hair, clothes, etc.); rumple

dis·hon'est a. not honest —**dis·hon'es·ty** n.

dis·hon'or n., v. shame; disgrace —**dis·hon'or·a·ble** a.

dish'wash'er n. person or machine that washes dishes

dis·il·lu'sion v. 1. to free from illusion 2. take away the idealism of

dis·in·cline' v. make unwilling

dis·in·fect' v. kill bacteria on —**dis·in·fect'ant** n.

dis·in·gen'u·ous (-jen'-) a. not candid

dis·in·her'it v. deprive of an inheritance

dis·in·te·grate v. separate into parts; break up —**dis·in·te·gra'tion** n.

dis·in·ter·est·ed a. 1. impartial 2. indifferent

dis·joint' v. 1. put out of joint 2. dismember

disk n. 1. thin, flat, circular thing 2. disc

dis·like' v., n. (have) a feeling of not liking

dis·lo·cate v. 1. put out of joint 2. disarrange —**dis·lo·ca'tion** n.

dis·lodge' v. force from its place

dis·loy'al a. not loyal —**dis·loy'al·ty** n.

dis·mal (diz'-) a. dreary

dis·man'tle v. take apart

dis·may' v. make afraid; daunt —n. loss of courage

dis·mem'ber v. cut or tear apart

dis·miss' v. 1. request or allow to leave 2. discharge 3. set aside —**dis·miss'al** n.

dis·mount' v. 1. get off 2. take from its mounting

dis·o·be'di·ence n. refusal to obey —**dis·o·be'di·ent** a.

dis·o·bey' v. refuse or fail to obey

dis·or'der n. 1. confusion 2. commotion; riot 3. ailment —v. cause disorder in

dis·or'der·ly a. 1. untidy 2. unruly; riotous

dis·or'gan·ize v. throw into confusion —**dis·or'gan·i·za'tion** n.

dis·o'ri·ent v. 1. cause to lose one's bearings 2. confuse mentally

dis·own' v. to refuse to acknowledge as one's own

dis·par'age v. belittle —**dis·par'age·ment** n.

dis'pa·rate (-rit) a. not alike

dis·par'i·ty n. [pl. -TIES] difference; unlikeness

dis·pas'sion·ate (-it) a. free from emotion or bias

dis·patch' v. 1. send 2. finish quickly 3. kill —n. 1. speed 2. message 3. news story —**dispatch'er** n.

dis·pel' v. [-PELLED, -PELLING] scatter and drive away

dis·pen'sa·ble a. not important

dis·pen'sa·ry n. [pl. -RIES] place in a school, etc. for getting medicines or first aid

dis'pen·sa'tion n. 1. distribution 2. system of administration 3. release from an obligation

dis·pense' v. 1. distribute 2. prepare and give out —

dispense with do without —**dis·pen'ser** n.

dis·perse' v. scatter —**dispers'al** n. —**dis·per'sion** n.

dis·pir'it·ed a. dejected

dis·place' v. 1. move from its usual place 2. replace

displaced person one forced from his country, esp. by war

dis·place'ment n. 1. a displacing 2. amount of a fluid displaced by floating object

dis·play' v. to show; exhibit —n. exhibition

dis·please' v. annoy; offend —**dis·pleas'ure** (-plezh'-) n. dissatisfaction

dis·port' v. 1. to play 2. amuse (oneself)

dis·pose' v. 1. arrange 2. incline mentally —**dispose of** 1. settle 2. get rid of —**dis·pos'a·ble** a. —**dis·pos'al** n.

dis·pos'er n. one that disposes 2. kitchen device for grinding up garbage

dis'po·si'tion (-zish'ən) n. 1. arrangement 2. management of affairs 3. a getting rid of 4. control 5. tendency 6. one's temperament

dis·pos·sess' v. force to give up property; oust

dis'pro·por'tion n. lack of proportion

dis·prove' v. prove false

dis'pu·ta'tious a. fond of arguing

dis·pute' v., n. 1. debate 2. quarrel —**in dispute** not settled —**dis·pu'ta·ble** a. —**dis·pu'tant** n.

dis·qual'i·fy v. [-FIED, -FYING] make ineligible

dis·qui'et v. make uneasy

dis'qui·si'tion n. treatise

dis·re·gard' v. ignore —n. lack of attention

dis·ro·pair' n. worn state

dis·rep'u·ta·ble a. 1. not reputable 2. not fit to be seen —**dis·rep'u·ta·bly** adv.

dis·re·pute' n. bad reputation

dis·re·spect' n. lack of respect —**dis're·spect'ful** a.

dis·robe' v. undress

dis·rupt' v. 1. break apart 2. disturb —**dis·rup'tion** n.

dis·sat'is·fy v. [-FIED, -FYING] make discontented —**dis'sat·is·fac'tion** n.

dis·sect' v. 1. cut apart so as to examine 2. analyze closely —**dis·sec'tion** n.

dis·sem'ble v. feign; pretend

dis·sem'i·nate v. spread widely —**dis·sem'i·na'tion** n.

dis·sen'sion n. disagreement or quarreling

dis·sent' v. disagree —n. difference of opinion

dis'ser·ta'tion n. formal discourse; thesis

dis·serv'ice n. harm

dis'si·dence n. disagreement —**dis'si·dent** a., n.

dis·sim'i·lar a. not alike

dis'si·pate v. 1. vanish or dispel 2. squander 3. indulge in wild, harmful pleasure —**dis'si·pa'tion** n.

dis·so'ci·ate (-sō'shē-) v. sever association (with)

dis'so·lute a. dissipated and immoral

dis'so·lu'tion n. a dissolving or breaking up

dis·solve' v. 1. melt 2. pass or make pass into solution 3.

break up 4. end 5. disappear or make disappear

dis'so·nance n. lack of harmony, esp. in sound; discord —**dis'so·nant** a.

dis·suade' (-swād') v. cause to turn from a purpose

dis'taff n. staff for holding flax, wool, etc. in spinning —a. female

dis'tance n. 1. length between two points 2. aloofness 3. far-away place

dis'tant a. 1. far apart; remote 2. away 3. aloof

dis·taste' n. dislike

dis·taste'ful a. unpleasant

dis·tem'per n. virus disease of young dogs

dis·tend' v. swell

dis·till' v. subject to or obtain by distillation

dis'til·la'tion n. process of purifying a mixture by heating it and condensing the resulting vapor

dis·till'er·y n. [pl. -IES] place for distilling alcoholic liquors —**dis·till'er** n.

dis·tinct' a. 1. not alike 2. separate 3. clear; plain

dis·tinc'tion n. 1. a keeping distinct 2. quality that differentiates or indicates superiority 3. fame

dis·tinc'tive a. making distinct

dis·tin'guish (-tiŋ'gwish) v. 1. perceive or show a difference 2. classify 3. make famous —**dis·tin'guish·a·ble** a.

dis·tin'guished a. famous

dis·tort' v. 1. twist out of

shape 2. misrepresent —**dis·tor′tion** n.

dis·tract′ v. 1. divert (the mind, etc.) 2. confuse

dis·trac′tion n. 1. confusion 2. cause of confusion 3. diversion 4. mental distress

dis·traught (dis trôt′) a. 1. harassed 2. crazed

dis·tress′ v., n. trouble, pain, worry, etc.

dis·trib′ute v. 1. deal out 2. spread out 3. arrange —**dis′tri·bu′tion** n.

dis·trib′u·tor n. 1. one who distributes, deals in a product, etc. 2. device distributing electricity to spark plugs in a gasoline engine

dis′trict n. 1. division of a state, etc. 2. region

district attorney prosecuting attorney of a district

dis·trust′ n. lack of trust —v. to doubt; mistrust

dis·turb′ v. 1. break up the quiet or settled order of 2. make uneasy 3. interrupt —**dis·turb′ance** n.

dis·u′nite v. divide; separate

dis·use′ (-yōōs′) n. lack of use

ditch n. channel dug out for drainage, etc. —v. [Sl.] get rid of

dith′er n. excited state

ditto mark mark (″) in lists showing the item above is to be repeated

dit′ty (dit′-) n. [pl. -TIES] short, simple song

di·u·ret′ic (dī′-) n. drug or substance that increases flow of urine

di·ur′nal a. daily

di′va (dē′-) n. prima donna

di·van (dī′van) n. large sofa

dive v. [alt. pt. DOVE] 1. plunge head first into water 2. submerge 3. plunge suddenly or deeply —n. 1. sudden plunge 2. [Col.] cheap saloon

di·verge′ (-vurj′) v. 1. branch off 2. deviate

di·vers (-vərz) a. various

di·verse′ a. 1. different 2. varied

di·ver′si·fy v. [-FIED, -FYING] vary

di·ver′sion n. 1. a diverting 2. pastime; amusement

di·ver′si·ty n. [pl. -TIES] variety

di·vert′ v. 1. turn aside (from) 2. amuse

di·ver′tic·u·li′tis (dī′-) n. inflammation of sac opening out from intestine

di·vest′ v. strip (of)

di·vide′ v. 1. separate into parts 2. apportion 3. Math. separate into equal parts by a divisor —n. ridge —**di·vis′i·ble** a.

div′i·dend n. 1. number to be divided 2. sum divided among stockholders, etc. 3. bonus

div′i·na′tion n. foretelling the future or the unknown

di·vine′ a. 1. of God or a god 2. supremely good —n. clergyman —v. 1. prophesy 2. guess

divining rod forked stick alleged to dip when held over underground water

di·vin′i·ty (-vin′-) n. 1. a being divine 2. [pl. -TIES] a god

di·vi′sion n. 1. a dividing 2.

thing that divides **3.** segment, group, etc. **4.** section of an army corps

di·vi′sive (-vī′-) *a.* causing disagreement

di·vi′sor *n.* number by which the dividend is divided

di·vorce′ *n.* **1.** legal dissolution of a marriage — *v.* separate from, as by divorce

di·vor′cée′, di·vor′cee′ (-sā′, -sē′) *n.* divorced woman

div′ot (div′-) *n.* turf dislodged in hitting a golf ball

di·vulge′ *v.* make known

diz′zy *a.* [-ZIER, -ZIEST] **1.** giddy; confused **2.** causing dizziness —**diz′zi·ly** *adv.* —**diz′zi·ness** *n.*

DNA basic material of chromosomes that transmits hereditary pattern

do *v.* [DID, DONE, DOING] **1.** perform (an action) **2.** finish **3.** cause **4.** deal with as required **5.** have as one's work **6.** get along **7.** be adequate —**do away with 1.** get rid of **2.** kill —**do without** get along without —**have to do with** relate to —**make do** get along with what is available —**do′er** *n.*

Do′ber·man pin′scher (-shər) large dog with short, dark hair

doc·ile (däs′'l) *a.* easy to train —**do·cil′i·ty** *n.*

dock *n.* **1.** landing pier; wharf **2.** water between piers **3.** place for the accused in a courtroom **4.** coarse weed —*v.* **1.** bring or come to a dock **2.** cut short **3.** deduct from

dock′et *n.* list of cases to be tried by a law court

dock′yard *n.* place with docks for building or repairing ships

doc′tor *n.* **1.** person with the highest degree from a university **2.** physician or surgeon — *v.* [Col.] **1.** try to heal **2.** tamper with

doc·tri·naire′ (-ner′) *a.* adhering strictly to a doctrine

doc′trine (-trĭn) *n.* something taught, as a religious tenet

doc′u·ment *n.* written record relied on as evidence —*v.* support by documents

doc′u·men′ta·ry *a.* **1.** of or supported by documents **2.** recording news events dramatically —*n.* [*pl.* -RIES] documentary film, etc.

dod′der *v.* shake as from old age

dodge *v.* **1.** move quickly aside **2.** avoid; evade —*n.* **1.** a dodging **2.** trick

do′do *n.* [*pl.* -DOS, -DOES] large extinct bird

doe (dō) *n.* female deer, etc. —**doe′skin** *n.*

does (duz) *pres. t. of* **do**: used with *he, she,* or *it*

does′n′t does not

doff *v.* take off; remove

dog *n.* **1.** domesticated animal of the wolf family **2.** mean fellow —*v.* [DOGGED, DOGGING] follow like a dog

dog′-ear′ *n.* turned-down corner of a page —**dog′-eared′** *a.*

dog′ged *a.* persistent

dog′ger·el *n.* trivial verse

do·gie, do·gy (dō′gē) n. [pl. -GIES] stray calf

dog′ma n. strict doctrine

dog·mat′ic a. 1. of a dogma 2. positive in stating opinion; arrogant —**dog·mat′i·cal·ly** adv. —**dog′ma·tism** n.

dog′wood n. tree with pink or white flowers

doi′ly n. [pl. -LIES] small mat, as of lace, to protect a table, etc.

do′ings n.pl. actions

dol′drums n.pl. 1. low spirits 2. dead calms in seas near equator

dole n. money paid to the unemployed by the government —v. give sparingly

dole′ful a. sad; sorrowful —**dole′ful·ly** adv.

doll n. child's toy made to resemble a person

dol′lar n. U.S. monetary unit, equal to 100 cents

dol·lop (däl′əp) n. small quantity of something soft

dol′ly n. [pl. -LIES] 1. doll 2. low, wheeled frame for moving heavy objects

dol′men n. monument with stone laid across upright stones

do′lor·ous a. sorrowful

dol′phin n. sea mammal with a beaklike snout

dolt (dōlt) n. stupid person —**dolt′ish** a.

-dom suf. 1. rank or domain of 2. state of being 3. group of

do·main′ (dō-) n. 1. territory under one ruler 2. field of activity

dome n. large, round roof

do·mes′tic a. 1. of home or family 2. of or made in one's country 3. tame —**do·mes′ti·cal·ly** adv. —**do·mes·tic′i·ty** n.

do·mes′ti·cate v. to tame —**do·mes′ti·ca′tion** n.

dom′i·cile (-sil) n. home

dom′i·nant a. ruling; prevailing

dom′i·nate v. 1. rule or control 2. rise high above —**dom′i·nance** n. —**dom′i·na′tion** n.

dom·i·neer′ v. rule harshly

do·min′ion n. 1. rule; power 2. governed territory

dom′i·noes n. game with tiles marked with dots

don v. [DONNED, DONNING] put on (clothes)

don n. Spanish gentleman

do′nate v. give; contribute —**do·na′tion** n.

done pp. of **do**

don′key n. [pl. -KEYS] horselike animal with long ears

don′ny·brook n. rowdy fight

do′nor n. one who donates

don′t do not

doo′dle v., n. scribble

doom n. 1. a judgment 2. fate 3. ruin —v. 1. condemn 2. destine; fate

dooms′day n. Judgment Day

door n. 1. movable panel for closing an entrance 2. entrance, with or without a door: also **door′way** —**out of doors** outdoors

door′bell n. bell rung by one wishing to enter

door′step n. step from outer door to path, lawn, etc.

dope n. [Sl.] 1. narcotic 2. information 3. stupid person —v. to drug

dor′mant a. 1. sleeping 2. quiet; inactive

dor′mer n. upright window structure in a sloping roof

dor′mi·to′ry n. [pl. -RIES] 1. room with many beds 2. building with many bedrooms

dor′mouse n. [pl. -MICE] small, squirrellike rodent

dor′sal a. of the back

do′ry n. [pl. -RIES] small, flat-bottomed fishing boat

dose n. amount of medicine taken at one time —v. give doses to —**dos′age** n.

do·sim′e·ter n. device that measures radiation absorbed

dos·si·er (däs′ē ā) n. documents about a person

dost (dust) [Ar.] do: used with thou

dot n. tiny mark or round spot —v. [DOTTED, DOTTING] mark with dots —**on the dot** [Col.] at the exact time

dot′age (dōt′ij) n. feebleness of old age

dot′ard n. one in his or her dotage

dote v. be too fond

doth (duth) [Ar.] does

dou′ble a. 1. of or for two 2. twice as much or as many —adv. twofold or twice —n. 1. twice as much or as many 2. a duplicate 3. Baseball hit putting the batter on second —v. 1. make or become double 2. fold 3. duplicate 4. turn back-ward 5. serve two purposes, etc.

double bass (bās) largest,

deepest-toned instrument of vi-olin family

dou′ble-cross′ v. [Sl.] betray —n. [Sl.] betrayal

dou′ble-deck′er n. 1. vehicle, etc. with upper deck 2. [Col.] two-layer sandwich

dou′ble-head′er n. two games played in succession

double play baseball play that puts out two players

double standard moral code stricter for women than men

dou′blet (dub′-) n. formerly, man's tight jacket

dou′bly adv. twice

doubt (dout) v. 1. be uncertain about 2. disbelieve —n. 1. wavering of belief 2. uncer-tainty —**no doubt** certainly —**doubt′ful** a.

doubt′less adv. certainly

douche (dōōsh) n. liquid jet for cleaning a body part —v. use a douche on

dough n. 1. thick mixture of flour, liquid, etc. for baking 2. [Sl.] money

dough′nut n. small fried cake, usually ring-shaped

dour (door, dour) a. gloomy

douse (dous) v. 1. thrust into liquid 2. drench 3. [Col.] extin-guish (a light)

dove (duv) n. kind of pigeon

dove′tail n. joint formed by fitting together wedge-shaped parts —v. join closely, as with dovetails

dow′a·ger (-jər) n. wealthy widow

dow′dy a. [-DIER, -DIEST] not neat or not stylish

dow′el n. peg fitted into holes to join two pieces

dow′er n. widow's inheritance —v. endow

down adv. 1. to or in a lower place, state, etc. 2. to a later time 3. in cash 4. in writing —a. 1. descending 2. in a lower place 3. gone, paid, etc. down 4. discouraged —prep. down toward, into, etc. —v. put down —n. 1. misfortune 2. soft feathers or hair 3. pl. high, grassy land 4. one of a series of football plays to advance the ball —**down with!** away with!

down′cast a. 1. directed downward 2. sad

down′er n. [Sl.] any sedative

down′fall n. sudden fall, as from power

down′grade n. downward slope —adv., a. downward —v. 1. demote 2. belittle

down′heart′ed a. sad

down′hill adv., a. down a slope; downward

down′pour n. heavy rain

down′right adv. thoroughly —a. 1. utter 2. plain

Down's syndrome congenital disease marked by mental deficiency

down′stairs a., adv. on or to lower floor —n. lower floor

down′swing n. 1. downward swing of golf club 2. downward trend

down′town a., adv. in or toward business section —n. business section

down′trod′den a. oppressed

down′ward adv., a. toward a lower place, etc.: also **down′-wards** adv.

down′y a. [-IER, -IEST] soft and fluffy

dow′ry n. [pl. -RIES] property a bride brings to her husband

dowse (douz) v. use divining rod

dox·ol′o·gy n. [pl. -GIES] hymn of praise to God

doze v., n. sleep; nap

doz′en n. set of twelve

Dr. Doctor

drab a. [DRABBER, DRABBEST] dull —**drab′ness** n.

drach′ma (drak′-) n. Greek monetary unit

draft n. 1. drink 2. rough sketch of a writing 3. plan 4. current of air 5. written order for money 6. selection for compulsory military service 7. depth of water a ship displaces —v. 1. select to serve 2. make a plan, outline, etc. for —a. drawn from a cask

draft·ee′ n. one drafted for military service

drafts′man n. [pl. -MEN] one who draws plans of structures or machinery

draft′y a. [-IER, -IEST] open to drafts of air

drag v. [DRAGGED, DRAGGING] 1. pull or be pulled with effort, esp. along the ground 2. search (a river bottom, etc.) as with a net 3. pass slowly —n. 1. hindrance 2. [Sl.] puff of a cigarette, etc. 3. [Sl.] something dull or boring 4. [Sl.] influence

drag′net n. 1. net dragged

along water bottom **2.** system for catching criminals

drag'on n. large, mythical reptile breathing out fire

drag'on·fly n. [pl. -FLIES] long insect with four wings

dra·goon' n. armed cavalryman —v. force to do something

drag race [Sl.] race of cars starting quickly on short course

drain v. **1.** draw off (liquid) gradually **2.** empty **3.** exhaust, as energy **4.** flow off —n. channel; pipe

drain'age (-ij) n. **1.** a draining or system for draining **2.** that which is drained off

drain'pipe n. large pipe carrying off water, sewage, etc.

drake (drāk) n. male duck

dram n. **1.** apothecaries' weight, 1/8 oz. **2.** small drink of alcoholic liquor

dra'ma n. **1.** a play **2.** art of writing and staging plays

dra·mat'ic a. **1.** of drama **2.** vivid, exciting, etc.

dra·mat'ics n. performing or producing of plays

dram'a·tist n. playwright

dram'a·tize v. **1.** make into a drama **2.** regard or show in a dramatic manner

drank pt. of drink

drape v. cover or hang as with cloth in loose folds —n. *usually in pl.* curtain

dra'per·y n. [pl. -IES] curtain

dras'tic a. severe; harsh

draught (draft) n., v., a. draft: Br. sp.

draughts (drafts) n.pl. game of checkers: Br.

draw v. [DREW, DRAWN, DRAWING] **1.** pull **2.** attract **3.** inhale **4.** take out; get **5.** come; move **6.** write (a check) **7.** deduce **8.** stretch **9.** make (lines, pictures, etc.) as with a pencil —n. **1.** stalemate **2.** thing that attracts

draw'back n. disadvantage

draw'bridge n. bridge that can be raised, lowered, or drawn aside

drawer (drôr) n. **1.** sliding box in a table, etc. **2.** pl. underpants

draw'ing n. **1.** art of sketching **2.** picture sketched

drawing card entertainment drawing large audience

drawing room parlor

drawl n. slow, prolonged manner of speech —v. speak with a drawl

drawn a. haggard

dray n. wagon for heavy loads

dread (dred) v. await with fear or distaste —n. fear —a. inspiring fear —**dread'ful** a.

dream n. **1.** images, etc. seen during sleep **2.** reverie **3.** fond hope —v. [alt. pt. & pp. DREAMED (dremt)] have dreams —**dream'y** [-IER, -IEST] a.

drear'y a. [-IER, -IEST] dismal —**drear'i·ness** n.

dredge n. apparatus for scooping up mud, etc. as in deepening channels —v. **1.** enlarge with a dredge **2.** sprinkle with flour

dregs n.pl. **1.** particles at the

bottom in a liquid 2. most worthless part

drench v. soak

dress v. 1. clothe 2. adorn 3. arrange (hair) 4. treat (a wound, etc.) 5. prepare, as a fowl —n. 1. clothes; attire 2. woman's garment —**dress'** **down** to scold —**dress'-** **mak'er** n.

dress'er n. chest of drawers with a mirror

dress'ing n. 1. bandages, etc. 2. salad sauce 3. stuffing for roast fowl

dress'y a. [-IER, -IEST] [Col.] elegant

drew (drōō) pt. of **draw**

drib'ble v. 1. flow in drops 2. drool 3. repeatedly bounce, kick, or tap (ball or puck) —n. a dribbling

drib'let n. small amount

dried pt. & pp. of **dry**

dri'er n. device or substance that dries

drift v. 1. be carried along, as by a current 2. pile up in heaps —n. 1. snow, etc. driven into a heap 2. trend 3. meaning —**drift'er** n.

drift'wood n. wood that has drifted ashore

drill n. 1. tool for boring 2. systematic training 3. seeding machine 4. coarse, twilled cloth —v. 1. bore with a drill 2. train systematically —**drill'er** n.

drink v. [DRANK, DRUNK, DRINKING] swallow (liquid) —n. 1. liquid for drinking 2. alcoholic liquor —**drink'a·ble** a.

drip v. [DRIPPED, DRIPPING] fall

or let fall in drops —n. a dripping

drip'-dry' a. of garments that need little ironing

drive v. [DROVE, DRIVEN, DRIVING] 1. force to go, do, pierce, etc. 2. operate, or go in, a vehicle 3. hit (ball) hard —n. 1. trip in a vehicle 2. paved road 3. energy 4. urge 5. campaign 6. mechanism that makes machine go —**drive at** to mean —**drive in** cause (baseball runner) to score —**driv'er** n.

drive'-in' n. place for eating, etc. in one's car

driv'el v. to slobber; drool —n. silly talk

drive'way n. path for cars

driz'zle v., n. rain in fine, misty drops

drogue (drōg) n. device towed behind aircraft to slow it

droll a. quaintly amusing —**droll'er·y** [pl. -IES] n.

drom'e·dar'y n. [pl. -IES] one-humped camel

drone n. 1. male honeybee 2. constant hum —v. 1. to hum 2. talk monotonously

drool v. drip saliva

droop v. 1. sink or bend down 2. lose vitality 3. become dejected —n. a drooping —**droop'y** [-IER, -IEST] a. —**droop'i·ly** adv.

drop n. 1. small, round mass, as of falling liquid 2. tiny amount 3. sudden fall 4. distance down —v. [DROPPED, DROPPING] 1. fall or let fall 2. to send 3. utter (a hint, etc.) —**drop in** visit —**drop out**

stop taking part —**drop'let** n.

drop'-off' n. 1. steep drop 2. decline, as in sales, etc.

drop'out n. student who leaves school before graduating

drop'per n. tube with bulb to release liquid in drops

drop'sy n. edema

dross n. rubbish; refuse

drought (drout) n. spell of dry weather: also **drouth** (drouth)

drove pt. of **drive** —n. herd of cattle, etc.

drown v. 1. die or kill by suffocation in water 2. muffle (sound, etc.)

drowse v. be sleepy; doze —**drow'sy** [-SIER, -SIEST] a.

drub v. [DRUBBED, DRUBBING] 1. thrash 2. defeat —**drub'bing** n.

drudge n. one who does hard or dull work —v. do such work —**drudg'er·y** n.

drug n. 1. medicinal substance 2. narcotic —v. [DRUGGED, DRUGGING] add or give a drug to

drug'gist n. pharmacist —**drug'store** n.

dru'id n. member of religious order in ancient British Isles and France

drum n. 1. hollow form covered with a membrane and used as a percussion instrument 2. container, as for oil 3. eardrum —v. [DRUMMED, DRUMMING] beat as on a drum —**drum up** solicit (business) —**drum'mer** n.

drum'lin n. long ridge or hill

drum major one who leads a marching band

drum'stick n. 1. stick for beating a drum 2. lower leg of a cooked fowl

drunk pp. of **drink** —a. overcome by alcoholic liquor —n. [Sl.] drunken person —**drunk'ard** n.

drunk'en a. intoxicated —**drunk'en·ness** n.

dry a. [DRIER, DRIEST] 1. not wet 2. lacking rain 3. thirsty 4. not sweet 5. matter-of-fact 6. dull —v. [DRIED, DRYING] make or become dry —**dry'ly** adv.

dry'ad n. tree nymph

dry'-clean' v. to clean (garments) with a solvent, as naphtha —**dry cleaner**

dry'er n. 1. a drier 2. appliance that dries clothes with heat

dry goods cloth (products)

dry ice carbon dioxide in a solid state

dry run [Sl.] practice; rehearsal

dry wall wall made of wallboard, etc. without wet plaster

du'al a. 1. of two 2. double

du·al'i·ty n. [pl. -TIES] a being two, or double

dub v. [DUBBED, DUBBING] 1. confer a title upon 2. insert (dialogue, etc.) in film sound track

du'bi·ous a. doubtful

du'cal a. of a duke

duc·at (duk'ət) n. a former European coin

duch'ess n. duke's wife

duch'y n. [pl. -IES] land ruled by a duke

duck n. 1. flat-billed, web-footed swimming bird 2. cloth like canvas but lighter —*v.* 1. dip under water briefly 2. bend suddenly, as to avoid a blow 3. [Col.] avoid

duck'bill *n.* platypus

duck'ling *n.* young duck

duck'pins *n.pl.* bowling game with small pins and balls

duct *n.* tube or channel for fluid —**duct'less** *a.*

duc'tile *a.* 1. that can be drawn thin 2. easily led

dud *n.* [Col.] 1. bomb or shell that fails to explode 2. failure

dude *n.* 1. dandy; fop 2. [Sl.] man or boy

dudg'eon (duj'ən) *n.* anger

due *a.* 1. owed 2. suitable 3. expected to arrive —*adv.* exactly —*n.* anything due —**due to** 1. caused by 2. [Col.] because of

du'el *n.* planned formal fight between two armed persons — *v.* fight a duel —**du'el·ist** *n.*

dues *n.pl.* 1. fee or tax 2. money paid for membership

du·et' *n.* musical composition for two performers

duf'fel bag large cloth bag for clothes, etc.: also **duffle bag**

duf'fer *n.* [Sl.] clumsy person

dug *pt.* & *pp.* of **dig**

dug'out *n.* 1. boat hollowed out of a log 2. a shelter, as in warfare, dug in the ground 3. shelter for baseball players

duke *n.* nobleman next in rank to a prince —**duke'dom** *n.*

dul'cet *a.* pleasant to hear

dul'ci·mer (-sə-) *n.* stringed musical instrument

dull *a.* 1. stupid 2. sluggish 3. boring 4. not sharp 5. not bright —*v.* make or become dull —**dul'ly** *adv.*

dull'ard *n.* stupid person

du'ly *adv.* properly

dumb *a.* 1. unable to talk 2. silent 3. [Col.] stupid — **dumb'ly** *adv.*

dumb'bell *n.* short bar joining two weights, used in exercising

dumb·found', dum·found' *v.* make speechless; amaze

dumb'wait'er *n.* small elevator for food, etc.

dum'my *n.* [*pl.* -MIES] 1. humanlike figure for displaying clothes 2. imitation 3. bridge partner's hand, played by winner of bid —*a.* sham

dump *v.* 1. unload in a heap 2. throw away —*n.* 1. place for dumping rubbish 2. place for storing ammunition, etc. —**in the dumps** dejected

dump'ling *n.* 1. piece of boiled dough 2. baked crust filled with fruit

dun *a.* dull grayish-brown —*v.* [DUNNED, DUNNING] demand money owed

dunce *n.* stupid person

dune *n.* hill of drifted sand

dung *n.* animal excrement

dun·ga·rees' *n.pl.* work pants of coarse cotton

dun'geon (-jən) *n.* dark underground prison

dunk *v.* dip (bread, etc.) into coffee, etc. before eating it

du'o *n.* [*pl.* -os] performers of a duet

du'o·de'num (-dē'-) *n.* first section of small intestine

dupe *n.* person easily tricked — *v.* deceive

du'plex n. house with two separate family units

du'pli·cate (-kit) a. 1. double 2. exactly alike —n. exact copy —v. (-kāt) 1. make a copy of 2. make happen again —**du'pli·ca'tion** n. —**du'pli·ca'tor** n.

du·plic'i·ty (-plis'-) n. [pl. -TIES] cunning deception

du'ra·ble a. lasting a long time —**du'ra·bil'i·ty** n.

du·ra'tion n. time that a thing continues or lasts

du·ress' n. coercion

dur'ing prep. 1. throughout 2. in the course of

du'rum n. hard wheat used for spaghetti, etc.

dusk n. evening twilight —**dusk'y** [-IER, -IEST] a.

dust n. 1. finely powdered matter, esp. earth 2. earth —v. 1. sprinkle with powder 2. wipe dust from —**bite the dust** be killed —**dust'y** [-IER, -IEST] a.

dust'pan n. pan into which floor dust is swept

Dutch a., n. (of) the people or language of the Netherlands —**go Dutch** [Col.] have each pay own expenses —**in Dutch** [Col.] in trouble

Dutch uncle [Col.] person who lectures one sternly

du'ti·ful a. showing respect; obedient: also **du'te·ous** —**du'ti·ful·ly** adv.

du'ty n. [pl. -TIES] 1. respect owed, as to parents 2. sense of

obligation, justice, etc. 3. thing one must do 4. tax, as on imports

dwarf n. unusually small being or thing —v. 1. stunt in growth 2. make seem small —a. stunted

dwell v. [DWELT or DWELLED, DWELLING] make one's home —**dwell on** (or **upon**) talk or think about at length

dwell'ing (place) residence

dwin'dle v. decrease

dyb·buk (dib'ək) n. dead person's spirit in Jewish folklore

dye n. coloring matter in solution —v. [DYED, DYEING] color with a dye —**dy'er** n.

dy'ing prp. of **die**

dy·nam'ic a. 1. of energy 2. energetic; forceful —**dy·nam'i·cal·ly** adv.

dy·nam'ics n. science of motions produced by forces

dy'na·mism n. forceful quality

dy'na·mite n. powerful explosive —v. blow up with dynamite

dy'na·mo n. [pl. -MOS] 1. generator: earlier term 2. dynamic person

dy'nas·ty n. [pl. -TIES] family line of rulers —**dy·nas'tic** a.

dys'en·ter'y (dis'-) n. disease characterized by bloody diarrhea

dys·func'tion (dis-) n. abnormal functioning

dys·lex'i·a (-lek'sē ə) n. impairment of reading ability

dys·pep'si·a n. indigestion

E

each *a., pron.* every one of two or more —*adv.* apiece

ea'ger *a.* keenly desiring

ea'gle *n.* large bird of prey with sharp vision

ea'gle-eyed' *a.* having keen vision

ear *n.* **1.** organ of hearing **2.** sense of hearing **3.** attention **4.** grain-bearing spike of a cereal plant —**play it by ear** [Col.] improvise

ear'drum *n.* thin membrane inside the ear

earl (url) *n.* British nobleman

ear'ly *adv., a.* [-LIER, -LIEST] **1.** near the beginning **2.** before the expected or usual time **3.** in the distant past or near future —**early on** at an early stage

ear'mark (ir'-) *v.* reserve for a special purpose

ear'muffs *n.pl.* warm coverings for the ears

earn *v.* **1.** receive for one's work **2.** get as deserved **3.** gain as profit

ear'nest *a.* serious or sincere —*n.* a pledge of money, etc. for binding a bargain —**in earnest 1.** serious **2.** with determination

earn'ings *n.pl.* **1.** wages **2.** profits, interest, etc.

ear'phone *n.* receiver for radio, etc., put to or into the ear

ear'ring *n.* ear ornament

ear'shot *n.* distance within which a sound can be heard

ear'split'ting *a.* very loud

earth *n.* **1.** the planet we live on **2.** land **3.** soil —**down to earth** practical

earth'en *a.* made of clay

earth'en·ware *n.* dishes, etc. made of baked clay

earth'ling *n.* human being

earth'ly *a.* **1.** terrestrial **2.** worldly **3.** conceivable

earth'quake *n.* a shaking of the crust of the earth

earth'work *n.* embankment or fortification

earth'worm *n.* common worm in soil

earth'y *a.* [-IER, -IEST] **1.** of or like earth **2.** coarse

ease *n.* **1.** comfort **2.** poise **3.** facility —*v.* **1.** to comfort **2.** relieve **3.** facilitate **4.** shift carefully

ea·sel (ē'z'l) *n.* a stand to hold an artist's canvas

ease'ment *n.* right one may have in another's land

eas'i·ly *adv.* **1.** with ease **2.** without a doubt **3.** very likely

east *n.* **1.** direction in which sunrise occurs **2.** region in this direction **3.** [E-] the Orient —*a., adv.* in, toward, or from the east —**east'er·ly** *a., adv.* —**east'ern** *a.* —**east'ern·er** *n.*

East'er *n.* spring Christian festival

east'ward *adv., a.* toward the east: also **east'wards** *adv.*

eas'y *a.* [-IER, -IEST] **1.** not difficult **2.** without worry, pain, etc. **3.** comfortable **4.** not stiff

5. not strict 6. unhurried —
adv. [Col.] easily —**take it
easy** [Col.] 1. refrain from
anger, etc. 2. relax —**eas'i-
ness** n.

eas'y·go'ing a. not worried,
rushed, or strict

eat v. [ATE, EATEN, EATING] 1.
chew and swallow (food) 2.
wear away, corrode, etc. 3.
make by eating 4. [Sl.] to
worry or bother

eats n.pl. [Col.] food

eaves (ēvz) n.pl. projecting
edge of a roof

eaves'drop [-DROPPED,
-DROPPING] listen secretly —
eaves'drop'per n.

ebb n., v. 1. flow back toward
the sea: said of the tide 2. decline

eb'on·y n. [pl. -IES] hard, dark,
tropical wood —a. black

e·bul'lient a. bubbling with
joy —**e·bul'lience** n.

ec·cen'tric a. 1. having its
axis off center 2. odd in conduct —n. eccentric person —
ec'cen·tric'i·ty (-tris'-) [pl.
-TIES] n.

ec·cle'si·as'tic n. clergyman
—a. ecclesiastical

ec·cle'si·as'ti·cal a. of the
church or clergy

ech'e·lon (esh'-) n. 1. steplike
formation of troops, ships, or
planes 2. level of command

ech·o (ek'ō) n. [pl. -OES] repe-
tition of a sound by reflection
of sound waves —v. 1. resound
2. repeat

é·clair (ā kler') n. oblong pastry filled with custard

é·clat (ā klä') n. 1. striking effect 2. fame

ec·lec'tic a. using various
sources —**ec·lec'ti·cism** n.

e·clipse' n. the obscuring of
the sun by the moon, or of the
moon by the earth's shadow —
v. surpass

e·clip'tic n. sun's apparent annual path

e'co·cide n. destruction of the
environment

e·col'o·gy n. science dealing
with organisms in their environment —**e'co·log'i·cal** a.
—**e·col'o·gist** n.

e'co·nom'ic a. 1. of the management of income, expendi-
tures, etc. 2. of economics

e'co·nom'i·cal a. thrifty —
e'co·nom'i·cal·ly adv.

e'co·nom'ics n. science that
deals with the production, distribution, and use of wealth —
e·con'o·mist n.

e·con'o·mize v. be thrifty

e·con'o·my n. [pl. -MIES] 1.
management of finances 2.
thrift 3. system of producing
and consuming wealth

e'co·sys'tem n. community of
animals and plants and the
related environment

ec'ru (-rōō) a., n. light tan

ec'sta·sy n. [pl. SIES] over-
powering joy —**ec·stat'ic** a.

ec·u·men'i·cal a. of or fur-
thering unity among churches,
esp. Christian churches

ec'u·men·ism n. movement to
unify churches, esp. Christian
churches: also **ec'u·men'i·
cism**

ec·'ze·ma (or eg zē'-) n. itchy, scaly skin disease

-ed suf. 1. having or being 2. pt. and pp. ending of many verbs

E'dam (cheese) mild yellow cheese

ed'dy n. [pl. -DIES] little whirlpool or whirlwind —v. [-DIED, -DYING] to whirl

e·de'ma (-dē'-) n. abnormal amount of fluid in the body

E'den n. Bible garden where Adam and Eve first lived

edge n. 1. blade's cutting side 2. brink 3. border 4. [Col.] advantage —v. 1. put an edge on 2. move sideways —**on edge** tense —**take the edge off** dull the force of

edg'ing n. trimming along an edge

edg'y a. [-IER, -IEST] tense

ed'i·ble a. fit to be eaten

e'dict n. public order

ed'i·fice (-fis) n. large, imposing building

ed'i·fy v. [-FIED, -FYING] instruct or improve morally — **ed'i·fi·ca'tion** n.

ed'it v. 1. revise, select, etc. (writing) for publication 2. be in charge of (a newspaper, etc.) 3. prepare (film, etc.) by cutting, etc. —**ed'i·tor** n.

e·di'tion n. 1. form in which a book is published 2. total copies of a book, etc. published at one time

ed'i·to'ri·al n. article in a newspaper, etc. stating the opinions of the editor or publisher —a. of an editor

ed'i·to'ri·al·ize' v. express editorial opinions

ed'u·cate v. develop the knowledge, skill, etc. of by schooling —**ed'u·ca'tor** n.

ed'u·ca'tion n. 1. teaching 2. knowledge developed by teaching 3. formal schooling —**ed'u·ca'tion·al** a.

-ee suf. 1. recipient of an action 2. one in a specified condition

eel n. snakelike fish

e'er (er) adv. [Poet.] ever

ee'rie, ee'ry a. [-RIER, -RIEST] weird; uncanny

ef·face' v. erase; wipe out

ef·fect' n. 1. a result 2. influence 3. meaning 4. pl. belongings —v. bring about — **in effect** 1. actually 2. in operation —**take effect** begin to act

ef·fec'tive a. 1. producing a desired result 2. in operation 3. impressive —**ef·fec'tive·ly** adv.

ef·fec'tu·al (-choo wal) a. effective (sense 1) —**ef·fec'tu·al·ly** adv.

ef·fem'i·nate (-nit) a. showing womanly traits; unmanly

ef·fer·vesce' v. to bubble — **ef'fer·ves'cent** a.

ef·fete' a. 1. sterile 2. decadent —**ef·fete'ness** n.

ef·fi·ca'cious a. effective (sense 1) —**ef'fi·ca·cy** n.

ef·fi'cient a. effective with a minimum of effort, expense, etc. —**ef·fi'cien·cy** n. —**ef·fi'cient·ly** adv.

ef'fi·gy n. [pl. -GIES] statue or

image; esp., a crude figure as for mock hanging

ef'flu·ent *n.* outflow of a sewer, etc.

ef'fort *n.* 1. use of energy to do something 2. attempt

ef·fron'ter·y *n.* impudence

ef·fu'sive *a.* expressing excessive emotion too openly

e·gal'i·tar'i·an *a.* advocating full equality for all

egg *n.* 1. oval body from which young of birds, fish, etc. are hatched 2. ovum —*v.* to urge (on)

egg'head' *n.* [Sl.] intellectual

egg'nog' *n.* drink made of eggs, milk, sugar, etc.

egg'plant' *n.* large, purple, pear-shaped vegetable

e·gis (ē'jis) *n.* aegis

eg·lan·tine (-tīn) *n.* pink rose with sweet-scented leaves

e'go *n.* 1. the self 2. conceit

e'go·cen'tric *a.* self-centered

e'go·ism *n.* 1. selfishness; self-interest 2. conceit —**e'go·ist** *n.* —**e'go·is'tic·a** *a.*

e'go·tism *n.* 1. excessive reference to oneself 2. conceit — **e'go·tist** *n.* —**e'go·tis'tic,** **e'go·tis'ti·cal** *a.*

ego trip self-fulfilling or vain experience

e·gre'gious (-jəs) *a.* flagrant

e'gress *n.* an exit

e'gret *n.* heron having long, white plumes

E·gyp'tian *n., a.* (native) of Egypt

eh (ā, e) *int.* sound expressing surprise, doubt, etc.

ei'der (ī'-) *n.* large sea duck

with soft, fine down (**eider down**)

eight *a., n.* one more than seven —**eighth** *a., n.*

eight'een' *a., n.* eight more than ten —**eight'eenth'** *a., n.*

eight'y *a., n.* [*pl.* **-IES**] eight times ten —**eight'i·eth** *a., n.*

ei·ther (ē'thər, ī'-) *a., pron.* one or the other (of two) — *con.* correlative used with *or* —*adv.* any more than the other

e·jac'u·late *v.* 1. eject (esp. semen) 2. exclaim suddenly — **e·jac·u·la'tion** *n.*

e·ject' *v.* throw out; expel

eke (ēk) *v.* barely manage to make (a living): with *out*

e·lab'o·rate *v.* add details —*a.* (-rit) in great detail

é·lan' (ā·län') *n.* spirited self-assurance; dash

e·lapse' *v.* pass, as time

e·las'tic *a.* 1. springing back to its original shape 2. recovering easily 3. adaptable —*n.* elastic band —**e·las'tic'i·ty** (-tis'-) *n.*

e·las'ti·cize *v.* make elastic

e·late' *v.* make proud, happy, etc. —**e·la'tion** *n.*

el'bow *n.* joint between the upper and lower arm —*v.* shove as with the elbows

elbow grease [Col.] hard work

el'bow·room' *n.* ample space

eld'er *a.* older —*n.* 1. older person 2. church official 3. shrub with dark berries

el'der·ber'ry *n.* [*pl.* **-RIES**] 1. the elder 2. its berry

eld'er·ly *a.* somewhat old

eld'est a. oldest

e·lect' a. 1. chosen 2. elected but not yet in office —v. select, esp. by voting

e·lec'tion n. 1. a choosing or choice 2. choosing by vote

e·lec'tion·eer' v. canvass votes in an election

e·lec'tive a. 1. filled by election 2. optional —n. optional subject in school

e·lec'tor n. 1. qualified voter 2. member of the electoral college

e·lec'tor·al college assembly that formally elects the U.S. president

e·lec'tor·ate (-it) n. the body of qualified voters

e·lec'tric, e·lec'tri·cal a. of, charged with, or worked by electricity

e·lec'tri'cian (-shən) n. one who installs and repairs electrical apparatus

e·lec'tric'i·ty (-tris'-) n. 1. form of energy with magnetic, chemical, and radiant effects 2. electric current

e·lec'tri·fy v. [-FIED, -FYING] 1. equip for the use of electricity 2. thrill

e·lec'tro·car'di·o·gram' n. tracing showing electrical changes in the heart

e·lec'tro·car'di·o·graph' n. instrument for making electrocardiograms

e·lec'tro·cute (-kyōot) v. kill by electricity —e·lec'tro·cu'tion n.

e·lec'trode n. terminal of an electric source

e·lec'tro·en·ceph'a·lo·gram' n. tracing showing electrical changes in the brain

e·lec'tro·en·ceph'a·lo·graph' n. instrument for making electroencephalograms

e·lec'trol'y·sis (-trăl'ə-) n. 1. breakdown into ions of a chemical compound in solution by electrical current 2. eradication of unwanted hair with an electrified needle

e·lec'tro·lyte (-līt) n. substance which in solution conducts electric current —e·lec'tro·lyt'ic (-lit'-) a.

e·lec'tro·mag'net n. soft iron core made magnetic by an electric current —e·lec'tro·mag·net'ic a.

electromagnetic wave wave generated by an oscillating electric charge

e·lec'tro·mo'tive a. producing an electric current

e·lec'tron (-trän) n. negatively charged particle in an atom

e·lec·tron'ic a. 1. of electrons 2. produced or done by the action of electrons

e·lec·tron'ics n. science of electronic action

electron microscope device using electrons to enlarge the image of an object

electron tube electronic device used in radio, etc.

e·lec'tro·plate' v. coat with metal by electrolysis

e·lec'tro·ther'a·py n. treatment of disease using electricity, as by diathermy

el'ee·mos'y·nar'y (-i mäs'ə-) a. of, for, or by charity

el'e·gant a. 1. tastefully luxurious 2. [Col.] excellent —**el'·e·gance** *n.*

el'e·gy (-jē) *n.* [pl. -GIES] poem lamenting a dead person —**el'·e·gi'ac** (-jī'-) *a.*

el'e·ment *n.* 1. natural environment 2. basic part or feature 3. *Chem.* substance that cannot be separated into different substances except by nuclear disintegration —the **elements** wind, rain, etc. —**el'e·men'tal** *a.*

el'e·men'ta·ry *a.* of fundamentals; introductory

elementary school school of the first 6 (or 8) grades

el'e·phant *n.* huge, thick-skinned mammal with a long trunk and ivory tusks

el'e·phan'tine (-tēn, -tīn) *a.* huge, clumsy, etc.

el'e·vate *v.* 1. raise 2. raise in rank 3. elate

el'e·va'tion *n.* 1. high place 2. height, as above sea level

el'e·va'tor *n.* 1. suspended cage for hoisting or lowering goods or people 2. warehouse for grain

el·ev'en *a., n.* one more than ten —**el·ev'enth** *a., n.*

elf *n.* [pl. ELVES] small fairy —**elf'in** *a.*

e·lic'it (-lis'-) *v.* draw forth

el·ide' *v.* slur over

el'i·gi·ble (-jə-) *a.* qualified —*n.* eligible person —**el'i·gi·bil'i·ty** *n.*

e·lim'i·nate *v.* 1. remove 2. excrete —**e·lim'i·na'tion** *n.*

e·lite, é·lite (i lēt', ā-) *n.* best or most powerful part of a group

e·lit'ism *n.* government or control by an elite —**e·lit'ist** *a., n.*

e·lix'ir (-lik'sər) *n.* drug in alcoholic solution

elk *n.* large deer

ell *n.* 1. extension at right angles to main part 2. L-shaped joint 3. former measure of length equal to 45 inches

el·lipse' *n.* closed curve that is a symmetrical oval

el·lip'sis *n.* 1. omission of words 2. mark (...) indicating this

el·lip'ti·cal *a.* 1. of an ellipse 2. of ellipsis

elm *n.* tall shade tree

el'o·cu'tion *n.* art of public speaking

e·lon'gate *v.* lengthen —**e'lon·ga'tion** *n.*

e·lope' *v.* run away to marry —**e·lope'ment** *n.*

el'o·quent *a.* vivid or forceful in expression —**el'o·quence** *n.*

else *a.* 1. different; other 2. in addition —*adv.* 1. otherwise 2. if not

else'where *adv.* in or to some other place

e·lu'ci·date *v.* explain —**e·lu'·ci·da'tion** *n.*

e·lude' *v.* escape; evade

e·lu'sive *a.* hard to grasp; baffling

elves *n.* pl. of elf

e·ma'ci·ate (-shē-) *v.* make thin —**e·ma'ci·a'tion** *n.*

em'a·nate *v.* come or issue —**em'a·na'tion** *n.*

e·man'ci·pate *v.* set free or

liberate —e·man'ci·pa'tion n. —e·man'ci·pa'tor n.

e·mas'cu·late v. 1. castrate 2. weaken —e·mas'cu·la'tion n.

em·balm' (-bäm') v. preserve (a dead body)

em·bank'ment n. bank of earth, etc. as to keep back water

em·bar'go n. [pl. -GOES] legal restriction of commerce or shipping

em·bark' v. 1. go aboard a ship, airplane, etc. 2. begin; start —em'bar·ka'tion n.

em·bar'rass v. 1. make feel self-conscious 2. cause to be in debt —em·bar'rass·ment n.

em'bas·sy n. [pl. -SIES] staff or headquarters of an ambassador

em·bat'tled a. ready for battle

em·bed' v. [-BEDDED, -BED-DING] set firmly (in)

em·bel'lish v. 1. decorate 2. add details, often untrue —em·bel'lish·ment n.

em'ber n. glowing piece of coal or wood

em·bez'zle v. steal (money entrusted) —em·bez'zle·ment n. —em·bez'zler n.

em·bit'ter v. make bitter

em·bla'zon v. 1. decorate 2. display openly

em'blem n. visible symbol; sign —em'blem·at'ic a.

em·bod'y v. [-IED, -YING] 1. give form to 2. include —em·bod'i·ment n.

em·bold'en v. cause to be bold

em'bo·lism n. obstruction of a blood vessel

em·boss' v. decorate with raised designs

em·bou·chure (äm boo shoor') n. way of putting lips on mouthpiece of a wind instrument

em·brace' v. 1. hug lovingly 2. adopt, as an idea 3. include —n. an embracing —em·brace'a·ble a.

em·broi'der v. ornament with needlework —em·broi'der·y [pl. -IES] n.

em·broil' v. get involved

em'bry·o n. [pl. -os] animal or plant in earliest stages of development —em'bry·on'ic a.

em·cee' v. [-CEED, -CEEING] n. [Col.] (act as) master of ceremonies

e·mend' v. correct, as a text —e'men·da'tion n.

em'er·ald n. green jewel

e·merge' v. come out; appear —e·mer'gence n. —e·mer'gent a.

e·mer'gen·cy n. [pl. -CIES] sudden occurrence demanding quick action

e·mer'i·tus a. retired, but keeping one's title

em'er·y n. hard corundum used for grinding, etc.

e·met'ic n., a. (substance) causing vomiting

em'i·grate v. leave one country to settle in another —em'i·grant a., n. —em'i·gra'tion n.

é·mi·gré, e·mi·gré (ä ma grā', em'a grā) n. one forced to flee for political reasons

em'i·nent a. prominent or high —em'i·nence n.

em·i·nent domain right of a government to take private property for public use

e·mir (i mir') *n.* Muslim ruler

em·is·sar·y *n.* [*pl.* -IES] one sent on a mission

e·mit' *v.* [EMITTED, EMITTING] 1. send out; discharge 2. utter —**e·mis'sion** *n.*

e·mol·li·ent *n., a.* (medicine) for soothing the skin

e·mol·u·ment (-yoo-) *n.* salary; payment

e·mote' *v.* [Col.] show emotion dramatically

e·mo·tion *n.* strong feeling, as of love, fear, anger, *etc.*

e·mo·tion·al *a.* 1. showing emotion 2. easily aroused 3. appealing to emotions

e·mo·tion·al·ize *v.* deal with in an emotional way

em·pa·thize *v.* feel empathy (*with*)

em·pa·thy *n.* identification with another

em·per·or *n.* ruler of an empire

em·pha·sis *n.* [*pl.* -SES (-sēz)] 1. stress; importance 2. stress on a syllable

em·pha·size *v.* to stress

em·phat·ic *a.* 1. using emphasis 2. forcible —**em·phat'i·cal·ly** *adv.*

em·phy·se·ma (-fə-) *n.* disease of the lungs

em·pire *n.* group of countries under one sovereign

em·pir·i·cal *a.* based on experiment or experience —**em·pir'i·cism** *n.*

em·place'ment *n.* position from which to fire heavy guns

em·ploy' *v.* 1. use 2. keep busy 3. have or have as workers —*n.* employment

em·ploy·ee, em·ploy·e (-ē) *n.* person working for another for pay

em·ploy·er *n.* one who employs others for pay

em·ploy·ment *n.* 1. an employing or being employed 2. work; occupation

em·pow·er *v.* 1. authorize 2. enable

em·press *n.* 1. woman ruler of an empire 2. emperor's wife

emp·ty *a.* [-TIER, -TIEST] 1. with nothing or no one in it 2. worthless —*v.* [-TIED, -TYING] 1. make or become empty 2. pour out —*n.* [*pl.* -TIES] empty bottle, *etc.* —**emp'ti·ness** *n.*

em·py·re·an (-pi-) *n.* 1. highest heaven 2. the sky

e·mu *n.* ostrichlike bird

em·u·late *v.* try to equal or surpass —**em·u·la'tion** *n.*

e·mul·si·fy *v.* [-FIED, -FYING] form into an emulsion

e·mul·sion *n.* one liquid suspended in another; spec., oil suspended in watery liquid

en- *pref.* 1. to put on 2. to make 3. in or into

-en *suf.* 1. make or become 2. get or give 3. made of

en·a·ble *v.* make able

en·act' *v.* 1. pass, as a law 2. act out —**en·act'ment** *n.*

en·am·el *n.* 1. glassy coating fused to metal 2. white coating of teeth 3. hard, glossy paint —*v.* coat with enamel

en·am·el·ware *n.* enameled kitchen utensils, *etc.*

en·am'or v. fill with love; charm

en bloc (bläk) all together

en·camp' v. set up, or put in, a camp —en·camp'ment n.

en·cap'su·late v. 1. enclose in a capsule 2. condense

en·case' v. enclose

-ence suf. act, state, or result: also -ency

en·ceph·a·li'tis n. inflammation of the brain

en·chant' v. charm; delight

en·cir'cle v. surround

en'clave n. foreign land inside another country

en·close' v. 1. surround; shut in 2. insert in an envelope —en·clo'sure n.

en·code' v. put (a message) into code

en·co'mi·um n. high praise

en·com'pass v. 1. surround 2. contain

en'core (än'-) int. again! —n. further performance in response to applause

en·coun'ter v. 1. meet unexpectedly 2. fight —n. 1. unexpected meeting 2. fight

en·cour'age v. 1. give courage or hope to 2. help —en·cour'age·ment n.

en·croach' v. intrude (on)

en·crust' v. incrust

en·cum'ber v. 1. hinder 2. burden —en·cum'brance n.

en·cy'cli·cal (-sik'-) n. papal letter to bishops

en·cy'clo·pe'di·a n. book or set of books on one or all branches of knowledge: also sp. en·cy'clo·pae'di·a —en·cy'-clo·pe'dic a.

end n. 1. limit 2. last part; finish 3. destruction 4. tip 5. purpose 6. result —v. finish; stop —a. final —make (both) ends meet manage to spend within one's income

en·dan'ger v. put in danger

en·dear' v. make beloved

en·dear'ment n. affection

en·deav'or v. try hard —n. earnest attempt

en·dem'ic a. prevalent in a place, as a disease

end'ing n. 1. last part 2. death

en'dive n. salad plant

end'less a. 1. eternal 2. lasting too long 3. with the ends joined to form a ring

end'most a. farthest

en'do·crine gland any of the ductless glands that regulate bodily functions

en·dorse' v. 1. sign on the back of (a check) 2. approve 3. recommend in return for a fee —en·dorse'ment n.

en·dow' v. 1. provide with some quality 2. give money to —en·dow'ment n.

en·dur'ance n. ability to last, stand pain, etc.

en·dure' v. 1. stand (pain, etc.) 2. tolerate 3. last

end'ways adv. 1. upright 2. with the end foremost 3. lengthwise Also end'wise

en'e·ma n. therapeutic flushing of the rectum

en'e·my n. [pl. -MIES] person or nation hostile to another; foe

en·er·get'ic a. vigorous; having energy

en·er·gize v. give energy to

en·er·gy n. [pl. -GIES] 1. vigor; power 2. capacity to do work

en·er·vate v. weaken

en·fee·ble v. weaken

en·fold' v. 1. wrap up 2. embrace

en·force' v. 1. impose by force 2. make people obey (a law) — **en·force'ment** n.

en·fran·chise' v. 1. free from slavery 2. give the right to vote

en·gage' v. 1. bind by a promise of marriage 2. involve oneself 3. hire 4. attract and hold 5. enter into conflict with 6. interlock; mesh

en·gaged' a. 1. betrothed 2. occupied 3. involved in combat 4. meshed

en·gage'ment n. 1. betrothal 2. appointment 3. battle 4. performance

en·gag'ing a. charming

en·gen·der (-jen'-) v. cause

en·gine n. 1. machine using energy to develop mechanical power 2. locomotive

en·gi·neer' n. 1. one trained in engineering 2. locomotive driver —v. manage skillfully

en·gi·neer'ing n. practical use of sciences in industry, building, etc.

Eng·lish a. of the people or language of England —n. 1. language of the people of England, the U.S., etc. 2. people of England 3. [sometimes e-] spinning motion given to a ball —the English people of England

en·grave' v. cut (designs) on (a metal plate, etc.), as for printing —en·grav'er n.

en·grav'ing n. 1. engraved plate, design, etc. 2. printed impression from this

en·gross' v. take the full attention of

en·gulf' v. swallow up

en·hance' v. make greater

e·nig·ma n. baffling matter, person, etc. —e'nig·mat'ic, e'nig·mat'i·cal a.

en·join' v. 1. to command 2. prohibit by law

en·joy' v. 1. get pleasure from 2. have the use of —enjoy oneself have a good time — **en·joy'a·ble** a. —**en·joy'ment** n.

en·large' v. 1. make larger 2. discuss at greater length (with on or upon) —en·large'ment n.

en·light'en v. 1. free from ignorance, prejudice, etc. 2. inform —en·light'en·ment n.

en·list' v. 1. enroll in an army, etc. 2. engage in a cause —en·list'ment n.

en·liv'en v. liven up

en masse (mas) as a whole

en·mesh' v. catch as in meshes of a net; entangle

en·mi·ty n. ill will

en·no·ble v. dignify

en·nui (än'wē) n. boredom

e·nor·mi·ty n. [pl. -TIES] 1. great wickedness 2. outrageous act

e·nor'mous a. huge; vast

e·nough' a., adv. as much as is needed —n. amount needed —int. no more!

en·plane' v. board an airplane

en·quire' v. inquire —en·quir'y [pl. -IES] n.

en·rage' v. put into a rage

en·rap'ture v. fill with delight

en·rich' v. make rich or richer —en·rich'ment n.

en·roll' v. put or be put in a list, as a member, etc. —en·roll'ment n.

en route (än rōōt') on the way

en·sconce' v. place snugly

en·sem·ble (än säm'-) n. 1. total effect 2. costume of matching parts 3. group of musicians playing together

en·shrine' v. hold as sacred

en·shroud' v. hide

en·sign (-sīn) n. 1. flag 2. (-s'n) lowest-ranking navy officer

en·si·lage (-s'l ij) n. green fodder in silo

en·slave' v. make a slave of

en·snare' v. catch as in a snare

en·sue' v. follow; result

en·tail' v. make necessary

en·tan·gle v. trap; confuse —en·tan'gle·ment n.

en·tente (än tänt') n. agreement between nations

en·ter v. 1. come or go in 2. put in a list, etc. 3. join 4. begin —enter into 1. take part in 2. form a part of —enter on (or upon) begin

en'ter·prise (-priz) n. 1. important undertaking 2. energy and boldness

en'ter·pris'ing a. full of energy and boldness

en'ter·tain' v. 1. amuse 2. act as host to 3. consider, as an idea —en'ter·tain'er n. —en'ter·tain'ment n.

en·thrall' v. fascinate

en·throne' v. place on throne

en·thuse' v. [Col.] act or make enthusiastic

en·thu'si·asm n. eager interest —en·thu'si·ast n. —en·thu'si·as'tic a.

en·tice' v. tempt —en·tice'ment n.

en·tire' a. complete; whole —en·tire'ly adv. —en·tire'ty n.

en·ti·tle v. 1. give a title to 2. give a right to

en'ti·ty n. [pl. -TIES] thing having real existence

en·tomb' v. put in a tomb; bury

en'to·mol'o·gy n. study of insects

en·tou·rage (än'too räzh') n. retinue; attendants

en'trails n.pl. inner organs; spec., intestines

en'trance (-trəns) n. 1. act of entering 2. door, gate, etc. 3. permission to enter —v. (-trans') to delight

en'trant n. one who enters

en·trap' v. [-TRAPPED, -TRAP·PING] catch in a trap

en·treat' v. ask earnestly

en·treat'y n. [pl. -IES] earnest request; prayer

en·tree, en·trée (än'trā) n. main dish

en·trench' v. set securely

en·tre·pre·neur (än'trə prə nur') n. one who organizes and operates a business

en'tro·py n. 1. energy available for work 2. tendency of energy system to run down

en·trust' v. assign the care of (to)

en'try n. [pl. -TRIES] 1. entrance 2. item in a list, etc. 3. contestant

en·twine' (-twīn') v. twist together or around

e·nu'mer·ate v. name one by one —e·nu'mer·a'tion n.

e·nun'ci·ate (-sē-) v. 1. to state 2. pronounce (words)

en'u·re'sis (-rē'-) n. inability to control urination

en·vel'op v. 1. wrap up 2. surround —en·vel'op·ment n.

en've·lope n. covering, esp. for a letter

en·ven'om v. 1. put venom into 2. fill with hate

en·vi'ron·ment n. surroundings —en·vi'ron·men'tal a.

en·vi'ron·men'tal·ist n. person working to solve environmental problems

en·vi'rons n.pl. suburbs

en·vis'age (-viz'-) v. imagine

en·vi'sion v. imagine

en'voy n. 1. messenger 2. diplomatic official

en'vy n. 1. discontent and ill will over another's advantages, etc. 2. object of such feeling —v. [-VIED, -VYING] feel envy toward —en'vi·a·ble a. —en'vi·ous a.

en'zyme (-zīm) n. catalyst formed in body cells

e'on (ē'-) n. very long time

ep'au·let (ep'ə-) n. shoulder ornament on a uniform

e·pee, é·pée (e pā') n. rigid sword for fencing

e·pergne (i purn') n. a footed dish for candy, flowers, etc.

e·phem'er·al a. short-lived

ep'ic n. long poem about a hero's deeds —a. heroic

ep'i·cen'ter n. earth's surface directly above point of origin of earthquake

ep'i·cure n. one with a fine taste for foods and liquors —ep'i·cu·re'an a.

ep'i·dem'ic a. spreading rapidly among people —n. an epidemic disease

ep'i·der'mis n. outermost layer of the skin

ep'i·glot'tis n. thin lid covering windpipe during swallowing

ep'i·gram n. witty saying

ep'i·lep'sy n. disease marked by convulsive fits, etc. —ep'i·lep'tic a., n.

ep'i·logue, ep'i·log (-lôg) n. part added at the end of a novel, play, etc.

e·pis'co·pal a. of or governed by bishops

ep'i·sode n. incident —ep'i·sod'ic a.

e·pis'tle (-pis''l) n. 1. letter 2. [E-] Bible letter of an Apostle

ep'i·taph n. inscription on a tomb

ep'i·thet n. word or phrase characterizing a person, etc.

e·pit'o·me (-mē) n. 1. typical part or thing 2. summary —e·pit'o·mize v.

ep'och (-ək) n. period marked by certain events, etc. —ep'och·al a.

ep·ox'y n. [pl. -IES] resin used in strong glues, enamels, etc.

Ep′som salts (or **salt**) type of salt used as a cathartic

eq·ua·ble (ek′wə‑) *a.* even; calm —**eq′ua·bly** *adv.*

e′qual *a.* of the same quantity, value, rank, etc. —*n.* person or thing that is equal —*v.* be, or do something, equal to — **equal to** capable of — **e·qual′i·ty** *n.* —**e′qual·ize** *v.* —**e′qual·ly** *adv.*

equal sign (or **mark**) sign (=) indicating equality

e′qua·nim′i·ty *n.* composure

e·quate′ *v.* treat, regard, or express as equal

e·qua′tion *n.* **1.** an equating **2.** equality of two quantities as shown by the equal sign

e·qua′tor *n.* imaginary circle around the earth, equally distant from N. and S. poles

e·ques′tri·an *a.* of horses or horsemanship —*n.* rider or acrobat on horseback

equi‑ *pref.* equal; equally

e′qui·dis′tant *a.* equally distant

e′qui·lat′er·al *a.* having all sides equal

e′qui·lib′ri·um *n.* state of balance

e′quine *a.* of a horse

e′qui·nox *n.* time when the sun crosses the equator, making night and day of equal length everywhere —**e′qui·noc′tial** (‑shəl) *a.*

e·quip′ *v.* [**-QUIPPED**, **-QUIP- PING**] fit out, as for an undertaking —**e·quip′ment** *n.*

eq′ui·page (‑pij) *n.* horse and carriage with servants

eq′ui·poise *n.* equilibrium

eq′ui·ta·ble *a.* fair; just

eq′ui·ta′tion *n.* horsemanship

eq′ui·ty *n.* **1.** fairness **2.** value of property beyond amount owed on it

e·quiv′a·lent *a.* equal in quantity, measure, meaning, etc. — *n.* equivalent thing

e·quiv′o·cal *a.* **1.** purposely ambiguous **2.** doubtful — **e·quiv′o·cate** *v.*

-er *suf.* **1.** one that **2.** living in **3.** repeatedly

e′ra *n.* period of time

e·rad′i·cate *v.* wipe out — **e·rad′i·ca′tion** *n.*

e·rase′ *v.* rub out, as writing — **e·ras′a·ble** *a.* —**e·ras′er** *n.*

e·ra′sure (‑shər) *n.* the place where something was erased

ere *con., prep.* [Ar. or Poet.] before

e·rect′ *a.* upright —*v.* **1.** construct; build **2.** set upright — **e·rec′tion** *n.*

e·rec′tile *a.* that becomes rigid when filled with blood

erg *n.* unit of work

er·mine (ur′mən) *n.* weasel with white fur in winter

e·rode′ *v.* wear away —**e·ro′- sion** *n.*

e·rot′ic *a.* causing sexual feelings or desires

e·rot′i·ca *n.pl.* erotic books, pictures, etc.

err (ur) *v.* **1.** be wrong **2.** violate a moral code

er′rand (er′-) *n.* short trip to do a thing

er′rant *a.* wandering

er·rat′ic *a.* irregular; odd

er·ra′tum (‑rät′-) *n.* [*pl.* **-TA** (‑tə)] printing error

er·ro'ne·ous *a.* wrong —**er·ro'ne·ous·ly** *adv.*

er'ror *n.* 1. mistake; blunder 2. mistaken belief 3. sin 4. baseball misplay

er·satz' (ur'zäts) *a.* substitute and inferior

erst'while *a.* former

e·ruct' *v.* to belch —**e·ruc'ta' tion** *n.*

er'u·dite *a.* learned; scholarly —**er'u·di'tion** *n.*

e·rupt' *v.* 1. burst forth 2. break out in a rash —**e·rup'tion** *n.*

-ery *suf.* 1. a place to or for 2. act or product of 3. condition of 4. collection of

er'y·sip'e·las (er'ə-) *n.* acute skin disease

es'ca·late *v.* 1. rise 2. expand 3. increase —**es'ca·la'tion** *n.*

es'ca·la'tor *n.* moving stairway on an endless belt

es·cal'lop, es·cal'op *n., v.* scallop

es'ca·pade *n.* reckless adventure or prank

es·cape' *v.* 1. get free 2. slip away from 3. avoid harm 4. leak away —*n.* 1. act or means of escape 2. a leakage —**es·cap·ee'** *n.*

es·cape'ment *n.* notched wheel regulating movement in a clock, etc.

es·cap'ism *n.* tendency to escape reality by fantasy —**es·cap'ist** *n., a.*

es'ca·role *n.* plant with leaves used in salads

es·carp'ment *n.* cliff

es·chew' *v.* shun; avoid

es'cort *n.* one or more persons accompanying another person to protect, honor, etc. —*v.* (i skôrt') go with as an escort

es'crow *n.* state of a deed held by a third party until conditions are fulfilled

es·cutch'eon (-ən) *n.* shield bearing a coat of arms

Es'ki·mo *n.* [*pl.* -mos] one of a people living in Greenland, arctic N. America, etc. —*a.* of these people

Eskimo dog strong dog used by Eskimos to pull sleds

e·soph'a·gus (-säf'-) *n.* [*pl.* -GI (-jī)] passage between the pharynx and stomach

es'o·ter'ic *a.* known by few

ESP extrasensory perception

es'pa·dril'le *n.* flat canvas shoe with rope sole

es·pal'ier (-yər) *n.* tree growing flat on lattice

es·pe'cial *a.* special; chief —**es·pe'cial·ly** *adv.*

Es'pe·ran'to (-rän'-) *n.* artificial international language

es'pi·o·nage (-näzh) *n.* a spying

es·pla·nade' (or -näd') *n.* a public walk

es·pouse' (-spouz') *v.* 1. marry 2. support (an idea or cause) —**es·pous'al** *n.*

es·pres'so *n.* coffee made by forcing steam through finely ground coffee beans

es·py' (-pī') *v.* [-PIED, -PYING] catch sight of; see

Es·quire' (-kwīr) *n.* title of courtesy put after a man's surname: abbrev. **Esq.**

es·say' *v.* to try —*n.* (es'ā) 1. a try 2. short personal writing on one subject —**es′say·ist** *n.*

es′sence *n.* **1.** basic nature **2.** substance in concentrated form **3.** perfume

es·sen′tial (-shəl) *n.* something necessary —*a.* necessary —**es·sen′tial·ly** *adv.*

es·tab′lish *v.* **1.** set up; fix **2.** ordain, as a law **3.** to found **4.** prove

es·tab′lish·ment *n.* **1.** a business **2.** [E-] group that holds power

es·tate′ *n.* **1.** one's possessions **2.** piece of land with a residence

es·teem′ *v.* value highly —*n.* high regard

es′ter *n.* organic salt

es′thete *n.* aesthete —**es·thet′ic** *a.*

es′ti·ma·ble *a.* worthy of esteem

es′ti·mate *v.* figure roughly, as size or cost —*n.* (-mit) **1.** rough calculation **2.** opinion —**es′ti·ma′tion** *n.*

es·trange′ *v.* make unfriendly —**es·trange′ment** *n.*

es′tro·gen (-trə jən) *n.* female sex hormone

es′tu·ar′y *n.* [*pl.* -IES] wide mouth of a river

et cet′er·a (set′-) and so forth: abbrev. **etc.**

etch *v.* put a design on metal plates or glass with acid, often for making prints —**etch′ing** *n.*

e·ter′nal *a.* **1.** everlasting **2.** forever the same **3.** seeming never to stop —**e·ter′nal·ly** *adv.*

eth′ane *n.* gaseous hydrocarbon used as fuel

e′ther *n.* **1.** upper regions of space **2.** an anesthetic

e·the′re·al *a.* **1.** light; delicate **2.** heavenly

eth′i·cal *a.* **1.** of ethics **2.** proper; right

eth′ics *n.pl.* moral standards; system of morals

eth′nic *a.* of any of the many peoples of mankind —*n.* member of a nationality group in a larger community —**eth′ni·cal·ly** *adv.*

eth·nic′i·ty (-nis′-) *n.* ethnic affiliation

eth·nol′o·gy *n.* study of the world's peoples and cultures —**eth′no·log′i·cal** *a.*

e′thos (ē′thäs) *n.* characteristic habits, attitudes, etc. of group

eth′yl *n.* carbon-hydrogen radical of common alcohol, etc.

eth′yl·ene (-ēn) *n.* flammable, smelly gaseous hydrocarbon

e′ti·ol′o·gy (ē′tē-) *n.* cause assigned, as for a disease

et′i·quette (-ket) *n.* social forms; good manners

é′tude (ā′-) *n.* Mus. instrumental piece stressing a technique

et′y·mol′o·gy *n.* [*pl.* -GIES] **1.** origin of a word **2.** study of word origins

eu′ca·lyp′tus (yōō′-) *n.* an aromatic evergreen of Australia

Eu′cha·rist (-kə-) *n.* Holy Communion

eu′chre (-kər) *n.* card game played with 32 cards

eu·gen′ics *n.* any plan for improving the human race by heredity control —**eu·gen′ic** *a.*

eu′lo·gy *n.* [*pl.* -GIES] praise — **eu′lo·gize** *v.*

eu′nuch *n.* castrated man

eu′phe·mism *n.* mild word replacing an offensive one

eu·pho′ni·ous *a.* pleasant sounding —**eu′pho·ny** *n.*

eu·pho′ri·a *n.* feeling of well being —**eu·phor′ic** *a.*

eu·re′ka *int.* cry of triumph

Eu·ro·pe′an *n., a.* (native) of Europe

eu·ryth′mics *n.pl.* rhythmical body movements to music

Eu·sta′chi·an tube (-shē ən) tube between middle ear and pharynx

eu·tha·na′sia (-zhə) *n.* painless death to end suffering

e·vac′u·ate *v.* 1. make empty 2. discharge (excrement) 3. remove 4. withdraw (from) — **e·vac′u·a′tion** *n.*

e·vade′ *v.* avoid by deceit, indirect answer, etc. —**e·va′sion** *n.* —**e·va′sive** *a.*

e·val′u·ate *v.* find the value of —**e·val′u·a′tion** *n.*

ev′a·nes′cent *a.* fleeting

e′van·gel′i·cal *a.* 1. of the Gospels or New Testament 2. of churches that stress salvation by faith

e·van′gel·ist *n.* 1. [E-] Gospel writer 2. revivalist preacher — **e·van′gel·ism** *n.*

e·vap′o·rate *v.* 1. change into vapor 2. condense by heating 3. vanish —**e·vap′o·ra′tion** *n.*

eve *n.* 1. [Poet.] evening 2.

evening before a holiday 3. time just before

e′ven *a.* 1. flat; level 2. constant; uniform 3. calm 4. equal 5. divisible by two 6. exact —*adv.* 1. indeed 2. exactly 3. still —*v.* make or become even —**even if** though —**e′ven·ly** *adv.*

e′ven-hand′ed *a.* impartial; fair

eve′ning *n.* end of day and beginning of night

e·vent′ *n.* 1. an occurrence 2. sports contest in a series —**in the event of** in case of

e·ven-tem′pered *a.* calm

e·vent′ful *a.* full of events; important

e·ven′tu·al (-choo-) *a.* final — **e·ven′tu·al·ly** *adv.*

e·ven′tu·al′i·ty *n.* [*pl.* -TIES] possible outcome

e·ven′tu·ate *v.* happen in the end; result

ev′er *adv.* 1. always 2. at any time 3. at all

ev′er·glade *n.* swampy land

ev′er·green′ *n., a.* (tree or plant) having green leaves all year

ev′er·last′ing *a.* eternal

ev′er·more′ *adv.* forever; constantly

ev′er·y *a.* 1. each of a group 2. all possible —**every other** each alternate —**every so often** [Col.] occasionally — **ev′er·y·bod′y, ev′er·y·one′** *pron.* —**ev′er·y·thing′** *pron.* —**ev′er·y·where′** *adv.*

e·vict′ *v.* put (a tenant) out by law —**e·vic′tion** *n.*

ev′i·dence *n.* 1. sign; indication 2. proof —v. make evident

ev'i·dent a. easy to see; clear —ev'i·dent·ly adv.

e'vil a. 1. morally bad 2. harmful —n. wickedness —e'vil·do'er n. —e'vil·ly adv.

e·vince' v. show plainly (a quality, feeling, etc.)

e·vis'cer·ate v. remove the entrails from —e·vis'cer·a'tion n.

e·voke' v. call forth; produce —ev'o·ca'tion n.

ev'o·lu'tion n. 1. an evolving 2. theory that all species developed from earlier forms —ev'o·lu'tion·ar'y a. —ev'o·lu'tion·ist n.

e·volve' v. develop gradually; unfold

ewe (yōō) n. female sheep

ew'er (yōō'-) n. large, wide-mouthed water pitcher

ex- pref. former

ex·ac'er·bate (-as'-) v. aggravate; irritate —ex·ac'er·ba'tion n.

ex·act' a. strictly correct; precise —v. 1. demand and get 2. extort —ex·act'i·tude n. —ex·act'ly adv.

ex·act'ing a. strict; hard

ex·ag'ger·ate (-aj'ər-) v. make seem greater than it really is; overstate —ex·ag'ger·a'tion n.

ex·alt' v. 1. raise in dignity 2. praise 3. fill with joy —ex'al·ta'tion n.

ex·am' n. [Col.] examination

ex·am'ine v. 1. inspect 2. test by questioning —ex·am'i·na'tion n.

ex·am'ple n. 1. sample 2. case that serves as warning 3. illustration 4. model

ex·as'per·ate v. annoy; vex —ex·as'per·a'tion n.

ex'ca·vate v. 1. make a hole in 2. unearth 3. dig out —ex'ca·va'tion n. —ex'ca·va'tor n.

ex·ceed' v. 1. go beyond (a limit) 2. surpass

ex·ceed'ing a. extreme —ex·ceed'ing·ly adv.

ex·cel' v. [-CELLED, -CELLING] be better than

Ex'cel·len·cy n. [pl. -CIES] title of honor

ex'cel·lent a. unusually good —ex'cel·lence n.

ex·cel'si·or n. wood shavings used for packing

ex·cept' prep. leaving out; but —v. exclude —except for if it were not for

ex·cep'tion n. 1. person or thing excluded 2. case to which a rule does not apply 3. objection —take exception to object

ex·cep'tion·al a. 1. unusual 2. needing special education because handicapped —ex·cep'tion·al·ly adv.

ex'cerpt n. passage selected from a book, etc. —v. (ik surpt') select; extract

ex·cess' n. 1. more than is needed 2. surplus —a. (ek'ses) extra —ex·ces'sive a. —ex·ces'sive·ly adv.

ex·change' v. 1. to trade; barter 2. interchange —n. 1. an exchanging 2. thing exchanged

3. place for exchanging 4. area telephone system 5. value of one currency in terms of another —**ex·change′a·ble** *a.*

ex·cheq′uer (-chek′ər) *n.* 1. treasury 2. funds

ex′cise *n.* tax on certain goods within a country: also **excise tax** —*v.* (ik sīz′) cut out —**ex·ci′sion** (-sizh′ən) *n.*

ex·cit′a·ble *a.* easily excited —**ex·cit′a·bil′i·ty** *n.*

ex·cite′ *v.* 1. make active 2. arouse; stir the feelings of —**ex·cite′ment** *n.*

ex·claim′ *v.* utter sharply —**ex′cla·ma′tion** *n.* —**ex·clam′a·to′ry** *a.*

exclamation mark (or **point**) mark of punctuation (!)

ex·clude′ *v.* keep out or shut out —**ex·clu′sion** *n.*

ex·clu′sive *a.* 1. not shared 2. snobbish —**exclusive of** not including; ignoring —**ex·clu′sive·ly** *adv.*

ex′com·mu′ni·cate *v.* expel from communion with a church —**ex′com·mu′ni·ca′tion** *n.*

ex·co′ri·ate *v.* to denounce harshly —**ex·co′ri·a′tion** *n.*

ex′cre·ment *n.* waste matter from the bowels

ex·cres′cence *n.* outgrowth, esp. an abnormal one

ex·crete′ *v.* eliminate (waste) from the body —**ex·cre′tion** *n.* —**ex·cre′to·ry** *a.*

ex·cru′ci·at′ing (-shē ãt′-) *a.* 1. very painful; agonizing 2. meticulous

ex′cul·pate *v.* exonerate —**ex′cul·pa′tion** *n.*

ex·cur′sion *n.* 1. short trip, esp. for pleasure 2. round trip at reduced rates

ex·cuse′ (ik skyo͞oz′) *v.* 1. apologize for 2. overlook (a fault) 3. release from a duty 4. let leave 5. justify —*n.* (-skyo͞os′) 1. apology 2. something that excuses 3. pretext —**ex·cus′a·ble** *a.*

ex′e·cra·ble *a.* 1. detestable 2. very inferior

ex′e·crate *v.* 1. denounce 2. loathe; abhor —**ex′e·cra′tion** *n.*

ex′e·cute *v.* 1. carry out; do 2. put to death legally 3. make valid (a will, deed, etc.) —**ex′e·cu′tion** *n.*

ex′e·cu′tion·er *n.* official who executes (*v.* 2)

ex·ec′u·tive *a.* 1. having to do with managing 2. administering laws, etc. —*n.* one who administers affairs

ex·ec′u·tor *n.* one who carries out the provisions of another's will

ex·em′plar (-plär) *n.* model; pattern

ex·em′pla·ry *a.* serving as a model or example

ex·em′pli·fy *v.* [-FIED, -FYING] show by example

ex·empt′ *v.* set free from a rule or obligation —*a.* freed from a usual rule, duty, etc. —**ex·emp′tion** *n.*

ex′er·cise *n.* 1. active use 2. activity to develop the body, a skill, etc. 3. *pl.* program, as at a graduation ceremony —*v.* 1. use 2. do or give exercises 3.

exert (influence, etc.) **4.** disturb

ex·ert′ v. **1.** put into action **2.** apply (oneself) with great effort

ex·er′tion n. **1.** act of exerting **2.** effort

ex·hale′ v. breathe forth — **ex′ha·la′tion** n.

ex·haust′ (ig zôst′) v. **1.** use up **2.** drain **3.** go into thoroughly **4.** tire out —n. **1.** discharge from an engine **2.** pipe for this —**ex·haust′i·ble** a. —**ex·haus′tion** n.

ex·haus′tive a. thorough

ex·hib′it (ig zib′-) v., n. show; display —**ex·hib′i·tor** n.

ex′hi·bi′tion (ek′sə bi′-) n. **1.** a (public) showing **2.** that which is shown

ex′hi·bi′tion·ist n. one who likes to show off —**ex′hi·bi′tion·ism** n.

ex·hil′a·rate (ig zil′-) v. make lively; stimulate —**ex·hil′a·ra′tion** n.

ex·hort′ (ig zôrt′) v. urge earnestly —**ex′hor·ta′tion** n.

ex·hume′ v. dig out of the earth

ex′i·gen·cy n. [pl. -CIES] **1.** urgency **2.** pressing situation

ex·ig′u·ous a. scanty

ex·ile (eg′zil) n. **1.** a prolonged, often enforced, living away from one's country **2.** person in exile —v. send into exile

ex·ist′ v. **1.** be **2.** occur **3.** live —**ex·ist′ence** n.

ex·is·ten′tial (-shəl) a. of existence

ex′it n. **1.** a leaving **2.** a way out **3.** actor's departure from the stage

ex′o·dus n. **1.** departure **2.** [E-] departure of the Israelites from Egypt

ex of·fi·ci·o (ə fish′ē ō) [L.] by virtue of one's position

ex·on′er·ate v. to free from blame

ex·or′bi·tant a. excessive —**ex·or′bi·tance** n.

ex′or·cise, ex′or·cize v. drive out (an evil spirit), as by magic —**ex′or·cism** n.

ex·ot′ic a. **1.** foreign **2.** strangely beautiful, etc.

ex·pand′ v. **1.** spread out **2.** enlarge —**ex·pan′sion** n.

ex·panse′ n. wide extent

ex·pan′sive a. **1.** broad **2.** warm and open in talk, etc.

ex·pa′ti·ate (-pā′shē-) v. speak or write at length

ex·pa′tri·ate v. to exile —n. (-it) an exile

ex·pect′ v. **1.** look for as likely or due **2.** [Col.] suppose —**be expecting** [Col.] be pregnant —**ex·pect′an·cy** n. —**ex·pect′ant** a. —**ex′pec·ta′tion** n.

ex·pec′to·rant n. medicine to bring up phlegm

ex·pec′to·rate v. to spit

ex·pe′di·ent a. **1.** useful for the purpose **2.** based on self-interest —n. a means to an end —**ex·pe′di·en·cy** n.

ex·pe·dite′ v. speed up; facilitate —**ex′pe·dit′er** n.

ex′pe·di′tion n. **1.** a journey, as for exploration **2.** those on such a journey

ex′pe·di′tious a. efficient;

speedy; prompt —ex′pe·di′-tious·ly adv.

ex·pel′ v. [-PELLED, -PELLING] 1. force out 2. dismiss by authority

ex·pend′ v. spend; use up

ex·pend′a·ble a. expected to be used up or killed in military service

ex·pend′i·ture (-chər) n. 1. spending of money, time, etc. 2. amount spent

ex·pense′ n. 1. cost 2. pl. charges met with in one's work, etc.

ex·pen′sive a. high-priced

ex·pe′ri·ence n. 1. a living through an event 2. thing one has done or lived through 3. skill got by training, work, etc. —v. have experience of

ex·per′i·ment n., v. test to discover or prove something — ex·per′i·men′tal a. —ex·per′i·men·ta′tion n.

ex′pert a. very skillful —n. one with great skill or knowledge in a field

ex·per·tise′ (-tēz′) n. skill or knowledge of an expert

ex′pi·ate v. atone for —ex′pi·a′tion n.

ex·pire′ v. 1. die 2. end 3. exhale —ex′pi·ra′tion n.

ex·plain′ v. 1. make plain or understandable 2. give the meaning of 3. account for — ex′pla·na′tion n. —ex·plan′-a·to′ry a.

ex′ple·tive n. oath or exclamation

ex·pli·ca·ble a. that can be explained

ex′pli·cate v. make clear; explain fully

ex·plic′it (-plis′-) a. clearly stated; definite

ex·plode′ v. 1. burst noisily 2. discredit —ex·plo′sion n.

ex′ploit n. bold deed —v. (iks ploit′) 1. use to advantage 2. make unethical use of —ex′-ploi·ta′tion n.

ex·plore′ v. 1. investigate 2. travel in (a region) for discovery —ex′plo·ra′tion n. —ex·plor′a·to′ry a.

ex·plo′sive a. of or like an explosion —n. substance that can explode

ex·po′nent n. 1. interpreter 2. example or symbol 3. Math. symbol at the upper right of another to show the times the latter is to be a factor

ex′port v. (also ik spôrt′) send (goods) to another country for sale —n. something exported —ex′por·ta′tion n.

ex·pose′ v. 1. lay open, as to danger 2. reveal 3. subject photographic film to light

ex·po·sé′ (-zā′) n. disclosure of a scandal

ex′po·si′tion n. 1. explanation 2. public exhibition

ex·pos′i·to′ry a. explaining

ex·pos′tu·late v. reason with a person in protest

ex·po′sure n. 1. direction house faces 2. public appearance 3. time film is exposed 4. one picture

ex·pound′ v. explain fully

ex·press′ v. 1. put into words 2. show or symbolize 3. send by express 4. squeeze out (juice) —a. 1. explicit 2. exact 3. fast and direct —adv. by express —n. an express train, bus, delivery service, etc.

ex·pres'sion n. 1. an expressing or way of expressing 2. certain word or phrase 3. look, etc. that shows how one feels —**ex·pres'sion·less** a. —**ex·pres'sive** a.

ex·pres·sion·ism n. art, writing, etc. expressing inner experience

ex·press'way n. divided highway for high-speed traffic

ex·pro'pri·ate v. take (land, etc.) for public use —**ex·pro'pri·a'tion** n.

ex·pul'sion n. an expelling or being expelled

ex·punge' v. erase

ex'pur·gate v. delete (from) as a censor

ex'qui·site a. 1. beautiful, delicate, etc. 2. of highest quality 3. very keen

ex'tant a. still existing

ex·tem·po·re adv., a. without preparation: also **ex·tem'po·ra'ne·ous** a.

ex·tem'po·rize v. speak, do, etc. extempore

ex·tend' v. 1. prolong 2. expand 3. stretch forth 4. offer

ex·ten'sion n. 1. an extending 2. an addition

ex·ten'sive a. far-reaching; vast —**ex·ten'sive·ly** adv.

ex·tent' n. 1. size 2. scope 3. vast area

ex·ten'u·ate v. lessen the seriousness of (an offense)

ex·te'ri·or a. on or from the outside —n. the outside

ex·ter'mi·nate v. destroy entirely —**ex·ter'mi·na'tion** n. —**ex·ter'mi·na'tor** n.

ex·ter'nal a. 1. on or from the outside 2. superficial 3. foreign —**ex·ter'nal·ly** adv.

ex·tinct' a. no longer existing or active

ex·tinc'tion n. a dying out; annihilation

ex·tin'guish v. 1. put out (a fire) 2. destroy

ex'tir·pate v. 1. pull up by the roots 2. destroy completely

ex·tol', ex·toll' v. [-TOLLED, -TOLLING] praise highly

ex·tort' v. get (money) by threats, etc. —**ex·tor'tion** n.

ex'tra a. more than expected; additional —n. 1. extra person or thing 2. extra benefit 3. minor actor hired by the day —adv. especially

extra- pref. outside; besides

ex·tract' v. 1. pull out 2. get by pressing, distilling, etc. 3. select —n. (eks'trakt) 1. something extracted 2. a concentrate 3. excerpt —**ex·trac'tion** n.

ex'tra·cur·ric'u·lar a. not part of required curriculum

ex'tra·dite v. to return (a fugitive) —**ex'tra·di'tion** n.

ex·tra'ne·ous a. 1. from outside 2. not pertinent

ex·traor'di·nar'y (iks trôr'-) a. very unusual

ex·trap'o·late v. to estimate on basis of known facts —**ex·trap'o·la'tion** n.

ex'tra·sen'so·ry a. apart from normal sense perception

ex·trav'a·gant a. 1. excessive

2. wasteful —**ex·trav·a·gance** n.

ex·trav·a·gan'za n. spectacular show

ex·treme' a. 1. utmost 2. final 3. excessive 4. radical —n. extreme degree, state, etc. —**ex·treme'ly** adv.

ex·trem'i·ty (-trem'-) n. [pl. -TIES] 1. end 2. extreme need, danger, etc. 3. pl. hands and feet

ex'tri·cate v. set free

ex·trin'sic a. 1. not essential 2. external —**ex·trin'si·cal·ly** adv.

ex'tro·vert n. one not given to introspection

ex·trude' v. 1. force through a small opening 2. project —**ex·tru'sion** n.

ex·u'ber·ant a. 1. very lively and healthy 2. luxuriant —**ex·u'ber·ance** n.

ex·ude' v. 1. pass out in drops 2. to seem to radiate —**ex·u·da'tion** n.

ex·ult' v. rejoice greatly —**ex·ult'ant** a. —**ex·ul·ta'tion** n.

ex·ur'bi·a n. communities beyond the suburbs —**ex·ur'ban·ite** n., a.

eye n. 1. organ of sight 2. vision 3. a look 4. attention 5. power of judging by eyesight —v. [EYED, EYING or EYEING] look at

eye'ball n. ball-shaped part of the eye

eye'brow n. bony arch over the eye, or the hair on this

eye'ful n. [Sl.] striking person or thing

eye'glass·es n.pl. pair of lenses to help faulty vision

eye'lash n. hair on the edge of the eyelid

eye'let n. small hole, as for a hook, cord, etc.

eye'lid n. either of two folds of flesh that cover and uncover the eyeball

eye'sight n. power of seeing

eye'sore n. ugly sight

eye'tooth n. [pl. -TEETH] upper canine tooth

eye'wit'ness n. one who has seen something happen

F

fa'ble n. 1. brief tale having a moral 2. untrue story

fab'ric n. material made from fibers, as cloth

fab'ri·cate v. 1. make 2. make up (a lie, story, etc.) —**fab'ri·ca'tion** n.

fab'u·lous (-yoo-) a. 1. fictitious 2. incredible 3. [Col.] wonderful; fine —**fab'u·lous·ly** adv.

fa·çade, fa·cade (fə säd') n.

1. main face of a building 2. deceptive appearance

face n. 1. front of the head; countenance 2. (main) surface 3. appearance 4. dignity —v. 1. turn, or have the face turned, toward 2. confront —**make a face** to grimace —**on the face of it** apparently

face'less a. anonymous

face lifting 1. plastic surgery to remove wrinkles from the face 2. altering of an exterior Also **face lift**

face′·sav′ing *a.* preserving one's self-respect

fac′et (fas′-) *n.* 1. a surface of a cut gem 2. aspect —*v.* cut facets on

fa·ce·tious (fə sē′shəs) *a.* joking, esp. at the wrong time — **fa·ce′tious·ly** *adv.*

face value 1. value on a bill, bond, etc. 2. seeming value

fa′cial (-shəl) *a.* of or for the face —*n.* treatment of the skin of the face with massage, creams, etc.

facial tissue soft tissue paper used as a handkerchief, etc.

fac·ile (fas′′l) *a.* 1. easy 2. superficial

fa·cil′i·tate *v.* make easier

fa·cil′i·ty *n.* [*pl.* -TIES] 1. ease or skill 2. *pl.* means for doing something easily 3. building, etc. meant for some activity

fac·sim·i·le (fak sim′ə lē) *n.* exact copy

fact *n.* 1. actual happening 2. truth —**in fact** really

fac′tion *n.* 1. clique 2. dissension —**fac′tion·al** *a.* —**fac′tious** *a.*

fac·ti′tious *a.* forced or artificial

fac′tor *n.* 1. causal element 2. *Math.* any of the quantities multiplied together

fac′to·ry *n.* [*pl.* -RIES] building in which things are manufactured

fac·to′tum *n.* handyman

fac′tu·al (-choo-) *a.* of facts; real

fac′ul·ty *n.* [*pl.* -TIES] 1. natural power or aptitude 2. staff of teachers

fad *n.* passing fashion —**fad′dish** *a.*

fade *v.* 1. (make) lose color or strength 2. die out

fag *v.* [FAGGED, FAGGING] make tired —*n.* [Sl.] male homosexual

fag′ot, fag′got *n.* bundle of sticks or twigs

Fahr·en·heit (fer′ən hīt) *a.* of a thermometer on which the boiling point of water is 212°, the freezing point 32°

fail *v.* 1. fall short 2. weaken 3. become bankrupt 4. not succeed 5. neglect 6. stop operating 7. disappoint 8. not pass a test or course

fail′ing *n.* 1. failure 2. fault —**prep.** lacking

faille (fil) *n.* soft, ribbed fabric of silk or rayon

fail′-safe′ *a.* of a system for preventing accidental operation, as of nuclear weapons

fail′ure (-yər) *n.* 1. act of failing 2. one that fails

faint *a.* 1. weak, dim, etc. 2. weak and dizzy —*n.* state of temporary unconsciousness — *v.* fall into a faint —**faint′ly** *adv.* —**faint′ness** *n.*

fair *a.* 1. beautiful 2. blond 3. clear and sunny 4. just 5. according to the rules 6. average —*adv.* in a fair way —*n.* exposition with exhibits, amusements, etc. —**fair′ly** *adv.* — **fair′ness** *n.*

fair′y *n.* [*pl.* -IES] tiny imaginary being in human form, with magic powers

faith n. 1. unquestioning belief, esp. in religion 2. particular religion 3. loyalty

faith'ful a. 1. loyal 2. exact — **faith'ful·ly** adv.

faith'less a. disloyal

fake v., n., a. sham —**fak'er** n.

fa·kir (fa kir') n. Muslim or Hindu religious mendicant

fal'con (fal'-) n. hawk trained to hunt —**fal'con·ry** n.

fall v. [FELL, FALLEN, FALLING] 1. to drop or descend 2. tumble 3. occur 4. sin 5. be divided (into) —n. 1. a falling 2. autumn 3. overthrow or ruin 4. amount of what has fallen 5. pl. a waterfall —**fall back** retreat —**fall off** lessen or worsen —**fall on** (or **upon**) to attack —**fall out** quarrel —**fall through** fail —**fall to** begin

fal'la·cy (fal'-) n. [pl. -CIES] 1. false idea; error 2. false reasoning —**fal·la'cious** a.

fal'li·ble a. liable to error —**fal'li·bil'i·ty** n.

Fal·lo'pi·an tube either of two tubes that carry ova to the uterus

fall'out n. 1. descent to earth of radioactive particles after a nuclear explosion 2. these particles

fal·low (fal'ō) a. 1. plowed but unplanted 2. inactive

false a. 1. not true 2. lying 3. unfaithful 4. not real 5. misleading —adv. in a false way —**false'ly** adv. —**false'ness** n. —**fal'si·fy** [-FIED, -FYING] v. —**fal'si·ty** n.

false'hood n. a lie or lying

fal·set'to n. artificial, high-pitched singing

fal'ter (fôl'-) v. 1. stumble 2. stammer 3. waver

fame n. great reputation

fa·mil'ial (-yəl) a. of or common to a family

fa·mil'iar (-yər) a. 1. friendly; intimate 2. too intimate 3. closely acquainted (with) 4. well-known —**fa·mil'i·ar'i·ty** n. —**fa·mil'iar·ize'** v.

fam'i·ly n. [pl. -LIES] 1. parents and their children 2. relatives 3. lineage 4. group of related things

fam'ine (-ən) n. 1. widespread food shortage 2. starvation

fam'ish v. be hungry; starve

fa'mous a. having fame

fan n. 1. device to move air for cooling, ventilating, etc. 2. [Col.] enthusiastic supporter —v. [FANNED, FANNING] 1. blow air toward 2. stir up 3. spread (out) 4. Baseball strike out

fa·nat'ic a. too enthusiastic or zealous: also **fa·nat'i·cal** —n. fanatic person; zealot —**fa·nat'i·cal·ly** adv. —**fa·nat'i·cism** n.

fan'ci·er n. person with a special interest, esp. plant or animal breeding

fan'cy n. [pl. -CIES] 1. playful imagination 2. notion, whim, etc. 3. a liking —a. [-CIER, -CIEST] 1. extravagant 2. elaborate 3. of superior quality —v. [-CIED, -CYING] 1. imagine 2. be fond of 3. suppose — **fan'ci·ful** a. —**fan'ci·ness** n.

fan'cy-free' a. 1. not married or engaged 2. carefree

fan′fare *n.* 1. blast of trumpets 2. showy display

fang *n.* long, pointed tooth

fan′ta·size *v.* have fantasies (about)

fan·tas′tic *a.* 1. unreal 2. grotesque 3. extravagant —**fan·tas′ti·cal·ly** *adv.*

fan′ta·sy *n.* [*pl.* **-SIES**] 1. fancy 2. illusion; reverie 3. fantastic poem, play, etc.

far *a.* [FARTHER, FARTHEST] distant —*adv.* 1. very distant 2. very much —**by far** very much —**(in) so far as** to the extent that

far′a·way′ *a.* distant

farce *n.* 1. exaggerated comedy 2. absurd thing —**far′ci·cal** *a.*

fare *v.* get along —*n.* 1. transportation charge 2. paying passenger 3. food

fare·well′ *int.* goodbye —*n.* good wishes at parting —*a.* (-wel′) parting; final

far′fetched′ *a.* not reasonable; strained

far′-flung′ *a.* extensive

fa·ri′na (-rē′-) *n.* flour or meal eaten as cooked cereal

farm *n.* land used to raise crops or animals —*v.* 1. cultivate (land) 2. let out (work or workers) on contract

farm′er *n.* one who manages or runs a farm

farm′hand′ *n.* hired farm worker

farm′house *n.* house on a farm

farm′ing *n.* business of running a farm; agriculture

farm′yard′ *n.* yard around or enclosed by farm buildings

far′-off′ *a.* distant

far′-out′ *a.* [Col.] nonconformist; avant-garde

far′-reach′ing *a.* having wide range, influence, etc.

far′sight′ed *a.* 1. planning ahead 2. seeing far objects better than near ones —**far′sight′ed·ness** *n.*

far′ther *a.* 1. more distant 2. additional —*adv.* 1. at or to a greater distance or extent 2. in addition

far′thest *a.* most distant —*adv.* at or to the greatest distance

fas′ci·nate *v.* hold spellbound; captivate —**fas′ci·na′tion** *n.*

fas·cism (fash′iz′m) *n.* militaristic dictatorship —**fas′cist** *n., a.*

fash′ion *n.* 1. kind; sort 2. manner 3. current style —*v.* 1. make; form 2. fit (*to*) —**after a fashion** to some extent

fash′ion·a·ble *a.* stylish

fast *a.* 1. firm 2. loyal 3. unfading 4. rapid; quick 5. ahead of time 6. of loose morals —*adv.* 1. firmly 2. thoroughly 3. rapidly —*v.* abstain from food —*n.* period of fasting

fas·ten (fas′'n) *v.* 1. attach 2. make secure; fix —**fas′ten·er** *n.*

fas′ten·ing *n.* thing used to fasten

fast′-food′ *a.* of a business, as a drive-in, that serves food prepared quickly

fas·tid′i·ous *a.* not easy to please; particular

fast′-talk′ *v.* [Col.] persuade with fast, smooth talk

fast time daylight-saving time

fat a. [FATTER, FATTEST] 1. oily; greasy 2. plump 3. profitable 4. [Sl.] desirable and important —n. oily substance found in animal tissue and plant seeds

fa'tal a. 1. causing death 2. disastrous —**fa'tal·ly** adv.

fa'tal·ism n. belief that all events are destined by fate —**fa'tal·ist** n. —**fa'tal·is'tic** a.

fa·tal'i·ty n. [pl. -TIES] death caused by disaster

fate n. 1. power supposedly making events inevitable 2. one's lot in life 3. outcome 4. death; ruin —**fate'ful** a.

fat'ed a. destined

fa'ther n. 1. male parent 2. [F-] God 3. founder; creator 4. Christian priest —v. beget, found, etc. —**fa'ther·hood** n. —**fa'ther·less** a. —**fa'ther·ly** a.

fa'ther-in-law n. [pl. FATHERS-IN-LAW] father of one's wife or husband

fa'ther·land n. one's native land

fath'om (fath'-) n. Naut. six feet —v. understand

fa·tigue' (-tēg') n. 1. weariness 2. [pl.] soldiers' work clothing —v. to weary

fat'ten v. make or get fat

fat'ty a. [-TIER, -TIEST] 1. of or containing fat 2. like fat; greasy

fat'u·ous (fach'-) a. foolish

fau'cet n. device with valve to draw liquid from a pipe

fault n. 1. flaw 2. error 3. blame —**find fault (with)** criticize —**fault'less** a.

fault'y a. [-IER, -IEST] defective

faun n. Roman deity, half man and half goat

fau'na n. the animals of a certain region

faux pas (fō'pä') [pl. FAUX PAS (päz')] social blunder

fa'vor n. 1. approval 2. partiality 3. kind act 4. small gift —v. 1. show favor toward 2. support; advocate 3. resemble Also Br. sp. favour —**in favor of** approving —**fa'vor·a·ble** a.

fa'vor·ite a., n. preferred (one) —**fa'vor·it·ism** n.

fawn v. 1. show affection as by licking 2. flatter servilely —n. 1. baby deer 2. pale brown

faze v. [Col.] disturb

fear n. 1. anxious anticipation of danger, pain, etc. 2. awe —v. 1. be afraid (of) 2. be in awe (of) —**fear'ful** a. —**fear'less** a.

fear'some a. 1. dreadful 2. frightened

fea'si·ble (fē'-) a. 1. possible 2. probable 3. suitable —**fea'si·bil'i·ty** n.

feast n. 1. religious festival 2. banquet —v. 1. have a feast (for) 2. delight

feat n. bold and daring deed

feath'er n. 1. one of the outgrowths covering a bird 2. kind —**feath'er·y** a.

feath'er·bed'ding n. use of extra workers to make more jobs, as by union contract

fea'ture (-chər) n. 1. pl. form of the face or its parts 2. special part, article, etc. **3.** main attraction —v. make a feature of

Feb'ru·ar'y n. second month

fe'ces (-sēz) n.pl. excrement

feck'less a. **1.** ineffective **2.** careless

fe'cund a. fertile

fed'er·al a. **1.** of a union of states under a central government **2.** of the central government, esp. [F-] of the U.S. — **fed'er·al·ism** n. —**fed'er·al·ist** a., n.

fed'er·al·ize' v. **1.** unite in a federal union **2.** put under federal authority

fed'er·ate v. unite in a federation

fed'er·a'tion n. union of states or groups; league

fe·do'ra n. man's felt hat

fee n. charge for some service or right

fee'ble a. weak; not strong — **fee'bly** adv.

fee'ble·mind'ed a. mentally retarded

feed v. [FED, FEEDING] **1.** give food to **2.** supply as fuel, material, etc. **3.** gratify **4.** eat —n. fodder —**feed'er** n.

feed'back' n. transfer of part of the output back to the input, as of information

feel v. [FELT, FEELING] **1.** touch **2.** have a feeling (of) **3.** be aware of **4.** believe **5.** be or seem to be **6.** grope —n. **1.** sense of touch **2.** way a thing feels —**feel like** [Col.] have a desire for —**feel up to** [Col.] feel able to

feel'er n. **1.** antenna or other organ of touch **2.** remark or offer made to elicit opinions

feel'ing n. **1.** sense of touch **2.** sensation **3.** an emotion **4.** pl. sensitiveness **5.** sympathy **6.** opinion

feet n. pl. of **foot**

feign (fān) v. **1.** make up (an excuse) **2.** pretend

feint (fānt) n. pretended attack, as in boxing —v. make a feint

feld'spar n. hard, crystalline mineral

fe·lic'i·tate (-lis'-) v. congratulate —**fe·lic'i·ta'tion** n.

fe·lic'i·tous a. appropriate

fe·lic'i·ty n. [pl. -TIES] **1.** happiness **2.** apt and pleasing expression

fe'line a. of or like a cat —n. a cat

fell pt. of **fall** —v. **1.** knock down **2.** cut down —a. cruel; terrible

fel'low n. **1.** an associate **2.** an equal **3.** a mate **4.** [Col.] man or boy —a. associated —**fel'low·ship** n.

fel'on n. criminal

fel'o·ny n. [pl. -NIES] major crime —**fe·lo'ni·ous** a.

felt n. fabric made of fibers pressed together

fe'male a. **1.** designating or of the sex that bears offspring **2.** feminine —n. female person or animal

fem'i·nine a. of or like women —**fem'i·nin'i·ty** n.

fem'i·nism n. movement to win equal rights for women — **fem'i·nist** n., a.

fe'mur (fē'-) n. thighbone

fen n. swamp; bog

fence n. 1. barrier of posts, wire, etc. 2. dealer in stolen goods —v. 1. enclose with a fence 2. engage in fencing

fenc′ing n. sport of fighting with foils or swords —**fenc′er** n.

fend v. ward (off) —**fend for oneself** manage by oneself

fend′er n. guard over an automobile wheel

fer′ment n. 1. thing causing fermentation 2. agitation —v. (fər ment′) 1. undergo or cause fermentation (in) 2. excite or be excited

fer′men·ta′tion n. chemical change caused by yeast, bacteria, etc.

fern n. nonflowering plant with fronds

fe·ro′cious (-shəs) a. savage; fierce —**fe·roc′i·ty** n.

fer′ret n. kind of weasel —v. search out

fer′ric, **fer′rous** a. of iron

Fer′ris wheel large, revolving wheel with hanging seats to ride in at an amusement park

fer′rule (-əl) n. metal ring or cap around the end of a cane, etc. to strengthen it

fer′ry v. [-RIED, -RYING] take across a river, etc. in a boat — n. [pl. -RIES] boat (in full, **ferryboat**) used for ferrying

fer′tile (fur′-) a. 1. producing abundantly 2. able to produce young, fruit, etc. —**fer·til′i·ty** n.

fer′ti·lize v. 1. make fertile 2. spread fertilizer on 3. make

fruitful by introducing a male germ cell

fer′ti·liz′er n. chemicals, etc. to enrich the soil

fer′ule (-əl) n. flat stick or ruler used to punish a child

fer′vent a. intense; ardent

fer′vid a. fervent

fer′vor n. ardor; zeal

fes′tal a. joyous; merry

fes′ter v. 1. form pus 2. rankle

fes′ti·val n. time or day of celebration

fes′tive a. joyous; merry

fes·tiv′i·ty n. [pl. -TIES] 1. gaiety 2. pl. festive proceedings

fes·toon′ n. garland, etc. hanging in loops —v. adorn with festoons

fe′ta (cheese) (fet′ə) white, soft cheese made in Greece

fetch v. 1. go after and bring back; get 2. sell for

fetch′ing a. attractive

fete, fête (fāt) n. festival; outdoor party —v. honor with a fete

fet′id a. stinking

fet′ish n. 1. object thought to have magic power 2. nonsexual object that arouses sexual desire —**fet′ish·ism** n.

fet′lock n. 1. tuft of hair above a horse's hoof in back 2. leg joint bearing this tuft

fet′ter n. ankle shackle —v. restrain as with fetters

fet′tle n. condition; trim

fe′tus (fēt′əs) n. 1. unborn young 2. human offspring in the womb after the end of the third month —**fe′tal** a.

feud (fyōod) n. deadly quarrel

as between families —v. engage in a feud

feu'dal·ism (fyōō'-) n. medieval system with lords, vassals, and serfs —**feu'dal** a.

fe'ver n. 1. abnormally high body temperature 2. disease marked by high fever 3. great excitement —**fe'ver·ish** a.

few a. not many —pron., n. a small number

fi·an·cé (fē'än sā') n. man to whom a woman is betrothed

fi'an·cée (-sā') n. woman to whom a man is betrothed

fi·as·co (fē as'kō) n. [pl. -COES, -COS] utter failure

fi'at n. a decree

fib n. petty lie —v. [FIBBED, FIBBING] tell a fib —**fib'ber** n.

fi'ber, fi'bre (-bər) n. 1. threadlike part forming organic tissue 2. threadlike part or parts used for weaving, etc. —**fi'brous** a.

Fi'ber·glas' trademark for material made of filaments of glass —n. [f-] this material: also **fiberglass**

fi·bril·la'tion (fib'rə-) n. rapid series of contractions of heart, causing weak heartbeats

fi'broid (fī'-) a. like or composed of fibrous tissue

fi·bro'sis n. abnormal growth of fibrous connective tissue in an organ, part, etc.

fib'u·la (-yoo-) n. [pl. -LAE (-lē), -LAS] thinner bone of lower leg

fick'le a. changeable

fic'tion n. literary work or works with imaginary charac-

ters and events —**fic'tion·al** a.

fic·ti'tious a. imaginary

fic'tive a. 1. of fiction 2. imaginary

fid'dle n. [Col.] violin —v. 1. [Col.] play a violin 2. fidget —**fid'dler** n.

fi·del'i·ty n. faithfulness

fidg'et (fij'-) v. make nervous movements —**fidg'et·y** a.

fie (fī) int. shame!

field n. 1. piece of open land, esp. one for crops, grazing, etc. 2. expanse 3. playing field 4. sphere of knowledge or activity 5. all entrants in a contest —v. stop or catch and return (a baseball, etc.) —**field'er** n.

field glasses portable, telescopic eyeglasses

field goal 1. Basketball basket toss from play, scoring two points 2. Football goal kicked from the field, scoring three points

field hand hired farm worker

fiend (fēnd) n. 1. devil 2. [Col.] addict —**fiend'ish** a.

fierce a. 1. savage; wild 2. violent 3. intense —**fierce'ly** adv.

fi'er·y a. [-IER, -IEST] 1. flaming, hot, etc. 2. ardent

fi·es'ta n. festival

fife n. small, shrill flute

fif'teen' a., n. five more than ten —**fif'teenth'** a., n.

fifth a. preceded by four others —n. 1. one after the fourth 2. one of five equal parts 3. fifth of a gallon

fif'ty a., n. [pl. -TIES] five times ten —**fif'ti·eth** a., n.

fig 199 filth

fig *n.* 1. sweet fruit with seed-filled pulp 2. tree it grows on 3. trifle

fight *n., v.* [FOUGHT, FIGHTING] struggle; battle; contest

fight'er *n.* 1. one that fights 2. fast combat airplane

fig'ment *n.* thing imagined

fig'ur·a·tive *a.* using metaphors, similes, etc.

fig'ure *n.* 1. outline; shape 2. person 3. likeness of a person or thing 4. illustration 5. design 6. a number 7. sum of money —*v.* 1. compute 2. be conspicuous 3. [Col.] believe; consider —**figure on** rely on —**figure out** solve

fig'ure·head' *n.* 1. carved figure on a ship's bow 2. leader with no real power

figure of speech a vivid expression, as a metaphor or simile

fig'u·rine' (-rēn') *n.* statuette

fil'a·ment *n.* threadlike part

fil'bert *n.* hazelnut

filch *v.* steal (something trivial)

file *n.* 1. container for keeping papers in order 2. orderly arrangement of papers, etc. 3. line of persons or things 4. ridged tool for scraping, etc. —*v.* 1. put papers, etc. in order 2. move in a file 3. smooth or grind with a file

fi·let mi·gnon (fi lā' min yōn') thick cut of lean beef tenderloin broiled

fil'i·al (-ē əl) *a.* of or suitable to a son or daughter

fil'i·bus'ter *n.* obstruction of a bill in a legislature, as by a long speech —*v.* obstruct a bill in this way

fil'i·gree *n.* lacelike work of fine wire

fil'ings *n.pl.* small pieces scraped off with a file

fill *v.* 1. make or become full 2. put into or hold (a job or office) 3. supply things ordered —*n.* anything that fills —**fill in** 1. make complete 2. substitute —**fill out** 1. make or become larger, etc. 2. complete (a blank form)

fil·let', fi·let' (-lā') *n.* boneless piece of fish or meat —*v.* to bone (fish, etc.)

fill'ing *n.* thing used to fill something else

filling station service station

fil'lip *n.* stimulus; tonic

fil'ly *n.* [*pl.* -LIES] young mare

film *n.* 1. thin coating 2. flexible cellulose material used in photography 3. movie —*v.* 1. cover with a film 2. make a movie of

film'strip *n.* strip of film with stills of pictures, charts, etc. on some subject

film'y *a.* [-IER, -IEST] 1. gauzy; thin 2. blurred

fil'ter *n.* 1. thing used for straining out particles, etc. from a fluid, etc. 2. device absorbing certain light rays —*v.* 1. pass through a filter 2. remove with a filter 3. pass slowly —**fil·tra'tion** *n.*

filter tip cigarette with a tip of cellulose, etc. to filter the smoke

filth *n.* 1. foul dirt 2. obscenity

—**filth'i·ness** n. —**filth'y** [-IER, -IEST] a.

fin n. **1.** winglike, membranous organ on a fish **2.** thing like this

fi·na'gle (-nā'-) v. [Col.] use, or get by, trickery —**fi·na'gler** n.

fi'nal a. **1.** last **2.** conclusive —n. **1.** pl. last of a series of contests **2.** final examination —**fi·nal'i·ty** n. —**fi'nal·ly** adv. —**fi'nal·ist** n.

fi·na'le (-nä'lē) n. last part of a musical work

fi'nal·ize v. make final

fi·nance' (or fi'nans) n. **1.** pl. funds **2.** science of managing money matters —v. supply money for —**fi·nan'cial** a. —**fin·an·cier'** (-sir') n.

finch n. small songbird, as the canary or sparrow

find v. [FOUND, FINDING] **1.** come upon; discover **2.** get by searching **3.** learn **4.** recover (a thing lost) **5.** decide —n. something found

fine a. **1.** excellent **2.** not heavy or coarse **3.** clear and bright **4.** very small **5.** sharp **6.** subtle; delicate **7.** elegant —adv. [Col.] very well —n. money paid as a penalty —v. cause to pay a fine

fine arts painting, sculpture, music, etc.

fin'er·y (fin'-) n. showy clothes

fi·nesse' n. skill, esp. in handling delicate situations

fin'ger n. any of the parts (five with the thumb) at the end of the hand —v. to handle —**fin'·ger·nail** n.

fin'ger·board n. part of a stringed instrument against which the strings are pressed

fin'ger·print n. impression of the lines of a finger tip —v. take the fingerprints of

fin'ick·y a. too particular; fussy: also **fin'i·cal**

fi·nis (fin'is, fē nē') n. [pl. -NISES] the end; finish

fin'ish v. **1.** to end **2.** complete **3.** use up **4.** perfect; polish —n. **1.** last part; end **2.** polish or perfection **3.** way a surface is finished

fi'nite a. having limits

Finn n. Finnish person

Fin'nish a., n. (of) the people or language of Finland

fiord (fyôrd) n. sea inlet bordered by steep cliffs

fir n. evergreen tree of the pine family

fire n. **1.** flame **2.** thing burning **3.** ardor **4.** discharge of firearms **1.** make burn **2.** excite **3.** shoot (a gun, etc.) **4.** [Col.] discharge from a job —**on fire** burning —**under fire** under attack

fire'arm n. rifle, pistol, etc.

fire'bomb n. incendiary bomb

fire'crack·er n. noisy explosive rolled in paper

fire engine truck equipped for fire fighting

fire escape outside stairway to escape a burning building

fire'fly n. [pl. -FLIES] winged beetle with a glowing abdomen

fire'man n. [pl. -MEN] **1.** one who fights fires **2.** stoker

fire'place n. place built in a wall for a fire

fire′plug n. street hydrant

fire′proof v., a. (make) not easily destroyed by fire

fire′wood n. wood used as fuel

fire′works n.pl. firecrackers, rockets, etc. for noisy or brilliant displays

firm a. 1. solid 2. fixed; stable 3. strong and steady 4. definite —v. make firm —n. business company —**firm′ly** adv. —**firm′ness** n.

fir′ma·ment n. [Poet.] sky

first a. 1. before any others 2. earliest 3. foremost —adv. 1. before any others 2. for the first time —n. 1. first one 2. beginning

first aid emergency care for injuries —**first′-aid′** a.

first′-class′ a. of the highest quality —adv. with the best accommodations

first′hand′ a., adv. from the source; direct

first lady [often F- L-] wife of the U.S. president

first lieutenant military officer ranking just above second lieutenant

first′ly adv. in the first place

first′-rate′ a. excellent

firth n. narrow inlet of the sea

fis′cal a. financial —**fis′cal·ly** adv.

fish n. [pl. FISH; for different kinds, FISHES] 1. coldblooded animal with gills and fins, living in water 2. flesh of fish used as food —v. 1. catch fish 2. angle (for) —**fish′er·man** [pl. -MEN] n. —**fish′er·y** [pl. -IES] n.

fish′hook′ n. hook for catching fish

fish′y a. [-IER, -IEST] 1. like a fish 2. [Col.] questionable

fis·sion (fish′ən) n. 1. a split ting apart 2. nuclear fission

fis·sure (fish′ər) n. a cleft or crack

fist n. clenched hand

fis′ti·cuffs n.pl. boxing

fit v. [FITTED or FIT, FITTED, FITTING] 1. be suitable to 2. be the proper size, etc. (for) 3. adjust to fit 4. equip —a. [FITTER, FITTEST] 1. suited 2. proper 3. healthy —n. 1. way of fitting 2. seizure as of coughing 3. outburst —**fit′ness** n.

fit′ful a. not regular

fit′ting a. proper —n. 1. adjustment 2. pl. fixtures

five a., n. one more than four

fix v. 1. fasten or set firmly 2. determine 3. adjust 4. repair 5. prepare (food, etc.) 6. [Col.] influence by bribery, etc. —n. [Col.] predicament —**fix up** [Col.] 1. repair 2. set in order · fixed a.

fix·a′tion n. obsession

fix′ings n.pl. [Col.] accessories; trimmings

fix′ture (-chər) n. usually pl. any of the attached furnishings of a house

fizz v., n. (make) a hissing, bubbling sound

fiz′zle v. 1. to fizz 2. [Col.] fail —n. 1. fizzing sound 2. [Col.] failure

fjord (fyôrd) n. fiord

flab n. [Col.] sagging flesh

flab′ber·gast v. [Col.] amaze

flab'by *a.* [-BIER, -BIEST] 1. limp and soft 2. weak

flac·cid (flak'sid) *a.* flabby

flag *n.* 1. cloth with designs, etc. used as a symbol, as of a nation, or as a signal 2. iris (flower) —*v.* [FLAGGED, FLAGGING] 1. to signal with flags 2. grow weak

flag·el·late (flaj'-) *v.* to whip —**flag'el·la'tion** *n.*

flag'on (flag'-) *n.* container for liquids

flag'pole *n.* pole for flying a flag: also **flag'staff**

fla'grant *a.* glaringly bad —**fla'gran·cy** *n.*

flag'stone *n.* a flat, paving stone

flail *n.* implement used to thresh grain by hand —*v.* 1. use a flail 2. beat

flair *n.* 1. aptitude; knack 2. [Col.] sense of style

flak *n.* 1. fire of antiaircraft guns 2. criticism: also **flack**

flake *n.* 1. soft, thin mass 2. chip or peeling —*v.* form into flakes

flak'y *a.* [-IER, -IEST] 1. made of, or breaking into, flakes 2. [Sl.] very odd

flam·boy'ant *a.* showy

flame *n.* tongue(s) of fire; blaze —*v.* burst into flame

fla·men'co (-men'kō) *n.* Spanish gypsy music or dancing

flame'out *n.* failure of combustion in jet engine in flight

fla·min'go *n.* [*pl.* -GOS, -GOES] pink, long-legged wading bird

flam'ma·ble *a.* easily set on fire

flange (flanj) *n.* projecting rim on a wheel, etc.

flank *n.* 1. side of an animal between the ribs and the hip 2. side of anything —*v.* be at, or go around, the side of

flan'nel *n.* soft, napped cloth of wool, etc.

flan·nel·ette', **flan'nel·et'** (-et') *n.* soft, fleecy, cotton cloth

flap *n.* 1. flat, loose piece 2. motion or sound of a swinging flap 3. [Sl.] a commotion —*v.* [FLAPPED, FLAPPING] flutter

flare *v.* 1. blaze up 2. spread outward —*n.* 1. bright, unsteady blaze 2. brief, dazzling signal light 3. sudden outburst 4. a curving outward

flare'-up' *n.* sudden outburst

flash *v.* 1. send out a sudden, brief light 2. sparkle 3. move suddenly —*n.* 1. sudden, brief light 2. an instant 3. bit of late news

flash'back *n.* interruption in a story by a return to some earlier episode

flash'bulb *n.* bulb giving brief, bright light, for taking photographs

flash'cube *n.* rotating cube with flashbulbs in four sides

flash'light *n.* portable electric light

flash'y *a.* [-IER, -IEST] gaudy; showy

flask *n.* kind of bottle

flat *a.* [FLATTER, FLATTEST] 1. smooth and level 2. broad and thin 3. lying spread out 4. absolute 5. tasteless 6. dull 7. emptied of air 8. *Mus.* below

true pitch —*adv.* in a flat way
  n. 1. flat surface or part 2.
deflated tire 3. *Mus.* note one
half step below another: symbol (♭) 4. apartment —*v.*
[FLATTED, FLATTING] make or
become flat .

flat'bed *n.* truck or trailer with
a platform without sides

flat'car *n.* railroad freight car
without sides or roof

flat'fish *n.* fish with a very
broad, flat body

flat'foot *n.* foot with the instep arch flattened

flat'ten *v.* make or become flat
or flatter

flat'tor *v.* 1. praise insincerely
2. gratify the vanity of —**flat'-
ter·y** *n.*

flat'u·lent (flach'ə-) *a.* having
or making gas in the stomach
—**flat'u·lence** *n.*

flat'ware *n.* flat tableware

flaunt (flônt) *v.* show off

fla'vor *n.* taste of a substance
—*v.* give flavor to —**fla'vor-
ful** *a.* —**fla'vor·less** *a.*

fla'vor·ing *n.* added essence,
etc. that flavors food

flaw *n.* defect; fault —
flaw'less *a.*

flax *n.* plant with fibers that
are spun into linen thread

flax'en *a.* pale yellow

flay *v.* 1. strip the skin from 2.
criticize harshly

flea *n.* small jumping insect
that is parasitic

flea market outdoor bazaar for
selling secondhand goods

fleck *n., v.* spot

fledg'ling *n.* young bird just
able to fly

flee *v.* [FLED, FLEEING] escape
swiftly, as from danger

fleece *n.* wool covering a sheep
—*v.* to swindle

fleec'y *a.* [-IER, -IEST] of or
like fleece, soft and light

fleet *n.* 1. group of warships
under one command 2. any
similar group, as of trucks, etc.
—*a.* swift

fleet'ing *a.* passing swiftly

flesh *n.* 1. tissue between the
skin and bones 2. pulp of
fruits and vegetables 3. body
—**flesh'y** [-IER, -IEST] *a.*

flesh'ly *a.* [-LIER, -LIEST] 1. of
the body 2. sensual 3. fleshy

flex *v.* 1. bend, as an arm 2.
contract, as a muscle

flex'i·ble *a.* 1. easily bent; pliable 2. adaptable —**flex'i·bil'-
i·ty** *n.*

flick *n.* 1. light, quick stroke 2.
[Sl.] movie —*v.* strike, throw,
etc. with such a stroke

flick'er *v.* move, burn, or shine
unsteadily —*n.* dart of flame
or light

fli'er *n.* 1. aviator 2. small
handbill

flight *n.* 1. act or power of flying 2. distance flown 3. group
of things flying together 4.
trip by airplane 5. set of stairs
6. a fleeing

flight'less *a.* not able to fly

flight'y *a.* [-IER, -IEST] 1. frivolous; irresponsible 2. foolish;
silly

flim'sy *a.* [-SIER, -SIEST] 1.
easily broken 2. ineffectual

flinch *v.* draw back, as from a
blow

fling v. throw with force —n. 1. a flinging 2. brief, wild time of fun 3. lively dance 4. [Col.] a try

flint n. a hard quartz

flip v. [FLIPPED, FLIPPING] 1. toss with a quick jerk 2. turn over 3. [Sl.] lose self-control —n. a flipping —**flip one's lid** [Sl.] go berserk

flip'pant a. saucy

flip'per n. 1. flat limb adapted for swimming, as in seals 2. paddlelike device worn on each foot by swimmers

flip side [Col.] reverse side (of a phonograph record)

flirt v. 1. play at love 2. trifle 3. move jerkily —n. one who plays at love

flir·ta'tion n. frivolous love affair —**flir·ta'tious** a.

flit v. [FLITTED, FLITTING] move lightly and rapidly

float n. 1. thing that stays on the surface of a liquid 2. flat, decorated vehicle in a parade —v. 1. stay on the surface of a liquid 2. drift gently in air, etc. 3. put into circulation, as a bond issue 4. arrange for (a loan)

flock n. group, esp. of animals —v. gather in a flock

flock'ing n. tiny fibers put on wallpaper, etc. as a velvetlike surface: also **flock**

floe (flō) n. large sheet of floating ice

flog v. [FLOGGED, FLOGGING] beat, thrash, or whip

flood n. 1. overflowing of water on land 2. great outpouring —v. 1. to overflow 2. put too much water, fuel, etc. in

flood'light n. lamp casting a very bright, broad light —v. [alt. pt. & pp. -LIT] illuminate by a floodlight

floor n. 1. bottom surface of a room, etc. 2. story in a building 3. permission to speak —v. 1. furnish with a floor 2. knock down

floor'ing n. material for making a floor

floor show show with singers, dancers, etc., as in a nightclub

flop v. [FLOPPED, FLOPPING] 1. move, drop, or flap about clumsily 2. [Col.] fail —n. a flopping —**flop'py** a.

flo'ra n. plants of a certain region

flo'ral a. of or like flowers

flor'id a. 1. ruddy 2. flashy

flo'rist n. one who grows or sells flowers

floss n. 1. soft, silky fibers 2. soft, loosely twisted thread 3. dental floss —v. use dental floss on —**floss'y** a.

flo·til'la n. small fleet

flot'sam n. floating debris or cargo of a shipwreck

flounce v. move with quick, flinging motions —n. ruffle

floun'der v. struggle or speak clumsily —n. kind of edible flatfish

flour n. powdery substance ground from grain, esp. wheat —**flour'y** a.

flour'ish (flur'-) v. 1. thrive 2. be in one's prime 3. brandish —n. 1. sweeping motion or stroke 2. fanfare

flout v. mock or scorn

flow v. 1. move as water does 2. move smoothly 3. proceed 4. be plentiful 5. hang loose — n. a flowing or thing that flows

flow'er n. 1. petals and pistil of a plant 2. a plant grown for its blossoms 3. best part —v. 1. produce blossoms 2. become its best

flow'er·pot n. container with earth for a plant to grow in

flow'er·y a. showy in expression

flown pp. of fly

flu n. 1. influenza 2. respiratory or intestinal infection caused by a virus

flub v. [FLUBBED, FLUBBING] [Col.] bungle —n. [Col.] blunder

fluc'tu·ate v. keep changing, as prices —**fluc'tu·a'tion** n.

flue n. shaft in a chimney

flu'ent a. speaking or writing easily —**flu'en·cy** n. —**flu'ent·ly** adv.

fluff n. loose, soft mass —v. 1. make fluffy 2. bungle

fluff'y a. [-IER, -IEST] soft and light

flu'id a. 1. able to flow 2. not fixed —n. liquid or gas —**flu·id'i·ty** n.

fluke n. 1. anchor blade 2. [Col.] stroke of luck

flung pt. & pp. of fling

flunk v. [Col.] to fail

flunk'y n. [pl. -IES] low, servile person

flu'o·res'cent a. giving off cool light —**flu'o·res'cence** n.

fluor'i·date (flôr'-, floor'-) v. add fluorides to (water) to reduce tooth decay —**fluor'i·da'tion** n.

flu'o·ride n. fluorine salt

flu'o·rine (-rēn) n. yellowish gas, a chemical element

fluor'o·scope (floor'ə-) n. kind of X-ray machine

flur'ry n. [pl. -RIES] 1. gust of wind, rain, or snow 2. sudden commotion; fuss —v. [-RIED, -RYING] confuse

flush v. 1. to redden in the face 2. start up from cover, as a bird 3. wash out —n. 1. a blush; glow 2. a washing out 3. hand of cards all in the same suit —a. 1. well supplied 2. level (with) 3. direct —adv. 1. so as to be level 2. directly

flus'ter v. make confused

flute n. 1. tubelike wind instrument 2. groove in a column shaft —**flut'ed** a. **flut'ist** n.

flut'ter v. wave, move, or beat rapidly and irregularly —n. 1. a fluttering 2. confusion —**flut'ter·y** a.

flux n. 1. a flowing 2. constant change 3. substance used to help metals fuse

fly v. [FLEW, FLOWN, FLYING] 1. move through the air by using wings 2. wave or float in the air 3. move swiftly 4. flee 5. [pt. & pp. FLIED] hit a fly in baseball 6. travel in or pilot (aircraft) —n. [pl. FLIES] 1. flap concealing buttons, etc. in a garment 2. baseball batted high 3. winged insect 4. fish lure like a fly

fly'catch'er n. small bird that catches flying insects

fly'er n. flier

flying colors notable success

flying fish fish with winglike fins that glides in the air

flying saucer unidentified flying object

fly'leaf n. blank leaf at the front or back of a book

fly'pa'per n. sticky paper set out to catch flies

fly'wheel n. wheel that regulates a machine's speed

FM frequency modulation

foal (fōl) n. young horse —v. give birth to (a foal)

foam n. 1. bubbly mass on liquids 2. spongy mass made from rubber, plastic, etc. —v. form foam —**foam'y** [-IER, -IEST] a.

fob n. pocket-watch chain or ornament on it

fo'cus n. [pl. -CUSES, -CI (-sī)] 1. point where rays of light meet 2. adjustment of lens distance for clear image 3. center of activity —v. 1. bring into focus 2. concentrate —**fo'cal** a.

fod'der n. coarse food for cattle, horses, etc.

foe n. enemy

fog n. 1. thick mist 2. mental confusion —v. [FOGGED, FOGGING] make or become foggy

fog'gy a. [-GIER, -GIEST] 1. full of fog 2. blurred 3. confused —**fog'gi·ness** n.

fog'horn n. horn blown to warn ships in a fog

fo'gy n. [pl. -GIES] one who is old-fashioned or conservative: also **fo'gey** [pl. -GEYS]

foi'ble n. small weakness in character

foil v. thwart —n. 1. thin fencing sword 2. thin sheet of metal 3. one that enhances another by contrast

foist v. impose by fraud

fold v. 1. double up on itself 2. intertwine 3. wrap up —n. 1. folded layer 2. pen for sheep

-fold suf. times as many

fold'a·way a. that can be folded together and stored

fold'er n. 1. folded sheet of cardboard to hold papers 2. booklet of folded sheets

fo'li·age (-ij) n. plant leaves

fo'li·o n. [pl. -OS] largest regular size of book

folk n. [pl. FOLK, FOLKS] people —a. of the common people

folk'lore n. beliefs, legends, etc. of a people

folk song song made and handed down among the common people —**folk singer**

folk'sy a. [-SIER, -SIEST] [Col.] friendly or sociable

fol'li·cle (-k'l) n. small sac or gland, as in the skin

fol'low v. 1. come or go after 2. go along 3. take up (a trade) 4. result (from) 5. obey 6. pay attention to 7. understand —**follow out** (or **up**) carry out fully —**follow through** continue and finish a stroke or action

fol'low·er n. 1. one who follows another's teachings 2. attendant

fol'low·ing *a.* next after —*n.* group of followers

fol'ly *n.* [*pl.* -LIES] foolish state, action, belief, etc.

fo·ment' (fō-) *v.* incite

fond *a.* loving; tender —**fond of** liking —**fond'ly** *a.*

fon'dle *v.* to caress

fon·due', fon·du' *n.* melted cheese, etc. for dipping bread cubes

font *n.* **1.** basin for holy water **2.** bowl of water for baptism

food *n.* substance taken in by an animal or plant to enable it to live and grow

food poisoning any sickness caused by eating food contaminated by bacteria, chemicals, etc.

fool *n.* **1.** silly person **2.** dupe —*v.* **1.** be silly or playful **2.** trick

fool'har'dy *a.* [-DIER, -DIEST] foolishly daring; rash

fool'ish *a.* silly; unwise

fool'proof *a.* simple, safe, etc.

foot *n.* [*pl.* FEET] **1.** end part of the leg, on which one stands **2.** bottom; base **3.** measure of length, 12 inches **4.** unit of meter in verse —*v.* [Col.] pay (a bill) —**foot it** [Col.] to walk —**on foot** walking —**under foot** in the way

foot'ball *n.* **1.** game played on a field with an inflated leather ball **2.** this ball

foot'hill *n.* low hill at the foot of a mountain

foot'hold *n.* place for the feet, as in climbing

foot'ing *n.* **1.** secure placing of the feet **2.** basis for relationship

foot'lights *n.pl.* lights at the front of a stage floor

foot'loose *a.* free to go where or do as one likes

foot'man *n.* [*pl.* -MEN] male servant assisting a butler

foot'note *n.* note at the bottom of a page

foot'print *n.* mark left by a foot

foot'rest *n.* support for foot or feet

foot'step *n.* **1.** sound of a step **2.** footprint

foot'stool *n.* stool for a seated person's feet

fop *n.* vain man fussy about his clothes, etc. —**fop'pish** *a.*

for *prep.* **1.** in place of **2.** in the interest of **3.** in favor of **4.** with the purpose of **5.** in search of **6.** meant to be received, used, etc. by **7.** with respect to **8.** because of **9.** to the extent or duration of **10.** at the price of —*con.* because

for'age (-ij) *n.* fodder —*v.* to search for food

for'ay (-ā) *n., v.* raid

for·bear' *v.* [-BORE, -BORNE, -BEARING] **1.** refrain (from) **2.** control oneself —**for·bear'ance** *n.*

for·bid' *v.* [-BADE (-bad') or -BAD, -BIDDEN, -BIDDING] not permit; prohibit

for·bid'ding *a.* frightening

force *n.* **1.** strength; power; energy **2.** coercion **3.** effectiveness **4.** organized group, as an army —*v.* **1.** make do something; compel **2.** break open **3.**

impose, produce, etc. by force
—force′ful *a.*

forced *a.* 1. compulsory 2. not natural

for′ceps *n.* [*pl.* -CEPS] small tongs or pincers

for′ci·ble *a.* with force —for′ci·bly *adv.*

ford *n.* shallow place in a river —*v.* cross at a ford

fore *adv., a.* in or toward the front part —*n.* the front —*int.* Golf shout warning that one is about to hit the ball

fore- *pref.* before; in front

fore′arm *n.* arm between the elbow and wrist

fore′bear *n.* ancestor

fore·bode′ *v.* foretell

fore′cast *v.* [-CAST or -CASTED, -CASTING] predict —*n.* prediction —fore′cast′er *n.*

fore·cas·tle (fōk′s'l, fōr′kas'l) *n.* forward deck or front part of a ship

fore·close′ *v.* take away the right to redeem (a mortgage) —fore·clo′sure *n.*

fore′fa′ther *n.* ancestor

fore′fin′ger *n.* finger nearest the thumb

fore′front *n.* extreme front

fore′go′ing *a.* preceding

fore·gone′ *a.* 1. previous 2. previously determined

fore′ground *n.* part of a scene nearest the viewer

fore′hand *n.* a stroke, as in tennis, made with the palm of the hand turned forward

fore′head *n.* part of the face above the eyebrows

for′eign (-in) *a.* 1. of or from another country 2. not characteristic —for′eign-born′ *a.*

for′eign·er *n.* person from another country

foreign minister cabinet member in charge of foreign affairs

fore′knowl′edge *n.* knowledge of something beforehand

fore′leg *n.* front leg of animal

fore′man *n.* [*pl.* -MEN] 1. man in charge of workers 2. chairman of a jury

fore′most *a., adv.* first

fore′noon *n.* time before noon

fo·ren′sic *a.* of or suitable for public debate

fore·or·dain′ *v.* predestine

fore·run′ner *n.* person or thing foretelling something

fore·see′ *v.* [-SAW, -SEEN, -SEEING] see beforehand —fore·see′a·ble *a.*

fore·shad′ow *v.* presage

fore·short′en *v.* shorten some lines in drawing to make some parts seem farther away

fore′sight *n.* 1. power to foresee 2. prudence

fore′skin *n.* fold of skin over the end of the penis

for′est *n.* tract of land covered with trees —*v.* to plant with trees

fore·stall′ *v.* prevent by acting beforehand

for′est·a′tion *n.* planting or care of forests

for′est·er *n.* one trained in forestry

for′est·ry *n.* science of the care of forests

fore·tell′ *v.* [-TOLD, -TELLING] predict

fore′thought *n.* foresight

for·ev'er adv. 1. for all time 2. at all times

fore·warn' v. warn beforehand

fore'word n. preface

for'feit (-fit) n. penalty —v. lose as a penalty —**for'fei·ture** (-chər) n.

forge n. 1. furnace for heating metal to be wrought 2. smith's shop —v. 1. to shape by heating and hammering 2. counterfeit (a signature) 3. advance slowly

for'ger·y n. [pl. -IES] crime of forging documents, signatures, etc. 2. anything forged

for·get' v. [-GOT, -GOTTEN or -GOT, -GETTING] 1. be unable to remember 2. neglect

for·get'-me-not' n. plant with small, blue flowers

for·give' v. [-GAVE, -GIVEN, -GIVING] give up wanting to punish; pardon —**for·give'ness** n. —**for·giv'ing** a.

for·go' v. [-WENT, -GONE, -GOING] do without

fork n. 1. pronged instrument for lifting 2. place of branching —v. to branch —**fork'ful** [pl. -FULS] n.

fork'lift n. device with prongs slid under loads to lift them

for·lorn' a. 1. deserted 2. wretched; miserable

form n. 1. shape; figure 2. mold 3. kind; type 4. style; customary behavior 5. document to be filled in —v. 1. to shape 2. develop (habits) 3. constitute —**form'less** a.

for'mal a. 1. according to custom, rule, etc. 2. stiff; prim 3. for use at ceremonies 4. requiring formal clothes —n. 1. formal dance 2. woman's evening dress —**for'mal·ly** adv.

form·al'de·hyde (-hīd) n. disinfectant and preservative

for·mal'i·ty n. 1. an observing of customs, rules, etc. 2. [pl. -TIES] formal act

for'mal·ize v. 1. to shape 2. make formal

for'mat n. general arrangement, as of a book

for·ma'tion n. 1. a forming 2. thing formed; structure —**form'a·tive** a.

for'mer a. 1. of the past 2. being the first mentioned

for'mer·ly adv. in the past

for'mi·da·ble a. 1. causing fear 2. hard to handle

for'mu·la n. [pl. -LAS, -LAE (-lē)] 1. fixed expression or rule 2. fortified milk for a baby 3. set of symbols expressing a mathematical formula, chemical compound, etc. —**for'mu·late** v. —**for'mu·la'tion** n.

for'ni·ca'tion n. sexual intercourse between unmarried people —**for'ni·cate** v.

for·sake' v. [-SOOK, -SAKEN, -SAKING] abandon; desert

for·swear' v. 1. swear to give up 2. commit perjury

for·syth'i·a (-sith'-) n. shrub with yellow flowers

fort n. fortified place for military defense

forte (fôrt) n. what one does well

for'te (-tā, -tē) a., adv. Mus. loud

forth *adv.* 1. forward 2. out into view

forth·com·ing *a.* 1. about to appear 2. ready at hand

forth·right' *a.* frank

forth·with' *adv.* at once

for·ti·fi·ca'tion *n.* 1. a fortifying 2. a fort

for'ti·fy *v.* [-FIED, -FYING] 1. strengthen 2. add alcohol to (wine) 3. add vitamins, etc. to (milk)

for·tis'si·mo *a., adv. Mus.* very loud

for'ti·tude *n.* calm courage

fort'night *n.* [Chiefly Br.] two weeks

for'tress *n.* fortified place

for·tu'i·tous *a.* 1. accidental 2. lucky

for'tu·nate (-chə nit) *a.* 1. lucky 2. favorable —**for'tu·nate·ly** *adv.*

for'tune *n.* 1. luck; fate 2. one's future lot, good or bad 3. good luck 4. wealth

for'tune·tell'er *n.* one claiming to foretell others' future —**for'tune·tell'ing** *n.*

for'ty *a., n.* [*pl.* -TIES] four times ten —**for'ti·eth** *a., n.*

fo'rum *n.* meeting for public discussion

for'ward *a.* 1. at, to, or of the front 2. advanced 3. bold —*adv.* ahead: also **forwards** —*v.* 1. promote 2. send on

fos'sil *n.* 1. hardened plant or animal remains, as in rock 2. old-fashioned person —*a.* 1. of a fossil 2. taken from the earth 3. antiquated

fos'sil·ize *v.* 1. change into a fossil 2. make or become outdated, rigid, etc.

fos'ter *v.* 1. bring up 2. promote —*a.* in a family but not by birth or adoption

fought *pt. & pp.* of **fight**

foul *a.* 1. stinking 2. very dirty 3. stormy 4. outside the rules or limits 5. [Col.] unpleasant —*n.* foul hit, blow, etc. —*v.* 1. make filthy 2. obstruct 3. entangle 4. make a foul —**foul up** [Col.] bungle —**foul'ness** *n.*

foul'-up' *n.* [Col.] mix-up

found *pt. & pp.* of **find** —*v.* 1. to base 2. establish; set up —**found'er** *n.*

foun·da'tion *n.* 1. establishment or basis 2. base of a wall, house, etc. 3. philanthropic fund or institution

foun'der *v.* 1. fall or go lame 2. fill and sink, as a ship

found'ling *n.* deserted child

found'ry *n.* [*pl.* -RIES] place where metal is cast

fount *n.* fountain

foun'tain *n.* 1. spring of water 2. jet of water or basin for it 3. source

foun'tain·head' *n.* source

fountain pen pen getting ink from its own reservoir

four *a., n.* one more than three —**fourth** *a., n.*

four'score' *a., n.* eighty

four'some *n.* group of four people

four'square' *a.* 1. firm 2. frank —*adv.* frankly

four'teen' *a., n.* four more than ten —**four'teenth'** *a., n.*

fowl *n.* 1. any bird 2. a domestic bird, as the chicken

fox *n.* 1. small, wild, doglike animal 2. its fur 3. sly, crafty person —*v.* slyly trick

fox'glove *n.* digitalis (*sense* 1)

fox'hole *n.* hole dug as protection against gunfire

fox terrier small terrier with smooth or wiry coat

fox trot ballroom dance

fox'y *a.* [-IER, -IEST] 1. sly; crafty 2. [Sl.] attractive, stylish, etc.

foy'er *n.* entrance hall

fra'cas (frā'-) *n.* brawl

frac'tion *n.* 1. part of a whole, as 3/4, 1/2, etc. 2. small part —**frac'tion·al** *a.*

frac'tious *a.* unruly

frac'ture *n.* a break, esp. in a bone —*v.* to break; crack

frag'ile (fraj'-) *a.* easily broken —**fra·gil'i·ty** *n.*

frag'ment *n.* 1. part broken away 2. incomplete part —**frag'men·tar'y** *a.*

fra'grant *a.* sweet-smelling —**fra'grance** *n.*

frail *a.* 1. fragile 2. delicate or weak —**frail'ty** [*pl.* -TIES] *n.*

frame *v.* 1. make, form, build, etc. 2. put into words 3. enclose in a border 4. [Col.] falsify evidence to make seem guilty —*n.* 1. framework 2. framing border or case 3. mood 4. one film exposure —*a.* having a wooden framework

frame'-up *n.* [Col.] falsifying of evidence to make seem guilty

frame'work *n.* supporting or basic structure

franc *n.* Fr. monetary unit

fran'chise (-chīz) *n.* 1. special right 2. right to vote

fran'gi·ble (-jə-) *a.* breakable

frank *a.* outspoken; candid —*v.* send (mail) free —**frank'ly** *adv.* —**frank'ness** *n.*

frank'furt·er (-fər tər) *n.* smoked sausage; wiener: also [Col.] **frank**

frank'in·cense *n.* gum resin burned as incense

fran'tic *a.* wild with anger, worry, pain, etc. —**fran'ti·cal·ly** *adv.*

frap·pé (fra pā') *n.* dessert of partly frozen fruit juices

fra·ter'nal *a.* 1. brotherly 2. of a fellowship society

fra·ter'ni·ty *n.* [*pl.* -TIES] 1. brotherliness 2. college social club for men 3. group with like interests

frat'er·nize *v.* be friendly —**frat'er·ni·za'tion** *n.*

fraud *n.* 1. trickery 2. intentional deception 3. a trick 4. impostor

fraud'u·lent *a.* 1. using fraud 2. done by fraud —**fraud'u·lence** *n.*

fraught *a.* filled (*with*)

fray *n.* quarrel or fight —*v.* make or become ragged

fraz'zle *v.* [Col.] wear out —*n.* [Col.] frazzled state

freak *n.* 1. abnormal animal or plant 2. [Sl.] devotee; fan —*a.* abnormal —**freak out** [Sl.] have hallucinations, etc. —**freak'ish** *a.*

freck'le *n.* small brown spot on the skin —*v.* to spot with freckles

free *a.* [FREER, FREEST] 1. not under another's control 2. loose, clear, unrestricted, etc. 3. generous 4. frank 5. without cost —*adv.* 1. without cost 2. in a free way —*v.* [FREED, FREEING] make free —**free from** (or **of**) without

free′boot′er *n.* a pirate

free′dom *n.* 1. independence 2. liberty 3. ease of movement 4. frankness 5. a right

free fall unchecked fall through the air, esp. part of parachutist's jump before parachute opens

free′-for-all′ *n.* brawl

free′-lance′ *a.* selling services to individual buyers

free′load′er *n.* [Col.] one always imposing on others for free food, etc.

free′think′er *n.* religious skeptic

free′way′ *n.* multiple-lane highway with interchanges

freeze *v.* [FROZE, FROZEN] 1. change into, or become covered with, ice 2. make or become very cold 3. kill or damage by cold 4. make or become motionless 5. make or become unfriendly 6. fix (prices, etc.) at a set level —*n.* a freezing —**freeze out** [Col.] keep out by a cold manner, competition, etc.

freeze′-dry′ *v.* [-DRIED, -DRYING] preserve (food) by freezing quickly and drying

freez′er *n.* refrigerator for freezing and storing foods

freight (frāt) *n.* 1. goods transported 2. transportation of goods or its cost 3. train for freight

freight′er *n.* ship for freight

French *a., n.* (of) the people or language of France

French dressing salad dressing of vinegar, oil, etc.

French fried fried in deep fat

French fries [Col.] potatoes cut in strips and French fried

French horn brass-wind horn with a coiled tube

fre·net′ic *a.* frantic

fren′zy *n.* [*pl.* -ZIES] wild excitement —**fren′zied** *a.*

fre′quen·cy *n.* [*pl.* -CIES] 1. frequent occurrence 2. number of times anything recurs in a given period

frequency modulation changing of the frequency of the radio wave according to the signal being broadcast

fre′quent *a.* 1. occurring often 2. constant —*v.* (frē kwent′) go to habitually

fres′co *n.* [*pl.* -COES, -COS] painting done on wet plaster

fresh *a.* 1. not spoiled, stale, worn out, etc. 2. new 3. refreshing 4. not salt: said of water 5. [Sl.] bold; insolent

fresh′en *v.* make or become fresh, clean, etc.

fresh′et *n.* flooded stream

fresh′man *n.* [*pl.* -MEN] first-year student in high school or college

fresh′wa′ter *a.* living in water that is not salty

fret *v.* [FRETTED, FRETTING] to worry 1. worry 2. ridge on the fingerboard of a banjo, guitar, etc.

fret′ful *a.* irritable

fret′work *n.* ornate openwork

fri′a·ble *a.* easily crumbled

fri′ar *n.* R.C.Ch. member of a religious order

fric′as·see′ (-sē′) *n.* stewed pieces of meat

fric′tion *n.* 1. rubbing of one object against another 2. conflict —**fric′tion·al** *a.*

Fri′day *n.* sixth day of the week

fried *pt. & pp. of* **fry**

friend *n.* 1. person one knows well and likes 2. ally — **friend′ship** *n.*

friend′ly *a.* [-LIER, -LIEST] kindly; helpful

frieze (frēz) *n.* decorative band around a wall, etc.

frig·ate (frig′it) *n.* fast sailing warship

fright *n.* sudden fear

fright′en *v.* 1. make afraid 2. drive (*away*) with fear

fright′ful *a.* 1. causing fright 2. shocking 3. [Col.] unpleasant 4. [Col.] great

frig·id (frij′id) *a.* very cold — **fri·gid′i·ty** *n.*

frill *n.* 1. ruffle 2. [Col.] fancy ornament —**frill′y** *a.*

fringe *n.* 1. border, as of loose threads 2. minor part —*v.* be or make a fringe for —*a.* 1. at the outer edge 2. additional 3. minor

fringe benefit payment other than wages, as in pension, insurance, etc.

frip′per·y *n.* [*pl.* -IES] showy display, clothes, etc.

frisk *v.* 1. to frolic 2. [Sl.] search for weapons, etc.

frisk′y *a.* [-IER, -IEST] lively — **frisk′i·ness** *n.*

frit′ter *v.* waste (money, etc.) bit by bit —*n.* small cake of fried batter

friv′o·lous *a.* 1. trivial 2. silly —**fri·vol′i·ty** (-väl′-) [*pl.* -TIES] *n.*

frizz *v.* form into tight curls: also **friz′zle** —**friz′zy** *a.*

fro *adv.* back: only in **to and fro,** back and forth

frock *n.* 1. dress 2. robe

frog *n.* 1. leaping web-footed animal 2. braided loop —**frog in the throat** hoarseness

frol′ic *n.* 1. lively party 2. fun —*v.* [ICKED, -ICKING] 1. have fun 2. romp about

frol′ic·some *a.* playful

from *prep.* 1. beginning at 2. out of 3. originating with 4. out of the possibility, reach, etc. of 5. as not being like 6. because of

frond *n.* fern or palm leaf

front *n.* 1. forward part 2. first part 3. land along a street, ocean, etc. 4. outward behavior —*a.* of or at the front —*v.* to face —**front′al** *a.*

front′age *n.* 1. front part of a building 2. land bordering a street, etc.

fron·tier′ (-tir′) *n.* 1. border of a country 2. new or unexplored field —**fron·tiers′man** [*pl.* -MEN] *n.*

fron′tis·piece *n.* picture facing the title page

front′-run′ner *n.* leading contestant

frost *n.* 1. temperature causing freezing 2. frozen dew or vapor

—*v.* cover with frost or frosting —**frost'y** [-IER, -IEST] *a.*

frost'bite *n.* injury from intense cold —**frost'bit'ten** *a.*

frost'ing *n.* 1. icing 2. dull finish on glass

froth *n.* 1. foam 2. trifling ideas, etc. —*v.* to foam —**froth'y** [-IER, -IEST] *a.*

fro'ward (frō'-) *a.* stubborn

frown *v.* 1. contract the brows 2. look with disapproval (*on*) —*n.* a frowning

frow'zy *a.* [-ZIER, -ZIEST] slovenly

froze *pt. of* freeze

fro'zen *pp. of* freeze

fruc'tose *n.* sugar found in sweet fruit, honey, etc.

fru'gal *a.* thrifty or sparing —**fru·gal'i·ty** *n.*

fruit *n.* 1. pulpy, edible product of a plant or tree 2. result; product

fruit'cake *n.* rich cake with fruit, nuts, etc.

fruit'ful *a.* productive

fru·i'tion (-ish'ən) *n.* 1. the bearing of fruit 2. fulfillment

fruit'less *a.* unsuccessful

frump *n.* dowdy woman —**frump'ish, frump'y** *a.*

frus·tra'tion *n.*

fry *v.* [FRIED, FRYING] cook in hot fat or oil —*n.* young fish —**small fry** 1. children 2. insignificant people

fry'er *n.* 1. utensil for deep-frying foods 2. tender chicken for frying

fuch'sia (fyōō'shə) *n.* plant with purplish-red flowers —*a.* purplish-red

fudge *n.* soft candy made of butter, sugar, etc. —*v.* to fake or cheat

fu'el *n.* thing burned for heat or power —*v.* supply with or get fuel

fu'gi·tive *a.* 1. fleeing 2. fleeting —*n.* one who has fled from the law, etc.

fugue (fyōōg) *n.* musical work in which theme is developed by parts in counterpoint

-ful *suf.* 1. full of 2. having the qualities of 3. apt to 4. quantity that will fill

ful'crum *n.* support on which a lever turns

ful·fill', ful·fil' *v.* [-FILLED, -FILLING] 1. carry out or complete (a promise, duty, etc.) 2. satisfy (a condition) —**ful·fill'ment, ful·fil'ment** *n.*

full *a.* 1. containing all there is space for 2. having a great deal (*of*) 3. complete 4. having reached the greatest amount, etc. 5. round 6. flowing —*n.* greatest amount, etc. —*adv.* 1. completely 2. exactly —**full'-ness** *n.*

full'blown' *a.* matured

full dress formal dress

full'-fledged' *a.* fully developed; of full status

full house poker hand with three of a kind and a pair

full'-scale' *a.* to the utmost degree

full'-time' *a.* of work, etc. using all one's regular working hours

full'y *adv.* 1. thoroughly 2. at least

ful'mi·nate (ful'-) v. 1. explode 2. shout forth

ful'some (fool'-) a. disgusting, esp. because excessive

fum'ble v. grope or handle clumsily —n. a fumbling

fume (fyōōm) n. offensive smoke or vapor —v. 1. give off fumes 2. show anger

fu'mi·gate v. fill with fumes so as to kill vermin, germs, etc.

fun n. 1. lively, amusing play 2. source of amusement — **make fun of** ridicule

func·tion n. 1. special or typical action, use, duty, etc. 2. formal ceremony or social affair —v. do its work —**func'tion·al** a.

func·tion·ar'y n. [pl. -IES] an official

fund n. 1. supply; store 2. money set aside for a purpose 3. pl. ready money —v. provide for by a fund

fun'da·men'tal a., n. basic (thing)

fun'da·men'tal·ism n. religious beliefs based literally on the Bible —**fun'da·men'tal·ist** n., a.

fu'ner·al n. ceremonies for burial or cremation of the dead

funeral director manager of place (**funeral home** or **parlor**) for funerals

fu·ne're·al a. sad; gloomy

fun'gus n. [pl. -GI (-jī), -GUSES] any of the mildews, molds, mushrooms, etc. —**fun'gous** a.

funk n. [Col.] 1. panic 2. depressed mood

fun'nel n. 1. slim tube with a cone-shaped mouth 2. ship's smokestack —v. pour as through a funnel

fun'ny a. [-NIER, -NIEST] 1. amusing 2. [Col.] odd 3. [Col.] tricky

fur n. soft, thick hair on an animal —a. of fur —**fur'ry** [-RIER, -RIEST] a.

fur'be·low (-lō) n. fancy trimming

fu'ri·ous (fyoor'ē-) a. 1. very angry 2. very great

furl (furl) v. roll up tightly, as a flag

fur'long n. 1/8 of a mile

fur'lough (-lō) n. a military leave of absence —v. grant a furlough to

fur'nace (-nis) n. structure in which heat is produced

fur'nish v. 1. put furniture into 2. supply

fur'nish·ings n.pl. 1. furniture and fixtures, as for a house 2. things to wear

fur'ni·ture n. chairs, beds, etc. in a room, etc.

fu·ror (fyoor'ôr) n. 1. fury 2. widespread enthusiasm 3. uproar

fur'ri·er n. one who processes, or deals in, furs

fur'ring n. thin wood strips put on a wall, floor, etc. before boards or plaster

fur'row n. 1. groove made in the ground by a plow 2. deep wrinkle —v. make furrows in

fur'ther a. 1. additional 2. more distant —adv. 1. to a greater extent 2. in addition 3. at or to a greater distance —v. promote —**fur'ther·ance** n.

fur·ther·more adv. besides

fur·thest a. most distant —adv. at or to the greatest distance or extent

fur·tive (-tiv) a. done or acting in a stealthy way

fu·ry (fyoor'ē) n. 1. wild rage 2. violence

fuse (fyooz) v. melt (together) —n. 1. wick that is lighted to set off an explosive 2. safety device that breaks an electric circuit when the current is too strong

fu·se·lage (-läzh, -lij) n. body of an airplane

fu·sil·lade' n. simultaneous discharge of many guns

fu·sion n. 1. a melting together 2. blending 3. nuclear fusion

fuss n. 1. nervous, excited state 2. [Col.] quarrel 3. [Col.] showy display —v. 1. bustle about or worry over trifles 2. whine, as a baby

fuss'y a. [-IER, -IEST] 1. worrying over trifles 2. hard to please 3. with too many details —**fuss'i·ness** n.

fus'ty a. [-TIER, -TIEST] 1. musty 2. old-fashioned —**fu·til'·i·ty** n.

fu'tile (-til) a. useless —**fu·til'·i·ty** n.

fu'ture (-chər) a. that is to be or come —n. 1. time that is to come 2. what is going to be; prospects —**fu'tur·is'tic** a.

fu·tu'ri·ty (-toor'ə-) n. [pl. -TIES] 1. the future 2. future condition

fuzz n. loose, light particles; fine hairs —**the fuzz** [Sl.] the police —**fuzz'y** [-IER, -IEST] a.

G

gab n., v. [GABBED, GABBING] [Col.] chatter

gab·ar·dine (-ər dēn) n. cloth with a diagonal weave

gab'ble v., n. jabber

gab'by a. [-BIER, -BIEST] [Col.] talkative

ga'ble n. triangular wall enclosed by the sloping ends of a roof —**ga'bled** a.

gad v. [GADDED, GADDING] roam about restlessly

gad'a·bout n. [Col.] restless seeker after fun, etc.

gad'fly' n. [pl. -FLIES] 1. large, stinging fly 2. annoying person

gadg'et (gaj'-) n. small mechanical device

gaff n. large hook on a pole for landing fish

gaffe (gaf) n. a blunder

gag v. [GAGGED, GAGGING] 1. retch or cause to retch 2. keep from speaking, as with a gag —n. 1. something put into the mouth to prevent speech 2. [Sl.] joke

gage n. 1. pledge 2. challenge 3. gauge —v. gauge

gag'gle n. 1. flock of geese 2. any group

gai'e·ty (gā'-) n. 1. cheerfulness 2. merriment

gai'ly adv. 1. merrily 2. brightly

gain n. 1. increase 2. profit —v. 1. earn 2. win 3. get as an addition or advantage 4. reach 5. make progress —**gain on** draw nearer to, as in a race

gain'ful a. profitable —**gain'ful·ly** adv.

gain·say' v. [-SAID, -SAYING] deny or contradict

gait n. manner of walking or running

gal n. [Col.] girl

ga'la n. a celebration —a. festive

gal·ax·y n. [pl. -IES] very large group of stars —**ga·lac'tic** a.

gale n. 1. strong wind 2. outburst, as of laughter

gall (gôl) n. 1. bile 2. tumor on plant tissue 3. [Col.] impudence —v. annoy

gal'lant a. 1. brave and noble 2. polite to women

gal'lant·ry n. [pl. -RIES] 1. heroic courage 2. courtesy

gall bladder sac attached to the liver, in which excess bile is stored

gal'le·on n. large Spanish ship of 15th-16th centuries

gal'ler·y n. [pl. -IES] 1. covered walk 2. outside balcony 3. theater balcony 4. place for art exhibits

gal'ley n. [pl. -LEYS] 1. ancient sailing ship with oars 2. ship's kitchen

gal'li·vant v. gad about for pleasure

gal'lon n. 4 quarts

gal'lop n. fastest gait of a horse —v. go or make go at a gallop

gal'lows n. [pl. -LOWSES, -LOWS] structure for hanging condemned persons

gall'stone n. small solid mass sometimes formed in the gall bladder

ga·lore' adv. in great plenty

ga·losh', ga·loshe' n. high, warmly lined rubber overshoe

gal·van'ic a. of electric current, esp. from a battery

gal'va·nize v. 1. excite 2. plate (metal) with zinc

gam'bit n. opening move in chess

gam'ble v. 1. play games of chance for money 2. take a risk 3. bet —n. risk, chance —**gam'bler** n.

gam'bol v., n. frolic

game n. 1. amusement or sport with competing players 2. a plan 3. wild animals hunted for sport 4. [Col.] risky business —v. gamble —a. 1. plucky 2. ready (for) 3. [Col.] lame —**the game is up** failure is certain

game plan long-range strategy

gam'ete (-ēt) n. reproductive cell

gam'in n. 1. homeless child 2. girl with saucy charm

gam'ma rays strong electromagnetic radiation from a radioactive substance

gam'ut n. the entire range, esp. of a musical scale

gam'y a. [-IER, -IEST] 1. strongly flavored 2. slightly tainted

gan'der n. 1. male goose 2. [Sl.] a look

gang n. group working or acting together —**gang up on** [Col.] attack as a group

gan'gling *a.* thin, tall, and awkward: also **gan'gly**

gan'gli·on (-ən) *n.* [*pl.* -GLIA, -GLIONS] mass of nerve cells

gang'plank *n.* movable ramp from a ship to the dock

gan'grene *n.* decay of body tissue from lack of blood supply —**gan'gre·nous** *a.*

gang'ster *n.* member of a gang of criminals

gang'way *n.* 1. passageway 2. gangplank —*int.* clear the way!

gant'let (gônt'-) *n.* punishment of being beaten as one runs between two rows of men

gan'try *n.* [*pl.* -TRIES] wheeled framework with a crane

gaol (jāl) *n.* jail: Br. sp.

gap *n.* 1. opening or break 2. mountain pass 3. blank space 4. lag; disparity

gape *v.* 1. open wide 2. stare with the mouth open

gar *n.* long fish with a long snout: also **gar'fish**

ga·rage' (-räzh', -räj') *n.* shelter or repair shop for automobiles, etc.

garb *n.* clothing; style of dress —*v.* clothe

gar'bage (-bij) *n.* waste parts of food

gar'ble *v.* distort (a story, etc.)

gar'den *n.* 1. plot for flowers, vegetables, etc. 2. fertile area 3. public park —*v.* make, or work in, a garden —**gar'den·er** *n.*

gar·de'nia (-dēn'yə) *n.* waxy white flower

Gar·gan'tu·an *a.* huge

gar'gle *v.* rinse the throat —*n.* liquid for gargling

gar'goyle *n.* gutter spout in the form of a sculptured grotesque creature

gar'ish (ger'-) *a.* gaudy

gar'land *n.* wreath of flowers, leaves, etc. —*v.* decorate with garlands

gar'lic *n.* strong-smelling plant bulb, used to season —**gar'lick·y** *a.*

gar'ment *n.* piece of clothing

gar'ner *v.* gather and store

gar'net *n.* deep-red gem

gar'nish *v.* decorate (food) —*n.* decoration for food

gar'nish·ee' *v.* attach (a debtor's wages, etc.) to pay the debt

gar'ret *n.* attic

gar'ri·son *n.* fort or the troops in it —*v.* provide with troops

gar·rote' (-rät') *n.* cord, thong, etc. used in strangling —*v.* execute or attack with a garrote

gar'ru·lous (gar'-) *a.* talking much —**gar·ru'li·ty** *n.*

gar'ter *n.* elastic band to hold up a stocking

gas *n.* 1. fluid substance that can expand; vapor 2. mixture of gases used as fuel 3. [Col.] gasoline 4. [Col.] automobile accelerator —*v.* [GASSED, GASSING] attack or kill with gas —**gas'e·ous** *a.*

gash *v.* cut deep into —*n.* deep cut

gas'ket *n.* rubber or metal ring sealing a joint, etc.

gas'o·line, gas'o·lene (-lēn) *n.* liquid fuel from petroleum

gasp v. catch the breath with effort —n. a gasping

gas station service station

gas'sy a. [-SIER, -SIEST] flatulent

gas'tric a. of the stomach

gas·tri'tis n. inflammation of the stomach

gas·tron'o·my n. art of good eating —gas'tro·nom'i·cal a.

gas'tro·pod (păd) n. kind of mollusk, as a snail or slug

gate n. 1. hinged door in a fence or wall 2. number of paid admissions

gate'-crash'er n. [Col.] one who attends without invitation or payment

gate'way n. 1. entrance with a gate 2. entrance or access

gath'er v. 1. bring or come together; collect 2. infer 3. draw into pleats —n. a pleat

gath'er·ing n. 1. meeting; crowd 2. folds in cloth

gauche (gōsh) a. tactless

gau'cho n. [pl. -CHOS] South American cowboy

gaud'y (gôd'-) a. [-IER, -IEST] showy but tasteless —gaud'i·ly adv.

gauge (gāj) n. 1. standard measure 2. device for measuring 3. distance between railway rails 4. size of shotgun bore 5. thickness of wire, etc. —v. 1. to measure 2. to estimate; judge

gaunt (gônt) a. haggard; thin

gaunt'let n. 1. long glove with a flaring cuff 2. gantlet — **throw down the gauntlet** challenge

gauze (gôz) n. loosely woven material —gauz'y a.

gave pt. of **give**

gav'el (gav'-) n. chairman's small mallet

ga·votte' (-vät') n. 17th-c. dance like the minuet

gawk v. stare stupidly

gawk'y a. [-IER, -IEST] clumsy; ungainly

gay a. 1. joyous and lively 2. bright 3. [Sl.] homosexual

gaze v. look steadily; stare —n. steady look

ga·ze'bo (-zē'-, -zä'-) n. [pl. -BOS, -BOES] summerhouse or a balcony with windows

ga·zelle' n. swift antelope

ga·zette' n. newspaper

gaz·et·teer' n. dictionary of geographical names

gear n. 1. equipment 2. system of toothed wheels that mesh 3. such a wheel —v. 1. connect by gears 2. adjust

gear'shift' n. device for changing transmission gears

gee (jē) int. [Sl.] exclamation of surprise, etc.

geese n. pl. of **goose**

gee'zer n. [Sl.] eccentric old man

Gei·ger counter (gī'gər) instrument for measuring radioactivity

gei·sha (gā'shə) n. Japanese woman entertainer

gel (jel) n. jellylike substance formed by a colloidal solution

gel'a·tin (jel'-) n. jellied substance extracted from bones, hoofs, vegetables, etc. —ge·lat′i·nous a.

geld (geld) v. castrate (a horse, etc.) —geld′ing n.

gel′id (jel′-) a. frozen

gem n. precious stone

Gem′i·ni 3rd sign of the zodiac; Twins

gen·darme (zhän′därm′) n. armed policeman in France

gen′der (jen′-) n. classification of words as masculine, feminine, or neuter

gene (jēn) n. unit of heredity in chromosomes

ge′ne·al′o·gy (jē′nē äl′-) n. history of ancestry —ge′ne·a·log′i·cal a.

gen′er·al a. 1. of or for all 2. widespread 3. usual 4. not specific —n. high-ranking army officer —in general usually —gen′er·al·ly adv.

gen′er·al′i·ty n. [pl. -TIES] nonspecific or vague idea or statement

gen′er·al·ize′ v. talk in generalities —gen′er·al·i·za′tion n.

gen′er·ate v. cause to be; produce —gen′er·a′tive a.

gen·er·a′tion n. 1. production 2. all persons born about the same time 3. average time (30 years) between generations

gen′er·a′tor n. machine for changing mechanical into electrical energy

ge·ner′ic (jə-) a. 1. inclusive; general 2. of a genus 3. not a trademark —ge·ner′i·cal·ly adv.

gen′er·ous a. 1. giving read-

ily; unselfish 2. ample —gen′er·os′i·ty n.

gen′e·sis n. 1. origin 2. [G-] first book of the Bible

ge·net′ics n. study of heredity —ge·net′ic a.

gen′ial (jēn′-) a. kindly; amiable —ge′ni·al′i·ty n.

ge·nie (jē′nē) n. jinni

gen′i·tals n.pl. external sex organs —gen′i·tal a.

gen′i·tive a., n. Gram. (in) the case showing possession or origin

gen′ius (jēn′-) n. 1. great mental or creative ability 2. person having this

gen′o·cide (jen′-) n. systematic killing of a whole people

gen·re (zhän′rə) n. kind or type

gen·teel′ a. (overly) polite, refined, etc.

gen′tian (-shən) n. plant with blue, fringed flowers

gen′tile (-tīl) a., n. [also G-] non-Jewish (person)

gen·til′i·ty n. politeness

gen′tle a. 1. mild; moderate 2. kindly; patient —gen′tly adv.

gen′tle·folk n.pl. well-bred people: also gentlefolks

gen′tle·man n. [pl. -MEN] 1. well-bred, courteous man 2. any man: polite term

gen′try n. people just below the nobility

gen′u·flect′ v. bend the knee, as in worship —gen′u·flec′tion n.

gen′u·ine (-in) a. 1. real; true 2. sincere

ge′nus (jē′-) n. [pl. GENERA

(jen′ər ə), sometimes GENUSES] class; kind, esp. in biology

ge·o·des·ic *a.* of a dome formed by short, straight bars in a patterned grid

ge·o·det·ic *a.* of the measurement of the earth

ge·og·ra·phy *n.* science of the earth's surface, its divisions into continents and countries, etc. —**ge′o·graph′i·cal, ge′o·graph′ic** *a.*

ge·ol·o·gy *n.* science of the earth's crust and of rocks and fossils **ge′o·log′i·cal** (-läj′-) *a.* —**ge·ol′o·gist** *n.*

ge′o·mag·net′ic *a.* of the magnetic properties of the earth

ge·om′e·try *n.* branch of mathematics dealing with plane and solid figures —**ge′o·met′ric, ge′o·met′ri·cal** *a.*

ge′o·phys′ics *n.* science of the effects of weather, tides, etc. on the earth —**ge′o·phys′i·cal** *a.*

geor·gette (jôr jet′) *n.* thin, crinkled fabric, for dresses, etc.

ge·ra′ni·um (jə rā′-) *n.* plant with showy flowers

ger·bil (jur′b'l) *n.* small rodent with long hind legs

ger′i·at′rics (jer′-) *n.* branch of medicine dealing with diseases of old age

germ *n.* 1. microscopic, disease-causing organism 2. seed, bud, etc. 3. origin

Ger′man *n., a.* (native or language) of Germany

ger·mane′ (jar-) *a.* relevant

ger·ma′ni·um *n.* rare element used in transistors

ger′mi·cide *n.* anything used to destroy germs

ger′mi·nal *a.* in earliest stage of growth

ger′mi·nate *v.* sprout, as from a seed —**ger′mi·na′tion** *n.*

ger′on·tol′o·gy (jer′-) *n.* study of aging —**ger′on·tol′o·gist** *n.*

ger′ry·man′der *v.* divide (voting area) unfairly to benefit one party

ger′und (jer′-) *n.* verbal noun ending in *-ing*

ges·ta′tion (jes-) *n.* pregnancy

ges·tic′u·late (jes-) *v.* to gesture

ges′ture (-char) *n.* movement of part of the body, to express ideas, feelings, etc. —*v.* make gestures

get *v.* [GOT, GOT or GOTTEN, GETTING] 1. come to have; obtain 2. come, go, or arrive 3. make or become 4. bring 5. [Col.] *a)* be obliged *b)* possess *c)* baffle *d)* understand —**get along** manage: also **get by** —**get around** circumvent —**get away** escape —**get over** recover from —**get through** 1. finish 2. manage to survive —**get together** 1. assemble 2. [Col.] reach an agreement —**get up** rise (from sleep, etc.)

get′a·way *n.* 1. a starting, as in a race 2. an escape

get′-to·geth′er *n.* informal gathering

gew·gaw (gyōō′gô) *n.* trinket

gey·ser (gī′zər) *n.* gushing hot spring

ghast·ly (gast′lē) *a.* [-LIER,

-LIEST] 1. horrible 2. pale as a ghost

gher'kin (gur'-) *n.* small pickle

ghet·to (get'ō) *n.* [*pl.* -TOS, -TOES] section of a city lived in by members of a minority group

ghost *n.* supposed disembodied spirit of a dead person — **ghost'ly** *a.*

ghost'writ'er *n.* writer of speeches, etc. for another, who pretends to be the author — **ghost'write** *v.*

ghoul (gōōl) *n.* supposed evil spirit that feeds on the dead — **ghoul'ish** *a.*

GI (jē'ī') *a.* government issue, as military clothing —*n.* [Col.] enlisted soldier

gi'ant *n.* person or thing of great size, strength, etc. —*a.* like a giant

gib'ber (jib'-) *v.* speak incoherently

gib'ber·ish *n.* confused talk

gib'bet (jib'-) *n.* a gallows

gib'bon (gib'-) *n.* small, slender, long-armed ape

gibe (jīb) *v., n.* taunt

gib'let (jib'-) *n.* edible internal part of a fowl

gid'dy (gid'-) *a.* [-DIER, -DIEST] 1. dizzy 2. frivolous —**gid'di·ness** *n.*

gift *n.* 1. a present 2. a giving 3. natural ability

gift'ed *a.* talented

gig (gig) *n.* [Sl.] job for jazz musician

gi·gan'tic (jī-) *a.* huge

gig'gle *v.* laugh in a nervous, silly way —*n.* such a laugh

gig'o·lo (jig'-) *n.* [*pl.* -LOS] man paid to escort woman

Gi·la monster (hē'lə) stout, poisonous lizard

gild *v.* [alt. pt. & pp. GILT] 1. overlay with gold 2. make better than it is

gill (gil) *n.* breathing organ of a fish

gill (jil) *n.* 1/4 pint

gilt *n.* surface layer of gold

gilt'edged' *a.* of highest value, as securities

gim'bals (gim'-) *n.pl.* pair of free-swinging balls that keep ship's compass level

gim'crack (jim'-) *n.* object that is showy but useless

gim'let (gim'-) *n.* small tool for making holes

gim'mick *n.* 1. [Col.] tricky or deceptive device 2. [Sl.] attention-getting ruse

gimp (gimp) *n.* [Col.] a limp — **gimp'y** *a.*

gin (jin) *n.* 1. an alcoholic liquor 2. machine for separating cotton from the seeds

gin'ger (jin'-) *n.* spice from the root of a tropical herb

ginger ale nonalcoholic drink flavored with ginger

gin'ger·bread *n.* cake flavored with ginger

gin'ger·ly *a.* careful or timid —*adv.* carefully or timidly

gin'ger·snap *n.* crisp ginger cookie

ging'ham (giŋ'əm) *n.* cotton cloth in stripes or checks

gin'gi·vi'tis (jin'jə vī'-) *n.* inflammation of gums

gink·go (giŋ'kō) *n.* [*pl.* -GOES] tree with fan-shaped leaves

Gip'sy n. [pl. -SIES] Gypsy

gi·raffe' n. large African animal with a very long neck

gird (gurd) v. [alt. pt. & pp. GIRT] 1. encircle 2. prepare for action

gird'er n. large beam for supporting a floor, etc.

gir'dle n. 1. a belt 2. light, flexible corset

girl n. female child or young woman —**girl'ish** a.

girl scout member of the **Girl Scouts**, girls' club stressing healthful activities

girth n. 1. horse's belly band 2. circumference

gist (jist) n. main point

give v. [GAVE, GIVEN, GIVING] 1. hand over; deliver 2. cause to have 3. produce 4. utter 5. act as host of 6. to sacrifice 7. perform 8. bend, etc. from pressure —n. a bending, etc. under pressure —**give away** [Col.] expose —**give forth** (or **off**) emit —**give in** yield —**give out** 1. make public 2. distribute 3. become worn out —**give up** 1. relinquish 2. stop

give'a·way n. [Col.] thing given away or sold cheap

giv'en a. 1. bestowed 2. accustomed 3. stated

glz'mo, gis'mo (giz'-) n. [pl. -MOS] [Sl.] gadget or gimmick

giz'zard n. muscular second stomach of a bird

gla·cé (gla sā') a. candied, as fruit

gla'cier (-shər) n. large mass of ice moving slowly down a slope —**gla'cial** a.

glad a. [GLADDER, GLADDEST]

1. happy 2. causing joy 3. pleased —**glad'ly** adv.

glad'den v. make glad

glade n. clearing in a forest

glad'i·a'tor n. in ancient Rome, a fighter in public shows 2. any fighter

glad'i·o'lus n. plant with tall spikes of funnel-shaped flowers: also **glad'i·o'la**

glam'or·ize (-īz) v. to make glamorous

glam'our, glam'or n. bewitching charm —**glam'or·ous, glam'our·ous** a.

glance v. 1. strike and go off at an angle 2. look briefly —n. a glimpse

gland n. body organ that secretes a substance —**glan'du·lar** (-jə-) a.

glare v. 1. shine with a dazzling light 2. stare fiercely —n. 1. dazzling light 2. fierce stare 3. glassy surface, as of ice

glar'ing a. flagrant

glass n. 1. hard, brittle substance, usually transparent 2. drinking vessel, mirror, etc. made of this 3. pl. eyeglasses or binoculars

glass'ware n. glass articles

glass'y a. [-IER, -IEST] 1. like glass 2. expressionless

glau·co'ma (glô-) n. eye disease

glaze v. 1. furnish with glass 2. give a glossy finish to 3. cover with a sugar coating —n. glassy coating

gla'zier (-zhər) n. one who fits glass in windows

gleam n. 1. faint glow of light

2. brief show, as of hope —v. send out a gleam

glean v. collect, as grain left by reapers —**glean′er** n.

glee n. joy —**glee′ful** a.

glee club singing group

glen n. secluded valley

glib a. [GLIBBER, GLIBBEST] fluent, esp. in a shallow way

glide v. move or descend smoothly and easily —n. smooth, easy flow or descent

glid′er n. engineless airplane carried by air currents 2. porch swing

glim′mer v. give a faint, flickering light —n. such a light

glimpse n. brief, quick view —v. catch a glimpse of

glint v., n. gleam

glis·ten (glis′'n) v. shine with reflected light, as wet surface —n. a glistening

glit′ter v. be showy; sparkle —n. 1. sparkling light 2. bits of glittering material

gloam′ing n. twilight

gloat v. feel or show malicious pleasure

glob (gläb) n. rounded lump

glob′al·ism (glō′-) n. worldwide outlook

globe n. 1. ball-shaped thing 2. the earth, or a model of it —**glob′al** a.

globe′-trot′ter n. world traveler

glob′u·lar (gläb′yə-) a. 1. spherical 2. of globules

glob′ule n. small drop

glock·en·spiel (gläk′ən spēl) n. instrument with tuned metal bars played with hammers

gloom n. 1. darkness 2. dark place 3. sadness —**gloom′y** [-IER, -IEST] a.

glo′ri·fy v. [-FIED, -FYING] 1. give glory to; honor 2. make seem greater —**glo′ri·fi·ca′tion** n.

glo′ri·ous a. 1. full of glory 2. splendid

glo′ry n. [pl. -RIES] 1. great praise or fame 2. splendor 3. heavenly bliss —v. [-RIED, -RYING] exult (in)

gloss n. 1. surface polish or brightness 2. explanation; footnote —v. smooth (over), as an error —**gloss′y** [-IER, -IEST] a.

glos′sa·ry n. [pl. -RIES] list of difficult terms with definitions, as for a book

glos′so·la′li·a (gläs′-) n. speaking of unintelligible sounds in religious ecstasy

glot′tis n. opening between the vocal cords —**glot′tal** a.

glove n. 1. covering for the hand with sheaths for the fingers 2. baseball mitt 3. padded mitt for boxing —**gloved** a.

glow v. 1. give off bright or steady light 2. be elated 3. be bright with color —n. 1. bright or steady light 2. brightness, warmth, etc.

glow′er (glou′-) v. stare with sullen anger —n. sullen stare; scowl

glow′worm n. luminescent insect or larva

glu′cose n. the sugar in fruits and honey

glue n. thick, adhesive liquid —v. stick together as with glue —**glue′y** a.

glum *a.* [GLUMMER, GLUMMEST] gloomy

glut *v.* [GLUTTED, GLUTTING] feed, fill, or supply to excess — *n.* excess

glu·ten (glōōt'ʼn) *n.* sticky protein substance in wheat flour

glu'ti·nous *a.* sticky

glut'ton *n.* one who eats too much —**glut'ton·ous** *a.*

glut'ton·y *n.* overeating

glyc'er·in, glyc·er·ine (glis'-) *n.* commercial name for glycerol

glyc'er·ol (-ôl) *n.* colorless, syrupy liquid used in lotions, etc.

gly·co·gen (glī'kə jən) *n.* body tissue substance that changes to sugar

gnarl (närl) *n.* knot on a tree — *v.* to twist —**gnarled** *a.*

gnash (nash) *v.* grind (the teeth) together

gnat (nat) *n.* small insect

gnaw (nô) *v.* 1. wear away by biting 2. torment —**gnaw'ing** *a.*

gneiss (nīs) *n.* rock like granite formed in layers

gnome (nōm) *n.* dwarf

gnu (nōō) *n.* African antelope

go *v.* [WENT, GONE, GOING] 1. move along; pass or proceed 2. depart 3. work, as a clock 4. be or become 5. fit or suit 6. belong in a place —*n.* [*pl.* GOES] 1. a success 2. [Col.] energy 3. [Col.] a try —**go back on** [Col.] break, as a promise —**go off** explode —**go out** 1. be extinguished 2. go to social affairs, etc. —**go over** 1. examine 2. do again —**go**

through 1. endure 2. search —**go under** fail —**let go** release one's hold

goad (gōd) *n.* 1. pointed stick 2. spur —*v.* urge on

goal *n.* 1. place where a race, trip, etc. ends 2. end striven for 3. place to put the ball or puck to score

goal'keep'er *n.* player guarding goal: also **goal'ie, goal'tend'er**

goat *n.* cud-chewing horned animal

goat·ee' *n.* pointed beard on a man's chin

goat'herd *n.* herder of goats

goat'skin *n.* (leather made from) skin of goat

gob *n.* 1. [Col.] lump or mass 2. [Sl.] U.S. sailor

gob'ble *n.* cry of a male turkey —*v.* 1. make this cry 2. eat greedily —**gob'bler** *n.*

gob'ble·dy·gook' *n.* [Sl.] pompous wordage with little meaning

go'-be·tween' *n.* one acting between two persons

gob'let *n.* stemmed glass

gob'lin *n.* evil spirit

God *n.* 1. monotheistic creator and ruler of the universe 2. [g-] any divine being —**god'dess** *n.fem.* —**god'like** *a.*

god'child *n.* person (**god'daugh'ter** or **god'son**) that a godparent sponsors

god'hood *n.* state of being a god

god'less *a.* 1. irreligious 2. wicked

god'ly *a.* [-LIER, -LIEST] devoted to God; devout

god'par'ent n. spiritual sponsor (**god'fa'ther** or **god'-moth'er**) of an infant, esp. at baptism

god'send n. something unexpected but much needed

gog'gle v. stare with bulging eyes —n. pl. large spectacles to protect the eyes against dust, etc.

go'ing n. 1. departure 2. degree of ease in traveling —a. working

goi'ter, goi'tre n. enlargement of the thyroid gland

gold n. 1. yellow, precious metal, a chemical element 2. money; wealth 3. bright yellow —**gold'en** a.

golden ager [Col.] retired person 65 or older

gold'en·rod n. plant with long, yellow flower clusters

gold'-filled' a. of cheap metal overlaid with gold

gold'finch n. small, yellow American songbird

gold'fish n. small yellowish fish, kept in ponds, etc.

gold'smith n. skilled maker of gold articles

golf n. outdoor game in which a small ball is driven, with special clubs, into holes

go'nad n. ovary or testicle

gon'do·la n. boat used on canals of Venice —**gon·do·lier'** (-lir') n.

gone pp. of **go**

gon'er n. [Col.] person sure to die, be ruined, etc.

gong n. metal disk that resounds loudly when struck

gon·or·rhe·a (gän'ə rē'ə) n. venereal disease

goo'ber n. peanut

good a. [BETTER, BEST] 1. having proper qualities 2. beneficial 3. of moral excellence 4. skilled 5. enjoyable, happy, etc. 6. considerable —n. 1. worth or virtue 2. benefit —**make good** 1. repay 2. succeed

good'bye', good'-bye' int., n. farewell: also **goodby, good-by**

Good Friday Friday before Easter

good'-heart'ed a. kind

good'-look'ing a. handsome

good'ly a. [-LIER, -LIEST] rather large

good'-na'tured a. pleasant

good'ness n. being good; kindness, virtue, etc.

goods n.pl. 1. personal property 2. wares 3. fabric

good'y n. [pl. -IES] [Col.] thing good to eat

goof (g⊖of) n. [Sl.] 1. stupid person 2. blunder —v. [Sl.] 1. to blunder 2. waste time (with off) —**goof'y** [-IER, -IEST] a.

gook (gook) n. [Sl.] sticky or slimy substance

goon (g⊖on) n. [Sl.] 1. hired thug 2. stupid person

goose n. [pl. GEESE] 1. long-necked water bird like a large duck 2. silly person —**cook one's goose** [Col.] spoil one's chances

goose'ber'ry n. [pl. -RIES] sour berry used for jam, etc.

goose flesh (or **pimples**)

rough skin caused by fear, cold, etc.

go'pher (-fər) *n.* burrowing rodent

gore *n.* 1. clotted blood 2. tapered cloth inserted to add width —*v.* 1. pierce as with a tusk 2. insert gores in —**gor'y** [-IER, -IEST] *a.*

gorge *n.* 1. deep, narrow pass 2. resentment, disgust, etc. — *v.* eat or stuff greedily

gor'geous *a.* magnificent

go·ril'la *n.* largest of the apes, native to Africa

gor'mand·ize *v.* eat like a glutton

gosh *int.* call of surprise

gos'ling *n.* young goose

gos'pel *n.* 1. [*often* G-] teachings of Jesus and the Apostles 2. belief proclaimed as true

gos'sa·mer *n.* filmy cobweb or cloth —*a.* filmy

gos'sip *n.* 1. one who chatters about others 2. such idle talk —*v.* indulge in gossip —**gos'sip·y** *a.*

got *pt. & pp.* of **get**

got'ten alt. *pp.* of **get**

Gou·da cheese (gou'də) mild cheese

gouge (gouj) *n.* 1. chisel for cutting grooves 2. such a groove —*v.* 1. scoop out as with a gouge 2. [Col.] overcharge —**goug'er** *n.*

gou·lash (gōō'läsh) *n.* stew seasoned with paprika

gou·ra·mi (goor'ə mē, goo rä'mē) *n.* brightly colored fish, often kept in aquariums

gourd (gôrd, goord) *n.* 1. bulb-shaped fruit of a trailing plant 2. its dried shell hollowed out for use

gour·mand (goor'mənd) *n.* one who likes to eat

gour·met (goor'mā) *n.* judge of fine foods and drinks

gout *n.* disease with painful swelling of the joints

gov'ern *v.* 1. control 2. influence; determine —**gov'ern·a·ble** *a.*

gov'ern·ess *n.* woman hired to teach children at home

gov'ern·ment *n.* 1. control; rule 2. system of ruling 3. those who rule —**gov'ern·men'tal** *a.*

gov'er·nor *n.* 1. one who governs; esp., head of a State 2. device to control engine speed automatically

gown *n.* 1. woman's dress 2. long robe, as for a judge

grab *v.* [GRABBED, GRABBING] snatch suddenly —*n.* a grabbing

grab'by *a.* [-BIER, -BIEST] avaricious

grace *n.* 1. beauty of form, movement, etc. 2. favor; good will 3. delay granted for payment due 4. prayer of thanks at a meal 5. God's love for man —*v.* [GRACED, GRACING] dignify or adorn —**in the good graces of** in favor with —**grace'ful** *a.* —**grace'ful·ly** *adv.*

grace'less *a.* 1. ignorant of propriety 2. clumsy

gra'cious *a.* charming, kind, polite, pleasing, etc.

grack'le *n.* small blackbird

gra·da'tion n. 1. arrangement in steps 2. stage in a series

grade n. 1. degree in a scale of rank or quality 2. slope 3. any of the school years through the 12th 4. a mark or rating as on a test —v. 1. classify; sort 2. give a grade (n. 4) to 3. make (ground) sloped or level

grade crossing place where a road crosses a railroad

grade school school of the first 6 (or 8) grades

gra'di·ent n. slope, or degree of slope

grad'u·al a. little by little —**grad'u·al·ly** adv.

grad'u·al·ism n. principle of gradual social change

grad'u·ate (-it) n. one who has completed a course of study at a school or college —v. (-āt) 1. give a diploma to (a graduate) 2. become a graduate 3. mark with degrees for measuring —**grad'u·a'tion** n.

graf·fi'to (-fē'-) n. [pl. -TI (-tē)] crude drawing or writing on wall in public place

graft n. 1. shoot, etc. of one plant inserted in another to grow 2. transplanting of skin, etc. 3. dishonest gain of money by public officials —v. insert (a graft)

gra'ham a. made of whole-wheat flour

Grail n. in legend, cup used by Jesus

grain n. 1. seed of wheat, corn, etc. 2. cereal plants 3. particle, as of salt or sand 4. smallest unit of weight 5. natural markings on wood, leather, etc.

grain'y a. [-IER, -IEST] 1. of wood that shows grain 2. granular —**grain'i·ness** n.

gram n. metric unit of weight (1/28 of an ounce)

-gram suf. 1. a writing or drawing 2. given number of grams

gram'mar n. system of speaking and writing a language —**gram·mar'i·an** n. —**grammat'i·cal** a.

gran'a·ry n. [pl. -RIES] building for storing grain

grand a. great in size, beauty, importance, etc.; splendid, imposing, etc. —n. [Sl.] a thousand dollars

grand'child n. [pl. -CHILDREN] child (**granddaughter** or **grandson**) of one's son or daughter

gran'deur (-jər) n. 1. great size, beauty, etc.; splendor 2. nobility

grandfather clock clock in tall, upright case

gran·dil'o·quent a. bombastic

gran'di·ose (-ōs) a. 1. very grand 2. too grand

grand jury jury with power to indict persons for trial

grand'par'ent n. parent (**grandfather** or **grandmother**) of one's father or mother

grand piano large piano with a horizontal case

grand slam 1. Baseball home run hit with a runner on each base 2. Bridge winning of all tricks in a deal

grand'stand n. structure for spectators of outdoor sports

grange n. 1. farm 2. [G-] association of farmers

gran·ite (-it) n. very hard crystalline rock

gran'ny n. [pl. -NIES] [Col.] 1. grandmother 2. fussy person

gran·o'la n. breakfast cereal of oats, honey, nuts, etc.

grant v. 1. consent to or give 2. concede 3. transfer legally —n. something granted —**take for granted** consider as a fact

grant'-in-aid' n. [pl. GRANTS-] grant of funds by a foundation, etc. to an artist, scientist, etc.

gran'u·lar a. of or like grains or granules

gran'u·late v. form into granules —**gran'u·la'tion** n.

gran'ule n. small grain

grape n. small, round fruit growing in clusters

grape'fruit n. large citrus fruit with a yellow rind

grape hyacinth small plant with blue, bell-shaped flowers

grape'vine n. 1. woody vine with grapes 2. rumor

graph n. diagram showing changes in value

-graph suf. 1. that writes 2. thing written

graph'ic a. 1. vivid; in lifelike detail 2. of the arts of drawing, printing, etc. —**graph'i·cal·ly** adv.

graph'ics n. 1. graphic arts 2. design in graphic arts

graph'ite n. soft, black carbon in pencils, etc.

graph·ol'o·gy (gra făl'-) n. study of handwriting —**graph·ol'o·gist** n.

grap'nel n. device with hooks or claws for grasping

grap'ple n. 1. grapnel 2. grip in wrestling —v. 1. grip and hold 2. struggle

grasp v. 1. grip; seize 2. comprehend —n. 1. a grip 2. control 3. power to grasp

grasp'ing a. greedy

grass n. 1. green plant grown for lawns 2. cereal plant 3. pasture 4. [Sl.] marijuana —**grass'y** [-IER, -IEST] a.

grass'hop'per n. leaping insect with long hind legs

grass roots [Col.] 1. common people 2. basic support

grate v. 1. form into particles by scraping 2. rub with a harsh sound 3. irritate —n. 1. frame of bars to hold fuel 2. framework of bars over an opening

grate'ful a. thankful

grat'i·fy v. [-FIED, -FYING] 1. please 2. indulge —**grat'i·fi·ca'tion** n.

grat'ing n. grate

gra'tis (grat'is) adv., a. free

grat'i·tude n. thankful appreciation

gra·tu'i·tous a. 1. free of charge 2. uncalled-for

gra·tu'i·ty n. [pl. -TIES] gift of money for a service

grave a. 1. serious 2. solemn —n. burial place, esp. a hole in the ground

grav'el (grav'-) n. bits of rock —v. cover with gravel

grav'el·ly a. 1. covered with gravel 2. hoarse or rasping

grav'en (grāv'-) a. carved

grave'stone n. tombstone

grave′yard n. cemetery

grav′id (grav′-) a. pregnant

grav′i·tate v. be attracted

grav′i·ta′tion n. *Physics* force of mutual attraction between masses —**grav·i·ta′tion·al** a.

grav′i·ty n. 1. seriousness 2. weight 3. *Physics* gravitation; esp., the pull on bodies toward earth's center

gra′vy n. [pl. **-VIES**] 1. juice from cooking meat 2. sauce made from this juice

gray n. mixture of black and white —a. 1. of this color 2. dreary —**gray′ish** a.

gray′beard n. old man

gray matter 1. grayish nerve tissue of the brain 2. [Col.] intelligence

graze v. 1. feed on growing grass, etc. 2. rub lightly in passing —n. a grazing

grease n. 1. melted animal fat 2. thick, oily lubricant —v. put grease on —**greas′y** [**-IER**, **-IEST**]

grease′paint n. greasy stage makeup

great a. 1. much larger, more, or better than average 2. being one generation removed —n. *usually pl.* distinguished person —**great′ly** adv.

Great Dane large dog with short hair

Gre′cian (-shən) a. Greek

greed n. excessive desire, esp. for wealth

greed′y a. [**-IER**, **-IEST**] 1. wanting too much 2. gluttonous —**greed′i·ly** adv.

Greek n., a. (native or language) of Greece

green n. 1. color of grass 2. pl. leafy vegetables 3. smooth turf —a. 1. of the color green 2. unripe 3. inexperienced —**green′ness** n.

green′belt n. area around a city, reserved for parks or farms

green′er·y n. green foliage

green′-eyed′ a. very jealous

green′horn n. beginner

green′house n. heated glass building for growing plants

green thumb knack for growing plants

greet v. 1. to welcome 2. address, meet, or receive in a certain way

greet′ing n. act or words of one who greets

gre·gar′i·ous a. sociable

gre·nade′ n. small bomb usually thrown by hand

gren·a·dier′ (-dir′) n. British soldier of a special regiment

gren′a·dine (-dēn) n. syrup made from pomegranates

grew pt. of **grow**

grey n., a. gray: Br. sp.

grid n. 1. grate (n. 2) 2. device in an electron tube, for controlling the flow of electrons

grid′dle n. flat pan for cooking pancakes, etc.

grid′i·ron n. 1. framework of bars on which to broil 2. football field

grief n. deep sorrow —**come to grief** fail

griev′ance (grēv′-) n. complaint or a basis for it

grieve v. be or make sad

griev′ous a. 1. causing grief 2.

severe 3. deplorable **—griev'-ous·ly** adv.

grif'fin n. mythical beast, part eagle and part lion

grill n. 1. gridiron 2. restaurant serving grilled foods **—v.** 1. broil 2. question relentlessly

grille (gril) n. open grating forming a screen

grim a. [GRIMMER, GRIMMEST] 1. stern; harsh 2. repellent; ghastly **grim'ly** adv.

gri·mace (gri mās') n. twisting of the facial features **—v.** make grimaces

grime n. sooty dirt **—grim'y** [-IER, -IEST] a.

grin v. [GRINNED, GRINNING] smile broadly **—n.** broad smile

grind v. [GROUND, GRINDING] 1. crush into bits 2. sharpen, smooth, etc. by friction 3. rub harshly 4. work by cranking **—n.** 1. hard work 2. student who studies hard

grind'stone n. revolving stone for sharpening, etc. **—keep one's nose to the grindstone** work steadily

grip n. 1. firm hold 2. hand-clasp 3. a handle 4. valise **—v.** [GRIPPED, GRIPPING] hold firmly

gripe v. 1. cause pain in the bowels of n. 2. [Sl.] annoy 3. [Sl.] complain **—n.** [Sl.] complaint

gris'ly (griz'-) a. [-LIER, -LIEST] ghastly

grist n. grain to be ground

gris'tle (-'l) n. cartilage

grit n. 1. rough bits of sand, etc. 2. stubborn courage **—v.** [GRITTED, GRITTING] grind (the teeth) **—grit'ty** [-TIER, -TIEST] a.

grits n.pl. coarsely ground grain

griz'zled, griz'zly a. gray

grizzly bear large, ferocious N. American bear

groan v., n. (utter) a deep sound of pain, etc.

gro'cer n. storekeeper who sells food, etc.

gro'cer·y n. [pl. -IES] 1. store of a grocer 2. pl. goods sold by a grocer

grog n. rum and water

grog'gy a. [-GIER, -GIEST] dazed

groin n. fold where the abdomen joins either thigh

groom n. 1. man who tends horses 2. bridegroom **—v.** 1. make neat 2. train

groove n. 1. narrow furrow 2. channel 3. routine **—v.** make a groove in

groov'y a. [-IER, -IEST] [Sl.] very pleasing

grope v. feel or search about blindly

gross a. 1. flagrant 2. coarse 3. total **—n.** 1. overall total 2. [pl. GROSS] twelve dozen **—v.** [Col.] earn before deductions

gross national product value of a nation's output of goods and services

gro·tesque' (-tesk') a. 1. distorted 2. absurd

grot'to n. [pl. -TOES, -TOS] 1. cave 2. cavelike shrine, place, etc.

grouch n. [Col.] 1. one who grumbles 2. sulky mood **—grouch'y** [-IER, -IEST] a.

ground pt. & pp. of grind —n. 1. land; earth 2. pl. tract of land 3. often pl. cause or basis 4. background 5. pl. dregs —a. of or on the ground —v. 1. set or keep on the ground 2. base 3. instruct (in)

ground crew group of workers who maintain aircraft

ground'er n. baseball batted on the ground

ground'hog n. woodchuck

ground'less a. without reason

ground rule 1. Baseball rule for a specific ballpark 2. any basic rule

ground'swell n. violent rolling of the ocean

ground'work n. foundation

group n. persons or things gathered or classed together —v. form into a group

group'ie n. [Col.] fan of rock groups

grouse n. game bird —v. [Col.] complain

grout n. thin mortar

grove n. small group of trees

grov'el (gruv'-) v. 1. crawl abjectly 2. behave humbly

grow v. [GREW, GROWN, GROWING] 1. develop 2. increase in size, quantity, etc. 3. become 4. raise (crops) —**grow up** to mature

growl n. rumbling sound, as of an angry dog —v. make this sound

grown'-up' a., n. adult

growth n. 1. a growing 2. something that grows 3. abnormal mass of tissue

grub v. [GRUBBED, GRUBBING] 1. dig or dig up 2. work hard —n. 1. wormlike larva, esp. of a beetle 2. [Sl.] food

grub'by a. [-BIER, -BIEST] dirty; untidy

grub'stake n. [Col.] money advanced for an enterprise

grudge v. begrudge —n. resentment; ill will

gru'el n. thin cereal broth

gru'el·ing, gru'el·ling a. very tiring; exhausting

grue'some a. causing horror or loathing

gruff a. 1. rough or surly 2. hoarse —**gruff'ly** adv.

grum'ble v. mutter in discontent —**grum'bler** n.

grump'y a. [-IER, -IEST] peevish; surly

grun'gy (-jē) a. [-GIER, -GIEST] [Sl.] dirty, messy, etc.

grunt v., n. (utter with) the deep sound of a hog

gua'no (gwä'nō) n. manure of bats or sea birds

guar·an·tee' (gar-) n. 1. pledge to replace something sold if faulty 2. assurance 3. pledge or security for another's debt or obligation —v. 1. give a guarantee for 2. to promise Also **guar'an·ty** [pl. -TIES] —**guar'an·tor** n.

guard v. 1. protect; defend 2. keep from escape 3. take precautions (against) —n. 1. person or thing that guards 2. careful watch

guard'ed a. 1. kept safe 2. cautious

guard'house n. Mil. jail

guard'i·an n. 1. one legally in charge of a minor, etc. 2. cus-

todian —*a.* protecting —
guard′i·an·ship′ *n.*

guard′rail *n.* protective railing

gua′va (gwä′-) *n.* yellow tropical fruit

gu′ber·na·to′ri·al *a.* of a governor or his or her office

guer·ril′la, gue·ril′la (gə ril′-) *n.* fighter who makes raids behind enemy lines

guess *v.* 1. estimate; judge 2. suppose —*n.* a surmise

guess′work *n.* 1. a guessing 2. view based on this

guest *n.* 1. one entertained at another's home, etc. 2. paying customer, as at a hotel —*a.* 1. for guests 2. performing by invitation

guf·faw′ *n., v.* laugh in a loud, coarse burst

guid′ance (gīd′-) *n.* 1. leadership 2. advice

guide *v.* 1. show the way to 2. control —*n.* person or thing that guides

guide′book *n.* book for tourists

guided missile war missile guided by radio or radar

guide′line *n.* principle for directing policies, etc.

guild (gild) *n.* association to promote mutual interests

guile (gīl) *n.* deceit

guil·lo·tine (gil′ə tēn) *n.* instrument for beheading

guilt *n.* 1. fact of having committed an offense 2. painful feeling that one has done a wrong

guilt′y *a.* [-IER, -IEST] having or showing guilt —**guilt′i·ly** *adv.*

guin·ea (gin′ē) *n.* former English coin equal to 21 shillings

guinea fowl (or **hen**) speckled domestic fowl

guinea pig small rodent used in experiments

guise (gīz) *n.* assumed or false appearance

gui·tar′ (gi-) *n.* musical instrument with strings that are plucked or strummed

gulch *n.* deep narrow valley

gulf *n.* 1. ocean area partly enclosed by land 2. wide chasm 3. vast separation

gull *n.* 1. gray and white sea bird 2. a dupe —*v.* to cheat

gul′let *n.* esophagus

gul′li·ble *a.* easily tricked —**gul′li·bil′i·ty** *n.*

gul′ly *n.* [*pl.* -LIES] narrow ravine

gulp *v.* swallow greedily or hastily —*n.* a gulping

gum *n.* 1. sticky substance from some plants 2. an adhesive 3. chewing gum 4. flesh around base of the teeth —*v.* [GUMMED, GUMMING] make sticky —**gum′my** [-MIER, -MIEST] *a.*

gum′bo *n.* soup made with okra pods

gum′drop *n.* chewy candy

gump′tion *n.* [Col.] initiative

gun *n.* weapon for shooting projectiles —*v.* [GUNNED, GUNNING] shoot or hunt with a gun

gun′fire *n.* firing of guns

gung′-ho′ *a.* enthusiastic

gunk *n.* [Sl.] thick, messy substance

gun′man n. [pl. **-MEN**] armed gangster

gun′ner·y n. the making or firing of large guns —**gun′ner** n.

gun′ny·sack n. sack made of coarse fabric

gun′play n. exchange of gunshots

gun′pow′der n. explosive powder used in guns, etc.

gun′ship n. armed helicopter

gun′shot n. shot fired from a gun

gun′smith n. one who makes or repairs small guns

gun·wale (gun′′l) n. upper edge of a boat's side

gup′py n. [pl. **-PIES**] tiny tropical fish

gur′gle n. bubbling sound —v. make this sound

gu·ru (goor′ōō) n. Hindu spiritual adviser or teacher

gush v. 1. flow copiously 2. talk too emotionally —n. a gushing —**gush′y** [**-IER, -IEST**] a.

gush′er n. spouting oil well

gus′set n. triangular piece inserted in a garment

gust n. 1. sudden rush of air 2. sudden outburst —**gust′y** [**-IER, -IEST**] a.

gus′ta·to′ry a. of the sense of taste

gus′to n. zest; relish

gut n. 1. intestine 2. cord made of intestines 3. pl. [Sl.]

courage —v. [**GUTTED, GUTTING**] 1. eviscerate 2. destroy the interior of —a. [Sl.] 1. basic 2. easy

gut′less a. [Sl.] lacking courage

guts′y a. [**-IER, -IEST**] courageous, forceful, etc.

gut′ta-per′cha n. rubberlike substance from some trees

gut′ter n. channel to carry off rain water, etc.

gut′tur·al a. sounded in the throat; rasping

guy (gī) n. 1. guiding or steadying wire or rope 2. [Sl.] man or boy

guz′zle v. drink greedily

gym n. [Col.] gymnasium

gym·na′si·um (jim-) n. place for physical training and sports

gym·nas′tics n.pl. exercises for the muscles —**gym′nast** n. —**gym·nas′tic** a.

gyn·e·col′o·gy (gīn′ə-) n. medical science of women's diseases —**gyn′e·col′o·gist** n.

gyp (jip) n., v. [**GYPPED, GYPPING**] [Col.] swindle

gyp′sum n. calcium sulfate, a white chalky mineral

Gyp′sy n. [pl. **-SIES**] [also **g-**] one of a wandering people

gy′rate (jī′-) v. to whirl —**gy·ra′tion** n.

gy′ro·scope n. wheel mounted in a ring and spinning rapidly, used as a stabilizer

H

ha *int.* exclamation of surprise, triumph, etc.

ha'be·as cor'pus [L.] writ requiring a court to decide the legality of a prisoner's detention

hab'er·dash'er *n.* dealer in men's hats, shirts, etc. —**hab'·er·dash'er·y** [*pl.* -IES] *n.*

ha·bil'i·ments *n.pl.* attire

hab'it *n.* 1. distinctive costume 2. custom 3. fixed practice

hab'it·a·ble *a.* fit to live in

hab'i·tat *n.* natural living place

hab'i·ta'tion *n.* dwelling

hab'it-form'ing *a.* leading to the formation of a habit or addiction

ha·bit'u·al (-bich'ŏŏ-) *a.* 1. done by habit 2. steady 3. usual —**ha·bit'u·al·ly** *adv.*

ha·bit'u·ate *v.* accustom

hab'i·tu·é (-ā) *n.* constant frequenter of a place

hack *v.* 1. chop roughly 2. cough harshly —*n.* 1. gash 2. harsh cough 3. old worn-out horse 4. literary drudge 5. [Col.] taxicab

hack'les *n.pl.* hairs on a dog's back that bristle

hack'neyed *a.* trite; stale

hack'saw *n.* saw for cutting metal: also **hack saw**

had *pt.* & *pp.* of **have**

had'dock *n.* small ocean fish used as food

Ha·des (hā'dēz) *n. often* h-] [Col.] hell

had'n't had not

haft *n.* handle, as of an ax

hag *n.* ugly old woman

hag'gard *a.* having a wasted, worn look; gaunt

hag'gle *v.* argue about terms, price, etc.

hah (hä) *int.* ha

hai·ku (hī'kōō) *n.* three-line Japanese poem

hail *n.* 1. greeting 2. frozen raindrops *—n.* shower of or like hail *—int.* shout of greeting, etc. *—v.* 1. cheer 2. shout to 3. pour down (like) hail —**hail from** be from

hail'stone *n.* piece of hail

hair *n.* 1. threadlike outgrowth from the skin 2. growth of these, as on the head 3. very small space, degree, etc. —**split hairs** quibble

hair'breadth *n.* very short distance —*a.* very narrow

hair'cut *n.* act or style of cutting the hair

hair'do (-dōō) *n.* [*pl.* -DOS] hair style

hair'dress'er *n.* one who arranges (women's) hair

hair'line *n.* 1. thin line 2. outline of hair above the forehead

hair'piece *n.* wig

hair'pin *n.* wire for keeping hair in place —*a.* U-shaped

hair'-rais'ing *a.* [Col.] horrifying

hair'y *a.* [-IER, -IEST] 1. covered with hair 2. [Sl.] difficult, upsetting, etc.

hal'cy·on (-sē-) *a.* tranquil

hale *a.* healthy; robust —*v.* drag; haul

half *n.* [*pl.* HALVES] either of the two equal parts of a thing —*a.* 1. being a half 2. partial —*adv.* 1. to the extent of a half 2. [Col.] partly —**one's better half** [Sl.] one's spouse

half'-breed' *n.* one with parents of different races: also **half'-caste'**

half brother (or **sister**) brother (or sister) by one parent only

half'-heart'ed *a.* with little enthusiasm or interest

half'track *n.* army vehicle with a continuous tread instead of rear wheels

half'way' *a.* 1. midway between points 2. partial —*adv.* to the halfway point

half'-wit' *n.* stupid person — **half'-wit'ted** *a.*

hal'i·but *n.* large flatfish

hal'i·to'sis *n.* bad-smelling breath

hall *n.* 1. public building with offices 2. large room for meetings, shows, etc. 3. vestibule 4. passageway

hal·le·lu'jah, hal·le·lu'iah (-yə) *int.* praise the Lord!

hall'mark *n.* mark of quality

hal'low *v.* make or regard as holy —**hal'lowed** *a.*

Hal'low·een', Hal'low·e'en' *n.* evening of Oct. 31

hal·lu'ci·nate *v.* have hallucinations

hal·lu'ci·na'tion *n.* apparent perception of sights, etc. not really present —**hal·lu'ci·na·to'ry** *a.*

hal·lu'ci·no·gen *n.* drug that produces hallucinations

hall'way *n.* corridor

ha'lo *n.* [*pl.* -LOS, -LOES] ring of light

halt *v.* 1. to stop 2. hesitate — *n.* stop —**the halt** those who are lame

hal'ter *n.* 1. rope to tie an animal 2. woman's backless upper garment

halve (hav) *v.* 1. divide into halves 2. reduce to half

halves *n.* pl. of **half** —**by halves** halfway —**go halves** share expenses equally

hal'yard (-yərd) *n.* rope for raising a flag, etc.

ham *n.* 1. upper part of a hog's hind leg 2. [Col.] amateur radio operator 3. [Sl.] actor who overacts

ham'burg·er *n.* 1. ground beef 2. cooked patty of such meat Also **ham'burg**

ham'let *n.* small village

ham'mer *n.* tool with a metal head for pounding —*v.* pound, drive, shape, etc. as with a hammer

ham'mock (-ək) *n.* bed of canvas, etc. swung from poles

ham'per *v.* hinder; impede — *n.* large basket

ham'ster *n.* ratlike animal, used in experiments

ham'string *n.* tendon back of the knee —*v.* disable

hand *n.* 1. end of the arm beyond the wrist 2. side or direction 3. active part 4. handwriting 5. applause 6. help 7. hired worker 8. pointer on a clock 9. cards held by a player in a card game —*a.* of, for, or by the hand —**at hand** near —**hand in hand** together —**hands down** easily —**on hand** available —**upper hand** the advantage

hand'bag *n.* woman's purse

hand'ball *n.* game in which players hit a ball against a wall with the hand

hand'bill *n.* printed notice passed out by hand

hand'book *n.* handy book of instructions

hand'cuff *n.* one of a pair of shackles for the wrists —*v.* put handcuffs on

hand'ful *n.* [*pl.* -FULS] **1.** as much as a hand will hold **2.** a few **3.** one that is hard to manage

hand'gun *n.* firearm held with one hand, as a pistol

hand'i·cap *n.* **1.** difficulty or advantage given to some contestants to equalize their chances **2.** hindrance —*v.* [-CAPPED, -CAPPING] hinder

hand'i·craft *n.* work calling for skill with the hands

hand'i·work *n.* result of one's actions

hand'ker·chief *n.* small cloth for wiping the nose, etc.

han'dle *n.* part of tool, etc. by which it is held —*v.* **1.** touch, lift, etc. with the hand **2.** manage **3.** deal with **4.** deal in

han'dle·bar *n.* often *pl.* curved metal bar for steering a bicycle, etc.

hand'made' *a.* made by hand, not by machine

hand'out *n.* **1.** gift, as to a beggar **2.** leaflet handed out

hand'pick *v.* choose with care

hand'rail *n.* rail, as along a stairway

hand'shake *n.* gripping of hands in greeting, etc.: also **hand'clasp**

hand'some *a.* **1.** good-looking in a manly or impressive way **2.** sizable **3.** gracious

hand'spring *n.* a turning over in midair with the hands touching the ground

hand'-to-hand' *a.* at close quarters

hand'-to-mouth' *a.* with just enough to live on

hand'writ'ing *n.* writing done by hand

hand'y *a.* [-IER, -IEST] **1.** nearby **2.** easily used **3.** clever with the hands —**hand'i·ly** *adv.*

hand'y·man *n.* [*pl.* -MEN] man who does odd jobs

hang *v.* [HUNG or (for *v.* 3) HANGED, HANGING] **1.** attach or be attached from above **2.** attach so as to swing freely **3.** kill by suspending from a rope about the neck **4.** attach to walls **5.** droop —*n.* **1.** way a thing hangs **2.** way a thing is done **3.** meaning —**hang around** [Col.] loiter around —**hang back** hesitate, as from shyness

hang'ar *n.* aircraft shelter

hang'dog *a.* abject; cowed

hang'er *n.* that on which something is hung

hang'man *n.* [*pl.* -MEN] man who hangs convicted criminals

hang′nail *n.* bit of torn skin next to a fingernail

hang′o′ver *n.* sickness resulting from being drunk

hang′-up′ *n.* [Sl.] problem one finds hard to cope with

hank *n.* skein of yarn

hank′er *v.* long (*for*) —**hank′-er·ing** *n.*

Ha·nu·ka (khä′noo kä, -kə) *n.* Jewish festival

hap′haz′ard *a.* not planned; random —*adv.* by chance

hap′less *a.* unlucky

hap′pen *v.* 1. take place 2. occur by chance 3. have the luck or occasion —**happen on** (or **upon**) to chance to find

hap′pen·ing *n.* event

hap′py *a.* [-PIER, -PIEST] 1. showing pleasure or joy 2. lucky 3. apt —**hap′pi·ly** *adv.* —**hap′pi·ness** *n.*

hap′py-go-luck′y *a.* easygoing

ha·ra-ki·ri (hä′rə kir′ē) *n.* Japanese ritual suicide

ha·rangue′ (-raŋ′) *v., n.* (address in) a noisy speech

har·ass (hə ras′, har′əs) *v.* trouble or attack constantly —**har·ass′ment** *n.*

har·bin·ger (här′bin jər) *n.* forerunner

har′bor *n.* protected inlet for ships —*v.* 1. to shelter 2. hold in the mind

hard *a.* 1. firm or solid 2. powerful 3. difficult to do, understand, etc. 4. harsh 5. interfering with lathering 6. energetic 7. ambitious and harmful —*adv.* 1. with energy 2. with strength 3. sharply —**hard and fast** strict

hard′-bit′ten *a.* tough

hard′-boiled′ *a.* 1. boiled until solid 2. unfeeling

hard′-core′ *a.* absolute

hard′en *v.* make or become hard

hard hat 1. protective helmet 2. [Sl.] worker wearing a hard hat

hard′head′ed *a.* 1. shrewd 2. stubborn

hard′heart′ed *a.* cruel

har′di·hood *n.* boldness, vigor, etc.

hard′-line′ *a.* aggressive

hard′ly *adv.* 1. barely 2. not likely

hard′-nosed′ *a.* [Sl.] tough and stubborn

hard sell high-pressure salesmanship

hard′ship *n.* thing hard to bear, as poverty, pain, etc.

hard′tack *n.* unleavened bread in hard wafers

hard′ware *n.* 1. metal articles, as tools, nails, etc. 2. mechanical, magnetic, and electronic devices of a computer

hard′wood *n.* tough timber with a compact texture

har′dy *a.* [-DIER, -DIEST] 1. bold and resolute 2. robust —**har′di·ness** *n.*

hare (her) *n.* rabbit, esp. one of the larger kind

hare′brained′ *a.* foolish

hare′lip′ *n.* congenital cleft of the upper lip

ha·rem (her′əm) *n.* 1. quarters for the women in a Muslim's house 2. these women

hark *v.* [Poet.] listen

hark′en *v.* hearken

har′lot *n.* a prostitute

harm *n., v.* hurt; damage — **harm′ful** *a.* —**harm′less** *a.*

har·mon′ic (-män′-) *n. Mus.* of or in harmony

har·mon′i·ca *n.* small wind instrument with metal reeds

har′mo·nize *v.* 1. be, sing, etc. in harmony 2. bring into harmony

har′mo·ny *n.* 1. pleasing agreement of parts 2. agreement in ideas, action, etc. 3. pleasing combination of musical tones —**har′mo′ni·ous** *a.*

har′ness *n.* straps, etc. for hitching a horse to a wagon, etc. —*v.* 1. put harness on 2. control for use

harp *n.* stringed musical instrument played by plucking —*v.* keep talking or writing (*on*) —**harp′ist** *n.*

har·poon′ *n.* barbed shaft for spearing whales —*v.* strike with a harpoon

harp′si·chord *n.* early keyboard instrument

har′ri·dan *n.* shrewish old woman

har′row *n.* frame with spikes or disks for breaking up plowed land —*v.* 1. draw a harrow over 2. distress —**har′-row·ing** *a.*

har′ry *v.* [-RIED, -RYING] harass; torment

harsh *a.* 1. rough to the eye, ear, taste, etc. 2. cruel or severe —**harsh′ly** *adv.* — **harsh′ness** *n.*

hart *n.* male European deer

har′vest *n.* 1. a season's crop or the gathering of it 2. season for this —*v.* gather (a crop)

has *pres. t. of* **have**: used with *he, she, it*

has′-been′ *n.* [Col.] one whose popularity is past

hash *n.* 1. cooked mixture of chopped meat and vegetables 2. a muddle —**hash over** [Col.] to discuss at length

hash′ish (-ēsh) *n.* narcotic made from Indian hemp

has′n′t has not

hasp *n.* clasplike fastening for a door, lid, etc.

has′sle *n.* [Col.] squabble; argument —*v.* 1. [Col.] have a hassle 2. [Sl.] harass

has′sock *n.* firm cushion used as a footstool, etc.

hast [Ar.] *have*: with *thou*

haste *n.* a hurry or rush — **make haste** to hurry

has′ten *v.* to hurry

hast′y *a.* [-IER, -IEST] done with haste —**hast′i·ly** *adv.*

hat *n.* head covering, often with a brim

hatch *v.* 1. bring or come forth from (an egg) 2. contrive (a plot) —*n.* hatchway or its lid

hatch′back′ *n.* automobile with rear lid over wide storage area

hatch′er·y *n.* [*pl.* -IES] place for hatching eggs

hatch′et *n.* short ax

hatch′way′ *n.* opening in a ship's deck, or in a floor

hate *v.* dislike strongly —*n.* strong dislike: also **ha′tred**

hate′ful *a.* deserving hate

hath [Ar.] has

haugh′ty (hô′-) *a.* [-TIER, -TIEST] scornfully proud —

haugh′ti·ly adv. —**haugh′ti-ness** n.

haul v. **1.** pull; drag **2.** transport by truck, etc. —n. **1.** amount caught, won, etc. **2.** distance one travels

haunch n. hip, rump, and upper thigh

haunt v. **1.** visit often **2.** recur often to —n. place often visited

haunt′ed a. supposedly frequented by ghosts

haunt′ing a. not easily forgotten

hau·teur (hō tur′) n. scornful pride

have v. [HAD, HAVING] **1.** hold; possess **2.** experience **3.** hold mentally **4.** get; take **5.** beget **6.** engage in **7.** cause to do, be, etc. **8.** permit **9.** be forced *Have* is an important helping verb —n. rich person or nation —**have on** be wearing

ha′ven n. shelter; refuge

have′-not′ n. person or nation with little wealth

have′n′t have not

hav′er·sack n. bag for provisions, worn on the back

hav′oc n. great destruction —**play havoc with** ruin

hawk n. bird of prey —v. **1.** peddle (goods) in the streets **2.** clear the throat

haw′ser n. cable for anchoring or towing a ship

haw′thorn n. small tree with red berries

hay n. grass, clover, etc. cut and dried for fodder

hay fever allergy to pollen that affects one like a cold

hay′mow (-mou) n. pile of hay in a barn

hay′stack n. pile of hay outdoors

hay′wire a. [Sl.] wrong or crazy

haz′ard n. **1.** risk; danger **2.** obstacle on a golf course —v. to risk

haz′ard·ous a. dangerous

haze n. **1.** mist of fog, smoke, etc. **2.** vagueness

ha′zel n. **1.** tree bearing small nut (**ha′zel·nut**) **2.** reddish brown

ha′zy a. [-ZIER, -ZIEST] **1.** foggy or smoky **2.** vague

H′-bomb′ n. hydrogen bomb

he pron. **1.** the male mentioned **2.** anyone

head n. **1.** part of the body beyond the neck **2.** mind **3.** top or front part **4.** froth on beer, etc **5.** position of leadership **6.** leader **7.** crisis **8.** poise —a. **1.** chief **2.** at the head —v. **1.** to lead **2.** set out; go —**head off** intercept —**head over heels** completely —**not make head or tail of** not to understand —**over one's head** beyond one's understanding —**turn one's head** make one vain

head′ache n. pain in the head

head′first adv. **1.** with the head first **2.** rashly

head′ing n. **1.** title; caption **2.** direction in which a ship, etc. is moving

head′light n. light at the front of a vehicle

head′line n. title of newspaper article —v. feature

head′long *a., adv.* **1.** with the head first **2.** rash(ly)

head′-on′ *a., adv.* with the head or front foremost

head′quar′ters *n.pl.* center of operations; main office

head′room *n.* space overhead

head start early start or other competitive advantage

head′stone *n.* grave marker

head′strong *a.* obstinate

head′wa′ters *n.pl.* sources of a river

head′way *n.* progress

head′y *a.* [-IER, -IEST] **1.** intoxicating **2.** rash

heal *v.* cure or mend

health *n.* **1.** soundness of body and mind **2.** condition of body or mind

health′ful *a.* helping to produce or maintain health

health′y *a.* [-IER, -IEST] **1.** having or showing good health **2.** healthful

heap *n., v.* pile; mass

hear *v.* [HEARD, HEARING] **1.** receive (sounds) through the ear **2.** listen to **3.** be told —**hear from** get a letter, etc. from —**not hear of** not permit

hear′ing *n.* **1.** ability to hear **2.** chance to be heard **3.** formal meeting to hear testimony **4.** distance a sound will carry

heark′en (härk′-) *v.* listen

hear′say *n.* gossip; rumor

hearse (hurs) *n.* vehicle to carry a body to the grave

heart *n.* **1.** organ that circulates the blood **2.** vital part **3.** love, sympathy, courage, etc. **4.** figure shaped like ♥ **5.** playing card so marked —**by heart**

by memorization —**take to heart 1.** consider seriously **2.** be troubled by

heart′ache *n.* sorrow

heart attack coronary thrombosis

heart′break *n.* great sorrow

heart′burn *n.* burning sensation in the stomach

heart′en *v.* encourage

heart′felt *a.* sincere

hearth (härth) *n.* **1.** floor of a fireplace **2.** home

heart′less *a.* unkind

heart′-rend′ing *a.* causing much grief or pity

heart′sick *a.* very sad

heart′strings *n.pl.* deepest feelings

heart′-to-heart′ *a.* intimate

heart′y *a.* [-IER, -IEST] **1.** cordial **2.** vigorous **3.** strong and healthy **4.** nourishing —**heart′i·ly** *adv.*

heat *n.* **1.** hotness, or the perception of it **2.** strong feeling **3.** single race, etc. in a series **4.** sexual excitement of animals —*v.* make or become hot —**heat′er** *n.*

heat′ed *a.* hot **2.** impassioned —**heat′ed·ly** *adv.*

heath *n.* **1.** tract of open wasteland **2.** shrub that grows on heaths, as heather or brier

hea·then (hē′*th*ən) *a., n.* (of) one not a Jew, Christian, or Muslim

heath′er (he*th*′-) *n.* low plant with purple flowers

heave *v.* [alt. *pp.* HOVE] **1.** lift, or lift and throw, with effort **2.** make (a sigh) with effort **3.** swell up **4.** rise and fall in rhythm 5. vomit —n. act of heaving —**heave to** Naut. to stop

heav′en n. 1. Theol. [H-] place where God and his angels are 2. pl. sky 3. state of bliss —**heav′en·ly** a.

heav′y a. [-IER, -IEST] 1. weighing much 2. very great, intense, etc. 3. sorrowful 4. using large machines to produce basic materials —n. [pl. -IES] stage villain —**heav′i·ly** adv. —**heav′i·ness** n.

heav′y-du′ty a. made to withstand hard use

heav′y-hand′ed a. awkward

heav′y-heart′ed a. sad

heav′y-set′ a. stout; stocky

He′brew n. language of ancient and modern Israel —a. of the Jews

heck′le v. annoy with questions, taunts, etc. —**heck′ler** n.

hec·tare (hek′ter) n. 10,000 square meters

hec′tic a. feverish, frenzied, etc. —**hec′ti·cal·ly** adv.

hedge n. 1. dense row of shrubs 2. a hedging —v. 1. put a hedge around 2. avoid direct answers 3. avoid betting loss by offsetting bets

hedge′hog n. porcupine

he′don·ist (hē′-) n. pleasure-seeker —**he′don·ism** n. —**he′don·is′tic** a.

heed n. careful attention —v. pay heed (to) —**heed′ful** a. —**heed′less** a.

heel n. 1. back part of the foot 2. part of shoe, etc. at the heel —v. 1. furnish with heels 2.

follow closely 3. lean to one side, as a ship

heft n. [Col.] heaviness —v. [Col.] 1. to lift 2. guess weight of by lifting —**heft′y** a.

he·gem′o·ny (hi jem′-) n. dominance of one nation over others

heif′er (hef′-) n. young cow

height (hīt) n. 1. highest point or degree 2. distance from bottom to top 3. altitude 4. pl. high place

height′en v. make or become higher, greater, etc.

hei′nous (hā′-) a. outrageous

heir (er) n. one who inherits another's property, etc. —**heir′ess** n.fem.

heir′loom n. a possession handed down in a family

heist (hīst) n. [Sl.] a robbery —v. [Sl.] to rob or steal

held pt. & pp. of **hold**

hel′i·cop′ter n. aircraft with a horizontal propellor above the fuselage

he′li·o·cen′tric (hē′-) a. having the sun as center

he′li·o·trope′ n. plant with clusters of purple flowers

hel′i·port n. flat area for helicopters to land and take off

he′li·um n. very light, nonflammable gas, a chemical element

he′lix (hē′-) n. [pl. -LIXES, -LICES (hel′ə sēz)] spiral —**hel′i·cal** a.

hell n. Theol. place of torment for sinners after death —**hell′ish** a.

he′ll 1. he will 2. he shall

Hel·len′ic a. Greek

hell'gram·mite (-mīt) *n.* fly larva used as fish bait

hel'lion (-yən) *n.* [Col.] person fond of mischief; rascal

hel·lo' *int.* exclamation of greeting

helm *n.* **1.** tiller or wheel to steer a ship **2.** control

hel'met *n.* protective head covering of metal, etc.

helms'man *n.* [*pl.* -MEN] man who steers a ship

help *v.* **1.** give assistance (to); aid **2.** remedy **3.** avoid **4.** serve —*n.* **1.** aid; assistance **2.** remedy **3.** one that helps **4.** hired helper or helpers — **help'er** *n.* —**help'ful** *a.*

help'ing *n.* portion of food served to one person

help'less *a.* **1.** unable to help oneself **2.** unprotected

help'mate *n.* wife or husband: also **helpmeet**

hel'ter-skel'ter *adv., a.* in or showing haste or confusion

hem *v.* [HEMMED, HEMMING] **1.** fold the edge of and sew down **2.** surround or confine **3.** clear the throat audibly —*n.* hemmed edge —**hem and haw** hesitate in speaking

hem'a·tite *n.* kind of iron ore

he·ma·tol'o·gy (hē′-) *n.* study of blood and its diseases —**he'ma·tol'o·gist** *n.*

hem'i·sphere *n.* **1.** half a sphere **2.** any of the halves (N or S, E or W) of the earth

hem'lock *n.* **1.** evergreen tree **2.** poisonous weed

hemo- *pref.* blood

he'mo·glo'bin *n.* coloring matter of red blood cells

he'mo·phil'i·a *n.* prolonged bleeding due to failure of blood to clot

hem'or·rhage (-ij) *n.* heavy bleeding —*v.* bleed heavily

hem'or·rhoids *n.pl.* swollen veins near the anus

hemp *n.* tall plant with fibers used to make rope, etc.

hem'stitch *n.* ornamental stitch, used esp. at a hem

hen *n.* female of the chicken or certain other birds

hence *adv.* **1.** from this place or time **2.** therefore

hence'forth' *adv.* from now on: also **hence'for'ward**

hench'man *n.* [*pl.* -MEN] trusted helper

hen'na *n.* reddish-brown dye from a tropical shrub

hen'peck *v.* to domineer over (one's husband)

hep *a.* [Sl.] hip

he·pat'ic *a.* of the liver

hep'a·ti'tis *n.* inflammation of the liver

her *pron.* objective case of **she** —*a.* of her

her'ald *n.* **1.** messenger **2.** forerunner —*v.* foretell

her'ald·ry *n.* **1.** study of coats of arms, etc. **2.** pomp —**he·ral'dic** *a.*

herb *n.* nonwoody plant, now esp. one used as seasoning or in medicine

herb'age *n.* pasturage; grass

herb'al·ist *n.* one who grows or sells herbs

her'bi·cide *n.* chemical used to kill plants, esp. weeds

her·biv'o·rous *a.* plant-eating

her·cu·le'an *a.* [*often* H-] having or involving great strength, courage, etc.

herd *n.* cattle, etc. feeding or living together —*v.* form into a herd or group

herds'man *n.* [*pl.* -MEN] one who tends a herd

here *adv.* **1.** in, at, or to this place **2.** at this point; now —*n.* this place

here'a·bout' *adv.* near here: also **here'a·bouts'**

here·af'ter *adv.* from now on —*n.* state after death

here·by' *adv.* by this means

he·red'i·tar'y *a.* of, or passed down by, heredity or inheritance

he·red'i·ty *n.* passing on of characteristics to offspring or descendants

here·in' *adv.* in this place, matter, writing, etc.

her'e·sy (her'-) *n.* [*pl.* -SIES] unorthodox opinion or religious belief —**her'e·tic** *n.* —**he·ret'i·cal** *a.*

here·to·fore' *adv.* until now

her'it·a·ble (her'-) *a.* that can be inherited

her'it·age *n.* tradition, etc. handed down from the past

her·met'ic (har-) *a.* airtight: also **her·met'i·cal** —**her·met'i·cal·ly** *adv.*

her'mit *n.* one who lives alone in a secluded place —**her'mit·age** (-ij) *n.*

her'ni·a *n.* rupture, as of the abdominal wall

her'ni·ate *v.* form a hernia

he'ro *n.* [*pl.* -ROES] **1.** brave, noble man **2.** central male character in a story —**he·ro'ic**

a. —**her·o·ine** (her'ə win) *n.fem.* —**her'o·ism** *n.*

her'o·in (her'-) *n.* narcotic

her'on *n.* wading bird

hero sandwich meat, cheese, etc. in long, sliced roll

her·pes (hur'pēz) *n.* blisters on skin caused by virus

her'ring *n.* food fish of the Atlantic

her'ring·bone' *n.* pattern of parallel, slanting lines

hers *pron.* that or those belonging to her

her·self' *pron.* intensive or reflexive form of **she**

hertz *n.* [*pl.* HERTZ] international unit of frequency

hes'i·tate (hez'-) *v.* **1.** feel unsure; waver **2.** pause —**hes'i·tant** *a.* —**hes'i·tan·cy** *n.* —**hes'i·ta'tion** *n.*

het'er·o·dox' *a.* unorthodox, as in religious beliefs —**het'er·o·dox'y** *n.*

het'er·o·ge'ne·ous *a.* **1.** dissimilar **2.** varied

het'er·o·sex'u·al *a.* of or having sexual desire for those of the opposite sex —*n.* heterosexual person

heu·ris'tic (hyoo-) *a.* helping to learn, as by self-teaching

hew *v.* [alt. pp. HEWN] **1.** chop, as with an ax **2.** conform (*to* a rule, principle, etc.)

hex *n.* something thought to bring bad luck —*v.* cause bad luck to

hex'a·gon *n.* figure with six angles and six sides —**hex·ag'o·nal** *a.*

hey (hā) *int.* exclamation to get attention, etc.

hey′day n. peak period

hi int. word of greeting

hi·a′tus (hī ā′-) n. gap

hi·ba′chi (-bä′chē) n. charcoal-burning cooking grill

hi′ber·nate v. spend the winter in a sleeplike state —**hi′ber·na′tion** n.

hi·bis′cus n. plant with large, colorful flowers

hic′cup, **hic′cough** (-kəp) n. muscle spasm that stops the breath —v. to make a hiccup

hick n. [Col.] unsophisticated country person

hick′o·ry n. [pl. -RIES] 1. hardwood tree 2. its nut

hide v. [HID, HIDDEN or HID, HIDING] 1. put, or be, out of sight 2. keep secret —n. animal skin or pelt

hide′a·way n. [Col.] a secluded place

hide′bound′ a. narrow-minded

hid′e·ous a. very ugly

hide′out′ n. [Col.] hiding place, as for gangsters

hie v. [HIED, HIEING or HYING] hasten

hi′er·ar′chy (-kē) n. [pl. -CHIES] (rule by) clergy or officials in graded ranks

hi′er·o·glyph′ic (-glif′-) a., n. (of) picture writing, as of the ancient Egyptians

hi′-fi′ a. of high fidelity —n. phonograph, etc. having high fidelity

high a. 1. tall 2. to, at, or from a height 3. above others in rank, size, cost, etc. 4. raised in pitch; shrill 5. elated —adv. in or to a high level, degree, etc. —n. 1. high level, degree,

etc. 2. gear arrangement giving greatest speed —**high′ly** adv.

high′ball n. liquor mixed with soda water, etc.

high′brow n., a. [Col.] intellectual

high′fa·lu′tin a. [Col.] pompous: also **highfaluting**

high fidelity accurate reproduction of sound

high′-flown′ a. too showy

high frequency radio frequency between 3 and 30 megahertz

high′hand′ed a. arrogant

high′land n. mountainous region

high′light n. brightest or most interesting part, scene, etc.

high′-mind′ed a. having high ideals or principles

high′ness n. 1. height 2. [H-] title of royalty

high′-pres′sure a. using persuasive methods

high′-rise′ n. tall building

high school school of grades 10, 11, and 12, and sometimes grade 9

high seas ocean waters not belonging to any nation

high′-spir′it·ed a. lively

high′-strung′ a. excitable

high′-ten′sion a. carrying a high voltage

high′way n. main road

high′way′man n. [pl. -MEN] highway robber

hi′jack v. 1. steal (goods in transit) by force 2. force (aircraft) to fly unscheduled route

hike v. 1. take a long walk 2. [Col.] raise —n. a hiking

hi·lar'i·ous a. 1. noisily merry 2. funny —hi·lar'i·ty n.

hill n. mound of land —hill'y [-IER, -IEST] a.

hill'bil'ly n. [pl. -LIES] [Col.] native of mountains or backwoods in South

hill'ock n. small hill

hilt n. handle of a sword, dagger, etc.

him pron. objective case of he

him·self' pron. intensive or reflexive form of he

hind (hīnd) a. back; rear —n. female of the red deer

hin'der v. keep back; stop or thwart —hin'drance n.

hind'most a. farthest back

hind'sight n. recognition, after the event, of what one should have done

Hin'du n. native or language of India —a. 1. of Hindus 2. of Hinduism

Hin'du·ism n. main religion of India

hinge n. joint on which a door, etc. swings —v. 1. attach by a hinge 2. depend

hint n. slight indication —v. give a hint

hin'ter·land n. remote area

hip n. part between the upper thigh and the waist —a. [HIPPER, HIPPEST] [Sl.] 1. sophisticated 2. of hippies

hip'pie n. [Sl.] young person alienated from conventional society

hip'po·drome n. arena

hip'po·pot'a·mus n. [pl. -MUSES, -MI (-mī')] large, thick-skinned animal of Africa

hire v. pay for the services or use of —n. amount paid in hiring

hire'ling n. one who will do almost anything for pay

hir'sute (hur'-) a. hairy

his pron. that or those belonging to him —a. of him

hiss n. a prolonged s sound —v. 1. make this sound 2. disapprove of by hissing

his'to·ry n. [pl. -RIES] study or record of past events —his·to'ri·an n. —his·tor'i·cal, his·tor'ic a.

his'tri·on'ics n.pl. dramatics —his'tri·on'ic a.

hit v. [HIT, HITTING] 1. come against with force; bump 2. give a blow (to); strike 3. affect strongly 4. come (on or upon) —n. 1. a blow 2. collision 3. successful song, play, etc. 4. base hit —hit'ter n.

hit'-and-run' a. of a car driver who leaves after hitting a victim: also hit'-skip'

hitch v. 1. move with jerks 2. fasten with a hook, knot, etc. —n. 1. a tug; jerk 2. hindrance 3. kind of knot 4. [Sl.] time served, as in military service

hitch'hike' v. travel by asking for rides from motorists —hitch'hik'er n.

hith'er adv. to this place

hith'er·to adv. until now

hive n. 1. colony of bees or its shelter 2. place full of busy people 3. pl. skin allergy with raised, itching patches

hoa'gy, hoa'gie (-gē) n. [pl. -GIES] hero sandwich

hoard n. hidden supply —v. accumulate and store away (money, etc.)

hoar′frost *n.* frozen dew

hoarse *a.* sounding rough and husky

hoar′y *a.* [-IER, -IEST] 1. white 2. white-haired and old 3. very old

hoax (hōks) *n.* a trick; practical joke —*v.* to fool

hob′ble *v.* 1. to limp 2. hamper by tying the legs —*n.* a limp

hob′by *n.* [*pl.* -BIES] pastime activity

hob′by·horse *n.* stick with horse's head; child's toy

hob′gob′lin *n.* 1. elf 2. bugbear

hob′nail *n.* broad-headed nail for shoe soles

hob′nob *v.* [-NOBBED, -NOBBING] be friendly (*with*)

ho′bo *n.* [*pl.* -BOS, -BOES] a vagrant; tramp

hock *n.* hind-leg joint that bends backward —*v.* [Sl.] pawn

hock′ey *n.* team game played on ice skates

ho′cus-po′cus *n.* 1. magic tricks 2. trickery

hod *n.* 1. trough for carrying bricks, etc. 2. coal scuttle

hodge′podge *n.* a jumble

hoe *n.* garden tool with a thin blade at the end of a long handle —*v.* [HOED, HOEING] cultivate with a hoe

hoe′down *n.* lively dance

hog *n.* 1. pig 2. [Col.] greedy person —*v.* [HOGGED, HOGGING] [Sl.] take all of

hogs′head *n.* large barrel

hog′tie *v.* [-TIED, -TYING or -TIEING] [Col.] to hinder from action

hog′wash *n.* insincere words

hoi pol·loi (pə loi′) [Gr.] the common people

hoist *v.* raise, esp. with a crane, etc. —*n.* apparatus for lifting

hoke *v.* [Sl.] treat in a sentimental or contrived way — **hok′ey** *a.*

ho′kum *n.* [Sl.] nonsense

hold *v.* [HELD, HOLDING] 1. keep in the hands 2. keep in a certain position 3. keep back 4. occupy 5. have (a meeting, etc.) 6. contain 7. regard 8. remain unyielding —*n.* 1. grip 2. strong influence 3. ship's interior below deck —**get hold of** acquire; take —**hold forth** preach; lecture —**hold out** 1. endure 2. [Col.] refuse to give —**hold up** 1. delay 2. rob

hold′ing *n. often pl.* property owned

hold′o′ver *n.* [Col.] one still here from former time

hold′up *n.* 1. a delay 2. robbery

hole *n.* 1. hollow place 2. burrow 3. an opening, tear, etc. —**hole up** [Col.] 1. hibernate, as in a hole 2. hide —**in the hole** [Col.] owing money

hol′i·day (häl′ə-) *n.* 1. religious festival 2. work-free day, usually set aside by law

hol′i·ness *n.* 1. a being holy 2. [H-] title of the Pope

hol′ler *v., n.* [Col.] shout

hol′low *a.* 1. having a cavity within it 2. concave; sunken 3.

insincere 4. deep-toned and dull —n. 1. cavity 2. small valley —v. make or become hollow

hol'ly n. [pl. -LIES] evergreen shrub with red berries

hol'ly·hock n. tall plant with large, showy flowers

hol·o·caust (häl'ə kôst) n. 1. great destruction, esp. of people or animals by fire 2. [H-] destruction of Jews by Nazis

hol'o·graph (häl'-) n. document handwritten by author

hol'ster n. leather pistol case

ho'ly a. [-LIER, -LIEST] 1. sacred 2. sinless 3. deserving reverence or worship

Holy Communion church rite in which bread and wine are received as (symbols of) the body and blood of Jesus

Holy Ghost (or **Spirit**) third person of the Trinity

hom·age (häm'ij, äm'-) n. anything done to show honor or respect

home n. 1. place where one lives 2. household or life around it 3. living place for the aged, etc. —a. 1. domestic 2. central —adv. 1. at or to home 2. to the target — **home'less** a. —**home'made'** a.

home'land n. native land

home'ly a. [-LIER, -LIEST] 1. simple 2. plain; ugly

home plate Baseball last base touched in scoring a run

home run Baseball hit by which the batter scores a run: also **hom'er**

home'sick a. longing for home —**home'sick'ness** n.

home'spun n. cloth made of yarn spun at home —a. plain or simple

home'stead n. 1. a home and its grounds 2. public land granted as a farm

home'stretch' n. part of race track just before finish line

home'ward adv., a. toward home: also **home'wards** adv.

home'work n. schoolwork done outside the classroom

hom'i·cide (-sīd) n. 1. a killing of one person by another 2. one who kills another —**hom'i·ci'dal** a.

hom'i·let'ics n. art of writing and preaching sermons

hom'i·ly n. [pl. -LIES] sermon

hom'i·ny n. coarsely ground dry corn

homo- pref. same; equal

ho'mo·ge'ne·ous (-jē'nē-) a. 1. similar 2. made up of similar parts

ho·mog'e·nize (-mäj'-) v. make uniform throughout

hom'o·graph n. word with the same spelling as another but different in meaning

hom'o·nym n. word pronounced like another but having a different meaning and, usually, spelling

Ho·mo sa'pi·ens (hō'mō sā'pē enz) man; human being

ho'mo·sex'u·al a. of or having sexual desire for those of the same sex —n. homosexual person

hone n. fine whetstone —v. sharpen on a hone

hon′est *a.* **1.** not cheating, stealing, or lying; upright **2.** sincere or genuine **3.** frank and open —**hon′est·ly** *adv.* —**hon′es·ty** *n.*

hon′ey *n.* sweet, syrupy substance that is made by bees (**honeybees**)

hon′ey·comb *n.* structure of wax cells made by bees to hold their honey, etc. —*v.* fill with holes

hon′ey·dew mel′on kind of melon with a whitish rind

hon′ey·moon *n.* vacation for a newly married couple —*v.* have a honeymoon

hon′ey·suck′le *n.* vine with small, fragrant flowers

honk *n.* **1.** call of a wild goose **2.** sound of an auto horn —*v.* make this sound

hon′ky-tonk′ *n.* [Sl.] cheap, noisy nightclub

hon·or (än′ər) *n.* **1.** high regard **2.** good reputation **3.** adherence to right principles **4.** glory or credit **5.** [H-] title of certain officials **6.** something showing respect **7.** source of respect or fame —*v.* **1.** treat with respect or high regard **2.** confer an honor on **3.** accept as valid

hon′or·a·ble *a.* deserving honor —**hon′or·a·bly** *adv.*

hon′o·rar′i·um *n.* fee paid for professional services

hon′or·ar′y *a.* done, given, or held as an honor

hon·or·if′ic *a.* signifying honor, as a title

hon′our *n.* honor: Br. sp.

hood *n.* **1.** covering for the head and neck **2.** cover over an automobile engine — **hood′ed** *a.*

-hood *suf.* **1.** state or quality **2.** whole group of

hood′lum (hood′-) *n.* [Col.] ruffian; criminal

hoo′doo *n.* [*pl.* -DOOS] [Col.] bad luck or its cause

hood′wink *v.* deceive

hoof *n.* [*pl.* HOOFS, HOOVES] horny covering on the feet of cattle, horses, etc.

hook *n.* **1.** bent piece of metal used to catch or hold something **2.** fishhook **3.** sharp curve or curving motion —*v.* catch, fasten, hit, etc. with a hook —**hook up** connect, as a radio —**off the hook** [Col.] out of trouble

hook′ah *n.* tobacco pipe for drawing smoke through water

hook′up *n.* connection of parts, as in radio

hook′worm *n.* a small intestinal roundworm

hoo′li·gan *n.* ruffian

hoop *n.* large, circular band

hoop′la (-lä) *n.* [Sl.] excitement

hoop skirt woman's skirt worn over hoop framework

hoo·ray′ *int., n.* hurrah

hoose′gow (-gou) *n.* [Sl.] jail

hoot *n.* **1.** cry an owl makes **2.** shout of scorn —*v.* utter a hoot or hoots

hoot′en·an′ny *n.* [*pl.* -NIES] folk singers' show or party

hop *v.* [HOPPED, HOPPING] leap on one foot, or with all feet at once —*n.* **1.** a hopping **2.** [Col.] a dance **3.** [Col.] short plane flight **4.** *pl.* dried cones of a vine, used to flavor beer, etc.

hope *n.* **1.** trust that what is wanted will happen **2.** object of this —*v.* want and expect — **hope'ful** *a.* —**hope'less** *a.*

hop'per *n.* trough from which material is conveyed

hop'sack'ing *n.* coarse cloth

hop'scotch *n.* children's hopping game

horde *n.* a crowd; pack

hore'hound *n.* medicine or candy made from a bitter plant

ho·ri'zon (-rī'-) *n.* line where sky and earth seem to meet

hor'i·zon'tal *a.* **1.** parallel to the horizon **2.** level

hor'mone *n.* substance that is formed by a gland and stimulates an organ —**hor·mo'nal** *a.*

horn *n.* **1.** bonelike growth on the head of a cow, etc. **2.** brass-wind musical instrument —**horned** *a.*

hor'net *n.* large wasp

horn'pipe *n.* sailor's dance

horn'y *a.* [**-IER, -IEST**] **1.** hard; callous **2.** [Sl.] lustful

hor'o·scope *n.* chart of the zodiac used by astrologers

hor·ren'dous *a.* horrible

hor'ri·ble *a.* **1.** causing horror **2.** [Col.] very bad, ugly, etc. — **hor'ri·bly** *adv.*

hor'rid *a.* horrible

hor'ri·fy *v.* [**-FIED, -FYING**] **1.** make feel horror **2.** [Col.] shock greatly

hor'ror *n.* **1.** strong fear or dislike **2.** cause of this

hors d'oeu·vre (ôr' durv') [*pl.* D'OEUVRES] appetizer

horse *n.* **1.** large animal domesticated for pulling loads, carrying a rider, etc. **2.** supporting frame on legs

horse'back *adv., n.* (on) the back of a horse

horse chestnut 1. tree with large brown seeds **2.** its seed

horse'hair *n.* stiff fabric made from hair of horse's mane or tail

horse'man *n.* [*pl.* **-MEN**] skilled rider of horses —**horse'man·ship** *n.*

horse'play *n.* rough play

horse'pow'er *n.* unit of power output, as of engines

horse'rad'ish *n.* plant with a pungent edible root

horse'shoe *n.* **1.** U-shaped, flat metal plate nailed to a horse's hoof **2.** *pl.* game of tossing horseshoes at a stake

hor'ta·to'ry *a.* exhorting

hor'ti·cul'ture *n.* art of growing flowers, fruits, etc. —**hor'ti·cul'tur·al** *a.*

ho·san'na (-zan'-) *int.* shout of praise to God

hose *n.* **1.** [*pl.* HOSE] stocking **2.** flexible tube to convey liquids

ho'sier·y (-zhər-) *n.* stockings

hos'pice (-pis) *n.* shelter for travelers

hos'pi·ta·ble *a.* friendly to guests —**hos'pi·tal'i·ty** *n.*

hos'pi·tal *n.* place of medical care for ill and hurt

hos'pi·tal·ize' *v.* put in a hospital —**hos'pi·tal·i·za'tion** *n.*

host *n.* **1.** man who entertains

guests 2. great number 3. wafer used in Eucharist

hos·tage (häs'tij) *n.* person held as a pledge

hos'tel *n.* lodging place

host'ess *n.* 1. woman who entertains guests 2. woman in charge of seating in a restaurant

hos'tile *a.* 1. of or like an enemy 2. unfriendly

hos·til'i·ty *n.* [*pl.* -TIES] 1. enmity 2. *pl.* warfare

hos'tler *n.* one caring for horses in stable or inn

hot *a.* [HOTTER, HOTTEST] 1. high in temperature; very warm 2. spicy; peppery 3. angry, violent, eager, etc. 4. electrically charged 5. close behind 6. [Sl.] fresh or new 7. [Sl.] just stolen —**hot'ly** *adv.*

hot'bed *n.* glass-covered bed of earth, for forcing plants

hot'-blood'ed *a.* excitable

hot cake pancake

hot dog [Col.] wiener

ho·tel' *n.* place with rooms, food, etc. for travelers

hot'head'ed *a.* easily angered —**hot'head** *n.*

hot'house *n.* greenhouse

hot line phone or telegraph line for emergencies

hot plate small, portable stove

hot rod [Sl.] car with supercharged engine —**hot rodder** *n.*

hound *n.* breed of hunting dog —*v.* keep pursuing

hour *n.* 1. 1/24 of a day; 60 minutes 2. a particular time —**hour'ly** *a.*, *adv.*

hour'glass *n.* instrument for measuring time by the flow of sand in it

hou·ri (hoor'ē) *n.* nymph in Muslim paradise

house *n.* 1. building to live in 2. family 3. building for specified use 4. business firm 5. theater 6. legislative assembly —*v.* (houz) cover, shelter, lodge, etc. —**keep house** take care of a home

house'break'ing *n.* breaking into another's house to steal

house'bro'ken *a.* trained to live in a house, as a dog

house'hold *n.* 1. all those living in one house 2. home and its affairs

house'hold'er *n.* 1. owner of a house 2. head of a household

house'keep'er *n.* woman who manages a home

house'warm'ing *n.* party after moving into a new home

house'wife *n.* [*pl.* -WIVES] woman in charge of her own household

house'work *n.* work of cleaning, cooking, etc. in a house

hous'ing (houz'-) *n.* 1. shelter or lodging; houses 2. enclosing frame, box, etc.

hov'el (huv'-) *n.* small, miserable dwelling

hov'er *v.* 1. flutter in the air near one place 2. linger close by

how *adv.* 1. in what way 2. in what condition 3. why 4. to what extent

how'dah (-də) *n.* seat on the back of an elephant or camel

how·ev'er *adv.* 1. by whatever means 2. to whatever degree —*con.* nevertheless

how'itz·er *n.* short cannon

howl *n.* 1. long, wailing cry of a wolf, dog, etc. 2. similar cry, as of pain —*v.* 1. utter a howl 2. laugh in scorn, mirth, etc.

howl'er *n.* [Col.] funny blunder

how'so·ev'er *adv.* however

hoy'den *n.* tomboy

hua·ra·ches (hə rä'chēz) *n.pl.* flat sandals

hub *n.* 1. center of a wheel 2. center of activity, etc.

hub'bub *n.* tumult

hu'bris (hyōō'-) *n.* arrogance

huck'le·ber'ry *n.* [*pl.* -RIES] edible dark-blue berry

huck'ster *n.* peddler

hud'dle *v.* 1. crowd close together 2. draw (oneself) up tightly —*n.* 1. confused crowd or heap 2. [Sl.] private conference 3. *Football* grouping of a team to get signals

hue *n.* color; tint —**hue and cry** loud outcry

huff *v.* to blow; puff —*n.* burst of anger —**huff'y** [-IER, -IEST] *a.*

hug *v.* [HUGGED, HUGGING] 1. embrace 2. keep close to —*n.* embrace

huge *a.* very large; immense —**huge'ly** *adv.*

hu·la (hōō'lä) *n.* native Hawaiian dance: also **hula-hula**

hulk *n.* 1. body of an old, dismantled ship 2. big, clumsy person or thing —**hulk'ing** *a.*

hull *n.* 1. outer covering of a seed or fruit 2. main body of a

ship or aircraft —*v.* remove the hulls from

hul'la·ba·loo' *n.* clamor

hum *v.* [HUMMED, HUMMING] 1. sing with closed lips 2. make a low, steady murmur 3. [Col.] be full of activity —*n.* humming sound

hu'man *a.* of or like a person or people —*n.* a person: also **human being** —**hu'man·ly** *adv.*

hu·mane' *a.* kind, merciful, etc. —**hu·mane'ly** *adv.*

hu'man·ism *n.* system of thought based on interests and ideals of humankind —**hu'man·ist** *n.*

hu·man·i·tar'i·an *n.* one devoted to promoting the welfare of humanity —*a.* helping humanity

hu·man'i·ty *n.* 1. a being human or humane 2. the human race —**the humanities** studies of literature, philosophy, etc.

hu'man·ize *v.* make human or humane —**hu'man·i·za'tion** *n.*

hu'man·kind *n.* people

hu'man·oid *a.* nearly human —*n.* nearly human creature

hum'ble *a.* 1. not proud; modest 2. lowly; unpretentious —*v.* make humble —**hum'bly** *adv.*

hum'bug *n.* fraud; sham

hum'drum *a.* monotonous

hu'mer·us *n.* bone of upper arm

hu'mid *a.* damp; moist

hu·mid'i·fy *v.* [-FIED, -FYING]

to make humid —**hu·mid′i·fi′er** n.

hu·mid′i·ty n. 1. dampness 2. amount of moisture in the air

hu′mi·dor n. jar for keeping tobacco moist

hu·mil′i·ate v. lower the pride or dignity of; mortify —**hu·mil′i·a′tion** n.

hu·mil′i·ty n. humbleness

hum′ming·bird n. tiny bird able to hover

hum′mock (-ək) n. rounded hill

hu′mor n. 1. comical quality, talk, etc. 2. ability to see or express what is funny 3. mood 4. whim —v. indulge Br. sp. **humour** —**out of humor** disagreeable —**hu′mor·ist** n. —**hu′mor·ous** a.

hump n. rounded bulge —v. to arch; hunch —**over the hump** [Col.] past the hard part

hump′back n. (person having) a back with a hump

hu′mus n. dark soil made up of decayed leaves, etc.

hunch v. arch into a hump —n. 1. a hump 2. [Col.] a feeling that something is going to happen

hunch′back n. humpback

hun′dred a., n. ten times ten —**hun′dredth** a., n.

hun′dred·weight n. unit of weight, 100 pounds

hung pt. & pp. of **hang**

hun′ger n. need or craving for food 2. strong desire —v. feel hunger (for) —**hun′gry** [-GRIER, -GRIEST] a. —**hun′gri·ly** adv.

hunk n. [Col.] large piece

hun′ker v. to squat —n. pl. haunches or buttocks

hunt v. 1. search out (game) to catch or kill 2. search; seek 3. chase —n. a chase or search —**hunt′er** n.

hur′dle n. 1. frame for jumping over in a race 2. obstacle —v. 1. jump over 2. overcome (an obstacle)

hur′dy-gur′dy n. [pl. -DIES] barrel organ

hurl v. throw with force or violence —**hurl′er** n.

hurl′y-burl′y n. turmoil

hur·rah′ int., n. shout of joy, approval, etc.

hur·ray′ int., n. hurrah

hur′ri·cane (hur′-) n. violent storm from the tropics

hur′ry v. [-RIED, -RYING] move, act, etc. with haste; rush —n. rush; haste —**hur′ried·ly** adv.

hurt v. [HURT, HURTING] 1. cause pain or injury to 2. damage 3. offend 4. have pain —n. pain, injury, or harm —**hurt′ful** a.

hur′tle v. move or throw swiftly or with violence

hus′band (huz′-) n. married man —v. manage thriftily

hus′band·ry n. 1. thrifty management 2. farming

hush v. make or become silent —n. silence; quiet —int. be silent!

hush puppy cornmeal fritter

husk n. dry covering of some fruits and seeds —v. remove the husk from

husk′y a. [-IER, -IEST] 1. hoarse 2. big and strong —n. [also H-] Eskimo dog

hus'sy *n.* [*pl.* -SIES] bold or shameless woman

hus'tings *n.* (place for) political campaigning

hus·tle (hus''l) *v.* **1.** shove roughly **2.** move, work, etc. quickly or energetically —*n.* a hustling

hut *n.* shedlike cabin

hutch *n.* **1.** chest or cupboard **2.** pen or coop for small animals

hy'a·cinth *n.* plant with spikes of flowers

hy'brid *n.* offspring of two animals or plants of different species, etc.

hy'brid·ize *v.* produce hybrids; crossbreed —**hy'brid·i·za'tion** *n.*

hy'dra *n.* tiny freshwater polyp

hy·dran·gea (hī drān'jə) *n.* shrub with large clusters of flowers

hy'drant *n.* large pipe with a valve for drawing water from a water main

hy·drau'lic (-drô'-) *a.* **1.** worked by force of a moving liquid **2.** of hydraulics

hy·drau'lics *n.* study and use of the mechanical properties of liquids

hydro- *pref.* **1.** water **2.** hydrogen

hy'dro·car'bon *n.* compound of hydrogen and carbon

hy'dro·chlo'ric acid acid formed from hydrogen and chlorine

hy'dro·e·lec'tric *a.* of the production of electricity by water power —**hy'dro·e·lec'tric'i·ty** *n.*

hy'dro·foil *n.* (winglike structure on) watercraft that skims just above water at high speed

hy'dro·gen *n.* colorless gas, the lightest chemical element

hy'dro·gen·at'ed *a.* treated with hydrogen

hydrogen bomb very destructive atomic bomb

hydrogen peroxide liquid bleach and disinfectant

hy·drol'y·sis *n.* chemical reaction of a compound with water that produces a weak acid or base or both

hy'dro·pho'bi·a *n.* rabies

hy'dro·plane *n.* **1.** small, high-speed motorboat with hydrofoils **2.** seaplane

hy'dro·pon'ics *n.* science of growing plants in liquid mineral solutions

hy'dro·ther'a·py *n.* treatment of disease by external use of water

hy·drox'ide *n.* substance containing the radical OH

hy·e'na *n.* wolflike animal of Africa and Asia

hy'giene (-jēn) *n.* set of principles for health

hy'gi·en'ic *a.* **1.** of hygiene or health **2.** sanitary

hy·grom'e·ter *n.* device for measuring humidity

hy'men *n.* membrane covering part of the opening of the vagina in a virgin

hymn (him) *n.* song of praise, esp. a religious one

hym'nal *n.* book of hymns: also **hymn'book**

hype *n.* [Sl.] sensational publicity —*v.* [Sl.] **1.** stimulate, as with a drug **2.** promote in a sensational way

hyper- *pref.* over; excessive

hy·per·bo·le (-bə lē) *n.* exageration for effect —**hy'per·bol'ic** *a.*

hy'per·crit'i·cal *a.* too critical

hy'per·sen'si·tive *a.* too sensitive

hy'per·ten'sion *n.* abnormally high blood pressure

hy'per·thy'roid *a.* of or having excessive activity of the thyroid gland

hy'phen *n.* mark (-) used between parts or syllables of a word

hy'phen·ate *v.* join or write with a hyphen —**hy'phen·a'tion** *n.*

hyp·no'sis *n.* sleeplike state in which one responds to the hypnotist's suggestions —**hyp·not'ic** *a.*

hyp'no·tism *n.* practice of inducing hypnosis —**hyp'no·tist** *n.*

hyp'no·tize *v.* induce hypnosis in

hypo- *pref.* **1.** under **2.** less than; deficient in

hy'po·chon'dri·ac' (-kän'-) *n.* one who suffers from abnormal anxiety over his or her health

hy·poc'ri·sy *n.* [*pl.* -SIES] condition of being, or action of, a hypocrite

hyp'o·crite (-krit) *n.* one who pretends to be good, pious, kind, etc. without really being so —**hyp'o·crit'i·cal** *a.*

hy'po·der'mic *a.* injected under the skin —*n.* syringe and needle for giving hypodermic medical or drug injections

hy·pot'e·nuse *n.* side of right-angled triangle opposite the right angle

hy·poth'e·sis *n.* [*pl.* -SES (-sēz)] tentative explanation

hy'po·thet'i·cal *a.* based on a hypothesis; supposed

hy'po·thy'roid *a.* of or having deficient activity of thyroid gland

hys·sop (his'əp) *n.* fragrant plant of mint family

hys·ter·ec'to·my (his'-) *n.* [*pl.* -MIES] surgical removal of the uterus

hys·te'ri·a *n.* outbreak of wild emotion —**hys·ter'i·cal** *a.*

hys·ter'ics *n.pl.* hysteria

I

I *pron.* person speaking or writing

i′bex *n.* wild goat

i′bis *n.* large wading bird

-ible *suf.* **1.** that can or should be **2.** tending to

-ic, -ical *suf.* **1.** of or having to do with **2.** like **3.** produced by **4.** containing

ICBM intercontinental ballistic missile

ice *n.* **1.** water frozen solid by cold **2.** frozen dessert of fruit juice, sugar, etc. —*v.* **1.** change into ice **2.** cool with ice **3.** cover with icing —**iced** *a.*

ice′berg *n.* great mass of ice afloat in the sea

ice′box *n.* refrigerator, esp. one in which ice is used

ice′break′er *n.* sturdy boat for breaking through ice

ice cream frozen cream dessert

ice milk frozen dessert less rich than ice cream

ice skate shoe with a metal runner for skating on ice —**ice′-skate′** *v.*

ich′thy·ol′o·gy (ik′thē-) *n.* study of fishes —**ich′thy·ol′o·gist** *n.*

i′ci·cle *n.* hanging stick of ice

ic′ing *n.* sweet, soft coating for cakes; frosting

i′con *n.* sacred image or picture

i·con′o·clast *n.* one who attacks venerated institutions or ideas

-ics *suf.* art or science

i′cy *a.* [ICIER, ICIEST] **1.** full of or covered with ice **2.** very cold —**i′ci·ly** *adv.* —**i′ci·ness** *n.*

id *n.* part of mind thought to be source of psychic energy

I'd **1.** I had **2.** I would

i·de′a *n.* **1.** mental conception; thought or belief **2.** plan; scheme

i·de′al *n.* **1.** conception of something in its perfect form **2.** perfect model —*a.* thought of as, or being, an ideal —**i·de′al·ly** *adv.*

i·de′al·ism *n.* conception of, or striving for, an ideal —**i·de′al·ist** *n.* —**i′de·al·is′tic** *a.*

i·de′al·ize *v.* regard or show as perfect —**i·de′al·i·za′tion** *n.*

i·den′ti·cal *a.* the same —**i·den′ti·cal·ly** *adv.*

i·den′ti·fy *v.* [-FIED, -FYING] **1.** show to be a certain one **2.** associate closely (*with*) —**i·den′ti·fi·ca′tion** *n.*

i·den′ti·ty *n.* [*pl.* -TIES] **1.** state or fact of being the same **2.** individuality

i′de·ol′o·gy *n.* [*pl.* -GIES] system of beliefs, as of a group —**i′de·o·log′i·cal** *a.*

id′i·o·cy *n.* [*pl.* -CIES] **1.** great stupidity **2.** idiotic act or remark

id′i·om *n.* **1.** set phrase with a special meaning **2.** usual way of expression in words —**id′i·o·mat′ic** *a.*

id′i·o·path′ic *a.* of a disease with unknown cause

id'i·o·syn'cra·sy n. [pl. -SIES] personal oddity

id'i·ot n. person who is mentally very deficient —**id'i·ot'ic** a. —**id'i·ot'i·cal·ly** adv.

i'dle a. 1. useless 2. baseless 3. not busy or working 4. lazy —v. 1. loaf 2. be or make idle 3. operate motor in neutral —**i'dler** n. —**i'dly** adv.

i'dol n. image or object worshiped or adored

i·dol'a·try n. worship of idols —**i·dol'a·ter** n. —**i·dol'a·trous** a.

i'dol·ize v. adore as an idol

i·dyll, i·dyl (ī'd'l) n. short poem about pleasant rural life —**i·dyl'lic** (-dil'-) a.

i.e. that is to say

if con. 1. in case that 2. although 3. whether —**as if** as it would be if

ig'loo n. [pl. -LOOS] Eskimo hut made of snow blocks

ig'ne·ous a. 1. of fire 2. produced by great heat

ig·nite' v. 1. set fire to 2. catch on fire

ig·ni'tion n. 1. an igniting 2. electrical system for igniting the gases in an engine

ig·no'ble a. not noble; base

ig'no·min'y n. shame; disgrace —**ig'no·min'i·ous** a.

ig'no·ra'mus n. [pl. -MUSES] ignorant person

ig'no·rant a. 1. showing lack of knowledge 2. unaware —**ig'no·rance** n.

ig·nore' v. pay no attention to

i·gua'na (-gwä'-) n. large tropical lizard

ilk n. kind; sort

ill a. [WORSE, WORST] 1. bad 2. sick —n. evil or disease —adv.

I'll 1. I shall 2. I will

ill'-ad·vised' a. unwise

ill'-bred' a. rude; impolite

il·le'gal a. against the law —**il'le·gal'i·ty** n. —**il·le'gal·ly** adv.

il·leg'i·ble (-lej'-) a. hard or impossible to read

il·le·git'i·mate (-mit) a. 1. born of unwed parents 2. contrary to law, rules, etc. —**il'le·git'i·ma·cy** n.

ill'-fat'ed a. unlucky

ill'-got'ten a. obtained unlawfully or dishonestly

il·lib'er·al a. 1. stingy 2. narrow-minded

il·lic'it (-lis'-) a. unlawful; improper

il·lim'it·a·ble a. without limit; immeasurable

il·lit'er·ate (-it) a. unable to read —n. illiterate person —**il·lit'er·a·cy** n.

ill'-man'nered a. impolite; rude

ill'ness n. sickness; disease

il·log'i·cal a. not logical

ill'-suit'ed a. not appropriate

ill'-timed' a. done at the wrong time

ill'-treat' v. treat unkindly, unfairly, etc. —**ill'-treat'ment** n.

il·lu'mi·nate v. 1. light up 2. explain 3. decorate —**il·lu'mi·na'tion** n.

il·lu'mine v. light up

ill'-use' (-yōoz') v. abuse —n.

(-yo͞os') cruel treatment: also **ill-usage**

il·lu'sion n. 1. false idea 2. misleading appearance —**il·lu'sive, il·lu'so·ry** a.

il'lus·trate v. 1. explain, as by examples 2. furnish (books, etc.) with pictures —**il'lus·tra'tion** n. —**il·lus'tra·tive** a. —**il'lus·tra'tor** n.

il·lus'tri·ous a. famous

ill will hate; dislike

I'm I am

im'age (-ij) n. 1. a representation, as a statue 2. reflection in a mirror, etc. 3. mental picture; idea 4. copy —v. reflect

im'age·ry n. 1. images 2. descriptions

im·ag'i·nar'y a. existing only in the imagination

im·ag·i·na'tion n. 1. power to form mental pictures or ideas 2. thing imagined —**im·ag'i·na'tive** a.

im·ag'ine v. 1. conceive in the mind 2. suppose —**im·ag'i·na·ble** (-nə b'l) a.

im·bal'ance n. lack of balance in proportion, force, etc.

im'be·cile (-s'l) a. stupid —n. person who is mentally deficient —**im·be·cil'ic** a. —**im'be·cil'i·ty** n.

im·bed' v. embed

im·bibe' v. 1. drink (in) 2. absorb into the mind

im·bro'glio (-brōl'yō) n. [pl. -GLIOS] involved misunderstanding or disagreement

im·bue' (-byo͞o') v. 1. saturate 2. dye 3. fill, as the mind

im'i·tate v. 1. copy or mimic 2. resemble —**im'i·ta'tion** n., a.

im·mac'u·late (-yə lit) a. 1. perfectly clean 2. without a flaw 3. pure; sinless

im'ma·nent a. present everywhere: said of God

im'ma·te'ri·al a. 1. unimportant 2. spiritual

im·ma·ture' a. not fully grown or developed —**im'ma·tu'ri·ty** n.

im·meas'ur·a·ble a. boundless; vast —**im·meas'ur·a·bly** adv.

im·me'di·a·cy n. direct relation to present time, place, etc.

im·me'di·ate (-it) a. 1. closest 2. instant 3. direct —**im·me'di·ate·ly** adv.

im·me·mo'ri·al a. very old

im·mense' a. vast; huge —**im·men'si·ty** n.

im·merse' v. 1. plunge into a liquid 2. engross —**im·mer'sion** n.

im'mi·grant n. one who immigrates —a. immigrating

im'mi·grate v. enter a country, etc. in order to settle there —**im'mi·gra'tion** n.

im'mi·nent a. likely to happen without delay —**im'mi·nence** n.

im·mo'bile a. not moving or movable —**im'mo·bil'i·ty** n. —**im·mo'bi·lize** v.

im·mod'er·ate (-it) a. without restraint; excessive

im·mod'est a. 1. indecent 2. not shy —**im·mod'est·ly** adv. —**im·mod'es·ty** n.

im·mor'al a. not moral; esp., unchaste —**im·mor'al·ly** adv.

im·mo·ral'i·ty *n.* 1. a being immoral 2. [*pl.* -TIES] immoral act; vice

im·mor'tal *a.* 1. living forever 2. having lasting fame —*n.* immortal being —**im'mor·tal'i·ty** *n.*

im·mov'a·ble *a.* 1. firmly fixed 2. unyielding

im·mune' (-myōōn') *a.* exempt from or protected against something bad, as a disease, etc. —**im·mu'ni·ty** *n.*

im'mu·nize *v.* make immune, as by inoculation —**im'mu·ni·za'tion** *n.*

im'mu·nol'o·gy *n.* study of immunity to disease or of allergies

im·mure' (i myoor') *v.* to shut up within walls

im·mu'ta·ble *a.* unchangeable —**im·mu'ta·bly** *adv.*

imp *n.* 1. young demon 2. mischievous child —**imp'ish** *a.*

im'pact *n.* (force of) a collision

im·pact'ed *a.* describing a tooth lodged tight in jaw

im·pair' *v.* make worse, less, etc. —**im·pair'ment** *n.*

im·pa'la (-pä'lə) *n.* reddish African antelope

im·pale' *v.* pierce through with something pointed

im·pal'pa·ble *a.* that cannot be felt or easily perceived

im·pan'el *v.* choose (a jury) from a jury list

im·part' *v.* 1. give 2. tell

im·par'tial *a.* fair; just —**im'par·ti·al'i·ty** *n.*

im·pass'a·ble *a.* that cannot be traveled over

im'passe (-pas) *n.* deadlock

im·pas'sioned *a.* passionate; fiery

im·pas'sive *a.* calm

im·pas'to (-päs'-) *n.* painting with paint laid thickly on the canvas

im·pa'tient *a.* annoyed because of delay, etc. —**im·pa'tience** *n.*

im·peach' *v.* try (an official) on a charge of wrongdoing —**im·peach'ment** *n.*

im·pec'ca·ble *a.* flawless

im'pe·cu'ni·ous *a.* having no money; poor

im·ped'ance (-pēd'-) *n.* resistance in an electric circuit to flow of an alternating current

im·pede' *v.* hinder

im·ped'i·ment *n.* thing that impedes; spec., a speech defect

im·ped'i·men'ta *n.pl.* encumbrances

im·pel' *v.* [-PELLED, -PELLING] 1. drive forward 2. force

im·pend' *v.* be imminent —**im·pend'ing** *a.*

im·pen'e·tra·ble *a.* that cannot be penetrated

im·pen'i·tent *a.* not ashamed

im·per'a·tive *a.* 1. necessary; urgent 2. of the mood of a verb expressing a command

im'per·cep'ti·ble *a.* not easily perceived; subtle —**im'per·cep'ti·bly** *adv.*

im·per'fect *a.* 1. not complete 2. not perfect; faulty —**im·per'fect·ly** *adv.*

im'per·fec'tion *n.* 1. a being imperfect 2. fault

im·pe'ri·al *a.* 1. of an empire, emperor, or empress 2. majestic 3. authoritative 4. superior

—*n.* small, pointed chin beard

imperial gallon Br. gallon, equal to 1 1/5 U.S. gallons

im·pe·ri·al·ism *n.* policy of forming and maintaining an empire, as by subjugating territories, etc. —**im·pe'ri·al·ist** *a., n.*

im·per'il *v.* endanger

im·pe'ri·ous *a.* 1. domineering 2. urgent —**im·pe'ri·ous·ly** *adv.*

im·per'ish·a·ble *a.* indestructible

im·per'ma·nent *a.* not permanent

im·per·son·al *a.* 1. without reference to any one person 2. not existing as a person 3. of a verb in the third person singular, usually with *it* for subject —**im·per'son·al·ly** *adv.*

im·per'son·ate *v.* 1. assume the role of 2. mimic —**im·per'son·a'tion** *n.*

im·per'ti·nent *a.* 1. not relevant· 2. insolent —**im·per'ti·nence** *n.*

im·per·turb'a·ble *a.* calm; impassive

im·per'vi·ous *a.* 1. incapable of being penetrated 2. not affected by (with *to*)

im·pe·ti'go (-tī'-) *n.* skin disease with pustules

im·pet'u·ous (-pech'-) *a.* impulsive; rash —**im·pet'u·os'·i·ty** *n.*

im'pe·tus *n.* 1. force of a moving body 2. stimulus

im·pinge' (-pinj') *v.* 1. strike, hit, etc. (*on* or *upon*) 2. encroach (*on* or *upon*)

im'pi·ous (-pē-) *a.* not pious —**im·pi'e·ty** (-pī'-) *n.*

im·plac'a·ble (-plak'ə-, -plā'kə-) *a.* not to be appeased

im·plant' *v.* 1. plant firmly 2. inculcate 3. insert within the body

im·plau'si·ble *a.* not plausible

im'ple·ment *n.* tool or instrument —*v.* put into effect —**im'ple·men·ta'tion** *n.*

im'pli·cate *v.* show to be a party to a crime, etc.

im·pli·ca'tion *n.* 1. an implying or implicating 2. something implied

im·plic'it (-plis'-) *a.* 1. implied 2. absolute

im·plode' *v.* burst inward —**im·plo'sion** *n.*

im·plore' *v.* 1. ask earnestly for 2. beg to do something —**im·plor'ing·ly** *adv.*

im·ply' *v.* [-PLIED, -PLYING] 1. involve necessarily 2. hint; suggest

im·po·lite' *a.* discourteous

im·pol'i·tic *a.* unwise

im·pon'der·a·ble *a.* not measurable or explainable —*n.* anything imponderable

im·port' *v.* 1. bring (goods) into a country 2. signify —*n.* (im'pôrt) 1. thing imported 2. meaning 3. importance —**im'por·ta'tion** *n.*

im·por'tant *a.* 1. having much significance 2. having power or authority —**im·por'tance** *n.*

im·por·tune' (-tōōn') *v.* urge repeatedly —**im·por'tu·nate** (-chə nit) *a.* —**im'por·tu'ni·ty** [*pl.* -TIES] *n.*

im·pose' *v.* put on (a burden,

tax, etc.) —**impose on** (or **upon**) **1.** take advantage of **2.** cheat —im′**po·si′tion** n.

im·**pos′ing** a. impressive

im·**pos′si·ble** a. that cannot exist, be done, etc. —im·**pos′-si·bil′i·ty** [pl. -TIES] n.

im·**pos′tor** n. cheat pretending to be what he is not

im′**po·tent** a. **1.** lacking power; helpless **2.** unable to engage in sexual intercourse: said of males —im′**po·tence** n.

im·**pound′** v. seize by law

im·**pov′er·ish** v. make poor

im·**prac′ti·ca·ble** a. that cannot be put into practice

im·**prac′ti·cal** a. not practical

im′**pre·cate** v. to curse —im′**pre·ca′tion** n.

im·**pre·cise′** a. not precise; vague

im·**preg′na·ble** a. that cannot be overcome by force

im·**preg′nate** v. **1.** make pregnant **2.** saturate —im′**preg·na′tion** n.

im′**pre·sa′ri·o** (-sä′-) n. [pl. -OS] manager, as of concerts

im·**press′** v. **1.** to stamp **2.** affect the mind or emotions of **3.** fix in the memory —n. (im′pres) an imprint

im·**pres′sion** n. **1.** a mark **2.** effect produced on the mind **3.** vague notion **4.** amusing impersonation

im·**pres′sion·a·ble** a. sensitive; easily influenced

im·**pres′sion·ism** n. art, music, etc. reproducing the immediate, overall impression — im·**pres′sion·ist** a., n.

im·**pres′sive** a. eliciting wonder or admiration

im′**pri·ma′tur** (-mät′ər) n. permission, esp. to publish

im·**print′** v. mark or fix as by pressing —n. (im′print) **1.** a mark; print **2.** characteristic effect

im·**pris′on** v. put in prison

im·**prob′a·ble** a. unlikely

im·**promp′tu** a., adv. without preparation; offhand

im·**prop′er** a. **1.** not suitable **2.** incorrect **3.** not in good taste —im·**prop′er·ly** adv.

im·**pro′pri·e·ty** n. [pl. -TIES] improper act

im·**prove′** v. make or become better or more valuable —im·**prove′ment** n.

im·**prov′i·dent** a. unthrifty

im′**pro·vise′** v. **1.** compose and perform without preparation **2.** make or do with whatever is at hand —im·**prov′i·sa′tion** n.

im·**pru′dent** a. rash; indiscreet —im·**pru′dence** n.

im′**pu·dent** a. insolent —im′**pu·dence** n.

im·**pugn′** (-pyoon′) v. to challenge as false

im′**pulse** n. **1.** driving force; impetus **2.** sudden inclination to act —im·**pul′sive** a.

im·**pu′ni·ty** n. freedom from punishment or harm

im·**pure′** a. **1.** dirty **2.** immoral **3.** adulterated —im·**pu′ri·ty** [pl. -TIES] n.

im·**pute′** v. to attribute

in prep. **1.** contained by **2.** wearing **3.** during **4.** at the end of **5.** not beyond **6.** out of a group of **7.** amidst **8.** affected by **9.** with regard to **10.** using **11.** because of **12.** into —*adv.* **1.** to the inside **2.** to or at a certain place —*a.* **1.** that is in power **2.** inside **3.** gathered, counted, etc. **4.** [Col.] currently smart, popular, etc. —*n.* **1.** *pl.* those in power **2.** [Col.] special influence or favor —**have it in for** [Col.] hold a grudge against —**in that** because —**in with** associated with

in- *pref.* 1. in, into, or toward **2.** no, not, or lacking: for list below add *not* or *lack* of to meaning of base word

in'a·bil'i·ty
in'ac·ces'si·ble
in·ac'cu·ra·cy
in·ac'cu·rate
in·ac'tion
in·ac'tive
in·ad'e·qua·cy
in·ad'e·quate
in'ad·mis'si·ble
in'ad·vis'a·ble
in·an'i·mate
in·ap'pli·ca·ble
in'ap·pro'pri·ate
in·apt'
in'ar·tis'tic
in'au·di·ble
in'aus·pi'cious
in·ca'pa·ble
in·cau'tious
in'ci·vil'i·ty
in'com·bus'ti·ble
in·com·men'su·rate
in'com·mu'ni·ca·ble
in'com·pre·hen'si·ble
in'con·ceiv'a·ble
in'con·clu'sive

in'con·sist'en·cy
in'con·sist'ent
in'con·tro·vert'i·ble
in'cor·rect'
in·cur'a·ble
in·dec'o·rous
in·de·fin'a·ble
in'dis·cern'i·ble
in'dis·pu'ta·ble
in'dis·tinct'
in'dis·tin'guish·a·ble
in'di·vis'i·ble
in·ed'i·ble
in'ef·fec'tive
in'ef·fec'tu·al
in·ef'fi·ca·cy
in'e·las'tic
in·el'i·gi·ble
in'e·qual'i·ty
in·eq'ui·ta·ble
in·eq'ui·ty
in'ex·act'
in'ex·cus'a·ble
in'ex·pe'di·ent
in'ex·pen'sive
in·fer'tile
in'har·mo'ni·ous
in·hos'pi·ta·ble
in·hu·mane'
in'ju·di'cious
in·op'er·a·ble
in·op'por·tune'
in·sep'a·ra·ble
in'sig·nif'i·cance
in'sig·nif'i·cant
in·sol'v·a·ble
in'suf·fi'cient
in'sur·mount'a·ble
in'sus·cep'ti·ble
in·var'i·a·ble

in ab·sen'tia (-shə) although not present
in·ac'ti·vate *v.* make no longer active

in'ad·vert'ent a. 1. not attentive 2. due to oversight —**in'ad·vert'ence** n.

in·al'ien·a·ble (-āl'yən-) a. that cannot be taken away

in·ane' a. lacking sense; silly —**in·an'i·ty** n.

in·ar·tic'u·late a. 1. speaking or spoken unclearly 2. mute 3. not expressed

in·as·much' as 1. because 2. to the extent that

in·at·ten'tion n. failure to pay attention; negligence —**in'at·ten'tive** a.

in·au'gu·ral (-ô'gyə-) a. 1. of an inauguration 2. first —n. 1. speech at an inauguration 2. inauguration

in·au'gu·rate v. 1. formally induct into office 2. begin; open —**in·au'gu·ra'tion** n.

in'board adv., a. inside the hull of a boat —n. marine motor mounted inboard

in'born' a. present at birth; natural

in'bound' a. going inward

in'bred' a. 1. natural 2. resulting from inbreeding

in'breed' v. [-BRED, -BREED-ING] 1. breed by continually mating from the same stock 2. make or become too refined

in·cal'cu·la·ble a. too great to be calculated

in'can·des'cent a. 1. glowing with heat 2. very bright —**in'can·des'cence** n.

in'can·ta'tion n. words chanted in magic spells

in·ca·pac'i·tate (-pas'-) v. make unable or unfit

in·ca·pac'i·ty n. [pl. -TIES] 1. lack of capacity, power, etc. 2. legal incapacitation

in·car'cer·ate v. imprison —**in·car'cer·a'tion** n.

in·car'nate (-nit) a. in human form; personified —v. (-nāt) 1. give bodily form to 2. be the type of —**in·car'na'tion** n.

in·cen'di·ar'y a. 1. causing fires 2. stirring up strife —n. one who willfully sets fire to property

in·cense' n. 1. substance burned to produce a pleasant odor 2. this odor —v. (in sens') enrage

in·cen'tive n. motive or stimulus

in·cep'tion n. a beginning

in·ces'sant a. constant

in'cest n. sexual intercourse between close relatives —**in·ces'tu·ous** a.

inch n. measure of length, 1/12 foot —v. move very slowly, by degrees —**every inch** in all respects

in·cho'ate (-kō'it) a. 1. just begun 2. not yet clearly formed

in'ci·dence n. range of occurrence or effect

in'ci·dent n. 1. event, esp. a minor one 2. minor conflict

in'ci·den'tal a. 1. happening along with something more important 2. minor —n. 1. something incidental 2. pl. miscellaneous items —**in'ci·den'tal·ly** adv.

in·cin'er·ate v. burn to ashes —**in·cin'er·a'tion** n.

in·cin'er·a'tor n. furnace for burning trash

in·cip′i·ent *a.* just beginning to exist or appear

in·cise′ (-sīz′) *v.* cut into; engrave

in·ci′sion (-sizh′ən) *n.* 1. a cutting into 2. a cut; gash

in·ci′sive (-sī′siv) *a.* piercing; acute

in·ci′sor (-zər) *n.* any of the front cutting teeth

in·cite′ *v.* urge to action —**in·cite′ment** *n.*

in·clem′ent *a.* stormy

in′cli·na′tion *n.* 1. a bending or sloping 2. slope 3. bias; tendency 4. preference

in·cline′ (in klīn′) *v.* 1. lean; bend; slope 2. tend 3. have a preference 4. influence —*n.* (in′klīn) a slope

in·close′ *v.* enclose

in·clude′ *v.* have or take in as part of a whole; contain —**in·clu′sion** *n.*

in·clu′sive *a.* 1. including everything 2. including the limits mentioned

in·cog′ni·to (in′käg nē′tō, in käg′ni tō) *adv., a.* disguised under a false name

in′co·her′ent (-hir′-) *a.* 1. not logically connected 2. having incoherent speech, etc. —**in′co·her′ence** *n.*

in′come *n.* money one gets as wages, salary, rent, etc.

in′com·mu·ni·ca′do (-kä′-) *a.* not allowed to communicate

in·com′pa·ra·ble *a.* beyond comparison; matchless

in′com·pat′i·ble *a.* unable to be together harmoniously — **in′com·pat′i·bil′i·ty** *n.*

in·com′pe·tent *n., a.* (a

person) without adequate skill or knowledge —**in·com′pe·tence** *n.*

in′com·plete′ *a.* 1. lacking a part or parts 2. unfinished 3. not perfect

in′con·gru·ous *a.* 1. lacking harmony 2. unsuitable —**in′con·gru′i·ty** *n.*

in′con·se·quen′tial *a.* unimportant

in′con·sid′er·a·ble *a.* small

in′con·sid′er·ate (-it) *a.* without thought for others

in′con·sol′a·ble *a.* that cannot be comforted or cheered

in′con·spic′u·ous *a.* attracting little attention

in·con′stant *a.* changeable, fickle, irregular, etc. —**in·con′stan·cy** *n.*

in′con·test′a·ble *a.* certain

in·con′ti·nent *a.* unable to control one's actions, natural functions, etc. —**in·con′ti·nence** *n.*

in′con·ven′ience *n.* 1. lack of comfort, etc. 2. inconvenient thing —*v.* cause bother, etc. to —**in′con·ven′ient** *a.*

in·cor′po·rate *v.* 1. combine; include 2. merge 3. form (into) a corporation —**in·cor′po·ra′tion** *n.*

in′cor·ri·gi·ble *a.* too bad to be reformed

in′cor·rupt′i·ble *a.* that cannot be corrupted, esp. morally

in·crease′ *v.* make or become greater, larger, etc. —*n.* (in′krēs) 1. an increasing 2. amount of this

in·creas′ing·ly *adv.* more and more

in·cred'i·ble *a.* too unusual to be believed

in·cred'u·lous *a.* showing doubt —**in'cre·du'li·ty** *n.*

in'cre·ment *n.* 1. an increasing 2. amount of this

in·crim'i·nate *v.* involve in, or make appear guilty of, a crime

in·crust' *v.* cover with, or form into, a crust

in'cu·bate (-kya-) *v.* 1. sit on and hatch (eggs) 2. keep in a favorable environment for developing —**in'cu·ba'tion** *n.*

in'cu·ba'tor *n.* 1. heated container for hatching eggs 2. similar device in which premature babies are kept

in·cul'cate *v.* fix in the mind, as by insistent urging

in·cum'bent *a.* resting (*on* or *upon* one) as a duty —*n.* holder of an office, etc.

in·cur' *v.* [-CURRED, -CURRING] bring upon oneself

in·cur'sion *n.* raid

in·debt'ed *a.* 1. in debt 2. owing gratitude

in·debt'ed·ness *n.* 1. a being indebted 2. amount owed

in·de'cent *a.* 1. improper 2. obscene —**in·de'cen·cy** *n.*

in'de·ci'pher·a·ble *a.* illegible

in'de·ci'sion *n.* inability to decide —**in'de·ci'sive** *a.*

in·deed' *adv.* certainly —*int.* exclamation of surprise, doubt, sarcasm, etc.

in'de·fat'i·ga·ble *a.* not tiring; tireless

in'de·fen'si·ble *a.* that cannot be defended or justified

in·def'i·nite (-nit) *a.* 1. having no exact limits 2. not precise in meaning 3. not certain

in·del'i·ble *a.* that cannot be erased, washed out, etc.

in·del'i·cate (-kit) *a.* lacking propriety; coarse

in·dem'ni·fy *v.* [-FIED, -FYING] repay for or insure against loss —**in·dem'ni·ty** *n.*

in·dent' *v.* 1. to notch, dent, etc. 2. space in from the regular margin

in'den·ta'tion *n.* 1. a notch, dent, etc. 2. spacing in from the margin: also **in·den'tion**

in·den'ture *v.* bind by a contract to work for another

in'de·pend'ent *a.* not ruled, controlled, supported, etc. by others —**in'de·pend'ence** *n.*

in'-depth' *a.* thorough

in'de·scrib'a·ble *a.* beyond the power of description

in'de·struct'i·ble *a.* that cannot be destroyed

in'de·ter'mi·nate (-nit) *a.* not definite; vague

in'dex *n.* [*pl.* -DEXES, -DICES (-də sēz)] 1. forefinger: also **index finger** 2. indication 3. alphabetical list of names, etc. in a book showing pages where they can be found

In'di·an *n., a.* 1. (native) of India 2. (member) of any of the aboriginal races of the Western Hemisphere: also **American Indian**

in'di·cate *v.* 1. point out; show 2. be a sign of —**in'di·ca'tion** *n.* —**in·dic'a·tive** *a.* —**in'di·ca'tor** *n.*

in·dict' (-dīt') *v.* charge with a crime —**in·dict'ment** *n.*

in·dif'fer·ent *a.* 1. neutral 2. unconcerned 3. of no importance 4. fair; average —in·dif'fer·ence *n.*

in·dig'e·nous (-dij'-) *a.* native

in'di·gent *a.* poor; needy —*n.* indigent person —in'di·gence *n.*

in'di·gest'i·ble *a.* not easily digested

in'di·ges'tion *n.* difficulty in digesting food

in·dig'nant *a.* angry at unjust or mean action —in'dig·na'tion *n.*

in·dig'ni·ty *n.* [*pl.* -TIES] an insult to one's pride

in'di·go *n.* 1. blue dye 2. deep violet-blue

in'di·rect' *a.* 1. not straight 2. not immediate —in'di·rect'ly *adv.*

in'dis·creet' *a.* unwise

in'dis·cre'tion *n.* indiscreet act or remark

in'dis·crim'i·nate (-nit) *a.* making no distinctions

in'dis·pen'sa·ble *a.* absolutely necessary

in'dis·posed' *a.* 1. slightly ill 2. unwilling

in'dis·sol'u·ble *a.* that cannot be dissolved or destroyed

in'di·vid'u·al *n.* single person, thing, or being —*a.* 1. single 2. of, for, or typical of an individual —in'di·vid'u·al·ly *adv.*

in'di·vid'u·al·ism *n.* leading of one's life in one's own way —in'di·vid'u·al·ist *n.*

in'di·vid'u·al'i·ty *n.* distinct characteristics

in·doc'tri·nate *v.* teach a doc-trine or belief to —in·doc'tri·na'tion *n.*

in'do·lent *a.* idle; lazy —in'do·lence *n.*

in·dom'i·ta·ble *a.* unyielding; unconquerable

in'door' *a.* being, belonging, done, etc. in a building

in'doors' *adv.* in or into a building

in·du'bi·ta·ble *a.* that cannot be doubted

in·duce' *v.* 1. persuade 2. bring on; cause 3. draw (a conclusion) from facts

in·duce'ment *n.* 1. an inducing 2. motive; incentive

in·duct' *v.* 1. install in an office, a society, etc. 2. bring into the armed forces

in·duct·ee' *n.* one inducted, esp. into the armed forces

in·duc'tion *n.* 1. an inducting 2. a coming to a general conclusion from particular facts

in·dulge' *v.* 1. satisfy a desire 2. gratify the wishes of —in·dul'gence *n.* —in·dul'gent *a.*

in·dus'tri·al *a.* having to do with industries or people working in industry

in·dus'tri·al·ist *n.* owner or manager of a large industry

in·dus'tri·al·ize' *v.* build up industries in

industrial park area zoned for industry and business

in·dus'tri·ous *a.* working hard and steadily

in'dus·try *n.* [*pl.* -TRIES] 1. steady effort 2. any branch of manufacture or trade

-ine *suf.* of or like

in·e′bri·ate v. make drunk — n. (-it) drunkard —**in·e′bri·a′tion** n.

in·ef′fa·ble a. 1. inexpressible 2. too sacred to be spoken

in′ef·fi′cient a. 1. not efficient 2. incapable —**in′ef·fi′cien·cy** n.

in·el′e·gant a. crude; coarse

in′e·luc′ta·ble a. not to be avoided or escaped

in·ept′ a. 1. unfit 2. foolish 3. awkward; clumsy —**in·ept′i·tude, in·ept′ness** n.

in·ert′ a. 1. unable to move 2. dull; slow 3. without active properties

in·er′tia (-sha) n. 1. tendency of matter to remain at rest, or to continue moving in a fixed direction 2. unwillingness to act

in′es·cap′a·ble a. that cannot be escaped

in·es′ti·ma·ble a. too great to be estimated

in·ev′i·ta·ble a. certain to happen —**in·ev′i·ta·bil′i·ty** n.

in′ex·haust′i·ble (-ig zôst′-) a. 1. that cannot be used up or emptied 2. tireless

in·ex′o·ra·ble a. unrelenting —**in·ex′o·ra·bly** adv.

in′ex·pe′ri·enced a. lacking experience or skill

in·ex′pert a. not skillful

in·ex′pli·ca·ble a. that cannot be explained

in′ex·press′i·ble a. that cannot be expressed

in′ex·tin′guish·a·ble a. that cannot be put out or stopped

in·ex′tri·ca·ble a. 1. that one

cannot get free from 2. that cannot be disentangled

in·fal′li·ble a. 1. never wrong 2. dependable

in′fa·mous a. 1. notorious 2. scandalous

in′fa·my (-fə mē) n. 1. disgrace 2. great wickedness

in′fant n. baby —a. 1. of infants 2. in an early stage — **in′fan·cy** n. —**in′fan·tile** a.

in′fan·try n. soldiers trained to fight on foot —**in′fan·try·man** [pl. -MEN] n.

in·farct′ (-färkt′) n. area of dying tissue: also **in·farc′tion** n.

in·fat′u·ate (-fach′ʊ-) v. inspire with foolish love or affection —**in·fat′u·a′tion** n.

in·fect′ v. make diseased

in·fec′tion n. infectious disease

in·fec′tious a. 1. caused by microorganisms in the body 2. tending to spread to others

in′fe·lic′i·tous (-lis′-) a. unsuitable; not apt

in·fer′ (-fur′) v. [-FERRED, -FERRING] conclude by reasoning —**in′fer·ence** n.

in·fe′ri·or a. 1. lower in space, order, status, etc. 2. poor in quality —**in·fe′ri·or′i·ty** n.

in·fer′nal a. of hell; hellish

in·fer′no n. [pl. -NOS] hell

in·fest′ v. overrun in large numbers

in′fi·del n. one who rejects (a) religion

in′fi·del′i·ty n. unfaithfulness

in′field n. Baseball 1. area enclosed by base lines 2. players (**infielders**) positioned there

in′fight′ing n. personal conflict within a group

in·fil′trate v. 1. filter or pass through 2. penetrate gradually or stealthily —**in′fil·tra′tion** n.

in′fi·nite (-nit) a. 1. lacking limits; endless 2. vast

in·fin·i·tes′i·mal a. too small to be measured

in·fin′i·tive n. form of a verb without reference to person, tense, etc.

in·fin′i·ty n. unlimited space, time, or quantity

in·firm′ a. weak; feeble

in·firm′i·ty n. [pl. -TIES] physical weakness or defect

in·fir′ma·ry n. [pl. -RIES] hospital

in·flame′ v. 1. arouse, excite, etc. 2. make red, sore, and swollen —**in′flam·ma′tion** n. —**in·flam′ma·to′ry** a.

in·flam′ma·ble (-flam′-) a. 1. flammable 2. easily excited

in·flate′ v. make swell out, as with gas

in·fla′tion n. 1. an inflating 2. increase in the currency in circulation resulting in a fall in its value and a rise in prices —**in·fla′tion·ar′y** a.

in·flect′ v. 1. vary the tone of (the voice) 2. change the form of (a word) to show tense, etc. —**in·flec′tion** n.

in·flex′i·ble a. stiff, fixed, unyielding, etc.

in·flict′ v. cause to suffer (a wound, punishment, etc.) —**in·flic′tion** n.

in′flight′ a. done while an aircraft is in flight

in′flo·res′cence n. 1. producing of blossoms 2. flowers

in′flu·ence n. 1. power to affect others 2. one with such power —v. have an effect on —**in′flu·en′tial** a.

in′flu·en′za n. acute, contagious virus disease

in′flux n. a flowing in

in·form′ v. give information (to) —**in·form′er** n.

in·for′mal a. 1. not following fixed rules 2. casual, relaxed, etc. 3. not requiring formal dress 4. colloquial —**in·for·mal′i·ty** [pl. -TIES] n. —**in·for′mal·ly** adv.

in·form′ant n. person who gives information

in′for·ma′tion n. news or knowledge imparted —**in·form′a·tive** a.

infra- pref. below

in·frac′tion n. violation of a law, etc.

in·fran′gi·ble (-jə-) a. unbreakable

in′fra·red′ a. of those invisible rays having a penetrating, heating effect

in′fra·struc′ture n. basic installations and facilities

in·fre′quent a. happening seldom; rare

in·fringe′ v. break (a law, etc.) —**infringe on** (or **upon**) encroach on (one's rights) —**in·fringe′ment** n.

in·fu′ri·ate v. enrage

in·fuse′ v. 1. instill 2. inspire 3. to steep —**in·fu′sion** n.

-ing suf. used to form the present participle

in·gen′ious (-jēn′-) a. clever; resourceful —**in′ge·nu′i·ty** (-jə nōō′-) n.

in·gé·nue (an'zhə nōō') *n.* role of an inexperienced young woman in a play, etc.

in·gen'u·ous (-jen'-) *a.* 1. frank 2. naive

in·glo'ri·ous *a.* disgraceful

in·got (iŋ'gət) *n.* mass of metal cast as a bar, etc.

in·grained' *a.* firmly fixed

in'grate *n.* ungrateful person

in·gra'ti·ate (-shē-) *v.* get (oneself) into another's favor

in·grat'i·tude *n.* lack of gratitude

in·gre'di·ent *n.* component part of a mixture

in'gress *n.* entrance

in'grown *a.* grown inward, esp. into the flesh

in·hab'it *v.* live in

in·hab'it·ant *n.* person or animal inhabiting a place

in·hal'ant *n.* medicine, etc. to be inhaled

in'ha·la'tor *n.* 1. apparatus used to inhale medicinal vapors 2. respirator

in·hale' *v.* breathe in —**in'ha·la'tion** *n.*

in·hal'er *n.* 1. respirator 2. inhalator (*sense* 1)

in·her'ent (-hir'-, -her'-) *a.* inborn; natural; basic

in·her'it *v.* 1. receive as an heir 2. have by heredity —**in·her'it·ance** *n.*

in·hib'it *v.* restrain; check —**in'hi·bi'tion** *n.*

in·hu'man *a.* cruel, brutal, etc. —**in'hu·man'i·ty** *n.*

in·im'i·cal *a.* 1. hostile 2. adverse; harmful

in·im'i·ta·ble *a.* that cannot be imitated

in·iq'ui·ty (-ik'wə-) *n.* 1. wickedness 2. [*pl.* -TIES] wicked or unjust act —**in·iq'ui·tous** *a.*

in·i'tial (i nish'əl) *a.* first —*n.* first letter of a name —*v.* mark with one's initials —**in·i'tial·ly** *adv.*

in·i'ti·ate (i nish'ē-) *v.* 1. begin to use 2. teach the fundamentals to 3. admit as a new member —**in·i'ti·a'tion** *n.*

in·i'ti·a·tive *n.* 1. first step 2. ability to get things started 3. introduction of legislation by voters' petitions

in·ject' *v.* 1. force (a fluid) into tissue, etc. with a syringe, etc. 2. throw in; insert —**in·jec'tion** *n.*

in·junc'tion *n.* order or command, esp. of a court

in·jure *v.* 1. do harm to; hurt 2. wrong or offend

in·ju'ri·ous *a.* harmful

in'ju·ry *n.* [*pl.* -RIES] harm or wrong

in·jus'tice *n.* 1. a being unjust 2. unjust act

ink *n.* colored liquid for writing, printing, etc. with ink —*v.* mark or color with ink

ink'blot *n.* pattern of blots of ink used in a psychological test

ink'ling *n.* hint or notion

ink'y *a.* [-IER, -IEST] dark

in'land *a., adv.* in or toward a country's interior

in'-law *n.* [Col.] a relative by marriage

in'lay *v.* [-LAID, -LAYING] decorate a surface with pieces of wood, etc. set in —*n.* [*pl.*

-LAYS] 1. inlaid decoration 2. filling in a tooth

in'let n. narrow strip of water going into land

in'mate n. one kept in a prison, hospital, etc.

in'most a. 1. farthest within 2. most secret

inn n. hotel or restaurant

in'nate a. inborn; natural

in'ner a. 1. farther in 2. more secret

inner city crowded or blighted central section of a city

in'ner·most a. inmost

in'ner·sole n. insole

in'ning n. Baseball round of play in which both teams have a turn at bat

in'no·cent a. 1. without sin 2. not guilty 3. harmless 4. artless —n. innocent person —**in'no·cence** n.

in·noc'u·ous a. harmless

in'no·va'tion n. new method, device, etc. —**in'no·va'tor** n.

in'nu·en'do n. [pl. -DOES, -DOS] hint or sly remark

in·nu'mer·a·ble a. too numerous to be counted

in·oc'u·late v. inject a vaccine so as to immunize —**in·oc'u·la'tion** n.

in·of·fen'sive a. causing no harm or annoyance

in·op'er·a·tive a. not working or functioning

in·or'di·nate (-nit) a. excessive

in'or·gan'ic a. not living; not animal or vegetable

in'put n. what is put in, as power into a machine, information into a computer, etc.

in'quest n. judicial inquiry, as by a coroner

in·quire' v. 1. ask; question 2. investigate (into) —**in·quir'y** [pl. -IES] n.

in'qui·si'tion n. 1. investigation 2. strict suppression, as of heretics by a tribunal —**in·quis'i·tor** n.

in·quis'i·tive a. asking many questions; prying

in'roads n.pl. injurious encroachments

in·sane' a. 1. mentally ill 2. of or for insane people 3. very foolish —**in·san'i·ty** n.

in·sa'tia·ble (-sha b'l) a. that cannot be satisfied

in·scribe' v. mark or engrave (words, etc.) on —**in·scrip'tion** n.

in·scru'ta·ble a. that cannot be understood

in'sect n. small animal with six legs, as a fly

in·sec'ti·cide n. substance used to kill insects

in·se·cure' a. 1. not safe 2. anxious 3. not firm —**in·se·cu'ri·ty** n.

in·sem'i·nate v. 1. fertilize; impregnate 2. imbue —**in·sem'i·na'tion** n.

in·sen'sate a. 1. not feeling 2. unfeeling; cold

in·sen'si·ble a. 1. unconscious 2. unaware

in·sen'si·tive a. not sensitive or responsive —**in·sen'si·tiv'i·ty** n.

in·sert' v. put into something else —n. (in'sart) thing inserted —**in·ser'tion** n.

in·set' v. set in —n. (in'set) something inserted

in'shore' adv., a. near or in toward the shore

in'side' n. 1. inner side or part 2. pl. [Col.] the viscera —a. 1. internal 2. secret —adv. (in sīd') 1. within 2. indoors —prep. (in sīd') 1. within 2. indoors —**inside of** within the time of

in'sid'er n. one having confidential information

in·sid'i·ous a. sly, treacherous, tricky, etc.

in'sight' n. understanding of a thing's true nature

in·sig'ni·a n.pl. badges, emblems, etc., as of rank or membership

in·sin·cere' a. deceptive or hypocritical —**in'sin·cer'i·ty** n.

in·sin'u·ate' v. 1. hint; imply 2. to get in artfully —**in·sin'·u·a'tion** n.

in·sip'id a. tasteless; dull

in·sist' v. 1. demand strongly 2. maintain a stand —**in·sist'·ence** n. —**in·sist'ent** a.

in·so·far' adv. to the degree that (with as)

in'sole' n. 1. inside sole 2. extra, removable inside sole

in'so·lent a. showing disrespect —**in'so·lence** n.

in·sol'u·ble a. that cannot be solved or dissolved

in·sol'vent a. bankrupt —**in·sol'ven·cy** n.

in·som'ni·a n. abnormal inability to sleep —**in·som'·ni·ac** (-ak) n.

in'so·much' adv. 1. to such an extent 2. inasmuch

in·sou'ci·ant (-sōō'sē-) a. calm; carefree

in·spect' v. 1. look at carefully 2. examine officially —**in·spec'tion** n. —**in·spec'tor** n.

in·spire' v. 1. stimulate, as to a creative effort 2. arouse (a feeling) 3. inhale —**in·spi·ra'·tion** n.

in'stant·ly adv.

in·sta·bil'i·ty n. lack of firmness, determination, etc.

in·stall', in·stal' v. 1. put formally in office 2. establish in a place 3. fix in place for use —**in·stal·la'tion** n.

in·stall'ment, in·stal'ment n. any of the several parts of a payment, serial, etc.

installment plan system by which debts, as for purchases, are paid in installments

in'stance n. 1. example 2. occasion 3. instigation

in'stant a. 1. immediate 2. quick to prepare —n. moment —**in'stant·ly** adv.

in'stan·ta'ne·ous a. done or happening in an instant

in·stead' adv. in place of the other

in'step' n. upper surface of the arch of the foot

in'sti·gate' v. urge on to an action; incite —**in'sti·ga'tion** n. —**in'sti·ga'tor** n.

in·still', in·stil' v. 1. put in drop by drop 2. put (an idea, etc.) in gradually

in'stinct n. 1. inborn tendency to do a certain thing 2. knack —**in·stinc'tive** a.

in'sti·tute' v. 1. establish 2. start —n. organization for promoting art, science, etc.

in·sti·tu·tion n. 1. establishment 2. established law, custom, etc. 3. organization having social or educational purpose 4. [Col.] person or thing long established —**in'sti·tu'tion·al** a.

in·sti·tu·tion·al·ize' v. 1. make into an institution 2. place in an institution

in·struct' v. 1. teach 2. to order or direct —**in·struc'tion** n. —**in·struc'tive** a. —**in·struc'tor** n.

in'stru·ment n. 1. means; agent 2. tool or device for doing exact work 3. device producing musical sound

in'stru·men'tal a. 1. serving as a means 2. of, for, or by musical instruments

in'stru·men·tal'i·ty n. [pl. -TIES] means; agency

in'sub·or'di·nate (-nit) a. disobedient

in'sub·stan'tial (-shəl) a. 1. unreal 2. weak or flimsy

in·suf'fer·a·ble a. intolerable

in'su·lar a. 1. of an island 2. narrow in outlook

in'su·late v. 1. protect with a material to prevent the loss of electricity, heat, etc. 2. set apart —**in'su·la'tion** n. —**in'su·la'tor** n.

in'su·lin n. pancreatic hormone used to treat diabetes

in'sult n. act or remark meant to hurt one's feelings —v. (in sult') subject to an insult

in·su'per·a·ble a. that cannot be overcome

in·sur'ance (-shoor'-) n. 1. an insuring 2. contract whereby a company guarantees payment for a loss, death, etc. 3. amount for which a thing is insured

in·sure' v. 1. make sure 2. protect 3. get or give insurance on

in·sured' n. person insured against loss

in·sur'er n. company that insures others against loss

in·sur'gent a. rising up in revolt; rebelling —n. a rebel —**in·sur'gence** n.

in'sur·rec'tion n. rebellion

in·tact' a. kept whole

in·tagl'io (-tal'yō) n. [pl. -IOS] design carved below the surface

in'take n. 1. amount taken in 2. place in a pipe, etc. where fluid is taken in

in·tan'gi·ble (-jə-) a. 1. that cannot be touched 2. representing value, as stocks 3. vague —n. something intangible

in'te·ger (-jər) n. whole number

in'te·gral a. 1. essential to completeness 2. entire

in'te·grate v. 1. form into a whole; unify 2. desegregate —**in'te·gra'tion** n.

integrated circuit electronic circuit on a chip of semiconductor material

in·teg'ri·ty n. 1. honesty, sincerity, etc. 2. wholeness

in·teg'u·ment n. skin, rind, shell, etc.

in'tel·lect n. 1. ability to reason 2. high intelligence 3. very intelligent person

in·tel·lec'tu·al *a.* 1. of the intellect 2. needing or showing high intelligence —*n.* one with intellectual interests

in·tel·loo'tu·al·ize' *v.* examine rationally, not emotionally

in·tel'li·gence *n.* 1. ability to learn, or solve problems 2. news or information 3. those who gather secret information, as for the police

in·tel'li·gent *a.* clever, wise, etc.

in·tel'li·gi·ble *a.* that can be understood; clear

in·tem'per·ate (-it) *a.* 1. not moderate; excessive 2. drinking too much liquor

in·tend' *v.* 1. to plan; purpose 2. to mean

in·tend'ed *n.* [Col.] one's prospective wife or husband

in·tense' *a.* 1. very strong, great, deep, etc. 2. very emotional

in·ten'si·fy *v.* [-FIED, -FYING] make or become more intense —**in·ten·si·fi·ca'tion** *n.*

in·ten'si·ty *n.* [*pl.* -TIES] 1. great energy or vehemence 2. amount of force or energy

in·ten'sive *a.* 1. thorough 2. *Gram.* emphasizing

in·tent' *a.* firmly fixed in attention or purpose —*n.* purpose; intention —**to all intents and purposes** in almost every respect

in·ten'tion *n.* thing intended or planned; purpose —**in·ten'tion·al** *a.*

in·ter' (-tur') *v.* [-TERRED, -TERRING] bury

inter- *pref.* 1. between; among 2. with each other

in·ter·breed' *v.* [-BRED, -BREEDING] hybridize

in·ter·cede' (-sēd') *v.* 1. plead for another 2. mediate —**in'ter·ces'sion** *n.*

in·ter·cept' *v.* seize or interrupt on the way —**in'ter·cep'tion** *n.*

in·ter·change' *v.* 1. exchange 2. alternate —*n.* (in'tər chānj) 1. an interchanging 2. traffic entrance or exit on a freeway —**in'ter·change'a·ble** *a.*

in'ter·col·le'giate *a.* between or among colleges

in'ter·com *n.* communication system, as between rooms

in'ter·con·nect' *v.* connect with one another

in'ter·con·ti·nen'tal *a.* able to travel between continents

in'ter·course *n.* 1. dealings between people, countries, etc. 2. sexual union

in'ter·de·nom'i·na'tion·al *a.* between or among religious denominations

in'ter·de·pend'ence *n.* mutual dependence

in·ter·dict' *v.* 1. prohibit 2. restrain —*n.* prohibition —**in'ter·dic'tion** *n.*

in'ter·est *n.* 1. feeling of curiosity or concern 2. thing causing this feeling 3. share in something 4. welfare; benefit 5. group with a common concern 6. (rate of) payment for the use of money —*v.* have the interest or attention of

in'ter·est·ed *a.* 1. influenced

by personal interest 2. feeling or showing interest

in'ter·est·ing *a.* exciting curiosity or attention

in'ter·face *n.* surface forming a common boundary between two parts

in·ter·fere' *v.* 1. come between; intervene 2. meddle —interfere with hinder —in'ter·fer'ence *n.*

in'ter·im *n.* time between; meantime —*a.* temporary

in·te'ri·or *a.* 1. inner 2. inland 3. private —*n.* 1. interior part 2. domestic affairs of a country

in·ter·ject' *v.* throw in between; insert

in·ter·jec'tion *n.* 1. an interjecting 2. thing interjected 3. *Gram.* exclamation

in·ter·lace' *v.* join as by weaving together

in·ter·lard' *v.* intersperse

in·ter·line' *v.* write between the lines of

in·ter·lock' *v.* lock together

in·ter·loc'u·to·ry *a. Law* not final, as a decree

in'ter·lop'er *n.* intruder

in'ter·lude *n.* thing that fills time, as music between acts of a play

in·ter·mar'ry *v.* [-RIED, -RY-ING] marry, as persons of different races, religions, etc. —in'ter·mar'riage *n.*

in'ter·me'di·ar'y *a.* intermediate —*n.* [*pl.* -IES] go-between

in'ter·me'di·ate (-it) *a.* in the middle; between

in·ter'ment *n.* burial

in'ter·mez'zo (-met'sō) *n.* [*pl.* -ZOS, -ZI (-sē)] short musical piece

in·ter'mi·na·ble *a.* lasting, or seeming to last, forever

in'ter·min'gle *v.* mix together

in'ter·mis'sion *n.* interval, as between acts of a play

in·ter·mit'tent *a.* periodic; recurring at intervals

in·tern' *n.* 1. doctor in training at a hospital 2. apprentice teacher, etc. Also sp. interne —*v.* (in turn') 1. serve as an intern 2. confine in an area —in·tern'ment *n.*

in·ter'nal *a.* 1. inner 2. for inside the body 3. intrinsic 4. domestic

in·ter'nal·ize *v.* make part of one's own thinking, etc.

in'ter·na'tion·al *a.* 1. among nations 2. for all nations —in'ter·na'tion·al·ize' *v.*

in'ter·ne'cine (-nē'sin) *a.* destructive to both sides

in'ter·nist *n.* non-surgical doctor

in'ter·of'fice *a.* between offices of an organization

in'ter·per'son·al *a.* between persons

in'ter·plan'e·tar'y *a.* between planets

in'ter·play *n.* action or influence on each other

in·ter'po·late *v.* to insert (extra words, etc.)

in·ter·pose' *v.* place or come between; interrupt

in·ter'pret *v.* explain or translate —in·ter'pre·ta'tion *n.* —in·ter'pret·er *n.* —in·ter'pre·tive *a.*

in'ter·ra'cial *a.* among or for persons of different races

in'ter·re·lat'ed *a.* closely connected with one another

in·ter'ro·gate (-ter'-) *v.* question formally —in·ter'ro·ga'tion *n.*

in'ter·rog'a·tive *n., a.* (word) asking a question

in·ter·rupt' *v.* 1. break in on (talk, etc.) 2. obstruct —in'ter·rup'tion *n.*

in'ter·scho·las'tic *a.* between or among schools

in'ter·sect' *v.* 1. divide by passing across 2. cross each other

in'ter·sec'tion *n.* 1. an intersecting 2. place where two roads, etc. meet or cross

in'ter·sperse' *v.* to scatter among other things

in'ter·state' *a.* between or among states of a country

in·ter'stice (-stis) *n.* crevice

in'ter·twine' *v.* twist together

in'ter·ur'ban *a.* going between towns or cities

in'ter·val *n.* 1. space between things 2. time between events 3. difference in musical pitch —at intervals now and then

in'ter·vene' *v.* 1. come or be between 2. come in so as to help settle something

in'ter·ven'tion *n.* 1. an intervening 2. interference in the affairs of others

in'ter·view *n.* 1. meeting of people, as to confer, ask questions, etc. 2. published account of this —*v.* have an interview with —in'ter·view·ee' *n.* —in'ter·view'er *n.*

in·tes'tate *a.* not having made a will

in·tes'tine (-tin) *n. usually pl.* alimentary canal from the stomach to the anus —in·tes'ti·nal *a.*

in'ti·mate *v.* hint —*a.* (-mit) 1. most personal 2. very familiar —*n.* intimate friend —in'ti·ma·cy [*pl.* -CIES] *n.* —in'ti·ma'tion *n.*

in·tim'i·date *v.* make afraid as with threats —in·tim'i·da'tion *n.*

in'to *prep.* 1. toward and within 2. to the form, state, etc. of 3. so as to strike 4. [Col.] involved in

in·tol'er·a·ble *a.* too painful to be endured

in·tol'er·ant *a.* unwilling to tolerate others' beliefs, etc. —in·tol'er·ance *n.*

in'to·na'tion *n.* 1. manner of producing tones with accurate pitch 2. variations in pitch within an utterance

in·tone' *v.* utter in a chant

in to'to (tō'tō) [L.] as a whole

in·tox'i·cate *v.* 1. make drunk 2. excite greatly —in·tox'i·cant *n.* —in·tox'i·ca'tion *n.*

intra- *pref.* within; inside

in·trac'ta·ble *a.* unruly

in'tra·mu'ral *a.* among members of a school or college

in·tran'si·gent (-jənt) *a.* refusing to compromise —in·tran'si·gence *n.*

in·tran'si·tive *a.* not taking a direct object, as some verbs

in'tra·ve'nous *a.* into or within a vein

in·trep'id *a.* fearless

in'tri·cate (-kit) *a.* hard to follow because complicated —in'tri·ca·cy [*pl.* -CIES] *n.*

in·trigue' (-trēg') *v.* 1. plot secretly 2. excite the curiosity of —*n.* 1. secret plot 2. secret love affair

in·trin'sic *a.* real; essential — in·trin'si·cal·ly *adv.*

in·tro·duce' *v.* 1. insert 2. bring into use 3. make acquainted with 4. give experience of 5. begin

in'tro·duc'tion *n.* 1. an introducing 2. preliminary section of a book, etc.

in'tro·duc'to·ry *a.* preliminary

in'tro·spec'tion *n.* a looking into one's own thoughts, feelings, etc. —in'tro·spec'tive *a.*

in'tro·vert *n.* one more interested in his inner feelings than in external events

in·trude' *v.* force oneself upon others without welcome —in·trud'er *n.* —in·tru'sion *n.* —in·tru'sive *a.*

in·tu·i'tion (-ish'ən) *n.* immediate knowledge of something without conscious reasoning —in·tu'i·tive *a.*

in'un·date *v.* flood —in'un·da'tion *n.*

in·ure' (-yoor') *v.* accustom to pain, trouble, etc.

in·vade' *v.* 1. enter forcibly or hostilely 2. intrude upon —in·vad'er *n.* —in·va'sion *n.*

in'va·lid *n.* one who is ill or disabled

in·val'id *a.* not valid; null

in·val'i·date *v.* make invalid; deprive of legal force

in·val'u·a·ble *a.* priceless

in·vec'tive *n.* strong critical or abusive language

in·veigh' (-vā') *v.* talk or write bitterly (*against*)

in·vei'gle (-vē'-, -vā'-) *v.* trick or lure into an action

in·vent' *v.* 1. produce (a new device) 2. think up —in·ven'tor *a.*

in·ven'tion *n.* 1. an inventing 2. power of inventing 3. something invented —in·ven'tive *a.*

in'ven·to·ry *n.* [*pl.* -RIES] complete list or stock of goods

in·verse' (*or* in'vurs) *a.* inverted; directly opposite —*n.* inverse thing

in·vert' *v.* 1. turn upside down 2. reverse —in·ver'sion *n.*

in·ver'te·brate *n., a.* (animal) having no backbone

in·vest' *v.* 1. install in office 2. furnish with authority 3. put (money) into business, etc. for profit —in·ves'tor *n.*

in·ves'ti·gate *v.* search (into); examine —in·ves'ti·ga'tor *n.*

in·ves'ti·ga'tion *n.* careful search; systematic inquiry

in·ves'ti·ture *n.* formal investing, as with an office

in·vest'ment *n.* 1. an investing 2. money invested 3. that in which money is invested

in·vet'er·ate (-it) *a.* firmly fixed; habitual

in·vid'i·ous *a.* offensive, as an unfair comparison

in·vig'or·ate *v.* fill with energy; enliven

in·vin'ci·ble *a.* unconquerable —in·vin'ci·bil'i·ty *n.*

in·vi'o·la·ble a. not to be profaned or injured

in·vi'o·late (-lit) a. kept sacred or unbroken

in·vis'i·ble (-viz'-) a. 1. not visible 2. out of sight 3. imperceptible —**in·vis'i·bil'i·ty** n. —**in·vis'i·bly** adv.

in'vi·ta'tion n. 1. an inviting 2. message used in inviting

in'vi·ta'tion·al a. only for those invited to take part

in·vite' v. 1. ask (a person) to come somewhere or do something 2. request 3. give occasion for 4. tempt —n. [Col.] invitation

in·vit'ing a. tempting

in·vo·ca'tion n. prayer for blessing, help, etc.

in'voice n. itemized list of goods shipped to a buyer, stating prices, etc.

in·voke' v. call on (God, etc.) for help, etc.

in·vol'un·tar'y a. 1. not done by choice 2. not consciously controlled

in'vo·lu'tion n. 1. entanglement 2. intricacy

in·volve' v. 1. complicate 2. draw into difficulty, etc. 3. include 4. require 5. occupy the attention of —**in·volve'ment** n.

in·vul'ner·a·ble a. 1. that cannot be injured 2. proof against attack

in'ward a. 1. internal 2. directed toward the inside —adv. 1. toward the inside 2. into the mind or soul Also **in'wards** adv. —**in'ward·ly** adv.

i'o·dine n. chemical element used in medicine, etc.

i'o·dize v. treat with iodine

i'on n. electrically charged atom or group of atoms

-ion suf. 1. act or state of 2. result of

i'on·ize v. dissociate into ions or become electrically charged —**i'on·i·za'tion** n.

i·on'o·sphere n. outer layers of earth's atmosphere

i·o'ta (ī-) n. a jot

IOU signed note acknowledging a debt

-ious suf. having; characterized by

ip'e·cac (-kak) n. emetic made from a plant root

ip'so fac'to [L.] by the fact (or act) itself

IQ, I.Q. number showing one's level of intelligence, based on a test

i·ras'ci·ble (-ras'ə-) a. easily angered

i·rate' a. angry

ire n. anger

ir'i·des'cent a. showing a play of rainbowlike colors —**ir'i·des'cence** n.

i'ris n. 1. colored part of the eye, around the pupil 2. plant with sword-shaped leaves and showy flowers

I'rish a., n. (of) the people or language of Ireland

irk (urk) v. annoy; tire

irk'some a. annoying

i'ron n. 1. strong metal that is a chemical element 2. device used for pressing cloth 3. pl. iron shackles —a. 1. of iron 2. strong —v. press with a hot iron —**iron out** smooth away

i′ron·clad *a.* **1.** covered with iron **2.** difficult to change or break

i·ron′i·cal *a.* **1.** opposite of what is meant or expected **2.** using irony Also **i·ron′ic**

iron lung large respirator enclosing the body

i′ro·ny *n.* [*pl.* -NIES] **1.** expression in which what is meant is the opposite of what is said **2.** event that is the opposite of what is expected

ir·ra′di·ate *v.* **1.** shine (upon) **2.** enlighten **3.** radiate **4.** expose to X-rays

ir·ra′tion·al *a.* **1.** lacking the power to reason **2.** senseless; absurd

ir·rec′on·cil′a·ble *a.* that cannot be reconciled or made to agree

ir·re·deem′a·ble *a.* that cannot be bought back, changed, converted, etc.

ir·ref′u·ta·ble (-ref′yoo-, -ri fyo͞o′-) *a.* that cannot be disproved

ir·reg′u·lar *a.* **1.** not conforming to rule, standard, etc. **2.** not straight or uniform —**ir·reg′u·lar′i·ty** *n.*

ir·rel′e·vant *a.* not to the point —**ir·rel′e·vance** *n.*

ir·re·li′gious *a.* **1.** not religious **2.** profane

ir′re·me′di·a·ble *a.* that cannot be remedied or corrected

ir·rep′a·ra·ble *a.* that cannot be repaired or remedied

ir′re·press′i·ble *a.* that cannot be held back

ir′re·proach′a·ble *a.* blameless; faultless

ir′re·sist′i·ble *a.* that cannot be resisted

ir·res′o·lute *a.* not resolute; wavering —**ir·res′o·lu′tion** *n.*

ir′re·spec′tive *a.* regardless (*of*)

ir′re·spon′si·ble *a.* lacking a sense of responsibility

ir′re·triev′a·ble *a.* that cannot be recovered

ir·rev′er·ent *a.* showing disrespect

ir′re·vers′i·ble *a.* **1.** that cannot be reversed **2.** that cannot be annulled

ir·rev′o·ca·ble *a.* that cannot be undone or changed —**ir·rev′o·ca·bly** *adv.*

ir′ri·gate *v.* **1.** supply with water by means of ditches, etc. **2.** wash out (a body cavity) —**ir′ri·ga′tion** *n.*

ir′ri·ta·ble *a.* easily irritated or angered —**ir′ri·ta·bil′i·ty** *n.*

ir′ri·tate *v.* **1.** to anger; annoy **2.** make sore —**ir′ri·tant** *a.,* *n.* —**ir′ri·ta′tion** *n.*

ir·rupt′ *v.* **1.** burst (into) **2.** increase abruptly in population

is pres. t. of **be**: used with *he, she,* or *it*

-ise -ize: Br. sp.

-ish *suf.* **1.** like; like that of **2.** somewhat

i′sin·glass (ī′z'n-) *n.* **1.** gelatin made from fish bladders **2.** mica

Is·lam (is′läm, iz′-) *n.* Muslim religion, founded by Mohammed

is·land (ī′lənd) *n.* land mass

surrounded by water —**is'·land·er** *n.*

isle (īl) *n.* small island

is·let (ī'lit) *n.* very small island

ism *n.* doctrine, theory, system, etc. whose name ends in *-ism*

-ism *suf.* 1. theory or doctrine of 2. act or result of 3. condition or qualities of 4. an instance of

is'n't is not

i'so·bar (-so-) *n.* line on a map connecting points of equal barometric pressure

i'so·late *v.* place alone —**i'so·la'tion** *n.*

i'so·la'tion·ist *n.* one who believes his or her country should not get involved with other countries

i'so·mer (-sə-) *n.* chemical compound whose molecules have same atoms as another, but differently arranged

i'so·met'ric *a.* 1. of equal measure 2. of exercises in which muscles tense against each other

i·sos·ce·les (ī säs'ə lēz) *a.* designating a triangle with two equal sides

i'so·tope *n.* any of two or more forms of an element with different atomic weights

Is·rae·li (iz rā'lē) *n., a.* (native or inhabitant) of modern Israel

Is·ra·el·ite (iz'rē ə līt') *n.* one of the people of ancient Israel

is·sue (ish'ōō) *n.* 1. result 2. offspring 3. point under dispute 4. an issuing or amount issued —*v.* 1. emerge 2. result 3. put out; give out 4. publish —**at issue** disputed —**take**

issue disagree —**is'su·ance** *n.*

-ist *suf.* 1. one who practices 2. adherent of

isth·mus (is'məs) *n.* strip of land connecting two larger bodies of land

it *pron.* the animal or thing mentioned *It* is also used as an indefinite subject or object

I·tal'ian *n., a.* (native or language) of Italy

i·tal'ic *a.* of type in which the letters slant upward to the right —*n.* this type —**i·tal'i·cize** *v.*

itch *n.* 1. tingling of the skin, with the desire to scratch 2. restless desire —*v.* have an itch —**itch'y** [-IER, -IEST] *a.*

-ite *suf.* 1. inhabitant of 2. adherent of

i'tem *n.* 1. article; unit 2. bit of news

i'tem·ize *v.* list the items of

it'er·ate *v.* repeat —**it'er·a'tion** *n.*

i·tin'er·ant *a.* traveling —*n.* traveler

i·tin'er·ar·y *n.* [*pl.* -IES] 1. route 2. plan of a journey

-itis *suf.* inflammation of

its *a.* of it

it's 1. it is 2. it has

it·self' *pron.* intensive or reflexive form of it

-ity *suf.* state or quality

I've I have

-ive *suf.* 1. of or having the nature of 2. tending to

i'vo·ry *n.* [*pl.* -RIES] 1. hard, white substance in elephants' tusks, etc. 2. creamy white

ivory tower a place of mental withdrawal from reality and action

i'vy n. [pl. IVIES] 1. climbing evergreen vine 2. any similar climbing plant

-ize suf. 1. make or become 2. unite with 3. engage in

J

jab v., n. [JABBED, JABBING] punch or poke

jab'ber v. talk quickly or foolishly —n. chatter

ja·bot (zha bō′) n. [pl. -BOTS, (-bōz′)] front ruffle on a blouse

jack n. 1. man or boy 2. device to lift something 3. playing card with a page boy's picture 4. Naut. small flag 5. small metal piece tossed in game of jacks 6. electric plug-in receptacle 7. [Sl.] money —v. raise as with a jack

jack'al n. wild dog of Asia, Africa, etc.

jack'ass n. 1. male donkey 2. fool

jack'daw n. European black bird

jack'et n. 1. short coat 2. outer covering

jack'-in-the-box' n. box from which a figure springs up when the lid is lifted: child's toy

jack'-in-the-pul'pit n. plant with a hooded flower spike

jack'knife n. [pl. -KNIVES] 1. large pocketknife 2. dive made by touching one's feet, then straightening out —v. bend like a half-open jackknife

jack'-o'-lan'tern n. hollow pumpkin cut to look like a face and used as a lantern

jack'pot n. cumulative stakes, as in a poker game

jack rabbit large hare of western N. America

Jac·quard (jə kärd′) n. fabric with a figured weave

jade n. 1. hard, green stone 2. worn-out horse 3. loose woman —v. tire or satiate

jade'ite n. variety of jade

jade plant house plant with thick leaves

jag'ged a. having sharp points; notched or ragged

jag'uar (-wär) n. animal like a large leopard

jai a·lai (hī′lī) game like handball, played with a racket

jail n. prison for short-term confinement —v. put or keep in jail —**jail'er, jail'or** n.

ja·lop'y n. [pl. -IES] [Sl.] old, worn-out automobile

jal'ou·sie (-ə sē) n. window or door made of slats fixed as in a Venetian blind

jam v. [JAMMED, JAMMING] 1. cram; stuff 2. crush or crowd 3. wedge tight 4. make (radio broadcasts) hard to hear by sending signals on the same wavelength 5. [Sl.] to improvise jazz —n. 1. a jamming 2. [Col.] difficult situation 3. spread made by boiling fruit and sugar

jamb (jam) n. side post of a doorway

jam·bo·ree′ n. 1. [Col.] noisy

revel 2. large gathering of boy scouts

jan·gle v., n. (make or cause to make) a harsh, inharmonious sound

jan·i·tor n. one who takes care of a building —**jan′i·to′ri·al** a.

Jan·u·ar·y n. first month

Jap·a·nese n. [pl. **-NESE**] native or language of Japan a. of Japan

jar v. [JARRED, JARRING] 1. make a harsh sound 2. jolt —n. 1. jolt 2. wide-mouthed container

jar·di·niere (-d'n ir′) n. large flower pot

jar·gon n. special vocabulary of some work, class, etc.

jas·mine (-min) n. shrub with fragrant flowers

jas′per n. colored quartz

jaun·dice (jôn′dis) n. disease that turns the skin, eyeballs, etc. yellow —v. make bitter with envy

jaunt n. short pleasure trip

jaun′ty a. [-TIER, -TIEST] perky, easy, and carefree

jave·lin (jav′-) n. light spear thrown in contests

jaw n. either of the two bony parts that hold the teeth —v. [Sl.] to talk

jaw′bone n. lower bone of jaw —v. try to persuade by using one's influence

jaw′break′er n. 1. machine for crushing rocks 2. hard candy 3. [Sl.] word that is hard to pronounce

jay n. 1. bird of the crow family 2. blue jay

jay′walk v. [Col.] cross a street heedlessly —**jay′walk′er** n.

jazz n. popular American music with strong rhythms

jazz′y a. [-IER, -IEST] [Sl.] lively, flashy, etc.

jeal′ous (jel′-) a. 1. resentfully suspicious or envious 2. watchful in guarding —**jeal′ous·y** [pl. -IES] n.

jeans n.pl. trousers of twilled cotton cloth or denim

jeep n. small, rugged, orig. military automobile

jeer v., n. ridicule

Je·ho′vah n. God

je·june′ a. childish

je·ju′num n. middle part of the small intestine

jell v. 1. become, or make into, jelly 2. become definite

jel′ly n. [pl. -LIES] 1. soft, gelatinous food made from cooked fruit syrup 2. gelatinous substance

jel′ly·bean n. small, bean-shaped candy

jel′ly·fish n. jellylike sea animal with tentacles

jel′ly·roll n. thin cake spread with jelly and rolled up

jeop′ard·ize (jep′-) v. to risk; endanger

jeop′ard·y n. risk; danger

jerk n. 1. sharp pull 2. muscular twitch 3. [Sl.] stupid person —v. 1. move with a jerk 2. twitch —**jerk′y** [-IER, -IEST] a.

jer′kin n. snug, usually sleeveless jacket

jerk′wa′ter a. [Col.] small or unimportant, as a town

jer'ky n. strips of meat dried in the sun

jer'sey n. **1.** soft, knitted cloth **2.** [pl. -SEYS] upper garment of this

jest v., n. **1.** joke **2.** ridicule —**jest'er** n.

Je'sus founder of the Christian religion

jet v. [JETTED, JETTING] **1.** shoot out in a stream **2.** to travel by jet aircraft —n. **1.** liquid or gas shot out in a stream **2.** spout that shoots a jet **3.** jet-propelled airplane **4.** black mineral —a. **1.** jet-propelled **2.** black

jet lag fatigue, etc. from adjusting to different time zone after traveling by jet

jet'lin'er n. commercial jet passenger plane

jet'port n. airport with long runways for jet aircraft

jet propulsion propulsion by gases from a rear vent or vents —**jet'-pro·pelled'** a.

jet'sam n. cargo thrown overboard to lighten a ship

jet'ti·son v. **1.** throw (goods) overboard to lighten a ship **2.** discard

jet'ty n. [pl. -TIES] **1.** wall built into the water **2.** landing pier

Jew n. **1.** descendant of people of ancient Israel **2.** believer in Judaism —**Jew'ish** a.

jew'el n. **1.** gem **2.** small gem used as a watch bearing

jew'el·er, jew'el·ler n. one who deals in jewelry

jew'el·ry n. jewels or ornaments set with jewels

jib n. triangular sail ahead of all other sails

jibe (jīb) v. **1.** shift a sail, or the course, of a ship **2.** [Col.] be in accord **3.** to gibe —n. gibe

jif'fy n. [pl. -FIES] [Col.] an instant

jig n. **1.** lively dance **2.** device to guide a tool —v. [JIGGED, JIGGING] dance (a jig) —**in jig time** [Col.] very quickly

jig'ger n. glass of 1 1/2 ozs. for measuring liquor

jig'gle v. move in slight jerks —n. a jiggling

jig'saw n. saw with a narrow blade set in a frame

jigsaw puzzle picture cut in pieces to be fitted together again

jilt v. reject (a lover)

Jim Crow [Col.] discrimination against black people

jim'my n. [pl. -MIES] short crowbar used by burglars —v. [-MIED, -MYING] pry open

jim'son weed poisonous weed with trumpet-shaped flowers

jin'gle v. make light, ringing sounds —n. **1.** jingling sound **2.** light verse or song with easy rhythm

jin'go·ism n. warlike chauvinism —**jin'go·ist** n.

jin·ni (ji nē') n. [pl. JINN] imaginary being in Muslim legend

jin·rik'i·sha (-rik'shô) n. two-wheeled oriental carriage that is pulled by a man, esp. formerly

jinx n. [Col.] person or thing

supposed to cause bad luck —
v. [Col.] cause bad luck to

jit·ter·y *a.* nervous or restless
—**the jitters** nervous feeling

jive *n.* 1. [Sl.] foolish, insincere
talk 2. jazz: earlier word

job *n.* 1. piece of work 2. employment; work —*a.* done by
the job —*v.* [JOBBED, JOBBING]
handle (goods) as a middleman
—**job'hold'er** *n.*

job'ber *n.* one who buys goods
in quantity and sells them to
dealers

job lot goods, often of various
sorts, for sale as one quantity

jock [Sl.] 1. disc jockey 2. athlete

jock'ey *n.* [*pl.* -EYS] racehorse
rider —*v.* maneuver for advantage

jo·cose' *a.* joking; playful —
jo·cos'i·ty (-käs'-) *n.*

joc'u·lar *a.* joking; full of fun
—**joc'u·lar'i·ty** *n.*

joc'und *a.* genial; gay

jodh·purs (jäd'pərz) *n.pl.* riding breeches

jog *v.* [JOGGED, JOGGING] 1.
nudge; shake 2. move at a
slow, steady, jolting pace —*n.*
1. nudge 2. jogging pace 3.
part that changes direction
sharply

jog'gle *v., n.* jolt; jounce

join *v.* 1. connect; unite 2.
become a part or member (of)

join'er *n.* 1. carpenter of interior woodwork 2. [Col.] one
who joins many clubs

joint *n.* 1. place where two
things are joined 2. one of the
parts of a jointed whole 3.
large cut of meat with the

bone in 4. [Sl.] cheap bar, etc.
5. [Sl.] marijuana cigarette —
a. 1. common to two or more
2. sharing with another —*v.*
connect by a joint —**out of
joint** 1. dislocated 2. disor-
dered —**joint'ly** *adv.*

joist *n.* any of the parallel tim-
bers holding up planks of a
floor, etc.

joke *n.* 1. anything said or
done to arouse laughter 2.
thing not to be taken seriously
—*v.* make jokes —**jok'ing·ly**
adv.

jok'er *n.* 1. one who jokes 2.
deceptive clause, as in a contract 3. extra playing card
used in some games

jol'ly *a.* [-LIER, -LIEST] merry;
gay —*v.* [-LIED, -LYING] [Col.]
coax into good humor —**jol'-
li·ty** *n.*

jolt *v., n.* 1. jar; jerk 2. shock
or surprise

jon'quil *n.* narcissus with yellow or white flower

josh *v.* [Col.] tease, fool, etc.

jos'tle *v.* shove roughly

jot *n.* very small amount —*v.*
[JOTTED, JOTTING] write (*down*)
briefly

jounce *v., n.* jolt or bounce —
jounc'y [-IER, -IEST] *a.*

jour'nal (jur'-) *n.* 1. diary 2.
record of proceedings 3. newspaper or magazine 4. book for
business records 5. part of an
axle, etc. that turns in a bearing

jour'nal·ism *n.* newspaper
writing and editing —**jour'nal-
ist** *n.* —**jour'nal·is'tic** *a.*

jour′ney *n.* [*pl.* -NEYS] a trip — *v.* travel

jour′ney·man *n.* [*pl.* -MEN] worker skilled at his trade

joust (joust, just) *n., v.* fight with lances on horseback

jo′vi·al *a.* gay; jolly —**jo′vi·al′i·ty** *n.* —**jo′vi·al·ly** *adv.*

jowl *n.* 1. cheek 2. fleshy, hanging part under the jaw

joy *n.* gladness; delight —**joy′ful** *a.* —**joy′ous** *a.*

joy ride [Col.] reckless, speedy ride in a car, just for fun

ju′bi·lant *a.* rejoicing —**ju′bi·la′tion** *n.*

ju′bi·lee *n.* 1. a 50th or 25th anniversary 2. time of rejoicing

Ju′da·ism *n.* Jewish religion

judge (juj) *v.* 1. hear and decide cases in a law court 2. determine the winner 3. appraise or criticize 4. think; suppose — *n.* one who judges

judg′ment, judge′ment *n.* 1. a deciding 2. legal decision 3. opinion 4. ability to make wise decisions

Judgment Day time of divine judgment of all people

ju·di′cial (jōō dish′əl) *a.* 1. of judges, courts, etc. 2. careful in thought

ju·di′ci·ar′y (-dish′ē-) *a.* of judges or courts —*n.* [*pl.* -IES] 1. part of government that administers justice 2. judges collectively

ju·di′cious (-dish′əs) *a.* showing good judgment —**ju·di′cious·ly** *adv.*

ju′do *n.* kind of wrestling used for self-defense

jug *n.* container for liquids, with a small opening and a handle

jug′ger·naut *n.* terrible, irresistible force

jug′gle *v.* 1. do tricks with (balls, etc.) 2. handle in a tricky way —**jug′gler** *n.*

jug′u·lar *n.* either of two large veins in the neck: in full, **jugular vein**

juice *n.* liquid from fruit or cooked meat —**juic′y** [-IER, -IEST] *a.*

ju·jit′su *n.* kind of wrestling using opponent's strength against him

ju′ju·be *n.* gelatinous, fruit-flavored candy

juke′box *n.* coin-operated phonograph

ju·li·enne′ (-lē en′) *a.* cut into strips: said of vegetables

Ju·ly′ *n.* seventh month

jum′ble *v., n.* (mix in) a confused heap

jum′bo *a.* very large

jump *v.* 1. spring from the ground, etc. 2. leap or make leap over 3. move or change suddenly 4. rise or raise suddenly, as prices —*n.* 1. a jumping 2. distance jumped 3. sudden move or change — **jump at** accept eagerly — **jump′er** *n.*

jump′er *n.* 1. sleeveless dress worn over a blouse, etc. 2. *often pl.* wire or cable for a temporary electrical connection

jump suit lounging suit like a coverall

jump′y *a.* [-IER, -IEST] 1. moving jerkily 2. nervous

jun'co n. [pl. -cos] small bird with gray or black head

junc'tion n. 1. a joining 2. place where things join

junc'ture (-chər) n. 1. junction 2. point of time

June n. sixth month

jun'gle n. dense forest in the tropics

jun'ior a. 1. the younger: written Jr. 2. of lower rank, etc. —n. high school or college student in the next-to-last year

junior college school with courses two years beyond high school

ju'ni·per n. small evergreen with berrylike cones

junk n. 1. old metal, paper, etc. 2. Chinese ship with flat bottom 3. [Col.] rubbish —v. [Col.] to discard

junk'er n. [Sl.] dilapidated car

jun'ket n. 1. pleasure trip 2. milk thickened as curd

junk'ie, junk'y n. [pl. -IES] [Sl.] narcotics addict

jun·ta (hoon'tə) n. military group seizing political power: also **jun·to** (jun'tō) [pl. -TOS]

ju'ris·dic'tion n. (range of) authority, as of a court

ju'ris·pru'dence n. 1. science

or philosophy of law 2. a system of laws

ju'rist n. an expert in law

ju'ror n. member of a jury: also **ju'ry·man** [pl. -MEN]

ju'ry n. [pl. -RIES] group of people chosen to give a decision, esp. in a law case

just a. 1. right or fair 2. righteous 3. well-founded 4. correct; exact —adv. 1. exactly 2. only 3. barely 4. a very short time ago 5. [Col.] really —**just the same** [Col.] nevertheless —**just'ly** adv.

jus'tice n. 1. a being just 2. reward or penalty as deserved 3. the upholding of what is just 4. a judge

justice of the peace local magistrate in minor cases

jus'ti·fy v. [-FIED, -FYING] 1. show to be just, right, etc. 2. to free from guilt —**jus'ti·fi'a·ble** a. —**jus'ti·fi·ca'tion** n.

jut v. [JUTTED, JUTTING] stick out

jute n. strong fiber used to make burlap, rope, etc.

ju'ven·ile (-və n'l, -nīl) n. child or young person —a. 1. young; immature 2. of or for juveniles

jux·ta·pose (juk stə pōz') v. put side by side —**jux'ta·po·si'tion** n.

K

kad'dish (käd'-) *n.* Jewish mourner's prayer

Kai·ser (kī'zər) *n.* title of former Austrian and German rulers

kale *n.* a cabbage with spreading, curled leaves

ka·lei·do·scope (-lī'-) *n.* small tube containing bits of colored glass that change patterns as the tube is turned —**ka·lei'do·scop'ic** (-skäp'-) *a.*

kan·ga·roo' *n.* leaping animal of Australia

ka·o·lin *n.* white clay, used in making porcelain, paper, etc.

ka·pok (-päk) *n.* silky fibers from tropical trees, used for stuffing pillows, etc.

ka·put' (kə poot') *a.* [Sl.] ruined, destroyed, etc.

kar'a·kul *n.* curly black fur from the fleece of Asian lambs

kar'at *n.* carat

ka·ra'te *n.* self-defense by blows with side of open hand

kar'ma *n.* fate

kart *n.* small motorized vehicle, used in racing

ka'ty·did *n.* insect resembling the grasshopper

kay'ak (kī'-) *n.* Eskimo canoe

kay'o *v.* [Sl.] knock out in boxing

ka·zoo' *n.* toy instrument to hum into for musical buzzing

ke·bab (kə bäb') *n.* small pieces of meat broiled on a skewer

keel *n.* center piece along the bottom of a ship —**keel over** [Col.] turn or fall over

keen *a.* 1. sharp 2. piercing 3. perceptive; acute 4. eager 5. intense 6. [Sl.] excellent — **keen'ly** *adv.*

keep *v.* [KEPT, KEEPING] 1. fulfill; observe 2. protect; take care of 3. preserve 4. retain 5. continue 6. hold and not let go 7. refrain —*n.* food and shelter —**keep to oneself** 1. avoid others 2. refrain from telling — **keep'er** *n.*

keep'ing *n.* care or protection —**in keeping with** in conformity with

keep'sake *n.* souvenir

keg *n.* small barrel

kelp *n.* brown seaweed

ken *n.* range of knowledge —*v.* [KENNED, KENNING] [Scot.] to know

ken'nel *n.* 1. doghouse 2. *often pl.* place where dogs are bred or kept

kerb *n.* curb: Brit. sp.

ker'chief *n.* 1. cloth worn around the head or neck 2. handkerchief

ker'nel *n.* 1. grain or seed 2. soft, inner part of a nut or fruit pit

ker'o·sene, ker'o·sine (-sēn) *n.* oil distilled from petroleum

kes'trel *n.* European falcon

ketch *n.* sailing vessel

ketch'up *n.* thick sauce of tomatoes, spices, etc.

ket'tle *n.* 1. pot used in cooking 2. teakettle

ket'tle·drum n. hemispheric copper drum with an adjustable parchment top

key n. 1. device for working a lock 2. lever pressed in operating a piano, typewriter, etc. 3. thing that explains, as a code 4. controlling factor 5. mood or style 6. low island 7. Mus. scale based on a certain keynote —a. controlling —v. bring into harmony —**key up** excite —**key'hole** n.

key'board n. row or rows of keys of a piano, typewriter, etc.

key'note n. 1. Mus. lowest, basic note of a scale 2. basic idea

key'stone n. top, supporting stone of an arch

kha·ki (kak'ē) a., n. yellowish-brown (uniform)

kib·butz' (-boots') n. [pl. -BUTZIM] (kē'boo tsēm') Israeli collective farm

kib'itz·er n. [Col.] onlooker who gives unwanted advice

ki'bosh n. [Sl.] end —**put the kibosh on** check, squelch, etc.

kick v. 1. strike (out) with the foot 2. recoil, as a gun 3. [Col.] complain —n. 1. a kicking 2. [Col.] thrill

kick'back n. [Sl.] forced or secret rebate

kick'off n. kick in football that begins play

kick'stand n. metal bar on a bicycle that pivots to hold it upright

kid n. 1. young goat 2. leather from its skin: also **kid'skin** 3. [Col.] child —v. [KIDDED,

KIDDING] [Col.] tease, fool, etc. —**kid'der** n.

kid'dy, kid'die n. [pl. -DIES] [Col.] child

kid'nap v. [-NAPPED, -NAPPING] seize and hold a person, esp. for ransom —**kid'nap'per** n.

kid'ney n. [pl. -NEYS] urine-forming gland

kidney bean seed of common garden bean

kiel·ba·sa (kēl bä'sə) n. [pl. -SI (-sē), -SAS] smoked Polish sausage

kill v. 1. make die; slay 2. destroy 3. spend (time) idly 4. turn off (an engine) —n. 1. a killing 2. animal or animals killed —**kill'er** n.

kill'ing n. 1. murder 2. [Col.] sudden great profit

kill'-joy' n. spoiler of pleasure for others

kiln (kil, kiln) n. oven for baking bricks, etc.

ki·lo (kē'lō, kil'ō) n. [pl. -LOS] kilogram

kilo- pref. one thousand

kil'o·cy'cle n. kilohertz: earlier name

kil'o·gram n. 1,000 grams

kil'o·hertz n. 1,000 hertz

ki·lo·me·ter (ki läm'ə tər, kil'ə mēt'ər) n. 1,000 meters

kil'o·watt n. 1,000 watts

kilt n. skirt worn by men of the Scottish Highlands

kil'ter n. [Col.] working order: chiefly in **out of kilter**

ki·mo·no (-nə) n. [pl. -NOS] Japanese robe

kin n. relatives; family

kind n. sort; variety —a. gentle, generous, etc. —**in kind** in the same way —**kind of** [Col.] somewhat —**kind'ness** n.

kin'der·gar'ten n. class or school for children about four to six years old

kind'heart'ed a. kind

kin'dle v. 1. set on fire 2. start burning 3. excite

kin'dling n. bits of wood, etc. for starting a fire

kind'ly a. [-LIER, -LIEST] 1. kind 2. pleasant —adv. 1. graciously 2. favorably 3. please —**kind'li·ness** n.

kin'dred n. relatives; kin —a. related or similar

kine n. [Ar.] cows; cattle

ki·net'ic a. of motion

kin'folk n.pl. family; relatives: also **kinfolks**

king n. 1. male ruler of a state 2. playing card with a king's picture 3. chess piece that has to be captured

king'dom n. country ruled by a king or queen

king'fish'er n. fish-eating diving bird

king'-size' a. [Col.] larger than usual size

kink n. 1. curl or twist 2. painful muscle cramp 3. queer notion —v. form or cause kinks —**kink'y** [-IER, -IEST] a.

kin'ship n. 1. family relationship 2. close connection

kins'man n. [pl. -MEN] male relative —**kins'wom'an** [pl. -WOMEN] n.fem.

kip'per n. salted and dried or smoked herring

kirk (kurk) n. Scottish church

kis'met (kiz'-) n. fate

kiss v. caress with the lips in affection or greeting —n. 1. act of kissing 2. kind of candy

kit n. 1. set of tools, supplies, parts, etc. 2. box or bag for the set

kitch'en n. place for preparing and cooking food

kitch·en·ette', **kitch·en·et'** n. small kitchen

kitch'en·ware n. kitchen utensils

kite n. 1. kind of hawk 2. light frame covered with paper, tied to a string, and flown in the wind

kith and kin friends and relatives

kit'ten n. young cat

kit'ten·ish a. coy

kit'ty n. [pl. -TIES] 1. kitten 2. stakes in a poker game

kit'ty-cor'nered a., adv. cater-cornered

ki·wi (kē'wē) n. [pl. -WIS] flightless bird of New Zealand

klep'to·ma'ni·a n. persistent impulse to steal —**klep'to·ma'ni·ac** n.

knack n. special ability

knack'wurst (näk'-) n. thick sausage

knap'sack n. bag to carry supplies on the back

knave n. dishonest person; rogue —**knav'ish** a.

knav'er·y n. dishonesty

knead v. press and squeeze

knee n. joint between thigh and lower leg —v. hit with the knee

knee'cap n. movable bone at the front of the knee

knee'-deep' a. very much involved

kneel v. [KNELT or KNEELED, KNEELING] rest on the bended knee or knees

knell n. slow tolling of a bell, as at a funeral

knew pt. of know

knick′ers n.pl. breeches gathered below the knees: also **knick′er·bock′ers**

knick′knack n. small, showy article

knife n. [pl. KNIVES] sharp cutting blade set in a handle —v. 1. stab with a knife 2. [Col.] injure by treachery —**under the knife** [Col.] undergoing surgery

knight (nīt) n. 1. medieval, chivalrous soldier 2. British man holding honorary rank 3. chessman like a horse's head — v. make a knight

knight′hood n. 1. chivalry 2. knights collectively

knit v. [KNITTED or KNIT, KNITTING] 1. make by looping yarn with needles 2. draw or grow together

knit′wear n. knitted clothing

knob n. round handle, etc. — **knob′by** [-BIER, -BIEST] a.

knock v. 1. hit; strike; rap 2. make a thumping noise 3. to bump 4. [Col.] find fault with —n. 1. hit; blow 2. thumping noise 3. [Col.] adverse criticism —**knock about** wander about —**knock down** take apart —**knock off** 1. [Col.] stop working 2. [Col.] deduct 3. [Sl.] kill or overcome — **knock out** make unconscious —**knock together** make hastily

knock′er n. small knob, etc. on a door for knocking

knock′-kneed′ a. having legs that bend inward at the knees

knock′out n. 1. [Sl.] very attractive person or thing 2. boxing victory when an opponent can no longer fight

knock′wurst n. knackwurst

knoll n. little hill; mound

knot n. 1. lump in tangled thread, etc. 2. a tying together of string, rope, etc. 3. small group 4. hard lump in wood where a branch has grown 5. one nautical mile per hour —v. [KNOTTED, KNOTTING] form a knot (in)

knot′ty a. [-TIER, -TIEST] 1. full of knots 2. puzzling

know v. [KNEW, KNOWN, KNOWING] 1. be informed (about) 2. be aware (of) 3. be acquainted with

know′-how′ n. [Col.] technical skill

know′ing a. 1. having knowledge 2. shrewd; cunning

knowl′edge n. things known or learned —**knowl′edge·a·ble** a.

knuck′le n. joint of a finger — **knuckle down** work hard — **knuckle under** surrender

ko·a′la n. tree dwelling marsupial of Australia

kohl·ra·bi (kōl rä′bē) n. [pl. -BIES] kind of cabbage

kook (kōōk) n. [Sl.] silly, eccentric person —**kook′y, kook′ie** a.

Ko·ran′ (kō-) n. sacred book of Muslims

ko·sher *a.* fit to eat according to Jewish dietary laws

kow·tow (kou′tou′) *v.* show great deference (*to*)

ku·chen (kōō′kən) *n.* breadlike cake, with raisins, etc.

ku·dos (kōō′däs) *n.* [Col.] credit for achievement; fame

kum·quat (-kwät) *n.* small, oval, orangelike fruit

kung fu (kooŋ′fōō′) system of self-defense like karate

L

lab *n.* [Col.] laboratory

la′bel *n.* card, etc. marked and attached to an object to show its contents, etc. —*v.* 1. attach a label to 2. classify as

la′bi·al *a.* of the lips

la′bi·um *n.* [*pl.* -BIA] liplike fold of the vulva

la′bor *n.* 1. work 2. task 3. all workers 4. process of childbirth —*v.* 1. work hard 2. move with effort 3. suffer (*under* a false idea, etc.) 4. develop in too great detail

lab′o·ra·to′ry *n.* [*pl.* -RIES] place for scientific work or research

la′bored *a.* with effort

la′bor·er *n.* a worker, esp. an unskilled worker

la·bo′ri·ous *a.* difficult

labor union association of workers to further their interests

la′bour *n., v.* labor: Br. sp.

la·bur′num *n.* shrub with drooping yellow flowers

lab′y·rinth *n.* maze

lac (lak) *n.* resinous source of shellac

lace (lās) *n.* 1. string used to fasten parts of a shoe, etc. 2. openwork fabric woven in fancy designs —*v.* 1. fasten with a lace 2. intertwine 3. whip

lac′er·ate (las′-) *v.* to tear jaggedly —**lac′er·a′tion** *n.*

lace′work *n.* lace, or any openwork like it

lach′ry·mose (lak′-) *a.* tearful; sad

lack *n.* state of not having enough or any —*v.* have little or nothing of

lack′a·dai′si·cal (-dā′-) *a.* showing lack of interest

lack′ey *n.* [*pl.* -EYS] 1. menial male servant 2. toady

lack′lus′ter *a.* dull

la·con′ic (-kän′-) *a.* concise; brief

lac′quer (lak′ər) *n.* a varnish, often like enamel —*v.* coat with lacquer

la·crosse′ *n.* ball game using long-handled rackets

lac′te·al *a.* of or like milk

lac′tic *a.* 1. of milk 2. of an acid in sour milk

lac′tose *n.* sugar found in milk

la·cu′na (-kyōō′-) *n.* [*pl.* -NAS, -NAE (-nē)] gap; space

lac′y *a.* [-IER, -IEST] of or like lace —**lac′i·ness** *n.*

lad *n.* boy; youth

lad′der *n.* series of rungs framed by two sidepieces for climbing up or down

lade v. [alt. pp. LADEN] to load

lad'en a. 1. loaded 2. burdened; afflicted

lad'ing n. a load; cargo

la'dle n. long-handled, cuplike spoon for dipping —v. dip out with a ladle

la'dy n. [pl. -DIES] 1. well-bred, polite woman 2. any woman — a. female —**la'dy·like** a.

la'dy·bug n. small beetle with a spotted back

la'dy·fin'ger n. small, finger-shaped spongecake

la'dy·like a. refined; well-bred

la'dy·love n. sweetheart

la'dy·slip'per n. orchid with flowers like slippers

lag v. [LAGGED, LAGGING] fall behind —n. 1. a falling behind 2. amount of this

la·ger (beer) (lä'gər) n. a beer aged for several months

lag'gard a. backward; slow — n. one who falls behind

la·gniappe, la·gnappe (lan yap') n. gratuity

la·goon' n. 1. shallow lake joined to a larger body of water 2. water inside an atoll

laid (läd) pt. & pp. of **lay**

lain pp. of **lie** (recline)

lair (ler) n. animal's den

lais·sez faire (les'ā fer') noninterference

la'i·ty n. all lay people, as a group

lake n. large inland body of water

lam n. [Sl.] headlong flight —v. [LAMMED, LAMMING] [Sl.] flee

la'ma (lä'-) n. Buddhist priest or monk in Tibet

la'ma·ser'y n. [pl. -IES] monastery of lamas

La·maze' (-mäz') n. training program in natural childbirth

lamb (lam) n. 1. young sheep 2. its flesh as food 3. gentle, innocent person

lam·baste' (-bāst') v. [Sl.] beat or scold soundly

lam'bent a. 1. flickering 2. glowing softly 3. light and graceful

lame a. 1. crippled 2. stiff and painful 3. poor; ineffectual — v. make lame

la·mé (la mā') n. cloth interwoven with metal threads

lame duck elected official whose term goes beyond a re-election defeat

la·mel'la n. [pl. -LAE (-ē), -LAS] thin plate, layer, etc.

la·ment' v. feel or show deep sorrow for —n. 1. a lamenting 2. elegy; dirge —**lam'en·ta·ble** a. —**lam'en·ta'tion** n.

lam'i·na n. [pl. -NAE (-nē), -NAS] thin scale or layer

lam'i·nate v. form of or into thin layers —**lam'i·nat'ed** a. —**lam'i·na'tion** n.

lamp n. 1. device for producing light 2. such a device set in a stand

lamp'black n. fine soot used as a black pigment

lam·poon' n. written satirical attack —v. to attack in a lampoon

lamp'post n. post supporting a street lamp

lam'prey (-prē) n. eellike water animal

la·nai (lä nī') n. veranda

lance n. 1. long spear 2. lancet —v. cut open with a lancet

lan′cer n. cavalry soldier armed with a lance

lan′cet n. surgical knife

land n. 1. solid part of earth's surface 2. country or region 3. ground; soil 4. real estate —v. 1. put or go on shore or land 2. arrive at a place, port, etc. 3. catch 4. [Col.] get or secure 5. [Col.] deliver (a blow)

land′ed a. 1. owning land 2. consisting of land

land′fall n. sighting of land

land′fill n. disposing of garbage by burying

land′hold′er n. land owner

land′ing n. 1. a coming to shore 2. pier; dock 3. platform at the end of stairs 4. an alighting

land′locked a. 1. surrounded by land 2. confined to fresh water

land′lord n. man who rents land, houses, rooms, etc. to others —land′la′dy n.fem.

land′lub′ber n. one with little experience at sea

land′mark n. 1. identifying feature of a locality 2. important event

land′mass n. continent

land′-of′fice business [Col.] booming business

land′scape n. (picture of) natural scenery —v. plant lawns, bushes, etc. on

land′slide n. 1. sliding of rocks or earth down a slope 2. overwhelming victory

lane n. 1. narrow path, road, etc. 2. path designated for ships, aircraft, cars, etc.

lan′guage n. 1. speech or writing 2. any means of communicating, as a set of computer symbols 3. speech of a nation, group, etc.

lan′guid (-gwid) a. 1. weak 2. listless; sluggish

lan′guish (-gwish) v. 1. become weak 2. long; pine —lan′guish·ing a.

lan′guor (-gar) n. lack of vigor —lan′guor·ous a.

lank a. tall and lean

lank′y a. [-IER, -IEST] awkwardly tall and lean

lan′o·lin n. fatty substance obtained from wool

lan′tern n. transparent case holding a light

lan′tern-jawed′ a. having long, thin jaws and sunken cheeks

lan′yard (-yərd) n. short rope used on ships

lap n. 1. front part from the waist to the knees of a seated person 2. place in which one is cared for 3. one circuit of a race track 4. overlapping part —v. [LAPPED, LAPPING] 1. fold or wrap 2. lay or extend partly over 3. dip up with the tongue 4. splash lightly —lap up [Col.] accept eagerly

la·pel′ n. fold-back part at the upper front of a coat

lap′i·dar′y n. [pl. -IES] one who cuts and polishes gems

lap′is laz′u·li (-yoo lī) azure, opaque semiprecious stone

lap robe heavy blanket, etc. laid over the lap

lapse n. 1. small error 2. a falling into a lower condition 3. passing, as of time —v. 1. fall into a certain state 2. deviate from virtue 3. become void

lar'board (-bərd) n., a. left; port

lar'ce·ny n. theft —**lar'ce·nous** a.

larch n. kind of pine tree

lard n. melted fat of hogs —v. cover with lard

lard'er n. (place for keeping) food supplies

large a. of great size or amount —adv. in a large way —**at large** 1. free; not jailed 2. in general 3. representing no particular district —**large'ness** n.

large'ly adv. mainly

large'-scale' a. extensive

lar·gess, lar·gesse (lär jes') n. generous giving

lar'go (lär'-) a., adv. Mus. slow and stately

lar'i·at (lar'-) n. 1. rope for tethering 2. lasso

lark n. 1. any of various songbirds 2. frolic or spree —v. to play or frolic

lark'spur n. delphinium

lar'va n. [pl. -VAE (-vē), -VAS] insect in the earliest stage after hatching —**lar'val** a.

lar'yn·gi'tis (lar'ən jī'-) n. inflammation of the larynx

lar'ynx (-iŋks) n. upper end of the trachea

la·sa·gna (lə zän'yə) n. wide noodles baked with layers of cheese, ground meat, etc.

las·civ'i·ous (lə siv'-) a. showing or exciting lust

la·ser (lā'zər) n. device that concentrates light rays in an intense beam

lash n. 1. striking part of a whip 2. a stroke as with a whip 3. eyelash —v. 1. strike or drive as with a lash 2. swing sharply 3. tie with a rope, etc. 4. censure or rebuke —**lash out** 1. strike out violently 2. speak angrily

lass n. young woman

las'si·tude n. weariness

las'so n. [pl. -SOS, -SOES] rope with a sliding noose, for catching cattle, etc. —v. catch with a lasso

last a. 1. after all others 2. only remaining 3. most recent 4. least likely 5. conclusive —adv. 1. after all others 2. most recently 3. finally —n. 1. last one 2. footlike form for making shoes —v. 1. go on, stay in use, etc. 2. be enough for —**at (long) last** finally

last hurrah final attempt or appearance

last'ly adv. in conclusion

last straw final trouble causing defeat, anger, etc.

latch n. fastening for a door, window, etc.; esp., a bar that fits into a notch —v. fasten with a latch —**latch onto** [Col.] get or obtain

late a. 1. after the expected time 2. near the end of a period 3. recent 4. recently dead —adv. 1. after the expected time 2. near the end of a period 3. recently —**of late** recently

late'ly adv. recently

la'tent a. undeveloped

lat′er·al a. sideways

la′tex n. milky fluid in certain plants and trees

lath (lath) n. framework for plaster, as thin strip of wood

lathe (lāth) n. machine for shaping wood, metal, etc., with a cutting tool —v. shape on a lathe

lath′er (lath′-) n. 1. foam formed by soap and water 2. foamy sweat 3. [Sl.] excited state —v. cover with or form lather —lath′er·y a.

Lat′in n. 1. language of ancient Rome 2. speaker of a Latin language —a. of or derived from Latin

lat′i·tude n. 1. extent 2. freedom of opinion, action, etc. 3. distance in degrees from the equator

la·trine′ (-trēn′) n. toilet for the use of many people

lat′ter a. 1. nearer the end 2. last mentioned of two

lat′tice n. structure of crossed strips of wood, etc.

lat′tice·work n. 1. lattice 2. lattices collectively

laud (lôd) v., n. praise —**laud′-a·to′ry** a.

laud′a·ble a. praiseworthy

laud′a·num n. solution of opium in alcohol

laugh v. make vocal sounds showing mirth, scorn, etc. —n. act of laughing —**laugh at 1.** be amused by 2. make fun of

laugh′a·ble a. amusing or ridiculous

laugh′ing·stock n. object of ridicule

laugh′ter n. action or sound of laughing

launch (lônch) v. 1. send into space 2. set afloat 3. begin 4. plunge (into) —n. large motorboat

launch pad platform for launching a rocket, etc.

laun′der v. wash or wash and iron (clothes, etc.) —**laun′-dress** n.fem.

Laun′dro·mat service mark for self-service laundry —n. [l-] such a laundry

laun′dry n. [pl. -DRIES] 1. place for laundering 2. things (to be) laundered —**laun′dry-man** [pl. -MEN] n.

lau′rel n. 1. evergreen with large, glossy leaves 2. pl. fame; victory

la·va (lä′və, lav′ə) n. rock from a volcano

lav′a·to′ry n. [pl. -RIES] 1. washbowl 2. room with toilet and washbowl

lav′en·der n. 1. fragrant mint plant 2. pale purple

lav′ish a. 1. very generous 2. very abundant —v. give or spend freely

law n. 1. any of the rules of conduct made by a government 2. obedience to these 3. profession of lawyers 4. fundamental rule 5. series of natural events always happening the same way —**the law** [Col.] the police

law′-a·bid′ing a. obeying the law

law′break′er n. one who violates the law

law′ful a. legal (sense 1)

law'less *a.* 1. not regulated by law 2. disobeying law

law'mak'er *n.* one who makes laws

lawn *n.* grass cut short

lawn mower machine to cut lawn grass

law'suit *n.* case before a court for decision

law'yer *n.* person licensed to represent others legally

lax *n.* 1. not tight 2. not strict —**lax'i·ty** *n.*

lax'a·tive *n., a.* (medicine) making the bowels move

lay *v.* [LAID, LAYING] 1. put down on something 2. set in place 3. put or place 4. produce (an egg) 5. settle; allay 6. bet 7. devise 8. present —*n.* 1. position; arrangement 2. short poem —*a.* of or for laymen —**lay aside, lay away,** or **lay by** save for future use —**lay off** 1. discharge temporarily 2. [Sl.] cease —**lay out** spend —**lay over** stop before going on —**lay up** confine to a sickbed

lay *pt.* of **lie** (recline)

lay'er *n.* single thickness

lay·ette' (-et') *n.* complete outfit for a newborn baby

lay'man *n.* [*pl.* -MEN] one not belonging to the clergy or to a given profession

lay'off' *n.* temporary unemployment

lay'out' *n.* arrangement

lay'o'ver *n.* stop in a journey

laze *v.* idle or loaf

la'zy *a.* [-ZIER, -ZIEST] 1. not willing to work 2. sluggish —**la'zi·ly** *adv.* —**la'zi·ness** *n.*

Lazy Su'san revolving food tray

leach *v.* extract (a soluble substance) from something

lead (lēd) *v.* [LED, LEADING] 1. direct or guide as by going before 2. be at the head of 3. go or pass 4. bring as a result 5. move first in a game, etc. 6. live; spend —*n.* 1. role or example of a leader 2. first place 3. distance ahead 4. clue 5. leading role —**lead off** begin —**lead on** lure —**lead up to** prepare the way for

lead (led) *n.* 1. heavy, soft metal, a chemical element 2. graphite used in pencils

lead'en *a.* 1. of lead 2. heavy 3. gloomy

lead'er *n.* guiding head. —**lead'er·ship** *n.*

lead'ing (lēd'-) *a.* 1. that leads; guiding 2. chief

leaf *n.* [*pl.* LEAVES] 1. flat, thin, usually green part growing from a plant stem 2. sheet of paper, etc. —*v.* turn the pages of

leaf'let *n.* 1. small leaf 2. folded printed sheet

leaf'y [-IER, -IEST] having many leaves

league (lēg) *n.* 1. association of nations, groups, etc. 2. unit of distance, about 3 miles —*v.* join in a league

leak *v.* 1. pass or let pass out or in accidentally 2. become known gradually —*n.* accidental crack that allows leaking —**leak'y** [-IER, -IEST] *a.*

leak'age *n.* 1. a leaking 2. amount that leaks

lean v. 1. bend or slant 2. rely (on) 3. tend 4. rest against something —a. 1. with little or no fat 2. meager —**lean′ness** n.

lean′ing n. tendency

lean′-to′ n. [pl. -TOS] structure whose sloping roof abuts a wall, etc.

leap v. [alt. pt. & pp. LEAPT] 1. jump (over) 2. accept eagerly (with at) —n. a jump

leap′frog n. game in which players leap over the backs of others —v. [-FROGGED, -FROGGING] leap or skip (over)

leap year every fourth year, having 29 days in February

learn v. 1. get knowledge or skill by study 2. hear (of) 3. memorize

learn′ed (-id) a. having or showing much learning

learn′ing n. (acquiring of) knowledge or skill

lease n. contract by which property is rented —v. give or get by a lease

leash n. strap or chain for holding a dog, etc. in check

least a. smallest —adv. in the smallest degree —n. smallest in degree, etc. —**at least** at any rate

leath′er (leth′-) n. animal skin that has been tanned

leath′er·y a. tough and flexible

leave v. [LEFT, LEAVING] 1. let remain 2. have remaining after one 3. bequeath 4. go away (from) —n. 1. permission 2. permitted absence from duty —**leave out** omit —**take one's leave** depart

leav′en (lev′-) n. 1. yeast, etc. used to make dough rise 2. permeating influence —v. affect with leaven

leaves n. pl. of **leaf**

leav′ings n.pl. remnants

lech′er n. lustful, grossly sensual man —**lech′er·ous** a.

lec′i·thin (les′-) n. fatty compound in living cells

lec′tern n. reading stand

lec′ture n. 1. informative talk 2. a scolding —v. 1. give a lecture (to) —**lec′tur·er** n.

led pt. & pp. of **lead** (guide)

ledge n. 1. shelf 2. projecting ridge of rocks

ledg′er n. book of final entry for transactions

lee a., n. (on) the side away from the wind

leech n. 1. bloodsucking worm 2. one who clings like a parasite —v. cling (onto) thus

leek n. onionlike vegetable

leer n. malicious or suggestive grin —v. look with a leer

leer′y a. wary; suspicious

lees (lēz) n.pl. sediment

lee′ward (also Naut. lōō′ərd) a. away from the wind —n. lee side —adv. toward the lee

lee′way n. [Col.] 1. margin of time, money, etc. 2. room for freedom of action

left a. of that side toward the west when one faces north —n. 1. left side 2. [often L-] liberal or radical party, etc. —adv. toward the left

left pt. & pp. of **leave**

left′-hand′ed a. 1. using the left hand more easily 2. for the left hand **3.** insincere —*adv.* with the left hand

left'ist *n., a.* liberal or radical

left'o·ver *n.* something left over, as from a meal

leg *n.* **1.** limb used for standing and walking **2.** thing like a leg in shape or use **3.** stage, as of a trip —**pull someone's leg** [Col.] fool one

leg'a·cy *n.* [pl. -CIES] something handed down to one, esp. by a will

le'gal *a.* **1.** of, based on, or permitted by law **2.** of lawyers —**le·gal'i·ty** *n.* —**le'gal·ly** *adv.*

le·gal·ese' (-ēz') *n.* special legal words, often thought incomprehensible by laymen

le'gal·ize *v.* make lawful

legal tender money legally acceptable for payment

leg'ate (-it) *n.* papal envoy

le·ga'tion *n.* envoy and his or her staff and headquarters

le·ga'to (-gä'-) *a., adv. Music* in a smooth, even style

leg'end (lej'-) *n.* **1.** traditional tale **2.** notable person **3.** inscription, title, etc. —**leg'end·ar'y** *a.*

leg'er·de·main' (lej'-) *n.* sleight of hand

leg'gings *n.pl.* coverings for protecting the legs

leg'horn *n.* [often L-] a kind of small chicken

leg'i·ble *a.* that can be read —**leg'i·bly** *adv.*

le'gion (-jən) *n.* **1.** large body of soldiers **2.** great number

le·gion·naire' (-er') *n.* member of a legion

leg'is·late *v.* **1.** make laws **2.** bring (about) by laws —**leg'is·la'tion** *n.* —**leg'is·la'tive** *a.* —**leg'is·la'tor** *n.*

leg'is·la'ture *n.* group of persons who make laws

le·git'i·mate (-jit'ə mit) *a.* **1.** born of a married couple **2.** lawful **3.** reasonable **4.** justifiable **5.** conforming to accepted rules, etc. —**le·git'i·ma·cy** *n.*

le·git'i·mize *v.* legalize, authorize, justify, etc.

leg'man' *n.* [pl. -MEN] assistant who does routine work outside the office

leg·ume (leg'yōōm) *n.* plant with pods, as the pea and bean —**le·gu'mi·nous** *a.*

lei (lā, lā'ē) *n.* [pl. LEIS] garland or wreath of flowers

lei·sure (lē'zhər) *a., n.* free (time) for rest, play, etc. —**lei'sure·ly** *a.* slow —*adv.* in an unhurried manner

lem'ming *n.* small rodent

lem'on *n.* **1.** small, sour, yellow citrus fruit **2.** [Sl.] something defective

lem'on·ade' *n.* drink of lemon juice, sugar, and water

le'mur (lē'-) *n.* small mammal related to the monkey

lend *v.* [LENT, LENDING] **1.** let another use (a thing) temporarily **2.** let out (money) at interest **3.** impart —**lend'er** *n.*

length *n.* **1.** distance from end to end **2.** extent in space or time **3.** long stretch —**at length** finally

length'en *v.* make or become longer

length'wise *adv., a.* in the di-

rection of the length: also
length′ways

length′y a. [-IER, -IEST] long;
esp., too long

le′ni·ent a. merciful; gentle —
le′ni·en·cy n.

lens n. 1. curved piece of glass,
plastic, etc. for adjusting light
rays passing through it: used
in cameras, telescopes, etc. 2.
similar part of the eye

Lent n. period of 40 weekdays
before Easter

lent pt. and pp. of **lend**

len′til n. small edible seed of a
pealike plant

Le′o 5th sign of the zodiac;
Lion

le′o·nine a. like a lion

leop′ard (lep′-) n. large, black-
spotted, wildcat of Asia and
Africa

le′o·tard n. tightfitting garment, as for a dancer

lep′er n. one having leprosy

lep′re·chaun (-kôn) n. Irish
fairy said to be able to reveal
hidden treasure

lep′ro·sy n. disease with skin
ulcers, scaling, etc.

les′bi·an (lez′-) n. homosexual
woman

le·sion (lē′zhən) n. injury of
an organ or tissue

less a. not so much, so great,
etc. —adv. to a smaller extent
—n. a smaller amount —prep.
minus

-less suf. 1. without 2. that
does not 3. that cannot be

les·see′ n. one to whom
property is leased

less′en v. make or become less

less′er a. smaller, less, etc.

les′son n. 1. exercise for a student to learn 2. something
learned by experience

les′sor n. one giving a lease

lest con. for fear that

let v. [LET, LET′TING] 1. allow;
permit 2. leave 3. rent 4.
cause to flow, as blood —n.
hindrance —**let down** 1. lower
2. disappoint —**let off** deal le-
niently with —**let on** [Col.]
show one is aware —**let up** 1.
relax 2. cease

let′down n. disappointment

le′thal a. fatal; deadly

leth·ar·gy n. lack of energy —
le·thar′gic (-thär′-) a.

let′ter n. 1. a character of the
alphabet 2. message sent by
mail 3. literal meaning 4. pl.
literature —v. mark with letters

let′tered a. 1. well-educated 2.
marked with letters

let′ter·head n. 1. name, etc.
of a person or firm as a heading on letter paper 2. sheet of
this paper

let′ter·per′fect a. entirely correct

let′tuce n. plant with crisp,
green leaves used in salads

let′up n. [Col.] 1. a slackening
2. stop; pause

leu·ke′mi·a (loo-) n. disease
characterized by an abnormal
increase in the white blood
corpuscles

lev′ee n. river embankment to
prevent flooding

lev′el n. 1. instrument for de-
termining the horizontal 2.
horizontal plane, line, etc. 3.
height 4. position, rank, etc. —

a. 1. flat and even 2. even in height (*with*) —*v.* 1. make or become level 2. demolish 3. raise and aim (a gun) —**level with** [Sl.] be honest with —**lev'el·er** *n.*

lev'el-head'ed *a.* sensible

lev'er (or lē'vər) *n.* bar turning on a fulcrum, used to lift or move weights

lev'er·age (-ij) *n.* action or power of a lever

le·vi'a·than (-vī'-) *n.* 1. *Bible* sea monster 2. huge thing

Le·vis (lē'vīz) *trademark for* denim trousers

lev'i·ta'tion *n.* illusion of raising an unsupported body in the air —**lev'i·tate** *v.*

lev'i·ty *n.* improper gaiety; frivolity

lev'y [-IED, -YING] 1. impose (a tax, etc.) 2. enlist (troops) 3. wage (war) —*n.* [*pl.* -IES] a levying or something levied

lewd (lōōd) *a.* indecent

lex'i·cog'ra·phy *n.* work of writing a dictionary —**lex'i·cog'ra·pher** *n.*

lex'i·con *n.* dictionary

li'a·bil'i·ty *n.* [*pl.* -TIES] 1. a being liable 2. *pl.* debts 3. disadvantage

li'a·ble *a.* 1. legally responsible 2. subject to 3. likely (*to*)

li·ai·son (lē'ə zän, -zōn) *n.* 1. communication between military units 2. illicit love affair

li'ar *n.* one who tells lies

lib *n.* liberation

li·ba'tion *n.* 1. wine or oil poured in honor of a god 2. alcoholic drink

li'bel *n.* statement in writing that may unjustly hurt a reputation —*v.* make a libel against —**li'bel·ous** *a.*

lib'er·al *a.* 1. generous 2. not strict 3. tolerant 4. favoring reform —*n.* one who favors reform —**lib'er·al·ism** *n.*

liberal arts literature, philosophy, history, etc.

lib'er·al'i·ty *n.* [*pl.* -TIES] 1. generosity 2. tolerance

lib'er·al·ize *v.* make or become liberal

lib'er·ate *v.* 1. set free; release 2. secure equal rights for —**lib'er·a'tion** *n.* —**lib'er·a'tor** *n.*

lib'er·tar'i·an *n.* advocate of full civil liberties

lib'er·tine (-tēn) *n.* sexually promiscuous man

lib'er·ty *n.* [*pl.* -TIES] 1. freedom from slavery, etc. 2. a particular right 3. excessive familiarity 4. leave given to a sailor —**at liberty** 1. not confined 2. permitted (*to*) —**take liberties** 1. be impertinent 2. deal inaccurately (*with* facts, etc.)

li·bid'i·nous *a.* lustful

li·bi'do (-bē'-, -bī'-) *n.* sexual urge

Li'bra (lī'-, lē'-) 7th sign of the zodiac; Scales

li·brar'i·an *n.* one trained in library science

li'brar·y *n.* [*pl.* -IES] collection of books or a place for it

li·bret'to *n.* [*pl.* -TOS, -TI (-tē)] text of an opera, etc. —**li·bret'tist** *n.*

lice *n.* pl. of **louse**

li'cense *n.* 1. legal permit 2.

freedom from rules **3.** freedom that is abused —*v.* permit formally Br. sp. **li'cence**

li·cen'tious (-shəs) *a.* morally unrestrained

li·chen (lī'kən) *n.* mosslike plant growing on rocks, trees, etc.

lic'it (lis'-) *a.* lawful

lick *v.* **1.** pass the tongue over **2.** [Col.] beat or conquer —*n.* **1.** a licking **2.** small quantity —**lick up** consume by licking

lic'o·rice (-ər ish) *n.* black flavoring from a plant root

lid *n.* **1.** movable cover **2.** eyelid —**lid'ded** *a.*

lie *v.* [LAY, LAIN, LYING] **1.** be horizontal or rest horizontally **2.** be or exist —*n.* position; lay

lie *v.* [LIED, LYING] make a false statement knowingly —*n.* thing said in lying

lie detector polygraph

liege (lēj) *n.* feudal lord or vassal

lien (lēn) *n.* legal claim on another's property until a debt is paid

lieu (lōō) *n.* place —**in lieu of** instead of

lieu·ten'ant *n.* **1.** deputy **2.** army officer ranking below a captain **3.** low-ranking naval officer —**lieu·ten'an·cy** [*pl.* -CIES] *n.*

lieutenant governor elected State official who may substitute for a governor

life *n.* [*pl.* LIVES] **1.** active existence of plants and animals **2.** living things **3.** time of being alive **4.** way of living **5.** a biography **6.** liveliness — **life'like** *a.*

life'boat *n.* small rescue boat carried by a ship

life'guard *n.* swimmer employed to prevent drownings

life jacket (or **vest**) life preserver like a jacket or vest

life'less *a.* **1.** inanimate **2.** dead **3.** dull

life'long *a.* lasting for life

life preserver device for keeping a body afloat

life'sav·er *n.* [Col.] help in time of need

life'-size' *a.* as big as the thing represented

life style individual's whole way of living

life'time *n.* length of time one lives or a thing lasts

lift *v.* **1.** bring higher; raise **2.** go up; rise **3.** [Sl.] steal —*n.* **1.** a lifting **2.** lifting force **3.** raising of one's spirits **4.** help; aid **5.** ride in the direction one is going **6.** [Br.] elevator

lift'off *n.* vertical takeoff of a spacecraft, etc.

lig'a·ment *n.* connective tissue for bones or organs

lig'a·ture *n.* **1.** a thing for tying, as surgical thread **2.** letters united, as *th*

light *n.* **1.** radiant energy by which one sees **2.** brightness **3.** lamp, lantern, etc. **4.** daylight **5.** thing to ignite something **6.** aspect **7.** knowledge —*a.* **1.** bright **2.** pale; fair **3.** not heavy **4.** not important **5.** easy to bear or do **6.** happy **7.** dizzy **8.** moderate **9.** producing small products —*adv.* **1.** palely

2. lightly —v. [LIGHTED or LIT, LIGHTING] 1. ignite 2. cause to give off light 3. furnish with light 4. brighten 5. be lighted 6. come to rest 7. happen (on or upon) —in the light of considering —make light of treat as trivial

light'en v. make or become brighter, less heavy, etc.

light'er n. 1. person or thing that ignites something 2. barge for loading or unloading large ships

light'-fin'gered a. thievish

light'head'ed a. 1. dizzy 2. flighty

light'heart'ed a. cheerful — light'heart'ed·ly adv. — light'heart'ed·ness n.

light'house n. tower with a light to guide ships

light'ing n. act or manner of giving light

light'ly adv. 1. gently 2. to a small degree 3. nimbly 4. cheerfully 5. carelessly

light'-mind'ed a. frivolous

light'ning n. flash of light in the sky from a discharge of atmospheric electricity

lightning bug firefly

lightning rod metal rod to divert lightning

light'-year' n. distance that light travels in a year, about 6 trillion miles

lik'a·ble, like'a·ble a. pleasant, friendly, etc.

like a. similar; equal —prep. 1. similar(ly) to 2. typical of 3. in the mood for 4. indicative of 5. as for example —con. [Col.] 1. as 2. as if —v. 1. be fond of; enjoy 2. wish —n. 1. an equal 2. pl. preferences —and the like and other of the same kind —like crazy (or mad) [Col.] wildly

-like suf. like

like'li·hood n. probability

like'ly a. 1. credible 2. probable; expected 3. suitable — adv. probably

like'-mind'ed a. having the same ideas, tastes, etc.

lik'en (lîk'-) v. compare

like'ness n. 1. a being like 2. picture; copy

like'wise adv. 1. in the same way 2. also; too

lik·ing (lîk'iŋ) n. 1. fondness 2. preference; taste

li'lac n. shrub with tiny, pale-purple flower clusters

lilt n. light, swingy rhythm

lil'y n. [pl. -IES] plant with trumpet-shaped flowers

lil'y-liv'ered a. cowardly

lily of the valley [pl. LILIES OF THE VALLEY] plant with a spike of bell-shaped flowers

li'ma bean [also L- b-] large, flat, edible bean in pods

limb n. 1. arm, leg, or wing 2. large tree branch

lim'ber v., a. (make or become) flexible

lim'bo n. place of oblivion

Lim'burg·er (cheese) soft, strong-smelling cheese

lime n. 1. white substance obtained from limestone 2. green, lemonlike fruit

lime'light n. prominent position before the public

lim'er·ick n. rhymed, funny poem of five lines

lime'stone *n.* rock used in building, making lime, etc.

lim'it *n.* **1.** point where something ends **2.** *pl.* bounds **3.** greatest amount allowed —*v.* set a limit to —**lim'i·ta'tion** *n.*

lim'it·ed *a.* **1.** restricted **2.** making a restricted number of stops

lim·ou·sine' (-ə zēn) *n.* large, luxury automobile

limp *v., n.* (walk with) lameness —*a.* not firm

lim'pet *n.* shellfish that clings to rocks, etc.

lim'pid *a.* perfectly clear

lin'den *n.* tree with heart-shaped leaves

line *n.* **1.** cord, rope, etc. **2.** wire, pipe, etc. **3.** long, thin mark **4.** boundary **5.** outline **6.** row or series **7.** conformity **8.** transportation system **9.** route; course **10.** stock of goods **11.** short letter **12.** *Football* players in the forward row —*v.* **1.** mark with lines **2.** form a line along **3.** put, or serve as, a lining in —**hold the line** stand firm —**line up** form a line

lin·e·age (lin'ē ij) *n.* line of descent; ancestry

lin'e·al *a.* **1.** directly descended **2.** linear

lin'e·a·ment (-mənt) *n.* distinctive facial feature

lin'e·ar *a.* **1.** of a line or lines **2.** of length

line'man *n.* [*pl.* -MEN] **1.** person who repairs telephone or electric power lines **2.** *Football* player in the line

lin'en *n.* **1.** cloth of flax **2.** *often pl.* sheets, tablecloths, etc. of linen or cotton

lin'er (lin'-) *n.* **1.** ship or airplane of a line (*sense* 8) **2.** cosmetic applied in a fine line

line'up' *n.* row of persons or things

lin'ger (lin'gər) *v.* **1.** continue to stay **2.** loiter

lin·ge·rie' (län zhə rā') *n.* women's underwear

lin'go (lin'-) *n.* [*pl.* -GOES] unfamiliar jargon

lin'guist *n.* **1.** one adept in several languages **2.** specialist in linguistics

lin·guis'tics *n.pl.* science of (a) language

lin'i·ment *n.* medicated liquid for the skin

lin'ing *n.* material covering an inner surface

link *n.* **1.** loop in a chain **2.** part in a chainlike series **3.** thing that connects —*v.* join; connect

link'age *n.* **1.** a linking **2.** series of links

links *n.pl.* place where golf is played

li·no'le·um *n.* hard, smooth floor covering

lin'seed' oil yellow oil from seed of flax

lint *n.* bits of thread, fluff, etc. from cloth —**lint'y** [-IER, -IEST] *a.*

lin'tel *n.* horizontal piece over a door or window

li'on *n.* **1.** large animal of the cat family, found in Africa and SW Asia **2.** very strong or brave person 3. celebrity —**li'-on·ess** n.fem.

li'on·heart'ed a. very brave

li'on·ize v. treat as a celebrity

lip n. 1. upper or lower edge of the mouth 2. thing like a lip, as a cup's rim

lip reading recognition of words by watching a speaker's lips —**lip'-read'** v.

lip'stick n. small stick of rouge to color the lips

liq'ue·fy (-wə-) v. [-FIED, -FY-ING] change to a liquid

li·queur' (-kur') n. sweet alcoholic liquor

liq'uid (-wid) a. 1. readily flowing 2. readily changed into cash —n. substance that flows easily

liq'ui·date v. 1. settle the accounts of (a business) 2. pay (a debt) 3. change into cash 4. get rid of, as by killing —**liq'ui·da'tion** n.

liq'uor (-ər) n. alcoholic drink, as whiskey

li·ra (lir'ə) n. [pl. -RE (-ā), -RAS] It. monetary unit

lisle (līl) n. fabric woven of strong cotton thread

lisp v. substitute the sounds "th" and "th" for the sounds of s and z —n. act or sound of lisping

lis·some (lis'əm) a. lithe

list n. series of names, words, etc. set forth in order —v. put in a list

list v. to tilt to one side, as a ship —n. a listing

lis·ten v. 1. try to hear 2. pay attention

list'ing n. 1. making of a list 2. entry in a list

list'less a. indifferent because ill, sad, etc.

lists n.pl. area where knights jousted

lit pt. & pp. of **light**

lit'a·ny n. [pl. -NIES] prayer with responses

li'ter (lē'-) n. metric unit of capacity (61.025 cu. in.): Br. sp. **li'tre**

lit'er·a·cy n. ability to read and write

lit'er·al a. 1. precise; exact; strict 2. prosaic 3. restricted to fact —**lit'er·al·ly** adv.

lit'er·ar'y a. having to do with literature

lit'er·ate (-it) a. educated; esp., able to read and write

lit'er·a·ture (-char) n. 1. all the valuable writings of a specific time, nation, etc. 2. all writings on some subject

lithe (līth) a. bending easily

lith'i·um (lĭth'-) n. soft, white chemical element

lith'o·graph (lĭth'-) n. print made by lithography

li·thog'ra·phy n. printing from stone or metal treated with grease and water

lit'i·gant n. party to a lawsuit

lit'i·gate v. to contest in a lawsuit —**lit'i·ga'tion** n.

lit'mus paper treated paper that turns blue in bases and red in acids

lit'ter n. 1. portable couch 2. stretcher 3. young borne at one time by a dog, cat, etc. 4. things lying about in disorder —v. make untidy

lit·ter·bug *n.* one who litters public places with rubbish, etc.

lit·tle *a.* [LITTLER or LESS or LESSER, LITTLEST or LEAST] 1. small in size or amount 2. short; brief 3. not important —*adv.* [LESS, LEAST] 1. slightly 2. not at all —*n.* small amount or short time —**little by little** gradually

lit·to·ral *a.* of or along the shore

lit·ur·gy *n.* [*pl.* -GIES] ritual for public worship —**li·tur'gi·cal** *a.*

liv·a·ble *a.* 1. fit or pleasant to live in 2. endurable Also **live'a·ble**

live (liv) *v.* 1. have life 2. stay alive; endure 3. pass one's life in a certain way 4. have a full life 5. feed (*on*) 6. reside

live (līv) *a.* 1. having life 2. energetic 3. of interest now 4. still burning 5. unexploded 6. carrying electrical current 7. in person 8. recorded at a public performance

live·li·hood *n.* means of supporting oneself

live·long (liv'-) *a.* whole

live·ly *a.* [-LIER, -LIEST] 1. full of life 2. exciting 3. cheerful 4. having much bounce —**live'li·ness** *n.*

liv·en (liv'-) *v.* cheer (*up*)

liv·er (liv'-) *n.* organ in vertebrates that makes bile

liv·er·wurst *n.* sausage made of ground liver

liv·er·y *n.* [*pl.* -IES] 1. uniform as of a servant 2. business of renting horses and carriages

lives *n.* pl. of **life**

live·stock *n.* animals kept or raised on a farm

liv·id *a.* 1. black-and-blue 2. grayish-blue

liv·ing *a.* 1. having life 2. in active use 3. of persons alive 4. true; lifelike 5. of life —*n.* 1. a being alive 2. livelihood 3. way that one lives —**the living** those that are still alive

living room room for lounging, entertaining, etc.

living wage wage high enough to live on in some comfort

liz·ard *n.* reptile with a long tail and four legs

lla·ma (lä'-) *n.* S. American camellike animal

lo *int.* look! see!

load *n.* 1. amount carried 2. burden 3. *often pl.* [Col.] great amount —*v.* 1. put (a load) in or on 2. burden 3. supply in large quantities 4. put ammunition into

load'star *n.* lodestar

load'stone *n.* lodestone

loaf *n.* [*pl.* LOAVES] bread, etc. baked in one piece —*v.* waste time —**loaf'er** *n.*

loam *n.* rich soil

loan *n.* 1. act of lending 2. something lent, esp. money at interest —*v.* lend

loath (lōth) *a.* reluctant

loathe (lōth) *v.* abhor

loath·ing (lōth'-) *n.* intense dislike

loath·some (lōth'-) *a.* disgusting

lob *v.* [LOBBED, LOBBING] toss or hit (a ball) in a high curve

lob·by *n.* [*pl.* -BIES] 1. entrance hall 2. group of lobbyists for the same interest —*v.* [-BIED, -BYING] act as a lobbyist

lob′by·ist *n.* one who tries to get legislators to support certain measures

lobe *n.* rounded projection

lob′ster *n.* edible sea animal with a pair of large pincers

lobster tail edible tail of any of various crayfish

lo′cal *a.* 1. of a particular place or area —*n.* 1. bus, etc. making all stops 2. branch, as of a labor union —**lo′cal·ly** *adv.*

lo·cale′ (-kal′) *n.* a place or setting for events, etc.

lo·cal′i·ty *n.* [*pl.* -TIES] place or district

lo′cal·ize *v.* limit or trace to a certain place

lo′cate *v.* 1. establish in a certain place 2. find or show the position of 3. [Col.] settle (*in a place*)

lo·ca′tion *n.* 1. a locating 2. position; place

loch (läk) *n.* [Scot.] 1. lake 2. arm of the sea

lock *n.* 1. device for fastening a door, etc. as with a key 2. part of a canal between gates 3. curl of hair —*v.* 1. fasten with a lock 2. shut (*in* or *out*) 3. jam or link together

lock′er *n.* 1. chest, closet, etc. that can be locked 2. large compartment for freezing and storing foods

lock′et *n.* little case worn on a necklace

lock′jaw′ *n.* tetanus

lock′out′ *n.* a locking out of

employees to force agreement to employer's terms

lock′smith′ *n.* one who makes or repairs locks and keys

lock′up′ *n.* jail

lo′co *a.* [Sl.] crazy; insane

lo·co·mo′tion *n.* act or power of moving about

lo′co·mo′tive *n.* engine for a railroad train

lo′cust *n.* 1. grasshopperlike insect 2. cicada 3. tree with white flowers

lo·cu′tion (-kyōo′-) *n.* phrase or phraseology

lode *n.* vein or stratum of metallic ore

lode′star′ *n.* star by which one directs one's course

lode′stone′ *n.* strongly magnetic iron ore

lodge *n.* 1. a house for special use 2. chapter of a society —*v.* 1. to house or dwell for a time 2. put in 3. come to rest

lodg′er *n.* one who lives in a room rented from another

lodg′ing *n.* 1. place to live 2. *pl.* rented rooms

loft *n.* 1. space below a roof 2. upper story of a warehouse, etc. 3. gallery 4. height of a lofted ball —*v.* send (a ball) high into the air

loft′y *a.* [-IER, -IEST] 1. very high 2. noble 3. haughty — **loft′i·ness** *n.*

log *n.* 1. section cut from a tree trunk 2. daily record of a ship's or an aircraft's progress —*v.* [LOGGED, LOGGING] 1. cut down trees and remove the logs 2. to record in a log 3. sail or fly (a certain distance)

lo′gan·ber′ry n. [pl. -RIES] purple-red berry

log′a·rithm n. exponent showing power to which one number must be raised to produce another

loge (lōzh) n. theater box

log′ger·head n. stupid fellow —at loggerheads in disagreement

log′ic (läj′-) n. 1. science of reasoning 2. (correct) reasoning —lo·gi·cian (lō jish′ən) n.

log′i·cal a. 1. using or used in logic 2. expected as a result —log′i·cal·ly adv.

lo·gis′tics (-jis′-) n. military science of moving and supplying troops

log′jam n. 1. logs jammed up in a stream 2. piled-up work that obstructs progress

log′roll′ing n. mutual exchange of favors, esp. among lawmakers

lo·gy (lō′gē) a. [-GIER, -GIEST] [Col.] dull or sluggish

-logy suf. science or study of

loin n. 1. lower back from ribs to hipbone 2. pl. hips and lower abdomen

loin′cloth n. cloth worn about the loins, as by some tribes

loi′ter v. 1. spend time idly 2. move slowly

loll v. 1. lounge about 2. droop or let hang loosely

lol′li·pop, lol′ly·pop n. piece of candy on a stick

lol′ly·gag v. [-GAGGED, -GAGGING] [Col.] waste time aimlessly

lone a. by oneself or itself

lone′ly a. [-LIER, -LIEST] 1. alone and unhappy 2. unfrequented —lone′li·ness n.

lon′er (lōn′-) n. one who avoids the company of others

lone′some a. having or causing a lonely feeling

long a. 1. measuring much 2. in length 3. of great length 4. tedious 5. far-reaching 6. well-supplied —adv. 1. for a long time 2. for the time of 3. at a remote time —v. to wish earnestly; yearn —as (or so) long as 1. while 2. since 3. provided that —before long soon

long′-dis′tance a. to or from distant places —adv. by long-distance telephone

long distance telephone service for long-distance calls

lon·gev′i·ty (-jev′-) n. long life

long′-faced′ a. glum

long′hair′ a. [Col.] of intellectuals or their tastes

long′hand′ n. ordinary handwriting

long′ing n. earnest desire

lon′gi·tude (län′jə-) n. distance, in degrees, east or west of a line through Greenwich, England

lon′gi·tu′di·nal (-tōō′-) a. 1. of length 2. of longitude

long jump Sports jump for distance, made from a stationary position or a running start

long′-lived′ (-līvd′, -livd′) a. having a long life span

long′-play′ing a. of a phonograph record playing at 33 1/3 revolutions per minute

long′-range′ a. covering a long distance or time

long'shore'man n. [pl. -MEN] one whose work is loading and unloading ships

long'-term' a. for or extending over a long time

long ton 2,240 pounds

long'ways adv. lengthwise

long'-wind'ed (-win'did) a. 1. speaking at great length 2. tiresomely long

look v. 1. direct the eyes so as to see 2. search 3. seem 4. be facing —n. 1. act of looking 2. appearance 3. pl. [Col.] personal appearance —int. 1. see! 2. pay attention! —**look after** care for —**look down on** regard with contempt —**look for** expect —**look forward to** anticipate —**look into** investigate —**look out** be careful —**look over** examine —**look up** 1. search for in a book 2. [Col.] call on —**look up to** admire

looking glass glass mirror

look'out' n. 1. careful watching 2. guard; sentry 3. [Col.] concern

look'-see' n. [Sl.] quick look

loom (lōōm) n. machine for weaving —v. come into sight suddenly

loon n. ducklike bird

loon'y a. [-IER, -IEST] [Sl.] crazy; demented

loop n. figure of a line, etc. curving back to cross itself —v. make a loop

loop'hole n. means of evading something

loose (lōōs) a. 1. free 2. not firm or tight 3. inexact 4. sexually immoral 5. [Col.] relaxed —adv. loosely —v. 1. free 2. make less tight, etc. 3. release —**loose'ly** adv. —**loos'en** v.

loot n., v. plunder

lop v. [LOPPED, LOPPING] cut off

lope (lōp) v., n. (move with) a long swinging stride

lop'sid'ed a. heavier, lower, etc. on one side

lo·qua'cious (-kwā'shəs) a. very talkative —**lo·quac'i·ty** (-kwas'-) n.

lord n. 1. master 2. [L-] God 3. [L-] Jesus Christ 4. British nobleman

lore n. knowledge

lor·gnette' (-nyet') n. eyeglasses on a handle

lor'ry n. [pl. -RIES] [Br.] motor truck

lose (lōōz) v. [LOST, LOSING] 1. become unable to find 2. have taken from one by accident, death, etc. 3. fail to keep 4. fail to have, get, etc. 5. fail to win 6. wander from —**lose oneself** become engrossed —**los'er** n.

loss (lôs) n. 1. a losing, or damage, etc. from this 2. person, thing, etc. lost

lost a. 1. ruined 2. missing or mislaid 3. not gained or won 4. having wandered astray 5. wasted

lot n. 1. deciding of a matter by chance 2. fate 3. piece of land 4. group 5. often pl. [Col.] great amount —adv. very much

lo'tion n. liquid for softening or healing the skin

lot'ter·y n. [pl. -IES] game in

which numbered chances on prizes are sold

lo'tus *n.* tropical waterlily

loud *a.* 1. strong in sound 2. noisy 3. [Col.] flashy —*adv.* in a loud way —**loud'ly** *adv.* —**loud'ness** *n.*

loud-mouthed (loud'moutht, -mouthd) *a.* talking in a loud, irritating way

loud'speak'er *n.* device, as in a radio, for changing electric waves into sound and amplifying it

lounge (lounj) *v.* 1. sit in a relaxed way 2. to be idle —*n.* 1. room furnished for lounging 2. couch

louse *n.* [*pl.* LICE] small insect parasite —**louse up** [Sl.] to spoil; ruin

lous·y (lou'zē) *a.* [-IER, -IEST] 1. infested with lice 2. [Sl.] disgusting 3. [Sl.] inferior 4. [Sl.] well supplied (*with*)

lout *n.* stupid fellow

lou'ver (lōō'-) *n.* 1. an opening with boards slanted to let in air and keep out rain 2. such a board

love *n.* 1. strong affection 2. object of this 3. *Tennis* score of zero —*v.* feel love (for) —in love feeling love —**make love** 1. woo, embrace, etc. 2. have sexual intercourse —**lov'a·ble**, **love'a·ble**. —**love'less** *a.* —**lov'er** *n.*

love'lorn *a.* pining from love

love'ly *a.* [-LIER, -LIEST] 1. beautiful 2. [Col.] very enjoyable —**love'li·ness** *n.*

love seat small sofa for two

lov'ing *a.* feeling or expressing love —**lov'ing·ly** *adv.*

loving cup large drinking cup with two handles, often given as a prize

low (lō) *a.* 1. not high 2. below others in rank, size, cost, etc. 3. gloomy 4. deep in pitch 5. vulgar 6. not loud —*adv.* in or to a low level, etc. —*n.* 1. low level, degree, etc. 2. gear arrangement giving least speed 3. moo —*v.* moo —**lay low** kill —**lie low** stay hidden —**low'ness** *n.*

low'brow *n.*, *a.* [Col.] nonintellectual

low'down *n.* [Sl.] true, pertinent facts (with *the*) —*a.* (-doun') contemptible

low'er (lou'-) *a.* 1. below in place, rank, etc. 2. less in amount, degree, etc. —*v.* 1. let or put down 2. make or become less in amount, value, etc.

low'er (lou'-) *v.* 1. to scowl 2. appear threatening —**low'er·ing** *a.*

lower case small-letter type used in printing, rather than capital letters

low frequency radio frequency between 30 and 300 kilohertz

low'-key' *a.* of low intensity, tone, etc.: also **low'-keyed'**

low'land *n.* land lower than land around it

low'ly *a.* 1. of low rank 2. humble —**low'li·ness** *n.*

low'-mind'ed *a.* having a coarse, vulgar mind

low profile unobtrusive presence or concealed activity

lox *n.* 1. smoked salmon 2.

liquid oxygen, used in rocket fuel

loy'al a. faithful to one's friends, country, etc. —**loy'-al·ly** adv. —**loy'al·ty** [pl. -**TIES**] n.

loy'al·ist n. supporter of the government during a revolt

loz·enge (läz'inj) n. cough drop, candy, etc.

LP trademark for a long-playing record —n. long-playing record

LSD chemical compound used as a psychedelic drug

lu·au (lōō ou') n. Hawaiian feast

lub'ber n. clumsy person

lube n. 1. lubricating oil 2. [Col.] lubrication

lu'bri·cant a. that lubricates — n. oil, grease, etc.

lu'bri·cate v. apply oil or grease to reduce friction —**lu'-bri·ca'tion** n.

lu'cid (-sid) a. 1. clear 2. sane 3. shining —**lu·cid'i·ty** n. —**lu'cid·ly** adv.

luck n. 1. chance; fortune 2. good fortune —**luck out** [Col.] be lucky —**luck'less** a.

luck'y a. [-**IER**, -**IEST**] having, resulting in, or thought to bring good luck —**luck'i·ly** adv.

lu'cra·tive a. profitable

lu'cre (-kər) n. riches; money: chiefly derogatory

lu'cu·brate (-kyoo-) v. work or study hard, esp. late at night —**lu'cu·bra'tion** n.

lu'di·crous (-krəs) a. so incongruous as to be funny — **lu'di·crous·ly** adv.

luff v. head a ship toward the wind

lug v. [**LUGGED, LUGGING**] carry with effort —n. 1. earlike handle or support 2. heavy nut to keep a wheel on an axle

lug'gage n. suitcases, trunks, etc.

lu·gu'bri·ous a. mawkishly mournful —**lu·gu'bri·ous·ly** adv.

luke'warm' a. 1. slightly warm 2. lacking enthusiasm

lull v. 1. soothe by gentle sound or motion 2. calm —v. move short period of calm

lull'a·by n. [pl. -**BIES**] song for lulling a baby to sleep

lum·ba'go n. pain in the lower back

lum'bar (-bər) a. of or near the loins

lum'ber n. wood sawed into beams, boards, etc. —v. move heavily

lum'ber·jack n. man who cuts timber for the sawmill

lum'ber·man n. [pl. -**MEN**] 1. lumberjack 2. lumber dealer

lu'mi·nar'y n. [pl. -**IES**] famous person

lu'mi·nes'cence n. giving off of light without heat —**lu'mi·nes'cent** a.

lu'mi·nous a. bright; shining —**lu'mi·nos'i·ty** n.

lum'mox n. [Col.] clumsy, stupid person

lump n. 1. mass of something 2. a swelling 3. pl. [Col.] hard blows, criticism, etc. —a. in a lump or lumps —v. 1. group together 2. treat or deal with in a mass 3. [Col.] put up with anyhow —**lump'y** [-IER, -IEST] *a.*

lump sum total sum paid at one time

lu'nar *a.* of the moon

lu'na·tic *a.* 1. insane 2. utterly foolish —*n.* insane person — **lu'na·cy** *n.*

lunch *n.* midday meal —*v.* eat lunch

lunch'eon (-ən) *n.* formal lunch

lunch·eon·ette' *n.* small restaurant serving light lunches

luncheon meat meat processed in loaves, etc., ready to eat

lung *n.* spongelike organ in the chest for breathing

lunge (lunj) *n.* 1. sudden thrust 2. forward plunge —*v.* make a lunge

lung'fish' *n.* fish having lungs as well as gills

lu'pine *n.* plant with spikes of rose, white, or blue flowers

lu'pus *n.* disease with skin lesions

lurch *v.* 1. sway suddenly to one side 2. stagger —*n.* 1. lurching movement 2. danger; trouble: only in **leave in the lurch**

lure *n.* 1. thing that attracts 2. fish bait —*v.* attract; entice

lu'rid *a.* 1. shocking 2. glowing strangely

lurk *v.* stay or be hidden, ready to attack

lus'cious (lush'əs) *a.* 1. delicious 2. pleasing

lush *a.* of or having luxuriant growth

lust *n.* 1. strong sexual desire 2. strong desire, as for power

—*v.* feel an intense desire — **lust'ful** *a.*

lus'ter *n.* 1. gloss; brightness 2. brilliant fame —**lus'trous** (-trəs) *a.*

lust'y *a.* [-IER, -IEST] vigorous; robust —**lust'i·ly** *adv.*

lute *n.* stringed, guitarlike instrument

lut'ist *n.* lute player: also **lu'-ta·nist**

lux·u'ri·ant (lug zhoor'-) *a.* 1. growing in abundance 2. richly ornamented —**lux·u'ri·ance** *n.*

lux·u'ri·ate *v.* 1. live in luxury 2. revel (*in*)

lux·u'ri·ous *a.* 1. giving a feeling of luxury 2. fond of luxury —**lux·u'ri·ous·ly** *adv.*

lux'u·ry *n.* [*pl.* -RIES] 1. enjoyment of the best and most costly things 2. any of these things, often not needed

-ly *suf.* 1. like 2. in a specified way, or at a specified time or place 3. in sequence 4. every

lye (lī) *n.* strong alkaline substance, used in cleaning

ly'ing *prp.* of **lie**

ly'ing-in' *a., n.* (of or for) childbirth

lymph (limf) *n.* clear, yellowish body fluid —**lym·phat'ic** *a.*

lynch *v.* kill by mob action, without lawful trial

lynx *n.* N. American wildcat

ly·on·naise' (-ə nāz') *a.* made with fried, sliced onions

lyre (līr) *n.* ancient instrument like a small harp

lyr'ic (lir'-) *a.* 1. suitable for singing 2. expressing the poet's emotions **3.** of or having a high voice —n. **1.** lyric poem **2.** pl. words of a song

lyr'i·cal a. **1.** lyric **2.** very enthusiastic, etc. —**lyr'i·cal·ly** adv.

M

ma n. [Col.] mother

ma'am n. [Col.] madam

ma·ca'bre (-kä'bra) a. grim and horrible

mac·ad'am n. **1.** small broken stones, often with tar or asphalt, used to make some roads **2.** such a road —**mac·ad'am·ize** v.

mac'a·ro'ni (-nē) n. tubes of flour paste, cooked for food

mac·a·roon' n. cookie made with almonds or coconut

ma·caw' n. large parrot

Mace (mās) trademark for a combined tear gas and nerve gas

mace n. **1.** heavy spiked club **2.** official's staff **3.** spice made from ground nutmeg shell

mac'er·ate (mas'-) v. soften by soaking

ma·che·te (ma shet'ē) n. large, heavy knife

Mach'i·a·vel'li·an (mak'-) a. crafty, deceitful, etc.

mach'i·na'tion (mak'-) n. wily or evil scheme

ma·chine' n. **1.** device with moving parts, for doing work **2.** group in control of a political party —a. of or done by machines —v. to shape, etc. by machinery

machine gun automatic gun

ma·chin'er·y n. **1.** machines **2.** working parts

ma·chin'ist n. one who makes or operates machines

Mach number (mäk) number for the ratio of airspeed to the speed of sound

ma·cho (mä'chō) a. [Sp.] masculine, virile, etc.

mack'er·el n. edible fish of the N. Atlantic

Mack'i·naw coat short, heavy coat, often plaid: also **mackinaw** n.

mack'in·tosh n. raincoat of rubberized cloth

mac'ra·mé (-mā) n. coarse yarn, cord, etc. knotted in designs

mac'ro·cosm n. universe

ma'cron (-krən) n. pronunciation mark (¯)

mad a. [MADDER, MADDEST] **1.** insane **2.** frantic **3.** foolish **4.** infatuated **5.** having rabies **6.** angry —**mad'ly** adv. —**mad'ness** n.

mad'am n. **1.** polite title for a woman **2.** woman in charge of a brothel

mad'ame (-əm) n. [pl. MESDAMES (mā däm')] married woman: Fr. for Mrs.

mad'cap n. reckless person

mad'den v. make mad —**mad'den·ing** a.

mad'der n. **1.** vine with berries **2.** red dye made from its root

made pt. & pp. of **make**

ma'de·moi·selle' (-ma zel') n.

unmarried woman: Fr. for *Miss*

made'-to-or'der *a.* made to customer's specifications

made'-up' *a.* 1. invented; false 2. with cosmetics applied

mad'house *n.* 1. insane asylum 2. place of turmoil

mad'man *n.* [*pl.* -MEN] insane person —**mad'wom'an** [*pl.* -WOMEN] *n.fem.*

Ma·don'na *n.* picture or statue of the mother of Jesus

ma·dras (mad'rəs, mə dras') *n.* fine cotton cloth, usually striped

mad'ri·gal *n.* part song without accompaniment

mael'strom (māl'-) *n.* violent whirlpool

ma·es'tro (mīs'-, mä es'-) *n.* [It.] master, as in music

Ma·fi·a, Maf·fi·a (mä'fē ə) *n.* secret society of criminals

mag·a·zine' (-zēn') *n.* 1. periodical publication 2. storage place, as for military supplies 3. supply chamber, as in a rifle, camera, etc.

ma·gen'ta (-jen'-) *n.* purplish red

mag'got *n.* wormlike larva —**mag'got·y** *a.*

Ma·gi (mā'jī) *n.pl.* wise men in the Bible

mag'ic *n.* 1. use of charms, spells, etc. 2. sleight of hand —*a.* produced by or as if by magic: also **mag'i·cal** —**mag'i·cal·ly** *adv.*

ma·gi'cian (-jish'ən) *n.* one who does magic

mag·is·te'ri·al (maj'-) *a.* authoritative

mag'is·trate (maj'-) *n.* official administering the law —**mag'is·tra·cy** *n.*

mag·nan'i·mous (mag-) *a.* generous in forgiving; noble —**mag'na·nim'i·ty** *n.*

mag'nate (-nāt) *n.* influential person in business

mag·ne'sia (-zhə) *n.* white powder (magnesium oxide) used as a laxative

mag·ne'si·um (-zē-) *n.* light, silvery metal, a chemical element

mag'net *n.* piece of iron, steel, etc. that attracts iron or steel

magnetic tape thin plastic tape magnetized for recording sound, video material, etc.

mag'net·ism *n.* 1. properties of magnets 2. personal charm —**mag·net'ic** *a.*

mag'net·ize *v.* 1. make a magnet of 2. to charm

mag·ne'to (-nē'-) *n.* [*pl.* -TOS] small electric generator

mag'ne·tom'e·ter *n.* device for measuring magnetic forces

mag·nif'i·cent *a.* 1. grand and stately; splendid 2. exalted —**mag·nif'i·cence** *n.*

mag'ni·fy *v.* [-FIED, -FYING] 1. increase apparent size of, as with a lens 2. exaggerate —**mag'ni·fi·ca'tion** *n.* —**mag'ni·fi'er** *n.*

mag'ni·tude *n.* 1. greatness of size, extent, or importance 2. loudness of sound 3. brightness of a star

mag·no'li·a *n.* tree with large, fragrant flowers

mag'pie *n.* noisy bird of the crow family

Mag'yar (-yär) *n.* person or language of Hungary

ma·ha·ra'jah *n.* in India, a prince, formerly the ruler of a native state —**ma·ha·ra'ni, ma·ha·ra'nee** *n.fem.*

ma·hat'ma *n.* in India, wise and holy person

mah'-jongg' (-jôn') *n.* Chinese game played with small tiles: also **mahjong**

ma·hog'a·ny *n.* reddish-brown wood of a tropical tree

ma·hout' (-hout') *n.* in India, elephant driver

maid *n.* 1. unmarried, esp. young, woman 2. woman or girl servant

maid'en *n.* young unmarried woman —*a.* 1. of or for a maiden 2. unmarried 3. first; earliest —**maid'en·hood** *n.* — **maid'en·ly** *a.*

maid'en·hair' *n.* delicate fern

mail *n.* 1. letters, etc. sent by postal service 2. postal system 3. metal mesh armor —*a.* of mail —*v.* send by mail — **mail'box** *n.*

mail carrier one who carries and delivers mail

mail'man *n.* [*pl.* **-MEN**] mail carrier

maim *v.* cripple; disable

main *a.* chief; leading; principal —*n.* 1. chief pipe in a system 2. [Poet.] ocean —**in the main** mostly —**with might and main** with all one's strength —**main'ly** *adv.*

main'land *n.* main part of a continent

main'line *n.* principal road —

v. [Sl.] inject (a narcotic drug) directly into a large vein

main'spring *n.* chief spring in a clock, etc.

main'stay *n.* main support

main'stream *n.* major trend, line of thought, etc.

main·tain' *v.* 1. keep up; carry on 2. keep in repair 3. declare to be true 4. support

main'te·nance *n.* 1. a maintaining 2. means of support

maî·tre d'hô·tel (met'r' dô'-tel') [Fr.] chief of waiters

maize (māz) *n.* corn

maj'es·ty *n.* 1. grandeur; dignity 2. [M-] title for a sovereign —**ma·jes'tic** *a.* — **ma·jes'ti·cal·ly** *adv.*

ma·jol'i·ca (mə jäl'-) *n.* Italian glazed pottery

ma'jor *a.* 1. greater in size, rank, etc. 2. *Mus.* half tone higher than the minor —*n.* 1. military officer above a captain 2. main study —*v.* specialize (*in* a subject)

ma'jor·do'mo *n.* [*pl.* **-MOS**] man in charge of a great house

ma·jor·ette' *n.* girl who leads a marching band: also **drum majorette**

major general officer above brigadier general

ma·jor'i·ty *n.* 1. more than half 2. full legal age

make *v.* [MADE, MAKING] 1. bring into being; build, create, etc. 2. cause to be 3. amount to; equal 4. acquire; earn 5. cause success of 6. execute, do, etc. 7. force; compel 8. arrive at 9. [Col.] get a place on (a team) —*n.* 1. act of making 2.

style or build —**make away with** steal —**make believe** pretend —**make for** go toward —**make it** [Col.] achieve a certain thing —**make out 1.** see **2.** succeed —**make over** change —**make up 1.** put together **2.** invent **3.** compensate **4.** stop quarreling **5.** put on cosmetics —**make up to** flatter —**mak′er** n.

make′-be·lieve′ n. pretense — a. pretended

make′shift a., n. (as) a temporary substitute

make′up′, make′-up′ n. **1.** way a thing is put together **2.** cosmetics

mal- pref. bad or badly

mal′ad·just′ed a. badly adjusted, as to environment —**mal′ad·just′ment** n.

mal·a·droit′ a. clumsy

mal′a·dy n. [pl. -DIES] illness; disease

ma·laise′ (ma lāz′) n. vague illness

mal′a·mute (-myo͞ot) n. breed of sled dog used by Eskimos

mal′a·prop·ism n. ridiculous misuse of words

ma·lar′i·a n. disease with chills and fever, carried by mosquitoes

ma·lar′key, ma·lar′ky n. [Sl.] nonsensical talk

mal′a·thi′on (-thī′-) n. kind of organic insecticide

mal·con·tent a., n. dissatisfied (person)

male a. **1.** of the sex that fertilizes the ovum **2.** of, like, or for men or boys —n. a male person, animal, or plant

mal′e·dic′tion n. a curse

mal′e·fac′tor n. evildoer —**mal′e·fac′tion** n.

ma·lev′o·lent a. wishing harm to others —**ma·lev′o·lence** n.

mal·fea′sance (-fē′z′ns) n. wrongdoing in public office

mal·for·ma′tion n. faulty formation —**mal·formed′** a.

mal·func′tion v. fail to work as it should —n. failure

mal′ice (-is) n. ill will; wish to harm —**ma·li′cious** (-shəs) a.

ma·lign′ (-līn′) v. speak evil of —a. evil; harmful

ma·lig′nant a. **1.** evil **2.** very harmful **3.** likely to cause death —**ma·lig′nan·cy** n.

ma·lin′ger v. feign illness to escape duty —**ma·lin′ger·er** n.

mall n. **1.** shaded public walk **2.** shop-lined street for pedestrians only **3.** enclosed shopping center

mal′lard n. wild duck

mal′le·a·ble a. that can be hammered or pressed into shape —**mal′le·a·bil′i·ty** n.

mal′let n. hammer with a wooden head

mal′low n. family of plants including the hollyhock

mal·nour′ished a. improperly nourished

mal′nu·tri′tion n. faulty diet; lack of nourishment

mal′oc·clu′sion n. faulty position of teeth so that they do not meet properly

mal·o′dor·ous a. having a bad smell; stinking

mal·prac′tice n. improper practice, as by a doctor

malt n. barley, etc. soaked and dried for use in brewing and distilling

mal·treat' v. to abuse —**mal·treat'ment** n.

mam'ma, ma'ma n. mother: child's word

mam'mal n. any vertebrate the female of which suckles its offspring —**mam·ma'li·an** (-mā'-) a., n.

mam·mog'ra·phy n. X-ray technique to detect breast tumors

mam'mon n. riches as an object of greed

mam'moth n. huge, extinct elephant —a. huge

man n. [pl. MEN] 1. human being; person 2. adult male person 3. human race 4. piece used in chess, checkers, etc. —v. [MANNED, MANNING] furnish with men for work, etc. —**as one man** in unison —**to a man** with no exception

man'a·cle n., v. handcuff

man'age v. 1. to control or guide 2. have charge of 3. succeed in doing 4. carry on business 5. contrive to get along —**man'age·a·ble** a. —**man'age·ment** n. —**man'ag·er** n.

man'a·ge'ri·al (-jir'ē-) a. of a manager

ma·ña'na (mä nyä'nä) adv., n. [Sp.] tomorrow

man·a·tee' n. large mammal living in tropical waters

man'da·rin n. 1. formerly, high Chinese official 2. [M-] main Chinese dialect

man'date n. 1. an order; command 2. will of voters as expressed in elections 3. formerly, commission given to a nation to administer a region 4. such a region

man'da·to'ry a. 1. of a mandate 2. required; commanded

man'di·ble n. lower jaw

man'do·lin n. musical instrument with from four or five pairs of strings

man'drake n. poisonous plant with a forked root

man'drel, man'dril n. spindle in a lathe to support work

man'drill n. large African baboon

mane n. long hair on the neck of a horse, lion, etc.

man'-eat'er n. animal that eats human flesh

ma·nège' (-nezh') n. art of riding and training horses

ma·neu'ver (-nōō'-) n. 1. planned movement of troops, warships, etc. 2. scheme —v. 1. perform maneuvers 2. get, etc. by some scheme —**ma·neu'ver·a·ble** a.

man'ga·nese n. grayish metal in alloys, a chemical element

mange (mānj) n. skin disease of animals —**man'gy** [-GIER, -GIEST] a.

man'ger (mān'jər) n. box from which livestock feed

man'gle v. 1. mutilate by hacking, etc. 2. botch 3. press in a mangle —n. machine with rollers for ironing

man'go n. [pl. -GOES, -GOS] yellow-red tropical fruit

man'grove n. tropical tree with branches that send down roots to form trunks

man'han·dle v. to handle roughly

man'hole n. hole for entering a sewer, etc.

man'hood n. 1. time of being a man 2. manly qualities 3. men collectively

man'-hour' n. time unit equal to one hour of work done by one person

man'hunt n. hunt for a fugitive

ma'ni·a n. 1. wild insanity 2. obsession —**man'ic** a.

ma'ni·ac n. violently insane person —**ma·ni'a·cal** (-nī'ə k'l) a.

man'ic-de·pres'sive a. having alternating periods of mania and mental depression

man'i·cure v., n. (take) care of the fingernails —**man'i·cur'ist** n.

man'i·fest a. obvious —v. reveal; show —n. list of a ship's cargo —**man'i·fes·ta'tion** n.

man'i·fes'to n. [pl. -TOES] public declaration

man'i·fold a. of many parts, sorts, etc. —n. pipe with several outlets, as for carrying exhaust from an engine

man'i·kin n. mannequin

ma·nip'u·late v. 1. handle skillfully 2. manage unfairly or dishonestly —**ma·nip'u·la'tion** n.

man'kind' n. 1. human race 2. (-kīnd) all human males

man'ly a. [-LIER, -LIEST] of, like, or fit for a man —**man'li·ness** n.

man'-made' a. artificial; synthetic

man'na n. thing provided as by a miracle

man'ne·quin (-kin) n. 1. woman who models clothes 2. model of the human body

man'ner n. 1. way; style 2. habit 3. pl. (polite) ways of behaving 4. kind; sort

man'ner·ism n. (affected) peculiarity of manner

man'ner·ly a. polite

man of letters writer or scholar in field of literature

man'-of-war' n. warship

man'or n. large estate

man'pow'er n. 1. human strength 2. collective strength of a nation, etc.

man'sard (roof) (-särd) roof with two slopes on each side

manse n. residence of a minister or clergyman

man'sion n. large, imposing house

man'slaugh'ter n. unintentional killing of a person

man'tel n. frame around or shelf above a fireplace

man·til'la n. woman's scarf for the hair and shoulders

man'tis n. predatory insect with forelegs held as if praying

man'tle n. 1. sleeveless cloak 2. thing that covers —v. 1. to cover 2. to blush

man'tra (-trə) n. Hindu hymn or text chanted as a prayer

man'u·al a. made or done by hand —n. 1. handbook 2. military weapons drill —**man'u·al·ly** adv.

man·u·fac'ture n. making of goods by machinery —v. make, esp. by machinery —**man′u·fac′tur·er** n.

man′u·mit v. [-MITTED, -MITTING] free from slavery —**man′u·mis′sion** n.

ma·nure′ n. animal waste as fertilizer —v. put manure on

man′u·script n. 1. written or typed book, article, etc. 2. writing as opposed to print —a. 1. handwritten or typewritten 2. written with printlike letters

man′y a. [MORE, MOST] numerous —n., pron. large number (of persons or things)

map n. drawing of the earth's surface or of the sky —v. [MAPPED, MAPPING] 1. to make a map of 2. plan

ma′ple n. 1. large shade tree 2. its hard wood 3. flavor of syrup or sugar made from its sap

mar v. [MARRED, MARRING] damage; spoil

mar′a·bou (-bōō) n. (plumes of) a stork of Africa or India

ma·ra′ca (-rä′-) n. pebble-filled musical rattle

mar·a·schi·no cherries (mar′-ə skē′nō) cherries in flavored syrup

mar′a·thon n. 1. foot race of about 26 miles 2. any endurance contest

ma·raud′er (-rôd′-) n. raider —**ma·raud′ing** a.

mar′ble n. 1. hard limestone, white or colored 2. little ball of stone, glass, or clay, used in children's game —a. of or like marble —v. 1. make book edges look mottled like marble

2. cause (meat) to be streaked with fat

mar′ble·ize v. make look like marble

March n. third month

march v. 1. walk with regular steps 2. advance steadily —n. 1. a marching 2. progress 3. distance marched 4. marching music

mar′chion·ess (-shə nis) n. wife or widow of a marquess

Mar·di gras (mär′dē grä′) last day before Lent begins

mare (mer) n. female horse, mule, donkey, etc.

mar·ga·rine (mär′jə rin) n. a spread like butter, of vegetable oil and skim milk

mar′gin n. 1. edge, as the blank border of a page 2. extra amount in reserve 3. allowance for increase or error 4. difference between cost and selling price —**mar′gin·al** a.

ma·ri·a·chi (mär′ē ä′chē) n. 1. (member of) a strolling band in Mexico 2. its music

mar′i·gold (mar′-) n. plant with yellow or orange flowers

ma·ri·jua·na, ma·ri·hua·na (mar′ə wä′nə) n. 1. hemp plant 2. its dried leaves and flowers, smoked, esp. as cigarettes, for euphoric effect

ma·rim′ba n. kind of xylophone

ma·ri′na (-rē′-) n. small harbor with docks

mar′i·nade (mar-) n. spiced pickling solution for meat, fish, etc.

mar′i·nate v. steep (fish, meat, etc.) in marinade

ma·rine′ (-rēn′) *a.* of or in the sea, ships, etc. —*n.* member of the U.S. Marine Corps

mar′i·ner (mar′-) *n.* sailor

mar′i·o·nette′ *n.* puppet

mar′i·tal *a.* of marriage

mar′i·time *a.* 1. on or near the sea 2. of sailing

mar′jo·ram (mär′-) *n.* plant used for flavoring

mark *n.* 1. spot, scratch, etc. 2. sign or label 3. sign of quality 4. grade 5. impression 6. target; goal —*v.* 1. put a mark on 2. show by a mark 3. characterize 4. listen to 5. rate — **make one's mark** succeed — **mark′er** *n.*

mark′down *n.* price decrease

marked *a.* 1. having a mark 2. noticeable —**mark′ed·ly** *adv.*

mar′ket *n.* 1. place where goods are sold 2. store selling food 3. buying and selling 4. demand for (goods, etc.) —*v.* buy or sell —**mar′ket·a·ble** *a.* —**mar′ket·er, mar·ket·eer′** *n.* —**mar′ket·place** *n.*

mark′ing *n.* arrangement of marks, as on fur, etc.

marks′man *n.* [*pl.* -MEN] one who shoots well —**marks′man·ship** *n.*

mark′up *n.* price increase

mar′lin *n.* large, slender, deep-sea fish

mar′ma·lade *n.* preserve of oranges or other fruits

mar′mo·set *n.* small monkey

mar′mot *n.* thick-bodied rodent, as the woodchuck

ma·roon′ *n., a.* dark brownish red —*v.* put (a person) ashore in a lonely place

mar·quee′ (-kē′) *n.* rooflike projection over an entrance

mar′quess (-kwis) *n.* 1. British nobleman above an earl 2. marquis

mar′que·try (-kə-) *n.* fancy inlaid work in furniture, etc.

mar′quis (-kwis) *n.* nobleman above an earl or count —**mar·quise′** (-kēz′) *n.fem.*

mar·qui·sette′ (-ki-, -kwi-) *n.* thin, netlike cloth

mar′riage (mar′ij) *n.* 1. married life 2. wedding —**mar′riage·a·ble** *a.*

mar′row *n.* 1. soft core inside bones 2. central part

mar′ry *v.* [-RIED, -RYING] 1. join as husband and wife 2. take as spouse 3. unite

marsh *n.* swamp —**marsh′y** [-IER, -IEST] *a.*

mar′shal *n.* 1. highest ranking officer in some armies 2. Federal officer like a sheriff 3. head of a police or fire department —*v.* arrange (troops, ideas, etc.)

marsh′mal′low *n.* soft, white, spongy candy

mar·su′pi·al *n.* animal with a pouch for carrying its young

mart *n.* market

mar′ten *n.* 1. weasellike animal 2. its fur

mar′tial (-shəl) *a.* 1. of war 2. military 3. warlike

martial law military rule over civilians

mar′tin *n.* kind of swallow

mar·ti·net′ *n.* strict disciplinarian

mar′tyr (-tər) *n.* one who suffers or dies for his or her behefs —v. treat as a martyr — **mar'tyr·dom** n.

mar'vel n. wonderful thing — v. be amazed —**mar'vel·ous**, **mar'vel·lous** a.

Marx'ism n. doctrine of socialism —**Marx'ist**, **Marx'i·an** a., n.

mar'zi·pan n. candy of ground almonds, sugar, and egg white

mas·ca·ra (-kar'ə) n. cosmetic to color eyelashes

mas'con n. dense material beneath the moon's surface

mas'cot n. animal or thing kept for good luck

mas'cu·line a. of or like men —**mas·cu·lin'i·ty** n.

ma·ser (mā'zər) n. device that emits radiation in a narrow beam

mash n. 1. grain crushed in water for brewing, etc. 2. moist feed mixture for horses, etc. —v. crush into a soft mass

mask n. 1. cover to conceal or protect the face 2. molded likeness of the face 3. grotesque cover for the face —v. to cover or conceal as with a mask

mas'och·ist (-ə kist) n. one who gets pleasure from being hurt —**mas'och·ism** n. —**mas·och·is'tic** a.

ma'son n. construction worker in brick, stone, etc.

ma'son·ry n. mason's work

masque (mask) n. 1. masquerade (n. 1) 2. elaborate verse play

mas·quer·ade' (-kar-) n. 1. party with masks and costumes 2. disguise —v. be disguised

mass n. 1. quantity of matter 2. large number 3. size 4. main part 5. [M] R.C.Ch. service of the Eucharist —v. gather into a mass —a. of or for the masses —**the masses** the common people

mas'sa·cre (-kər) n. indiscriminate killing —v. kill in large numbers

mas·sage' (-säzh') n. rubbing and kneading of part of the body —v. give a massage to

mas·seur' (-sur') n. man whose work is massaging —**mas·seuse'** (-sooz') n.fem.

mas'sive a. 1. big and heavy 2. large and imposing

mass media newspapers, magazines, radio, and TV

mass number number of neutrons and protons in the nucleus of an atom

mass production production in large quantities

mast n. tall, upright pole on a ship, supporting sails

mas·tec'to·my (-tek'tə-) n. [pl. -MIES] surgical removal of a breast

mas'ter n. 1. man who rules others or is in control 2. expert —a. 1. of a master 2. chief; main —v. 1. control 2. become expert in

mas'ter·ful a. 1. domineering 2. expert; skillful: also **mas'ter·ly**

master key key that opens every one of a set of locks

mas'ter·mind n. very clever person

Master of Arts (or **Science**, etc.) advanced college degree

master of ceremonies person who presides at an entertainment, banquet, etc.

mas'ter·piece n. **1.** thing made or done with expert skill **2.** the greatest work of a person or group Also **masterwork**

mas'ter·y n. **1.** control **2.** victory **3.** expert skill

mast'head n. part of newspaper, etc. telling address, publisher, etc.

mas'ti·cate v. chew up —**mas'ti·ca'tion** n.

mas'tiff n. big, strong dog

mas'to·don n. extinct animal like the elephant

mas'toid a., n. (of) a bony projection behind the ear

mas'tur·bate v. practice genital self-excitation —**mas'tur·ba'tion** n.

mat n. **1.** flat piece, as of woven straw, for protecting a floor, etc. **2.** thick tangled mass **3.** border around a picture —v. [MATTED, MATTING] **1.** cover with a mat **2.** weave or tangle together **3.** frame (picture) with a mat

mat'a·dor n. bullfighter

match n. **1.** short sliver with a tip that catches fire by friction **2.** person or thing like another **3.** contest **4.** marriage —v. **1.** be equal (to) **2.** put in opposition **3.** get an equivalent for

match'less a. without equal

match'mak'er n. arranger of marriages

mate n. **1.** one of a pair **2.** husband or wife **3.** lower officer on a ship —v. join, as in marriage

ma·te'ri·al n. **1.** what a thing is made of **2.** fabric **3.** pl. tools, etc. needed to make something —a. **1.** physical **2.** of the body; not spiritual **3.** essential

ma·te'ri·al·ism n. **1.** concern with physical things only **2.** belief that everything has a physical cause —**ma·te'ri·al·is'tic** a.

ma·te'ri·al·ize' v. give or take material form —**ma·te'ri·al·i·za'tion** n.

ma·te'ri·al·ly adv. **1.** physically **2.** considerably

ma·te'ri·el' n. military supplies

ma·ter'nal (-tur'-) a. of, like, or from a mother —**ma·ter'nal·ly** adv.

ma·ter'ni·ty n. motherhood —a. **1.** for pregnant women **2.** for mothers and their new babies

math n. [Col.] mathematics

math'e·mat'ics n. science dealing with quantities and forms, their relationships, etc. —**math'e·mat'i·cal** a. —**math'e·ma·ti'cian** n.

mat·i·née', **mat·i·nee'** (-nā') n. afternoon performance of a play, etc.

mat'ins n.pl. morning prayer

ma'tri·arch (-ärk) n. woman who rules her family or tribe —**ma'tri·ar'chal** a.

ma·tric'u·late v. enroll, as in college —**ma·tric'u·la'tion** n.

mat'ri·mo'ny n. marriage — **mat'ri·mo'ni·al** a.

ma'trix n. [pl. -TRICES (-trə sēz), -TRIXES] that within which a thing develops

ma'tron n. 1. wife or widow 2. woman manager of domestic affairs, as of a prison

matte (mat) n. dull surface or finish —a. not glossy

mat'ted a. closely tangled

mat'ter n. 1. physical substance of a thing 2. thing or affair 3. occasion 4. content of thought 5. importance 6. trouble 7. pus 8. mail —v. be of importance —as a matter of fact really —no matter 1. not important 2. regardless of

mat'ter-of-fact' a. sticking to facts; literal

mat'ting n. woven straw, etc. used as for mats

mat'tock n. kind of pickax

mat'tress n. casing filled with cotton, springs, etc., for use on a bed

ma·ture' (-toor', -choor') a. 1. fully grown, developed, etc. 2. due for payment —v. make or become mature —ma·tu'ri·ty n.

mat·zo (mät'sə) n. [pl. -ZOT, -ZOTH (-sōt), -ZOS] (piece of) unleavened bread eaten at Passover

maud'lin (môd'-) a. foolishly sentimental

maul v. handle roughly

maun'der v. talk or move aimlessly

mau'so·le'um n. large, imposing tomb

mauve (mōv) n. pale purple

mav'er·ick n. 1. lost, unbranded calf 2. [Col.] political independent

maw n. throat, gullet, jaws, mouth, etc.

mawk'ish a. sentimental in a sickening way

maxi- pref. maximum, very large, very long

max·il'la n. [pl. -LAE (-ē)] upper jawbone —**max'il·lar'y** a.

max'im n. concise saying that is a rule of conduct

max'i·mize v. to increase to a maximum

max'i·mum a., n. greatest possible (quantity or degree) —**max'i·mal** (-m'l) a.

May n. fifth month

may v. [pt. MIGHT] be able, likely, permitted, etc. to

may'be adv. possibly

may'flow'er n. early spring flower

may'hem n. crime of maiming a person intentionally

may·on·naise' (-nāz') n. creamy salad dressing

may'or n. head of a city —**may'or·al·ty** n.

maze n. confusing network of paths

maz·el tov (mä'z'l tōv') [Heb.] good luck

ma·zur·ka (mə zur'kə) n. lively Polish dance

M.C. Master of Ceremonies

me pron. objective case of I

mead (mēd) n. alcoholic liquor made from honey

mead·ow (med'ō) n. level field of grass

mea·ger, mea·gre (mē′gər) *a.*
1. poor; scanty 2. thin

meal *n.* 1. any of the times for eating 2. food served then 3. coarsely ground grain —**meal′y** [-IER, -IEST] *a.*

meal′y-mouthed′ (-mouthd′) *adj.* not sincere

mean *v.* [MEANT (ment), MEANING] 1. intend 2. intend to express 3. signify 4. have a certain importance —*a.* 1. low in quality or rank 2. poor or shabby 3. ignoble, petty, unkind, etc. 4. stingy 5. halfway between extremes —*n.* 1. middle point 2. *pl.* that by which a thing is gotten or done 3. *pl.* wealth —**by all** (or **no**) **means** certainly (not) —**by means of** by using —**mean′ly** *adv.* —**mean′ness** *n.*

me·an·der *v.* 1. wind back and forth 2. wander idly

mean′ing *n.* what is meant, indicated, etc. —**mean′ing·ful** *a.* —**mean′ing·less** *a.*

mean′time *adv.*, *n.* (during) the intervening time: also **mean′while**

mea·sles (mē′z'lz) *n.* contagious disease, usually of children

mea·sly (mēz′lē) *a.* [-SLIER, -SLIEST] [Col.] slight, worthless, or skimpy

meas′ure *v.* 1. find out the extent, dimensions, etc. of 2. mark of a certain amount 3. be a thing for measuring 4. be of specified dimensions —*n.* 1. dimensions, capacity, etc. 2. unit of measuring 3. system of measuring 4. instrument for measuring 5. definite quantity 6. course of action 7. a law 8. notes and rests between two bars on a musical staff —**for good measure** as something extra —**measure up** be worthwhile —**meas′ur·a·ble** *a.* —**meas′ure·less** *a.*

meas′ure·ment *n.* 1. a measuring 2. quantity measured 3. system of measuring

meat *n.* 1. flesh of animals used as food 2. edible part 3. essence —**meat′y** [-IER, -IEST] *a.*

me·chan′ic (-kan′-) *n.* worker who repairs machines

me·chan′i·cal *a.* 1. of or run by machinery 2. machinelike —**me·chan′i·cal·ly** *adv.*

me·chan′ics *n.* 1. science of motion and the effect of forces on bodies 2. knowledge of machinery 3. technical aspect

mech′a·nism (mek′-) *n.* 1. working parts of a machine 2. system of interrelated parts 3. any process producing a result —**mech′a·nis′tic** *a.*

mech′a·nize *v.* 1. make mechanical 2. equip with machinery, trucks, etc. —**mech′a·ni·za′tion** *n.*

med′al *n.* 1. flat, inscribed piece of metal given as an honor or reward 2. disk bearing a religious symbol

med′al·ist *n.* one who wins a medal

me·dal′lion (-yan) *n.* 1. large medal 2. round, medallike design

med′dle *v.* interfere in

another's affairs —**med'dler** n. —**med'dle·some** a.

me'di·an n. alt. pl. of **medium**: see **medium** (n. 3)

me'di·an n., a. (number, point, etc.) in the middle

me'di·ate v. (try to) settle (differences) between two parties —**me'di·a'tion** n. —**me'di·a'tor** n.

med'ic n. [Col.] 1. doctor 2. military medical corpsman

Med'i·caid n. State and Federal program that pays certain medical expenses for low-income persons

med'i·cal a. having to do with the practice or study of medicine —**med'i·cal·ly** adv.

Med'i·care n. Federal program that pays certain medical expenses for older people

med'i·cate v. treat with medicine —**med'i·ca'tion** n.

me·dic'i·nal a. that is or is used as a medicine

med'i·cine (-s'n) n. 1. science of treating and preventing disease 2. drug, etc. used in treating disease

medicine man among N. American Indians, etc., a man supposed to have healing powers

me'di·e'val a. of or like the Middle Ages

me'di·o'cre (-kər) a. 1. ordinary; average 2. inferior —**me'di·oc'ri·ty** (-äk'-) [pl. -TIES] n.

med'i·tate v. 1. think deeply 2. plan —**med'i·ta'tion** n. —**med'i·ta'tive** a.

me'di·um a. intermediate in

amount, degree, etc. —n. [pl. -DIUMS, -DIA] 1. medium thing or state 2. thing through which a force acts 3. means, agency, etc.; esp., a means of communication that reaches the general public: also now called **media** [pl. -DIAS] 4. surrounding substance

med'ley n. [pl. -LEYS] 1. mixture of unlike things 2. musical piece made up of several songs

meek a. 1. patient and mild 2. easily imposed on

meer'schaum (-shəm) n. (tobacco pipe made of) white, claylike mineral

meet v. [MET, MEETING] 1. come upon 2. be present at the arrival of 3. be introduced (to) 4. come into contact (with) 5. come together 6. satisfy 7. pay —n. a meeting —a. [Rare] suitable

meet'ing n. 1. a coming together 2. a gathering of people 3. junction

mega- pref. 1. large, great 2. a million of

meg'a·hertz n. [pl. -HERTZ] one million hertz

meg'a·lo·ma'ni·a n. delusion of grandeur or power

meg'a·lop'o·lis (-läp'-) n. vast urban area

meg'a·phone n. funnel-shaped device to increase the volume of the voice

meg'a·ton n. explosive force of a million tons of TNT

mel'an·cho'li·a (-ən kō'-) n. extreme depression

mel'an·chol'y (-kăl'ē) n. sad-

ness and mental depression —
a. sad or saddening

mé·lange (mā länzh′) **n.** mixture; medley

mel′a·nin n. brownish-black pigment of hair, skin, etc.

Mel′ba toast very crisp, thinly sliced toast

meld **v.,** **n.** (show and declare) playing cards that make a score

me·lee, mê·lée (mā′lā′) **n.** brawling group fight

mel′io·rate (mēl′yə-) **v.** make or become better

mel·lif′lu·ous a. smooth and sweet, as sounds: also **mel·lif′lu·ent** —**mel·lif′lu·ence n.**

mel′low a. full, rich, gentle, etc.; not harsh —**v.** make or become mellow

me·lo′di·ous a. 1. having melody 2. pleasing to hear — **me·lo′di·ous·ly adv.**

mel′o·dra·ma n. sensational, extravagant drama —**mel′o·dra·mat′ic a.**

mel′o·dra·mat′ics n.pl. melodramatic behavior

mel′o·dy n. [pl. -DIES] 1. pleasing sounds in sequence 2. a tune, song, etc. 3. leading part in harmony —**me·lod′ic** (-läd′-) **a.** —**me·lod′i·cal·ly adv.**

mel′on n. large, juicy, manyseeded fruit

melt v. 1. change from solid to liquid, as by heat 2. dissolve 3. disappear or merge gradually 4. soften

mem′ber n. 1. distinct part, as

an arm 2. person in an organization

mem′ber·ship n. 1. state of being a member 2. all the members 3. number of members

mem′brane n. thin tissue lining an organ or part —**mem′bra·nous a.**

me·men′to n. [pl. -TOS, -TOES] souvenir

mem′o n. [pl. -os] [Col.] memorandum

mem′oirs (-wärz) **n.pl.** 1. an autobiography 2. personal record of important events

mem′o·ra·bil′i·a n.pl. things worth remembering

mem′o·ra·ble a. that is worth remembering —**mem′o·ra·bly adv.**

mem′o·ran′dum n. [pl. -DUMS, -DA] 1. short note to remind one of something 2. informal office communication

me·mo′ri·al n. anything meant to help people remember a person or event

me·mo′ri·al·ize′ v. commemorate

mem′o·rize v. commit to memory

mem′o·ry n. [pl. -RIES] 1. power or act of remembering 2. something or everything remembered 3. commemoration

men n. pl. of **man**

men′ace (-is) **n.** a threat —**v.** threaten; endanger —**men′ac·ing·ly adv.**

mé·nage (mā näzh′) **n.** household: also **menage**

me·nag'er·ie (-naj'-) *n.* collection of wild animals

mend *v.* 1. repair 2. make or become better, esp. in health 3. heal, as a fracture —*n.* mended place —**on the mend** improving —**mend'er** *n.*

men·da'cious (-dā'shəs) *a.* lying —**men·dac'i·ty** (-das'-) *n.*

men'di·cant *n.* beggar

men'folk *n.pl.* [Col.] men

me·ni'al *a.* servile —*n.* 1. servant 2. servile, low person —**me'ni·al·ly** *adv.*

men·in·gi'tis (-jī'-) *n.* inflammation of membranes of the brain and spinal cord

me·nis'cus *n.* 1. a crescent 2. upper surface of a column of liquid

men'o·pause *n.* permanent cessation of menstruation

men·o'rah *n. Judaism* candelabrum with seven (or nine) branches

men'ses (-sēz) *n.pl.* monthly flow of blood from the uterus

men'stru·ate *v.* have a flow of blood monthly from the uterus —**men'stru·al** *a.* —**men'stru·a'tion** *n.*

men·su·ra'tion (-shə-) *n.* a measuring

-ment *suf.* 1. result of 2. a means for 3. act of 4. state of being

men'tal *a.* 1. of or in the mind 2. ill in mind 3. for the mentally ill —**men'tal·ly** *adv.*

men·tal'i·ty *n.* mental power

mental retardation congenital lowness of intelligence

men'thol (-thôl) *n.* derivative of oil of peppermint —**men'tho·lat'ed** *a.*

men'tion *n.* 1. brief reference 2. a citing for honor —*v.* refer to briefly

men'tor *n.* wise adviser

men'u (-yōō) *n.* [*pl.* -US] list of foods at a meal

me·ow', me·ou' (-ou') *v., n.* (make) the sound of a cat

mer'can·tile *a.* of merchants or trade

mer'ce·nar'y *a.* working or done mainly for money —*n.* [*pl.* -IES] soldier paid to serve in a foreign army

mer'cer·ized *a.* treated, as cotton, to strengthen it

mer'chan·dise (-dīz) *v.* buy and sell —*n.* (or -dīs) things bought and sold

mer'chant *n.* 1. dealer in goods 2. storekeeper

mer'chant·man *n.* [*pl.* -MEN] ship used in commerce

merchant marine ships of a nation used in trade

mer·cu'ri·al (-kyoor'ē-) *a.* changeable, fickle, etc.

mer'cu·ry *n.* silvery liquid metal, a chemical element

mer'cy *n.* [*pl.* -CIES] 1. kindness; forbearance 2. power to forgive 3. a lucky thing or blessing —**at the mercy of** in the power of —**mer'ci·ful** *a.* —**mer'ci·less** *a.*

mercy killing euthanasia

mere *a.* [superl. MEREST] no more than; only

mere'ly *adv.* only; simply

mer'e·tri'cious *a.* flashy; tawdry

mer·gan'ser *n.* large duck

merge v. unite or combine so as to lose identity

merg'er n. a merging, as of several companies into one

me·rid'i·an n. 1. highest point 2. circle through the earth's poles

me·ringue' (-ran′) n. egg whites and sugar beaten stiff

me·ri'no (mə rē′-) n. [pl. -NOS] (silky wool of) a hardy breed of sheep

mer'it n. 1. worth; value 2. something deserving praise —v. deserve

mer'i·to'ri·ous a. deserving reward, praise, etc.

mer'maid (mur′-) n. imaginary creature like a woman with a fish's tail

mer'ry a. [-RIER, -RIEST] full of fun —**make merry** be festive —**mer'ri·ly** adv. —**mer'ri·ment** n.

mer'ry-go-round' n. revolving platform with seats, as in amusement parks

mer'ry·mak'ing n. fun; festivity —**mer'ry·mak'er** n.

me'sa (mā′-) n. high plateau with steep sides

mes'ca·line (-lēn) n. psychedelic drug got from a cactus plant (mescal)

mes·dames (mā däm′) n. pl. of **madam**, **madame**, or **Mrs.**

mesh n. 1. (cord or wire of) a net or network 2. netlike material, as for stockings 3. engagement of the teeth of gears —v. 1. entangle 2. interlock 3. engage, as gears

mes'mer·ize (mez′-) v. hypno-tize —**mes'mer·ism** n. —**mes'mer·ist** n.

mes·quite, mes·quit (mes kēt′) n. spiny shrub

mess n. 1. a jumble 2. trouble 3. untidy condition 4. communal meal as in the army —v. 1. make dirty, jumbled, etc. 2. meddle 3. bungle; botch (up) —**mess'i·ness** n. —**mess'y** [-IER, -IEST] a.

mes'sage n. 1. a communication 2. important idea —**get the message** [Col.] understand a hint

mes'sen·ger n. one who carries a message, etc.

mess hall room or building where soldiers, etc. regularly eat

Mes·si'ah 1. Judaism expected deliverer of the Jews 2. Christianity Jesus —**Mes·si·an'ic** (mes′ē-) a.

Messrs. (mes′ərz) pl. of **Mr.**

mes·ti'zo (-tē′-) n. [-ZOS, -ZOES] one of American Indian and Spanish parentage

met pt. & pp. of **meet**

me·tab'o·lism n. changing of food by organisms into energy, new cells, etc. —**met'a·bol'ic** (-bäl′-) a.

met'a·car'pus n. [pl. -PI (-pī)] part of the hand between the wrist and the fingers

met'al n. 1. shiny, usually solid, chemical element 2. an alloy —a. of metal —**me·tal'lic** a.

met'al·lur'gy n. science of refining metals —**met'al·lur'gi·cal** a. —**met'al·lur'gist** n.

met'a·mor'pho·sis n. [pl. -SES

(-sēz)] **1.** change in form **2.** any marked change

met'a·phor n. word for one thing used for another —**met'a·phor'i·cal** a. —**met'a·phor'i·cal·ly** adv.

met'a·phys'ics n. philosophy that deals with first principles —**met'a·phys'i·cal** a.

me·tas'ta·sis n. [pl. **-ses** (-sēz)] transfer of malignant cells in the body through the bloodstream —**me·tas'ta·size** v.

met'a·tar'sus n. [pl. **-si** (-sī)] part of the foot between the ankle and the toes —**met'a·tar'sal** a.

mete (mēt) v. allot

me'te·or n. **1.** streak of light seen when a meteoroid enters the earth's atmosphere **2.** meteoroid or meteorite —**me'te·or'ic** a.

me'te·or·ite' n. part of a meteoroid fallen to earth as a stone or metal mass

me'te·or·oid' n. small, solid body from outer space, seen as a meteor when falling to earth

me'te·or·ol'o·gy n. science of weather, climate, etc. —**me'te·or·o·log'i·cal** a. —**me'te·or·ol'o·gist** n.

me'ter n. **1.** rhythmic pattern in verse **2.** metric unit of length (39.37 in.) **3.** device to measure flow of fluid

meth'a·done (-dōn) n. synthetic narcotic drug used in medicine

meth'ane n. colorless, odorless, flammable gas

meth'a·nol (-nôl) n. poisonous

liquid used as fuel, antifreeze, etc.

me·thinks' v. [Ar.] it seems to me

meth'od n. **1.** way; process **2.** system —**me·thod'i·cal** a. —**me·thod'i·cal·ly** adv.

meth'od·ol'o·gy n. system of methods

me·tic'u·lous a. very careful about details; fussy

mé·tier (mā tyā') n. one's trade, craft

me'tre (-tər) n. meter: Br. sp.

met'ric a. **1.** of the meter (unit of length) **2.** of the metric system **3.** metrical

met'ri·cal a. **1.** of or composed in meter or verse **2.** used in measurement —**met'ri·cal·ly** adv.

met'ri·ca'tion n. a changing to the metric system

met'ri·cize (-sīz) v. to change to the metric system

metric system decimal system of weights and measures

met'ro·nome n. device that beats time at a set rate

me·trop'o·lis n. main or important city —**met'ro·pol'i·tan** a.

met'tle n. spirit; courage —**on one's mettle** ready to do one's best

met'tle·some a. spirited; ardent

mew v., n. meow

mewl v. to cry weakly, like a baby

mews n.pl. [Br.] stables or carriage houses, now often made into dwellings

Mex′i·can *n., a.* (native) of Mexico

mez′za·nine (-nēn) *n.* **1.** low story built between two main stories **2.** first few rows of balcony seats

mez′zo·so·pra′no (met′sō-) *n.* [*pl.* -NOS] voice or singer between soprano and contralto

mi·as′ma (mī az′-) *n.* vapor from swamps, once believed poisonous

mi·ca (mī′kə) *n.* mineral that forms into thin, heat-resistant layers

mice *n.* pl. of mouse

micro- *pref.* small

mi′crobe *n.* minute organism, esp. one causing disease

mi′cro·cosm *n.* universe on a small scale

mi′cro·fiche (-fēsh) *n.* film card on which greatly reduced microfilm is recorded

mi′cro·film *n.* film on which documents, etc. are recorded in a reduced size

mi′cro·groove *n.* very narrow needle groove on a phonograph record

mi·crom′e·ter *n.* instrument for measuring very small distances, angles, etc.

mi′cron *n.* one millionth of a meter

mi′cro·or′gan·ism *n.* microscopic organism

mi′cro·phone *n.* instrument for changing sound waves into electric impulses

mi′cro·scope *n.* device for magnifying minute objects

mi′cro·scop′ic (-skäp′-) *a.* so small as to be invisible except through a microscope

mid, 'mid *prep.* [Poet.] amid

mid- *pref.* middle of

mid′air′ *n.* point not in contact with any surface

mid′day′ *n., a.* noon

mid′dle *a.* halfway between two points, etc. —*n.* middle point or part

mid′dle-aged′ *a.* in the time of life between youth and old age

Middle Ages period in Europe, c. 500–1450 A.D.

mid′dle·man *n.* [*pl.* -MEN] **1.** one who buys from a producer and sells at wholesale or retail **2.** go-between

middle school school with grades usually between 5th and 9th

mid′dling *a.* of middle size, quality, etc.

mid′dy *n.* [*pl.* -DIES] loose blouse with a sailor collar

midge *n.* small gnat

midg′et *n.* very small person —*a.* miniature

mid′land *a., n.* (of) the middle region of a country

mid′night *n.* twelve o'clock at night

mid′riff *n.* part of the body between the abdomen and the chest

mid′ship·man *n.* [*pl.* -MEN] naval officer trainee

midst *n.* the middle —*prep.* [Poet.] in the midst of —**in the midst of 1.** in the middle of **2.** during

mid′sum′mer *n.* period about June 21

mid'way *a., adv.* in the middle; halfway —*n.* location for sideshows, etc. at a fair

mid'wife *n.* [*pl.* **-WIVES**] woman who helps others in childbirth

mid'win'ter *n.* period about December 22

mien (mēn) *n.* one's manner

miff *v.* [Col.] offend

might (mīt) *v.* pt. of **may** —*n.* strength; force

might'y *a.* [**-IER, -IEST**] powerful, great, etc. —*adv.* [Col.] very —**might'i·ly** *adv.*

mi'graine (-grān) *n.* periodic headache

mi'grant *a.* migrating —*n.* farm laborer harvesting seasonal crops from place to place

mi'grate *v.* move from one place or region to another, as with the change in season — **mi·gra'tion** *n.* —**mi'gra·tor'y** *a.*

mi·ka'do (mi kä'-) *n.* [*pl.* **-DOS**] formerly, emperor of Japan

mike *n.* [Sl.] microphone

mil *n.* .001 of an inch

milch *a.* kept for milking

mild *a.* 1. gentle 2. having a soft, pleasant flavor —**mild'ly** *adv.*

mil'dew *n.* whitish fungus on plants, damp cloth, etc. —*v.* affect or be affected with mildew

mile *n.* unit of measure, 5,280 ft. The **nautical mile** is 6,076.1 ft.

mile'age *n.* 1. total miles traveled 2. allowance per mile for traveling expenses 3. average number of miles traveled, as per gallon of gasoline

mil'er *n.* contestant in mile races

mile'stone *n.* significant event

mi·lieu (mēl yōō') *n.* environment; esp., social setting

mil'i·tant *a.* ready to fight, esp. for some cause —*n.* militant person —**mil'i·tan·cy** *n.*

mil'i·ta·rism *n.* 1. warlike spirit 2. maintenance of strong armed forces —**mil'i·ta·rist** *n.* —**mil'i·ta·ris'tic** *a.*

mil'i·tar'y *a.* of soldiers, war, etc. —**the military** the army

mil'i·tate *v.* work (*against*)

mi·li'tia (-lish'ə) *n.* citizens trained for emergency military service

milk *n.* 1. white liquid secreted by female mammals for suckling their young 2. any liquid like this —*v.* 1. draw milk from (a mammal) 2. extract from —**milk'y** [**-IER, -IEST**] *a.* —**milk'i·ness** *n.*

milk'man *n.* [*pl.* **-MEN**] man who sells or delivers milk

milk of magnesia milky-white liquid used as laxative, etc.

milk'shake *n.* drink of milk, flavoring, and ice cream, shaken until frothy

milk'sop *n.* sissy

milk'weed *n.* plant with a milky juice

mill *n.* 1. place for grinding grain into flour 2. machine for grinding 3. factory 4. 1/10 of a cent —*v.* 1. grind by or in a mill 2. move (*around*) confusedly, as a crowd —**through**

the mill [Col.] through a painful experience —**mill′er** n.

mil′lage (-ij) n. taxation in mills per dollar of valuation

mil·len′ni·um n. [pl. -NIUMS, -NIA (-ə)] 1. Theol. 1000-year period of Christ's future reign on earth 2. period of peace and joy

mil′let n. cereal grass

milli- pref. 1/1000 part of

mil′li·gram n. one thousandth of a gram

mil′li·me′ter n. one thousandth of a meter

mil′li·ner n. one who makes or sells women's hats

mil′li·ner′y n. 1. women's hats 2. business of a milliner

mil′lion (-yən) n. a thousand thousands —**mil′lionth** a., n.

mil′lion·aire′ (-er′) n. one having at least a million dollars

mill′stone n. 1. flat, round stone used for grinding grain, etc. 2. heavy burden

mill′wright n. worker who installs or repairs heavy machinery

milt n. fish sperm

mime n. 1. representation of an action, etc. by gestures, not words 2. a mimic —v. to mimic

mim′e·o·graph′ n. machine for making stenciled copies of typewritten matter —v. make (such copies) of

mim′ic v. [-ICKED, -ICKING] 1. imitate, as in ridicule 2. copy closely —n. one who mimics — **mim′ic·ry** n.

mi·mo′sa n. flowering tree or shrub of warm climates

min·a·ret′ n. mosque tower

mince v. 1. cut into small pieces 2. lessen the force of (words) 3. act with affected daintiness —**minc′ing** a.

mince′meat n. pie filling of raisins, spices, suet, etc.

mind n. 1. center of thought, feeling, etc. 2. intellect 3. sanity 4. memory 5. opinion — v. 1. observe 2. obey 3. take care of 4. be careful about 5. object to —**bear** (or **keep**) in **mind** remember —**blow one's mind** [Sl.] stun, amaze, etc. — **have in mind** intend —**make up one's mind** reach a decision —**out of one's mind** frantic —**put in mind** remind

mind′ful a. aware (of)

mind′s eye the imagination

mine pron. that or those belonging to me —n. 1. large excavation from which to extract ores, coal, etc. 2. great source of supply 3. explosive device hidden under land or water —v. 1. dig (ores, etc.) from a mine 2. hide mines in

min′er n. one who works digging coal, etc. in a mine

min′er·al (min′-) n. ore, rock, etc. found naturally in the earth —a. of or containing minerals

mineral jelly petrolatum

min′er·al′o·gy n. science of minerals —**min′er·al′o·gist** n.

mineral oil oil from petroleum used as a laxative

mineral water water having mineral salts or gases

mi'ne·stro'ne (-strō'nē) *n.* [It.] thick vegetable soup

min'gle *v.* 1. mix or become mixed 2. join with others

mini- *pref.* miniature; very small; very short

min'i·a·ture (-char) *n.* 1. very small copy or model 2. tiny painting —*a.* minute

min'i·a·tur·ize' *v.* make in a small and compact form

min'i·bus *n.* very small bus

min'i·mize *v.* reduce to or estimate at a minimum

min'i·mum *n.* 1. smallest quantity possible 2. lowest degree reached —*a.* lowest or least possible: also **min'i·mal**

min'ing *n.* work of removing ores, etc. from a mine

min·ion (min'yan) *n.* 1. servile follower 2. subordinate official

min'is·cule (-as kyōol) *a.* minuscule: a misspelling

min'i·skirt *n.* skirt ending well above the knee

min'is·ter *n.* 1. head of a governmental department 2. diplomatic official below an ambassador 3. one who conducts religious services —*v.* give help (to); serve —**min'is·te'ri·al** *a.*

min'is·tra'tion *n.* a giving help or care; service

min'is·try *n.* [*pl.* -TRIES] 1. office of a clergyman 2. clergy 3. governmental department headed by a minister 4. a ministering

mink *n.* 1. weasellike mammal 2. its valuable fur

min'now (-ō) *n.* very small freshwater fish

mi'nor *a.* 1. lesser in size, rank, etc. 2. *Mus.* half tone lower than the major —*v.* have a secondary field of study (*in*) —*n.* 1. one under full legal age 2. secondary field of study

mi·nor'i·ty *n.* 1. smaller part or number 2. racial, religious, etc. group that differs from the larger group 3. time of being a minor

min'strel *n.* 1. traveling singer of the Middle Ages 2. member of a comic musical show (**minstrel show**) with performers' faces blackened

mint *n.* 1. place where the government makes coins 2. large amount 3. aromatic plant with leaves used for flavoring —*v.* coin (money)

min'u·end *n.* number from which another is to be subtracted

min·u·et' *n.* slow, stately dance of 18th century

mi'nus *prep.* less —*a.* 1. negative 2. less than —*n.* sign (-) showing subtraction or negative quantity

mi·nus'cule (-kyōol, min'as kyōol) *a.* tiny; minute

min'ute (-it) *n.* 1. 1/60 of an hour 2. moment 3. *pl.* official record —**the minute (that)** just as soon as

mi·nute' (mī nōot') *a.* 1. very small 2. exact —**mi·nute'ly** *adv.*

mi·nu'ti·ae (-nōo'shi ē) *n.pl.* trifling details

minx *n.* bold or saucy girl

mir'a·cle *n.* **1**. event that seems to contradict scientific laws **2**. remarkable thing —**mi·rac'u·lous** *a.*

mi·rage' (-räzh') *n.* optical illusion caused by refraction of light

mire *n.* deep mud or slush —*v.* stick or cause to get stuck as in mire

mir'ror *n.* coated glass that reflects images —*v.* reflect, as in a mirror

mirth *n.* gaiety with laughter —**mirth'ful** *a.*

mis- *pref.* wrong(ly); bad(ly)

mis'ad·ven'ture *n.* bad luck

mis'an·thrope *n.* one who hates all people: also **mis·an'thro·pist** —**mis·an·throp'ic** *a.* —**mis·an'thro·py** *n.*

mis·ap·ply' *v.* [-PLIED, -PLY-ING] apply badly or wrongly

mis'ap·pre·hend' *v.* understand wrongly —**mis'ap·pre·hen'sion** *n.*

mis'ap·pro'pri·ate *v.* use (funds, etc.) dishonestly — **mis'ap·pro'pri·a'tion** *n.*

mis'be·got'ten *a.* illegitimate

mis·be·have' *v.* behave badly —**mis'be·hav'ior** *n.*

mis·cal'cu·late *v.* misjudge —**mis'cal·cu·la'tion** *n.*

mis·car'ry *v.* [-RIED, -RYING] **1**. go wrong **2**. lose a fetus before full term —**mis·car'riage** *n.*

mis·cast' *v.* cast (an actor or a play) unsuitably

mis'ce·ge·na'tion (mis'i jə-) *n.* interracial marriage

mis'cel·la'ne·ous (-səl-) *a.* of various kinds; mixed

mis'cel·la'ny *n.* [*pl.* -NIES] collection of various kinds

mis·chance' *n.* bad luck

mis'chief *n.* **1**. harm or damage **2**. prank **3**. lively teasing

mis'chie·vous (-chi-) *a.* **1**. harmful **2**. prankish **3**. annoying with playful tricks

mis'ci·ble (mis'ə-) *a.* that can be mixed

mis·con·ceive' *v.* misunderstand —**mis'con·cep'tion** *n.*

mis·con'duct *n.* wrong conduct

mis·con·strue' *v.* misinterpret

mis'count' *v.* count incorrectly —*n.* incorrect count

mis'cre·ant *n.* villain

mis·deal' *v.* [-DEALT, -DEAL-ING] deal (playing cards) wrongly —*n.* wrong deal

mis·deed' *n.* crime, sin, etc.

mis'de·mean'or *n. Law* minor offense

mis·di·rect' *v.* direct wrongly or badly —**mis'di·rec'tion** *n.*

mi'ser *n.* stingy hoarder of money —**mi'ser·ly** *a.*

mis'er·a·ble *a.* **1**. in misery **2**. causing misery **3**. bad, poor, etc. —**mis'er·a·bly** *adv.*

mis'er·y *n.* [*pl.* -IES] pain, poverty, distress, etc.

mis·file' *v.* file in the wrong place

mis·fire' *v.* **1**. fail to go off **2**. fail to achieve an effect —*n.* a misfiring

mis·fit' *v.* fit improperly —*n.* **1**. improper fit **2**. (mis'fit) maladjusted person

mis·for'tune *n.* **1**. trouble **2**. mishap, calamity, etc.

mis·giv'ings *n.pl.* feelings of fear, doubt, etc.

mis·gov'ern *v.* govern badly — **mis·gov'ern·ment** *n.*

mis·guide' *v.* mislead

mis·han'dle *v.* abuse

mis'hap *n.* misfortune

mish'mash *n.* a jumble

mis·in·form' *v.* supply with wrong information —**mis'in·for·ma'tion** *n.*

mis·in·ter'pret *v.* interpret wrongly —**mis'in·ter·pre·ta'tion** *n.*

mis·judge' *v.* judge wrongly

mis·la'bel *v.* label wrongly

mis·lay' *v.* [-LAID, -LAYING] put in a place later forgotten

mis·lead' *v.* 1. lead astray 2. deceive

mis·man'age *v.* manage badly

mis·match' *v.* match badly — *n.* bad match

mis·name' *v.* give an inappropriate name to

mis·no'mer *n.* name wrongly applied

mi·sog'y·nist (-säj'-) *n.* one who hates women **mi·sog'y·ny** *n.*

mis·place' *v.* 1. put in a wrong place 2. bestow unwisely 3. mislay

mis·play' *v.* play wrongly —*n.* wrong play

mis'print *n.* printing error

mis·pri'sion (-prizh'ən) *n.* misconduct by a public official

mis·pro·nounce' *v.* pronounce wrongly

mis·quote' *v.* quote incorrectly

mis·read' *v.* [-READ (-red'), -READING] read wrongly and so misunderstand

mis·rep·re·sent' *v.* give a false idea of

mis·rule' *n.* bad government

miss *v.* 1. fail to hit, meet, do, see, hear, etc. 2. avoid 3. note or feel the loss of —*n.* failure to hit, etc.

miss *n.* [*pl.* MISSES] 1. [M-] title used before the name of an unmarried woman 2. young unmarried woman

mis'sal *n. R.C.Ch.* prayer book for Mass for the year

mis·shap'en *a.* deformed

mis'sile *n.* object to be thrown or shot

miss'ing *a.* absent; lost

mis·sion *n.* 1. special task or duty 2. group or station of missionaries 3. diplomatic delegation 4. group of specialists, etc. sent to a foreign country

mis'sion·ar'y *n.* [*pl.* -IES] person sent by a church to make converts, esp. abroad

mis'sive *n.* letter or note

mis·spell' *v.* spell incorrectly —**mis·spell'ing** *n.*

mis·spend' *v.* [-SPENT, -SPENDING] spend improperly or wastefully

mis·state' *v.* state wrongly — **mis·state'ment** *n.*

mis·step' *n.* 1. wrong step 2. mistake in conduct

mist *n.* mass of water vapor; thin fog —*v.* make or become misty

mis·take' *v.* [-TOOK, -TAKEN, -TAKING] understand or perceive wrongly —*n.* error

mis·tak'en *a.* wrong or incorrect

mis'ter *n.* 1. [M-] title before

a man's name: usually **Mr. 2.** [Col.] sir

mis·tle·toe *n.* evergreen plant with white berries

mis·treat' *v.* treat badly — **mis·treat'ment** *n.*

mis'tress *n.* **1.** woman in charge or control **2.** woman with whom a man is having an affair

mis·tri'al *n. Law* trial made void by an error, etc.

mis·trust' *n.* lack of trust —*v.* have no trust in; doubt —**mis·trust'ful** *a.*

mist'y *a.* [-IER, -IEST] **1.** like or covered with mist **2.** vague or indistinct

mis·un·der·stand' *v.* [-STOOD, -STANDING] understand incorrectly

mis·un·der·stand'ing *n.* **1.** failure to understand **2.** quarrel or disagreement

mis·use' (-yōoz') *v.* **1.** use improperly **2.** abuse —*n.* (-yōos') incorrect use

mite *n.* **1.** tiny, parasitic arachnid **2.** tiny amount

mi'ter *n.* **1.** tall cap of a bishop **2.** corner joint of two pieces cut at an angle

mit'i·gate *v.* make or become less severe —**mit'i·ga'tion** *n.*

mi·to'sis (mī-) *n.* process of cell division

mitt *n.* **1.** padded baseball glove **2.** [Sl.] hand

mit'ten *n.* glove without separate finger pouches

mix *v.* [alt. pt. & pp. MIXT] **1.** stir or come together in a single mass **2.** make by mixing ingredients **3.** combine **4.** get along together —*n.* mixture, or its ingredients —**mix up 1.** confuse **2.** involve (in) —

mixed *a.* **1.** blended **2.** of different kinds **3.** of both sexes **4.** confused

mix'ture (-chər) *n.* **1.** a mixing **2.** thing mixed

mix'-up' *n.* confusion

mne·mon'ic (nē-) *a.* of or helping the memory

moan (mōn) *n.* low, mournful sound —*v.* **1.** utter (with) a moan **2.** complain

moat *n.* deep, usually water-filled ditch around a castle

mob *n.* **1.** crowd, esp. a disorderly one **2.** [Sl.] gang of criminals —*v.* [MOBBED, MOBBING] crowd around, as to attack, annoy, etc.

mo'bile (-b'l, -bēl) *a.* **1.** readily movable or adaptable **2.** easy in changing one's social class —*n.* (-bēl) piece of abstract sculpture suspended to move in the air —**mo·bil'i·ty** *n.*

mobile home large trailer outfitted as a home

mo'bil·ize *v.* make or become ready, as for war —**mo'bil·i·za'tion** *n.*

moc'ca·sin *n.* heelless slipper of soft leather

mo'cha (-kə) *n.* kind of coffee —*a.* flavored with coffee and chocolate

mock *v.* **1.** ridicule **2.** mimic and deride —*a.* false

mock'er·y *n.* [*pl.* -IES] **1.** a mocking **2.** poor imitation

mock'ing·bird *n.* small bird with imitative call

mock'-up' n. model built to scale, often full-sized

mode n. 1. way of acting or doing 2. current fashion

mod'el n. 1. small copy of something 2. one to be imitated 3. style 4. one who poses for an artist 5. one who displays clothes by wearing them —a. 1. serving as a model 2. representative —v. 1. plan or form 2. work as a model

mod'er·ate (-it) a. 1. avoiding extremes 2. calm 3. medium —n. moderate person —v. (-āt) 1. make or become moderate 2. preside over (a meeting, etc.) —**mod'er·ate·ly** adv.

mod'er·a'tion n. 1. avoidance of extremes 2. calmness

mod'er·a'tor n. one who presides at a meeting, etc.

mod'ern a. 1. of recent times; up-to-date —n. modern person —**mod'ern·is'tic** a.

mod'ern·ize v. make or become modern —**mod'ern·i·za'tion** n.

mod'est a. 1. not vain or boastful 2. shy 3. decent 4. not extreme —**mod'es·ty** n.

mod'i·cum n. small amount

mod'i·fy v. [-FIED, -FYING] change or limit slightly —**mod'i·fi·ca'tion** n. —**mod'i·fi'er** n.

mod'ish (mōd'-) a. fashionable

mod·u·lar (mäj'ə lər) a. of modules

mod'u·late v. adjust or vary, as the pitch of the voice —**mod'u·la'tion** n.

mod'ule n. 1. any of a set of units to be fitted together 2. detachable unit with a specific function

mo'gul n. important person

mo'hair n. goat-hair fabric

Mo·ham'med·an a., n. Muslim —**Mo·ham'med·an·ism** n.

moi'e·ty n. [pl. -TIES] 1. half 2. indefinite part

moire (mwär) n. fabric with a wavy pattern: also **moi·ré** (mwä rā')

moist a. slightly wet

mois'ten (-'n) v. make moist

mois'ture (-chər) n. slight wetness

mois'tur·ize v. make moist —**mois'tur·iz'er** n.

mo'lar n. tooth for grinding

mo·las'ses n. dark syrup produced during sugar refining

mold (mōld) n. 1. hollow form in which a thing is shaped 2. thing shaped 3. pattern; model 4. furry, fungous growth —v. 1. make in a mold 2. shape 3. become moldy

mold'er v. crumble

mold'ing n. decorative strip of wood, etc.

mold'y a. [-IER, -IEST] 1. covered with mold (n. 4) 2. musty or stale

mole n. 1. small, dark, congenital spot on the skin 2. small, burrowing animal

mol'e·cule n. smallest particle of a substance that can exist alone —**mo·lec'u·lar** a.

mole'hill n. small ridge made by a burrowing mole

mole'skin n. 1. fur of the mole 2. napped cotton fabric

mo·lest' v. 1. to trouble or harm 2. make improper sexual advances to —**mo·les·ta'tion** n.

moll n. [Sl.] gangster's mistress

mol'li·fy v. [-FIED, -FYING] soothe; make calm

mol'lusk, mol'lusc n. invertebrate with a soft body enclosed in a shell, as an oyster

mol'ly·cod·dle n. man or boy used to being coddled —v. pamper; coddle

molt (mōlt) v. shed hair, skin, etc. before getting a new growth

mol'ten (mōl'-) a. melted by heat

mom n. [Col.] mother

mo'ment n. 1. brief period of, or certain point in, time 2. brief time of importance 3. importance

mo'men·tar'i·ly adv. 1. for a short time 2. at any moment

mo'men·tar'y a. lasting for only a moment

mo·men'tous a. very important

mo·men'tum n. impetus of a moving object

mom'my n. [pl. -MIES] mother: child's word

mon·arch (män'ərk) n. hereditary ruler —**mo·nar'chi·cal** (-när'ki-) a.

mon'arch·ist n. one who favors monarchical government

mon'arch·y n. [pl. -IES] government by a monarch

mon·as·ter'y n. [pl. -IES] residence for monks

mo·nas'tic a. of or like monks or nuns: also **mo·nas'ti·cal** —

n. monk —**mo·nas'ti·cism** n.

mon·au'ral (-ô'rəl) a. of sound reproduction using a single channel

Mon'day n. second day of the week

mon'e·tar'y (män'-) a. 1. of currency 2. of money

mon'ey n. [pl. -EYS, -IES] 1. metal coins or paper notes used as the legal medium of exchange 2. wealth —**in the money** [Sl.] wealthy —**make money** gain profits —**put money into** invest money in

mon'ey·bags n. [Col.] rich person

mon'eyed (-ēd) a. rich

mon'ey·mak'er n. something financially profitable —**mon'ey·mak'ing** a., n.

money order order for payment issued at a bank, etc.

Mon'gol·oid n., a. (member) of the large human group including most of the Asian people

mon'goose n. [pl. -GOOSES] ferretlike animal of India

mon'grel n., a. (animal or plant) of mixed breed

mon'i·tor n. 1. student who helps keep order, etc. 2. device for regulating performance of a machine, etc. 3. radio or TV receiver for checking on programs —v. watch, or check on

monk (muŋk) n. man who is a member of an ascetic religious order

mon'key n. [pl. -KEYS] small, long-tailed primate —v. [Col.] meddle; trifle

monkey business [Col.] foolishness, deceit, etc.

mon′key-shines *n.pl.* playful tricks or pranks

monkey wrench wrench with an adjustable jaw —**throw a monkey wrench into** [Col.] disrupt

monk's cloth heavy cloth with a weave like that of a basket

mon·o (män′ō) *n.* mononucleosis

mono- *pref.* one; alone

mon′o·cle (män′-) *n.* eyeglass for one eye

mo·nog′a·my *n.* practice of being married to only one person at a time —**mo·nog′a·mous** *a.*

mon′o·gram *n.* initials of a name, made into a design

mon′o·graph *n.* book or article on a single subject

mon′o·lith *n.* pillar, statue, etc. made of a single, large stone —**mon′o·lith′ic** *a.*

mon′o·logue, **mon′o·log** *n.* 1. long speech 2. skit for one actor only

mon′o·ma′ni·a *n.* excessive interest in one thing —**mon′o·ma′ni·ac** *n.*

mon′o·nu′cle·o′sis *n.* acute disease with fever, etc.

mon′o·phon′ic *a.* of sound reproduction using a single channel

mo·nop′o·lize *v.* get a monopoly or full control of

mo·nop′o·ly *n.* [*pl.* **-LIES**] 1. total control of a product or service 2. company having this —**mo·nop′o·lis′tic** *a.*

mon′o·rail *n.* railway with cars on a single rail

mon′o·syl′la·ble *n.* word of one syllable —**mon′o·syl·lab′ic** *a.*

mon′o·the·ism (-thē-) *n.* belief that there is only one God —**mon′o·the·is′tic** *a.*

mon′o·tone *n.* sameness of tone, pitch, color, etc.

mo·not′o·ny *n.* 1. lack of variety 2. tiresome sameness —**mo·not′o·nous** *a.*

mon·ox′ide *n.* oxide with one oxygen atom per molecule

mon·sieur (mə syur′) *n.* [*pl.* **MESSIEURS** (mes′ərz)] gentleman: Fr. for *Mr.*

Mon·si′gnor (-sēn′yər) *n.* R.C.Ch. title of high rank

mon·soon′ (-sōōn′) *n.* wind bringing rainy season to S Asia

mon′ster *n.* huge or abnormal plant or animal

mon′strous *a.* 1. horrible 2. huge 3. very abnormal —**mon·stros′i·ty** [*pl.* **-TIES**] *n.*

mon·tage′ (-täzh′) *n.* 1. composite picture 2. rapid sequence of superimposed movie scenes

Mon′tes·so′ri method (-sō′rē) method of teaching children, emphasizing training of senses

month *n.* any of the 12 divisions of the year

month′ly *a.* happening, appearing, etc. every month —*n.* [*pl.* **-LIES**] monthly periodical —*adv.* every month

mon′u·ment *n.* 1. memorial statue, building, etc. 2. famous work

mon'u·men'tal *a.* massive, enduring, etc.

moo *v., n.* (make) the vocal sound of a cow

mooch *v.* [Sl.] get by begging, imposition, etc. —**mooch'er** *n.*

mood (mood) *n.* **1.** state of mind **2.** predominant feeling **3.** verb form used to express a fact, wish, or order

mood'y *a.* [-IER, -IEST] **1.** changing in mood **2.** gloomy

moon *n.* body that revolves around a planet, spec. around the earth —*v.* look dreamy or listless

moon'beam *n.* ray of moonlight

moon'light *n.* light of the moon

moon'light'ing *n.* the holding of a second job along with a main job

moon'lit *a.* lighted by the moon

moon'scape *n.* surface of the moon

moon'shine *n.* **1.** moonlight **2.** [Col.] whiskey made illegally

moon'shot *n.* launching of a spacecraft to the moon

moon'stone *n.* milky-white gem

moon'struck *a.* **1.** crazed **2.** romantically dreamy

moon'walk *n.* a walking about on the moon's surface

Moor *n.* Muslim of NW Africa —**Moor'ish** *a.*

moor (moor) *n.* [Br.] open wasteland —*v.* to secure, as by cables, ropes, etc.

moor'ings *n.pl.* cables, or place, for mooring a ship

moose *n.* [*pl.* MOOSE] largest animal of the deer family

moot *a.* **1.** debatable **2.** hypothetical

mop *n.* rags, sponge, etc. on a stick, as for washing floors —*v.* [MOPPED, MOPPING] clean up, as with a mop —**mop up 1.** clear of beaten enemy forces **2.** [Col.] finish

mope *v.* be gloomy and apathetic —**mop'ey, mop'y** *a.*

mop'pet *n.* [Col.] little child

mo·raine' (-rān') *n.* heap of rocks, etc. left by a glacier

mor'al *a.* **1.** of or dealing with right and wrong **2.** good; virtuous **3.** giving sympathy, but no active help **4.** virtually such **5.** based on probability —*n.* **1.** moral lesson **2.** *pl.* moral rules or standards —**mor'al·ly** *adv.*

mo·rale' (-ral') *n.* degree of courage, discipline, etc.

mo·ral'i·ty *n.* **1.** moral quality **2.** virtue

mor'al·ize *v.* discuss moral questions —**mor'al·ist** *n.*

mo·rass' *n.* bog; swamp

mor'a·to'ri·um *n.* **1.** authorized delay in paying debts **2.** any authorized delay

mo'ray (eel) voracious, brilliantly colored eel

mor'bid *a.* **1.** diseased **2.** gloomy or unwholesome — **mor·bid'i·ty** *n.*

mor'dant *a.* sarcastic

more *a., n.* **1.** greater (in) amount or degree **2.** (something) additional —*adv.* **1.** to a greater degree **2.** in addition —**more or less** somewhat

more·o′ver adv. besides

mo′res (-rēz, -rāz) n.pl. customs with the force of law

morgue (môrg) n. place where bodies of accident victims, etc. are taken, as for autopsy

mor′i·bund a. dying

morn n. [Poet.] morning

morn′ing n. first part of the day, till noon

morning glory vine with trumpet-shaped flowers

mo·roc′co n. fine, soft leather made of goatskin

mo′ron n. person who is mentally somewhat deficient — **mo·ron′ic** a.

mo·rose′ (-rōs′) a. gloomy — **mo·rose′ly** adv.

mor′phine (-fēn) n. opium drug used to relieve pain

mor·phol′o·gy n. form and structure, as in biology

mor′row n. [Poet.] **1.** morning **2.** the following day

Morse code code of dots and dashes used in telegraphy

mor′sel n. bit, as of food

mor′tal a. **1.** that must die **2.** causing death **3.** very great; extreme —n. human being — **mor′tal·ly** adv.

mor·tal′i·ty n. **1.** a being mortal **2.** ratio of deaths to population; death rate

mor′tar n. **1.** bowl for pulverizing things with a pestle **2.** small cannon **3.** cement mixture used between bricks, etc.

mor′tar·board n. **1.** square board for carrying mortar **2.**

academic cap with square, flat top

mort·gage (môr′gij) n. deed pledging property as security for a debt —v. pledge by a mortgage

mor·ti′cian (-tish′ən) n. funeral director

mor′ti·fy v. [-FIED, -FYING] **1.** shame; humiliate **2.** control (desires) by fasting, etc. — **mor′ti·fi·ca′tion** n.

mor′tise (-tis) n. hole cut for a tenon to fit in

mor′tu·ar′y (-choo-, -tyoo-) n. [pl. -IES] funeral home

mo·sa′ic (-zā′-) n. design made of colored stones inlaid in mortar

mo′sey (-zē) v. [Sl.] amble along

Mos′lem n., a. Muslim

mosque (mäsk) n. Muslim place of worship

mos·qui′to (-kē′-) n. [pl. -TOES, -TOS] small biting insect that sucks blood

moss n. tiny green plant growing in clusters on rocks, etc. — **moss′y** [-IER, -IEST] a.

moss′back n. **1.** turtle's back covered with algae **2.** [Col.] conservative person

most a. **1.** greatest in amount or number **2.** almost all —n. the greatest amount or number —adv. to the greatest degree

most′ly adv. mainly; chiefly

mote n. speck, as of dust

mo′tel′ n. hotel for motorists

moth n. four-winged insect like a butterfly: its larvae eat wool and fur

moth'ball n. ball of naphthalene, camphor, etc.: its fumes repel moths —**in mothballs** in reserve

moth'er n. 1. female parent 2. woman head of a convent —a. 1. of or like a mother 2. native —v. be a mother to —**moth'er·hood** n. —**moth'er·less** a. —**moth'er·ly** a.

moth'er-in-law' n. [pl. MOTHERS-IN-LAW] mother of one's husband or wife

moth'er·land n. one's native land

moth'er-of-pearl' n. hard, shiny lining of some shells

mo·tif' (-tēf') n. main theme of an artistic work

mo·tile (-t'l) a. that can move —**mo·til'i·ty** n.

mo'tion n. 1. a moving; change of position 2. gesture 3. proposal made at a meeting —v. make, or direct by, gestures —**go through the motions** do something automatically —**in motion** moving —**mo'tion·less** a.

motion picture 1. series of pictures flashed on a screen in rapid succession so that things in them seem to move 2. play, etc. in this form

mo'ti·vate' v. provide with motive —**mo'ti·va'tion** n.

mo'tive n. reason for doing something —a. of motion

mot'ley a. of many different elements; varied

mo'to·cross' n. cross-country motorcycle race

mo'tor n. 1. machine using electricity to make something

work 2. engine, esp. a gasoline engine —a. 1. of or run by a motor 2. of or for motor vehicles 3. producing motion 4. of muscular movements —v. travel by automobile

mo'tor·bike n. [Col.] 1. bicycle with motor 2. light motorcycle

mo'tor·boat n. boat propelled by a motor

mo'tor·cade n. procession of cars

mo'tor·car n. automobile

mo'tor·cy'cle n. two-wheeled, engine-powered vehicle

mo'tor·ist n. car driver or rider

mo'tor·ize v. equip with a motor or motor vehicles

motor vehicle car, truck, bus, etc.

mot'tle v. mark with colored blotches —**mot'tled** a.

mot'to n. [pl. -TOES, -TOS] maxim or phrase, as used on seals, coins, etc., that shows one's ideals, etc.

mould (mōld) n., v. mold —**mould'y** [-IER, -IEST] a.

moult (mōlt) v. molt

mound n. heap of earth, etc. —v. heap up

mount v. 1. climb; go up 2. get up on 3. increase in amount 4. fix (a jewel or picture) on or in a mounting 5. arrange (a dead animal) for exhibit 6. place (a gun) in position —n. 1. act of mounting 2. horse to ride 3. mounting 4. mountain

moun'tain n. very high rise of land on the earth's surface

moun·tain·eer' *n.* 1. mountain dweller 2. mountain climber

mountain goat long-haired antelope of Rocky Mountains

mountain lion cougar

moun'tain·ous *a.* 1. full of mountains 2. very big

moun'te·bank *n.* charlatan

mount'ing *n.* a backing, support, setting, etc.

mourn (môrn) *v.* feel or express grief or sorrow (for) —**mourn'er** *n.* —**mourn'ful** *a.*

mourn'ing *n.* 1. grief at a death 2. mourners' black clothes

mouse *n.* [*pl.* MICE] 1. small rodent 2. timid person —**mous'y** [-IER, -IEST] *a.*

mousse (mōōs) *n.* chilled dessert made with egg white, gelatin, whipped cream, etc.

mous·tache' *n.* mustache

mouth *n.* [*pl.* MOUTHS (mouthz)] 1. opening in the face for taking in food and making sounds 2. any opening —*v.* (mouth) say affectedly —**down in the mouth** [Col.] unhappy —**mouth'ful** [*pl.* -FULS] *n.*

mouth organ harmonica

mouth'piece' *n.* 1. part held in or near the mouth 2. spokesman for others

mouth'wash *n.* liquid for rinsing the mouth

mouth'wa·ter·ing *a.* tasty

mouth'y *a.* [-IER, -IEST] talkative

mou·ton (mōō'tän) *n.* lamb fur made to resemble beaver, etc.

move *v.* 1. change the place of 2. set or keep in motion 3. change one's residence 4. be active or take action 5. cause 6. make progress 7. arouse emotionally 8. propose (a resolution) 9. be sold: said of goods —*n.* 1. movement or action 2. *Games* one's turn —**move up** be promoted —**on the move** [Col.] active —**mov'a·ble, move'a·ble** *a.*, *n.*

move'ment *n.* 1. a moving or way of moving 2. organized action toward a goal 3. moving parts of a clock, etc. 4. *Music* main division of a composition

mov'er *n.* one who moves furniture, etc. for those who change residences

mov'ie *n.* motion picture: also **moving picture**

mow (mō) *v.* [alt. *pp.* MOWN] 1. cut down (grass) 2. kill; knock down —**mow'er** *n.*

mow (mou) *n.* heap of hay, esp. in a barn

Mr. (mis'tər) [*pl.* MESSRS. (mes'ərz)] title used before a man's name

Mrs. (mis'iz) title used before a married woman's name

Ms. (miz) title used instead of *Miss* or *Mrs.*

much *a.* [MORE, MOST] great in quantity, degree, etc. —*adv.* 1. greatly 2. nearly —*n.* 1. great amount 2. something great

mu'ci·lage (-s'l ij) *n.* gluey or gummy adhesive —**mu'ci·lag'i·nous** (-laj'-) *a.*

muck *n.* 1. black earth 2. dirt; filth

muck'rake' *v.* expose corruption in politics and business — **muck′rak′er** n.

mu′cous (myōō′-) a. 1. of or secreting mucus 2. slimy

mucous membrane membrane lining body cavities

mu′cus (myōō′-) n. slimy secretion of mucous membranes

mud n. wet, soft earth

mud′dle v. 1. mix up; confuse 2. act confusedly —n. mess, confusion, etc.

mud′dle-head′ed a. confused —v.

mud′dy a. [-DIER, -DIEST] 1. full of or covered with mud 2. dull·3. clouded or obscure —v. [-DIED, -DYING] make or become muddy

mud′sling′ing n. unfair verbal attacks against opponent

mu·ez′zin (myōō-) n. Muslim crier of people to prayer

muff n. cylindrical covering to warm the hands —v. bungle; miss

muf′fin n. bread baked in a small cupcake mold

muf′fle v. 1. wrap up warmly 2. deaden (sound)

muf′fler n. 1. thick scarf 2. device to deaden noise

muf′ti n. civilian clothes

mug n. 1. heavy drinking cup 2. [Sl.] face —v. [MUGGED, MUGGING] 1. assault with intent to rob 2. [Sl.] grimace

mug′gy a. [-GIER, -GIEST] hot and humid

muk′luk n. Eskimo boot

mu·lat′to n. [pl. -TOES] one with a black parent and a white parent

mul′ber′ry n. [pl. -RIES] a tree with berrylike fruit

mulch v., n. (use) a cover of leaves, peat, etc. to keep plants from freezing

mulct (mulkt) v. take from by fraud

mule n. 1. offspring of a male donkey and a female horse 2. lounging slipper 3. cotton-spinning machine 4. [Col.] stubborn person

mul′ish (myōōl′-) a. stubborn

mull v. 1. [Col.] ponder 2. heat and flavor, as wine

mul′lein (-in) n. tall plant with downy leaves

mul′let n. an edible fish

mul′li·gan stew [Sl.] meat stew

mul′li·ga·taw′ny n. meat soup flavored with curry

mul′lion (-yən) n. vertical bar between windowpanes

multi- pref. 1. having many 2. many times

mul′ti·far′i·ous (-far′-) a. of many kinds; varied

mul′ti·ple a. having many parts, etc. —n. product of two numbers, one specified

mul′ti·ple-choice′ a. listing several answers to choose from

multiple sclerosis disease of nervous system

mul′ti·plex a. of a system for sending more than one signal over a single circuit

mul′ti·pli·cand′ n. the number that is to be multiplied by another

mul′ti·plic′i·ty (-plis′-) n. great number

mul′ti·ply v. [-PLIED, -PLYING]

1. to increase in number, degree, etc. **2.** find the product (of) by adding a certain number a certain number of times —**mul'ti·pli·ca'tion** n. — **mul'ti·pli·er** n.

mul'ti·stage a. operating by successive propulsion systems, as a missile or rocket

mul'ti·tude n. large number

mul'ti·tu'di·nous a. many

mum n. [Col.] chrysanthemum

mum a. silent

mum'ble v. speak or say indistinctly —n. mumbled utterance

mum'bo jum'bo meaningless ritual or talk

mum'mer n. actor, esp. one with a mask or disguise

mum'mer·y n. [pl. -IES] foolish ritual; false show

mum'mi·fy v. [-FIED, -FYING] make into or become a mummy

mum'my n. [pl. -MIES] ancient embalmed body

mumps n. disease in which the salivary glands swell

munch v. chew noisily

mun'dane a. **1.** of the world **2.** ordinary; commonplace

mu·nic'i·pal (-nis'-) a. of a city or town

mu·nic'i·pal'i·ty n. [pl. -TIES] city or town having local self-government

mu·nif'i·cent a. very generous —**mu·nif'i·cence** n.

mu·ni'tions n.pl. weapons and ammunition for war

mu·ral (myoor'əl) a. of or on a wall —n. picture painted on a wall

mur'der v. **1.** kill (a person) unlawfully and with malice **2.** spoil, as a performance —n. **1.** act of murdering **2.** [Col.] something hard to deal with — **mur'der·er** n. —**mur'der·ess** n.fem.

mur'der·ous a. **1.** of or like murder **2.** guilty of, or ready to, murder

murk n. darkness; gloom — **murk'y** [-IER, -IEST] a.

mur'mur n. **1.** low, steady sound **2.** mumbled complaint **3.** Med. strange sound around heart —v. **1.** make a murmur **2.** say in a low voice

mur'rain (-in) n. a plague, esp. of cattle

mus'ca·tel' n. wine made from kind of sweet grape (**muscat**)

mus'cle n. **1.** tissue forming the fleshy parts that move the body **2.** any single part of this tissue **3.** strength

mus'cle-bound' a. having some muscles enlarged and less elastic

mus'cu·lar a. **1.** of or done by muscle **2.** strong —**mus'cu·lar'i·ty** n.

muscular dys·tro·phy (dis'trə fē) disease in which muscles waste away

mus'cu·la·ture (-chər) n. muscular system of a body, limb, etc.

muse v. think deeply —n. spirit inspiring an artist

mu·se'um n. place for keeping artistic, historical, or scientific objects

mush n. **1.** thick, soft mass **2.**

boiled cornmeal **3.** [Col.]
maudlin sentimentality —*int.*
shout urging on sled dogs —*v.*
travel over snow —**mush'y**
[-IER, -IEST] *a.*

mush'room *n.* rapid-growing,
fleshy, umbrella-shaped fungus, often edible —*v.* grow rapidly

mu'sic *n.* **1.** songs, symphonies, etc. **2.** art of composing or performing these **3.** sequence of pleasing sounds —**face the music** [Col.] accept the consequences

mu'si·cal *a.* of, fond of, or set to music —*n.* light play or movie with songs and dancing —**mu'si·cal·ly** *adv.*

mu·si·cale' (-kal'-) *n.* social affair with musical program

mu·si'cian (-zish'ən) *n.* person skilled in music

mu·si·col'o·gy *n.* study of history- and forms of music —**mu·si·col'o·gist** *n.*

musk *n.* strong-smelling animal secretion, used in perfumes —**musk'i·ness** *n.* —**musk'y** [-IER, -IEST] *a.*

mus'kel·lunge (-lunj) *n.* [*pl.* -LUNGE] large pike: also **mus'kie** (-kē)

mus'ket *n.* long gun

mus·ket·eer' *n.* soldier armed with musket

musk'mel'on *n.* kind of sweet, juicy melon, as cantaloupe

musk'rat *n.* **1.** water rodent **2.** its fur

Mus'lim (muz'ləm) *n.* follower of Islam, religion of Mohammed —*a.* of Islam

mus'lin (muz'-) *n.* strong cotton cloth, as for sheets

muss *v.* make messy —*n.* mess —**muss'y** [-IER, -IEST] *a.*

mus'sel *n.* bivalve mollusk

must *v.* **1.** have to **2.** be likely or certain to —*n.* [Col.] thing that must be done

mus·tache' (məs tash', mus'-tash) *n.* hair grown out on the upper lip of men

mus'tang *n.* small, wild horse

mus'tard *n.* **1.** plant with yellow flowers **2.** yellow, spicy powder or paste made from its seeds

mus'ter *v.* **1.** bring or come together, as troops **2.** summon —*n.* a mustering

mus'ty *a.* [-TIER, -TIEST] stale and moldy

mu'ta·ble *a.* changeable

mu'tant (-tənt) *n.* animal or plant different from parents

mu·ta'tion (myōo tā'shən) *n.* a change, esp. a sudden variation in a plant or animal

mute *a.* **1.** silent **2.** not able to speak —*n.* **1.** a deaf-mute **2.** device to mute a musical instrument —*v.* soften the sound of

mu'ti·late *v.* cut off or damage part of —**mu'ti·la'tion** *n.* —**mu'ti·la'tor** *n.*

mu'ti·ny *v.* [-NIED, -NYING] revolt, as against one's military superiors —*n.* [*pl.* -NIES] such a revolt —**mu·ti·neer'** *n.* —**mu'ti·nous** *a.*

mutt *n.* [Sl.] mongrel dog

mut'ter *v.* **1.** speak or say indistinctly **2.** grumble —*n.* muttered utterance

mut′ton *n.* flesh of (grown) sheep used as food

mu′tu·al (-chōō-) *a.* 1. of or for one another 2. in common — **mu′tu·al·ly** *adv.*

muu·muu (mōō′mōō) *n.* long, loose Hawaiian dress

muz′zle *n.* 1. snout 2. device for an animal's mouth to prevent biting 3. front end of a gun barrel —*v.* 1. put a muzzle on 2. prevent from talking

my *pronominal a.* of me

my′e·li′tis (mī′ə-) *n.* inflammation of bone marrow or spinal cord

my′na, my′nah *n.* Asian starling

my·o′pi·a *n.* nearsightedness —**my·op′ic** *a.*

myr′i·ad (mir′-) *n.* great number —*a.* very many

myrrh (mur) *n.* resin used in incense, perfume, etc.

myr′tle (mur′-) *n.* 1. evergreen shrub 2. creeping evergreen plant

my·self′ *pron.* intensive or reflexive form of I

mys′ter·y (mis′-) *n.* [*pl.* -IES] 1. unexplained or unknown thing 2. obscurity or secrecy 3. story or play about a secret crime, etc. —**mys·te′ri·ous** *a.*

mys′tic *a.* 1. of mysticism 2. occult or mysterious —*n.* believer in mysticism

mys′ti·cal *a.* 1. spiritually symbolic 2. mystic

mys′ti·cism *n.* 1. belief that God can be known directly 2. obscure thinking

mys′ti·fy *v.* [-FIED, -FYING] perplex or puzzle —**mys′ti·fi·ca′tion** *n.*

mys·tique′ (mis tēk′) *n.* mystical attributes of or attitudes toward some person or thing

myth (mith) *n.* 1. traditional story explaining some phenomenon 2. fictitious person or thing —**myth′i·cal** *a.*

my·thol′o·gy (mi-) *n.* [*pl.* -GIES] 1. study of myths 2. myths of a certain people — **myth′o·log′i·cal** *a.*

N

nab *v.* [NABBED, NABBING] [Col.] seize or arrest

na·bob (nā′bäb) *n.* very rich or important person

na·cre (nā′kər) *n.* mother-of-pearl

na′dir (nā′-) *n.* 1. lowest point 2. the point directly beneath one

nag *v.* [NAGGED, NAGGING] 1. scold or urge constantly 2. keep troubling —*n.* 1. one who

nags: also **nag′ger** 2. inferior horse

nai·ad (nā′ad, nī′-) *n.* in myths, nymphs living in water

nail *n.* 1. horny layer at the ends of the fingers and toes 2. narrow, pointed piece of metal driven into pieces of wood to hold them —*v.* 1. fasten as with nails 2. [Col.] catch or hit

na·ive, na·ïve (nä ēv′) *a.* in-

nocent; simple —**na·ïve·té′,
na·ïve·te′** (-tā′) n.

na′ked a. 1. without clothing or covering 2. plain

nam′by-pam′by n. [pl. -BIES] insipid, indecisive person

name n. 1. word or words for a person, thing, or place 2. reputation 3. epithet, often abusive 4. appearance only —a. wellknown —v. 1. give a name to 2. mention or identify by name 3. appoint

name′less a. 1. without a name 2. obscure; vague

name′ly adv. that is to say

name′sake n. person named after another

nan′ny goat [Col.] female goat

nap v. [NAPPED, NAPPING] sleep briefly —n. 1. short sleep 2. fuzzy surface of fibers on cloth —**napped** a.

na·palm (nä′päm) n. jellylike gasoline used in flame throwers and fire bombs —v. to attack with this

nape n. back of the neck

naph′tha (naf′-) n. oily liquid used as a solvent, etc.

naph′tha·lene n. crystalline substance made from coal tar

nap′kin n. small piece of paper or cloth to protect clothes while eating

narc, nark (närk) n. [Sl.] police agent enforcing narcotics laws

nar·cis·sism n. self-love —**nar′cis·sist** n.

nar·cis·sus (när-) n. flowering bulbous plant

nar·cot′ic n. drug that causes deep sleep and lessens pain —a. of or like a narcotic

nar·rate (nar′āt, na rāt′) v. tell a story —**nar′ra·tor** n.

nar·ra′tion n. 1. a narrating 2. a narrative

nar′ra·tive a. in story form —n. story; account

nar′row a. 1. not wide 2. intolerant 3. limited in size, degree, etc. —v. lessen in width, extent, etc. —n. pl. narrow passage; strait —**nar′row·ly** adv.

nar′row-mind′ed a. bigoted

nar·whal (när′wǝl) n. small whale with a long tusk

nar·y (ner′ē) a. [Dial.] not any

na′sal (-z′l) a. of or through the nose

na′sal·ize v. speak with nasal sound —**na′sal·i·za′tion** n.

nas·cent (nas′′nt) n. 1. starting to be or develop

na·stur·tium (nǝ stur′shǝm) n. yellowish-red flower

nas′ty a. [-TIER, -TIEST] 1. dirty 2. obscene 3. unpleasant; mean —**nas′ti·ly** adv. —**nas′ti·ness** n.

na′tal a. of one's birth

na′tion n. 1. a people with history, language, etc. in common 2. people under one government

na′tion·al (nash′ǝn-) a. of a whole nation —n. citizen —**na′tion·al·ly** adv.

na′tion·al·ism n. 1. patriotism 2. advocacy of national independence —**na′tion·al·ist** a., n. —**na′tion·al·is′tic** a.

na′tion·al′i·ty n. [pl. -TIES] nation, esp. of one's birth or citizenship

na′tion·al·ize′ v. transfer control of to a government —**na'-tion·al·i·za'tion** n.

na'tion·wide a. throughout the whole nation

na'tive a. 1. belonging to a region or country by birth, source, etc. 2. being or of the place of one's birth 3. inborn 4. of the original people of a place —n. native person, animal, or plant

na'tive-born' a. born in a specified place

na·tiv'i·ty n. birth

nat'ty a. [-TIER, -TIEST] neat and stylish —**nat'ti·ly** adv.

nat'u·ral a. 1. of or dealing with nature 2. not artificial 3. innate 4. lifelike 5. to be expected 6. Mus. neither sharp nor flat —**nat'u·ral·ly** adv.

natural childbirth childbirth without anesthesia but with prior training

nat'u·ral·ism n. art or writing about people and things as they really are

nat'u·ral·ist n. 1. one who studies plants and animals 2. advocate of naturalism —**nat'u·ral·is'tic** a.

nat'u·ral·ize' v. confer citizenship upon (an alien) —**nat'u·ral·i·za'tion** n.

natural resources coal, oil, water power, etc.

natural sciences biology, chemistry, physics, etc.

na'ture n. 1. basic quality of a thing 2. inborn character 3. kind; sort 4. physical universe or [also N-] its forces 5. primi-

tive state of humankind 6. natural scenery

naught (nôt) n. 1. nothing 2. zero

naugh'ty a. [-TIER, -TIEST] 1. mischievous 2. not nice or proper —**naugh'ti·ly** adv. —**naugh'ti·ness** n.

nau'se·a (-shə, -sē ə) n. 1. feeling of wanting to vomit 2. disgust —**nau'se·ate** v. —**nau'seous** (-shəs) a.

nau'ti·cal a. of sailors, ships, or navigation —**nau'ti·cal·ly** adv.

nau'ti·lus n. tropical mollusk with spiral shell

na'val a. of or for a navy, its ships, etc.

nave n. main, long part of some churches

na'vel n. small abdominal scar where the umbilical cord was attached

nav'i·ga·ble a. 1. wide or deep enough for ship travel 2. that can be steered —**nav'i·ga·bil'i·ty** n.

nav'i·gate v. 1. travel through or on (air, sea, etc.) in a ship or aircraft 2. steer (a ship or aircraft) —**nav'i·ga'tor** n.

nav'i·ga'tion n. science of plotting courses for ships or aircraft

na'vy n. [pl. -VIES] 1. entire fleet of warships, etc. of a nation 2. very dark blue: also **navy blue**

navy bean small, white bean

nay n. 1. denial 2. negative vote or voter

Na·zi (nät'sē) n., a. (adherent)

of the German fascist party (1933–45) —**Na'zism** *n.*

neap tide lowest high tide, occurring twice a month

near *adv.* at a short distance — *a.* 1. close in distance, time, etc. 2. intimate 3. stingy —*v.* draw near to —*prep.* close to —**near'ness** *n.*

near'by' *a., adv.* near; close at hand

near'ly *adv.* almost

near miss result that is not quite successful

near'sight'ed *a.* seeing only near objects distinctly

neat *a.* 1. tidy; clean 2. skillful 3. trim in form 4. undiluted 5. [Sl.] nice —**neat'ly** *adv.* —**neat'ness** *n.*

neb'u·la *n.* [*pl.* -LAE (-lē), -LAS] cloudlike patch seen in the night sky —**neb'u·lar** *a.*

neb'u·lous *a.* vague

nec'es·sar'i·ly *adv.* 1. because of necessity 2. as a necessary result

nec'es·sar'y *a.* 1. that must be had or done; essential 2. inevitable —*n.* [*pl.* -IES] necessary thing

ne·ces'si·tate *v.* to make (something) necessary

ne·ces'si·ty *n.* [*pl.* -TIES] 1. great need 2. something necessary 3. poverty

neck *n.* 1. part that joins the head to the body 2. narrow part of bottle 3. narrow strip of land —*v.* [Sl.] to kiss and caress in making love —**neck and neck** very close —**stick one's neck out** take a chance of failing, losing, etc.

neck'er·chief *n.* kerchief worn around the neck

neck'lace (-lis) *n.* chain of gold, beads, etc. worn around the neck

neck'tie *n.* decorative neck band worn with a shirt

neck'wear *n.* neckties, scarfs, etc.

ne·crol'o·gy (ne kräl'-) *n.* list of people who have died

ne·cro'sis *n.* death or decay of tissue in some body part

nec'tar *n.* 1. in myths, the drink of the gods 2. sweet liquid in flowers 3. delicious drink

nec·tar·ine' (-ēn') *n.* smooth-skinned peach

nee, née (nā, nē) *a.* born

need *n.* 1. lack of something required; also, the thing lacking 2. poverty or distress —*v.* 1. have need of 2. be obliged —**if need be** if it is required —**need'less** *a.*

need'ful *a.* necessary; required

nee'dle *n.* 1. very slender, pointed piece, as for sewing, knitting, playing phonograph records, etc. 2. pointer of a compass 3. thin, short leaf of pine, spruce, etc. 4. sharp tube at the end of a hypodermic syringe —*v.* [Col.] goad; tease

nee'dle·point *n.* embroidery of woolen threads on canvas

nee'dle·work *n.* sewing, embroidery, crocheting, etc.

need'y *a.* [-IER, -IEST] very poor; destitute

ne'er (ner) *adv.* [Poet.] never

ne'er'-do-well' *n.* shiftless, irresponsible person

ne·far'i·ous (-fer'-) *a.* very wicked

no·gate' *v.* deny or nullify — **ne·ga'tion** *n.*

neg'a·tive *a.* 1. saying "no" 2. not positive 3. of the electricity made by friction on resin or wax 4. having an excess of electrons 5. being less than zero —*n.* 1. a negative word, reply, etc. 2. battery plate of lower potential 3. photographic plate or film in which light and shadow are reversed —**neg'a·tive·ly** *adv.*

neg·lect' *v.* 1. fail to do 2. fail to care for properly —*n.* a neglecting —**neg·lect'ful** *a.*

neg·li·gee' (-zhā'-) *n.* woman's dressing gown

neg'li·gent *a.* habitually careless —**neg'li·gence** *n.*

neg'li·gi·ble *a.* trivial

ne·go'ti·ate *v.* 1. discuss so as to agree on 2. arrange for (a loan, etc.) 3. transfer or sell 4. [Col.] get across —**ne·go'ti·a·ble** *a.* —**ne·go'ti·a'tion** *n.* — **ne·go'ti·a'tor** *n.*

Ne'gri·tude (neg'ro, nē'gro-) *n.* pride of blacks in their heritage

Ne'gro *n.* [*pl.* -GROES] member of one of the major groups of human beings: also called **black** —*a.* of this group — **Ne'groid** *a.*

neigh (nā) *v., n.* (utter) the cry of a horse

neigh'bor *n.* 1. one that lives or is near another 2. fellow human being —*a.* nearby —*v.* live or be near

neigh'bor·hood *n.* one part of

a city or the people in it —**in the neighborhood of** [Col.] near or nearly

neigh'bor·ly *a.* friendly

nei'ther (nē'thər, nī'-) *a., pron.* not one or the other (of two) —*con.* correlative used with *nor*

nem'e·sis *n.* 1. just punishment 2. unavoidable cause of one's defeat

neo- *pref.* new; recent

ne'o·co·lo'ni·al·ism *n.* exploiting of a supposedly independent region by a foreign power

ne·ol'o·gism (-jiz'm) *n.* new word or new meaning

ne'on *n.* inert gaseous chemical element, used in electric signs

ne'o·phyte (-fīt) *n.* novice

ne'o·plasm (-plaz'm) *n.* abnormal growth of tissue, as a tumor

neph'ew *n.* 1. son of one's brother or sister 2. son of one's brother-in-law or sister-in-law

ne·phri'tis (ne frīt'-) *n.* inflammation of the kidneys

nep'o·tism *n.* giving of jobs, etc. to relatives

nerve *n.* 1. cordlike fiber carrying impulses to and from the brain 2. courage 3. *pl.* nervousness 4. [Col.] impudence — **get on one's nerves** [Col.] make one irritable

nerve center 1. group of nerve cells working together 2. headquarters

nerve'-rack'ing *a.* very hard on one's patience: also **nerve'-wrack'ing**

nerv'ous *a.* 1. of nerves 2.

easily upset; restless **3.** fearful
—**ner'vous·ness** *n.*

nervous system all the nerve
cells and nervous tissues of an
organism

nerv'y *a.* [-IER, -IEST] **1.** bold
2. [Col.] impudent; brazen

-ness *suf.* quality; state

nest *n.* **1.** place where a bird or
other animal raises its young
2. cozy place **3.** set of things
in increasing sizes —*v.* make a
nest

nest egg money put aside

nes·tle (nes′'l) *v.* **1.** settle
down or hold close for comfort
2. lie sheltered **3.** rest snugly

net *n.* **1.** openwork fabric as of
string, for snaring fish, etc. **2.**
fine net to hold the hair **3.**
netlike cloth **4.** net amount —
a. **1.** of net **2.** left over after
deductions, etc. —*v.* [NETTED,
NETTING] **1.** to snare **2.** to gain

neth·er (neth′ər) *a.* under

net'ting *n.* net fabric

net'tle *n.* weed with stinging
hairs —*v.* annoy

net'work *n.* **1.** arrangement of
wires or threads as in a net **2.**
anything like this, as of roads
3. chain of radio or TV sta-
tions

neu'ral (noo′-) *a.* of a nerve or
nerves

neu·ral'gia (-jə) *n.* pain along
a nerve path

neu·ri'tis *n.* inflammation of
nerves —**neu·rit'ic** *a.*

neuro- *pref.* of nerves

neu·rol'o·gy *n.* branch of
medicine dealing with the
nervous system —**neu·rol'o·
gist** *n.*

neu·ron (noo′rän) *n.* nerve cell
and its processes

neu·ro'sis *n.* [*pl.* -SES (-sēz)]
mental disorder with abnor-
mally intense anxieties, obses-
sions, etc. —**neu·rot'ic** *a., n.*

neu'ter *a.* neither masculine
nor feminine —*v.* castrate or
spay (an animal)

neu'tral *a.* **1.** supporting neither side in a war or quarrel **2.**
not one or the other **3.** having
no decided color —*n.* **1.** neutral nation, etc. **2.** position of
disengaged gears —**neu·tral'·
i·ty** *n.*

neu'tral·ize *v.* counteract the
effectiveness of

neu'tron *n.* uncharged particle
of an atom

nev'er *adv.* **1.** at no time **2.** in
no case

nev'er·the·less' *adv.* however; in spite of that

new *a.* **1.** appearing, made, etc.
for the first time **2.** unfamiliar
3. fresh **4.** unused **5.** modern;
recent **6.** more **7.** beginning
again —*adv.* **1.** again **2.** recently

new blood new people as a
source of new ideas, vigor, etc.

new'born' *a.* **1.** just born **2.**
reborn

new'com'er *n.* recent arrival

new'fan'gled (-fang′g'ld) *a.*
new and strange; contemp-
tuous term

new'ly *adv.* recently

new'ly·wed *n.* recently married person

news (nooz, nyooz) *n.* **1.** new
information **2.** (reports of) recent events **3.** newscast —

make news do something reported as news

news′boy n. boy who sells or delivers newspapers

news′cast n. radio or television news broadcast — **news′cast′er** n.

news′let′ter n. bulletin of news issued regularly to a special group

news′man n. [pl. -MEN] one who gathers and reports news for a newspaper, TV station, etc.

news′pa′per n. daily or weekly news publication

news′print n. cheap paper used for newspapers, etc.

news′stand n. a stand for the sale of newspapers, etc.

news′wor′thy a. timely and important or interesting

news′y a. [-IER, -IEST] [Col.] having much news

newt n. small salamander

New Testament second part of the Christian Bible

New Year's Day January 1: also **New Year's**

next a. nearest; closest —adv. in the nearest time, place, etc. —prep. beside

next′-door′ a. in or at the next house, building, etc.

nex′us n. [pl. -USES, -US] connection or link

ni′a·cin n. nicotinic acid

nib n. 1. bird's beak 2. a point, esp. a pen point

nib′ble v. 1. eat with quick, small bites 2. take small bites from time to time —n. small bite

nibs n. [Col.] important, esp. a self-important, person

nice a. 1. pleasant, kind, good, etc. 2. precise; accurate 3. refined —**nice′ly** adv.

ni′ce·ty n. [pl. -TIES] 1. accuracy 2. refinement 3. small detail; fine point 4. something choice or dainty

niche (nich) n. 1. recess in a wall for a statue, etc. 2. especially suitable position

nick v. make a small cut, chip, etc. in or on —n. small cut, chip, etc. —**in the nick of time** exactly when needed

nick′el n. 1. rust-resistant metal, a chemical element 2. nickel and copper coin worth five cents

nick′name n. 1. substitute name, as "Slim" 2. familiar form of a proper name, as "Bob" —v. give a nickname to

nic′o·tine (-tēn) n. poisonous liquid in tobacco leaves

nic′o·tin′ic acid member of the vitamin B complex, found in protein foods

niece (nēs) n. 1. daughter of one's brother or sister 2. daughter of one's brother-in-law or sister-in-law

nig′gard n. stingy person; miser —a. stingy —**nig′-gard·ly** a., adv.

nigh (nī) adv., a., prep. [Chiefly Ar. or Dial.] near

night (nīt) n. period of darkness between sunset and sunrise

night blindness poor vision in near darkness or dim light

night′cap n. 1. cap worn in

bed 2. [Col.] alcoholic drink taken just before bedtime

night clothes clothes to be worn in bed, as pajamas

night'club *n.* place for eating, drinking, dancing, etc. at night

night crawl'er large earthworm that comes to the surface at night

night'fall *n.* close of the day

night'gown *n.* sleeping gown for women and children

night'hawk *n.* 1. night bird related to the whippoorwill 2. night owl

night'ie (-ē) *n.* [Col.] nightgown

night'in·gale *n.* European thrush that sings at night

night life pleasure-seeking activity at night, as in nightclubs

night'ly *a., adv.* (done or happening) every night

night'mare *n.* frightening dream or experience

night owl one who stays up late

night'shade *n.* belladonna or related plant

night'shirt *n.* kind of nightgown for men

night'spot *n.* [Col.] nightclub

night stand small bedside table

night stick long, heavy club carried by a policeman

night'time *n.* night

nil *n.* nothing

nim'ble *a.* quick in movement or thought —**nim'bly** *adv.*

nim'bus *n.* 1. rain cloud 2. halo

nin'com·poop *n.* fool

nine *a., n.* one more than eight —**ninth** *a., n.*

nine'teen' *a., n.* nine more than ten —**nine'teenth'** *a., n.*

nine'ty *a., n.* [*pl.* -TIES] nine times ten —**nine'ti·eth** *a., n.*

nin'ny *n.* [*pl.* -NIES] a fool

nip *v.* [NIPPED, NIPPING] 1. pinch or bite 2. pinch off 3. spoil, as by frost —*n.* 1. a bite 2. stinging cold 3. small drink of liquor —**nip and tuck** close as to outcome

nip'per *n.* 1. *pl.* pliers, pincers, etc. 2. claw of a crab or lobster

nip'ple *n.* 1. protuberance on a breast or udder 2. thing shaped like this

nip'py *a.* [-PIER, -PIEST] sharp; biting

nir·va'na (-vä'-) *n.* *Buddhism* perfect, passionless bliss

nit *n.* egg of a louse

ni'ter *n.* salt used in explosives, fertilizer, etc.: also, esp. Br., **ni'tre**

nit'-pick'ing *a., n.* finicky; fussy —**nit'-pick'er** *n.*

ni'trate *n.* salt of nitric acid

ni'tric acid corrosive acid containing nitrogen

ni'tro·cel'lu·lose (-lōs) *n.* pulplike substance, used in making explosives, etc.

ni'tro·gen (-jən) *n.* colorless, odorless gas, a chemical element —**ni·trog'e·nous** *a.*

ni'tro·glyc'er·in (-glis'ər in) *n.* thick explosive oil, used in dynamite: also **ni'tro·glyc'er·ine**

nit'ty-grit'ty *n.* [Sl.] basic facts, issues, etc.

nit'wit *n.* stupid person

nix *int.* [Sl.] no! stop!

no *adv.* 1. not at all 2. not so —a. not a —n. [*pl.* NOES, NOS] 1. refusal 2. negative vote

no·bil′i·ty *n.* [*pl.* -TIES] 1. noble state or rank 2. people of noble rank

no′ble *a.* 1. highly moral 2. grand; splendid 3. of high hereditary rank —*n.* person of high rank —**no′ble·ness** *n.* —**no′bly** *adv.*

no′ble·man *n.* [*pl.* -MEN] member of the nobility; peer

no′bod′y *pron.* no one —*n.* [*pl.* -IES] unimportant person

noc·tur′nal *a.* 1. of the night 2. done, happening, etc. at night

noc·turne *n.* romantic musical composition

nod *v.* [NODDED, NODDING] 1. bend the head quickly 2. show (assent) thus 3. let the head fall forward in dozing —*n.* a nodding

node *n.* 1. knob; swelling 2. point on a stem from which a leaf grows

nod·ule (näj′ool) *n.* small knot or rounded lump

No·ol, No·ël (nō el′) *n.* Christmas

no′-fault′ *a.* of automobile insurance that pays for damages without blame being fixed

nog′gin *n.* 1. small mug 2. [Col.] the head

no′-good′ *a.* [Sl.] despicable

noise *n.* sound, esp. a loud, unpleasant sound —*v.* spread (a rumor) —**noise′less** *a.*

noi·some *a.* 1. unhealthful 2. foul-smelling

nois′y *a.* [-IER, -IEST] 1. making noise 2. full of noise —**nois′i·ly** *adv.* —**nois′i·ness** *n.*

no′mad *n.* 1. member of a wandering tribe 2. wanderer —**no·mad′ic** *a.*

no′men·cla′ture (-klā′chər) *n.* system of names

nom′i·nal *a.* 1. in name only 2. relatively small —**nom′i·nal·ly** *adv.*

nom′i·nate *v.* 1. appoint to an office 2. name as a candidate —**nom′i·na′tion** *n.*

nom′i·na·tive *a., n. Gram.* (in) the case of the subject of a verb

nom·i·nee′ (-nē′) *n.* person who is nominated

non- *pref.* not (as in the list below)

non′ab·sorb′ent
non·ac′tive
non′ag·gres′sion
non′al·co·hol′ic
non′be·liev′er
non′bel·lig′er·ent
non·burn′a·ble
non′com·bus′ti·ble
non·com·mer′cial
non-Com′mu·nist
non′con·ta′gious
non′de·duct′i·ble
non′es·sen′tial
non′ex·empt′
non′ex·ist′ent
non·fac′tu·al
non·fad′ing
non·fat′
non·fa′tal
non·fic′tion
non′flam′ma·ble
non′flow′er·ing
non·fly′ing

non·func'tion·al
non·in·fla'tion·ar'y
non·in'ter·fer'ence
non·in·tox'i·cat·ing
non·ir'ri·tat·ing
non·ma·lig'nant
non·mil'i·tar·y
non·of·fi'cial
non·pay'ment
non·per'ish·a·ble
non·poi'son·ous
non·po·lit'i·cal
non·po'rous
non·pro·duc'tive
non·pro·fes'sion·al
non·prof'it·a·ble
non·re·li'gious
non·res·i·den'tial
non·re·sist'ant
non·re·turn'a·ble
non·smok'er
non·sup·port'ing
non·sus·tain'ing
non·tax'a·ble
non·tech'ni·cal
non·tox'ic

non·age (nän'ij) *n.* state of being under legal age
non·a·ligned' *a.* not aligned with either side in a conflict
nonce *n.* the present time
non·cha·lant' (-shə länt') *a.* casually indifferent —**non·cha·lance'** *n.*
non'com *n.* [Col.] noncommissioned officer
non·com'bat·ant *n.* **1.** civilian in wartime **2.** soldier not in combat
non'com·mis'sioned officer enlisted person in the armed forces: in U.S. Army, from corporal to sergeant

non'com·mit'tal *a.* not taking a definite stand
non'con·duc'tor *n.* thing that does not conduct electricity, heat, etc.
non'con·form'ist *n., a.* (one) not conforming to rules, customs, etc. —**non'con·form'i·ty** *n.*
non'de·script *a.* of no definite class or type
none *pron.* **1.** no one **2.** not any —*adv.* not at all
non·en'ti·ty *n.* [*pl.* **-TIES**] unimportant person
none'the·less' *adv.* nevertheless: also **none the less**
non'in·ter·ven'tion *n.* refusal by one nation to interfere in another's affairs
non·met'al *n.* element that is not a metal, as carbon —**non'me·tal'lic** *a.*
non·pa·reil' (-pə rel') *a.* unequaled; peerless
non·par'ti·san *a.* not of any single party, faction, etc.: also **non·par'ti·zan**
non·plus' *v.* [-PLUSED or -PLUSSED, -PLUSING or -PLUSSING] thoroughly bewilder
non·prof'it *a.* not for profit
non·res'i·dent *n., a.* (person) not living in the locality of his work, etc.
non·sec·tar'i·an *a.* not connected with a specific religion
non'sense *n.* absurd or meaningless words or acts —**non·sen'si·cal** *a.*
non'stop' *a., adv.* without a stop
non'sup·port' *n.* failure to support a legal dependent

non·un'ion *a.* not belonging to, or done by, a labor union

non·vi'o·lent *a.* not using violence —**non·vi'o·lence** *n.*

noo'dle *n.* **1.** flat strip of dry dough **2.** [Sl.] the head

nook (nŏŏk) *n.* **1.** corner **2.** small secluded spot

noon (nōōn) *n.* twelve o'clock in the daytime; midday: also **noon'day, noon'time**

no one no person

noose *n.* loop with a slipknot for tightening it

nor *con.* and not (either)

norm *n.* standard or model

nor'mal *a.* **1.** usual; natural **2.** average —*n.* what is normal; usual state —**nor'mal·cy, nor·mal'i·ty** *n.*

nor'mal·ly *adv.* **1.** in a normal way **2.** usually

north *n.* **1.** direction to the right of one facing the sunset **2.** region in this direction —*a., adv.* in, toward, or from the north —**north'er·ly** *a., adv.* —**north'ern** *a.* —**north'ern·er** *n.*

north'east' *n.* direction or region between north and east —*a., adv.* in, toward, or from the northeast —**north'east'er·ly** *a., adv.* —**north'east'ern** *a.*

north'east'ward *adv., a.* toward the northeast: also **north'east'wards** *adv.*

northern lights aurora borealis

North Pole northern end of the earth's axis

North Star bright star almost directly above the North Pole

north'ward *adv., a.* toward the north: also **north'wards** *adv.*

north'west' *n.* direction or region between north and west —*a., adv.* in, toward, or from the northwest —**north'west'er·ly** *a., adv.* —**north'west'ern** *a.*

north'west'ward *adv., a.* toward the northwest: also **north'west'wards** *adv.*

Nor·we'gian (-jən) *n., a.* (native or language) of Norway

nose *n.* **1.** part of the face with two openings for breathing and smelling **2.** sense of smell **3.** thing like a nose —*v.* **1.** find, as by smell **2.** push with the front forward **3.** meddle (in) —**nose out** defeat narrowly

nose'bleed *n.* bleeding from the nose

nose cone foremost part of a rocket or missile

nose dive **1.** swift downward plunge of an airplane, nose first **2.** any sharp drop, as of prices —**nose'-dive'** *v.*

nose drops medication put into the nose in drops

nose'gay *n.* small bunch of flowers

nos·tal'gia (-jə) *n.* a longing for something past or far away —**nos·tal'gic** *a.*

nos'tril *n.* either of two outer openings of the nose

nos'trum *n.* quack medicine

nos'y, nos'ey (nōz'-) *a.* [-IER, -IEST] [Col.] inquisitive

not *adv.* in no manner, degree, etc.

no'ta·ble *a., n.* remarkable or

outstanding (person) —**no′ta·bly** *adv.*

no′ta·rize *v.* certify (a document) as a notary

no′ta·ry *n.* [*pl.* -RIES] one authorized to certify documents, etc.: in full, **notary public**

no·ta′tion *n.* **1.** use of symbols to represent words, quantities, etc. **2.** system of symbols, as in music **3.** brief note

notch *n.* **1.** V-shaped cut **2.** [Col.] a step; degree —*v.* cut notches in

note *n.* **1.** brief writing, letter, etc. **2.** notice; heed **3.** explanation or comment **4.** written promise to pay **5.** musical tone or its symbol **6.** importance —*v.* **1.** to notice **2.** make a note of **3.** mention particularly — **compare notes** to exchange views

note′book *n.* book for keeping memorandums, etc.

not′ed *a.* renowned; famous

note′wor′thy *a.* outstanding; remarkable

noth′ing *n.* **1.** no thing **2.** unimportant person or thing **3.** zero **4.** nothingness —**for nothing 1.** free **2.** in vain **3.** without reason

noth′ing·ness *n.* **1.** nonexistence **2.** insignificance **3.** unconsciousness

no′tice *n.* **1.** announcement or warning **2.** short review **3.** attention **4.** formal warning of the time an agreement will end —*v.* **1.** mention **2.** observe —**take notice** observe

no′tice·a·ble *a.* **1.** easily seen

2. significant —**no′tice·a·bly** *adv.*

no′ti·fy *v.* [-FIED, -FYING] give notice to; inform —**no′ti·fi·ca′tion** *n.*

no′tion *n.* **1.** general idea **2.** belief; opinion **3.** whim **4.** *pl.* small wares

no·to′ri·ous *a.* widely known, esp. unfavorably —**no′to·ri′e·ty** *n.*

no′-trump′ *n.* Bridge a bid to play with no suit being trumps

not′with·stand′ing *prep.* in spite of —*adv.* nevertheless — *con.* although

nou·gat (nō′gat) *n.* candy made of sugar paste with nuts

nought (nôt) *n.* **1.** nothing **2.** zero

noun *n.* word that names a person, thing, etc.

nour′ish (nur′-) *v.* **1.** feed to promote life and growth **2.** foster; promote —**nour′ish·ment** *n.*

no·va (nō′va) *n.* [*pl.* -VAS, -VAE (-vē)] star that brightens intensely and then gradually dims

nov′el *a.* new and unusual —*n.* long fictional narrative

nov′el·ist *n.* writer of novels

nov′el·ty *n.* [*pl.* -TIES] **1.** newness **2.** novel thing **3.** small, cheap toy, etc.

No·vem′ber *n.* eleventh month

no·ve′na *n.* R.C.Ch. special prayers for nine days

nov′ice *n.* **1.** one in a religious order before taking final vows **2.** beginner

no·vi·ti·ate (nō vish'ē it) *n.* period of being a novice

No'vo·cain (-və kān) *trademark for* procaine

now *adv.* **1.** at this moment; at present **2.** at that time; then **3.** with things as they are —*con.* since —*n.* the present time —*a.* of the present time —**now and then** (or **again**) occasionally

now'a·days *adv.* in these days; at the present time

no'where *adv.* not in, at, or to any place —**nowhere near** not by a wide margin

no'wise *adv.* in no way: also **no'way, no'ways**

nox·ious (näk'shəs) *a.* harmful to health or morals

noz'zle *n.* small spout at the end of a hose, etc.

nu'ance (-äns) *n.* slight change in color, meaning, etc.

nub *n.* **1.** lump or small piece **2.** [Col.] gist

nub'by *a.* [-BIER, -BIEST] rough and knotty, as cloth

nu'cle·ar *a.* **1.** of, like, or forming a nucleus or nuclei **2.** of or using atomic energy, bombs, etc.

nuclear family family including parents and their children living in one household

nuclear fission splitting of nuclei of atoms, with the release of much energy, as in the atomic bomb

nuclear fusion fusion of nuclei of atoms, with the release of much energy, as in the hydrogen bomb

nuclear reactor device for creating controlled chain reaction in a fissionable fuel, as for producing energy

nu'cle·us *n.* [*pl.* -CLEI (-klē ī), -CLEUSES] central part, spec. of an atom of a living cell

nude *a.*, *n.* naked (figure)

nudge *v.* push gently, as with the elbow, to attract attention —*n.* gentle push

nud'ism *n.* practice or cult of going nude —**nud'ist** *a.*, *n.*

nug'get *n.* lump of gold ore

nui'sance (noo'-) *n.* annoying act, person, etc.

null (nul) *a.* without legal force: usually in phrase **null and void**

nul'li·fy *v.* [-FIED, -FYING] **1.** make null **2.** make useless **3.** cancel out —**nul'li·fi·ca'tion** *n.*

numb (num) *a.* not able to feel —*v.* make numb

num'ber *n.* **1.** symbol or word showing how many or what place in a series **2.** total **3.** *often pl.* many **4.** quantity **5.** single issue of a periodical **6.** one part of a program of entertainment **7.** form of a word showing it to be singular or plural —*v.* **1.** count **2.** give a number to **3.** include **4.** total or contain —**a number of** several or many —**beyond** (or **without**) **number** too numerous to be counted —**the numbers** illegal numbers lottery based on certain numbers published in newspapers

num'ber·less *a.* countless

nu'mer·al *n.* figure, letter, or word expressing a number

nu'mer·a'tor *n.* part above the line in a fraction

nu·mer'i·cal *a.* 1. of, or having the nature of, number 2. in or by numbers 3. expressed by numbers —**nu·mer'i·cal·ly** *adv.*

nu'mer·ol'o·gy *n.* divination by numbers

nu'mer·ous *a.* 1. very many 2. large in number

nu'mis·mat'ics *n.* study or collection of coins, medals, etc. —**nu·mis'ma·tist** *n.*

num'skull *n.* stupid person

nun *n.* woman devoted to a religious life, esp. one living in a convent under vows

nun'ci·o (-shē ō) *n.* [*pl.* -os] papal ambassador

nun'ner·y *n.* [*pl.* -IES] convent: former name

nup'tial (-shəl) *a.* of marriage or a wedding —*n. pl.* a wedding

nurse *n.* 1. one trained to care for the sick, help doctors, etc. 2. nursemaid —*v.* 1. take care of (an invalid, etc.) 2. try to cure; treat 3. suckle 4. protect or conserve 5. nourish

nurse'maid *n.* woman hired to care for a child or children

nurs'er·y *n.* [*pl.* -IES] 1. room set aside for children 2. place where parents may temporarily leave children to be cared for 3. place where trees and plants are raised for sale

nurs'er·y·man *n.* [*pl.* -MEN] one who owns or works for a nursery (*sense* 3)

nursery rhyme poem for children

nursery school prekindergarten school for young children

nursing home residence providing care for the infirm, chronically ill, disabled, etc.

nur'ture (-chər) *n.* 1. food 2. training; care —*v.* 1. nourish 2. train; rear

nut *n.* 1. dry fruit with a kernel, often edible, inside a hard shell 2. the kernel 3. small metal block for screwing onto a bolt, etc. 4. [Sl.] odd or silly person 5. [Sl.] devotee; fan

nut'crack'er *n.* device for cracking nutshells

nut'meat *n.* kernel of a nut

nut'meg *n.* aromatic seed grated and used as a spice

nut'pick *n.* small device for digging out nut kernels

nu'tri·a (-trē-) *n.* soft, brown fur of a S. American rodent

nu'tri·ent *a., n.* nutritious (substance)

nu'tri·ment *n.* food

nu·tri'tion (-trĭ'-) *n.* 1. process of taking in and assimilating food 2. food 3. study of diet and health —**nu'tri·tive** *a.*

nu·tri'tious *a.* nourishing

nuts *a.* [Sl.] crazy; silly —*int.* [Sl.] exclamation of disgust, scorn, etc. —**be nuts about** [Sl.] 1. be very enthusiastic about 2. be greatly in love with

nut'shell *n.* shell of a nut —**in a nutshell** in a few words

nut'ty *a.* [-TIER, -TIEST] 1. containing nuts 2. tasting like nuts 3. [Sl.] crazy, queer, enthusiastic, etc. —**nut'ti·ness** n.

nuz'zle v. 1. push against with the nose 2. snuggle

ny'lon n. 1. synthetic material made into thread, etc. 2. pl. stockings of this

nymph n. 1. minor Greek or Roman nature goddess 2. young insect not fully adult

O

O int. 1. exclamation in direct address 2. oh

oaf (ōf) n. stupid, clumsy fellow —**oaf'ish** a.

oak (ōk) n. 1. hardwood tree bearing acorns 2. its wood —**oak'en** a.

oak'um n. hemp fiber used to caulk seams in boats

oar n. pole with a broad blade at one end, for rowing —**oars'man** [pl. -MEN] n.

oar'lock n. device supporting an oar in rowing

o·a'sis n. [pl. -SES (-sēz)] fertile place with water in a desert

oat n. usually pl. 1. a cereal grass 2. its grain

oath n. 1. sworn declaration to tell the truth, etc. 2. word used in cursing

oat'meal n. ground or rolled oats, cooked as porridge

ob'bli·ga'to (-gä'-) n. [pl. -TOS, -TI (-tē)] elaborate musical accompaniment to a piece

ob'du·rate (-rət) a. 1. stubborn; unyielding 2. not repenting —**ob'du·ra·cy** n.

o·be'di·ent a. obeying or willing to obey —**o·be'di·ence** n. —**o·be'di·ent·ly** adv.

o·bei'sance (-bā'-, -bē'-) n. 1. bow, curtsy, etc. 2. homage; deference

ob'e·lisk n. tall, four-sided pillar tapering to its pyramidal top

o·bese' (-bēs') a. very fat —**o·bes'i·ty** n.

o·bey' v. 1. carry out orders (of) 2. be guided by

ob·fus'cate v. obscure; confuse —**ob·fus·ca'tion** n.

o·bit'u·ar'y n. [pl. -IES] notice of death, often with a short biography: also **o·bit** (ō'bit)

ob'ject n. 1. thing that can be seen or touched 2. person or thing to which action, etc. is directed 3. purpose; goal 4. Gram. word receiving the action of the verb or governed by a preposition —v. (əb jekt') feel or express opposition or disapproval —**ob·jec'tor** n.

ob·jec'tion n. 1. expression of opposition or disapproval 2. reason for objecting

ob·jec'tion·a·ble a. offensive; disagreeable

ob·jec'tive a. 1. real or actual; not subjective 2. without bias 3. Gram. of the case or an object of a preposition or verb —n. goal —**ob'jec·tiv'i·ty** n. —**ob·jec'tive·ly** adv.

object lesson practical example of some principle

ob·jet d'art (äb'zhā där') [pl. OBJETS D'ART (äb'zhā)] [Fr.]

small object of artistic value

ob·jur·gate v. rebuke; upbraid
—**ob′jur·ga′tion** n.

ob·late a. Geom. flattened at the poles

ob·la·tion n. sacrifice or offering to God or a god

ob·li·gate v. bind by a promise, sense of duty, etc.

ob·li·ga·tion n. 1. (binding power of) a contract, promise, etc. 2. a being indebted for a favor, etc.

ob·lig·a·to·ry a. legally or morally binding

o·blige′ (-blīj′) v. 1. compel, as by law or duty 2. make indebted; do a favor for

o·blig′ing a. helpful

ob·lique′ (-lēk′ or -līk′) a. 1. slanting 2. not direct —**ob·lique′ly** adv. —**ob·liq′ui·ty** (-lik′wə tē) n.

ob·lit′er·ate v. 1. blot out 2. destroy —**ob·lit′er·a′tion** n.

ob·liv′i·on n. 1. state of being forgotten 2. forgetfulness

ob·liv′i·ous a. unmindful

ob′long a. rectangular and longer than broad —n. oblong figure

ob′lo·quy (-kwē) n. widespread censure or disgrace

ob·nox′ious (-näk′shəs) a. offensive; very unpleasant

o′boe (-bō) n. double-reed woodwind instrument

ob·scene′ (äb sēn′) a. offensive to decency —**ob·scen′i·ty** (-sen′-) [pl. -**TIES**] n.

ob·scure′ a. 1. dim 2. not clear or distinct 3. not well-known —v. make obscure —**ob·scu′ri·ty** n.

ob′se·quies (-sə kwēz) n.pl. funeral rites

ob·se′qui·ous (-sē′kwē-) a. servile; fawning

ob·serv′ance n. 1. observing of a law, custom, etc. 2. customary act, rite, etc.

ob·serv′ant a. 1. attentive 2. perceptive; alert

ob·serv′a·to·ry n. [pl. -**RIES**] building for astronomical research

ob·serve′ v. 1. adhere to (a law, etc.) 2. celebrate (a holiday, etc.) 3. notice; watch 4. remark 5. examine scientifically —**ob·ser·va′tion** n. —**ob·serv′er** n.

ob·sess′ v. haunt in mind; preoccupy —**ob·ses′sive** a.

ob·ses′sion n. idea, etc. that obsesses one

ob·sid′i·an n. hard, dark, volcanic glass

ob′so·les′cent a. becoming obsolete —**ob′so·les′cence** n.

ob′so·lete a. no longer used

ob′sta·cle n. obstruction

ob·stet′rics n. branch of medicine dealing with childbirth —**ob·stet′ric, ob·stet′ri·cal** a. —**ob′ste·tri′cian** (-trish′ən) n.

ob′sti·nate (-nit) a. 1. stubborn 2. hard to treat or cure —**ob′sti·na·cy** n.

ob·strep′er·ous a. unruly

ob·struct′ v. 1. block 2. hinder —**ob·struc′tion** n. —**ob·struc′tive** a.

ob·tain′ v. 1. get by trying 2. prevail —**ob·tain′a·ble** a.

ob·trude′ v. 1. push out 2. to

force oneself upon others —**ob·tru'sive** *a.*

ob·tuse' *a.* **1.** more than 90°: said of an angle **2.** blunt **3.** slow to understand

ob·verse' *a.* facing the observer —*n.* (äb'vərs) front or main side of a coin, etc.

ob'vi·ate *v.* prevent, as by proper measures

ob'vi·ous *a.* easy to understand —**ob'vi·ous·ly** *adv.*

oc'a·ri'na (äk'ə rē'-) *n.* small, oval instrument with finger holes and a mouthpiece

oc·ca'sion *n.* **1.** happening **2.** special event **3.** opportunity **4.** cause —*v.* cause —**on occasion** sometimes

oc·ca'sion·al *a.* **1.** for special times **2.** infrequent —**oc·ca'sion·al·ly** *adv.*

Oc'ci·dent *n.* Europe and the Americas —**Oc'ci·den'tal** *a., n.*

oc·clude' *v.* close or shut

oc·clu'sion *n.* **1.** an occluding **2.** the way the upper and lower teeth come together

oc·cult' *a.* **1.** secret **2.** mysterious **3.** magical

oc'cu·pan·cy *n.* an occupying —**oc'cu·pant** *n.*

oc'cu·pa'tion *n.* **1.** an occupying **2.** work; vocation —**oc'cu·pa'tion·al** *a.*

oc'cu·py *v.* [-PIED, -PYING] **1.** take possession of **2.** dwell in **3.** take up (space, etc.) **4.** employ

oc·cur' *v.* [-CURRED, -CURRING] **1.** exist **2.** come to mind **3.** happen

oc·cur'rence *n.* event; incident

o·cean (ō'shən) *n.* **1.** body of salt water covering much of the earth **2.** one of its five main divisions **3.** great quantity —**o'ce·an'ic** *a.*

o'cean·og'ra·phy *n.* study of ocean environment, plants, animals, etc.

o'ce·lot (äs'ə-, ō'sə-) *n.* medium-sized, spotted wildcat

o·cher, o·chre (ō'kər) *n.* yellow or red clay pigment

o'clock' *adv.* by the clock

oc'ta·gon *n.* figure with eight sides and eight angles —**oc·tag'o·nal** *a.*

oc'tane number (or rating) number representing antiknock properties of a gasoline

oc'tave *n.* eight full steps of a musical scale

oc·tet', oc·tette' *n.* group of eight, esp. of musical performers

Oc·to'ber *n.* tenth month

oc'to·ge·nar'i·an (-ji-) *n., a.* (person) between 80 and 90 years old

oc'to·pus *n.* mollusk with soft body and eight arms

oc'u·lar (-yə-) *a.* of, for, or by the eye

oc'u·list *n.* ophthalmologist: earlier term

OD *v.* [OD'D, ODED; OD'ING, ODING] [Sl.] take an overdose, esp. a fatal one

odd *a.* **1.** having a remainder of one when divided by two **2.** left over, as from a pair **3.** with a few more **4.** occasional

5. peculiar; queer —**odd'ly** *adv.*

odd'ball *a., n.* [Sl.] strange or eccentric (person)

odd'i·ty *n.* 1. odd quality 2. [*pl.* -TIES] odd person or thing

odds *n.pl.* 1. advantage; favoring difference 2. betting ratio based on chances —**at odds** quarreling

odds and ends remnants

odds'-on' *a.* having a very good chance of winning

ode *n.* lyric poem with lofty, dignified style

o'di·ous *a.* disgusting

o'di·um *n.* 1. hatred 2. disgrace

o·dom'e·ter *n.* device that measures distance traveled

o'dor *n.* smell; aroma —**o'dor·ous** *a.*

o'dor·if'er·ous *a.* giving off an (esp. fragrant) odor

o'dour *n.* odor: Br. sp.

od·ys·sey (äd'ə sē) *n.* long journey with adventures

o'er (ôr) *prep., adv.* [Poet.] over

of *prep.* 1. coming or resulting from 2. by 3. separated from 4. made from 5. belonging to 6. having or containing 7. specified as 8. concerning; about 9. during

off *adv.* 1. farther away in space or time 2. so as to be no longer on 3. so as to be less —*prep.* 1. not on 2. dependent on 3. away from 4. below the standard of —*a.* 1. not on 2. on the way 3. away from work 4. below standard 5. provided for 6. wrong —*int.* go away!

v. [Sl.] kill; murder —**off and on** now and then

of'fal *n.* refuse; garbage

off'beat' *a.* [Col.] unusual, strange, etc.

off'-col'or *a.* 1. varying from the standard color 2. improper; risqué

of·fend' *v.* 1. commit an offense 2. make angry; displease —**of·fend'er** *n.*

of·fense' (*or* ô'fens) *n.* 1. sin or crime 2. an offending 3. an attacking 4. the side that attacks or seeks to score —**take offense** be offended

of·fen'sive *a.* 1. attacking 2. disgusting —*n.* position for attacking

of·fer *v.* 1. present or give 2. suggest 3. bid (a price, etc.) 4. present itself —*n.* thing offered

of'fer·ing *n.* 1. act of making an offer 2. something offered for sale, as a gift, etc.

of'fer·to·ry *n.* [*pl.* -RIES] 1. offering of bread and wine at Mass 2. collection of money at church service 3. prayers or music during this

off'hand' *adv.* without preparation —*a.* 1. said offhand 2. casual, rude, curt, etc. Also **off'hand'ed**

of'fice *n.* 1. a favor 2. post of authority 3. place for doing business 4. rite

of'fice·hold'er *n.* government official

of'fi·cer *n.* 1. one having a position of authority in business, the armed forces, etc. 2. police officer

of·fi'cial (-fish'əl) *a.* 1. authorized **2.** formal —*n.* one holding an office —**of·fi'cial·ly** *adv.*

of·fi'ci·ate *v.* **1.** perform the duties of an office **2.** perform the functions of a priest, rabbi, etc.

of·fi'cious (-fish'əs) *a.* meddlesome, esp. in a highhanded way

off'ing *n.* distant part of the sea —**in the offing** at some vague future time

off'-key' *a.* not harmonious

off'-lim'its *a.* not to be gone to by a group

off'-put'ting *a.* distracting, annoying, etc.: chiefly Br.

off'-sea'son *n.* time when usual activity is reduced

off'set' *v.* [-SET, -SETTING] compensate for —*n.* (ôf'set) printing process in which the inked impression is transferred from a rubber roller to paper

off'shoot' *n.* anything that comes from a main source

off'shore' *a., adv.* (moving) away from shore

off'side' *a.* not in proper position for play

off'spring' *n.* child or children

off'-white' *a.* grayish-white or yellowish-white

off year year of little production

oft *adv.* [Poet.] often

of·ten (ôf'n) *adv.* many times: also **of'ten·times**

o·gle (ō'g'l) *v.* look (at) flirtatiously —*n.* ogling look

o'gre (-gər) *n.* **1.** *Folklore* maneating giant **2.** cruel man

oh (ō) *int., n.* [*pl.* OH'S, OHS]

exclamation of surprise, fear, wonder, pain, etc.

ohm (ōm) *n.* unit of electrical resistance

-oid *suf.* like; resembling

oil *n.* **1.** any greasy liquid **2.** petroleum **3.** oil painting —*v.* lubricate with oil —*a.* of, from, or like oil

oil'cloth' *n.* cloth waterproofed with oil or paint

oil color paint made of pigment ground in oil

oil painting painting in oil colors

oil shale shale from which oil can be distilled

oil'skin' *n.* cloth made waterproof with oil

oil'y *a.* [-IER, -IEST] **1.** of oil **2.** greasy **3.** too suave

oink *n., int.* grunt of a pig —*v.* make this sound

oint'ment *n.* oily cream for healing the skin

OK, O.K. *a., adv., int.* all right —*n.* approval —*v.* [OK'D, O.K.'D] OK'ING, O.K.'ING] to approve Also *sp.* [Col.] **okay**

o'kra *n.* plant with green pods used in soups

old *a.* **1.** having lived or existed for a long time **2.** of a certain age **3.** not new **4.** former **5.** experienced **6.** of long standing —*n.* time long past —**old'ness** *n.*

Old English English before 1100 A.D.

old'-fash'ioned *a.* of the past; out-of-date

old hand experienced person

old hat [Sl.] stale

old'ie, old'y *n.* [*pl.* -IES] [Col.] old joke, song, etc.

old lady [Sl.] one's mother or wife

old'-line' *a.* long-established, conservative, etc.

old maid spinster

old man [Sl.] one's father or husband

old'ster *n.* [Col.] old or elderly person

Old Testament Bible of Judaism, or the first part of the Christian Bible

old'-tim'er *n.* [Col.] longtime member, worker, etc.

o·lé (ō lā') *int., n.* [Sp.] shout of approval, etc.

o'le·ag'i·nous (-aj'-) *a.* oily; unctuous

o'le·an'der *n.* flowering evergreen shrub

o'le·o·mar'ga·rine (-jə rin) *n.* margarine: also **o'le·o**

ol·fac'to·ry *a.* of the sense of smell

ol'i·gar·chy (-gärk'-) *n.* [*pl.* -IES] **1.** state rule by a few people **2.** these people —**ol'i·gar'chic** *a.*

ol'ive *n.* **1.** evergreen tree **2.** its small oval fruit **3.** yellowish green

om'buds·man *n.* [*pl.* -MEN] official who investigates complaints against government

o·me'ga *n.* last letter of the Greek alphabet

om·e·let, om·e·lette (äm'lit) *n.* eggs beaten up and cooked as a pancake

o'men *n.* sign of something to come

om'i·nous *a.* threatening

o·mis'sion (-mish'-) *n.* an omitting or thing omitted

o·mit' *v.* [OMITTED, OMITTING] **1.** leave out **2.** fail to do

omni- *pref.* all; everywhere

om'ni·bus *a.* providing for many things at once

om·nip'o·tent *a.* all-powerful —**om·nip'o·tence** *n.*

om·nip·res'ent *a.* present in all places at the same time

om·nis'cient (-nish'ənt) *a.* knowing all things —**om·nis'·cience** *n.*

om·niv'o·rous *a.* **1.** eating all foods **2.** taking in everything

on *prep.* **1.** held up by, covering, or attached to **2.** near to **3.** at the time of **4.** connected with **5.** in a state of **6.** by using **7.** concerning **8.** [Col.] at the expense of **9.** [Sl.] addicted to; using —*adv.* **1.** in a situation of touching, covering, or being held up by **2.** toward **3.** forward **4.** continuously **5.** into operation —*a.* in action —**on** *to* [Sl.] aware of the real meaning of

once *adv.* **1.** one time **2.** at any time **3.** formerly —*n.* one time —**at once 1.** immediately **2.** simultaneously

once'-o'ver *n.* [Col.] quick look, examination, etc.

on'com'ing *a.* approaching

one *a.* **1.** being a single thing **2.** united **3.** a certain **4.** some —*n.* **1.** lowest number **2.** single person or thing —*pron.* a person or thing

one'ness *n.* unity; identity

on'er·ous *a.* oppressive

one·self' *pron.* one's own self

—**be oneself** function normally —**by oneself** alone

one'-sid'ed *a.* 1. unequal 2. partial

one'-time' *a.* former

one'-track' *a.* [Col.] limited in scope

one'-way' *a.* in one direction only

on'go·ing *a.* progressing

on·ion (un'yən) *n.* edible bulb having a sharp taste

on'ion·skin' *n.* tough, thin, translucent, glossy paper

on·look'er *n.* spectator

on'ly *a.* 1. alone of its or their kind 2. best —*adv.* 1. and no other 2. (but) in the end 3. as recently as —*con.* [Col.] but —**only too** very

on'rush *n.* strong onward rush

on'set' *n.* 1. attack 2. start

on'slaught (-slôt) *n.* violent attack

on'to *prep.* 1. to and upon 2. [Sl.] aware of Also **on to**

o'nus *n.* 1. burden, unpleasant duty, etc. 2. blame

on'ward *adv.* forward: also **on'wards** —*a.* advancing

on'yx (-iks) *n.* kind of agate

ooze *v.* 1. flow out slowly 2. exude —*n.* 1. something that oozes 2. soft mud or slime

o'pal *n.* iridescent gem

o·paque' (-pāk') *a.* 1. not translucent 2. dull; dark 3. hard to understand —**o·pac'i·ty** (-pas'-) *n.*

o'pen *a.* 1. not closed, covered, etc. 2. not enclosed 3. unfolded 4. free to be entered, used, etc. 5. not restricted 6. available 7. frank —*v.* 1. cause

to be or become open 2. begin 3. start operating —**open to** glad to consider —**the open** 1. the outdoor world 2. public knowledge —**o'pen·er** *n.* — **o'pen·ly** *adv.*

o'pen-air' *a.* outdoor

o'pen-and-shut' *a.* easily decided

o'pen-end'ed *a.* unlimited

o'pen-eyed' *a.* with the eyes wide open, as in surprise

o'pen-faced' *a.* having a frank, honest face

o'pen-hand'ed *a.* generous

open house 1. informal home reception 2. time when an institution is open to visitors

o'pen·ing *n.* 1. open place 2. beginning 3. favorable chance 4. unfilled job

o'pen-mind'ed *a.* impartial

o'pen-work' *n.* ornamental work with openings in it

op'er·a *n.* play set to music and sung with an orchestra — **op'er·at'ic** *a.*

op'er·a·ble *a.* 1. feasible 2. that can be treated by surgery

op'er·ate *v.* 1. be or keep in action 2. have an effect 3. perform an operation 4. manage

op'er·a'tion *n.* 1. act or way of operating 2. being in action 3. one process in a series 4. surgical treatment for an illness

op'er·a'tion·al *a.* 1. of the operation of something 2. that can be operated 3. in use

op'er·a'tive *a.* 1. operating 2. effective

op'er·a'tor *n.* 1. one who

operates a machine 2. one engaged in business

op'er·et'ta *n.* short, amusing musical play

oph'thal·mol'o·gy (äf'-) *n.* branch of medicine dealing with diseases of the eye — **oph'thal·mol·o·gist** *n.*

o'pi·ate (-pē it) *n.* 1. narcotic drug containing opium 2. anything quieting

o·pine' *v.* think; suppose: usually humorous

o·pin'ion (-yan) *n.* 1. what one thinks true 2. estimation 3. expert judgment

o·pin'ion·at'ed *a.* obstinate in holding an opinion

o'pi·um *n.* narcotic drug made from a certain poppy

o·pos'sum *n.* small, treedwelling mammal

op·po'nent *n.* person against one in a fight, etc.

op·por·tune' *a.* 1. suitable 2. timely

op'por·tun'ism *n.* policy of advancing one's interests, using any means —**op'por·tun'ist** *n.* —**op'por·tun·is'tic** *a.*

op'por·tu'ni·ty *n.* [*pl.* -TIES] 1. fit time to do something 2. good chance

op·pose' *v.* 1. place opposite 2. fight or resist

op'po·site *a.* 1. entirely different 2. opposed to —*n.* anything opposed —*prep.* across from

op'po·si'tion *n.* 1. resistance, contrast, hostility, etc. 2. [*often* O-] political party opposing the party in power

op·press' *v.* 1. worry; trouble 2. keep down by cruel use of authority —**op·pres'sion** *n.* —**op·pres'sor** *n.*

op·pres'sive *a.* 1. causing discomfort 2. tyrannical 3. distressing

op·pro'bri·ous *a.* abusive

op·pro'bri·um *n.* 1. disgrace 2. reproachful contempt

opt *v.* make a choice (*for*) — **opt out** (*of*) choose not to be or continue in

op'tic *a.* of the eye

op'ti·cal *a.* 1. of vision 2. aiding sight 3. of optics

op·ti'cian (-tish'ən) *n.* maker or seller of eyeglasses

op'tics *n.* science dealing with light and vision

op'ti·mism *n.* tendency to take the most hopeful view — **op'ti·mist** *n.* —**op'ti·mis'tic** *a.*

op'ti·mum *n.* best or most favorable condition —*a.* most favorable; best: also **op'ti·mal**

op'tion *n.* 1. choice 2. right of choosing 3. something that can be chosen 4. right to buy, etc. at a fixed price within a certain time —**op'tion·al** *a.*

op·tom'e·trist *n.* one who tests eyes and fits eyeglasses — **op·tom'e·try** *n.*

op'u·lent *a.* 1. wealthy 2. abundant —**op'u·lence** *n.*

o'pus *n.* [*pl.* OPERA (äp'-), OPUSES] a work; esp., numbered musical work of a composer

or *con.* word introducing an alternative, synonym, etc.

-or *suf.* person or thing that

or·a·cle *n.* ancient Greek or Roman priest who acted as prophet —**o·rac′u·lar** *a.*

o′ral (ô′-) *a.* **1.** spoken **2.** of the mouth —**o′ral·ly** *adv.*

or′ange *n.* **1.** sweet, reddish-yellow citrus fruit **2.** reddish yellow

or·ange·ade′ *n.* drink of orange juice, water, and sugar

o·rang′u·tan *n.* humanlike ape

o·rate′ *v.* speak pompously

o·ra′tion *n.* formal speech, esp. at a ceremony

or′a·tor *n.* eloquent public speaker

or·a·to′ri·o *n.* [*pl.* -os] long, dramatic musical work, usually on a religious theme

or′a·to·ry *n.* skill in public speaking —**or′a·tor′i·cal** *a.*

orb *n.* (heavenly) sphere

or′bit *n.* path of one heavenly body around another —*v.* put or go in an orbit —**or′bit·al** *a.*

or′chard *n.* grove of fruit trees

or·ches·tra (-kis-) *n.* **1.** group of musicians playing together **2.** main floor of a theater —**or·ches′tral** *a.*

or′ches·trate *v.* arrange (music) for an orchestra —**or′ches·tra′tion** *n.*

or′chid (-kid) *n.* **1.** plant having flowers with three petals, one of which is lip-shaped **2.** this flower **3.** pale purple

or·dain′ *v.* **1.** to decree **2.** admit to the ministry

or·deal′ *n.* difficult or painful experience

or′der *n.* **1.** peaceful, orderly, or proper state **2.** monastic or fraternal brotherhood **3.** general condition **4.** command **5.** (request for) items to be supplied **6.** class; kind —*v.* **1.** arrange **2.** command **3.** request (supplies) —**in** (or **out of**) **order 1.** in (or out) of proper position **2.** in (or not in) working condition —**in order that** so that

or′der·ly *a.* **1.** neatly arranged **2.** well-behaved —*n.* [*pl.* -LIES] **1.** soldier acting as an officer's servant **2.** male hospital attendant —**or′der·li·ness** *n.*

or′di·nal number number used to show order in a series, as *first, second,* etc.

or′di·nance *n.* statute, esp. of a city government

or′di·nar′i·ly *adv.* usually

or′di·nar′y *a.* **1.** customary; usual **2.** common; average

or′di·na′tion *n.* an ordaining or being ordained

ord′nance *n.* **1.** artillery **2.** all military weapons, vehicles, etc.

or′dure (-jar) *n.* excrement

ore *n.* natural combination of minerals containing metal

o·reg′a·no *n.* plant with fragrant leaves used to season food

or′gan *n.* **1.** keyboard musical instrument using pipes, reeds, or electronic tubes **2.** animal or plant part with a special function **3.** agency or medium

or′gan·dy, or′gan·die *n.* [*pl.* -DIES] sheer, stiff cotton cloth

or·gan′ic *a.* **1.** of a body organ **2.** inborn **3.** systematically arranged **4.** of or from living matter **5.** of chemical compounds containing carbon **6.**

grown with only animal or vegetable fertilizers —**or·gan′i·cal·ly** adv.

or′gan·ism n. living thing

or′gan·ist n. player of the organ

or·gan·i·za′tion n. 1. act of organizing 2. group organized for some purpose

or′gan·ize v. 1. arrange according to a system 2. form into a group, union, etc. —**or′gan·iz′er** n.

or·gan′za n. stiff fabric of rayon, silk, etc.

or′gasm n. climax of a sexual act

or′gy (-jē) n. [pl. -GIES] wild merrymaking

o′ri·ent n. [O-] Asia —v. adjust (oneself) to a specific situation —**o′ri·en·ta′tion** n.

O′ri·en′tal a. of the Orient —n. native of the Orient

or′i·fice (-fis) n. mouth; opening

o·ri·ga·mi (ôr′ə gä′mē) n. Japanese art of folding paper to form flowers, etc.

or′i·gin n. 1. beginning 2. parentage 3. source

o·rig′i·nal a. 1. first 2. new; novel 3. inventive 4. being that from which copies are made —n. an original work, form, etc. —**o·rig′i·nal′i·ty** n. —**o·rig′i·nal·ly** adv.

o·rig′i·nate v. 1. create; invent 2. begin; start —**o·rig′i·na′tion** n. —**o·rig′i·na′tor** n.

o′ri·ole n. bird with bright orange and black plumage

Or′lon trademark for synthetic fiber —n. [o-] this fiber

or′na·ment (-mənt) n. decoration —v. (-ment′) decorate —**or′na·men′tal** a. —**or′na·men·ta′tion** n.

or·nate′ a. showy —**or·nate′ly** adv.

or′ner·y a. [Chiefly Dial.] 1. mean 2. obstinate —**or′ner·i·ness** n.

or·ni·thol′o·gy n. study of birds —**or·ni·thol′o·gist** n.

o′ro·tund a. 1. full and deep in sound 2. bombastic

or′phan n. child whose parents are dead —v. cause to be an orphan

or′phan·age n. institution that is a home for orphans

or′ris n. iris having a root (or′ris·root) pulverized for perfumery, etc.

or·tho·don′tics, or·tho·don′tia (-shə) n. dentistry of correcting tooth irregularities —**or·tho·don′tist** n.

or′tho·dox a. 1. holding to the usual or fixed beliefs; conventional 2. [O-] of a Christian church dominant in E Europe, W Asia, and N Africa —**or′tho·dox′y** n.

or·thog′ra·phy n. [pl. -PHIES] 1. correct spelling 2. spelling as a subject for study

or′tho·pe′dics n. surgery dealing with bones —**or′tho·pe′dic** a. —**or′tho·pe′dist** n.

-ory suf. 1. of or like 2. place or thing for

os′cil·late v. 1. swing to and fro 2. fluctuate —**os′cil·la′tion** n.

os·cil′lo·scope n. instrument

that shows an electrical wave on a fluorescent screen

os'cu·late (-kyə-) v. kiss —**os'·cu·la'tion** n.

-ose suf. full of; like

o·sier (ō'zhər) n. willow with branches used for baskets and furniture

-osis suf. 1. condition or action 2. diseased condition

os·mo'sis n. diffusion of fluids through a porous membrane

os'prey n. [pl. -PREYS] large, fish-eating hawk

os'si·fy v. [-FIED, -FYING] 1. change into bone 2. fix rigidly in a custom, etc. —**os'si·fi·ca'tion** n.

os·ten'si·ble a. seeming; apparent —**os·ten'si·bly** adv.

os·ten·ta'tion n. showiness —**os·ten·ta'tious** a.

os'te·op'a·thy n. school of medicine and surgery emphasizing the relation of muscles and bones to all other body systems —**os'te·o·path'** n.

os'tra·cize v. banish; shut out —**os'tra·cism** n.

os'trich n. large, nonflying bird

oth'er a. 1. being the one(s) remaining 2. different 3. additional —pron. 1. the other one 2. some other one —adv. otherwise —**the other day** (or **night,** etc.) not long ago; recently

oth'er·wise adv. 1. differently 2. in all other ways 3. if not; else —a. different

oth'er·world'ly a. apart from earthly interests

o'ti·ose a. 1. idle 2. futile 3. useless

ot'ter n. 1. weasellike animal 2. its fur

ot'to·man n. low, cushioned seat or footstool

ouch int. cry of pain

ought v. a helping verb showing: 1. duty 2. desirability 3. probability

oui (wē) adv. [Fr.] yes

ounce n. 1. unit of weight, 1/16 pound 2. fluid ounce, 1/16 pint

our a. of us

ours pron. that or those belonging to us

our·selves' pron. intensive or reflexive form of **we**

-ous suf. having; full of; characterized by

oust v. force out; expel

oust'er n. dispossession

out adv. 1. away from a place, etc. 2. outdoors 3. into being or action 4. completely 5. beyond a regular condition 6. into disuse 7. from a group 8. [Sl.] into unconsciousness —a. 1. not used, working, etc. 2. [Col.] having lost financially 3. [Col.] old-fashioned —n. 1. [Sl.] excuse 2. Baseball failure of a player to reach base safely —v. become known —prep. out of **on the outs** [Col.] on unfriendly terms —**out for** trying to do —**out of** 1. from inside of 2. beyond 3. from (material) 4. because of 5. having no 6. so as to deprive —**out to** trying to

out- pref. 1. outside 2. outward 3. better or more than

out'age *n.* accidental suspension of operation

out'-and-out' *a.* thorough

out'back *n.* remote, sparsely settled region

out'bal'ance *v.* be greater than in weight, value, etc.

out-bid' *v.* bid or offer more than (someone else)

out'board *a., adv.* outside the hull of a boat —*n.* portable gasoline engine mounted outboard

out'bound *a.* going outward

out'break *n.* a breaking out, as of disease or rioting

out'build'ing *n.* building apart from the main one

out'burst *n.* sudden show of feeling, energy, etc.

out'cast *a., n.* shunned or rejected (person)

out-class' *v.* surpass

out'come *n.* result

out'crop *n.* exposed rock layer

out'cry *n.* [*pl.* -CRIES] 1. a crying out 2. strong protest

out-dat'ed *a.* out-of-date

out-dis'tance *v.* get ahead of, as in a race

out-do' *v.* [-DID, -DONE, -DOING] exceed or surpass —**outdo oneself** do better than one expected to do

out'door *a.* in the open

out'doors' *adv.* in or into the open; outside —*n.* the outdoor world

out'er *a.* farther out or away

out'er·most *a.* farthest out

outer space space beyond the earth's atmosphere

out'er·wear *n.* garments worn over the usual clothing

out'field *n. Baseball* 1. area beyond the base lines 2. players (**outfielders**) positioned there

out'fit *n.* 1. equipment for some activity 2. clothes worn together 3. group of people associated in an activity —*v.* [-FITTED, -FITTING] equip

out-flank' *v.* go around and beyond the flank of (troops)

out-fox' *v.* outwit

out'go *n.* expenditure

out'go'ing *a.* 1. leaving 2. sociable

out-grow' *v.* [-GREW, -GROWN, -GROWING] 1. grow too large for 2. lose in maturing

out'growth *n.* 1. result 2. an offshoot

out-guess' *v.* outwit

out'house *n.* booth outdoors, used as a toilet

out'ing *n.* picnic, trip, etc.

out-land'ish *a.* 1. strange 2. fantastic

out-last' *v.* endure longer than

out'law *n.* notorious criminal —*v.* declare illegal

out'lay *n.* money spent

out'let *n.* 1. passage or way out 2. means of expression 3. market for goods

out'line *n.* 1. bounding line 2. sketch showing only outer lines 3. general plan —*v.* make an outline of

out-live' *v.* live longer than

out'look *n.* 1. viewpoint 2. prospect

out'ly'ing *a.* remote

out-mod'ed (-mōd'-) *a.* old-fashioned

out·num'ber v. be greater in number than

out'-of-date' a. no longer in style or use; old-fashioned

out'-of-door' a. outdoor

out'-of-doors' adv., n. outdoors

out'-of-the-way' a. 1. secluded 2. unusual

out'pa'tient n. hospital patient not an inmate

out'post n. remote settlement or military post

out'put n. 1. total quantity produced in a given period 2. information as from a computer 3. current or power delivered

out'rage (-rāj) n. 1. extremely vicious act 2. grave insult 3. great anger aroused by this — v. 1. commit an outrage against 2. cause outrage in

out·ra'geous a. very shocking

out'right' a. complete —adv. (out rīt′) 1. entirely 2. openly 3. at once

out'set n. beginning

out'side' n. 1. the exterior 2. area beyond —a. 1. outer 2. from some other 3. slight — adv. on or to the outside — prep. on or to the outside of

out·sid'er n. one not of a certain group

out'skirts' n.pl. outlying districts of a city, etc.

out·smart' v. [Col.] outwit

out'spo'ken a. frank; bold

out·stand'ing a. 1. prominent 2. unpaid

out'stretched' a. extended

out·strip' v. [-STRIPPED, -STRIPPING] excel

out'ward a. 1. outer 2. visible —adv. toward the outside: also **out'wards** —**out'ward·ly** adv.

out·wear' v. [-WORE, -WORN, -WEARING] 1. wear out 2. outlast

out·wit' v. [-WITTED, -WITTING] to overcome by cleverness

o'va n. pl. of ovum

o'val a., n. egg-shaped (thing)

o'va·ry n. [pl. -RIES] 1. female gland where ova are formed 2. part of a flower where the seeds form —**o·var'i·an** a.

o·va'tion n. loud and long applause or cheering

ov'en n. compartment for baking, drying, etc.

o'ver prep. 1. above 2. on; upon 3. across 4. during 5. more than 6. about —adv. 1. above or across 2. more 3. down 4. other side up 5. again —a. 1. finished 2. on the other side

over- pref. excessive or excessively (as in the list below)

o'ver·a·bun'dance
o'ver·ac'tive
o'ver·anx'ious
o'ver·bur'den
o'ver·cau'tious
o'ver·con'fi·dent
o·ver·cook'
o·ver·crit'i·cal
o·ver·crowd'
o'ver·ea'ger
o'ver·eat'
o'ver·em'pha·size
o'ver·es'ti·mate
o'ver·ex·ert'
o'ver·ex·pose'
o·ver·heat'

o'ver·in·dulge'
o'ver·load'
o'ver·pop'u·late
o'ver·price'
o'ver·pro·duc'tion
o·ver·ripe'
o'ver·sen'si·tive
o'ver·spend'
o'ver·stim'u·late
o'ver·stock'
o'ver·strict'
o'ver·sup·ply'
o'ver·tire'

o'ver·all' a. 1. from end to end 2. total

o'ver·alls' n.pl. loose work trousers with attached bib

o·ver·awe' v. subdue by inspiring awe

o'ver·bear'ing a. bossy

o'ver·board' adv. from a ship into the water —go overboard [Col.] go to extremes

o'ver·cast' a. cloudy; dark

o'ver·coat' n. coat worn over the usual clothing

o·ver·come' v. [-CAME, -COME, -COMING] get the better of; master

o·ver·do' v. [-DID, -DONE, -DOING] 1. do too much 2. cook too long 3. exaggerate

o·ver·dose' n. too large a dose —v. (ō vər dōs') take too large a dose

o·ver·drawn' a. drawn on in excess of the amount credited to one

o·ver·dress' v. dress too warmly, too showily, or too formally

o'ver·drive' n. gear that reduces an engine's power without reducing its speed

o·ver·due' a. past the time for payment, arrival, etc.

o'ver·flight' n. flight of an aircraft over foreign territory

o'ver·flow' v. 1. flood; run over 2. fill beyond capacity —n. (ō'vər flō) 1. an overflowing 2. vent for overflowing liquids

o·ver·grow' v. [-GREW, -GROWN, -GROWING] 1. grow over all of 2. grow too much

o'ver·hand' a., adv. with the hand held higher than the elbow

o·ver·haul' v. check thoroughly and make needed repairs

o'ver·head' a., adv. above the head —n. continuing business costs, as of rent

o·ver·hear' v. [-HEARD, -HEARING] hear (something spoken) without the speaker's knowledge

o·ver·joyed' a. delighted

o'ver·kill' n. ability of a supply of nuclear arms to kill more than a nation's total population

o·ver·land' a., adv. by or across land

o·ver·lap' v. [-LAPPED, -LAPPING] lap over

o·ver·lay' v. [-LAID, -LAYING] 1. spread over 2. cover with decorative layer

o·ver·look' v. 1. look down on 2. fail to notice 3. neglect 4. excuse

o'ver·ly adv. too much

o'ver·night' adv. during the night —a. (ō'vər nīt) of or for a night

o·ver·pass n. bridge over a river, road, etc.

o·ver·pow′er v. subdue

o·ver·rate′ v. estimate too highly

o·ver·re·act′ v. react in an overly emotional way

o·ver·ride′ v. [-RODE, -RIDDEN, -RIDING] 1. prevail over 2. nullify

o·ver·rule′ v. 1. set aside 2. prevail over

o·ver·run′ v. [-RAN, -RUN, -RUNNING] 1. spread out over 2. swarm over 3. extend beyond

o′ver·seas′ a., adv. 1. across or beyond the sea 2. foreign

o·ver·see′ v. [-SAW, -SEEN, -SEEING] supervise —**o′ver·se′er** n.

o′ver·shad′ow v. be more important than

o′ver·shoe′ n. boot worn over the regular shoe to ward off dampness, etc.

o′ver·sight′ n. 1. failure to see 2. careless omission

o·ver·sim′pli·fy v. [-FIED, -FYING] simplify to the point of distortion —**o′ver·sim′pli·fi·ca′tion** n.

o′ver·size′ a. 1. too large 2. larger than usual Also **o′ver·sized′**

o·ver·sleep′ v. [-SLEPT, -SLEEPING] sleep longer than intended

o′ver·stuffed′ a. upholstered with deep stuffing

o·vert′ (or o′vurt) a. 1. open; public 2. done openly

o·ver·take′ v. [-TOOK, -TAKEN,

-TAKING] 1. catch up with 2. come upon suddenly

o′ver·tax′ v. 1. tax too much 2. put a strain on

o·ver·throw′ v. [THREW, -THROWN, -THROWING] 1. turn over 2. conquer —n. (ō′vər thrō) defeat or destruction

o′ver·time′ n. 1. time beyond a set limit 2. pay for overtime work —a., adv. of or for overtime

o′ver·tone′ n. 1. Mus. higher tone heard faintly when a main tone is played 2. implication

o′ver·ture (-chər) n. 1. Mus. introduction 2. proposal

o·ver·turn′ v. 1. turn over 2. conquer

o·ver·ween′ing a. haughty

o·ver·weight′ a. above the normal or allowed weight

o·ver·whelm′ v. 1. cover over completely 2. crush —**o·ver·whelm′ing** a.

o·ver·work′ v. work too hard —n. (ō′vər wurk′) too much work

o·ver·wrought′ (-rôt′) a. too nervous or excited

o′vi·duct′ n. tube for passage of ova from ovary to uterus

o·void′ a. egg-shaped

o′vu·late (-vyə-) v. produce and discharge ova —**o·vu·la′tion** n.

o′vule n. 1. immature ovum 2. part of a plant that develops into a seed

o′vum n. [pl. -VA (-və)] female germ cell

owe v. 1. be in debt (to) for a

certain sum **2.** feel obligated to give

ow'ing (ō'-) *a.* due; unpaid **— owing to** resulting from

owl *n.* night bird of prey with large eyes **—owl'ish** *a.*

owl'et *n.* small or young owl

own *a.* belonging to oneself or itself *—n.* what one owns *—v.* **1.** possess **2.** confess **—on one's own** [Col.] by one's own efforts **—own'er** *n.* **— own'er·ship** *n.*

ox *n.* [*pl.* OXEN] **1.** a cud-chewing animal, as a cow, bull, etc. **2.** castrated bull

ox'blood *n.* deep red color

ox'bow (-bō) *n.* U-shaped part of yoke for ox

ox'ford (-fard) *n.* low shoe laced over the instep

ox'ide *n.* oxygen compound **—ox'i·da'tion** *n.*

ox'i·dize *v.* unite with oxygen **—ox'i·da'tion** *n.*

ox'y·gen *n.* colorless gas, commonest chemical element

ox'y·gen·ate *v.* combine or treat with oxygen **—ox'y·gen·a'tion** *n.*

oys'ter (ois'-) *n.* edible mollusk with hinged shell

o'zone *n.* **1.** form of oxygen with a strong odor **2.** [Sl.] pure, fresh air

P

pa *n.* [Col.] father

pace *n.* **1.** a step or stride **2.** rate of speed **3.** gait *—v.* **1.** walk back and forth across **2.** measure by paces **3.** set the pace for

pace'mak'er *n.* **1.** person, horse, car, etc. that leads the way **2.** electronic device placed in the body to regulate heartbeat

pach'y·derm (pak'-) *n.* large, thick-skinned animal

pach'y·san'dra *n.* low evergreen plant grown as ground cover

pa·cif'ic *a.* peaceful; calm

pac'i·fism (pas'-) *n.* opposition to all war **—pac'i·fist** *n.*

pac'i·fy *v.* [-FIED, -FYING] make calm **—pac'i·fi·ca'tion** *n.* **—pac'i·fi'er** *n.*

pack *n.* **1.** bundle of things **2.** package of a set number **3.** group of animals, etc. *—v.* **1.** put (things) in a pack, bundle, etc. **2.** crowd; cram **3.** fill tightly **4.** send (*off*) **5.** choose (a jury) dishonestly **—send packing** dismiss

pack'age *n.* packed thing *—v.* make a package of

pack'et *n.* **1.** small package **2.** boat traveling regular route with freight, mail, etc.: also **packet boat**

packing house plant where meats, etc. are packed for sale

pack rat rat that hides small articles in its nest

pack'sad'dle *n.* saddle with fasteners to secure a load

pact *n.* compact; agreement

pad *n.* **1.** soft stuffing or cushion **2.** sole of an animal's foot **3.** waterlily leaf **4.** paper sheets fastened at one edge *— v.* [PADDED, PADDING] **1.** stuff with material 2. walk softly 3. expand with something unnecessary or improper

pad'ding n. material used to pad

pad'dle n. 1. oar for a canoe 2. similar thing for games, etc. —v. 1. propel with a paddle 2. spank 3. move hands or feet about in water

paddle wheel wheel with boards around it for propelling a steamboat

pad'dock n. small enclosure for horses

pad'dy n. [pl. -DIES] rice field

pad'lock n. a lock with a U-shaped arm —v. fasten with a padlock

pa·dre (pä'drā) n. father: title for a priest

pae·an (pē'ən) n. song of joy

pa'gan n. a heathen —**pa'gan·ism** n.

page n. 1. one side of a leaf of a book, etc. 2. the leaf 3. boy attendant —v. 1. number the pages of 2. try to find (a person) by calling his name

pag·eant (paj'ənt) n. elaborate show, parade, play, etc. — **pag'eant·ry** n.

pag·i·na'tion (paj'-) n. numbering of pages

pa·go·da (pə-) n. towerlike temple of the Orient

paid pt. & pp. of **pay**

pail n. bucket —**pail'ful** n.

pain n. 1. hurt felt in body or mind 2. pl. great care —v. cause pain to —**pain'ful** a. —**pain'less** a.

pains'tak'ing a. careful

paint n. pigment mixed with oil, water, etc. —v. 1. make pictures (of) with paint 2. cover with paint —**paint'er** n. —**paint'ing** n.

pair n. two things, persons, etc. that match or make a unit — v. form pairs (of)

pais'ley, Pais·ley (pāz'-) a. having an elaborate pattern of swirls, etc.

pa·ja'mas n.pl. jacket and trousers for sleeping

pal n. [Col.] close friend

pal'ace n. 1. monarch's residence 2. magnificent building —**pa·la'tial** (-shəl) a.

pal'at·a·ble a. pleasing to the taste

pal'ate (-it) n. 1. roof of the mouth 2. taste

pa·la'ver n., v. talk

pale a. 1. white; colorless 2. not bright or intense —n. 1. pointed fence stake 2. boundary —v. turn pale

pa·le·on·tol'o·gy (pā'-) n. study of fossils —**pa'le·on·tol'o·gist** n.

pal·ette (-it) n. thin board on which artists mix paint

pal'frey (pôl'-) n. [pl. -FREYS] [Ar.] saddle horse

pal'in·drome (pal'-) n. word, phrase, or sentence that reads the same backward as forward

pal'ing (pāl'-) n. fence made of pales

pal·i·sade' (pal ə sād') n. 1. fence of large pointed stakes for fortification 2. pl. steep cliffs

pall (pôl) v. [PALLED, PALLING] become boring —n. dark covering as for a coffin

pall'bear'er n. bearer of a coffin at a funeral

pal'let n. 1. straw bed 2. movable platform used in a warehouse

pal'li·ate v. 1. relieve; ease 2. make seem less serious —**pal'li·a'tion** n. —**pal'li·a'tive** a., n.

pal'lid a. pale —**pal'lor** n.

palm (päm) n. 1. tall tropical tree topped with a bunch of huge leaves 2. its leaf: symbol of victory 3. inside of the hand —**palm off** get rid of, sell, etc. by fraud

pal·met'to n. [pl. -TOS, -TOES] small palm tree

palm'is·try n. fortunetelling from the lines, etc. on a person's palm —**palm'ist** n.

palm'y a. [-IER, -IEST] prosperous

pal'o·mi'no (-mē'-) n. [pl. -NOS] pale-yellow horse with white mane and tail

pal'pa·ble a. 1. that can be touched, felt, etc. 2. obvious —**pal'pa·bly** adv.

pal'pi·tate v. to throb —**pal'pi·ta'tion** n.

pal·sy (pôl'zē) n. paralysis in part of the body, often with tremors —**pal'sied** a.

pal·try (pôl'trē) a. [-TRIER, -TRIEST] trifling; petty —**pal'tri·ness** n.

pam'pas n.pl. treeless plains of Argentina

pam'per v. be overindulgent with

pam'phlet n. thin, unbound booklet

pan n. broad, shallow container used in cooking, etc. —v. [PANNED, PANNING] 1. wash (gravel) in a pan to separate (gold, etc.) 2. move TV or movie camera to view a panorama 3. [Col.] criticize adversely —**pan out** [Col.] turn out (well)

pan- pref. all; of all

pan'a·ce'a (-sē'-) n. supposed remedy for all diseases

pa·nache' (pə nash') n. dashing, elegant manner or style

pan'cake n. thin cake of batter fried in a pan

pan'chro·mat'ic (-krō'-) a. describing film sensitive to all colors

pan'cre·as n. gland that secretes a digestive juice —**pan'cre·at'ic** a.

pan'da n. white-and-black, bearlike animal of Asia

pan·dem'ic n., a. (disease) that is epidemic over a large region

pan'de·mo'ni·um n. wild disorder or noise

pan'der v. 1. act as a pimp 2. help others satisfy their desires —n. pimp

pane n. sheet of glass

pan'e·gyr'ic (-jir'-) n. speech or writing of praise

pan'el n. 1. flat section set off on a wall, door, etc. 2. board for instruments or controls 3. list of persons called for jury duty 4. group chosen for judging, discussing, etc. —v. provide with panels —**pan'el·ing** n. —**pan'el·ist** n.

pang n. sudden, sharp pain

pan'han'dle n. [also P-] strip

of land shaped like handle of a pan —v. [Sl.] beg on the streets

pan'ic n. sudden, wild fear —v. [-ICKED, -ICKING] fill with panic —**pan'ick·y** a.

pan'ic-strick'en a. badly frightened

pan·nier, pan·ier (pan'yər) n. basket for carrying loads on the back

pan'o·ply n. [pl. -PLIES] 1. suit of armor 2. splendid display — **pan'o·plied** a.

pan'o·ra·ma (-ra'-) n. 1. unlimited view 2. constantly changing scene

pan'sy n. [pl. SIES] small plant with velvety petals

pant v. 1. breathe in pants 2. long (for) 3. gasp out —n. 1. rapid, heavy breath

pan·ta·loons' n.pl. trousers

pan'the·ism n. doctrine that all forces of the universe are God —**pan'the·ist** n.

pan'the·on n. temple for all the gods

pan'ther n. 1. cougar 2. jaguar 3. leopard

pan'ties n.pl. women's or children's short underpants

pan'to·mime v., n. (make) use of gestures without words to present a play

pan'try n. [pl. -TRIES] a room for food, pots, etc.

pants n.pl. 1. trousers 2. drawers or panties

pant'suit' n. matched jacket and pants for women

pan'ty hose combined panties and hose

pap n. soft food

pa'pa n. father; child's word

pa'pa·cy (pā'-) n. position, authority, etc. of the Pope

pa'pal a. of the Pope or the papacy

pa·paw (pô'pô) n. tree with yellow fruit

pa·pa·ya (-pä'-) n. tropical palmlike tree with large, orange fruit

pa'per n. 1. thin material in sheets, used to write or print on, wrap, etc. 2. sheet of this 3. essay 4. newspaper 5. wallpaper 6. document 7. pl. credentials —a. of or like paper —v. cover with wallpaper —**pa'per·y** a.

pa'per·back' n. book bound in paper

pa'per·boy' n. boy who sells or delivers newspapers

pa'per·weight' n. object set on papers to hold them down

pa·pier-mâ·ché (pā'pər mə shā') n. wet paper pulp, molded into various objects

pa·pil'la n. [pl. -LAE (-ē)] small projection of tissue, as on the tongue

pa·poose' n. N. American Indian baby

pap·ri'ka (-rē'-) n. ground, mild, red seasoning

Pap test test for uterine cancer

pa·py'rus n. 1. paper made by ancient Egyptians from a water plant 2. this plant

par (pär) n. 1. equal rank 2. average 3. face value of stocks, etc. 4. expert score in golf

para- pref. 1. beside; beyond 2. helping; secondary

par·a·ble (par′-) *n.* short, simple story with a moral

pa·rab·o·la *n.* curve formed when a cone is sliced parallel to its side —**pa·ra·bol·ic** *a.*

par·a·chute (-shōōt) *n.* umbrellalike device used to slow down one dropping from an aircraft —*v.* drop by parachute —**par′a·chut·ist** *n.*

pa·rade′ *n.* 1. showy display 2. march or procession —*v.* 1. march in a parade 2. show off

par′a·digm (-dim) *n.* example

par′a·dise *n.* 1. place or state of great happiness 2. heaven

par′a·dox *n.* contradictory statement that is or seems false —**par′a·dox′i·cal** *a.*

par·af·fin *n.* white, waxy substance used for making candles, sealing jars, etc.

par′a·gon *n.* model of perfection or excellence

par′a·graph *n.* distinct section of a piece of writing, begun on a new line —*v.* arrange in paragraphs

par′a·keet *n.* small parrot

par′al·lax *n.* apparent change in object's position resulting from change in viewer's position

par′al·lel *a.* 1. in the same direction and at a fixed distance apart 2. similar —*n.* 1. parallel line, surface, etc. 2. one like another 3. circle parallel to the equator —*v.* be parallel with

par′al·lel′o·gram *n.* four-sided figure with opposite sides parallel and equal

pa·ral′y·sis *n.* 1. loss of power to move any part of the body

2. a crippling —**par′a·lyt′ic** (-lit′-) *a.*, *n.*

par′a·lyze (-līz) *v.* 1. cause paralysis in 2. make ineffective

par′a·me′ci·um (-shē əm) *n.* [*pl.* -CIA (-shē ə)] a freshwater protozoan

par′a·med′i·cal *a.* of medical auxiliaries, as nurses' aides, midwives, etc.

par′a·mil′i·tar′y *a.* of a private, often secret, military group

par′a·mount *a.* supreme

par′a·mour (-moor) *n.* illicit lover or mistress

par′a·noi′a *n.* mental illness of feeling persecuted —**par′a·noid** *a.*, *n.*

par′a·pet *n.* 1. wall for protection from enemy fire 2. low wall or railing along a balcony

par′a·pher·na′li·a *n.pl.* [*often with sing. v.*] belongings or equipment

par′a·phrase *n.* a rewording —*v.* reword

par′a·ple′gi·a (-plē′jē ə) *n.* paralysis of the lower body —**par′a·ple′gic** *a.*, *n.*

par′a·pro·fes′sion·al *n.* a worker trained to assist a professional

par′a·site *n.* plant or animal that lives on or in another —**par′a·sit′ic** *a.*

par′a·sol (-sôl) *n.* light umbrella used as a sunshade

par′a·thi′on (-thī′ən) *n.* a poisonous insecticide

par′a·thy′roid (-thī′-) *a.* of certain small glands near the thyroid

par′a·troops *n.pl.* unit of soldiers trained to parachute from airplanes behind enemy lines —**par'a·troop'er** n.

par'boil v. boil until partly cooked

par'cel (-s'l) n. 1. package 2. piece (of land) —v. apportion (with *out*)

parcel post postal branch which delivers parcels

parch v. 1. make hot and dry 2. make thirsty

parch'ment n. 1. skin of a sheep, etc. prepared as a surface for writing 2. paper like this 3. a document on parchment

par'don v. 1. to release from punishment 2. excuse; forgive —n. 1. act of pardoning 2. document granting pardon —**par'don·a·ble** a.

pare (per) v. 1. peel 2. reduce gradually

par'e·gor'ic n. medicine with opium, for diarrhea, etc.

par'ent n. 1. father or mother 2. source —**pa·ren'tal** a. —**par'ent·hood** n.

par'ent·age n. descent from parents or ancestors

pa·ren'the·sis n. [pl. -SES (-sēz')] 1. word of explanation put into a sentence 2. either of the marks () used to set this off —**par'en·thet'i·cal, par'en·thet'ic** a.

pa·re'sis n. brain disease caused by syphilis

par·fait (pär fā') n. ice-cream dessert in a tall glass

pa·ri'ah (-rī'-) n. outcast

par'ing n. strip peeled off

par'ish n. 1. part of a diocese under a priest, etc. 2. church congregation

pa·rish'ion·er n. member of a parish

par'i·ty n. equality of value at a given ratio between moneys, commodities, etc.

park n. public land for recreation or rest —v. leave (a vehicle) temporarily

par'ka n. hooded coat

Par'kin·son's disease disease causing tremors

park'way n. broad road lined with trees, bushes, etc.

parl'ance n. mode of speech

par'lay v. bet winnings on another race, etc.

par'ley (-lē) v., n. talk to settle differences, etc.

par'lia·ment (-lə-) n. legislative body, spec. [P-] of Great Britain, Canada, etc. —**par'lia·men'ta·ry** a.

par'lor n. 1. living room 2. business establishment, as a beauty *parlor* Br. sp. **par'lour**

Par'me·san cheese (-mə zän') a dry Italian cheese

pa·ro'chi·al (-kē əl) a. 1. of a parish 2. limited; narrow

par'o·dy n. [pl. -DIES] a farcical imitation of a work —v. [-DIED, -DYING] write a parody of

pa·role' n. release from prison on condition of future good behavior

par'ox·ysm (-ək siz'm) n. sudden attack or outburst

par·quet' (-kā') n. flooring of parquetry

par'quet·ry (-kə trē) n. inlaid flooring of geometric forms

par·ri·cide (par'ə sīd) *n.* **1.** act of murdering one's parent **2.** one who does this

par·rot *n.* brightly colored bird that can imitate speech —*v.* repeat or copy without full understanding

par·ry *v.* [-RIED, -RYING] **1.** ward off **2.** evade

parse *v.* analyze (a sentence) grammatically

par·si·mo·ny *n.* stinginess — **par·si·mo'ni·ous** *a.*

pars·ley *n.* plant with leaves used to flavor some foods

pars·nip *n.* sweet white root used as a vegetable

par·son *n.* minister or clergyman

par·son·age (-ij) *n.* dwelling that a church provides for its parson

part *n.* **1.** portion, piece, element, etc. **2.** duty **3.** role **4.** music for a certain voice or instrument in a composition **5.** *usually pl.* region **6.** dividing line formed in combing the hair **7.** one of the sides in a conflict —*v.* **1.** divide; separate **2.** go away from each other —*a.* less than a whole —**for the most part** mostly —**part** with give up —**take part** participate

par·take' *v.* [-TOOK, -TAKEN, -TAKING] have or take a share (of)

par·tial (-shəl) *a.* **1.** favoring one over another **2.** not complete —**partial to** fond of — **par'ti·al'i·ty** *n.* —**par'tial·ly** *adv.*

par·tic·i·pate (-tis'-) *v.* have

or take a share with others (*in*) —**par·tic'i·pant** *n.* —**par·tic'i·pa'tion** *n.*

par·ti·ci·ple *n.* verb form having the qualities of both a verb and adjective —**par'ti·cip'i·al** (-sip'ē əl) *a.*

par·ti·cle *n.* **1.** tiny fragment **2.** preposition, article, or conjunction

par·ti·col·ored *a.* having different colors in different parts

par·tic·u·lar *a.* **1.** of one; individual **2.** specific **3.** hard to please **4.** unusual —*n.* detail — **par·tic'u·lar'i·ty** *n.* —**par·tic'u·lar·ly** *adv.*

par·tic·u·late (-lit) *a.* of or formed of tiny, separate particles

part'ing *a., n.* **1.** dividing **2.** departing

par·ti·san (-z'n) *n.* **1.** strong supporter; adherent **2.** guerrilla —*a.* of a partisan Also **partizan** —**par'ti·san·ship'** *n.*

par·ti·tion (-tish'ən) *n.* **1.** division into parts **2.** thing that divides —*v.* divide into parts

part'ly *adv.* not fully

part'ner *n.* one who undertakes something with another; associate; mate —**part'ner·ship** *n.*

part of speech class of word, as noun, verb, etc.

par'tridge *n.* game bird, as the pheasant, quail, etc.

part song song for several voices, usually unaccompanied

part'-time' *a.* of a period of

work, study, etc. for less than a full schedule

par'tu·ri'tion n. childbirth

par'ty n. [pl. **-TIES**] 1. group working together for a political cause, etc. 2. social gathering 3. one involved in a lawsuit, crime, etc. 4. [Col.] person

party line 1. single circuit for two or more telephone users 2. a political party's policies

pas'chal (-k'l) a. of the Passover or Easter

pass v. 1. go by, beyond, etc. 2. go or change from one form, place, etc. to another 3. cease; end 4. die 5. approve or be approved 6. take a course, etc. successfully 7. cause or allow to go, move, qualify, etc. 8. spend time 9. happen 10. give as an opinion, judgment, etc. —n. 1. a passing 2. free ticket 3. brief military leave 4. narrow passage between mountains 5. motion of hands 6. [Sl.] bold attempt to kiss or embrace —**pass for** be accepted as —**pass out** 1. distribute 2. faint —**pass'a·ble** a. —**pass'a·bly** adv.

pas'sage n. 1. a passing 2. right to pass 3. voyage 4. road, opening, etc. 5. part of something written

pas'sage·way n. narrow way, as a hall, alley, etc.

pass'book n. bankbook

pas·sé (pa sā') a. out-of-date

pas'sen·ger n. one traveling in a train, car, etc.

pass'er·by' n. [pl. PASSERS-BY] one who passes by

pass'ing a. 1. that passes 2. fleeting 3. casual 4. meeting requirements —n. death —**in passing** incidentally

pas'sion n. 1. strong emotion, as hate, love, etc. 2. object of strong desire —**pas'sion·ate** a.

pas'sive a. 1. inactive, but acted upon 2. yielding; submissive —**pas·siv'i·ty** n.

passive resistance opposition to a law by refusal to comply or by nonviolent acts

pass'key n. key that fits a number of locks

Pass'o'ver n. Jewish holiday in the spring

pass'port n. government document identifying a citizen traveling abroad

pass'word n. secret word given to pass by a guard

past a. 1. gone by 2. of a former time —n. 1. history 2. time gone by —prep. beyond in time, space, etc. —adv. to and beyond

pas·ta (päs'ta) n. spaghetti, noodles, and other food made of flour paste

paste n. 1. moist, smooth mixture 2. adhesive mixture with flour, water, etc. —v. make adhere, as with paste —**past'y** a.

paste'board n. stiff material of pasted layers of paper

pas·tel' a. soft and pale —n. 1. crayon of ground pigment 2. soft, pale shade of color

pas'teur·ize (-char-, -tar-) v. kill bacteria in (milk, etc.) by heating —**pas'teur·i·za'tion** n.

pas·tiche' (-tēsh') n. artistic

composition made up of bits from several sources

pas'time n. way to spend spare time

pas'tor n. clergyman in charge of a congregation

pas'to·ral a. 1. of a pastor 2. simple and rustic

past participle participle used to indicate a past time

pas·tra·mi (pa strä'mē) n. spiced, smoked beef

pas·try (pās'trē) n. [pl. -TRIES] fancy baked goods

pas'ture (-chər) n. ground with grass for grazing: also **pas'tur·age** (-ij) —v. let (cattle) graze

pat n. 1. gentle tap with something flat 2. small lump, as of butter —v. [PATTED, PATTING] 1. give a gentle pat to 2. shape by patting —a. 1. suitable 2. glib —**stand pat** refuse to change

patch n. 1. piece of material used to mend a hole, etc. 2. bandage 3. spot 4. plot of land —v. 1. put a patch on 2. make crudely —**patch up** settle (a quarrel)

patch'work n. quilt made of odd patches of cloth

pate n. top of the head

pa·tel'la n. [pl. -LAS, -LAE (-lē)] kneecap

pat'ent n. document granting exclusive rights over an invention —a. 1. protected by patent 2. (pāt''nt) obvious —v. get a patent for

patent leather leather with a hard, glossy finish

pa·ter'nal a. 1. fatherly 2. on the father's side —**pa·ter'nal·**

ism n. —**pa·ter'nal·is'tic** a.

pa·ter'ni·ty n. fatherhood

path n. 1. way worn by footsteps 2. line of movement 3. course of conduct

pa·thet'ic a. arousing pity — **pa·thet'i·cal·ly** adv.

path'o·gen'ic a. producing disease

pa·thol'o·gy n. 1. study of the nature and effect of disease 2. abnormal variation from sound condition —**path'o·log'i·cal** (-läj'-) a. —**pa·thol'o·gist** n.

pa'thos n. the quality in a thing which arouses pity

path'way n. path

pa'tient a. 1. enduring pain, delay, etc. without complaint 2. tolerant 3. persevering —n. one receiving medical care — **pa'tience** n. —**pa'tient·ly** adv.

pat'i·na n. green oxidized coating on bronze or copper

pat'i·o n. [pl. -os] 1. courtyard 2. paved terrace near a house

pat·ois (-wä) n. [pl. -OIS (-wäz)] dialect of a region

pa'tri·arch (-ärk) n. 1. father and head of a family or tribe 2. dignified old man 3. bishop of Orthodox Eastern Church — **pa·tri·ar'chal** a.

pa·tri'cian (-shən) a., n. aristocratic (person)

pat'ri·mo'ny n. inheritance from one's father

pa'tri·ot n. one who shows love and loyalty for his or her country —**pa'tri·ot'ic** a. —**pa'tri·ot'i·cal·ly** adv. —**pa'tri·ot·ism** n.

pa·trol' v. [-TROLLED, -TROL-**

LING] make trips around in guarding —*n.* a patrolling, or a group that patrols

pa·trol'man *n.* [*pl.* -MEN] policeman who patrols a certain area

pa'tron *n.* 1. a sponsor 2. regular customer —**pa'tron·ess** *n.fem.*

pa'tron·age (-ij) *n.* 1. help given by a patron 2. customers, or their trade 3. political favors

pa'tron·ize' *v.* 1. sponsor 2. be condescending to 3. be a regular customer of

pat'ro·nym'ic (-nim'-) *n.* name showing descent from a given person

pat'sy *n.* [*pl.* -SIES] [Sl.] person easily imposed on

pat'ter *n.* 1. series of rapid taps 2. glib talk —*v.* make or utter (a) patter

pat'tern *n.* 1. one worthy of imitation 2. plan used in making things 3. design or decoration 4. usual behavior, procedure, etc. —*v.* copy as from a pattern

pat'ty *n.* [*pl.* -TIES] flat cake of ground meat, etc.

pau'ci·ty (pô'-) *n.* 1. fewness 2. scarcity

paunch *n.* protruding belly

paunch'y [-IER, -IEST] *a.*

pau'per *n.* very poor person —**pau'per·ism** *n.*

pause *v., n.* (make a) temporary stop

pave *v.* surface (a road, etc.) as with asphalt

pave'ment *n.* paved road

pa·vil'ion (-yən) *n.* 1. large tent 2. building for exhibits, etc., as at a fair

paw *n.* foot of an animal with claws —*v.* 1. touch, etc. with paws or feet 2. handle roughly

pawl *n.* catch for teeth of a ratchet wheel

pawn *v.* give as security for a loan —*n.* 1. chessman of lowest value 2. person subject to another's will

pawn'bro'ker *n.* one whose business is lending money on things pawned with him

pawn'shop *n.* pawnbroker's shop

pay *v.* [PAID, PAYING] 1. give (money) to (one) for goods or services 2. settle, as a debt 3. give, as a compliment 4. make, as a visit 5. be profitable (to) —*n.* wages —*a.* 1. operated by coins 2. paid for by fees —**pay back** 1. repay 2. retaliate —**pay for** suffer or atone for —**pay off** pay all that is owed —**pay out** [pt. & pp. PAYED OUT] let out, as a rope —**pay·ee'** *n.* —**pay'er** *n.* —**pay'ment** *n.*

pay'a·ble *a.* 1. that can be paid 2. due to be paid

pay'load *n.* 1. cargo 2. warhead of a missile 3. working parts of an artificial satellite

pay'mas'ter *n.* official in charge of paying employees

pay'off *n.* 1. reckoning or payment 2. [Col.] bribe 3. [Col.] climax

pay'roll *n.* 1. list of employees with amount due to each 2. total amount for this

pea *n.* plant with pods having round, edible seeds

peace *n.* **1.** freedom from war or strife **2.** agreement to end war **3.** law and order **4.** calm —**keep one's peace** be silent —**peace'a·ble** *a.*

peace'ful *a.* **1.** not fighting **2.** calm **3.** of a time of peace — **peace'ful·ly** *adv.*

peace'mak'er *n.* one who settles quarrels, etc.

peach *n.* **1.** round, juicy, orange-yellow fruit **2.** tree it grows on

pea'cock *n.* male of a large bird (**pea'fowl**), with a long, showy tail

pea jacket heavy coat worn by seamen

peak *n.* **1.** pointed end or top **2.** mountain with pointed summit **3.** highest point —*v.* come or bring to a peak

peak'ed *a.* thin and drawn

peal *n.* **1.** loud ringing of bell(s) **2.** loud, prolonged sound —*v.* ring; resound

pea'nut *n.* **1.** vine with underground pods and edible seeds **2.** the pod or a seed **3.** *pl.* [Sl.] trifling amount

peanut butter food paste made by grinding peanuts

pear *n.* **1.** soft, juicy, yellow or brown fruit **2.** tree it grows on

pearl (purl) *n.* **1.** smooth, roundish stone formed in oysters, used as a gem **2.** mother-of-pearl **3.** bluish gray — **pearl'y** [-IER, -IEST] *a.*

peas·ant (pez'-) *n.* farm worker of Europe, Asia, etc. — **peas'ant·ry** *n.*

peat (pēt) *n.* decayed plant matter in bogs, dried for fuel

peat moss peat made up of moss residues, used for mulch

peb'ble *n.* small, smooth stone —**peb'bly** [-BLIER, -BLIEST] *a.*

pe·can' (-kan', -kän') *n.* edible nut with a thin, smooth shell

pec'ca·dil'lo *n.* [*pl.* -LOES, -LOS] minor or petty sin

pec'ca·ry *n.* [*pl.* -RIES] wild piglike animal with tusks

peck *v.* strike as with a beak — *n.* **1.** stroke made as with a beak **2.** [Col.] quick kiss **3.** dry measure equal to 8 quarts — **peck at 1.** eat little of **2.** criticize constantly

pec'tin *n.* substance in some fruits causing jelly to form

pec'to·ral *a.* of the chest

pec'u·late *v.* embezzle

pe·cu'liar (-kyōōl'yər) *a.* **1.** of only one; exclusive **2.** special **3.** odd —**pe·cu'li·ar'i·ty** [*pl.* -TIES] *n.*

pe·cu'ni·ar'y (-kyōō'-) *a.* of money

ped'a·gogue, ped'a·gog *n.* teacher

ped'a·go'gy (-gō'jē) *n.* the art of teaching —**ped'a·gog'ic** (-gäj'-), **ped'a·gog'i·cal** *a.*

ped'al *n.* lever worked by the foot —*v.* work by pedals —*a.* of the foot

ped'ant *n.* one who stresses trivial points of learning —**pe·dan'tic** *a.* —**ped'ant·ry** *n.*

ped'dle *v.* go from place to place selling —**ped'dler** *n.*

ped'es·tal *n.* base, as of a column, statue, etc.

pe·des'tri·an *a.* **1.** going on

foot 2. dull and ordinary —*n.* one who goes on foot; walker

pe·di·at·rics (pē′-) *n.* medical care and treatment of babies and children —**pe′di·a·tri′cian** (-trish′ən) *n.*

ped′i·cab *n.* a three-wheeled carriage pedaled by the driver

ped′i·cure *n.* care of the toenails

ped′i·gree *n.* ancestry; descent —**ped′i·greed** *a.*

ped′i·ment *n.* ornamental triangular piece over a doorway

pe·dom′e·ter (-däm′-) *n.* device to indicate the distance walked

peek *v.* glance quickly and furtively —*n.* glance

peel *v.* 1. cut away (the rind, etc.) of 2. shed skin —*n.* rind or skin of fruit

peel′ing *n.* rind peeled off

peen *n.* end of hammer head opposite the striking surface

peep *v.* 1. make the chirping cry of a young bird 2. look through a small opening 3. peek 4. appear partially —*n.* 1. peeping sound 2. furtive glimpse —**peep′hole** *n.*

peer *n.* 1. an equal 2. British noble —*v.* look closely —**peer′age** (-ij) *n.*

peer′less *a.* without equal

peeve *v.* [Col.] make peevish —*n.* [Col.] annoyance

pee′vish *a.* irritable

pee′wee *n.* [Col.] something small

peg *n.* 1. short pin or bolt 2. step or degree 3. [Col.] a throw —*v.* [PEGGED, PEGGING]

1. fix or mark as with pegs 2. [Col.] throw —**peg away** work steadily

peign·oir (pān′wär′) *n.* a woman's loose dressing gown

pe′jo·ra′tion (pē′jə-) *n.* a worsening —**pe·jo′ra·tive** (pi jôr′-) *a.*

Pe·king·ese′ (-kə nēz′) *n.* [*pl.* -ESE] small dog with pug nose: also **Pe·kin·ese′**

pe′koe (-kō) *n.* a black tea

pelf *n.* mere wealth

pel′i·can *n.* water bird with a pouch in its lower bill

pel·la·gra (-lag′rə) *n.* disease caused by vitamin deficiency

pel′let *n.* 1. little ball 2. a bullet, small lead shot, etc.

pell′-mell′, pell′mell′ *adv.*, *a.* 1. in a jumble 2. in reckless haste

pel·lu′cid (-lōo′sid) *a.* clear

pelt *v.* 1. throw things at 2. beat steadily —*n.* skin of a fur-bearing animal

pel′vis *n.* cavity formed by bones of the hip and part of the backbone —**pel′vic** *a.*

pem′mi·can *n.* dried food concentrate of beef, dried fruit, etc.

pen *n.* 1. enclosure for animals 2. device for writing with ink 3. [Sl.] penitentiary —*v.* [PENNED (*for* 1 *also* PENT), PENNING] 1. enclose as in a pen 2. write with a pen

pe′nal *a.* of or as punishment

pe′nal·ize *v.* punish —**pe′nal·i·za′tion** *n.*

pen′al·ty *n.* [*pl.* -TIES] 1. punishment 2. handicap

pen′ance *n.* voluntary suffering to show repentance

pence *n.* [Br.] pl. of **penny**

pen′chant *n.* strong liking

pen′cil *n.* device with a core of graphite, etc. for writing, etc. —*v.* write with a pencil

pend *v.* await decision

pend′ant *n.* hanging object used as an ornament

pend′ent *a.* suspended

pend′ing *a.* not decided — *prep.* 1. during 2. until

pen′du·lous (-joo ləs) *a.* hanging freely

pen′du·lum *n.* weight hung so as to swing freely

pen′e·trate *v.* 1. enter by piercing 2. affect throughout 3. understand —**pen′e·tra·ble** *a.* —**pen′e·tra′tion** *n.*

pen′guin (-gwin) *n.* flightless bird of the antarctic

pen′i·cil′lin (-sil′-) *n.* antibiotic drug got from a mold

pen·in′su·la *n.* land area almost surrounded by water — **pen·in′su·lar** *a.*

pe′nis *n.* male sex organ

pen′i·tent *a.* willing to atone —*n.* penitent person —**pen′i·tence** *n.*

pen′i·ten′tia·ry (-shə-) *n.* [pl. -RIES] prison

pen′knife *n.* [pl. -KNIVES] small pocketknife

pen′man·ship *n.* handwriting

pen name pseudonym

pen′nant *n.* 1. long, narrow flag 2. championship

pen′non *n.* flag or pennant

pen′ni·less *a.* very poor

pen′ny *n.* 1. [pl. -NIES] cent 2. [pl. PENCE] Br. coin, formerly 1/12 shilling, now 1/100 pound

penny arcade public amusement hall with coin-operated games

pe·nol′o·gy (pē näl′-) *n.* study of prisons

pen′sion *n.* regular payment to a retired or disabled person —*v.* pay a pension —**pen′sion·er** *n.*

pen′sive (-siv) *a.* thoughtful; reflective

pent *a.* shut in; kept in

pen′ta·gon *n.* 1. figure with five angles and five sides 2. [P-] office building of Defense Department —**pen·tag′o·nal** *a.*

pen·tam′e·ter *n.* line of verse of five metrical feet

pen·tath′lon (-län) *n.* athletic contest with five different events

pent′house *n.* apartment on the roof of a building

pent′-up′ *a.* held back; curbed

pe·nu·che, pe·nu·chi (pə nōō′chē) *n.* fudgelike candy

pe·nul′ti·mate (-mit) *a.,* *n.* next to the last (one)

pe·nu′ri·ous *a.* stingy

pen′u·ry (-yə-) *n.* extreme poverty

pe′on (-än) *n.* Latin American worker —**pe′on·age** (-ij) *n.*

pe′o·ny *n.* [pl. -NIES] plant with large showy flowers

peo′ple *n.* [pl. -PLE] 1. human beings 2. populace 3. one's family 4. [pl. -PLES] a nation, race, etc. —*v.* populate

pep *n.* [Col.] energy —*v.* [PEPPED, PEPPING] [Col.] fill

with pep (with *up*) —**pep′py**
[-PIER, -PIEST] *a.*

pep′per *n.* 1. plant with a red
or green, hot or sweet pod 2.
the pod 3. spicy seasoning
made from berries (**pep-
percorns**) of a tropical plant
—*v.* 1. season with pepper (*n.*
3) 2. pelt with small objects

pepper mill hand mill used to
grind peppercorns

pep′per·mint *n.* mint plant
yielding an oily flavoring

pep′per·o′ni (-nē) *n.* highly
spiced Italian sausage

pep′per·y *a.* 1. fiery 2. hot-
tempered

pep′sin *n.* stomach enzyme
that helps digest proteins

pep′tic *a.* of digestion

per *prep.* 1. by means of 2. for
each

per·am′bu·late *v.* to walk
through or over

per·am′bu·la′tor *n.* [Br.] a
baby carriage

per annum by the year

per·cale′ (-kāl′) *n.* cotton cloth
used for sheets

per cap′i·ta for each person

per·ceive′ (-sēv′) *v.* 1. grasp
mentally 2. become aware (of)
through the senses —**per-
ceiv′a·ble** *a.*

per·cent′ *adv., a.* in or for
every hundred; symbol, %: also
per cent —*n.* [Col.] percentage

per·cent′age *n.* 1. rate per
hundred 2. portion 3. [Col.]
advantage

per·cen′tile (-tīl, -t′l) *n.* any of
100 equal divisions

per·cep′ti·ble *a.* that can be

perceived   —**per·cep′ti·bly**
adv.

per·cep′tion *n.* 1. ability to
perceive 2. knowledge got by
perceiving

per·cep′tive *a.* able to perceive readily

perch *n.* 1. small food fish 2. a
pole or branch that birds roost
on —*v.* rest on a perch

per·chance′ *adv.* [Ar.] 1. by
chance 2. perhaps

per′co·late *v.* 1. filter 2. make
in a percolator

per′co·la′tor *n.* pot in which
boiling water filters through
ground coffee

per·cus′sion (-kush′ən) *n.* hitting of one thing against
another

percussion instruments cym-
bals, drums, xylophones, etc. —
per·cus′sion·ist *n.*

per di·em (dē′əm, dī′-) daily

per·di′tion (-dish′ən) *n.* 1. hell
2. loss of one's soul

per′e·gri·na′tion (per′-) *n.* a
walking about

per·emp′to·ry *a.* 1. overbearing 2. not to be refused

per·en′ni·al *a.* 1. lasting a
year 2. living more than two
years 3. continuing for a long
time —*n.* plant living more
than two years —**per·en′ni-
al·ly** *adv.*

per′fect *a.* 1. complete 2. excellent 3. completely accurate
—*v.* (pər fekt′) make perfect —
per·fect′i·ble *a.* —**per·fec′-
tion** *n.* —**per′fect·ly** *adv.*

per·fec′tion·ist *n.* one who
strives for perfection

per′fi·dy *n.* [*pl.* -DIES]

treachery —per·fid'i·ous a.

per'fo·rate v. pierce with a hole or holes —per'fo·ra'tion n.

per·force' adv. necessarily

per·form' v. 1. do; carry out 2. act a role, play music, etc.

per·form'ance n. 1. act of performing 2. deed or feat 3. presentation, as of a play, music, etc.

performing arts arts, as drama and dance, performed before an audience

per·fume' (-fyoom') v. scent with perfume —n. (pur'fyoom) 1. fragrance 2. liquid with a pleasing odor

per·func'to·ry a. done without care or interest

per·go'la n. arbor with latticework roof

per·haps' adv. possibly; probably

per'i·gee (-jē) n. point nearest heavenly body in a satellite's orbit

per'il v., n. (put in) danger or risk —per'il·ous a.

pe·rim'e·ter n. 1. outer boundary of a figure or area 2. total length of this

pe'ri·od n. 1. portion of time 2. interval between related events 3. division of game, school day, etc. 4. the menses 5. mark of punctuation (.)

pe'ri·od'ic a. 1. recurring at regular intervals 2. intermittent

pe'ri·od'i·cal n. magazine published every week, month, etc. —a. periodic —pe·ri·od'i·cal·ly adv.

per·i·o·don'tal (per'ē ə dän'-t'l) a. around a tooth and affecting the gums

per'i·pa·tet'ic a. walking or moving about; itinerant

pe·riph'er·y n. [pl. -IES] outer boundary or part —pe·riph'er·al a.

per'i·scope n. tube with mirrors, etc., for seeing over or around an obstacle

per'ish v. be destroyed; die

per'ish·a·ble n., a. (food) liable to spoil

per'i·stal'sis (-stôl'-) n. action of intestines that moves food onward

per'i·to·ni'tis n. inflammation of the membrane (per'i·to·ne'um) lining the abdominal cavity

per'i·win'kle n. 1. myrtle (sense 2) 2. small snail with cone-shaped shell

per'jure v. tell a lie while under oath —per'jur·er n.

per'ju·ry n. [pl. -RIES] telling of a lie while under oath

perk v. 1. raise or liven (up) 2. make stylish or smart 3. [Col.] percolate (coffee) —perk'y [-IER, -IEST] a.

per'ma·frost n. permanently frozen subsoil

per'ma·nent a. lasting indefinitely —per'ma·nence n. —per'ma·nent·ly adv.

per'me·a·ble a. that can be permeated, as by fluids —per'me·a·bil'i·ty n.

per'me·ate v. diffuse; penetrate (through or among)

per·mis'si·ble a. allowable

per·mis'sion n. consent

per·mis'sive *a.* not restricting

per·mit' *v.* [-MITTED, -MITTING] allow —*n.* (pur'mit) document giving permission

per·mu·ta'tion *n.* 1. radical change 2. any of the combinations possible within a group

per·ni'cious (-nish'əs) *a.* very harmful or damaging

per'o·ra'tion *n.* last part or summation of a speech

per·ox'ide *n.* hydrogen peroxide

per·pen·dic'u·lar *a.* 1. at right angles to a given line or plane 2. vertical —*n.* perpendicular line

per'pe·trate *v.* do (something evil, wrong, etc.) —**per'pe·tra'tion** *n.* —**per'pe·tra'tor** *n.*

per·pet'u·al *a.* 1. lasting forever 2. constant —**per·pet'u·al·ly** *adv.*

per·pet'u·ate *v.* cause to continue or be remembered —**per·pet'u·a'tion** *n.*

per'pe·tu'i·ty *n.* existence forever

per·plex' *v.* confuse or puzzle —**per·plex'i·ty** *n.*

per'qui·site (-zit) *n.* something in addition to regular pay for one's work, as a tip

per se (sē, sā) by (or in) itself

per'se·cute *v.* torment continuously for one's beliefs, etc. — **per'se·cu'tion** *n.* —**per'se·cu'tor** *n.*

per·se·vere' (-vir') *v.* continue in spite of difficulty —**per·se·ver'ance** *n.*

Persian cat cat with long hair

Persian lamb karakul

per'si·flage (-fläzh) *n.* playful or joking talk

per·sim'mon *n.* orange-red, plumlike fruit

per·sist' *v.* continue insistently or steadily —**per·sist'ent** *a.* —**per·sist'ence** *n.*

per·snick'i·ty *a.* [Col.] fussy

per'son *n.* 1. human being 2. the body or self 3. *Gram.* any of the three classes of pronouns indicating the identity of the subject, as *I, you, he,* etc. —**in person** actually present

-person *suf.* individual (without regard to sex)

per'son·a·ble *a.* pleasing in looks and manner

per'son·age (-ij) *n.* (important) person

per'son·al *a.* 1. private; individual 2. of the body 3. of the character, conduct, etc. of a person 4. done in person 5. indicating person in grammar 6. other than real estate: said of property

personal effects personal belongings worn or carried

per'son·al'i·ty *n.* [*pl.* -TIES] 1. distinctive or attractive character of a person 2. notable person 3. *pl.* offensive remarks about a person

per'son·al·ize' *v.* have marked with one's name, etc.

per'son·al·ly *adv.* 1. in person 2. as a person 3. in one's opinion 4. directed at oneself

per·son'i·fy *v.* [-FIED, -FYING] 1. represent as a person 2. typify —**per·son'i·fi·ca'tion** *n.*

per·son·nel' n. persons employed in any work, etc.

per·spec'tive a. appearance of objects from their relative distance and positions 2. sense of proportion

per·spi·ca'cious a. having keen insight —**per'spi·cac'i·ty** (-kas'-) n.

per·spic'u·ous a. easily understood —**per'spi·cu'i·ty** n.

per·spire' v. to sweat —**per'spi·ra'tion** n.

per·suade' v. cause to do or believe by urging, etc. —**per·sua'sive** a.

per·sua'sion n. 1. a persuading 2. belief

pert a. saucy; impudent

per·tain' v. 1. belong 2. have reference

per·ti·na'cious a. persistent —**per'ti·nac'i·ty** (-nas'-) n.

per'ti·nent a. relevant; to the point —**per'ti·nence** n.

per·turb' v. alarm; upset —**per'tur·ba'tion** n.

pe·ruse' (-rōōz') v. read —**pe·rus'al** n.

per·vade' v. spread or be prevalent throughout —**per·va'sive** a.

per·verse' a. 1. stubbornly contrary 2. erring 3. wicked —**per·ver'si·ty** n.

per·vert' v. 1. lead astray; corrupt 2. to misuse 3. distort 4. debase —n. (pur'vərt) doer of abnormal sexual acts —**per·ver'sion** n.

pes'ky a. [-KIER, -KIEST] [Col.] annoying

pe·so (pā'sō) n. [pl. -sos] monetary unit of Mexico, Cuba, etc.

pes'si·mism n. tendency to expect the worst —**pes'si·mist** n. —**pes'si·mis'tic** a.

pest n. person or thing that causes trouble, etc.

pes'ter v. annoy; vex

pes'ti·cide n. chemical for killing insects, weeds, etc.

pes·tif'er·ous a. 1. noxious 2. [Col.] annoying

pes'ti·lence n. virulent or contagious disease —**pes'ti·lent** a.

pes'tle (-'l) n. tool used to pound or grind substances

pet n. 1. domesticated animal treated fondly 2. favorite 3. bad humor —a. 1. treated as a pet 2. particular 3. showing fondness —v. [PETTED, PETTING] stroke gently

pet'al n. leaflike part of a blossom

pet'cock n. small valve for draining pipes, etc.

pe'ter v. [Col.] fade or become weaker until gone (with *out*)

pe·tite' (-tēt') a. small and trim in figure

pe·tit four (pet'ē) tiny frosted cake

pe·ti'tion n. solemn, earnest request, esp. in writing —v. address a petition to

pet'rel n. small sea bird

pet'ri·fy' v. [-FIED, -FYING] 1. change into stony substance 2. stun, as with fear —**pet'ri·fac'tion** n.

pet'ro·chem'i·cal n. chemical derived from petroleum

pet'rol n. [Br.] gasoline

pet′ro·la′tum n. greasy, jelly-like substance used for ointments: also **petroleum jelly**

pe·tro′le·um n. oily liquid found in rock strata: it yields kerosene, gasoline, etc.

pet′ti·coat n. skirt worn under an outer skirt

pet′ti·fog′ger n. unethical lawyer handling petty cases

pet′ty a. [TIER, -TIEST] 1. of little importance 2. narrow-minded 3. low in rank —**pet′ti·ness** n.

petty cash fund for incidentals

petty officer naval enlisted person of same rank as non-commissioned army officer

pet′u·lant (pech′-) a. impatient or irritable —**pet′u·lance** n.

pe·tu′ni·a n. plant with funnel-shaped flowers

pew (pyōō) n. row of fixed benches in a church

pew′ter n. alloy of tin with lead, brass, or copper

pe·yo·te (pā ō′tē) n. mescal cactus plant

pha′e·ton (fā′-) n. light, four-wheeled carriage

pha′lanx n. massed group of individuals

phal′lus n. [pl. -LI (-lī), -LUSES] image of the penis —**phal′lic** a.

phan′tasm n. figment of the mind

phan·tas′ma·go′ri·a (-taz′-) n. rapidly changing series of things seen, as in a dream

phan′ta·sy n. [pl. -SIES] fantasy

phan′tom n. 1. ghost; specter 2. illusion —a. unreal

Phar·aoh (fer′ō) n. title of ancient Egyptian rulers

phar′i·see (far′-) n. person who is self-righteous —**phar′i·sa′ic** a.

phar′ma·ceu′ti·cal (fär′mə sōō′-) a. 1. of pharmacy 2. of or by drugs —n. a drug or medicine

phar′ma·cist n. one whose profession is pharmacy

phar′ma·col′o·gy n. study of drugs —**phar′ma·col′o·gist** n.

phar′ma·co·pe′ia (-kə pē′ə) n. official book listing drugs and medicines

phar′ma·cy n. [pl. -CIES] 1. science of preparing drugs and medicines 2. drugstore

phar′yn·gi′tis (far′in jī′-) n. inflammation of the pharynx

phar′ynx (far′inks) n. cavity between mouth and larynx —**pha·ryn′ge·al** (fə rin′jē-) a.

phase n. 1. aspect; side 2. one of a series of changes —v. 1. introduce in stages (with in) 2. terminate in stages (with out)

pheas′ant (fez′-) n. game bird with a long tail

phe′no·bar′bi·tal′ n. white compound used as a sedative

phe·nom′e·non n. [pl. -NA] 1. observable fact or event 2. anything very unusual —**phe·nom′e·nal** a.

phi′al (fī′-) n. vial

phi·lan′der v. make love insincerely —**phi·lan′der·er** n.

phi·lan′thro·py n. 1. desire to help mankind 2. [pl. -PIES] thing done to help mankind — **phil'an·throp'ic** (-thräp'-) *a*. —**phi·lan'thro·pist** *n*.

phi·lat'e·ly *n*. collection and study of postage stamps —**phil·lat'e·list** *n*.

phil'har·mon'ic *a*. loving music

phi·lip'pic *n*. bitter verbal attack

Phil'is·tine (-tēn) *n*. one who is smugly conventional

phil'o·den'dron *n*. tropical American climbing plant

phi·los'o·pher *n*. one learned in philosophy

phi·los'o·phize *v*. to reason like a philosopher

phi·los'o·phy *n*. [*pl*. -PHIES] 1. study of ultimate reality, ethics, etc. 2. system of principles 3. calmness —**phil'o·soph'ic, phil'o·soph'i·cal** *a*.

phil'ter, phil'tre (-tar) *n*. magic potion to arouse love

phle·bi'tis *n*. inflammation of a vein

phlegm (flem) *n*. mucus in the throat, as during a cold

phleg·mat'ic *a*. sluggish, unexcitable, etc.

phlox (fläks) *n*. plant with clusters of flowers

pho·bi·a *n*. irrational, persistent fear of something

phoe·be (fē'-) *n*. small bird

phoe'nix *n*. *Egyptian Myth* immortal bird

phone *n*., *v*. [Col.] telephone

pho'neme *n*. set of speech sounds heard as one sound

pho·net'ics *n*. study of speech sounds and the written representation of them —**pho·net'ic** *a*.

phon'ics (fän'-) *n*. phonetic method of teaching reading

pho'no·graph *n*. instrument that reproduces sound from grooved records

pho·nol'o·gy *n*. (study of) speech sounds in a language —**pho'no·log'i·cal** *a*. —**pho·nol'o·gist** *n*.

pho'ny *a*. [-NIER, -NIEST] [Col.] fake —*n*. [*pl*. -NIES] [Col.] fraud; fake Also **phoney**

phos'phate *n*. 1. salt of phosphoric acid 2. fertilizer containing phosphates 3. a flavored carbonated beverage

phos'pho·res'cent *a*. giving off light without heat —**phos'pho·res'cence** *n*.

phos'pho·rus *n*. phosphorescent, waxy, nonmetallic chemical element —**phos·phor'ic, phos'pho·rous** *a*.

pho'to *n*. [*pl*. -TOS] [Col.] a photograph

pho'to·cop'y *n*. [*pl*. -IES] copy, as of a page, made by photographic device (**photocopier**)

pho'to·e·lec'tric cell device, as for opening doors, in which light controls an electric circuit

pho'to·en·grav'ing *n*. reproduction of photographs in relief on printing plates —**pho'to·en·grav'er** *n*.

photo finish finish of a race so close the winner is known only by a photograph of the finish

pho'to·flash *a*. using a flashbulb synchronized with camera shutter

pho·to·gen'ic (-jen'-) *a.* attractive to photograph

pho'to·graph *n.* picture made by photography —*v.* take a photograph of —**pho·tog'ra·pher** *n.*

pho·tog'ra·phy *n.* process of producing images on a surface sensitive to light —**pho'to·graph'ic** *a.*

pho'to·off'set *n.* offset printing in which photographic copies are transferred to metal plates, then to a press roller

Pho'to·stat *trademark* for device for making photographic copies of printed matter, etc. —*n.* [p-] copy so made —*v.* [p-] make a photostat of

pho'to·syn'the·sis (-sin'-) *n.* formation of carbohydrates in plants by the action of sunlight

pho'to·syn'the·size *v.* produce by photosynthesis

phrase *n.* 1. short, colorful expression 2. group of words, not a sentence or clause, conveying a single idea —*v.* express in words

phra'se·ol'o·gy *n.* wording

phy·lac'ter·y *n.* [*pl.* -IES] small leather case holding Jewish Scripture text

phy'lum (fī'-) *n.* [*pl.* -LA] basic division of plants or animals

phys'ic (fiz'-) *n.* cathartic —*v.* [-ICKED, -ICKING] to dose with this

phys'i·cal *a.* 1. of matter 2. of physics 3. of the body —*n.* physical examination —**phys'i·cal·ly** *adv.*

physical education instruction

in the exercise and care of the body

physical science any science of inanimate matter, as physics or chemistry

physical therapy treatment of disease by massage, exercise, etc.

phy·si'cian (-zish'ən) *n.* doctor of medicine

phys'ics *n.* science that deals with matter and energy —**phys'i·cist** *n.*

phys'i·og'no·my *n.* [*pl.* -MIES] the face

phys'i·ol'o·gy *n.* science of the functions of living organisms —**phys'i·o·log'i·cal** *a.* —**phys'i·ol'o·gist** *n.*

phys'i·o·ther'a·py *n.* physical therapy

phy·sique' (-zēk') *n.* form or build of the body

pi (pī) *n.* symbol (π) for the ratio of circumference to diameter, about 3.1416

pi·a·nis'si·mo (pē'-) *a., adv. Mus.* very soft

pi·an'ist (*or* pē'-) *n.* piano player

pi·an'o *n.* [*pl.* -OS] keyboard instrument with hammers that strike steel wires: also **pi·an'o·forte** —*a., adv.* (-än'-) *Mus.* soft

pi·az'za *n.* 1. in Italy, public square 2. veranda

pi·ca·resque (pik ə resk') *a.* of adventurous vagabonds

pic·a·yune' *a.* trivial

pic'ca·lil'li *n.* relish of vegetables, mustard, etc.

pic'co·lo *n.* [*pl.* -LOS] small flute

pick *v.* **1.** scratch or dig at with something pointed **2.** gather, pluck, etc. **3.** choose; select **4.** provoke (a fight) —*n.* **1.** choice **2.** the best **3.** pointed tool for breaking up soil, etc. **4.** plectrum **5.** eat sparingly —**pick on** [Col.] criticize; tease —**pick out** choose —**pick up 1.** lift **2.** get, find, etc. **3.** gain (speed) **4.** improve **5.** [Col.] make an acquaintance, esp. for lovemaking —**pick'er** *n.*

pick'a·back *adv., a.* on the shoulders or back

pick'ax, pick'axe *n.* pick with one end of the head pointed, the other axlike

pick'er·el *n.* fish with a narrow, pointed snout

pick'et *n.* **1.** pointed stake **2.** soldier(s) on guard duty **3.** striking union member etc. stationed outside a factory, etc. —*v.* place or be a picket at

picket line line of people serving as pickets

pick'ings *n.pl.* scraps

pick'le *v.* preserve in vinegar, brine, etc. —*n.* **1.** cucumber, etc. so preserved **2.** [Col.] awkward situation

pick'pock'et *n.* one who steals from pockets

pick'up *n.* **1.** power of speeding up **2.** small truck **3.** [Col.] acquaintance **4.** device containing phonograph needle

pick'y *a.* [-IER, -IEST] [Col.] fussy

pic'nic *n.* pleasure outing with an outdoor meal —*v.* [-NICKED,] -NICKING] hold a picnic —**pic'-nick·er** *n.*

pi·cot (pē'kō) *n.* loop that is part of fancy edge on lace

pic'to·graph *n.* picturelike symbol used in a system of writing

pic·to'ri·al *a.* of or expressed in pictures

pic'ture *n.* **1.** likeness made by painting, photography, etc. **2.** description **3.** motion picture **4.** image on TV screen —*v.* **1.** make a picture of **2.** describe **3.** imagine

pic·tur·esque' (-esk') *a.* **1.** having natural beauty **2.** quaint **3.** vivid

pid'dle *v.* dawdle; trifle

pidg'in English (pij'-) mixture of English and Chinese

pie *n.* fruit, meat, etc. baked on or in a crust

pie'bald *a.* covered with spots or patches of two colors

piece *n.* **1.** part broken off or separated **2.** part complete in itself **3.** single thing —*v.* **1.** join (*together*) the pieces of **2.** add pieces to in repairing —**go to pieces 1.** fall apart **2.** lose self-control

piece'meal *a., adv.* (made or done) piece by piece

piece'work *n.* work which one is paid for by the piece

pied (pīd) *a.* spotted with various colors

pier (pir) *n.* **1.** landing place built out over water **2.** heavy, supporting column

pierce (pirs) *v.* **1.** pass through as a needle does **2.** make a

hole in 3. sound sharply —
pierc′ing a.

pi′e·ty n. devotion to religious
duties, etc.

pif′fle n. [Col.] triviality or
nonsense

pig n. 1. fat farm animal;
swine 2. greedy or filthy person —**pig′gish** a.

pi·geon (pij′ən) n. plump bird
with a small head

pi′geon·hole′ n. (put in) a
compartment, as in a desk, for
filing papers

pi′geon-toed′ a. having the
toes or feet turned in

pig′gy·back adv., a. 1. on the
shoulders or back 2. of or by a
system for transporting truck
trailers on railroad cars

pig′head′ed a. stubborn

pig iron molten iron

pig′ment n. coloring matter

pig′men·ta′tion n. coloration
in plants or animals

pig′my (-mē) a., n. [pl. -MIES]
pygmy

pig′pen n. pen for pigs: also
pig′sty [pl. -STIES]

pig′skin n. 1. leather made
from the skin of a pig 2. [Col.]
a football

pig′tail n. braid of hair hanging down the back

pike n. 1. slender, freshwater
fish 2. turnpike 3. metal-tipped spear

pik′er n. [Sl.] cheapskate

pi·laf, pi·laff (pi läf′) n.
boiled, seasoned rice with
meat, etc.

pi·las′ter n. column projecting
from a wall

pil′chard (-chərd) n. sardine

pile n. 1. mass of things
heaped together 2. pyre 3.
large building 4. thick nap, as
on a rug 5. heavy, vertical
beam v. 1. heap up 2. accumulate 3. crowd

piles n.pl. hemorrhoids

pile′up n. 1. accumulation 2.
collision of several cars

pil′fer v. steal; filch —**pil′fer·age** n.

pil′grim n. traveler to a holy
place —**pil′grim·age** n.

pill n. pellet of medicine to be
swallowed whole —**the pill**
[Col.] contraceptive drug for
women, in pill form

pil′lage (-ij) v., n. plunder

pil′lar n. upright support

pil′lion (-yən) n. extra seat on
a horse or motorcycle

pil′lo·ry n. [pl. -RIES] device
with holes for head and hands,
in which offenders were locked
—v. [-RIED, -RYING] expose to
public scorn

pil′low n. case containing soft
material, to support the head,
as in sleeping v. rest as on a
pillow

pil′low·case n. removable covering for a pillow: also **pil′-low·slip**

pi′lot n. 1. one whose job is
steering ships in harbors, etc.
2. one who flies an airplane 3.
guide —v. be pilot of, in, etc.
—a. serving as a trial unit in
testing

pi′lot·house n. enclosure for
helmsman on a ship

pilot light small gas jet kept
burning to light burners

pi·men′to n. [pl. -TOS] n.

sweet, red pepper: also **pi·mien'to** (-myen'-)

pimp v. act as a prostitute's agent —n. prostitute's agent

pim'ple n. small, sore swelling of the skin —**pim'ply** [-**PLIER**, -**PLIEST**] a.

pin n. 1. pointed piece of wire to fasten things together 2. peg, rod, or other device for holding things together 3. thing like a pin 4. ornament with a pin to fasten it 5. club at which a ball is bowled —v. [**PINNED**, **PINNING**] 1. fasten as with a pin 2. hold firmly —**pin down** 1. persuade to make a decision 2. establish (a fact)

pin'a·fore n. apronlike garment for girls

pin'ball machine game machine with pins and holes for scoring points made by rolling ball

pince-nez (pans'nā') n. [pl. -**NEZ** (-nāz')] eyeglasses held in place only by a spring gripping bridge of nose

pin'cers n.pl. 1. tool for gripping things 2. claw of a crab, etc. Also **pinch'ers**

pinch v. 1. squeeze between two surfaces 2. make look thin, gaunt, etc. 3. be stingy —n. 1. a squeeze 2. small amount 3. emergency

pinch'-hit' v. [-**HIT**, -**HITTING**] 1. bat in place of regular baseball player 2. substitute (for one) —**pinch hitter**

pin'cush'ion n. small cushion to stick pins in

pine n. 1. evergreen tree with cones and needle-shaped leaves

2. its wood —v. 1. waste (away) through grief, etc. 2. yearn

pine'ap'ple n. large, juicy tropical fruit

pin'feath'er n. undeveloped feather

ping n. sound of a bullet striking something sharply —v. strike with a ping

Ping'-Pong' trademark for table tennis equipment —n. [p- p-] table tennis

pin'ion (-yan) n. 1. small cogwheel 2. wing or wing feather —v. bind the wings or arms of

pink n. 1. plant with pale-red flowers 2. pale red 3. finest condition —v. cut a sawtoothed edge on (cloth) —a. 1. pale-red 2. [Col.] somewhat radical —**in the pink** [Col.] healthy

pink'eye n. contagious eye disease

pink'ie, pink'y n. [pl. -**IES**] smallest finger

pin'na·cle n. 1. slender spire 2. mountain peak 3. highest point

pi·noch·le, pi·noc·le (pē'nuk'l) n. card game using two of every card above the eight

pin'point v. show the precise location of

pin'prick n. 1. tiny hole made by a pin 2. minor annoyance

pin'set'ter n. person or machine that sets bowling pins: also **pin'spot'ter**

pin stripe fabric pattern of very narrow stripes

pint n. 1/2 quart

pin'to a., n. [pl. -TOS] piebald (horse)

pinto bean mottled kidney bean

pin'up a. that can be fastened to a wall —n. [Col.] pinup picture, esp. of a girl

pin'wheel n. 1. small plastic wheel that turns in the wind 2. kind of firework wheel

pi·o·neer' n. early settler, researcher, experimenter, etc. —v. be a pioneer

pi'ous a. having, showing, or pretending religious devotion —**pi'ous·ly** adv.

pip n. 1. seed of an apple, orange, etc. 2. spot on a playing card 3. disease of chickens

pipe n. 1. long tube for conveying water, gas, etc. 2. tube with a bowl at one end, for smoking tobacco 3. tube for making musical sounds —v. 1. utter in a shrill voice 2. convey (water, etc.) by pipes 3. play (a tune) on a pipe —**pip'er** n.

pipe'line' n. 1. line of pipes for water, gas, etc. 2. any means of conveying something

pip'ing n. 1. music made by pipes 2. shrill sound 3. pipe-like cloth trimming —**piping hot** so hot as to sizzle

pip'it n. small songbird

pip'pin n. kind of apple

pip'squeak n. [Col.] insignificant person or thing

pi·quant (pē'kənt) a. 1. agreeably pungent 2. stimulating —**pi'quan·cy** n.

pique (pēk) n. resentment at

being slighted —v. 1. offend 2. excite

pi·qué (pē kā') n. cotton fabric with vertical cords

pi·ra·nha (pi rän'yə) n. small voracious fish

pi'rate (-rət) n. 1. one who robs ships at sea 2. one who uses a copyrighted or patented work without authorization —v. be a pirate —**pi'ra·cy** n.

pi·ro·gi (pi rō'gē) n.pl. small pastry turnovers filled with meat, cheese, etc.

pir·ou·ette' (-oo wet') n. a whirling on the toes —v. [-ETTED, -ETTING] do a pirouette

pis'ca·to'ri·al a. of fishing

Pis·ces (pī'sēz) 12th sign of the zodiac; Fishes

pis'mire n. ant

pis·ta'chi·o (-tä'shē-) n. [pl. -OS] greenish nut

pis'til n. seed-bearing organ of a flower

pis'tol n. small firearm held with one hand

pis'ton n. disk or short cylinder that moves back and forth in a hollow cylinder: it pushes against or is pushed by a fluid

pit n. 1. stone of a plum, peach, etc. 2. hole in the ground 3. abyss 4. pitfall 5. enclosed area where animals are set to fight 6. small hollow in a surface 7. section for the orchestra in front of the stage —v. [PITTED, PITTING] 1. remove the pit (stone) from 2. mark with pits 3. set in competition (against)

pit′a·pat adv. with rapid, strong beating

pitch v. 1. set up (tents) 2. throw 3. act as baseball pitcher 4. plunge forward 5. set at some level, key, etc. 6. rise and fall, as a ship —n. 1. throw 2. point or degree 3. degree of slope 4. highness or lowness of a musical sound 5. black, sticky substance from coal tar, etc. 6. [Sl.] persuasive line of talk —**pitch in** [Col.] 1. begin working hard 2. contribute

pitch′blende n. dark, lustrous, uranium-bearing mineral

pitch′er n. 1. container for holding and pouring liquids 2. baseball player who pitches to the batters

pitch′fork n. large fork for lifting and tossing hay

pitch pipe small musical pipe making a fixed tone as a standard of pitch for singers, etc.

pit′e·ous a. deserving pity — **pit′e·ous·ly** adv.

pit′fall n. 1. covered pit as a trap 2. hidden danger

pith n. 1. soft, spongy tissue in the center of plant stems 2. essential part

pith′y a. [-IER, -IEST] full of meaning or force

pit′i·ful a. 1. arousing or deserving pity 2. contemptible Also **pit′i·a·ble** —**pit′i·ful·ly** adv.

pit′i·less a. without pity

pit′tance n. small amount, esp. of money

pit′ter-pat′ter n. rapid series of tapping sounds

pi·tu′i·tar′y a. of a small endocrine gland attached to the brain

pit′y n. 1. sorrow for another's misfortune 2. cause for sorrow or regret —v. [-IED, -YING] feel pity (for)

piv′ot n. 1. person or thing on which something turns or depends 2. pivoting motion —v. provide with or turn on a pivot —**piv′ot·al** a.

pix′ie, pix′y n. [pl. -IES] fairy; sprite

pi·zazz′, piz·zazz′ n. [Sl.] 1. vitality 2. dash, flair, etc.

piz′za (pēt′sə) n. [It.] baked dish of thin dough, tomatoes, cheese, etc.

piz·ze·ri·a (pēt′sə rē′ə) n. a place where pizzas are made and sold

piz·zi·ca·to (pit′sə kät′ō) adj. Mus. plucked, as violin strings

pj's (pē′jäz) n.pl. [Col.] pajamas

plac′ard v., n. (put up) a sign in a public place

pla′cate v. appease

place n. 1. space 2. region 3. city or town 4. residence 5. particular building, site, part, position, etc. 6. job or its duties 7. step in a sequence 8. seat, etc. reserved or occupied 9. second position at the finish in a race —v. 1. put in a certain place 2. identify by some relationship 3. find a job for 4. finish second in a race —**in place of** rather than —**take place** occur

pla·ce·bo (plə sē′bō) n. [pl. -BOS, -BOES] neutral medicine given to humor a patient

place′ment n. a placing, esp. in a job

pla·cen·ta n. [pl. -TAS, -TAE (-tē)] organ in the uterus to nourish the fetus —**pla·cen′tal** a.

plac′er (plas′-) n. gravel with gold, etc. in it

plac′id (plas′-) a. calm

plack′et n. slit at the waist of a skirt or dress

pla·gia·rize (-jə-) v. offer another's writings as one's own —**pla′gia·rism** n. —**pla′gia·rist** n.

plague (plāg) n. 1. affliction 2. deadly epidemic disease —v. vex; trouble

plaice (plās) n. kind of flatfish

plaid (plad) n., a. (cloth) with crisscross pattern

plain a. 1. clear 2. outspoken 3. obvious 4. simple 5. homely 6. not fancy 7. common —n. extent of flat land —adv. clearly —**plain′ly** adv. —**plain′ness** n.

plain′clothes man detective in civilian clothes on duty

plain′song n. very old church music chanted in unison

plaint n. complaint

plain′tiff n. one who brings a suit into a court of law

plain′tive a. sad; mournful

plait (plāt) v., n. 1. braid 2. pleat

plan n. 1. outline; map 2. way of doing; scheme; method —v. [PLANNED, PLANNING] 1. make a plan of or for 2. intend —**plan′ner** n.

plane a. flat —n. 1. flat surface 2. level or stage 3. airplane 4. carpenter's tool for leveling or smoothing —v. smooth or level with a plane

plan′et n. any of nine heavenly bodies revolving around the sun —**plan′e·tar′y** a.

plan′e·tar′i·um n. large domed room for projecting images of the heavens

plane tree American sycamore

plank n. 1. long, broad, thick board 2. a principle in a political platform —v. 1. cover with planks 2. broil and serve on a board 3. [Col.] set (down) heavily

plank′ton n. tiny animals and plants floating in bodies of water

plant n. 1. living thing that cannot move, as a tree, flower, etc. 2. factory —v. 1. put in the ground to grow 2. set firmly in place 3. establish 4. [Sl.] place (something) so as to trick, trap, etc.

plan′tain (-tin) n. 1. weed with broad leaves 2. plant with bananalike fruit

plan′tar (-tər) a. of the sole of the foot

plan·ta′tion n. estate with its workers living on it

plant′er n. 1. owner of plantation 2. machine that plants 3. container for plants

plaque (plak) n. 1. flat, decorative piece of wood or metal 2. thin film of bacteria on teeth

plas′ma *n.* fluid part of blood or lymph

plas′ter *n.* lime, sand, and water, mixed as a coating that hardens on walls —*v.* cover as with plaster

plaster of Paris paste of gypsum and water that hardens quickly

plas′tic *a.* 1. that shapes or can be shaped 2. of plastic —*n.* substance that can be molded and hardened —**plas′tic′i·ty** (-tis′-) *n.*

plas′ti·cize *v.* make plastic

plastic surgery surgical grafting of skin or bone

plat *n.* 1. map 2. plot (*n.* 1)

plate *n.* 1. shallow dish 2. plated dinnerware 3. cast of molded type 4. engraved illustration 5. home plate 6. denture —*v.* coat with metal

pla·teau′ (-tō′) *n.* 1. tract of high, level land 2. period of no progress

plat′en *n.* 1. plate that presses paper against printing type 2. typewriter roller on which keys strike

plat′form *n.* 1. raised horizontal surface 2. political party's stated aims

plat′i·num *n.* silvery, precious metal, a chemical element

plat′i·tude *n.* trite remark

pla·ton′ic *a.* not sexual but purely spiritual

pla·toon′ (-tōōn′) *n.* small group, as of soldiers

plat′ter *n.* large serving dish

plat′y·pus *n.* [*pl.* -PUSES, -PI (-pī)] small, egg-laying mammal with bill like duck's: also **duckbill platypus**

plau′dits (plô′-) *n.* applause

plau′si·ble *a.* credible —**plau′si·bil·i·ty** *n.*

play *v.* 1. have fun 2. do in fun 3. take part in a game or sport 4. perform on a musical instrument 5. trifle 6. cause 7. act in a certain way 8. act the part of —*n.* 1. recreation 2. fun 3. motion or freedom for motion 4. move in a game 5. drama —**play up** [Col.] emphasize —**play′er** *n.*

play′act′ *v.* 1. pretend 2. act in dramatic way

play′back *n.* playing of tape or disc just after recording it

play′bill *n.* program of a play

play′boy *n.* [Col.] rich man who dissipates much

play′ful *a.* full of fun; frisky —**play′ful·ly** *adv.* —**play′ful·ness** *n.*

play′go′er *n.* one who attends plays frequently

play′ground *n.* outdoor place for games and play

play′house *n.* 1. theater 2. small house for children to play in

playing cards cards in four suits for playing games

play′mate *n.* companion in recreation

play′-off′ *n.* final match that is played to break a tie

play on words pun

play′pen *n.* enclosure for infant to play in

play′thing *n.* toy

play′wright (-rīt) *n.* one who writes plays

pla′za (plä′zə, plaz′ə) n. 1. public square 2. shopping center 3. service area along a superhighway

plea n. 1. appeal; request 2. statement in defense

plead v. 1. beg; entreat 2. argue (a law case) 3. offer as an excuse

pleas′ant a. pleasing; agreeable —**pleas′ant·ly** adv.

pleas′ant·ry n. [pl. -RIES] 1. jocular remark 2. polite social remark

please v. 1. satisfy 2. be the wish of 3. be obliging enough to: used in polite requests —**pleased** a.

pleas′ing a. giving pleasure —**pleas′ing·ly** adv.

pleas′ure n. 1. delight or satisfaction 2. one's choice —**pleas′ur·a·ble** a.

pleat n. fold made by doubling cloth —v. make pleats in

ple·be′ian (-bē′ən) a., n. common (person)

pleb′i·scite (-sīt) n. direct popular vote on an issue

plec′trum n. [pl. -TRUMS, -TRA (-trə)] small device for plucking a banjo, etc.

pledge n. 1. thing given as security for a contract, etc. 2. promise —v. 1. give as security 2. promise

ple′na·ry (or plen′ə-) a. full or fully attended

plen′i·po·ten′ti·ar·y (-shē-) a. having full authority —n. [pl. -IES] ambassador

plen′i·tude n. 1. fullness 2. abundance

plen′ti·ful a. abundant: also

plen′te·ous —**plen′ti·ful·ly** adv.

plen′ty n. 1. prosperity 2. ample amount

pleth′o·ra n. overabundance

pleu·ri·sy (ploor′ə sē) n. inflammation of membrane lining the chest cavity

Plex′i·glas trademark for a transparent plastic —n. [p-] this plastic

plex′us n. network of blood vessels, nerves, etc.

pli′a·ble a. easily bent; flexible —**pli′a·bil′i·ty** n.

pli′ant a. 1. pliable 2. compliant —**pli′an·cy** n.

pli′ers n.pl. small pincers

plight (plīt) n. condition, esp. a bad or dangerous one —v. 1. pledge 2. betroth

plinth n. block at base of column, pedestal, etc.

plod v. [PLODDED, PLODDING] 1. trudge 2. work steadily —**plod′der** n.

plop n. sound of object falling into water —v. [PLOPPED, PLOPPING] fall with a plop

plot n. 1. piece of ground 2. diagram, plan, etc. 3. plan of action of a play, etc. 4. secret, esp. evil, scheme or plan —v. [PLOTTED, PLOTTING] 1. make a map, plan, etc. of 2. scheme —**plot′ter** n.

plov′er (pluv′-) n. shore bird with long, pointed wings

plow (plou) n. 1. implement for cutting and turning up soil 2. machine for removing snow —v. 1. use a plow (on) 2. make one's way through 3. plod 4. begin to work hard Also [Br.]

plough —**plow'man** [*pl.* -MEN] *n.*

plow'share *n.* blade of the plow

ploy *n.* action intended to outwit someone

pluck *v.* **1.** pull off or out **2.** snatch **3.** pull hair or feathers from **4.** pull at and release quickly —*n.* **1.** a pull **2.** courage

pluck'y *a.* [-IER, -IEST] brave; spirited

plug *n.* **1.** stopper **2.** cake of tobacco **3.** device for making electrical contact **4.** [Col.] free advertisement **5.** [Sl.] old, worn-out horse —*v.* [PLUGGED, PLUGGING] **1.** stop up with a plug **2.** [Sl.] hit with a bullet **3.** [Col.] advertise with a plug **4.** [Col.] work doggedly

plum *n.* **1.** smooth-skinned, juicy fruit **2.** bluish-red color **3.** choice thing

plum'age (plōōm'-) *n.* a bird's feathers

plumb (plum) *n.* weight on a line for checking a vertical wall or sounding a depth —*a.* perpendicular —*adv.* **1.** straight down **2.** [Col.] entirely —*v.* **1.** test with a plumb **2.** fathom; solve —**out of plumb** not vertical

plumb'er *n.* one who fits and repairs water pipes, etc. — **plumb'ing** *n.*

plume *n.* feather or tuft of feathers —*v.* **1.** adorn with plumes **2.** preen

plum'met *v.* fall straight downward —*n.* plumb

plump *a.* full and rounded —*v.*

drop heavily —*adv.* suddenly; heavily

plun'der *v.* rob by force —*n.* goods plundered

plunge *v.* **1.** thrust suddenly (*into*) **2.** dive or rush **3.** [Col.] gamble heavily —*n.* **1.** dive or fall **2.** [Col.] a gamble

plung'er *n.* **1.** rubber suction cup to open drains **2.** part that moves with plunging motion, as a piston

plunk *v.* **1.** strum (a banjo, etc.) **2.** put down heavily —*n.* sound of plunking —**plunk down** [Col.] pay

plu'ral *a.* more than one —*n.* *Gram.* word form designating more than one

plu·ral'i·ty *n.* **1.** majority **2.** excess of winner's votes over his nearest rival's

plu'ral·ize *v.* make plural

plus *prep.* added to —*a.* **1.** positive **2.** more than —*n.* **1.** sign (+) showing addition or positive quantity **2.** an advantage

plush *n.* fabric with a long pile —*a.* [Sl.] luxurious

plu·toc'ra·cy *n.* [*pl.* -CIES] government by the wealthy

plu'to·crat *n.* wealthy person with great influence —**plu'to·crat'ic** *a.*

plu·to'ni·um *n.* radioactive chemical element

ply *n.* [*pl.* PLIES] one layer in plywood, folded cloth, etc. —*v.* [PLIED, PLYING] **1.** work at (a trade) or with (a tool) **2.** keep supplying (*with*) **3.** travel back and forth (*between*)

ply'wood n. board made of glued layers of wood

P.M., p.m. after noon

pneu·mat'ic (noo̅-) a. 1. of or containing air or gases 2. worked by compressed air

pneu·mo'ni·a (noo̅-) n. acute disease of the lungs

poach (pōch) v. 1. cook (an egg without its shell) in water 2. hunt or fish illegally —**poach'er** n.

pock'et n. 1. little bag or pouch, esp. when sewed into clothing 2. pouchlike cavity or hollow 3. small area or group —a. that can be carried in a pocket —v. 1. put into a pocket 2. hide; suppress —**pock'et·ful** n.

pock'et·book n. purse

pock'et·knife n. [pl. -KNIVES] small knife with folding blades

pock'mark n. scar left by a pustule: also **pock**

pod n. shell of peas, beans, etc. containing the seeds

po·di'a·try (-dī'-) n. treatment of disorders of the feet —**po·di'a·trist** n.

po'di·um n. [pl. -DIA (-ə)] platform for an orchestra conductor

po'em n. piece of imaginative writing in rhythm, rhyme, etc.

po'et n. writer of poems

po'et·ry n. 1. writing of poems 2. poems 3. rhythms, deep feelings, etc. of poems —**po·et'ic, po·et'i·cal** a.

po·grom' (-gräm') n. organized massacre, as of Jews in Czarist Russia

poi n. pastelike Hawaiian food

poign·ant (poin'yant) a. 1. painful to the feelings 2. keen —**poign'an·cy** n.

poin·ci·a'na (poin'sē an'ə) n. tropical tree with red flowers

poin·set'ti·a (ʊr -ē·ə) n. plant with petallike red leaves

point n. 1. a dot 2. specific place or time 3. stage or degree reached 4. item; detail 5. special feature 6. unit, as of a game score 7. sharp end 8. cape (land) 9. purpose; object 10. essential idea 11. mark showing direction on a compass —v. 1. sharpen to a point 2. call attention (to) 3. show 4. aim —**at the point of** very close to —**beside the point** irrelevant —**to the point** pertinent

point'-blank' a., adv. 1. (aimed) straight at a mark 2. direct(ly)

point'ed a. 1. sharp 2. aimed at someone, as a remark 3. evident —**point'ed·ly** adv.

point'er n. 1. long, tapered rod for pointing 2. indicator 3. large hunting dog 4. [Col.] hint; suggestion

point'less a. without meaning —**point'less·ly** adv.

point of view way something is viewed or thought of

poise (poiz) n. 1. balance 2. ease and dignity of manner —v. balance

poi'son n. substance which can cause illness or death —v. 1. harm or kill with poison 2. put poison into 3. corrupt —**poi'son·ous** a.

poison ivy plant that can cause severe skin rash

poke v. 1. prod, as with a stick 2. make (a hole) by poking 3. search (about or around) 4. [Sl.] to hit 5. move slowly (along) —n. 1. jab; thrust 2. [Sl.] a blow with the fist 3. [Dial.] a sack —**poke fun (at)** ridicule

pok'er n. 1. gambling game with cards 2. iron bar for stirring a fire

pok'y, pok'ey a. [-IER, -IEST] [Col.] slow; dull

polar bear large white bear of arctic regions

po·lar'i·ty (-lar'-) n. [pl. -TIES] 1. property of having opposite magnetic poles 2. tendency to grow, think, etc. in contrary directions

po'lar·ize v. separate into opposed groups, viewpoints, etc. —**po'lar·i·za'tion** n.

Po'lar·oid trademark for a camera that produces a print within seconds

Pole n. Polish person

pole n. 1. long, slender piece of wood, metal, etc. 2. end of an axis, as of the earth 3. either of two opposed forces, as the ends of a magnet —v. propel (a boat) with a pole —**po'lar** a.

pole'cat' n. 1. weasellike animal of Europe 2. skunk

po·lem'ics n. art or practice of disputation —**po·lem'ic** a., n.

pole vault a leap for height by vaulting with aid of a pole — **pole'-vault'** v.

po·lice' n. 1. department of a city, etc. for keeping law and order 2. [with pl. v.] members of such a department —v. control, etc. with police

po·lice'man n. [pl. -MEN] member of a police force —**po·lice'wom'an** [pl. -WOMEN] n.fem.

police officer member of a police force

pol'i·cy n. [pl. -CIES] 1. governing principle, plan, etc. 2. insurance contract

pol'i·o·my'e·li'tis n. virus disease often resulting in paralysis: also **po'li·o**

Pol'ish (pōl'-) a., n. (of) the people or language of Poland

pol'ish (päl'-) v. 1. smooth and brighten, as by rubbing 2. refine (manners, etc.) —n. 1. surface gloss 2. elegance 3. substance used to polish

po·lite' a. 1. showing good manners 2. refined —**po·lite'ly** adv.

pol'i·tic a. 1. wise or shrewd 2. expedient, as a plan —v. [-TICKED, -TICKING] to campaign in politics

po·lit'i·cal a. of government, politics, etc. —**po·lit'i·cal·ly** adv.

pol'i·ti'cian (-tish'ən) n. one active in politics

pol'i·tics n. 1. science of government 2. political affairs 3. factional scheming for power

pol'i·ty n. [pl. -TIES] 1. system of government 2. a state

pol'ka (pōl'-) n. fast dance for couples

polka dot (pō'-) any of a pattern of dots on cloth

poll (pōl) *n.* **1.** a counting or listing as of voters **2.** number of votes recorded **3.** *pl.* voting place **4.** survey of opinion —*v.* **1.** take the votes or opinions of **2.** receive, as votes

pol'len *n.* powderlike sex cells on flower stamens

pol'li·nate *v.* put pollen on the pistil of —**pol'li·na'tion** *n.*

pol'li·wog *n.* tadpole

poll'ster *n.* one who takes public opinion polls

pol·lute' *v.* make unclean or impure —**pol·lu'tant** *n.* —**pol·lu'tion** *n.*

po'lo (-lō) *n.* team game played on horseback

pol·troon' *n.* coward

poly- *pref.* much; many

pol'y·clin'ic *n.* clinic for treatment of various kinds of diseases

pol'y·es'ter *n.* resin used in making plastics, fibers, etc.

po·lyg'a·my (-lĭg'ə mē) *n.* a being married to more than one person at one time —**po·lyg'a·mist** *n.* —**po·lyg'a·mous** *a.*

pol'y·gon *n.* figure with more than four angles and sides

pol'y·graph *n.* device measuring bodily changes, used on one suspected of lying

pol'y·mer (-mər) *n.* substance of giant molecules formed from smaller molecules of same kind —**po·lym'er·ize** (-lĭm'-) *v.*

pol'yp (-ĭp) *n.* **1.** slender water animal with tentacles **2.** growth on mucous membrane

pol'y·syl'la·ble *n.* word of more than three syllables —**pol'y·syl·lab'ic** *a.*

pol'y·tech'nic (-tĕk'-) *a.* giving instruction in many scientific and technical subjects

pol'y·the·ism (-thē-) *n.* belief in more than one god —**pol'y·the·is'tic** *a.*

pol'y·un·sat'u·rat'ed *a.* of fats with low cholesterol

pol'y·vi'nyl *a.* of any of a group of polymerized compounds

po·made' *n.* perfumed ointment for the hair

pome'gran·ate (păm'gran'-) *n.* round, red fruit with a hard rind and many seeds

pom'mel (pum'-) *n.* rounded, upward-projecting front part of a saddle —*v.* pummel

pomp *n.* stately or ostentatious display

pom'pa·dour (-dôr) *n.* hair style with the hair brushed up high from the forehead

pom'pa·no *n.* [*pl.* -NO, -NOS] food fish of the West Indies

pom'pon *n.* **1.** decorative tuft, as of silk **2.** small, round chrysanthemum

pom'pous *a.* pretentious —**pom·pos'i·ty** *n.*

pon'cho (-chō) *n.* [*pl.* -CHOS] cloak like a blanket

pond *n.* small lake

pon'der *v.* think deeply (about)

pon·der·o'sa pine yellow pine of western N. America

pon'der·ous *a.* heavy; clumsy

pone *n.* corn bread made in small ovals

pon·gee' (-jē') *n.* soft, silk cloth

pon'iard (-yard) *n.* dagger

Pon'tiff, pon'tiff *n.* the Pope —**pon·tif'i·cal** *a.*

pon·tif'i·cate *v.* be dogmatic or pompous

pon·toon' *n.* one of the floats supporting a bridge or airplane on water

po'ny *n.* [*pl.* -**NIES**] **1.** small horse **2.** small liqueur glass **3.** [Col.] translation of foreign work, used in doing schoolwork

po'ny·tail *n.* hair style in which hair hangs down in back

poo'dle *n.* curly-haired dog

pooh *int.* exclamation of contempt, disbelief, etc.

pool *n.* **1.** small pond **2.** puddle **3.** tank for swimming **4.** billiards on a table with pockets **5.** common fund of money, etc. —*v.* put into a common fund

poop *n.* raised deck at the stern of a sailing ship —*v.* [Sl.] make tired

poor *a.* **1.** having little money **2.** below average; inferior **3.** worthy of pity —**poor'ly** *adv.*

poor'-mouth' *v.* [Col.] complain about one's lack of money

pop *n.* **1.** light, explosive sound **2.** flavored soda water **3.** [Sl.] father —*v.* [**POPPED, POPPING**] **1.** make, or burst with, a pop **2.** cause to pop **3.** move, go, etc. suddenly **4.** bulge **5.** hit (a baseball) high into the infield —*a.* [Col.] popular

pop (**art**) realistic art style

pop'corn *n.* corn with kernels that pop when heated

Pope, pope *n.* head of the Roman Catholic Church

pop'gun *n.* toy gun that shoots pellets by compressed air

pop'lar (-lar) *n.* tall tree

pop'lin *n.* ribbed cloth

pop'o'ver *n.* hollow muffin

pop'py *n.* [*pl.* -**PIES**] plant with showy flowers

pop'py·cock *n.* nonsense

pop'u·lace (-lis) *n.* the common people

pop'u·lar *a.* **1.** of, by, or for people **2.** not expensive **3.** prevalent **4.** very well liked —**pop'u·lar'i·ty** *n.*

pop'u·lar·ize' *v.* make popular

pop'u·late *v.* inhabit

pop'u·la'tion *n.* total number of inhabitants

pop'u·lism *n.* any movement to advance interests of common people —**pop'u·list** *a.*, *n.*

pop'u·lous *a.* full of people

por'ce·lain (-s'l in) *n.* hard, fine, glazed ceramic ware

porch *n.* open or screen-enclosed room on the outside of a building

por'cine *a.* of or like pigs

por'cu·pine *n.* gnawing animal with long, sharp spines in its coat

pore *v.* study or ponder (*over*) —*n.* tiny opening, as in the skin, for absorbing or discharging fluids

pork *n.* flesh of a pig used as food

pork barrel [Col.] government grants for political favors

por·nog'ra·phy *n.* writings,

pictures, etc. intended to arouse sexual desire: also [Col.]

por'no, porn —**por'no·graph'ic** a.

por'ous a. full of pores or tiny holes —**po·ros'i·ty** n.

por'poise (-pəs) n. 1. small whale with blunt snout 2. dolphin

por'ridge n. cereal or meal boiled in water or milk

por'rin·ger (-jər) n. bowl for porridge, etc.

port n. 1. harbor 2. city with a harbor 3. sweet, dark-red wine 4. left side of a ship as one faces the bow 5. porthole 6. opening, as in a valve face

port'a·ble a. that can be carried —**port'a·bil'i·ty** n.

port'age n. 1. carrying of boats and supplies overland between waterways 2. route so used

por'tal n. doorway; gate

por·tend' v. be an omen or warning of —**por'tent** n. —**por·ten'tous** a.

por'ter n. 1. doorman 2. attendant who carries luggage, sweeps up, etc.

por'ter·house (steak) choice cut of beefsteak

port·fo'li·o n. [pl. -os] briefcase

port'hole n. window in a ship's side

por'ti·co n. [pl. -COES, -COS] porch consisting of a roof supported by columns

por·tiere', por·tière' (-tyer') n. curtain hung in a doorway

por'tion n. 1. part; share 2. a

dowry 3. one's destiny —v. divide or give out in portions

port'ly a. [-LIER, -LIEST] stout and stately

port·man'teau (-tō) n. [pl. -TEAUS, -TEAUX (-tōz)] kind of suitcase

por'trait n. painting, photograph, etc. of a person

por'trai·ture (-tri chər) n. art or practice of portraying

por·tray' v. 1. make a portrait of 2. describe 3. represent on the stage —**por·tray'al** n.

Por'tu·guese (-chə gēz) n. [pl. -GUESE] native or language of Portugal a. of Portugal

por'tu·lac'a (-chə lak'ə) n. plant with small flowers

pose (pōz) v. 1. present, as a question 2. assume a bodily posture, a false role, etc. n. assumed posture, etc. —**pos'er, po·seur'** (-zur') n.

posh (päsh) a. [Col.] luxurious and fashionable —**posh'ness** n.

pos'it (päz'-) v. postulate

po·si'tion n. 1. way of being placed 2. opinion 3. place; location 4. status 5. job —v. to place

pos'i·tive (päz'-) a. 1. explicit; definite 2. sure or too sure 3. affirmative 4. real; absolute 5. of the electricity made by friction on glass 6. having a deficiency of electrons 7. being more than zero 8. Gram. of an adjective or adverb in its uncompared degree —n. 1. something positive, as a degree, quality, etc. 2. battery plate of higher potential 3. photographic print or film in which light and shadow are as in original subject —**pos'i·tive·ly** *adv.*

pos'i·tron *n.* positive antiparticle of an electron

pos·se (päs'ē) *n.* body of men called to help a sheriff

pos·sess' *v.* 1. own 2. have as a quality, etc. 3. control — **pos·ses'sor** *n.*

pos·sessed' *a.* controlled as if by a demon; crazed

pos·ses'sion *n.* 1. a possessing 2. thing possessed 3. *pl.* property; wealth 4. territory ruled by another country

pos·ses'sive *a.* 1. showing or desiring possession 2. *Gram.* of a form, etc. indicating possession

pos'si·ble *a.* 1. that can be, can happen, etc. 2. permissible —**pos·si·bil'i·ty** [*pl.* -TIES] *n.* —**pos'si·bly** *adv.*

pos'sum *n.* [Col.] opossum — **play possum** feign sleep, ignorance, etc.

post *n.* 1. piece of wood, etc. set upright as a support 2. place where a soldier or soldiers are stationed 3. job; position 4. mail —*v.* 1. put up (a notice, etc.) 2. assign to a post 3. mail 4. inform

post- *pref.* after; following

post'age *n.* amount charged for mailing a letter, etc.

post'al *a.* of (the) mail

postal card card with printed postage stamp, to be sent by mail

post card card, often a picture card, sent by mail

post·date' *v.* 1. mark with a later date 2. be later than

post'er *n.* large sign or notice posted publicly

pos·te'ri·or *a.* 1. at the back 2. later —*n.* buttocks

pos·ter'i·ty *n.* all future generations

post exchange general store at an army camp

post'grad'u·ate *a.* of study after graduation

post'haste' *adv.* speedily

post'hu·mous (päs'choo məs) *a.* 1. after one's death 2. born after the father's death 3. published after the author's death —**post'hu·mous·ly** *adv.*

post'lude *n.* concluding musical piece

post'man *n.* [*pl.* -MEN] mail carrier

post'mark *v., n.* mark to show the date and place of mailing at the post office

post'mas'ter *n.* person in charge of a post office —**post'· mis'tress** *n.fem.*

postmaster general head of a government's postal system

post-mor'tem *a.* after death — *n.* autopsy

post·na'tal *a.* after birth

post office place where mail is sorted, etc.

post·op'er·a·tive *a.* after a surgical operation

post'paid' *a.* with the sender paying the postage

post·pone' *v.* put off; delay — **post·pone'ment** *n.*

post'script *n.* note added at the end of a letter, etc.

pos'tu·late (-chə lāt) *v.* 1. assume to be true, esp. for the sake of argument **2**. take for granted —*n*. (-lit) something postulated

pos'ture (-char) *n*. way one holds the body —*v*. pose

post'war' *a*. after the war

po'sy (-zē) *n*. [*pl*. -SIES] flower or bouquet

pot *n*. **1**. round container for cooking, etc. **2**. [Col.] all the money bet **3**. [Sl.] marijuana —*v*. [POTTED, POTTING] put into a pot —**go to pot** go to ruin

po'ta·ble *a*. drinkable

pot'ash *n*. white substance got from wood ashes

po·tas'si·um *n*. soft, white, metallic chemical element

po·ta'to *n*. [*pl*. -TOES] starchy tuber of a common plant, used as a vegetable

potato chip thin slice of potato fried crisp

pot'bel'ly *n*. [*pl*. -LIES] a protruding belly

po'tent *a*. **1**. powerful **2**. effective **3**. able to have sexual intercourse: said of a male

po'ten·tate *n*. person having great power; ruler, etc.

po·ten'tial (-shal) *a*. that can be; possible —*n*. **1**. something potential **2**. voltage at a given point in a circuit —**po·ten'ti·al'i·ty** (-shē al'-) [*pl*. -TIES] *n*. —**po·ten'tial·ly** *adv*.

poth'er (päth'-) *n*. fuss

pot'hold'er *n*. small pad for handling hot pots, etc.

po'tion *n*. a drink, esp. of medicine or poison

pot'luck' *n*. whatever the family meal happens to be

pot'pie' *n*. meat pie

pot·pour·ri (pō poo rē') *n*. mixture

pot'sherd *n*. piece of broken pottery

pot'shot *n*. **1**. easy shot **2**. random shot

pot'tage *n*. kind of thick soup

pot'ter *n*. one who makes pots, dishes, etc. of clay

potter's field graveyard for paupers or unknown persons

potter's wheel rotating disk upon which bowls, etc. are made from clay

pot'ter·y *n*. pots, dishes, etc. made of clay hardened by heat

pouch *n*. **1**. small sack or bag **2**. baglike part

poul'tice (pōl'-) *n*. hot, soft mass applied to a sore part of the body

poul'try *n*. domestic fowls

pounce *v*. leap or swoop down, as if to seize —*n*. a pouncing

pound *n*. **1**. unit of weight, 16 ounces **2**. Br. monetary unit **3**. enclosure for stray animals —*v*. **1**. hit hard **2**. beat to pulp, powder, etc. **3**. throb

pour *v*. **1**. flow or make flow steadily **2**. emit or utter profusely **3**. rain heavily

pout *v*. **1**. push out the lips, as in sullenness **2**. sulk —*n*. a pouting

pov'er·ty *n*. **1**. a being poor; need **2**. inadequacy

pov'er·ty-strick'en *a*. very poor

pow'der *n*. dry substance of fine particles —*v*. **1**. put pow-

der on 2. make into powder —
pow'der·y a.

pow'er n. 1. ability to do or
act 2. strength or energy 3.
authority 4. powerful person,
nation, etc. 5. result of multiplying a number by itself —v.
supply with power —a.
operated by electricity, fuel engine, etc. —**pow'er·less** a.

pow'er·ful a. strong; mighty
—**pow'er·ful·ly** adv.

power of attorney written authority to act for another

pow'wow' n. conference of or
with N. American Indians

pox n. 1. smallpox or chicken
pox 2. syphilis

prac'ti·ca·ble a. that can be
done —**prac'ti·ca·bil'i·ty** n.

prac'ti·cal a. 1. of or obtained
through practice 2. useful 3.
sensible 4. virtual —**prac'ti-
cal'i·ty** n. —**prac'ti·cal·ly**
adv.

prac'tice v. 1. do repeatedly so
as to gain skill 2. make a habit
of 3. work at as a profession —
n. 1. a practicing 2. acquired
skill 3. work or business of a
professional person Also, Br.
sp., **prac'tise**

prac'ticed a. skilled

prac·ti'tion·er n. one who
practices a profession, etc.

prag·mat'ic a. 1. practical 2.
tested by results —**prag·mat'-
i·cal·ly** adv.

prag'ma·tism n. pragmatic
behavior —**prag'ma·tist** n.

prai'rie (prer'ē) n. large area of
grassy land

prairie dog small squirrellike
animal

prairie schooner large covered
wagon

praise v. 1. say good things
about 2. worship —n. a praising —**praise'wor'thy** a.

prance v. 1. move along on the
hind legs, as a horse 2. strut —
pranc'er n.

prank n. mischievous trick —
prank'ish a. —**prank'ster** n.

prate v. talk foolishly

prat'tle v., n. chatter or bab-
ble

prawn n. shellfish like a
shrimp but larger

pray v. 1. implore 2. ask for by
prayer 3. say prayers

prayer n. 1. a praying 2. words
of worship or entreaty to God
3. thing prayed for —**pray'er-
ful** a.

praying mantis mantis

pre- pref. before

preach v. 1. give (a sermon) 2.
urge as by preaching —
preach'er n. —**preach'ment**
n.

pre·am'ble n. introduction

pre·ar·range' v. to arrange
beforehand

pre·car'i·ous a. not safe or
sure; risky

pre·cau'tion n. care taken
beforehand, as against danger
—**pre·cau'tion·ar'y** a.

pre·cede' (-sēd') v. go or come
before —**prec'e·dence** n.

prec'e·dent (pres'ə-) n. earlier
case that sets an example

pre'cept n. rule of ethics

pre·cep'tor n. teacher

pre'cinct (-siŋkt) n. 1. subdivision of a city, ward, etc. 2.
pl. grounds or environs

pre′cious *a.* **1.** of great value **2.** beloved **3.** too refined — **pre′cious·ly** *adv.*

prec′i·pice (-pis) *n.* steep cliff

pre·cip′i·tant *a.* precipitate

pre·cip′i·tate *v.* **1.** bring on; hasten **2.** hurl down **3.** to separate out as a solid from solution **4.** to condense and fall as rain, snow, etc. —*a.* (-tit) hasty; rash —*n.* precipitated substance

pre·cip′i·ta′tion *n.* **1.** a precipitating **2.** (amount of) rain, snow, etc.

pre·cip′i·tous *a.* **1.** steep **2.** hasty; rash

pré·cis (prā sē′) *n.* summary

pre·cise′ *a.* **1.** exact; definite; accurate **2.** strict; scrupulous —**pre·cise′ly** *adv.* —**pre·ci′sion** (-sizh′ən) *n.*

pre·clude′ *v.* make impossible, esp. in advance

pre·co′cious (-kō′shəs) *a.* advanced beyond one's age — **pre·coc′i·ty** (-käs′-) *n.*

pre·con·ceive′ *v.* form an opinion of beforehand —**pre′con·cep′tion** *n.*

pre′con·di′tion *v.* to prepare to react in a certain way under certain conditions

pre·cur′sor *n.* forerunner

pred′a·to′ry *a.* **1.** plundering **2.** preying on other animals — **pred′a·tor** *n.*

pre·de·cease′ *v.* die before someone else

pred′e·ces′sor *n.* one preceding another, as in office

pre·des′ti·na′tion *n.* doctrine that God decided in advance everything that would happen

pre·des′tine *v.* destine or determine beforehand

pre′de·ter′mine *v.* set or decide beforehand

pre·dic′a·ment *n.* difficult situation

pred′i·cate *v.* base upon facts, conditions, etc. —*a., n.* (-kit) *Gram.* (of) the word or words that make a statement about the subject

pre·dict′ *v.* tell about in advance —**pre·dict′a·ble** *a.* — **pre·dic′tion** *n.*

pre·di·gest′ *v.* treat (food) with enzymes so it will digest easily when eaten

pre′di·lec′tion (pred′′l-) *n.* special liking; partiality

pre·dis·pose′ *v.* make likely to get, etc.; incline —**pre′dis·po·si′tion** *n.*

pre·dom′i·nate *v.* be greater in amount, power, etc.; prevail —**pre·dom′i·nance** *n.* —**pre·dom′i·nant** *a.*

pre·em′i·nent *a.* most outstanding: also **pre-eminent** — **pre·em′i·nence** *n.*

pre·empt′ *v.* **1.** seize before anyone else can **2.** gain the right to buy public land by settling on it **3.** replace a scheduled radio or TV program Also **pre-empt** —**pre·emp′tion** *n.* —**pre·emp′tive** *a.*

preen *v.* **1.** clean and trim (its feathers): said of a bird **2.** groom (oneself)

pre′fab′ *n.* [Col.] prefabricated building

pre·fab′ri·cat′ed *a.* made in sections ready for quick assembly, as a house

pref·ace (-is) *n.* introduction to a book, speech, etc. —*v.* give or be a preface to —**pref'a·to·ry** *a.*

pre·fect' *n.* administrator —**pre'fec·ture** *n.*

pre·fer' *v.* [-FERRED, -FERRING] 1. like better 2. bring (charges) before a court —**pref'er·a·ble** *a.*

pref'er·ence *n.* 1. a preferring 2. thing preferred 3. advantage given to one over others —**pref·er·en'tial** (-shal) *a.*

pre·fer'ment *n.* promotion

pre'fix *n.* syllable or syllables added to the beginning of a word to alter its meaning

preg'nant *a.* 1. bearing a fetus in the uterus 2. filled (*with*) 3. full of meaning —**preg'nan·cy** [*pl.* -CIES] *n.*

pre·hen'sile *a.* adapted for grasping, as the hand

pre'his·tor'ic *a.* of times before recorded history

pre·judge' *v.* judge beforehand

prej'u·dice (-dis) *n.* 1. preconceived idea 2. hatred or intolerance of other races, etc. 3. disadvantage —*v.* 1. harm 2. fill with prejudice —**prej'u·di'cial** (-dish'əl) *a.*

prel'ate (-it) *n.* high-ranking clergyman —**prel'a·cy** *n.*

pre·lim'i·nar'y *a.* leading up to the main action —*n.* [*pl.* -IES] preliminary step

pre·lit'er·ate (-it) *a.* of a society lacking a written language

prel'ude *n.* preliminary part, as of a musical piece

pre·mar'i·tal *a.* before marriage

pre·ma·ture' *a.* before the proper or usual time

pre·med'i·tate *v.* think out or plan beforehand —**pre·med·i·ta'tion** *n.*

pre·mier (pri mir') *a.* foremost —*n.* prime minister

pre·mière' (-myer') *n.* first performance of a play, etc.

prem·ise (prem'is) *n.* 1. basic assumption 2. *pl.* piece of real estate —*v.* state as a premise; predicate

pre'mi·um *n.* 1. prize 2. extra charge 3. a payment 4. high value —**at a premium** valuable because of scarcity

pre'mo·ni'tion (prē'-) *n.* feeling of imminent evil —**pre·mon'i·to'ry** (-mänʹ-) *a.*

pre·na'tal *a.* before birth

pre·oc'cu·py *v.* [-PIED, -PYING] engross; absorb —**pre·oc'cu·pa'tion** *n.*

prep *a.* [Col.] preparatory —*v.* [PREPPED, PREPPING] prepare a patient for surgery

preparatory school private school that prepares students for college

pre·pare' *v.* 1. make or get ready 2. equip 3. put together —**prep'a·ra'tion** *n.* —**pre·par'a·to·ry** *a.* —**pre·par'ed·ness** *n.*

pre·pay' *v.* [-PAID, -PAYING] pay in advance

pre·pon'der·ate *v.* predominate —**pre·pon'der·ance** *n.* —**pre·pon'der·ant** *a.*

prep'o·si'tion (-zish'-) *n.* word that connects a noun or

pronoun to another word —
prep′o·si′tion·al a.

pre′pos·sess′ing a. making a
good impression

pre·pos′ter·ous a. absurd

pre·re·cord′ v. record (a TV or
radio program) for later broadcasting

pre·req′ui·site (-rek′wə zit)
n., a. (something) required
beforehand

pre·rog′a·tive n. exclusive
privilege

pres′age n. 1. warning 2. foreboding —v. (pri sāj′) 1. warn
about 2. predict

pre′school′ a. younger than
school age

pre·sci·ence (-shē-, presh′ē-)
n. foresight —**pre′sci·ent** a.

pre·scribe′ v. 1. to order 2.
order to take a certain medicine or treatment

pre′script n. prescribed rule —
pre·scrip′tive a.

pre·scrip′tion n. 1. a prescribing, esp. by a doctor 2.
medicine prescribed

pres′ence n. 1. a being present 2. one's surroundings 3.
one's appearance

pres′ent a. 1. being at a certain place 2. of or at this time
—n. 1. present time 2. gift —
v. (pri zent′) 1. introduce 2.
show 3. offer for consideration
4. give (to)

pre·sent′a·ble a. 1. fit to
present 2. properly dressed

pres′en·ta′tion n. 1. a presenting 2. thing presented

pre·sen′ti·ment n. premonition

pres′ent·ly adv. 1. soon 2.
now

pre·sent′ment n. presentation

present participle participle
expressing present or continuing action

pre·serve′ v. 1. keep from
harm, spoiling, etc. 2. maintain 3. prepare (food) as by
canning —n. 1. pl. fruit cooked
with sugar 2. place where
game or fish are maintained —
pre·serv′a·tive a., n. —
pres′er·va′tion n.

pre·set′ v. [PRESET, PRESET
TING] set (controls) beforehand

pre′-shrunk′ a. shrunk to
minimize further shrinkage in
laundering

pre·side′ (-zīd′) v. 1. act as
chairman 2. have control

pres′i·dent n. chief executive
of a republic, company, etc. —
pres′i·den·cy [pl. -CIES] n. —
pres′i·den′tial (-shəl) a.

press v. 1. push against;
squeeze 2. iron, as clothes 3.
force 4. entreat 5. urge on 6.
keep moving 7. crowd 8. distress —n. 1. pressure 2. crowd
3. machine for crushing, printing, etc. 4. newspapers 5.
journalists 6. publicity

press conference group interview of a celebrity by journalists

press′ing a. urgent

pres′sure (-shər) n. 1. a pressing 2. distress 3. strong influence 4. urgency 5. force of
weight —v. try to influence

pres′sur·ize v. keep nearly
normal air pressure inside
(aircraft, etc.) at high altitude

pres·ti·dig·i·ta·tion (-dij'-) n. sleight of hand

pres·tige' (-tēzh') n. earned fame and respect

pres·ti·gious (-tijʾəs) a. having prestige or distinction

pres'to adv., a. fast

pre·sume' v. 1. dare 2. suppose 3. take liberties —**pre·sump'tion** n. —**pre·sump'tive** a.

pre·sump·tu·ous (-choo wəs) a. too bold or daring

pre·sup·pose' v. to assume beforehand —**pre·sup·po·si'tion** n.

pre'teen' n. child nearly a teen-ager

pre·tend' v. 1. claim falsely 2. make believe 3. lay claim (with to)

pre·tense' n. 1. claim 2. false claim or show 3. a making believe

pre·ten'sion n. 1. claim 2. pretext 3. show; display

pre·ten'tious (-shəs) a. showy; flashy

pre'ter·nat'u·ral a. supernatural

pre'text n. false reason used to hide the real one

pret'ty a. [-TIER, -TIEST] attractive and dainty —adv. somewhat —**pret'ti·ly** adv. —**pret'ti·ness** n.

pret'zel n. hard, salted biscuit, twisted in a knot

pre·vail' v. 1. win out or be successful 2. become more common —**prevail upon** persuade

pre·vail'ing a. 1. superior 2. prevalent

prev'a·lent a. common; general —**prev'a·lence** n.

pre·var'i·cate v. evade the truth; lie —**pre·var'i·ca'tion** n. —**pre·var'i·ca'tor** n.

pre·vent' v. stop or keep from doing or happening —**pre·vent'a·ble, pre·vent'i·ble** a. —**pre·ven'tion** n.

pre·ven'tive a. that prevents —n. anything that prevents Also **pre·ven'ta·tive**

pre'view' n. advance showing of (scenes from) a movie

pre'vi·ous a. coming before; prior —**pre'vi·ous·ly** adv.

pre'war' a. before the war

prey (prā) n. 1. animal seized by another for food 2. victim —v. 1. hunt as prey 2. plunder; rob 3. harass Usually used with on or upon

price n. 1. sum asked or paid for a thing 2. value —v. get or put a price on

price'less a. beyond price

prick v. 1. pierce with a sharp point 2. pain sharply —n. 1. a pricking 2. sharp pain —**prick up one's (or its) ears** 1. raise the ears 2. listen closely

prick'le n. thorn or spiny point: also **prick'er** —v. tingle —**prick'ly** [-LIER, -LIEST] a.

pride n. 1. overhigh opinion of oneself 2. self-respect 3. satisfaction in one's achievements 4. person or thing one is proud of —**pride oneself on** be proud of

priest n. a person who conducts religious rites —**priest'ess** n.fem. —**priest'hood** n. —**priest'ly** a.

prig *n.* smug, moralistic person —**prig'gish** *a.*

prim *a.* [PRIMMER, PRIMMEST] stiffly proper —**prim'ly** *adv.*

pri·ma·cy *n.* supremacy

pri'ma don'na (prē'-) chief woman singer in an opera

pri'mal *a.* 1. first in time; original 2. chief

pri'mar·y *a.* 1. most important 2. basic 3. first in order —*n.* [*pl.* -IES] preliminary election —**pri·mar'i·ly** *adv.*

pri'mate *n.* 1. archbishop 2. member of the highest order of mammals; man, ape, etc.

prime *a.* first in rank, importance, or quality —*n.* best period or part —*v.* 1. make ready 2. pour water in (a pump) to get it working —**prim·er** (prim'ər) *n.*

prime minister chief official in some countries

prim·er (prim'ər) *n.* elementary textbook, esp. for reading

prime time hours when radio and TV have largest audience

pri·me'val (prī-) *a.* of the first age or ages

prim'i·tive *a.* 1. of earliest times 2. crude; simple —*n.* primitive person or thing

pri·mo·gen'i·ture (-jen'-) *n.* right of inheritance of eldest son

pri·mor'di·al (-dē-) *a.* primitive

primp *v.* groom oneself fussily: also **prink**

prim'rose *n.* plant with tube-like flowers in clusters

prince *n.* 1. monarch's son 2. ruler of a principality —**prin'cess** *n.fem.*

prince'ly *a.* [-LIER, -LIEST] 1. of a prince 2. generous

prin'ci·pal *a.* chief; main —*n.* 1. principal person or thing 2. head of a school 3. sum owed, etc. aside from interest —**prin'ci·pal·ly** *adv.*

prin·ci·pal'i·ty *n.* [*pl.* -TIES] land ruled by a prince

prin'ci·ple *n.* 1. basic truth, rule, action, etc. 2. rule of conduct 3. integrity 4. scientific law explaining a natural action 5. way a thing works —**prin'ci·pled** *a.*

print *n.* 1. cloth stamped with a design 2. impression made by inked type, plates, etc. 3. photograph —*v.* 1. impress inked type, etc. on paper 2. publish in print 3. write in letters resembling printed ones 4. make a photographic print —**print'er** *n.* —**print'ing** *n.*

printed circuit electrical circuit in fine lines on an insulating sheet

print'out *n.* printed or typed output of a computer

pri'or *a.* preceding in time, order, or importance —*n.* head of a monastery or order —**pri'or·ess** *n.fem.*

pri·or'i·ty *n.* [*pl.* -TIES] 1. precedence 2. prior right 3. something given prior attention

pri'o·ry *n.* [*pl.* -RIES] monastery run by prior, or convent run by prioress

prism *n.* clear glass, etc. of angular form, for dispersing light into its spectrum —**pris-mat'ic** a.

pris'on n. place of confinement —**pris'on·er** n.

pris'tine (-tēn) a. **1.** of the earliest period **2.** fresh and untouched

pri'vate a. **1.** of or for a particular person or group; not public **2.** secret **3.** not in public office —n. *Mil.* lowest rank of enlisted person —**pri'va·cy** n. —**pri'vate·ly** adv.

pri·va·teer' n. private ship commissioned to attack enemy ships

pri·va'tion n. lack of necessities

priv'et n. evergreen shrub

priv'i·lege (-lij) n. special right, favor, etc. —v. grant a privilege to

priv'y a. private —n. [pl. -IES] outhouse —**privy to** privately informed about

prize v. value highly —n. **1.** thing given to the winner of a contest, etc. **2.** valued possession

prize'fight n. professional boxing match —**prize'fight'er** n.

pro adv. on the affirmative side —n. **1.** [pl. PROS] reason or vote for **2.** [Col.] professional

pro- pref. **1.** in favor of **2.** before

prob'a·ble a. likely to occur or to be so —**prob·a·bil'i·ty** [pl. -TIES] n. —**prob'a·bly** adv.

pro'bate v. establish the validity of (a will) —a. of such action —n. a probating

pro·ba'tion n. **1.** trial of abil-

ity, etc. **2.** conditional suspension of a jail sentence —**pro·ba'tion·ar'y** a. —**pro·ba'-tion·er** n.

probation officer official who watches over persons on probation

probe n. **1.** slender instrument for exploring a wound **2.** investigation **3.** spacecraft used to get facts about an environment —v. **1.** explore with a probe **2.** investigate —**prob'er** n.

prob'i·ty (prō'bə-) n. honesty

prob'lem n. **1.** question to be solved **2.** difficult matter, etc.

prob'lem·at'ic a. **1.** of the nature of a problem **2.** uncertain Also **prob'lem·at'i·cal**

pro·bos'cis (prō bäs'is) n. elephant's trunk, or similar snout

pro'caine (-kān) n. drug used as a local anesthetic

pro·ce'dure (-jər) n. act or way of doing something —**pro·ce'dur·al** a.

pro·ceed' v. **1.** go on after stopping **2.** carry on some action **3.** take legal action (*against*) **4.** come forth (*from*)

pro·ceed'ing n. **1.** course of action **2.** pl. transactions **3.** pl. legal action

pro'ceeds n.pl. money from a business deal

proc'ess n. **1.** series of changes in developing **2.** act or way of doing something **3.** court summons **4.** projecting part —v. prepare by a special process

pro·ces'sion n. group moving forward, as in a parade

pro·ces'sion·al n. hymn or music for a procession

pro·claim' v. announce officially —**proc'la·ma'tion** n.

pro·cliv'i·ty n. [pl. -TIES] inclination; tendency

pro·cras'ti·nate v. put off; delay —**pro·cras'ti·na'tion** n. —**pro·cras'ti·na'tor** n.

pro·cre·ate v. produce (young) —**pro·cre·a'tion** n.

proc'tor n. college official supervising examinations

pro·cure' v. get; obtain; secure —**pro·cur'a·ble** a. —**pro·cure'ment** n.

pro·cur'er n. pimp

prod n., v. [PRODDED, PRODDING] goad or jab

prod'i·gal a. very wasteful or abundant —n. spendthrift —**prod'i·gal'i·ty** n.

pro·di'gious (-dij'əs) a. 1. amazing 2. enormous —**pro·di'gious·ly** adv.

prod'i·gy n. [pl. -GIES] remarkable person or thing; spec., a child of genius

pro·duce' v. 1. show 2. bring forth 3. manufacture 4. cause 5. get (a play, etc.) ready for the public —n. (präd'ōōs) farm products —**pro·duc'er** n. —**pro·duc'tion** n.

prod'uct n. 1. thing produced 2. result 3. result of multiplying numbers

pro·duc'tive a. 1. producing much 2. causing —**pro·duc·tiv'i·ty** n.

pro·fane' a. 1. not religious 2. scornful of sacred things —v. 1. treat irreverently; desecrate 2. debase; defile —**prof'a·na'-**

tion (präf'-) n. —**pro·fane'ly** adv.

pro·fan'i·ty n. [pl. -TIES] swearing

pro·fess' v. 1. declare openly 2. claim to have or be 3. declare one's belief in

pro·fes'sion n. 1. occupation requiring special study 2. its members 3. avowal

pro·fes'sion·al a. (one) of a profession, or (one) paid to play in games, etc. —**pro·fes'sion·al·ly** adv.

pro·fes'sor n. college teacher of the highest rank —**pro·fes·so'ri·al** a.

prof'fer v. n. offer

pro·fi'cient (prə fish'ənt) a. skilled —**pro·fi'cien·cy** n.

pro'file n. 1. side view of the face 2. outline

prof'it n. 1. gain; benefit 2. net income from business —v. benefit **prof'it·a·ble** a. —**prof'it·a·bly** adv. —**prof'it·less** a.

prof·it·eer' (-ir') n. one who makes excessive profits by charging very high prices —v. be a profiteer

prof'li·gate (-git) a. 1. dissolute 2. wasteful —**prof'li·ga·cy** n.

pro·found' a. 1. very deep 2. having intellectual depth 3. deeply felt 4. thoroughgoing —**pro·fun'di·ty** [pl. -TIES] n.

pro·fuse' (-fyōōs') a. abundant —**pro·fuse'ly** adv. —**pro·fu'sion** n.

pro·gen'i·tor (-jen'-) n. 1. ancestor 2. precursor

prog'e·ny (präj'-) n. offspring

prog·no'sis n. [pl. -SES (-sēz)] prediction

prog·nos'ti·cate v. predict —**prog·nos'ti·ca'tion** n.

pro'gram n. 1. list of things to be performed 2. plan or procedure 3. scheduled radio or TV broadcast 4. logical sequence of operations for an electronic computer —v. [-GRAMMED, -GRAMMING] 1. schedule in a program 2. prepare for use in programmed learning 3. plan a computer program for 4. furnish (a computer) with a program Br. sp. **pro'gramme**

programmed learning independent learning from a series of questions answered in a text

prog·ress (prə gres') v. advance, develop, or improve —n. (präg'res) a progressing

pro·gres'sion n. 1. a moving forward 2. succession

pro·gres'sive a. 1. progressing 2. favoring progress, reform, etc. —n. progressive person —**pro·gres'sive·ly** adv.

pro·hib'it v. 1. forbid, as by law 2. prevent —**pro·hib'i·tive, pro·hib'i·to'ry** a.

pro'hi·bi'tion n. a forbidding, esp. of the making or selling of liquor —**pro'hi·bi'tion·ist** n.

pro·ject' n. 1. scheme 2. undertaking —v. (prə jekt') 1. propose 2. stick out 3. cause (a shadow, image, etc.) to fall upon a surface —**pro·jec'tion** n.

pro·jec'tile (-t'l) n. object to be shot forth, as a bullet

pro·jec'tion·ist n. operator of a movie or slide projector

pro·jec'tor n. machine for projecting images on a screen

pro·lapse' v. fall or slip out of place —n. (prō'laps) prolapsed condition

pro·le·tar'i·at n. working class —**pro'le·tar'i·an** a., n.

pro·lif'er·ate v. increase rapidly —**pro·lif'er·a'tion** n.

pro·lif'ic a. 1. very productive 2. very creative —**pro·lif'i·cal·ly** adv.

pro·lix' a. wordy —**pro·lix'i·ty** n.

pro'logue (-lôg) n. introduction to a poem, play, etc.

pro·long' v. lengthen —**pro'·lon·ga'tion** n.

prom n. [Col.] dance, as of a particular school class

prom'e·nade' (-nād', -näd') n. 1. walk for pleasure 2. public place for walking —v. take a promenade

prom'i·nent a. 1. projecting 2. conspicuous 3. famous —**prom'i·nence** n.

pro·mis'cu·ous a. not discriminating, esp. in sexual liaisons —**prom'is·cu'i·ty** n.

prom·ise n. 1. agreement to do or not do something 2. sign as of future success —v. 1. make a promise of or to 2. cause to expect —**prom'is·ing** a.

prom'is·so'ry a. containing or being a promise

prom'on·to'ry n. [pl. -RIES] peak of high land jutting out into the sea

pro·mote' v. 1. raise in rank 2. further the growth or sale of

—pro·mo'tion n. —pro·mo'·tion·al a.

pro·mot'er n. one who organizes and furthers an undertaking

prompt a. 1. ready, punctual, etc. 2. done without delay —v. 1. urge into action 2. help with a cue 3. inspire — prompt'er v. —prompt'ly adv.

promp'ti·tude n. quality of being prompt

pro·mul'gate v. proclaim; publish —pro·mul·ga'tion n.

prone a. 1. lying face downward 2. apt or likely

prong n. projecting point, as of a fork —pronged a.

prong'horn n. deer having curved horns

pro'noun n. word used in place of a noun —pro·nom'i·nal a.

pro·nounce' v. 1. declare officially 2. utter the sounds of — pro·nounce'a·ble a.

pro·nounced' a. definite

pro·nounce'ment n. formal statement, as of an opinion

pron'to (prän'-) adv. [Sl.] at once; quickly

pro·nun·ci·a'tion n. act or way of pronouncing words

proof n. 1. convincing evidence 2. a test 3. strength of a liquor 4. trial print of a photograph 5. trial sheet printed from set type —a. strong enough to resist (against)

-proof suf. 1. impervious to 2. protected from

proof'read v. to read in order to correct errors —proof'read'er n.

prop n. 1. a support or aid 2. [Col.] propeller —v. [PROPPED, PROPPING] to support or lean against

prop·a·gan'da n. 1. systematic spreading of ideas 2. ideas so spread —prop'a·gan'dist a., n. —prop'a·gan'dize v.

prop'a·gate v. 1. produce offspring 2. raise; breed 3. spread (ideas) —prop·a·ga'tion n.

pro'pane n. hydrocarbon used as a fuel

pro·pel' v. [-PELLED, -PELLING] drive forward

pro·pel'lant, pro·pel'lent n. fuel for a rocket

pro·pel'ler n. bladed end of a revolving shaft for propelling a ship or aircraft

pro·pen'si·ty n. [pl. -TIES] natural tendency

prop'er a. 1. suitable; fit 2. correct 3. belonging (to) 4. decent 5. strictly so called 6. designating a noun naming a specific person, place, etc. — prop'er·ly adv.

prop'er·ty n. [pl. -TIES] 1. thing owned 2. characteristic 3. article used in a stage setting —prop'er·tied a.

proph'e·cy (-sē) n. [pl. -CIES] prediction

proph'e·sy (-sī) v. [-SIED, -SYING] predict; foretell

proph'et n. 1. leader regarded as divinely inspired 2. one who predicts

pro·phet'ic a. 1. of or like a prophet 2. like or containing a prophecy

pro'phy·lac'tic (-fǝ-) n., a.

(medicine, device, etc.) that prevents disease

pro·phy·lax'is n. [pl. -LAXES (-sēz)] cleaning of the teeth

pro·pin'qui·ty n. nearness

pro·pi'ti·ate (-pish'ē āt) v. appease —**pro·pi'ti·a'tion** n. —**pro·pi'ti·a·to'ry** a.

pro·pi'tious a. favorable

prop'jet n. turboprop

pro·po'nent n. supporter

pro·por'tion n. 1. part in relation to the whole 2. ratio 3. symmetry 4. pl. dimensions —v. 1. make symmetrical 2. make fit —**pro·por'tion·al, pro·por'tion·ate** (-it) a.

pro·pose' v. 1. suggest for considering 2. plan 3. offer marriage —**pro·pos'al** n.

prop'o·si'tion n. 1. a plan 2. [Col.] proposed deal, as in business 3. [Col.] problem to be dealt with 4. subject for discussion

pro·pound' v. suggest for consideration

pro·pri'e·tar'y a. held under a patent, etc.

pro·pri'e·tor n. owner —**pro·pri'e·tress** n.fem.

pro·pri'e·ty n. [pl. -TIES] 1. fitness 2. conformity with accepted behavior

pro·pul'sion n. a propelling or a force that propels —**pro·pul'sive** a.

pro·rate' v. divide or assess proportionally

pro·sa'ic a. commonplace

pro·sce'ni·um (-sē'-) n. [pl. -NIUMS, -NIA] arch framing a conventional stage

pro·scribe' v. 1. to outlaw 2. to exile 3. forbid the use, etc. of —**pro·scrip'tion** n.

prose n. nonpoetic language

pros'e·cute' v. 1. engage in 2. take legal action against —**pros'e·cu'tion** n. —**pros'e·cu'tor** n.

pros'e·lyte (-līt) n., v. convert —**pros'e·lyt·ize'** v.

pros'pect n. 1. outlook 2. something expected 3. pl. apparent chance for success 4. likely customer, etc. —v. search (for) —**pros'pec·tor** n.

pro·spec'tive a. expected

pro·spec'tus n. report outlining a new work, etc.

pros'per v. thrive

pros·per'i·ty n. wealth

pros'per·ous a. 1. successful 2. wealthy —**pros'per·ous·ly** adv.

pros'tate a. of a gland at the base of the bladder in males

pros·the·sis (präs'thə sis, präs thē'-) n. [pl. -SES (-sēz)] artificial body part —**pros·thet'ic** a.

pros'ti·tute n. woman who engages in sexual intercourse for pay —v. sell (one's talents, etc.) for base purposes —**pros'ti·tu'tion** n.

pros'trate a. 1. lying flat, esp. face downward 2. overcome —v. 1. lay flat 2. overcome —**pros·tra'tion** n.

pro·tag'o·nist n. main character or leading figure

pro'te·an a. readily taking on many forms

pro·tect' v. shield from harm —**pro·tec'tion** n. —**pro·tec'tive** a. —**pro·tec'tor** n.

pro·tec'tor·ate (-it) *n.* territory controlled and protected by a strong state

pro'té·gé (-ta zhā) *n.* one under another's patronage

pro·tein (-tēn) *n.* nitrogenous substance essential to diet

pro·test' *v.* 1. object 2. assert —*n.* (prō'test) objection —**prot'es·ta'tion** *n.*

Prot'es·tant *n.* Christian not of the Roman Catholic or Orthodox Eastern Church —**Prot'es·tant·ism** *n.*

proto- *pref.* original

pro'to·col *n.* code of etiquette among diplomats, etc.

pro'ton *n.* positive particle in the nucleus of an atom

pro'to·plasm *n.* essential matter of all living cells —**pro'to·plas'mic** *a.*

pro'to·type *n.* first thing of its kind

pro'to·zo'an *n.* [*pl.* -ZOA] one-celled animal

pro·tract' *v.* draw out; prolong —**pro·trac'tion** *n.*

pro·trac'tor *n.* device for drawing and measuring angles

pro·trude' *v.* jut out —**pro·tru'sion** *n.*

pro·tu'ber·ance *n.* bulge —**pro·tu'ber·ant** *a.*

proud *a.* 1. haughty 2. feeling or causing pride 3. splendid —**proud of** highly pleased with —**proud'ly** *adv.*

proud flesh excessive growth of flesh around a healing wound

prove *v.* [alt. pp. PROVEN] 1. test by experiment 2. establish as true —**prov'a·ble** *a.*

prov'e·nance *n.* origin; source

prov'en·der *n.* 1. fodder 2. [Col.] food

prov'erb *n.* short saying expressing an obvious truth —**pro·ver'bi·al** *a.*

pro·vide' *v.* 1. supply; furnish (with) 2. prepare (*for* or *against*) 3. stipulate —**pro·vid'er** *n.*

pro·vid'ed *con.* on condition (that): also **pro·vid'ing**

prov'i·dence *n.* 1. prudent foresight 2. guidance of God or nature 3. [P-] God

prov'i·dent *a.* 1. providing for the future 2. prudent or economical

prov'i·den'tial (-shəl) *a.* of or by divine providence

prov'ince *n.* 1. division of a country 2. *pl.* parts of a country outside major cities 3. sphere; field

pro·vin'cial (-shəl) *a.* 1. of a province 2. countrylike; rustic 3. narrow; limited —**pro·vin'cial·ism** *n.*

proving ground place for testing new equipment, etc.

pro·vi'sion *n.* 1. a providing 2. *pl.* stock of food 3. stipulation —*v.* supply with provisions

pro·vi'sion·al *a.* temporary

pro·vi'so *n.* [*pl.* -SOS, -SOES] condition or stipulation

prov'o·ca'tion *n.* 1. a provoking 2. thing that provokes —**pro·voc'a·tive** *a.*

pro·voke' *v.* 1. excite to action or feeling 2. to anger 3. stir up 4. evoke

pro'vost (-vōst) *n.* high executive official, as in some colleges

prow (prou) *n.* forward part of a ship

prow′ess *n.* **1.** bravery **2.** superior skill, etc.

prowl *v.* stalk furtively —**prowl′er** *n.*

prox·im′i·ty *n.* nearness

prox′y *n.* [*pl.* -IES] **1.** authority to act for another **2.** person so authorized

prude *n.* one overly modest —**prud′er·y** *n.* —**prud′ish** *a.*

pru′dent *a.* **1.** wisely careful; cautious **2.** managing carefully —**pru′dence** *n.* —**pru·den′tial** (-shəl) *a.*

prune *n.* dried plum —*v.* **1.** trim parts from (a plant) **2.** cut out (unnecessary parts)

pru′ri·ent *a.* exciting lust; lewd —**pru′ri·ence** *n.*

pry *n.* [*pl.* PRIES] lever or crowbar. —*v.* [PRIED, PRYING] **1.** raise with a pry **2.** get with difficulty **3.** look closely and inquisitively

psalm (säm) *n.* sacred song or poem —**psalm′ist** *n.*

pseudo- *pref.* sham; counterfeit

pseu·do·nym (sōō′də nim) *n.* fictitious name assumed by an author, etc.

pshaw (shô) *int., n.* exclamation of disgust, etc.

pso·ri′a·sis (sə-) *n.* skin disease with reddish patches

psych (sīk) *v.* [Sl.] probe behavior psychologically, so as to outwit or control (used with *out*)

psy·che (sī′kē) *n.* **1.** soul **2.** mind

psy·che·del·ic (sī′kə-) *a.* of or causing extreme changes in the conscious mind

psy·chi·a·try (sī kī′ə trē) *n.* branch of medicine dealing with mental illness —**psy′chi·at′ric** *a.* —**psy·chi′a·trist** *n.*

psy′chic (-kik) *a.* **1.** of the mind **2.** beyond known physical processes Also **psy′chi·cal**

psy′cho *n.* [Col.] psychopath —*a.* [Col.] psychopathic

psycho- *pref.* mind; mental processes: also **psych-**

psy′cho·a·nal′y·sis *n.* method of treating neuroses —**psy′cho·an′a·lyst** *n.* —**psy′cho·an′a·lyze** *v.*

psy·chol′o·gy *n.* science dealing with the mind and behavior —**psy′cho·log′i·cal** *a.* —**psy′cho·log′i·cal·ly** *adv.* —**psy·chol′o·gist** *n.*

psy′cho·path *n.* one suffering from emotional disorders with amoral or asocial behavior —**psy′cho·path′ic** *a.*

psy·cho′sis *n.* [*pl.* -SES (-sēz)] severe mental illness —**psy·chot′ic** *a., n.*

psy′cho·so·mat′ic *a.* of a physical disorder caused by emotional disturbance

psy′cho·ther′a·py *n.* treatment of mental illness —**psy′cho·ther′a·pist** *n.*

ptar·mi·gan (tär′mə gən) *n.* northern grouse

pter·o·dac′tyl (ter′-) *n.* extinct flying reptile

pto′maine (tō′-) *n.* substance in decaying matter

pub *n.* [Br. Col.] bar; tavern: in full, **public house**

pu'ber·ty (pyōō'-) *n.* time of maturing sexually

pu'bic (pyōō'-) *a.* of or near the genitals

pub'lic *a.* 1. of people as a whole 2. for everyone 3. known by all —*n.* the people, or a specific part of it —**in public** in open view —**pub'lic·ly** *adv.*

pub·li·ca'tion *n.* 1. printing and selling of books, etc. 2. thing published

public domain condition of being free from copyright or patent

pub'li·cist *n.* publicity agent

pub·lic'i·ty *n.* 1. public attention meant to bring one this 3. work of spreading this information

pub'li·cize *v.* give publicity to

public servant government official or employee

pub'lish *v.* 1. issue (a printed work) for sale 2. announce —**pub'lish·er** *n.*

puck *n.* hard rubber disk used in ice hockey

puck'er *n., v.* wrinkle

puck'ish *a.* mischievous

pud'ding *n.* soft food of flour, milk, eggs, etc.

pud'dle *n.* small pool of water

pudg'y *a.* [-IER, -IEST] short and fat

pueb'lo (pweb'-) *n.* [*pl.* -LOS] Southwestern Indian village

pu'er·ile (pyōō'-) *a.* childish —**pu'er·il'i·ty** *n.*

puff *n.* 1. brief burst of wind, etc. 2. draw at a cigarette 3. light pastry shell 4. soft pad 5. exaggerated praise —*v.* 1. blow in puffs 2. breathe rapidly 3. smoke 4. swell 5. praise unduly —**puff'y** [-IER, -IEST] *a.*

puff'ball *n.* round, white fungus

puf'fin *n.* northern seabird

pug *n.* small dog

pu'gil·ism (pyōō'jil-) *n.* sport of boxing —**pu'gil·ist** *n.* —**pu'gil·is'tic** *a.*

pug·na'cious (-shəs) *a.* eager to fight; quarrelsome —**pug·na'cious·ly** *adv.* —**pug·nac'i·ty** (-nas'-) *n.*

pug nose turned-up nose that is short and thick —**pug'nosed'** *a.*

puke (pyōōk) *v., n.* vomit

puk'ka *a.* 1. first-rate 2. genuine; real

pul'chri·tude *n.* beauty

pull *v.* 1. make move toward one 2. pluck out 3. rip 4. strain 5. [Col.] do 6. [Col.] draw out 7. move (*away, ahead,* etc.) —*n.* 1. act of pulling 2. difficult effort 3. handle, etc. 4. [Col.] influence 5. [Col.] drawing power —**pull for** [Col.] cheer on; encourage —**pull off** [Col.] accomplish —**pull through** [Col.] get over (an illness, etc.)

pul'let *n.* young hen

pul'ley *n.* [*pl.* -LEYS] wheel with a grooved rim in which a rope runs, to raise weights

Pull'man (car) railroad car with berths for sleeping

pull'out *n.* removal, withdrawal, etc.

pull'o'ver *n.* sweater, etc. to be pulled over the head

pul'mo·nar'y *a.* of the lungs

pulp n. 1. soft, inside part, as of fruit 2. moist wood fiber, ground to make paper —**pulp′y** [-IER, -IEST] a.

pul′pit n. clergyman's platform for preaching

pul′sate v. throb —**pul·sa′tion** n.

pulse n. regular beat, as of blood in the arteries

pul′ver·ize v. grind into powder

pu′ma (pyōō′-) n. cougar

pum′ice n. light, spongy rock, used for cleaning, etc.

pum′mel v. hit with repeated blows

pump n. 1. machine that forces fluids in or out 2. low-cut, strapless shoe —v. 1. move or empty (fluids) with a pump 2. move like a pump 3. [Col.] question persistently

pump′er·nick′el n. coarse, dark rye bread

pump′kin n. large, round, orange-yellow gourd

pun n. humorous use of different words that sound alike —v. [PUNNED, PUNNING] make puns —**pun′ner** n.

punch n. 1. tool for piercing, etc. 2. fruit drink 3. blow with the fist 4. [Col.] effective force —v. 1. pierce, etc. with a punch 2. hit with the fist

punch′-drunk′ a. [Col.] dazed

punch′y a. [-IER, -IEST] [Col.] 1. forceful 2. punch-drunk

punc·til′i·ous a. 1. careful in behavior 2. precise

punc′tu·al (-chōō wəl) a. on time —**punc′tu·al′i·ty** n.

punc′tu·ate v. 1. use periods, commas, etc. in (writing) 2. interrupt 3. emphasize —**punc′tu·a′tion** n.

punc′ture (-chər) n. hole made by a sharp point —v. pierce as with a point

pun′dit n. learned person

pun′gent (-jənt) a. 1. sharp in taste or smell 2. keen and direct —**pun′gen·cy** n.

pun′ish v. make suffer pain, loss, etc. as for a crime or offense —**pun′ish·a·ble** a.

pun′ish·ment n. 1. a punishing 2. penalty imposed 3. harsh treatment

pu′ni·tive a. of or inflicting punishment

punk n. 1. substance that smolders, used to light fireworks 2. [Sl.] insignificant young person —a. [Sl.] poor in quality

punt v. 1. kick a dropped football before it touches the ground 2. move (a boat) using a long pole —n. 1. a punting 2. square, flat-bottomed boat

pu′ny a. [-NIER, -NIEST] small or weak

pup n. young dog, sea', etc.

pu′pa (pyōō′-) n. [pl. -PAE (-pē), -PAS] insect just before the adult stage

pu′pil n. 1. person being taught 2. contractile opening in iris of the eye

pup′pet n. 1. doll moved by strings, etc. in a play 2. one controlled by another

pup′py n. [pl. -PIES] pup

pup tent small, portable tent

pur′chase (-chis) v. buy —n. 1. thing bought 2. act of buying 3. firm hold —**pur'chas·er** n.

pure a. 1. unmixed 2. clean 3. mere 4. faultless 5. chaste 6. abstract —**pure'ly** adv.

pu·rée (pyoo rā′) n. 1. food that is strained or whipped to smoothness 2. thick soup of this —v. make a purée of

pur'ga·tive (-ga-) a. purging —n. a cathartic

pur'ga·to·ry n. R.C.Ch. state or place for expiating sins after death

purge v. 1. cleanse; make pure 2. move (the bowels) 3. get rid of —n. 1. a purging 2. cathartic

pu·ri·fy v. [-FIED, -FYING] rid of impurities, guilt, sin, etc. —**pu·ri·fi·ca′tion** n.

pu'ri·tan n. one very strict in morals and religion —**pu'ri·tan'i·cal** a.

pu'ri·ty n. 1. freedom from adulterating matter, cleanness 2. chastity

purl v. invert (stitches) in knitting to form ribbing

pur'lieu (-lōō) n. 1. outlying part, as of a city 2. pl. suburbs

pur·loin′ v. steal

pur'ple n. bluish red —a. 1. bluish-red 2. ornate

pur·port′ v. seem or claim to mean or be —n. (pur′ pôrt) 1. meaning 2. intention

pur'pose n. 1. intention; aim 2. determination 3. end in view —**on purpose** intentionally —**pur'pose·ful** a. —**pur'pose·less** a.

pur'pose·ly adv. intentionally; deliberately

purr v., n. (make) the sound of a cat at ease

purse n. 1. small bag for money 2. woman's handbag 3. finances; money 4. prize money —v. to pucker

purs'er n. ship's officer in charge of accounts, etc.

pur·su'ant a. [Rare] following —**pursuant to** according to

pur·sue′ v. 1. try to overtake; chase 2. go on with 3. seek —**pur·su'ance** n.

pur·suit′ n. 1. a pursuing 2. occupation

pu'ru·lent (pyoo′-) a. of or discharging pus —**pu'ru·lence** n.

pur·vey′ (-vā′) v. supply (esp. food) —**pur·vey'or** n.

pur'view n. scope or extent, as of control, activity, etc.

pus n. yellowish matter forming in infections

push v. 1. move by pressing against 2. urge on 3. urge the use of —n. 1. a pushing 2. an advance —**push'er** n.

push'o·ver n. [Sl.] 1. anything easy to do 2. one easily persuaded, defeated, etc.

push′-up′, push'up n. exercise of raising one's prone body by pushing down on the palms

push'y a. [-IER, -IEST] [Col.] annoyingly aggressive

pu'sil·lan'i·mous a. cowardly; timid

puss n. cat: also **puss'y**

puss'y·foot n. [Col.] 1. move cautiously 2. avoid taking a stand

pussy willow willow with soft, silvery catkins

pus'tule (-chool) *n.* inflamed, pus-filled pimple

put *v.* [PUT, PUTTING] 1. make be in some place, state, relation, etc. 2. impose or assign 3. express 4. present for decision 5. bet (money) *on* 6. go (*in, out,* etc.) —*a.* [Col.] fixed —**put across** cause acceptance of —**put down** 1. repress 2. [Sl.] belittle or humiliate —**put off** postpone —**put on** 1. pretend 2. [Sl.] to hoax —**put out** 1. extinguish 2. inconvenience —**put up** 1. preserve (fruits, etc.) 2. give lodgings to 3. provide (money) —**put up with** tolerate

pu'ta·tive *a.* supposed

put'-down' *n.* [Sl.] belittling remark

put'-on' *n.* [Sl.] a hoax

pu're·fy *v.* [-FIED, -FYING] rot —**pu're·fac'tion** *n.*

pu'trid *a.* rotten; stinking

putt *v., n. Golf* (make) a stroke to get the ball into the hole

put'ter *v.* busy oneself futilely —*n.* club for putting

put'ty *n.* pliable substance to fill cracks, etc. —*v.* [-TIED, -TYING] fill with putty

puz'zle *v.* 1. perplex 2. exercise one's mind —*n.* 1. thing that puzzles 2. problem to test cleverness —**puz'zle·ment** *n.* —**puz'zler** *n.*

pyg'my *n.* [*pl.* -MIES] dwarf —*a.* very small

py·ja'mas *n.pl.* pajamas: Br. sp.

py'lon *n.* towerlike shaft

py·lo'rus *n.* [*pl.* -RI] opening from the stomach into intestines —**py·lor'ic** *a.*

py·or·rhe·a (pī'ə rē'ə) *n.* infection of the gums and tooth sockets

pyr'a·mid (pir'-) *n.* solid figure or structure with triangular sides meeting at a point —*v.* build up —**py·ram'i·dal** *a.*

pyre (pir) *n.* pile of wood for burning a dead body

py'ro·ma'ni·a *n.* compulsion to start fires —**py'ro·ma'ni·ac** *n., a.*

py'ro·tech'nics (-tek'-) *n.pl.* display of fireworks

py'thon *n.* large snake that crushes its prey to death

Q

quack *v.* utter the cry of a duck —*n.* 1. this cry 2. one who practices medicine fraudulently —**quack'er·y** *n.*

quad (kwäd) *n.* [Col.] 1. quadrangle 2. quadruplet

quad'ran·gle *n.* 1. plane figure with four angles and four sides 2. four-sided area surrounded by buildings

quad'rant *n.* quarter section of a circle

quad'ra·phon'ic *a.* using four channels to record and reproduce sound

quad·ren'ni·al *a.* lasting or occurring every four years

quad'ri·lat'er·al *a., n.* four-sided (figure)

qua·drille' n. square dance for four couples

quad·ru·ped n. four-footed animal

quad·ru·ple a. four times as much —v. make or become quadruple

quad·ru·plet (-drup'lit) n. any of four children born at one birth

quad·ru·pli·cate v. make four copies of —a. (-kit) made in four identical copies —n. one of these copies

quaff v. drink deeply —n. a quaffing

quag'mire n. a bog

qua'hog (kwô'-) n. edible, hard-shelled clam: also sp. **quahaug**

quail v. draw back in fear —n. game bird

quaint a. 1. pleasingly odd or old-fashioned 2. unusual; curious 3. whimsical **quaint'ly** adv. —**quaint'ness** n.

quake v. shake —n. 1. a quaking 2. earthquake

qual'i·fied a. 1. skilled; able 2. limited

qual'i·fi'er n. adjective or adverb

qual'i·fy v. [-FIED, -FYING] 1. make or be fit for a job, etc. 2. modify; limit 3. moderate — **qual'i·fi·ca'tion** n.

qual'i·ty n. [pl. -TIES] 1. characteristic 2. kind 3. degree of (excellence) —**qual'i·ta'tive** a.

qualm n. 1. sudden sickness 2. scruple; misgiving 3. twinge of conscience

quan'da·ry n. [pl. -RIES] state of perplexity; dilemma

quan'ti·ty n. [pl. -TIES] 1. amount 2. large amount 3. number or symbol expressing measure —**quan'ti·ta'tive** a.

quan'tum n. [pl. -TA] fixed, elemental unit of energy

quar'an·tine (-tēn) n. isolation to keep contagious disease from spreading —v. place under quarantine

quark n. assumed basic unit of matter

quar'rel v., n. (have) an argument or disagreement —**quar'rel·some** a.

quar'ry n. [pl. -RIES] 1. animal, etc. being hunted down 2. place where stone is excavated —v. [-RIED, -RYING] excavate from a quarry

quart n. 1. liquid measure, 1/4 gallon 2. dry measure, 1/8 peck

quar'ter n. 1. any of four equal parts; 1/4 2. coin worth 25 cents 3. district 4. pl. lodgings 5. mercy 6. particular source —v. 1. divide into quarters 2. provide lodgings for — **at close quarters** at close range —**cry quarter** beg for mercy

quar'ter·back n. Football back who calls signals

quar'ter·deck n. after part of a ship's top deck

quar'ter·ly a. occurring regularly four times a year —adv. once every quarter of the year —n. [pl. -LIES] publication issued quarterly

quar'ter·mas'ter n. 1. army

officer in charge of supplies 2. navy officer who tends to the compass, navigation, etc.

quar·tet′, quar·tette′ *n.* a musical composition for four performers

quar′to *n.* book-page size about 9 x 12 inches

quartz *n.* bright mineral

quartz crystal *Electronics* piece of quartz that vibrates at a particular frequency

qua·sar (kwā′zär) *n.* distant celestial object that emits radio waves

quash *v.* 1. annul 2. suppress

qua′si *a., adv.* seeming(ly)

quat′rain (kwät′-) *n.* stanza of four lines

qua′ver *v.* 1. tremble 2. be tremulous: said of the voice —*n.* tremulous tone

quay (kē) *n.* wharf

quea·sy (kwē′zē) *a.* [-SIER, -SIEST] 1. feeling nausea 2. squeamish

queen *n.* 1. wife of a king 2. woman monarch 3. female in an insect colony 4. playing card with a queen's picture 5. most powerful chess piece

queer *a.* 1. odd 2. [Col.] eccentric 3. [Sl.] homosexual —*v.* [Sl.] spoil the success of —*n.* [Sl.] queer person —**queer′ly** *adv.*

quell *v.* subdue or quiet

quench *v.* 1. extinguish 2. satisfy —**quench′less** *a.*

quer′u·lous (kwer′-) *a.* 1. fretful 2. complaining

que′ry (kwir′-) *n.* [*pl.* -RIES] a question —*v.* [-RIED, -RYING] to question

quest *n.* 1. a seeking 2. journey for adventure

ques′tion *n.* 1. inquiry 2. thing asked 3. doubt 4. problem 5. point being debated —*v.* 1. inquire 2. doubt 3. challenge —**out of the question** impossible —**ques′tion·er** *n.*

ques′tion·a·ble *a.* 1. doubtful 2. not well thought of

question mark mark of punctuation (?)

ques·tion·naire′ (-ner′) *n.* list of questions for gathering information

queue (kyōō) *n.* 1. pigtail 2. line of persons —*v.* line up in a queue

quib′ble *v.* evade a point by carping —*n.* petty evasion

quiche Lor·raine (kēsh lô ren′) [Fr.] custard pie made with cheese and bacon

quick *a.* 1. swift 2. prompt —*adv.* rapidly —*n.* 1. the living 2. sensitive flesh under the nails 3. one's deepest feelings —**quick′ly** *adv.*

quick′en *v.* 1. enliven 2. hasten

quick′-freeze′ *v.* [-FROZE, -FROZEN, -FREEZING] freeze (food) suddenly for storage

quick′ie (-ē) *n.* [Sl.] anything done or made quickly

quick′lime *n.* lime (*sense* 1)

quick′sand *n.* wet, deep sand that engulfs heavy things

quick′sil′ver *n.* mercury

quick′-tem′pered *a.* easily angered

quick′-wit′ted *a.* alert

quid *n.* piece of tobacco to be chewed

qui·es'cent (kwī-) *a.* quiet; inactive —**qui·es'cence** *n.*

qui'et *a.* 1. still 2. silent 3. gentle 4. not showy 5. not forward —*v.* make or become quiet —**qui'et·ly** *adv.* —**qui'et·ness** *n.*

qui'e·tude *n.* calmness

quill *n.* 1. large feather 2. pen made from this 3. spine of a porcupine

quilt *v., n.* (make) a bedcover stitched in layers

quince *n.* yellowish fruit

qui'nine (-nīn) *n.* alkaloid used in treating malaria

quin'sy (-zē) *n.* sore throat

quin·tes'sence *n.* 1. pure essence 2. perfect example

quin·tet', quin·tette' *n.* a musical composition for five performers

quin·tu'plet (-tup'lit) *n.* any of five children born at one birth

quip *v.* [QUIPPED, QUIPPING], *n.* (make) a witty remark —**quip'ster** *n.*

quire *n.* set of 24 or 25 sheets of the same paper

quirk *n.* 1. sudden twist 2. peculiarity

quirt *n.* riding whip with braided leather lash

quis'ling *n.* traitor

quit *v.* [QUIT, QUITTED, QUITTING] 1. give up 2. leave 3. stop 4. resign from one's job —*a.* free

quit'claim *n.* deed resigning a claim, as to property

quite *adv.* 1. completely 2. really 3. very or fairly —**quite a few** [Col.] many

quits *a.* on even terms —**call it quits** [Col.] 1. stop working, etc. 2. stop being friendly

quit'tance *n.* 1. discharge of a debt 2. recompense

quit'ter *n.* [Col.] one who gives up easily

quiv'er *v.* tremble —*n.* 1. tremor 2. case for arrows

quix·ot'ic *a.* idealistic but impractical

quiz *n.* [*pl.* QUIZZES] test of knowledge —*v.* [QUIZZED, QUIZZING] give a quiz to

quiz'zi·cal *a.* 1. comical 2. perplexed —**quiz'zi·cal·ly** *adv.*

quoit (kwoit) *n.* 1. ring thrown to encircle an upright peg 2. *pl.* game so played

quon'dam *a.* former

Quon'set hut (kwän'-) *trademark for* a metal shelter with a curved roof

quo'rum *n.* minimum number needed to transact business at an assembly

quo'ta *n.* share assigned to each one

quo·ta'tion *n.* 1. a quoting 2. words quoted 3. current price of a stock or bond

quotation marks marks ("...") around quoted words

quote *v.* 1. repeat (the words of) 2. state (the price of) —*n.* [Col.] 1. quotation 2. quotation mark —**quot'a·ble** *a.*

quoth (kwōth) *v.* [Ar.] said

quo'tient (-shənt) *n.* number got by dividing one number into another

R

rab′bi (-bī) *n.* [*pl.* -BIS, -BIES] ordained teacher of the Jewish law —**rab·bin′i·cal** *a.*

rab′bit *n.* burrowing rodent with soft fur and long ears

rab′ble *n.* a mob

rab′ble-rous′er *n.* person who tries to arouse people to violent action

rab′id *a.* 1. fanatical 2. of or having rabies

ra′bies *n.* disease of dogs, etc., transmitted by biting

rac·coon′ *n.* small, furry mammal with black-ringed tail

race *n.* 1. a competition, esp. of speed 2. swift current 3. division of mankind, esp. based on skin color 4. any group or class —*v.* 1. be in a race 2. enter (a horse, etc.) in a race 3. move swiftly —**rac′er** *n.* —**ra′cial** *a.*

race′horse *n.* horse bred and trained for racing

ra·ceme (rā sēm′) *n.* flower cluster

race track course for racing

race′way *n.* race track for harness races or one for drag races, etc.

rac′ism *n.* racial discrimination or persecution —**rac′ist** *a., n.*

rack *n.* 1. framework for holding things 2. ancient torture device 3. great torment 4. toothed bar meshing with a gearwheel —*v.* to torture —**rack one's brains** think hard

rack′et *n.* 1. noisy confusion 2. dishonest scheme 3. netted frame with a handle, used as a bat in tennis: also sp. **rac′quet**

rack·et·eer′ *n.* one who gets money by fraud, extortion, etc.

rac·on·teur′ (-tur′) *n.* one clever at telling stories

rac·y (rās′ē) *a.* [-IER, -IEST] 1. lively 2. risqué

ra′dar *n.* device for locating objects by their reflection of radio waves

ra′dar·scope *n.* screen that displays reflected radio beams picked up by radar

ra′di·al *a.* of or like a ray or rays

radial (ply) tire tire with ply cords at right angles to center line of tread

ra′di·ant *a.* 1. beaming 2. shining bright 3. issuing in rays —**ra′di·ance** *n.*

ra′di·ate *v.* 1. send out rays, as of heat or light 2. branch out as from a center

ra′di·a′tion *n.* 1. a radiating 2. rays sent out 3. nuclear particles

ra′di·a′tor *n.* device for radiating heat

rad′i·cal *a.* 1. basic 2. favoring extreme change —*n.* 1. one with radical views 2. *Chem.* group of atoms acting as one —**rad′i·cal·ism** *n.* —**rad′i·cal·ly** *adv.*

ra′di·o *n.* [*pl.* -OS] 1. way of sending sounds through space by electromagnetic waves 2. set for receiving radio waves 3.

broadcasting by radio —*a.* of radio —*v.* [-OED, -OING] send by radio

ra·di·o·ac'tive *a.* emitting radiant energy by the disintegration of atomic nuclei —**ra'di·o·ac·tiv'i·ty** *n.*

ra·di·o·gram' *n.* message sent by radio

ra·di·ol'o·gy *n.* medical use of radiant energy —**ra'di·ol'o·gist** *n.*

ra'di·o·ther'a·py *n.* treatment of disease by X-rays or rays from radioactive substance

rad'ish *n.* edible pungent root of a certain plant

ra'di·um *n.* radioactive metallic chemical element

ra'di·us *n.* -DII (-dē ī), -DIUSES] **1.** straight line from the center to the outside of a circle or sphere **2.** area within the sweep of such a line **3.** thicker bone of the forearm

raf'fi·a *n.* fiber from leaves of a palm, used in weaving

raff'ish *a.* **1.** disreputable **2.** tawdry

raf'fle *n.* lottery —*v.* offer as a prize in a raffle

raft *n.* **1.** floating platform of logs fastened together **2.** inflatable boat **3.** [Col.] large quantity

raft'er *n.* beam in a roof

rag *n.* **1.** piece of torn or waste cloth **2.** *pl.* tattered clothes —*v.* [RAGGED, RAGGING] tease or scold

rag'a·muf'fin *n.* dirty, ragged child

rage *n.* **1.** furious anger **2.** craze; fad —*v.* **1.** show violent anger **2.** be unchecked

rag'ged *a.* **1.** shabby and torn **2.** wearing shabby clothes **3.** uneven; shaggy —**run ragged** tire out —**rag'ged·y** *a.*

rag'lan *a.* designating a sleeve that continues in one piece to the collar

ra·gout (ra gōō') *n.* stew

rag'time *n.* early jazz

rag'weed *n.* common weed whose pollen causes hay fever

raid *n.* sudden attack or invasion —*v.* make a raid on

rail *n.* **1.** bar put between posts as a guard or support **2.** either of the bars of a railroad track **3.** railroad **4.** small wading bird —*v.* speak bitterly

rail'ing *n.* fence made of rails and posts

rail'ler·y *n.* playful teasing

rail'road *n.* **1.** road with steel rails for trains **2.** system of such roads —*v.* [Col.] rush through unfairly

rail'way *n.* **1.** [Br.] railroad **2.** track with rails for cars

rai'ment (rā'-) *n.* [Ar.] attire

rain *n.* **1.** water falling in drops from the clouds **2.** rapid falling of many small objects —*v.* **1.** fall as or like rain **2.** give in large quantities —**rain'y** [-IER, -IEST] *a.*

rain'bow *n.* arc of colors formed by sunshine on rain

rain'coat *n.* waterproof coat

rain'drop *n.* single drop of rain

rain'fall *n.* **1.** fall of rain **2.** amount of rain over an area during a given time

rain'storm *n.* storm with heavy rain

raise *v.* 1. lift up 2. increase in amount, degree, etc. 3. build or put up 4. bring up 5. collect 6. make grow 7. inspire 8. rear (children) —*n.* a pay increase

rai'sin *n.* sweet dried grape

ra·jah, ra·ja (rä′jə) *n.* prince in India

rake *n.* 1. long-handled tool with teeth at one end 2. debauched man 3. slanting, as of a floor —*v.* 1. gather (leaves, etc.) with a rake 2. search carefully 3. sweep with gunfire —**rake in** gather much rapidly

rake′-off *n.* [Sl.] illegal commission or share

rak'ish (rāk′-) *a.* jaunty

ral'ly *v.* [-LIED, -LYING] 1. regroup to set in order 2. gather for a common aim 3. revive —*n.* [-LIES] a rallying 2. mass meeting

ram *n.* 1. male sheep 2. battering ram —*v.* [RAMMED, RAMMING] 1. strike against with force 2. force into place

ram'ble *v.* 1. stroll; roam 2. talk or write aimlessly 3. spread, as vines —*n.* a stroll

ram'bler *n.* 1. one who rambles 2. climbing rose

ram·bunc'tious (-shəs) *a.* disorderly; unruly

ram'e·kin *n.* small baking dish

ram'i·fy *v.* [-FIED, -FYING] spread out into branches —**ram'i·fi·ca'tion** *n.*

ramp *n.* 1. sloping passage joining different levels 2. wheeled staircase for boarding an airplane

ram·page' *v.* rush wildly about —*n.* (ram′pāj) wild, angry action: usually in **on the** (or **a**) **rampage**

ramp'ant *a.* 1. raging; wild 2. rearing up

ram'part *n.* fortified embankment

ram'rod *n.* rod for ramming down a charge in a gun

ram'shack'le *a.* rickety

ran *pt.* of **run**

ranch *n.* 1. large farm for raising livestock 2. kind of one-story house: in full, **ranch house** —*v.* work on a ranch —**ranch'er, ranch'man** [*pl.* -MEN] *n.*

ran'cid *a.* stale, as oil or fat; spoiled

ran'cor *n.* bitter hate or ill will —**ran'cor·ous** *a.*

ran'dom *a.* haphazard —**at random** haphazardly

ran'dy *a.* [-DIER, -DIEST] amorous; lustful

rang *pt.* of **ring**

range *v.* 1. set in rows 2. roam about 3. extend 4. vary between set limits —*n.* 1. row or line, esp. of mountains 2. effective distance 3. extent 4. open land for grazing livestock 5. place for shooting practice 6. place for testing rockets in flight 7. limits of possible variation 8. cooking stove

rang'er *n.* 1. trooper who patrols a region 2. warden who patrols forests 3. [*often* R-] soldier trained for close-combat raids

rang'y *a.* [-IER, -IEST] long-limbed and thin

rank *n.* 1. row; line 2. class or grade 3. *pl.* enlisted soldiers —*v.* 1. place in, or hold, a certain rank 2. outrank —*a.* 1. growing wildly 2. bad in taste or smell 3. utter —**rank and file** *n.* 1. enlisted soldiers 2. common people

rank'ing *a.* 1. of highest rank 2. prominent

ran'kle *v.* cause mental pain, resentment, etc.

ran'sack *v.* 1. search thoroughly 2. plunder; loot

ran'som *n.* 1. the freeing of a captive by paying money 2. price asked —*v.* buy a captive's freedom

rant *v.* talk wildly; rave

rap *v.* [RAPPED, RAPPING] 1. strike or knock sharply 2. [Sl.] to chat —*n.* 1. quick, sharp knock 2. [Sl.] a chat

ra·pa'cious (-shəs) *a.* 1. greedy; voracious 2. predatory —**ra·pac'i·ty** *n.*

rape *n.* crime of sexually attacking a woman —*v.* commit rape on —**rap'ist** *n.*

rap'id *a.* swift —**ra·pid'i·ty** *n.*, —**rap'id·ly** *adv.*

rap'ids *n.pl.* part of a river with very swift current

ra·pi'er (-ē-) *n.* light, sharp sword

rap·ine (rap'in) *n.* plunder

rap·port' (-pôr', -pōrt') *n.* sympathetic relationship; harmony

rap·proche·ment (ra prōsh'-män) *n.* friendly relations

rap·scal'lion (-yən) *n.* rascal

rapt *a.* engrossed (*in*)

rap'ture *n.* ecstasy

rare *a.* 1. scarce; uncommon 2. very good 3. not dense 4. cooked very little —**rare'ness** *n.* —**rar'i·ty** [-TIES] *n.*

rare'bit *n.* Welsh rabbit

rar'e·fy *v.* [-FIED, -FYING] make or become less dense —**rar'e·fac'tion** *n.*

rare'ly *adv.* seldom

ras'cal *n.* 1. rogue 2. mischievous child —**ras·cal'i·ty** *n.*

rash *a.* too hasty; reckless —*n.* red spots on the skin —**rash'ly** *adv.*

rash'er *n.* slice of bacon

rasp *v.* 1. scrape harshly 2. irritate —*n.* 1. rough file 2. grating sound

rasp'ber·ry (raz'-) *n.* [*pl.* -RIES] 1. shrub with red or black berries 2. the berry

rat *n.* 1. long-tailed rodent, larger than a mouse 2. [Sl.] contemptible person —*v.* [RATTED, RATTING] [Sl.] inform on others —**smell a rat** suspect a plot

ratch'et *n.* wheel or bar with slanted teeth that catch on a pawl

rate *n.* 1. relative amount or degree 2. price per unit 3. rank —*v.* 1. appraise 2. rank 3. [Col.] deserve

rath'er *adv.* 1. preferably 2. with more reason 3. more truly 4. on the contrary 5. somewhat

raths'kel·ler (rät'skel'-) *n.* restaurant below street level

rat'i·fy *v.* [-FIED, -FYING] approve formally —**rat'i·fi·ca'-tion** *n.*

rat'ing (rāt'-) *n.* 1. rank 2. appraisal

ra'tio (-shō) n. [pl. -TIOS] relation of one thing to another in size, etc.

ra·ti·o·ci·na'tion (rash'ē ō'sə-) n. reasoning by logic

ra'tion (raʃ'-, rā'-) n. fixed share, as of food —v. give in rations —ra'tion·ing n.

ra'tion·al (raʃ'-) a. 1. able to reason 2. reasonable —ra'tion·al'i·ty n. —ra'tion·al·ly adv.

ra·tion·ale (rash ə nal') n. reasons or explanation

ra'tion·al·ism n. belief in reason as the only authority

ra'tion·al·ize' v. give plausible explanations for —ra'tion·al·i·za'tion n.

rat·tan' n. palm stems used in wickerwork, etc.

rat'tle v. 1. make or cause to make a series of sharp, short sounds 2. chatter 3. [Col.] upset —n. 1. a rattling 2. baby's toy that rattles

rat'tle·snake n. snake with a tail that rattles: also rat'tler

rat'trap n. 1. trap for rats 2. [Col.] run-down building

rau'cous (rô'-) a. 1. hoarse 2. loud and rowdy

raun'chy a. [-CHIER, -CHIEST] [Sl.] risqué, lustful, etc.

rav'age (-ij) v., n. ruin

rave v. 1. talk wildly 2. praise greatly —n. [Sl.] enthusiastic praise

rav'el v. untwist; fray —n. raveled part or thread

ra'ven n. large black crow —a. black and shiny

rav'e·nous a. greedily hungry —rav'e·nous·ly adv.

ra·vine' (-vēn') n. long, deep hollow in the earth

rav'ing a. 1. frenzied 2. [Col.] remarkable

ra·vi·o·li (rav'ē ō'lē) n. dough casings holding meat, cheese, etc.

rav'ish v. 1. fill with great joy 2. rape

rav'ish·ing a. delightful

raw a. 1. uncooked 2. unprocessed 3. inexperienced 4. sore and inflamed 5. cold and damp 6. [Sl.] unfair —raw'ness n.

raw'boned a. lean; gaunt

raw'hide n. untanned cattle hide

ray n. 1. thin beam of light 2. stream of radiant energy 3. tiny amount 4. broad, flat fish

ray'on n. fabric made from cellulose

raze v. demolish

ra'zor n. sharp-edged instrument for shaving

razz v. [Sl.] make fun of

raz'zle-daz'zle n. [Sl.] flashy display

re (rē) prep. regarding

re- pref. 1. back 2. again: for list below add again to meaning of base word

re·ad·just'
re·af·firm'
re·ap·pear'
re·ap·point'
re·arm'
re·as·sem'ble
re·as·sign'
re·born'
re·broad'cast
re·build'
re·cap'ture

re·con·sid′er
re·con·struct′
re·dis·cov′er
re·dou′ble
re·ooh′o
re·e·lect′
re·en·act′
re·en·list′
re·en′ter
re′ex·am′ine
re·fi·nance′
re·fu′el
re·heat′
re·hire′
re·in·vest′
re·kin′dle
re·lo′cate
re·make′
re·mar′ry
re·o′pen
re·or′der
re·phrase′
re·play′
re·print′
re·read′
re·route′
re·tell′
re·u·nite′

reach v. 1. extend the hand, etc. 2. touch 3. get to 4. influence 5. get in touch with 6. try to get —n. act or extent of reaching

re·act′ v. 1. respond to stimulus 2. return to an earlier state 3. act with another substance in a chemical change —**re·ac′tion** n.

re·act′ant n. any substance involved in a chemical reaction

re·ac′tion·ar′y n. [pl. -IES], a. ultraconservative

re·ac′ti·vate v. make or become active again —**re·ac·ti·va′tion** n.

re·ac′tor n. nuclear reactor

read v. [READ (red), READING] 1. understand or utter (written or printed matter) 2. study 3. register, as a gauge 4. [Sl.] understand a radio message —**read′er** n.

read′er·ship′ n. all the readers of a magazine, etc.

read′ing n. 1. act of one that reads 2. thing to be read 3. interpretation 4. amount registered by a meter, etc.

read′y (red′ē) a. [-IER, -IEST] 1. prepared to act 2. willing 3. available v. [-IED, -YING] prepare —**read′i·ly** adv. —**read′i·ness** n.

read′y-made′ a. ready for use or sale at once

re·a′gent n. chemical used to detect or measure another substance or cause a reaction

re′al a. 1. actual; true 2. genuine —adv. [Col.] very —**re′al·ly** adv.

real estate land, including buildings, etc. on it

re′al·ism n. awareness of things as they really are —**re′al·ist** n. —**re′al·is′tic** a. —**re′al·is′ti·cal·ly** adv.

re·al′i·ty n. [pl. -TIES] 1. state of being real 2. real thing; fact

re′al·ize v. 1. understand fully 2. make real 3. gain 4. be sold for (a given sum) —**re′al·i·za′tion** n.

real′-life′ a. actual

realm (relm) n. 1. kingdom 2. region; sphere

Re·al·tor *n.* certified real-estate broker

re·al·ty *n.* real estate

ream *n.* quantity of 480 to 516 sheets of paper —*v.* enlarge (a hole) —**ream·er** *n.*

re·an·i·mate *v.* give new life or vigor to —**re·an·i·ma·tion** *n.*

reap *v.* 1. cut and gather (grain, etc.) 2. obtain as reward of action, etc. —**reap·er** *n.*

re·ap·por·tion *v.* adjust the representation pattern of a (legislature) —**re·ap·por·tion·ment** *n.*

rear *n.* 1. back part or place 2. part of army farthest from combat —*a.* of or at the rear —*v.* 1. bring up; raise 2. rise on the hind legs 3. build; erect —**rear·ward** *a., adv.*

rear admiral naval officer above a captain

re·ar·range *v.* arrange in a different way —**re·ar·range·ment** *n.*

rea·son *n.* 1. explanation 2. cause 3. power to think 4. good sense 5. sanity —*v.* think or argue with logic —**rea·son·ing** *n.*

rea·son·a·ble *a.* 1. fair 2. sensible 3. not expensive —**rea·son·a·bly** *adv.*

re·as·sure *v.* restore to confidence —**re·as·sur·ance** *n.*

re·bate *v., n.* return (of) part of a payment

reb·el *n.* one who openly resists authority —*a.* rebellious —*v.* (ri bel') [-ELLED, -ELLING]

resist authority —**re·bel·lion** *n.* —**re·bel·lious** *a.*

re·bound' *v.* spring or bounce back; recoil —*n.* (rē'bound) a rebounding or a ball, etc. that rebounds

re·buff' *v., n.* snub

re·buke' *v.* scold sharply —*n.* sharp scolding

re'bus *n.* puzzle in which pictures stand for words

re·but' *v.* [-BUTTED, -BUTTING] contradict formally —**re·but'tal** *n.*

re·cal'ci·trant *a.* refusing to obey —**re·cal'ci·trance** *n.*

re·call' *v.* 1. call back 2. remember 3. revoke —*n.* (rē'kôl) 1. a recalling 2. removal of an official from office by popular vote

re·cant' *v.* renounce (one's beliefs) —**re·can·ta'tion** *n.*

re·cap' *v.* [-CAPPED, -CAPPING] put new tread on (worn tire) —*n.* (rē'kap) recapped tire

re·cede' *v.* move or slope backward

re·ceipt' (-sēt') *n.* 1. a receiving 2. written acknowledgment of sum received 3. *pl.* amount received —*v.* mark a bill paid

re·ceiv'a·ble *a.* due

re·ceive' *v.* 1. get; be given 2. greet (guests) 3. react to 4. learn (news, etc.) 5. hold

re·ceiv'er *n.* 1. one who receives 2. one holding in trust property in bankruptcy, etc. 3. apparatus that converts electrical signals into sound or light, as in radio or TV

re·cent a. of a short time ago —**re′cent·ly** adv.

re·cep·ta·cle n. container

re·cep·tion n. 1. a receiving or being received 2. social function 3. the receiving of signals on radio or TV

re·cep·tion·ist n. employee who receives callers, etc.

re·cep·tive a. ready to receive suggestions, etc.

re·cep·tor n. nerve ending that feels heat, pressure, pain, etc.

re·cess n. 1. hollow in a wall 2. break from work —v. (ri ses′) 1. take a recess 2. set back

re·ces·sion n. temporary falling off of business

re·ces·sion·al n. hymn at end of church service when clergy and choir march out

re·ces·sive a. tending to recede

re·cher·ché (rə sher′shā) a. 1. rare 2. too refined

rec′i·pe n. directions for preparing dish or drink

re·cip·i·ent n. one that receives

re·cip·ro·cal a. 1. done, etc. in return 2. mutual 3. reversed 4. complementary —n. complement, counterpart, etc. —**re·cip′ro·cal·ly** adv. —**rec·i·proc′i·ty** (-präs′-) n.

re·cit·al (-sīt′-) n. 1. account told 2. musical program

re·cite′ v. 1. repeat something memorized 2. narrate —**rec′i·ta′tion** n.

reck′less a. heedless; rash —

reck′less·ly adv. —**reck′less·ness** n.

reck′on v. 1. count 2. estimate 3. [Col.] suppose —**reckon with** deal with

reck′on·ing n. 1. a figuring out 2. settlement of accounts

re·claim′ v. 1. make (desert or wasteland) usable 2. recover (useful materials) from waste products —**rec′la·ma′tion** n.

re·cline′ v. lie down or lean back

re·cluse n. one who lives a secluded, solitary life

rec′og·nize′ v. 1. identify as known before 2. perceive 3. acknowledge; notice formally —**rec′og·ni′tion** n. —**rec′og·niz′a·ble** a.

re·coil′ v. 1. pull back 2. spring back, as a gun when fired —n. (rē′koil) a recoiling

rec·ol·lect′ v. remember —**rec′ol·lec′tion** n.

rec·om·mend′ v. 1. suggest as fit or worthy 2. advise —**rec′om·men·da′tion** n.

rec′om·pense′ v. pay or pay back —n. compensation

rec′on·cile′ (-sīl) v. 1. make friendly again 2. settle (a quarrel) 3. make agree or fit 4. make acquiescent (to) —**rec′on·cil′a·ble** a. —**rec·on·cil′i·a′tion** (-sil′-) n.

rec′on·dite a. abstruse

re·con·di′tion v. put back in good condition

re·con·nais·sance (-ə səns) n. a spying on an area

rec·on·noi′ter v. examine or spy on an area

re·cord′ v. 1. keep a written

account of 2. show on a dial, etc. 3. put sound on a grooved disc, tape, etc. —*n.* (rek'ərd) 1. official account 2. known facts 3. grooved disc with recorded sound 4. the best yet done — *a.* (rek'ərd) best

re·cord'er *n.* 1. official who keeps records 2. tape recorder 3. early form of flute

re·cord'ing *n.* phonograph record

re·count' *v.* narrate

re'-count' *v.* count again —*n.* (rē'kount) second count

re·coup' (-kōōp') *v.* make up for, as a loss

re'course *n.* 1. a turning for aid 2. source of aid

re·cov'er *v.* 1. get back; regain 2. become normal 3. keep from a fall 4. reclaim 5. *Sports* regain control of a fumbled ball, etc. —**re·cov'er·y** [*pl.* -IES] *n.*

recovery room hospital room where patients are first cared for after surgery

rec're·ant *a.* 1. cowardly 2. disloyal —*n.* 1. coward 2. traitor

rec're·a'tion *n.* refreshing play —**rec're·a'tion·al** *a.*

re·crim'i·nate *v.* accuse one's accuser —**re·crim'i·na'tion** *n.*

re·cru·des'cence *n.* a breaking out again, esp. of something bad —**re·cru·des'cent** *a.*

re·cruit' (-krōōt') *n.* new member, soldier, etc. —*v.* enlist (recruits) —**re·cruit'er** *n.*

rec'tal *a.* of, for, or near the rectum

rec'tan'gle *n.* four-sided figure with four right angles —**rec·tan'gu·lar** *a.*

rec'ti·fy *v.* [-FIED, -FYING] 1. to correct; amend 2. convert (alternating current) into direct current —**rec'ti·fi·ca'tion** *n.* —**rec'ti·fi'er** *n.*

rec'ti·lin'e·ar *a.* bounded or formed by straight lines

rec'ti·tude *n.* honesty

rec'tor *n.* head of some schools or parishes

rec'to·ry *n.* [*pl.* -RIES] rector's residence

rec'tum *n.* lowest part of the intestine

re·cum'bent *a.* lying down

re·cu'per·ate *v.* to recover health, losses, etc. —**re·cu'per·a'tion** *n.*

re·cur' *v.* [-CURRED, -CURRING] 1. occur again 2. return in talk, etc. —**re·cur'rence** *n.* —**re·cur'rent** *a.*

re·cy'cle (-sī'-) *v.* 1. pass through a cycle again 2. use again and again, as the same water, paper, etc.

red *n.* color of blood 2. [R-] communist —*a.* [REDDER, REDDEST] of the color red —**red'dish** *a.* —**red'ness** *n.*

red'cap *n.* porter in a railroad or bus station

red carpet very grand or impressive welcome (used with *the*) —**red'-car'pet** *a.*

red'coat *n.* British soldier in a uniform with a red coat

red'den *v.* make or become red

re·deem' *v.* 1. buy back 2. pay off 3. turn in for a prize 4. free, as from sin 5. atone

for —re·deem'a·ble a. —re·
deem'er n. —re·demp'tion
n.

red'-hand'ed a. while commit-
ting a crime

red'head n. person with red
hair —red'head'ed a.

red herring something used to
divert attention from the basic
issue

red'-hot' a. 1. glowing hot 2.
very excited 3. very new

red'-let'ter a. memorable

red man N. American Indian

re·do' v. [-DID, -DONE, -DOING]
1. do again 2. redecorate

red'o·lent a. 1. fragrant 2.
smelling (of) 3. suggesting —
red'o·lence n.

re·doubt' (-dout') n. fortified
stronghold

re·doubt'a·ble a. 1. formida-
ble 2. commanding respect

re·dound' v. have a result

re·dress' v. correct and make
up for —n. (rē'dres) a redress-
ing

red snapper ocean food fish

red tape rules and details that
waste time and effort

re·duce' v. 1. lessen; decrease
2. change the form of 3. lower,
as in rank 4. lose weight —re·
duc'tion n.

re·dun'dant a. 1. excess; su-
perfluous 2. wordy —re·dun'-
dan·cy [-CIES] n.

red'wood n. 1. giant evergreen
2. its reddish wood

reed n. 1. a hollow-stemmed
grass 2. musical pipe made of
this 3. vibrating strip in some
musical instruments —reed'y
[-IER, -IEST] a.

reef n. ridge of sand, rock, etc.
near the surface of water —v.
take in part of a sail

reek v., n. (emit) a strong, offensive smell

reel n. 1. spool or frame on
which thread, film, etc. is
wound 2. amount wound on it
3. lively dance —v. 1. sway,
stagger, etc., as from dizziness
2. whirl; spin —reel in wind
on a reel —reel off tell, write,
etc. fluently —reel out unwind from a reel

re·en'try, re-en'try n. [pl.
-TRIES] a coming back, as of a
spacecraft into the earth's atmosphere

ref n., v. referee

re·fec'tion n. light meal

re·fec'to·ry n. [pl. -RIES] dining hall

re·fer' v. [-FERRED, -FERRING]
1. go to, or direct someone to,
for aid, information, etc. 2. al-
lude (to)

ref·er·ee' n. 1. one chosen to
decide something 2. judge in
certain sports —v. act as referee (in)

ref'er·ence n. 1. a referring 2.
relation or connection 3. mention of a source of information
4. such a source 5. recommendation, or person giving it
—make reference to mention

ref·er·en'dum n. submission
of a law to direct popular vote

re·fer'ral n. 1. a referring or
being referred 2. person referred to another person

re·fill' v. fill again —n. (rē'fil)
1. unit to refill a special con-

tainer 2. a refilling of a prescription

re·fine′ v. free from impurities, coarseness, crudeness, etc. —**re·fine′ment** n.

re·fined′ a. 1. purified 2. cultivated or elegant

re·fin′er·y n. [pl. -IES] plant for purifying materials

re·flect′ v. 1. throw back, as an image or sound 2. result in (credit, etc.) 3. think seriously (on or upon) 4. cast blame (on or upon) —**re·flec′tion** n.

re·flec′tive a. —**re·flec′tor** n.

re′flex a., n. (designating or of) an involuntary reaction to a stimulus

re·flex′ive a. 1. designating a verb whose subject and object are the same 2. designating a pronoun used as object of such a verb

re·form′ v. 1. improve 2. behave or make behave better —n. improvement

ref′or·ma′tion n. 1. a reforming 2. [R-] 16th-century movement establishing the Protestant churches

re·form′a·to·ry n. [pl. -RIES] institution for reforming young lawbreakers

re·form′er n. one who seeks political or social reform

re·fract′ v. bend (a light ray, etc.) —**re·frac′tion** n.

re·frac′to·ry a. obstinate

re·frain′ v. hold back —n. repeated verse of a song

re·fresh′ v. make fresh or stronger; renew or revive

re·fresh′ing a. 1. that re-

freshes 2. pleasingly new or different

re·fresh′ment n. 1. a refreshing 2. pl. food or drink

re·frig′er·ate (-frij′-) v. make cold, as for preserving —**re·frig′er·ant** a., n. —**re·frig′er·a′tion** n.

re·frig′er·a·tor n. box or room for refrigerating

ref′uge (-yōōj) n. protection from danger or pursuit

ref·u·gee′ (-jē′) n. one who flees to seek refuge

re·ful′gent (-ful′jənt) a. shining; radiant

re·fund′ v. give back (money, etc.) —n. (rē′fund) amount refunded

re·fur′bish v. renovate

re·fuse′ (-fyōōz′) v. 1. reject 2. decline (to do, etc.) —n. (ref′yōōs) rubbish —**re·fus′al** n.

re·fute′ v. prove wrong —**ref′u·ta′tion** n.

re·gain′ v. get back; recover

re′gal a. royal

re·gale′ v. entertain, as with a feast

re·ga′li·a n.pl. insignia or decorations, as of a rank

re·gard′ n. 1. concern 2. affection and respect 3. reference 4. pl. good wishes —v. 1. gaze upon 2. think of; consider 3. concern —**as regards** concerning —**re·gard′ful** a.

re·gard′ing prep. about

re·gard′less adv. [Col.] without regard for objections, etc.; anyway —**regardless of** in spite of

re·gat′ta (-gät′-) n. boat race

re·gen'er·ate v. 1. give new lift to; renew 2. improve —a. (-it) renewed or improved —**re·gen'er·a'tion** n.

re'gent (-jənt) n. interim ruler in place of a monarch —**re'gen·cy** [pl. -CIES] n.

reg'i·cide (rej'-) n. killer or killing of a king

re·gime (rə zhēm', rā-) n. political or ruling system

reg'i·men (rej'-) n. system of diet, exercise, etc.

reg'i·ment n. section of an army division —v. control with strict discipline —**reg'i·men'tal** a. —**reg'i·men·ta'tion** n.

re'gion n. area, division, or part —**re'gion·al** a.

re'gion·al·ism n. 1. regional quality or character 2. word, etc. peculiar to some region

reg'is·ter n. 1. list of names, etc. 2. book in which this is kept 3. recording device, as for cash transactions 4. device for adjusting passage of air 5. musical range —v. 1. enter in a list 2. show 3. make an impression —**reg'is·trant** (-trənt) n. —**reg'is·tra'tion** n.

registered nurse trained nurse who has passed a State examination

reg'is·trar (-trär) n. keeper of records, as in a college

re·gress' v. go backward —**re·gres'sion** n. —**re·gres'sive** a.

re·gret' v. [-GRETTED, -GRETTING] be sorry for (a mistake, etc.) —n. sorrow, esp. over one's acts or omissions —**re·gret'ful** a. —**re·gret'ta·ble** a.

reg'u·lar a. 1. according to rule; orderly 2. customary or established 3. consistent 4. functioning in a normal way 5. properly qualified 6. [Col.] thorough; complete 7. [Col.] pleasant, friendly, etc. —n. regular player, etc. —**reg'u·lar'i·ty** n. —**reg'u·lar·ly** adv.

reg'u·late v. 1. control 2. adjust to a standard, etc. 3. adjust so as to make work accurately —**reg'u·la'tive, reg'u·la·to'ry** a. —**reg'u·la'tor** n.

reg'u·la'tion n. 1. a regulating 2. rule —a. usual

re·gur'gi·tate (-jə-) v. bring up from the stomach —**re·gur'gi·ta'tion** n.

re·ha·bil'i·tate v. restore to earlier state, condition, etc. —**re·ha·bil'i·ta'tion** n.

re·hash' v. go over again —n. (rē'hash) a rehashing

re·hearse' (-hurs') v. 1. recite 2. practice for a performance —**re·hears'al** n.

reign (rān) n. (period of) a sovereign's rule —v. 1. rule as sovereign 2. prevail

re·im·burse' v. pay back —**re·im·burse'ment** n.

rein (rān) n. 1. usually pl. strap hooked to a bit for controlling a horse 2. pl. means of controlling, etc. —**give (free) rein to** free from restraint

re'in·car·na'tion n. rebirth (of the soul) in another body —**re'in·car'nate** v.

rein'deer (rān'-) n. [pl. -DEER] large northern deer

re·in·force' v. strengthen —**re'in·force'ment** n.

re·in·state' v. restore —**re'in·state'ment** n.

re·it'er·ate v. repeat —**re·it'er·a'tion** n.

re·ject' v. 1. refuse to accept 2. discard —n. (rē'jekt) thing or person rejected —**re·jec'·tion** n.

re·joice' v. be or make happy —**re·joic'ing** n.

re·join' v. 1. join again 2. answer —**re·join'der** n.

re·ju've·nate v. make feel or seem young again —**re·ju've·na'tion** n.

re·lapse' v. fall back into a past state —n. a relapsing

re·late' v. 1. narrate 2. connect, as in meaning 3. have reference (to)

re·lat'ed a. connected, as by origin, kinship, etc.

re·la'tion n. 1. a relating or being related 2. kinship 3. a relative 4. pl. dealings, as between people —**in** (or **with**) **relation to** concerning; regarding —**re·la'tion·ship** n.

rel'a·tive a. 1. related 2. relevant 3. comparative —n. related person —**rel'a·tive·ly** adv.

rel'a·tiv'i·ty n. 1. a being relative 2. Physics theory of the relative character of velocity, mass, etc., and the interdependence of matter, time, and space

re·lax' v. 1. loosen up 2. rest, as from work —**re·lax·a'tion** n.

re'lay n. fresh group of workers, runners, etc. —v. (ri lā') get and pass on

relay race a race between teams, each member of which goes part of the distance

re·lease' v. 1. set free 2. allow to be issued —n. 1. a releasing 2. device to release a catch 3. a book, news item, etc. released to the public

rel'e·gate v. 1. exile 2. put into a lower position 3. assign —**rel'e·ga'tion** n.

re·lent' v. become less stern

re·lent'less a. 1. pitiless 2. persistent

rel'e·vant a. pertinent —**rel'e·vance, rel'e·van·cy** n.

re·li'a·ble a. that can be relied on —**re·li'a·bil'i·ty** n. —**re·li'a·bly** adv.

re·li'ance n. trust or confidence —**re·li'ant** a.

rel'ic n. 1. something from the past 2. venerated remains, etc. of a saint

re·lief' n. 1. a relieving 2. thing that relieves 3. public aid, as to the poor 4. projection, as sculpture, from a flat surface —a. designating a baseball pitcher who replaces another during a game

re·lieve' v. 1. to ease; comfort 2. give aid to 3. free by replacing 4. bring a pleasant change to

re·li'gion n. 1. belief in God or gods 2. system of worship

re·li'gious a. 1. devout 2. of or about religion 3. very careful —n. nun or monk

re·lin'quish v. let go

rel'ish n. 1. pleasing flavor 2.

enjoyment 3. pickles, etc. served with a meal —v. enjoy

re·live' v. experience (a past event) again, as in the imagination

re·luc'tant a. unwilling —re·luc'tance n. —re·luc'tant·ly adv.

re·ly' v. [-LIED, -LYING] trust; depend (on or upon)

rem n. [pl. REM] a standard unit of absorbed radiation

re·main' v. 1. be left when part is gone 2. stay 3. continue

re·main'der n. 1. those remaining 2. what is left when part is taken away, as in subtraction

re·mains' n.pl. 1. part left 2. dead body

re·mand' v. send back

re·mark' v., n. (make) a brief comment or observation

re·mark'a·ble a. unusual —re·mark'a·bly adv.

re·me'di·al a. corrective

rem'e·dy n. [pl. -DIES] thing that corrects, etc. —v. [-DIED, -DYING] to correct, cure, etc.

re·mem'ber v. 1. think of again 2. recall 3. bear in mind

re·mem'brance n. 1. a remembering 2. souvenir

re·mind' v. cause to remember —re·mind'er n.

rem'i·nis'cence n. 1. memory 2. pl. account of remembered events —rem·i·nisce' v. —rem'i·nis'cent a.

re·miss' a. careless

re·mit' v. [-MITTED, -MITTING] 1. forgive 2. refrain from exacting 3. slacken 4. send

money —re·mis'sion n. —re·mit'tance n.

rem'nant n. part left over

re·mod'el v. rebuild

re·mon'strate v. say in protest —re·mon'strance n.

re·morse' n. deep sense of guilt —re·morse'ful a. —re·morse'less a.

re·mote' a. 1. distant 2. slight —re·mote'ly adv.

remote control control of aircraft, missiles, etc. from a distance, as by radio waves

re·move' v. 1. take away 2. dismiss 3. get rid of —re·mov'al n.

re·mu'ner·ate v. pay for; reward —re·mu'ner·a'tion n. —re·mu'ner·a·tive a.

ren'ais·sance (-ǝ säns) n. rebirth; revival: also re·nas'cence —re·nas'cent a.

re'nal a. of the kidneys

rend v. [RENT, RENDING] tear; split apart

ren'der v. 1. submit 2. give in return 3. cause to be 4. perform 5. translate 6. melt (fat) —ren·di'tion n.

ren·dez·vous (rän'dā vōō) n. appointed meeting (place) —v. meet as agreed

ren'e·gade n. traitor

re·nege (ri nig') v. 1. go back on a promise 2. play a card not of the suit called for

re·new' v. 1. make new again 2. begin again 3. replenish (a supply) —re·new'al n.

re·nounce' v. 1. give up (a claim, etc.) 2. disown —re·nounce'ment n.

ren'o·vate v. make like new;

restore —ren′o·va′tion n. —ren′o·va′tor n.

re·nown′ n. great fame —re·nowned′ a.

rent n. 1. payment for the use of property 2. a rip —v. get or give rent for —for rent available to be rented —rent′er n.

rent′al n. 1. rate of rent 2. thing for rent —a. of or for rent

re·nun′ci·a′tion n. a renouncing, as of a right

re·pair′ v. 1. fix; mend 2. make amends for 3. go (to) —n. a repairing or being repaired

rep′a·ra′tion n. 1. a making of amends 2. compensation, as for war damage

rep·ar·tee′ n. quick, witty reply; banter

re·past′ n. a meal

re·pa′tri·ate v. return to the country of birth, citizenship, etc. —re·pa′tri·a′tion n.

re·pay′ v. [-PAID, -PAYING] pay back —re·pay′ment n.

re·peal′ v. revoke; annul (a law) —n. revocation

re·peat′ v. say or do again —n. 1. a repeating 2. anything repeated —re·peat′ed·ly adv. —re·peat′er n.

re·pel′ v. [-PELLED, -PELLING] 1. force back 2. disgust 3. cause (insects, etc.) to stay away 4. be resistant to (water, dirt, etc.) —re·pel′lent a., n.

re·pent′ v. feel sorry for (a sin, etc.) —re·pent′ance n. —re·pent′ant a.

re′per·cus′sion (-kush′ən) n.

1. echo 2. reaction, often an indirect one

rep′er·toire′ (-twär) n. stock of plays, songs, etc. that a company, singer, etc. is prepared to perform: also rep′er·to′ry [pl. -RIES]

rep′e·ti′tion n. 1. a repeating 2. thing repeated —rep′e·ti′tious a. —re·pet′i·tive a.

re·pine′ v. feel or express discontent (at)

re·place′ v. 1. put back 2. take the place of 3. put another in place of —re·place′ment n.

re·plen′ish v. fill again —re·plen′ish·ment n.

re·plete′ a. filled —re·ple′tion n.

rep′li·ca n. exact copy

re·ply′ v. [-PLIED, -PLYING] respond or answer —n. [pl. -PLIES] answer

re·port′ v. 1. give an account of 2. tell as news; announce 3. denounce (an offender, etc.) to one in authority 4. present oneself —n. 1. statement or account 2. rumor 3. formal presentation of facts 4. loud explosive noise —re·port′ed·ly adv.

report card periodic written report on a student's progress

re·port′er n. one who gathers and reports news

re·pose′ v. 1. to place for rest 2. rest 3. lie dead 4. place (trust, etc.) in someone —n. 1. rest 2. sleep 3. calm; peace

re·pos′i·to′ry n. [pl. -RIES] place where things may be put for safekeeping

re·pos·sess' v. get possession of again; spec., take back from a defaulting buyer

rep·re·hend' v. scold or blame —**rep're·hen'si·ble** a.

rop·re·sent' v. 1. portray or describe 2. symbolize 3. act in place of 4. be an example or equivalent of

rep're·sen·ta'tion n. 1. a representing 2. legislators collectively 3. likeness, picture, etc. 4. often pl. statement of claims, facts, etc. —**rep're·sen·ta'tion·al** a.

rep're·sent'a·tive a. 1. representing 2. typical example n. 1. typical example 2. one chosen to act for others 3. [R-] Congressional or State legislator

re·press' v. 1. hold back 2. subdue 3. force (painful ideas, etc.) into the unconscious —**re·pres'sion** n. —**re·pres'sive** a.

re·prieve' v. 1. delay the execution of (one sentenced to die) 2. give temporary relief to —n. a reprieving or being reprieved

rep'ri·mand n., v. rebuke

re·pris'al n. injury done for injury received

re·proach' v. blame; rebuke —n. 1. disgrace 2. a scolding or blaming —**re·proach'ful** a.

rep'ro·bate a. depraved —n. depraved person

re·pro·duce' v. produce copies, offspring, etc. —**re'pro·duc'tion** n. —**re'pro·duc'tive** a.

re·proof' n. a reproving; rebuke: also **re·prov'al**

re·prove' v. find fault with

rep·tile n. coldblooded, creeping vertebrate, as a snake, lizard, etc. —**rep·til'i·an** a.

re·pub'lic n. government by elected representatives —**re·pub'li·can** a., n.

re·pu'di·ate v. disown; cast off —**re·pu'di·a'tion** n.

re·pug'nant a. 1. opposed 2. distasteful; offensive —**re·pug'nance** n.

re·pulse' v. 1. repel 2. rebuff —**re·pul'sion** n.

re·pul'sive a. disgusting

rep'u·ta·ble a. having a good reputation

rep'u·ta'tion n. 1. others' opinion of one 2. favorable estimation 3. fame

re·pute' v. consider to be —n. 2. thing asked for —v. ask for reputation —**re·put'ed** a. —**re·put'ed·ly** adv.

re·quest' n. 1. an asking for 2. thing asked for —v. ask for

Re'qui·em, re'qui·om (rek'-wē-, räk'-) n. R.C.Ch. Mass for the dead

re·quire' v. 1. to demand 2. to need —**re·quire'ment** n.

req'ui·site (rek'wə zit) a. required; necessary —n. something requisite

req'ui·si'tion n. written order —v. demand or take

re·quite' v. repay for —**re·quit'al** n.

re·route' v. send by a different route

re'run n. showing of a movie or TV program after the first showing

re·scind' (-sind') v. cancel; repeal (a law, etc.) —**re·scis'sion** (-sizh'ən) n.

res'cue v. free or save —n. a rescuing —**res'cu·er** n.

re·search' (or rē'sûrch) n. careful study in a subject —v. do research

re·sec'tion n. surgical removal of part of an organ, etc.

re·sem'ble v. be like —**re·sem'blance** n.

re·sent' v. feel anger at —**re·sent'ful** a. —**re·sent'ment** n.

res'er·va'tion n. 1. a reserving, as of a hotel room 2. public land set aside as for Indians

re·serve' v. keep back; set aside —n. 1. thing reserved 2. limitation 3. reticence 4. pl. troops subject to call —**in re·serve** reserved for later use —**re·served'** a.

res'er·voir (-vwär) n. 1. place for storing water 2. large supply

re·side' v. 1. live (in or at) 2. be present (in)

res'i·dence n. 1. a residing 2. home —**res'i·dent** a., n. —**res'i·den'tial** (-shal) a.

res'i·due n. part that is left —**re·sid'u·al** a.

re·sign' (-zīn') v. give up (a claim, position, etc.) —**resign oneself** (to) submit (to); accept —**res'ig·na'tion** n. —**re·signed'** a.

re·sil'ient (-zil'-) a. bouncing back; elastic —**re·sil'ience, re·sil'ien·cy** n.

res'in n. 1. substance from trees used in varnish, etc. 2. rosin —**res'in·ous** a.

re·sist' v. 1. withstand 2. fight against —**re·sist'er** n.

re·sist'ance n. 1. power to resist 2. opposition to another force —**re·sist'ant** a.

re·sis'tor n. device in an electrical circuit providing resistance

re·sole' v. put a new sole on (a shoe, etc.)

res'o·lute a. firm; determined —**res'o·lute'ly** adv.

res'o·lu'tion n. 1. a resolving 2. formal statement, as of a group 3. determination

re·solve' v. 1. decide 2. solve 3. change —n. fixed purpose —**re·solved'** a.

res'o·nant a. 1. resounding 2. intensifying sound 3. vibrant; sonorous —**res'o·nance** n.

res'o·na'tor n. device that produces resonance

re·sort' v. 1. go often 2. turn for help (to) —n. 1. place for a vacation, etc. 2. source of help

re·sound' (-zound') v. make a loud, echoing sound

re·sound'ing a. 1. reverberating 2. complete

re·source' (or rē'sôrs) n. 1. ready supply 2. pl. wealth 3. resourcefulness

re·source'ful a. able to handle problems, etc. —**re·source'ful·ness** n.

re·spect' v. 1. think highly of 2. show consideration for —n. 1. honor 2. consideration 3. pl. regards 4. reference —**re·spect'ful** a. —**re·spect'ful·ly** adv.

re·spect'a·ble a. 1. of good reputation 2. of moderate quality or size 3. presentable —**re·spect'a·bil'i·ty** n.

re·spect'ing *prep.* concerning

re·spec'tive *a.* of or for each separately —**re·spec'tive·ly** *adv.*

res·pi·ra'tion *n.* act or process of breathing —**res'pi·ra·to·ry** *a.*

res'pi·ra·tor *n.* device to aid breathing artificially

res'pite (-pit) *n.* 1. a delay 2. period of relief or rest

re·splend'ent *a.* dazzling —**re·splend'ence** *n.*

re·spond' *v.* 1. to answer 2. react 3. react favorably

re·sponse' *n.* 1. a reply 2. reaction —**re·spon'sive** *a.*

re·spon'si·ble *a.* 1. obliged to do or answer for 2. involving duties 3. accountable 4. dependable —**re·spon·si·bil'i·ty** [*pl.* -TIES] *n.*

rest *n.* 1. sleep 2. ease or inactivity 3. peace 4. support 5. pause 6. remainder —*v.* 1. sleep 2. get, or be at, ease 3. become still 4. lie or lay 5. depend —**lay to rest** bury —**rest'ful** *a.*

res'tau·rant (-tə-) *n.* place for buying and eating meals

res·ti·tu'tion *n.* 1. a giving back 2. reimbursement

res'tive *a.* restless or unruly

rest'less *a.* 1. uneasy 2. disturbed 3. active 4. discontented

re·store' *v.* 1. give back 2. return to a former position, condition, etc. —**res'to·ra'tion** *n.* —**re·stor'a·tive** *a., n.*

re·strain' *v.* hold back from action; suppress

re·straint' *n.* 1. a restraining 2. thing that restrains 3. self-control

re·strict' *v.* limit; confine —**re·stric'tion** *n.* —**re·stric'tive** *a.*

rest'room *n.* public room with toilets and washbowls: also **rest room**

re·struc'ture *v.* to plan a new structure or organization for

re·sult' *v.* 1. happen as an effect 2. end (*in*) —*n.* 1. what is caused; outcome 2. mathematical answer —**re·sult'ant** *a., n.*

re·sume' *v.* 1. take again 2. continue after interruption —**re·sump'tion** *n.*

ré·su·mé (rez'oo mā, rā'zoo-) *n.* summary, esp. of employment experience

re·sur'face *v.* 1. put a new surface on 2. come to the surface again

re·sur'gent *a.* rising again —**re·sur'gence** *n.*

res·ur·rect' *v.* bring back to life, use, etc. —**res'ur·rec'tion** *n.*

re·sus'ci·tate (-sus'ə-) *v.* revive, as one almost dead —**re·sus'ci·ta'tion** *n.*

re'tail *n.* sale of goods in small amounts to consumers —*a.* of such sale —*adv.* at retail prices —*v.* sell at retail —**re'tail·er** *n.*

re·tain' *v.* 1. keep in possession, use, etc. 2. keep in mind 3. hire (a lawyer)

re·tain'er *n.* 1. one that retains 2. servant to a rich person or family 3. fee paid to hire a lawyer

re·take' v. [-TOOK, -TAKEN, -TAKING] take again —n. (rē'tāk) scene photographed again

re·tal'i·ate v. return injury for injury —re·tal'i·a'tion n. —re·tal'i·a·to'ry a.

re·tard' v. slow down; delay —re·tar·da'tion n.

re·tard'ant n. substance that delays chemical reaction

re·tard'ate n. mentally retarded person

re·tard'ed a. slow in development, esp. mentally

retch v. strain to vomit

re·ten'tion n. 1. a retaining 2. ability to retain —re·ten'tive a.

ret'i·cent a. disinclined to speak —ret'i·cence n.

ret'i·na n. [pl. -NAS, -NAE (-nē)] part at the back of the eyeball, on which images are formed

ret'i·nue (-'n ōō) n. attendants on a person of rank

re·tire' v. 1. withdraw or retreat 2. withdraw from one's career, etc. 3. go to bed 4. pay off (bonds, etc.) 5. *Baseball* put out (a batter, side, etc.) —re·tir'ee' n. —re·tire'ment n.

re·tired' a. 1. secluded 2. no longer working

re·tir'ing a. shy; modest

re·tool' v. adapt (factory machinery) for different use

re·tort' v. reply sharply or cleverly —n. 1. sharp or clever reply 2. container for distilling, etc.

re·touch' v. touch up

re·trace' v. go back over

re·tract' v. 1. draw back or in 2. withdraw, as a charge —re·trac'tion n.

re'tread' v., n. recap

re·treat' n. 1. withdrawal, esp. under attack 2. quiet place 3. period of contemplation —v. withdraw

re·trench' v. economize

ret'ri·bu'tion n. deserved punishment

re·trieve' (-trēv') v. 1. get back or bring back 2. make good (a loss or error) 3. recover (data) stored in computer 4. bring back killed or wounded game: said of hunting dogs —re·triev'al n.

re·triev'er n. dog trained to retrieve game

ret'ro·ac'tive a. effective as of a prior date

ret'ro·fire v. fire a retrorocket

ret'ro·grade a. 1. moving backward 2. getting worse

ret'ro·gress v. move backward, esp. into a worse state —ret'ro·gres'sion n.

ret'ro·rock'et n. small rocket on spacecraft fired opposite to flight direction to reduce landing speed

ret'ro·spect n. contemplation of the past —ret'ro·spec'tion n.

ret'ro·spec'tive a. looking back on the past —n. show of works of an artist's lifetime

ret'si·na, ret'zi·na (-si na) n. Greek wine flavored with pine resin

re·turn' v. 1. go or come back 2. bring or send back 3. repay, as a visit 4. yield (profit) 5.

reelect —n. 1. a returning 2. something returned 3. recurrence 4. requital 5. often pl. yield or profit 6. often pl. official report, as of an election 7. income tax form —a. of, for, or given as a return —in **return** as a return

re·u'ni·fy v. [-FIED, -FYING] unify again after being divided —re·u'ni·fi·ca'tion n.

re·un'ion n. a coming together again

rev v. [REVVED, REVVING] [Col.] increase speed of an engine (used with *up*)

re·vamp' v. renovate; redo

re·veal' v. 1. make known, as a secret 2. show

re·veil·le (rev'a lē) n. Mil. morning signal to wake up

rev'el v. 1. make merry 2. take pleasure (*in*) —n. merrymaking —rev'el·ry [pl. -RIES] n.

rev·e·la'tion n. 1. a revealing 2. striking disclosure

re·venge' v., n. harm in return —re·venge'ful a.

rev'e·nue n. government's income from taxes, etc.

re·ver'ber·ate v. reecho —re·ver'ber·a'tion n.

re·vere' v. show deep respect or love for —rev'er·ence n. —rev'er·ent a.

rev'er·end a. respected: [R-] clergyman's title

rev'er·ie n. daydreaming

re·vers' (-vir') n. [pl. -VERS (-virz')] lapel

re·verse' a. opposite —n. 1. the opposite 2. the back of a coin, etc. 3. change for the

worse 4. gear for reversing —v. 1. turn about or inside out 2. revoke 3. go or make go in the opposite direction —re·ver'sal n. —re·vers'i·ble a.

re·vert' v. go back to a former state, owner, etc. —re·ver'sion n.

rev'er·y n. [pl. -IES] reverie

re·view' n. 1. general survey 2. reexamination 3. a criticism of a book, play, etc. 4. formal inspection —v. 1. survey 2. study again 3. inspect formally 4. write a review of (a book, etc.) —re·view'er n.

re·vile' v. use abusive language (to or about) —re·vile'ment n.

re·vise' v. change, esp. after reading —re·vi'sion n.

re·viv'al n. 1. a reviving 2. meeting to stir up religious feeling —re·viv'al·ist n.

re·vive' v. return to life, health, use, popularity, etc.

re·voke' v. put an end to; cancel —rev'o·ca·ble a. —rev'o·ca'tion n.

re·volt' v. 1. to rebel 2. disgust or be disgusted —n. a rebellion —re·volt'ing a.

rev'o·lu'tion n. 1. movement in an orbit 2. a turning around an axis; rotation 3. complete cycle 4. complete change 5. overthrow of a government, etc. —rev'o·lu'tion·ar'y a., n. [pl. -IES] —rev'o·lu'tion·ist n.

rev'o·lu'tion·ize' v. make a drastic change in

re·volve' v. 1. rotate 2. move in an orbit 3. think about

re·volv′er *n.* pistol with a revolving cylinder for bullets

re·vue′ *n.* musical show

re·vul′sion *n.* disgust

re·ward′ *n.* 1. thing given in return for something done 2. money offered for capturing a criminal —*v.* give a reward to or for

re·wind′ *v.* [-WOUND, -WIND-ING] wind (film or tape) back on reel

re·word′ *v.* put into other words

re·write′ *v.* [-WROTE, -WRIT-TEN, -WRITING] 1. revise 2. write (news turned in) so it may be published

rhap′so·dize (rap′-) *v.* speak or write ecstatically

rhap′so·dy *n.* [*pl.* -DIES] 1. ecstatic speech or writing 2. musical piece of free form — **rhap·sod′ic, rhap·sod′i·cal** *a.*

rhe·a (rē′ə) *n.* large, ostrichlike bird

rhe′o·stat *n.* device for regulating electric current

rhe′sus (monkey) small, brownish monkey of India

rhet′o·ric *n.* effective or showy use of words —**rhe·tor′i·cal** *a.* —**rhet′o·ri′cian** (-rish′ən) *n.*

rhetorical question question with an obvious answer

rheum (rōōm) *n.* watery discharge from nose, eyes, etc.

rheumatic fever disease with fever, aching joints, etc.

rheu′ma·tism *n.* painful condition of the joints, etc. —**rheu·mat′ic** *a.,* *n.* —**rheu′ma·toid** *a.*

rheumatoid arthritis chronic disease with swollen joints

Rh factor antigen group in some human blood

rhine′stone (rīn′-) *n.* artificial gem of glass, etc.

rhi·ni′tis *n.* inflammation of nasal membrane

rhi′no *n.* [*pl.* -NOS] [Col.] rhinoceros

rhi·noc′er·os (-näs′-) *n.* large mammal with one or two horns on the snout

rhi′zome *n.* creeping stem with leaves near its tips and roots growing underneath

rho·do·den′dron (rō′-) *n.* shrub with showy flowers

rhom′boid *n.* parallelogram with oblique angles and only opposite sides equal

rhom′bus *n.* [*pl.* -BUSES, -BI] equilateral parallelogram with oblique angles

rhu′barb (rōō′-) *n.* 1. plant with edible leafstalks 2. [Sl.] heated argument

rhyme (rīm) *n.* 1. likeness of end sounds in words 2. verse using this —*v.* make (a) rhyme

rhythm (rith′m) *n.* pattern of regular beat, accent, etc. — **rhyth′mic, rhyth′mi·cal** *a.* —**rhyth′mi·cal·ly** *adv.*

rib *n.* 1. any of the curved bones around the chest 2. anything riblike —*v.* [RIBBED, RIBBING] 1. form with ribs 2. [Sl.] tease

rib′ald *a.* coarsely joking — **rib′ald·ry** *n.*

rib′bon *n.* 1. narrow strip, as of silk, etc. 2. *pl.* shreds 3.

inked strip of cloth for typewriter, etc.

ri'bo·fla'vin (rī'-) *n.* vitamin B₂, found in milk, eggs, etc.

rice *n.* a food grain grown in warm climates

rich *a.* 1. wealthy 2. well supplied 3. costly 4. full of fats or sugar 5. full and deep 6. producing much —**the rich** wealthy people —**rich'ly** *adv.* —**rich'ness** *n.*

rich'es *n.pl.* wealth

rick *n.* stack of hay, etc.

rick'ets *n.* disease causing a softening of the bones

rick'et·y *a.* weak; shaky

rick'rack' *n.* flat, zigzag braid for trimming dresses, etc.

rick'shaw, rick'sha *n.* jin-rikisha

ric·o·chet (rik'ə shā') *n., v.* [-CHETED (-shād), -CHETING (-shā'iŋ)] rebound at an angle

rid *v.* [RID or RIDDED, RIDDING] free or relieve of — **get rid of** dispose of —**rid'dance** *n.*

rid'dle *n.* puzzling question, thing, etc. —*v.* perforate

ride (rīd) *v.* [RODE, RIDDEN, RIDING] 1. sit on and make go 2. move along, as in a car 3. be carried along on or by 4. move or float on water 5. dominate 6. [Col.] tease —*n.* 1. a riding 2. thing to ride at an amusement park

rid'er *n.* 1. one who rides 2. addition to a document

rid'er·ship *n.* passengers of a transportation system

ridge *n.* 1. crest 2. narrow, raised strip —*v.* form into ridges

ridge'pole *n.* beam at the ridge of a roof, to which rafters are attached

rid'i·cule *n.* remarks meant to make fun of another —*v.* make fun of

ri·dic'u·lous *a.* foolish; absurd —**ri·dic'u·lous·ly** *adv.*

rife *a.* 1. widespread; common 2. abounding

riff *n.* constantly repeated musical phrase in jazz

rif'fle *n.* 1. ripple in a stream 2. way of shuffling cards

riff'raff' *n.* people thought of as low, common, etc.

ri'fle *n.* gun with spiral grooves in the barrel —*v.* rob —**ri'fle·man** [*pl.* -MEN] *n.*

rift *n., v.* crack; split

rig *v.* [RIGGED, RIGGING] 1. equip or assemble 2. arrange dishonestly —*n.* 1. equipment 2. arrangement of sails 3. a tractor-trailer

rig'ging *n.* ropes, etc. to work the sails of a ship

right *a.* 1. straight 2. just and good 3. correct 4. suitable 5. normal 6. of the side meant to be seen 7. of that side toward the east when one faces north —*n.* 1. what is right 2. right side 3. power or privilege 4. [*often* R-] conservative party, etc. —*adv.* 1. directly 2. properly 3. completely 4. toward the right 5. exactly 6. correctly —*v.* set right —**right away** at once —**right'ly** *adv.*

right angle 90-degree angle

right·eous (rī'chəs) *a.* 1. virtuous 2. morally right —**right'-**

eous·ly *adv.* —right'eous-
ness *n.*

right'ful *a.* 1. fair 2. having a
lawful claim —right'ful·ly
adv.

right'-hand'ed *a.* 1. using the
right hand more easily 2. for
the right hand —*adv.* with the
right hand

right'ist *n., a.* conservative or
reactionary

right'-mind'ed *a.* having
sound principles

right of way legal right to
proceed, pass over, etc.

rig'id (rij'-) *a.* 1. stiff and firm
2. severe; strict —ri·gid'i·ty
n. —rig'id·ly *adv.*

rig'ma·role *n.* nonsense

rig'or *n.* strictness; hardship —
rig'or·ous *a.*

rig'or mor'tis stiffening of
muscles after death

rile *v.* [Col.] to anger

rill *n.* little brook

rim *n.* 1. edge, esp. of something round 2. outer part of
wheel —*v.* [RIMMED, RIMMING]
form a rim around

rime *n., v.* rhyme

rime *n.* white frost

rind *n.* firm outer layer

ring *v.* [RANG, RUNG, RINGING]
1. make, or cause to make, the
sound of a bell 2. seem 3. resound 4. call by telephone 5.
encircle —*n.* 1. sound of a bell
2. band for the finger 3. hollow circle 4. group with selfish
aims 5. enclosed area 6.
prizefighting (with *the*) —
ring'er *n.*

ring'lead'er *n.* leader of a
group, as of lawbreakers

ring'let *n.* long curl

ring'mas'ter *n.* director of circus performances

ring'side *n.* place beside the
ring at boxing match

ring'worm *n.* skin disease

rink *n.* smooth area of wood or
ice for skating

rinse *v.* 1. wash lightly 2.
wash soap from —*n.* rinsing or
liquid for this

ri'ot *v.* take part in mob violence —*n.* 1. mob violence 2.
brilliant display (of color) 3.
[Col.] something very funny —
run riot 1. act wildly 2. grow
profusely —ri'ot·er *n.* —ri'ot-
ous *a.*

rip *v.* [RIPPED, RIPPING] 1. tear
apart roughly 2. become torn
3. sever threads (of a seam) 4.
saw (wood) along the grain —
n. torn place —rip off [Sl.] to
steal, cheat, etc.

rip cord cord pulled to open
parachute during descent

ripe *a.* 1. ready to be harvested, eaten, etc. 2. ready —
rip'en *v.* —ripe'ness *n.*

rip'-off' *n.* [Sl.] a stealing,
cheating, etc.

ri·poste, ri·post (ri pōst') *n.*
sharp retort

rip'ple *v.* form small surface
waves —*n.* small wave

rip'saw *n.* saw for cutting
wood along the grain

rise *v.* [ROSE, RISEN, RISING] 1.
stand up 2. come or go up 3.
appear above the horizon, as
the sun 4. attain higher level,
rank, etc. 5. increase 6. expand, as dough with yeast 7.
begin 8. revolt —*n.* 1. ascent

2. upward slope **3.** increase **4.** origin

ris′er *n.* vertical piece between steps

ris·i·bil′i·ty (riz′-) *n.* laughter

risk *n.* chance of harm, loss, etc. —*v.* **1.** put in danger **2.** take the chance of —**risk′y** [-IER, -IEST] *a.*

ris·qué′ (-kā′) *a.* almost indecent

rite *n.* ceremonial act

rit′u·al (rich′ōō-) *a.* of a rite —*n.* system of rites —**rit′u·al·ism** *n.* —**rit′u·al·ly** *adv.*

ri′val *n.* competitor —*a.* **1.** competing **2.** equal in some way —*v.* compete with —**ri′val·ry** [*pl.* -RIES] *n.*

riv′en *a.* split

riv′er *n.* large stream —**riv′er·side** *n.*, *a.*

river basin area drained by a river and its tributaries

riv′et *n.* metal bolt used to fasten by hammering the ends into heads —*v.* fasten firmly —**riv′et·er** *n.*

riv′u·let *n.* little stream

roach (rōch) *n.* cockroach

road *n.* **1.** way made for traveling **2.** *pl.* place for anchoring ships near shore —**road′side** *n.*, *a.*

road′bed *n.* foundation for railroad tracks or highway

road′block *n.* blockade

road runner desert bird of southwestern U.S.

road′show *n.* touring theatrical show

roam *v.* wander about; rove

roan *a.* reddish-brown, etc.

thickly sprinkled with white —*n.* roan horse

roar *v.*, *n.* **1.** (make) a loud, deep, rumbling sound **2.** (burst out in) loud laughter

roast *v.* **1.** cook (meat, etc.) in an oven or over an open fire **2.** process (coffee) by heat **3.** [Col.] criticize —*n.* **1.** roasted meat **2.** cut of meat for roasting **3.** picnic with roasted food —*a.* roasted —**roast′er** *n.*

rob *v.* [ROBBED, ROBBING] take property from unlawfully by force —**rob′ber** *n.* —**rob′ber·y** [*pl.* -IES] *n.*

robe *n.* **1.** long, loose, outer garment **2.** covering —*v.* dress in a robe

rob′in *n.* red-breasted N. American thrush

ro′bot *n.* mechanical device that operates like a human being

ro·bust′ *a.* strong and healthy —**ro·bust′ness** *n.*

rock *n.* **1.** mass or pieces of stone **2.** popular music based on jazz, folk music, etc. —*v.* move back and forth —**on the rocks** [Col.] **1.** ruined; bankrupt **2.** served over ice cubes —**rock′i·ness** *n.* —**rock′y** [-IER, -IEST] *a.*

rock′-and-roll′ *n.* popular music with strong, regular beat

rock bottom lowest level

rock′-bound′ *a.* covered with rocks

rock′er *n.* chair mounted on curved pieces for rocking: also **rocking chair**

rocker panel panel below automobile door

rock'et n. projectile propelled by the thrust of escaping gases

rock'et·ry n. building and launching of rockets

rock salt common salt in masses

rock wool fibrous insulation made from molten rock

ro·co·co (rə kō′kō) a. full of elaborate decoration

rod n. 1. straight stick or bar 2. pole for fishing 3. scepter 4. linear measure, 5 1/2 yds. 5. [Sl.] pistol

rode pt. of **ride**

ro'dent n. gnawing mammal, as a rat, rabbit, etc.

ro·de·o (or rō dā′ō) n. [pl. -DEOS] public exhibition of the skills of cowboys

roe (rō) n. 1. fish eggs 2. [pl. ROE, ROES] small deer

roent·gen (rent′gən) n. unit for measuring radiation of X-rays

rogue (rōg) n. 1. scoundrel 2. mischievous person —**ro'guish** (-gish) a.

rogues' gallery police collection of pictures of criminals

roil v. 1. make muddy or cloudy 2. displease; vex

roist'er v. revel; carouse —**roist'er·er** n.

role, rôle (rōl) n. 1. part played by an actor 2. function assumed by someone

roll v. 1. move by turning 2. move on wheels 3. wind into a ball or cylinder 4. flatten with a roller 5. rock 6. trill —n. 1. a rolling 2. scroll 3. list of names 4. small cake of bread 5. a swaying motion 6. slight swell on a surface 7. loud, echoing sound —**roll'er** n.

roller coaster ride with cars on tracks that dip and curve sharply

roller skate frame or shoe with four small wheels, for gliding on a floor, etc. —**roll'er·skate'** v.

rol'lick·ing a. lively and carefree

roll'ing pin cylinder used to roll out dough

roll'-top' a. of a desk having a flexible, sliding top

ro'ly-po'ly a. pudgy

ro·maine' (-mān′) n. lettuce with long leaves in a head

Ro'man a. 1. of Rome 2. [r-] of type with non-slanting letters —n. 1. [r-] this type 2. native of Rome

Roman Catholic 1. of the Christian church headed by the Pope 2. member of this church

ro·mance' a. [R-] of any language derived from Latin —n. 1. tale of love, adventure, etc. 2. exciting quality 3. love affair —v. [Col.] make love to

Roman numerals Roman letters used as numerals: I=1, V=5, X=10, L=50, C=100, D=500, M=1,000

ro·man'tic a. 1. of romance 2. visionary 3. full of feelings of romance —n. romantic person —**ro·man'ti·cal·ly** adv. —**ro·man'ti·cism** n.

ro·man'ti·cize' v. treat or act in romantic way

romp v. play boisterously —n. a romping

romp'ers *n.pl.* loose, one-piece outer garment for a small child

rood (rōōd) *n.* crucifix

roof *n.* [*pl.* ROOFS] outside top covering of a building —*v.* cover as with a roof

roof'ing *n.* material for roofs

roof'top *n.* roof of building

rook (rook) *n.* 1. European crow 2. chess piece moving horizontally or vertically —*v.* cheat

rook'ie *n.* [Sl.] beginner

room *n.* 1. enough space 2. space set off by walls 3. *pl.* living quarters —*v.* to lodge —**room'er** *n.* —**room'ful** *n.* —**room'mate** *n.* —**room'y** [-IER, -IEST] *a.*

roost *n.* perch for birds —*v.* perch on a roost

roost'er *n.* male chicken

root *n.* 1. underground part of a plant 2. embedded part, as of a tooth 3. cause 4. quantity multiplied by itself —*v.* 1. take root 2. place firmly 3. dig (up, out) with the snout 4. rummage about 5. [Col.] support a team, etc. —**take root** 1. grow by putting out roots 2. become fixed

root beer carbonated drink made of root extracts

rope *n.* strong cord of twisted strands —*v.* 1. mark off with a rope 2. catch with a lasso —**know the ropes** [Col.] know procedures —**rope in** [Sl.] entice

Roque'fort cheese (rōk'-) strong cheese with bluish mold

ro'sa·ry *n.* [*pl.* -RIES] string of beads used when praying

rose *n.* 1. a shrub with prickly stems and sweet-smelling flowers 2. this flower 3. pinkish red —**rose'bud** *n.* —**rose'-bush** *n.* —**rose'-col'ored** *a.*

ro·sé (rō zā') *n.* a pink wine

ro'se·ate *a.* rose-colored

rose'mar'y *n.* plant with fragrant leaves, used in cooking

ro·sette' *n.* roselike ornament

rose'wood *n.* reddish wood

Rosh Ha·sha·na (rōsh' hə shō'nə) Jewish New Year

ros'in (räz'-) *n.* hard resin

ros'ter (räs'-) *n.* list; roll

ros'trum *n.* [*pl.* -TRUMS, -TRA] speakers' platform

ros'y *a.* [-IER, -IEST] 1. rose-red or pink 2. bright or promising —**ros'i·ly** *adv.* —**ros'i·ness** *n.*

rot *v.* [ROTTED, ROTTING] decay, spoil —*n.* 1. a rotting 2. plant disease 3. [Sl] nonsense

ro'ta·ry *a.* 1. rotating 2. having rotating parts

ro'tate *v.* 1. turn around, as a wheel 2. alternate —**ro·ta'-tion** *n.*

rote *n.* fixed routine —**by rote** by memory alone

ro·tis'ser·ie *n.* grill with an electrically turned spit

ro'tor (-tər) *n.* rotating airfoils on a helicopter

rot'ten *a.* 1. decayed 2. foul-smelling 3. corrupt 4. [Sl.] very bad —**rot'ten·ness** *n.*

ro·tund' *a.* round; plump —**ro·tun'di·ty** *n.*

ro·tun'da *n.* round building with a dome

rou·é (rōō ā') *n.* rake (*n.* 2)

rouge (rōōzh) *n.* 1. cosmetic to

redden cheeks and lips 2. red polish for jewelry —v. put rouge on

rough a. 1. not smooth; uneven 2. disorderly 3. harsh 4. stormy 5. lacking comforts 6. approximate 7. [Col.] difficult —n. 1. something rough 2. part of a golf course with uncut grass —adv. in a rough way —v. 1. treat roughly (with up) 2. shape roughly —**rough it** live without comforts —**rough'ly** adv. —**rough'ness** n.

rough'age (-ij) n. coarse food

rough'en v. make or become rough

rough'-hew' v. [alt. pp. -HEWN] form or form roughly: also **roughhew**

rough'house v. [Sl.] play or fight boisterously

rough'neck n. [Sl.] a rowdy

rou·lette (rōō let') n. gambling game played with a ball in a whirling bowl

round a. 1. that forms a circle or curve 2. complete 3. that is a whole number 4. vigorous —n. 1. thing that is round 2. a round 3. pl. regular circuit 4. single gunshot 5. outburst 6. period of action or time 7. simple song for three or four voices —v. 1. make round 2. finish 3. turn 4. pass around —adv. 1. in a circle 2. through a cycle 3. from one to another 4. in the opposite direction —prep. 1. so as to encircle 2. near 3. in a circuit through —**round'ly** adv. —**round'ness** n.

round'a·bout a. indirect

round'house n. round building for repairing and storing locomotives

round'-shoul'dered a. having the shoulders stooped

round steak a cut from a round of beef

round table 1. circular table 2. group discussion

round'-the-clock' a., adv. continuous(ly)

round trip trip to a place and back

round'up n. a bringing together, esp. of cattle

round'worm n. hookworm or similar unsegmented worm

rouse v. 1. excite 2. wake

roust'a·bout n. unskilled, transient worker

rout n. 1. confused flight 2. crushing defeat —v. 1. make flee 2. defeat 3. force out 4. gouge out

route (rōōt, rout) n. course traveled, as to make deliveries —v. send by a certain route

rou·tine' n. regular procedure —a. regular; customary —**rou·tine'ly** adv.

rove v. roam —**rov'er** n.

row (rō) n. 1. line of people, seats, etc. 2. a trip by rowboat —v. move (in) a boat with oars

row (rou) n., v. quarrel; brawl

row'boat n. boat to row

row'dy a. [-DIER, -DIEST] rough, disorderly, etc. —n. [pl. -DIES] rowdy person —**row'dy·ism** n.

row'el (rou'-) n. small wheel with points, as on a spur

roy'al a. 1. of a monarch, kingdom, etc. 2. fit for a monarch —**roy′al·ist** *a., n.* —**roy′al·ly** *adv.*

roy′al·ty *n.* [*pl.* -TIES] 1. royal rank, person, or persons 2. set payment for use of copyright or patent

R.S.V.P. please reply

rub *v.* [RUBBED, RUBBING] 1. move over a surface with pressure and friction 2. spread on, erase, injure, etc. by rubbing 3. smooth or polish by rubbing —*n.* 1. a rubbing 2. difficulty; trouble —**rub down** to massage —**rub the wrong way** to irritate

ru·ba·to (rōō bät′ō) *a., adv.* not in strict musical tempo

rub′ber *n.* 1. elastic substance 2. *pl.* overshoes 3. deciding game in a series —**rub′ber·y** *a.*

rub′ber·ize *v.* impregnate with rubber

rubber stamp 1. stamp of rubber inked for printing 2. [Col.] automatic approval

rub′bish *n.* 1. worthless material; trash 2. nonsense

rub′ble *n.* broken stones, bricks, etc.

rub′down *n.* a massage

rube *n.* [Sl.] uncouth rustic

ru·bel′la *n.* contagious disease with red skin spots

ru′bi·cund *a.* reddish

ru′ble *n.* monetary unit of U.S.S.R.

ru′bric *n.* 1. section in red in prayer book 2. rule; direction

ru′by *n.* [*pl.* -BIES] deep-red precious stone

ruck′sack *n.* knapsack

ruck′us *n.* [Col.] noisy confusion

rud′der *n.* steering piece at ship's stern or aircraft's tail —**rud′der·less** *a.*

rud′dy *a.* [-DIER, -DIEST] 1. healthily red 2. reddish —**rud′di·ness** *n.*

rude *a.* 1. coarse; crude 2. impolite 3. primitive —**rude′ly** *adv.* —**rude′ness** *n.*

ru′di·ment *n.* 1. first principle of a subject 2. trace —**ru′di·men′ta·ry** *a.*

rue *v.* 1. regret 2. feel remorse —*n.* 1. [Ar.] sorrow 2. strong-scented herb —**rue′ful** *a.* —**rue′ful·ly** *adv.*

ruff *n.* 1. high, frilled collar 2. raised ring of feathers or fur about an animal's neck

ruf′fi·an *n.* brutal, lawless person

ruf′fle *v.* 1. to ripple 2. make ruffles in or on 3. make (feathers, etc.) stand up 4. disturb —*n.* narrow, pleated cloth trimming

rug *n.* floor covering of thick fabric in one piece

rug′by *n.* game from which football developed

rug′ged *a.* 1. uneven; rough 2. harsh; severe 3. not refined 4. strong —**rug′ged·ly** *adv.*

ru′in *n.* 1. anything destroyed, etc. 2. *pl.* remains of this 3. downfall; destruction —*v.* bring or come to ruin —**ru′in·a′tion** *n.* —**ru′in·ous** *a.*

rule *n.* 1. a set guide for conduct, etc. 2. custom; usage 3. government 4. ruler (*sense* 2) —*v.* 1. to guide 2. govern 3.

decide officially 4. mark lines (on) —**as a rule** usually —**rule out** exclude

rule of thumb crude but practical method

rul'er n. 1. one who governs 2. straight-edged strip for drawing lines, measuring, etc.

rul'ing a. that rules —n. official decision of a court

rum n. alcoholic liquor made from molasses, etc.

rum'ba n. Cuban dance

rum'ble v. make a deep, rolling sound —n. 1. a rumbling sound 2. [Sl.] fight between teen-age gangs

ru'mi·nant a. cud-chewing —n. cud-chewing mammal

ru'mi·nate v. 1. chew the cud 2. meditate —**ru'mi·na'tion** n.

rum·mage (rum'ij) v. to search thoroughly

rummage sale sale of miscellaneous articles

rum'my n. card game

ru'mor n. unconfirmed report or story —v. spread as a rumor

rump n. 1. animal's hind part 2. buttocks

rum'ple n., v. wrinkle

rum'pus n. [Col.] uproar

run v. [RAN, RUN, RUNNING] 1. go by moving the legs fast 2. go, move, etc. easily 3. make a quick trip 4. compete (in) 5. ravel 6. spread over 7. discharge pus, etc. 8. continue 9. get past 10. operate 11. follow (a course) 12. undergo 13. publish 14. cause to run —n. 1. act or period of running 2. trip 3. brook 4. a kind 5. en-

closed area 6. freedom 7. a ravel 8. *Baseball* point scored by a circuit of the bases —**in the long run** ultimately —**run across** happen on —**run down** 1. stop 2. knock down, capture, or kill 3. disparage —**run out** expire —**run out of** use up —**run over** 1. ride over 2. overflow

run'a·round n. [Col.] series of evasions

run'a·way n. person or animal that runs away —a. 1. running away 2. out of control 3. easily won

run'-down a. 1. not wound, as a watch 2. in poor condition —n. quick summary

rung pp. of **ring** —n. rodlike step of a ladder, etc.

run'-in' n. [Col.] quarrel

run'ner n. 1. one that runs 2. long, narrow rug 3. ravel 4. either of the pieces on which a sled slides

run'ner-up' n. [pl. -NERS-UP] the second to finish in a contest

run'ning n. act of one that runs —a. 1. that runs 2. measured straight 3. continuous —adv. in succession

running mate lesser candidate, as for vice-president

run'ny a. [-NIER, -NIEST] 1. flowing too freely 2. discharging mucus

run'off n. a deciding contest

run'-of-the-mill' a. ordinary

runt n. stunted animal or plant

run'-through' n. complete rehearsal

run'way n. a landing strip

ru·pee' *n.* monetary unit of India, Pakistan, etc.

rup'ture (-char) *n.* 1. a breaking apart 2. hernia —*v.* 1. burst 2. induce a hernia

ru'ral *a.* of or living in the country —**ru'ral·ism** *n.*

ruse (rōōz) *n.* artful trick

rush *v.* 1. move, push, attack, etc. swiftly 2. hurry —*n.* 1. a rushing 2. busyness 3. grassy marsh plant

rush hour time when traffic is heavy

rusk *n.* (piece of) sweet bread toasted brown

rus'set *n.* yellowish (or reddish) brown

Rus'sian *n., a.* (native or language) of Russia

rust *n.* 1. reddish-brown coating formed on iron, etc. 2. a reddish brown 3. plant disease —*v.* 1. form rust on 2. deteriorate, as through disuse —**rust'y** [-IER, -IEST] *a.*

rus'tic *a.* 1. rural 2. plain or rough —*n.* country person **ruo'ti·cal·ly** *adv.* —**rus·tic'i·ty** (-tis'-) *n.*

rus·tle (rus'l) *v.* 1. [Col.] steal cattle 2. make soft, rubbing sounds —*n.* these sounds — **rustle up** [Col.] get together —**rus'tler** *n.*

rut *n.* 1. groove as made by wheels 2. fixed routine 3. heat (*n.* 4) —*v.* [RUTTED, RUTTING] make ruts in

ru'ta·ba'ga *n.* yellow turnip

ruth'less *a.* without pity — **ruth'less·ly** *adv.*

-ry *suf.* see **-ery**

rye (rī) *n.* 1. cereal grass 2. its grain, used for flour 3. whiskey made from thio grain

S

Sab'bath *n.* day of rest and worship: Saturday for Jews, Sunday for many Christians

sab·bat'i·cal *n.* period of absence with pay for study, travel, etc., as for teachers

sa'ber, sa'bre *n.* cavalry sword

sa'ble *n.* weasellike animal with dark fur

sab'o·tage (-täzh) *n.* destruction of factories, etc. as by enemy agents or strikers —*v.* destroy by sabotage

sab·o·teur' (-tur') *n.* one who commits sabotage

sac *n.* pouchlike part

sac'cha·rin (sak'ə-) *n.* sugar substitute

sac'cha·rine (-rin) *a.* too sweet —*n.* saccharin

sac'er·do'tal (sas'-) *a.* of priests

sa·chet' (sa shā') *n.* small bag of perfumed powder

sack *n.* 1. a bag, esp. a large coarse one 2. plunder 3. [Sl.] dismissal (with *the*) 4. [Sl.] bed —*v.* 1. put in sacks 2. plunder 3. [Sl.] fire (a person)

sack'cloth *n.* coarse cloth worn to show sorrow

sack'ing *n.* coarse cloth for making sacks

sac'ra·ment *n.* sacred Christian rite, as Communion — **sac'ra·men'tal** a.

sa'cred a. 1. consecrated to a god or God 2. venerated 3. inviolate —**sa'cred·ly** adv. —**sa'cred·ness** n.

sac'ri·fice v. 1. offer (something) to a deity 2. give up something for another 3. take a loss in selling —n. a sacrificing —**sac'ri·fi'cial** (-fish'al) a.

sac'ri·lege (-lij) n. desecration of sacred things —**sac'ri·le'gious** (-li'jas) a.

sac'ris·ty n. [pl. -TIES] room in a church for sacred vessels, etc.

sa'cro·il'i·ac (or sak'rō-) n. joint between the hipbone and the fused bottom vertebra

sac'ro·sanct (-saŋkt) a. very holy

sad a. [SADDER, SADDEST] showing or causing sorrow; unhappy —**sad'ly** adv. —**sad'ness** n.

sad'den v. make or become sad

sad'dle n. seat for a rider on a horse, bicycle, etc. —v. 1. put a saddle on 2. burden —**in the saddle** in control

sad'dle·bag n. 1. bag hung behind a horse's saddle 2. similar bag on a bicycle, etc.

saddle shoes white oxfords with dark band over the instep

sad'ist (sad'-) n. one who gets pleasure from hurting others —**sad'ism** n. —**sa·dis'tic** a.

sa·fa'ri (-fä'rē) n. hunting trip, esp. in Africa

safe a. 1. free from danger 2. unharmed 3. trustworthy 4. cautious —n. metal box with a lock —**safe'ly** adv.

safe'-con'duct n. permission to travel safely

safe'-de·pos'it a. of a bank box, etc. for storing valuables: also **safe'ty-de·pos'it**

safe'guard n. protection; precaution —v. protect

safe'keep'ing n. protection

safe'ty n. [pl. -TIES] 1. security 2. device for preventing an accident

safety glass glass that resists shattering

safety match match that strikes only on a prepared surface

safety pin bent pin with the point held in a guard

safety razor razor with a detachable blade held between guards

saf'flow'er n. plant whose seeds yield an edible oil

saf'fron n. orange-yellow dye and seasoning

sag v. [SAGGED, SAGGING] 1. sink in the middle 2. hang unevenly 3. lose strength —n. place that sags

sa'ga (sä'-) n. long story of heroic deeds

sa·ga'cious (-gā'shas) a. very wise or shrewd —**sa·gac'i·ty** (-gas'-) n.

sage a. very wise —n. 1. very wise man 2. green leaves used as seasoning 3. sagebrush

sage'brush n. shrub of the western plains of the U.S.

Sag'it·ta'ri·us (saj'i ter'ē-) 9th sign of the zodiac; Archer

said pt. & pp. of **say** —*a.* aforesaid; named before

sail *n.* 1. canvas sheet to catch the wind and move a vessel 2. boat trip —*v.* 1. move by means of sails 2. travel on water 3. glide —**sail into** [Col.] attack vigorously —**set sail** begin a trip by boat

sail'boat *n.* boat propelled by sails

sail'fish *n.* ocean fish with a tall dorsal fin

sail'or *n.* 1. enlisted man in the navy 2. one who sails

saint *n.* 1. holy person 2. person who is very charitable, patient, etc. —**saint'ly** [-LIER, -LIEST] *a.* —**saint'li·ness** *n.*

saith (seth) [Ar.] says

sake *n.* 1. motive; cause 2. behalf

sa·ke (sä'kē) *n.* Japanese alcoholic drink

sa·laam' (-läm') *n.* Oriental greeting of bowing low

sal'a·ble, sale'a·ble *a.* that can be sold

sa·la'cious (-lā'shəs) *a.* obscene

sal'ad *n.* vegetables, fruit, etc., with salad dressing

salad dressing oil, vinegar, spices, etc. put on a salad

sal'a·man'der *n.* lizardlike amphibian

sa·la·mi (-lä'mē) *n.* spiced, salted sausage

sal'a·ry *n.* [*pl.* -RIES] fixed payment at regular intervals for work —**sal'a·ried** *a.*

sale *n.* 1. a selling 2. special selling of goods at reduced prices

sales'clerk *n.* person employed to sell goods in a store

sales'man *n.* [*pl.* -MEN] man employed to sell goods — **sales'wom'an** [*pl.* -WOMEN] *n.fem.* —**sales'man·ship** *n.*

sales'per'son *n.* salesclerk

sales slip bill of sale

sal'i·cyl'ic acid pain-relieving compound, as in aspirin

sa'li·ent (sā'-) *a.* 1. prominent; conspicuous 2. jutting —*n.* salient part —**sa'li·ence** *n.*

sa·line (-līn) *a.* salty —**sa·lin'i·ty** *n.*

sa·li'va *n.* watery fluid secreted by glands in the mouth —**sal'i·var'y** *a.*

sal'low *a.* sickly yellow

sal'ly *n.* [*pl.* -LIES] 1. sudden rush forward 2. quip 3. short trip —*v.* [LIED, -LYING] start (*forth*) briskly

salm'on (sam'-) *n.* large, edible ocean fish

sal'mo·nel'la *n.* [*pl.* -LAE (-ē) -LAS] bacillus that causes typhoid fever, food poisoning, etc.

sa·lon' (-län) *n.* 1. parlor 2. gathering of notables

sa·loon' *n.* 1. public place where liquor is sold and drunk 2. large public room

salt *n.* 1. white substance found in the earth, sea water, etc., used to flavor food 2. compound formed from an acid 3. [Col.] sailor —*a.* containing salt —*v.* add salt to —**with a grain of salt** allowing for exaggeration —**salt'y** [-IER, -IEST] *a.*

salt′cel′lar n. 1. small dish for salt 2. saltshaker

salt·ine′ (-ēn′) n. flat, salted cracker

salt lick rock salt for animals to lick

salt′pe′ter n. niter

salt′shak′er n. salt container with holes on top

salt′wa′ter a. of or living in salt water or the sea

sa·lu′bri·ous a. healthful

sal′u·tar′y a. 1. healthful 2. beneficial

sal′u·ta′tion n. act or form of greeting

sa·lute′ n. formal gesture, act, etc. expressing respect —v. 1. greet with a salute 2. commend

sal′vage (-vij) n. 1. rescue of a ship, etc. from shipwreck 2. reclaimed property or goods —v. 1. save from shipwreck, etc. 2. utilize (damaged goods, etc.)

sal·va′tion n. 1. a saving or being saved 2. one that saves 3. saving of the soul

salve (sav) n. 1. soothing ointment 2. anything that soothes —v. soothe

sal′ver n. tray

sal′vo n. [pl. -VOS, -VOES] discharge of a number of guns together

sam′ba n. Brazilian dance, or the music for it

same a. 1. being the very one 2. alike 3. unchanged 4. before-mentioned —pron. the same person or thing —adv. in like manner —all (or just) the same nevertheless —same′ness n.

sam′o·var (-vär) n. metal urn to heat water for tea

sam′pan n. small Oriental boat, rowed with a scull

sam′ple n. 1. part typical of a whole 2. example —v. take a sample of

sam′pler n. 1. collection of representative selections 2. cloth embroidered with designs, etc.

san′a·to′ri·um n. [Chiefly Br.] sanitarium

sanc′ti·fy v. to make holy or free from sin —sanc′ti·fi·ca′tion n.

sanc′ti·mo′ni·ous a. pretending to be pious —sanc′ti·mo′ny n.

sanc′tion n. 1. authorization 2. approval 3. pl. punitive measures against a nation —v. 1. authorize 2. confirm

sanc′ti·ty n. 1. holiness 2. sacredness

sanc′tu·ar′y n. [pl. -IES] 1. holy place, as a church 2. place of refuge

sanc′tum n. 1. sacred place 2. one′s own private room

sand n. 1. loose grains of disintegrated rock 2. pl. area of sand —v. smooth or polish, as with sandpaper —sand′er n.

san′dal n. shoe with sole tied to the foot by straps

san′dal·wood n. tree with sweet-smelling wood

sand′bag n. sand-filled bag for ballast, etc. —v. [-BAGGED, -BAGGING] 1. put sandbags around 2. [Col.] force into doing something

sand bar ridge of sand along a shore: also **sandbank**

sand'blast v. clean with a blast of air and sand

sand'box n. box with sand, as for children to play in

sand'hog n. laborer in underground or underwater construction

sand'lot a. of baseball games, etc. played by amateurs

sand'man n. supposed bringer of sleep to children

sand'pa'per n. paper coated with sand —v. smooth with sandpaper

sand'pip'er (-pīp'-) n. shore bird with a long bill

sand'stone n. kind of rock much used in building

sand'storm n. windstorm with clouds of blown sand

sand'wich n. slices of bread with meat, etc. between them —v. squeeze between

sand'y a. [-IER, -IEST] 1. of or like sand 2. dull yellow

sane a. 1. mentally healthy 2. sensible —**sane'ly** adv.

sang pt. of **sing**

san'gui·nar'y (-gwi-) a. 1. of or with bloodshed 2. bloodthirsty

san'guine a. 1. blood-red 2. cheerful

san'i·tar'i·um n. institution for invalids, etc.

san'i·tar'y a. 1. of health 2. clean and healthful

sanitary napkin absorbent pad worn during menstruation

san'i·ta'tion n. 1. hygienic conditions 2. sewage disposal

san'i·tize v. make sanitary

san'i·ty n. soundness of mind or judgment

sank pt. of **sink**

sap n. 1. juice of a plant 2. vigor 3. [Sl.] a fool —v. [SAPPED, SAPPING] 1. undermine 2. weaken

sa'pi·ent (sā'-) a. wise —**sa'pi·ence** n.

sap'ling n. young tree

sap·phire (saf'īr) n. deep-blue precious stone

sap'py a. [-PIER, -PIEST] [Sl.] foolish

sap'suck'er n. small woodpecker

sa·ran' n. plastic for wrapping material, fabric, etc.

sar'casm n. taunting, ironical remark —**sar·cas'tic** a.

sar·co'ma n. [pl. -MAS, -MATA (-mə tə)] malignant tumor

sar·coph'a·gus n. [pl. -GI (-jī'), -GUSES] stone coffin

sar·dine' n. small herring preserved in oil

sar·don'ic a. bitterly sarcastic

sa·ri (sä'rē) n. long cloth wrapped around the body as a garment by Hindu women

sa·rong' n. skirtlike garment of East Indies

sar'sa·pa·ril'la (or sas'pə-) n. root-flavored drink

sar·to'ri·al a. 1. of tailors 2. of men's dress

sash n. 1. band worn over the shoulder or around the waist 2. sliding frame for glass in a window

sass n. [Col.] impudent talk —v. [Col.] talk impudently to

sas'sa·fras n. tree whose root bark is used for flavoring

sass'y a. [-IER, -IEST] [Col.] impudent

sat pt. & pp. of **sit**

Sa·tan n. the Devil

sa·tan'ic a. wicked

satch'el n. small traveling bag

sate v. 1. satisfy fully 2. satiate

sa·teen' n. satinlike cotton

sat'el·lite n. 1. small planet revolving around a larger one 2. man-made object orbiting in space 3. small state dependent on a larger one

sa'ti·ate (-shē-) v. give too much to, causing disgust —**sa·ti'e·ty** n.

sat'in n. smooth and glossy silk, nylon, or rayon cloth

sat'in·wood n. a tree yielding smooth wood used in fine furniture

sat'ire n. 1. use of ridicule, irony, etc. to attack vice or folly 2. literary work in which this is done —**sa·tir'i·cal** (-tir'-), **sa·tir'ic** a. —**sat'i·rist** n.

sat'i·rize v. attack with satire

sat·is·fac'tion n. 1. a satisfying 2. source of pleasure 3. settlement of debt

sat'is·fac'to·ry a. satisfying

sat'is·fy v. [-FIED, -FYING] 1. fulfill the needs and desires of 2. fulfill the requirements of 3. convince 4. pay in full

sa·to'ri (sä tō'rē) n. Buddhism spiritual enlightenment

sa'trap (sā'-, sat'-) n. petty tyrant

sat'u·rate (sach'oo-) v. 1. soak thoroughly 2. fill completely —**sat'u·ra'tion** n.

Sat'ur·day n. seventh day of the week

sat'ur·nine (-nīn) a. gloomy

sat'yr n. Gr. Myth. woodland god with goat's legs

sauce n. 1. tasty liquid or soft dressing for food 2. mashed, stewed fruit 3. impudence

sauce'pan n. metal cooking pot with a long handle

sau'cer n. shallow dish, esp. one for holding a cup

sau'cy a. [-CIER, -CIEST] 1. impudent 2. lively and bold —**sau'ci·ly** adv. —**sau'ci·ness** n.

sau·er·bra·ten (sour'brä't'n) n. beef marinated before cooking

sau·er·kraut (sour'krout) n. chopped, fermented cabbage

sau'na n. Finnish bath with exposure to hot, dry air

saun'ter (sôn'-) v., n. stroll

sau·sage (sô'sij) n. chopped, seasoned pork, etc., often stuffed into a casing

sau·té (sō tā', sô-) v. [-TÉED, -TÉING] fry quickly in a little fat

sau·terne (sō turn') n. a white table wine

sav'age a. 1. wild 2. fierce; untamed 3. primitive; barbarous 4. cruel; pitiless —n. brutal or crude person —**sav'age·ly** adv. —**sav'age·ry** n.

sa·vant (sə vänt') n. learned person

save v. 1. rescue; keep safe 2. keep or store up for future use 3. avoid waste (of) —prep., con. except; but

sav'ing a. 1. economizing or

economical 2. redeeming —*n.*
1. reduction in time, cost, etc.
2. *pl.* money saved

sav′ior, sav′iour (-yar) *n.* one who saves or rescues —**the Saviour** (or **Savior**) Jesus Christ

sa·voir-faire (sav′wär fer′) *n.* social poise; tact

sa′vor *n.* special taste, smell, or quality —*v.* 1. have the savor (of) 2. taste with delight

sa′vor·y *a.* [-IER, -IEST] 1. tasting or smelling good 2. pleasant, agreeable, etc.

sav′vy *n.* [Sl.] shrewdness or understanding

saw pt. of **see** —*n.* 1. thin, metal blade with sharp teeth, for cutting 2. proverb —*v.* cut with a saw —**saw′yer** *n.*

saw′dust *n.* fine bits of wood formed in sawing wood

sawed′-off′ *a.* short or shortened

saw′horse *n.* rack to hold wood while sawing it: also **saw′buck**

sax′o·phone *n.* single-reed, metal wind instrument

say *v.* [SAID, SAYING] 1. speak 2. state 3. suppose —*n.* 1. chance to speak 2. power to decide —**that is to say** in other words

say′ing *n.* proverb

say′-so′ *n.* [Col.] 1. (one's) word, assurance, etc. 2. power to decide

scab *n.* 1. crust over a healing sore 2. strikebreaker —*v.* [SCABBED, SCABBING] 1. form a scab 2. be a scab

scab′bard *n.* sheath for a sword, dagger, etc.

sca′bies (-bēz) *n.* itch caused by mites

scab′rous *a.* 1. scaly 2. indecent, shocking, etc.

scads *n.pl.* [Col.] very large number or amount

scaf′fold *n.* 1. framework to hold workmen, painters, etc. 2. platform on which criminals are executed

scald (skôld) *v.* 1. burn with hot liquid or steam 2. heat almost to a boil —*n.* burn caused by scalding

scale *n.* 1. series of gradations or degrees 2. ratio of distances on a map, etc. 3. any of the thin, hard plates on fish, etc. 4. flake 5. either pan of a balance 6. *often pl.* weighing machine 7. *Mus.* series of consecutive tones —*v.* 1. climb up 2. set according to a scale 3. scrape scales from 4. flake off in scales —**scal′y** [-IER, -IEST] *a.* —**scal′i·ness** *n.*

scal′lion (-yan) *n.* green onion

scal′lop *n.* 1. edible mollusk 2. any of the curves forming a fancy edge —*v.* 1. edge in scallops 2. bake with a milk sauce, etc.

scalp *n.* skin on top of the head —*v.* 1. cut the scalp from 2. buy (tickets, etc.) for later sale at higher prices —**scalp′er** *n.*

scal′pel *n.* sharp knife used in surgery, etc.

scamp *n.* rascal

scam′per *v.* run quickly —*n.* quick dash

scam'pi (-pē) n. [pl. -PI, -PIES] large, edible prawns

scan v. [SCANNED, SCANNING] 1. look at quickly 2. examine 3. show meter in verse —n. a scanning

scan'dal n. 1. disgrace or thing that disgraces 2. gossip

scan'dal·ize v. outrage one's feeling of decency

scan'dal·mon'ger (-muŋ'gər) n. one who spreads gossip

scan'dal·ous a. 1. shameful 2. spreading slander

scant a. not enough

scant'y a. [-IER, -IEST] barely or not enough —**scant'i·ly** adv. —**scant'i·ness** n.

scape'goat n. one who is blamed for others' mistakes

scape'grace n. rogue

scap'u·la n. [pl. -LAE (-lē), -LAS] shoulder bone

scar n. mark left after a wound has healed —v. [SCARRED, SCARRING] mark with or form a scar

scar'ab (skar'-) n. 1. black beetle 2. its carved image

scarce a. 1. not common 2. hard to get —**make oneself scarce** [Col.] go or stay away —**scarce'ness** n.

scarce'ly adv. 1. hardly 2. probably not or certainly not

scar'ci·ty n. [pl. -TIES] 1. inadequate supply 2. rarity

scare v. 1. fill with sudden fear 2. become frightened —n. sudden fear —**scare away** (or **off**) drive away (or off) by frightening —**scare up** [Col.] produce or gather quickly

scare'crow n. figure set up to scare birds away

scarf n. [pl. SCARFS, SCARVES] 1. piece of cloth worn about the neck, head, etc. 2. long, narrow covering for a table, etc.

scar'let n. bright red

scarlet fever contagious disease with fever and a rash

scar'y a. [-IER, -IEST] [Col.] 1. frightening 2. easily frightened

scat v. [Col.] go away!

scath'ing (skāth'-) a. harsh; bitter —**scath'ing·ly** adv.

scat'ter v. 1. throw about 2. move in several directions

scat'ter·brain n. person incapable of clear thinking

scatter rug small rug

scav'eng·er (-inj-) n. 1. one who collects refuse 2. animal that eats decaying matter —**scav'enge** v.

sce·nar'i·o (si-) n. [pl. -OS] 1. movie script 2. outline for proposed action

scene n. 1. place; setting 2. view 3. division of a play 4. show of emotion 5. [Col.] locale for an activity

scen'er·y n. [pl. -IES] 1. painted backdrops for a stage play 2. outdoor views

sce'nic (sē'-) a. 1. of scenery 2. picturesque

scent (sent) v. 1. to suspect 2. to perfume —n. 1. odor 2. perfume 3. sense of smell

scep'ter (sep'-) n. staff as a symbol of a ruler's power: chiefly Br. sp. **sceptre**

scep'tic (skep'-) *n.* skeptic: chiefly Br. sp.

sched·ule (skej'ool) *n.* 1. timetable 2. timed plan 3. list of details —*v.* place in a schedule

scheme *n.* 1. plan; system 2. plot; intrigue 3. diagram —*v.* plot —**schem'er** *n.* —**sche·mat'ic** *a.*

scher·zo (sker'tsō) *n.* [*pl.* -zos, -zi (-tsē)] lively musical movement in 3/4 time

schism (siz'm) *n.* split, esp. in a church, over doctrine — **schis·mat'ic** *a.*

schist (shist) *n.* rock in layers

schiz·o·phre'ni·a (skit'sə-) *n.* severe mental illness —**schiz'o·phren'ic** *a., n.*

schmaltz (shmälts) *n.* [Sl.] highly sentimental music, etc.

schnapps (shnäps) *n.* [*pl.* SCHNAPPS] strong liquor

schnau'zer (shnou'-) *n.* small terrier

schol'ar (skäl'-) *n.* 1. learned person 2. student —**schol'ar·ly** *a.*

schol'ar·ship *n.* 1. knowledge; learning 2. money given to help a student

scho·las'tic *a.* of schools, students, teachers, etc.

school *n.* 1. place for teaching and learning 2. its students and teachers 3. education 4. group with the same beliefs 5. group of fish —*v.* train; teach —*a.* of, in, or for school

school board group in charge of local public schools

school'ing *n.* training or education

school'mate *n.* person going to the same school at the same time as another

school'teach'er *n.* person teaching in a school

schoon'er *n.* ship with two or more masts

schwa (shwä) *n.* 1. vowel sound in an unaccented syllable 2. symbol (ə) for this

sci·at'ic (sī-) *a.* of or in the hip or its nerves

sci·at'i·ca (sī-) *n.* neuritis in the hip and thigh

sci'ence *n.* systemized knowledge or a branch of it —**sci'en·tif'ic** *a.* —**sci'en·tif'i·cal·ly** *adv.*

science fiction highly imaginative fiction involving scientific phenomena: also **sci'-fi'** *n.*

sci'en·tist *n.* expert in science

scim'i·tar, scim'i·ter (sim'-) *n.* curved sword

soin·til'la (sin-) *n.* 1. a spark 2. tiny bit; least trace

scin'til·late *v.* 1. sparkle 2. be clever and witty —**scin'til·la'tion** *n.*

sci·on (sī'ən) *n.* 1. bud or shoot 2. descendant

scis'sors (siz'-) *n.pl.* cutting tool with two pivoted blades

scle·ro'sis (skli-) *n.* abnormal hardening of body tissues

scoff *n.* scornful remark —*v.* mock or jeer (at)

scold *v.* find fault with angrily —*n.* one who scolds

sconce (skäns) *n.* wall bracket for candles

scone *n.* small tea cake

scoop *n.* 1. small, shovellike untensil 2. bucket of a dredge, etc. 3. a scooping 4. amount scooped —v. 1. take up with a scoop 2. hollow out

scoot v. [Col.] scurry off

scoot'er n. 1. child's two-wheeled vehicle 2. small motorcycle

scope n. 1. range of understanding, action, etc. 2. room for freedom of action

-scope suf. for seeing

scorch v. 1. burn slightly 2. parch —n. surface burn

score n. 1. points made in a game, etc. 2. grade on a test 3. piece of music showing all parts 4. scratch or mark 5. twenty 6. pl. very many 7. debt 8. grievance —v. 1. make a score or scores, as in a game 2. evaluate 3. achieve 4. keep score 5. upbraid —**scor'er** n.

score'board n. large board posting scores, etc., as in a stadium

score'less a. having scored no points

scorn n. contempt; disdain —v. 1. treat with scorn 2. refuse —**scorn'ful** a. —**scorn'ful·ly** adv.

Scor'pi·o 8th sign of the zodiac; Scorpion

scor'pi·on n. arachnid with a poisonous sting in the tail

Scot (skät) n. native or inhabitant of Scotland

Scotch (skäch) n. whisky made in Scotland —a. Scottish —v. [s-] put an end to

Scotch tape trademark for a thin, transparent adhesive tape

scot'-free' a. unpunished

Scot'tie, Scot'ty n. [pl. -TIES] [Col.] Scottish terrier

Scot'tish a., n. (of) the people or language of Scotland

Scottish (or Scotch) terrier short-legged terrier with wiry hair

scoun'drel n. villain

scour v. 1. to clean by rubbing with abrasives 2. go through thoroughly, as in search

scourge (skurj) n., v. 1. whip 2. torment; plague

scout n. 1. one sent to spy, search, etc. 2. Boy Scout or Girl Scout —v. spy, search, etc.

scout'mas'ter n. adult leader of a troop of Boy Scouts

scow n. flat-bottomed boat

scowl v. look angry, sullen, etc. —n. scowling look

scrag'gly a. [-GLIER, -GLIEST] rough; jagged

scram v. [SCRAMMED, SCRAMMING] [Sl.] get out

scram'ble v. 1. climb, crawl, etc. hurriedly 2. struggle for something 3. mix together, as eggs while cooking —n. a scrambling

scrap n. 1. fragment 2. discarded material 3. pl. bits of food —a. discarded —v. [SCRAPPED, SCRAPPING] 1. discard 2. [Sl.] fight —**scrap'per** n. —**scrap'py** [-PIER, -PIEST] a.

scrap'book n. book in which to paste pictures, etc.

scrape v. 1. rub smooth or rub away 2. scratch 3. gather bit by bit —n. 1. scraped place 2. harsh sound 3. predicament —**scrap'er** n.

scrap'heap n. pile of discarded material or things

scratch v. 1. cut the surface 2. scrape or dig with one's nails 3. scrape noisily 4. cross out — n. mark from scratching —a. for hasty notes, etc. —**from scratch** from nothing — **scratch'y** [-IER, -IEST] a.

scrawl v. write carelessly —n. poor handwriting

scraw'ny a. [-NIER, -NIEST] lean; thin —**scraw'ni·ness** n.

scream v., n. (make) a loud, shrill cry or noise

screech v., n. (make) a loud, high shriek —**screech'y** [-IER, -IEST] a.

screen n. 1. thing used to shield, conceal, etc. 2. wire mesh in a frame 3. surface for showing movies, etc. —v. 1. conceal or shelter 2. sift or sift out

screen'play n. script for a motion picture

screw n. 1. naillike fastener with a spiral groove 2. propeller —v. 1. to turn; twist 2. fasten, as with a screw

screw'ball n. [Sl.] erratic or unconventional person

screw'driv'er n. tool for turning screws

screw'y a. [-IER, -IEST] [Sl.] 1. crazy 2. eccentric

scrib'ble v. 1. write carelessly 2. draw marks —n. scribbled writing

scribe n. writer; author

scrim'mage (skrim'ij) n. Football 1. play that follows the pass from center 2. a practice game —v. take part in a scrimmage

scrimp v. spend or use as little as possible

scrip n. certificate redeemable for stocks, money, etc.

script n. 1. handwriting 2. working copy of a play, etc.

Scrip'ture (-char) n. 1. often pl. the Bible 2. [s-] any sacred writing —**Scrip'tur·al** a.

scrod (skräd) n. young codfish or haddock, filleted to cook

scrof'u·la (skräf'-) n. tuberculosis of the lymphatic glands

scroll n. 1. roll of parchment, paper, etc. with writing on it 2. coiled or spiral design

scro'tum n. skin pouch containing the testicles

scrounge v. [Col.] 1. get by begging or sponging 2. hunt around for and take; pilfer

scrub v. [SCRUBBED, SCRUBBING] rub hard, as in washing —n. 1. a scrubbing 2. growth of stunted trees or bushes —a. 1. inferior 2. undersized — **scrub'by** [-BIER, -BIEST] a.

scruff n. nape of the neck

scrump'tious (-shəs) a. [Col.] very pleasing

scrunch v. 1. crunch, crush, etc. 2. huddle, squeeze, etc. — n. crunching sound

scru'ple n. a doubt as to what is right, proper, etc. —v. hesitate (at) from doubt

scru'pu·lous a. 1. showing scruples 2. precise

scru'ti·nize v. examine closely —**scru'ti·ny** n.

scu'ba n. diver's equipment

with compressed-air tanks for breathing under water

scud *v.* [SCUDDED, SCUDDING] move swiftly

scuff *v.* 1. scrape with the feet 2. wear a rough place on —*n.* worn spot

scuf′fle *n.* rough, confused fight —*v.* be in a scuffle

scull *n.* 1. large oar at the stern of a boat 2. light rowboat for racing —*v.* propel with a scull

scul′ler·y *n.* [*pl.* -IES] room for rough kitchen work

sculp′ture *v.* carve wood, stone, etc. into statues, etc. —*n.* art of sculpturing or work sculptured —**sculp′tor** *n.* —**sculp′tur·al** *a.*

scum *n.* 1. surface impurities on a liquid 2. vile people —**scum′my** [-MIER, -MIEST] *a.*

scup′per *n.* side opening for water to run off a deck

scurf *n.* scales shed by skin

scur′ril·ous *a.* vulgarly abusive —**scur·ril′i·ty** [*pl.* -TIES] *n.*

scur′ry *n., v.* [-RIED, -RYING] scamper

scur′vy *a.* [-VIER, -VIEST] low; mean —*n.* disease due to vitamin C deficiency

scut′tle *n.* bucket for coal —*v.* 1. scamper 2. cut holes in (a ship) to sink it

scut′tle·butt *n.* [Col.] rumor

scythe (*sith*) *n.* long-bladed tool to cut grass, etc.

sea *n.* 1. the ocean 2. a smaller body of salt water 3. large body of fresh water 4. heavy

wave —**at sea** 1. on the open sea 2. bewildered

sea anemone sea polyp with gelatinous body

sea′board *n.* land along the sea: also **sea′coast**

sea′far′er (-fer′-) *n.* sea traveler; esp., a sailor —**sea′far′-ing** *a., n.*

sea′food *n.* ocean fish or shellfish used as food

sea′go′ing *a.* 1. made for use on the open sea 2. seafaring

sea gull gull (*n.* 1)

sea horse small fish with a head like that of a horse

seal *n.* 1. sea mammal with flippers 2. its fur 3. official design stamped on a letter, etc. 4. thing that seals —*v.* 1. certify as with a seal 2. close tight 3. settle finally

seal′ant *n.* substance, as a wax, used for sealing

sea level mean level of the sea's surface

sea lion N. Pacific seal

seam *n.* 1. line where two pieces are sewed or welded together 2. layer of ore or coal —*v.* join with a seam

sea′man *n.* [*pl.* -MEN] 1. sailor 2. navy enlisted person —**sea′man·ship** *n.*

seam′stress *n.* woman whose work is sewing

seam′y *a.* [-IER, -IEST] unpleasant or sordid

sé·ance (sā′äns) *n.* spiritualists' meeting

sea′plane *n.* airplane which can land on water

sea′port *n.* port for ocean ships

sear *a.* withered —*v.* **1.** wither **2.** burn the surface of

search *v.* **1.** look through or examine to find something **2.** probe —*n.* a searching

search'light *n.* **1.** strong light **2.** device to project it

search warrant writ authorizing a police search

sea'shell *n.* mollusk shell

sea'shore *n.* land along the sea: also **sea'side**

sea'sick'ness *n.* nausea caused by a ship's rolling — **sea'sick** *a.*

sea'son *n.* **1.** any of the four divisions of the year **2.** special or fitting time —*v.* **1.** to flavor **2.** age **3.** accustom —**sea'son·al** *a.*

sea'son·a·ble *a.* timely

sea'son·ing *n.* flavoring for food

seat *n.* **1.** place to sit **2.** thing or part one sits on; chair, etc. **3.** the buttocks **4.** right to sit as a member **5.** chief location —*v.* **1.** set on a seat **2.** have seats for

seat belt straps across the hips to protect a seated passenger from abrupt jolts

sea urchin small sea animal with a spiny shell

sea'way *n.* inland waterway for ocean-going ships

sea'weed *n.* any sea plant

sea'wor'thy *a.* fit for travel on the sea: said of a ship

se·ba'ceous (-shəs) *a.* of or secreting fat, etc.

se·cede' (-sēd') *v.* withdraw formally from a group, etc. — **se·ces'sion** *n.*

se·clude' *v.* isolate —**se·clu'sion** *n.*

sec'ond *a.* **1.** next after the first **2.** another, like the first —*n.* **1.** one that is second **2.** thing not of the first quality **3.** assistant **4.** 1/60 of a minute —*v.* support (a suggestion, motion, etc.) —*adv.* in the second place, etc. —**sec'ond·ly** *adv.*

sec'ond·ar'y *a.* **1.** second in order **2.** less important **3.** derivative

secondary school school, as high school, coming after elementary school

sec'ond-class' *a.* **1.** of the class, rank, etc. next below the highest **2.** inferior

sec'ond-guess' *v.* [Col.] use hindsight in judging

sec'ond-hand' *a.* **1.** not from the original source **2.** used before

second lieutenant *Mil.* commissioned officer of the lowest rank

second nature deeply fixed, acquired habit

sec'ond-rate' *a.* inferior

sec'ond-string' *a.* [Col.] playing as a substitute at a specified position, as in sports

second thought change in thought after reconsidering

se'cret *a.* **1.** kept from being known by others **2.** hidden —*n.* secret fact, etc. —**se'cre·cy** *n.* —**se'cret·ly** *adv.*

sec're·tar'i·at *n.* staff headed by a secretary

sec're·tar'y *n.* [*pl.* -IES] **1.** one who keeps records, writes letters, etc. for a person or group

2. head of a department of government **3.** tall desk —**sec're·tar'i·al** *a.*

se·crete' *v.* **1.** hide **2.** make (a body substance), as a gland

se·cre·tive (*or* si krē'-) *a.* not frank or open —**se·cre·tive·ly** *adv.*

sect *n.* group having the same beliefs, esp. in religion

sec·tar'i·an *a.* **1.** of or like a sect **2.** narrow-minded

sec'tion *n.* **1.** portion **2.** distinct part —*v.* divide into sections —**sec'tion·al** *a.*

sec'tor *n.* **1.** part of a circle like a pie slice **2.** district for military operations

sec'u·lar *a.* not connected with church or religion

sec'u·lar·ize' *v.* to change from religious to civil control

se·cure' *a.* **1.** free from danger, care, etc. **2.** firm; stable **3.** sure —*v.* **1.** make secure **2.** get —**se·cure'ly** *adv.*

se·cu'ri·ty *n.* [*pl.* -TIES] **1.** secure state or feeling **2.** protection **3.** thing given as a pledge of repayment, etc. **4.** *pl.* stocks, bonds, etc.

se·dan' *n.* closed automobile with front and rear seats

se·date' *a.* quiet and dignified —*v.* to dose with a sedative —**se·date'ly** *adv.*

sed'a·tive *a.* making one calmer —*n.* sedative medicine —**se·da'tion** *n.*

sed'en·tar'y *a.* characterized by much sitting

Se·der (sā'dər) *n.* feast on the eve of Passover

sedge *n.* coarse, grasslike plant of marshes

sed'i·ment *n.* **1.** matter that settles from a liquid **2.** matter deposited by water, etc. —**sed'i·men·ta·ry** *a.*

se·di'tion (-dish'ən) *n.* stirring up of rebellion —**se·di'tious** *a.*

se·duce' *v.* **1.** lead astray **2.** entice into unlawful sexual intercourse, esp. for the first time —**se·duc'er** *n.* —**se·duc'tion** *n.* —**se·duc'tive** *a.*

sed'u·lous *a.* diligent

see *v.* [SAW, SEEN, SEEING] **1.** look at **2.** understand **3.** find out **4.** make sure **5.** escort **6.** meet; visit with **7.** consult **8.** have the power of sight —*n.* office or district of a bishop —**see through 1.** perceive truly **2.** finish **3.** help through difficulty —**see to** attend to

seed *n.* [*pl.* SEEDS, SEED] **1.** the part of a plant from which a new one will grow **2.** source **3.** sperm —*v.* **1.** plant with seed **2.** take the seeds from —**seed'less** *a.*

seed'ling *n.* young plant grown from a seed

seed money money to begin a project or attract more funds for it

seed'y *a.* [-IER, -IEST] **1.** full of seeds **2.** shabby; untidy

see'ing con. considering

seek *v.* [SOUGHT, SEEKING] **1.** search for **2.** try to get

seem *v.* to look; appear (to be)

seem'ing *a.* not actual —**seem'ing·ly** *adv.*

seem'ly *a.* [-LIER, -LIEST] suitable, proper, etc.

seep *v.* leak through; ooze — **seep'age** *n.*

seer *n* prophet

seer'suck·er *n.* crinkled fabric

see'saw *n.* balanced plank ridden at the ends for swinging up and down —*v.* move up and down or back and forth

seethe (sē*th*) *v.* boil

seg'ment *n.* section —*v.* divide into segments

seg're·gate *v.* set apart — **seg're·ga'tion** *n.*

seine (sān) *n.* fishing net

seis'mic (sīz'-) *a.* of an earthquake

seis'mo·graph *n.* instrument to record earthquakes

seize *v.* 1. take suddenly or by force 2. attack 3. capture 4. grasp —**sei'zure** *n.*

sel'dom *adv.* rarely

se·loot' *a.* 1. chosen with care 2. excellent 3. exclusive —*v.* choose; pick out —**se·lec'tion** *n.* —**se·lec'tive** *a.*

selective service compulsory military training

se·lect'man *n.* [*pl.* -MEN] New England town official

self *n.* [*pl.* SELVES] one's own person, welfare, etc.

self- *pref.* of, by, in, to, or with oneself or itself (as in the list below)

  self'-ap·point'ed
  self'-de·cep'tion
  self'-de·ni'al
  self'-dis'ci·pline
  self'-ed'u·cat'ed
  self'-em·ployed'
  self'-es·teem'

  self'-ex·plan'a·to'ry
  self'-ex·pres'sion
  self'-in·dul'gence
  self'-pit'y
  self'-pres·er·va'tion
  self'-re·li'ance
  self'-re·spect'
  self'-sat'is·fied
  self'-seal'ing
  self'-sup·port'ing
  self'-taught'

self'-ad·dressed' *a.* addressed to oneself

self'-as·sur'ance *n.* confidence in oneself

self'-cen'tered *a.* selfish

self'-con'fi·dent *a.* sure of oneself —**self'-con'fi·dence** *n.*

self'-con'scious *a.* ill at ease —**self'-con'scious·ly** *adv.*

self'-con·tained' *a.* 1. self-controlled 2. reserved 3. self-sufficient

self'-con'tra·dic'to·ry *a.* having elements that contradict each other

self'-con·trol' *n.* control of one's emotions, actions, etc. — **self'-con·trolled'** *a.*

self'-de·fense' *n.* defense of oneself or of one's rights, etc.

self'-de·struct' *v.* destruct

self'-de·ter'mi·na'tion *n.* 1. free will 2. right to choose one's government

self'-ev'i·dent *a.* evident without proof

self'-gov'ern·ment *n.* government of a group by its own members —**self'-gov'ern·ing** *a.*

self'-im'age *n.* one's idea of oneself, one's worth, etc.

self'-im·por'tance *n.* pompous conceit —**self'-im·por'tant** *a.*

self'-in'ter·est *n.* proper or sometimes selfish interest in one's own welfare

self'ish *a.* caring too much about oneself —**self'ish·ly** *adv.* —**self'ish·ness** *n.*

self'less *a.* unselfish

self'-love' *n.* excessive regard for oneself, one's own interests, etc.

self'-made' *a.* successful, rich, etc. through one's own efforts

self'-pos·ses'sion *n.* full control over one's actions, etc. —**self'-pos·sessed'** *a.*

self'-re·straint' *n.* self-control —**self'-re·strained'** *a.*

self'-right'eous *a.* feeling more righteous than others

self'same *a.* identical

self'-serv'ice *n.* practice of serving oneself in a store, cafeteria, etc.

self'-serv'ing *a.* serving one's selfish interests

self'-styled' *a.* so called by oneself

self'-suf·fi'cient *a.* independent —**self'-suf·fi'cien·cy** *n.*

self'-sus·tain'ing *a.* 1. supporting oneself 2. able to continue once begun

self'-willed' *a.* stubborn

self'-wind'ing *a.* wound automatically, as some watches

sell *v.* [SOLD, SELLING] 1. exchange for money 2. offer for sale 3. be sold (*for*) —**sell out** 1. get rid of completely by selling 2. [Col.] betray

sell'out *n.* [Col.] 1. a selling

out; betrayal 2. show, game, etc. for which all the seats have been sold

sel'vage, sel'vedge (-vij) *n.* edge woven to prevent raveling

se·man'tics *n.* study of words —**se·man'tic** *a.*

sem'a·phore (-fôr) *n.* flags or lights for signaling

sem'blance *n.* 1. outward form 2. deceiving appearance

se'men *n.* reproductive fluid of the male

se·mes'ter *n.* either of the terms in a school year

sem'i (-ī) *n.* [Col.] truck tractor with trailer attached

semi- *pref.* 1. half 2. partly 3. twice in some period

sem'i·an'nu·al *a.* happening, coming, etc. every half year

sem'i·cir'cle *n.* half circle

sem'i·co'lon *n.* mark of punctuation (;)

sem'i·con·duc'tor *n.* substance, as silicon, used as in transistors to control current flow

sem'i·fi'nal *n.*, *a.* (contest) just before the finals

sem'i·nar *n.* supervised course of research

sem'i·nar'y *n.* [*pl.* -IES] 1. school for women 2. school to train ministers, etc.

sem'i·pre'cious *a.* of gems that are less valuable than precious gems

sem'i·pri'vate *a.* of a hospital room with two, three, or sometimes four beds

sem'i·skilled' *a.* of or doing manual work requiring little training

sem'i·week'ly *a., adv.* twice a week

sen'ate *n.* 1. lawmaking assembly 2. [S-] upper branch of Congress or of a State legislature —sen'a·tor *n.* —sen'a·to'ri·al *a.*

send *v.* [SENT, SENDING] 1. cause to go or be carried 2. impel; drive 3. [Sl.] thrill — send for summon —send'er *n.*

send'-off' *n.* [Col.] farewell demonstration for someone starting on a trip, etc.

se'nile (-nīl) *a.* 1. of old age 2. weak in mind and body —se·nil'i·ty *n.*

sen'ior *a.* 1. older: written *Sr.* 2. of higher rank, etc. 3. of or for seniors —*n.* high school or college student in the last year

senior citizen elderly person, esp. one retired

sen·ior'i·ty *n.* status gained by length of service

sen'na *n.* laxative derived from a cassia plant

se·ñor' (-nyôr') *n.* gentleman: Sp. for *Mr.*

se·ño'ra *n.* married woman: Sp. for *Mrs.* or *Madam*

se·ño·ri'ta (-rē'-) *n.* unmarried woman: Sp. for *Miss*

sen·sa'tion *n.* 1. sense impression or the power to receive it 2. generalized feeling 3. exciting thing

sen·sa'tion·al *a.* shocking — sen·sa'tion·al·ism *n.*

sense *n.* 1. power to see, hear, taste, feel, etc. 2. sound judgment 3. meaning —*v.* perceive —in a sense to some extent

—make sense be intelligible

sense'less *a.* 1. unconscious 2. foolish or stupid

sen'si·bil'i·ty *n.* [*pl.* -TIES] 1. power of feeling 2. *pl.* delicate feelings

sen'si·ble *a.* 1. reasonable; wise 2. aware 3. noticeable — sen'si·bly *adv.*

sen'si·tive *a.* 1. quick to feel, notice, etc. 2. susceptible to stimuli 3. tender or sore 4. touchy —sen'si·tiv'i·ty *n.*

sen'si·tize *v.* make sensitive

sen'sor *n.* device to measure body heat, pulse, etc.

sen'so·ry *a.* of the senses

sen'su·al (-shoo-) *a.* 1. of or enjoying the pleasures of the body 2. of sexual pleasures — sen'su·al·ly *adv.* —sen'su·al'i·ty *n.*

sen'su·ous *a.* having to do with the senses

sent *pt.* & *pp.* of send

sen'tence *n.* 1. group of words stating something 2. court decision 3. punishment —*v.* pronounce punishment on

sen·ten'tious (-shas) *a.* 1. pithy 2. pompously boring

sen'tient (-shont) *a.* conscious

sen'ti·ment *n.* 1. a feeling 2. opinion 3. tender feelings 4. maudlin emotion —sen'ti·men'tal *a.* —sen'ti·men'tal·ist *n.* —sen'ti·men·tal'i·ty *n.* —sen'ti·men'tal·ly *adv.*

sen'ti·men'tal·ize *v.* treat or think of in a sentimental way

sen'ti·nel *n.* guard; sentry

sen'try *n.* [*pl.* -TRIES] guard posted to protect a group

se′pal *n.* leaf at the base of a flower

sep′a·rate *v.* **1.** divide; set apart **2.** keep apart **3.** go apart —*a.* (-rit) set apart; distinct —**sep′a·ra·ble** *a.* —**sep′a·rate·ly** *adv.* —**sep′a·ra′tion** *n.* —**sep′a·ra′tor** *n.*

sep′a·ra·tism *n.* advocacy of separation, racially, politically, etc.

se′pi·a *n., a.* reddish brown

sep′sis *n.* blood infection —**sep′tic** *a.*

Sep·tem′ber *n.* ninth month

septic tank underground tank into which house waste drains

sep′tum *n.* [*pl.* -TUMS, -TA] dividing part in the nose, a fruit, etc.

se·pul′cher (-kər) *n.* tomb: Br. sp. **sepulchre**

se·pul′chral (-krəl) *a.* **1.** of burial, etc. **2.** gloomy **3.** deep, as sound

se′quel (-kwəl) *n.* **1.** result **2.** book that continues an earlier book

se′quence *n.* **1.** succession or the order of this **2.** series **3.** resulting event **4.** scene; episode

se·ques′ter *v.* hide; isolate — **se′ques·tra′tion** *n.*

se′quin *n.* small, shiny disk for decorating cloth

se·quoi′a (-kwoi′-) *n.* giant evergreen tree

se·rag′lio (si räl′yō) *n.* [*pl.* -LIOS] harem (*sense* 1)

se·ra′pe (sə rä′pē) *n.* bright-colored blanket used as man's garment in Mexico, etc.

ser′aph (ser′-) *n.* [*pl.* -APHS,

-APHIM] angel of the highest rank —**se·raph′ic** *a.*

ser·e·nade′ *v., n.* (perform) music sung or played at night, esp. by a lover

ser′en·dip′i·ty *n.* the making of lucky discoveries by chance

se·rene′ *a.* undisturbed; calm —**se·rene′ly** *adv.* —**se·ren′i·ty** *n.*

serf *n.* feudal farmer, almost a slave —**serf′dom** *n.*

serge (surj) *n.* twilled, worsted fabric

ser′geant (sär′jant) *n.* **1.** low-ranking police officer **2.** non-commissioned officer above a corporal

ser′geant-at-arms′ *n.* [*pl.* SERGEANTS-AT-ARMS] one who keeps order, as in a court

se′ri·al *a.* of, in, or published in a series —*n.* serial story — **se′ri·al·i·za′tion** *n.* —**se′ri·al·ize′** *v.*

serial number one of a series of numbers given for identification

se′ries *n.* [*pl.* SERIES] number of similar things coming one after another

se′ri·ous *a.* **1.** earnest **2.** important **3.** dangerous

ser′mon *n.* **1.** religious speech by a clergyman **2.** serious talk on duty, etc.

ser′pent *n.* snake

ser′pen·tine (-tēn) *a.* winding

ser′rate *a.* edged like a saw

ser′ried *a.* placed or located close together

se′rum (sir′-) *n.* **1.** yellowish fluid in blood **2.** antitoxin from the blood of an immune animal —**se′rous** *a.*

ser′vant *n.* one hired to work in another's home

serve *v.* **1.** be a servant to **2.** aid **3.** do official service **4.** spend a prison term **5.** offer (food, etc.) to **6.** be used by **7.** meet the needs of **8.** deliver **9.** hit a ball to start play —*n.* a serving of the ball in tennis, etc. —**serve (someone) right** be what someone deserves —**serv′er** *n.*

serv′ice *n.* **1.** a serving **2.** governmental work **3.** armed forces **4.** work done for others **5.** religious ceremony **6.** set of silverware, etc. **7.** aid **8.** system providing water, gas, etc. **9.** serving in tennis, etc. —*v.* **1.** supply **2.** repair —of service helpful —**serv′ice·a·ble** *a.*

serv′ice·man *n.* [*pl.* -MEN] member of the armed forces

service mark term used like a trademark by supplier of services

service station place selling gasoline, oil, etc.

ser′vile (-v′l) *a.* humbly submissive —**ser·vil′i·ty** *n.*

ser′vi·tude *n.* **1.** slavery **2.** work imposed as punishment for crime

ser′vo·mech′a·nism *n.* automatic remote control system

ses′a·me *n.* flat, edible seeds of an East Indian plant

ses′qui·cen·ten′ni·al *a.* of a period of 150 years

ses′sion *n.* meeting of a court, legislature, class, etc.

set *v.* [SET, SETTING] **1.** put; place **2.** put in the proper condition, position, etc. **3.** make or become firm or fixed **4.** establish; fix **5.** sit on eggs, as a hen **6.** start **7.** mount (gems) **8.** furnish (an example) **9.** sink below the horizon **10.** fit (words) to music —*a.* **1.** fixed **2.** obstinate **3.** ready —*n.* **1.** way in which a thing is set **2.** scenery for a play **3.** group of like persons or things **4.** assembled parts, as of a radio —**set about** (or **in, to**) begin —**set forth** state —**set off 1.** show off by contrast **2.** explode —**set on** (or **upon**) attack —**set up 1.** erect **2.** establish

set′back *n.* relapse

set·tee′ *n.* small sofa

set′ter *n.* long-haired hunting dog

set′ting *n.* **1.** that in which a thing is set **2.** position of a set dial **3.** time, place, etc., as of a story **4.** surroundings

set′tle *v.* **1.** put in order **2.** set in place firmly or comfortably **3.** go to live in **4.** deposit sediment, etc. **5.** calm **6.** decide **7.** pay, as a debt **8.** come to rest **9.** sink **10.** become localized, as pain **11.** reach an agreement (*with* or *on*) —**set′tler** *n.*

set′tle·ment *n.* **1.** a settling **2.** colony **3.** village **4.** agreement or payment **5.** community center for those in need

set'-to' n. [pl. -TOS] [Col.] fight or argument

set'up n. 1. details or makeup of organization, plan, equipment, etc. 2. glass, ice, soda water, etc. for an alcoholic drink

sev'en a., n. one more than six —**sev'enth** a., n.

sev'en·teen' a., n. seven more than ten —**sev'en·teenth'** a., n.

sev'en·ty a., n. [pl. -TIES] seven times ten —**sev'en·ti·eth** a., n.

sev'er v. cut off; separate —**sev'er·ance** n.

sev'er·al a. 1. more than two but not many 2. separate —n. several persons or things —**sev'er·al·ly** adv.

se·vere' a. 1. harsh; strict 2. grave 3. very plain 4. intense —**se·vere'ly** adv. —**se·ver'i·ty** n.

sew (sō) v. [SEWED, SEWN or SEWED, SEWING] fasten, make, etc. by means of needle and thread —**sew'er** n. —**sew'ing** n.

sew·age (soō'ij) n. waste matter carried off by sewers

sew'er n. underground drain for water and waste matter

sex n. 1. either of the two divisions of organisms, male or female 2. character of being male or female 3. attraction between the sexes 4. sexual intercourse

sex'ism n. unfair treatment of one sex by the other, esp. of women by men —**sex'ist** a., n.

sex'tant n. ship's instrument for navigation

sex'ton n. official who maintains church property

sex'u·al a. of sex, the sexes, sex organs, etc. —**sex'u·al'i·ty** n. —**sex'u·al·ly** adv.

sex'y a. [-IER, -IEST] [Col.] exciting sexual desire

shab'by a. [-BIER, -BIEST] 1. worn out 2. clothed poorly 3. mean —**shab'bi·ly** adv. —**shab'bi·ness** n.

shack n. shanty

shack'le n. metal fastening for a prisoner's wrist or ankle —v. 1. put shackles on 2. restrain

shad n. saltwater fish

shade n. 1. partial darkness caused by cutting off light rays 2. device to cut off light 3. degree of darkness of a color 4. small difference 5. pl. [Sl.] sunglasses —v. 1. screen from light 2. change slightly —**shad'y** [-IER, -IEST] a.

shad'ing n. 1. a shielding against light 2. slight variation

shad'ow n. 1. shade cast by a body blocking light rays 2. sadness 3. small amount —v. follow in secret —**shad'ow·y** a.

shad'ow-box' v. spar with imaginary boxing opponent

shaft n. 1. arrow or spear, or its stem 2. long, slender part or thing 3. bar transmitting motion to a mechanical part 4. vertical opening 5. long, narrow passage sunk in the earth

shag n. long nap on cloth —v. [SHAGGED, SHAGGING] chase

after and retrieve, as baseballs in batting practice

shag'gy a. [-GIER, -GIEST] 1. having long, coarse hair 2. unkempt 3. having a rough nap

shah n. ruler of Iran

shake v. [SHOOK, SHAKEN, SHAKING] 1. move quickly up and down, back and forth, etc. 2. tremble 3. weaken, disturb, upset, etc. 4. clasp (another's hand), as in greeting —n. 1. a shaking 2. a wood shingle 3. [Col.] milkshake 4. pl. [Col.] trembling —**shake off** get rid of —**shake up** 1. mix by shaking 2. jar 3. reorganize

shak'y [-IER, -IEST] a.

shake'down n. 1. [Sl.] extortion of money 2. thorough search —a. for testing equipment

shak'er n. 1. device used in shaking 2. [S-] member of celibate religious sect

shake'-up' n. reorganization

shak'o (shak'-) n. [pl. -OS] high, stiff military dress hat

shale n. rock of hard clay

shall v. [pt. SHOULD] a helping verb showing: 1. futurity 2. determination or obligation

shal·lot' n. onionlike plant

shal'low a. 1. not deep 2. lacking depth of character —n. shoal

shalt [Ar.] shall: used with *thou*

sham n., a. (something) false or fake —v. [SHAMMED, SHAMMING] pretend

sham'ble v. walk clumsily —n. pl. scene of great destruction

shame n. 1. guilt, embarrassment, etc. felt for a wrong act 2. dishonor 3. a misfortune —v. 1. make ashamed 2. dishonor 3. force by a sense of shame —**shame'ful** a.

shame'faced a. 1. bashful 2. ashamed

shame'less a. showing no shame or modesty

sham·poo' v. wash (the hair, etc.) —n. a shampooing, or soap, etc. for this

sham'rock n. cloverlike plant with three leaflets

shang'hai (-hī) v. [-HAIED, -HAIING] to kidnap for service aboard ship

shank n. 1. the leg, esp. between the knee and ankle 2. part between tool handle and working part —**shank of the evening** early evening

shan't shall not

shan'tung' n. silk fabric

shan'ty n. [pl. -TIES] small, shabby dwelling

shape n. 1. outer form 2. definite form 3. [Col.] condition —v. form or adapt —**shape up** [Col.] 1. come to definite form 2. behave as one should —**take shape** become definite —**shape'less** a.

shape'ly a. [-LIER, -LIEST] well-shaped

shard n. piece of broken pottery

share n. 1. part each gets or has 2. equal part of stock of a corporation —v. 1. give in shares 2. have a share (*in*) 3. use in common with

share'crop v. [-CROPPED, -CROPPING] work (land) for a

share of the crop —**share'-crop'per** n.

share'hold'er n. owner of share(s) of corporation stock

shark n. 1. a large, fierce fish 2. swindler 3. [Sl.] expert

shark'skin n. smooth, silky cloth

sharp a. 1. having a fine point or cutting edge 2. abrupt 3. distinct 4. clever or shrewd 5. vigilant 6. harsh or intense 7. sly; deceitful 8. pungent 9. brisk 10. *Mus.* above the true pitch —n. *Mus.* a note one half step above another: symbol·(♯) —adv. 1. in a sharp way 2. precisely —**sharp'ly** adv. —**sharp'ness** n.

sharp'en v. make or become sharp —**sharp'en·er** n.

sharp'er n. swindler; cheat

sharp'-eyed' a. having keen sight or perception

sharp'shoot'er n. good marksman

sharp'-tongued' a. sarcastic; highly critical

sharp'-wit'ted a. thinking quickly

shat'ter v. 1. break into pieces 2. damage badly

shat'ter·proof a. that will resist shattering

shave v. [alt. pp. SHAVEN] 1. cut thin slices from 2. cut the hair or beard (of) to the skin —n. act of shaving —**close shave** [Col.] narrow escape

shav'er n. 1. one who shaves 2. instrument for shaving, esp. by electricity 3. [Col.] lad

shav'ing n. 1. act of one who shaves 2. thin piece shaved off

shawl n. cloth covering for the head and shoulders

shay n. [Dial.] light carriage

she pron. the female mentioned

sheaf n. [pl. SHEAVES] bundle of stalks, papers, etc.

shear v. [alt. pp. SHORN] 1. cut or cut off as with shears 2. clip hair from —n. pl. large scissors

sheath (shēth) n. 1. case for a knife blade, etc. 2. any covering like this

sheathe (shēth) v. put into or cover with a sheath

she-bang' n. [Col.] affair, thing, contrivance, etc.

shed n. small shelter or storage place —v. [SHED, SHEDDING] 1. make flow 2. radiate 3. throw or cast off

sheen n. luster; gloss

sheep n. [pl. SHEEP] cud-chewing animal with heavy wool

sheep'ish a. bashful or embarrassed

sheep'skin n. 1. leather or parchment made from skin of sheep 2. [Col.] a diploma

sheer v. to swerve —a. 1. very thin 2. absolute 3. very steep —adv. completely

sheet n. 1. large cloth of cotton, etc. used on beds 2. piece of paper 3. broad, thin piece of glass, etc. 4. broad expanse, as of ice 5. rope to control a sail

sheet'ing n. cloth material for sheets

sheik, sheikh (shēk) n. Arab chief

shek'el n. ancient Hebrew coin

shelf n. [pl. SHELVES] 1. thin,

flat board for holding things **2.** ledge or reef —**on the shelf** out of use

shell *n.* **1.** hard outer covering, as of an egg **2.** narrow rowboat for racing **3.** missile from a large gun **4.** cartridge —*v.* **1.** remove the shell from **2.** bombard —**shell out** [Col.] pay (money)

she'll 1. she shall **2.** she will

shel·lac', **shel·lack'** *n.* thin varnish of resin and alcohol —*v.* [SHELLACKED, SHELLACKING] **1.** put shellac on **2.** [Sl.] to beat

shell'fish *n.* aquatic animal with a shell

shel'ter *n.* something that covers or protects —*v.* give shelter to

shelve *v.* **1.** put on a shelf **2.** lay aside

shelv'ing *n.* **1.** material for shelves **2.** shelves

she·nan'i·gan *n. usually pl.* [Col.] trickery; mischief

shep'herd *n.* **1.** one who herds sheep **2.** religious leader —*v.* be a shepherd —**shep'herd·ess** *n.fem.*

sher'bet *n.* frozen dessert of fruit juice, milk, etc.

sher'iff *n.* chief law officer of a county

sher'ry *n.* [*pl.* -RIES] a yellow or brown wine

shib'bo·leth *n.* password

shield *n.* **1.** armor carried on the arm **2.** thing that protects —*v.* protect

shift *v.* **1.** move or change from one person, place, direction, etc. to another **2.** get along —

n. **1.** a shifting **2.** relief crew of workers **3.** time at work **4.** trick **5.** gearshift

shift'less *a.* lazy

shift'y *a.* [-IER, -IEST] tricky; evasive

shill *n.* [Sl.] one who pretends to buy or bet, to lure others

shil·le'lagh (-lā'le) *n.* cudgel

shil'ling *n.* former British coin, 1/20 of a pound

shil'ly-shal'ly (-shal'e) *v.* [-LIED, -LYING] hesitate

shim *n.* wedge for filling space

shim'mer *v., n.* (shine with) a wavering light

shim'my *n., v.* [-MIED, -MY-ING] shake or wobble

shin *n.* front of the leg between knee and ankle —*v.* [SHINNED, SHINNING] climb, as a rope, with hands and legs: also **shin'ny** [-NIED, -NYING]

shin'bone *n.* tibia

shin'dig *n.* [Col.] party, dance, etc.

shine *v.* [SHONE or SHINED, SHINING] **1.** be or make be bright **2.** excel **3.** [pt. & pp. SHINED] make shiny by polishing —*n.* **1.** brightness **2.** polish

shin'gle *n.* **1.** piece of wood, slate, etc. for roofing **2.** [Col.] small signboard **3.** coarse gravel on beach —*v.* put shingles on (a roof)

shin'gles *n.* virus skin disease along a nerve

shin'guard *n.* padded guard for shin worn in sports

shin'splints *n.* muscle strain of lower leg

shin'y *a.* [-IER, -IEST] bright; shining

ship *n.* 1. large vessel for deep water 2. aircraft —*v.* [SHIPPED, SHIPPING] 1. put or go in a ship 2. transport 3. take in (water) over ship's side —on **shipboard** on a ship —ship'-load *n.* —ship'ment *n.* —ship'per *n.*

-ship *suf.* 1. state of 2. rank of 3. skill as

ship'mate *n.* fellow sailor

ship'shape *a.* neat; trim

ship'wreck *v., n.* (cause) loss or ruin of a ship

ship'yard *n.* place where ships are built and repaired

shire *n.* [Br.] county

shirk *v.* neglect (a duty) —shirk'er *n.*

shirr *v.* 1. pull stitches tight in rows 2. bake (eggs) with crumbs

shirt *n.* 1. upper garment for men 2. undershirt

shirt'waist *n.* woman's blouse tailored like a shirt

shish' ke-bab' (kə bäb') dish of kebabs, esp. lamb

shiv'er *v.* 1. shake or tremble 2. shatter —*n.* 1. a trembling 2. sliver

shoal *n.* 1. school of fish 2. shallow place in water

shock *n.* 1. sudden blow or jar 2. sudden emotional upset 3. effect of electric current on the body 4. impairment of blood circulation 5. bundle of grain 6. thick mass of hair —*v.* 1. astonish; horrify 2. give an electric shock to

shock'proof *a.* able to stand shock without damage

shod'dy *a.* [-DIER, -DIEST] inferior —shod'di·ness *n.*

shoe *n.* 1. outer covering for the foot 2. horseshoe 3. part of a brake that presses on the wheel —*v.* [SHOD, SHOEING] put shoes on —fill one's **shoes** take one's place

shoe'horn *n.* device to help slip a shoe on the foot

shoe'lace *n.* lace (*n.* 1)

shoe'string *n.* 1. shoelace 2. small amount of capital —*a.* near the ankles, as a baseball catch

shoe tree form put in a shoe to hold its shape

shone pt. & pp. of **shine**

shoo *int.* go away! —*v.* drive away by crying "shoo"

shoo'-in' *n.* [Col.] one expected to win easily

shook pt. of **shake**

shoot *v.* [SHOT, SHOOTING] 1. send out, or move, with force, speed, etc. 2. fire a bullet, etc. from 3. wound or kill with a bullet, etc. 4. to photograph 5. score (a point, etc.) in sports 6. grow rapidly 7. variegate —*n.* new growth; sprout or twig —shoot'er *n.*

shop *n.* 1. place where things are sold 2. manufacturing place —*v.* [SHOPPED, SHOPPING] look at or buy goods in shops —shop'per *n.*

shop'lift'er *n.* one who steals from store counters

shopping center complex of stores with common parking area

shop'talk *n.* 1. specialized words for certain work 2. talk about work after hours

shore *n.* 1. land next to water 2. prop; support —*v.* prop (*up*)

short *a.* 1. not measuring much 2. not tall 3. brief 4. brusque 5. less than enough 6. rich in shortening, as pastry —*n.* 1. short movie 2. *pl.* short pants 3. short circuit —*adv.* abruptly or briefly —*v.* short-circuit —**in short** briefly —**short'ness** *n.*

short'age *n.* 1. lack; deficiency 2. deficit

short'cake *n.* light biscuit or sweet cake

short·change' *v.* [Col.] give less change than is due

short circuit side circuit of low resistance that deflects electric current —**short'-cir'cuit** *v.*

short'com'ing *n.* defect

short'cut *n.* 1. shorter route 2. way of saving time, etc.

short'en *v.* make or become short or shorter

short'en·ing *n.* fat used to make baked goods flaky

short'hand *n.* system of symbols for writing fast

short'-hand'ed *a.* short of workers or helpers

short'horn *n.* kind of cattle with short, curved horns

short'-lived' (-līved', -livd') *a.* having a short life span

short'ly *adv.* 1. briefly 2. soon 3. curtly

short shrift little attention —**make short shrift of** deal with quickly

short'sight'ed *a.* lacking in foresight

short'stop *n. Baseball* infielder between second and third base

short subject short movie

short'-tem'pered *a.* easily angered

short'wave' *n.* radio wave 60 meters or less in length

short'-wind'ed (-win'did) *a.* easily put out of breath

shot *pt.* & *pp.* of **shoot** —*n.* 1. act of shooting 2. range; scope 3. attempt 4. throw, etc., as of a ball 5. projectile(s) for a gun 6. ball used in the shot put 7. marksman 8. photograph 9. hypodermic injection 10. drink of liquor —*a.* [Col.] worn out

shot'gun *n.* gun for firing small shot at close range

shot put athletic contest for throwing heavy metal ball —**shot'-put'ter** *n.*

should (shood) *pt.* of **shall** *Should* is used to express obligation, probability, etc.

shoul'der *n.* 1. part of the body to which an arm or foreleg is connected 2. edge of a road —*v.* 1. push with the shoulder 2. assume the burden of

shout *v., n.* (utter) a loud, sudden cry or call

shove *v.* 1. push along a surface 2. push roughly —*n.* a push

shov'el *n.* tool with a broad scoop and a handle —*v.* move or dig with a shovel —**shov'el·ful** [*pl.* -FULS] *n.*

show *v.* [*pp.* SHOWN or SHOWED] 1. bring into sight;

reveal 2. appear 3. be noticeable 4. guide 5. point out 6. prove; explain 7. finish third in a race —n. 1. a display, performance, etc. 2. pompous display 3. pretense 4. third position at the finish in a race —**show off** make a display of —**show up 1.** expose 2. arrive —**show'case** n. —**show'-room** n.

show'boat n. boat with theater and actors who play river towns

show'down n. [Col.] disclosure of facts to force a settlement

show'er (shou'-) n. 1. brief fall of rain 2. any sudden fall or flow 3. party with gifts for a bride, etc. 4. bath for the body with fine water spray: in full **shower bath** —v. 1. to spray with water 2. give, or fall, abundantly 3. take a shower bath —**show'er·y** a.

show'man n. [pl. -MEN] one who produces shows skillfully —**show'man·ship** n.

show'piece n. a fine example

show'y a. [-IER, -IEST] 1. of striking appearance 2. gaudy; flashy —**show'i·ly** adv. —**show'i·ness** n.

shrap'nel n. fragments of an exploded artillery shell

shred n. 1. torn strip 2. fragment —v. [SHREDDED or SHRED, SHREDDING] cut or tear into shreds

shrew n. 1. small, mouselike mammal 2. nagging woman —**shrew'ish** a.

shrewd a. clever or sharp in practical affairs —**shrewd'ly** adv. —**shrewd'ness** n.

shriek (shrēk) v., n. (utter) a loud, piercing cry

shrike n. shrill-voiced bird of prey

shrill a. high-pitched and piercing in sound —**shrill'ness** n. —**shril'ly** adv.

shrimp n. 1. small, long-tailed, edible shellfish 2. [Col.] small person

shrine n. saint's tomb or other sacred place

shrink v. [SHRANK or SHRUNK, SHRUNK or SHRUNKEN, SHRINKING] 1. lessen in amount 2. to contract 3. draw back —**shrink'age** n.

shriv'el v. dry up; wither

shroud n. 1. cloth used to wrap a corpse 2. cover; veil 3. pl. ropes supporting ship's masts —v. hide; cover

shrub n. bush

shrub'ber·y n. shrubs collectively

shrug v. [SHRUGGED, SHRUGGING] draw up the shoulders in a gesture of doubt, indifference, etc. —n. this gesture

shuck v., n. husk; shell

shud'der v. shake, as in horror —n. a shuddering

shuf'fle v. 1. walk with feet dragging 2. mix or jumble together —n. a shuffling

shuf'fle·board n. game in which disks are pushed toward numbered squares

shun v. [SHUNNED, SHUNNING] keep away from

shunt v. 1. move to one side 2.

switch or shift —n. a shunting or means of shunting

shush int. be quiet! —v. say "shush" to

shut v. [SHUT, SHUTTING] 1. close (a door, etc.) 2. prevent entrance to 3. confine (in a room, etc.) 4. fold up (an umbrella, etc.) —a. closed —**shut down** cease operating —**shut off** prevent passage of or on —**shut up** 1. enclose 2. [Col.] stop talking

shut'eye n. [Sl.] sleep

shut'-in' a. confined indoors by illness —n. invalid

shut'out n. prevention of the opposing team from scoring

shut'ter n. 1. movable window cover 2. light-controlling device on a camera lens

shut'tle n. 1. device to carry thread back and forth in weaving 2. bus, plane, etc. making short trips back and forth —v. move rapidly to and fro

shut'tle·cock n. feathered cork ball in badminton

shy a. [SHYER or SHIER, SHYEST or SHIEST] 1. timid 2. bashful 3. distrustful 4. [Sl.] lacking —v. [SHIED, SHYING] 1. be startled 2. hesitate 3. fling sideways —**shy'ly** adv. —**shy'ness** n.

shy'ster (shī'-) n. [Sl.] dishonest lawyer

Si·a·mese' twins pair of twins born joined

sib'i·lant a., n. hissing (sound) —**sib'i·lance** n.

sib'ling n. a brother or sister

sib'yl n. prophetess of ancient Greece or Rome

sic v. [SICKED, SICKING] to incite (a dog) to attack

sick a. 1. having disease; ill 2. nauseated 3. of or for sick people 4. disgusted 5. [Col.] morbid —**the sick** sick people —**sick'ish** a.

sick v. sic

sick bay ship's hospital

sick'bed n. sick person's bed

sick'en v. make or become sick —**sick'en·ing** a.

sick'le n. curved blade with a short handle, for cutting tall grass

sick'ly a. [-LIER, -LIEST] 1. in poor health 2. faint or weak

sick'ness n. 1. a being sick 2. disease 3. nausea

sick'room n. sick person's room

side n. 1. right or left half 2. a bounding line 3. a surface 4. aspect 5. relative position 6. party; faction 7. line of descent —a. 1. of, at, or to a side 2. secondary —**side with** support a faction —**take sides** support one faction

side arms weapons worn at the side or waist

side'board n. dining-room cabinet for linen, china, etc.

side'burns n.pl. hair on the cheeks, beside the ears

side dish separate dish along with the main course of food

side'kick n. [Sl.] 1. close friend 2. partner

side'light n. bit of incidental information

side'line n. secondary line of merchandise, work, etc.

side'long *adv., a.* toward or to the side

si·de're·al *a.* of or measured by the stars

side'show *n.* circus show apart from the main show

side'split'ting *a.* very hearty or very funny

side'step *v.* [-STEPPED, -STEPPING] avoid as by stepping aside

side'swipe *v.* hit along the side in passing —*n.* such a glancing blow

side'track *v.* turn aside from a course, subject, etc.

side'walk *n.* path for pedestrians alongside a street

side'wall *n.* side of a tire, between tread and wheel rim

side'ways *a., adv.* 1. to or from one side 2. side first Also **side'wise**

sid'ing *n.* 1. outside boards, etc. on a building 2. short railroad track off the main track

si'dle *v.* move sideways cautiously

siege (sēj) *n.* 1. encircling of a place to effect its capture 2. persistent attack

si·es'ta *n.* brief rest or nap, esp. in the afternoon

sieve (siv) *n.* strainer with many small holes

sift *v.* 1. pass through a sieve 2. examine (evidence, etc.) with care 3. to separate

sigh *v.* 1. let out a deep breath, as in sorrow 2. long (*for*) —*n.* a sighing

sight *n.* 1. something seen 2. act or power of seeing 3. range of vision 4. aiming device 5.

[Col.] anything that looks unpleasant, odd, etc. —*v.* 1. to see 2. aim (a gun, etc.) —**at** (or **on**) **sight** as soon as seen

sight'ed *a.* not blind

sight'less *a.* blind

sight'ly *a.* [-LIER, -LIEST] pleasing to look at

sight'see·ing *n.* visiting of places of interest

sign *n.* 1. mark or symbol 2. meaningful gesture 3. signboard, road marker, etc. 4. trace; vestige —*v.* 1. write one's name (on) 2. engage by written contract —**sign off** stop broadcasting —**sign'er** *n.*

sig'nal *n.* 1. gesture, device, etc. to warn, order, etc. 2. in radio, etc., electrical impulses sent or received —*a.* notable —*v.* make signals (to)

sig'nal·ize *v.* 1. make noteworthy 2. point out

sig'nal·ly *adv.* notably

sig·na·to'ry *n.* [*pl.* -RIES] nation signing a pact, etc.

sig'na·ture *n.* one's name written by oneself

sign'board *n.* board bearing advertising

sig'net *n.* small official seal

sig·nif'i·cance *n.* 1. meaning 2. importance —**sig·nif'i·cant** *a.*

sig'ni·fy *v.* [-FIED, -FYING] 1. to mean 2. make known, as by a sign —**sig'ni·fi·ca'tion** *n.*

si'lage (-lij) *n.* green fodder preserved in a silo

si'lence *n.* absence of sound —*v.* 1. make silent 2. repress —*int.* be silent!

si'lent *a.* 1. not speaking 2.

still; quiet **3.** inactive —**sil′·lent·ly** *adv.*

sil·hou·ette′ (-oo wet′) *v., n.* (make) a dark shape against a light background

sil′i·ca *n.* glassy mineral found as sand, etc.

sil′i·con *n.* chemical element forming silica, etc.

sil′i·cone *n.* silicon compound resistant to water, etc.

sil′i·co′sis *n.* chronic lung disease from inhaling silica dust

silk *n.* thread or fabric of soft fiber made by silkworms — **silk′en, silk′y** [-IER, -IEST] *a.*

silk′worm *n.* moth caterpillar that spins silk fiber

sill *n.* bottom of a door frame or window frame

sil′ly *a.* [-LIER, -LIEST] foolish; absurd —**sil′li·ness** *n.*

si′lo *n.* [*pl.* -LOS] tower for storing green fodder

silt *n.* fine particles of soil floating in or left by water —*v.* fill with silt

sil′ver *n.* **1.** white, precious metal, a chemical element **2.** silver coins **3.** silverware **4.** grayish white —*a.* of silver —*v.* cover as with silver —**sil′ver·y** *a.*

sil′ver·fish *n.* wingless insect found in damp places

silver lining hope or comfort in the midst of despair

sil′ver·smith *n.* one who makes things of silver

sil′ver·tongued′ *a.* eloquent

sil′ver·ware *n.* tableware of or plated with silver

sim′i·an *n.* ape or monkey

sim′i·lar *a.* nearly alike —

sim′i·lar′i·ty [*pl.* -TIES] *n.* —**sim′i·lar·ly** *adv.*

sim′i·le (-lē) *n.* a likening of dissimilar things

si·mil′i·tude *n.* likeness

sim′mer *v., n.* (keep at or near) a gentle boiling

si′mon-pure′ *a.* genuine

sim′o·ny (sim′-) *n.* buying or selling of sacred things

sim·pa′ti·co (-pä′-) *a.* compatible or congenial

sim′per *v.* smile in a silly way —*n.* silly smile

sim′ple *a.* **1.** having only one or a few parts **2.** easy to do or understand **3.** plain **4.** natural **5.** common **6.** foolish

simple interest interest computed on principal alone

sim′ple-mind′ed *a.* **1.** naive **2.** foolish **3.** mentally retarded

sim′ple·ton *n.* fool

sim·plic′i·ty (-plis′-) *n.* [*pl.* -TIES] **1.** simple quality **2.** plainness

sim′pli·fy *v.* [-FIED, -FYING] make less complex —**sim′pli·fi·ca′tion** *n.*

sim·plis′tic *a.* making complex problems seem very simple —**sim·plis′ti·cal·ly** *adv.*

sim′ply *adv.* **1.** in a simple way **2.** merely **3.** completely

sim′u·late *v.* **1.** pretend **2.** look or act like —**sim′u·la′tion** *n.*

si′mul·ta′ne·ous *a.* done, etc. at the same time —**si′mul·ta′ne·ous·ly** *adv.*

sin *n.* **1.** breaking of religious or moral law **2.** offense or fault —*v.* [SINNED, SINNING] commit a sin —**sin′ful** *a.* —**sin′ner** *n.*

since *adv., prep.* **1.** from then until now **2.** at some time between then and now —*con.* **1.** after the time that **2.** because

sin·cere´ *a.* **1.** without deceit **2.** genuine —**sin·cere´ly** *adv.* —**sin·cer´i·ty** *n.*

si´ne·cure (sī´-) *n.* well-paid job with little work

sin´ew (-yōō) *n.* **1.** tendon **2.** strength —**sin´ew·y** *a.*

sing *v.* [SANG, SUNG, SINGING] **1.** make musical sounds with the voice, etc. **2.** perform by singing **3.** hum, buzz, etc. **4.** tell in song —*n.* [Col.] group singing —**sing´er** *n.*

singe (sinj) *v.* [SINGED, SINGEING] burn superficially —*n.* a singeing

sin´gle *a.* **1.** one only **2.** of or for one person or family **3.** unmarried **4.** whole —*v.* **1.** select from others (often with *out*) **2.** *Baseball* hit a single —*n.* **1.** single person or thing **2.** *Baseball* hit by which the batter reaches first base **3.** *pl.* tennis game with only two players —**sin´gle·ness** *n.*

single file column of persons one behind the other

sin´gle-hand´ed *a.* without help

sin´gle-mind´ed *a.* with only one aim or purpose

sin´gly *adv.* **1.** alone **2.** one by one **3.** unaided

sing´song *n.* rise and fall of tone in unvarying cadence

sin´gu·lar *a.* **1.** unique **2.** exceptional **3.** unusual —*n. Gram.* word form designating

only one —**sin´gu·lar´i·ty** *n.* —**sin´gu·lar·ly** *adv.*

sin´is·ter *a.* **1.** threatening **2.** wicked or evil

sink *v.* [SANK or SUNK, SUNK, SINKING] **1.** go or put beneath the surface of water, etc. **2.** go down slowly **3.** become lower **4.** pass gradually (*into* sleep, etc.) **5.** invest **6.** defeat —*n.* **1.** basin with a drainpipe **2.** area of sunken land —**sink in** [Col.] be understood fully

sink´er *n.* lead weight used on a fishing line

sinking fund fund built up to pay off a debt

sin´u·ous *a.* **1.** bending or winding in or out **2.** crooked

si´nus *n.* [*pl.* -NUSES] any air cavity in the skull opening into the nasal cavities

si´nus·i´tis *n.* inflammation of the sinuses

-sion *suf.* act, state, or result of

sip *v.* [SIPPED, SIPPING] drink a little at a time —*n.* small amount sipped

si´phon *n.* tube for carrying liquid from one container to another below it —*v.* drain through a siphon

sir *n.* **1.** [*sometimes* S-] polite title for a man **2.** [S-] title for a knight or baronet

sire *n.* male parent —*v.* be the male parent of

si´ren *n.* **1.** warning device with a wailing sound **2.** seductive woman

sir´loin *n.* choice cut of beef from the loin

si·roc´co (-räk´-) *n.* [*pl.* -COS]

hot wind blowing from N Africa into S Europe

sir'up *n.* syrup

sis *n.* [Col.] sister

si'sal *n.* strong rope fiber

sis'sy *n.* [*pl.* -SIES] [Col.] 1. effeminate boy or man 2. timid or cowardly person —**sis'si·fied** *a.*

sis'ter *n.* 1. female related to one by having the same parents 2. female fellow member 3. nun —**sis'ter·hood** *n.* —**sis'ter·ly** *a.*

sis'ter-in-law' *n.* [*pl.* SISTERS-IN-LAW] 1. sister of one's spouse 2. brother's wife

sit *v.* [SAT, SITTING] 1. rest on one's buttocks or haunches 2. perch 3. be in session 4. pose, as for a portrait 5. be located 6. baby-sit —**sit down** take a seat —**sit in (on)** take part —**sit'ter** *n.*

si·tar' (-tär') *n.* lutelike instrument of India

sit'-down' *n.* strike, demonstration, etc. in which participants refuse to leave: also **sit'-in'**

site *n.* location or scene

sit'ting *n.* 1. session, as of court 2. time of being seated

sitting duck [Col.] easy target; one easily attacked

sit'u·ate (sich'oo-) *v.* put or place; locate

sit'u·a'tion *n.* 1. location 2. condition 3. job

six *a., n.* one more than five — **sixth** *a., n.*

six'teen' *a., n.* six more than ten —**six'teenth'** *a., n.*

six'ty *a., n.* [*pl.* -TIES] six

times ten —**six'ti·eth** *a., n.*

siz'a·ble, size'a·ble *a.* fairly large

size *n.* 1. dimensions 2. any of a series of measures, often numbered 3. pasty glaze: also **siz'ing** —*v.* 1. arrange by size (*n.* 2) 2. apply size (*n.* 3) —**size up** [Col.] 1. to estimate 2. meet requirements

siz'zle *v.* to hiss when hot —*n.* such a sound

skate *n.* 1. ice skate 2. roller skate 3. fish with a broad, flat body —*v.* glide or roll on skates —**skat'er** *n.*

skeet *n.* trapshooting from different angles

skein (skān) *n.* coil of yarn or thread

skel'e·ton *n.* framework, as of the bones of a body —**skel'e·tal** *a.*

skep'tic *n.* one who questions matters generally accepted

skep'ti·cal *a.* doubting; questioning

skep'ti·cism *n.* 1. skeptical attitude 2. doubt about religious doctrines

sketch *n.* 1. rough drawing or design 2. outline 3. short, light story, play, etc. —*v.* make a sketch (of) —**sketch'y** [-IER, -IEST] *a.*

skew *v., a.* slant

skew'er *n.* long pin to hold meat together as it cooks —*v.* pierce with skewers

ski (skē) *n.* [*pl.* SKIS] long, flat runner fastened to the shoe for snow travel —*v.* glide on skis —**ski'er** *n.*

skid *n.* 1. plank, log, etc. on

which to support or slide something heavy **2.** low, movable platform for holding loads **3.** act of skidding —*v.* [SKID-DED, SKIDDING] slide or slip, as on ice —**be on (or hit) the skids** [Sl.] meet failure

skid'dy *a.* [-DIER, -DIEST] having a slippery surface

skid row city area where vagrants, etc. gather

skiff *n.* small sailboat

ski lift endless cable with seats, for carrying skiers

skill *n.* **1.** great ability **2.** art or craft involving use of the hands or body —**skilled** *a.* — **skill'ful, skil'ful** *a.*

skil'let *n.* frying pan

skim *v.* [SKIMMED, SKIMMING] **1.** take floating matter from a liquid **2.** read quickly **3.** glide lightly (over)

skim milk milk with the cream removed

skimp *v.* [Col.] scrimp

skimp'y *a.* [-IER, -IEST] [Col.] barely enough; scanty

skin *n.* **1.** tissue covering the body **2.** pelt **3.** covering like skin, as fruit rind —*v.* [SKINNED, SKINNING] **1.** remove the skin from **2.** injure by scraping **3.** [Col.] swindle — **get under one's skin** [Col.] irritate one

skin diving underwater swimming with special equipment —**skin'-dive'** *v.*

skin'flint *n.* miser

skin'ny *a.* [-NIER, -NIEST] very thin —**skin'ni·ness** *n.*

skin'ny-dip' *n., v.* [-DIPPED,

-DIPPING] [Col.] swim in the nude

skip *v.* [SKIPPED, SKIPPING] **1.** move by hopping on alternate feet **2.** leap lightly (over) **3.** bounce **4.** omit **5.** [Col.] leave hurriedly —*n.* act of skipping

skip'per *n.* ship's captain

skir'mish *n.* (take part in) a small, brief battle

skirt *n.* **1.** part of a dress, coat, etc. below the waist **2.** woman's garment that hangs from the waist —*v.* go along the edge (of)

skit *n.* short, funny play

skit'tish *a.* **1.** lively; playful **2.** very nervous

skiv'vy *n.* [*pl.* -VIES] [Sl.] **1.** man's short-sleeved undershirt **2.** *pl.* men's underwear

skul·dug'ger·y, skull·dug'-ger·y *n.* [Col.] mean trickery

skulk *v.* move or lurk in a stealthy way

skull *n.* bony framework of the head

skunk *n.* small mammal that ejects a smelly liquid

sky *n.* [*pl.* SKIES] *often pl.* upper atmosphere or space around the earth

sky'cap *n.* porter at an air terminal

sky diving parachute jumping involving free fall

sky'lark *n.* lark famous for its song —*v.* romp or frolic

sky'light *n.* window in a roof or ceiling

sky'line *n.* outline of a city, etc. seen against the sky

sky'rock'et *n.* firework rocket —*v.* rise fast

sky'scrap'er n. very tall building

sky'ward a., adv. toward the sky: also **sky'wards** adv.

slab n. flat, thick piece

slack a. 1. loose 2. not busy 3. slow; sluggish —n. slack part or time —**slack off** (or **up**) slacken

slack'en v. 1. slow down 2. loosen

slack'er n. one who shirks

slacks n.pl. trousers

slag n. smelting refuse

slain pp. of slay

slake v. 1. satisfy (thirst) 2. mix (lime) with water

slam v. [SLAMMED, SLAMMING] shut, hit, etc. with force —n. heavy impact

slan'der n. spoken falsehood harmful to another —v. speak slander against —**slan'derous** a.

slang n. vigorous, short-lived, informal language

slant v., n. 1. incline; slope 2. (show) a special attitude

slap n. a blow with something flat —v. [SLAPPED, SLAPPING] strike with a slap

slap'dash a., adv. hurried(ly), careless(ly), etc.

slap'-hap'py a. [Sl.] 1. dazed 2. silly or giddy

slap'stick n. crude comedy

slash v. 1. cut at with a knife 2. cut slits in 3. reduce —n. a slashing; cut

slat n. narrow strip

slate n. 1. bluish-gray rock in thin layers 2. tile, etc. of slate 3. list of candidates —v. designate

slat'tern n. slovenly or sluttish woman —**slat'tern·ly** a., adv.

slaugh'ter (slô'-) v. 1. kill (animals) for food 2. kill (people) brutally or in large numbers —n. a slaughtering

slaugh'ter·house n. place for butchering animals

slave n. 1. human being owned by another 2. one dominated by some habit, person, etc. — v. work like a slave; drudge

slave driver merciless taskmaster

slav'er (slav'-) v. drool

slav'er·y (slāv'-) n. 1. condition of slaves 2. ownership of slaves 3. drudgery

Slav'ic (släv'-) a. of the Russians, Poles, Slovaks, etc.

slav'ish a. 1. servile 2. blindly imitating

slaw (slô) n. coleslaw

slay v. [SLEW, SLAIN, SLAYING] kill by violent means —**slay'er** n.

slea'zy (slē'-) a. [-ZIER, -ZIEST] flimsy; thin

sled n. vehicle with runners, for snow —v. [SLEDDED, SLEDDING] ride a sled

sledge n. 1. long, heavy hammer: also **sledge'ham'mer** 2. sled or sleigh

sleek a. 1. glossy 2. well-groomed 3. suave —v. make sleek

sleep n. natural regular rest, as at night —v. [SLEPT, SLEEPING] to be in a state of sleep —**sleep off** rid oneself of by sleeping —**sleep'less** a.

sleep'er n. 1. one who sleeps

2. railway car with berths 3. an unexpected success

sleeping bag warmly lined, zippered bag for sleeping in outdoors

sleep′y a. [-IER, -IEST] 1. drowsy 2. dull; idle

sleet n. partly frozen rain —v. to shower as sleet

sleeve n. 1. part of a garment covering the arm 2. protective cover —**sleeve′less** a.

sleigh (slā) n. light vehicle on runners, for travel on snow

sleight of hand (slīt) 1. skill in doing tricks with the hands 2. such tricks

slen′der a. 1. long and thin 2. small in size or force

slen′der·ize v. make or become slender

slept pt. & pp. of **sleep**

sleuth (slooth) n. [Col.] detective

slew pt. of **slay** —n. [Col.] large number or amount

slice n. 1. thin, broad piece cut off 2. share —v. cut into slices or as a slice —**slic′er** n.

slick v. 1. make smooth 2. [Col.] make smart, neat, etc. (up) —a. 1. smooth 2. slippery 3. clever —n. smooth area, as of oil on water

slick′er n. loose, waterproof coat

slide v. [SLID, SLIDING] 1. move along a smooth surface 2. glide 3. slip —n. 1. a sliding 2. inclined surface to slide on 3. transparent plate for projection on a screen 4. fall of rock, etc. down a slope —**let slide** fail to attend to properly

slide fastener fastener with interlocking tabs worked by a sliding part

slide rule device for calculating that looks like a ruler

sliding scale schedule of costs, etc. that varies with given conditions

slight a. 1. slender 2. unimportant 3. small or weak —v. 1. neglect 2. treat as unimportant or with disrespect —n. a slighting —**slight′ly** adv. —**slight′ness** n.

slim a. [SLIMMER, SLIMMEST] 1. long and thin 2. small —v. [SLIMMED, SLIMMING] make or become slim

slime n. soft, wet, sticky matter —**slim′y** [-IER, -IEST] a.

sling n. 1. device for hurling stones 2. band or looped cloth for raising or supporting —v. [SLUNG, SLINGING] hurl as with a sling

sling′shot n. Y-shaped piece with elastic band for shooting stones, etc.

slink v. [SLUNK, SLINKING] move in a sneaking way

slink′y a. [-IER, -IEST] [Sl.] sinuous in line or movement

slip v. [SLIPPED, SLIPPING] 1. go quietly 2. put or pass smoothly or quickly 3. slide accidentally 4. escape from 5. become worse 6. err —n. 1. a slip 2. space between piers 6. dock for ships 7. woman's sleeveless undergarment 3. a falling down 4. error 5. plant stem or root, for planting, etc. 6. small piece of paper

slip′knot n. knot that can slip along a rope

slip'page (-ij) *n.* a slipping

slipped disk ruptured disk between vertebrae

slip'per *n.* light, low shoe

slip'per·y *a.* [-IER, -IEST] 1. that can cause slipping 2. tending to slip 3. tricky

slith'er (slith'-) *v.* slide or glide along

sliv'er *n.* thin, pointed piece cut or split off —*v.* cut or split into slivers

slob *n.* [Col.] sloppy or coarse person

slob'ber *v., n.* drool

sloe *n.* dark-blue fruit

slog *v.* [SLOGGED, SLOGGING] plod

slo'gan *n.* motto or phrase, as for advertising purposes

sloop *n.* boat with one mast

slop *n.* 1. spilled liquid 2. slush 3. watery food 4. *often pl.* liquid waste —*v.* [SLOPPED, SLOPPING] splash

slope *n.* 1. rising or falling surface, line, etc. 2. amount of this —*v.* have a slope

slop'py *a.* [-PIER, -PIEST] 1. slushy 2. [Col.] careless 3. [Col.] overly sentimental —**slop'pi·ly** *adv.* —**slop'pi·ness** *n.*

slosh *v.* to splash

slot *n.* 1. narrow opening 2. [Col.] position —*v.* 1. make a slot in 2. [Col.] place in a series

sloth (slôth, slōth) *n.* 1. laziness 2. S. American animal living in trees —**sloth'ful** *a.*

slouch *n.* 1. lazy person 2. drooping posture —*v.* have a drooping posture

slough (sluf) *v.* to shed; discard

slough (slou) *n.* swamp

slov'en (sluv'-) *n.* slovenly person

slov'en·ly *a.* careless or untidy

slow *a.* 1. taking longer than usual 2. low in speed 3. behind the right time 4. stupid 5. sluggish —*v.* make or become slow —*adv.* in a slow way —**slow'ly** *adv.* —**slow'ness** *n.*

slow'-mo·tion *a.* designating a movie or TV tape showing action slowed down

slow'poke *n.* [Sl.] slow person

sludge *n.* 1. mud or mire 2. slimy waste

slue *n., v.* turn or swerve

slug *n.* 1. small mollusk 2. bullet 3. false coin 4. [Sl.] drink of liquor —*v.* [SLUGGED, SLUGGING] [Col.] hit hard —**slug'ger** *n.*

slug'gard *n.* lazy person

slug'gish *a.* slow-moving

sluice (slōōs) *n.* water channel or gate to control it —*v.* wash with water as from a sluice

slum *n.* populous area with very poor living conditions

slum'ber *v., n.* sleep

slump *v.* 1. fall suddenly 2. slouch —*n.* sudden fall

slur *v.* [SLURRED, SLURRING] 1. pass over quickly 2. pronounce indistinctly 3. insult —*n.* 1. a slurring 2. insult

slurp v. [Sl.] drink or eat noisily —n. [Sl.] loud sipping or sucking sound

slush n. 1. partly melted snow 2. soft mud 3. sentimentality —**slush′y** a.

slut n. immoral woman —**slut′tish** a.

sly a. [SLIER or SLYER, SLIEST or SLYEST] 1. cunning; crafty 2. playfully mischievous —**on the sly** secretly —**sly′ly, sli′ly** adv.

smack n. 1. slight taste 2. sharp noise made by parting the lips suddenly 3. sharp slap 4. loud kiss 5. fishing boat —v. 1. have a trace 2. make a smack with one's lips 3. slap loudly —adv. directly

small a. 1. little in size, extent, etc. 2. trivial 3. mean; petty —n. small part —**small′ish** a.

small arms firearms of small caliber, as pistols or rifles

small′pox n. contagious disease with fever and sores

smart v. 1. cause or feel stinging pain 2. suffer —a. 1. that smarts 2. brisk; lively 3. bright; clever 4. neat 5. stylish —**smart′ly** adv.

smart al′eck, smart al′ec [Col.] offensively conceited person

smart bomb [Sl.] bomb guided to a target electronically

smart′en v. make or become smarter

smash v. 1. break violently 2. crash 3. destroy —n. 1. a smashing 2. wreck; collision 3. popular success

smash′up n. violent collision

smat′ter·ing n. 1. a little knowledge 2. small number

smear v. 1. make greasy, dirty, etc. 2. spread 3. slander —n. a smearing

smear′case n. cottage cheese

smell v. [alt. pt. & pp. SMELT] 1. catch the odor of 2. sniff 3. have an odor —n. 1. power to smell 2. thing smelled; odor

smell′y a. [-IER, -IEST] having a bad smell

smelt n. small, silvery food fish —v. melt (ore or metal) so as to remove the impurities —**smelt′er** n.

smidg·en (smij′ən) n. [Col.] small amount; bit: also **smidg′in**

smile v. 1. show pleasure, amusement, etc. by curving the mouth upward 2. show with a smile —n. act of smiling

smirch v. 1. soil or stain 2. dishonor —n. smear

smirk v. smile in a conceited or complacent way —n. smug smile

smite v. [SMOTE, SMITTEN, SMITING] 1. hit or strike hard 2. affect strongly

smith n. one who makes or repairs metal objects

smith·er·eens′ (smith-) n.pl. [Col.] fragments

smith′y n. [pl. -IES] blacksmith's shop

smock n. loose, protective outer garment

smog n. fog and smoke

smoke n. vapor, as from something burning —v. 1. give off smoke 2. use cigarettes, a pipe, etc. **3.** cure (meats, etc.) with smoke **4.** drive out or stupefy with smoke —**smoke out** force out of hiding —**smoke'less** a. —**smok'er** n. —**smok'y** [-IER, -IEST] a.

smoke'stack n. tall chimney

smol'der v. **1.** burn without flame **2.** exist suppressed Also sp. **smoulder**

smooch n., v. [Sl.] kiss

smooth a. **1.** having no roughness or bumps; even **2.** with no trouble **3.** ingratiating —v. make smooth —adv. in a smooth way —**smooth'ly** adv. —**smooth'ness** n.

smor'gas·bord (-gəs-) n. variety of tasty foods served buffet style

smoth'er (smuth'-) v. **1.** suffocate **2.** cover thickly **3.** stifle (a yawn)

smudge n. **1.** dirty spot **2.** fire with dense smoke **3.** such smoke used to protect plants from frost —v. to smear —**smudg'y** a.

smug a. [SMUGGER, SMUGGEST] too self-satisfied —**smug'ly** adv. —**smug'ness** n.

smug'gle v. bring in or take out secretly or illegally —**smug'gler** n.

smut n. **1.** dirt **2.** obscene matter **3.** plant disease —**smut'ty** [-TIER, -TIEST] a.

snack n. light meal —v. eat lightly

snaf'fle n. horse's bit with a joint in the middle

snag n. **1.** sharp projection **2.** tear made by this **3.** hidden difficulty or obstacle —v. [SNAGGED, SNAGGING] **1.** tear on a snag **2.** hinder

snail n. mollusk with a spiral shell

snake n. **1.** long, legless reptile **2.** treacherous person —v. twist like a snake —**snak'y** [-IER, -IEST] a.

snap v. [SNAPPED, SNAPPING] **1.** bite or grasp (at) suddenly **2.** speak sharply (with at) **3.** break suddenly **4.** make a cracking sound **5.** move sharply **6.** take a snapshot of —n. **1.** sharp sound **2.** brief period of cold weather **3.** fastening that clicks shut **4.** [Sl.] easy job —a. **1.** quick **2.** easy —**snap out of it** recover quickly —**snap'per** n.

snap'pish a.

snap'drag'on n. plant with saclike, two-lipped flowers

snap'py a. [-PIER, -PIEST] [Col.] **1.** brisk or lively **2.** stylish; smart

snap'shot n. picture taken with a hand camera

snare n. **1.** trap for small animals **2.** dangerous lure **3.** wire or gut across the bottom of a drum —v. to trap

snarl v. **1.** growl, baring the teeth **2.** speak sharply **3.** tangle —n. **1.** a snarling **2.** tangle; disorder

snatch v. seize; grab —n. **1.** brief time **2.** fragment

sneak v. move, do, etc. secretly —n. one who sneaks —a. without warning —**sneak'y** [-IER, -IEST] a.

sneak'er n. shoe with a cloth upper and a soft rubber sole

sneer v. show scorn —n. sneering look or remark

sneeze v. expel breath from the nose and mouth in a sudden, uncontrolled way —n. act of sneezing

snick'er v., n. (give) a silly, partly stifled laugh

snide a. slyly malicious

sniff v. inhale forcibly through the nose, as in smelling —n. act of sniffing

snif'fle v., n. sniff to check mucus flow —**the sniffles** [Col.] head cold

snif'ter n. goblet with a small opening, as for brandy

snig'ger v., n. snicker

snip v. [SNIPPED, SNIPPING] cut in a quick stroke —n. small piece cut off

snipe n. wading bird —v. shoot at from a hidden place —**snip'er** n.

snip'pet n. 1. small, snipped piece 2. piece of information

snip'py a. [-PIER, -PIEST] [Col.] insolently curt

snitch v. [Sl.] 1. steal 2. tattle (on)

sniv'el v. 1. cry and sniffle 2. whine

snob n. one who disdains his supposed inferiors —**snob'ber·y** n. —**snob'bish** a.

snood n. kind of hair net

snoop v. [Col.] pry in a sneaky way —n. [Col.] one who snoops

snoot'y a. [-IER, -IEST] [Col.] snobbish

snooze v., n. [Col.] nap

snore v. breathe noisily while asleep —n. a snoring

snor'kel n. breathing tube for swimming underwater

snort v. 1. force breath audibly from the nose 2. express contempt by this —n. 1. snorting 2. [Sl.] quick drink of liquor

snot n. 1. nasal mucus: vulgar term 2. [Sl.] impudent young person —**snot'ty** [-TIER, -TIEST]

snout n. projecting nose and jaws of an animal

snow n. flakes of frozen water vapor from the sky —v. 1. fall as snow 2. cover with snow (with in, under) 3. [Sl.] deceive —**snow under** 1. overwhelm, as with work 2. defeat —**snow'y** [-IER, -IEST] a.

snow'ball n. ball of packed snow —v. increase rapidly

snow'bound a. shut in or blocked off by snow

snow'drift n. pile of snow heaped up by the wind

snow'fall n. fall of snow or the amount of this

snow'flake n. single snow crystal

snow'mo·bile n. motor vehicle for snow travel, with runners and tractor treads

snow'plow n. plowlike machine for removing snow

snow'shoe n. racketlike footgear for walking on snow

snow'storm n. storm with a heavy snowfall

snow'suit n. child's lined garment, often with a hood

snow tire tire with a deep tread for added traction

snub v. [SNUBBED, SNUBBING] 1. treat with scorn 2. check abruptly (a rope, etc.) —*n.* a slight —*a.* short and turned up, as a nose

snuff *v.* put out (a candle, etc.) *n.* powdered tobacco —**up to snuff** [Col.] up to the usual standard

snug *a.* [SNUGGER, SNUGGEST] 1. cosy 2. compact 3. tight in fit

snug'gle *v.* cuddle; nestle

so *adv.* 1. in such a way 2. to such a degree 3. very 4. therefore 5. more or less 6. also 7. then 8. [Col.] very much —**con.** 1. in order (that) 2. [Col.] with the result that —*int.* word showing surprise —*a.* true —**and so on (or forth)** and the rest

soak *v.* 1. make wet 2. stay in liquid 3. [Col.] charge excessively —**soak up** absorb

soap *n.* substance that makes suds in water for washing —*v.* rub with soap [Sl.] not acceptable —**soap'y** [-IER, -IEST] *a.*

soap'box *n.* improvised platform for public speaking

soap opera [Col.] melodramatic daytime TV serial drama

soar *v.* fly high in the air

sob *v.* [SOBBED, SOBBING] weep aloud with short gasps —*n.* act of sobbing

so'ber *a.* 1. not drunk 2. serious; sedate 3. plain —*v.* make or become sober —**so·bri'e·ty** *n.*

so'-called' *a.* called thus, but usually inaccurately

soc'cer *n.* kind of football

so'cia·ble (-shə-) *a.* friendly; agreeable —**so'cia·bil'i·ty** *n.* —**so'cia·bly** *adv.*

so'cial *a.* 1. of society 2. living in groups 3. sociable 4. of social work *n.* a party —**so'·cial·ly** *adv.*

so'cial·ism *n.* public ownership of the means of production —**so'cial·ist** *n., a.* —**so'·cial·is'tic** *a.*

so'cial·ite *n.* person prominent in fashionable society

so'cial·ize *v.* 1. put under public ownership 2. [Col.] take part in social affairs

social security federal insurance for old age, unemployment, etc.

social science study of social structure, as sociology

social work work of clinics, agencies, etc. to improve living conditions

so·ci'e·ty *n.* [*pl.* -TIES] 1. community of people 2. all people 3. companionship 4. organized group 5. the wealthy, dominant class

so'ci·ol'o·gy (-sē-) *n.* science of social relations, organization, and change —**so'ci·o·log'i·cal** *a.* —**so'ci·ol'o·gist** *n.*

sock *n.* 1. short stocking 2. [Sl.] a blow —*v.* [Sl.] hit with force

sock'et *n.* hollow part into which something fits

sock'eye *n.* red salmon

sod *n.* earth surface with grass —*v.* [SODDED, SODDING] cover with sod

so'da *n.* 1. sodium bicarbonate

2. soda water **3.** confection of soda water and ice cream

soda cracker crisp cracker

soda pop flavored, carbonated soft drink

soda water carbonated water

sod′den *a.* soaked or soggy

so′di·um *n.* silver-white metallic chemical element

sodium bi·car′bon·ate (-it) baking soda

sodium chloride common salt

sodium hydroxide lye

sodium nitrate a clear salt used in explosives, etc.

sod′om·y *n.* sexual intercourse held to be abnormal, as between males

so′fa *n.* couch with back and arms

sofa bed sofa that can be opened into a bed

soft *a.* **1.** not hard; easy to crush, cut, etc. **2.** not harsh; mild, gentle, etc. **3.** without minerals that hinder lathering **4.** weak **5.** nonalcoholic **6.** easy **7.** not bright: said of color or light —*adv.* gently — **soft′ly** *adv.* —**soft′ness** *n.*

soft′ball *n.* game like baseball, played with a larger and softer ball

soft′-boiled′ *a.* boiled briefly to keep the egg's yolk soft

soft drink nonalcoholic, esp. carbonated drink

sof′ten *v.* make or become soft —**sof′ten·er** *n.*

soft′heart′ed *a.* **1.** compassionate **2.** lenient

soft landing safe landing, as of a spacecraft on the moon

soft′-ped′al *v.* [Col.] make less emphatic; tone down

soft sell subtle selling

soft soap [Col.] smooth talk or flattery —**soft′-soap′** *v.*

soft′ware *n.* programs, data, etc. for a computer

soft′y *n.* [*pl.* -**IES**] [Col.] overly sentimental or trusting person

sog′gy *a.* [-**GIER**, -**GIEST**] very wet and heavy; soaked

soil *n.* earth or ground, esp. the surface layer —*v.* make or become dirty

soi·ree, soi·rée (swä rā′) *n.* an evening party

so′journ *n., v.* visit, as in a foreign land

sol′ace (-is) *n.* relief or comfort —*v.* comfort

so′lar *a.* of or having to do with the sun

so·lar′i·um *n.* [*pl.* -**IA**] glassed-in room for sunning

solar system the sun and all its planets

sold pt. & pp. of **sell**

sol·der (säd′ər) *n.* metal alloy for joining metal parts —*v.* join with solder

sol′dier (-jər) *n.* member of an army, esp. an enlisted person —*v.* be a soldier

sole *n.* **1.** bottom of the foot, or of a shoe **2.** sea flatfish —*v.* put a sole on (a shoe) —*a.* one and only

sole′ly *adv.* **1.** alone **2.** only

sol′emn *a.* **1.** formal **2.** serious —**sol′emn·ly** *adv.*

so·lem′ni·ty *n.* [*pl.* -**TIES**] **1.** solemn ritual **2.** seriousness

sol′em·nize *v.* celebrate or perform formally

so'le·noid n. coil of wire acting like a magnet

so·lic'it (-lis'-) v. **1.** appeal to for **2.** entice or lure —**so·lic'i·ta'tion** n.

so·lic'i·tor n. **1.** one who solicits trade, etc. **2.** [Br.] lawyer not a barrister **3.** lawyer for a city, etc.

so·lic'i·tous a. **1.** showing concern **2.** anxious

so·lic'i·tude n. concern

sol'id a. **1.** firm or hard **2.** not hollow **3.** three-dimensional **4.** of one piece, color, etc. **5.** unanimous **6.** dependable —n. **1.** firm or hard substance **2.** three-dimensional object —**so·lid'i·ty** n.

sol'i·dar'i·ty n. firm unity

so·lid'i·fy v. [-FIED, -FYING] make or become solid, hard, etc. —**so·lid'i·fi·ca'tion** n.

so·lil'o·quy (-kwē) n. [pl. -QUIES] a talking to oneself —**so·lil'o·quize** v.

sol'i·taire (-ter) n. **1.** gem set by itself **2.** card game for one person

sol'i·tar'y a. **1.** alone; lonely **2.** single

sol'i·tude n. a being alone

so'lo n. [pl. -LOS] piece of music for one performer —a. for one performer —v. perform a solo —**so'lo·ist** n.

sol'stice (-stis) n. longest day (June 21 or 22) or shortest day (Dec. 21 or 22)

sol'u·ble a. **1.** that can be dissolved **2.** solvable —**sol'u·bil'i·ty** n.

sol·ute (säl'yo͞ot) n. substance dissolved

so·lu'tion n. **1.** solving of a problem **2.** explanation or answer **3.** liquid with something dissolved in it

solve v. find the answer to —**solv'a·ble** a.

sol'vent a. **1.** able to pay one's debts **2.** able to dissolve a substance —n. substance used to dissolve another —**sol'ven·cy** n.

som'ber a. **1.** dark and gloomy **2.** sad

som·bre'ro (-brer'ō) n. [pl. -ROS] broad-brimmed hat

some a. **1.** certain but unspecified **2.** of indefinite quantity **3.** about —pron. indefinite quantity —adv. **1.** approximately **2.** [Col.] somewhat **3.** [Col.] to a great extent

-some suf. tending to (be)

some'bod'y n. [pl. -IES] important person —pron. person not named or known

some'day adv. sometime

some'how adv. in some way

some'one pron. somebody

som·er·sault (sum'ər sôlt) v., n. (perform) a turning of the body, heels over head

some'thing n. **1.** thing not named or known **2.** a bit **3.** [Col.] important person or thing —adv. **1.** somewhat **2.** [Col.] really

some'time adv. at some unspecified time —a. former

some'times adv. at times

some'what n. some part, amount, etc. —adv. a little

some'where adv. in, to, or at some unnamed place

som·nam'bu·lism *n.* act of walking while asleep

som'no·lent *a.* sleepy —**som'no·lence** *n.*

son *n.* male in relation to his parents

so·na'ta (-nä'-) *n.* piece of music for one or two instruments

song *n.* **1.** music, or poem, to be sung **2.** singing sound

song'bird *n.* bird that makes vocal sounds like music

song'ster *n.* singer —**song'stress** *n.fem.*

son'ic (sän'-) *a.* of or having to do with sound

sonic barrier large increase of air resistance as an aircraft nears the speed of sound

sonic boom explosive sound of supersonic jets overhead

son'-in-law' *n.* [*pl.* SONS-IN-LAW] husband of one's daughter

son'net *n.* 14-line poem

so·no'rous (-nôr'əs) *a.* **1.** resonant **2.** full, deep, or rich in sound —**so·nor'i·ty** *n.*

soon *adv.* **1.** in a short time **2.** quickly **3.** early **4.** readily

soot (soot) *n.* black particles in smoke —**soot'y** [-IER, -IEST] *a.*

soothe (sooth) *v.* **1.** make calm, as by kindness **2.** ease, as pain —**sooth'ing·ly** *adv.*

sooth'say'er (sooth'-) *n.* one who pretends to prophesy

sop *n.* **1.** something given to appease **2.** bribe —*v.* [SOPPED, SOPPING] soak (*up*)

soph'ist (säf'-) *n.* one who uses clever, specious reasoning

so·phis'ti·cat·ed (-kāt'id) *a.*

1. worldly-wise **2.** highly complex or developed —**so·phis'ti·cate** (-kit) *n.* —**so·phis'ti·ca'tion** *n.*

soph'is·try *n.* [*pl.* -TRIES] misleading but clever reasoning

soph'o·more *n.* second-year student in high school or college

soph'o·mor'ic *a.* immature

sop'o·rif'ic (säp'-) *n., a.* (drug) causing sleep

sop'py *a.* [-PIER, -PIEST] **1.** very wet: also **sop'ping 2.** [Col.] maudlin

so·pra'no *n.* [*pl.* -NOS] highest voice of women or boys

sor'cer·y *n.* supposed use of evil, supernatural power —**sor'cer·er** *n.* —**sor'cer·ess** *n.fem.*

sor'did *a.* **1.** dirty **2.** wretched **3.** base; mean

sore *a.* **1.** painful **2.** sad **3.** irritating **1.** [Col.] angry —*n.* infected spot on the body —**sore'ness** *n.*

sore'ly *adv.* greatly

sor'ghum (-gəm) *n.* grass grown for grain, syrup, etc.

so·ror'i·ty *n.* [*pl.* -TIES] social club for women

sor'rel *n.* **1.** reddish brown **2.** horse of this color

sor'row *v., n.* (feel) sadness —**sor'row·ful** *a.*

sor'ry *a.* [-RIER, -RIEST] **1.** full of sorrow, regret, etc. **2.** inferior **3.** wretched

sort *n.* kind; class —**of sorts** or **of a sort** of an inferior kind —**out of sorts** [Col.] cross; ill-humored —**sort of** [Col.] somewhat

sor'tie (-tē) *n.* raid by besieged troops

SOS signal of distress

so'-so' *a., adv.* fair or fairly well: also **so so**

sot *n.* habitual drunkard

souf·flé (sōō flā') *n.* food made puffy by being baked with beaten egg whites

sought *pt. & pp.* of **seek**

soul *n.* 1. spiritual part of a person 2. emotional warmth, etc. 3. vital part 4. person

soul'ful *a.* feeling deeply

sound *n.* 1. that which is heard 2. strait or inlet of the sea —*v.* 1. (cause) to make a sound 2. seem 3. measure the depth of water 4. seek the opinion of (with *out*) —*a.* 1. free from defect; healthy, secure, sensible, etc. 2. deep or thorough —*adv.* deeply — **sound'ly** *adv.* —**sound'ness** *n.*

sound barrier sonic barrier

sounding board person used to test ideas on

sound'proof *v., a.* (make) impervious to sound

sound track sound record along one side of a movie film

soup *n.* liquid food with meat, vegetables, etc. in it

soup'y *a.* [-IER, -IEST] 1. like soup 2. [Col.] foggy

sour *a.* 1. having an acid taste 2. fermented 3. unpleasant — *v.* make or become sour — **sour'ness** *n.*

source *n.* 1. starting point 2. place of origin

sour grapes scorning of something impossible to get or do

souse *n.* 1. pickled food 2. brine 3. [Col.] drunkard —*v.* 1. to pickle 2. soak in liquid

south *n.* 1. direction to the left of one facing the sunset 2. region in this direction —*a., adv.* in, toward, or from the south —**south'er·ly** *a., adv.* —**south'ern** *a.* —**south'ern·er** *n.*

south'east' *n.* direction or region between south and east —*a., adv.* in, toward, or from the southeast —**south'east'er·ly** *a., adv.* —**south'east'ern** *a.*

south'east'ward *adv., a.* toward the southeast: also **south'east'wards** *adv.*

south'paw' *n.* [Sl.] left-handed person, esp. a baseball pitcher

South Pole southern end of the earth's axis

south'ward *adv., a.* toward the south: also **south'wards** *adv.*

south'west' *n.* direction or region between south and west —*a., adv.* in, toward, or from the southwest —**south'west'er·ly** *a., adv.* —**south'west'ern** *a.*

south'west'ward *adv., a.* toward the southwest: also **south'west'wards** *adv.*

sou·ve·nir (sōō və nir') *n.* thing kept as a reminder

sov·er·eign (säv'rən) *a.* 1. chief; supreme 2. independent —*n.* 1. monarch 2. former British gold coin

sov'er·eign·ty *n.* [*pl.* -TIES] 1.

rule of a sovereign 2. independent political authority

so′vi·et *n.* elected governing council, as in the U.S.S.R.

sow (sou) *n.* adult female pig

sow (sō) *v.* [SOWED, SOWN (sōn) or SOWED, SOWING] scatter, or plant with, seed for growing

soy *n.* sauce from soybeans

soy′bean *n.* seed of a plant of the pea family

spa (spä) *n.* resort (having) a mineral spring

space *n.* 1. limitless expanse containing all things 2. distance or area 3. room for something 4. interval of time —*v.* divide by spaces

space′craft *n.* [*pl.* -CRAFT] vehicle for outer-space travel, exploration, etc.

spaced′-out′ *a.* [Sl.] under the influence of a drug, etc.: also **spaced, space′y**

space heater small heating unit for a room

space′man *n.* [*pl.* -MEN] astronaut

space′port *n.* center for launching spacecraft

space′ship *n.* rocket-propelled vehicle for travel in outer space

space′suit *n.* garment pressurized for use by spacemen

spa′cious (-shəs) *a.* having more than enough space; vast

spade *n.* 1. flat-bladed digging tool 2. playing card marked with a ♠ —*v.* dig with a spade

spade′work *n.* preparatory work, esp. when tiresome

spa·ghet′ti (-get′ē) *n.* (cooked) strings of dried flour paste

span *n.* 1. nine inches 2. extent 3. period of time —*v.* extend over

span′gle *n.* shiny decoration, as a sequin —*v.* decorate with spangles

span′iel (-yəl) *n.* dog with large drooping ears

Span′ish *a., n.* (of) the people or language of Spain

spank *v., n.* slap on the buttocks

spank′ing *adv.* [Col.] wholly or completely

spar *n.* pole supporting a ship's sail —*v.* [SPARRED, SPARRING] box cautiously 2. wrangle

spare *v.* 1. refrain from killing, etc. 2. save or free from something 3. use frugally 4. give up conveniently —*a.* 1. extra 2. free 3. meager 4. lean —*n.* 1. extra thing 2. *Bowling* a knocking down of all the pins with two rolls of the ball

spare′ribs *n.pl.* thin end of pork ribs

spar′ing *a.* frugal

spark *n.* 1. small glowing piece from a fire 2. particle 3. flash from an electrical discharge across a gap —*v.* 1. make sparks 2. excite

spar′kle *v.* 1. give off sparks 2. glitter 3. effervesce —*n.* glitter —**spar′kler** *n.*

spark plug piece in an engine cylinder, that ignites the fuel mixture

spar′row *n.* small songbird

sparse (spärs) *a.* thinly spread

—**sparse′ly** adv. —**sparse′-ness, spar′si·ty** n.

Spar′tan a. warlike, severe, disciplined, etc.

spasm n. 1. involuntary muscular contraction 2. short, sudden burst of activity —**spas-mod′ic** a.

spas′tic n., a. (one) having muscular spasms

spat pt. & pp. of **spit** —n. 1. [Col.] brief quarrel 2. cloth ankle covering

spate n. unusually large outpouring, as of words

spa′tial (-shəl) a. of, or existing in, space

spat′ter v. 1. spurt out in drops 2. splash —n. mark made by spattering

spat′u·la (spach′ə-) n. tool with a broad, flexible blade

spawn (spôn) n. 1. eggs of fishes, etc. 2. offspring —v. produce (spawn)

spay v. sterilize (a female animal)

speak v. [SPOKE, SPOKEN, SPOKEN] 1. to talk 2. tell; express 3. make a request (for) 4. make a speech 5. use (a language) in speaking

speak′er n. 1. one who speaks 2. device for changing electrical waves into sound

spear n. long, slender sharp-pointed weapon —v. pierce or stab as with a spear

spear′head n. leading person or group, as in an attack —v. take the lead in

spear′mint n. fragrant mint

spe′cial a. 1. distinctive 2. unusual 3. highly valued 4. for a

certain use 5. specific —n. special thing —**spe′cial·ly** adv.

spe′cial·ize v. concentrate on a certain type of study, work, etc. —**spe′cial·ist** n. —**spe′-cial·i·za′tion** n.

spe′cial·ty n. [pl. -TIES] 1. special feature, interest, etc. 2. special article

spe′cie (spē′shē) n. metal money

spe′cies n. [pl. -CIES] distinct kind of plant or animal

spe·cif′ic a. definite; explicit —**spe·cif′i·cal·ly** adv.

spec′i·fi·ca′tion (spes′-) n. 1. a specifying 2. usually pl. detailed description

spec′i·fy v. [-FIED, -FYING] state explicitly

spec′i·men n. sample

spe′cious (-shəs) a. plausible but not genuine

speck n. small spot or bit —v. mark with specks

speck′le n., v. speck

specs n.pl. [Col.] 1. eyeglasses 2. specifications

spec′ta·cle n. 1. unusual sight 2. public show 3. pl. eyeglasses

spec·tac′u·lar a. showy; striking —n. elaborate show or display

spec·ta′tor n. a person who watches

spec′ter n. ghost: Br. sp. **spectre** —**spec′tral** a.

spec′tro·scope n. instrument that forms spectra for study

spec′trum n. [pl. -TRA, -TRUMS] 1. row of colors formed by diffraction 2. continuous range or entire extent

spec′u·late v. 1. ponder 2. engage in a risky venture on the chance of making huge profits —**spec'u·la'tion** n. —**spec'u·la'tor** n.

speech n. 1. act or way of speaking 2. power to speak 3. something said 4. public talk —**speech'less** a.

speed n. 1. rapid motion 2. rate of movement 3. [Sl.] amphetamine compound —v. [SPED, SPEEDING] 1. move fast 2. aid —**speed up** to increase in speed —**speed'er** n. —**speed'y** [-IER, -IEST] a.

speed'boat n. fast motorboat

speed·om'e·ter n. device to indicate speed

speed'ster n. very fast driver, runner, etc.

speed'way n. track for racing automobiles or motorcycles

spe·le·ol'o·gy n. scientific study of caves

spell n. 1. supposedly magic words 2. fascination; charm 3. period of work, duty, etc. 4. [Col.] fit of illness —v. 1. give in order the letters of (a word) 2. mean; signify 3. [Col.] relieve (another)

spell'bind v. [-BOUND, -BINDING] cause to be spellbound —**spell'bind'er** n.

spell'bound a. fascinated

spell'down n. spelling match

spell'er n. 1. one who spells words 2. spelling textbook

spell'ing n. 1. act of one who spells words 2. way a word is spelled

spend v. [SPENT, SPENDING] 1. use up 2. pay out (money) 3. pass (time) —**spend'er** n.

spend'thrift n. one who wastes money —a. wasteful

sperm n. 1. semen 2. any of the reproductive cells in it

sperm whale large, toothed whale of warm seas

spew v. 1. throw up; vomit 2. gush forth

sphere n. 1. globe; ball 2. place or range of action —**spher'i·cal** (sfer'-) a.

sphe'roid n. almost spherical body

sphinx (sfiņks) n. 1. [S-] statue in Egypt with a lion's body and man's head 2. one difficult to know or understand

spice n. 1. any aromatic seasoning 2. stimulating quality —v. add spice to —**spic'y** [-IER, -IEST] a.

spick'-and-span' a. 1. new or fresh 2. neat and clean

spi'der n. arachnid that spins webs —**spi'der·y** a.

spiff'y a. [-IER, -IEST] [Sl.] spruce or dapper

spig·ot (spig'ət, spik'-) n. faucet or tap

spike n. 1. sharp-pointed projection 2. long, heavy nail 3. ear of grain 4. long flower cluster —v. 1. fasten or pierce as with a spike 2. thwart (a scheme, etc.)

spill v. [alt. pt. & pp. SPILT] 1. let run over 2. overflow 3. shed (blood) 4. [Col.] make fall —n. [Col.] a fall

spill'way n. channel for excess water

spin v. [SPUN, SPINNING] 1. twist fibers into thread 2. make a web, cocoon, etc. 3.

tell (a story) 4. whirl 5. move fast —n. 1. whirling movement 2. fast ride

spin'ach (-ich) n. plant with dark-green, edible leaves

spi'nal a. of the spine

spinal column long row of connected bones in the back

spinal cord of nerve tissue in the spinal column

spin'dle n. 1. rod used in spinning thread 2. rod that acts as an axis

spin'dly a. [-DLIER, -DLIEST] long or tall and thin: also **spin'dling**

spine n. 1. thorn, quill, etc. 2. spinal column —**spin'y** [-IER, -IEST] a.

spine'less a. 1. having no spine 2. weak or cowardly

spin'et n. small upright piano

spinning wheel simple spinning machine driven by a large wheel

spin'off n. secondary benefit, product, etc.

spin'ster n. unmarried, older woman

spi'ral a. circling around a center —n. spiral curve or coil —v. move in a spiral

spire n. tapering, pointed part, as of a steeple

spi·re'a n. plant with clusters of small, white flowers

spir'it n. 1. soul 2. ghost, angel, etc. 3. usually pl. mood 4. courage 5. loyalty 6. essential quality 7. usually pl. alcoholic liquor —v. carry away secretly

spir'it·ed a. lively

spir'it·u·al a. 1. of the soul 2.

religious; sacred —n. Negro religious song —**spir'it·u·al'i·ty** n.

spir·it·u·al·ism n. seeming communication with the dead —**spir'it·u·al·ist** n.

spit n. 1. thin rod to roast meat on 2. shoreline narrowed to a point 3. saliva —v. [SPIT or SPAT, SPITTING] to eject (saliva, etc.) from the mouth

spite n. malice —v. annoy; hurt —in spite of regardless of —**spite'ful** a.

spit·toon' n. container to spit into; cuspidor

splash v. dash liquid, etc. on —n. 1. a splashing 2. spot made by splashing —**make a splash** [Col.] attract great attention

splash'down n. landing of a spacecraft on water

splash'y a. [-IER, -IEST] [Col.] spectacular

splat'ter n., v. splash

splay v., a. spread out

spleen n. 1. large abdominal organ 2. malice; spite —**splenet'ic** a.

splen'did a. magnificent; grand —**splen'dor** n.

splice v. join the ends of (rope, wire, film, etc.) as by weaving, soldering, etc. —n. joint made by splicing

splint n. strip of wood, etc. to hold a broken bone in place

splin'ter n. thin, sharp piece —v. split in splinters

split v. [SPLIT, SPLITTING] separate into parts —n. break; crack —a. divided

split'-lev'el a. having adjacent

floor levels staggered about a half story apart

split′ting a. severe, as a headache

splotch n., v. spot; stain — **splotch′y** [-IER, -IEST] a.

splurge n. [Col.] 1. showy display, etc. 2. spending spree — v. [Col.] 1. show off 2. spend money freely

splut′ter v. 1. make spitting sounds 2. speak confusedly — n. a spluttering

spoil v. [alt. pt. & pp. SPOILT] to damage, ruin, decay, etc. — n. pl. plunder —**spoil′age** (-ij) n.

spoke pt. of **speak** —n. rod from hub to rim

spo′ken pp. of **speak** —a. oral; voiced

spokes′man n. [pl. -MEN] one who speaks for another for a group

sponge n. 1. absorbent substance made from a sea animal, plastic, etc. 2. the sea animal —v. 1. clean, etc. with a sponge 2. [Col.] live off others —**spon′gy** [-GIER, -GIEST] a.

sponge bath bath taken by using a wet sponge or cloth without getting one wet

sponge′cake n. light, spongy cake without shortening

spon′sor n. 1. promoter; supporter 2. godparent 3. advertiser who pays for a radio or TV program —v. be sponsor for

spon·ta′ne·ous a. without effort 2. within or by itself — **spon′ta·ne′i·ty** n.

spoof n. [Sl.] 1. a hoax 2. light satire —v. [Sl.] 1. to fool 2. satirize playfully

spook n. [Col.] ghost — **spook′y** [-IER, -IEST] a.

spool n. cylinder upon which thread, etc. is wound

spoon n. 1. small bowl with a handle, used in eating 2. spoonlike fishing lure — **spoon′ful** [pl. -FULS] n.

spoor (spoor) n. wild animal's trail or track

spo·rad′ic a. not regular — **spo·rad′i·cal·ly** adv.

spore n. tiny reproductive cell of mosses, ferns, etc.

sport n. 1. athletic game 2. fun 3. abnormal plant or animal 4. [Col.] showy, flashy fellow —v. 1. [Col.] to display 2. play —a. for play or casual wear

sport′ing a. 1. of sports 2. fair 3. risky

sports a. of or for athletic games

sports (or sport) car low, small automobile with a high-compression engine

sports′man n. [pl. -MEN] 1. participant in sports 2. one who plays fair —**sports′man·like** a.

sport′y a. [-IER, -IEST] [Col.] flashy or showy

spot n. 1. stain; mark 2. place —v. [SPOTTED, SPOTTING] 1. mark with spots 2. [Col.] see —a. made at random —**hit the spot** [Col.] satisfy a craving — **on the spot** [Sl.] in trouble or danger —**spot′less** a.

spot′-check′ v. check at random —n. such a checking

spot′light n. 1. strong beam of

light, or lamp that throws it **2.** public notice

spot'ty *a.* [-TIER, -TIEST] **1.** spotted **2.** not uniform

spouse *n.* husband or wife

spout *n.* **1.** pipe, etc. by which a liquid pours **2.** stream of liquid —*v.* **1.** shoot out with force **2.** talk loudly and pompously

sprain *v.* twist a muscle or ligament in a joint —*n.* injury caused by this

sprang *pt.* of spring

sprat *n.* small herring

sprawl *v.* sit or spread out in a relaxed or awkward way —*n.* sprawling position

spray *n.* **1.** mist or stream of tiny liquid drops **2.** branch with leaves, flowers, etc. **3.** device for spraying —*v.* apply, or emit in, a spray

spray can in which gas under pressure sprays out the contents

spray gun device that sprays a liquid, as paint

spread *v.* [SPREAD, SPREADING] **1.** open out **2.** extend in time or space **3.** make known **4.** cover **5.** push or be pushed apart —*n.* **1.** act or extent of spreading **2.** cloth cover **3.** butter, jam, etc.

spree *n.* **1.** lively time **2.** drinking bout

sprig *n.* little twig

spright'ly *a.* [-LIER, -LIEST] gay; lively —*adv.* briskly

spring *v.* [SPRANG *or* SPRUNG, SPRUNG, SPRINGING] **1.** leap **2.** grow; develop **3.** snap back or shut **4.** make or become bent,

split, etc. **5.** make known —*n.* **1.** a leap **2.** resilience **3.** resilient coil of wire, etc. **4.** flow of water from the ground **5.** source **6.** season after winter —*a.* of, for, or in the spring (*n.* 6) —**spring'y** [-IER, -IEST] *a.*

spring'board *n.* springy board, as to dive from

sprin'kle *v.* **1.** scatter drops of or on **2.** rain lightly —*n.* a sprinkling

sprint *v., n.* race at full speed over a short distance —**sprint'er** *n.*

sprite *n.* elf, fairy, etc.

sprock'et *n.* any tooth in a series on a wheel made to fit the links of a chain

sprout *v.* begin to grow —*n.* new growth; shoot

spruce *n.* evergreen tree —*a.* neat and trim —*v.* make or become spruce (with *up*)

sprung *pp.* & *alt. pt.* of spring

spry *a.* [SPRIER *or* SPRYER, SPRIEST *or* SPRYEST] lively

spud *n.* [Col.] potato

spume *n.* foam; froth

spun *pt.* & *pp.* of spin

spunk *n.* [Col.] courage —**spunk'y** [-IER, -IEST] *a.*

spur *n.* **1.** pointed device on a shoe to prick a horse **2.** stimulus **3.** projecting part —*v.* [SPURRED, SPURRING] **1.** prick with spurs **2.** urge on —**on the spur of the moment** abruptly and impulsively

spu'ri·ous (spyoor'-) *a.* false; not genuine

spurn *v.* reject in scorn

spurt *v.* **1.** shoot forth; squirt

2. make a sudden effort —*n.* a spurting

sput'nik *n.* Russian man-made satellite

sput'ter *v.* **1.** speak in a fast, confused way **2.** spit out bits **3.** make hissing sounds —*n.* a sputtering

spu'tum *n.* saliva spat out

spy *v.* [SPIED, SPYING] **1.** watch closely and secretly **2.** see —*n.* [*pl.* SPIES] one who spies, esp. to get another country's secrets

spy'glass *n.* small telescope

squab (skwäb) *n.* young pigeon

squab'ble *v., n.* quarrel over a small matter

squad *n.* **1.** small group of soldiers **2.** any small group

squad car police patrol car

squad'ron *n.* unit of warships, military aircraft, etc.

squal'id *a.* **1.** foul; unclean **2.** wretched —**squal'or** *n.*

squall *n.* **1.** brief, violent windstorm **2.** harsh, loud cry —*v.* cry loudly

squan'der *v.* spend or use wastefully

square *n.* **1.** rectangle with all sides equal **2.** area with streets on four sides **3.** tool for making right angles **4.** product of a number multiplied by itself **5.** [Sl.] person who is square (*a.* 6) —*v.* **1.** make square **2.** make straight, even, etc. **3.** settle; adjust **4.** multiply by itself —*a.* **1.** shaped like a square **2.** forming a right angle **3.** straight, level, or even **4.** just; fair **5.** [Col.] satisfying, as a meal **6.** [Sl.] old-fashioned,

unsophisticated, etc. —*adv.* in a square way —**square'ly** *adv.* —**square'ness** *n.*

square dance dance in which couples form in a square, do figures, etc.

square root quantity which when squared will produce a given quantity

squash *v.* **1.** press into a soft, flat mass **2.** suppress —*n.* **1.** a squashing **2.** game played in a walled court with rackets **3.** fleshy vegetable growing on a vine

squat *v.* [SQUATTED or SQUAT, SQUATTING] **1.** crouch **2.** settle on land without title to it —*a.* short and heavy or thick: also **squat'ty** —*n.* position of squatting —**squat'ter** *n.*

squaw *n.* American Indian woman, esp. a wife

squawk *v.* **1.** utter a loud, harsh cry **2.** [Sl.] complain loudly —*n.* a squawking —**squawk'er** *n.*

squeak *v.* make a sharp, high-pitched sound —*n.* such a sound —**narrow** (or **close**)

squeak [Col.] narrow escape —**squeak through** (or **by**) [Col.] get through, etc. with difficulty —**squeak'y** [-IER, -IEST] *a.*

squeal *v.* **1.** utter a long, shrill cry **2.** [Sl.] act as an informer —*n.* a squealing —**squeal'er** *n.*

squeam'ish *a.* **1.** easily nauseated **2.** easily shocked **3.** fastidious

squee'gee (-jē) *n.* rubber-edged tool to wash windows

squeeze v. 1. press hard 2. extract by pressure 3. force by pressing 4. hug —n. 1. a squeezing 2. a hug 3. crush 4. period of scarcity, hardship, etc. —**squeez′er** n.

squelch n. [Col.] crushing retort —v. [Col.] suppress or silence completely

squib n. short, witty verbal attack

squid n. long, slender sea mollusk with ten arms

squint v. 1. peer with eyes partly closed 2. be cross-eyed —n. a squinting

squire n. 1. English country gentleman 2. man escorting a woman —v. escort

squirm v. twist and turn

squir′rel n. tree-dwelling rodent with a bushy tail

squirt v. shoot out (a liquid) in a jet; spurt —n. 1. jet of liquid 2. [Col.] insignificant person

stab v. [STABBED, STABBING] pierce or wound as with a knife —n. 1. a thrust, as with a knife 2. a try

sta′bi·lize v. 1. make stable, or firm 2. keep from changing —sta′bi·li·za′tion n. —sta′bi·liz′er n.

sta′ble a. not apt to change; firm —n. building for horses or cattle —v. keep in a stable —sta·bil′i·ty n.

stac·ca·to (stə kä′tō) a., adv. Mus. with abrupt tones

stack n. 1. orderly pile 2. smokestack 3. pl. series of bookshelves —v. pile in a stack

sta′di·um n. place for outdoor

games, surrounded by tiers of seats

staff n. [pl. STAFFS; also for senses 1 & 3, STAVES] 1. stick or rod used for support, etc. 2. group of people assisting a leader 3. the five lines on and between which music is written —v. provide with workers

stag n. full-grown male deer —a. for men only —adv. unaccompanied by a woman

stage n. 1. platform, esp. one on which plays are presented 2. the theater 3. part of a journey 4. period in growth or development 5. any of the successive units for propelling a missile, spacecraft, etc. —v. 1. present as on a stage 2. carry out

stage′coach n. former horse-drawn public coach for long trips

stage′hand n. one who sets up scenery, furniture, etc. for a stage play

stage′-struck′ a. eager to become an actor or actress

stag′ger v. 1. (cause to) totter, reel, etc. 2. shock 3. arrange alternately —n. a staggering

stag′nant a. 1. not flowing, therefore foul 2. sluggish

stag′nate v. become stagnant —**stag·na′tion** n.

staid (stād) a. sober; sedate

stain v. 1. discolor; spot 2. dishonor 3. color (wood, etc.) with a dye —n. 1. a spot; mark 2. dishonor 3. dye for wood, etc. —**stain′less** a.

stainless steel alloyed steel almost immune to rust and corrosion

stair *n.* **1.** one of a series of steps between levels **2.** *usually pl.* flight of stairs: also **stair'case, stair'way**

stake *n.* **1.** pointed stick to be driven in the ground **2.** *often pl.* money, etc. risked as in a wager —*v.* **1.** mark the boundaries of **2.** gamble **3.** [Col.] furnish with money or resources —**at stake** being risked —**stake out** put under police surveillance

sta·lac'tite *n.* stick of lime hanging from a cave roof

sta·lag'mite *n.* stick of lime built up on a cave floor

stale *a.* **1.** no longer fresh **2.** trite **3.** out of condition

stale'mate *n.* deadlock

stalk *v.* **1.** stride haughtily **2.** advance grimly **3.** track secretly —*n.* **1.** a stalking **2.** plant stem

stall *n.* **1.** section for one animal in a stable **2.** market booth **3.** [Col.] evasive trick —*v.* **1.** keep in a stall **2.** stop **3.** delay by evading

stal'lion (-yən) *n.* uncastrated male horse

stal'wart *a.* strong or brave —*n.* stalwart person

sta'men *n.* pollen-bearing part of a flower

stam'i·na *n.* endurance

stam'mer *v., n.* pause or halt in speaking

stamp *v.* **1.** put the foot down hard **2.** pound with the foot **3.** cut out with a die **4.** impress a design on **5.** put a stamp on —

n. **1.** a stamping **2.** gummed piece of paper, as for postage **3.** stamped mark **4.** machine tool or die for stamping —**stamp out 1.** crush by treading on forcibly **2.** suppress or put down

stam·pede' *n.* sudden, headlong rush, as of a herd —*v.* move in a stampede

stamp'ing ground [Col.] favorite gathering place

stance *n.* **1.** way one stands **2.** attitude taken in a given situation

stanch *a., v.* staunch

stan'chion (-chən) *n.* upright support

stand *v.* [STOOD, STANDING] **1.** be or get in an upright position **2.** place or be placed **3.** hold a certain opinion **4.** halt **5.** endure or resist —*n.* **1.** a halt **2.** a position **3.** view, opinion, etc. **4.** platform, rack, counter, etc. **5.** a growth (of trees) —**stand by** be ready to help —**stand for 1.** represent **2.** [Col.] tolerate —**stand out** to project, be prominent, etc. —**stand up 1.** rise to a standing position **2.** prove valid, durable, etc. **3.** [Sl.] fail to keep a date with

stand'ard *n.* **1.** flag, banner, etc. **2.** thing set up as a rule or model **3.** upright support —*a.* **1.** that is a standard or rule **2.** typical

stand'ard·ize *v.* make standard or uniform

standard time official civil time for a region: the 24 time zones are one hour apart

stand′by n. [pl. -BYS] person or thing that is dependable, a possible source, etc.

stand′-in′ n. a substitute

stand′ing n. 1. status or rank 2. duration —a. 1. upright 2. continuing

stand′off n. a tie in a contest

stand′off′ish a. aloof

stand′point n. viewpoint

stand′still n. a stop or halt

stank alt. pt. of **stink**

stan′za n. group of lines making a section of a poem

staph′y·lo·coc′cus n. [pl. -COCCI (-kāk′sī)] kind of spherical bacteria

sta′ple n. 1. main product, part, etc. 2. basic trade item, as flour, etc. 3. fiber of cotton, etc. 4. U-shaped piece of metal used to fasten —v. fasten with a staple —a. regular or principal —**sta′pler** n.

star n. 1. heavenly body seen as a point of light at night 2. flat figure with five or more points 3. asterisk 4. one who excels, as in acting —v. [STARRED, STARRING] 1. mark with stars 2. present in, or play, a leading role —**star′ry** [-RIER, -RIEST] a.

star′board (-bǝrd) n. right side of a ship, etc. as one faces the bow

starch n. 1. white food substance in potatoes, cereals, etc. 2. powdered form of this —v. stiffen (laundry) with starch —**starch′y** [-IER, -IEST] a.

star′dom n. status of a star in the movies, etc.

stare v. gaze steadily —n. long, steady look

star′fish n. small, star-shaped sea animal

star′gaze v. 1. gaze at the stars 2. to daydream

stark a. 1. rigid, as a corpse 2. sharply outlined 3. bleak 4. sheer; utter —adv. wholly —**stark′ly** adv.

stark′-nak′ed a. entirely naked

star′light n. light given by the stars —**star′lit** a.

star′ling n. bird with shiny, black feathers

star′ry-eyed′ a. with sparkling eyes

star′-span′gled a. studded with stars

start v. 1. begin to go, do, etc. 2. set in motion 3. jump or jerk —n. 1. a starting 2. jump or jerk 3. place or time of beginning 4. lead; advantage —**start′er** n.

start out (or **off**) begin a trip, etc. —**start′er** n.

star′tle v. 1. frighten suddenly 2. surprise

starve v. 1. suffer or die from lack of food 2. cause to starve 3. suffer great need (with *for*) —**star·va′tion** n.

stash v. [Col.] hide away —n. [Sl.] something hidden

state n. 1. the way a person or thing is 2. formal style 3. nation 4. [often S-] a unit of a federal government —v. express in words

stat′ed a. fixed; set

state′ly a. [-LIER, -LIEST] grand or dignified

state′ment n. 1. a stating 2.

something stated 3. report, as of money owed

state′room *n.* private room in a ship or railroad car

states′man *n.* [*pl.* -MEN] man skillful in government

stat′ic *a.* 1. at rest 2. of electricity caused by friction —*n.* 1. electrical disturbances in radio or TV reception 2. [Sl.] adverse criticism

sta′tion *n.* 1. assigned place 2. stopping place 3. place for radio or TV transmission 4. social rank —*v.* assign to a station

sta′tion·ar′y (-er′-) *a.* not moving or changing

sta′tion·er′y (-er′-) *n.* writing materials

station wagon automobile with a back end that opens

sta·tis′tics *n.pl.* 1. analysis of numerical data 2. the data — **sta·tis′ti·cal** *a.* —**stat′is·ti′cian** (-tish′ən) *n.*

stat′u·ar′y (-wer′-) *n.* statues

stat·ue (stach′ $\overline{oo}$) *n.* likeness done in stone, metal, etc.

stat·u·esque′ (-wesk′) *a.* stately; imposing

stat·u·ette′ *n.* small statue

stat·ure (stach′ər) *n.* 1. person's height 2. level of attainment

sta′tus *n.* 1. rank 2. condition

status quo (kwō) [L.] existing state of affairs

status symbol a possession regarded as a sign of social status

stat′ute (stach′-) *n.* a law

stat′u·to′ry *a.* authorized, or punishable by statute

staunch (stônch) *a.* firm, loyal, etc. —*v.* check the flow of (blood, etc.) from (a wound, etc.)

stave *n.* 1. any of the wood side strips of a barrel 2. staff (*n.* 1) 3. stanza —*v.* [STAVED or STOVE, STAVING] smash —**stave off** hold off

staves (stāvz) *n.* 1. alt. pl. of **staff** 2. pl. of **stave**

stay *v.* 1. remain 2. dwell 3. stop or delay 4. support —*n.* 1. a staying 2. prop 3. guy rope 4. stiffening strip

stay′ing power endurance

stead (sted) *n.* place filled by a substitute

stead′fast *a.* constant; firm

stead′y *a.* [-IER, -IEST] 1. firm 2. regular 3. calm 4. reliable —*v.* [-IED, -YING] make or become steady

steak *n.* slice of meat or fish

steal *v.* [STOLE, STOLEN, STEALING] 1. take dishonestly and secretly 2. move stealthily 3. *Baseball* advance to (a base) as while a pitch is being delivered —*n.* [Col.] great bargain

stealth (stelth) *n.* secret or furtive action —**stealth′i·ly** *adv.* —**stealth′y** [-IER, -IEST] *a.*

steam *n.* water changed to a vapor by boiling: source of heat and power —*a.* using steam —*v.* 1. expose to steam 2. give off steam 3. move by steam power —**steam′y** *a.*

steam′boat *n.* small steamship

steam′er *n.* thing run by steam

steam′roll′er *n.* heavy steam-driven roller —*v.* move, crush, override, etc. as (with) a steamroller

steam'ship *n.* ship driven by steam

steed *n.* horse: literary term

steel *n.* hard alloy of iron with carbon —*a.* of steel —*v.* make strong —**steel'y** *a.*

steel wool steel shavings used for cleaning, etc.

stool'yard *n.* weighing scale

steep *a.* 1. having a sharp rise or slope 2. [Col.] excessive —*v.* soak

stee'ple *n.* high tower

stee'ple-chase *n.* horse race over a course with obstacles

steer *v.* guide; direct —*n.* male of beef cattle; ox

steer'age *n.* formerly, part of a ship for passengers paying the lowest fare

stein (stīn) *n.* beer mug

stel'lar *a.* 1. of or like a star 2. chief 3. excellent

stem *n.* 1. stalk of a plant, flower, etc. 2. stemlike part 3. prow of a ship 4. root of a word —*v.* [STEMMED, STEM-MING] 1. remove the stem of 2. advance against 3. stop 4. derive

stench *n.* offensive smell

sten'cil *n.* sheet cut with letters, etc. to print when inked over —*v.* mark with a stencil

ste·nog'ra·phy *n.* transcription of dictation in shorthand —**ste·nog'ra·pher** *n.* —**sten'o·graph'ic a.**

sten·to'ri·an *a.* very loud

step *n.* 1. single movement of the foot, as in walking, or the distance covered 2. footstep 3.

way of stepping 4. stair tread 5. degree; rank 6. act or process in a series —*v.* [STEPPED, STEPPING] 1. move with a step 2. press the foot down —*in* (or *out of*) step (not) in rhythm with others —**step up** 1. advance 2. increase in rate —**take steps** do the things needed

step'child *n.* stepparent's son

step'child *n.* spouse's child (**stepdaughter** or **stepson**) by a former marriage

step'-down' *n.* decrease, as in amount, intensity, etc.

step'lad'der *n.* four-legged ladder with flat steps

step'par'ent *n.* spouse (**stepfather** or **stepmother**) of one's remarried parent

steppe *n.* great plain

step'ping-stone *n.* 1. stone to step on, as in crossing a stream 2. means of bettering oneself

step'sis'ter *n.* stepparent's daughter

step'-up' *n.* increase, as in amount, intensity, etc.

ster'e·o *n.* [*pl.* -OS] stereophonic record player, radio system, etc.

ster'e·o·phon'ic *a.* of sound reproduced to show directions it came from

ster'e·o·scope' *n.* device for giving three-dimensional effect to pictures

ster'e·o·type' *v.* express in a set, trite form —*n.* such a form or pattern

ster·ile (ster'l) *a.* 1. unable to

reproduce itself 2. free of germs —ster·il′i·ty n.

ster′i·lize v. make sterile —ster′i·li·za′tion n.

ster′ling (stur′-) a. 1. (made) of silver at least 92.5% pure 2. of British money 3. excellent —n. 1. sterling silver 2. British money

stern a. severe; unyielding —n. rear end of a ship, etc.

ster′num n. front chest bone to which ribs are joined; breastbone

ster′oid n. any of a group of compounds including cortisone, etc.

steth′o·scope n. instrument for hearing chest sounds

ste′ve·dore n. one hired to load and unload ships

stew (stōō, styōō) v. 1. cook by boiling slowly 2. worry —n. meat with vegetables, cooked in this way

stew′ard n. 1. one put in charge of funds, supplies, etc. 2. attendant on a ship, etc. —stew′ard·ship n.

stew′ard·ess n. woman steward, esp. on an airplane

stick n. 1. small branch broken or cut off 2. long, thin piece, as of wood —v. [STUCK, STICKING] 1. pierce 2. attach or be attached as by pinning or gluing 3. project (out) 4. become fixed, jammed, etc. 5. persevere 6. hesitate 7. [Col.] puzzle —stick up for [Col.] defend —the sticks [Col.] rural districts

stick′er n. gummed label

stick′-in-the-mud′ n. [Col.] one who resists change

stick′le·back n. small fish with sharp spines on its back

stick′ler n. one who is stubbornly fussy

stick′pin n. ornamental pin worn in a necktie, etc.

stick shift car gearshift, operated manually by a lever

stick′up n. [Sl.] robbery

stick′y a. [-IER, -IEST] adhesive —stick′i·ness n.

stiff a. 1. hard to bend or move 2. thick; dense 3. strong, as a wind 4. harsh 5. difficult 6. tense —stiff′ly adv.

stiff′en v. make or become stiff

stiff′-necked′ a. stubborn

sti′fle v. 1. suffocate 2. suppress; restrain

stig′ma n. pl. -MAS, -MATA (-mät′ə)) 1. sign of disgrace 2. pl. marks like the crucifixion wounds of Jesus 3. upper tip of a pistil

stig′ma·tize v. mark as disgraceful

stile n. step or steps for climbing over a fence or wall

sti·let′to (-tō) n. [pl. -TOS, -TOES] small, thin dagger

still a. 1. quiet 2. motionless 3. calm —n. device to distill liquor —adv. 1. until then or now 2. even; yet 3. nevertheless —con. nevertheless —v. make or become still —still′-ness n.

still′born′ a. dead at birth

still life painting of inanimate objects, as fruit

stilt n. supporting pole, esp.

one of a pair for walking high off the ground

stilt′ed *a.* pompous

stim′u·lant *n.* thing that stimulates, as a drug

stim′u·late *v.* make (more) active —**stim′u·la′tion** *n.*

stim′u·lus *n.* [*pl.* **-LI** (-lī)] anything causing activity

sting *v.* [STUNG, STINGING] 1. hurt with a sting 2. cause or feel sharp pain —*n.* 1. a stinging, or pain from it 2. sharp-pointed organ, as in insects and plants, that pricks, etc. —**sting′er** *n.*

stin′gy (-jē) *a.* [-GIER, -GIEST] miserly; grudging

stink *v.* [STANK or STUNK, STUNK, STINKING] have a strong, unpleasant smell —*n.* such a smell; stench

stint *v.* restrict to a small amount —*n.* 1. limit 2. assigned task

sti′pend *n.* regular payment

stip′ple *v.* paint or draw in small dots

stip′u·late *v.* specify as an essential condition

stir *v.* [STIRRED, STIRRING] 1. move, esp. slightly 2. move around as with a spoon 3. excite —*n.* 1. a stirring 2. commotion

stir′rup *n.* ring hung from a saddle as a footrest

stitch *n.* 1. single movement or loop made by a needle in sewing, knitting, etc. 2. sudden pain —*v.* sew

stock *n.* 1. tree trunk 2. ancestry 3. biological breed 4. rifle part holding the barrel 5. *pl.*

frame with holes for feet and hands, once used for punishment 6. frame to hold an animal for shoeing 7. livestock 8. goods on hand 9. shares in a business —*v.* supply or keep in stock *a.* 1. kept in stock 2. common —**in** (or **out of**) **stock** (not) available —**take** (or **put**) **stock in** [Col.] have faith in

stock·ade′ *n.* defensive wall or enclosure of tall stakes

stock′bro′ker *n.* broker for stocks and bonds

stock car standard automobile, modified for racing

stock exchange (or **market**) place of sale for stocks and bonds

stock′hold′er *n.* one owning stock in a given company

stock′ing *n.* knitted covering for the leg and foot

stocking cap long, tapered, knitted cap

stock′pile *v., n.* (accumulate) a reserve supply

stock′-still′ *a.* motionless

stock′y *a.* [-IER, -IEST] short and heavy

stock′yard *n.* place to pen livestock till slaughtered

stodg′y *a.* [-IER, -IEST] dull; uninteresting

sto′gie, sto′gy (-gē) *n.* [*pl.* -GIES] long, thin, inexpensive cigar

sto′ic *a., n.* stoical (person)

sto′i·cal *a.* indifferent to joy, grief, pain, etc. —**sto′i·cism** *n.*

stoke *v.* stir up and feed fuel to (a fire) —**stok′er** *n.*

stole pt. of **steal** —*n.* woman's

long scarf worn around the shoulders

stol´en pp. of **steal**

stol´id (stäl´-) a. unexcitable

stom´ach n. 1. digestive organ into which food passes 2. abdomen 3. appetite 4. inclination —v. tolerate

stom´ach-ache n. pain in the stomach or abdomen

stomp v. to stamp (v. 1, 2)

stone n. 1. solid nonmetallic mineral matter of rock 2. piece of this 3. seed of certain fruits 4. abnormal stony mass in the kidney, etc. 5. [pl. STONE] [Br.] 14 pounds —v. throw stones at

stoned a. [Sl.] under the influence of liquor, a drug, etc.

stone's throw short distance

ston´y a. [-IER, -IEST] 1. full of stones 2. unfeeling

stood pt. & pp. of **stand**

stooge n. [Col.] lackey; foil

stool n. 1. single seat with no back or arms 2. feces

stoop v. 1. bend the body forward 2. degrade oneself —n. 1. position of stooping 2. small porch

stop v. [STOPPED, STOPPING] 1. close by filling, shutting off, etc. 2. cease; end; halt 3. block; obstruct 4. stay —n. 1. a stopping 2. place stopped at 3. obstruction, plug, etc. — **stop off** stop for a while — **stop´page** n.

stop´cock n. valve to regulate the flow of a liquid

stop´gap n. temporary substitute

stop´light n. 1. traffic light, esp. when red 2. rear light on

a vehicle that lights up when the brakes are applied

stop´o´ver n. brief stop at a place during a journey

stop´per n. something inserted to close an opening

stop´watch n. watch with a hand that can be started and stopped instantly

stor´age (-ij) n. 1. a storing 2. place for, or cost of, storing goods

storage battery battery capable of being recharged

store n. 1. supply; stock 2. establishment where goods are sold —v. put aside for future use —**in store** set aside for the future

store´house n. warehouse

store´keep´er n. person in charge of a store

store´room n. room where things are stored

stork n. large, long-legged wading bird

storm n. 1. strong wind with rain, snow, etc. 2. any strong disturbance 3. strong attack —v. 1. blow violently, rain, etc. 2. rage 3. rush or attack violently —**storm´y** [-IER, -IEST] a.

storm door (or window) door (or window) put outside the regular one as added protection

sto´ry n. [pl. -RIES] 1. telling of an event 2. fictitious narrative 3. one level of a building 4. [Col.] falsehood

sto´ry-book n. book of stories, esp. one for children

sto'ry·tell'er *n.* one who narrates stories

stout *a.* 1. brave 2. firm; strong 3. fat —*n.* strong, dark beer —**stout'ly** *adv.*

stove alt. pt. & pp. of **stave** —*n.* apparatus for heating, cooking, etc.

stove'pipe *n.* metal pipe to carry off stove smoke

stow (stō) *v.* pack or store away —**stow away** hide aboard a ship, etc. for a free ride —**stow'a·way** *n.*

strad'dle *v.* 1. sit or stand astride 2. take both sides of (an issue) —*n.* a straddling —**strad'dler** *n.*

strafe *v.* attack with machine guns from aircraft

strag'gle *v.* 1. wander from the group 2. spread out unevenly —**strag'gler** *n.*

straight *a.* 1. not crooked, bent, etc. 2. direct 3. in order 4. honest 5. undiluted 6. [Sl.] conventional —*adv.* 1. in a straight line 2. directly —*n.* poker hand of any five cards in sequence —**straight away** (or **off**) without delay —**straight'en** *v.*

straight face facial expression showing no emotion

straight'for'ward *a.* 1. direct 2. honest

straight'way *adv.* at once

strain *v.* 1. stretch tight or to the utmost 2. strive hard 3. sprain 4. filter —*n.* 1. a straining or being strained 2. excessive demand on one's emotions, etc. 3. ancestry 4. inherited tendency 5. trace; streak 6. tune —**strain'er** *n.*

strait *n. often pl.* 1. narrow waterway 2. distress

strait'en *v.* impoverish

strait'jack'et *n.* coatlike device for restraining a person

strait'-laced' *a.* strict

strand *v.* 1. many of the threads, wires, etc. that form a string, cable, etc. 2. string, as of pearls 3. shore —*v.* put into a helpless position

strange *a.* 1. unfamiliar 2. unusual 3. peculiar; odd —**strange'ly** *adv.*

stran'ger *n.* 1. newcomer 2. person not known to one

stran'gle *v.* 1. choke to death 2. suppress —**stran'gler** *n.*

strap *n.* narrow strip of leather, etc., as for binding things —*v.* [STRAPPED, STRAPPING] fasten with a strap —**strap'less** *a.*

strapped *a.* [Col.] without money

strap'ping *a.* [Col.] robust

strat'a·gem (-jəm) *n.* 1. plan, scheme, etc. for deceiving an enemy in war 2. tricky ruse or move to gain an end

strat'e·gy *n.* [*pl.* -GIES] 1. science of military operations 2. artful managing 3. plan —**stra·te'gic** *a.* —**stra·te'gi·cal·ly** *adv.* —**strat'e·gist** *n.*

strat'i·fy *v.* [-FIED, -FYING] form in layers —**strat'i·fi·ca'tion** *n.*

strat'o·sphere *n.* atmospheric zone from 6 to 15 miles above the earth's surface

stra'tum *n.* [*pl.* -TA, -TUMS] 1.

any of a series of layers, as of rock 2. level of society

stra′tus (strā′-) *n.* [*pl.* **-TI** (-tī)] long, low, gray cloud layer

straw *n.* 1. grain stalk or stalks after threshing 2. tube for sucking a drink

straw′ber′ry *n.* [*pl.* **-RIES**] small, red, juicy fruit of a vine-like plant

straw boss [Col.] person having subordinate authority

straw vote unofficial poll of public opinion

stray *v.* 1. wander; roam 2. deviate —*a.* 1. lost 2. isolated —*n.* one that strays, esp. a lost domestic animal

streak *n.* 1. long, thin mark 2. layer 3. tendency in behavior 4. period, as of luck —*v.* 1. mark with streaks 2. go fast

stream *n.* 1. small river 2. steady flow, as of air —*v.* 1. flow in a stream 2. move swiftly

stream′er *n.* long, narrow flag or strip

stream′line *v., a.* (make) streamlined

stream′lined *a.* 1. shaped to move easily in air, etc. 2. made more efficient

street *n.* 1. road in a city 2. people living, working, etc. along a given street

street′car *n.* passenger car on rails along streets

street′walk′er *n.* prostitute

street′wise′ *a.* [Col.] experienced in living in urban areas where crime is common

strength *n.* 1. force; power 2. durability 3. intensity 4. potency —**on the strength of** based or relying on —**strength′en** *v.*

stren′u·ous *a.* needing or showing much energy

strep′to·coc′cus *n.* [*pl.* **-COCCI** (-kăk′sī)] kind of spherical bacteria

strep′to·my′cin (-mī′sin) *n.* antibiotic drug

stress *n.* 1. strain; pressure 2. importance; emphasis 3. special force on a syllable, etc. — *v.* 1. strain 2. accent 3. emphasize

stretch *v.* 1. reach out 2. draw out to full extent 3. strain 4. exaggerate —*n.* 1. a stretching 2. ability to be stretched 3. extent

stretch′er *n.* 1. person or thing that stretches 2. canvas-covered frame to carry the sick

strew *v.* [alt. pp. STREWN] 1. scatter 2. cover as by scattering

stri′at·ed *a.* striped

strick′en *a.* struck, wounded, afflicted, etc.

strict *a.* 1. exact or absolute 2. rigidly enforced or enforcing —**strict′ly** *adv.* —**strict′ness** *n.*

stric′ture (-chər) *n.* 1. strong criticism 2. abnormal narrowing of a body passage

stride *v.* [STRODE, STRIDDEN, STRIDING] walk with long steps —*n.* 1. long step 2. *usually pl.* progress

stri′dent *a.* shrill; grating

strife *n.* a fight or quarrel

strike *v.* [STRUCK, STRUCK or STRICKEN, STRIKING] 1. hit 2.

sound by hitting some part **3.** ignite (a match) **4.** make by stamping **5.** attack **6.** reach or find **7.** occur to **8.** assume (a pose) **9.** take down or apart **10.** stop working until demands are met —*n.* **1.** a striking **2.** *Baseball* a pitched ball struck at but missed, etc. **3.** *Bowling* a knocking down of all the pins with the first ball —**strike out 1.** erase **2.** *Baseball* put or go out on three strikes —**strike up** begin — **strik'er** *n.*

strik'ing *a.* very attractive, impressive, etc.

string *n.* **1.** thick thread, etc. used as for tying **2.** number of things on a string or in a row **3.** thin cord bowed, etc. to make music, as on a violin **4.** [Col.] *usually pl.* condition attached to a plan, offer, etc. — *v.* [STRUNG, STRINGING] **1.** provide with strings **2.** put on a string **3.** extend —**pull strings** use influence to gain advantage —**string'y** *a.*

string bean thick bean pod, eaten as a vegetable

strin'gent (-jont) *a.* strict

strip *v.* [STRIPPED, STRIPPING] **1.** take off the clothing, covering, etc. (of) **2.** dispossess of (honors, etc.) **3.** plunder; rob **4.** make bare **5.** break the teeth of (a gear, etc.) —*n.* long, narrow piece, as of tape, etc.

stripe *n.* **1.** narrow band of different color or material **2.** kind; sort —*v.* mark with stripes

strip'ling *n.* a youth

strive *v.* [STROVE *or* STRIVED, STRIVEN *or* STRIVED, STRIVING] **1.** try very hard **2.** struggle

strobe (light) electronic tube emitting rapid, brilliant flashes of light

strode pt. of **stride**

stroke *n.* **1.** sudden blow, attack, action, etc. **2.** a single movement of the arm, a tool, etc. **3.** striking sound —*v.* draw one's hand, etc. gently over

stroll *n.* leisurely walk —*v.* **1.** take a stroll **2.** wander

stroll'er *n.* **1.** one who strolls **2.** chairlike baby carriage

strong *a.* **1.** powerful **2.** healthy **3.** durable **4.** intense —**strong'ly** *adv.*

strong'-arm' *a.* [Col.] using physical force —*v.* [Col.] use force upon

strong'box *n.* heavily made box or safe for valuables

strong'hold *n.* fortress

stron·ti·um (strän'shē əm) *n.* chemical element with a very dangerous radioactive isotope (**strontium 90**) produced by nuclear-reactor fuels

strove pt. of **strive**

struck pt. & pp. of **strike**

struc'ture (-chər) *n.* **1.** thing built **2.** plan, design, etc. — **struc'tur·al** *a.*

stru'del *n.* pastry of thin dough filled with apples, etc., rolled up, and baked

strug'gle *v.* **1.** fight **2.** strive —*n.* a struggling

strum *v.* [STRUMMED, STRUMMING] pluck, as a guitar

strum'pet *n.* prostitute

strung pt. & pp. of **string**

strut v. [STRUTTED, STRUTTING] walk arrogantly —n. 1. strutting walk 2. rod used as a support

strych·nine (strik′nin) n. poisonous drug used in small doses as a stimulant

stub n. 1. short, leftover or blunt part 2. part of a ticket, bank check, etc. kept as a record —v. [STUBBED, STUBBING] bump (one's toe)

stub′ble n. 1. short grain stumps 2. short growth

stub′born a. obstinate — **stub′born·ness** n.

stub′by a. [-BIER, -BIEST] short and thick

stuc′co n. [pl. -COES, -COS] plaster or cement for surfacing walls, etc. —v. [-COED, -COING] cover with stucco

stuck pt. & pp. of **stick**

stuck′-up′ a. [Col.] snobbish

stud n. 1. decorative nail 2. removable button 3. upright support in a wall 4. breeding stallion —v. [STUDDED, STUDDING] be set thickly with

stu′dent n. one who studies

stud′ied a. done on purpose

stu′di·o n. [pl. -OS] 1. artist's work area 2. place for producing movies, or radio or TV programs

studio couch couch that opens into a full-sized bed

stu′di·ous a. 1. fond of study 2. attentive

stud′y v. [-IED, -YING] 1. learn by reading, thinking, etc. 2. investigate carefully 3. read (a book, etc.) intently —n. [pl.

-IES] 1. act of studying 2. branch of learning 3. pl. education 4. deep thought 5. place to study

stuff n. 1. material; substance 2. objects; things 3. worthless objects; junk 4. [Col.] ability, skill, etc. —v. 1. fill 2. cram — **stuff′ing** n.

stuffed shirt [Sl.] pompous, pretentious person

stuff′y a. [-IER, -IEST] 1. poorly ventilated 2. stopped up 3. [Col.] dull

stul′ti·fy v. [-FIED, -FYING] make seem foolish, etc.

stum′ble v. 1. walk unsteadily; trip 2. speak confusedly 3. come by chance —n. a stumbling

stumbling block difficulty

stump n. part left after cutting off the rest —v. 1. make a speaking tour 2. walk heavily 3. [Col.] perplex

stun v. [STUNNED, STUNNING] 1. make unconscious, as by a blow 2. shock deeply

stung pt. & pp. of **sting**

stunk pp. & alt. pt. of **stink**

stun′ning a. [Col.] very attractive

stunt v. keep from growing — n. daring show of skill

stu·pe·fy v. [-FIED, -FYING] stun —**stu′pe·fac′tion** n.

stu·pen′dous a. overwhelming

stu′pid a. 1. not intelligent 2. foolish 3. dull —**stu·pid′i·ty** n. [pl. -TIES]

stu′por n. dazed condition

stur′dy a. [-DIER, -DIEST] 1. firm 2. strong

stur′geon (-jən) n. food fish

stut'ter *n.*, *v.* stammer

sty *n.* [*pl.* STIES] pigpen

sty, stye (stī) *n.* [*pl.* STIES] swelling on the rim of the eyelid

style *n.* 1. way of making, writing, etc. 2. excellence of expression 3. fashion —*v.* 1. name 2. design the style of

styl'ish *a.* fashionable

styl'ize *v.* design or depict according to a style rather than nature

sty'lus *n.* 1. pointed writing tool 2. phonograph needle

sty·mie (stī'mē) *v.* [-MIED, -MIEING] obstruct; block

styp'tic (stip'-) *a.* that halts bleeding; astringent

styptic pencil piece of a styptic substance to stop minor bleeding

suave (swäv) *a.* smoothly polite —**suav'i·ty** *n.*

sub- *pref.* 1. under 2. somewhat 3. being a division

sub'com'pact *n.* automobile model smaller than a compact

sub·con'scious *a.*, *n.* (of) one's feelings, wishes, etc. of which one is unaware

sub·cu·ta'ne·ous *a.* beneath the skin

sub·di·vide' *v.* 1. divide again 2. divide (land) into small sections for sale —**sub'di·vi'sion** *n.*

sub·due' *v.* 1. get control over 2. make less intense

sub'ject *a.* 1. under the authority or control of another 2. liable to; contingent upon —*n.* 1. one controlled by another 2. topic of discussion or study 3. *Gram.* word or words about which something is said —*v.* (səb jekt') 1. bring under the control of 2. make undergo —**sub·jec'tion** *n.*

sub·jec'tive *a.* of one's feelings rather than from facts —**sub'jec·tiv'i·ty** *n.*

sub'ju·gate *v.* conquer

sub'lease' *n.* lease granted by a lessee —*v.* (sub lēs') grant or hold a sublease of

sub·let' *v.* [-LET, -LETTING] 1. sublease 2. let out work one has contracted to do

sub'li·mate *v.* 1. to sublime 2. to express (unacceptable impulses) in acceptable forms —**sub'li·ma'tion** *n.*

sub·lime' *a.* noble; lofty —*v.* purify (a solid) by heating and then condensing —**sub·lim'i·ty** *n.*

sub·lim'i·nal *a.* below the threshold of awareness

sub'ma·chine' gun portable, automatic firearm

sub·mar'gin·al *a.* below minimum standards

sub'ma·rine' (-rēn) *n.* warship operating under water

submarine sandwich hero sandwich

sub·merge' *v.* put or go under water —**sub·mer'gence** *n.*

sub·merse' *v.* submerge —**sub·mers'i·ble** *a.*, *n.* —**sub·mer'sion** *n.*

sub·mis'sion *n.* 1. a submitting 2. obedience —**sub·mis'sive** *a.*

sub·mit' *v.* [-MITTED, -MITTING] 1. present for consideration, etc. 2. surrender

sub·nor'mal *a.* below normal, esp. in intelligence

sub·or'di·nate (-nit) *a.* lower in rank; secondary —*n.* subordinate person —*v.* (-nāt) make subordinate

sub·orn' *v.* induce (another) to commit perjury

sub·poe'na, sub·pe'na (sə pē'-) *n.* legal paper ordering one to appear in court —*v.* order with a subpoena

sub·scribe' *v.* 1. give support or consent (to) 2. promise to contribute (money) 3. agree to take and pay for a periodical, etc. (with *to*) —**sub·scrip'tion** *n.*

sub'se·quent *a.* following

sub·ser'vi·ent *a.* servile

sub·side' *v.* 1. sink lower 2. become quieter

sub·sid'i·ar'y (-er'ē) *a.* helping in a lesser way —*n.* [*pl.* -IES] company controlled by another

sub'si·dize *v.* support with a subsidy

sub'si·dy *n.* [*pl.* -DIES] grant of money, as from a government to a private enterprise

sub·sist' *v.* continue to live or exist

sub·sist'ence *n.* 1. a subsisting 2. means of support, esp. the barest means

sub'soil' *n.* layer of soil beneath the surface soil

sub·son'ic (-sän'-) *a.* moving at a speed less than sound

sub'stance *n.* 1. essence 2. physical matter 3. central meaning 4. wealth

sub·stand'ard *a.* below standard

sub·stan'tial (-shəl) *a.* 1. material 2. strong 3. large 4. wealthy 5. in essentials

sub·stan'ti·ate (-shē-) *v.* prove to be true or real

sub'sti·tute *n.* one that takes the place of another —*v.* use as or be a substitute —**sub'sti·tu'tion** *n.*

sub'ter·fuge *n.* scheme used to evade something

sub'ter·ra'ne·an *a.* 1. underground 2. secret

sub'ti·tle *n.* 1. secondary title 2. line of dialogue, etc. shown as on a movie screen

sub·tle (sut''l) *a.* 1. keen; acute 2. crafty 3. delicate 4. not obvious —**sub'tle·ty** [*pl.* -TIES] *n.* —**sub'tly** *adv.*

sub·tract' *v.* take away, as one number from another —**sub·trac'tion** *n.*

sub'urb *n.* district, town, etc. on the outskirts of a city —**sub·ur'ban** *a.*

sub·ur'ban·ite *n.* person living in a suburb

sub·ur'bi·a (-bē·ə) *n.* suburbs or suburbanites collectively

sub·vert' *v.* overthrow (something established) —**sub·ver'sion** *n.* —**sub·ver'sive** *a., n.*

sub'way' *n.* underground electric railroad in a city

suc·ceed' *v.* 1. come next after 2. have success

suc·cess' *n.* 1. favorable result 2. gaining of wealth, fame, etc. 3. successful one —**suc·cess'ful** *a.* —**suc·cess'ful·ly** *adv.*

suc·ces'sion *n.* 1. a coming

after another 2. series —**suc·ces′sive** *a.*

suc·ces′sor *n.* one who succeeds another, as in office

suc·cinct′ (-siŋkt′) *a.* terse

suc′cor *v., n.* help

suc′co·tash *n.* lima beans and corn kernels cooked together

suc′cu·lent *a.* juicy

suc·cumb′ (-kum′) *v.* 1. give in; yield 2. die

such *a.* 1. of this or that kind 2. whatever 3. so much —*pron.* such a one —**such as** for example

suck *v.* 1. draw into the mouth 2. suck liquid from 3. dissolve in the mouth —*n.* act of sucking

suck′er *n.* 1. one that sucks or clings 2. freshwater fish 3. sprout 4. lollipop 5. [Sl.] dupe

suck′le *v.* give or get milk from the breast or udder

suck′ling *n.* unweaned child or young animal

su′crose *n.* sugar found in sugar cane, sugar beets, etc.

suc′tion *n.* creation of a vacuum that sucks in fluid, etc. —*a.* worked by suction

sud′den *a.* 1. unexpected 2. hasty —**sud′den·ly** *adv.*

suds *n.pl.* foam on soapy water —**suds′y** *a.*

sue *v.* 1. begin a lawsuit against 2. petition

suede (swād) *n.* 1. leather with one side buffed into a nap 2. cloth like this

su′et *n.* hard animal fat

suf′fer *v.* 1. undergo or endure (pain, loss, etc.) 2. tolerate —**suf′fer·ance** *n.*

suf·fice′ (-fīs′) *v.* be enough

suf·fi′cient *a.* enough —**suf·fi′cien·cy** *n.* —**suf·fi′cient·ly** *adv.*

suf′fix *n.* syllable or syllables added at the end of a word to alter its meaning, etc.

suf′fo·cate *v.* 1. kill by cutting off air 2. die from lack of air 3. stifle —**suf′fo·ca′tion** *n.*

suf′frage (rij) *n.* right to vote

suf·fuse′ (-fyōōz′) *v.* overspread, as with color

sug′ar *n.* sweet carbohydrate found in sugar cane, etc.

sugar beet beet with a white root of high sugar content

sugar cane tall tropical grass grown for its sugar

sug′ar-coat′ *v.* 1. coat with sugar 2. make seem more pleasant

sug·gest′ *v.* 1. bring to mind 2. propose as a possibility 3. imply —**sug·ges′tion** *n.*

sug·gest′i·ble *a.* readily influenced by suggestion

sug·ges′tive *a.* suggesting ideas, esp. indecent ideas

su′i·cide *n.* 1. act of killing oneself intentionally 2. one who commits suicide —**su′i·ci′dal** *a.*

suit *n.* 1. coat and trousers (or skirt) 2. any of the four sets of playing cards 3. lawsuit 4. a suing, pleading, etc. —*v.* 1. be suitable for 2. make suitable 3. please —**follow suit** follow the example set

suit′a·ble *a.* appropriate; fitting —**suit′a·bly** *adv.*

suit′case *n.* traveling bag

suite (swēt) *n.* **1.** group of connected rooms **2.** set of matched furniture

suit'or *n.* man who courts a woman

su·ki·ya·ki (-kē yä'kē) *n.* Japanese dish of thinly sliced meat and vegetables

sul'fa *n.* of a family of drugs used in combating certain bacterial infections

sul'fate *n.* salt of sulfuric acid

sul'fide *n.* compound of sulfur

sul'fur *n.* yellow solid substance, a chemical element — **sul·fu'ric** (-fyoor'ik), **sul·fu'rous** *a.*

sulfuric acid corrosive liquid, used in making dyes, etc.

sulk *v.* be sulky —*n. often pl.* sulky mood

sulk'y *a.* [-IER, -IEST] sullen; glum —*n. [pl.* -IES] light, two-wheeled carriage —**sulk'i·ly** *adv.*

sul'len *a.* **1.** showing ill humor by morose withdrawal **2.** gloomy —**sul'len·ly** *adv.*

sul'ly *v.* [-LIED, -LYING] soil, stain, defile, etc.

sul'phur *n.* sulfur: Br. sp.

sul'tan *n.* Muslim ruler

sul'try *a.* [-TRIER, -TRIEST] **1.** hot and humid **2.** inflamed, as with passion

sum *n.* **1.** amount of money **2.** summary **3.** total —*v.* [SUMMED, SUMMING] to total — **sum up** summarize

su·mac, su·mach (shoo'mak, soo'-) *n.* plant with lance-shaped leaves and red fruit

sum'ma·rize *v.* make or be a summary of

sum'ma·ry *n. [pl.* -RIES] brief report; digest —*a.* **1.** concise **2.** prompt —**sum·ma'ri·ly** *adv.*

sum·ma'tion *n.* final summarizing of arguments, as in a trial

sum'mer *n.* warmest season of the year —*a.* of or for summer —*v.* pass the summer —**sum'mer·y** *a.*

sum'mer·house *n.* small, open structure in a garden, etc.

summer sausage hard, dried sausage, not spoiling easily

sum'mit *n.* highest point

sum'mon *v.* **1.** call together **2.** send for **3.** rouse

sum'mons *n.* official order to appear in court

sump'tu·ous (-choo əs) *a.* **1.** costly; lavish **2.** splendid

sun *n.* **1.** incandescent body about which the planets revolve **2.** heat or light of the sun —*v.* [SUNNED, SUNNING] expose to sunlight

sun'bathe (-bā*th*) *v.* expose the body to direct sunlight — **sun bath**

sun'beam *n.* beam of sunlight

sun'bon·net *n.* bonnet for shading the face, neck, etc. from the sun

sun'burn *n.* inflammation of the skin from exposure to the sun —*v.* [alt. pt. & pp. SUNBURNT] give or get a sunburn

sun'burst *n.* **1.** sudden sunlight **2.** decoration representing the sun's rays

sun'dae (-dē) *n.* ice cream covered with syrup, nuts, etc.

Sun'day *n.* first day of the week

sun'der *v.* break apart

sun'di·al *n.* instrument that shows time by the shadow cast by the sun

sun'down *n.* sunset

sun'dries (-drēz) *n.pl.* sundry items

sun'dry *a.* various

sun'fish *n.* 1. small freshwater fish 2. large sea fish

sun'flow'er *n.* tall plant with big, daisylike flowers

sung *pp.* of sing

sun'glass'es *n.pl.* eyeglasses with tinted lenses

sunk *pp. & alt. pt.* of sink

sunk'en *a.* 1. sunk in liquid 2. depressed; hollow

sun'lamp *n.* ultraviolet-ray lamp

sun'light *n.* light of the sun

sun'lit *a.* lighted by the sun

sun'ny *a.* [-NIER, -NIEST] 1. full of sunshine 2. cheerful

sun'rise *n.* daily rising of the sun in the east

sun'set *n.* daily setting of the sun in the west

sun'shine *n.* 1. shining of the sun 2. light from the sun — **sun'shin'y** *a.*

sun'spot *n.* temporary dark spot on the sun

sun'stroke *n.* illness from overexposure to the sun

sun'suit *n.* short pants with a bib and shoulder straps, worn by young children

sun'tan *n.* skin darkened by exposure to the sun

sup *v.* [SUPPED, SUPPING] have supper

su'per *a.* 1. outstanding 2. extreme or excessive

super- *pref.* 1. over; above 2. superior to 3. greater than others 4. extra

su'per·an'nu·at'ed *a.* 1. retired on a pension 2. too old to work or use

su·perb' *a.* excellent; grand

su'per·charge' *v.* increase an engine's power

su'per·cil'i·ous (-sil'-) *a.* disdainful; haughty

su'per·fi'cial (-fish'əl) *a.* 1. of or on the surface 2. shallow; hasty —**su'per·fi'cial·ly** *adv.*

su·per'flu·ous *a.* unnecessary —**su'per·flu'i·ty** *n.*

su'per·high'way *n.* expressway

su'per·hu'man *a.* 1. divine 2. greater than normal

su'per·im·pose' *v.* put on top of something else

su'per·in·tend' *v.* direct or manage —**su'per·in·tend'ent** *n.*

su·pe'ri·or *a.* 1. higher in rank, etc. 2. above average 3. haughty —*n.* one that is superior —**superior to** unaffected by —**su·pe'ri·or'i·ty** *n.*

su·per'la·tive *a.* of the highest degree; supreme —*n.* 1. highest degree 2. third degree in the comparison of adjectives and adverbs

su'per·man *n.* [*pl.* -MEN] seemingly superhuman man

su'per·mar'ket *n.* large, self-service food store

su'per·nat'u·ral *a.* beyond known laws of nature —**the**

supernatural supernatural things

su·per·nu·mer·ar·y *a., n.* [*pl.* -IES] extra (person or thing)

su·per·scribe' *v.* write on the top or outside of

su·per·script *n.* figure, letter, or symbol written above and to the side of another

su·per·sede' *v.* replace, succeed, or supplant

su·per·son·ic *a.* moving faster than sound

su'per·star *n.* famous athlete, entertainer, etc.

su·per·sti'tion *n.* belief or practice based on fear or ignorance —**su'per·sti'tious** *a.*

su·per·struc'ture *n.* 1. part above a ship's deck 2. upper part of a building

su'per·tank'er *n.* extremely large oil tanker

su·per·vene' *v.* happen unexpectedly

su'per·vise *v.* oversee or direct (work, etc.) —**su'per·vi'sion** *n.* —**su'per·vi'sor** *n.* —**su'per·vi'so·ry** *a.*

su·pine' *a.* 1. lying on the back 2. lazy

sup'per *n.* evening meal

supper club expensive nightclub

sup·plant' *v.* take the place of, esp. by force

sup'ple *a.* flexible; adaptable

sup'ple·ment *n.* something added —*v.* add to —**sup'ple·men'tal**, **sup'ple·men'ta·ry** *a.*

sup'pli·cate *v.* implore —**sup'pli·ant**, **sup'pli·cant** *n.*, *a.* —**sup'pli·ca'tion** *n.*

sup·ply' *v.* [-PLIED, -PLYING] 1. furnish; provide 2. make up for —*n.* [*pl.* -PLIES] 1. amount available 2. *pl.* materials —**sup·pli'er** *n.*

sup·port' *v.* 1. hold up 2. help 3. provide for 4. help prove —*n.* 1. a supporting 2. that which supports

sup·port'ive *a.* giving support, help, or approval

sup·pose' *v.* 1. take as true; assume 2. guess; think 3. expect —**sup·posed'** *a.* —**sup'po·si'tion** *n.*

sup·pos'i·to·ry *n.* [*pl.* -RIES] medicated substance put in the rectum or vagina

sup·press' *v.* 1. put down by force 2. keep back; conceal —**sup·pres'sion** *n.*

sup'pu·rate (-yoo-) *v.* form or discharge pus

su'pra·na'tion·al *a.* of, for, or above all or a number of nations

su·prem'a·cy *n.* supreme power or authority

su·preme' *a.* 1. highest in rank, power, or degree 2. highest in quality, achievement, etc. 3. final

sur·cease' *n.* end or cessation

sur'charge *n.* 1. extra charge 2. overload —*v.* put a surcharge in or on

sure *a.* 1. reliable; certain 2. without doubt 3. bound to happen or do —*adv.* [Col.] surely —**for sure** certainly —**sure enough** [Col.] without doubt

sure'-fire' *a.* [Col.] sure to be successful

sure'-foot'ed *a.* not likely to stumble, slip, err, etc.

sure'ly *adv.* **1.** with confidence **2.** without doubt

sure'ty *n.* [*pl.* -TIES] **1.** security **2.** guarantor of another's debts

surf *n.* ocean waves breaking on a shore or reef

sur·face *n.* **1.** outside of a thing **2.** any face of a solid **3.** outward look —*a.* superficial —*v.* **1.** give a surface to **2.** rise to the surface

surf'board *n.* long board used in the sport of surfing

sur·feit (-fit) *n.* **1.** excess, as of food **2.** sickness caused by this —*v.* overindulge

surf'ing *n.* sport of riding the surf on a surfboard

surge *n.* **1.** large wave of water, or its motion **2.** any sudden, strong increase —*v.* move in a surge

sur·geon (-jən) *n.* doctor who specializes in surgery

sur·ger·y *n.* **1.** treatment of disease or injury by operations **2.** a room for this —**sur'gi·cal** *a.*

sur'ly *a.* [-LIER, -LIEST] bad-tempered; uncivil

sur·mise (-mīz') *n., v.* guess

sur·mount' *v.* **1.** overcome **2.** climb over **3.** rise above —**sur·mount'a·ble** *a.*

sur'name *n.* family name

sur·pass' *v.* **1.** excel **2.** go beyond the limit of

sur'plice (-plis) *n.* loose, white tunic worn by clergy and choir

sur'plus *n.* quantity over what is needed or used —*a.* forming a surplus

sur·prise' *v.* **1.** come upon unexpectedly **2.** astonish —*n.* **1.** a surprising or being surprised **2.** thing that surprises —**sur·pris'ing** *a.*

sur·re'al·ism *n.* art depicting the unconscious mind —**sur·re'al·ist** *a., n.*

sur·ren'der *v.* **1.** give oneself up **2.** give up; abandon —*n.* act of surrendering

sur·rep·ti'tious (-tish'əs) *a.* secret; stealthy

sur'rey *n.* [*pl.* -REYS] light, four-wheeled carriage

sur'ro·gate *n.* a substitute

sur·round' *v.* encircle on all sides

sur·round'ings *n.pl.* things, conditions, etc. around a person or thing

sur'tax *n.* extra tax on top of the regular tax

sur·veil'lance (-vāl'-) *n.* watch kept over a person

sur·vey' *v.* **1.** examine in detail **2.** determine the form, boundaries, etc. of a piece of land —*n.* (sur'vā) [*pl.* -VEYS] **1.** general or comprehensive study **2.** act of surveying an area —**sur·vey'or** *n.*

sur·vey'ing *n.* science or work of making land surveys

sur·vive' *v.* **1.** outlive **2.** continue to live —**sur·viv'al** *n.* —**sur·vi'vor** *n.*

sus·cep'ti·ble (sə sep'-) *a.* easily affected; sensitive

sus·pect' *v.* **1.** believe to be guilty on little evidence **2.** distrust **3.** surmise —*n.* (sus'pekt) one suspected

sus·pend' *v.* **1.** exclude, stop,

etc. for a time 2. hold back (judgment, etc.) 3. hang from a support —**sus·pen'sion** n.

sus·pend'ers n.pl. shoulder straps to hold up trousers

sus·pense' n. tense uncertainty

suspension bridge bridge suspended by anchored cables from supporting towers

sus·pi'cion n. 1. a suspecting or being suspected 2. feeling of one who suspects 3. trace —**sus·pi'cious** a.

sus·tain' v. 1. maintain; prolong 2. provide for 3. support 4. suffer 5. uphold as valid 6. confirm

sus'te·nance n. 1. means of livelihood 2. nourishment

su'ture (-chər) n. stitching up of a wound, or stitch so used

su'ze·rain (-rin) n. state having some control over another state

svelte (svelt) a. 1. slender; lithe 2. suave

swab (swäb) n. 1. a mop 2. piece of cotton, etc. used to medicate or clean the throat, etc. —v. [SWABBED, SWABBING] clean with a swab

swad'dle v. formerly, wrap (a baby) in narrow bands of cloth

swag n. [Sl.] loot

swage (swāj) n. tool for shaping or bending metal

swag'ger v. 1. walk with a bold stride 2. brag loudly —n. swaggering walk

swain (swān) n. [Poet.] lover

swal'low v. 1. pass (food, etc.) from the mouth into the stomach 2. take in; absorb 3.

tolerate 4. suppress —n. 1. act of swallowing 2. amount swallowed 3. small, swift-flying bird

swam pt. of swim

swa·mi (swä'mē) n. Hindu religious teacher

swamp n. piece of wet, spongy ground; marsh —v. 1. flood with water 2. overwhelm —**swamp'y** a.

swamp buggy vehicle for traveling over swampy ground

swan n. large water bird with a long graceful neck

swank a. [Col.] ostentatiously stylish: also **swank'y**

swan song last act, final work, etc. of a person

swap (swäp) n., v. [SWAPPED, SWAPPING] [Col.] trade

sward n. grass-covered soil

swarm n. 1. colony of bees 2. large, moving mass, crowd, or throng —v. move in a swarm

swarth'y a. [-IER, -IEST] dark-skinned

swash'buck'ler (swäsh'-) n. swaggering fighting man

swas'ti·ka (swäs'-) n. cross with arms bent clockwise: Nazi emblem

swat v. [SWATTED, SWATTING], n. [Col.] (hit with) a quick, sharp blow —**swat'ter** n.

swatch n. sample bit of cloth

swath (swäth) n. a strip cut by a scythe, mower, etc.

swathe (swāth) v. 1. wrap up in a bandage 2. envelop

sway v. 1. swing from side to side or to and fro 2. incline 3. influence —n. 1. a swaying 2. influence

swear v. [SWORE, SWORN, SWEARING] **1.** make a solemn declaration or promise **2.** curse **3.** make take an oath —**swear off** renounce

swear'word n. profane or obscene word or phrase

sweat n. **1.** salty liquid given off through the skin **2.** moisture collected on a surface —v. [SWEAT or SWEATED, SWEATING] **1.** give forth sweat **2.** work so hard as to cause sweating —**sweat out** [Sl.] wait anxiously for or through —**sweat'y** [-IER, -IEST] a.

sweat'er n. knitted garment for the upper body

sweat shirt heavy jersey worn to absorb sweat

sweat'shop n. shop having long hours of work at low wages

Swed'ish a., n. (of) the people or language of Sweden

sweep v. [SWEPT, SWEEPING] **1.** clean, or clear away, with a broom **2.** carry away or pass over swiftly **3.** reach in a long line —n. **1.** a sweeping **2.** range or extent —**sweep'ing** a.

sweep'ings n.pl. things swept up

sweep'stakes n. [pl. -STAKES] lottery on a horse race

sweet a. **1.** tasting of sugar **2.** pleasant **3.** gratifying **4.** friendly, kind, etc. **5.** fresh —n. sweet food —**sweet'en** v. —**sweet'ly** adv.

sweet'bread n. calf's pancreas or thymus, used as food

sweet'bri'er, sweet'bri'ar n. eglantine

sweet corn kind of corn cooked and eaten before it is ripe

sweet'en·er n. sugar substitute, as saccharin

sweet'heart n. loved one

sweet'meat n. a candy

sweet pea climbing plant with fragrant flowers

sweet pepper 1. red pepper producing a large, mild fruit **2.** the fruit

sweet potato thick, yellow root of a tropical vine

sweet'-talk' v. [Col.] to flatter

sweet tooth [Col.] fondness or craving for sweets

swell v. [alt. pp. SWOLLEN] **1.** bulge **2.** increase in size, force, etc. **3.** fill, as with pride —n. **1.** a swelling **2.** large wave —a. [Sl.] excellent

swell'head n. [Col.] conceited person

swell'ing n. **1.** swollen part **2.** increase

swel'ter v. feel oppressed with great heat

swel'ter·ing a. very hot

swept pt. & pp. of **sweep**

swerve v., n. (make) a quick turn aside

swift a. **1.** moving fast **2.** prompt —n. swallowlike bird —**swift'ly** adv.

swig v. [SWIGGED, SWIGGING] [Col.] drink in large gulps —n. large gulp

swill v. drink greedily —n. garbage fed to pigs

swim v. [SWAM, SWUM, SWIMMING] **1.** move in water

by moving the limbs, fins, etc.
2. float on a liquid 3. overflow
4. be dizzy —n. a swimming —
swim'mer n.

swimming hole deep place in
a creek, etc. used for swimming

swim'suit n. garment worn for
swimming

swin'dle v. defraud; cheat —n.
a swindling

swine n. [pl. SWINE] pig or hog
—**swin'ish** a.

swing v. [SWUNG, SWINGING] 1.
sway back and forth 2. turn,
as on a hinge 3. strike (at) 4.
be suspended 5. [Col.] cause to
come about successfully 6. [Sl.]
be ultra-fashionable, esp. in
seeking pleasure —n. 1. a
swinging 2. sweeping blow 3.
musical rhythm 4. seat hanging from ropes —**swing'er** n.

swipe n. [Col.] hard, sweeping
blow —v. 1. [Col.] hit with a
swipe 2. [Sl.] steal

swirl v., n. whirl; twist

swish v., n. (move with) a
hissing or rustling sound

Swiss a. of Switzerland

Swiss chard chard

Swiss (**cheese**) pale-yellow
cheese with large holes

Swiss steak round steak
pounded with flour and
braised

switch n. 1. thin stick used for
whipping 2. control device for
an electric circuit 3. movable
section of railroad track 4.
shift; change —v. 1. to whip
2. jerk 3. turn a light, etc. on
or off 4. move a train to

another track 5. shift 6. [Col.]
change or exchange

switch'-blade' knife large
jackknife opened by a spring
release

switch'board n. control panel
for electric switches

switch'-hit'ter n. baseball
player who bats left-handed or
right-handed

swiv'el n. fastening with free-
turning parts —v. turn as on a
swivel

swiz'zle stick small rod for
stirring mixed drinks

swol'len alt. pp. of **swell** —a.
bulging

swoon v., n. faint

swoop v. sweep down or
pounce upon —n. a swooping

sword (sôrd) n. weapon with a
handle and a long blade

sword'fish n. large ocean fish
with a swordlike jaw

sword'play n. the act or skill
of using a sword

swore pt. of **swear**

sworn pp. of **swear** —a. bound
by an oath

swum pp. of **swim**

syc'a·more (sik'-) n. shade
tree with shedding bark

syc'o·phant n. flatterer

syl·lab'i·fy (sil-) v. [-FIED,
-FYING] divide into syllables:
also **syl·lab'i·cate** —**syl·lab'-
i·fi·ca'tion** n.

syl'la·ble n. 1. single vocal
sound 2. written form of this
—**syl·lab'ic** a.

syl'la·bus n. [pl. -BUSES, -BI
(-bī)] summary or outline

syl'lo·gism (-jiz'm) n. two
premises and a conclusion

sylph (silf) *n.* slender, graceful woman or girl

syl'van *a.* of, living in, or covered with trees

sym'bol *n.* object, mark, etc. that represents another object, an idea, etc. —**sym·bol'ic, sym·bol'i·cal** *a.* —**sym'bol·ize** *v.*

sym'bol·ism *n.* **1.** use of symbols **2.** set of symbols **3.** symbolic meaning

sym'me·try *n.* balance of opposite parts in position or size —**sym·met'ri·cal** *a.*

sym·pa·thet'ic *a.* **1.** of, in, or feeling sympathy **2.** of the nervous system regulating the response to alarm —**sym·pa·thet'i·cal·ly** *adv.*

sym'pa·thize *v.* share, feel, or show sympathy

sym'pa·thy *n.* [*pl.* -THIES] **1.** sameness of feeling **2.** agreement **3.** compassion

sym'pho·ny *n.* [*pl.* -NIES] **1.** harmony of sounds, color, etc. **2.** full orchestra or composition for it —**sym·phon'ic** *a.*

sym·po'si·um *n.* [*pl.* -UMS, -A (-ə)] meeting for discussion of some subject

symp'tom *n.* indication or sign, as of disease —**symp·to·mat'ic** *a.*

syn'a·gogue (-gôg) *n.* building where Jews worship

syn'chro·nize (siŋ'krə-) *v.* **1.** move or occur at the same time or rate **2.** make agree in time or rate

syn'co·pate *v. Mus.* shift the beat to unaccented notes —**syn'co·pa'tion** *n.*

syn'di·cate (-kit) *n.* **1.** business association of bankers, corporations, etc. **2.** association of criminals controlling gambling, etc. **3.** organization selling news stories, etc. —*v.* (-kāt) publish through a syndicate

syn'drome *n.* set of symptoms characterizing a disease or condition

syn'od *n.* council of churches or church officials

syn'o·nym *n.* word meaning the same as another —**syn·on'y·mous** *a.*

syn·op'sis *n.* [*pl.* -SES (-sēz)] summary

syn'tax *n.* way words are arranged in a sentence —**syn·tac'ti·cal** *a.*

syn'the·sis *n.* [*pl.* -SES (-sēz)] combining of parts into a whole —**syn'the·size** *v.*

syn'the·siz'er *n.* electronic device producing musical sounds without instruments

syn·thet'ic *a.* **1.** of or using synthesis **2.** artificial; not natural —*n.* synthetic thing —**syn·thet'i·cal·ly** *adv.*

syph'i·lis *n.* infectious venereal disease —**syph'i·lit'ic** *a., n.*

sy·ringe (sə rinj') *n.* ball with a tube, for ejecting fluids

syr'up *n.* sweet, thick liquid, as of sugar boiled in water —**syr'up·y** *a.*

sys'tem *n.* **1.** whole formed of related things **2.** set of organized facts, rules, etc. **3.** orderly way of doing things —**sys'tem·a·tize'** *v.*

sys·tem·at'ic *a.* orderly; me-

thodical —**sys'tem·at'i·cal·ly**
adv.

sys·tem'ic *a.* of or affecting
the body as a whole

sys'to·le (-tə lē) *n.* usual
rhythmic contraction of the
heart, esp. of the ventricles —
sys·tol'ic *a.*

T

tab *n.* small flap or tag —**keep
tab** (or **tabs**) **on** [Col.] keep
informed about

tab'by *n.* [*pl.* -BIES] pet cat

tab'er·nac·le *n.* large place of
worship

ta'ble *n.* 1. flat surface set on
legs 2. table set with food 3.
orderly list or arrangement —
v. postpone —**turn the tables**
reverse a situation

tab'leau (-lō) *n.* [*pl.* -LEAUX
(-lōz), -LEAUS] scene by persons
posing in costume

ta'ble·cloth *n.* cloth for covering a table at meals

ta'ble-hop' *v.* [-HOPPED, -HOP-
PING] leave one's table and
visit about at other tables

ta'ble·land *n.* plateau

ta'ble·spoon *n.* spoon holding
1/2 fluid ounce —**ta'ble-
spoon'ful** [*pl.* -FULS] *n.*

tab'let *n.* 1. flat, inscribed
piece of stone, metal, etc. 2.
writing pad 3. flat, hard cake
of medicine

table tennis game like tennis,
played on a table

ta'ble·ware *n.* dishes, forks,
etc. used for eating

tab'loid *n.* newspaper with
sensational news stories

ta·boo' *n.* [*pl.* -BOOS] sacred or
social prohibition —*v.* prohibit
Also **tabu**

tab'u·lar *a.* of or arranged in a
table or list

tab'u·late *v.* put in tabular
form —**tab'u·la'tion** *n.*

tac'it (tas'-) *a.* not expressed
openly, but implied

tac'i·turn (tas'-) *a.* usually silent —**tac'i·tur'ni·ty** *n.*

tack *n.* 1. short, flat-headed
nail 2. course of action 3.
ship's direction relative to position of sails —*v.* 1. fasten with
tacks 2. add 3. change course

tack'le *n.* 1. equipment 2. set
of ropes and pulleys 3. a tack-
ling —*v.* 1. undertake 2. *Football* bring down (the ball
carrier)

tack'y *a.* [-IER, -IEST] 1. sticky
2. [Col.] shabby

ta·co (tä'kō) *n.* [*pl.* -COS] fried
tortilla filled with chopped
meat, lettuce, etc.

tact *n.* skill in dealing with
people —**tact'ful** *a.*

tac'tic *n.* skillful method

tac'tics *n.* science of battle
maneuvers —**tac'ti·cal** *a.* —
tac·ti'cian (-tish'ən) *n.*

tad'pole *n.* larva of a frog or
toad, living in water

taf'fe·ta *n.* stiff silk cloth

taf'frail *n.* rail around a ship's
stern

taf'fy *n.* a chewy candy

tag *n.* 1. hanging end 2. card,
etc. attached as a label 3. epi-

thet **4.** children's chasing game —v. [TAGGED, TAGGING] **1.** provide with a tag **2.** touch as in game of tag **3.** [Col.] follow closely

tail n. **1.** appendage at rear end of animal's body **2.** hind or end part **3.** often pl. reverse side of a coin —v. [Col.] follow closely —a. at or from the rear —**tail'less** a.

tail'gate n. hinged board at the back of a truck, etc. —v. drive too closely behind (another vehicle)

tail'light n. red light at the back of a vehicle

tai'lor n. one who makes or repairs clothes —v. **1.** make by a tailor's work **2.** form, alter, etc. to suit

tail'pipe n. exhaust pipe at the rear of a car or truck

tail'spin n. sharp downward plunge of a plane with the tail spinning in circles

taint v. **1.** spoil; rot **2.** make corrupt or depraved —n. trace of contamination

take v. [TOOK, TAKEN, TAKING] **1.** grasp **2.** capture, seize, win, etc. **3.** obtain, select, assume, etc. **4.** use, consume, etc. **5.** buy; rent **6.** travel by **7.** deal with **8.** occupy **9.** derive from **10.** write down **11.** photograph **12.** require **13.** engage in **14.** understand **15.** have or feel **16.** carry, lead, etc. **17.** remove **18.** subtract **19.** [Sl.] cheat; trick —n. amount taken —**take after** act or look like —**take in 1.** admit; receive **2.** make smaller **3.** understand **4.**

trick —**take over** begin managing —**take to** become fond of —**take up 1.** make tighter or shorter **2.** absorb **3.** engage in

take'-off n. **1.** a leaving the ground, as in flight **2.** [Col.] mocking imitation

take'o'ver n. usurpation of power in a nation, firm, etc.

tak'ing a. attractive; winning —n. pl. profits

tal'cum (powder) n. powder for the body and face made from a soft mineral (**talc**)

tale n. **1.** story **2.** lie **3.** gossip

tale'bear'er n. one who spreads scandal, etc.; gossip

tal'ent n. **1.** ancient unit of weight or money **2.** special, natural ability —**tal'ent·ed** a.

tal'is·man n. [pl. -MANS] anything regarded as having magic power

talk v. **1.** say words; speak **2.** gossip **3.** confer **4.** discuss —n. **1.** a talking **2.** conversation **3.** speech **4.** conference **5.** gossip —**talk back** answer impertinently —**talk'er** n.

talk'a·tive a. talking a great deal: also **talk'y**

talk'ing-to' n. [Col.] a scolding

tall a. high, as in stature

tal'low n. hard animal fat used in candles and soap

tal'ly n. [pl. -LIES] record, account, etc. —v. **1.** record; score **2.** add **3.** agree

tal'ly-ho' int. fox hunter's cry

Tal·mud (täl'mood, tal'mad) n. body of early Jewish religious and civil law

tal'on n. claw of a bird of prey

tam *n.* tam-o'-shanter

ta·ma'le (-mä'le) *n.* [Mex. Sp.] peppery chopped meat cooked in corn husks

tam'a·rack *n.* swamp larch

tam·bou·rine' (-bə rēn') *n.* small, shallow drum with metal disks around it

tame *v.* 1. trained from a wild state 2. gentle 3. not lively; dull —*v.* make tame — **tame'ly** *adv.* —**tam'er** *n.*

tam'-o'-shan'ter *n.* flat, round Scottish cap

tamp *v.* pack down by tapping —**tamp'er** *n.*

tam'per *v.* 1. make secret, illegal arrangements (*with*) 2. interfere (*with*)

tam'pon (-pän) *n.* plug of cotton put into a wound, etc. to stop bleeding

tan *n.* yellowish brown —*a.* [TANNER, TANNEST] yellowish-brown —*v.* [TANNED, TANNING] 1. make (hide) into leather by soaking in tannic acid 2. produce a suntan in 3. [Col.] whip severely

tan'a·ger (-ə jər) *n.* American songbird

tan'bark *n.* tree bark containing tannic acid

tan'dem *adv.* one behind another; in single file

tang *n.* strong taste or odor — **tang'y** [-IER, -IEST] *a.*

tan'ge·lo (-jə-) *n.* [*pl.* -LOS] fruit that is a hybrid of the tangerine and grapefruit

tan'gent (-jənt) *a.* touching a curve at one point —*n.* a tangent curve, line, etc. —**go off at** (or **on**) **a tangent** change suddenly to another line of thought or action —**tan·gen'tial** (-jen'shəl) *a.*

tan·ge·rine' (-jə rēn') *n.* small, loose-skinned orange

tan'gi·ble (-jə-) *a.* 1. real or solid 2. definite

tan'gle *v.* 1. make or become knotted, confused, etc. 2. catch, as in a snare —*n.* tangled mass or condition

tan'go *n.* [*pl.* -GOS] South American dance —*v.* dance the tango

tank *n.* 1. large container for liquid or gas 2. armored vehicle carrying guns

tank'ard *n.* large drinking cup, often with a hinged lid

tank'er *n.* ship for transporting liquids, esp. oil

tank truck motor truck for transporting gasoline, etc.

tan'ner *y* *n.* [*pl.* -IES] place where leather is made by tanning hides —**tan'ner** *n.*

tan'nic acid acid used in tanning, dyeing, etc.: also **tan'nin** *n.*

tan'sy *n.* [*pl.* -SIES] plant with small, yellow flowers

tan'ta·lize *v.* show but withhold something; tease

tan'ta·mount *a.* equal (*to*)

tan'trum *n.* fit of temper

tap *v.* [TAPPED, TAPPING] 1. hit lightly 2. make a hole in 3. draw off, as liquid 4. connect into —*n.* 1. light blow 2. faucet or spigot 3. plug or cork 4. place for connection

tap dance dance done with sharp taps of the foot, toe, or heel —**tap'-dance'** *v.*

tape n. narrow strip of cloth, paper, etc. —v. 1. bind with a tape 2. record on tape

tape measure tape with marks for measuring

ta′per v. decrease or lessen gradually in thickness, loudness, etc. —n. 1. a tapering 2. slender candle

tape recorder recording device using magnetic tape

tap′es·try n. [pl. -TRIES] cloth with woven designs

tape′worm n. tapelike worm found in the intestines

tap′i·o′ca n. starchy substance from cassava roots

ta′pir n. hoglike animal

tap′room n. barroom

tap′root n. main root

taps n. bugle call for lights to be put out

tar n. 1. black liquid distilled from wood or coal 2. [Col.] sailor —v. [TARRED, TARRING] cover with tar —**tar′ry** a.

ta·ran′tu·la (-choo-) n. large, hairy spider

tar′dy a. [-DIER, -DIEST] 1. slow 2. late —**tar′di·ness** n.

tare (ter) n. 1. weed 2. container's weight

tar′get n. thing aimed at, shot at, or attacked

tar′iff (tar′-) n. 1. tax on exports or imports 2. list of prices, charges, etc.

tar′nish v. stain; discolor —n. dullness; stain

ta′ro (tä′-) n., [pl. -ROS] tropical plant with an edible root

ta·rot (tar′ō) n. [often T-] any of a set of fortunetelling cards

tar·pau′lin (-pô′-) n. water-proofed canvas

tar′pon n. large ocean fish

tar′ra·gon (tar′-) n. herb with fragrant leaves

tar′ry (tar′-) v. [-RIED, -RYING] 1. linger 2. delay

tart a. 1. sour; acid 2. sharp in meaning —n. pastry filled with jam, etc. —**tart′ly** adv. —**tart′ness** n.

tar′tan n. plaid cloth

tar′tar n. hard deposit forming on the teeth

tartar sauce mayonnaise with chopped pickles, olives, etc.

task n. work that must be done —v. burden; strain —**take to task** scold

task force group, esp. a military unit, assigned a task

task′mas′ter n. one who assigns severe tasks

tas′sel n. 1. bunch of threads hanging from a knob 2. tuft of corn silk

taste v. 1. notice or test the flavor of in one's mouth 2. eat or drink sparingly 3. have a certain flavor 4. to experience —n. 1. sense for telling flavor 2. flavor 3. small amount 4. sense 5. liking —**in bad (or good) taste** showing a bad (or good) sense of fitness, etc. —**taste′ful** a. —**taste′less** a.

taste bud taste organ in the tongue

tast′y a. [-IER, -IEST] that tastes good —**tast′i·ness** n.

tat v. [TATTED, TATTING] do tatting

tat′ter n. 1. rag; shred 2. pl.

ragged clothes —**tat′tered** *a.*

tat′ter·de·mal′ion (-di mäl′-yən) *n.* person in ragged clothing

tat′ting *n.* fine lace made by looping and knotting thread

tat′tle *v.* 1. tell secrets 2. gossip —**tat′tler** *n.*

tat′tle·tale *n.* talebearer

tat·too′ *v.* [-TOOED, -TOOING] make designs on the skin —*n.* [*pl.* -TOOS] 1. tattooed design 2. steady beating, as of a drum

taught (tôt) *pt.* & *pp.* of **teach**

taunt (tônt) *v.* mock; tease —*n.* scornful remark

taupe (tōp) *n.* dark, brownish gray

Tau′rus (tôr′-) 2nd sign of the zodiac; Bull

taut (tôt) *a.* 1. that is tightly stretched 2. tense 3. tidy

tau·tol′o·gy (tô-) *n.* use of a redundant word, phrase, etc.

tav′ern *n.* saloon or inn

taw′dry *a.* [-DRIER, -DRIEST] gaudy and cheap

taw′ny *a.* [-NIER, -NIEST] brownish-yellow or tan

tax *n.* 1. compulsory payment to a government 2. burden; strain —*v.* 1. levy, or make pay, a tax 2. burden 3. accuse; charge —**tax′a·ble** *a.* —**tax·a′tion** *n.* —**tax′pay′er** *n.*

tax′i *n.* [*pl.* -IS] taxicab —*v.* [-IED, -IING or -YING] 1. go in a taxicab 2. move along the ground or water, as an airplane

tax′i·cab *n.* automobile for passengers who pay

tax′i·der′my *n.* art of stuffing animal skins —**tax′i·der′mist** *n.*

tax·on′o·my *n.* classification of animals and plants

TB, T.B., tb, t.b. tuberculosis

T′-bone′ steak beefsteak with a T-shaped bone

tea *n.* 1. leaves of an Asiatic shrub 2. drink made from these 3. afternoon party with tea —**tea′cup** *n.*

tea′ber′ry *n.* [*pl.* -RIES] wintergreen

teach *v.* [TAUGHT, TEACHING] give lessons to or in —**teach′er** *n.*

teak *n.* East Indian tree

tea′ket′tle *n.* kettle with a spout, used to heat water

teal (tēl) *n.* 1. wild duck 2. dark grayish blue

team *n.* 1. two or more animals harnessed together 2. group working or playing together —*v.* join in a team —**team′work′** *n.*

team′mate′ *n.* one on the same team

team′ster *n.* truck driver

tea′pot *n.* pot with spout and handle for brewing tea

tear (ter) *v.* [TORE, TORN, TEARING] 1. pull apart, up, etc. by force 2. make by tearing 3. lacerate 4. disrupt; split 5. move fast —*n.* 1. a tearing 2. torn place —**tear down** wreck

tear (tir) *n.* drop of liquid from the eye —**in tears** weeping —**tear′ful** *a.*

tear′drop *n.* a tear

tear gas gas that blinds the eyes with tears

tea′room *n.* restaurant that

serves tea, light lunches, etc.

tease v. **1.** annoy by poking fun at, etc. **2.** fluff up, as hair —n. one who teases

tea'sel (-z'l) n. bristly plant with prickly flowers

tea'spoon n. small spoon — **tea'spoon'ful** [pl. -FULS] n.

teat (tēt) n. nipple on a breast or udder

tech'ni·cal (tek'-) a. **1.** dealing with industrial arts or skills **2.** of a specific art, science, etc. **3.** of technique — **tech'ni·cal·ly** adv.

tech'ni·cal·i·ty n. [pl. -TIES] **1.** technical detail **2.** minute formal point

tech·ni'cian (-nish'ən) n. one skilled in a technique

tech·nique' (-nēk') n. method of procedure, as in art

tech·nol'o·gy n. study of applied arts and sciences — **tech'no·log'i·cal** a.

ted'dy bear child's stuffed toy that looks like a bear

te'di·ous a. tiring; boring

te'di·um n. a being tedious

tee n. Golf **1.** small peg to rest the ball on **2.** starting place for each hole —v. [TEED, TEEING] place (a ball) on a tee —**tee off 1.** play a golf ball from a tee **2.** [Sl.] make angry

teem v. **1.** abound; swarm **2.** pour, as rain

teen n. **1.** pl. years of one's age from 13 through 19 **2.** teenager

teen'-age' a. **1.** in one's teens **2.** of or for persons in their teens Also **teenage** —**teen'-ag'er** n.

tee'ny (-nē) a. [-NIER, -NIEST] [Col.] tiny: also **teen'sy, tee'-ny-wee'ny**

tee'pee n. tepee

tee shirt T-shirt

tee'ter v., n. seesaw

tee'ter-tot'ter n., v. seesaw

teeth n. pl. of tooth

teethe (tēth) v. have teeth cutting through the gum

tee·to'tal·er n. one who never drinks liquor

Tef'lon trademark for nonsticking coatings as on cooking utensils

tel'e·cast v. [-CAST or -CASTED, -CASTING] broadcast over television —n. television broadcast —**tel'e·cast'er** n.

tel'e·gram n. message sent by telegraph

tel'e·graph n. device or system for sending messages by electric signals through a wire or radio —v. send a message by telegraph —**te·leg'ra·pher** n. —**tel'e·graph'ic** a. —**te·leg'ra·phy** n.

tel'e·me'ter n. device for transmitting data about temperature, etc. from a remote point —**te·lem'e·try** n.

te·lep'a·thy n. supposed communication between minds without help of speech, sight, etc. —**tel'e·path'ic** a.

tel'e·phone n. device or system for talking over distances through wires —v. talk (to) by telephone

tel'e·pho'to a. designating a camera lens that produces a large image of a distant object

tel'e·scope n. device with

lenses that magnify distant objects —v. slide or force one part into another —**tel'e·scop'ic** (-skäp'-) a.

tel'e·vise (-vīz) v. transmit by television

tel'e·vi'sion n. 1. way of sending pictures through space by radio waves to a receiving set 2. such a set

tell v. [TOLD, TELLING] 1. report; narrate 2. put into words 3. show 4. inform 5. recognize 6. order —**tell off** [Col.] criticize sharply

tell'er n. 1. one who tells 2. cashier at a bank

tell'ing a. forceful

tell'tale a. revealing what is meant to be secret

tem'blor n. earthquake

te·mer'i·ty (-mer'-) n. rashness; boldness

tem'per v. 1. make less intense 2. make hard, as steel — n. 1. state of mind 2. self-control 3. rage

tem'per·a n. painting with pigments mixed with size, casein, or egg

tem'per·a·ment n. (moody or excitable) disposition —**tem'per·a·men'tal** a.

tem'per·ance n. 1. self-restraint; moderation 2. abstinence from liquor

tem'per·ate (-it) a. 1. moderate; self-restrained 2. not very hot or very cold

tem'per·a·ture (-chər) n. 1. degree of hotness or coldness 2. fever

tem'pered a. having a certain kind of temper

tem'pest n. wild storm —**tem·pes'tu·ous** (-choo-) a.

tem'plate (-plit) n. pattern for making an exact copy

tem'ple n. 1. a building for worship service or for some special purpose 2. area near eye and ear

tem'po n. [pl. -POS, -PI (-pē)] rate of speed, esp. for playing music

tem'po·ral a. 1. worldly 2. of or limited by time

tem'po·rar'y a. lasting only a while —**tem'po·rar'i·ly** adv.

tempt v. 1. entice, esp. to an immoral act 2. provoke 3. incline strongly —**temp·ta'tion** n.

tem·pu·ra (tem'poo rä) n. Japanese dish of deep-fried shrimp, fish, vegetables, etc.

ten a., n. one more than nine —**tenth** a., n.

ten'a·ble a. that can be defended or believed

te·na'cious (-shəs) a. 1. holding firmly 2. retentive 3. stubborn —**te·nac'i·ty** (-nas'-) n.

ten'ant n. occupant (who pays rent) —**ten'an·cy** n.

tend v. 1. take care of 2. be apt; incline 3. lead

tend'en·cy n. [pl. -CIES] a being likely to move or act in a certain way

ten'der a. 1. soft or delicate 2. sensitive 3. loving 4. young — n. 1. thing offered, as in payment 2. car with locomotive's coal 3. one who tends —v. give to one to take —**ten'der·ly** adv.

ten'der·foot n. [pl. -FOOTS,

-FEET] newcomer, esp. one not used to hardships

ten'der·heart'ed *a.* quick to feel compassion

ten'der·ize *v.* make (meat) tender

ten'der·loin *n.* tenderest part of a loin of meat

ten'don *n.* cord of tissue binding a muscle to a bone

ten'dril *n.* threadlike, clinging part of a climbing plant

ten'e·ment *n.* an apartment house, esp. one in poor condition

ten'et *n.* principle or belief

ten'nis *n.* game played by hitting a ball over a net with a racket

tennis shoe sneaker

ten'on *n.* projecting part to fit in a mortise

ten'or *n.* 1. highest male voice 2. general tendency 3. general meaning

ten'pins *n.* bowling

tense *a.* 1. taut 2. anxious —*v.* make or become tense —*v.* verb form showing time

ten'sile (-s'l) *a.* 1. of or under tension 2. able to be stretched

ten'sion *n.* 1. a stretching 2. stress from this 3. nervous strain 4. strained relations 5. voltage

tent *n.* canvas shelter

ten'ta·cle *n.* slender growth on an animal's head, for feeling, grasping, etc.

ten'ta·tive *a.* not final

ten'ter·hook *n.* hooked nail —**on tenterhooks** in anxious suspense

ten'u·ous *a.* 1. thin; fine 2. not dense 3. flimsy

ten'ure *n.* right or duration of holding a position, etc.

te'pee *n.* cone-shaped tent

tep'id *a.* lukewarm

te·qui'la (-kē'-) *n.* alcoholic liquor distilled from an agave

term *n.* 1. fixed time period 2. *pl.* conditions of a contract, etc. 3. *pl.* personal relationship 4. work or phrase 5. either part of a fraction, etc. —*v.* name —**come to terms** arrive at an agreement —**in terms of** regarding; concerning

ter'ma·gant (-gənt) *n.* nagging woman

ter'mi·nal *a.* 1. of or at the end 2. final 3. close to causing death —*n.* 1. end (part) 2. main station, as for buses

ter'mi·nate *v.* 1. stop; end 2. form the end of —**ter'mi·na'tion** *n.*

ter'mi·nol'o·gy *n.* [*pl.* -GIES] special words or phrases

term insurance life insurance that expires after a specified period

ter'mi·nus *n.* [*pl.* -NI (-nī), -NUSES] 1. an end, limit, etc. 2. end of a transportation line

ter'mite *n.* antlike insect that eats wood

tern *n.* gull-like sea bird

ter'race (-ris) *n.* 1. patio 2. flat mound with sloping side 3. row of houses on this —*v.* make a terrace of

ter'ra cot'ta brown-red earthenware or its color

terra fir'ma solid ground

ter·rain' *n.* area of land with regard to its fitness for use

ter·ra·pin *n.* freshwater turtle

ter·rar'i·um *n.* [*pl.* -IUMS, -IA] glass enclosure for small plants or land animals

ter·raz'o (-razʹō, -rätʹsō) *n.* polished flooring of small marble chips set in cement

ter·res'tri·al *a.* 1. worldly 2. of the earth 3. of, or living on, land

ter'ri·ble *a.* 1. causing terror 2. extreme 3. [Col.] very bad —**ter'ri·bly** *adv.*

ter'ri·er *n.* breed of small, lively dog

ter·rif'ic *a.* 1. terrifying 2. [Col.] very great, etc.

ter'ri·fy *v.* [-FIED, -FYING] fill with terror

ter'ri·to·ry *n.* [*pl.* -RIES] 1. area under rule of a nation, etc. 2. part of a country, etc. not having full status 3. region 4. assigned area 5. sphere of action, etc. —**ter'ri·to'ri·al** *a.*

ter'ror *n.* great fear, or cause of this

ter'ror·ism *n.* use of force or threats to intimidate, esp. as a political policy —**ter'ror·ist** *n., a.*

ter'ror·ize *v.* 1. terrify 2. coerce by terrorism

ter'ry (cloth) cloth having a pile of uncut loops

terse *a.* concise; to the point —**terse'ly** *adv.*

ter'ti·ar'y (-shē-) *a.* third

test *n.* 1. examination or trial to determine a thing's value, one's knowledge, etc. 2. event, etc. that tries one's qualities —

v. subject to, or be rated by, a test

tes'ta·ment *n.* 1. [T-] either part of the Bible 2. testimonial 3. legal will

tes'ta·tor *n.* one who has made a will

tes'ti·cle *n.* male sex gland

tes'ti·fy *v.* [-FIED, -FYING] 1. give evidence in court 2. indicate

tes'ti·mo'ni·al *n.* 1. statement of recommendation 2. thing given as a tribute

tes'ti·mo'ny *n.* [*pl.* -NIES] 1. statement of one who testifies in court 2. indication

tes'tis *n.* [*pl.* -TES (-tēz)] testicle

tes·tos'ter·one (-tästʹtə rōn) *n.* male sex hormone

test tube tubelike glass container

tes'ty *a.* [-TIER, -TIEST] irritable; touchy

tet'a·nus *n.* acute infectious disease

tête-à-tête (tātʹə tātʹ) *a., n.* (of) a private talk between two people

teth'er (tethʹ-) *n.* 1. rope or chain tied to an animal to confine it 2. limit of one's abilities, etc. —*v.* fasten with a tether

tet'ra *n.* tropical fish

tet'ra·eth'yl lead lead compound added to gasoline to prevent engine knock

text *n.* 1. an author's words 2. main part of a printed page 3. textbook 4. Biblical passage 5. topic —**tex'tu·al** (-choo-) *a.*

text′book *n.* book used in teaching a subject

tex′tile *n.* woven fabric —*a.* 1. of weaving 2. woven

tex′ture (-chər) *n.* 1. look and feel of a fabric 2. structure —**tex′tur·al** *a.*

thal′a·mus *n.* [*pl.* -MI (-mī)] gray matter at the base of the brain

than *con.* compared to

thank *v.* give thanks to

thank′ful *a.* showing thanks —**thank′ful·ly** *adv.*

thank′less *a.* ungrateful or unappreciated

thanks *n.pl.* expression of gratitude —*int.* I thank you —**thanks to** 1. thanks be given to 2. because of

thanks′giv′ing *n.* 1. thanks to God 2. [T-] U.S. holiday: 4th Thursday in November

that *pron.* [*pl.* THOSE] 1. the one mentioned 2. the farther one or other one 3. who, whom, or which 4. where 5. when —*a.* being that one —*con. That* is used to introduce certain dependent clauses —*adv.* to that extent —**at that** [Col.] 1. at that point: also **with that** 2. even so —**that is** 1. to be specific 2. in other words

thatch *n.* 1. roof of straw, etc. 2. material for this: also **thatch′ing** —*v.* cover as with thatch

thaw *v.* 1. melt, as ice 2. become unfrozen 3. become warmer —*n.* period of thawing weather

the *a., definite article* that or

this one in particular or of a certain kind —*adv.* that much or by that much

the′a·ter, the′a·tre *n.* 1. place where plays, movies, etc. are shown 2. scene of events 3. dramatic art

the·at′ri·cal *a.* 1. of the theater 2. dramatic 3. melodramatic

thee (thē) *pron.* objective case of **thou**

theft *n.* act of stealing

their *a.* of them

theirs *pron.* that or those belonging to them

the′ism (thē′-) *n.* belief in a god or gods —**the′ist** *n., a.*

them *pron.* objective case of **they**

theme *n.* 1. topic 2. short essay 3. main melody 4. recurring or identifying song, as in a film —**the·mat′ic** (thē-) *a.*

them·selves′ *pron.* intensive or reflexive form of **they**

then *adv.* 1. at that time 2. next 3. in that case 4. besides —*a.* being such at that time —*n.* that time

thence *adv.* from that place or time

thence′forth′ *adv.* from that time on: also **thence′for′-ward**

the·oc′ra·cy (thē-) *n.* [*pl.* -CIES] (a) government by a church

the·ol′o·gy (thē-) *n.* study of God and of religious beliefs —**the′o·lo′gi·an** *n.* —**the′o·log′i·cal** *a.*

the′o·rem *n. Math.* statement (to be) proved

the·o·ret·i·cal *a.* based on theory, not on practice

the·o·rize *v.* form a theory; speculate —**the·o·rist** *n.*

the·o·ry *n.* [*pl.* -RIES] 1. explanation based on scientific study and reasoning 2. principles of an art or science 3. guess, conjecture, etc.

ther·a·peu·tic (-pyōō'-) *a.* serving to cure or heal

ther·a·peu·tics *n.* therapy

ther·a·py *n.* [*pl.* -PIES] method of treating disease —**ther·a·pist** *n.*

there *adv.* 1. at, in, or to that place 2. at that point 3. in that respect —*n.* that place —(**not**) **all there** (not) mentally sound

there·a·bouts *adv.* near that place, time, amount, etc.: also **there·a·bout**'

there·af·ter *adv.* after that

there·by' *adv.* 1. by that means 2. connected with that

there·fore *adv.* for this or that reason

there·in' *adv.* in that place, matter, writing, etc.

there·of' *adv.* 1. of that 2. from that as a cause

there·on' *adv.* 1. on that 2. thereupon

there·to' *adv.* to that place, thing, etc.

there·to·fore' *adv.* up to that time

there·up·on' *adv.* 1. just after that 2. because of that

there·with' *adv.* 1. with that or this 2. just after that

ther·mal *a.* 1. of heat 2. designating a blanket, etc. loosely knitted to retain body heat

thermal pollution harmful discharge of heated liquids into lakes, rivers, etc.

ther·mo·dy·nam·ics *n.* science that deals with transforming heat into mechanical energy —**ther·mo·dy·nam·ic** *a.*

ther·mom·e·ter *n.* device for measuring temperature

ther·mo·nu·cle·ar *a.* of or using the heat energy released in nuclear fusion

ther·mo·plas·tic *a.* soft and moldable when heated —*n.* thermoplastic substance

ther·mos (**bottle**) container for keeping liquids at the same temperature

ther·mo·stat *n.* device for regulating temperature

the·sau·rus (-sô'-) *n.* book containing lists of synonyms or related words

these *pron., a.* pl. of **this**

the·sis *n.* [*pl.* -SES (-sēz)] 1. statement to be defended 2. research paper, esp. one written to obtain a master's degree

Thes·pi·an, thes·pi·an *a.* dramatic —*n.* actor

thews *n.pl.* [*sing.* THEW] muscles or sinews

they *pron.* 1. the ones mentioned 2. people

they'll (thāl) 1. they will 2. they shall

they're (ther) they are

they've (thāv) they have

thi·a·mine (-mēn) *n.* vitamin B₁, found in liver, etc.

thick *a.* 1. great in extent from

side to side 2. as measured from side to side 3. dense 4. not clear 5. [Col.] stupid 6. [Col.] very friendly —n. the thickest part —**thick′ly** adv. —**thick′ness** n.

thick′en v. make or become thick, thicker, or more complex —**thick′en·ing** n.

thick′et a. thick growth of shrubs or small trees

thick′set′ a. thick in body

thick′-skinned′ a. unfeeling

thief n. [pl. **THIEVES**] one who steals

thieve v. steal —**thiev′ish** a.

thiev·er·y n. [pl. **-IES**] theft

thigh n. the leg between the knee and the hip

thim′ble n. protective cap worn on the finger in sewing — **thim′ble·ful** n.

thin a. [**THINNER, THINNEST**] 1. small in extent from side to side 2. lean; slender 3. sparse 4. watery 5. weak 6. transparent; flimsy —v. [**THINNED, THINNING**] make or become thin —**thin′ness** n.

thine pron. [Ar.] yours —a. [Ar.] your

thing n. 1. real object or substance 2. a happening, act, event, etc. 3. matter or affair 4. pl. belongings 5. item, detail, etc. 6. [Col.] person 7. [Col.] issue 8. [Col.] fear 9. [Col.] what one wants to do — **see things** [Col.] have hallucinations

think v. [**THOUGHT, THINKING**] 1. form in or use the mind 2. consider 3. believe 4. have an opinion (of) 5. remember (of or

about) 6. conceive (of) —**think up** invent, plan, etc. — **think′er** n.

think tank [Sl.] group organized for intensive research

thin′ner n. substance added to thin paint, etc.

thin′-skinned′ a. sensitive

third a. preceded by two others —n. 1. third one 2. one of three equal parts

third′-class′ a. of the class, etc. next below the second

third degree [Col.] cruel treatment to force confession

third dimension 1. depth 2. quality of seeming real

third′-rate′ a. inferior

third world [often T- W-] underdeveloped countries

thirst n. 1. need or craving for water 2. strong desire —v. feel thirst —**thirst′y** [**-IER, -IEST**] a.

thir′teen′ a., n. three more than ten —**thir′teenth′** a., n.

thir′ty a., n. [pl. **-TIES**] three times ten —**thir′ti·eth** a., n.

this a., pron. [pl. **THESE**] (being) the one mentioned or nearer —adv. to this extent

this′tle n. prickly plant

thith′er (thith′-) adv. there

tho, tho′ (thō) con., adv. though

thong n. strip of leather used as lace, strap, etc.

tho′rax n. 1. chest (sense 3) 2. middle segment of an insect

thorn n. short, sharp point on a plant stem —**thorn′y** a.

thor·ough (thur′ō) a. 1. complete 2. very exact

thor'ough·bred n., a. (an animal) of pure breed

thor'ough·fare n. main highway

thor'ough·go'ing a. very thorough

those a., pron. pl. of **that**

thou pron. [Ar.] you (sing. subject of v.)

though con. 1. although 2. yet 3. even if —adv. however

thought pt. & pp. of **think** —n. 1. act or way of thinking 2. idea, plan, etc. 3. attention; consideration

thought'ful a. 1. full of thought 2. considerate

thought'less a. 1. careless 2. inconsiderate 3. rash

thou'sand a., n. ten hundred —**thou'sandth** a., n.

thrash v. 1. thresh 2. beat 3. toss about violently —**thrash out** settle by discussion

thrash'er n. thrushlike songbird

thread n. 1. fine cord of spun cotton, silk, etc. 2. something threadlike, as in length or sequence 3. spiral ridge of a screw, etc. —v. 1. put a thread through (a needle) 2. make (one's way)

thread'bare a. 1. shabby 2. stale; trite

threat n. 1. warning of plan to harm 2. sign of danger

threat'en v. make or be a threat

three a., n. one more than two

three'-di·men'sion·al a. having depth or thickness

three'fold a. 1. having three parts 2. having three times as

much or as many —adv. three times as much or as many

three'score' a. sixty

thresh v. beat out (grain) from its husk —**thresh'er** n.

thresh'old n. 1. sill of a door 2. beginning point

threw pt. of **throw**

thrice adv. three times

thrift n. careful managing of money, resources, etc. —**thrift'i·ly** adv. —**thrift'less** a. —**thrift'y** [-IER, -IEST] a.

thrill v., n. (feel or make feel) great excitement

thrive v. [THRIVED or THROVE, THRIVED or THRIVEN, THRIV-ING] 1. be successful 2. grow luxuriantly

throat n. 1. front of the neck 2. upper passage from mouth to stomach or lungs

throb v. [THROBBED, THROB-BING] 1. beat or vibrate strongly 2. feel excitement —n. 1. a throbbing 2. strong beat

throe (thrō) n. pang of pain

throm·bo'sis n. a clotting in the circulatory system

throne n. 1. official chair, as of a king 2. his power

throng n., v. crowd

throt'tle n. valve to control fuel mixture —v. 1. choke 2. suppress

through prep. 1. from end to end of 2. by way of 3. to places in 4. throughout 5. by means of 6. because of —adv. 1. in and out of 2. all the way 3. entirely —a. 1. open; free 2. to the end without stops 3. finished

through·out' *adv., prep.* in every part (of)

through'way *n.* expressway: also **thru'way**

throw *v.* [THREW, THROWN, THROWING] 1. send through the air from the hand 2. make fall 3. put suddenly 4. move (a switch, etc.) 5. direct, cast, etc. 6. [Col.] lose deliberately 7. [Col.] give (a party, etc.) 8. [Col.] confuse or disconcert — *n.* 1. a throwing 2. distance thrown —**throw in** add free —**throw off** 1. get rid of, expel, emit, etc. 2. mislead —**throw together** assemble hastily —**throw up** 1. give up 2. vomit

throw'a·way *n.* designed to be discarded

throw'back *n.* (a) return to an earlier type

throw rug small rug

thru *prep., adv., a.* through

thrush *n.* any of a large group of songbirds

thrust *v.* [THRUST, THRUSTING] push with sudden force —*n.* 1. sudden push 2. stab 3. forward force 4. basic meaning

thud *v., n.* [THUDDED, THUDDING] (hit with) a dull sound

thug *n.* rough criminal

thumb *n.* short, thick finger nearest the wrist —*v.* [Col.] solicit (a ride) in hitchhiking —**all thumbs** clumsy

thumb'nail *n.* nail of the thumb —*a.* brief

thumb'tack *n.* tack with a wide, flat head

thump *n.* 1. a blow with a heavy, blunt object 2. its dull sound —*v.* hit or pound with a thump

thun'der *n.* loud noise after lightning —*v.* 1. cause thunder 2. shout loudly —**thun'der·ous** *a.*

thun'der·bolt *n.* flash of lightning and its thunder

thun'der·cloud *n.* storm cloud producing thunder

thun'der·show'er *n.* shower with thunder and lightning

thun'der·storm *n.* storm with thunder and lightning

thun'der·struck *a.* amazed

Thurs'day *n.* fifth day of the week

thus *adv.* 1. in this way 2. to this or that degree 3. therefore

thwack *v., n.* whack

thwart *v.* block; hinder

thy *a.* [Ar.] your

thyme (tīm) *n.* plant of the mint family

thy'mus (thī'-) *n.* small gland near the throat

thy'roid *a., n.* (of) a gland secreting a growth hormone

thy·self' *pron.* [Ar.] yourself

ti·ar·a (tē er'ə) *n.* woman's crownlike headdress

tib'i·a *n.* [*pl.* -AE (-ē), -AS] thicker bone of the lower leg

tic *n.* involuntary, repeated muscle spasm

tick *n.* 1. light clicking sound 2. blood-sucking insect —*v.* make a ticking sound

tick'er *n.* 1. one that ticks 2. telegraphic device recording stock prices on paper tape 3. [Sl.] heart

tick'et *n.* 1. printed card entitling one to a theater seat, etc.

2. tag, label, etc. **3.** list of a party's candidates **4.** [Col.] court summons for a traffic violation —*v.* **1.** put a ticket on **2.** give a ticket to

tick′ing *n.* cloth holding a pillow's contents

tick′le *v.* **1.** stroke lightly and make twitch or laugh **2.** feel tickled **3.** amuse; delight —*n.* a tickling

tick′ler *n.* file for noting items to be remembered

tick′lish *a.* **1.** sensitive to tickling **2.** touchy

tid′al *a.* of, having, or caused by a tide

tidal wave destructive wave sent inshore as by an earthquake

tid′bit *n.* choice morsel

tide *n.* **1.** rise and fall of the ocean twice a day **2.** trend —*v.* help (*over*) a difficulty

tide′land *n.* **1.** land covered by tide **2.** *pl.* land under territorial waters of a country

tide′wa′ter *n.* **1.** water affected by tide **2.** seaboard

ti′dings *n.pl.* news

ti′dy *a.* [-DIER, -DIEST] **1.** neat; orderly **2.** [Col.] quite large —*v.* [-DIED, -DYING] make tidy

tie *v.* [TIED, TYING] **1.** fasten with string, rope, etc. **2.** make (a knot) **3.** bind in any way **4.** to equal, as in a score —*n.* **1.** thing that ties or joins **2.** necktie **3.** contest with equal scores —*a.* made equal —**tie down** confine; restrict —**tie up 1.** moor to a dock **2.** hinder **3.** make be in use, busy, etc.

tie′-dye′ *n.* dyeing method that affects only exposed areas —*v.* dye in this way

tie′-in′ *n.* connection

tier (tir) *n.* any of a series of rows, one above another

tie′-up′ *n.* **1.** temporary stoppage, as of traffic **2.** connection

tiff *n.* slight quarrel

ti′ger *n.* large, striped jungle cat —**ti′gress** *n.fem.*

tight *a.* **1.** made to keep water, air, etc. out or in **2.** fitting closely or too closely **3.** taut **4.** difficult **5.** [Col.] stingy **6.** [Sl.] drunk —*adv.* **1.** closely **2.** firmly —**tight′ly** *adv.*

tight′en *v.* make or become tighter

tight′fist′ed *a.* stingy

tight′-lipped′ *a.* secretive

tight′rope *n.* taut rope on which acrobats perform

tights *n.pl.* tight garment from the waist to the feet

tight′wad *n.* [Sl.] miser

til′de *n.* diacritical mark (˜)

tile *n.* thin piece of baked clay, stone, plastic, etc. for roofing, flooring, etc. —*v.* cover with tiles

till *prep.*, *con.* until —*v.* cultivate land for crops —*n.* drawer for money

till′er *n.* bar or handle to turn a boat's rudder

tilt *v.*, *n.* **1.** slope; tip **2.** joust —**at full tilt** at full speed

tim′ber *n.* **1.** wood for building houses, etc. **2.** wooden beam **3.** trees

tim′bre (tam′bər, tim′-) *n.* the

distinctive sound of a voice or musical instrument

time n. 1. period; duration 2. the right instant, hour, etc. 3. the passing hours, days, etc.; or, system of measuring them 4. an occasion 5. set period of work, or pay for this 6. tempo or rhythm —v. 1. choose a right time for 2. measure the speed of —a. 1. of time 2. set to work at a given time 3. of paying in installments —**at times** occasionally —**do time** [Col.] serve a prison term —**from time to time** now and then —**in time** 1. eventually 2. before it is too late —**make time** go, do, etc. rapidly —**on time** 1. not late 2. by installment payments

time′-hon′ored a. honored because of long existence

time′keep′er n. one who records time played, as in games, or hours worked

time′less a. eternal

time′ly a. [-LIER, -LIEST] at the right time

time′out′ n. temporary suspension of play in sports

time′piece′ n. clock; watch

tim′er n. device for controlling timing

times prep. multiplied by

time′ta′ble n. schedule of arrivals and departures

time′worn′ a. 1. worn out 2. trite

tim′id a. shy; easily frightened —**ti·mid′i·ty** n.

tim′ing n. regulation of time or speed for effectiveness

tim′or·ous a. timid

tim′o·thy n. a tall grass used for fodder

tim′pa·ni (-nē) n.pl. kettledrums

tin n. soft, silvery metal, a chemical element

tinc′ture (-chər) n. solution of medicine in alcohol —v. tinge

tin′der n. any dry, easily ignited material

tin′der·box′ n. 1. highly flammable building, etc. 2. potential source of war, etc.

tine n. prong, as of a fork

tin′foil′ n. thin sheet of tin

tinge (tinj) n. 1. tint 2. slight trace —v. give a tinge to

tin′gle v. sting slightly; prickle —n. a tingling

tink′er n. mender of pots and pans —v. 1. mend clumsily 2. to putter

tin′kle n. ring of a small bell —v. make a tinkle

tin′ny a. [-NIER, -NIEST] 1. of tin 2. like tin, as in sound, look, etc.

tin plate thin sheets of iron or steel plated with tin

tin′sel n. 1. thin strips of metal foil, for decorating 2. showy, cheap thing

tin′smith n. one who works with tin: also **tin′ner**

tint n. 1. light color 2. a shading of a color —v. give a tint to

ti′ny a. [-NIER, -NIEST] very small

-tion suf. 1. act of 2. state of being 3. thing that is

tip n. 1. a point or end 2. thing fitted to an end 3. light blow; tap 4. secret information 5.

warning 6. gratuity 7. slant —
v. [TIPPED, TIPPING] 1. make
or put a tip on 2. give a tip 3.
overturn 4. slant 5. [Col.] give
secret information to (often
with *off*) —**tip one's hand**
[Sl.] reveal a secret, etc. unintentionally

tip'-off' *n.* a tip (*n.* 4 & 5)

tip'ple *v.* drink liquor

tip'ster *n.* [Col.] one who sells
tips, as on horse races

tip'sy *a.* [-SIER, -SIEST] 1. unsteady 2. drunk

tip'toe *n.* tip of a toe —*v.*
[-TOED, -TOEING] walk carefully
on one's tiptoes —**on tiptoe 1.**
eager(ly) 2. silently; stealthily

tip'top *a., adv., n.* (at) the
highest point

ti'rade *n.* long, angry speech

tire *v.* make or become weary,
bored, etc. —*n.* hoop or rubber
tube around a wheel

tired *a.* 1. weary; exhausted 2.
trite; stale

tire'less *a.* not becoming tired

tire'some *a.* tiring; boring

tis·sue (tish'ōō) *n.* 1. light,
thin cloth 2. soft, absorbent
paper 3. tissue paper 4. cellu-
lar material of organisms

tissue paper thin, soft paper

ti'tan *n.* giant —**ti·tan'ic** *a.*

tit for tat this for that

tithe (tīth) *v., n.* (pay) a tenth
part of one's income

ti·tian (tish'ən) *n., a.* reddish
yellow

tit'il·late *v.* excite pleasurably
—**tit'il·la'tion** *n.*

ti'tle *n.* 1. name of a book, picture, etc. 2. word showing rank

or occupation 3. legal right 4.
championship —*v.* to name

tit'mouse *n.* [*pl.* -MICE] small,
dull-colored bird

tit'ter *v., n.* giggle

tit'tle *n.* small bit; jot

tit'u·lar *a.* 1. in name only 2.
of or having a title

tiz'zy *n.* [*pl.* -ZIES] [Col.] frenzied excitement

TNT, T.N.T. an explosive

to *prep.* 1. toward 2. as far as
3. on, onto, or against 4. until
5. causing 6. with 7. in each
To may indicate an infinitive
or a receiver of action —*adv.*
1. forward 2. shut

toad *n.* froglike land animal

toad'stool *n.* poisonous mush-
room

toad'y *n.* [*pl.* -IES] servile flatterer —*v.* [-IED, -YING] be a
toady (to)

toast *v.* 1. brown by heating,
as bread 2. warm 3. drink in
honor of —*n.* 1. toasted bread
2. a toasting —**toast'er** *n.*

toast'mas·ter *n.* one who presides at a banquet

to·bac'co *n.* [*pl.* -COS] plant
with leaves dried for smoking,
chewing, etc.

to·bog'gan *n.* flat, runnerless
sled —*v.* 1. coast on a tobog-
gan 2. decline rapidly

toc'sin *n.* alarm bell

to·day' *adv.* 1. during this day
2. nowadays —*n.* this day or
time

tod'dle *v.* walk unsteadily, as a
child —**tod'dler** *n.*

tod'dy *n.* [*pl.* -DIES] whiskey,
etc. mixed with hot water,
sugar, etc.: also **hot toddy**

to-do (tə dōō′) n. [Col.] a fuss; commotion

toe n. any of five end parts of the foot —v. [TOED, TOEING] touch with the toes —**on one's toes** [Col.] alert —**toe the line** (or **mark**) follow orders strictly —**toe′nail** n.

toe dance dance performed on the tips of the toes

toe′hold n. slight footing or advantage

tof′fee, tof′fy n. taffy

to′ga n. loose garment worn in ancient Rome

to·geth′er adv. 1. in one group or place 2. at the same time 3. so as to meet, agree, etc.

to·geth′er·ness n. spending of much time together, as by family members

tog′gle switch switch with a lever to open or close an electric circuit

togs n.pl. [Col.] clothes

toil v. 1. work hard 2. go with effort —n. hard work

toi′let n. 1. fixture to receive body waste 2. bathroom 3. one's grooming or dressing: also **toi·lette** (twä let′)

toilet paper (or **tissue**) soft paper used after evacuation

toi′let·ry n. [pl. -RIES] soap, cosmetics, etc.

toilet water cologne

toils n.pl. snare or net

toil′some a. laborious

toke n., v. [Sl.] puff on a cigarette, esp. of marijuana

to′ken n. 1. sign or symbol 2. keepsake 3. metal disk, as for fare —a. pretended

to′ken·ism n. token recognition of rights to jobs, etc., as for Negroes, women, etc.

told pt. & pp. of **tell**

tole n. lacquered or enameled metalware, as for lamps

tol′er·a·ble a. 1. endurable 2. fairly good; passable —**tol′er·a·bly** adv.

tol′er·ance n. 1. a tolerating, as of another's ways 2. ability to resist a drug's effects 3. variation allowed from standard —**tol′er·ant** a.

tol′er·ate v. 1. put up with 2. permit 3. respect (others' beliefs, practices, etc.)

toll (tōl) n. 1. charge on a turnpike, for a long-distance phone call, etc. 2. number lost, etc. —v. ring with slow, regular strokes, as a bell

toll′gate n. gate where tolls are paid

toll road road on which tolls must be paid

tom′a·hawk n. light ax used by N. American Indians

to·ma′to n. [pl. -TOES] red, round, juicy vegetable

tomb (tōōm) n. vault or grave for the dead

tom′boy n. girl who behaves like an active boy

tomb′stone n. stone marking a tomb or grave

tom′cat n. male cat

tome (tōm) n. large book

tom′fool′er·y n. [pl. -IES] foolish behavior; silliness

to·mor′row adv., n. (on) the day after today

tom′-tom′ n. primitive drum

ton n. 2,000 pounds

tone *n.* **1.** vocal or musical sound, spec. as to pitch **2.** style, character, feeling, etc. **3.** shade or tint **4.** healthy condition, as of muscles —**tone down** give a less intense tone to —**ton'al** *a.*

tone arm arm containing the pickup of a phonograph

tongs *n.pl.* device for seizing, lifting, etc., made of two long, hinged arms

tongue *n.* **1.** movable muscle in the mouth, used in eating and speaking **2.** act or manner of speaking **3.** language **4.** tonguelike part

tongue'-lash'ing *n.* [Col.] harsh reprimand

tongue'-tied' *a.* speechless from amazement, confusion, etc.

tongue twister phrase or sentence hard to say fast

ton'ic *n.* medicine, etc. that invigorates

to-night' *adv., n.* (on) this night

ton'nage (-ij) *n.* **1.** amount in tons of shipping, etc. **2.** carrying capacity of a ship

ton'sil *n.* either of two oval masses of tissue at the back of the mouth

ton'sil-lec'to-my *n.* [*pl.* -MIES] surgical removal of the tonsils

ton'sil-li'tis *n.* inflammation of the tonsils

ton-so'ri-al *a.* of a barber or barbering

ton'sure *n.* shaven crown of a priest's or monk's head

too *adv.* **1.** also **2.** more than enough **3.** very

took *pt.* of **take**

tool *n.* **1.** instrument, implement, etc. used for some work **2.** stooge —*v.* shape or work with a tool

toot *v., n.* (make) a short blast on a horn, etc.

tooth *n.* [*pl.* TEETH] **1.** any of a set of bony structures in the jaws, used for biting and chewing **2.** toothlike part, as of a saw, gear, etc. —**tooth and nail** with all one's strength —**tooth'ache** *n.* —**tooth'brush** *n.*

tooth'paste *n.* paste for brushing the teeth

tooth'pick *n.* pointed stick for picking food from between the teeth

tooth'some *a.* tasty

tooth'y *a.* [-IER, -IEST] having prominent teeth

top *n.* **1.** highest point or surface **2.** uppermost part or covering **3.** highest degree or rank **4.** toy that spins round —*a.* of, at, or being the top —*v.* [TOPPED, TOPPING] **1.** provide with a top **2.** be at the top of **3.** surpass; exceed —**on top of 1.** resting upon **2.** besides —**top off** complete

to'paz *n.* yellow gem

top'coat *n.* light overcoat

top'-draw'er *a.* of first importance

top'er (tōp'-) *n.* drunkard

top'-flight' *a.* [Col.] first-rate

top hat man's tall, black hat

top'-heav'y *a.* too heavy at the top and, thus, unstable

top'ic *n.* subject of an essay, speech, etc.

top'i·cal *a.* of current or local interest

top'knot *n.* tuft of hair or feathers on top of the head

top'less *a.* without a top covering, as a dancer with breasts exposed

top'·lev'el *a.* of or by persons of the highest rank

top'mast *n.* second mast above the deck of a ship

top'most *a.* uppermost

top'-notch' *a.* [Col.] first-rate

to·pog'ra·phy *n.* 1. surface features of a region 2. science of showing these, as on maps —**top'o·graph'i·cal, top'o·graph'ic** *a.*

top'ping *n.* something put on top of something else

top'ple *v.* (make) fall over

top'sail *n.* sail next above the lowest sail on a mast

top'-se'cret *a.* designating or of the most secret information

top'side *adv.* on or to an upper deck or the main deck of a ship

top'soil *n.* upper layer of soil, usually richer

top'sy-tur'vy *adv., a.* 1. upside down 2. in disorder

to·rah (tō'ra) *n.* Jewish scriptures; specif. [T-] first 5 books of the Bible

torch *n.* 1. portable flaming light 2. device that makes a very hot flame, as in welding 3. [Br.] flashlight —**torch'light** *n.*

tore *pt.* of **tear** (pull apart)

tor'e·a·dor' *n.* bullfighter

tor'ment *n.* great pain —*v.* (tôr ment') make suffer —**tor·men'tor** *n.*

torn *pp.* of **tear** (pull apart)

tor·na'do *n.* [*pl.* -DOES] violent wind with a whirling, funnel-shaped cloud

tor·pe'do *n.* [*pl.* -DOES] large, cigar-shaped, underwater projectile —*v.* destroy or ruin

tor'pid *a.* dull; sluggish —**tor'por** *n.*

torque (tôrk) *n.* force that gives a twisting motion

tor'rent *n.* swift, violent stream —**tor·ren'tial** (-shəl) *a.*

tor'rid *a.* 1. very hot 2. passionate; ardent

tor'sion *n.* a twisting or being twisted

torsion bar metal bar having resilience under torsion

tor'so *n.* [*pl.* -SOS] human body minus head and limbs

tort (tôrt) *n. Law* wrongful act or damage

torte (tôrt) *n.* rich cake

tor·til'la (-tē'ə) *n.* flat, unleavened cake of cornmeal

tor'toise (-təs) *n.* turtle, esp. one living on land

tortoise shell yellow-and-brown shell of some turtles

tor'tu·ous (-choo-) *a.* full of twists and turns

tor'ture (-chər) *n.* 1. inflicting of great pain 2. great pain —*v.* 1. subject to torture 2. twist; distort

To'ry *n.* [*pl.* -RIES] 1. British loyalist in American Revolution 2. [*often* t-] a conservative

toss *v.* 1. throw lightly from the hand 2. fling or be flung about **3.** jerk upward —*n.* a tossing

toss'up *n.* **1.** flipping of a coin to decide something **2.** even chance

tot *n.* young child

to'tal *n.* the whole amount; sum —*a.* **1.** entire; whole **2.** complete —*v.* **1.** add up to **2.** [Sl.] demolish —**to·tal'i·ty** *n.* —**to'tal·ly** *adv.*

to·tal'i·tar'i·an *a.* designating or of a dictatorship

tote *v.* [Col.] carry; haul

to'tem pole pole carved with animals or objects symbolic of a N. American Indian tribe

tot'ter *v.* **1.** rock as if about to fall **2.** stagger

tou·can (tōō'kan) *n.* tropical bird with a large beak

touch *v.* **1.** put the hand, etc. on, so as to feel **2.** bring or come into contact **3.** tap lightly **4.** handle; use **5.** concern **6.** arouse pity, etc. in **7.** treat in passing (with *on* or *upon*) —*n.* **1.** a touching **2.** way things feel **3.** sense of this **4.** small bit **5.** contact —**touch up** improve by minor changes

touch and go risky situation

touch'down' *n.* goal scored in football, for six points

touched *a.* **1.** emotionally affected **2.** slightly demented

touch'ing *a.* arousing tender emotions; moving

touch'stone' *n.* criterion

touch'y *a.* [-IER, -IEST] **1.** irritable **2.** precarious

tough *a.* **1.** hard to chew, cut, break, etc. **2.** strong or rough

3. very difficult —*n.* ruffian —**tough'en** *v.*

tou·pee (tōō pā') *n.* man's small wig for a bald spot

tour *n.* long trip, as to see sights, put on plays, etc. —*v.* go on a tour (through) —**tour'ist** *n., a.*

tour'ism *n.* tourist travel

tour'na·ment *n.* **1.** series of contests for a championship **2.** knights' jousting contest

tour'ney *n.* [*pl.* -NEYS] tournament

tour'ni·quet (-kit) *n.* device for compressing a blood vessel to stop bleeding

tou·sle (tou'z'l) *v.* muss

tout (tout) *v.* [Col.] **1.** praise highly **2.** sell tips on (race horses) —*n.* [Col.] one who touts

tow *v.* pull by a rope or chain —*n.* a towing

toward (tôrd) *prep.* **1.** in the direction of **2.** concerning **3.** facing **4.** just before **5.** for Also **towards**

tow'el *n.* piece of cloth or paper to wipe things dry

tow'el·ing, tow'el·ling *n.* material for making towels

tow'er *n.* high structure, often part of another building —*v.* rise high

tow'head' (tō'-) *n.* person with light yellow hair

tow·hee (tou'hē, tō'-) *n.* small N. American sparrow

tow'line' *n.* rope, etc. for towing

town *n.* **1.** small city **2.** business center —**go to town** [Sl.] act fast and efficiently —**on**

the town [Col.] out for a good time

town crier one who formerly cried public announcements through the streets

town hall town building housing offices of officials, etc.

town house two-story dwelling in a complex of such houses

town meeting meeting of the voters of a town

town'ship n. 1. part of a county 2. U.S. land unit six miles square

towns'man n. [pl. -MEN] one who lives in a town

towns'peo'ple n.pl. people of a town: also **towns'folk**

tow'path n. path by a canal

tow'rope n. rope for towing

tox·e'mi·a n. condition in which the blood contains toxins or poisons

tox'ic a. 1. of or caused by a toxin 2. poisonous

tox'in n. poison, esp. from bacteria, viruses, etc.

toy n. thing to play with —a. small —v. play (with)

trace n. 1. mark or track left 2. small bit 3. harness strap connecting to vehicle —v. 1. follow (the trail or course of) 2. draw, outline, etc. —**trac'er** n.

trac'er·y n. [pl. -IES] design of interlacing lines

tra·che·a (trā'kē ə) n. [pl. -AE (-ē), -AS] air passage from the larynx to the bronchial tubes

trac'ing n. something traced

track n. 1. footprint, wheel rut, etc. 2. path, trail, or course 3. running sports, etc. 4. pair of

rails a train runs on —v. 1. follow the track of 2. leave footprints in —**keep** (or **lose**) **track of** keep (or fail to keep) informed about

tract n. 1. large stretch of land 2. system of bodily organs 3. pamphlet

trac'ta·ble a. manageable

trac'tion n. 1. power to grip a surface 2. a pulling

trac'tor n. 1. motor vehicle to pull farm machines, etc. 2. truck to haul a trailer

trac'tor-trail'er n. coupled tractor and trailer, used in trucking

trade n. 1. skilled work 2. buying and selling 3. an exchange —v. 1. buy and sell 2. exchange

trade'-in' n. thing used as part payment

trade'mark n. special mark or name (**trade name**) put on a product

trade'-off' n. exchange of a benefit for one more desirable

trades'man n. [pl. -MEN] [Chiefly Br.] storekeeper

trade union labor union

trade wind wind that blows toward the equator

trading post store in an outpost, where trading is done

trading stamp stamp premium redeemable for merchandise

tra·di'tion n. 1. custom, etc. handed down from the past 2. such handing down —**tra·di'tion·al** a.

tra·duce' v. to slander

traf'fic n. 1. vehicles moving along streets, etc. 2. amount of

business done 3. trade (n. 2) —
v. [-FICKED, -FICKING] do business, esp. illegally

traffic circle circular road at the intersection of several streets

traffic light (or **signal**) set of signal lights to regulate traffic

tra·ge'di·an n. actor or writer of tragedy —**tra·ge'di·enne'** n.fem.

trag'e·dy n. [pl. -DIES] 1. serious play with a sad ending 2. tragic event

trag'ic a. 1. of or like tragedy 2. disastrous —**trag'i·cal·ly** adv.

trail v. 1. drag or lag behind 2. follow or drift behind 3. dwindle —n. 1. thing trailing behind 2. beaten path 3. mark; scent

trail'blaz'er n. 1. one who blazes a trail 2. pioneer in any field

trail'er n. wagon or van pulled by a car or truck, sometimes used as a home

trailer park area designed for trailers, esp. mobile homes: also **trailer camp** (or **court**)

train n. 1. thing that drags behind 2. procession 3. connected series 4. locomotive with cars —v. 1. guide the development of 2. instruct or prepare 3. aim —**train·ee'** n. —**train'ing** n.

traipse (trãps) v. [Dial. or Col.] to walk, tramp, etc.

trait n. characteristic

trai'tor n. disloyal person —**trai'tor·ous** a.

tra·jec'to·ry n. [pl. -RIES]

curved path of a missile, etc.

tram'mel n., v. (thing) to hinder or restrain

tramp v. 1. walk, or step, heavily 2. roam about —n. 1. vagrant 2. a tramping 3. [Sl.] loose woman

tram'ple v. step hard on or crush underfoot

tram'po·line (-pə lēn) n. sheet of canvas stretched on a frame, used in tumbling

trance n. state of shock, hypnosis, or deep thought

tran'quil a. calm; quiet —**tran·quil'li·ty, tran·quil'i·ty** n. —**tran'quil·ly** adv.

tran'quil·ize, tran'quil·lize v. make tranquil

tran'quil·iz'er n. drug used to tranquilize the emotionally disturbed, etc.: also **tran'quil·liz'er**

trans- pref. over, across, beyond

trans·act' v. do; complete

trans·ac'tion n. 1. a transacting 2. business deal

tran·scend' (-send') v. exceed —**tran·scend'ent** a.

tran'scen·den'tal a. 1. transcendent 2. supernatural 3. abstract

tran·scribe' v. 1. write or type out 2. record for rebroadcast

tran'script n. written or type-written copy

tran·scrip'tion n. 1. a transcribing 2. transcript 3. recording made for radio or TV broadcasting

tran'sept n. shorter part of a cross-shaped church

trans·fer' v. [-FERRED, -FER-

RING] move or change from one person, place, etc. to another —*n.* 1. a transferring 2. ticket letting one change to another bus, etc. —**trans·fer'·a·ble** *a.* —**trans·fer'ence** *n.*

trans·fig'ure *v.* 1. transform 2. make seem glorious —**trans·fig'u·ra'tion** *n.*

trans·fix' *v.* pierce through

trans·form' *v.* change the form or condition of —**trans'·for·ma'tion** *n.*

trans·form'er *n.* device that changes voltage

trans·fuse' *v.* 1. imbue; fill 2. transfer blood to another —**trans·fu'sion** *n.*

trans·gress' *v.* 1. break a law; do wrong 2. go beyond —**trans·gres'sion** *n.* —**trans·gres'sor** *n.*

tran'sient (-shant) *a.* temporary —*n.* one who stays only a short time

tran·sis'tor *n.* 1. device used to control current flow 2. radio equipped with transistors

tran'sit *n.* 1. passage across 2. a conveying

tran·si'tion *n.* a passing from one condition, place, etc. to another

tran'si·tive *a.* taking a direct object, as some verbs

tran'si·to'ry *a.* temporary

trans·late' *v.* put into another language, form, etc. —**trans·la'tion** *n.* —**trans·la'tor** *n.*

trans·lu'cent *a.* letting a little light pass through

trans·mis'si·ble *a.* capable of being transmitted

trans·mis'sion *n.* 1. a trans-

mitting 2. car part sending power to wheels

trans·mit' *v.* [-MITTED, -MITTING] 1. transfer 2. pass or convey 3. send out radio or TV signals —**trans·mit'tal** *n.*

trans·mit'ter *n.* 1. one that transmits 2. apparatus for transmitting signals in radio, TV, etc.

trans·mute' *v.* change from one form, nature, etc. into another

tran'som *n.* small window above a door or window

trans·par'ent *a.* 1. that can be seen through; clear 2. obvious —**trans·par'en·cy** [*pl.* -CIES] *n.*

tran·spire' (-spīr') *v.* 1. become known 2. happen

trans·plant' *v.* 1. remove from one place and plant, settle, etc. in another 2. *Surgery* graft (tissue, an organ, etc.) —*n.* (trans'plant) something transplanted

trans·port' *v.* 1. carry from one place to another 2. carry away with emotion —*n.* (trans'pôrt) ship, airplane, etc. for transporting —**trans'por·ta'tion** *n.*

trans·pose' *v.* 1. to interchange 2. *Mus.* change the key of —**trans'po·si'tion** *n.*

trans·sex'u·al *n.* one who identifies with the opposite sex or has had sex-change surgery

trans·verse' (-vurs') *a.* situated, placed, etc. across

trap *n.* 1. device for catching animals 2. tricky ruse 3. bend in a drainpipe —*v.* [TRAPPED,

TRAPPING] 1. catch in a trap 2. set traps for animals —**trap'-per** n.

trap'door n. hinged or sliding door in a roof or floor

tra·peze' n. swinglike bar for acrobats

trap'e·zoid n. figure with two of four sides parallel

trap'pings n.pl. adornments

trap'shoot'ing n. sport of shooting at clay disks sprung into the air from throwing devices (**traps**)

trash n. rubbish —**trash'y** [-IER, -IEST] a.

trau·ma (trô'-) n. 1. bodily injury 2. emotional shock with lasting psychic effects —**trau·mat'ic** a.

trav·ail (or trə vāl') n. 1. labor 2. agony

trav'el v. 1. make a journey (through) 2. move or pass —n. a traveling; trip —**trav'el·er** n.

trav'e·logue, trav'e·log (-lôg) n. illustrated lecture or movie of travels

trav·erse (or trə vurs') v. to cross —a. of drapes drawn by pulling cords

trav·es·ty n. [pl. -TIES] farcical imitation —v. [-TIED, -TYING] make a travesty of

trawl (trôl) n. a large dragnet —v. fish with a trawl

trawl'er n. boat for trawling

tray n. flat, low-sided server to carry things

treach·er·ous (trech'-) a. 1. disloyal 2. not safe or reliable —**treach'er·y** n.

trea·cle (trē'k'l) n. [Br.] molasses

tread (tred) v. [TROD, TRODDEN or TROD, TREADING] 1. walk on, along, over, etc. 2. trample —n. 1. way or sound of treading 2. part for treading or moving on —**tread water** [pt. usually TREADED] stay upright in water by moving the legs up and down

trea·dle (tred'-) n. foot pedal to operate a wheel, etc.

tread'mill n. 1. device worked by treading an endless belt 2. seemingly aimless routine

trea·son (trē'z'n) n. betrayal of one's country —**trea'son·a·ble, trea'son·ous** a.

treas'ure n. 1. accumulated money, jewels, etc. 2. valued person or thing —v. 1. save up 2. value greatly

treas'ure-trove' n. treasure found hidden, its owner unknown

treas'ur·y n. [pl. -IES] 1. place where money is kept 2. funds of a state, corporation, etc. —**treas'ur·er** n.

treat v. 1. deal with or act toward 2. pay for the food, etc. of 3. subject to a process, medical care, etc. —n. 1. food, etc. paid for by another 2. thing giving pleasure —**treat'ment** n.

trea·tise (trē'tis) n. a formal writing on a subject

trea·ty n. [pl. -TIES] agreement between nations

tre'ble (treb'-) a. 1. triple 2. of or for the treble —n. 1. *Mus.*

highest part 2. high-pitched voice or sound —v. to triple

tree n. large, woody plant with one main trunk and many branches —v. [TREED, TREE-ING] chase up a tree

tre'foil n. 1. plant with three-part leaves 2. design like such a leaf

trek v. [TREKKED, TREKKING], n. (make) a slow, hard journey

trel'lis n. lattice on which vines, etc. are grown

trem'ble v. 1. shake from cold, fear, etc. 2. quiver or vibrate —n. act or fit of trembling

tre·men'dous a. 1. very large 2. [Col.] wonderful

trem'o·lo n. [pl. -LOS] tremulous effect of repeating the same tone

trem'or n. a trembling, shaking, etc.

trem'u·lous a. trembling

trench n. 1. deep furrow 2. ditch, esp. one dug for cover in battle

trench'ant a. incisive; keen

trench coat belted raincoat in a military style

trench'er·man n. [pl. -MEN] heavy eater

trench foot foot disorder from exposure to wet and cold

trench mouth infectious disease of the mouth

trend v., n. (have) a general direction or tendency

trend'y a. [-IER, -IEST] [Col.] of or in the latest style

trep'i·da'tion n. fear

tres'pass v. 1. enter another's property unlawfully 2. sin —n.

a trespassing —**tres'pass·er** n.

tress n. lock of hair

tres'tle n. 1. framework support, as for a bridge 2. sawhorse

trey (trā) n. playing card with three spots

tri- pref. three

tri'ad n. group of three

tri'al n. 1. hearing and deciding of a case in a law court 2. attempt 3. test 4. hardship, suffering, etc.

trial and error the making of repeated tests or trials, as to find a solution

trial balloon something done to test public opinion

tri'an·gle n. three-sided figure with three angles —**tri·an'gu·lar** a.

tribe n. 1. group of people living together under a chief 2. group or class —**trib'al** a. —**tribes'man** [pl. -MEN] n.

trib'u·la'tion n. great misery or distress

tri·bu'nal n. law court

trib'une n. champion of the people

trib'u·tar'y n. [pl. -IES] river that flows into a larger one

trib'ute n. 1. forced payment, as by a weak nation to a stronger 2. gift, speech, etc. showing respect

tri·cen·ten'ni·al (-sen-) n. 300th anniversary

trich'i·no'sis (trik'-) n. disease caused by worms in the intestines and muscles

trick n. 1. something done to fool, cheat, etc. 2. prank 3.

clever act or skillful feat **4.** turn at work **5.** personal mannerism **6.** cards played in one round —*v.* fool or cheat — **trick′er·y** *n.* —**trick′ster** *n.*

trick′le *v.* **1.** flow in drops or a thin stream **2.** move slowly — *n.* slow, small flow

trick′y *a.* [-IER, -IEST] **1.** deceitful **2.** difficult

tri′col′or *n.* flag having three colors

tri′cy·cle (-si k'l) *n.* child's three-wheeled vehicle

tri′dent *n.* three-pronged spear

tried *pt. & pp. of* **try** —*a.* tested or trustworthy

tri′fle *n.* **1.** thing of little value **2.** small amount —*v.* **1.** act jokingly **2.** toy (*with*)

tri′fling *a.* unimportant

trig′ger *n.* lever pressed in firing a gun

trig′o·nom′e·try *n.* mathematics dealing with relations between sides and angles of triangles —**trig′o·no·met′ric** *n.*

trill *v., n.* (sing or play with) a rapid alternation of two close notes

tril′lion *n.* thousand billions — **tril′lionth** *a., n.*

tril′o·gy (-jē) *n.* [*pl.* -GIES] set of three novels, etc.

trim *v.* [TRIMMED, TRIMMING] **1.** clip, lop, etc. **2.** decorate **3.** put (sails) in order **4.** [Col.] defeat —*n.* **1.** good condition **2.** decoration —*a.* [TRIMMER, TRIMMEST] **1.** orderly; neat **2.** in good condition —**trim′mer** *n.*

trim′ming *n.* **1.** decoration **2.**

pl. parts trimmed off **3.** [Col.] a beating, defeat, etc.

Trin′i·ty *n.* Father, Son, and Holy Spirit or Holy Ghost as one God

trin′ket *n.* small ornament

tri·o (trē′ō) *n.* [*pl.* -OS] musical composition for three performers

trip *v.* [TRIPPED, TRIPPING] **1.** move with light, rapid steps **2.** stumble or make stumble **3.** err or cause to err —*n.* **1.** a journey **2.** [Sl.] pleasing or exciting experience

tri·par′tite (trī-) *a.* **1.** having three parts **2.** between three parties, as a treaty

tripe *n.* **1.** stomach of a cow, etc. used as food **2.** [Sl.] anything worthless; nonsense

trip′ham′mer *n.* heavy power-driven hammer, alternately raised and dropped

tri′ple *a.* **1.** of or for three **2.** three times as much or as many —*n. Baseball* hit putting the batter on third —*v.* **1.** make or become triple **2.** hit a triple —**tri′ply** *adv.*

tri′plet *n.* any of three children born at one birth

trip′li·cate *v.* make three copies of —*a.* (-kit) made in three identical copies —*n.* one of these copies

tri′pod *n.* three-legged stool, support, etc.

trite *a.* worn-out; stale

tri′umph *n.* victory; success — *v.* gain victory or success —**tri·um′phal** *a.* —**tri·um′phant** *a.*

tri·um'vi·rate (-rit) *n.* government by three persons

triv'et *n.* 1. three-legged stand for holding pots 2. short-legged plate for holding hot dishes

triv'i·a *n.pl.* trifles

triv'i·al *a.* unimportant — **triv'i·al'i·ty** [*pl.* -TIES] *n.*

tro'che (-kē) *n.* small medicinal lozenge

trod *pt.* & *alt. pp. of* **tread**

trod'den *alt. pp. of* **tread**

trog·lo·dyte (träg'lə dīt) *n.* 1. cave dweller 2. hermit

troll (trōl) *v.* 1. fish with a moving line 2. sing loudly —*n. Folklore* cave-dwelling giant or dwarf

trol'ley *n.* [*pl.* -LEYS] 1. overhead device that sends electric current to a streetcar 2. electric streetcar: also **trolley car**

trol'lop *n.* prostitute

trom'bone *n.* brass-wind instrument with a sliding tube

troop *n.* 1. group of persons 2. *pl.* soldiers 3. cavalry unit —*v.* move in a group

troop'er *n.* 1. cavalryman 2. mounted policeman 3. [Col.] State policeman

tro'phy *n.* [*pl.* -PHIES] souvenir of victory, etc.; prize

trop'ic *n.* 1. either of two parallels of latitude (**Tropic of Cancer** and **Tropic of Capricorn**) north and south of the equator 2. [*also* T-] *pl.* hot region between these latitudes — **trop'i·cal** *a.*

tro'pism *n.* tendency to grow or turn in response to a stimulus, as light

trop'o·sphere *n.* atmosphere

from the earth's surface to about 6 to 12 miles above

trot *v.* [TROTTED, TROTTING] go at a trot —*n.* 1. running gait of a horse 2. slow, jogging run —**trot'ter** *n.*

troth *n.* [Ar.] 1. promise, esp. to marry 2. truth

trou·ba·dour (trōō'bə dôr) *n.* medieval lyric poet

trou'ble (tru'-) *n.* 1. worry, distress, bother, etc. 2. disturbance 3. difficulty —*v.* be or give trouble to —**trou'ble·some** *a.*

trou'ble-mak'er *n.* one who makes trouble for others

trou'ble-shoot'er *n.* worker who finds and fixes what is out of order

trough (trôf) *n.* 1. long, narrow, open container, as for feeding animals 2. long, narrow hollow

trounce *v.* 1. beat; flog 2. [Col.] defeat

troupe (trōōp) *n.* troop of actors, etc. —**troup'er** *n.*

trou'sers *n.pl.* man's two-legged outer garment

trous·seau (trōō'sō) *n.* [*pl.* -SEAUX (-sōz), -SEAUS] bride's outfit of clothes, linen, etc.

trout *n.* freshwater food fish of the salmon family

trow'el (trou'-) *n.* 1. flat tool for smoothing 2. scooplike tool for digging

troy (**weight**) system of weights for gold, silver, etc. in which 12 ozs. = 1 lb.

tru'ant *n.* 1. pupil who stays away from school without leave 2. one who shirks his duties —**tru'an·cy** n.

truce n. cessation of fighting by mutual agreement

truck n. 1. large motor vehicle for carrying loads 2. wheeled frame 3. vegetables raised for market 4. [Col.] dealings —v. carry on a truck —**truck'er** n.

truck farm farm where vegetables are grown for market

truck'le v. be servile

truc'u·lent a. 1. fierce 2. rude —**truc'u·lence** n.

trudge v. walk wearily

true a. 1. loyal 2. not false 3. accurate .4. lawful 5. real; genuine —adv. exactly —n. that which is true (with the) —**tru'ly** adv.

true'-blue' a. very loyal

truf'fle n. fleshy, edible underground fungus

tru'ism n. an obvious truth

trump n. (playing card of) a suit ranked highest —v. take with a trump —**trump up** devise deceitfully

trump'er·y n. [pl. -IES] showy but worthless thing

trum'pet n. brass-wind instrument with a flared end —v. proclaim loudly

trun'cate v. cut off a part —**trun·ca'tion** n.

trun'cheon (-chən) n. short, thick club

trun'dle v. roll along

trundle bed low bed on small wheels

trunk n. 1. main stem of a tree 2. body, not including the head and limbs 3. long snout of an elephant 4. large box for clothes, etc. 5. pl. men's shorts for boxing or swimming 6. car compartment for spare tire, luggage, etc.

trunk line main line of a railroad, telephone system, etc.

truss v. tie, fasten, or tighten —n. supporting framework or device

trust n. 1. belief in the honesty, reliability, etc. of another 2. one trusted 3. responsibility 4. custody 5. credit (n. 4) 6. property managed for another 7. monopolistic group of corporations —v. 1. have trust in 2. put in the care of 3. believe 4. hope 5. let buy on credit —**trust'ful** a. —**trust'wor'thy** a.

trus·tee' n. 1. one put in charge of another's property 2. member of a controlling board —**trus·tee'ship** n.

trust fund money, stock, etc. held in trust

trust'y a. [-IER, -IEST] dependable —n. [pl. -IES] a convict with privileges

truth n. 1. a being true, honest, etc. 2. that which is true 3. established fact —**truth'ful** a.

try v. [TRIED, TRYING] 1. conduct the trial of in a law court 2. test 3. afflict 4. attempt —n. [pl. TRIES] attempt; effort —**try on** test the fit of —**try out** 1. test by using 2. test one's fitness as for a team

try'ing a. hard to bear

try'out n. [Col.] test of fitness

tryst (trist) *n.* appointment to meet made by lovers

tsar (tsär, zär) *n.* czar

T'-shirt' *n.* short-sleeved, pull-over undershirt

T square T-shaped ruler

tsu·na·mi (tsōō nä′mē) *n.* [*pl.* -MIS] huge sea wave

tub *n.* **1.** large, open container **2.** bathtub

tu′ba *n.* large, deep-toned brass-wind instrument

tub′by (-ē) *a.* [-BIER, -BIEST] fat and short

tube *n.* **1.** slender pipe for fluids **2.** cylinder with a screw cap, for paste, etc. **3.** electron tube —**tu′bu·lar** *a.*

tu′ber *n.* thickened part of an underground stem —**tu′ber·ous** *a.*

tu′ber·cle *n.* **1.** small, round projection **2.** hard growth

tu·ber′cu·lo′sis *n.* wasting disease, esp. of the lungs —**tu·ber′cu·lar, tu·ber′cu·lous** *a.*

tuck *v.* **1.** gather up in folds **2.** push the edges of something under **3.** cover snugly **4.** press into a small space —*n.* sewed fold

tuck′er *v.* [Col.] tire (*out*)

-tude *suf.* like -NESS

Tues′day *n.* third day of the week

tuft *n.* bunch of hairs, grass, etc. growing or tied together —*v.* form in tufts

tug *v.* [TUGGED, TUGGING] pull; drag —*n.* **1.** hard pull **2.** tug-boat

tug′boat *n.* small boat for towing or pushing ships

tug of war contest with two teams pulling at a rope

tu·i′tion (tōō wish′ən) *n.* fee or charge for instruction, as at college

tu′lip *n.* bulb plant with a cup-shaped flower

tulle (tōōl) *n.* fine netting for veils, etc., made of silk, etc.

tum′ble *v.* **1.** fall or move suddenly or clumsily **2.** toss about **3.** do acrobatics —*n.* **1.** a fall **2.** disorder

tum′ble·down *a.* dilapidated

tum′bler *n.* **1.** drinking glass **2.** acrobat **3.** part of a lock moved by a key

tum′ble·weed *n.* plant that breaks off and is blown about

tu′mid *a.* **1.** swollen; bulging **2.** inflated; pompous

tum′my *n.* [*pl.* -MIES] stomach: child's word

tu′mor *n.* abnormal growth in or on the body

tu′mult *n.* **1.** uproar **2.** confusion —**tu·mul′tu·ous** (-chōō wəs) *a.*

tun *n.* large cask

tu′na *n.* large ocean fish with oily flesh: also **tuna fish**

tun′dra *n.* large arctic plain without trees

tune *n.* **1.** melody **2.** *Mus.* right pitch **3.** agreement —*v.* **1.** put in tune (*n.* 2) **2.** give a tuneup to —**tune in** adjust a radio or TV set to receive a station —**tun′er** *n.*

tune′ful *a.* full of melody

tune′up, tune′-up′ *n.* an adjusting, as of an engine, to the proper condition

tung′sten *n.* heavy, metallic

tu′nic *n.* 1. loose gown worn in ancient Greece and Rome 2. long, belted blouse

tun′ing fork two-pronged steel device struck to sound a tone in perfect pitch

tun′nel *n.* underground passageway —*v.* make a tunnel

tun′ny *n.* [*pl.* -NIES] tuna

tur′ban *n.* Muslim headdress, a scarf wound round the head

tur′bid *a.* 1. muddy or cloudy 2. confused

tur′bine (-bin, -bīn) *n.* engine driven by the pressure of air, steam, or water on the vanes of a wheel

tur′bo·jet *n.* jet engine in which the energy of the jet operates a turbine which drives the air compressor

tur′bo·prop *n.* turbojet engine whose turbine shaft drives a propeller

tur′bot (-bət) *n.* large, edible European flatfish

tur′bu·lent *a.* 1. disorderly 2. agitated —**tur′bu·lence** *n.*

tu·reen′ *n.* large, deep dish with a lid, for soup, etc.

turf *n.* 1. top layer of earth with grass 2. peat 3. horse racing, or a track for horse racing: usually with *the*

tur′gid (-jid) *a.* 1. swollen 2. pompous —**tur·gid′i·ty** *n.*

Turk *n.* native of Turkey

tur′key *n.* [*pl.* -KEYS] 1. large bird with a spreading tail 2. its flesh, used as food

turkey buzzard dark-colored American vulture

Turk′ish *n., a.* (language) of Turkey

tur′mer·ic (-mər ik) *n.* plant whose powdered root is used for seasoning, etc.

tur′moil *n.* tumult; commotion; confusion

turn *v.* 1. revolve or rotate 2. change in position or direction 3. make or perform 4. reverse 5. change in feelings, etc. 6. change in form, etc. 7. drive, set, etc. 8. wrench or twist 9. divert; deflect 10. upset 11. depend 12. reach or pass 13. become 14. become sour —*n.* 1. a turning around 2. change in position or direction 3. short walk, ride, etc. 4. bend; twist 5. chance; try 6. deed 7. natural inclination 8. style; form 9. sudden shock —**in** (or **out of**) **turn** in (or not in) proper order —**turn down** reject —**turn in** 1. hand in 2. [Col.] go to bed —**turn off** 1. shut off 2. [Sl.] cause to be bored, etc. —**turn on** 1. make go on 2. [Sl.] make or become elated, etc. —**turn out** 1. shut off 2. come 3. make 4. result —**turn over** 1. ponder 2. transfer —**turn to** apply to for help —**turn up** happen, appear, etc.

turn′a·bout *n.* reversal

turn′a·round *n.* 1. turnabout 2. wide area for turning a car around

turn′buck′le *n.* metal loop used as a coupling

turn′coat *n.* traitor

turn′ing point point in time for a decisive change

tur'nip n. 1. plant with an edible, round root 2. the root

turn'key n. [pl. -KEYS] jailer

turn'off n. 1. a turning off 2. place to turn off, as a road ramp

turn'out n. gathering of people

turn'o·ver n. 1. small pie with crust folded over 2. rate of replacement of workers, goods, etc.

turn'pike n. expressway or toll road

turn'stile n. gate admitting only one at a time

turn'ta·ble n. round, revolving platform

tur'pen·tine n. oil from certain conifers, used in paints, etc.

tur'pi·tude n. vileness

tur'quoise (-koiz, -kwoiz) n. greenish-blue gem

tur'ret n. 1. small tower on a building 2. armored dome, as on a tank 3. lathe part holding cutting tools

tur'tle n. hard-shelled land and water reptile

tur'tle·dove n. wild dove

tur'tle·neck n. 1. high, snug, turned-down collar 2. pullover sweater with such a collar

tusk n. long, projecting tooth, as of an elephant

tus'sle n., v. struggle

tus'sock (-ək) n. thick tuft or clump of grass, etc.

tu'te·lage (-lij) n. 1. instruction 2. protection

tu'tor n. private teacher —v. teach —**tu·to'ri·al** a.

tut·ti-frut·ti (to͞o'tē fro͞o'tē) n.,

a. (ice cream, etc.) made with mixed fruits

tux·e'do n. [pl. -DOS] man's semiformal suit

TV (tē'vē') n. [pl. TVS, TV'S] television or a television set

TV dinner precooked dinner frozen in a tray, heated, and served

twad'dle n. nonsense

twain n., a. [Ar.] two

twang n. 1. sharp, vibrating sound 2. nasal sound —v. make, or utter with, a twang

'twas it was

tweak v., n. (give) a sudden, twisting pinch to (the nose, etc.)

tweed n. 1. rough wool fabric 2. pl. clothes of tweed

tweet v., n. chirp

tweet'er n. small loudspeaker for reproducing high-frequency sounds

tweez'ers n.pl. small pincers for plucking hairs, etc.

twelve a., n. two more than ten —**twelfth** a., n.

twen'ty a., n. [pl. -TIES] two times ten —**twen'ti·eth** a., n.

twice adv. 1. two times 2. two times as much

twid'dle v. twirl or play with idly

twig n. small branch

twi'light n. 1. dim light after sunset 2. gradual decline

twill n. cloth woven with parallel diagonal lines

twin n. 1. either of two born at the same time 2. either of two very much alike   a. being a twin or twins

twine n. strong cord made of

twisted strands —v. **1.** interweave **2.** wind around

twinge (twinj) v., n. (have) a sudden pain or a qualm

twin'kle v. **1.** sparkle **2.** light up —n. a twinkling

twirl v., n. spin; twist

twist v. **1.** wind together or around something **2.** force out of shape **3.** pervert meaning of **4.** sprain **5.** rotate **6.** curve — n. **1.** something twisted **2.** a twisting

twist'er n. tornado; cyclone

twit v. [TWITTED, TWITTING], taunt; tease

twitch v. pull or move with a sudden jerk —n. sudden, spasmodic motion

twit'ter v. **1.** chirp rapidly **2.** tremble excitedly —n. a twittering

two a., n. one more than one —**in two** in two parts

two'-bit' a. [Sl.] cheap

two bits [Col.] twenty-five cents

two'-faced' a. deceitful

two'-fist'ed a. [Col.] virile

two'fold a. **1.** having two parts **2.** having twice as much or as many —adv. twice as much or as many

two'-ply' a. having two layers, strands, etc.

two'some n. couple

two'-time' v. [Sl.] be unfaithful to

two'-way' a. allowing passage in two directions

-ty suf. quality of; condition of

ty·coon' (tī-) n. [Col.] powerful industrialist

ty'ing prp. of **tie**

tyke (tīk) n. [Col.] small child

tym·pan'ic membrane (tim-) eardrum

tym'pa·num n. **1.** cavity beyond the eardrum **2.** eardrum

type n. **1.** kind or sort **2.** model; example **3.** metal piece or pieces for printing **4.** printed letters, etc. —v. **1.** classify **2.** write with a typewriter

type'cast v. [-CAST, -CASTING] cast repeatedly as the same type of actor

type'script n. typewritten matter

type'set v. [-SET, -SETTING] set in type —**type'set'ter** n.

type'write v. [-WROTE, -WRITTEN, -WRITING] type (v. 2)

type'writ'er n. keyboard machine for making printed letters on paper

ty'phoid n. infectious disease with intestinal disorder: also **typhoid fever**

ty·phoon' (tī-) n. cyclonic storm, esp. in the W. Pacific

ty'phus n. infectious disease with fever, skin rash, etc.: also **typhus fever**

typ'i·cal (tip'-) a. **1.** being a true example of its kind **2.** characteristic —**typ'i·cal·ly** adv.

typ'i·fy v. [-FIED, -FYING] be typical of; exemplify

typ'ist n. one who operates a typewriter

ty'po n. [pl. -POS] [Col.] error made in setting type or in typing

ty·pog'ra·phy n. **1.** setting of,

and printing with, type **2.** style, design, etc. of matter printed from type —**ty·pog′ra·pher** n. —**ty·po·graph′i·cal** a.

tyr·an·nize (tir′-) v. **1.** govern as a tyrant **2.** oppress

ty·ran′no·saur (-ə sôr′) n. huge, two-footed dinosaur

tyr·an·ny (-nē) n. **1.** government of a tyrant **2.** cruel and unjust use of power —**ty·ran′ni·cal** a.

ty′rant (ti′-) n. **1.** absolute ruler **2.** cruel, unjust ruler

ty′ro n. [pl. -ROS] novice

tzar (tsär, zär) n. czar

U

u·biq′ui·tous (yōō bik′wə-) a. everywhere at the same time —**u·biq′ui·ty** n.

U′-boat′ n. German submarine

ud′der n. large, milk-secreting gland of cows, etc.

UFO (yōō′fō′, yōō ef ō′) n. [pl. UFOS, UFO's] unidentified flying object

ugh int. exclamation of disgust, horror, etc.

ug′ly a. [-LIER, -LIEST] **1.** unpleasant to see **2.** bad **3.** dangerous —**ug′li·ness** n.

u·kase (yōō′kās, yōō kāz′) n. official decree

u·ku·le·le (yōō′kə la′lē) n. a kind of small guitar

ul′cer n. open sore, as on the skin —**ul′cer·ate** v. —**ul′cer·ous** a.

ul′na n. [pl. -NAE (-nē), -NAS] larger bone of the forearm

ul·te′ri·or a. beyond what is expressed

ul′ti·mate (-mit) a. **1.** farthest **2.** final **3.** basic —n. final point or result —**ul′ti·mate·ly** adv.

ul·ti·ma′tum n. final offer or demand

ultra- pref. **1.** beyond **2.** extremely

ul′tra·ma·rine′ (-mə rēn′) a. deep-blue

ul′tra·son′ic a. above the range of sound audible to the human ear

ul′tra·sound′ n. ultrasonic waves, used in medical diagnosis and therapy, etc.

ul′tra·vi′o·let a. of the invisible rays just beyond the violet end of the spectrum

um′bel n. cluster of flowers with stalks of equal length

um′ber n. reddish brown

um·bil′i·cal cord cord connecting a fetus with the placenta

um′brage (-brij) n. resentment and displeasure

um·brel′la n. cloth screen on a folding frame, carried for protection against rain

um′pire n. **1.** one who judges a dispute **2.** an official in certain sports —v. act as umpire

un- pref. **1.** not **2.** reversing action See list below

   un·a′ble
   un·a·bridged′
   un′ac·com′pa·nied

un·af·fect'ed
un·a·fraid'
un·aid'ed
un·a·shamed'
un·at·trac'tive
un·au'thor·ized
un·a·vail'a·ble
un·bear'a·ble
un·bi'ased
un·break'a·ble
un·bro'ken
un·but'ton
un·changed'
un·civ'i·lized
un·clas'si·fied
un·clean'
un·con·trol'la·ble
un·con·ven'tion·al
un·dam'aged
un·de·feat'ed
un·de·served'
un·de·sir'a·ble
un·de·vel'oped
un·dis'ci·plined
un·dis·cov'ered
un·dis·turbed'
un'di·vid'ed
un·earned'
un·ed'u·cat'ed
un·e·mo'tion·al
un·e·vent'ful
un·ex·plained'
un·ex·plored'
un·fair'
un·fast'en
un·fa'vor·a·ble
un·fit'
un·fore·seen'
un·for·giv'a·ble
un·ful·filled'
un·fur'nished
un·grate'ful
un·harmed'

un·heed'ed
un·hurt'
un·i·den'ti·fied
un·im·por'tant
un·in·hab'it·ed
un·in·sured'
un·in'jured
un·in·tel'li·gi·ble
un·in·ten'tion·al
un·in'ter·est·ing
un·in·vit'ed
un·lace'
un·list'ed
un·man'age·a·ble
un·marked'
un·mar'ried
un·mo·lest'ed
un·named'
un·no'ticed
un·ob·tru'sive
un·oc'cu·pied
un·of·fi'cial
un·o'pened
un·or'gan·ized
un·or'tho·dox
un·paid'
un·paved'
un·planned'
un'pre·dict'a·ble
un·prej'u·diced
un·pre·pared'
un·pre·ten'tious
un·pro·tect'ed
un're·al·is'tic
un·re·lat'ed
un're·li'a·ble
un·ripe'
un·safe'
un'sat·is·fac'to·ry
un·sat'is·fied
un·sat'u·rat'ed
un·seen'
un·self'ish
un'so·lic'it·ed

un·sound'
un·spoiled'
un·suit'a·ble
un·tamed'
un·tir'ing
un·touched'
un·tried'
un·trou'bled
un·true'
un·want'ed
un·war'rant·ed
un·wa'ry
un·wed'
un·will'ing
un·wor'thy
un·yield'ing

un'ac·count'a·ble *a.* 1. inexplicable 2. not responsible

un'ac·cus'tomed *a.* 1. not accustomed (*to*) 2. unusual

u·nan'i·mous *a.* without dissent —u'na·nim'i·ty *n.* —u·nan'i·mous·ly *adv.*

un'ap·proach'a·ble *a.* 1. aloof 2. without equal

un·armed' *a.* having no weapon

un'as·sum'ing *a.* modest

un'at·tached' *a.* 1. not attached 2. not engaged or married

un'a·vail'ing *a.* useless

un·a·ware' *a.* not aware —*adv.* unawares

un·a·wares' *adv.* 1. unintentionally 2. by surprise

un·bal'anced *a.* 1. not in balance 2. mentally ill

un·bar' *v.* [-BARRED', -BARRING'] unbolt; open

un·be·com'ing *a.* 1. not suited 2. not proper

un·be·lief' *n.* lack of belief, esp. in religion —un'be·liev'er *n.*

un'be·liev'a·ble *a.* incredible

un·bend' *v.* [-BENT' or -BENDED, -BENDING] 1. relax 2. straighten

un·bend'ing *a.* 1. rigid; stiff 2. firm; unyielding

un·blush'ing *a.* not ashamed

un·bolt' *v.* withdraw the bolt of (a door, etc.); open

un·born' *a.* 1. not born 2. yet to be; future

un·bos'om *v.* tell (secrets)

un·bound'ed *a.* not restrained

un·bri'dled *a.* 1. with no bridle on 2. uncontrolled

un·bur'den *v.* relieve by disclosing (guilt, etc.)

un·called'-for' *a.* unnecessary and out of place

un·can'ny *a.* 1. weird 2. unusually good, acute, etc.

un'cer·e·mo'ni·ous *a.* 1. informal 2. curt; abrupt

un·cer'tain *a.* 1. not sure or certain 2. vague 3. not steady or constant —un·cer'tain·ty [*pl.* -TIES] *n.*

un·char'i·ta·ble *a.* harsh or severe, as in opinion

un'cle *n.* 1. brother of one's father or mother 2. husband of one's aunt

un·coil' *v.* unwind

un·com'fort·a·ble *a.* 1. feeling or causing discomfort 2. ill at ease

un'com·mit'ted *a.* not pledged or taking a stand

un·com'mon *a.* 1. not usual 2. extraordinary

un'com·pro·mis'ing *a.* unyielding; firm

un·con·cern' n. lack of interest or worry; indifference —**un·con·cerned'** a.

un'con·di'tion·al a. absolute

un·con'scion·a·ble (-shan-) a. 1. unscrupulous 2. unreasonable

un·con'scious a. 1. not conscious 2. not aware (of) 3. unintentional

un·count'ed a. 1. not counted 2. innumerable

un·couth' a. rude; crude

un·cov'er v. 1. disclose 2. remove the cover from

unc'tion n. 1. an anointing 2. anything soothing

unc'tu·ous (-choo-) a. 1. oily 2. insincerely earnest

un·cut' a. 1. not shaped, as a gem 2. not abridged

un·daunt'ed a. fearless

un·de·cid'ed a. 1. not decided 2. not having decided

un'de·ni'a·ble a. that cannot be denied

un'der prep. 1. lower than; below; beneath 2. covered by 3. less than 4. below and across 5. subject to 6. undergoing —adv. 1. in or to a lower position 2. so as to be covered —a. lower

under- pref. 1. below 2. less than usual or proper

un'der·a·chieve' v. fail to do as well as expected

un·der·age' a. below the legal age

un'der·arm' a. 1. for the armpit 2. underhand (a. 1)

un'der·brush' n. small trees, bushes, etc. in a forest

un'der·car'riage n. supporting frame

un'der·clothes' n.pl. underwear: also **un'der·cloth'ing**

un'der·cov'er a. secret

un'der·cur'rent n. underlying tendency, opinion, etc.

un'der·de·vel'oped a. inadequately developed economically

un'der·dog' n. one that is expected to lose

un'der·es'ti·mate v. make too low an estimate

un·der·foot' adv., a. 1. under the feet 2. in the way

un'der·gar'ment n. piece of underwear

un'der·go' v. [-WENT, -GONE, -GOING] experience; endure

un'der·grad'u·ate n. college student who does not yet have a degree

un'der·ground' a., adv. 1. beneath the earth's surface 2. (in) secret —n. (-ground') secret revolutionary movement

un'der·growth' n. underbrush

un'der·hand' a. 1. with the hand held below the elbow 2. underhanded —adv. 1. with an underhand motion 2. in an underhanded way

un'der·hand'ed a. sly, deceitful, etc.

un·der·lie' v. [-LAY, -LAIN, -LYING] 1. lie beneath 2. support

un'der·line' v. 1. draw a line under 2. stress

un'der·ling n. a subordinate

un'der·ly'ing a. basic

un·der·mine' v. 1. dig beneath 2. weaken gradually

un·der·neath' adv., prep. under; below

un·der·pants n.pl. undergarment of short pants

un·der·pass n. road under a railway or highway

un·der·pin'ning n. support

un·der·priv'i·leged a. poor; needy

un·der·rate' v. rate too low

un·der·score' v. underline

un·der·sec're·tar'y n. [pl. -IES] assistant secretary

un·der·sell' v. [-SOLD, -SELLING] sell for less than

un·der·shirt n. collarless undergarment worn under a shirt

un·der·shorts n.pl. short underpants

un·der·shot a. with the lower part extending past the upper

un·der·stand' v. [-STOOD, -STANDING] 1. get the meaning (of) 2. take as a fact 3. know the nature, etc. of 4. sympathize with —**un'der·stand'a·ble** a.

un·der·stand'ing n. 1. comprehension 2. intelligence 3. mutual agreement

un·der·state' v. say with little or no emphasis

un·der·stud'y v. [-IED, -YING], n. [pl. -IES] (be ready to) substitute for an actor

un·der·take' v. [-TOOK, -TAKEN, -TAKING] 1. begin (a task, etc.) 2. promise

un·der·tak'er n. funeral director

un·der·tak'ing n. 1. task 2. promise

un·der·things n.pl. women's or girls' underwear

un'der·tone n. 1. low tone 2. underlying quality, etc.

un'der·tow n. strong flow of water back under breaking waves

un'der·wa'ter a. beneath the surface of the water

un'der·wear n. clothing worn next to the skin

un'der·weight a. weighing too little

un'der·world n. 1. criminal world 2. Hades

un'der·write v. [-WROTE, -WRITTEN, -WRITING] 1. agree to finance 2. write insurance for —**un'der·writ'er** n.

un·do' v. [-DID, -DONE, -DOING] 1. open, untie, etc. 2. cancel or destroy

un·do'ing n. 1. a bringing to ruin 2. cause of ruin

un·done' a. 1. not done 2. ruined

un·doubt'ed a. certain

un·dress' v. take the clothes off

un·due' a. more than is proper

un·du·late v. 1. move in waves 2. have or give a wavy form —**un'du·la'tion** n.

un·du'ly adv. 1. unjustly 2. excessively

un·dy'ing a. eternal

un·earth' v. 1. dig up from the earth 2. find

un·earth'ly a. 1. supernatural 2. weird

un·eas'y a. [-IER, -IEST] 1. uncomfortable 2. awkward —**un·eas'i·ness** n.

un·em·ployed' a. 1. without a job 2. idle —**un'em·ploy'ment** n.

un·e'qual *a.* 1. not equal in size, value, etc. 2. not adequate (*to*)

un·e'qualed, un·e'qualled *a.* without equal

un'e·quiv'o·cal *a.* straightforward; clear

un·e'ven *a.* 1. not even, smooth, equal, etc. 2. odd

un'ex·pect'ed *a.* not expected; sudden —**un'ex·pect'ed·ly** *adv.*

un·fail'ing *a.* 1. inexhaustible 2. always reliable

un·faith'ful *a.* 1. not faithful 2. adulterous

un'fa·mil'iar *a.* 1. strange 2. not acquainted (*with*)

un·feel'ing *a.* 1. insensible 2. hardhearted; cruel

un·feigned' (-fānd') *a.* real; genuine

un·fin'ished *a.* 1. incomplete 2. not painted, etc.

un·flap'pa·ble *a.* [Col.] not easily excited

un·flinch'ing *a.* steadfast

un·fold' *v.* 1. spread out 2. make or become known

un·for'tu·nate *a., n.* unlucky or unsuccessful (person)

un·found'ed *a.* not based on fact or reason

un·friend'ly *a.* not friendly, kind, or favorable

un·furl' *v.* unfold

un·gain'ly *a.* awkward

un·gov'ern·a·ble *a.* unruly

un·gra'cious *a.* 1. rude 2. unpleasant

un·guard'ed *a.* 1. unprotected 2. frank; candid 3. careless

un'guent (-gwant) *n.* salve

un'gu·late (-lit) *a.* having hoofs —*n.* ungulate mammal

un·hand' *v.* let go of

un·hap'py *a.* [-PIER, -PIEST] 1. unlucky 2. sad; wretched

un·health'y *a.* [-IER, -IEST] 1. not well 2. harmful to health 3. dangerous

un·heard' *a.* not heard or listened to

un·heard'-of' *a.* never known or done before

un·hinge' *v.* 1. remove from the hinges 2. unbalance (the mind)

un·ho'ly *a.* [-LIER, -LIEST] 1. not sacred 2. wicked; sinful

un·horse' *v.* make fall from a horse

uni- *pref.* having only one

u'ni·corn *n.* mythical horse with a horn in its forehead

u'ni·form *a.* 1. never changing 2. all alike —*n.* special clothes for some group —*v.* dress in a uniform —**u'ni·form'i·ty** *n.*

u'ni·fy' *v.* [-FIED, -FYING] make into one —**u'ni·fi·ca'tion** *n.*

u'ni·lat'er·al *a.* 1. of one side only 2. involving only one of several parties

un'im·peach'a·ble *a.* that cannot be doubted

un·in'ter·est·ed *a.* not interested; indifferent

un'ion *n.* 1. a uniting 2. group of nations or states united 3. marriage 4. labor union

un'ion·ize *v.* organize into a labor union

u·nique' (-nēk') *a.* 1. one and only 2. without equal 3. unusual

u'ni·son *n.* 1. *Mus.* sameness of pitch 2. agreement

u'nit *n.* 1. single part of a whole 2. special part 3. a standard measure 4. one

u·nite' *v.* 1. put together as one; combine 2. join together (*in*)

u'ni·ty *n.* [*pl.* -TIES] 1. a being united 2. harmony; agreement 3. complex of related parts

u'ni·ver'sal *a.* 1. of or for all 2. present everywhere —**u'ni·ver·sal'i·ty** *n.*

u'ni·ver'sal·ly *adv.* 1. in every case 2. everywhere

u'ni·verse *n.* 1. space and all things in it 2. the world

u'ni·ver'si·ty *n.* [*pl.* -TIES] school made up of colleges and, often, graduate schools

un·just' *a.* not just or right

un·kempt' *a.* untidy; messy

un·kind' *a.* 1. inconsiderate 2. harsh, cruel, etc.

un·known' *a., n.* unfamiliar or unidentified (person or thing)

un·law'ful *a.* against the law

un·lead'ed *a.* not mixed with tetraethyl lead, as gasoline

un·learn'ed *a.* not educated

un·leash' *v.* release as from a leash

un·less' *con.* except if

un·let'tered *a.* 1. ignorant 2. illiterate

un·like' *a.* not alike —*prep.* not like

un·like'ly *a.* 1. not likely 2. not likely to succeed

un·lim'it·ed *a.* without limits or bounds

un·load' *v.* 1. remove (a load) 2. take a load from 3. get rid of

un·lock' *v.* open by undoing a lock

un·luck'y *a.* [-IER, -IEST] having or bringing bad luck

un·make' *v.* [-MADE, -MAKING] 1. undo 2. ruin 3. depose

un·man' *v.* [-MANNED, -MANNING] deprive of manly courage —**un·man'ly** *a.*

un·manned' *a.* operating solely by remote control

un·mask' *v.* 1. remove a mask (from) 2. expose

un'mis·tak'a·ble *a.* that cannot be mistaken; clear —**un'mis·tak'a·bly** *adv.*

un·mit'i·gat'ed *a.* 1. not lessened 2. absolute

un·nat'u·ral *a.* 1. abnormal 2. artificial

un·nec'es·sar'y *a.* not necessary or required —**un·nec'es·sar'i·ly** *adv.*

un·nerve' *v.* make lose nerve, courage, etc.

un·num'bered *a.* 1. countless 2. not numbered

un·pack' *v.* take things out of a trunk, box, etc.

un·par'al·leled *a.* that has no equal or counterpart

un·pleas'ant *a.* offensive; disagreeable

un·pop'u·lar *a.* not liked by the public or the majority

un·prec'e·dent'ed *a.* having no precedent; unique

un·prin'ci·pled *a.* without good principles

un·print'a·ble *a.* not fit to be printed

un'pro·fes'sion·al *a.* violating a profession's ethics

un·qual'i·fied *a.* 1. lacking qualifications 2. absolute

un·ques'tion·a·ble *a.* certain —**un·ques'tion·a·bly** *adv.*

un·quote' *int.* that ends the quotation

un·rav'el *v.* 1. undo the threads of 2. make clear

un·read' (-red') *a.* not having been read

un·re'al *a.* fantastic

un·rea'son·a·ble *a.* 1. not reasonable 2. excessive

un're·gen'er·ate (-it) *a.* stubbornly defiant

un·re·lent'ing *a.* 1. refusing to relent 2. cruel

un·rest' *n.* 1. restlessness 2. angry discontent

un·ri'valed, un·ri'valled *a.* having no rival or equal

un·roll' *v.* open (something rolled up)

un·ruf'fled *a.* calm; smooth

un·rul'y *a.* [-IER, -IEST] not obedient or orderly

un·sa'vor·y *a.* 1. tasting or smelling bad 2. disgusting

un·scathed' (-skāthd') *a.* uninjured

un·scram'ble *v.* make ordered or intelligible

un·screw' *v.* detach or loosen by removing screws

un·scru'pu·lous *a.* without scruples; dishonest

un·seal' *v.* to open

un·sea'son·a·ble *a.* not usual for the season

un·seat' *v.* 1. throw from a seat 2. remove from office

un·seem'ly *a.* improper

un·set'tle *v.* disturb, displace, or disorder

un·sight'ly *a.* ugly

un·skilled' *a.* having or requiring no special skill

un·skill'ful *a.* clumsy

un'so·phis'ti·cat'ed *a.* simple, ingenuous, etc.

un·speak'a·ble *a.* inexpressibly bad, evil, etc.

un·sta'ble *a.* 1. not fixed, firm, etc. 2. changeable 3. emotionally unsettled

un·stead'y *a.* unstable

un·struc'tured *a.* loose, free, open, etc.

un·strung' *a.* nervous; upset

un·stuck' *a.* loosened or freed from being stuck

un·stud'ied *a.* spontaneous; natural

un'sub·stan'tial (-shəl) *a.* not solid, firm, real, etc.

un·sung' *a.* not honored

un·tan'gle *v.* free from tangles; straighten out

un·taught' *a.* 1. uneducated 2. got without teaching

un·think'a·ble *a.* that cannot be considered

un·think'ing *a.* thoughtless

un·ti'dy *a.* [-DIER, -DIEST] slovenly; messy

un·tie' *v.* [-TIED, -TYING] unfasten (something tied or knotted)

un·til' *prep.* 1. up to the time of 2. before —*con.* 1. to the time or degree that 2. before

un·time'ly *a.* 1. premature 2. at the wrong time —*adv.* too soon —**un·time'li·ness** *n.*

un·to' *prep.* [Ar.]

un·told' *a.* 1. not told or revealed 2. very great

un·to·ward' (-tôrd') *a.* 1. unfortunate 2. hard to control

un·truth' *n.* lie; falsehood — **un·truth'ful** *a.*

un·tu'tored *a.* uneducated

un·used' *a.* 1. not in use 2. never used before 3. unaccustomed (*to*)

un·u'su·al *a.* not usual; rare — **un·u'su·al·ly** *adv.*

un·ut'ter·a·ble *a.* that cannot be spoken or described

un·var'nished *a.* 1. not varnished 2. plain; simple

un·veil' *v.* remove a veil from; disclose

un·well' *a.* not well; sick

un·whole'some *a.* 1. harmful to body or mind 2. unhealthy

un·wield'y (-wēld'ē) *a.* [-IER, -IEST] 1. hard to handle because of size, etc 2. clumsy — **un·wield'i·ness** *n.*

un·wind' *v.* [-WOUND, -WINDING] 1. undo (something wound) 2. become unwound 3. become relaxed

un·wise' *a.* lacking wisdom

un·wit'ting *a.* 1. not knowing 2. not intentional

un·wont'ed *a.* unusual; rare

un·wrap' *v.* [-WRAPPED, -WRAPPING] take off the wrapping of

un·writ'ten *a.* 1. not in writing 2. observed through custom, as some rules

up *adv.* 1. to, in, or on a higher place, level, etc. 2. to a later time 3. upright 4. into action, discussion, etc. 5. aside; away 6. so as to be even 7. so as to be tightly bound 8. completely —*prep.* up to, toward,

along, on, in, etc. —*a.* 1. put, brought, going, or gone up 2. in an active or excited state 3. at an end 4. [Col.] going on 5. *Baseball* at bat. —*v.* [UPPED, UPPING] [Col.] increase —**on the up and up** [Sl.] honest —**up on** [Col.] well-informed about —**ups and downs** good periods and bad periods —**up to** [Col.] 1. doing or scheming 2. capable of 3. as many as 4. as far as 5. dependent upon

up'-and-com'ing *a.* 1. promising 2. gaining prominence

up'beat' *a.* cheerful

up·braid' *v.* scold

up'bring'ing *n.* training received as a child

up'com'ing *a.* coming soon

up-date' *v.* make up-to-date

up·end' *v.* set on end

up'-front' *a.* [Col.] 1. forthright 2. in advance

up'grade' *n.* upward slope —*v.* raise in grade or rank

up·heav'al *n.* 1. a heaving up 2. quick, violent change

up'hill' *a., adv.* 1. upward 2. with difficulty

up·hold' *v.* 1. support 2. confirm; sustain

up·hol'ster *v.* to fit out (furniture) with coverings, etc. —**up·hol'ster·y** *n.*

up'keep' *n.* 1. maintenance 2. cost of maintenance

up·lift' *v.* 1. lift up 2. raise to a better level —*n.* (up'lift) a lifting up

up·on' *prep., adv.* on, or up and on

up'per *a.* higher in place, rank, etc. —*n.* 1. part of a shoe above the sole 2. [Sl.] drug, a stimulant

upper hand position of advantage or control

up′per·most a. highest in place, power, etc. —adv. in the highest place; first

up·raise′ v. raise up; lift

up′right a. 1. standing up; erect 2. honest; just —adv. in an upright position —n. upright pole, beam, etc.

up′ris′ing n. a revolt

up′roar′ n. loud, confused noise or condition

up·roar′i·ous a. 1. making an uproar 2. boisterous

up·root′ v. 1. pull up by the roots 2. remove entirely

up·set′ v. [-SET, -SETTING] 1. overturn 2. disturb or distress 3. defeat unexpectedly —n. (up′set) an upsetting —a. 1. overturned 2. disturbed

up′shot′ n. result; outcome

up′side down′ 1. with the top part underneath 2. in disorder —**up′side-down′** a.

up·stage′ v. draw attention away from

up′stairs′ adv., a. to or on an upper floor —n. upper floor or floors

up·stand′ing a. honorable

up′start′ n. presumptuous newcomer

up′stream′ adv., a. against the current of a stream

up′swing n. upward trend

up′take n. taking up —**quick (or slow) on the uptake** [Col.] quick (or slow) to understand

up·tight′, up′tight′ a. [Sl.] very tense, nervous, etc.

up′-to-date′ a. 1. using the latest facts, ideas, etc. 2. keeping up with what is most recent

up′turn n. upward trend

up′turned′ a. turned up

up′ward adv., a. toward a higher place, position, etc.: also **up′wards** adv. —**up·ward(s) of** more than

u·ra′ni·um n. radioactive metallic chemical element

ur′ban a. of or in a city

ur·bane′ a. suave; refined : **ur·ban′i·ty** n.

ur′ban·ize′ v. change from rural to urban —**ur′ban·i·za′tion** n.

ur′chin n. small mischievous child, esp. a boy

-ure suf. 1. act, result, or means of 2. state of being

u·re′a n. substance found in urine

u·re′mi·a n. toxic condition caused by kidney failure —**u·re′mic** a.

u·re′ter n. tube from a kidney to the bladder

u·re′thra n. duct for discharge of urine from bladder

urge v. 1. insist on 2. force onward 3. plead with 4. incite —n. impulse

ur′gent a. 1. needing quick action 2. insistent —**ur′gen·cy** n.

u′ri·nal n. fixture in which to urinate

u′ri·nar′y a. of the organs that secrete or discharge urine

u′ri·nate v. discharge urine from the body

u′rine n. waste fluid from the kidneys, which passes through the bladder

urn n. **1.** footed vase **2.** container with a faucet

us pron. the objective case of **we**

us′a·ble, use′a·ble a. that can be used

us′age n. **1.** treatment **2.** custom; habit **3.** the way a word, phrase, etc. is used

use (yōōz) v. **1.** put into action **2.** treat **3.** consume —n. (yōōs) **1.** a using or being used **2.** power or right to use **3.** need to use **4.** utility or function — **used to 1.** did once **2.** familiar with —**us′er** n.

used a. not new; secondhand

use′ful a. that can be used; helpful —**use′ful·ness** n.

use′less a. worthless

ush′er v. show the way to or bring in —n. **1.** one who ushers **2.** bridegroom's attendant

u·su·al a. in common use; ordinary —**u·su·al·ly** adv.

u·surp′ v. take by force or without right —**u′sur·pa′tion** n. —**u·surp′er** n.

u′su·ry (yōō′zhoo-) n. lending of money at an excessive interest rate —**u′su·rer** n. — **u·su′ri·ous** a.

u·ten′sil n. tool or container, esp. one for kitchen use

u′ter·us n. hollow female organ in which a fetus grows —**u′ter·ine** (-in) a.

u·til′i·tar′i·an (-ter′-) a. **1.** useful or practical **2.** stressing usefulness over beauty, etc.

u·til′i·ty n. [pl. -TIES] **1.** usefulness **2.** water, gas, etc. for public use **3.** company providing this

utility room room containing laundry appliances, etc.

u′ti·lize v. put to use —**u′ti·li·za′tion** n.

ut′most a. **1.** most distant **2.** greatest or highest —n. the most possible

U·to′pi·a, u·to′pi·a n. any imaginary place where all things are perfect —**U·to′pi·an, u·to′pi·an** a., n.

ut′ter a. complete; absolute — v. express with the voice — **ut′ter·ly** adv.

ut′ter·ance n. **1.** an uttering **2.** something said

ut′ter·most a., n. utmost

u′vu·la (yōō′vyə-) n. [-LAS, -LAE (-lē)] small part hanging down above the back of the tongue

V

va'cant *a.* 1. empty; unoccupied 2. free from work 3. stupid —**va'can·cy** [*pl.* -CIES] *n.*

va'cate *v.* 1. make a place empty 2. annul

va·ca'tion *v., n.* rest from work, study, etc. —**va·ca'tion·er, va·ca'tion·ist** *n.*

vac'ci·nate *v.* inoculate with a vaccine —**vac'ci·na'tion** *n.*

vac'cine (-sēn) *n.* preparation injected for immunity to a disease

vac'il·late (vas'-) *v.* 1. waver 2. fluctuate 3. show indecision —**vac'il·la'tion** *n.*

vac'u·ous *a.* 1. empty 2. stupid; senseless —**va·cu'i·ty** [*pl.* -TIES] *n.*

vac'u·um *n.* 1. completely empty space 2. space with most of the air or gas taken out —*a.* of, having, or working by a vacuum —*v.* use a vacuum cleaner

vacuum cleaner machine that cleans by suction

vacuum-packed *a.* packed in airtight container to keep fresh

vacuum tube electron tube

vag'a·bond *n.* 1. wanderer 2. vagrant

va·ga'ry (-ger'-) *n.* [*pl.* -IES] odd action or idea

va·gi'na (-jī'-) *n.* canal leading to the uterus —**vag'i·nal** *a.*

va'grant *n.* homeless wanderer; tramp —*a.* 1. nomadic 2. wayward —**va'gran·cy** *n.*

vague (vāg) *a.* indefinite; un-

clear —**vague'ly** *adv.* —**vague'ness** *n.*

vain *a.* 1. conceited 2. futile 3. worthless —**in vain** 1. without success 2. profanely —**vain'ly** *adv.*

vain'glo'ry *n.* boastful pride —**vain'glo'ri·ous** *a.*

val'ance (val'əns) *n.* short drapery forming a border

vale *n.* [Poet.] valley

val'e·dic'to·ry *n.* farewell speech, as at graduation —**val'e·dic·to'ri·an** *n.*

va'lence *n.* *Chem.* combining capacity of an element

val'en·tine *n.* sweetheart or card for St. Valentine's Day

val'et (val'it, -ā) *n.* male servant to another man

val'iant (-yənt) *a.* brave

val'id *a.* 1. true or sound 2. having legal force

val'i·date *v.* 1. make legally valid 2. prove to be valid

va·lid'i·ty *n.* a being valid in law or in argument, etc.

va·lise' (-lēs') *n.* suitcase

val'ley *n.* [*pl.* -LEYS] 1. low land between hills 2. land drained by a river system

val'or *n.* courage; bravery —**val'or·ous** *a.*

val'u·a·ble *a.* 1. having value 2. worth much money 3. highly important —*n. usually pl.* valuable thing

val'u·a'tion *n.* 1. the fixing of a thing's value 2. value set on a thing

val'ue *n.* 1. importance, desirability, utility, etc. **2.** worth in money **3.** buying power **4.** *pl.* standards —*v.* **1.** set the value of **2.** think highly of —**val'ue·less** *a.*

valve *n.* **1.** device in a pipe, etc. to control the flow by a flap, lid, etc. **2.** membrane that controls the flow of body fluids

vamp *n.* part of a shoe over the instep

vam'pire *n.* **1.** one who preys on others **2.** bat that lives on other animals' blood: also **vampire bat**

van *n.* **1.** vanguard **2.** large closed truck

van'dal *n.* one who maliciously destroys things

van'dal·ize *v.* destroy maliciously —**van'dal·ism** *n.*

Van·dyke' (**beard**) (-dīk') short, pointed beard

vane *n.* **1.** device that swings to show wind direction **2.** blade of a windmill, etc.

van'guard *n.* **1.** front part of an army **2.** leading group or position in a movement

va·nil'la *n.* **1.** orchid with pods (**vanilla beans**) **2.** flavoring made from these pods

van'ish *v.* disappear

van'i·ty *n.* [*pl.* -TIES] **1.** a being vain, or conceited **2.** futility **3.** small table with a mirror

van'quish *v.* conquer

van'tage *n.* **1.** favorable position **2.** position giving a clear view: also **vantage point**

vap'id *a.* tasteless; dull

va'por *n.* **1.** thick mist, as fog

or steam **2.** gas formed by heating a liquid or solid —**va'por·ous** *a.*

va'por·ize *v.* change into vapor —**va'por·i·za'tion** *n.* —**va'por·iz'er** *n.*

var'i·a·ble (ver'ē-) *a.* that varies or can be varied —*n.* variable thing

var'i·ance *n.* **1.** a varying **2.** degree of change —**at variance** not in agreement

var'i·ant *a.* slightly different —*n.* variant form

var'i·a'tion *n.* **1.** change in form, etc. **2.** amount of change **3.** variant thing

var'i·col'ored *a.* of several or many colors

var'i·cose *a.* abnormally swollen, as veins

var'ied *a.* **1.** of different kinds **2.** changed

var'i·e·gat'ed *a.* **1.** marked with different colors **2.** varied

va·ri'e·ty *n.* [*pl.* -TIES] **1.** change **2.** kind; sort **3.** number of different kinds

var'i·ous *a.* **1.** of several kinds **2.** several or many **3.** individual

var'mint *n.* [Dial.] objectionable person or animal

var'nish *n.* **1.** resinous liquid forming a glossy surface **2.** surface smoothness —*v.* **1.** cover with varnish **2.** make superficially attractive

var'si·ty *n.* [*pl.* -TIES] school's team in contests

var'y *v.* [-IED, -YING] **1.** make or become different; change **2.** differ **3.** give variety to **4.** depart (*from*)

vas'cu·lar (-kyə-) *a.* of vessels carrying blood, etc.

vase *n.* open container for flowers, etc.

vas·ec'to·my *n.* [*pl.* -MIES] surgical removal of ducts carrying sperm

Vas'e·line (-lēn) *a trademark for* petrolatum —*n.* [v-] petrolatum

vas'sal *n.* 1. feudal tenant 2. subordinate, servant, etc.

vast *a.* very great in size, degree, etc. —**vast'ly** *adv.* — **vast'ness** *n.*

vat *n.* large tank or cask

vaude·ville (vôd'vil) *n.* stage show with song and dance acts, skits, etc.

vault *n.* 1. arched roof or ceiling 2. arched room 3. burial chamber 4. room for keeping money, etc. as in a bank —*v.* 1. provide with a vault 2. leap over, balancing on a pole or the hands

vaunt *n., v.* boast

veal *n.* meat from a calf

veer *v., n.* shift; turn

veg'e·ta·ble (vej'-) *n.* 1. plant eaten raw or cooked 2. any plant

veg'e·tar'i·an *n.* one who eats no meat —*a.* 1. of vegetarians 2. of vegetables only

veg'e·tate' *v.* 1. grow as plants 2. lead a dull, inactive life

veg'e·ta'tion *n.* plant life

ve'he·ment *a.* 1. showing strong feeling 2. violent —**ve'he·mence** *n.*

ve'hi·cle (-ə k'l) *n.* 1. device for conveying persons or things 2. means of communicating

thoughts, etc. —**ve·hic'u·lar** *a.*

veil (vāl) *n.* 1. piece of thin fabric worn by women over the face or head 2. thing that conceals —*v.* 1. cover with a veil 2. conceal

veiled *a.* 1. wearing a veil 2. hidden 3. not openly expressed

vein (vān) *n.* 1. blood vessel going to the heart 2. line in a leaf or an insect's wing 3. fissure of mineral in rock 4. colored streak 5. distinctive quality 6. mood —*v.* mark as with veins

veld, veldt (velt) *n.* S. African grassy land

vel'lum *n.* fine parchment

ve·loc'i·ty *n.* speed

ve·lour, ve·lours (və loor') *n.* [*pl.* -LOURS] fabric with a soft nap like velvet

ve·lure' *n.* velvet or a fabric like velvet

vel'vet *n.* fabric of silk, rayon, etc. with a soft, thick pile — **vel'vet·y** *a.*

vel·vet·een' *n.* cotton cloth with a nap like velvet

ve'nal *a.* open to bribery —**ve·nal'i·ty** *n.*

vend *v.* sell (goods) —**ven'dor, vend'er** *n.*

ven·det'ta *n.* feud, as between families

vending machine a coin-operated machine for selling small articles

ve·neer' *n.* 1. thin, covering layer, as of fine wood 2. superficial appearance —*v.* cover with a veneer

ven'er·a·ble *a.* worthy of re-

spect because of age, etc. —
ven′er·a·bil′i·ty n.

ven′er·ate v. show deep respect for —**ven′er·a′tion** n.

ve·ne′re·al a. of or passed on by sexual intercourse

Ve·ne′tian blind, ve·ne′tian blind window blind of thin slats adjustable to any angle

venge′ance n. revenge —**with a vengeance** 1. with great force 2. very much

venge′ful a. seeking revenge

ve′ni·al a. pardonable

ven′i·son n. flesh of deer

ven′om n. 1. poison of some snakes, spiders, etc. 2. malice

ven′om·ous a. 1. poisonous 2. spiteful; malicious

ve′nous a. 1. of veins 2. of blood carried in veins

vent n. 1. outlet 2. release 3. opening to let gas, etc. out 4. vertical slit in a garment —v. let out

ven′ti·late v. 1. circulate fresh air in 2. make an opening for the escape of gas, etc. —**ven′ti·la′tion** n.

ven′ti·la·tor n. opening, etc. for replacing foul air

ven′tral a. of, near, or on the belly

ven′tri·cle n. either lower chamber of the heart

ven·tril′o·quism n. art of making one's voice seem to come from another point —**ven·tril′o·quist** n.

ven′ture (-char) n. risky undertaking —v. 1. place in danger 2. dare to do, say, etc.

ven′ture·some a. 1. daring; bold 2. risky

ven′tur·ous a. venturesome

ven′ue (-yoō) n. locality of a crime or where a legal case is tried

ve·ra′cious (-shəs) a. 1. honest 2. accurate 3. true

ve·rac′i·ty (və ras′ə tē) n. 1. honesty 2. accuracy 3. truth

ve·ran′da, ve·ran′dah n. open, roofed porch

verb n. word expressing action or being

ver′bal a. 1. of or in words 2. in speech 3. like or derived from a verb —**ver′bal·ly** adv.

ver′bal·ize v. 1. use words for communication 2. express in words

verbal noun noun derived from a verb

ver·ba′tim adv., a. word for word

ver·be′na n. ornamental plant with showy flowers

ver′bi·age (-ij) n. wordiness

ver·bose′ (-bōs′) a. wordy —**ver·bos′i·ty** (-bäs′-) n.

ver′dant a. covered with green vegetation

ver′dict n. decision, as of a jury in a law case

ver′di·gris (-grēs, -gris) n. greenish coating on brass, copper, or bronze

ver′dure (-jər) n. 1. green vegetation 2. color of this

verge n. edge, brink, or margin (of) —v. 1. be on the verge; border (on) 2. incline (to or toward) 3. change (into)

ver·i·fy (ver′ə fī) v. [-FIED, -FYING] 1. prove to be true 2. test the accuracy of —**ver′i·fi·ca′tion** n.

ver'i·ly *adv.* [Ar.] really

ver'i·si·mil'i·tude *n.* appearance of being real

ver'i·ta·ble *a.* true; real

ver'i·ty (-tē) *n.* [*pl.* -TIES] (a) truth

ver·mi·cel·li (vur'mə sel'ē, -chel'ē) *n.* pasta that is like thin spaghetti

ver·mil·ion (vər mil'yən) *n.* bright red

ver'min *n.* [*pl.* -MIN] 1. small, destructive animal, as a louse or rat 2. vile person

ver·mouth' (-mōōth') *n.* a fortified white wine

ver·nac'u·lar *a., n.* (of) the everyday speech of a country or place

ver'nal *a.* 1. of or in the spring 2. springlike

ver'sa·tile (-t'l) *a.* able to do many things well **—ver'sa·til'i·ty** *n.*

verse *n.* 1. poetry 2. stanza 3. short division of a Bible chapter

versed *a.* skilled

ver'si·fy *v.* [-FIED, -FYING] 1. write poetry 2. tell in verse **—ver'si·fi·ca'tion** *n.* **—ver'si·fi'er** *n.*

ver'sion *n.* 1. translation 2. account; report

ver'sus *prep.* 1. against 2. in contrast with

ver'te·bra *n.* [*pl.* -BRAE (-brē), -BRAS] any single bone of the spinal column

ver'te·brate *n., a.* (animal) having a spinal column

ver'tex *n.* [*pl.* -TEXES, -TICES (-tə sēz')] highest point; top

ver'ti·cal *n., a.* (line, plane, etc.) that is straight up and down

ver'ti·go *n.* dizzy feeling

verve *n.* vigor; enthusiasm

ver'y *a.* 1. complete; absolute 2. same 3. actual **—adv.** 1. extremely 2. truly

ves'i·cle *n.* small membranous cavity, sac, or cyst

ves'per *n.* [*also* V-] *usually pl.* evening prayer or service

ves'sel *n.* 1. container 2. ship or boat 3. tube of the body, as a vein

vest *n.* short, sleeveless garment, esp. one worn under a man's suit coat **—v.** 1. clothe 2. place (authority, etc.) in 3. put (a person) in control of, as power

ves'ti·bule (-byōōl) *n.* 1. small entrance hall 2. enclosed passage

ves'tige (-tij) *n.* a trace or mark, esp. of something gone **—ves·tig'i·al** *a.*

vest'ing *n.* retention by an employee of pension rights, etc., when changing jobs, etc.

vest'ment *n.* garment, esp. one for a clergyman

vest'pock'et *a.* very small

ves'try *n.* [*pl.* -TRIES] 1. church meeting room 2. lay church group with certain powers **—ves'try·man** [*pl.* -MEN] *n.*

vet *n.* 1. veterinarian 2. veteran

vetch *n.* plant grown for fodder

vet'er·an *a.* experienced **—n.** 1. former member of the armed forces 2. long-time employee, etc.

vet·er·i·nar'i·an n. doctor for animals

vet·er·i·nar'y a. of the medical care of animals —n. [pl. -IES] veterinarian

ve'to n. [pl. -TOES] 1. power, or right, to prohibit or reject 2. use of this —v. [-TOED, -TOING] use a veto on

vex v. annoy; disturb —**vex·a'tion** n. —**vex·a'tious** a.

vi·a (vī'ə, vē'ə) prep. by way of

vi'a·ble a. 1. able to exist 2. workable

vi'a·duct n. bridge held up by a series of towers

vi'al n. small bottle

vi'and n. 1. article of food 2. pl. fine food

vibes n.pl. 1. [Col.] vibraphone 2. [Sl.] one's (good or bad) emotional reaction

vi'brant a. 1. quivering 2. resonant 3. energetic —**vi'bran·cy** n.

vi'bra·phone n. an instrument like a marimba, with electrically operated valves

vi'brate v. 1. oscillate 2. move rapidly back and forth; quiver 3. resound 4. be emotionally stirred —**vi·bra'tion** n. —**vi'bra·tor** n.

vi·bra'to (-brä'-) n. [pl. -TOS] pulsating effect made by slight wavering of a tone

vic'ar n. 1. Anglican priest with a stipend 2. R.C.Ch. deputy of a bishop, etc.

vic'ar·age (-ij) n. vicar's residence

vi·car'i·ous (-ker'-) a. 1. felt by imagined participation 2.

taking another's place —**vi·car'i·ous·ly** adv.

vice n. 1. bad or evil conduct 2. bad or evil habit 3. prostitution 4. trivial fault

vice- pref. substitute or subordinate

vice'-pres'i·dent n. officer next in rank to a president

vice'roy n. deputy ruler for a sovereign

vi·ce ver'sa (vī'sē, vīs') the other way around

vi·cin'i·ty n. [pl. -TIES] 1. nearness 2. nearby area

vi·cious (vish'əs) a. 1. evil 2. unruly 3. malicious; spiteful —**vi'cious·ly** adv. —**vi'cious·ness** n.

vi·cis'si·tudes n.pl. unpredictable changes in life, fortune, etc.; ups and downs

vic'tim n. 1. one killed, hurt, etc. 2. one cheated, tricked, etc.

vic'tim·ize v. make a victim of

vic'tor n. winner or conqueror

vic·to'ri·ous a. having won a victory; conquering

vic'to·ry n. [pl. -RIES] success in war or any struggle

vict'uals (vit'lz) n.pl. [Dial. or Col.] food

vi·cu'na (-kōōn'yə, -ə) n. 1. S. American animal 2. its soft, shaggy wool

vid'e·o a. n. (of) television

video tape magnetic tape for recording TV programs

vie v. [VIED, VYING] compete (with) as in a contest

view (vyōō) n. 1. a looking 2. range of vision 3. mental survey 4. scene 5. opinion 6. aim;

goal —v. 1. look at or see 2. consider —**in view of** because of —**with a view to** with the purpose or hope of

view'er n. 1. one who views 2. device for looking at slides

view'point' n. mental position from which views are judged

vig'il n. 1. watchful staying awake 2. watch kept 3. eve of a religious festival

vig'i•lant (vij'-) a. watchful —**vig'i•lance** n.

vig'i•lan'te n. one of a group illegally organized to punish crime

vi•gnette' (vin yet') n. 1. short literary sketch 2. picture that shades off at the edges

vig'or n. active force; strength and energy —**vig'or•ous** a. —**vig'or•ous•ly** adv.

vik'ing n. [also V-] early Scandinavian pirate

vile a. 1. evil; wicked 2. disgusting 3. lowly or bad

vil'i•fy v. [-FIED, -FYING] defame or slander

vil'la n. country house or estate, esp. a large one

vil'lage n. small town —**vil'lag•er** n.

vil'lain (-lən) n. evil or wicked person —**vil'lain•ous** a.

vil'lain•y n. [pl. -IES] 1. evil 2. a villainous act

vim n. energy; vigor

vin'di•cate v. 1. clear from criticism, blame, etc. 2. justify —**vin'di•ca'tion** n.

vin•dic'tive a. 1. revengeful in spirit 2. done in revenge

vine n. 1. plant with a stem that grows along the ground or climbs a support 2. the stem of such a plant

vin'e•gar n. sour liquid made by fermenting cider, wine, etc. —**vin'e•gar•y** a.

vine'yard (vin'-) n. land where grapevines are grown

vin'tage (-tij) n. 1. wine of a certain region and year 2. earlier model —a. 1. of choice vintage 2. of a past period

vint'ner n. wine merchant

vi•nyl (vi'n'l) a. of a group of chemical compounds used in making plastics

vi•o'la (vē-, vī-) n. instrument like, but larger than, the violin —**vi•o'list** n.

vi'o•late v. 1. break (a law, etc.) 2. rape 3. desecrate 4. disturb —**vi'o•la'tion** n. —**vi'o•la'tor** n.

vi'o•lence n. 1. physical force used to injure 2. powerful force 3. violent act 4. harm done by violating rights

vi'o•lent a. 1. acting with or having great physical force 2. furious 3. intense

vi'o•let n. delicate spring flower, usually bluish-purple

vi'o•lin' n. four-stringed instrument played with a bow —**vi'o•lin'ist** n.

vi'o•lon•cel'lo n. [pl. -LOS] cello

vi'per n. 1. venomous snake 2. treacherous person

vi•ra'go n. [pl. -GOES, -GOS] shrewish woman

vi'ral (vi'rəl) a. involving or caused by a virus

vir'gin n. person, esp. a young woman, who has not had sexual intercourse —*a.* chaste, pure, untouched, etc. —**vir·gin′i·ty** *n.*

vir′gi·nal *a.* virgin

Vir·gin′ia creeper woodbine

Virginia reel American reel danced by couples facing in two lines

Vir′go 6th sign of the zodiac; Virgin

vir′ile *a.* 1. masculine 2. strong, vigorous, etc. —**vi·ril′i·ty** *n.*

vir′tu·al (-choo-) *a.* being so in effect if not in fact —**vir′tu·al·ly** *adv.*

vir′tue *n.* 1. moral excellence 2. good quality, esp. a moral one 3. chastity —**by** (*or* **in**) **virtue of** because of —**vir′tu·ous** *a.* —**vir′tu·ous·ly** *adv.*

vir·tu·o′so *n.* [*pl.* -sos] musician, etc. having great skill —**vir′tu·os′i·ty** *n.*

vir′u·lent *a.* 1. deadly 2. full of hate —**vir′u·lence** *n.*

vi′rus *n.* very small infective agent that causes disease

vi·sa (vē′zə) *n.* endorsement on a passport, granting entry into a country

vis·age (viz′ij) *n.* the face

vis-à-vis (vē′zə vē′) *a., adv.* face to face —*prep.* 1. opposite to 2. in relation to

vis·cer·a (vis′ər ə) *n.pl.* internal organs of the body —**vis′cer·al** *a.*

vis·cid (vis′id) *a.* viscous

vis′count (vī′-) *n.* nobleman above a baron —**vis′count·ess** *n.fem.*

vis′cous (-kəs) *a.* thick, syr-

upy, and sticky —**vis·cos′i·ty** *n.*

vise (vis) *n.* device with adjustable jaws for holding an object firmly

vis·i·bil′i·ty (viz′-) *n.* 1. a being visible 2. distance within which things can be seen

vis′i·ble *a.* that can be seen; evident —**vis′i·bly** *adv.*

vi·sion (vizh′ən) *n.* 1. power of seeing 2. something seen in a dream, trance, etc. 3. mental image 4. foresight

vi′sion·ar′y *a., n.* [*pl.* -IES] idealistic and impractical (person)

vis′it *v.* 1. go or come to see 2. stay with as a guest 3. afflict 4. [Col.] chat —*n.* a visiting —**vis′i·tor** *n.*

vis·it·a′tion *n.* 1. official visit as to inspect 2. punishment sent by God

vi′sor (-zər) *n.* 1. movable part of a helmet, covering the face 2. brim on a cap for shading the eyes

vis′ta *n.* view; scene

vis′u·al (vizh′oo-) *a.* 1. of or used in seeing 2. visible

vis′u·al·ize′ *v.* form a mental image of

vi′tal *a.* 1. of life 2. essential to life 3. fatal 4. very important 5. full of life —*n. pl.* 1. vital organs, as the heart, brain, etc. 2. essential parts —**vi′tal·ly** *adv.*

vi·tal′i·ty *n.* 1. energy; vigor 2. power to survive

vi′tal·ize *v.* give life *or* vigor to

vital signs pulse, respiration, and body temperature

vital statistics data on births, deaths, etc.

vi·ta·min *n.* any of certain substances vital to good health: some of the vitamins are: —**vitamin A**, found in carrots, eggs, etc. —**vitamin B (complex)** including vitamin B₁ (see **thiamine**), vitamin B₂ (see **riboflavin**), **nicotinic acid**, and vitamin B₁₂, vitamin used in treating anemia —**vitamin C**, found in citrus fruits —**vitamin D**, found esp. in fish-liver oils

vi·ti·ate (vish'ē-) *v.* corrupt; spoil —**vi·ti·a'tion** *n.*

vit're·ous *a.* of or like glass

vit'ri·fy *v.* [-FIED, -FYING] change into glass by heating

vit'ri·ol *n.* 1. sulfuric acid 2. metal sulfate 3. caustic speech, etc. —**vit'ri·ol'ic** *a.*

vi·tu'per·ate *v.* berate

vi·va'cious (-shas) *a.* spirited; lively —**vi·vac'i·ty** *n.*

viv'id *a.* 1. full of life 2. bright; intense 3. strong; active —**viv'id·ly** *adv.*

viv'i·fy *v.* [-FIED, -FYING] give life to

vi·vip'a·rous (vī-) *a.* bearing living young

viv'i·sec'tion *n.* surgery on living animals for medical research

vix'en *n.* 1. female fox 2. shrewish woman

vi·zier (vi zir') *n.* in Muslim countries, a high government official

vo·cab'u·lar'y *n.* [*pl.* -IES] all the words used by a person,

group, etc. or listed in a dictionary, etc.

vo'cal *a.* 1. of or by the voice 2. speaking freely —**vo'cal·ly** *adv.*

vocal cords membranes in the larynx that vibrate to make voice sounds

vo·cal'ic *a.* of or like a vowel or vowels

vo'cal·ist *n.* singer

vo'cal·ize *v.* speak or sing

vo·ca'tion *n.* one's profession, trade, or career —**vo·ca'tion·al** *a.*

vo·cif'er·ous (-sif'-) *a.* loud; clamorous

vo·cif'er·ate *v.* shout loudly

vod'ka *n.* colorless alcoholic liquor made from grain

vogue (vōg) *n.* 1. current fashion 2. popularity

voice *n.* 1. sound made through the mouth 2. ability to make such sound 3. sound like this 4. right to express one's opinion, etc. 5. expression —*v.* utter or express

void *a.* 1. empty; vacant 2. lacking 3. of no legal force —*n.* empty space —*v.* 1. to empty 2. cancel 3. defecate or urinate

voile (voil) *n.* thin fabric

vol'a·tile (-t'l) *a.* 1. quickly evaporating 2. changeable —**vol'a·til'i·ty** *n.*

vol·ca'no *n.* [*pl.* -NOES, -NOS] mountain formed by erupting molten rock —**vol·can'ic** *a.*

vo·li'tion *n.* act or power of using the will

vol'ley *n.* [*pl.* -LEYS] 1. discharge of a number of weapons together 2. return of a tennis

ball before it hits the ground
—*v.* **1.** to discharge as in a volley **2.** return (the ball) as a
volley

vol·ley·ball *n.* game between
teams hitting a large, light ball
back and forth over a net with
the hands

volt (vōlt) *n.* unit of electromotive force

volt·age (-ij) *n.* electromotive
force, shown in volts

vol·ta·ic (väl-, vōl-) *a.* of or
producing electricity by chemical action

vol·u·ble *a.* talkative

vol·ume *n.* **1.** a book **2.** cubic
measure **3.** amount **4.** loudness
of sound

vo·lu·mi·nous *a.* **1.** filling
volumes **2.** large; full

vol·un·tar·y *a.* **1.** by choice; of
one's own free will **2.** controlled by the will —**vol'un-
tar'i·ly** *adv.*

vol·un·teer' *v.* offer, give, etc.
of one's own free will —*n.* one
who volunteers

vo·lup'tu·ous *a.* sensual

vom'it *v., n.* (have) matter
from the stomach ejected
through the mouth

voo'doo *n.* [*pl.* -DOOS] primitive religion of the West Indies

vo·ra·cious (vô rā'shəs) *a.* **1.**
greedy **2.** very eager

vor'tex *n.* [*pl.* -TEXES, -TICES
(-tə sēz)] **1.** whirlpool **2.** whirlwind

vo'ta·ry *n.* [*pl.* -RIES] wor-
shiper; devotee

vote *n.* **1.** decision or choice
shown on a ballot, etc. **2.** all
the votes **3.** the right to vote
—*v.* **1.** cast a vote **2.** decide by
vote —**vot'er** *n.*

vo'tive *a.* given or done to fulfill a vow or promise

vouch *v.* give or be a guarantee, etc. (*for*)

vouch'er *n.* a paper serving as
proof of payment, etc.

vouch·safe' *v.* be kind enough
to grant

vow *v., n.* (make) a solemn
promise or statement

vow'el *n.* speech sound of the
letters *a, e, i, o, u*

voy'age *n., v.* journey by ship,
aircraft, etc.

vul'can·ize *v.* treat rubber to
make it stronger and more
elastic

vul'gar *a.* **1.** popular **2.** lacking
culture; crude **3.** vernacular **4.**
obscene —**vul'gar·ly** *adv.*

vul'gar·ism *n.* **1.** word or
phrase used widely but regarded as nonstandard or obscene **2.** vulgarity

vul·gar'i·ty *n.* **1.** vulgar state
or quality **2.** [*pl.* -TIES] vulgar
act, word usage, etc.

vul'ner·a·ble *a.* **1.** that can be
hurt, attacked, etc. **2.** easily
hurt; sensitive —**vul'ner·a·
bil'i·ty** *n.*

vul'ture (-chər) *n.* **1.** large bird
that lives chiefly on carrion **2.**
greedy, ruthless person

vul'va *n.* external female sex
organs

W

wab'ble *n., v.* wobble

wack'y *a.* [-IER, -IEST] [Sl.] erratic; irrational

wad *n.* 1. small, soft mass 2. small lump —*v.* [WADDED, WADDING] 1. roll into a wad 2. stuff as with padding

wad'ding *n.* any soft material used in padding, packing, etc.

wad'dle *v., n.* walk with short steps, swaying from side to side

wade *v.* 1. walk through water, mud, etc. 2. proceed with difficulty 3. cross by wading 4. [Col.] attack with vigor (with *in* or *into*)

wad'er *n.* 1. one who wades 2. *pl.* high, waterproof boots, often with trousers

wading bird long-legged shore bird that wades in shallows

wa'fer *n.* 1. thin, crisp cracker 2. dislike thing

waf'fle *n.* crisp cake baked between two flat, studded plates (**waffle iron**)

waft *v.* carry or move (sounds, odors, etc.) lightly over water or through the air —*n.* 1. odor, sound, etc. carried through the air 2. wafting motion

wag *v.* [WAGGED, WAGGING] move rapidly back and forth or up and down —*n.* 1. a wagging 2. a wit; comic

wage *v.* take part in —*n.* often *pl.* money paid for work done

wag'er *n., v.* bet

wag'gish *a.* 1. roguishly merry 2. said, done, etc. in jest

wag'gle *v.* wag abruptly

wag'on *n.* four-wheeled vehicle, esp. for hauling —**on** (or **off**) **the wagon** [Sl.] no longer (or once again) drinking alcoholic liquor

waif *n.* homeless child

wail *v.* make a loud, sad cry, as in grief —*n.* such a cry

wain'scot *n.* wall paneling of wood —*v.* panel with wood

waist *n.* 1. body part between the ribs and the hips 2. waistline 3. narrow part of any object that is wider at the ends

waist'band *n.* band fitting around the waist, as on slacks or a skirt

waist'coat (or wes'kət) *n.* [Br.] man's vest

waist'line *n.* line at the narrowest part of the waist

wait *v.* 1. remain (until something expected happens) 2. be ready 3. remain undone 4. serve food at a meal (with *at* or *on*) 5. await —*n.* act or time of waiting —**wait on** (or **upon**) 1. be a servant to 2. serve (a customer)

wait'er *n.* man who serves food at table —**wait'ress** *n. fem.*

wait'ing *a.* 1. that waits 2. of or for a wait —*n.* 1. act of one that waits 2. period of waiting

waiting list list of applicants, as for a vacancy

waiting room room where people wait, as in a bus station

waive *v.* **1.** give up, as a right **2.** postpone

waiv′er *n. Law* waiving of a right, claim, etc.

wake *v.* [WOKE or WAKED, WAKED, WAKING] **1.** come or bring out of a sleep **2.** become alert (*to*) **3.** stir up —*n.* **1.** all-night vigil over a corpse **2.** track or trail left behind

wake′ful *a.* **1.** watchful **2.** unable to sleep

wak′en *v.* to wake

wale *n.* **1.** welt **2.** ridge, as on corduroy

walk *v.* **1.** go on foot at moderate speed **2.** walk along, over, with, etc. —*n.* **1.** way of walking **2.** stroll; hike **3.** path for walking **4.** sphere of activity, occupation, etc. —**walk away** (or **off**) **with 1.** steal **2.** win easily —**walk′er** *n.*

walk′ie-talk′ie *n.* portable radio for sending and receiving

walking stick stick carried when walking; cane

walk′out *n.* labor strike

walk′up *n.* apartment house without an elevator

wall *n.* upright structure that encloses, divides, etc. —*v.* divide, or close up, with a wall

wal′la·by *n.* [*pl.* -BIES, -BY] small kangaroo

wall′board *n.* fibrous material in thin slabs for making or covering walls

wal′let *n.* flat case for carrying money, cards, etc.

wall′eye *n.* N. American freshwater food fish

wall′flow′er *n.* [Col.] shy or unpopular person

wal′lop *v.* [Col.] **1.** hit hard **2.** defeat completely —*n.* [Col.] hard blow

wal′low *v.* **1.** roll around in mud or filth, as pigs do **2.** indulge oneself fully (*in*)

wall′pa′per *v., n.* (apply) paper for covering walls or ceilings

wall′-to-wall′ *a.* **1.** covering a floor completely **2.** [Col.] all-inclusive

wal′nut *n.* **1.** tree bearing an edible nut in a hard shell **2.** its nut **3.** its wood

wal′rus *n.* large seallike animal with two tusks

waltz *n.* **1.** ballroom dance in 3/4 time **2.** music for this —*v.* dance a waltz

wam′pum (wäm′-) *n.* beads used as money by N. American Indians

wan (wän) *a.* **1.** sickly pale **2.** weak

wand *n.* slender rod, as one of supposed magic power

wan′der *v.* **1.** roam idly about **2.** go astray; stray **3.** meander —**wan′der·er** *n.*

wan′der·lust *n.* strong urge to wander or travel

wane *v.* **1.** get smaller, weaker, etc. **2.** approach the end —*n.* a waning

wan′gle *v.* [Col.] get by persuasion, tricky means, etc.

want *v.* **1.** wish for; desire **2.** need **3.** lack **4.** crave —*n.* **1.** lack; need **2.** poverty **3.** desire; craving

want ad [Col.] advertisement for something wanted

want'ing *a.* **1.** lacking **2.** inadequate *—prep.* minus

wan'ton *a.* **1.** sexually loose **2.** senseless, malicious, etc. **3.** recklessly ignoring justice, etc. *—n.* wanton person

wap·i·ti (wäp'ə tē) *n.* elk of N. America

war *n.* **1.** armed conflict, as between nations **2.** any fight *—v.* [WARRED, WARRING] **1.** carry on war **2.** contend; strive *—* **war'like** *a.*

war'ble *v.* sing with trills, runs, etc., as a bird *—n.* a warbling *—***war'bler** *n.*

ward *n.* **1.** one under the care of a guardian **2.** division of a hospital **3.** voting district of a city *—v.* turn aside; fend (*off*)

ward'en *n.* **1.** one who takes care of something **2.** head official of a prison

ward'er *n.* watchman; guard

ward'robe *n.* **1.** closet for clothes **2.** all one's clothes

ware *n.* **1.** *usually pl.* thing for sale **2.** pottery

ware'house *n.* building where goods are stored

war'fare *n.* war or any conflict

war'head *n.* front part of a bomb, etc., with the explosive

war'horse *n.* [Col.] veteran of many struggles

war'lock *n.* male equivalent of a witch

warm *a.* **1.** moderately hot **2.** that keeps body heat in **3.** enthusiastic **4.** kind and loving *—v.* make or become warm *—* **warm'ly** *adv.*

warm'blood'ed *a.* **1.** having a

relatively constant body temperature **2.** ardent

warm'heart'ed *a.* kind; loving

war'mon·ger (-muŋ'gər) *n.* one who tries to cause war

warmth *n.* **1.** a being warm **2.** strong feeling; ardor

warn *v.* **1.** tell of danger; advise to be careful **2.** inform; let know *—***warn'ing** *n., a.*

warp *v.* **1.** bend or twist out of shape **2.** distort *—n.* **1.** a warping or twist **2.** long threads in a loom

war'rant *n.* **1.** justification **2.** legal writ authorizing an arrest, search, etc. *—v.* **1.** authorize **2.** justify

warrant officer officer just above enlisted man

war'ran·ty *n.* [*pl.* -TIES] guarantee (*n.* 1)

war'ren *n.* area in which rabbits breed

war'ri·or *n.* soldier

war'ship *n.* ship for combat

wart *n.* small, hard growth on the skin *—***wart'y** *a.*

war·y (wer'ē) *a.* [-IER, -IEST] on guard; cautious *—*wary of careful of *—***war'i·ly** *adv.*

was pt. of **be**: used with *I* and *he, she,* or *it*

wash *v.* **1.** clean with water **2.** wash clothes **3.** flow over or against **4.** remove by washing **5.** coat thinly *—n.* **1.** a washing **2.** clothes washed, or to be washed **3.** rush of water **4.** eddy from propeller, oars, etc. *—a.* that can be washed *—* **wash'a·ble** *a.*

wash'-and-wear *a.* needing

little or no ironing after washing

wash'board *n.* ridged board to scrub clothes on

wash'bowl' *n.* bowl for washing the hands and face: also **wash'ba'sin**

wash'cloth *n.* small cloth to wash the face or body

washed'-up' *a.* 1. [Col.] tired 2. [Sl.] having failed

wash'er *n.* 1. machine for washing 2. flat ring used to make a bolt, nut, etc. fit tight 3. one who washes

wash'ing *n.* 1. act of one that washes 2. clothes, etc. to be washed

washing machine machine for washing clothes, etc.

wash'out' *n.* 1. washing away of soil, etc. by water 2. [Sl.] a failure

wash'room *n.* restroom

wash'stand *n.* plumbing fixture with a washbowl

wash'tub *n.* tub, often with faucets and a drain, to wash clothes, etc.

was'n't was not

wasp *n.* flying insect: some have a sharp sting

wasp'ish *a.* bad-tempered

was·sail (wäs'l) *n.* former toast in drinking healths

waste *v.* 1. use up needlessly 2. fail to take advantage of 3. wear away 4. lose strength or weaken 5. destroy —*a.* 1. barren or wild, as land 2. left over 3. excreted from the body —*n.* 1. a wasting 2. wasted matter; refuse, etc. 3. waste land —**go to waste** be wasted —**lay**

waste devastate —**waste'ful** *a.*

waste'bas'ket *n.* container for discarded paper, etc.

waste'pa'per *n.* paper thrown away after use

wast'rel (wāst'-) *n.* one who wastes; esp., a spendthrift

watch *n.* 1. act of guarding or observing 2. guard, or period of guard duty 3. small clock for wrist or pocket 4. *Naut.* period of duty, or crew on duty —*v.* 1. keep vigil 2. observe 3. guard or tend 4. be alert (for) —**watch out** be alert or careful —**watch'ful** *a.*

watch'band *n.* band for holding a watch on the wrist

watch'dog *n.* 1. dog kept to guard property 2. one that watches to prevent waste, etc.

watch'man *n.* [*pl.* -MEN] person hired to guard

watch'tow'er *n.* high tower from which a sentinel watches for enemies, etc.

watch'word *n.* slogan

wa'ter *n.* 1. colorless liquid of rivers, lakes, etc. 2. water solution 3. body secretion, as urine —*v.* 1. supply with water 2. dilute with water 3. fill with tears 4. secrete saliva —*a.* of, for, in, or by water

water buffalo oxlike work animal of S Asia

wa'ter·col'or *n.* 1. paint made by mixing pigment and water 2. a picture painted with such paints

wa'ter-cooled' *a.* cooled by circulating water

wa·ter·course *n.* river, brook, canal, etc.

wa·ter·craft *n.* [*pl.* -CRAFT] any water vehicle

wa·ter·cress *n.* water plant with leaves used in salads

wa·ter·fall *n.* steep fall of water, as from a cliff

wa·ter·fowl *n.* swimming bird

wa·ter·front *n.* land or docks at the edge of a river, harbor, etc.

wa·ter·lil'y *n.* [*pl.* -IES] water plant with large, showy flowers

wa·ter·logged' *a.* soaked or filled with water

wa·ter·mark *n.* 1. mark showing how high water has risen 2. design pressed into paper — *v.* mark (paper) with a watermark

wa·ter·mel'on *n.* large melon with juicy, red pulp

water moccasin large, poisonous snake of southeastern U.S.

wa·ter·proof *v., a.* (make) impervious to water

wa·ter·shed *n.* 1. area a river system drains 2. ridge between two such areas

wa·ter·ski' *v.* be towed over water on skilike boards

wa·ter·spout *n.* whirling water funnel rising from sea

water table level below which the ground is saturated with water

wa·ter·tight *a.* 1. so tight no water can get through 2. that cannot be refuted, etc.

water tower elevated tank for water storage, etc.

wa·ter·way *n.* navigable river, lake, canal, etc.

wa·ter·works *n.pl.* system of reservoirs, pumps, etc. supplying water to a city

wa·ter·y *a.* 1. of, like, or full of water 2. diluted

watt (wät) *n.* unit of electric power —**watt'age** *n.*

wat·tle (wät'-) *n.* 1. sticks woven with twigs 2. flap of skin hanging from the throat of a turkey, etc.

wave *v.* 1. move to and fro 2. wave the hand, etc., or signal thus 3. arrange in curves —*n.* 1. curving swell moving along on the ocean, etc. 2. wavelike vibration 3. curve, as in the hair 4. a waving, as of the hand —**wav'y** [-IER, -IEST] *a.*

wave'length *n.* distance between any point in a wave, as of light or sound, to the same point in the next wave

wa'ver *v.* 1. flutter, falter, flicker, etc. 2. show indecision —*n.* a wavering

wax *n.* 1. plastic substance secreted by bees 2. substance like this, as paraffin —*v.* 1. put polish or wax on 2. get larger, stronger, etc. 3. become —**wax'y** [-IER, -IEST], **wax'en** *a.*

wax bean bean with long, edible, yellow pods

wax (or waxed) paper paper made moisture-proof by a wax coating

wax'works *n.* exhibition of human figures made of wax

way *n.* 1. road or route 2. movement forward 3. method, manner, etc. 4. distance 5. direction 6. particular 7. wish;

will 8. *pl.* framework on which a ship is built —*adv.* [Col.] far —**by the way** incidentally —**by way of 1.** passing through 2. as a means of giving way 1. yield 2. break down —**under way** moving ahead

way'far'er (-fer'-) *n.* traveler, esp. on foot —**way'far'ing** *a., n.*

way·lay' *v.* [-LAID, -LAYING] ambush

way'-out' *a.* [Col.] very unusual or unconventional

ways and means methods of raising money

way'side' *n.* edge of a road

way'ward (-ward) *a.* 1. willful; disobedient 2. irregular —**way'ward·ness** *n.*

we *pron.* persons speaking or writing

weak *a.* lacking strength, power, etc.; not strong, effective, etc. —**weak'en** *v.*

weak'-kneed' *a.* cowardly; timid

weak'ling *n.* weak person

weak'ly *a.* [-LIER, -LIEST] sickly —*adv.* in a weak way

weak'ness *n.* 1. a being weak 2. fault 3. special liking

weal (wēl) *n.* 1. skin welt 2. welfare; well-being

wealth *n.* 1. riches 2. large amount —**wealth'y** [-IER, -IEST] *a.*

wean *v.* 1. stop suckling 2. withdraw (a person) from a certain habit, etc.

weap·on (wep'ən) *n.* 1. thing used for fighting 2. means of attack or defense

weap'on·ry *n.* weapons or their production

wear *v.* [WORE, WORN, WEARING] 1. have on the body as clothes 2. make or become damaged by use 3. hold up in use 4. tire or exhaust —*n.* 1. clothing 2. impairment

wear and tear (ter) loss and damage resulting from use

wea'ry *a.* [-RIER, -RIEST] 1. tired 2. bored —*v.* [-RIED, -RYING] make or become weary —**wea'ri·ness** *n.* —**wea'ri·some** *a.*

wea·sel (wē'z'l) *n.* small, flesh-eating mammal —*v.* [Col.] be evasive or misleading

weath'er (we*th*'-) *n.* 1. condition of the atmosphere as to temperature, humidity, etc. 2. storm, rain, etc. —*v.* 1. pass through safely 2. be exposed to sun, rain, etc.

weath'er-beat'en *a.* roughened, etc. by the weather

weath'er·man *n.* [*pl.* -MEN] weather forecaster

weath'er·proof *v., a.* (make) able to stand exposure to the weather

weath'er·strip *n.* strip of metal, felt, etc. for covering joints to keep out drafts, etc.: also **weath'er·strip'ping**

weather vane vane (sense 1)

weave *v.* [WOVE or WEAVED, WOVEN or WEAVED, WEAVING] 1. make (cloth) by interlacing (threads), as on a loom 2. twist or move from side to side or in and out —*n.* pattern of weaving

web *n.* 1. network, esp. one

spun by a spider 2. skin joining the toes of a duck, frog, etc. —v. [WEBBED, WEBBING] join by a web

web′bing n. strong fabric woven in strips

web′foot n. [pl. -FEET] foot with webbed toes —**web′foot′ed** a.

wed v. [WEDDED, WEDDED or WED, WEDDING] 1. marry 2. unite

we′d (wēd) 1. we had 2. we should 3. we would

wed′ding n. ceremony of marrying

wedge n. piece of wood, etc. tapering to a thin edge —v. 1. force apart or fix in place with a wedge 2. pack (in)

wed′lock n. matrimony

Wednes·day (wenz′dē, -dā) n. fourth day of the week

wee a. 1. very small; tiny 2. very early

weed n. unwanted plant, as in a lawn —v. 1. remove weeds 2. take (out) as useless, etc.

weeds n.pl. black clothes for mourning

weed′y a. [-IER, -IEST] 1. full of weeds 2. like a weed

week n. 1. period of seven days, esp. Sunday through Saturday 2. hours or days of work in this period

week′day n. any day of the week except Sunday and, often, Saturday

week′end′, week′-end′ n. Saturday and Sunday —v. spend the weekend

week′ly a. 1. lasting a week 2. done, etc. once a week —adv.

once a week —n. [pl. -LIES] periodical coming out once a week

weep v. [WEPT, WEEPING] 1. shed (tears) 2. mourn (for)

weep′ing n. act of one who weeps —a. 1. that weeps 2. having drooping branches

weep′y a. [-IER, -IEST] weeping or inclined to weep

wee′vil n. beetle whose larvae feed on grain, etc.

weft n. woof in weaving

weigh (wā) v. 1. determine the heaviness of, as on a scale 2. have a certain weight 3. consider well 4. burden (with down) 5. hoist (an anchor)

weight n. 1. quantity weighing a definite amount 2. heaviness 3. amount of heaviness 4. unit of heaviness 5. body used for its heaviness 6. burden 7. importance or influence —v. to burden; load down —**weight′y** [-IER, -IEST] a.

weight′less a. having little or no apparent weight

weight lifting athletic exercise or sport of lifting barbells

weir (wir) n. fencelike barrier in a stream, etc., for catching fish

weird (wird) a. 1. mysterious 2. bizarre

weird′o n. [pl. -OS] [Sl.] bizarre person or thing

wel′come a. 1. gladly received 2. freely permitted 3. under no obligation —n. a welcoming —v. greet or receive with pleasure

weld v. unite by melting together —n. welded joint

wel'fare *n.* health, happiness, and comfort —**on welfare** receiving government aid because of poverty, etc.

well *n.* 1. natural spring 2. hole dug in the earth to get water, oil, etc. 3. hollow shaft 4. source —*v.* gush or flow —*adv.* [BETTER, BEST] 1. in a pleasing, good, or right way 2. prosperously 3. much 4. thoroughly —*a.* in good health —*int.* exclamation of surprise, etc. —**as well (as)** 1. in addition (to) 2. equally (with)

we'll (wēl) 1. we shall 2. we will

well'-ap·point'ed *a.* excellently furnished

well'-be'ing *n.* welfare

well'-bred' *a.* showing good manners; courteous

well'-dis·posed' *a.* friendly or receptive

well'-done' *a.* 1. done with skill 2. thoroughly cooked

well'-fixed' *a.* [Col.] rich

well'-found'ed *a.* based on facts or good judgment

well'-ground'ed *a.* having a thorough basic knowledge of a subject

well'-heeled' *a.* [Sl.] rich

well'-in·formed' *a.* having extensive knowledge of a subject or many subjects

well'-known' *a.* famous or familiar

well'-man'nered *a.* polite

well'-mean'ing *a.* with good intentions —**well'-meant'** *a.*

well'-nigh' *adv.* almost

well'-off' *a.* 1. fortunate 2. prosperous

well'-read' *a.* having read much

well'spring *n.* 1. spring 2. continual source

well'-to-do' *a.* wealthy

well'-worn' *a.* much worn or used

Welsh *a., n.* (of) the people or language of Wales

welsh *v.* [Sl.] fail to pay a debt, etc. —**welsh'er** *n.*

Welsh rabbit (or **rarebit**) melted cheese on toast

welt *n.* 1. leather strip in the seam between shoe sole and upper 2. ridge raised on the skin by a blow

wel'ter *v.* wallow —*n.* confusion

wen *n.* benign skin tumor

wench *n.* young woman: derogatory or humorous

wend *v.* proceed or go on

went *pt.* of **go**

wept *pt.* & *pp.* of **weep**

were *pt.* of **be**, used with *you*, *we*, and *they*

we're (wir) we are

weren't were not

were·wolf (wir'woolf) *n.* [*pl.* -WOLVES] *Folklore* person changed into a wolf

west *n.* 1. direction in which sunset occurs 2. region in this direction 3. [W-] the Occident —*a., adv.* in, toward, or from the west —**west'er·ly** *a., adv.* —**west'ern** *a.* —**west'ern·er** *n.*

west'ward *adv., a.* toward the west: also **west'wards** *adv.*

wet *a.* [WETTER, WETTEST] 1. covered or soaked with water 2. rainy 3. not dry yet —*n.*

water, rain, etc. —v. [WET or WETTED, WETTING] make or become wet —all wet [Sl.] wrong

wet'back n. [Col.] Mexican who illegally enters the U.S.

wet blanket one who lessens the gaiety of others

wet suit close-fitting, rubber suit for skindivers

we've we have

whack v., n. [Col.] hit or slap with a sharp sound

whale n. huge, fishlike sea mammal —v. 1. hunt for whales 2. [Col.] beat

whale'bone n. horny substance from a whale's jaw

whal'er n. man or ship engaged in hunting whales

wham int. sound imitating a heavy blow —n. heavy blow or impact

wham'my n. [pl. -MIES] [Sl.] a jinx

wharf n. [pl. WHARVES, WHARFS] platform at which ships dock to load, etc.

what pron. 1. which thing, event, etc.? 2. that which —a. 1. which or which kind of 2. as much or as many as 3. how great! —adv. 1. how? 2. partly —int. exclamation of surprise, etc. —what for? why? —what if suppose

what·ev'er pron. 1. anything that 2. no matter what 3. what —a. 1. of any kind 2. no matter what

what'not n. set of open shelves, as for bric-a-brac

what'so·ev'er pron., a. whatever

wheal (hwēl) n. weal (sense 1)

wheat n. cereal grass with seed ground for flour, etc.

whee'dle v. coax

wheel n. 1. round disk turning on an axle 2. pl. [Sl.] automobile —v. 1. move on wheels 2. turn, revolve, etc.

wheel'bar'row n. single-wheeled cart with handles

wheel'base n. distance from front to rear axle

wheel'chair n. chair mounted on wheels, as for an invalid

wheeze v., n. (make) a whistling, breathy sound

whelk n. large sea snail with a spiral shell

whelp n. puppy or cub —v. give birth to whelps

when adv. at what time? —con. 1. at what time 2. at which time 3. at the time that 4. as soon as 5. although —pron. what or which time

whence adv. from where

when·ev'er adv. [Col.] when —con. at whatever time

where adv. 1. in or to what place? 2. in what way? 3. from what source? —con. 1. at what place 2. at which place 3. to the place that —pron. 1. what place 2. the place to which

where'a·bouts adv. at what place? —n. location

where·as' con. 1. because 2. while on the contrary

where·by' con. by which

where'fore adv. [Ar.] why? —con. therefore —n. the reason

where·in' con. in which

where·of *adv., con.* of what, which, or whom

where·on' *con.* on which

where·up·on' *con.* at or upon which

wher·ev'er *adv.* [Col.] where? —*con.* in, at, or to whatever place

where·with' *con.* with which

where·with·al *n.* necessary means, esp. money

whet *v.* [WHETTED, WHETTING] 1. sharpen, as by grinding 2. stimulate

wheth'er *con.* 1. if it is true or likely that 2. in either case that

whet'stone *n.* abrasive stone for sharpening knives

whew (hyōō) *int.* exclamation of relief, surprise, etc.

whey (hwā) *n.* watery part of curdled milk

which *pron.* 1. what one (or ones) of several? 2. the one or ones that 3. that —*a.* 1. what one or ones 2. whatever

which·ev'er *pron., a.* any one (of two or more); no matter which

whiff *n.* 1. light puff of air 2. slight odor

while *n.* period of time —*con.* 1. during the time that 2. although —*v.* spend (time) pleasantly

whi·lom (hwī'ləm) *a.* former

whim *n.* sudden notion

whim'per *v., n.* (make) a low, broken cry

whim'sy (-zē) *n.* [*pl.* -SIES] 1. whim 2. fanciful humor — **whim'si·cal** *a.*

whine *v., n.* (make) a long, high cry, as in complaining

whin'ny *v.* [-NIED, -NYING], *n.* [*pl.* -NIES] (make) a low, neighing sound

whip *v.* [WHIPPED, WHIPPING] 1. move suddenly 2. strike, as with a strap 3. beat (cream, etc.) into a froth 4. [Col.] defeat —*n.* 1. rod with a lash at one end 2. dessert of whipped cream, fruit, etc. —**whip up** 1. rouse (interest, etc.) 2. [Col.] prepare quickly

whip'cord *n.* strong worsted cloth with diagonal ribs

whip'lash *n.* severe jolting of the neck back and forth

whip'per·snap'per *n.* insignificant but impertinent person

whip'pet *n.* small, swift dog

whip'poor·will *n.* N. American bird active at night

whir, whirr *v.* [WHIRRED, WHIRRING] fly or revolve with a buzzing sound —*n.* this sound

whirl *v.* 1. move or spin rapidly 2. seem to spin —*n.* 1. a whirling 2. confused condition

whirl'i·gig (-gig) *n.* child's toy that whirls or spins

whirl'pool *n.* water in violent, whirling motion

whirl'wind *n.* air whirling violently and moving forward —*a.* speedy

whisk *v.* move, pull, etc. with a quick, sweeping motion —*n.* this motion

whisk broom small broom

whisk'er *n.* 1. *pl.* hair on a

man's face 2. long hair, as on a cat's upper lip

whis'key n. [pl. **-KEYS, -KIES**] strong liquor made from grain: also, esp. for Br. and Can. usage, **whis'ky** [pl. **-KIES**]

whis'per v. **1.** say very softly **2.** tell furtively, as in gossip — n. a whispering

whist n. card game like bridge

whis'tle v. **1.** make, or move with, a high, shrill sound **2.** blow a whistle —n. **1.** device for making whistling sounds **2.** a whistling

whistle stop small town

whit n. least bit; jot

white a. **1.** of the color of snow **2.** pale **3.** pure; innocent **4.** having light skin —n. **1.** color of pure snow **2.** a white thing, as egg albumen **3.** light-skinned person; Caucasoid — **white'ness** n.

white ant termite

white'cap n. wave with its crest broken into foam

white'-col'lar a. of office and professional workers

white elephant useless thing expensive to maintain

white'fish n. white lake fish of the salmon family

white flag white banner, a signal of truce or surrender

white goods household linens, as sheets, towels, etc.

white lead poisonous lead compound, used in paint

white lie lie about a trivial matter

whit'en v. make or become white

white'wall n. tire with a white band on the sidewall

white'wash n. mixture of lime, water, etc. as for whitening walls —v. **1.** cover with whitewash **2.** conceal the faults of

whith'er (hwith'-) adv. where?

whit'ing (hwīt'-) n. sea fish of the cod family

whit'ish a. somewhat white

whit'tle v. **1.** cut shavings from wood with a knife **2.** reduce gradually

whiz, whizz v. [WHIZZED, WHIZZING] **1.** make the hissing sound of a thing rushing through air **2.** speed by —n. **1.** whizzing sound **2.** [Sl.] expert

who pron. **1.** what person? **2.** which person **3.** that

whoa (hwō) int. stop!: command to a horse

who·ev'er pron. **1.** any person that **2.** no matter who

whole a. **1.** not broken, damaged, etc. **2.** complete **3.** not divided up **4.** healthy —n. **1.** entire amount **2.** thing complete in itself —**on the whole** in general —**whole'ness** n.

whole'heart'ed a. sincere

whole'sale n. sale of goods in large amounts, as to retailers —a. **1.** of such sale **2.** extensive —adv. **1.** at wholesale prices **2.** extensively —v. sell at wholesale —**whole'sal'er** n.

whole'some a. **1.** healthful **2.** improving mind or character **3.** having health or vigor — **whole'some·ness** n.

who'll 1. who shall **2.** who will

whol'ly *adv.* completely

whom *pron.* obj. case of **who**

whoop *v., n.* (utter) a loud shout, cry, etc.

whooping cough infectious disease, esp. of children

whop'per *n.* [Col.] 1. any large thing 2. big lie

whop'ping *a.* [Col.] very large or great

whore (hôr) *n.* prostitute

whorl (hwôrl, hwurl) *n.* design of circular ridges

who's 1. who is 2. who has

whose *pron.* that or those belonging to whom —*a.* of whom or of which

who'so·ev'er *pron.* whoever

why *adv.* for what reason or purpose? —*con.* 1. because of which 2. reason for which —*n.* [*pl.* WHYS] the reason —*int.* exclamation of surprise, etc.

wick *n.* piece of cord, etc. for burning, as in a candle

wick'ed *a.* 1. evil 2. unpleasant 3. mischievous 4. [Sl.] showing great skill

wick'er *n.* 1. long, thin twigs or strips 2. wickerwork —*a.* made of wicker

wick'er·work *n.* baskets, etc. made of wicker

wick'et *n.* 1. small door, gate, or window 2. wire arch used in croquet

wide *a.* 1. great in width, amount, degree, etc. 2. of a specified width 3. far from the goal —*adv.* 1. over or to a large extent 2. so as to miss what is aimed at; astray — **wide'ly** *adv.*

wide'-a·wake' *a.* 1. completely awake 2. alert

wide'-eyed' *a.* with the eyes opened wide, as in surprise

wid'en *v.* make or become wider

wide'spread' *a.* occurring over a wide area

wid'ow *n.* woman whose husband has died —*v.* make a widow of —**wid'ow·hood** *n.*

wid'ow·er *n.* man whose wife has died

width *n.* 1. distance from side to side 2. piece of a certain width

wield (wēld) *v.* 1. handle with skill 2. use (power, etc.)

wie'ner (wē'-) *n.* frankfurter

wife *n.* [*pl.* WIVES] married woman —**wife'ly** *a.*

wig *n.* false covering of hair for the head

wig'gle *v., n.* twist and turn from side to side —**wig'gly** [-GLIER, -GLIEST] *a.*

wig'wag *v.* [-WAGGED, -WAGGING] 1. wag 2. send messages by visible code

wig'wam *n.* cone-shaped tent of N. American Indians

wild *a.* 1. in its natural state 2. not civilized 3. unruly 4. stormy 5. enthusiastic 6. reckless 7. missing the target — *adv.* in a wild way —*n.* *usually pl.* wilderness

wild'cat *n.* 1. fierce animal of the cat family 2. fierce, aggressive person —*a.* 1. risky 2. unauthorized —*v.* [-CATTED, -CATTING] drill for oil in an area formerly unproductive

wil'der·ness *n.* wild region

wild'-eyed' *a.* 1. staring wildly 2. very foolish

wild'fire *n.* rapidly spreading fire, hard to put out

wild'fowl *n.* wild bird, esp. a game bird: also **wild fowl**

wild'-goose' chase futile pursuit, search, or endeavor

wild'life *n.* wild animals

wild rice 1. aquatic grass 2. its edible grain

wile *n.* sly or beguiling trick —*v.* beguile; lure

will *n.* 1. wish; desire 2. strong purpose 3. power of choice 4. attitude 5. legal document disposing of one's property after death —*v.* 1. decide 2. control by the will 3. bequeath —**at will** when one wishes

will *v.* [pt. WOULD] helping verb showing: 1. futurity 2. determination or obligation 3. willingness 4. ability or capacity

will'ful *a.* 1. done deliberately 2. stubborn Also sp. **wil'ful** —**will'ful·ly** *adv.* —**will'ful·ness** *n.*

will'ing *a.* 1. consenting 2. doing or done gladly —**will'ing·ly** *adv.* —**will'ing·ness** *n.*

will'-o'-the-wisp' *n.* anything elusive

wil'low *n.* tree with narrow leaves

wil'low·y *a.* slender

will'pow'er *n.* self-control

wil'ly-nil'ly *adv.* (happening) whether one wishes it or not

wilt *v.* 1. make or become limp 2. make or become weak

wi'ly *a.* [-LIER, -LIEST] crafty; sly —**wi'li·ness** *n.*

win *v.* [WON, WINNING] 1. gain a victory 2. get by work, effort, etc. 3. persuade —*n.* [Col.] victory

wince *v.* shrink or draw back slightly —*n.* a wincing

winch *n.* machine for hoisting by a chain wound on a drum

wind (wīnd) *v.* [WOUND, WINDING] 1. turn, coil, or twine around 2. cover, or tighten, by winding 3. move or go indirectly —*n.* a turn —**wind up** 1. finish; settle 2. make very tense

wind (wind) *n.* 1. air in motion 2. gales 3. breath 4. smell —*v.* put out of breath —**get wind of** hear of —**in the wind** happening or about to happen

wind'break *n.* fence, trees, etc. protecting a place from the wind

wind'ed *a.* out of breath

wind'fall *n.* unexpected gain, as of money

wind instrument *Mus.* instrument played by blowing air, esp. breath, through it

wind'lass (-ləs) *n.* winch

wind'mill *n.* machine operated by the wind's rotation of a wheel of vanes

win'dow *n.* 1. opening for light and air in a building, car, etc. 2. windowpane

win'dow-pane *n.* pane of glass in a window

win'dow-shop' *v.* [-SHOPPED, -SHOPPING] look at goods in store windows without buying

win'dow·sill n. sill of a window

wind'pipe n. trachea

wind'shield n. in cars, etc., glass shield in the front

wind'up (wīnd'-) n. **1.** end **2.** *Baseball* swinging of the arm before pitching

wind'ward a., adv., n. (in or toward) the direction from which the wind blows

wind'y a. [-IER, -IEST] **1.** with much wind **2.** talky

wine n. fermented juice of grapes or of other fruits —v. entertain with wine

wing n. **1.** organ used by a bird, insect, etc. in flying **2.** thing like a wing in use or position **3.** political faction —v. **1.** to fly **2.** send swiftly **—on the wing** in flight **—take wing** fly away **—under one's wing** under one's protection, etc. **—winged** a. **—wing'less** a.

wing'span n. distance between tips of an airplane's wings

wing'spread n. **1.** distance between tips of fully spread wings **2.** wingspan

wink v. **1.** close and open the eyelids quickly **2.** do this with one eye, as a signal **3.** twinkle —n. **1.** a winking **2.** an instant **—wink at** pretend not to see

win'ner n. one that wins

win'ning a. **1.** victorious **2.** charming —n. **1.** a victory **2.** pl. something won

win'now (-ō) v. **1.** blow the chaff from grain **2.** sort out

win·o (wīn'ō) n. [pl. -os] [Sl.] alcoholic who drinks cheap wine

win'some (-səm) a. charming

win'ter n. **1.** coldest season of the year **2.** period of decline, etc. —a. of or for winter —v. spend the winter

win'ter·green n. **1.** evergreen plant **2.** oil made from its leaves, used for flavoring

win'ter·ize v. put into condition for winter

win·try (win'trē) a. [-TRIER, -TRIEST] of or like winter

wipe v. **1.** clean or dry by rubbing **2.** rub (a cloth, etc.) over something —n. a wiping **—wipe out 1.** remove **2.** kill **3.** destroy **—wip'er** n.

wire n. **1.** metal drawn into a long thread **2.** telegraph or telegram **3.** finish line of a race —a. made of wire —v. **1.** furnish or fasten with a wire or wires **2.** telegraph

wire'hair n. fox terrier with a wiry coat: also **wire-haired terrier**

wire'less a. operating by electric waves, not with conducting wire —n. **1.** wireless telegraph or telephone **2.** [Chiefly Br.] radio

wire service agency sending news stories by telegraph to newspapers, etc.

wire'tap v. [-TAPPED, -TAPPING] tap (telephone wire) to get information secretly —n. device for wiretapping

wir'ing n. system of wires, as for carrying electricity

wir'y a. [-IER, -IEST] **1.** like

wire; stiff **2.** lean and strong —
wir′i·ness *n.*

wis′dom *n.* **1.** a being wise; good judgment **2.** knowledge

wisdom tooth back tooth on each side of each jaw

wise *a.* **1.** having good judgment **2.** informed or learned **3.** shrewd **4.** [Sl.] insolent, fresh, etc. —*n.* manner; way — **wise′ly** *adv.*

-wise *suf.* **1.** in a certain direction, position, or manner **2.** with regard to

wise′a′cre *n.* one pretending to be wiser than he or she is

wise′crack *v., n.* [Sl.] (make) a flippant remark

wish *v.* **1.** to want; desire **2.** express a desire concerning **3.** request —*n.* **1.** a wishing **2.** something wished for **3.** request

wish′bone *n.* forked bone in front of a bird's breastbone

wish′ful *a.* showing a wish

wish′y-wash′y *a.* [Col.] **1.** weak **2.** showing indecision

wisp *n.* **1.** slight thing or bit **2.** something delicate, frail, etc. — **wisp′y** [-IER, -IEST] *a.*

wis·te′ri·a *n.* twining vine with clusters of flowers

wist′ful *a.* expressing vague yearnings —**wist′ful·ly** *adv.*

wit *n.* **1.** the ability to make clever remarks **2.** one having this ability **3.** good sense **4.** *pl.* powers of thinking —**to wit** namely

witch *n.* woman supposed to have evil, magic power

witch′craft *n.* power or practices of witches

witch doctor one practicing primitive medicine involving magic

witch′er·y *n.* **1.** witchcraft **2.** bewitching charm

witch hazel lotion made from a plant extract

with *prep.* **1.** against **2.** near to; in the care or company of **3.** into **4.** as a member of **5.** concerning **6.** compared to **7.** as well as **8.** in the opinion of **9.** as a result of **10.** by means of **11.** having or showing **12.** to; onto **13.** from **14.** after

with·draw′ (-drô′) *v.* [-DREW, -DRAWN, -DRAWING] **1.** take back **2.** move back **3.** remove oneself *(from)* —**with·draw′al** *n.*

with·drawn′ *a.* shy, reserved, etc.

with′er (with′-) *v.* **1.** wilt **2.** make or become weakened or decayed **3.** make feel embarrassed

with′ers (with′-) *n.pl.* highest part of a horse's back

with·hold′ *v.* [-HELD, -HOLDING] **1.** keep back; restrain **2.** refrain from granting **3.** deduct from wages

with·in′ *adv.* in or to the inside —*prep.* **1.** inside **2.** not beyond —*n.* the inside

with·out′ *adv.* on the outside —*prep.* **1.** outside **2.** lacking **3.** avoiding

with·stand′ *v.* [-STOOD, -STANDING] resist; endure

wit′less *a.* stupid; foolish

wit′ness *n.* **1.** one who saw and can testify to a thing **2.** testimony **3.** attesting signer

—v. 1. see 2. act as a witness of 3. be proof of 4. be present at —**bear witness** testify

wit'ti·cism n. witty remark

wit'ty a. [-TIER, -TIEST] cleverly amusing

wives n. pl. of **wife**

wiz'ard n. 1. magician 2. [Col.] one very skilled

wiz'ard·ry n. magic

wiz'ened a. dried up and wrinkled

wob'ble v. 1. move unsteadily from side to side 2. vacillate — n. a wobbling —**wob'bly** a.

woe n. grief or trouble

woe'be·gone a. showing woe

woe'ful a. 1. sad 2. causing woe 3. pitiful —**woe'ful·ly** adv.

wok (wäk) n. bowl-shaped cooking pan for frying, etc.

woke pt. of **wake**

wolf n. [pl. WOLVES] 1. wild, doglike animal 2. cruel or greedy person —v. eat greedily —**cry wolf** give a false alarm —**wolf'ish** a.

wolf'hound n. breed of large dog

wol·ver·ine' (-ēn') n. stocky, flesh-eating animal

wom'an n. [pl. WOMEN] adult female person

wom'an·hood n. 1. time of being a woman 2. womanly qualities 3. women collectively

wom'an·ish a. like a woman

wom'an·kind n. women in general

wom'an·ly a. 1. womanish 2. of, like, or fit for a woman

womb (wōōm) n. uterus

wom'bat (wäm'-) n. burrowing marsupial like a small bear

wom'en·folk (-fōk) n.pl. [Col.] women

won pt. of **win**

won'der n. 1. amazing thing; marvel 2. feeling caused by this —v. 1. feel wonder 2. be curious or doubtful about

won'der·ful a. 1. causing wonder 2. [Col.] excellent

won'der·land n. imaginary land full of wonders

won'der·ment n. amazement

won'drous a. wonderful — adv. surprisingly Now literary

wont (wônt, wônt) a. accustomed (to) —n. habit

won't will not

wont'ed a. customary; accustomed

woo v. seek to win, esp. as one's spouse

wood n. 1. hard substance under a tree's bark 2. lumber 3. often pl. forest —a. 1. of wood; wooden 2. of the woods —**out of the woods** [Col.] out of difficulty, danger, etc. — **wood'ed** a.

wood alcohol poisonous alcohol used as fuel, etc.

wood'bine n. climbing vine with blue berries

wood'chuck n. N. American burrowing animal

wood'cut n. print made from a wood engraving

wood'en a. 1. made of wood 2. lifeless, dull, etc.

wood'land n., a. forest

wood'peck'er n. bird that pecks holes in bark

wood'wind a., n. (of) any of

the wind instruments, as the clarinet, oboe, flute, etc.

wood'work n. wooden doors, frames, moldings, etc.

wood'work'ing n. art or work of making things of wood

wood'y a. [-IER, -IEST] 1. tree-covered 2. of or like wood

woof (woof) n. threads woven across the warp in a loom

woof'er n. large loudspeaker for reproducing low-frequency sounds

wool n. 1. soft, curly hair of sheep, goats, etc. 2. yarn or cloth made of this

wool'en, wool'len a. of wool —n. pl. woolen goods

wool'gath'er·ing n. daydreaming

wool'ly a. [-LIER, -LIEST] 1. of, like, or covered with wool 2. rough and uncivilized 3. confused Also sp. **wooly**

wooz·y (wōōz'ē) a. [-IER, -IEST] [Col.] dizzy, as from drink

word n. 1. a sound or sounds as a speech unit 2. letter or letters standing for this 3. brief remark 4. news 5. promise 6. password 7. command 8. pl. speech 9. pl. lyrics 10. pl. quarrel —v. express in words —**in a word** briefly

word'ing n. choice and arrangement of words

word'y a. [-IER, -IEST] using too many words —**word'i·ness** n.

wore pt. of **wear**

work n. 1. effort of doing or making; labor 2. occupation, trade, etc. 3. task; duty 4. thing made, done, etc. 5. pl.

factory 6. workmanship —v. [alt. pt. & pp. WROUGHT] 1. do work; toil 2. function 3. cause to work 4. be employed 5. bring about 6. come or bring to some condition 7. solve (a problem) 8. make (one's way) by effort —**at work** working —**the works** 1. working parts (of) 2. [Col.] everything: also **the whole works** —**work off** get rid of —**work on** 1. influence 2. try to persuade —**work out** 1. develop 2. result 3. have a workout —**work up** 1. advance 2. develop 3. excite —**work'er** n.

work'a·ble a. practicable

work'a·day a. ordinary

work'book n. book of exercises for students

work'day n. day or part of a day during which work is done

work'horse n. steady, responsible worker

work'house n. prison where petty offenders are made to work

work'ing a. 1. that works 2. of or used in work 3. enough to get work done

work'ing·man n. [pl. -MEN] worker, esp. in industry; laborer —**work'ing·wom'an** [pl. -WOMEN] n.

work'man n. [pl. -MEN] 1. workingman 2. craftsman

work'man·like a. done well

work'man·ship n. worker's skill, or the quality of work shown

work'out n. strenuous exercise, practice, etc.

work'shop n. room or building where work is done

world n. 1. the earth 2. the universe 3. people generally 4. [also **W-**] some part of the earth 5. any sphere or domain 6. individual outlook 7. secular life 8. often pl. large amount

world'ly a. [-LIER, -LIEST] 1. secular 2. devoted to the pleasures, etc. of this world 3. worldly-wise

world'ly-wise' a. wise in the ways of the world

worm n. 1. long, slender creeping animal 2. thing like a worm 3. pl. disease caused by worms —v. 1. move like a worm 2. get in a sneaky way —**worm'y** a.

worm'wood n. bitter herb

worn pp. of wear

worn'-out' a. 1. no longer usable 2. very tired

wor'ri·some a. 1. causing worry 2. tending to worry

wor'ry v. [-RIED, -RYING] 1. make, or be, troubled or uneasy 2. annoy 3. shake with the teeth —n. [pl. -RIES] 1. troubled feeling 2. cause of this —**wor'ri·er** n.

wor'ry·wart n. one who worries too much

worse a. 1. more evil, bad, etc. 2. inferior 3. more ill 4. less satisfactory —adv. in a worse way —n. that which is worse —**worse off** in worse circumstances

wors'en v. make or become worse

wor'ship n. 1. prayer, service, etc. in reverence to a deity 2. intense love or admiration —v. 1. show reverence for 2. admire greatly 3. take part in worship service

worst a. 1. most evil, bad, etc. 2. of the lowest quality —adv. in the worst way —n. that which is worst —**(in) the worst way** [Sl.] very much

wor·sted (woos'tid) n. wool fabric with a smooth surface

worth n. 1. value or merit 2. equivalent in money 3. quantity for a given sum —a. 1. deserving 2. equal in value to —**worth'less** a.

worth'-while' a. worth the time or effort spent

wor'thy a. [-THIER, -THIEST] 1. having worth or value 2. deserving —n. worthy person —**wor'thi·ness** n.

would (wood) pt. of will: used to express futurity, a wish, a request, etc.

would'-be' a. wishing, pretending, or meant to be

wound (wōond) n. 1. injury to body tissue 2. injury to the feelings, etc. —v. injure; hurt

wound (wound) pt. & pp. of wind (turn)

wove pt. of weave

wo'ven pp. of weave

wow int. expression of surprise, pleasure, etc.

wrack (rak) n. destruction

wraith (rāth) n. ghost

wran'gle (raŋ'-) v., n. quarrel; dispute

wran'gler n. cowboy who herds livestock —**wran'gle** v.

wrap v. [WRAPPED or WRAPT, WRAPPING] 1. wind or fold (a

covering) around 2. enclose in paper, etc. —*n.* 1. outer garment 2. *pl.* secrecy —**wrapped up in** absorbed in —**wrap up** [Col.] conclude

wrap'per *n.* 1. that in which something is wrapped; covering 2. woman's dressing gown

wrap'ping *n.* often *pl.* material for wrapping something

wrap'-up' *n.* [Col.] concluding, summarizing report

wrath *n.* great anger; rage —**wrath'ful** *a.*

wreak (rēk) *v.* 1. to inflict (vengeance, etc.) 2. to give vent to (anger, etc.)

wreath (rēth) *n.* [*pl.* WREATHS (rē*th*z)] twisted ring of leaves, etc.

wreathe (rē*th*) *v.* 1. encircle 2. decorate with wreaths

wreck *n.* 1. remains of a thing destroyed 2. run-down person 3. a wrecking —*v.* 1. destroy or ruin 2. dismantle; tear down —**wreck'age** (-ij) —**wreck'er** *n.*

wren *n.* small songbird

wrench *n.* 1. sudden, sharp twist 2. injury caused by a twist 3. tool for turning nuts, bolts, etc. —*v.* 1. twist or jerk sharply 2. injure with a twist 3. distort

wrest *v.* take by force

wres'tle *v.* 1. struggle with (an opponent) trying to throw him 2. contend (*with*) —*n.* struggle —**wres'tler** *n.* —**wres'tling** *n.*

wretch *n.* 1. very unhappy person 2. person despised

wretch'ed *a.* 1. very unhappy

2. distressing 3. poor in quality 4. despicable

wrig'gle *v.* twist and turn, or move along thus —*n.* a wriggling —**wrig'gler** *n.*

wring *v.* [WRUNG, WRINGING] 1. squeeze and twist 2. force out by this means 3. get by force —**wring'er** *n.*

wrin'kle *n.* 1. small crease or fold 2. [Col.] clever idea —*v.* form wrinkles (in)

wrist *n.* joint between the hand and forearm

writ *n.* formal court order

write *v.* [WROTE, WRITTEN, WRITING] 1. form (words, letters, etc.) 2. produce (writing or music) 3. write a letter —**write off** cancel, as a debt —**writ'er** *n.*

writhe (rī*th*) *v.* twist and turn, as in pain

wrong *a.* 1. not right or just 2. not true or correct 3. not suitable 4. mistaken 5. out of order 6. not meant to be seen —*adv.* incorrectly —*n.* something wrong —*v.* treat unjustly

wrong'do'ing *n.* unlawful or bad behavior —**wrong'do'er** *n.*

wrong'ful *a.* unjust, unlawful, etc. —**wrong'ful·ly** *adv.*

wrong'head'ed *a.* stubborn

wroth (rôth) *a.* angry

wrought (rôt) *a.* 1. made 2. shaped by hammering

wrought iron tough, malleable iron used for fences, etc. —**wrought'-i'ron** *a.*

wrought'-up' *a.* excited

wrung *pt.* & *pp.* of **wring**

wry *a.* [WRIER, WRIEST] 1.

twisted or distorted **2.** ironic —
wry'ly *adv.* —**wry'ness** *n.*

wy'vern *n. Heraldry* two-legged dragon with wings

X

Xe'rox (zï'-) *trademark for a* process of copying printed material electrically —*v.* reproduce by this process

Xmas *n.* Christmas

X'-ray *n.* **1.** ray that can penetrate solid matter **2.** photograph made with X-rays —*a.*
of, by, or having to do with X-rays —*v.* examine, treat, or photograph with X-rays Also **X ray, x-ray, x ray**

xy'lem (zï'-) *n.* woody plant tissue

xy'lo·phone (zï'-) *n.* musical instrument of a row of wooden bars struck with hammers

Y

-y *suf.* **1.** full of or like **2.** rather **3.** apt to **4.** state of being **5.** act of

yacht (yät) *n.* small ship —*v.* sail in a yacht —**yachts'man** [*pl.* **-MEN**] *n.*

yak *v.* [YAKKED, YAKKING] [Sl.] talk much or idly —*n.* **1.** [Sl.] a yakking **2.** [Sl.] a laugh **3.** wild ox of Asia

yam *n.* **1.** starchy, edible root of a tropical plant **2.** [South] large sweet potato

yam'mer *v.* whine or complain

yank *v., n.* [Col.] jerk

Yan'kee *n.* **1.** U.S. citizen **2.** native of a northern State

yap *v.* [YAPPED, YAPPING] **1.** make a sharp, shrill bark **2.** [Sl.] talk noisily and stupidly —*n.* **1.** sharp, shrill bark **2.** [Sl.] jabber **3.** [Sl.] the mouth

yard *n.* **1.** measure of length, three feet **2.** ground around a building **3.** enclosed place **4.** slender spar

yard'age *n.* distance or length in yards

yard'stick *n.* **1.** measuring stick one yard long **2.** standard for judging

yarn *n.* **1.** spun strand of wool, cotton, etc. **2.** [Col.] tale or story

yaw *v., n.* turn from the course, as of a ship

yawl *n.* kind of sailboat

yawn *v.* open the mouth widely, as when one is sleepy —*n.* a yawning

yaws *n.pl.* tropical, infectious skin disease

ye (yē) *pron.* [Ar.] you —*a.* (*tha*) [Ar.] the

yea (yā) *adv.* **1.** yes **2.** truly —*n.* vote of "yes"

yeah (ya, ye) *adv.* [Col.] yes

year *n.* **1.** period of 365 days (366 in leap year) or 12 months **2.** *pl.* age **3.** *pl.* a long time

year'book *n.* book with data of the preceding year

year′ling *n.* animal in its second year

year′ly *a.* 1. every year 2. of a year —*adv.* every year

yearn (yurn) *v.* feel longing — **yearn′ing** *n.*

year′-round′ *a.* open or in use throughout the year

yeast (yēst) *n.* 1. moist mass of fungi that causes fermentation 2. yeast dried and pressed into cakes —**yeast′y** *a.*

yell *v., n.* scream; shout

yel′low *a.* 1. of the color of ripe lemons 2. [Col.] cowardly 3. sensational —*n.* yellow color —*v.* make or become yellow — **yel′low·ish** *a.*

yellow fever tropical disease carried by a mosquito

yellow jacket bright-yellow wasp or hornet

yelp *v., n.* (utter) a short, sharp cry or bark

yen *n.* 1. [Col.] deep longing 2. monetary unit of Japan

yeo′man (yō′-) *n.* [*pl.* -MEN] 1. U.S. Navy clerk 2. [Br.] small-farm owner

yes *adv.* 1. it is so 2. not only that, but more —*n.* [*pl.* YESES] 1. consent 2. affirmative vote

yes man [Sl.] one who always approves what his superior says

yes′ter·day *n.* 1. day before today 2. recent time —*adv.* on the day before today

yet *adv.* 1. up to now 2. now 3. still 4. nevertheless —*con.* nevertheless

yew *n.* evergreen tree

Yid′dish *n.* German dialect using the Hebrew alphabet

yield (yēld) *v.* 1. produce; give 2. surrender 3. concede; grant 4. give way to force —*n.* amount produced

yield′ing *a.* flexible; submissive

yip *n., v.* [YIPPED, YIPPING] [Col.] yelp or bark

yo′del *v.* sing with abrupt, alternating changes to the falsetto —*n.* a yodeling

yo′ga *n.* Hindu discipline for uniting self with supreme spirit through various exercises

yo′gi (-gē) *n.* [*pl.* -GIS] one who practices yoga

yo′gurt, yo′ghurt (-gərt) *n.* thick, semisolid food made from fermented milk

yoke *n.* 1. frame for harnessing together a pair of oxen, etc. 2. thing that binds or unites 3. servitude 4. part of a garment at the shoulders —*v.* 1. harness to 2. join together

yo′kel *n.* person from the country: contemptuous term

yolk (yōk) *n.* yellow part of an egg

Yom Kip·pur (yäm kip′ər) Jewish holiday and day of fasting

yon *a., adv.* [Ar.] yonder

yon′der *a., adv.* over there

yore *adv.* [Obs.] long ago

you *pron.* 1. the person or persons spoken to 2. a person or people generally

you'd 1. you had 2. you would

you'll 1. you will 2. you shall

young *a.* 1. in an early stage of life or growth 2. fresh —*n.* young offspring —**with young** pregnant —**young′ish** *a.*

young′ster *n.* child

your *a.* of you

you're you are

yours *pron.* that or those belonging to you

your·self′ *pron.* [*pl.* -SELVES] intensive or reflexive form of **you**

yours truly [Col.] I or me

youth *n.* **1.** state or quality of being young **2.** adolescence **3.** young people **4.** young man

youth′ful *a.* **1.** young **2.** of or fit for youth **3.** fresh **4.** new; early

you've you have

yowl *v.*, *n.* howl; wail

yo′-yo′ *n.* [*pl.* -YOS] spoollike toy reeled up and let down by a string

yuc′ca *n.* lilylike plant

yule *n.* Christmas

yule′tide *n.* Christmas time

yum′my *a.* [-MIER, -MIEST] [Col.] very tasty; delicious

Z

za′ny *a.* [-NIER, -NIEST] of or like foolish or comical person —*n.* [*pl.* -NIES] such a person —**za′ni·ness** *n.*

zap *v.* [ZAPPED, ZAPPING] [Sl.] move, strike, kill, etc. with sudden speed —*n.* [Sl.] pep

zeal *n.* intense enthusiasm

zeal′ot (zel′-) *n.* one showing zeal, esp. fanatic zeal

zeal′ous (zel′-) *a.* full of zeal —**zeal′ous·ly** *adv.*

ze′bra *n.* striped African animal related to the horse

ze·bu (zē′byōō) *n.* oxlike animal with a hump

ze′nith *n.* **1.** point in the sky directly overhead **2.** highest point

zeph·yr (zef′ər) *n.* breeze

zep′pe·lin *n.* rigid airship

ze′ro *n.* [*pl.* -ROS, -ROES] **1.** the symbol 0 **2.** point marked 0 in a scale **3.** nothing —*a.* of or at zero —**zero in on** concentrate on

zero hour 1. the time an attack is to begin **2.** crucial point

zero population growth condition in which the birth rate equals the death rate

ze′ro-sum′ *a.* of a situation in which a gain for one means a loss for another

zest *n.* **1.** stimulating quality **2.** keen enjoyment —**zest′ful** *a.*

zig′zag *n.* line with sharp turns back and forth —*a.*, *adv.* in a zigzag —*v.* [-ZAGGED, -ZAGGING] to move or form in a zigzag

zilch *n.* [Sl.] nothing; zero

zil′lion *n.* [Col.] very large, indefinite number

zinc *n.* bluish-white metal, a chemical element

zing *n.* [Sl.] shrill, whizzing sound

zin′ni·a *n.* plant having colorful flower clusters

zip *v.* [ZIPPED, ZIPPING] **1.** make a short, sharp hissing sound **2.** [Col.] move fast **3.** fasten with a zipper —*n.* **1.** a zipping sound **2.** [Col.] energy; vigor

ZIP code mail delivery system using code numbers for zones

zip'per *n.* fastener consisting of interlocking tabs worked by a sliding part

zip'py *a.* [-PIER, -PIEST] [Col.] full of energy; brisk

zir'con *n.* transparent gem

zith'er *n.* stringed instrument, played by plucking

zo'di·ac *n.* imaginary belt along the sun's apparent path divided into twelve parts, or signs, named for constellations

zom'bie, zom'bi *n.* animated corpse in folklore

zone *n.* **1.** any of the five areas into which the earth is divided according to climate **2.** area set apart in some way —*v.*

mark off into zones —**zoned** *a.*

zonked *a.* [Sl.] drunk or stupefied, as from a drug

zoo *n.* place with wild animals on exhibition

zoological garden zoo

zo·ol'o·gy *n.* science of animal life —**zo'o·log'i·cal** *a.* —**zo·ol'o·gist** *n.*

zoom *v.* **1.** make a loud, buzzing sound **2.** climb sharply **3.** rise rapidly **4.** focus with a zoom lens —*n.* a zooming

zoom lens system of lenses adjustable for close or distant shots always in focus

zuc·chi·ni (zoo kē'nē) *n.* a cucumberlike squash

zwie·back (swē'bak, swī'-) *n.* biscuit that is sliced and toasted after baking

ABBREVIATIONS

A. answer
A.A. Associate in Arts
A.B. Bachelor of Arts
ab, a.b. *Baseball* at bat
AC, A.C. alternating current
acc., acct. account
ADC, A.D.C. Aid to Dependent Children
adm. Admiral
A.E.C., AEC Atomic Energy Commission
AFB Air Force Base
agcy. agency
AK Alaska
AL, Ala. Alabama
Alas. Alaska
alt. alteration; altitude
A.M. Master of Arts
amp. ampere
anon. anonymous
ans. answer
Apr. April
apt(s). apartment(s)
AR, Ark. Arkansas
ar., arr. arrival; arrives
Ariz. Arizona
Assn. Association
assoc. associate
asst. assistant
Atl. Atlantic
Attn., attn. attention
atty. attorney
Aug. August
Aus. Austria
Aust., Austl., Austral. Australia
aux. auxiliary
av. average; avoirdupois
Ave. Avenue
avg. average
AZ Arizona

b. born
B.A. Bachelor of Arts

bal. balance
bap., bapt. baptized
Bapt. Baptist
bar. barometer
bb, b.b. *Baseball* base on balls
bbl(s). barrel(s)
bch(s). bunch(es)
bd. board; bond
bdl(s). bundle(s)
bg(s). bag(s)
Belg. Belgian; Belgium
Bib. Bible; Biblical
bibliog. bibliography
biog. biography
bk. bank; book
bl. bale(s)
B/L bill of lading
bldg. building
Blvd. boulevard
b.p. boiling point
br. branch
Br., Brit. British
bro(s). brother(s)
B.S. Bachelor of Science
B/S bill of sale
bskt. basket
B.t.u. British thermal unit(s)
bu. bushel(s)
Bur. Bureau
bus. business
BX base exchange

C, C. Celsius
C., c. catcher; cent; center; centimeter; century; circa; college; copyright; cup
CA California
Cal. California; calorie(s)
cal. calorie(s)
Calif. California
Can. Canada
Canad. Canadian
C & W Country and Western

cap. capital
Capt. Captain
c.c. carbon copy; cubic centimeter (also **cc.**)
cent. century
cf. center field(er); compare
cg, cg., cgm, cgm. centigram(s)
Ch., ch. chapter; church
chap. chapter
chg(d). charge(d)
CIA Central Intelligence Agency
cm, cm. centimeter(s)
CO Colorado; Commanding Officer (also **C.O.**)
Co. company; county
c/o in care of
C.O.D. collect on delivery
Col. Colonel
Colo. Colorado
Com. Commander; Commission
Cong. Congress
Conn. Connecticut
cont. continued
Corp. Corporal; Corporation
CPA, C.P.A. Certified Public Accountant
cr. credit
CST, C.S.T. Central Standard Time
CT Connecticut
ct(s). cent(s)
cu. cubic
cwt. hundredweight
C.Z., CZ Canal Zone

d. daughter(s); degree; diameter; died; dose
D.A. District Attorney
Dan. Danish
dba, d.b.a. doing business as
DC, D.C. direct current; District of Columbia
D.D. Doctor of Divinity
D.D.S. Doctor of Dental Surgery

DE Delaware
Dec. December
dec. deceased
Del. Delaware
Dem. Democrat; Democratic
Den. Denmark
dept. department
dim. diminutive
dir. director
disc. discount
dist. distributor; district
div. division
D.J., DJ disc jockey
DOE Department of Energy
DOT Department of Transportation
doz. dozen(s)
DP, D.P. displaced person
Dr. Doctor; Drive
dr. dram(s)
DST, D.S.T. Daylight Saving Time
Du. Dutch
dup. duplicate
DWI, D.W.I. driving while intoxicated
dz. dozen(s)

E *Baseball* error(s)
E, E., e, e. east; eastern
e *Football* end
ea. each
econ. economics
ed. edition; editor; education
EEC, E.E.C. European Economic Community
e.g. for example
EKG electrocardiogram
elem. elementary
elev. elevation
enc., encl. enclosure
ency., encycl. encyclopedia
ENE, E.N.E. east-northeast
Eng. England; English

eng. engineer; engraver
Ens. Ensign
EPA Environmental Protection Agency
Epis. Episcopal; Episcopalian
eq. equal; equivalent
equiv. equivalent
ERA *Baseball* earned run average; Equal Rights Amendment
ESE, E.S.E. east-southeast
ESP extrasensory perception
esp., espec. especially
Esq. Esquire
EST, E.S.T. Eastern Standard Time
est. established; estimated
et al. and others
etc. et cetera
et seq. and the following
ETV educational television
Eur. Europe; European
ex. example; except; exchange; export; extra
exec. executive
ext. extension; exterior; extra

F, F. Fahrenheit; Friday
F, f. fathom; female; forward
FBI, F.B.I. Federal Bureau of Investigation
FCC, F.C.C. Federal Communications Commission
FDA, F.D.A. Food and Drug Administration
Feb. February
Fed. Federal; Federation
fem. feminine
ff. following
FHA, F.H.A. Federal Housing Administration
FICA Federal Insurance Contributions Act
fig. figuratively; figure(s)
Fin. Finland; Finnish

FL, Fla. Florida
fl. flourished; fluid
F.O.B., f.o.b. free on board
f.p. freezing point
Fr. Father; French; Friar
Fri. Friday
Ft. Fort
ft. foot, feet
FTC, F.T.C. Federal Trade Commission
fut. future
fwd. forward
FYI for your information

G., g. gram(s)
g goal(s); goalkeeper; guard
GA, Ga. Georgia
gal(s). gallon(s)
Gen. General
Ger. German; Germany
GHQ General Headquarters
gi. gill(s)
gm. gram(s)
G.M. General Manager
GOP, G.O.P. Grand Old Party (Republican Party)
Gov. Governor
govt. government
G.P. general practitioner
Gr. Greece; Greek
gr. grain(s); gram(s)
grad. graduate; graduated
gram. grammar
Gr. Brit. Great Britain
gt. great
guar. guaranteed

H., h., h height; high; *Baseball* hit(s); hour(s)
hdqrs. headquarters
HEW Department of Health, Education, and Welfare
hf. half
hgt. height

HI Hawaii
H.M.S. His (or Her) Majesty's Ship
Hon. honorable
HP, H.P., hp, h.p. horsepower
HQ, H.Q., hq, h.q. headquarters
hr, h.r., HR home run(s)
hr(s). hour(s)
H.R. House of Representatives
H.R.H. His (or Her) Royal Highness
H.S. high school
ht. heat; height
HUD Department of Housing and Urban Development
Hung. Hungarian; Hungary
Hwy., hwy. highway
Hz, hz hertz

I., i. island(s)
IA, Ia. Iowa
ibid. in the same place
ICC, I.C.C. Interstate Commerce Commission
ID, I.D. identification
ID, Ida. Idaho
i.e. that is
IL, Ill. Illinois
illus. illustrated; illustration
imp. imperial; import
IN Indiana
in. inch(es)
inc. income; incorporated; increase
incl. including; inclusive
Ind. Indiana
ind. independent; index; industrial
inf. infantry; infinitive; information
ins. inches; insurance
insp. inspected; inspector
Inst. Institute; Institution
instr. instructor

int. interest; interior; international (also **intl.**)
inv. invoice
Ir. Ireland; Irish
I.R.A. Irish Republican Army
IRS, I.R.S. Internal Revenue Service
Is., is. island(s); isle(s)
It. Italian; Italy
ital. italic type
IV, i.v. intravenous

Jan. January
jct. junction
J.D. Doctor of Laws
J.P. justice of the peace
Jr., jr. junior

K., k. karat
Kans., Kan. Kansas
kg, kg. kilogram(s)
kHz kilohertz
K.K.K., KKK Ku Klux Klan
kl, kl. kiloliter(s)
km, km. kilometer(s)
KO, K.O. *Boxing* knockout
KS Kansas
kt. karat
kw, kw. kilowatt(s)
kwh, K.W.H., kw.-hr. kilowatt-hour
KY, Ky. Kentucky

L., l. lake; left; length; liter(s)
LA, La. Louisiana
lab. laboratory
Lat. Latin
lat. latitude
lb(s). pound(s)
L.D.S. Latter-day Saints
Legis. Legislature
lf. left field(er)
lg. large
lgth. length

Lieut. Lieutenant
liq. liquid
lit. liter(s); literature
LL.B. Bachelor of Laws
LL.D. Doctor of Laws
loc. cit. in the place cited
log. logarithm
long. longitude
LPN, L.P.N. Licensed Practical Nurse
Lt. Lieutenant
Ltd., ltd. limited
Luth. Lutheran
lv. leave(s)

M. Monday (also **M**); Monsieur
M., m. male; married; mile(s); minute(s)
m, m. meter(s)
MA Massachusetts
M.A. Master of Arts
mach. machinery
mag. magazine; magnitude
Maj. Major
Mar. March
masc. masculine
Mass. Massachusetts
max. maximum
M.C. Master of Ceremonies
MD, Md. Maryland
M.D. Doctor of Medicine
mdse. merchandise
ME, Me. Maine
mech. mechanical; mechanics
med. medical; medicine; medium
met. metropolitan
Meth. Methodist
Mex. Mexican; Mexico
mfg. manufacturing
mfr. manufacturer
mg, mg. milligram(s)
Mgr. Manager
MHz, Mhz megahertz
MI Michigan

mi. mile(s)
Mich. Michigan
mil. military
min. minimum; minute(s)
Minn. Minnesota
misc. miscellaneous
Miss. Mississippi
mkt. market
ml, ml. milliliter(s)
Mlle. Mademoiselle
mm, mm. millimeter(s)
Mme. Madame
MN Minnesota
MO, Mo. Missouri
mo. month
M.O., MO mode of operation; money order (also **m.o.**)
mod. moderate; modern
Mon. Monday
Mont. Montana
mos. months
M.P. Member of Parliament; Military Police
m.p. melting point
mpg, m.p.g. miles per gallon
mph, m.p.h. miles per hour
MS manuscript (also **ms.**); Mississippi; multiple sclerosis
M.S. Master of Science
MSS, mss. manuscripts
MST, M.S.T. Mountain Standard Time
MT Montana
Mt., mt. mount; mountain
mtg. meeting; mortgage
mts. mountains
mun. municipal
mus. museum; music

N, N, n, n. north; northern
N., n. navy; new; number
NASA National Aeronautics and Space Administration
natl. national

NATO North Atlantic Treaty Organization
N.B., n.b. note well
NC, N.C. North Carolina; no charge
ND, N.D., N. Dak. North Dakota
NE Nebraska
NE, N.E. Northeast; Northeastern
Nebr., Neb. Nebraska
neg. negative
Neth. Netherlands
neut. neuter
Nev. Nevada
N.F., n/f no funds
NH, N.H. New Hampshire
NJ, N.J. New Jersey
NM, N.M., N. Mex. New Mexico
No., no. number
Norw. Norway; Norwegian
Nos., nos. numbers
Nov. November
N.P. notary public
NRC, N.R.C. Nuclear Regulatory Commission
nt. wt. net weight
NV Nevada
NW, N.W. northwest; northwestern
NY, N.Y. New York
N.Z. New Zealand

O. Ocean; Ohio
O., o. old; *Baseball* out(s)
OAS, O.A.S. Organization of American States
ob. he (or she) died
Obs., obs. obsolete; observatory
Oct. October
off. office; officer; official
OH Ohio
OK, Okla. Oklahoma
OMB, O.M.B. Office of Management and Budget

op. cit. in the work cited
OPEC Organization of Petroleum Exporting Countries
opp. opposite
OR Oregon
orch. orchestra
ord. order; ordinance
Oreg. Oregon
orig. original
OT, o.t. overtime
OTB offtrack betting
oz(s). ounce(s)

P., p. pitcher; pressure
p. page; part; penny; pint
PA, Pa. Pennsylvania
P.A. public-address system
Pac. Pacific
par. paragraph
pass. passenger
pat. patent; patented
pc. piece
pct. percent
pd. paid
P.D. police department
Pen., pen. peninsula
Penn., Penna. Pennsylvania
per. period; person
pers. person; personal
Pfc, Pfc., PFC Private First Class
pg. page
Ph. D. Doctor of Philosophy
phys. physical; physician
pk. pack; park; peak; peck
pkg. package(s)
pl. place; plural
P.M. Postmaster; Prime Minister
po, po *Baseball* putout
P.O., p.o. post office
Pol. Poland; Polish
polit. political; politics
pop. popular; population
Port. Portugal; Portuguese
pos. positive

POW, P.O.W. prisoner of war
P.P., p.p. parcel post
ppd. postpaid
pr. pair(s); price
P.R., PR public relations; Puerto Rico
prec. preceding
pref. preferred
prelim. preliminary
prep. preparatory
Pres. President
Presb. Presbyterian
prin. principal
priv. private
prob. problem
Prof. Professor
prop. proprietor
Prot. Protestant
Prov. Province
ps. pieces
P.S., PS postscript
PSI pollutant standard index
PST, P.S.T. Pacific Standard Time
pt. part; pint(s); point
pub. public; publisher
Pvt. Private
PX post exchange

Q. question
q. quart; quarter; question
qb. *Football* quarterback
qr. quarter
qt. quantity; quart(s)
ques. question
quot. quotation
q.v. which see

R., r. radius; right; river; *Baseball* run(s)
RA Regular Army
RAdm. Rear Admiral
r & b, R & B rhythm and blues
R & D research and development
rb *Football* running back

rbi, r.b.i., RBI *Baseball* runs batted in
R.C. Roman Catholic
rcpt. receipt
Rct. Recruit
Rd., rd. road; rod
R.D. rural delivery
rec. receipt; record; recorded
recd., rec'd. received
ref. referee; reference; reformed; refund
reg. regiment; region; registered; regular; regulation
rel. relative; religion
Rep. Representative; Republic; Republican
rep. report; reporter
res. reserve; residence
ret. retired; returned
Rev. Reverend
rev. revenue; revised; revolution
rf. right field(er)
RI, R.I. Rhode Island
rm. ream; room
RN, R.N. Registered Nurse
Rom. Roman; Romania
ROTC, R.O.T.C. Reserve Officers Training Corps
rpm, r.p.m. revolutions per minute
rpt. report
R.R., RR railroad
R.S.V.P., r.s.v.p. please reply
Rt., rt. right
Russ. Russian
Rwy., Ry. Railway

S, S., s, s. south; southern
S, S. Saturday; Sunday
s. second(s); singular; son
SALT Strategic Arms Limitation Talks
Sat. Saturday
SC, S.C. South Carolina

sch. school
Scot. Scotland; Scottish
SD, S.D., S. Dak. South Dakota
SE, S.E. southeast; southeastern
sec. second(s); secretary; section(s)
sect. section
secy., sec'y. secretary
Sem. Seminary
Sen., sen. senate; senator
Sept. September
seq. the following
serv. service
Sgt, Sgt. Sergeant
shpt. shipment
shr. share(s)
sing. singular
SO, S.O. *Baseball* strikeout(s)
Soc., soc. socialist; society
sol. solution
SOP, S.O.P. standard operating procedure
Sp. Spain; Spanish
sp. special; spelling
spec. special; specification
sq. square
Sr. Senior; Sister
S.R.O. standing room only
SS, S.S. social security; steamship; Sunday School
SS. Saints
ss, ss. *Baseball* shortstop
SST supersonic transport
St. Saint; Strait; Street
Ste. Sainte
sub. substitute; suburb
Sun. Sunday
sup. supplement; supply
Supt., supt. Superintendent
surg. surgeon; surgery
SW, S.W. southwest; southwestern
Sw., Swed. Sweden; Swedish
Switz. Switzerland

syn. synonym
syst. system

T Thursday; Tuesday
T. tablespoon(s)
t *Football* tackle
t. teaspoon(s); temperature; time; ton(s)
tab. table(s); tablet(s)
tbs. tablespoon(s)
TD, td touchdown
te *Football* tight end
tech. technical; technology
tel. telegram; telephone
temp. temperature
Tenn. Tennessee
Tex. Texas
Th., Thur., Thurs. Thursday
tinct. tincture
TKO, T.K.O. *boxing* technical knockout
TN Tennessee
tpk. turnpike
tr. translated; translator; transpose
trans. translated; translator
treas. treasurer; treasury
tsp. teaspoon(s)
Tu., Tue., Tues. Tuesday
Turk. Turkey; Turkish
twp. township
TX Texas

U. Union; United; University
UHF, U.H.F. ultrahigh frequency
U.K. United Kingdom
ult. ultimately
UN, U.N. United Nations
Univ. University
U.S., US United States
USA, U.S.A. United States of America; United States Army
USAF, U.S.A.F. United States Air Force

USDA United States Department of Agriculture
USMC, U.S.M.C. United States Marine Corps
USN, U.S.N. United States Navy
U.S.S. United States Ship
U.S.S.R., USSR Union of Soviet Socialist Republics
UT, Ut. Utah

V, v volt(s); volume
v. verse; version; versus
VA, V.A. Veterans Administration
VA, Va. Virginia
var. variant; variety
VD, V.D. venereal disease
VHF, V.H.F. very high frequency
VI, V.I. Virgin Islands
VIP, V.I.P. very important person
viz. that is; namely
vol(s). volume(s)
V.P., VP Vice-President
vs. versus
VT, Vt. Vermont

W Wednesday
W, W, w, w. west; western
W. Wednesday; Welsh

W., w. watt(s); width; won
w. week(s); wife; with
WA Washington
WAC Women's Army Corps
Wash. Washington
Wed. Wednesday
WI Wisconsin
W.I. West Indies
Wis., Wisc. Wisconsin
wk(s). week(s); work(s)
wkly. weekly
WNW, W.N.W. west-northwest
wr *Football* wide receiver
wrnt. warrant
WSW, W.S.W. west-southwest
wt. weight
WV, W. Va. West Virginia
WY, Wyo. Wyoming

XL extra large

y. yard(s); year(s)
yd(s). yard(s)
Y.M.C.A., YMCA Young Men's Christian Association
yr(s). year(s)
Yugo. Yugoslavia
Y.W.C.A., YWCA Young Women's Christian Association

Z., z. zero; zone

NATIONS OF THE WORLD

Nation	Area sq. mi.	(sq. km.)	Population*	Capital
Afghanistan.....	250,000	(657,500)	14,448	......Kabul
Albania.........	11,101	(28,748)	2,906	......Tirana
Algeria	949,753	(2,460,500)	21,351	......Algiers
Andorra.........	190	(465)	45	......Andorra
Angola..........	481,351	(1,246,700)	7,770	......Luanda
Antigua and Barbuda.	171	(442)	80	......St. John's
Argentina........	1,072,237	(2,777,815)	30,097	......Buenos Aires
Australia........	2,969,227	(7,692,300)	15,462	......Canberra
Austria.........	32,375	(83,853)	7,579	......Vienna
Bahamas........	5,380	(13,934)	228	......Nassau
Bahrain.........	260	(673)	409	......Manama
Bangladesh......	55,598	(144,020)	99,585	......Dacca
Barbados.......	166	(430)	252	......Bridgetown
Belgium........	11,800	(30,562)	9,872	......Brussels
Belize..........	8,867	(22,966)	158	......Belmopan
Benin..........	43,483	(112,620)	3,910	......Porto Novo
Bhutan.........	18,000	(46,620)	1,417	......Thimphu
Bolivia.........	424,160	(1,098,580)	6,037	......La Paz; Sucre
Botswana.......	220,000	(569,800)	1,038	......Gaborone
Brazil..........	3,290,000	(8,521,100)	134,380	......Brasilia
Brunei..........	2,226	(5,765)	218	......Bandar Seri Begawan
Bulgaria	42,758	(110,743)	8,969	......Sofia
Burkina Faso....	108,880	(281,999)	6,733	......Ouagadougou
Burma..........	261,789	(678,033)	36,196	......Rangoon
Burundi........	10,747	(27,834)	4,691	......Bujumbura
Cameroon	183,568	(475,439)	9,506	......Yaoundé
Canada	3,851,809	(9,976,140)	25,142	......Ottawa
Cape Verde......	1,557	(4,033)	300	......Praia
Central African Republic.....	242,936	(626,777)	2,585	......Bangui
Chad...........	496,000	(1,284,000)	5,116	......N'Djamena
Chile...........	292,258	(756,945)	11,655	......Santiago
China..........	3,704,400	(9,597,000)	1,034,907	......Peking
Colombia........	440,000	(1,139,600)	28,248	......Bogotá
Comoros........	718	(1,862)	455	......Moroni
Congo..........	132,000	(341,580)	1,745	......Brazzaville
Costa Rica......	19,700	(51,022)	2,693	......San José
Cuba...........	44,206	(114,477)	9,995	......Havana

* in thousands

618

Nation	Area sq. mi.	(sq. km.)	Population*	Capital
Cyprus	3,572	(9,247)	662	Nicosia
Czechoslovakia	49,365	(127,877)	15,466	Prague
Denmark	16,631	(43,074)	5,112	Copenhagen
Djibouti	8,500	(23,000)	289	Djibouti
Dominica	305	(790)	74	Roseau
Dominican Republic	18,712	(48,464)	6,416	Santo Domingo
Ecuador	104,506	(270,669)	9,091	Quito
Egypt	386,198	(1,000,258)	47,049	Cairo
El Salvador	8,236	(21,393)	4,123	San Salvador
Equatorial Guinea	10,820	(28,023)	275	Malabo
Ethiopia	472,000	(1,222,480)	31,998	Addis Ababa
Fiji	7,073	(18,319)	686	Suva
Finland	130,160	(337,113)	4,873	Helsinki
France	212,650	(550,761)	54,872	Paris
Gabon	102,317	(265,000)	958	Libreville
Gambia	4,003	(10,367)	725	Banjul
Germany, East	41,757	(108,150)	16,718	East Berlin
Germany, West	95,930	(248,457)	61,387	Bonn
Ghana	92,100	(238,538)	13,804	Accra
Greece	51,182	(132,560)	9,984	Athens
Grenada	133	(344)	113	St. George's
Guatemala	42,042	(108,889)	7,956	Guatemala
Guinea	95,000	(246,050)	5,579	Conakry
Guinea-Bissau	13,948	(36,125)	842	Bissau
Guyana	83,000	(214,970)	837	Georgetown
Haiti	10,714	(27,749)	5,803	Port-au-Prince
Honduras	43,289	(112,150)	4,424	Tegucigalpa
Hungary	35,900	(92,981)	10,681	Budapest
Iceland	39,758	(103,000)	239	Reykjavik
India	1,211,000	(3,136,475)	746,388	New Delhi
Indonesia	736,000	(1,906,230)	169,442	Jakarta
Iran	636,000	(1,647,240)	43,820	Tehran
Iraq	172,000	(445,500)	15,000	Baghdad
Ireland	26,599	(68,893)	3,575	Dublin
Israel	7,993	(20,701)	3,855	Jerusalem
Italy	116,303	(301,223)	56,998	Rome
Ivory Coast	124,500	(322,455)	9,178	Abidjan

+ in thousands

Nation	Area sq. mi.	(sq. km.)	Popula-tion*	Capital
Jamaica	4,411	(11,424)	2,388	Kingston
Japan	147,470	(381,947)	119,896	Tokyo
Jordan	37,100	(96,088)	2,689	Amman
Kampuchea	69,982	(181,300)	6,118	Phnom Penh
Kenya	224,900	(582,488)	19,362	Nairobi
Kiribati	263	(681)	61	Tarawa
Korea, North	47,225	(122,370)	19,630	Pyongyang
Korea, South	38,002	(98,447)	41,999	Seoul
Kuwait	7,780	(20,150)	1,758	Kuwait
Laos	91,430	(236,803)	3,732	Vientiane
Lebanon	4,000	(10,360)	2,601	Beirut
Lesotho	11,716	(30,344)	1,474	Maseru
Liberia	43,000	(111,369)	2,160	Monrovia
Libya	679,536	(1,759,998)	3,684	Tripoli
Liechtenstein	62	(160)	27	Vaduz
Luxembourg	999	(2,590)	366	Luxembourg
Madagascar	228,000	(590,517)	•9,645	Antananarivo
Malawi	45,747	(118,484)	6,829	Lilongwe
Malaysia	128,553	(332,952)	15,330	Kuala Lumpur
Maldives	115	(298)	173	Malé
Mali	464,873	(1,204,121)	7,562	Bamako
Malta	121	(313)	356	Valletta
Mauritania	432,076	(1,119,367)	1,623	Nouakchott
Mauritius	720	(1,867)	1,018	Port Louis
Mexico	764,000	(1,978,750)	77,659	Mexico
Monaco	½	(1.5)	28	Monaco
Mongolia	604,103	(1,564,619)	1,860	Ulan Bator
Morocco	254,748	(659,797)	23,565	Rabat
Mozambique	303,762	(786,762)	13,413	Maputo
Nauru	8	(21)	8	
Nepal	56,136	(145,391)	16,578	Kathmandu
Netherlands	15,748	(41,160)	14,437	Amsterdam
New Zealand	103,736	(268,675)	3,238	Wellington
Nicaragua	57,100	(147,888)	2,914	Managua
Niger	490,000	(1,269,000)	6,284	Niamey
Nigeria	356,669	(923,773)	88,148	Lagos
Norway	124,968	(323,750)	4,145	Oslo
Oman	105,000	(271,950)	1,009	Muscat
Pakistan	307,374	(796,095)	96,628	Islamabad
Panama	29,201	(75,650)	2,101	Panama

---

* in thousands

Nation	Area sq. mi.	(sq. km.)	Popula- tion*	Capital
Papua New Guinea.......	178,656	(462,840)	3,353	.... Port Moresby
Paraguay	157,047	(406,750)	3,623	.... Asunción
Peru	496,222	(1,285,209)	19,157	...........Lima
Philippines	115,707	(299,679)	55,528	.... Manila
Poland	120,700	(312,612)	36,887	.... Warsaw
Portugal	36,391	(94,276)	10,045	.... Lisbon
Qatar	4,000	(10,360)	276	..........Doha
Romania	91,699	(237,499)	22,683	...... Bucharest
Rwanda	10,169	(26,338)	5,836	.... Kigali
San Marino.....	24	(62)	23	......San Marino
Sao Tome and Principe.......	372	(964)	89	...... Sao Tome
Saudi Arabia	899,766	(2,331,000)	10,794	.... Riyadh
Senegal	76,124	(197,160)	6,541	.... Dakar
Seychelles	156	(404)	66	.... Victoria
Sierra Leone	27,925	(72,326)	3,805	.... Freetown
Singapore	233	(603)	2,531	...... Singapore
Solomon Islands........	11,500	(29,785)	263	.... Honiara
Somalia	246,155	(637,541)	6,393	..... Mogadiscio
South Africa....	471,867	(1,222,480)	31,698	...... Pretoria; Cape Town
Spain	195,988	(507,606)	38,435	.... Madrid
Sri Lanka	25,332	(65,610)	15,925	.... Colombo
St. Christopher- Nevis	100	(259)	44	...... Basseterre
St. Lucia	238	(616)	120	.... Castries
St. Vincent	150	(389)	138	..... Kingstown
Sudan	967,500	(2,505,813)	21,103	...... Khartoum
Suriname	63,020	(163,265)	370	..... Paramaribo
Swaziland	6,704	(17,366)	651	...... Mbabane
Sweden	173,000	(448,070)	8,335	..... Stockholm
Switzerland	15,943	(41,292)	6,477	.... Bern
Syria	71,981	(186,480)	10,075	..... Damascus
Taiwan..........	13,892	(35,981)	19,117	.... Taipei
Tanzania........	364,590	(944,281)	21,202	.. Dar es Salaam
Thailand........	197,949	(512,820)	51,724	.... Bangkok
Togo	21,995	(56,980)	2,926	...........Lomé
Tonga...........	269	(697)	106	...... Nuku'alofa

* in thousands

Nation	Area sq. mi.	(sq. km.)	Population*	Capital
Trinidad and Tobago	1,980	(5,128)	1,168	.... Port-of-Spain
Tunisia	63,378	(164,149)	7,202	.... Tunis
Turkey	295,923	(766,640)	50,207	.... Ankara
Tuvalu	10	(26)	8	.... Funafuti
Uganda	91,076	(235,885)	14,819	.... Kampala
United Arab Emirates	32,000	(82,880)	1,523	.....Abu Dhabi
United Kingdom	94,200	(243,977)	56,023	.........London
United States....	3,615,211	(9,363,396)	236,413	...... Washington
Uruguay	72,000	(186,997)	2,926	..... Montevideo
U.S.S.R..........	8,649,490	(22,402,076)	274,860	........Moscow
Vanuatu..........	5,700	(14,763)	130	.... Vila
Vatican City.....	1/5	(.438)	1	
Venezuela	352,143	(912,050)	18,552	.... Caracas
Vietnam	127,300	(329,707)	59,030	.... Hanoi
Western Samoa	1,133	(2,934)	162	.... Apia
Yemen, Democratic....	110,971	(287,490)	2,147	.... Aden
Yemen Arab Republic	75,270	(195,000)	5,902	............San'a
Yugoslavia	99,000	(256,410)	22,997	.... Belgrade
Zaire............	905,063	(2,344,102)	32,158	.... Kinshasa
Zambia	290,724	(752,975)	6,554	........Lusaka
Zimbabwe	150,820	(390,622)	8,325	.... Harare

CONTINENTS

	Area* (approximate)		Population*
	sq.mi	sq.km.	(1981 est.)
Africa......................	11,600	30,044	484,000
Antarctica.................	5,500	14,245	— — —
Asia	17,000	44,030	2,713,000
Europe	3,800	9,842	679,000
North America	9,400	24,346	376,000
South America	6,800	17,612	246,000

* in thousands

THE STATES
OF THE UNITED STATES

State	Date Admitted	Area sq. mi.	Area (sq. km.)	Population[1] 1980 Census
Alabama (AL)[2]	1819	51,609	(133,667)	3,890
Alaska (AK).............	1959	589,757	(1,527,470)	400
Arizona (AZ)	1912	113,909	(295,024)	2,718
Arkansas (AR).........	1836	53,104	(137,539)	2,286
California (CA)	1850	158,693	(411,015)	23,669
Colorado (CO)	1876	104,247	(270,000)	2,889
Connecticut (CT).......	1788[3]	5,009	(12,973)	3,108
Delaware (DE).........	1788[3]	2,057	(5,328)	595
Dist. of Columbia (DC)	1790[4]	67	(174)	638
Florida (FL)...........	1845	58,560	(151,670)	9,740
Georgia (GA)	1788[3]	58,876	(152,489)	5,464
Hawaii (HI)	1959	6,450	(16,706)	965
Idaho (ID).............	1890	83,557	(216,413)	944
Illinois (IL)...........	1818	56,400	(146,076)	11,418
Indiana (IN)...........	1816	36,291	(93,994)	5,490
Iowa (IA)..............	1846	56,290	(145,791)	2,913
Kansas (KS)...........	1861	82,264	(213,064)	2,363
Kentucky (KY)	1792	40,395	(104,623)	3,661
Louisiana (LA)........	1812	48,523	(125,675)	4,204
Maine (ME)	1820	33,215	(86,027)	1,125
Maryland (MD)........	1788[3]	10,577	(27,394)	4,216
Massachusetts (MA) ...	1788[3]	8,257	(21,386)	5,737
Michigan (MI).........	1837	58,216	(150,779)	9,258
Minnesota (MN).......	1858	84,068	(217,736)	4,077
Mississippi (MS)......	1817	47,716	(123,584)	2,521
Missouri (MO).........	1821	69,686	(180,487)	4,917
Montana (MT).........	1889	147,138	(381,087)	787
Nebraska (NE)	1867	77,227	(200,018)	1,570
Nevada (NV)	1864	110,540	(286,299)	799
New Hampshire (NH)...	1788[3]	9,304	(24,097)	921
New Jersey (NJ).......	1787[3]	7,836	(20,295)	7,364
New Mexico (NM)......	1912	121,666	(315,115)	1,300
New York (NY)........	1788[3]	49,576	(128,402)	17,557
North Carolina (NC)...	1789[3]	52,586	(136,198)	5,874
North Dakota (ND)	1889	70,665	(183,022)	653
Ohio (OH).............	1803	41,222	(106,765)	10,797
Oklahoma (OK)........	1907	69,919	(181,090)	3,025
Oregon (OR)...........	1859	96,981	(251,181)	2,633

[1]in thousands [2]Abbreviations to be used with ZIP code [3]One of the 13 original States [4]Established by Congress

State	Date Admitted	Area sq. mi.	(sq. km.)	Population[1] 1980 Census
Pennsylvania (PA)[2]	1787[3]	45,333	(117,412)	11,867
Rhode Island (RI)	1790[3]	1,214	(3,144)	947
South Carolina (SC).....	1788[3]	31,055	(80,432)	3,119
South Dakota (SD).......	1889	77,047	(199,552)	690
Tennessee (TN)	1796	42,244	(109,412)	4,591
Texas (TX)	1845	267,338	(692,405)	14,228
Utah (UT)..............	1896	84,916	(219,932)	1,461
Vermont (VT)...........	1791	9,609	(24,887)	511
Virginia (VA)...........	1788[3]	40,817	(105,716)	5,346
Washington (WA)	1889	68,192	(176,617)	4,130
West Virginia (WV)......	1863	24,181	(62,629)	1,950
Wisconsin (WI)	1848	56,154	(145,439)	4,705
Wyoming (WY)	1890	97,914	(253,597)	471

[1]in thousands   [2]Abbreviations to be used with ZIP code
[3]One of the 13 original States

CAPITALS OF THE STATES

STATE	CAPITAL	STATE	CAPITAL
Alabama	Montgomery	Montana	Helena
Alaska	Juneau	Nebraska	Lincoln
Arizona	Phoenix	Nevada	Carson City
Arkansas	Little Rock	New Hampshire	Concord
California	Sacramento	New Jersey............	Trenton
Colorado	Denver	New Mexico	Santa Fe
Connecticut	Hartford	New York	Albany
Delaware	Dover	North Carolina	Raleigh
Florida	Tallahassee	North Dakota.........	Bismark
Georgia	Atlanta	Ohio	Columbus
Hawaii	Honolulu	Oklahoma	Oklahoma City
Idaho	Boise	Oregon	Salem
Illinois	Springfield	Pennsylvania	Harrisburg
Indiana	Indianapolis	Rhode Island	Providence
Iowa	Des Moines	South Carolina	Columbia
Kansas..............	Topeka	South Dakota..........	Pierre
Kentucky	Frankfort	Tennessee	Nashville
Louisiana	Baton Rouge	Texas	Austin
Maine.............	Augusta	Utah..............	Salt Lake City
Maryland	Annapolis	Vermont	Montpelier
Massachusetts	Boston	Virginia	Richmond
Michigan...........	Lansing	Washington	Olympia
Minnesota...........	St. Paul	West Virginia	Charleston
Mississippi	Jackson	Wisconsin	Madison
Missouri	Jefferson City	Wyoming	Cheyenne

THE LARGEST CITIES IN
THE UNITED STATES

1980 Census Figures

New York, N.Y.	7,071,030	Albuquerque, N. Mex.	331,767
Chicago, Ill.	3,005,072	Tucson, Ariz.	330,537
Los Angeles, Cal.	2,966,763	Newark, N.J.	329,248
Philadelphia, Pa.	1,688,210	Charlotte, N.C.	314,447
Houston, Tex.	1,594,086	Omaha, Nebr.	311,681
Detroit, Mich.	1,203,339	Louisville, Ky.	298,451
Dallas, Tex.	904,078	Birmingham, Ala.	284,413
San Diego, Cal.	875,504	Wichita, Kans.	279,272
Baltimore, Md.	786,775	Sacramento, Cal.	275,741
San Antonio, Tex.	785,410	Tampa, Fla.	271,523
Phoenix, Ariz.	764,911	St. Paul, Minn.	270,230
Indianapolis, Ind.	700,807	Norfolk, Va.	266,979
San Francisco, Cal.	678,974	Virginia Beach, Va.	262,199
Memphis, Tenn.	646,356	Rochester, N.Y.	241,741
Washington, D.C.	637,651	Akron, O.	237,177
San Jose, Cal.	636,550	St. Petersburg, Fla.	236,893
Milwaukee, Wis.	636,212	Jersey City, N.J.	223,532
Cleveland, O.	573,822	Anaheim, Cal.	221,847
Columbus, O.	564,871	Baton Rouge, La.	219,486
Boston, Mass.	562,994	Richmond, Va.	219,214
New Orleans, La.	557,182	Fresno, Cal.	218,202
Jacksonville, Fla.	540,898	Colorado Springs, Colo.	215,150
Seattle, Wash.	493,846	Shreveport, La.	205,815
Denver, Colo.	491,396	Lexington, Ky.	204,165
Nashville, Tenn.	455,651	Santa Ana, Cal.	203,713
St. Louis, Mo.	453,085	Dayton, O.	203,588
Kansas City, Mo.	448,159	Jackson, Miss.	202,895
El Paso, Tex.	425,259	Mobile, Ala.	200,452
Atlanta, Ga	425,022	Yonkers, N.Y.	195,351
Pittsburgh, Pa.	423,938	Des Moines, Ia.	191,003
Oklahoma City, Okla.	403,213	Knoxville, Tenn.	183,139
Cincinnati, O.	385,457	Grand Rapids, Mich.	181,843
Fort Worth, Tex.	385,141	Montgomery, Ala.	178,157
Minneapolis, Minn.	370,951	Lubbock, Tex.	173,979
Portland, Oreg.	366,383	Anchorage, Alas.	173,017
Honolulu, Hawaii	365,048	Fort Wayne, Ind.	172,196
Tulsa, Okla.	360,919	Lincoln, Nebr.	171,932
Buffalo, N.Y.	357,870	Spokane, Wash.	171,300
Toledo, O.	354,635	Riverside, Cal.	170,876
Miami, Fla.	346,931	Madison, Wis.	170,616
Austin, Tex.	345,496	Huntington Beach, Cal.	170,505
Oakland, Cal.	339,288	Syracuse, N.Y.	170,105

LARGEST METROPOLITAN AREAS
OF THE UNITED STATES

1980 Census Figures

New York, N.Y.—N.J. 9,119,737
Los Angeles—Long Beach, Cal. 7,477,657
Chicago, Ill. 7,102,328
Philadelphia, Pa.—N.J. 4,716,818
Detroit, Mich. 4,352,762
San Francisco—Oakland, Cal. 3,252,721
Washington, D.C.—Md.—Va. 3,060,240
Dallas—Fort Worth, Tex. 2,974,878
Houston, Tex. 2,905,350
Boston, Mass. 2,763,357
Nassau—Suffolk, N.Y. 2,605,813
St. Louis, Mo.—Ill. 2,355,276
Pittsburgh, Pa. 2,263,894
Baltimore, Md. 2,174,023
Minneapolis—St. Paul, Minn.—Wis. 2,114,256
Atlanta, Ga. 2,029,618
Newark, N.J. 1,965,304
Anaheim—Santa Ana—Garden Grove, Cal. 1,931,570
Cleveland, Ohio 1,898,720
San Diego, Cal. 1,861,846
Miami, Fla. 1,625,979
Denver—Boulder, Colo. 1,619,921
Seattle—Everett, Wash. 1,606,765
Tampa—St. Petersburg, Fla. 1,569,492
Riverside—San Bernardino—Ontario, Cal. 1,557,080
Phoenix, Ariz. 1,508,030
Cincinnati, Ohio—Ky.—Ind. 1,401,403
Milwaukee, Wis. 1,397,143
Kansas City, Mo.—Kans. 1,327,020
San Jose, Cal. 1,295,071
Buffalo, N.Y. 1,242,573
Portland, Oreg.—Wash. 1,242,187
New Orleans, La. 1,186,725
Indianapolis, Ind. 1,166,929
Columbus, Ohio 1,093,293
San Antonio, Tex. 1,071,954
Fort Lauderdale—Hollywood, Fla. 1,014,043
Sacramento, Cal. 1,014,002
Rochester, N.Y. 971,879
Salt Lake City—Ogden, Utah 936,255
Providence—Warwick—Pawtucket, R.I.—Mass. ... 919,216
Memphis, Tenn.—Ark.—Miss. 912,887

NATIONAL PARKS
OF THE UNITED STATES

Name	Location	Acreage
Acadia	Southern Maine	38,522
Arches	East central Utah	73,379
Big Bend	Southwestern Texas	708,118
Bryce Canyon	Southwestern Utah	35,835
Canyonlands	Southeastern Utah	337,570
Capitol Reef	South central Utah	241,874
Carlsbad Caverns	Southeastern New Mexico	46,755
Crater Lake	Southwestern Oregon	160,290
Everglades	Southern Florida	1,398,800
Glacier	Northwestern Montana	1,013,595
Grand Canyon	Northern Arizona	1,218,375
Grand Teton	Northwestern Wyoming	310,516
Great Smoky Mountains	Western North Carolina and Eastern Tennessee	517,368
Guadalupe Mountains	Western Texas	76,293
Haleakala	Island of Maui, Hawaii	28,660
Hawaii Volcanoes	Island of Hawaii	229,177
Hot Springs	West central Arkansas	5,801
Isle Royale	Island in Lake Superior (Michigan)	571,796
Kings Canyon	East central California	460,136
Lassen Volcanic	Northern California	106,372
Mammoth Cave	Southwest central Kentucky	52,129
Mesa Verde	Southwestern Colorado	52,036
Mount McKinley	South central Alaska	1,939,493
Mount Rainier	West central Washington	235,404
North Cascades	Northern Washington	504,780
Olympic	Northwestern Washington	908,692
Petrified Forest	Eastern Arizona	93,493
Platt	Southern Oklahoma	912
Redwood	Northwestern California	62,211
Rocky Mountain	North central Colorado	263,793
Sequoia	East central California	386,823
Shenandoah	Northern Virginia	190,591
Virgin Islands	St. John Island, V.I.	14,490
Voyageurs	Northern Minnesota	219,128
Wind Cave	Southwestern South Dakota	28,060
Yellowstone	Northwestern Wyoming, Southern Montana, and Eastern Idaho	2,219,823
Yosemite	East central California	760,917
Zion	Southwestern Utah	146,547

PRESIDENTS OF THE UNITED STATES

Name	Lived	Birth-Place	In Office	Party
George Washington	1732-1799	Va.	1789-1797	Fed.
John Adams	1735-1826	Mass.	1797-1801	Fed.
Thomas Jefferson	1743-1826	Va.	1801-1809	Rep.
James Madison	1751-1836	Va.	1809-1817	Rep.
James Monroe	1758-1831	Va.	1817-1825	Rep.
John Quincy Adams	1767-1848	Mass.	1825-1829	Rep.
Andrew Jackson	1767-1845	N.C.	1829-1837	Dem.
Martin Van Buren	1782-1862	N.Y.	1837-1841	Dem.
William H. Harrison	1773-1841	Va.	1841	Whig
John Tyler	1790-1862	Va.	1841-1845	Dem.
James K. Polk	1795-1849	N.C.	1845-1849	Dem.
Zachary Taylor	1784-1850	Va.	1849-1850	Whig
Millard Fillmore	1800-1874	N.Y.	1850-1853	Whig
Franklin Pierce	1804-1869	N.H.	1853-1857	Dem.
James Buchanan	1791-1868	Pa.	1857-1861	Dem.
Abraham Lincoln	1809-1865	Ky.	1861-1865	Rep.
Andrew Johnson	1808-1875	N.C.	1865-1869	Rep.
Ulysses S. Grant	1822-1885	Ohio	1869-1877	Rep.
Rutherford B. Hayes	1822-1893	Ohio	1877-1881	Rep.
James A. Garfield	1831-1881	Ohio	1881	Rep.
Chester A. Arthur	1830-1886	Vt.	1881-1885	Rep.
Grover Cleveland	1837-1908	N.J.	1885-1889 1893-1897	Dem.
Benjamin Harrison	1833-1901	Ohio	1889-1893	Rep.
William McKinley	1843-1901	Ohio	1897-1901	Rep.
Theodore Roosevelt	1858-1919	N.Y.	1901-1909	Rep.
William H. Taft	1857-1930	Ohio	1909-1913	Rep.
Woodrow Wilson	1856-1924	Va.	1913-1921	Dem.
Warren G. Harding	1865-1923	Ohio	1921-1923	Rep.
Calvin Coolidge	1872-1933	Vt.	1923-1929	Rep.
Herbert Hoover	1874-1964	Iowa	1929-1933	Rep.
Franklin D. Roosevelt	1882-1945	N.Y.	1933-1945	Dem.
Harry S Truman	1884-1972	Mo.	1945-1953	Dem.
Dwight D. Eisenhower	1890-1969	Tex.	1953-1961	Rep.
John F. Kennedy	1917-1963	Mass.	1961-1963	Dem.
Lyndon B. Johnson	1908-1973	Tex.	1963-1969	Dem.
Richard M. Nixon	1913-	Cal.	1969-1974	Rep.
Gerald R. Ford	1913-	Neb.	1974-1977	Rep.
Jimmy Carter	1924-	Ga.	1977-1981	Dem.
Ronald Reagan	1911-	Ill.	1981-	Rep.

WEIGHTS AND MEASURES

Linear

12 inches	= 1 foot	1 centimeter	=	0.3937 inch
3 feet	= 1 yard	1 inch	=	2.5400 centimeters
5½ yards	= 1 rod	1 foot	=	0.3048 meter
40 rods	= 1 furlong	1 meter	=	39.3701 inches
8 furlongs	= 1 mile	1 yard	=	0.9144 meter
1,760 yards	= 1 mile	1 kilometer	=	0.6213 mile
5,280 feet		1 mile	=	1.6093 kilometers

Liquid

8 grams	= 1 ounce	1 centiliter	=	0.3381 ounce
4 ounces	= 1 gill	1 deciliter	=	3.3814 ounces
4 gills	= 1 pint	1 quart	=	0.9464 liter
2 pints	= 1 quart	1 liter	=	1.0567 quarts
4 quarts	= 1 gallon	1 gallon	=	3.7854 liters
31½ gallons	= 1 barrel	1 decaliter	=	2.6417 gallons

Dry

33.60 cu. inches	= 1 pint	1 liter	=	0.9081 quart
2 pints	= 1 quart	1 quart	=	1.1012 liters
8 quarts	= 1 peck	1 decaliter	=	0.2838 bushel
4 pecks	= 1 bushel	1 bushel	=	35.2390 liters

Square

144 sq. inches	= 1 sq. foot			
9 sq. feet	= 1 sq. yard			
30¼ sq. yards	= 1 sq. rod			
160 sq. rods	= 1 acre			
640 acres	= 1 sq. mile			
	1 sq. inch	=	6.452 sq. centimeters	
	1 sq. centimeter	=	0.155 sq. inch	
	1 sq. foot	=	929.034 sq. centimeters	
	1 sq. meter	=	1.196 sq. yards	
	1 sq. mile	=	2.590 sq. kilometers	
	1 sq. kilometer	=	0.386 sq. mile	

Cubic

1,728 cu. inches	= 1 cu. foot			
27 cu. feet	= 1 cu. yard			
16 cu. feet	= 1 cord foot			
8 cord feet	= 1 cord			
128 cu. feet				
	1 cu. inch	=	16.3872 cu. centimeters	
	1 cu. centimeter	=	0.06102 cu. inch	
	1 cu. foot	=	0.0283 cu. meter	
	1 cu. meter	=	35.314 cu. feet	
	1 cu. yard	=	0.7646 cu. meter	

Circular			Nautical	
60 seconds = 1 minute			6 feet = 1 fathom	
60 minutes = 1 degree			100 fathoms = 1 cable's length	
90 degrees = 1 quadrant			10 cables' length = 1 nautical mile	
180 degrees = 1 semicircle			1 nautical mile = 1,852 kilometers	
360 degrees = 1 circle			3 nautical miles = 1 league	

WEIGHT (AVOIRDUPOIS)

27.34 grains = 1 dram	1 centigram =	0.1543 grain
16 drams = 1 ounce	1 grain =	0.0648 gram
437.5 grains = 1 ounce	1 gram =	0.35274 ounce
16 ounces = 1 pound	1 ounce =	28.3495 grams
7,000 grains = 1 pound	1 kilogram =	2.2046 pounds
100 pounds = 1 hundredweight	1 pound =	0.4535 kilograms
2,000 pounds = 1 short ton	1 metric ton =	2,204.6 pounds
2,240 pounds = 1 long ton	1 short ton =	907.18 kilograms

TEMPERATURE

Fahrenheit		Celsius
32°F	freezing point of water	0°C
212°F	boiling point of water	100°C
98.6°F	body temperature	37°C

COMMON METRIC PREFIXES

mega-	meaning "one million"	as in **megaton**
kilo-	meaning "one thousand"	as in **kiloliter**
hecto-	meaning "one hundred"	as in **hectogram**
deca-	meaning "ten"	as in **decameter**
deci-	meaning "one tenth"	as in **deciliter**
centi-	meaning "one hundredth"	as in **centigram**
milli-	meaning "one thousandth"	as in **millimeter**
micro-	meaning "one millionth"	as in **microgram**